VOLUME TWO

IN SEARCH OF AMERICA
COMMUNITY / NATIONAL IDENTITY / DEMOCRACY

VOLUME TWO

IN SEARCH OF AMERICA
COMMUNITY / NATIONAL IDENTITY / DEMOCRACY

Edited by

DAVID H. FOWLER
Carnegie-Mellon University

EUGENE D. LEVY
Carnegie-Mellon University

JOHN W. BLASSINGAME
Yale University

JACQUELYN S. HAYWOOD
University of California, Riverside

The Dryden Press
Holt, Rinehart and Winston, Inc.
New York Chicago San Francisco Atlanta Dallas

Cover:
Andrew Carnegie   Carnegie Library, Pittsburgh
Eleanor Roosevelt   Acme Photo
Dwight D. Eisenhower   United Press International Photo
Malcolm X   John Launois, Black Star

Text Design and Maps by PLASENCIA DESIGN ASSOCIATES, INC., New York

Copyright acknowledgments for art appearing in text are given on page 638

Copyright © 1972 by Holt, Rinehart and Winston, Inc.
All rights reserved
Library of Congress Catalog Card Number: 78-182143
ISBN: 0-03-074130-0
Printed in the United States of America
4 5   061   9 8 7 6 5 4 3 2

Preface

In Search of America, Volume II, is a book about important themes in American history: the nature of social and political identity, the evolution of democratic political systems in an urban industrial society, the emergence of the American nation as a world power, the evolution of a mass production economy, and the continued growth of the ideal and practice of social equality.

This book is intended, as a textbook, to serve as the core of an introductory college course in American history, but in most ways it is unlike a conventional text. It uses source materials and interpretive readings much more than historical narratives. Its materials are arranged as problems. It explores selected themes in depth rather than attempting comprehensive coverage. It concentrates as much on the formulating of ideas as on transmitting information. While the book can also be used effectively as an adjunct to a textbook or other core materials, its readings will prove most effective when discussed in class.

Each of the book's five chapters deals in a major way with at least one or more of the selected themes of democracy, growth as a world power, urban-industrial expansion, and equality; chapter introductions suggest these points of emphasis. Each of the thirty-six topics in this volume constitutes a historical problem, as defined in its introduction, and is designed to be read as a single assignment. The editors have prepared a separate *Guide to Study* which the student will find to be of considerable value, especially in preparing for class discussion. The guide provides study questions and exercises that help him to analyze the historical problems inherent in the readings as well as to sharpen other skills. Since *In Search of America* has been planned to make it possible for students with varying abilities to deal effectively with the same set of historical problems, assignments in the guide suggest three reading options of varying length and sophistication for each topic.

In Search of America is the product of an experimental course in American history designed, under a grant from the

Carnegie Corporation of New York, to develop more effective approaches to the teaching of history. Without this assistance the project would scarcely have been possible, and we thank the many individuals associated with the Carnegie Corporation who have encouraged and supported our efforts.

Those who have collaborated with us in a Cooperative Program in History include representatives from predominantly black colleges and universities, a Catholic college, and other private and state-related institutions. Versions of the course upon which this book is based have been taught at Alabama State University (Ala.), Carnegie-Mellon University (Pa.), Fayetteville State College (N.C.), Fontbonne College (Mo.), Grambling College (La.), Hampton Institute (Va.), Howard University (D.C.), Johnson State College (Vt.), Norfolk State College (Va.), Southern University (La.), Texas Southern University (Tex.), and Virginia State College (Va.). We are indebted to these institutions for their help, and to other institutions and individuals for joining in an experiment in testing reading skills.

Colleagues who have been especially helpful in providing criticism and other assistance are Lorenzo Battle, Emma Brown, Olive Brown, Lena Brown, Henry Cobb, Sister Dolorita Dougherty, William Doyle, Noel Gray, Lou Holloway, William McCree, Alvin McNeil, Herbert Marshall, J. Reuben Sheeler, Charles Simmons, Virginius Thornton, and Norman Walton. We also thank Seymour Mandelbaum for creative suggestions at the inception of the project, Nancy Mason and Richard Kammer for valuable work on the *Guide to Study*, Richard Kammer for preparing the index to this book, and Ruth Corrigan for great help in procuring library materials.

Among the many persons who have helped to further the work in American history of the Cooperative Program, we wish especially to thank Helen Prine for her devoted efforts over several years, and as well, Gita Braude, Nancy Dent, Marian Feeney, Beatrice Goldszer, Barbara Hale, Rebecca Harper, Martel Montgomery, Natalie McKenna, Margaret Neff, Celia Reisman, Barbara Tardy, and Mary Zarroli.

A pioneering work of this sort requires creative backing from its publishers. To Tobi Zausner we are indebted for imaginative pictorial research; to Raymond Gill for conscientious and concerned editing, and to Clifford Snyder for his vision and support. To all the above and to others we are properly grateful.

November 1971

DAVID H. FOWLER
EUGENE D. LEVY
JOHN W. BLASSINGAME
JACQUELYN S. HAYWOOD

Contents

Preface vi

Chapter 6
A NEW INDUSTRIAL SOCIETY, 1865-1920   1

TOPIC 38   ECONOMIC CHANGE AND AMERICAN
WAVES OF LIFE   3
181   The Impact of Industrial Technology   3

TOPIC 39   AMERICAN VALUES IN THE
NEW ERA   15
182   Success through Self-Improvement (1900)   16
183   Boyhood in a Small Town in the 1880s   19
184   A Middle-Class View of Labor and
        Immigrants (1877)   23
185   A Social Prophet Foretells the Future (1887)   27
186   The Justification of Concentrated Wealth (1902)   31

TOPIC 40   ANDREW CARNEGIE AND THE
GROWTH OF THE STEEL INDUSTRY   33
187   The Background of an Industrialist   34
188   The Characteristics of Industrial Leaders
        in the 1870s   37
189   The Meaning of Steel in Industrial America   38
190   Competition in the Steel Industry (1897)   40
191   The Creation of the United States Steel
        Corporation (1901)   41
192   Competition and Steel Prices (1886-1910)   45
193   The Steel Industry in the Twentieth Century   46
Portfolio-Portraits of the Industrial Era   51

TOPIC 41   THE CONFLICT OF LABOR
AND CAPITAL   59
194   Unions and the Workingman (1880-1920)   60
195   The Homestead Strike of 1892   64
196   The Rights of Capital Must Prevail (1892)   71

197	The Homestead Strike: A Labor Leader's View (1892)	72
198	Homestead, Fifteen Years Later	74

TOPIC 42 THE IMMIGRANTS   77
199	Thirty-Eight Million New Americans	77
200	Immigration: The View from Europe	81
201	The Immigrant's Future and His Past	85
202	"What Do You Want of Us Poor Jews?"	86
203	A Question of Identity	89

TOPIC 43 REACTIONS TO THE IMMIGRANTS   93
204	The American and the Immigrant	93
205	The "Barbarian" Invasion of America (1912)	98
206	America, the Melting Pot of Nations (1912)	100
207	Theodore Roosevelt on the Immigrant as an American	103
208	America: A Federation of Cultures (1916)	104

TOPIC 44 THE AGRARIAN REVOLT   108
209	The Farmer in an Industrialized Society (1865–1900)	109
210	The Farmer's View: "The Octopus" (1901)	114
211	The Populist Position (1892)	115
212	"What's the Matter with Kansas?" (1896)	119
213	The Meaning of Populism for America's Future (1896)	122

Portfolio–The Last Days of the Frontier

TOPIC 45 THE PROGRESSIVE APPROACH TO REFORM   133
214	Reform—Progressive Style	133
215	Roosevelt and the Progressives	136
216	Politics in the City—Old Style (1905)	140
217	Politics in the City—New Style (1914)	141
218	Theodore Roosevelt on Progressive Goals	142
219	Another Progressive View of Morality (1909)	144
220	The Theme of Conservation (1910)	146
221	The Church and Social Reform (1907)	148
222	The Supreme Court in the Progressive Era (1905)	149

TOPIC 46 PROGRESSIVES AND THE REGULATION OF BIG BUSINESS   152
223	Business and Government at the Turn of the Century	152
224	Business Concentration as a Positive Goal (1901)	154
225	"Who Owns the United States?" (1904)	156
226	Roosevelt on the Trusts (1911)	159
227	Woodrow Wilson on the Trusts (1912)	162
228	The Businessman and the Progressive Movement	164

Chapter 7
Boom, Bust, Depression, Recovery: Responses to Economic Change, 1920–1945   169

TOPIC 47 THE NEW ERA   171
229	Government and the Economy in the 1920s	172
230	The Impact of the Automobile	175
231	Henry Ford and his "Tin Lizzie"	178
232	The Impact of the Radio (1924)	180
233	The Rise of a Consumer Economy	181
234	Flight from the City	184

TOPIC 48 SOCIAL CHANGE AND CONFLICT   187
235	Tensions of the Twenties	187
236	The Older Generation Looks at the Jazz Age (1925)	188
237	The City, the Elite, and Liquor (1923)	189
238	The Ku Klux Klan Interpreted (1925)	192
239	Politics and Social Values in the 1928 Election	194
240	The Making of a Hero (1927)	196
241	The Younger Generation Looks at the Jazz Age (1927)	199

TOPIC 49 BLACKS AND WHITES IN THE TWENTIES — 202
- 242 The Struggle for Equality and Identity — 202
- 243 A Black Youth in the South During the 1920s — 207
- 244 The New Emancipation: The Migration North — 211
- 245 A Northern Ghetto—Chicago — 212
- 246 Working for a Better Future: The N.A.A.C.P. — 216
- 247 Marcus Garvey and the Appeal to Black Identity — 217
- 248 The Young Negro Speaks Out (1926) — 220

TOPIC 50 CRASH AND DEPRESSION, 1929–1933
- 249 Disaster Strikes the Economy — 222
- Portfolio—The Movies: Dreams and Reality for the Millions — 223
- 250 Hoover Explains His Policies — 234
- 251 The Deepening Crisis (1932) — 236
- 252 Family Life and the Depression — 241
- 253 A Liberal Glance at Roosevelt's Plans (1932) — 243
- 254 Roosevelt: Nothing To Fear but Fear Itself (1933) — 245

TOPIC 51 THE CREATION OF THE NEW DEAL — 248
- 255 A Plea for a Planned Economy (1932) — 248
- 256 The Need for Public Investment (1932) — 250
- 257 The New Deal Attacks the Crisis (1933) — 251
- 258 Frances Perkins: The Roosevelt I Knew — 255
- 259 Hoover Denounces the New Deal (1935) — 257
- 260 An Attack on Capitalism (1935) — 259
- 261 Huey Long: Share Our Wealth (1935) — 260

TOPIC 52 THE SEARCH FOR SECURITY — 264
- 262 Roosevelt: The Goal of Social Justice (1935) — 266
- 263 Social Security for All (1935) — 267
- 264 A Critique of Social Security (1937) — 269
- 265 The Unionization of Big Steel (1937) — 271
- 266 Jones & Laughlin Steel Corporation Basic Contract (1937) — 274
- 267 Aliquippa Celebrates (1937) — 275
- 268 An Evaluation of the New Deal — 276

Chapter 8
The United States Becomes a World Power — 281

TOPIC 53 AMERICAN DESTINY AND OVERSEAS EXPANSION — 284
- 269 The Force of Nationalism — 286
- 270 Josiah Strong: The Anglo-Saxon Mission (1885) — 290
- 271 Nationalism, Expansion, and Hawaii (1893) — 292
- 272 The Question of Conspiracy — 294
- 273 Further Thoughts on Annexation — 295
- 274 Triumph of Liberty or Insult to the Flag? — 297
- 275 Carl Schurz: Big Navies and Aggression — 297
- 276 Grover Cleveland: "An Armed Invasion" — 298

TOPIC 54 POWER IN THE CARIBBEAN AND PACIFIC — 300
- 277 Sea Power and American Strategy — 300
- 278 American Policy in Two Hemispheres — 302
- 279 *The Nation* Denounces the Panama Affair (1903) — 307
- 280 A Poet Celebrates the Panama Affair (1904) — 307
- 281 Latin Americans Consider the Panama Affair (1904) — 308
- 282 Roosevelt Defends His Actions in Panama — 310
- 283 The Realities of Power in the Pacific (1905) — 313
- 284 Roosevelt Explains His Policy toward Japan — 314

TOPIC 55 THE FAILURE OF NEUTRALITY — 317
- 285 The Origins of World War One — 317
- 286 Wilson: The Choice Is Ours (1914) — 319
- 287 Roosevelt: Morality and Self-Preservation — 321
- 288 Early Challenges to Neutrality — 322
- 289 An American Diplomat Views the British (1914) — 325
- 290 An American Diplomat Views the Germans (1915) — 325
- 291 Submarine Warfare Results in an American Warning (1917) — 326

292 Germany Attempts an Alliance with Mexico (1917) 328
293 A Senator Pleads for Peace (1917) 328
294 Wilson Calls for War (1917) 330

TOPIC 56 VERSAILLES:
THE PROSPECT OF COLLECTIVE SECURITY 333
295 Victory and the Making of Peace (1918-1920) 333
296 The Versailles Treaty and Collective Security 338
297 Irish Nationalism and the Treaty (1919) 339
298 Senator Lodge Attacks the
 League of Nations (1919) 341
299 Wilson Defends the League of Nations (1919) 343
300 Woodrow Wilson: A Prophet Ahead of His Time 346
301 Wilson's Goals: Tragic and Unachievable 347

TOPIC 57 THE SECOND FAILURE OF
NEUTRALITY: WORLD WAR II 349
302 The Coming of the Second World War (1919-1939) 349
303 A Guarded Plea for Neutrality (1939) 352
304 American Response to Nazi Victories:
 "The Arsenal of Democracy" (1940) 354
305 Lindbergh: Avoid Defeat through
 True Neutrality (1941) 357
306 Beginning of an Undeclared Naval War (1941) 360
307 Public Sentiment: Anti-Nazi but Antiwar
 (1940-1941) 362

TOPIC 58 WAR WITH JAPAN: INEVITABLE
RESULT OR DIPLOMATIC FAILURE? 366
308 Japan: The First Modern Power in Asia 366
309 Ambassador Grew Advocates a Hard Line (1940) 368
310 Grew Suggests Easing Pressure on Japan (1941) 371
311 Public Sentiment Increasingly Opposes Japanese
 Expansion (1941) 372
312 Breakdown of Negotiations:
 A Diplomatic Failure? 373

313 Breakdown of Negotiations:
 An Inevitable Result? 379

Chapter 9
The Reconstruction of World Politics, 1941-1971   385

TOPIC 59 THE WAR AND THE NUCLEAR AGE 387
314 The United States in World War II (1941-1945) 387
315 Planning the Peace 392
316 The Bomb That Changed the World 394
317 Why the United States Dropped the Bomb 396
318 Alternatives to the Bomb 399

TOPIC 60 THE COLD WAR 406
319 The Cold War (1945-1949) 406
320 Where Are We Headed? (1946) 408
321 The Russian Menace (1947) 409
322 The Sources of Soviet Conduct (1947) 412
323 A Dissent on Containment (1947) 414
324 The North Atlantic Treaty (1949) 418

TOPIC 61 TROUBLE IN EAST ASIA,
1950-1954 420
325 China, Korea, and the Cold War 420
326 The United States Acts To Defend
 South Korea (1950) 424
327 Conference at Wake Island (1950) 428
328 American Intervention: The Chinese View 430
329 Chinese Intervention: The American View 431
330 Decision on Vietnam (1954) 434

TOPIC 62 EISENHOWER, DULLES, AND
AMERICAN POWER 438
331 The Eisenhower Era (1953-1960) 438
332 The United States Backs a Revolution (1954) 442

333	Guatemala's Tragedy		444	TOPIC 66 AMERICAN RESPONSIBILITIES
334	The Soviet Union Suppresses a Revolution (1956)		446	IN THE 1970s	497
335	The Suez Crisis (1956)		446	354 Senator Fulbright: The Arrogance of Power	497
336	Applying the Eisenhower Doctrine: Lebanon (1958)		448	355 Robert Wolfe: American Capitalism and Imperialism	499
337	Cold War and the Necessity of Peace (1958)		450	356 Irving Kristol: We Must Remain a Policeman	502
				357 Walter Lippmann: Beyond Our National Limits	507

TOPIC 63 McCARTHY AND COMMUNISM: LOYALTY OR CONFORMITY?   452

338 The Rise and Fall of Senator McCarthy   452
339 McCarthy: The Conspiracy against America   455
340 A Defense of Conformity (1954)   457
341 The Long Trial of John Paton Davies   459
342 The Legacy of McCarthyism (1961)   462

Chapter 10
A Troubled Society, 1945–1972   513

TOPIC 67 FROM RAGS TO RICHES, 1945–1960   515
358 Coping with Prosperity   515
359 Back to 1929?   520
360 The Changing Distribution of Wealth   521
361 The Capitalism of the Proletariat?   524
362 The Organization Man (1956)   526
363 Facts and Fictions of U.S. Capitalism (1959)   529

TOPIC 64 CUBA AND REVOLUTION IN THE AMERICAS

343 Nuclear Confrontation in the Americas   469
344 Kennedy and Cuba (1962)   470
345 Fidel Castro: "A Grave Threat to the United States"   473
346 Teetering on the Brink   476
347 The Future of Democracy in the Americas   477

TOPIC 68 THE ATTACK ON JIM CROW   532
364 Black and White in America (1930–1954)   532
365 *Brown* v. *Board of Education* (1954)   536
366 The Significance of the Supreme Court Decision   538
Portfolio-A Second Reconstruction   540
367 Mixed Schools and Mixed Blood   548
368 The Little Rock Crisis (1957)   551
369 How Long, How Long . . . ?   554

TOPIC 65 THE DECISION TO INTERVENE IN VIETNAM   482

348 Vietnam: Central Issue of the 1960s   482
349 Retaliation in the Gulf of Tonkin (1964)   484
350 I. F. Stone: Brainwashing the Public   485
351 Further Light on the Gulf of Tonkin Episode   488
352 State Department: Aggressive War from the North (1965)   489
353 I. F. Stone: Civil War in the South (1965)   494

TOPIC 69 DIRECT ACTION AND CIVIL RIGHTS   556
370 Black Activism (1955–1965)   556
371 The Sit-In Movement   560
372 "Negroes with Guns"   562

373	Malcolm X	565	386 Fighting Poverty in the 1970s	604
374	Mississippi Summer (1964)	569		

TOPIC 70 INTEGRATION, SEPARATION, AND BLACK POWER — 573

- 375 The New Mood of Black Americans — 573
- 376 Riots in the Cities (1967) — 577
- 377 The White Backlash — 581
- 378 The Black Manifesto (1969) — 584
- 379 Towards Integration as a Goal — 585
- 380 Blacks in the United States (1969) — 588

TOPIC 71 THE PROBLEM OF POVERTY — 591

- 381 The Emergence of the "Great Society" (1961–1968) — 593
- 382 Poverty in America — 596
- 383 Is There Really a New Poor? — 599
- 384 The Poor: A Conservative View — 601
- 385 The War on Poverty (1964) — 602

TOPIC 72 YOUTH AND THE NEW POLITICS — 608

- 387 The New Radicals — 609
- 388 Another View of America (1956) — 612
- 389 Revolt at Berkeley (1964) — 613
- 390 You Don't Need a Weatherman to Know Which Way the Wind Blows — 615
- 391 On Madness and Violence (1970) — 618
- 392 Thoughts on a Troubled El Dorado (1970) — 621

TOPIC 73 THE FUTURE OF THE NATIONAL COMMUNITY — 625

- 393 The Lessons of the Past: Historians View America in the 1970s — 626

Acknowledgements — 639
Index — 641

List of Maps

The U.S. Railroad Network, 1890	111
The Disappearing Frontier	123
The Growing Airline Network	198
Colonial Empires to 1914	284
American Overseas Expansion up to 1917	304
The European Nations Divide for War	321
Main American Actions in the Final Allied Offensive, 1918	334
The Peace Settlement: Europe in 1920	338
The Furthest Expansion of German Power: Europe in 1942	353
Japanese Expansion, 1895–1942	367
The Allies on the Offensive: Europe and the Middle East, 1942–1945	389
The Allies on the Offensive: Asia and the Pacific	390
The Korean War	423
The IndoChina Scene	483
The Tonkin Gulf Incident	486

VOLUME TWO
IN SEARCH OF AMERICA
COMMUNITY / NATIONAL IDENTITY / DEMOCRACY

Chapter 6

A New Industrial Society, 1865–1920

Between 1865 and 1920 the United States became the world's foremost industrial nation. The dramatic rise in American productivity was the result of many factors, among which were the speedy mechanization that everywhere accompanied the Industrial Revolution, the exploitation of unsurpassed natural resources, the labor and ingenuity of a population richly endowed with vigor and skills, and the existence of a vast market—people to whom goods could be sold—within the nation's borders.

The readings in this chapter deal in part with the reasons why the American economy grew so fast and the related problem of why cities grew so fast at the expense of rural areas. Most of the readings, however, are concerned with the effects of the urban-industrial change on the American people. Here one should recall the themes mentioned earlier. A mass production economy was closely related to mass consumption. Life became more abundant for many people in many ways. But were the fruits of the immense gains in industrial and agricultural production spread evenly among Americans? Or did some people get a far larger share than others?

The rapid transformation of the base of American society from rural to urban, with its accompanying tide of immigrants, and the transformation of the base of economic life from small organizations to large, created exciting opportunities for many persons. Many others, however, were unsure whether the changes were making life better or worse. And to many others the transformations were cruel and embittering.

These situations were full of paradox and conflict. The new industrial society demanded collective activity. Yet this was the era when great individual enterprisers like Andrew Carnegie and John D. Rockefeller seemed to many persons to be characteristic figures. Was individual achievement the rule or the exception? Mass production also demanded closely managed cooperation between employers and workers. Yet violence in labor disputes rose to an unprecedented height. Did such giant cooperative economic efforts necessarily bring conflict with them?

Some Americans demanded social, economic, and political changes to cope with the conditions of the new industrial era. Others, content with their rewards or fearful of added uncertainties, resisted. Their battles filled the literature of the day and played a growing part in public life. The following readings examine some of these controversies, which occurred both inside and outside the framework of conventional political action.

This chapter, dealing with the years between the eras of the Civil War and World War I, generally treats political matters as reflections of economic and social questions. There is good reason for the subordination of the narrative of national politics. Through most of the years before 1900 the control of Congress and the Presidency shifted between national political parties which had little desire to make policies that would affect the nation deeply. National political leadership reached a low ebb at a time when the most burning questions were those of the protective tariff and the money supply rather than those of human rights or state-federal conflicts. The appearance of Theodore Roosevelt and Woodrow Wilson as national leaders in a new era of reform after 1900 changed this picture somewhat. Yet most of the ideas and actions which brought significant or dramatic change to American politics took place in the realms of local or state government. We must grant that democratic ideas and the habits of political action continued as important elements in the American experience. Nevertheless, the historical developments most worthy of intensive study in this era are those of the economic and social relationships of urban industrialism.

TOPIC 38

ECONOMIC CHANGE AND AMERICAN WAYS OF LIFE

During the last century such sweeping changes occurred in the United States that Americans of the 1870s and those of the 1970s might find it hard to comprehend each other's worlds. Those of the 1870s lived in times of dramatic developments in business and industry, in the midst of revolutions in transportation and communications. Yet while industrialization and urbanization had already progressed greatly in parts of Europe and the American Northeast, probably few Americans realized that they were approaching the end of an era ten thousand years old. Through this era most humans lived by growing crops and animals and the farmer served as the necessary standard by which all other men and occupations were measured.

On the other hand, Americans of the 1970s, characteristically urban in residence and outlook, find it increasingly difficult to relate their own experiences to those of their ancestors who lived in an agricultural society. The town and city dweller, beset by a deteriorating physical and social environment, sees the agricultural American past as less and less relevant to his life and problems.

How did this transformation in outlook and way of life come about? As in the case of any complex historical development, many elements, including population, ideas, and institutions, need to be taken into account. The one reading that makes up this topic concentrates, however, on the factor that was most crucial of all: the technology that grew out of the scientific revolution in the modern Western world. No factor was more important in making most Americans children of industry, business, and the city, rather than children of the soil.

Reading 181

The Impact of Industrial Technology

In the following analysis, economist Robert L. Heilbroner examines the ways in which changes in technology have affected the patterns of production and consumption which had been a central part of life in recent American history.

From Robert L. Heilbroner, *The Making of Economic Society* © 1962. Reprinted by permission of Prentice-Hall, Inc., Englewood Cliffs, New Jersey. Pp. 101–125. Subheadings added and footnote omitted by the editors.

I

A New Period of History

With this chapter, we enter a new major period of economic history. Formerly we have dealt largely with the past, giving only an occasional glance to later echoes of the problems we have encountered. Commencing with this chapter, our focus turns toward and into the actual present. We have reached the stage of economic history whose nearest boundary is our own time. Simultaneously, our point of geographic focus shifts. As economic history enters the mid-nineteenth century, the dynamic center of events comes increasingly to be located in the United States. Not only do we now begin to enter the modern world, but the economic trends in which we will be interested take us directly into our own society.

What will be the theme of this chapter? Essentially it will be a continuation of a motif we began with the Industrial Revolution—the impact of technology on economic society.

Looking back, we can see that the burst of inventions which marked "the" Revolution was not in any sense the completion of an historic event. Rather, it was merely the inception of a process of technological change which would continually accelerate down to the present time.

We can distinguish three or even four stages of this continuous process. The "first" Industrial Revolution was largely concentrated in new textile machinery, improved methods of coal production and iron manufacture, revolutionary agricultural techniques, and steam power. It was succeeded in the middle years of the nineteenth century by a "second" Industrial Revolution: a clustering of industrial inventions centering on steel, on railroad and steamship transportation, on agricultural machinery, and chemicals. By the early years of the twentieth century there was a third wave of inventions: electrical power, automobiles, the gasoline engine. In our own time there is a fourth: the revolution of electronics, air travel, automation, and, of course, nuclear energy.

It is difficult, perhaps impossible, to exaggerate the impact of this continuing industrial revolution. Now advancing rapidly, now slowly; now on a broad front, now on a narrow salient; now in the most practical of inventions, again in the purest of theoretical discoveries, the cumulative application of science and technology to the productive process was *the* great change of the nineteenth and twentieth centuries. The initial Industrial Revolution was thus in retrospect a kind of discontinuous leap in human history; a leap as important as that which had lifted the first pastoral settlements above the earlier hunting communities. We have already noted that in the factory the new technology brought a new working place for man, but its impact was vastly greater than that alone. The enormously heightened powers of transportation and communication, the far more effective means of wresting a crop from the soil, the hugely enhanced ability to apply power for lifting, hauling, shaping, binding, cutting—all this conspired to bring about a literal remaking of the human environment, and by no means an entirely benign one.

II
The Impact of One Invention

In this book we cannot do more than inquire into some of the economic consequences of the incursion of industrial technology into modern society, but it may help us gain some insight into the dimensions of that penetrative process if we follow for a short distance the repercussions of a single invention.

Let us therefore look in on the Paris Exposition of 1867, where curious visitors are gathered around an interesting exhibit: a small engine in which illuminating gas and air are introduced into a combustion chamber and ignited by a spark. The resulting explosion pushes a piston; the piston turns a wheel. There is but one working stroke in every four, and the machine requires a large flywheel to regularize its movement, but as the historian Allan Nevins writes, the effect of the machine "was comparable to the sudden snapping on of an electric globe in a room men had been trying to light with smoky candles."* It was the world's first internal combustion engine.

It was not long before the engine, invented by Dr. N. A. Otto of Germany, was a regular feature of the American landscape. Adapted to run on gasoline, a hitherto uninteresting by-product of kerosene manufacture, it was an ideal stationary power plant. Writes Nevins, "Soon every progressive farm, shop, and feed-mill had its one-cylinder engine chugging away, pumping water, sawing wood, grinding meal, and doing other small jobs."* By 1900 there were more than 18,500 internal combustion engines in the United States; and whereas the most powerful model in the Chicago World's Fair in 1893 was 35 horsepower, at the Paris Exposition seven years later it was 1,000 horsepower.

In itself the internal combustion engine was an extraordinary means of increasing and diffusing and making mobile a basic requirement of material progress: power. And soon the new engine opened the way for a yet more startling advance. In 1886, Charles E. Duryea of Chicopee, Massachusetts, had already decided that the gasoline engine was a far more promising power source than steam for a self-propelling road vehicle. By 1892 he and his brother had produced the first gas-powered "automobile," a weak and fragile toy. The next model in 1893 was a better one, and by 1896 the Duryea brothers actually sold thirteen cars. In that same year, a thirty-two-year-old mechanic called Henry Ford sold his first "quadricycle." The history of the automobile industry had begun.

Its growth was phenomenal. By 1905 there were 121 establishments making automobiles, and 10,000 wage earners were employed in the industry. By 1923 the number of plants had risen to 2,471, making the industry the largest in the country. In 1960 its annual payroll was as large as the national income of

---

Ford, the Times, the Man, the Company (New York: Scribner's, 1954), I, p. 96.

Study in Power, John D. Rockefeller (New York: Scribner's, 1953), II, p. 109.

It did not take long for the automobile to penetrate small town America. This family scene was taken in Redwood Falls, Minnesota, in 1902. The photograph reveals the early technology of the automobile, with its buggy body and belt drive, the latter customary on stationary gasoline and steam engines.

the United States in 1890. Not only that, but the automobile industry had become the single greatest customer for sheet steel, zinc, lead, rubber, leather. It was the buyer of one out of every three radios produced in the nation. It absorbed twenty-five billion pounds of chemicals a year. It was the second largest user of engineering talent in the country, bowing only to national defense. It was the source of one-sixth of all the patents issued in the nation and the object of one-tenth of all consumer spending in the country. In fact, it has been estimated that no less than one job out of every seven and one business out of every six owed their existences directly or indirectly to the car.

Even this impressive array of figures by no means exhausts the impact of the internal combustion engine and its vehicular mounting. Because of the existence of the car, some fifty thousand towns managed to flourish without rail or water connections, an erstwhile impossibility. Seven out of ten workers no longer lived within walking distance of their places of employment but drove to work. Of the nation's freight tonnage, 76 percent no longer moved by rail but by truck. To an extraordinary extent, our entire economy was "mobilized"—which is to say, dependent for its very functioning on the existence of wheeled, self-propelled transportation. If by some strange occurrence our automotive fleet were put out of commission—say by a spontaneous change in the nature of the gasoline molecule, rendering it incombustible—the effect would be as grave and as socially disastrous as a catastrophic famine in the Middle Ages.

III

The General Impact of Technology

We dwell on the impact of the car, not because it was the most significant of technological changes. Before the car, there had been the startling economic transformation of the train, and after it would come the no less totally transforming effects of electronic communication. Rather, we touch on the profound economic implications of the automobile to illustrate the diffuse effects of all industrial technology—effects which economics often cannot measure and which exceed its normal area of study but which must, nonetheless, be borne in mind as the ever-present and primary reality of the technological revolution itself. Let us mention a few

5

of these general effects on the society in which we live.

The first has been a *vast increase in the degree of urbanization of society*. To an extraordinary extent ... technology has enchanced the ability of the farmer to support the nonfarmer. As a result, society has more and more taken on the aspects and problems of the city rather than the country. In 1790 only twenty-four towns and cities in all of the United States numbered more than 2,500, and together they accounted for only 6 percent of the population. By 1860 the 392 biggest cities held 20 percent of the population; and by the late 1950's, 168 great metropolitan areas from Boston through Washington, D.C., along the eastern seaboard had become virtually one huge, loosely connected city with 60 percent of the nation's people. Industrial technology has literally refashioned the human environment, bringing with it all the gains—and all the terrible problems—of city life on a mass scale.

Second, *the steady growth of industrial technology has radically lessened the degree of economic independence of the average citizen*. In our opening chapter we noted the extreme vulnerability of the "unsupported" inhabitant of a modern society, dependent on the work of a thousand others to sustain his own existence. This, too, we can now trace to the effect of the continuing industrial revolution. Technology has not only moved men off the soil and into the city, but has vastly increased the specialized nature of work. Unlike the "man of all trades" of the early nineteenth century—the farmer who could perform so many of his necessary tasks himself—the typical factory worker or office worker is trained and employed to do only one small part of a social operation which now achieves staggering complexity. Technology has vastly increased the degree of economic interdependence of the modern community and has made the solution of the economic problem hinge on the smooth coordination of an ever-widening network of delicately connected activities.

Third, and stemming from these changes, *the expansion of industrial technology has profoundly altered the kinds of skills demanded of the economic population*. It is obvious that the inventory of skills we possessed in 1800 would never suffice to operate the social "machine" of 1960. But even in the much shorter time span since 1900, the required distribution of skills has significantly changed, as the table [1] below shows.

Note how different is our profile of occupations today from the not too distant past. We have already commented on the sharp drop in the number of people needed to feed the nation, but we can also see a shift within the "blue collar" group from unskilled to skilled and semi-skilled jobs, as more people labor with capital equipment than with their hands. In addition, as the sharp increase in the number of managers and clerical workers indicates, a swifter and more complex production process requires ever more people to coordinate and oversee the actual making of goods. In 1899 there was one "nonproduction" employee for every thirteen production workers; in 1954, one for every four. And finally we note that the sheer volume of production makes selling a much more important and complicated task and enforces a rise in the number of persons whose jobs are concerned with the distribution of goods rather than their output.

What we have seen by no means covers the over-all impact of technology on the structure—much less the operation—of our economic society, but it will serve as a useful backdrop against which to proceed. We shall return again to the general impact of technology. It is now time to look more deeply into its more immediate and specific manifestation—the startling increases in production which it made possible.

TABLE 1 OCCUPATIONAL DISTRIBUTION OF THE LABOR FORCE, 1900–1960*

	% OF LABOR FORCE 1900	1960
Managerial & Professional		
Professional & technical workers	4.1	11.8
Managers, officials & proprietors (nonfarm)	5.9	10.9
White Collar		
Clerical workers	3.1	14.9
Sales workers	4.8	6.5
Blue Collar		
Skilled workers & foremen	10.3	12.9
Semi-skilled workers	12.8	18.6
Unskilled workers	12.4	4.9
Household & other service workers	8.9	12.7
Farm		
Farmers and farm managers	20.0	4.2
Farm laborers	17.6	2.6

*1900 figures calculated from *Historical Statistics of the United States*, Series D 72–122, p. 74; 1960 figures from *Stat. Abstract 1960*, p. 216. Totals do not add to 100% owing to rounding.

IV

The Effect on Output

[We have investigated] one of the most important problems in economics: the power of industrial capital to raise output. Now we

TABLE 2 PRODUCTION OF SELECTED COMMODITIES AND SERVICES IN THE UNITED STATES
(YEAR INDICATED OR NEAREST AVAILABLE DATE)

	1860	1880	1900	1920	1940	1959
Corn (1,000 bu.)	838,793	1,706,673	2,661,978	3,070,604	2,457,146	4,361,170
Wheat (1,000 bu.)	173,105	502,257	599,315	843,277	814,646	1,128,151
Bituminous coal (1,000 tons)	9,057	50,757	212,316	568,667	460,772	410,446
Petroleum (1,000 bbls.)	500	26,286	63,621	442,929	1,353,214	2,574,590
Copper (short tons)	8,064	30,240	303,059	612,275	878,086	830,435
Cement (1,000 bbls.)	1,100	2,073	17,231	97,079	132,864	351,653
Steel capacity (1,000 tons)		(est.) 900	23,276	60,220	81,619	147,634
Paper and paperboard (1,000 tons)	n.a.*	n.a.	2,782	7,671	16,557	34,051
Number of nonfarm houses built (1 family or more)	n.a.	n.a.	189,000	247,000	602,600	1,379,000
Av. no. daily local telephone calls, Bell System (in thou.)		237	4,773	31,836	79,040	204,491
Pieces of mail handled (millions)	n.a.	3,747	7,130	23,055	27,749	61,247
Total horsepower, prime movers (1,000 h.p.)	13,763	26,314	65,045	453,450	2,759,018	7,143,723**

*Not available.
**1955.
Source: *Historical Statistics of the United States; United States Statistical Abstract, 1960.*

must pursue the problem further by following the actual effect of the continuing industrial revolution on production. Let us begin by acquainting ourselves with some of the statistics of output in the United States over the past century.

The [above] table . . . gives us a first view of the trend. Here is the output record of an assortment of goods and services by twenty-year intervals over the last century.

A first glance cannot fail to be impressive: fivefold, tenfold, even thousandfold increases in output are visible in our table. Some items have latterly declined; note, for instance, the dip in coal production before the onslaughts of oil. But the main line of march is clear enough.

Yet, how representative are these items? Which of their many rates of increase should we take as reflecting the nation as a whole? Clearly, a larger sampling of the national output would soon involve us in a hopeless mass of statistics. A table comprising thousands of items would be necessary to give us a panorama of production, and the eye would fail before the task. If we want to grasp the overall trend of national output, we must find a more convenient way of doing so. How shall we derive it?

V

Gross National Product

Perhaps we should begin by admitting that there is no fully satisfactory way of measuring economic growth in a dynamic economy. And for a very good reason: we are not measuring comparable things. Output not only grows but *changes;* new items appear, old ones disappear; quality, style, durability, all vary from year to year. At best, any measurement must be an approximation, a general guideline to the past.

For the reasons we have just given, economists use a different yardstick from the one above, a yardstick which concerns not just the tonnages and barrels and bushels of physical production, but the *values* of those outputs—that is, the actual amount of money for which the bushels, barrels, and tons of output were sold. We can imagine a gigantic cash register which rings up a sum every time a final good or service is sold in the economy. At the end of the year, the total on the cash register would tell us the total value of the final output of all kinds of goods and services in the nation. This sum is called *Gross National Product* (or GNP, as it is often abbreviated).

Note that we talk about sales of only *final* goods. This is because we do not want to double-count in measuring total output. For example, some wheat is sold to millers who process it into flour which is sold to bakers, who, in turn, bake it into bread for sale in a grocery store. If we counted the value of the sale of wheat, and then of the sale of flour, and then of the sale of bread, we should be counting the wheat and the flour more than once. Wheat and flour are products which enter into the final good, bread. Therefore, their value is already included when we simply take the value of bread. Most goods incorporate many such products bought in an earlier stage of production: a car, for instance, includes steel and rubber and upholstery, all of which were produced and sold to the automobile manufacturing company. Whatever they cost is included in the price the customer pays for a car.

The only way to be reasonably sure that we are not double-counting when we sum up the nation's production is to include the value of *final products* only.

What are these final products? Economists class them into four general categories:

1. *Consumption goods.* These are the goods and services bought by individuals for their private use and enjoyment. They include such items as food and clothing, doctors' bills, travel expenses, etc. They do not, however, include individuals' purchases of new houses.
2. *Gross domestic private investment.* This covers additions to our stock of real wealth. Here we find not only private purchases of houses, but commercial construction, business purchases of capital goods of all kinds, and additions to inventories. We use the term *net*

investment if we subtract from the gross figure an allowance for *depreciation*—the value of the capital annually used up in the process of production.
3. *Net exports.* This category measures the value of goods and services produced here and sold abroad, less the value of goods and services produced abroad and sold here. In other words, it represents the net disposal of our production to foreign buyers.
4. *Government purchases.* Here we find that portion of our annual output bought by local, state or federal government: purchases and pay for the armed forces, teachers' salaries, road construction, etc.

. . . We shall see that this division of GNP into main component parts serves a very useful function, for these categories of output often behave differently as the economy grows. For the moment, however, it is enough that we understand the basic make-up of GNP as a measuring stick for the over-all trend of output.

VI
The Trend of Gross National Product

What does Gross National Product look like over the period we have been studying? The first line of figures in the table [3] below, gives us the value of our GNP over the twenty-year intervals of our previous scrutiny. Still, the figures do not give us much of a basis for comparison, since the *prices* in which GNP is toted up each year are not the same. Clearly, if prices are higher in one year than another, Gross National Product will be a bigger number, even though actual output in tonnage may not be larger at all. So in the second line of our table we also show the approximate relative value of the dollars of former years compared with those of 1960. In the last line of the table we have multiplied GNP in its original or current dollar values with this series of "corrected" dollar values. This gives us GNP in "constant" prices, or in "real terms"—that is, with price variations

TABLE 3 GROSS NATIONAL PRODUCT IN CURRENT AND CONSTANT PRICES SELECTED YEARS

	1880	1900	1920	1940	1960
Gross National Product measured in the prices at which it was actually bought* (billions)	$ 9.18	$17.3	$ 88.9	$100.6	$504.4
Approximate value of past dollars in terms of 1960†	3.27	3.89	1.53	2.24	1.00
Gross National Product measured in dollars of 1960 purchasing power (billions)	30.0	67.3	136.0	225.4	504.4

*Historical Statistics, Series F104 and F1. Figures for 1880 and 1900 are nearest five-year averages.
†Computed from *Historical Statistics*, Series F5.

washed out. These are the comparative totals we are looking for.*

Now we are beginning to see the sweep of advance. If we look at the last line of the table above *we can see that GNP in real terms more or less doubled every twenty years.* Here is the basis for the huge advance in living standards. . . . .

While we are still interested in the producing, rather than the consuming side of the question, let us proceed one step more. If we take the last line of our previous table and compare it with the number of people who produced that Gross National Product, we see still another highly significant fact illustrated by our next table [4].

Now the full impact of industrial technology on output begins to emerge. Not only did our real GNP increase nearly seventeen-fold over the period, but *total output rose about four-and-a-half times as fast as our working force.* And even this does not yet state the case fully. In 1880, the average work week was seventy hours. Today it is forty hours. Our output per person *per hour* has risen almost twice as fast as our over-all employment figures indicate.

What we have here is the historical reality of a process. . .—the extraordinary increase in productivity which stems from industrialization. On this productivity, it must now be obvious, hangs the vast difference which divides the industrial nations of the West from

*A word of warning is in order about these figures. All attempts to convert the GNP of one period into an "equivalent" GNP of another period are made approximate, at best, because the different components of GNP often display different price movements. The "corrected" figures are useful and roughly indicative, but they should not be thought of as precise translations across the years.

TABLE 4 GNP AND EMPLOYED WORKERS

	1880	1900	1920	1940	1960	% INCREASE 1880 / 1960
GNP in 1960 dollars (billions)	30.0	67.3	136.0	225.4	504.4	1681
Employed workers* (millions)	17.4	29.1	42.4	47.5	66.7	384

*Historical Statistics, 1880-1920, D36; 1940, D5; 1960. Economic Indicators.

the unindustrialized nations of the South and East or, for that matter, of the pre-Industrial Revolution West, itself. Not all of the profoundly revolutionary effect of the continuing industrial revolution was a consequence of its huge leverage on productivity, but without that leverage the surrounding changes would never have taken place.

VII
Economies of Large-Scale Production

Thus far we have treated the rise in productivity and output mainly on a national scale. Yet the dynamics of growth were no less startling—and perhaps even more significant—when followed at the level of the individual industrial plant itself. For no small part of the burst in output which began in the 1860's and 1870's in America was the result of a new technique of production, a technique which would develop into, and finally be called, *mass production.*

The technological aspects of mass production are in themselves a subject of fascinating interest. Allan Nevins describes an early Ford assembly-line process.

> Just how were the main assembly lines and lines of component production and supply kept in harmony? For the chassis alone, from 1000 to 4000 pieces of each component had to be furnished every day at just the right point and right minute; a single failure, and the whole mechanism would come to a jarring standstill. . . . Superintendents had to know every hour just how many components were being produced and how many were in stock. Whenever danger of shortage appeared, the shortage chaser—a familiar figure in all automobile factories—flung himself into the breach. Counters and checkers reported to him. Verifying in person any ominous news, he mobilized the foreman concerned to repair deficiencies. Three times a day he made typed reports in manifold to the factory clearing-house, at the same time chalking on blackboards in the clearing house office a statement of results in each factory-production department and each assembling department.*

Such systematizing in itself resulted in astonishing increases in productivity. With each operation analyzed and subdivided into its simplest components, with a steady stream of work passing before stationary men, with

*Ford, the Times, the Man, the Company, I, p. 507.

a relentless but manageable pace of work, the total time required to assemble a car dropped astonishingly. Within a single year the time required to assemble a motor fell from 600 minutes to 226 minutes; to build a chassis, from 12 hours and 28 minutes to one hour and 33 minutes. A stop-watch man was told to observe a three-minute assembly in which men assembled rods and piston, a simple operation. The job was divided into three jobs, and half the men turned out the same output as before.*

But what interests us in the context of our study are not the technical achievements of mass production as much as its economic results. Mass production is not only a method of increasing productivity; it is a way of vastly reducing cost. Even though the costly equipment needed for mass production increases the over-all expenses of production, it increases output even faster, so that cost *per item* drops considerably.

Imagine, for instance, a small plant which turns out 1,000 items a day with the labor of ten men and a small amount of equipment. Suppose each man is paid $10, each item before manufacture costs 10¢, and the daily amount of "overhead"—that is, the daily share of costs such as rent, plant maintenance, office salaries, and wear-and-tear on equipment—comes to $100. Then our total daily cost of production is $300 per day ($100 of payroll, $100 of raw material cost, and $100 of overhead). Divided among 1,000 items of output, our cost per item is 30¢.

Now imagine that our product lends itself to mass production techniques. Our payroll may then jump to $1,000 and with our much larger plant and equipment, our daily overhead to $5,000. Nevertheless, mass production may have boosted output as much as 100 times. Then our total daily cost of production will be $16,000 ($1,000 of payroll, $5,000 of overhead, and $10,000 of raw material costs). Divided among our 100,000 items of output, our cost per item has fallen to 16¢. Despite a quintupling of over-all expense, our cost per unit has almost halved.

This is not a far-fetched example of what economists call *the economies of large-scale production*. A glance at the following table [5] shows how mass production techniques did, in fact, boost output of Ford cars by more than one hundred times while reducing their cost by seven-eighths.

TABLE 5

DATE	UNIT SALES OF FORD CARS	PRICE OF TYPICAL MODEL
1907-08	6,398	$2,800 (Model K) touring
1908-09	10,607	850 (Model T) touring
1909-10	18,664	950 (Model T) touring
1910-11	34,528	780 (Model T) touring
1911-12	78,440	690 (Model T) touring
1912-13	168,304	600 (Model T) touring
1913-14	248,307	550 (Model T) touring
1914-15	221,805 (10 mos.)	490 (Model T) touring
1915-16	472,350	440 (Model T) touring
1916-17	730,041	360 (Model T) touring

*Compiled from Nevins, *Ford, the Times, the Man, the Company*, pp. 644, 646-647.

Nor do the dynamics of the industrial process come to a halt with these formidable economies of large-scale production. With this technological achievement comes as well a new factor of primary importance for the market system itself. That factor is *size*.

It is not difficult to see why. Once a firm—by virtue of adroit management, improved product, advantages of location, or whatever other reason—steps out decisively in front of its competitors in size, *the economies of large-scale production operate to push it out still further in front*. Bigger size means lower cost. Lower cost means bigger profits. Bigger profits mean the ability to grow to still larger size. Thus the techniques of large-scale manufacture bring about a situation which threatens to alter the whole meaning of competition. From a mechanism which prevents any single firm from dominating the market, competition now becomes a force which may drive an ever-larger share of the market into the hands of the largest and most efficient producer.

VIII

The Great Entrepreneurs

We shall have much more to say about the economics of the drive to bigness. Yet, it may be helpful if we look once again at the actual historic scene in which this internal growth took place. For the processes of economic change described in this chapter did not occur in a vacuum. They were brought about by a social "type" and a business milieu which powerfully accelerated and abetted the process of industrial enlargement, much as the "New Men" had speeded along the initial industrializing process in England in the late eighteenth century.

The agents of change during the late nineteenth century in America were very much the descendants of their industrial forebears a century earlier. Like Arkwright and Watt, many of the greatest American entrepreneurs were men of humble origin endowed with

*Ibid., pp. 504, 506.

an indomitable drive for business success. There was Carnegie in steel, Harriman in railroads, Rockefeller in oil, Frick in coke, Armour and Swift in meat packing, McCormick in agricultural machinery—to mention but a few. To be sure, the *typical* businessman was very different from these Horatio Alger stereotypes of the business hero. Economic historians, such as F. W. Taussig, looking back over the careers of the business leaders of the late nineteenth century, have discovered that the average entrepreneur was not a poor, industrious immigrant lad, but the son of well-circumstanced people often in business affairs themselves. Nor was the average businessman nearly so successful as a Carnegie or a Rockefeller.

Yet in nearly every line of business, at least *one* "captain of industry" appeared who dominated the field by his personality and ability. Though few achieved their supreme degree of pecuniary success, the number who climbed into the "millionaire class" was impressive. In 1880 it had been estimated that there were 100 millionaires in the country. By 1916 the number had grown to 40,000.

Interesting and significant differences distinguish the nineteenth century business leaders from those of a century earlier. The captains of industry were not typically men whose leadership rested on inventive or engineering skills. With the growth of large-scale production, the engineering functions became the province of salaried production experts, of second-echelon plant managers. What was required now was the master touch in guiding industrial strategy, in making or breaking alliances, choosing salients for advance, or overseeing the logistics of the whole operation. More and more the great entrepreneurs were concerned with the strategy of finance, of competition, of sales, rather than with the cold technics of production itself.

Then, too, we must make note of the entrepreneurial tactics and tone of the period. In a phrase which has stuck, Matthew Josephson once called the great men of business in this era "the robber barons." In many ways, they did indeed resemble the predatory lords of the medieval era. For example, in the 1860's a small group of California entrepreneurs under the guiding hand of Collis Huntington performed the astonishing feat of building a railroad across the hitherto impassible Rockies and Sierras. Aware that Huntington and his associates would thereby have a monopolistic control of all rail traffic to California, the Congress authorized the construction of three competing lines. But the legislators had not taken the measure of the wily pioneers. Before their own line was completed, they secretly bought the charter of one competitive line; and when the second proved somewhat harder to buy out, they simply built it out, recklessly flinging their lines into its territory until it, too, was forced to surrender. Thereafter it was no great trick to buy out the third, having first blocked it at a critical mountain pass. Only one competitive source of transportation remained: the Pacific Mail Steamship Company. Fortunately, this was owned by the obliging Jay Gould, a famous robber baron in his own right; and for the payment of a proper tribute, he agreed to eliminate San Francisco as a cargo port. There was now *no* way of bringing goods across the nation into Southern California except those which the Huntington group controlled. Counting the smaller lines and subsidiaries which passed into their grasp, *nineteen* rail systems, in all, came under their domain. It was not surprising that to the residents of California the resulting unified system was known as "the Octopus" and that its average freight rate was the highest in the nation.

And it was not just the railroad industry that used economic power to create a monopoly position. In whisky and in sugar, in tobacco and cattlefeed, in wire nails, steel hoops, electrical appliances, tin plate, in matches and meat there was an Octopus similar to that which fastened itself on California. One commentator of the late 1890's pictured the American citizen born to the profit of the Milk Trust and dying to that of the Coffin Trust.

If the robber barons milked the public as consumers (and to an even greater extent bilked them as stockholders), they also had no compunctions about cutting each other down to size. In the struggle for financial control of the Albany and Susquehanna Railroad, for instance, James Fisk and J. P. Morgan found themselves in the uncomfortable position of each owning a terminal at the end of a single line. Like their feudal prototypes, they resolved the controversy by combat, mounting locomotives at each end and running them full tilt into each other—after which the losers still did not give up, but retired, ripping up the line and tearing down trestles as they went. In similar spirit the Huntington group that built the Central Pacific hired General David Colton to run a subsidiary enterprise for them, and the General wrote to his employers:

> I have learned one thing. We have got *no true* friends outside of us five. We cannot depend upon a human soul outside of ourselves, and hence we must all be good-natured, stick together, and keep to our own counsels.

Whereupon he proceeded to swindle his true friends out of several millions.*

IX
The Change in Market Structure

It is impossible to consider the period of history in which we are concerned without taking into account the social type of the robber baron and the milieu in which he operated. Bold, aggressive, acquisitive, competitive, the great entrepreneur was a natural agent to speed along a process for which the technology of the day prepared the way. Under the joint impact of his personal drive for aggrandizement and the self-feeding potentialities of the burgeoning economies of large-scale production, a profound change in market structure swept over the country. In industry after industry there was visible a dramatic concentration of production into a few large business units rather than numerous small ones.

By 1900, the number of textile mills, although still large, had dwindled by a third from the 1880's; the number of manufacturers of agricultural implements had fallen by 60 per cent over the same period, and the number of leather manufacturers by three quarters. In the locomotive industry, two companies ruled the roost in 1900, contrasted with nineteen in 1860. The biscuit and cracker industry changed from a scatter of small companies to a market in which one producer had 90 per cent of the industry's capacity by the turn of the century. Meanwhile in steel there was the colossal U.S. Steel Corporation, which alone turned out over half the steel production of the nation. In oil, the Standard Oil Company tied up between 80 to 90 per cent of the nation's output. In tobacco, the American Tobacco Company controlled 75 per cent of the output of cigarettes and 25 per cent of cigars. Similar control rested with the American Sugar Company, the American Smelting and Refining Company, the United Shoe Machinery Company, and dozens more.

From an over-all view, the change was even more impressive. In the early 1800's, according to the calculations of Myron W. Watkins, no single plant controlled as much as 10 per cent of the output of a manufacturing industry. By 1904, seventy-eight enterprises controlled over half the output of their industries, fifty-seven controlled 60 per cent or more, and twenty-eight controlled 80 per cent or more. From industry to industry this degree of "concentration" varied—from no significant concentration at all in printing and publishing, for instance, to the highly concentrated market structure of industries like copper or rubber. But there was no mistaking the overall change. In 1896, railroads excepted, there were not a dozen $10,000,000 companies in the nation. By 1904, there were over 300 of them with a combined capitalization of over $7,000,000,000. Together these giants controlled over two-fifths of the industrial capital of the nation and affected four-fifths of its important industries.

Clearly something akin to a major revolution in market structure had taken place. Let us examine more closely the course of events which led up to it.

X
The Change in Competition

The initial impact of the trend to big business was an unexpected one. Rather than diminishing the degree of competitiveness of the market structure, it extended and intensified it. In the largely agricultural handicraft and small factory economy of the early nineteenth century, "the" market consisted mainly of small, localized markets, each insulated from the next by the high cost of transportation and each supplied by local producers who had neither the means nor the motivation to invade the market on anything resembling a national scale.

The rise of mass production radically changed this fragmented market structure and, with it, the type of competition within the market. As canals and railroads opened the country and as new manufacturing techniques vastly increased output, the parochial quality of the market system changed. More and more, one unified and interconnected market bound together the entire nation, and the petty semi-monopolies of local suppliers were invaded by products from large factories in distant cities.

Quickly, a second development followed. As the new production techniques gained momentum, aggressive businessmen typically not only built, but overbuilt. "As confident entrepreneurs raced to take advantage of every ephemeral rise in prices, of every ad-

---

*With all this buccaneering went, as well, another identifying mark of the times: conspicuous consumption. Frederick Townsend Martin, a repentant member of the gilded set, has written in his memoirs of parties at which cigarettes were wrapped in money for the pleasure of inhaling wealth; of a dog presented with a $15,000 diamond collar; of an infant resting in a $10,000 cradle attended by four doctors who posted regular bulletins on its (excellent) health; of the parade of fabulous châteaux stuffed with fabulous works of art on New York's Fifth Avenue; and of the collection of impecunious European royalty as sons-in-law of the rich.

vance in tariff schedules, of every new market opened by the railroads and puffed up immigration," write Thomas Cochran and William Miller in a history of these industrializing times, "they recklessly expanded and mechanized their plants, each seeking the greatest share of the new melon."*

The result was a phenomenal burst in output but, simultaneously, a serious change in the nature of competition. Competition now became not only more extensive, but more *expensive*. As the size of the plant and the complexity of equipment grew, so did the "fixed charges" of a business enterprise—the interest on borrowed capital, the depreciation of capital assets, the cost of administrative staff, the rent of land, and "overhead," generally. These costs tended to remain fairly constant, regardless of whether sales were good or bad. Unlike the payment of wages to a working force, which dropped when men were fired, there was no easy way to cut down the steady drain of payments for these fixed expenditures. The result was that the bigger the business, the more vulnerable was its economic health when competition cut into its sales.

The ebullience of the age—plus the steady growth of a technology that *required* massive investments—made competition increasingly drastic. As growing giant businesses locked horns, railroad against railroad, steel mill against steel mill, each sought to assure the coverage of its fixed expenses by gaining for itself as much of the market as it could. The outcome was the steady growth of cutthroat competition among massive producers, replacing the more restricted, local competition

The Age of Enterprise (New York: Harper & Row, revised ed., 1961), p. 139.

of the small business, small market world. On the railroads, for example, constant rate-wars were fought in the 1870's. In the oil fields, the coal fields, among the steel and copper producers, similar price-wars repeatedly broke out as producers sought to capture the markets they needed to achieve a profitable level of production. All this was unquestionably favorable to the consumer, as indeed competitive situations always are, but it threatened literal bankruptcy for the competing enterprises themselves—bankruptcy on a multi-million dollar scale.

XI
The Limitation of Competition

In these circumstances, it is not difficult to understand the next phase of economic development. The giants decided not to compete.

But how were they to avoid competition? Since common law made it illegal to sign a contract binding a competitor to fixed prices or production schedules, there seemed no alternative but voluntary cooperation: trade associations, "gentleman's agreements," or "pools," informal treaties to divide the market. By the 1880's there were a cordage pool and a whiskey pool, a coal pool, a salt pool, and endless rail pools, all calculated to relieve the individual producers from the mutually suicidal game of all-out competition. But to little avail. The division of the market worked well during good times; but when bad times approached, the pools broke down. As sales fell, the temptation to cut prices was irresistible, and thus began the old, ruinous game of competition all over again.

The robber baron ethics of the day contributed to the difficulties. "A starving man will usually get bread if it is to be had," said James J. Hill, a great railway magnate, "and a starving railway will not maintain rates."* Typically, at a meeting of rail heads called to agree upon a common freight schedule, the president of one road slipped out, during a brief recess, to wire the new rates to his road, so that it might be the first to undercut them. (By chance, his wire was intercepted, so that when the group next met it was forced to recognize that even among thieves there is not always honor.)

During the 1880's, a more effective device for control became available. In 1879, Samuel Dodd, lawyer for the new Standard Oil Company, had a brilliant idea for regulating the murderous competition that regularly wracked the oil industry. He devised the idea of a trust. Stockholders of companies that wished to join in the Standard Oil Trust were asked to surrender their actual shares to the board of directors of the new trust. Thereby they would give up working control over their companies, but in return they would get "trust certificates" which entitled them to the same share in the profits as their shares earned. In this way, the Standard Oil directors wielded control over all the associated companies, while the former stockholders shared fully in the profits.

In time, as we shall see, the trusts were declared to be illegal. But by then still more effective devices were discovered. One was the *merger*, the coming together of two corporations to form a new, bigger one. In manufacturing and mining, alone, there were forty-three mergers in 1895 (affecting 41 million dollars worth of corporate assets); twenty-six mergers in 1896, sixty-nine mergers

*Cochran and Miller, *The Age of Enterprise*, p. 141.

in 1897; in 1898 there were 303—and *1,208 mergers combined some $2,263,000,000 corporate assets* in 1899.† Another great wave of mergers occurred in the 1920's. In all, from 1895 to 1929, some $20 billions of industrial corporate wealth were merged into larger units.

Another effective means of limiting competition was the *holding company*. In 1888, New Jersey passed a law permitting one corporation to buy stock in another; a few years later, it permitted a New Jersey corporation to do business anywhere. Thus the legal foundation was laid for a central corporation which could control subsidiary enterprises by the simple means of buying a controlling share of their stock. By 1911, when the Standard Oil combine was finally dissolved, Standard Oil of New Jersey had used this device to acquire direct control over seventy companies and indirect control over thirty more.

Yet we must not think that it was only the movement toward trustification and merger which brought about the emergence of the giant firm with its ability to limit—or eliminate—competition. Equally, perhaps more, important was simply the process of internal growth. Ford and General Motors, General Electric and A. T. & T., DuPont and Carnegie Steel (later the core of U.S. Steel) grew essentially because their market was expanding and they were quick, able, efficient, and aggressive enough to grow faster than any of their competitors. All of them gobbled up some small businesses along the way, and most of them benefited from agreements not to compete. But their gradual emergence to a position of dominance within their industries was not, in the last analysis, attributable to these facts. It was the dynamism of their own business leadership, coupled with a production technique which made enormous size both possible and profitable.

---

†*Historical Statistics of the United States* (Washington, D.C.: U.S. Bureau of the Census), Series V, 30, 31.

TOPIC 39

AMERICAN VALUES IN THE NEW ERA

Through their technology and business organization Americans of the late nineteenth century held the keys to both the gold and the grime of urban-industrial life. Yet the ways they made use of technology and conducted business depended in part on their values.

Some of these values were old and familiar. They were derived from the heritage of an individualistic Protestant Christianity which encouraged men to see worldly success as a sign of God's favor rather than as devotion to Mammon. The virtues of individual initiative and self-reliance celebrated by Thomas Jefferson and Ralph Waldo Emerson, the chief philosophers of American democracy, remained secular ideals. In applying these values to the marketplace, Americans extolled free economic competition, as both an important element in democratic opportunity and as the best way to ensure the greatest economic good of the greatest number of persons. In their pursuit of prosperity, few Americans questioned the desirability of exploiting their natural resources to the utmost. Nor did many question the right of the employer to extort the most possible labor from his employee for the lowest wage the latter would take. Finally, the fact that most Americans still were farmers, living in the countryside, strongly influenced the way they interpreted all these values.

One newer idea deserves mention. This was the notion that economic competition among humans formed only a part of the larger world of nature and that economic success or failure represented the same sort of outcome of natural "laws" as did survival by animals and plants against their rivals. This idea grew greatly in popularity and legitimacy as one result of the profound influence of naturalists like Charles Darwin. In his *The Origin of Species* (1859), Darwin showed how certain species of plants and animals, and certain individuals within species, survived and dominated other species or individuals by virtue of characteristics which gave them special advantages within their own environments. His *The Descent of Man* (1871) made explicit his conclusions that man evolved from animal ancestors rather than from the special creation of God, which is the creed of the major religions. Darwin's account thus struck hard at the traditional Christian belief in the story of Adam's and Eve's parentage of all mankind.

For the moment, those who applied Darwin's ideas enthusiastically to the explanation of man's history and civilization saw little more than his linking of humans to the rest of nature. The "survival of the fittest" seemed to them an adequate doctrine for explaining the fate of individuals, groups, nations, and races. For the moment most forgot the gap between man and the rest of nature represented by human consciousness, which set humans in a unique place where the laws of jungle survival might not apply so clearly.

Success through Self-Improvement (1900)

The doctrine that self-improvement and hard work led to success of all kinds, put forth so persuasively by Benjamin Franklin in the eighteenth century, proved even more appealing in the booming economy and swiftly changing society of the United States in the nineteenth century. Cases of poor boys who became rich or famous may not have been characteristic of American life, but they were common enough—and publicized enough—so that many people believed that a man could achieve anything that his talents allowed. No better example could be found of this self-made man than Booker T. Washington (1856-1915), born a slave in Virginia, who became an internationally famous educator, the chief spokesman for black Americans, and an adviser to Presidents on problems affecting blacks. In his autobiography, published in 1900, Washington recalls his intense drive for self-improvement and success.

From Booker T. Washington, *Up From Slavery* (New York, 1924), pp. 63-69, 72-75, 96-98.

I

Struggle against Poverty

At the end of my first year at Hampton I was confronted with another difficulty. Most of the students went home to spend their vacation. I had no money with which to go home, but I had to go somewhere. In those days very few students were permitted to remain at the school during vacation. It made me feel very sad and homesick to see the other students preparing to leave and starting for home. I not only had no money with which to go home, but I had none with which to go anywhere.

In some way, however, I had gotten hold of an extra, second-hand coat which I thought was a pretty valuable coat. This I decided to sell, in order to get a little money for travelling expenses. I had a good deal of boyish pride, and I tried to hide, as far as I could, from the other students the fact that I had no money and nowhere to go. I made it known to a few people in the town of Hampton that I had this coat to sell, and, after a good deal of persuading, one coloured man promised to come to my room to look the coat over and consider the matter of buying it. This cheered my drooping spirits considerably. Early the next morning my prospective customer appeared. After looking the garment over carefully, he asked me how much I wanted for it. I told him I thought it was worth three dollars. He seemed to agree with me as to price, but remarked in the most matter-of-fact way: "I tell you what I will do; I will take the coat, and I will pay you five cents, cash down, and pay you the rest of the money just as soon as I can get it." It is not hard to imagine what my feelings were at the time.

With this disappointment I gave up all hope of getting out of the town of Hampton for my vacation work. I wanted very much to go where I might secure work that would at least pay me enough to purchase some much-needed clothing and other necessities. In a few days practically all the students and teachers had left for their homes, and this served to depress my spirits even more.

After trying for several days in and near the town of Hampton, I finally secured work in a restaurant at Fortress Monroe. The wages, however, were very little more than my board. At night, and between meals, I found considerable time for study and reading; and in this direction I improved myself very much during the summer.

When I left school at the end of my first year, I owed the institution sixteen dollars that I had not been able to work out. It was my greatest ambition during the summer to save money enough with which to pay this debt. I felt that this was a debt of honour, and that I could hardly bring myself to the point of even trying to enter school again till it was paid. I economized in every way that I could think of—did my own washing, and went without necessary garments—but still I found my summer vacation ending and I did not have the sixteen dollars.

One day, during the last week of my stay in the restaurant, I found under one of the tables a crisp, new ten-dollar bill. I could hardly contain myself, I was so happy. As it was not my place of business I felt it to be the proper thing to show the money to the proprietor. This I did. He seemed as glad as I was, but he coolly explained to me that, as it was his place of business, he had a right to keep the money, and he proceeded to do so. This, I confess, was another pretty hard blow to me. I will not say that I became discouraged, for as I now look back over my life I do not recall that I ever became discouraged over anything that I set out to accomplish. I have begun everything with the idea that I could succeed, and I never had much patience with the multitudes of people who are always ready to explain why one cannot succeed. I have always had a high regard for the man who could tell me how to succeed. I determined to face the situation just as it was. At the end of the week I went to the treasurer of the Hampton Institute, General J. F. B. Marshall, and told him frankly my condition. To my gratification he told me that I could reenter the institution, and that he would trust me to pay the debt when I could. During the second year I continued to work as a janitor.

II
Education at Hampton

The education that I received at Hampton out of the text-books was but a small part of what I learned there. One of the things that impressed itself upon me deeply, the second year, was the unselfishness of the teachers. It was hard for me to understand how any individuals could bring themselves to the point where they could be so happy in working for others. Before the end of the year, I think I began learning that those who are happiest are those who do the most for others. This lesson I have tried to carry with me ever since.

I also learned a valuable lesson at Hampton by coming into contact with the best breeds of live stock and fowls. No student, I think, who has had the opportunity of doing this could go out into the world and content himself with the poorest grades.

Perhaps the most valuable thing that I got out of my second year was an understanding of the use and value of the Bible. Miss Nathalie Lord, one of the teachers, from Portland, Me., taught me how to use and love the Bible. Before this I had never cared a great deal about it, but now I learned to love to read the Bible, not only for the spiritual help which it gives, but on account of it as literature. The lessons taught me in this respect took such a hold upon me that at the present time, when I am at home, no matter how busy I am, I always make it a rule to read a chapter or a portion of a chapter in the morning, before beginning the work of the day.

Whatever ability I may have as a public speaker I owe in a measure to Miss Lord. When she found out that I had some inclination in this direction, she gave me private lessons in the matter of breathing, emphasis, and articulation. Simply to be able to talk in public for the sake of talking has never had the least attraction for me. In fact, I consider that there is nothing so empty and unsatisfactory as mere abstract public speaking; but from my early childhood I have had a desire to do something to make the world better, and then to be able to speak to the world about that thing.

The debating societies at Hampton were a constant source of delight to me. These were held on Saturday evening; and during my whole life at Hampton I do not recall that I missed a single meeting. I not only attended the weekly debating society, but was instrumental in organizing an additional society. I noticed that between the time when supper was over and the time to begin evening study there were about twenty minutes which the young men usually spent in idle gossip. About twenty of us formed a society for the purpose of utilizing this time in debate or in practice in public speaking. Few persons ever derived more happiness or benefit from the use of twenty minutes of time than we did in this way.

At the end of my second year at Hampton, by the help of some money sent me by my mother and brother John, supplemented by a small gift from one of the teachers at Hampton, I was enabled to return to my home in Malden, West Virginia, to spend my vacation. When I reached home I found that the salt-furnaces were not running, and that the coal-mine was not being operated on account of the miners being out on a "strike." This was something which, it seemed, usually occurred whenever the men got two or three months ahead in their savings. During the strike, of course, they spent all that they had saved, and would often return to work in debt at the same wages, or would move to another mine at considerable expense. In either case, my observations convinced me that the miners were worse off at the end of a strike. Before the days of strikes in that section of the country, I knew miners who had considerable money in the bank, but as soon as the professional labour agitators got control, the savings of even the more thrifty ones began disappearing. . . .

III
The Dignity of Labor

Three weeks before the time for the opening of the term at Hampton, I was pleasantly surprised to receive a letter from my good friend Miss Mary F. Mackie, the lady principal, asking me to return to Hampton two weeks before the opening of the school, in order that I might assist her in cleaning the buildings and getting things in order for the new school year. This was just the opportunity I wanted. It gave me a chance to secure a credit in the treasurer's office. I started for Hampton at once.

During these two weeks I was taught a lesson which I shall never forget. Miss Mackie was a member of one of the oldest and most cultured families of the North, and yet for two weeks she worked by my side cleaning windows, dusting rooms, putting beds in order, and what not. She felt that things would not be in condition for the opening of school unless every window-pane was perfectly clean, and she took the greatest satisfaction in helping to clean them herself. The work which I have described she did every year that I was at Hampton.

It was hard for me at this time to understand how a woman of her education and social standing could take such delight in performing such service, in order to assist in the elevation of an unfortunate race. Ever since then I have had no patience with any school for my race in the South which did not teach its students the dignity of labour.

During my last year at Hampton every minute of my time that was not occupied with my duties as janitor was devoted to hard study. I was determined, if possible, to make such a record in my class as would cause me to be placed on the "honour roll" of Commencement speakers. This I was successful in doing. It was June of 1875 when I finished the regular course of study at Hampton. The greatest benefits that I got out of my life at the Hampton Institute, perhaps, may be classified under two heads:—

First was contact with a great man, General S. C. Armstrong, who, I repeat, was, in my opinion, the rarest, strongest, and most beautiful character that it has ever been my privilege to meet.

Second, at Hampton, for the first time, I learned what education was expected to do for an individual. Before going there I had a good deal of the then rather prevalent idea among our people that to secure an education meant to have a good, easy time, free from all necessity for manual labour. At Hampton I not only learned that it was not a disgrace to labour, but learned to love labour, not alone for its financial value, but for labour's own sake and for the independence and self-reliance which the ability to do something which the world wants done brings. At that institution I got my first taste of what it meant to live a life of unselfishness, my first knowledge of the fact that the happiest individuals are those who do the most to make others useful and happy.

IV
Search for a Career

I was completely out of money when I graduated. In company with other Hampton students, I secured a place as a table waiter in a summer hotel in Connecticut, and managed to borrow enough money with which to get there. I had not been in this hotel long before I found out that I knew practically nothing about waiting on a hotel table. The head waiter, however, supposed that I was an accomplished waiter. He soon gave me charge of a table at which there sat four or five wealthy and rather aristocratic people. My ignorance of how to wait upon them was so apparent that they scolded me in such a severe manner that I became frightened and left their table, leaving them sitting there without food. As a result of this I was reduced from the position of waiter to that of a dish-carrier.

But I determined to learn the business of waiting, and did so within a few weeks and was restored to my former position. I have had the satisfaction of being a guest in this hotel several times since I was a waiter there.

At the close of the hotel season I returned to my former home in Malden, and was elected to teach the coloured school at that place. This was the beginning of one of the happiest periods of my life. I now felt that I had the opportunity to help the people of my home town to a higher life. I felt from the first that mere book education was not all that the young people of that town needed. I began my work at eight o'clock in the morning, and, as a rule, it did not end until ten o'clock at night. In addition to the usual routine of teaching, I taught the pupils to comb their hair, and to keep their hands and faces clean, as well as their clothing. I gave special attention to teaching them the proper use of the tooth-brush and the bath. In all my teaching I have watched carefully the influence of the tooth-brush, and I am convinced that there are few single agencies of civilization that are more far-reaching. . . .

About this time the experiment was being tried for the first time, by General Armstrong, of educating Indians at Hampton. Few people then had any confidence in the ability of the Indians to receive education and to profit by it. General Armstrong was anxious to try the experiment systematically on a large scale. He secured from the reservations in the Western states over one hundred wild and for the most part perfectly ignorant Indians, the greater proportion of whom were young men. The special work which the General desired me to do was to be a sort of "house father" to the Indian young men—that is, I was to live in the building with them and have the charge of their discipline, clothing, rooms, and so on. This was a very tempting offer, but I had become so much absorbed in my work in West Virginia that I dreaded to give it up. However, I tore myself away from it. I did not know how to refuse to perform any service that General Armstrong desired of me.

On going to Hampton, I took up my residence in a building with about seventy-five Indian youths. I was the only person in the building who was not a member of their race. At first I had a good deal of doubt about my ability to succeed. I knew that the average

Indian felt himself above the white man, and, of course, he felt himself far above the Negro, largely on account of the fact of the Negro having submitted to slavery—a thing which the Indian would never do. The Indians, in the Indian Territory, owned a large number of slaves during the days of slavery. Aside from this, there was a general feeling that the attempt to educate and civilize the red men at Hampton would be a failure. All this made me proceed very cautiously, for I felt keenly the great responsibility. But I was determined to succeed. It was not long before I had the complete confidence of the Indians, and not only this, but I think I am safe in saying that I had their love and respect. I found that they were about like any other human beings; that they responded to kind treatment and resented ill-treatment. They were continually planning to do something that would add to my happiness and comfort. The things that they disliked most, I think, were to have their long hair cut, to give up wearing their blankets, and to cease smoking; but no white American ever thinks that any other race is wholly civilized until he wears the white man's clothes, eats the white man's food, speaks the white man's language, and professes the white man's religion.

Boyhood in a Small Town in the 1880s

Frederic C. Howe (1867-1940), who was born and grew up in Meadville, Pennsylvania, went on to become a distinguished lawyer, writer, and public servant. His autobiography, published in 1925, gives a revealing picture of some of the details and qualities of life in a small American town in the late nineteenth century.

Reprinted by permission of Quadrangle Books from *The Confessions of a Reformer* by Frederic C. Howe, copyright © 1967 by Quadrangle Books, Inc. Pp. 9-10, 15-19, 20-21.

I

Family Background

There was nothing in my inheritance to make me want the world any different. None of my ancestors ever crusaded. They took no part in the Revolutionary War; they were not Abolitionists; they escaped service in the Civil War. My mother's people were Quakers in a direct line of descent from the little band of settlers which Gustavus Adolphus sent out from Sweden in the early days of the seventeenth century to build a Swedish colony on the shores of Delaware Bay. There was no meeting-house in Meadville, and, like many Quakers, my mother's family had joined the Methodist church. Her grandparents were farmers who had drifted west till they came to rest in the very centre of what was later the town of Meadville, Pa. There my grandfather laid off a big city block and settled his five children around him.

My paternal ancestors came from the north of Ireland in the eighteenth century. They were what is known as Scotch-Irish, which means that they were Scotch Presbyterians who went over to Ireland and took the land away from the Irish and gave them their Scotch brand of religion in exchange. Like my mother's people, they came to this country poor, to get a new start in life. Only those who had little to lose came to America in those days, in sailing-ships which often took months in the crossing. They settled in northeastern Pennsylvania, and when other settlers trod on their heels they packed up their few possessions and trekked to the western part of the State. My father came to Meadville as a young man and there he married my mother. There I was born and lived to my twenty-fifth year.

Neither of my parents had any interest in reform. They did not want the world changed. It was a comfortable little world, Republican in politics, careful in conduct, Methodist in religion. Religion to me was a matter of attending church, of listening to long and tedious sermons, of irritable empty Sunday afternoons, church sociables, and Wednesday-evening prayer-meetings. To the older people it meant rivalry with Presbyterians and serious differences about the minister, the choir, and the power of a rich trustee who contributed generously to the church. Life revolved about our church, which was the finest in town. My father was president of its board of trustees. The neighbors whose opinions counted belonged mostly to it, although they might be Presbyterians. Unitarians were beyond some pale. Church activities and sectarian points of view bulked large in our lives, even though my mother had a gentle Quaker tolerance and kindliness and my father a quiet broadmindedness which was unusual in the community. Fellow churchmen did not understand his going across the public square on Sunday evenings to hear a Unitarian minister who had formerly been a Methodist and had renounced Methodism. The apostasy of Doctor Townsend had been in the nature of a public disgrace, hardly less than a crime. Lifelong friends shunned him. Yet my father, without discussion or

The flavor of American middle class life in the 1890s is captured in these views of life in Wisconsin.

defense of his action, forsook his own pew of a Sunday evening and went to hear strange doctrine. . . .

II

A Sectarian Education

When my sisters and I finished high school we went to Allegheny College, not because we had any love of learning but because it was the proper thing to do. The income from my father's business was somehow stretched to suffice for all of us. Allegheny was one of the two colleges in Meadville that gave to the town the modest name of the "Athens of the West." Allegheny was thoroughly sectarian. Progress toward a degree was made easy for men who said they were going into the church or into foreign missions. Many of our professors were retired ministers or missionaries, who knew none too much about their subjects. Professions of faith were rather more important than scholarship, and revival meetings were the great events of the winter. I found study a bore. None of the subjects stirred in me the least enthusiasm and I cut classes as often as I dared. I was never able to make head or tail of the sciences, mathematics, Latin, and Greek. As far as I can recall, I went through college without having an enthusiasm awakened, yet I wanted to know things, to be admitted to the secrets of life. My classmates seemed to get as little out of the course as I did. Because the college failed to satisfy us, we created activities of our own. Mine were in college journalism. I planned in class and fraternity politics to get the posts

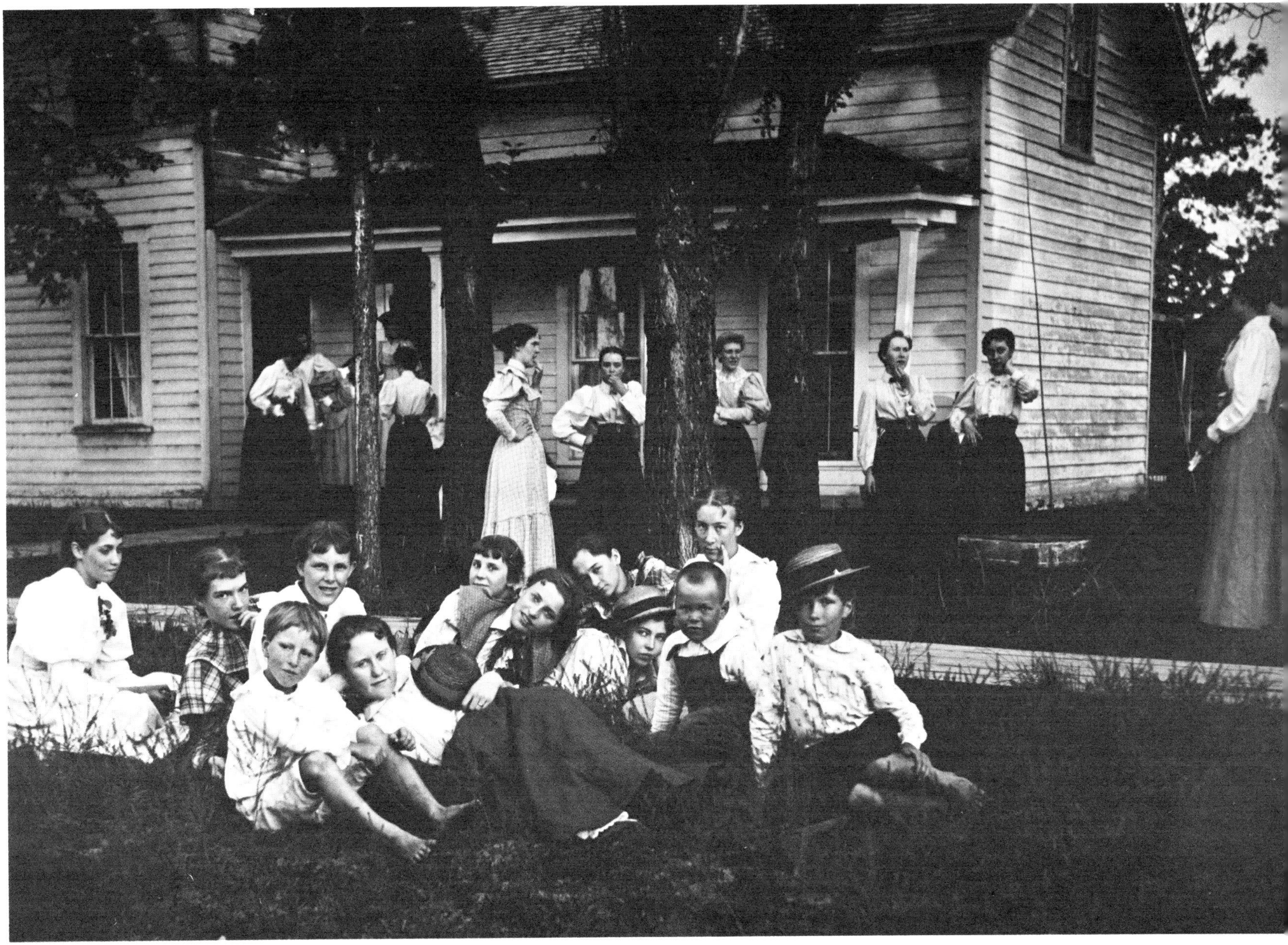

I wanted. The first thrill of my academic life came from getting out the commencement edition of the college weekly. I worked on it day and night. I could hardly wait for the summer vacation to end to take up the work again. The furtive and forbidden amusements of theatre-going, card-playing, and dancing were but slightly diverting as compared with the joy of working over an editorial column.

The winter revival meetings at the college found me inwardly rebellious, outwardly passive. They were thoroughly organized. Freshmen and sophomores were allotted to the seniors, who took us on long walks, during which they inquired about our souls. Night after night they herded us into the Stone church. There revivalists prayed, worked on our fears, made us feel that we were eternally damned if we went without their particular brand of religion. Under the influence of Moody and Sankey hymns I went to the mourners' bench the second winter. I crept forward to be prayed for by strangers for sins of which I was ignorant and for a salvation that seemed at best dreary. I did what relatives, friends, and older college students expected me to do. I had no conviction of sin, no sense of guilt, or of being abandoned. And nothing happened. The great change that was promised did not come over me. Convinced of my own callousness, and rather sick at heart because of it, I found myself hating every one engaged in the proceedings and wishing heartily to escape. I had gone through the ordeal of being prayed for, of confessing a desire for regeneration, and had found no relief; no heavenly manna had fallen my way. I was resentful of religion, and deliberately refused from that time on to attend revival meetings, scandalizing and grieving my teachers and friends.

III

Emancipation versus Conformity

Physical escape from the embraces of evangelical religion did not mean moral escape. From that religion my reason was never emancipated. By it I was conformed to my generation and made to share its moral standards and ideals. It was with difficulty that realism got lodgment in my mind; early assumptions as to virtue and vice, goodness and evil remained in my mind long after I had tried to discard them. This is, I think, the most characteristic influence of my generation. It explains the nature of our reforms, the regulatory legislation in morals and economics, our belief in men rather than in institutions and our messages to other peoples. Missionaries and battleships, anti-saloon leagues and Ku Klux Klans, Wilson and Santo Domingo are all a part of that evangelistic psychology that makes America what she is.

This particular brand of evangelistic morality became bone of my bone, flesh of my flesh. It was a morality of duty, of careful respectability. It was the code of a small town, of the Sunday-school, of my church. I had no rights as to my own life; danger lurked in doing what I wanted, even though what I wanted was innocent. One's desires were to be suspected; they were in some way related to lustful things, and lust in thought was as bad as in deed. One might hate Democrats, Unitarians, persons outside of one's own church; one could be sharp in business, possibly corrupt in politics, but one could not forget that life was a serious business, that duty should be always before one's eyes, that one should be diligent in things distasteful, and that self-fulfillment meant getting on in the world, being assiduous to church-going, rather exhibitive in attendance on revivals, the holding to one's particular church denomination, and the avoidance of even the appearance of careless morals, drinking or association with men of questionable opinions.

The important thing was to live as other men lived, do as other men did, avoid any departure from what other men thought. Not to conform was dangerous to one's reputation. Men who had strange ideas, who protested, who thought for themselves, were quietly ostracized. When people passed their houses there were side glances between the men; some remarks that sounded very damning to me at that time. There were other men, bankers and department-store keepers, of whom stories were whispered about women they had been seen with, of their trips to New York, of sharp advantages they had taken of other men. But these things did not seem to matter so much as did dissension from established ideas. It was a distinction to be stopped by them on the street, to be nodded to from their carriages, to be called by one's given name. Somehow they seemed to be permitted to do things that other men did not do. They had a freedom from their neighbors, from a code of living that was always demanding something unpleasant of me.

I conformed, but departed when I dared. In town and at college I resisted claims made upon me; decisions made by others; the dulness of classrooms, of chapel exercises, of conformity. I did not fit in as other boys did, and was conscious of questionings on the part of neighbors, my college professors, most of whom were friends of my family.

It was rumored that when I came up for a degree and various professors made unfavorable comments in faculty meeting on my scholarship and attendance, President David

H. Wheeler asked how long I had been at Allegheny.

"Five years," he commented, on hearing the secretary's reply. "Well, any one who can stay at this institution for five years deserves a degree." And to that estimate of the worth of sectarian education pronounced by a man of genuine culture who was oddly out of place in it, I owe perhaps my bachelor's degree....

At Chautauqua* I heard some lectures on political economy by Richard T. Ely, of Johns Hopkins [University]. They made me want to know more about the big world outside of my little home town. I met John H. Finley, later president of the College of the City of New York and now on the New York *Times,* who was then a student at Johns Hopkins and was doing editorial work on *The Chautauquan,* a periodical published by the Assembly. John Finley, I realized suddenly, was doing what I most wanted to do. He was writing for a newspaper. And I found that I had a definite ambition. I would become an editorial writer on a city newspaper. In order to be that I felt that I should know something about economics, history, politics. Apparently Johns Hopkins was the place where one should study these things. Therefore I would go to Johns Hopkins. I had saved a few hundred dollars; that would be enough for a start and I would work my way through. For the first time in my life I had a definite, serious desire to do something, not because somebody expected me to do it or because it was there to do, but because I genuinely wanted it. I was also under the glamour of a Ph.D.

*Chautauqua, New York, where during each summer the Chautauqua Assembly held a wide variety of educational and cultural programs—Eds.

degree. It seemed to me a hallmark of intellectual power. It might open doors to wealth and distinction. And I was not indifferent to wealth. Men in Meadville were comfortable on nine hundred dollars a year; few made more than twelve hundred out of their business. Given the magical degree, I might in time earn fifteen hundred dollars a year. And that would be a princely income.

A Middle-Class View of Labor and Immigrants (1877)

The chief problem of an increasing number of Americans in the late nineteenth century was holding a steady job at decent pay. The concentration of workingmen and women in growing industrial centers made it harder for them to find work, when hundreds or thousands of them were laid off or discharged during a business depression. The economic power of a large corporation gave it the ability to keep wages low so long as the labor supply was plentiful, and industrial employers generally welcomed the huge flow of immigrants from Europe after the Civil War. Workers responded to these conditions by organizing unions on a national scale to give them bargaining power in dealing with employers. Such organizations provoked alarm on the part of many middle-class Americans, who worried that economic power in the hands of the lower classes might lead to socialism, anarchy, and revolution. In 1877 such fears seemed to be coming true, when railroads reduced wages in the aftermath of a depression. Railway workers, through strikes, virtually tied up rail transportation throughout the nation. Almost at once violence broke out as state militia and federal troops clashed with the strikers. Rioting broke out in Baltimore, Pittsburgh, Chicago, and St. Louis; nine persons were killed in Martinsburg, West Virginia, and twenty-six in Pittsburgh. In an editorial appearing two weeks later, the periodical *The Nation* speaks for what was probably a large part of the middle-class citizens.

From *The Nation,* XXV (August 2, 1877), pp. 68–69.

I

The Late Riots

It is impossible to deny that the events of the last fortnight constitute a great national disgrace, and have created a profound sensation throughout the civilized world. They are likely to impress the foreign imagination far more than the outbreak of the Civil War, because the probability that the slavery controversy would end in civil war or the disruption of the Union had been long present to people's minds both at home and abroad. Slavery, too, was well known to be an accident, and by no means a natural product of American institutions, and its horrors and inconsistencies did not really seriously shake the general confidence in the soundness and solidity of American polity, strong and numerous as were the attempts made for that purpose. There has for fifty years been throughout Christendom a growing faith that outside the area of slave-soil the United States had—of

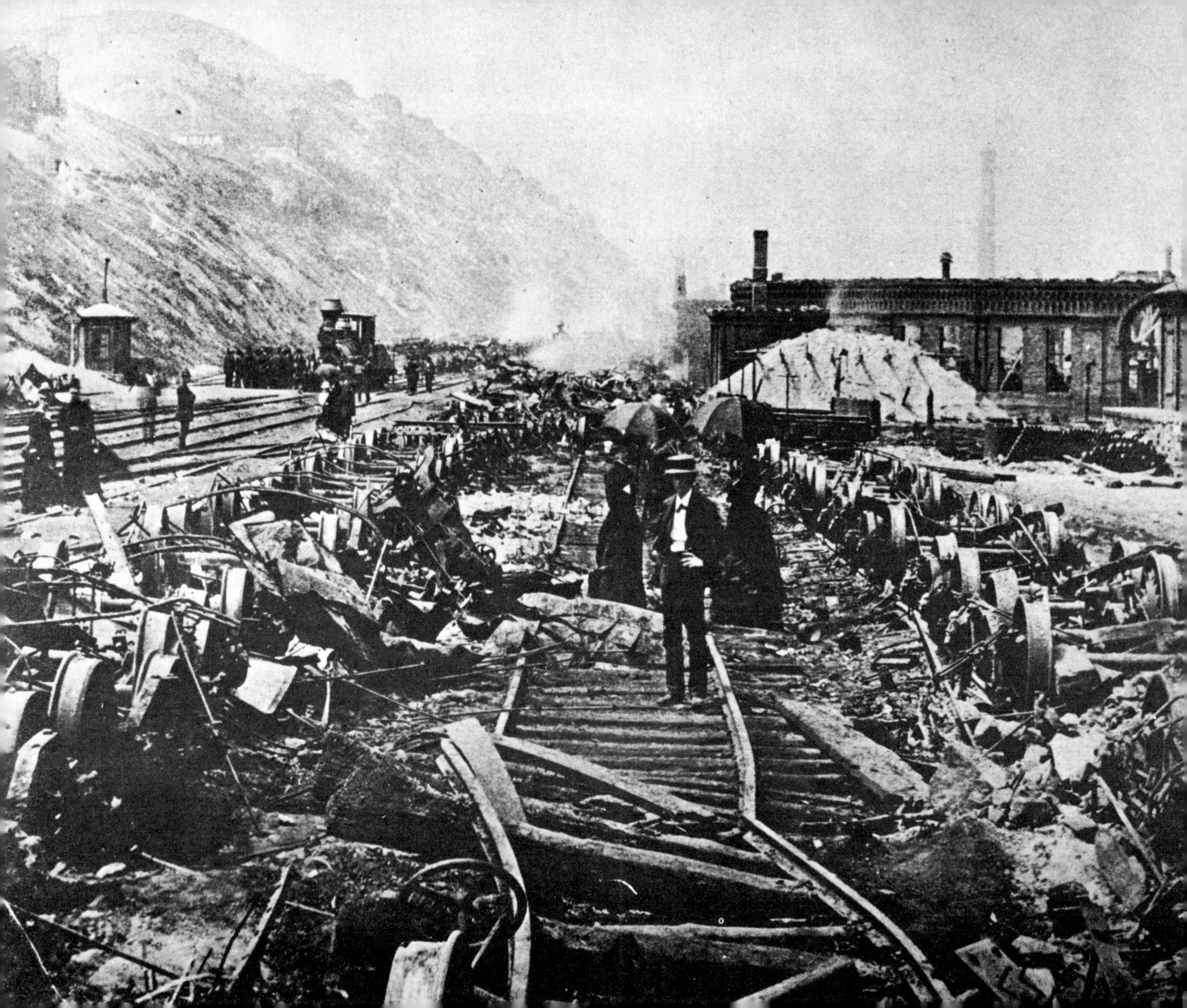

Urban violence is nothing new to America, as this illustration of Pittsburgh's railroad yards shortly after the riots of 1877 makes clear. The hundreds of burnt boxcars and the gutted shell of the roundhouse give mute testimony to the intensity of the hostility between workers and owners.

course with the help of great natural resources—solved the problem of enabling labor and capital to live together in political harmony, and that this was the one country in which there was no proletariat and no dangerous class, and in which the manners as well as legislation effectually prevented the formation of one. That the occurrences of the last fortnight will do, and have done, much to shake or destroy this faith, and that whatever weakens it weakens also the fondly-cherished hopes of many millions about the future of the race, there is unhappily little question. We have had what appears a widespread rising, not against political oppression or unpopular government, but against society itself. What is most curious about it is that it has probably taken people here nearly as much by surprise as people in Europe. The optimism in which most Americans are carefully trained, and which the experience of life justifies to the industrious, energetic and provident, combined with the long-settled political habit of considering riotous poor as the products of a monarchy and aristocracy, and impossible in the absence of "down-trodden masses," has concealed from most of the well-to-do and intelligent classes of the population the profound changes which have during the last thirty years been wrought in the composition and character of the population, especially in the great cities. Vast additions have been made to it within that period, to whom American political and social ideals appeal but faintly, if at all, and who carry in their very blood traditions which give universal suffrage an air of menace to many of the things which civilized men hold most dear. So complete has this illusion been that up to the day of the outbreak at Martinsburg thousands, even of the most reflective class, were gradually ridding themselves of the belief that force would be much longer necessary, or, indeed, was now necessary in the work of government....

II

Police and Militia Inadequate

Another illusion which the riots have dispelled is that the means provided by the several States for the protection of life and property, in the shape of police and militia, are at all adequate. Riots on the scale on which they have taken place during the past fortnight put almost as much strain on the nerves and on the discipline of the force called on to suppress them as the operations of regular warfare. A lawful enemy forms an organization which keeps to itself in a defined position, and its attacks are controlled by rules with which men are more or less familiar, and dictated by motives which can be guessed, and the force of which can be weighed. A mob, on the other hand, is essentially irrational, and its conduct has all the fitfulness and incomprehensibleness of that of a wild beast, and is just as merciless and destructive. It requires, therefore, to be met by a coolness and cohesiveness, and a presence of mind, which are not often called for in actual campaigning. Nothing can supply these things but *the habit* of obedience—not simply intellectual readiness to obey, as part of a contract, but the habitual readiness to obey a particular man, produced by obeying him every day on all sorts of small matters, and the familiarity with his person and character which results from living under his orders. This regular troops have; this even the best militia has not and cannot have....

III

Protection of Order and Property

The kindest thing which can be done for the great multitudes of untaught men who have been received on these shores, and are daily arriving, and who are torn perhaps even more here than in Europe by wild desires and wilder dreams, is to show them promptly that society as here organized, on individual freedom of thought and action, is impregnable, and can be no more shaken that the order of nature. The most cruel thing is to let them suppose, even for one week, that if they had only chosen their time better, or had been better led or better armed, they would have succeeded in forcing it to capitulate. In what way better provision, in the shape of public force, should be made for its defence we have no space left to discuss, but that it will not do to be caught again as the rising at Martinsburg caught us; that it would be fatal to private and public credit and security to allow a state of things to subsist in which 8,000 or 9,000 day-laborers of the lowest class can suspend, even for a whole day, the traffic and industry of a great nation, merely as a means of extorting ten or twenty cents a day more wages from their employers, we presume everybody now sees. Means of prompt and effectual prevention—so plainly effectual that it will never need to be resorted to—must be provided, either by an increase of the standing army or some change in the organization of the militia which will improve its discipline and increase its mobility. There are, of course, other means of protection against labor-risings than physical ones, which ought not to be neglected, though we doubt if they can be made to produce much effect on the present generation. The exercise of greater watchfulness over their tongues by philanthropists, in devising schemes of social improvement, and in affecting to treat all things as open to discussion, and every question as having two sides, for purposes of legislation as well as for purposes of speculation, is one of them. Some of the talk about the laborer and his rights that we have listened to on the platform and in literature during the last fifteen years, and of the capacity even of the most grossly ignorant, such as the South Carolina field-hand, to reason upon and even manage the interests of a great community, has been enough, considering the sort of ears on which it now falls, to reduce our great manufacturing districts to the condition of the Pennsylvania mining regions, and put our very civilization in peril. Persons of humane tendencies ought to remember that we live in a world of stern realities, and that the blessings we enjoy have not been showered upon us like the rain from heaven. Our superiority to the Ashantees or the Kurds is not due to right thinking or right feeling only, but to the determined fight which the more enlightened part of the community has waged from generation to generation against the ignorance and brutality, now of one class and now of another. In trying to carry on the race to better things nobody is wholly right or wise. In all controversies there are wrongs on both sides, but most certainly the presumptions in the labor controversy have always been in favor of the sober, orderly, industrious, and prudent, who work and accumulate and bequeath. It is they who brought mankind out of the woods and caves, and keep them out; and all discussion which places them in a position of either moral or mental inferiority to those who contrive not only to own nothing, but to separate themselves from property-holders in feeling or interest, is mischievous as well as foolish, for it strikes a blow at the features of human character which raise man above the beasts.

A Social Prophet Foretells the Future
(1887)

By 1887 the problems of conflict between workingmen and employers had become so serious that many Americans feared that social revolution lay ahead. Not many persons recognized, however, the relationship between the growth of large-scale businesses and the growth of the labor organizations which were so often blamed for industrial strife. In his utopian novel, *Looking Backward,* published in 1887, reformer Edward Bellamy (1850–1898) asks what might happen if a nineteenth-century Bostonian (Mr. West) were to fall asleep and awake in the year 2000. His host in 2000, a Dr. Leete, serves as the spokesman for Bellamy's analysis of American society in the late 1800s.

From Edward Bellamy, *Looking Backward, 2000–1887* (Boston, 1926), pp. 49–58. Copyright © 1926 by Sylvester Baxter.

I

Life Styles of the Future

"It was in 1887 that you fell into this sleep, I think you said."

"Yes, May 30th, 1887."

My companion regarded me musingly for some moments. Then he observed, "And you tell me that even then there was no general recognition of the nature of the crisis which society was nearing? Of course, I fully credit your statement. The singular blindness of your contemporaries to the signs of the times is a phenomenon commented on by many of our historians, but few facts of history are more difficult for us to realize, so obvious and unmistakable as we look back seem the indications, which must also have come under your eyes, of the transformation about to come to pass. I should be interested, Mr. West, if you would give me a little more definite idea of the view which you and men of your grade of intellect took of the state and prospects of society in 1887. You must, at least, have realized that the widespread industrial and social troubles, and the underlying dissatisfaction of all classes with the inequalities of society, and the general misery of mankind, were portents of great changes of some sort."

"We did, indeed, fully realize that," I replied. "We felt that society was dragging anchor and in danger of going adrift. Whither it would drift nobody could say, but all feared the rocks."

"Nevertheless," said Dr. Leete, "the set of the current was perfectly perceptible if you had but taken pains to observe it, and it was not toward the rocks, but toward a deeper channel."

"We had a popular proverb," I replied, "that 'hindsight is better than foresight,' the force of which I shall now, no doubt, appreciate more fully than ever. All I can say is, that the prospect was such when I went into that long sleep that I should not have been surprised had I looked down from your house-top to-day on a heap of charred and moss-grown ruins instead of this glorious city."

Dr. Leete had listened to me with close attention and nodded thoughtfully as I finished speaking. "What you have said," he observed, "will be regarded as a most valuable vindication of Storiot, whose account of your era has been generally thought exaggerated in its picture of the gloom and confusion of men's minds. That a period of transition like that should be full of excitement and agitation was indeed to be looked for; but seeing how plain was the tendency of the forces in operation, it was natural to believe that hope rather than fear would have been the prevailing temper of the popular mind."

"You have not yet told me what was the answer to the riddle which you found," I said. "I am impatient to know by what contradiction of natural sequence the peace and prosperity which you now seem to enjoy could have been the outcome of an era like my own."

"Excuse me," replied my host, "but do you smoke?" It was not till our cigars were lighted and drawing well that he resumed. "Since you are in the humor to talk rather than to sleep, as I certainly am, perhaps I cannot do better than to try to give you enough idea of our modern industrial system to dissipate at least the impression that there is any mystery about the process of its evolution. The Bostonians of your day had the reputation of being great askers of questions, and I am going to show my descent by asking you one to begin with. What should you name as the most prominent feature of the labor troubles of your day?"

"Why, the strikes, of course," I replied.

"Exactly; but what made the strikes so formidable?"

"The great labor organizations."

"And what was the motive of these great organizations?"

"The workmen claimed they had to organize to get their rights from the big corporations," I replied.

"That is just it," said Dr. Leete; "the organization of labor and the strikes were an effect, merely, of the concentration of capital in greater masses than had ever been known before. Before this concentration began, while as yet commerce and industry were conducted by innumerable petty concerns with small capital, instead of a small number of great concerns with vast capital, the individual workman was relatively important and independent in his relations to the employer. Moreover, when a little capital or a new idea was enough to start a man in business for himself, workingmen were constantly becoming employers and there was no hard and fast line between the two classes. Labor unions were needless then, and general strikes out of the question. But when the era of small concerns with small capital was succeeded by that of the great aggregations of capital, all this was changed. The individual laborer, who had been relatively important to the small employer, was reduced to insignificance and powerlessness over against the great corporation, while at the same time the way upward to the grade of employer was closed to him. Self-defense drove him to union with his fellows.

"The records of the period show that the outcry against the concentration of capital was furious. Men believed that it threatened society with a form of tyranny more abhorrent than it had ever endured. They believed that the great corporations were preparing for them the yoke of a baser servitude than had ever been imposed on the race, servitude not to men but to soulless machines incapable of any motive but insatiable greed. Looking back, we cannot wonder at their desperation, for certainly humanity was never confronted with a fate more sordid and hideous than would have been the era of corporate tyranny which they anticipated.

"Meanwhile, without being in the smallest degree checked by the clamor against it, the absorption of business by ever larger monopolies continued. In the United States there was not, after the beginning of the last quarter of the century, any opportunity whatever for individual enterprise in any important field of industry, unless backed by a great capital. During the last decade of the century, such small businesses as still remained were fast-failing survivals of a past epoch, or mere parasites on the great corporations, or else existed in fields too small to attract the great capitalists. Small businesses, as far as they still remained, were reduced to the condition of rats and mice, living in holes and corners, and counting on evading notice for the enjoyment of existence. The railroads had gone on combining till a few great syndicates controlled every rail in the land. In manufactories, every important staple was controlled by a syndicate. These syndicates, pools, trusts, or whatever their name, fixed prices and crushed all competition except when combinations as vast as themselves arose. Then a struggle, resulting in a still greater consolidation, ensued. The great city bazaar crushed its country rivals with branch stores, and in the city itself absorbed its smaller rivals till the business of a whole quarter was concentrated under one roof, with a hundred former proprietors of shops serving as clerks. Having no business of his own to put his money in, the small capitalist, at the same time that he took service under the corporation, found no other investment for his money but its stocks and bonds, thus becoming doubly dependent upon it.

"The fact that the desperate popular opposition to the consolidation of business in a few powerful hands had no effect to check it proves that there must have been a strong economical reason for it. The small capitalists, with their innumerable petty concerns, had in fact yielded the field to the great aggregations of capital, because they belonged to a day of small things and were totally incompetent to the demands of an age of steam and telegraphs and the gigantic scale of its enterprises. To restore the former order of things, even if possible, would have involved returning to the day of stage-coaches. Oppressive and intolerable as was the regime of the great consolidations of capital, even its victims, while they cursed it, were forced to admit the prodigious increase of efficiency which had been imparted to the national industries, the vast economies effected by concentration of management and unity of organization, and to confess that since the new system had taken the place of the old the wealth of the world had increased at a rate before undreamed of. To be sure this vast increase had gone chiefly to make the rich richer, increasing the gap between them and the poor; but the fact remained that, as a means merely of producing wealth, capital had been proved efficient in proportion to its consolidation. The restoration of the old system with the subdivision of capital, if it were possible, might indeed bring back a greater equality of conditions, with more individual dignity and freedom, but it would be at the price of general poverty and the arrest of material progress.

II

Reforms of the Future

"Was there, then, no way of commanding the services of the mighty wealth-producing principle of consolidated capital without bowing down to a plutocracy like that of Carthage? As soon as men began to ask themselves these questions, they found the answer ready for them. The movement toward the conduct of business by larger and larger aggregations of capital, the tendency toward monopolies, which had been so desperately and vainly resisted, was recognized at last, in its true significance, as a process which only needed to complete its logical evolution to open a golden future to humanity.

"Early in the last century the evolution was completed by the final consolidation of the entire capital of the nation. The industry and commerce of the country, ceasing to be conducted by a set of irresponsible corporations and syndicates of private persons at their caprice and for their profit, were intrusted to a single syndicate representing the people, to be conducted in the common interest for the common profit. The nation, that is to say, organized as the one great business corporation in which all other corporations were absorbed; it became the one capitalist in the place of all other capitalists, the sole employer, the final monopoly in which all previous and lesser monopolies were swallowed up, a monopoly in the profits and economies of which all citizens shared. The epoch of trusts had ended in The Great Trust. In a word, the people of the United States concluded to assume the conduct of their own business, just as one hundred odd years before they had assumed the conduct of their own government, organizing now for industrial purposes on precisely the same grounds that they had then organized for political purposes. At last, strangely late in the world's history, the obvious fact was perceived that no business is so essentially the public business as the industry and commerce on which the people's livelihood depends, and that to entrust it to private persons to be managed for private profit is a folly similar in kind, though vastly greater in magnitude, to that of surrendering the functions of political government to kings and nobles to be conducted for their personal glorification."

"Such a stupendous change as you describe," said I, "did not, of course, take place without great bloodshed and terrible convulsions."

"On the contrary," replied Dr. Leete, "there was absolutely no violence. The change had been long foreseen. Public opinion had become fully ripe for it, and the whole mass of the people was behind it. There was no more possibility of opposing it by force than by argument. On the other hand the popular sentiment toward the great corporations and those identified with them had ceased to be one of bitterness, as they came to realize their necessity as a link, a transition phase, in the evolution of the true industrial system. The most violent foes of the great private monopolies were now forced to recognize how invaluable and indispensable had been their office in educating the people up to the point of assuming control of their own business. Fifty years before, the consolidation of the industries of the country under national control would have seemed a very daring experiment to the most sanguine. But by a series of object lessons, seen and studied by all men, the great corporations had taught the people an entirely new set of ideas on this subject. They had seen for many years syndicates handling revenues greater than those of states, and directing the labors of hundreds of thousands of men with an efficiency and economy unattainable in smaller operations. It had come to be recognized as an axiom that the larger the business the simpler the principles that can be applied to it; that, as the machine is truer than the hand, so the system, which in a great concern does the work of the master's eye in a small business, turns out more accurate results. Thus it came about that, thanks to the corporations themselves, when it was proposed that the nation should assume their functions, the suggestion implied nothing which seemed impracticable even to the timid. To be sure it was a step beyond any yet taken, a broader generalization, but the very fact that the nation would be the sole corporation in the field would, it was seen, relieve the undertaking of many difficulties with which the partial monopolies had contended."

The Justification of Concentrated Wealth (1902)

One of the most remarkable circumstances in American life of the late 1800s was the appearance of a large number of rich men who had gained their wealth in business. Some persons found this circumstance an inspiration; it revealed the promise of American life and offered models for young men to emulate. Others deplored the glaring contrasts between the very rich and the poor and argued that huge concentrations of wealth, in the hands of individuals or small groups, were making the United States a plutocracy, a country governed by the rich. William Graham Sumner (1840-1910), a professor at Yale University, explained in an article written in 1902 why he thought this concentration of wealth a good thing.

From Albert G. Keller and Maurice R. Davie, eds., *Essays of William Graham Sumner* (New Haven, 1934), Vol. II, pp. 163, 168-172. Copyright © 1934 by Yale University Press.

The concentration of wealth I understand to include the aggregation of wealth into large masses and its concentration under the control of a few. In this sense the concentration of wealth is indispensable to the successful execution of the tasks which devolve upon society in our time. Every task of society requires the employment of capital, and involves an economic problem in the form of the most expedient application of material means to ends. Two features most prominently distinguish the present age from all which have preceded it: first, the great scale on which all societal undertakings must be carried out; and second, the transcendent importance of competent management, that is, of the personal element in direction and control. . . .

It is a consequence of the principle just stated that at every point in the history of civilization it has always been necessary to concentrate capital in amounts large relatively to existing facts. In low civilization chiefs control what capital there is, and direct industry; they may be the full owners of all the wealth or only the representatives of a collective theory of ownership. This organization of industry was, at the time, the most efficient, and the tribes which had it prospered better than others. In the classical states with slavery and in the mediaeval states with serfdom, the great achievements which realized the utmost that the system was capable of were attained only where wealth was concentrated in productive enterprises in amounts, and under management, which were at the maximum of what the system and the possibilities of the time called for. If we could get rid of some of our notions about liberty and equality, and could lay aside this eighteenth century philosophy according to which human society is to be brought into a state of blessedness, we should get some insight into the might of the societal organization: what it does for us, and what it makes us do. Every day that passes brings us new phenomena of struggle and effort between parts of the societal organization. What do they all mean? They mean that all the individuals and groups are forced against each other in a ceaseless war of interests, by their selfish and mutual efforts to fulfill their career on earth within the conditions set for them by the state of the arts, the facts of the societal organization, and the current dogmas of world philosophy. As each must win his living, or his fortune, or keep his fortune, under these conditions, it is difficult to see what can be meant in the sphere of industrial or economic effort by a "free man." It is no wonder that we so often hear angry outcries about being "slaves" from persons who have had a little experience of the contrast between the current notions and the actual facts.

In fact, what we all need to do is to be taught by the facts in regard to the notions which we ought to adopt, instead of looking at the facts only in order to pass judgment on them and make up our minds how we will change them. If we are willing to be taught by the facts, then the phenomena of the concentration of wealth which we see about us will convince us that they are just what the situation calls for. They ought to be because they are, and because nothing else would serve the interests of society.

I am quite well aware that, in what I have said, I have not met the thoughts and feelings of people who are most troubled about the "concentration of wealth." I have tried to set forth the economic necessity for the concentration of wealth; and I maintain that this is the controlling consideration. Those who care most about the concentration of wealth are indifferent to this consideration; what strikes them most is the fact that there are some rich men. I will, therefore, try to show that this fact also is only another economic justification of the concentration of wealth.

I often see statements published, in which the objectors lay stress upon the great *inequalities* of fortune, and, having set forth the contrast between rich and poor, they rest their case. What law of nature, religion, ethics, or the state is violated by inequalities of fortune? The inequalities prove nothing. Others argue that great fortunes are won by privileges created by law and not by legitimate enterprise and ability. This statement is true, but it is entirely irrelevant; we have to discuss the concentration of wealth within the facts of the institutions, laws, usages, and customs which our ancestors have bequeathed to us and which we allow to stand. If it is proposed to change any of these parts of the societal order, that is a proper subject of discussion, but it is aside from the concentration of wealth. So long as tariffs, patents, etc., are part of the system in which we live, how can it be expected that people will not take advantage of them; what else are they for? As for franchises, a franchise is only an x until it has been developed. It never develops itself; it requires capital and skill to develop it. When the enterprise is in the full bloom of prosperity the objectors complain of it, as if the franchise, which never was anything but an empty place where something might be created, had been the completed enterprise. It is interesting to compare the exploitation of the telephone with that of the telegraph fifty years earlier. The latter was, in its day, a far more wonderful invention, but the time and labor required to render it generally available were far greater than what has been required for the telephone, and the fortunes which were won from the former were insignificant in comparison with those which have been won from the latter. Both the public and the promoters acted very differently in the two cases. In these later times promoters seize with avidity upon an enterprise which contains promise, and they push it with energy and ingenuity, while the public is receptive to "improvements"; hence the modern methods offer very great opportunities, and the rewards of those men who can "size up" a situation and develop its controlling elements with sagacity and good judgment are very great. It is well that they are so, because these rewards stimulate to the utmost all the ambitious and able men, and they make it certain that great and useful inventions will not long remain unexploited as they did formerly. Here comes, then, a new reaction on the economic system; new energy is infused into it, with hope and confidence. We could not spare it and keep up the air of contentment and enthusiastic cheerfulness which characterizes our society. No man can acquire a million without helping a million men to increase their little fortunes all the way down through all the social grades. In some points of view it is an error that we fix our attention so much upon the very rich and overlook the prosperous mass, but the compensating advantage is that the great successes stimulate emulation the most powerfully.

What matters it then that some millionaires are idle, or silly, or vulgar; that their ideas are sometimes futile and their plans grotesque, when they turn aside from money-making? How do they differ in this from any other class? The millionaires are a product of natural selection, acting on the whole body of men to pick out those who can meet the requirement of certain work to be done. In this respect they are just like the great statesmen, or scientific men, or military men. It is because they are thus selected that wealth—both their own and that intrusted to them—aggregates under their hands. Let one of them make a mistake and see how quickly the concentration gives way to dispersion. They may fairly be regarded as the naturally selected agents of society for certain work. They get high wages and live in luxury, but the bargain is a good one for society. There is the intensest competition for their place and occupation. This assures us that all who are competent for this function will be employed in it, so that the cost of it will be reduced to the lowest terms; and furthermore that the competitors will study the proper conduct to be observed in their occupation. This will bring discipline and the correction of arrogance and masterfulness.

ANDREW CARNEGIE AND THE GROWTH OF THE STEEL INDUSTRY

The boom in American iron and steel production in the late nineteenth century reveals a great deal about the process of industrialization as well as about Americans' attitudes toward related social changes. The materials themselves were symbolic. Iron, and increasingly steel, formed the rails, bridges, engines, machines, and buildings from which the new society was constructed. The mode of manufacture also symbolized the rapid technological changes of the era. The new Bessemer and open hearth processes revolutionized the manufacture of steel, making it possible to produce a strong, cheap material in large quantities.

Those who led these ventures in iron and steel were characteristic entrepreneurs of the era. Such leaders built personal empires in transportation, manufacturing, communications, and finance, making their own fortunes but risking them in the process, often displaying callousness and rapacity toward competitors and the public as well as boldness, shrewdness, and hard work. The iron and steel industry had its share of the great entrepreneurs, including the man who was both a poor immigrant boy who became wealthy, famous, and powerful, and a great capitalist who concerned himself with the social implications of wealth. This was Andrew Carnegie.

Growth in iron and steel production also was a symbol of the United States' rise to power as the leading industrial nation. Great Britain, where the Industrial Revolution had begun in the eighteenth century, had long led the world in producing iron and steel, but in the late nineteenth century first the United States and then Germany surpassed Britain in this field.

Finally, the iron and steel industry provides an excellent example of two important economic trends of the time. The first was the purchase or construction of facilities by a company which gave it control of all materials and processes from raw materials (in this case, iron ore, coal, and other minerals) to finished products. This was "vertical integration." The second was "horizontal integration," or the combination of competing producers through purchase or merger, so as to create an enterprise with vastly increased economic power, perhaps enough power to dominate the production, sales, pricing, and labor policies of a whole industry.

Combinations in other industries, such as oil, sugar, tobacco, and farm machinery, especially where combination led to the fixing of higher prices and discrimination against some users or buyers in favor of others, led to public protests and legislation to regulate the so-called "trusts." As will be seen in the following readings, the iron and steel industry never reached the point of concentration where one firm totally dominated it. However, the creation of the United States Steel Corporation in 1901, with Andrew Carnegie's company as its keystone, did give that firm so much power that the federal government tried—unsuccessfully—to break it up.

The Background of an Industrialist

Andrew Carnegie (1835–1919) was probably one of the best known of the great industrialists of the late nineteenth century. Soon after the Civil War he saw that steel would replace iron as a basic product in the American economy. Beginning in 1868, Carnegie and his partners built a steel empire which by 1900 produced the bulk of most steel products in the United States. Carnegie also saw himself as a public spokesman, and he wrote many articles on social and economic topics for popular magazines. In later life Carnegie became America's best-known philanthropist, giving millions of dollars, largely to educational institutions and for the establishment of public libraries. In the following selection, originally published in 1896, Carnegie offers an engaging version of his own childhood.

From Andrew Carnegie, "How I Served My Apprenticeship," in *The Gospel of Wealth and Other Timely Essays* (New York, 1933), pp. vii–ix, xi–xii, xiii, xiv, xvi–xix. Copyright © 1933 by Doubleday, Doran and Company.

I

Emigration to America

It is a great pleasure to tell how I served my apprenticeship as a business man. But there seems to be a question preceding this: Why

Andrew Carnegie was sixteen when he and his younger brother sat for this photograph. At the time he was a messenger boy in a Pittsburgh telegraph office.

did I become a business man? I am sure that I should never have selected a business career if I had been permitted to choose.

The eldest son of parents who were themselves poor, I had, fortunately, to begin to perform some useful work in the world while still very young in order to earn an honest livelihood, and was thus shown even in early boyhood that my duty was to assist my parents and, like them, become, as soon as possible, a bread-winner in the family. What I could get to do, not what I desired, was the question.

When I was born my father was a well-to-do master weaver in Dunfermline, Scotland. He owned no less than four damask-looms and employed apprentices. This was before the days of steam-factories for the manufacture of linen. A few large merchants took orders, and employed master weavers, such as my father, to weave the cloth, the merchants supplying the materials.

As the factory system developed hand-loom weaving naturally declined, and my father was one of the sufferers by the change. The first serious lesson of my life came to me one day when he had taken in the last of his work to the merchant, and returned to our little home greatly distressed because there was no more work for him to do. I was then just about ten years of age, but the lesson burned into my heart, and I resolved then that the wolf of poverty should be driven from our door some day, if I could do it.

The question of selling the old looms and starting for the United States came up in the family council, and I heard it discussed from day to day. It was finally resolved to take the plunge and join relatives already in Pittsburg. I well remember that neither father nor mother thought the change would be otherwise than a great sacrifice for them, but that "it would be better for the two boys."

In after life, if you can look back as I do and wonder at the complete surrender of their own desires which parents make for the good of their children, you must reverence their memories with feelings akin to worship.

On arriving in Allegheny City (there were four of us: father, mother, my younger brother, and myself) my father entered a cotton factory. I soon followed, and served as a "bobbin-boy," and this is how I began my preparation for subsequent apprenticeship as a business man. I received one dollar and twenty cents a week, and was then just about twelve years old.

I cannot tell you how proud I was when I received my first week's own earnings. One dollar and twenty cents made by myself and given to me because I had been of some use in the world! No longer entirely dependent upon my parents, but at last admitted to the family partnership as a contributing member and able to help them! I think this makes a man out of a boy sooner than almost anything else, and a real man, too, if there be any germ of true manhood in him. It is everything to feel that you are useful.

I have had to deal with great sums. Many millions of dollars have since passed through my hands. But the genuine satisfaction I had from that one dollar and twenty cents outweighs any subsequent pleasure in money-getting. It was the direct reward of honest, manual labor; it represented a week of very hard work—so hard that, but for the aim and end which sanctified it, slavery might not be much too strong a term to describe it.

For a lad of twelve to rise and breakfast every morning, except the blessed Sunday morning, and go into the streets and find his way to the factory and begin to work while it was still dark outside, and not be released until after darkness came again in the evening, forty minutes' interval only being allowed at noon, was a terrible task.

But I was young and had my dreams, and something within always told me that this would not, could not, should not last—I should some day get into a better position. Besides this, I felt myself no longer a mere boy, but quite a little man, and this made me happy....

It seems, nowadays, a matter of universal desire that poverty should be abolished. We should be quite willing to abolish luxury, but to abolish honest, industrious, self-denying poverty would be to destroy the soil upon which mankind produces the virtues which enable our race to reach a still higher civilization than it now possesses.

II

The Road to Success

I come now to the third step in my apprenticeship, for I had already taken two, as you see—the cotton factory and then the bobbin factory; and with the third—the third time is the chance, you know—deliverance came. I obtained a situation as messenger boy in the telegraph office of Pittsburg when I was fourteen. Here I entered a new world....

Having a sensitive ear for sound, I soon learned to take messages by the ear, which was then very uncommon—I think only two persons in the United States could then do it. Now every operator takes by ear, so easy is it to follow and do what any other boy can—if you only have to. This brought me into notice, and finally I became an operator, and received the, to me, enormous recompense of twenty-five dollars per month—three hundred dollars a year! . . .

The Pennsylvania Railroad shortly after this was completed to Pittsburg, and that genius, Thomas A. Scott, was its superintendent. He often came to the telegraph office to talk to his chief, the general superintendent, at Altoona, and I became known to him in this way.

When that great railway system put up a wire of its own, he asked me to be his clerk and operator; so I left the telegraph office—in which there is great danger that a young man may be permanently buried, as it were—and became connected with the railways.

The new appointment was accompanied by what was, to me, a tremendous increase of salary. It jumped from twenty-five to thirty-five dollars per month. Mr. Scott was then receiving one hundred and twenty-five dollars per month, and I used to wonder what on earth he could do with so much money. . . .

A very important incident in my life occurred when, one day in a train, a nice, farmer-looking gentleman approached me, saying that the conductor had told him I was connected with the Pennsylvania Railroad, and he would like to show me something. He pulled from a small green bag the model of the first sleeping-car. This was Mr. Woodruff, the inventor.

Its value struck me like a flash. I asked him to come to Altoona the following week, and he did so. Mr. Scott with his usual quickness, grasped the idea. A contract was made with Mr. Woodruff to put two trial cars on the Pennsylvania Railroad. Before leaving Altoona Mr. Woodruff came and offered me an interest in the venture, which I promptly accepted. But how I was to make my payments rather troubled me, for the cars were to be paid for in monthly instalments after delivery, and my first monthly payment was to be two hundred and seventeen dollars and a half.

I had not the money, and I did not see any way of getting it. But I finally decided to visit the local banker and ask him for a loan, pledging myself to repay at the rate of fifteen dollars per month. He promptly granted it. Never shall I forget his putting his arm over my shoulder, saying, "Oh, yes, Andy; you are all right!"

I then and there signed my first note. Proud day this; and surely now no one will dispute that I was becoming a "business man." I had signed my first note, and, most important of all,—for any fellow can sign a note,—I had found a banker willing to take it as "good."

My subsequent payments were made by the receipts from the sleeping-cars, and I really made my first considerable sum from this investment in the Woodruff Sleeping-car Company, which was afterwards absorbed by Mr. Pullman—a remarkable man whose name is now known over all the world.

Shortly after this I was appointed superintendent of the Pittsburg division, and returned to my dear old home, smoky Pittsburg. Wooden bridges were then used exclusively upon the railways, and the Pennsylvania Railroad was experimenting with a bridge built of cast-iron. I saw that wooden bridges would not do for the future, and organized a company in Pittsburg to build iron bridges.

Here again I had recourse to the bank, because my share of the capital was twelve hundred and fifty dollars, and I had not the money; but the bank lent it to me, and we began the Keystone Bridge Works, which proved a great success. This company built the first great bridge over the Ohio River, three hundred feet span, and has built many of the most important structures since.

This was my beginning in manufacturing; and from that start all our other works have grown, the profits of one building the other. My "apprenticeship" as a business man soon ended, for I resigned my position as an officer of the Pennsylvania Railroad Company to give exclusive attention to business.

I was no longer merely an official working for others upon a salary, but a full-fledged business man working upon my own account.

I never was quite reconciled to working for other people. At the most, the railway officer has to look forward to the enjoyment of a stated salary, and he has a great many people to please; even if he gets to be president, he has sometimes a board of directors who cannot know what is best to be done; and even if this board be satisfied, he has a board of stockholders to criticize him, and as the property is not his own he cannot manage it as he pleases.

I always liked the idea of being my own master, of manufacturing something and giving employment to many men. There is only one thing to think of manufacturing if you are a Pittsburger, for Pittsburg even then had asserted her supremacy as the "Iron City," the leading iron- and steel-manufacturing city in America.

So my indispensable and clever partners, who had been my boy companions, I am delighted to say, . . . began business, and still continue extending it to meet the ever-growing and ever-changing wants of our most progressive country, year after year.

Always we are hoping that we need expand no farther; yet ever we are finding that to stop expanding would be to fall behind; and even to-day the successive improvements and inventions follow each other so rapidly that we see just as much yet to be done as ever.

Reading 188

When the manufacturer of steel ceases to grow he begins to decay, so we must keep on extending. The result of all these developments is that three pounds of finished steel are now bought in Pittsburg for two cents, which is cheaper than anywhere else on the earth, and that our country has become the greatest producer of iron in the world.

And so ends the story of my apprenticeship and graduation as a business man.

The Characteristics of Industrial Leaders in the 1870s

Was Andrew Carnegie the rule or the exception? Those who wrote and spoke at the time treated him as an example of the openness of American society to the man of talent and energy, no matter what his social or national background. There were other examples of poor immigrants who won fame and fortune in this period of almost explosive economic growth. The commentators of the day, noting a shift of population from rural to urban areas, also tended to picture business leaders as boys who had left their farm homes to seek their fortunes in the city. The following reading offers some statistics about the actual characteristics of leaders in three key industries in the 1870s.

Reprinted by permission of the publishers from pp. 197, 202–203, "The American Industrial Elite of the 1870's" by Frances Gregory and Irene Neu in *Men in Business*, edited by William Miller. Cambridge, Mass.: Harvard University Press, Copyright, 1952, by the President and Fellows of Harvard College.

American Industrial Leaders of the 1870s in Textiles, Railroads and Steel

TABLE 1 THEIR REGION OF BIRTH

BIRTHPLACE*	TEXTILES	RAILROADS	STEEL	TOTAL
	%	%	%	%
New England	90	39	24	51
Middle Atlantic	1	40	50	29
East North Central	1	4	7	4
South	1	6	1	3
West	..	1	..	1
U.S., Unspecified	..	..	4	2
United States	93	90	86	90
Foreign	7	10	14	10
Total cases (= 100%)	87	80	80	247

*These are census regions. Combined in "South" are south Atlantic, south central, west south central, in "West" west north central, mountain, Pacific.

TABLE 2 THEIR FATHER'S OCCUPATION

OCCUPATION	TEXTILES	RAILROADS	STEEL	TOTAL
	%	%	%	%
Businessman	57	49	48	51
Professional	7	16	16	13
Farmer	19	31	27	25
Public Official	2	4	..	3
Worker	15	..	11	8
Total cases (= 100%)	67	70	57	194

TABLE 3 THE HIGHEST EDUCATIONAL LEVEL THEY ACHIEVED

EDUCATION	TEXTILES	RAILROADS	STEEL	TOTAL
	%	%	%	%
Grammar School	25	22	43	30
High School	31	48	20	33
College	44	30	37	37
Total cases (= 100%)	59	64	60	183

TABLE 4 THEIR AGE ON GOING TO WORK

AGE	TEXTILES	RAILROADS	STEEL	TOTAL
	%	%	%	%
15 or under	30	23	18	23
16–18	21	35	38	32
19 and over	49	42	44	45
Total cases (= 100%)	57	62	57	176

The Meaning of Steel in Industrial America

Steel provides the material framework for modern industrial society. In the following excerpt, Burton Hendrick, a biographer of Andrew Carnegie, vividly describes both the rapid expansion of the steel industry in the late 1800s and the impact of steel on crucial areas of the American economy.

From Burton J. Hendrick, *The Life of Andrew Carnegie* (New York, 1932), pp. 308-311, 312-313. Copyright © 1932 by Burton J. Hendrick. Subheadings added by the editors.

I

Rise of American Steel Production

Meanwhile, through these eventful eighteen eighties, the great steel age was coming into its own. Year by year the United States was playing a more important part in producing the metal that was directing the forces of the modern world. American steel, a "hothouse plant," as the English called it when Carnegie began his labors, was rapidly developing into the hardiest of growths. The revolution in the relative positions of America and Europe came so suddenly that it had virtually the character of an explosion. As recently as 1873 British steel makers had looked upon the United States chiefly as a dumping ground for a surplus output that could not be consumed at home or exported elsewhere. They even made a particular product, called "American rails," unfit for their own country and useful only on the ramshackle roads of the undeveloped prairie. Up to the early seventies American mills almost meekly accepted this inferiority. In 1875, however, the situation began to change. The great mineral resources of the Lake Superior fields, the able management that went into American mills, the skill of American workmen, above all, the market afforded by an expanding country, found expression in the growing proportions of the American steel trade. The progress of railroad building, which absorbed nearly the entire product of the steel mills in this early period, was the sufficient explanation. By 1885 the United States had a greater mileage than the whole of Europe. More than two-fifths of all the railroads in the world were found in the American Republic. A rich harvest, this, for European steel makers, but practically all the business fell into the lap of Carnegie and a half dozen other ironmasters. So sudden, almost ferocious, was the conquest, that British rivals were taken unaware. In the year 1881 the English works presented a melancholy spectacle. In most of them stood mountains of pig iron—unsold and unsaleable. These stores had been prepared for the American market. They advertised the news that America was making its own steel. Trade statistics for 1880 more emphatically forced the lesson home. In 1872, when Carnegie became actively interested, the United States produced 94,000 tons of Bessemer rails; in 1880 the output had grown to 954,000. America was making a greater tonnage than the land in which the steel rail had had its origin. The performance meant a revolution: the ultimate transference of economic power from the Old World to the New. A paper by Captain Jones, presented to the British Iron and Steel Institute in 1881, told the story in detail. In a little less than two months the two converters of the Edgar Thomson Works had turned out nearly 125,000 tons of steel ingots—about doubling the record of its largest English competitor. There was not a boastful word in the Captain's paper; he unfolded, with the utmost simplicity, the annals of the Edgar Thomson Works—the works which, for three years, from 1878 to 1881, had manufactured more steel than any of its rivals either in Britain or America. The genial Captain, at the end of his paper, acknowledged the debt of Americans to British scientists and inventors. "While your metallurgists," he said, "as well as those of France and Germany, have been devoting their time and talents to the discovery of new processes, we have swallowed the information so generously tendered through the printed reports of the Institute, and have selfishly devoted ourselves to beating you in output."

II

The Development of Products

Even while Captain Jones was presenting these statistics, new forces were at work that were ultimately to make insignificant the achievement he was describing. The time was approaching when the United States would manufacture not only more steel than any other country, but more than all the rest of the world combined. New uses were being discovered for this material, which Bessemer and his co-workers had hardly dreamed of. The fact was becoming plain that everything which had for centuries been made of iron could now be made more satisfactorily and more cheaply of steel. The needs of railroads still held the preeminent place. Trains were becoming longer, locomotives and cars larger,

Billowing clouds of black smoke symbolized economic prosperity to nineteenth century Americans. This sketch of Pittsburgh in 1871 shows the dismal conditions, but bustling activity, which industrial prosperity produced.

their capacity to transport the products of farms and factories consequently greater. Carnegie had himself played a conspicuous part in removing the wooden railroad bridges of the primitive day and replacing them with iron. Now iron bridges in their turn were being supplanted by steel. For a hundred other everyday uses—farming implements, machinery, tools, boiler plates, axles, shafts, wire, nails, screws, bolts—the ancient metal was giving place to the new. The world had marvelled when iron was substituted for wood in building ships; the innovation, however, proved short lived, for steel quickly took its place. The new American navy, an outcome of Cleveland's first administration, was built entirely of steel. The Western cowboys now began enclosing their rampageous herds with steel barbed wire; Southern planters were bundling their cotton bales with steel ties; farmers in the arid lands were irrigating their fields with the assistance of steel tubes and siphons; oil drillers were sending their wares to market through steel pipe lines; American tools, especially saws, all made of steel, were flooding the markets of the world; American business was transacted largely on steel typewriters—a discovery of the late seventies; and a considerable part of the nation had taken to coursing along the highways on lofty bi-

39

cycles, made of steel. Hardly a day passed that some new use for the all pervasive metal was not found.

But a utility more grandiose than all, a development that was to change the aspect of American cities, now made a tentative appearance. In one of his meetings with Gladstone the British statesman showed Carnegie a photograph that had aroused his curiosity. It pictured an office building under construction in an American city. The puzzling point was that the usual procedure had apparently been reversed; instead of extending the walls from the ground upward, the walls began several stories in the air and were descending to the ground. The upper half of the structure seemed to stand, almost unsupported, between earth and heaven, like a huge Mahomet's coffin. What kind of a topsy-turvy country was this whose praises Carnegie was always chanting? The explanation involved a considerable discourse on American architecture. American skyscrapers had indeed revolutionized the age-long principles of construction. From time immemorial the walls of buildings had supported the floors; in the monster that had aroused Gladstone's interest the floors supported the walls. Yet one simple fact explained the mystery; the walls played no essential function in the American system, all the serious labor being performed by a steel frame. . . .

The Home Insurance Building, designed by Mr. W. L. B. Jenney, was the parent of an enormous progeny—as distinctive an American contribution to architecture as is the Gothic to the architecture of medieval Europe. Though this aspiring edifice reared its height for ten stories, the walls at the bottom were no thicker than at the top. The external covering was actually not a wall at all—it performed no part, that is, in supporting the building. Mr. Jenney had contrived simply a huge cage of steel. The apparent walls were merely curtains, giving privacy and safety to the tenants and keeping out the rain and the cold. The monstrous thing was a kind of Eiffel Tower, enclosed in masonry. The circumstance that had so astonished Gladstone was therefore easily accounted for. As the steel floors and columns supported the gossamer brick work that masqueraded as walls, they could be put in place anywhere and at any time.

In this explanation Carnegie probably took more than an artistic satisfaction. The coming of the skyscraper was an important factor in his fortune. In the eighties the demand for steel rails diminished, chiefly because the fervent building of railroads that had marked the twenty years preceding 1885 began to slacken. The revelation of an entirely unexpected new outlet for steel products in construction thus further reinforced his position. The Homestead works, originally built for rolling rails, was transformed into a plant for fabricating other forms rapidly growing in demand; above all, for beams and girders needed by a new architectural epoch. The youthful Charles M. Schwab, placed at its head, began to roll immense quantities of structural shapes—to perform the same services for the modern American city that his mentor, Captain Jones, had performed for American railroads. The very first skyscraper—the Home Insurance Building referred to above—was, in its essential iron and steel, manufactured in the Homestead mill. The contract originally called for iron. When the sixth floor was reached Mr. Jenney, the architect, received a letter from Carnegie, Phipps & Co., suggesting that the remaining stories be made of steel. The advice was adopted and so it stands today. For this pioneer, started in May, 1884, and finished in the fall of 1885, is still in existence and as sturdy at the present time as when it was opened. The prophecies made by the fearful—that it would collapse in a hard storm, that its metal skeleton would waste away with rust, that a new physical horror, electrolysis, would devour its vitals—have been disproved. Some day—for in America even skyscrapers are not immortal—it will probably be taken down. When that hour comes, every beam and girder and column recovered from the encasing brick and mortar will be found to bear, deeply indented in steel, the word "Carnegie."

Competition in the Steel Industry (1897)

By the 1890s Carnegie Steel Company was not the only steel company in America, but it was the largest. If a nineteenth-century businessman, such as Andrew Carnegie, triumphed in the fierce competitive business struggles of the period, he usually took great pride in his achievement. Nevertheless, many businessmen quickly abandoned their love of competition as soon as other companies drove down the price of a product to the point where it threatened to reduce profits for them. The following "pool agreement" is an example of what a number of steel companies did when they were faced with competition in the sale of a particular steel product—the structural steel I-beam.

From U.S. House of Representatives, *Hearings Before the Committee on Investigation of United States Steel Corporation* (Washington, D.C., 1911), Vol. III, p. 1813.

The Creation of the United States Steel Corporation (1901)

This agreement, made and entered into this 1st day of January, 1897, by and between the Passaic Rolling Mill Co., Pottsville Iron & Steel Co., A. & P. Roberts Co., Cambria Iron Co., Phoenix Iron Co., New Jersey Steel & Iron Co., Universal Construction Co., the Carnegie Steel Co. (Ltd.), Cleveland Rolling Mill Co., Jones & Laughlin Steel Co. (Ltd.).

Witnesseth that the above said parties have mutually agreed to and with each other to form an association to be known as the Structural Steel Association of the United States.

First. Each of the above parties named, being manufacturers and sellers of steel I beams and channels of sizes not less than 3 inches in depth, shall, by reason of such manufacture and sale, be entitled to membership in this association, and each of the parties hereto shall be entitled to such portion of all sales by parties hereto of I beams and channels of sizes not less than 3 inches in depth (except I beams and channels for use in car construction and deck or bulb beams) as is allotted to it under the following table [1].

TABLE 1

	PERCENT
The Carnegie Steel Co. (Ltd.)	49 3/8
Jones & Laughlin (Ltd.)	12 7/8
A. & P. Roberts Co.	11 1/2
Passaic Rolling Mill Co.	6
Phoenix Iron Co.	5
Cambria Iron Co.	5
Universal Construction Co.	4 1/4
Pottsville Iron & Steel Co.	3
Cleveland Rolling Mill Co.	3
	100

The emergence of great combinations, controlling most of the production in many of America's major industries, was one of the most significant economic, social, and political facts of the era. Sometimes a combination consisted of separate companies controlled by a single group of trustees. The nickname "trust," applied to such a combination, was also used freely to describe combinations in which one company owned many others or in which many companies were merged into one giant corporation. The following selection from an official government report details the creation of a "trust" in the steel industry when the Carnegie Steel Company became a part of the first billion-dollar company, the United States Steel Corporation.

From U.S. Commissioner of Corporations, *Report on the Steel Industry*, Part I, (Washington, D.C., 1911), pp. 82–85, 99–101, 103–104. Subheadings added by the editors.

I
Reasons for Consolidation

While the failure of the various pools in the iron and steel trade to establish permanently effective control over the production and prices of iron and steel products was undoubtedly an important cause of outright consolidation as a surer method of restricting or eliminating competition, consolidation was not, however, resorted to for this purpose alone. The underlying causes of consolidation in the steel industry, which were substantially the same as those operating in other great industries, may be defined as follows:

1. The restriction of competition.
2. Integration; that is, the linking-up of productive processes through the acquisition, under one control, of raw materials and manufacturing plants (and in some cases transportation facilities), and through extensions and coordination of manufacturing processes.
3. The creation of a great amount of inflated securities.

The first of these causes, namely, the restriction or elimination of competition, was undoubtedly the most potent. . . .

The second cause, namely, the integration of industry (that is, the opportunity of securing economies and commercial advantages through larger and more highly coordinated enterprises), also had considerable influence in the formation of certain types of consolidation. This was especially true in the steel industry, where such integration has been introduced to an exceptional degree, extending from ownership and production of the primary raw materials to the manufacture of the finished product, and involving extraordinary improvements in methods of operation. . . .

The importance of . . . [the] stock-market factor in the consolidation movement, whether in the iron and steel industry or in other industries, is too often overlooked. Consolidation, while in large measure an outgrowth of technical and industrial conditions, was by no means exclusively so. Instead, there was frequently a marked reluctance on the part of owners to dispose of the businesses which they had built up, and in many cases the controlling inducement to sell out was the enormous price obtainable in the securities of these great consolidations.

The profits from this source were of two kinds—first, those made by the manufacturers who took stock in the new consolidations for the property or businesses which they transferred; and, second, those made by the promoters of these companies. In most cases the profit depended upon the issue and sale to the public of stocks and securities of a par value greatly in excess of the aggregate values of the assets of the consolidations thus formed; in other cases, the fact that a consolidation was so comprehensive as to give a substantial monopoly in a particular branch of the business made it possible for the former owners to realize a liberal profit by retaining the inflated securities thus created, and receiving the dividends paid thereon.

The huge "commissions," so called, obtained by the promoters of some of these concerns are discussed elsewhere. They frequently amounted to millions of dollars. Out of the proceeds of such stock commissions usually some organization expenses had to be met, but in the main these commissions were intended as compensation to the promoters of these consolidations. It should be noted that the size of these commissions frequently was fixed by the promoters themselves, since they determined the capitalization of the consolidated company.

II

Primary and Secondary Producers

The preceding discussion has shown that a remarkable condition had been reached in the iron and steel industry by the close of the year 1900. In the first place, the manufacture of crude and semifinished steel was largely in the hands of a comparatively few great concerns. The manufacture of several of the more finished lines, such as wire and wire products, tin plate, sheets, and tubes, moreover, had been substantially transferred to another group of consolidations, each of which with few exceptions had a more or less monopolistic position. These latter concerns were in great measure dependent upon the larger steel makers for a supply of their raw material, namely, semifinished steel. The larger steel concerns, on the other hand, were chiefly engaged in the manufacture of crude and semifinished steel or of heavier finished steel products, such as rails and structural material, which did not bring them directly in conflict with the group of concerns making the more elaborated products.

The relationships of the companies in these two groups to one another have already been partly indicated in the preceding discussion. These relationships had, however, such a vital bearing upon the organization of the Steel Corporation that they may be briefly summarized at this point.

The large consolidations which were subsequently merged into the Steel Corporation may be conveniently grouped in two classes—(1) the "primary group," or those making chiefly semifinished steel and heavy steel products, and (2) the "secondary group," consisting of those making lighter and more elaborated products.

The primary group of companies comprised the Carnegie Company, the Federal Steel Company, and the National Steel Company. Of these, the Carnegie Company was, of course, the most important. As already shown, it was a highly integrated concern, completely independent as to the production of its raw materials, and also pig iron and crude steel. It also had very important transportation facilities. The company, however, depended to a considerable extent for the marketing of its semifinished steel products (which comprised a very large portion of its total output) upon other steel manufacturers, who used such semifinished steel as their raw material. Some of its most important customers, in fact, were concerns in the second group of consolidations just noted. . . .

The principal concerns in the secondary group were the American Steel and Wire Company, the National Tube Company, the American Tin Plate Company, the American Sheet Steel Company, the American Steel Hoop Company, and the American Bridge Company.

The American Steel and Wire Company, it will be remembered, originally had a substantially monopolistic control of the production of wire products in the United States. Its position with respect to its chief raw material, namely, steel billets, was not nearly so strong. Instead it purchased a very large proportion of its billet requirements. While the subsequent efforts of the company toward further integration through purchases of iron-ore and coking-coal properties, and the erection of additional blast furnaces, considerably improved its position in this respect, nevertheless it was not thoroughly integrated in 1900, and was still very largely dependent upon the large steel makers. However, it contemplated carrying the processes of integration much further by the erection of additional steel works of large capacity. . . .

III

From Carnegie Steel to U.S. Steel

In the year 1900 the prospective loss of business for the great steel-producing companies, accompanied by a slackened activity in the trade, developed an exceedingly acute situation. The Federal Steel Company prepared to take up the manufacture of several lines of finished products, namely, structural material, universal plates, and tubes. In the summer of the same year it was reported that the Carnegie Company would go into the manufacture of wire rods on an extensive scale, thus "invading" the territory of the secondary group. This action was generally regarded as a blow at the American Steel and Wire Company, which had just threatened to erect additional blast furnaces and a large steel plant. Reports of further important plans of the Carnegie Company for extending its lines of production of finished products were current during the year 1900, and early in 1901 the definite announcement was made that the company was about to take up the manufacture of steel tubes in a new plant of enormous capacity, to be constructed at Conneaut Harbor, Ohio. This announcement, moreover, was made in such a way that it could be interpreted only as a declaration on the part of the Carnegie interests that they did not propose to submit idly to the loss of tonnage threatened by the plans of some of the larger consolidations making finished products, which previously had been among their largest customers. Not only was this the interpretation of the company's move placed on it by the trade, but it was expressly stated in a newspaper article as representing the attitude of Mr. Carnegie himself. This will be seen from the following excerpt:

> Mr. Carnegie's personal view of the situation may be authoritatively stated as follows: . . .
> The National Tube Company formerly obtained its steel billets from the Carnegie Company, but decided to erect blast furnaces and mills to supply itself. Naturally, the Carnegie Company then announced that it would be forced to erect mills to finish its own product into tubes.*

The intention of the Carnegie interests to extend their manufacture of finished lines had, indeed, been contemplated for some time. In an interview in the London Iron and Coal Trades Review of May 12, 1899, Mr. Carnegie was quoted as saying:

> Yes, we have been erecting several new departments, including what I believe will be the largest axle factory in the world. Why, it may be asked, should steel makers make plates for other firms to work up into boilers, when they can manufacture the boilers themselves? Or beams and girders for bridges, when they can turn out and build up the completed article, or plates for pipes when they can make the pipes? I think the next step to be taken by steel makers will be to furnish finished articles ready for use. In the future the most successful firms will be those that go the farthest in this direction.

Furthermore this proposed entrance of the Carnegie concern into the tube business was regarded by the trade as the forerunner of still further projects. In fact, the announcement was almost immediately followed by a well-defined report that the Carnegie Company would at once invade the field of the American Sheet Steel Company by the erection of a sheet plant at Duquesne, capable of turning out 60,000 tons of sheets annually. Simultaneously there were reports that the company would speedily take up the manufacture of tin plate on a large scale.

This unmistakable evidence of an aggressive policy of retaliation on the part of the Carnegie concern, accompanied as it was by the important extensions into the manufacture of finished articles announced by the Federal Steel Company, revealed sharply the trend of the existing conditions, and naturally had a very disquieting effect in the trade and in financial circles. Both the trade journals and the financial press were filled with articles to the effect that a "battle of the giants" in the steel industry was at hand.

In such a contest it was apparent to all that the Carnegie Company, while likely at first to lose some business, might be expected in the long run to maintain, and even to increase, its dominating position in the industry. Its long established business, the modern character of its plants, its efficient technical and commercial organization, as well as its strong financial position, made it easily superior to any of its competitors. It had a distinct advantage in all these respects over even the Federal Steel Company, which was its largest rival, but whose plants were for the most part less modern and also widely separated geographically. There was no question that if the Carnegie Company, with its unlimited means and efficient organization, went into the manufacture of wire, tubes, sheets, or tin plate it would be more than able to hold its own against the respective large consolidations which produced those products, and which in their efforts to monopolize the business had been constrained to include in their respective organizations many plants of inferior character.

*New York Evening Post, January 21, 1901.

IV

The Financial Situation

This unsettled trade situation was aggravated because of the importance which the securities of several of these steel concerns had assumed in the stock market. A period of violent competition in the steel industry would inevitably have been followed by a great decline in the value of these securities. A still more important matter was that the financial backers of some of these steel concerns had extensive commitments in other directions, which might be jeopardized by such an acute struggle in the steel industry. From the standpoint of these financiers, therefore, the situation presented at once a great danger and a great opportunity.

From a financial point of view there were four important steel groups, which were more or less distinct, namely, the Morgan group, the Moore group, and the Carnegie and the Rockefeller interests. . . .

It is evident, therefore, that, both from the point of view of the iron and steel industry and that of the stock market, the threatened outbreak of violent competition between these rival interests involved serious consequences. It might have meant the sudden termination of the extraordinary period of speculative activity and profit. On the other hand, an averting of this conflict by a merger of the various great consolidations, if successfully financed, would be a tremendous "bull" argument. It would afford its promoters an opportunity for enormous stock-market profits through the sale of its securities. The advantages to these interests, through the concentration of profits in different stages of the industry under a single control, would also be considerable, and there was undoubtedly some advantage to be gained through the further integration which such a consolidation would render possible.

It was clear to everyone that no consolidation of this sort could be made successful unless it included the Carnegie Company, which was the most powerful factor in the situation, which had long been noted for its aggressive tactics, and which, as above shown, had precipitated this crisis. Moreover, there can be little doubt that many interests in the steel industry regarded Mr. Carnegie's personal influence as a menace to their success, and desired to secure his retirement from the trade. At the same time the enormous earning power of the Carnegie concern would be an exceedingly important consideration both in the profits of the new company and also in facilitating the flotation of its securities.

The primary solution of the situation, therefore, from the standpoint of these interests, was to buy out Mr. Carnegie. Mr. Carnegie's well-known willingness to sell made the problem largely one of terms. Negotiations were promptly undertaken and speedily concluded by arranging to take over his large interest in his concern in exchange for bonds of the new consolidation. On March 2, 1901, announcement was made by J. P. Morgan & Co., as bankers, that arrangements had been completed for the organization of the United States Steel Corporation to acquire control of the following concerns: Carnegie Company (of New Jersey), Federal Steel Company, American Steel and Wire Company, National Tube Company, National Steel Company, American Tin Plate Company, American Steel Hoop Company, and American Sheet Steel Company.

The preliminary incorporation papers of the new company, under New Jersey laws, had already been taken out. The terms offered the constituent companies . . . were speedily accepted by a great majority of the stockholders of these concerns, and, on April 1, 1901, within a very few weeks after the first serious intimation that negotiations were under way the United States Steel Corporation was definitely launched and in actual operation. The authorized capital stock was $1,100,000,000, equally divided between preferred and common shares. In addition there was a bond issue of $304,000,000 (exclusive of underlying indebtedness aggregating approximately $81,000,000, this including sundry mortgages and purchase-money obligations). About $425,000,000 of each class of stock and all of the bonds were issued for the companies named and for other purposes. Very soon after its organization the Corporation made three further important acquisitions, namely, the Lake Superior Consolidated Iron Mines, the Bessemer Steamship Company, and the American Bridge Company. It also acquired a one-sixth interest in the Oliver Iron Mining Company and the Pittsburg Steamship Company, the other five-sixths having been secured in the purchase of the Carnegie Company. During the following summer it purchased the Shelby Steel Tube Company. As a result of these acquisitions its issue of stock was increased to over $500,000,000 of each class, giving it an issued capitalization in stock alone of more than $1,000,000,000.

Thus, the threatened conflict in the steel industry was averted, while, as shown later, an unprecedented profit was reaped by the organization syndicate.

Reading 192

Competition and Steel Prices (1886-1910)

Table 1 gives the United States Steel Corporation's share of the market of various iron and steel products, and Table 2 indicates the average prices charged for these products from 1886 to 1910.

I. From U.S. Commissioner of Corporations, *Report on the Steel Industry*, Part I (Washington, D.C., 1911), p. 56; II. From U.S. House of Representatives, *Hearings Before the Committee on Investigation of United States Steel Corporation* (Washington, D.C., 1912), IV, pp. 2627-2628, 2633.

TABLE 1 PROPORTION OF OUTPUT OF SELECTED IRON AND STEEL PRODUCTS PRODUCED BY UNITED STATES STEEL CORPORATION AND BY INDEPENDENT COMPANIES IN 1901 AND 1910.

PRODUCTS	UNITED STATES STEEL CORPORATION'S PERCENTAGES 1901	1910	INDEPENDENT COMPANIES' PERCENTAGES 1901	1910
Pig iron	43.2	43.4	56.8	56.6
Steel ingots and castings*	65.7	54.3	34.3	45.7
Rails	59.8	58.9	40.2	41.1
Black plate produced in tin mills	79.8	52.9	20.2	47.1
Coated tin-mill products	73.1	61.1	26.9	38.9
Wire nails	68.1	55.5	31.9	44.5

*Steel ingots and castings were sold in the form of steel billets.

TABLE 2 PRICES OF SELECTED IRON AND STEEL PRODUCTS, 1886 to 1910.*

CALENDAR YEAR	PIG IRON [PER TON]	STEEL BILLETS [PER TON]	RAILS [PER TON]	WIRE NAILS [PER 100 LBS.]	TIN PLATE [PER 100 LBS.]
1886	$18.96	$31.75	$34.50	$ —	$ —
1887	21.37	32.55	37.08	3.15	—
1888	17.38	28.78	29.83	2.55	—
1889	18.00	29.45	29.25	2.49	—
1890	18.85	30.32	31.75	2.51	—
1891	15.95	25.32	29.92	2.04	—
1892	14.37	23.63	30.00	1.70	—
1893	12.87	20.44	28.12	1.49	—
1894	11.38	16.58	24.00	1.11	—
1895	12.72	18.48	24.33	1.69	—
1896	12.14	18.83	28.00	2.50	—
1897	10.13	15.08	19.58	1.45	—
1898	10.33	15.31	17.62	1.45	—
1899	19.03	31.12	28.12	2.60	4.06
1900	19.49	25.06	32.29	2.76	4.47
1901	15.93	24.13	27.33	2.41	4.00
1902	20.67	30.57	28.00	2.15	3.93
1903	18.98	27.91	28.00	2.13	3.74
1904	13.76	22.18	28.00	1.96	3.41
1905	16.36	24.03	28.00	1.93	3.50
1906	19.54	27.45	28.00	1.98	3.69
1907	22.84	29.25	28.00	2.18	3.90
1908	17.07	26.31	28.00	2.17	3.70
1909	17.41	24.62	28.00	2.00	3.50
1910	17.19	25.38	28.00	1.96	3.60

*U.S. House of Representatives, *Hearings Before the Committee on Investigation of United States Steel Corporation* (Washington, 1912), IV, 2627-2628, 2633.

The Steel Industry in the Twentieth Century

In 1911 a committee of the United States Congress began an investigation of the United States Steel Corporation. For more than a year the committee heard testimony from scores of witnesses, many of them from the upper echelons of the steel business. In August 1911, Charles Schwab (1862–1939), president of the Bethlehem Steel Company, appeared before the committee and offered his interpretation of both the past and the future of the steel industry. A few months later Andrew Carnegie who had retired from the steel business when he sold out in 1901, offered the committee his views on essentially the same question.

From U.S. House of Representatives, *Hearings Before the Committee on Investigation of the United States Steel Corporation* (Washington, D.C., 1911–1912), II, pp. 1289–1290, 1295; III, pp. 2416–2419.

I

Statement of Charles Schwab

[The Chairman] That was one of the things which made our friend, Mr. Andrew Carnegie, persona non grata with the older steel concerns, was it not—that he would sell and keep his mills running?

[Mr. Schwab] That is true; and I want to say that the policy of the Carnegie Co. for many years was to have nothing to do with any agreements of that sort,* but the conditions were somewhat different. We had a position to win in the steel trade then. There were older companies than the Carnegie Co., and longer established, like the Pennsylvania Steel, Federal Steel, Lackawanna Steel, Cambria Steel, Jones & Laughlin. Those were all older concerns. The policy of the Carnegie Co. was to demonstrate its position and to win a position for itself. And it is my belief, if Mr. Carnegie were in business now with his plant established, and his position established, and with the possibility that there is not likely to be any more great steel plants, any more than there is likely to be any other great trunk-line railroad, that there will be development and extension of the present businesses, it is my opinion his policy would have been somewhat different, and that he would not have made the great sacrifices in prices he then made.

[The Chairman] The other old companies—Jones & Laughlin, Lackawanna, Cambria, and the rest of them—had been in business for years and years, had they not?

[Mr. Schwab] Yes.

[The Chairman] And it was a safe, profitable business?

[Mr. Schwab] I will not say that. I think it is a very risky business.

[The Chairman] But these other concerns had managed to escape and accumulate some money?

[Mr. Schwab] They escaped, but many did not.

[The Chairman] And they would hitch up and jog along in an easy way, and Carnegie, with his talent and with the splendid personnel of his able lieutenants, among whom is the present president of the Bethlehem Steel Co.—

[Mr. Schwab] Thank you.

[The Chairman] Carnegie would improve methods, discover new ways of cheapening and facilitating the manufacture of steel by exhausting the ingenuity of the alchemist, and the chemist, and of the civil engineer, and by firing the ambition of young, aspiring men who

---

*Schwab is here referring to pool agreements, an example of which is given in Reading 190—Eds.

came into the business and who were given a share in it —and Carnegie dealt rather in men than in money when he wanted to increase his capitalization, did he not?

[Mr. Schwab] Yes.

[The Chairman] He took these strong, able men into the concern in preference to a man with any amount of money who wanted to buy shares; isn't that true?

[Mr. Schwab] Absolutely.

[The Chairman] And it was this strictly American, audacious, capable, aspiring set of men in the steel industry, who were like a bull in a china shop, and who kept the steel business, as you say, in an uncertain state, and enabled Carnegie to smash agreements to keep up the sharpest kind of competition and to develop the steel industry to the highest state of perfection known in the known world at the time he retired from business; is not that true?

[Mr. Schwab] Mr. Chairman, that is true. But I want to point out to you one radical difference as between that time and the present. I will illustrate it best by speaking of rails. At the time Mr. Carnegie went into the steel business it was costing about $60 to make a ton of rails, probably more. To-day, let us say, it costs $21 or $22 a ton. In those days there was a very great opportunity for the alchemist and the chemist and the civil engineer which does not exist to-day. The most skillful set of men money could buy could not cheapen the production of a ton of rails a dollar a ton to-day, with unlimited capital for its development. Now, that is the difference between Mr. Carnegie's policy in those days and the policy that, to my mind, ought to be adopted to-day. The day has gone by when these developments, which were so noteworthy and radical, can be made. There is little difference in the cost of manufacture as between different works to-day. Do I make that clear, Mr. Chairman?

[The Chairman] Yes. You mean the industry has reached a state of such perfection—

[Mr. Schwab (interposing)] Yes; that it is not possible. It would not be possible for Mr. Carnegie to-day, for example, to adopt successfully the methods of 20 years ago.

[The Chairman] I would not discuss so scientific a question with so able a scientist.

[Mr. Schwab] I thank you. You pay so many compliments I am inclined to be confidential.

[The Chairman] If there is anything on earth I am seriously desirous of doing, it is to get the confidence of the witness.

[Mr. Schwab] You have it.

[The Chairman] Because there is a great deal you know that I want to find out.

[Mr. Schwab] Yes. . . .

[Mr. Littleton] With such control as you speak of, could you avoid—in a very large sense—establishing the prices with such control?

[Mr. Schwab] The prices of iron and steel have naturally been established. I mean not necessarily by any agreement or by anything or that sort, but, if you will let me illustrate it, for example, by rails, which are the best known steel product, I do not think the price of rails has been changed for 12 or 15 years. It has been regarded by most manufacturers as a fair price. It is regarded by some as being too low; but as a general rule it is an established price for rails. No one ever thinks of questioning that price, and I have never been asked in our concern to make a different price. I would hesitate very much about changing the price, even in a small amount, because I feel that the establishment in Chicago, or elsewhere, would be obliged to do the same; and it is so with most of the great steel commodities to-day, that they have an established price that the people do not expect you to vary from. Indeed, in my experience, most of the buyers would rather buy their steel under those conditions than in open, destructive competition.

[Mr. Littleton] Who fixed the price at $28 a ton?

[Mr. Schwab] I do not know. I can not tell you, except that it has probably been going on for 15 years. I think that $28 a ton was probably fixed by a gentleman's agreement 15 years ago.

[Mr. Littleton] And it has perpetuated itself by custom?

[Mr. Schwab] By custom and usage. I can not be certain of that, but I think that is the case.

[Mr. Littleton] If it was fixed in that way and has perpetuated itself in that way, is it based upon this control or is it within your ability to keep it at $28 a ton?

[Mr. Schwab] I do not think there is any effort to keep it there. I think it naturally keeps itself there. . . .

II

Statement of Andrew Carnegie

[Mr. Beall] Mr. Carnegie, you were actively connected with the iron and steel business for about 40 years?

[Mr. Carnegie] Yes, Mr. Beall.

[Mr. Beall] You found it at the beginning of small proportions? You left it with the business of this country dominating the business of the world almost?

[Mr. Carnegie] In steel.

[Mr. Beall] You found them making iron only at the beginning?

[Mr. Carnegie] Yes, sir.

[Mr. Beall] In the early years of this business, Mr. Carnegie, it was thoroughly disintegrated, was it not; that is, one concern owned the ores and was mining them, another was carrying the ores to the furnaces, another was producing the iron and steel in its crudest form and selling that to some other concern that would refine it and make the finished product? Years went by and the process of integration occurred. When you left the field you would find the same concern owning the ores, transporting them to the mills, manufacturing the iron and steel in the crude form, and then on up to the highly finished product?

[Mr. Carnegie] Admirably stated. . . .

[Mr. Beall] Is it not a fact that when the business in any line gets into the hands of great combinations or great corporations, there is not the same tendency to development and to improvement that there would be if it were divided out into a number of hands?

[Mr. Carnegie] There I can speak my opinions. You are on ground where I stand.

[Mr. Beall] I would be glad to have your opinion.

[Mr. Carnegie] I do not believe that corporations can manage a business like partners. When we were partners I felt we could run around corporations. Take 35 men, young men, each one interested in a department and watching the spigot from which there might be a leak, and [you have] the Carnegie Steel Co. organization, of which I have spoken so much, as Mr. Perkins says—Mr. Perkins told me, not long ago, "Mr. Carnegie, I heard you make one statement once that I thought was positively foolish; I did not understand you; but I recognize now that you were right."

It is the same thing with a man who owns the land he tills. Take Europe to-day; take Britain; the farmers lease the land. Go to Iowa, where I went, when I was a young man, on a holiday, and there I saw the homes of triumphant democracy, every little bit of ground owned by a man and tilled by him. Great Caesar! What can a big farm do? Look at the failures of those enormous farms they have there. They were given up. They commenced to do farming on a large scale. The man that owns the ground he tills is the man equal of any other in this land of triumphant democracy, and I have loved Iowa ever since I went through there and saw what it meant.

It is the same in manufacturing. The best corporations that ever were formed will be beaten by such an organization as we had in the Carnegie Steel Co.

[Mr. Beall] Then I would judge that it would be your opinion that the progress would be more rapid if, instead of having one great corporation that is dominating any line of industry, you had three or four corporations of a fair sized capital, engaged in that production?

[Mr. Carnegie] I would not say that the greater corporation would not equal the smaller corporation. What I wish to say is that the corporation is not in it with the partners managing their own business. For instance, I want a great contract for rails. I remove to New York. Sidney Dillon, of the Union Pacific, was a personal friend of mine. Huntington was a friend. Dear Butler Duncan, that called on me the other day, was a friend. Those and other men were presidents of railroads. The Union Pacific had advertised for 70,000 tons of rails, the biggest order that had been given. It was to be decided at Omaha, and all my competitors, all the agents of those corporations, were out at Omaha, and those bids were to be opened. I walked over to Sidney Dillon. I was able to do the Union Pacific a favor once, and I did it, and I was elected a director in the Union Pacific, and I got them a loan on securities in Philadelphia, I think, for $600,000, and they elected Mr. George M. Pullman and myself directors. I had done him a favor, and I said, "Mr. Dillon, you have had some Carnegie rails. What is the report?" "Oh, first class; splendid rails, Mr. Carnegie." "I want you to do this for me: Your people are out there bidding on 70,000 tons of rails. I ask you to give me those rails, and I will promise you to take the lowest price that is bid." "All right, Carnegie."

What is the use of a corporation with hired people fighting against that?

Take Butler Duncan, who is a fellow Scotsman. He would no more have given anybody a rail but me than anything in the world.

Take Huntington; you know C. P. Huntington. He was hard up very often. He was a great man, but had a great deal of paper out. I knew his things were good. When he wanted credit, I gave it to him. If you help a man through that way, what chance has any paid agent going to those men? It was absurd.

[Mr. Beall] I notice in your testimony—

[Mr. Carnegie (interposing)] Excuse me for being so personal, Mr. Beall, I can not explain these things to you except from my own personal experience.

[Mr. Beall] In your testimony before the Ways and Means Committee two years ago I find this statement:

"If you want to keep this country ahead in steel, you can not depend upon great combinations. In the nature of the case they become conservative."

[Mr. Carnegie] Quite true—great corporations. I have illustrated that to you; but we became ourselves something of, well, not a corporation. I do not think there ever was a steel company that resembled the Carnegie Steel Co. That is my frank opinion.

[Mr. Beall] I think that opinion is shared pretty generally, Mr. Carnegie.

[Mr. Carnegie] I went to New York to be at headquarters. I was there. When there was anything needed, we were there. We built the first overhead railway in New York. I got the contract for the great bridge. Take the president of a great corporation walking in to see these men, "Hello, who is this?" He is here to-day; where may he be to-morrow? Out of the State. He is an employee.

Take me going to these fellows as brother capitalists that had helped them and asking them to give me a preference, and it was good business for them to do it.

[Mr. Beall] In your experience in the steel business you went through a good many periods of pretty active and severe competition, did you not?

[Mr. Carnegie] I do not think—

[Mr. Beall] Fierce competition?

[Mr. Carnegie] Oh, no; not fearful competition.

[Mr. Beall] From 1880 to 1890 there was a good deal of competition in your business, was there not?

[Mr. Carnegie] Oh, yes; competition.

[Mr. Beall] From 1890 to 1900 there was pretty severe competition?

[Mr. Carnegie] Yes; certainly. But do you notice that the Carnegie Steel Co. was always making money?

[Mr. Beall] Is it not a fact that the existence of that keen competition was always a spur to the Carnegie Steel Co. or the Carnegie Co. (Ltd.) to try to improve the methods and try to cheapen production and try to extend the market?

[Mr. Carnegie] Everything.

[Mr. Beall] In order that they might be the masters in that contest of competition?

[Mr. Carnegie] Undoubtedly, Mr. Beall. We were in a race.

[Mr. Beall] When you are in a race of that sort, is not that the very time when the people who are in the race are looking out for this means and that means of improving and developing the business in which they are engaged?

[Mr. Carnegie] Quite true.

Portraits of the Industrial Era

1 Mill workers' homes along muddy alleys crowd close against giant steel mills in Pittsburgh. This is one of a series of photographs taken by Lewis Hine to illustrate the Pittsburgh Survey, a pioneer community study commissioned by the Russell Sage Foundation. Pittsburgh then deserved in full its nickname of the "Smoky City." The writer Lincoln Steffens, who did some investigative reporting of Pittsburgh politics about this time, called the city "hell with the lid lifted."

The building of an urban industrial society depended on steel in the late nineteenth and early twentieth centuries. The drawing of Bessemer converters (2) shows the spectacular effect produced when air was forced into the converter under pressure so that its oxygen would combine with impurities, converting iron into steel. The molten metal was then drawn from the furnace and cast into various shapes as desired (3). The work of shaping iron or steel employed further machinery, such as the steam-operated triphammer (4), but a great deal of human muscle power was still needed for such tasks.

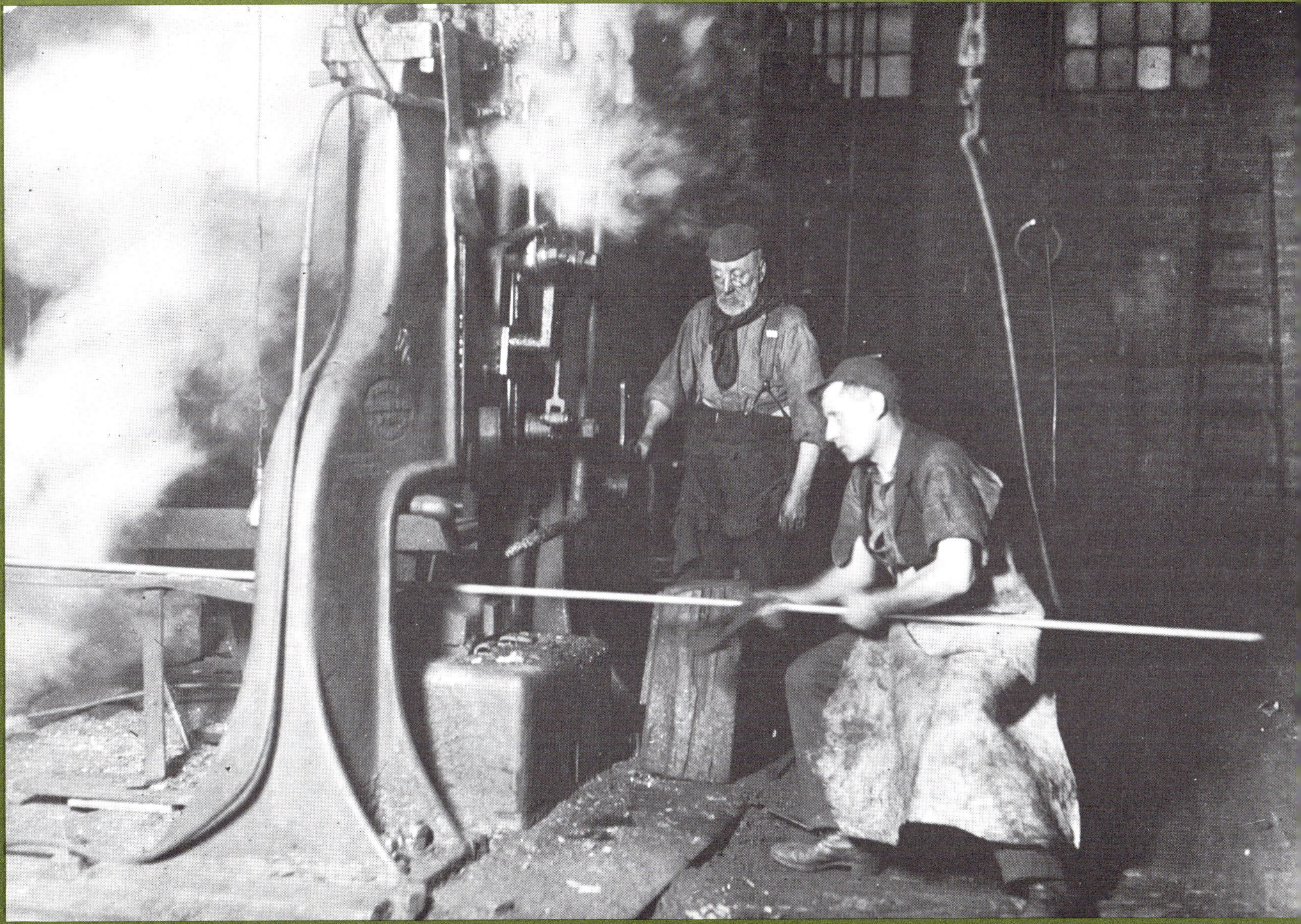

4

The process of industrialization in the Western world usually sharpened contrasts between wealth and poverty, power and impotence. Pittsburgh and the steel industry were not exceptions. At the banquet table (5), which was shaped like the cross-section of a railroad rail, of which the Carnegie Steel Company had made so many, sit eighty-nine officials of Carnegie companies on January 9, 1901. Many were already millionaires. While the guest of honor, Andrew Carnegie, was detained in New York and could not attend, he sent greetings predicting that the organization would become even greater. A few months after the banquet the Carnegie companies became the central element in the new United States Steel Corporation. In stark contrast, a few years later in Marianna, Pa., wives and children of men trapped in a coal mine disaster in 1908 (6) endure the agony of waiting for news of life or death. One hundred and fifty-four men died this time.

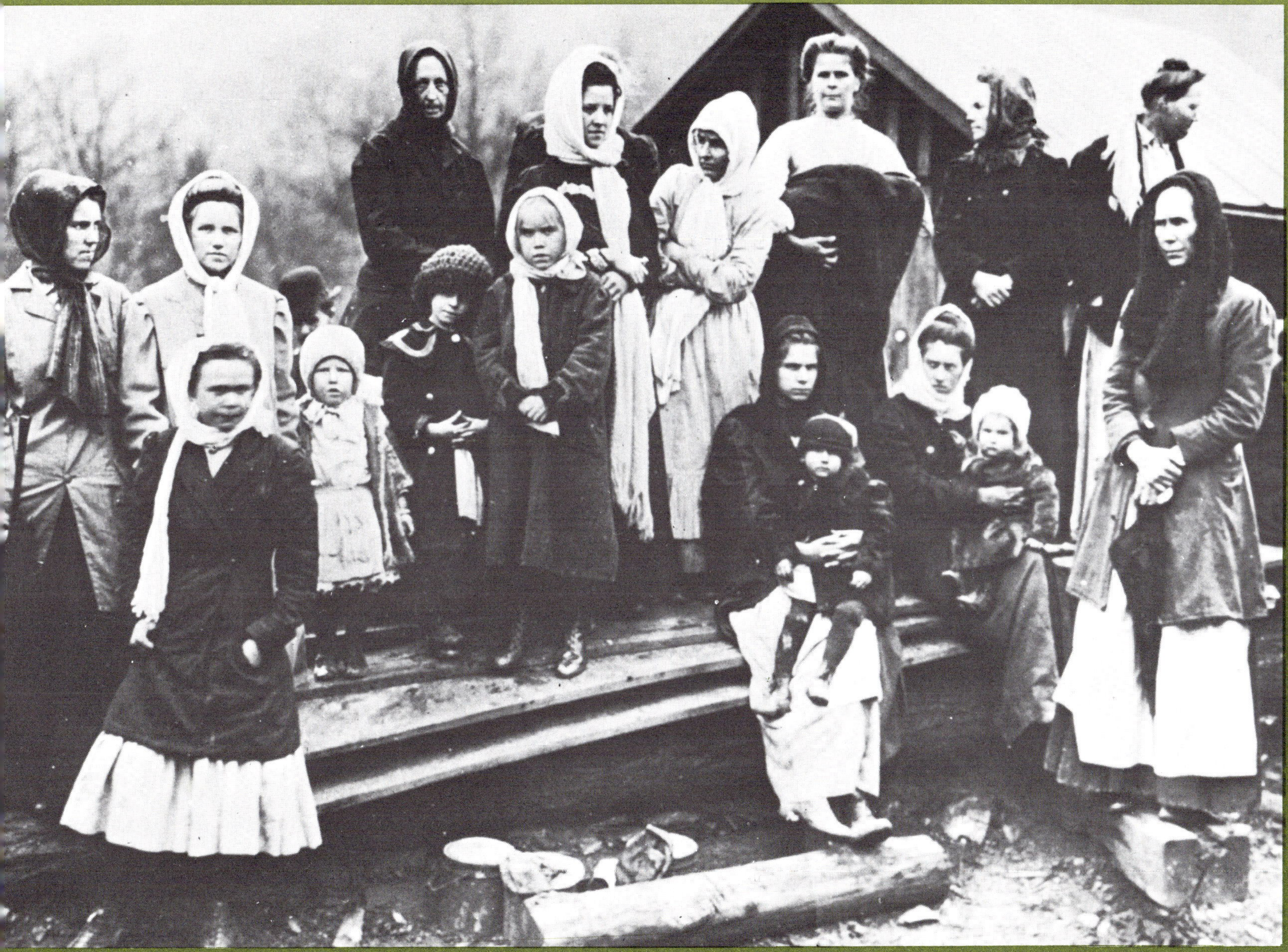

The elegant residence of Daniel M. Clemson (7) stood among many other mansions in the fashionable section along Fifth Avenue in Pittsburgh's East End. Clemson, a partner of Andrew Carnegie, was among those attending the banquet depicted in (5). In the days before electric power replaced them, two horses toil up a hill in Soho, a Pittsburgh working class district (8), with their burden of humanity riding on rails behind them.

The faces and names of a city reveal parts of its past. The steelworker (9) at U.S. Steel's (formerly Carnegie's) Homestead Works in 1908 may well have been one of the many new immigrants from Eastern Europe who poured in to work there. The young steelworker (10) is described as German, one of a large minority well established in Pittsburgh by then, as seen in the names of proprietors of small shops in (11). Both German and Irish groups in the city had long had numbers of flourishing political, social, and athletic organizations; the P. F. O'Toole Athletic Club probably served all three functions in varying degree.

12 The middle classes, who made up a substantial part of Pittsburgh's population, enjoyed their chance to escape from the smoke and cinders. Here (8) the Iron City Fishing Club settles down for a go at the trout. The presence of the ladies guaranteed a genteel tone to the occasion.

TOPIC 41

THE CONFLICT OF LABOR AND CAPITAL

As American industry grew in the late nineteenth century, relationships between workers and owners became more frequently bitter and violent. This topic deals for the most part with a bloody strike in 1892 at the Carnegie Steel Company's plant at Homestead, Pennsylvania, which reveals some of the problems of industrial labor relations in those years.

To say that labor relations in the late 1800s were becoming worse is not to say that they had been ideal earlier. Slavery had been a form of labor relations, and as long as slavery lasted it constituted a degrading, highly exploitative, and often cruel system of compelling work. The same was true, to a lesser extent, of indentured servitude until its decline in the early national period. Moreover, until the Civil War the vast majority of free workingmen and women did not belong to labor organizations but had to bargain individually with employers about wages and working conditions. Most Americans probably disapproved of labor organizations, and employers were often successful in getting the courts to declare strikes and boycotts illegal, as conspiracies to restrain trade.

For free workers, however, the perennial shortage of labor in the developing American economy, together with easy access to cheap land, made the United States a desirable place. The waves of immigrants sometimes created surpluses of labor which reduced wages temporarily. But in the long run the immigrants helped to stimulate demand for labor: by helping the economy to become more productive through their own hard work, by demanding, consuming, and paying for its products themselves, and by adding modest sums of money brought with them to the supply of capital available for investment in productive enterprises.

Conditions in Europe were more strained. There land was scarcer and more expensive, displaced farm workers created larger pools of surplus labor, driving wages down, and the lines between social classes and economic groups were more sharply drawn. The worsening of labor relations during industrialization encouraged the growth and popularity of radical doctrines, such as those of the German socialists Karl Marx and Friedrich Engels. Marx and Engels believed that conflict between propertied owners and propertyless workers was inevitable. They believed that in Europe, at least, this conflict would lead to a revolution ending in control of all property by the working class, in the name of the whole society. Other socialist spokesmen urged peaceful means such as legislation to achieve their ends; still others established utopian productive communities as models for a future society. Some radicals, called anarchists, despaired of reforming society and preached the violent destruction of all its institutions.

In the United States the conditions that made labor relations somewhat better than in Europe tended to slow the spread of radical ideas. Many a potential labor leader yearned to become an owner himself rather than to identify himself permanently with a labor movement. The booming growth of industry in the late nineteenth century did, however, encourage the rapid growth of unions, deepen the division of interest between employers and workers, and bring about occasional bloodshed between the antagonists.

Reading 194

Unions and the Workingman (1880-1920)

In the early 1800s workmen's organizations possessed strength only at the local level. After the Civil War, some unions, such as those of railway workers, attracted many members and succeeded in winning a few strikes affecting whole regions of the country. The first national organizations drawing members from a wide variety of occupations were the National Labor Union, which was founded in 1866 and had about 300,000 members before it lost strength in the 1870s, and the Noble Order of the Knights of Labor, which was founded in 1869 and had about 700,000 members before its decline in the late 1880s. In each case the leadership committed the national organization to broad political and economic reforms in which local unions had relatively little interest. The Knights of Labor suffered additionally from the fact that the public tended to confuse labor agitation with the anarchism of the day, a movement which caused occasional violence. The following reading considers the difficulties confronting the successors of these early labor groups as they tried to organize unions locally and nationally.

Forrest McDonald, *The Torch is Passed: The United States in the 20th Century,* 1968, Addison-Wesley, Reading, Mass., pp. 55-59. Subheadings added by the editors.

The Knights of Labor sought to organize all workers, regardless of job, skill, or race, into one union. The union reached its height in the mid-1880s, but rapidly lost ground to the largely craft-organized American Federation of Labor. In the above engraving, Frank J. Farrell, a black delegate representing a district local, introduces Terence V. Powderly, Grand Master Workman, to the 1886 convention of the Knights of Labor.

I
Obstacles to Unionization

In view of the obstacles that they faced, it is perhaps surprising that unions accomplished anything at all. From the outside, they were hemmed in by a mixed front of hostile business, an unsympathetic general public, and a legal and constitutional system that treated them as little short of subversive. From the inside they encountered equally formidable problems. For one thing, it proved virtually impossible to organize women and children—despite the almost unbelievably low wages, long hours, and harsh conditions that attended their work—and these constituted perhaps a third of the nonprofessional urban work force. For another, many native adult male workers, especially those recently migrated from the farms, were vaguely suspicious of unions on the grounds that they were somehow deleterious to a man's dignity, pride of craftsmanship, and hope of becoming wealthy—general impressions that were lent weight by the intimidation and propaganda sponsored by employers, and also by the all-too-frequent abuse of responsibility by dishonest business managers of union locals.

And there were other difficulties. Not the least of these was that a sizable minority of the nation's labor unions and leaders were committed to radicalism that, however noble in purpose, regularly brought the whole labor movement into public disfavor. The most violent of the radical labor organizations was the Industrial Workers of the World (better known as the IWW or simply as the "Wobblies"), formed in Chicago in 1905 through the merger of the Western Federation of Miners and the American Labor Union (organized in 1898 as a left-wing rival of the American Federation of Labor). The Wobblies, under the vigorous leadership of William D. "Big Bill" Haywood, won support among unskilled and migratory workers in the fruit-growing, shipping, and lumbering businesses in the West and, after a bloody but successful strike in Lawrence, Massachusetts, in 1912, among some textile workers. But their radical program—which included such exotic measures as the abolition of the wage system—and their open advocacy of violence, their use of sabotage, and their sit-down strikes in Akron rubber plants and Michigan lumber camps did the cause of labor more harm than good. The IWW was finally eliminated as a serious force just after World War I, when vigilante action and federal prosecution removed its leadership.

II
Socialists and Wobblies

The nonviolent radical wing of the labor movement was the Socialist party. Until 1897 the principal American socialist organization had been a revolutionary one: the Socialist Labor party, headed by the brilliant and militant Marxist Daniel De Leon, an immigrant from the British West Indies. But in that year a group of admirers of the British Fabian Socialists and the German Social Democrats—notably Eugene V. Debs, Victor Berger, and Morris Hillquit—formed a rival organization, the Social Democratic Party of America, which was committed to achieving socialism (government ownership of the means of production) gradually and through persuasion, the ballot-box, and other peaceful means. Three years later a large faction of De Leon's party bolted and joined the Social Democratic party, which changed its name to the Socialist Party of America. De Leon took his remaining followers into the IWW. The Socialist party steadily grew in strength, principally among German-Americans in the Middle West and among Jewish laborers in the garment industry in New York. The party won control of a number of cities, and reached its peak nationally in 1912, when Berger was elected to Congress from Milwaukee and Debs received 900,000 of the 15 million votes cast for president. But socialism failed to gain widespread regular support among American workers—partly because the leaders of the dominant labor organization were opposed to socialism, partly because some 50 percent of the union members were also members of the Catholic Church (which had condemned socialism in 1891), and partly because native Americans had such a deeply rooted tradition of respect for the sanctity of private property.

One position taken by the Wobblies and Socialists, however, was in certain respects considerably more realistic than that taken by the dominant American labor organization. The leading organization, the American Federation of Labor, insisted on the autonomy of each trade—that is, that each union represent only the workers in a single craft. This was reasonable enough for the skilled workers in the building trades and relatively small shops, but it was ill-suited for protecting the interests of unskilled workers and was unlikely to be effective in mining enterprises and factories employing thousands of workers who did routine functions. For the coal, steel, and textile industries, for example, and for the rapidly growing automobile industry, industry-wide unionization was far more rational than craft unionization and in the long run more successful.

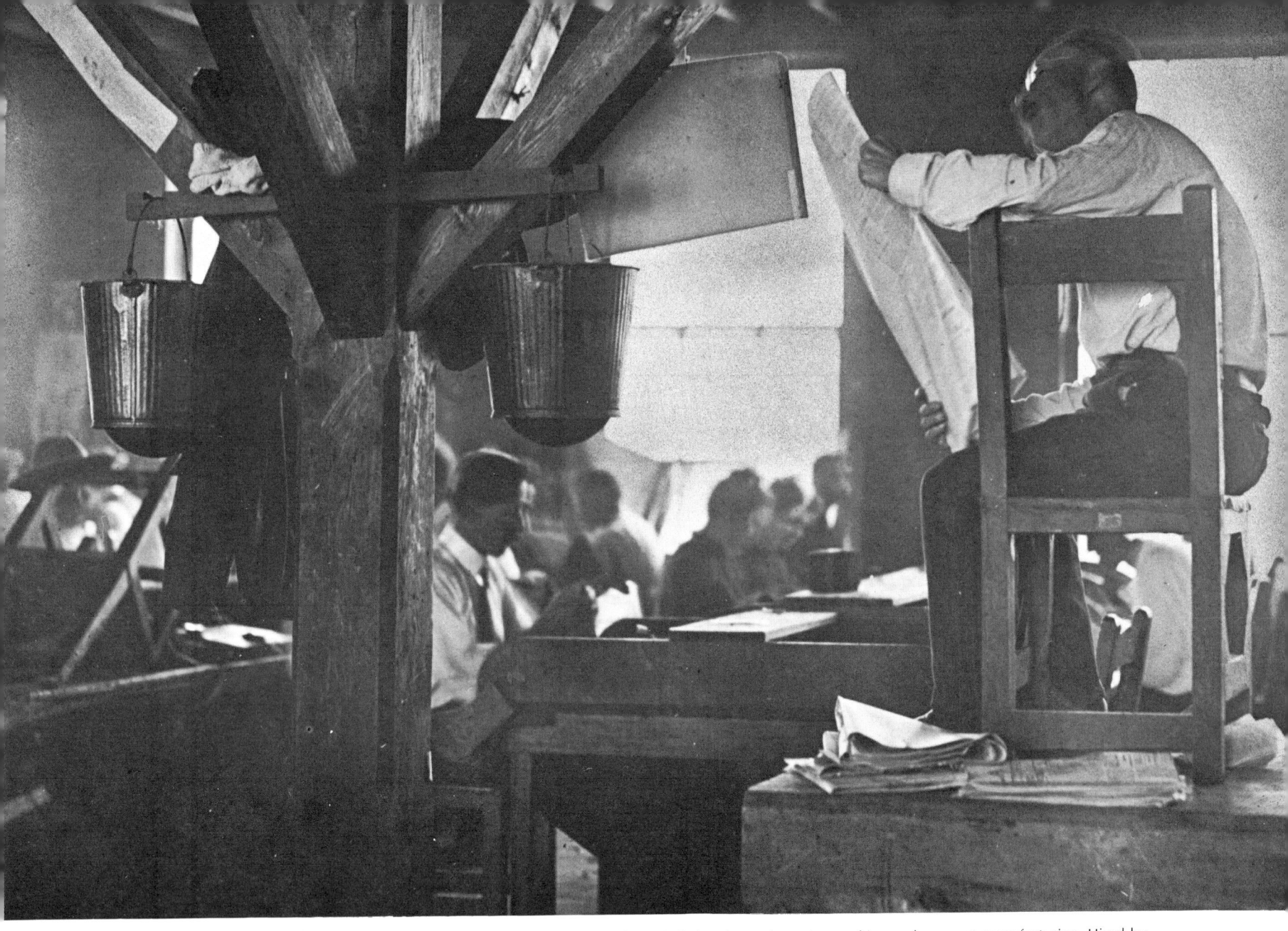

The reader in a cigar factory, 1909. The reader was a common figure in industries such as cigar making and garment manufacturing. Hired by the workers both to entertain and to enlighten, he read aloud from a wide selection of newspapers and magazines. The photo is by Lewis Hine, who captured many scenes of working class life in early twentieth century America.

But in these years efforts to organize along industrial lines failed, with but two significant exceptions: the United Mine Workers, whose membership leaped from roughly 20,000 in 1897 to more than 200,000 in 1901 and was well over 300,000 by 1911; and the unions in the clothing industry (the International Ladies Garment Workers, the United Garment Workers, and after 1914 the Amalgamated Clothing Workers), which were both industry-wide and theoretically socialist, and whose membership grew from 15,000 in 1897 to 78,000 in 1904, to almost 100,000 in 1910, and to more than 200,000 by 1916. Otherwise industry-wide organizers failed. Efforts to organize steel workers were brutally crushed in a series of strikes between 1901 and 1905; textile workers' unions had only scattered and short-lived success; and workers in the automotive, electrical machinery, and farm machinery industries failed to achieve organization at all.

III
Rise of the AFL

The union that met the greatest success, within the limits it imposed upon itself, was the American Federation of Labor, which was in fact not a single union but a federation of unions of skilled craftsmen. The guiding spirit of the AFL (and president for every year but one) from its founding in 1886 until his death in 1924 was Samuel Gompers of the cigar-makers union. Gompers had strong ideas about the proper course for the American labor movement, and his ideas had a lasting influence upon it. After long and serious study Gompers rejected Marxism and all other doctrinaire political programs, insisting that labor's sole objective should be "to get more." To the socialists he said "economically, you are unsound; socially you are wrong; and industrially you are an impossibility." He held that American labor would do better for itself by avoiding identification with political parties or movements of any kind, and concentrating instead on winning its "more" through collective bargaining.

Indeed, until 1908 Gompers believed that labor should generally oppose government action on behalf of workers, no matter how favorable it might appear—on the ground that government was and would likely remain under the domination of employers and their white-collar and farmer allies, and therefore was not to be trusted. Gompers made several minor exceptions (for example, he favored safety legislation and sometimes endorsed political candidates) but only three major ones: he approved of social legislation for the benefit of women, children, and seamen, for these workers could not be unionized, and he fought for legal restrictions on immigration and for legislative removal of legal barriers to unionization and collective bargaining.

Accordingly, most of the social legislation passed during the period was passed without the support of organized labor, and sometimes over its opposition. In New York, where the AFL was strongest, but also in Pennsylvania, Ohio, Illinois, and several other states, the union opposed laws establishing industrial commissions, fixing maximum hours and minimum wages, instituting public health measures, and setting up government-sponsored systems of unemployment and retirement insurance—because all such enactments reduced both the appeal of unions and the scope and potential yield of collective bargaining.

For all that, Gompers was probably right, for in the long run labor gained in both dignity and power by insisting on winning its way through collective bargaining at the conference table, rather than leaving its fate to the caprice of government and the self-interested generosity of employers. The record bore him out: at the turn of the century union membership was something over 860,000, by 1910 it had passed two million, and by 1920 it was more than five million, and on all three dates upwards of three-quarters of the union men were members of the American Federation of Labor. Throughout that period union members worked an average of ten hours less each week than did nonunion men in the same occupations, and were paid twice as much per hour.

IV
Legal Difficulties

The battle to overcome legal obstacles to collective bargaining was difficult enough to make any workers share Gompers' suspicion of the kind intentions of government. The courts had traditionally been unsympathetic if not outright hostile toward organized labor, and during the 1890's both federal and state courts freely issued injunctions restraining unions in disputes over wages, hours, and working conditions. The crowning legal blows came in two cases settled by the Supreme Court in 1908. In *Adair v. United States,* the Court sanctioned "yellow-dog contracts" (those requiring as a condition of employment that workers agree not to join a union) by striking down a statute outlawing them. In the Danbury Hatters Case (*Loewe v. Lawler*), instituted in 1902 and settled six years later, the Court held that a secondary boycott (refusal by members of one union to patronize a company being struck by another) was an illegal conspiracy in restraint of trade under the

Reading 195

Socialists and social reformers celebrated the cause of the working man on May Day (May 1). This illustration of 1894 heralds many reform causes, but its lush romanticism conveys little sense of social ills in need of cures.

meaning of the Sherman Antitrust Act, and ruled that the strikers were liable for civil damages. In subsequent labor disputes, strikes and attempts of unions to gain recognition were defeated through court action even before they could begin. In 1911 the workers in the cloak and suit industry—who were largely unorganized, but whose strike was directed by the International Ladies Garment Workers and whose cause was aided by the Boston attorney Louis D. Brandeis—made a breakthrough in an intermediate direction by negotiating an agreement with Hart, Schaffner & Marx that established machinery for settling disputes through arbitration. To Gompers and most other union leaders, however, compulsory arbitration was little more acceptable than having no negotiation at all. It was not until the 1930's that most legal barriers to unionization and collective bargaining were removed.

The Homestead Strike of 1892

In the late nineteenth century questions of labor and labor unions were bitterly controversial. Strikes were frequent and, as in the railroad strikes of 1877 (see Reading 184), violence often occurred. Although many of the strikes involved questions of wages and working conditions, just as frequently the key issue was more basic: the right of workers in a particular plant or industry to organize and act together against their employer. In the following selection Henry David, a historian of American labor, analyzes one of the best-known strikes of the era. It occurred at the Homestead, Pennsylvania, plant of the Carnegie Steel Company in 1892.

From Henry David, "Upheaval at Homestead," in Daniel Aaron, *America in Crisis*. Copyright © 1952 by Alfred A. Knopf, Inc. Reprinted by permission of the publisher. Pp. 136-142, 144-150, 152. Subheadings added by the editors.

I

The Union and the Mills

In 1892, when Carnegie Steel was formed, the Amalgamated Association of Iron and Steel Workers of America was the dominant labor organization in the industry. Its membership, its financial resources, and its collective agreements gave it a claim to recognition as the strongest union in the country. At its peak at the close of 1891, its two hundred and ninety lodges had over twenty-four thousand taxable members, exclusive of those holding traveling cards. This was roughly one tenth of the total number of workers in unions in the American Federation of Labor, with which the Amalgamated Association affiliated at the close of 1887. Its treasury closed 1891 with a balance of almost $150,000, and its total receipts the following year, out of which it disbursed all but $75,000, topped a quarter of a million.

By 1890, the Amalgamated had probably won greater gains in collective bargaining than any other union. At its height, it accounted for about one fourth of the one hundred thousand eligible workers in iron and steel. The larger group in its membership consisted of iron workers. In the Pittsburgh district its rolls included nearly half of the eligible steel workers. In steel, the union had made greater gains where the mills had first been organized in their iron-producing days. Where plants began their existence as steel mills, the Amalgamated found organization far more difficult. Thus, of the three major works in the Carnegie domain which were built as steel mills, only one, Homestead, was controlled by the Amalgamated. Duquesne had never been organized at the time of its acquisition in 1890, and the Edgar Thomson works had experienced two brief periods of unionization. West of the Alleghenies, the Amalgamated had secured wage and conditions-of-work agreements of a uniform character for most of the occupations represented by its membership through discussions with an employers' association, the Western Iron Conference. These regional agreements, which pointed toward uniform national wage-scales, constituted a measure of the union's unusual power.

When the Amalgamated Association was formed, in August 1876, roughly a quarter of a century after the first ephemeral organizations appeared among iron workers, a movement to bring the existing national unions of craft workers into a single body had been under way for several years. The oldest and largest of the unions that helped bring the Amalgamated into existence and that provided the core of its membership was the United Sons of Vulcan. Made up of iron puddlers, it had become a national organization in 1862, and it had won union recognition and a sliding-scale contract in Pittsburgh as early as 1865. The impulses to organization in the iron industry which marked the 1860's and '70's produced national unions in the Associated Brotherhood of Iron and Steel Heaters, Rollers and Roughers (1872), and the Iron and Steel Roll Hands of the United States (1873). These and the Sons of Vulcan created the Amalgamated Association. In 1877, the new organization had only 111 lodges and 3,755 members, almost all in iron. Membership grew rapidly up to 1882, when the loss of an extended strike resulted in a sharp drop. Four years later, the union entered a five-year period of steady expansion.

The strategic position in the manufacturing process occupied by its highly skilled members, who could not be rapidly replaced, constituted the union's initial source of strength. With the steady changes in technology, it would have been suicidal to restrict membership to the highly skilled alone, and the union admitted four classes of semiskilled workers in 1877. Twelve years later, after the leadership had attempted to open the organization to "all branches of labor directly interested in the manufacture of iron and steel," all workers except common laborers were made eligible for membership. All the lodges, however, did not open their doors. Some resisted the inclusion of semiskilled workers and helpers, even though membership was a function of the national body. Many also discriminated against foreign-born workers and against Negroes, who were made eligible for membership in 1881.

The unwillingness to organize the common laborers arose from a desire to maintain substantial wage differences between the unskilled and the skilled workers and to avoid wage disputes involving easily replaceable workers. The Amalgamated's jurisdictional boundaries excluded large numbers of workers in iron and steel for whom other trade unions existed, such as engineers, bricklayers, carpenters, firemen, and the like. The organized iron and steel workers not in the Amalgamated belonged, for the most part, to the Knights of Labor, which recruited without reference to skill or color. Conflicting jurisdictions invited conflicts between the organizations in the 1880's. In 1888, the Amalgamated prohibited co-membership in the Knights, while the latter established a National Trade District, No. 217, for Iron, Steel and Blast Furnacemen. Jurisdictional rivalry was exacerbated by wage factors, for the members of the K. of L. overwhelmingly worked for hourly and daily rates, while the wages of Amalgamated workers were based on tonnage. The special tax that the Amalgamated imposed to finance the Homestead strike encouraged a dissident group, made up of finishers in Pittsburgh and Youngstown plants, which left to found a rival union. Although the new organization had a very short life, its presence injured the Amalgamated at a critical juncture.

Its membership, the tradition of the earlier organizations, and the character of the industries contributed to the Amalgamated's conservative position with respect to social and economic theory and to its militant concern with wages, hours, conditions of work, and job control. The preamble to its constitution did not quarrel with capitalism or the tendency toward consolidation and combination, and offered organization as the means of maintaining a decent life for the workers in iron and steel. The constitution itself urged the members to protect "the business of all employers" who signed agreements with the union, but warned against construing this to mean permission to depart from the wage scale adopted or from the "established rules [and] customs" governing the work of the various occupations. . . .

II

The Union and Andrew Carnegie

Early in April 1892, two months before the three-year contract with the Amalgamated covering the Homestead plant was due to expire and before the final launching of Carnegie Steel, Andrew Carnegie drafted a notice addressed to its workers, which he submitted to Frick.* This notice stated that the formation of the new consolidation forced the management to adopt a uniform policy toward union recognition. "As the vast majority of our employees are Non-Union," wrote Carnegie, "the firm has decided that the minority must give way to the majority. These works will necessarily be Non-Union after the expiration of the present agreement." No reduction of wages would follow, for Carnegie represented the rates at the non-union Edgar Thomson and Duquesne works as more advantageous than at unionized Homestead, but he did admit that improvements at the latter plant would bring temporary reductions in the number employed. He closed with the pious observation that the refusal to deal with the union was "not taken in any spirit of hostility to labor organizations, but every man will see that the firm cannot run Union and Non-Union. It must be one or the other." Carnegie

*Henry Clay Frick, general manager of Carnegie Steel Company—Eds.

also proposed, if Frick agreed to announce that Homestead would no longer be a union mill, that it would be wise to "roll a large lot of plates ahead, which can be finished" in the event of a strike. Wage discussions with the union had been initiated early in the year, and Frick disregarded Carnegie's suggestion.

Had Andrew Carnegie, whom Mark Twain described as "the Human Being Unconcealed," never publicized the sympathetic attitudes he struck on the labor question and unionism, this proposed notice would have trivial significance. But his tender concern for humanity, his philanthropies, and his desire to improve the lot of the laboring classes had not been kept secret. He had spoken warmly of the glory and importance of manual toil, and urged that workers be given a larger share of the wealth they helped create. He had preached the ideal of copartnership between employees and employers. Two widely publicized articles in *The Forum* in April and August of 1886 had been exceptional in their sympathy with unionism and collective bargaining. Declaring that there were few offenses as heinous as strikebreaking, Carnegie proposed to amend the Decalogue by adding the injunction "Thou Shalt Not Take Thy Neighbor's Job!"

In his *Autobiography,* Carnegie later asserted that he had never employed a strikebreaker, and described his method for settling disputes: "My idea is that the Company should be known as determined to let the men at the works stop work; that it will confer freely with them and wait patiently until they decide to return to work, never thinking of trying new men—never." Up to the Homestead strike, declared Carnegie, his companies had never had a "serious" labor dispute, and he took great pride in the friendly and understanding "relations between ourselves and our men" for which he had been responsible for twenty-six years. There was, he observed, more than "the reward that comes from feeling that you and your employees are friends. . . . I believe that higher wages to men who respect their employers and are happy and content is a good investment, yielding, indeed, big dividends."

Carnegie's ambiguity makes it uncertain whether he really approved of unions which reached beyond the local plant. He showed little sympathy for organizations of larger scope, such as the Knights of Labor or the national affiliates of the A.F.L., but was, perhaps, prepared to live with a fragmented unionism. The history of industrial relations in the Carnegie enterprises before 1892 certainly is at odds with his pronouncements on labor questions.

As early as 1867, Carnegie joined with other iron manufacturers to import foreign workers when iron puddlers struck against wage cuts. Unionism was discouraged at the Edgar Thomson works, where organization first appeared in 1882. At the Beaver Fall mills two years later, the Amalgamated was defeated in a sharp struggle during which scabs from outside the district were used. . . .

III

Homestead

Homestead, some ten miles east of Pittsburgh on the left bank of the Monongahela River and about a mile below Braddock's crossing, had been founded in 1820. Containing less than six hundred people as late as 1879, it was the creation of the steel plant located there. By 1892, its population had climbed to between eleven and twelve thousand, and it displayed the characteristic ugliness and vitality of the steel town. The plant, with its normal output of twenty-five thousand tons a month, and almost four thousand workers, most of whom were foreign-born, set the terms of life for Homestead. Its workers did not regard themselves as badly off. Many owned their own homes. Labor in the mills was exhausting, reported one worker, but it enabled most of the workers to maintain a decent physical existence. He also spoke of those who were reduced to a life of grim "misfortune" by the many mill accidents. On June 1, 1892, there were employee savings amounting to $140,000 deposited with the company. Visitors were struck by the town's drabness and by its many saloons.

In January 1892, the management requested the eight lodges of the Amalgamated Association to prepare a new wage-scale. Several fruitless conferences followed the lodges' proposal to maintain the existing schedules, and at the end of May, Frick directed the superintendent of the Homestead works, John A. Potter, to present scales similar to those in effect at Edgar Thomson and Duquesne. These would have substantially reduced the earnings of the Homestead tonnage workers. Frick required a reply by June 24, and stated that after that the management would bargain individually and not collectively with the members of the Amalgamated, which opened its convention in Pittsburgh June 7. The convention approved a schedule of steel-mill scales and appointed a committee to negotiate with the Carnegie Company. On June 23, that committee conferred with Frick and Potter.

While Frick had given no public intimation that he regarded union recognition as a crucial issue, Carnegie, in letters from England, indicated his desire to operate Homestead as a non-union plant and to be relieved from the union working rules. The advantage earlier gained from encouraging uniform wage scales through collective bargaining had served its purpose. Frick did not share Carnegie's eagerness for a showdown with the union, but he was quite prepared to hold out for a settlement on his own terms.

Before arranging for what turned out to be the final conference with the union committee, Frick had been assured by the Pinkerton agency, in reply to his own inquiry, that it could supply an adequate number of men to guard the Homestead plant in the event of a strike. Earlier, a three-mile-long board fence topped by barbed wire had been built around the plant. Regularly spaced three-inch holes in the fence were later described by Frick as designed for observation purposes. To the workers, they seemed suited to a different use. At the extremes of the mill there had been erected platforms on which searchlights were to be mounted.

Three issues occupied the June 23 conference: the minimum selling-price of steel upon which the quarterly sliding-scale was to be based; the termination date of the new contract; and the tonnage rates for the open-hearth plants and 32-inch and 119-inch mills, which would immediately affect the wages of 325 workers. Wage agreements with the other employees were not at issue.

Frick wanted the sliding-scale base reduced to twenty-two dollars a ton for 4 × 4 billets, arguing that steel had been selling for less than the old minimum of twenty-five dollars since February, and that wages which were not limited by a maximum should also reflect declining prices. The union reduced its minimum from twenty-five to twenty-four dollars,

Homestead's Carnegie Mills lay before these strikers keeping watch over activity in the plant. On a "normal" working day a clear view such as this would have been impossible, so dense would have been the smoke.

and Frick increased his to twenty-three dollars during the conference. Frick insisted on a December 31 termination date for the contract, contending that this would facilitate contracts with steel purchasers. The union, prepared to sign a three- to five-year agreement, but anxious to avoid mid-winter strikes, held firm for a contract running to June 30, the date in effect for a dozen years.

Wages at Homestead ranged from a low of fourteen cents an hour for common labor to over fourteen dollars a day for a few highly skilled tonnage-workers. The proposed tonnage-rate reductions were justified on the ground that recent improvements had significantly increased output and that contemplated changes would boost it further. Of the 325 workers involved, 280 would be affected only by tonnage-rate changes, while the others would also suffer from the lower sliding-scale minimum. On the average, wages would be cut by eighteen per cent. A tableman estimated that his monthly wage would drop from $130 to $92. For some workers, a thirty-five per cent cut was at stake. It was widely believed that the new scales would soon be followed by wage cuts in the other departments and by reductions in the size of the work force. Frick later testified that he did not intend to reduce other rates until contemplated improvements were installed. The company's willingness to sign agreements with hourly-rate workers, its acceptance of the Amalgamated scale at a Pittsburgh mill, the building of the fence at Homestead, and other evidences persuaded the workers that Frick was preparing for a strike.

The conference on the 23rd ended in a stalemate, but the union expected that negotiations would continue. Two days later the management announced that there would be no further conferences, and Frick wrote to Robert A. Pinkerton requesting three hundred guards "for service at a Homestead mill as a measure of precaution against interference with our plan to start operation of the works on July 6, 1892." Frick asked for arms to be provided for the Pinkertons, and indicated that arrangements were being made to deputize them once they reached the plant. He patently knew that the Pinkertons were detested and feared, and that their arrival at Homestead was likely to cause trouble, for he directed that they be brought to the plant with the greatest secrecy. Frick later explained that his doubts concerning the ability of the sheriff to maintain order and protect property, based on what had happened during the 1889 strike, led him to employ the Pinkerton guards. . . .

IV

The Strike

Only the highlights of the strike, which continued until November, can be indicated. It is even impossible here to do justice to the events of July 6, which catapulted Homestead into fame. About two o'clock that morning, three hundred Pinkerton agents were loaded on two barges near Pittsburgh to be towed up the Monongahela River. Due to the strikers' warning system, the flotilla's movement was known long before it approached Homestead about 4 A.M. It was not at first known that the barges carried hated Pinkertons. The news flew through the town that scabs were arriving, and strikers, accompanied by their wives and children, raced out in the foggy morning to prevent them from entering

The strikers prevailed in their battle with the Pinkerton guards, but one week later the governor of Pennsylvania sent 8000 state militia troops into Homestead, an event which, in effect, broke the strike.

the plant by the landing at its rear. The barges tied up there before the townspeople broke through the fence blocking their approach to the wharf. The Pinkertons' attempt to land, which made known the cargo of the barges, was resisted. In the exchange of shots both sides suffered casualties. After the tug steamed off to carry several wounded Pinkertons back to Pittsburgh, the barges were in effect trapped off the landing. Another attempt to land before eight o'clock set off an exchange of gunfire lasting several hours. As the hours passed, recruits came into Homestead to strengthen the strikers, as did firearms and ammunition from Pittsburgh. Workers elsewhere wired offers of assistance, and from Texas there came a proffer of artillery.

The strikers early brought into play a twenty-pound brass breechloader, used by the town in holiday celebrations, and later employed a smaller cannon belonging to the Homestead Grand Army Post. Neither was effective against the barges. Sticks of dynamite hurled against them did little damage, and the attempt to set fire to the barges with a burning raft failed. The strikers set fire to oil and waste loaded on a railroad car and sent it down the tracks into the water, but it did not reach the barges. Later they unsuccessfully tried to destroy the barges with burning oil on the river.

The Pinkertons, who harrassed their besiegers with rifle and revolver fire, made their first truce offer at noon. Three hours later, at a hastily called mass meeting, Weihe, other Amalgamated officials, and O'Donnell pleaded with the strikers to permit the Pinkertons to land in safety. At the same time the Pinkertons decided that they had had enough, and at four o'clock the battle terminated, with the understanding that the Pinkertons were to receive, after being disarmed, safe passage out of Homestead. After they came ashore, the barges were set on fire, and the pledge of safety was violated. As the Pinkertons were marching into town between lines of enraged strikers and their wives and children, they were violently assaulted, and about half their number suffered injuries. The battle on the riverfront brought death to three Pinkertons and ten strikers. Some thirty Pinkertons were hospitalized, and an undetermined number of strikers were wounded.

The sheriff's frantic telegrams to Governor Robert E. Pattison for assistance brought, not the militia, but criticism of the sheriff. The governor even observed that bloodshed could have been avoided if the sheriff had accepted the Advisory Committee's proposal to guard the plant. Subsequent pleas by McCleary, who was unable to raise a deputy force, reports that the Advisory Committee was in complete control of the town, and the advice of a National Guard officer, whom he had dispatched to Homestead, finally led the governor to intervene. Late in the night of July 10, Pattison ordered Major General George R. Snowden to call out the entire militia force. Twelve hours later, the eight thousand officers and men of one of the country's best National Guard divisions began to march on Homestead. The Advisory Committee planned a formal reception for the troops, which was frustrated by their sudden appearance early in the morning of the 12th. Major General Snowden, who later declared that "revolution was proclaimed and entered upon" in Homestead, curtly refused the committee's pledge of assistance in maintaining order.

Immediately after the militia invested the town, the management took possession of the plant, and prepared to resume operations with non-union men. The furnaces were lit again for the first time on July 15, but no steel was made for a long time. The company experienced great difficulty in securing skilled workers. The strikebreakers lived at first as virtual prisoners within the plant, where they were housed and fed. Only later, after the sheriff built an adequate force of deputies, did the scabs venture to leave the mill and move about in Homestead. . . .

The spirit shown by the strikers, the support from organized labor, the degree of favorable public sentiment, and the inability of the management to secure enough skilled strikebreakers, encouraged the Advisory Committee to optimism. But by mid-October there were some two thousand men at work in the plant, about one fifth of them former employees, and it was clear that the strike was lost. A month later, the mechanics and laborers asked the union to terminate the struggle. They had stood firm up to then, but the refusal to call the strike off sent them back to the mill for jobs. Two days later, November 20, at a meeting of three hundred Amalgamated members, a resolution to declare the mill open was carried by a slight margin. The next day, the Advisory Committee disbanded.

The struggle cost three fifths of the strikers their jobs, and meant a wage loss of about $1,250,000. Without contributions of money, food, and clothing from the business people of Homestead and the Pittsburgh area, and assistance from the organized labor movement, it would have been far more difficult for the strikers to have held out as long as they did. The state met a charge of more than $440,000 to maintain the militia at Homestead for a period of ninety-five days. While the collapse of the strike was cheered in many newspapers, it was also observed that Carnegie Steel did not merit congratulations for the victory it had scored.

The Rights of Capital Must Prevail (1892)

The strike at Homestead, and particularly the seizure of the mill and the attack on the Pinkerton men by the workers, stirred up an enormous amount of controversy in the American press. The following selection by Julian Hawthorne (1846–1934), son of the writer Nathaniel Hawthorne, reflects the view of many middle-class Americans as they tried to reconcile the labor struggle with traditional American values.

From Julian Hawthorne, "Reflections on the Homestead Strike," *The Engineering Magazine*, III (1892), pp. 759–764. Subheadings added by the editors.

I

The Causes of the Strike

The recent disturbances at Homestead, while not differing in principle from other labor outbreaks, were marked by especial bitterness on the men's part, and by determination on the part of the firm; and several dramatic episodes have drawn the attention of the country to the struggle, and made it valuable as an object-lesson. We were confronted with a spectacle but nominally distinguishable from anarchy. Indeed avowed anarchy took a hand in the battle, in the attack on one of the firm's managers. In the daily press the series of events has been copiously though not often judiciously depicted and commented on; but the New York *Sun*, ignoring partisan politics and the temptations of an unworthy popularity, published a succession of remarkable editorials, stating the true issues forcibly and unflinchingly.

For my own part, I think the action of the discharged employés has been indefensible from the start, and that the firm, save on one occasion, has been in the right. I shall briefly outline what happened, and then consider what can be done to prevent the recurrence of such outbreaks hereafter.

There were three points of dispute between the men and the firm: (1) as to the minimum figures for a "sliding scale" of wages; (2) as to the time at which the yearly agreement regarding wages should be made; and (3) as to the amount of reduction in the pay of a certain class of Homestead laborers,—325 in number, out of a total of between 8000 and 9000 employés. Whether or not Hugh O'Donnell's unsupported assertion be true, that this reduction was to have been followed by similar reductions "all along the line," the fact remains, as stated by the New York *Times*, that—allowing for the claims of humanity—the legitimate rate of wages in any occupation *must* depend upon the supply of the particular kind of labor required in relation to the demand therefor. No basis of agreement was reached between the men and the firm, and the former were thereupon discharged, and the firm announced its determination to employ no more "Union" laborers. Pending the hiring of other laborers, the works were shut down. The town of Homestead consists mainly of dwellings hitherto occupied by the firm's men, but, of course, no more belonging to them after discharge than to me or to the reader. Nevertheless these unauthorized persons now seized upon both the town and the mills, and declared that, if they were not to work there at their own terms, no one else should, and that whoever attempted to do so risked his life.

We may observe here that it has been contended that the fact that Mr. Carnegie, the owner of Homestead, once said in certain articles in the *Forum* things inconsistent with the present attitude of the firm renders that attitude legally and economically untenable. He made five statements, one of which was a truism, while the other four were more or less foolish. The truism was that strikes and lockouts, like the duello, are a resort to force, which, whatever the issue in specific cases, establish no economic truth. He then asked consideration for the unwritten law, "Thou shalt not covet thy neighbor's job"; declared that non-union laborers were generally to be regarded with disfavor, and added that "to expect that one dependent on his wages for the necessaries of life shall stand peaceably by and see a new man employed in his stead was to expect much"; and finally, he agreed with Martin Irons, a labor agitator, that a little courtesy on the part of employers towards labor deputations would often avert a strike. In other words, a soft answer would not only turn away wrath, but would enable a laborer to live on wages which had a moment before been insufficient for that purpose! Now, it is doubtless annoying to Mr. Carnegie to be thus arraigned against himself, but neither his feelings nor his sayings are any more decisive of the question at issue than are anybody else's. The thing to be determined is the abstract or algebraic value of the situation, and thence to devise an equation for settling such differences henceforward.

II

The Rights of Business

The firm were in the position of a householder whose discharged servants bar him out of his own house, and will only admit him on his promise to reemploy them on their own terms and to forever renounce all servants but them. The firm duly appealed for redress to the sheriff, who, on being defied by the rebels, invoked the aid of the Government. While the latter was hesitating whether or not to send troops, the firm committed their single error; they hired the "Pinkerton Guards" to get possession of the mills and to safeguard their new laborers. But let it be noted that the strikers had not, under the circumstances, the remotest justification in resisting the Pinkertons. Nevertheless, under our theory of Government, the laws are an absolute protection to the individual in the maintenance of his rights, and no extraneous aids are necessary. The Pinkertons were resisted, and bloodshed and outrage followed. The killing of the Pinkertons was murder, because they represented the lawful owners of the property. The strikers were now like burglars who fortify a man's house against him and shoot him down on his attempt to enter. Troops, under General Snowden, arrived, and order was forcibly restored, though only so long as the troops should remain. At this juncture, Mr. Frick, the local manager of the business, was shot and stabbed by an avowed Anarchist, not without the explicit approval of individual strikers and of one member of the militia.* General Snowden took a gloomy view of the situation, believing we were on the brink of a war with the commune.

*On July 23, 1892, Alexander Berkman, an anarchist, recently arrived from New York, seriously wounded Henry Clay Frick, a Carnegie partner. Berkman had no connection with the strike and knew none of the strike leaders—Eds.

Formerly employers were masters and laborers slaves. Now men may work or not, as they choose. Natural law, however, still makes work obligatory. Except capital be invested for productive purposes, the capitalist as well as the laborer must starve. Wealth is a fund acquired by help of labor in industries organized by capitalists. Not the capitalist, but the necessity of self-support forces the laborer into the factories. They have neither means nor ability to organize industries for themselves. Either party may terminate the connection, and the laborer may also use argument and persuasion, not amounting to force, to deter others from taking his place. But the right of employers to conduct their business in their own way, and of "scabs" to replace "Union" men, is sacred, and to be upheld, at need, by the whole force of the State. The "rights" arrogated by labor unions can be conceded only in so far as they do not clash with the fundamental rights of the individual. On no plea may ex-employés take possession of their late employer's works. If such a thing as human property in anything exists, then the Carnegies own Homestead and the only alternative of supporting them in that ownership is the acceptance of Anarchy....

The remedy for "Homestead," then, and solution of all else insoluble disagreements between Labor and Capital, is to give the underpaid laborer free recourse to the unused land. The public domain of the United States is ample to afford relief to our laboring population for generations to come. But that magnificent domain has been blighted and sterilized by inadequate legislation and selfish chicanery. It is no new idea, indeed, that occupancy and use should be the basis of land legislation. But the laws framed for that end are, in the first place, not thoroughgoing enough, and in the second place, such as they are, they are too easily evaded,—their letter observed, while their spirit is violated. More stringent laws, and more searching enforcement of them are needed. Not a few statesmen and scholars, who think straight and see clear, have demanded it. Even in the English Parliament, a bill recently introduced, constraining the landlords of Great Britain to sell vacant and unused land in small lots to purchasers who guaranteed to work it,—the price to be fixed by juries under the supervision of borough officers,—came within fifty votes of being made law. The drift of the times is in this direction, and the spirit of the age demands it.

The Homestead Strike: A Labor Leader's View
(1892)

One of the best-known labor leaders of the 1880s and 1890s was Terence V. Powderly (1849–1924), Grand Master Workman of the Knights of Labor, the largest and most powerful labor union of its day. Though there had been trouble between the Knights of Labor and the Amalgamated Association, Powderly nevertheless defended the actions of the workers at Homestead and urged a policy which he believed would give a fair chance to workers in a similar situation in the future.

From Terence V. Powderly, "A Knight of Labor's View," *North American Review,* CLV

(1892), pp. 370–374. Subheadings added by the editors.

I
The Rights of the Worker

The principle involved in the Homestead trouble is the same as that by which the founders of this republic were governed in rebelling against the British government. To have accepted decisions, decrees, and laws without question, and without a voice in their making, would have stamped the colonists as slaves. To accept, without inquiring the why or wherefore, such terms and wages as the Carnegie Steel Company saw fit to offer would stamp the brand of inferiority upon the workmen of Homestead. Independence is worth as much to the workingman as it can be to the employer. The right to sell his labor in the highest market is as dear to the workman as the right of the manufacturer to sell the product of that labor can possibly be to the latter. It is folly to assert that the workman has no right to a voice in determining what the minimum rate of compensation shall be. If the manufacturer is permitted to invade the market place and undersell competitors a reduction in the wages of his employees must inevitably follow. It was to protect the manufacturer as well as the workman that the Amalgamated Association insisted on a minimum rate of pay. The fixing of that rate imposed no hardship on the manufacturer; it gave no competitor the advantage over him, for the majority of mills were operated under the Amalgamated scale, and this of itself fixed a rate below which manufacturers would not sell. The minimum rate was therefore as advantageous to the manufacturer as to the workman in the steel trade. The question at issue between the Carnegie Steel Company and the steel workers does not so much concern the price as the right to a voice in fixing that price.

Individual employers no longer exist; the day no longer dawns on the employer taking his place in the shop among the men. When that condition of workshop life existed employer and employee experienced a feeling of lasting friendship for each other; the interests of each were faithfully guarded by the other. Now the employer of men may be three thousand miles away from the workshop; he may be a part of a syndicate or corporation which deals with the employees through a special agent or superintendent, whose desire to secure the confidence and good will of the corporation may cause him to create friction in order to demonstrate that he is vigilant in looking after the interests of those to whom he looks for favors. The corporation, composed of many men, is an association of capital which delegates its authority to an agent whose duty it is to deal with the workmen and make terms with them. The Amalgamated Association, and all other bodies of organized workmen, stand in the same relation to the men as the corporation does to the capitalists whose money is invested. One invests money, that is, his capital; the other invests his labor, which to him is not only his capital but his all. That the workman should have the same right to be heard through his legitimately appointed agent, the officer of the labor organization, that the corporation has to be heard through the superintendent or agent, is but equity. This is the bone of contention at Homestead, and in fact everywhere else where a labor organization attempts to guard the right of its members. . . .

II
Future Plans

What would have averted this trouble at Homestead, is asked? Industries which are protected by tariff laws should be open to inspection by government officials. When the managers of such concerns seek to absorb all of the protection the government should interfere on behalf of the workingmen. If we must have protection let us see to it that it protects the man who works.

At the hands of the law-making power of State and nation the Knights of Labor demand "the enactment of laws providing for arbitration between employers and employed, and to enforce the decision of the arbitrators." It should be a law in every State that in disputed cases the employer should be obliged to select two arbitrators and the employees two, these four to select the fifth; this arbitration commission to have access to all books, papers, and facts bearing on the question at issue from both sides. It goes without saying that the commission should be made up of reasonable, well-disposed men, and that publicity would not be given to such information as they might become possessed of.

An established board of arbitration, appointed by a governor or other authority, is simply no board of arbitration at all, for the reason that the workmen would have no voice in its selection, and the other side, having all the money and influence, would be tempted to "fix" such a board preparatory to engaging in a controversy with workingmen. For either side to refuse to appoint its arbitrators should be held to be cause for their appointment by the Governor of the State. No strike or lockout should be entered upon before the decision of the board of

Reading 198

arbitrators. Provisions for appeal from the decision of the arbitrators should be made in order to prevent intimidation or money from influencing the board.

In no case should the introduction of an armed force, such as the Pinkerton detective agency arms and equips, be tolerated. The system which makes one man a millionaire makes tramps and paupers of thousands. The thousands go down to the brothels and slums, where they sprout the germs of anarchy and stand ready for any deed of desperation. The millionaire becomes more arrogant and unreasonable as his millions accumulate. Victimizing and blacklisting are the concomitants of the rule of industrial establishments by our millionaire "lords of industry," and these measures furnish recruits for the army of greed when organized labor enters its protest against such acts of injustice as has made tramps of other men under like circumstances. The employer who is satisfied with a reasonable profit will not fear to intrust his case to such a board of arbitrators as I have described. The employer who refuses arbitration fears for the justice of his cause. He who would acquire legitimately need not fear investigation; he who would steal must do it in the dark in order to be successful.

Homestead, Fifteen Years Later

The Homestead mills, along with most of the steel industry, were not unionized after the failure of the 1892 strike. In 1901, the mills, with the rest of Carnegie Steel, became a part of the United States Steel Corporation. In 1907 Margaret Byington, a New York social worker, did a year-long field study of the community of Homestead and in doing so provided a picture of the steel workers fifteen years after the great strike.

From Margaret Byington, *Homestead: The Households of a Mill Town* (New York, 1910), pp. 171–175. Subheadings added by the editors.

I

Working in the Mills

I spoke of the twelve-hour day spent in tumult and in heat, the heavy work, the periodic intensity of labor at the rolls and the furnaces for the skilled steel workers. The onlooker, fascinated by the picturesqueness of it all, sees in the great dim sheds a wonderful revelation of the creative powers of man. To the worker this fascination is gone; heat and grime, noise and effort are his part in the play. The spectacular features may serve only to heighten the over-strain which accompanies continuous processes whenever, as here, the full twenty-four hours is split between two shifts. In the open-hearth department in Homestead in October, 1907, 1517 men worked a twelve-hour day, as against 93 who worked ten. In the Bessemer department, there were nine men who worked an eight-hour day, 19 who worked eleven; the remaining 153 worked the full twelve. In the rolling mills some common laborers were employed eleven hours, but the men in the processes were dividing the twenty-four hours of the day and night between two shifts. (The normal day of the yard laborer was ten hours.) These long hours restrict the development of the individual. They give the men in the two shifts little time for outside interests. The week that a man works on the night turn, from 5.30 p.m. to 7.30 a.m., he has plainly small time to do anything but eat and get such sleep as he can. The other week he has, of course, such leisure as falls to any ten-hour worker. This alternation of shifts lets the men out of consecutive night work, but it interferes with that regularity of meals and of sleep which physicians tell us is essential to health. When a man sleeps in the daytime alternate weeks, it means continual change and adjustment. One week he has supper at 4.30 p.m., works all night, has breakfast at 8 a.m., and has a more or less broken sleep during the day. The alternate week he has supper at 6 p.m., breakfast at 6.30, and a good night's sleep between. Sometimes when sons who are in the mill are on the opposite shift from the father, the family cannot even meet for meals. The irregularity in hours not only adds in the long run to the fatigue of the work and breaks into the family life, but also makes weekly engagements, such as lodge meetings, impossible, and prevents the men from taking much part in other activities.

Some local ministers said they believed that this stiff routine tends to develop steadiness on the part of the mill workers; one clergyman, for instance, told me that most of the hard drinking he knew was among men who had irregular work either as teamsters or in the building trades. Yet the existence of the fifty or more saloons in Homestead indicates that drinking is a prevalent form of excitement in the town. And exhaustion, coupled with the thirst occasioned by the heat in the mills, is at least partly responsible for the number of men who seek stimulus from drink.

A further depressing result of the overwork in the mills is the mental fatigue which ac-

Steel workers peer into Lewis Hine's camera, Homestead, 1909. One senses in these men the kind of stolid strength necessary to endure twelve hours a day in the mills.

companies it. The men are too tired to take an active part in family life; they are usually ready after smoking a pipe to go to bed. They have small interest in outside matters and consequently make little effort to increase the provision of amusements in the town, a condition from which their wives and children suffer. Again, with the broken Sunday, which is due either to work on that day or to work Saturday night or Sunday night, it is easy to drift away from church, and many ministers find it almost impossible to secure the attendance of the men. One man who usually had to work at least part time on Saturday night said to me that he was far too tired to get up to go to church on Sunday morning. In the year of our study one man in five worked on seven days in the seven in the steel mills of Allegheny County.

II

What the Worker Thinks

All this is bound up with perhaps the most serious outcome of conditions in the mill, the tendency to develop in the men a spirit of taking things as they come. As we noted in the chapter dealing with the growth of Homestead, while the industry has attained a marvelous degree of efficiency the town as a political unit has failed. Men weary with long hours of work, men who have been refused any share in determining the conditions under which they work, are not prompted to seize opportunities for improving the conditions under which they live. Their habitual suppression industrially has meant a loss of initiative. Somehow it is easier to pay a neighbor fifty cents a month for the privilege of bringing drinking water three times a day from his well, than to insist that the borough provide a wholesome supply.

There is, therefore, in the routine of life outside the mill, little to stimulate these men to mental alertness, nor did my talks with them give me the impression that their work within it tended to supply this want. At different points in the process are men upon whose experience and judgment rest heavy responsibilities. But where individual skill was formerly a constant element, little by little that skill, as well as much of the crudest manual labor, is being transferred to the machines. As you watch a crane pick up "buggies" of scrap iron, empty them into a furnace, and then move on to repeat the operation, you feel that the machine itself must be alive until you see the man who pulls lever after lever with strong, steady hand. The demands upon this man's faculties during working hours are not those which had to be met by the old time craftsmen in metals. Improvements in process are, some of them, the result of the men's practical suggestions, which are welcomed eagerly by the superintendents, tested, and when practicable adopted. I was told that the recompense in most instances is small—sometimes a gift of money. Evidence, however, of quickness and ingenuity undoubtedly increases the possibility of promotion. The exceptional man may become an influential official, and the officials of the Steel Corporation state that there is as keen a demand for prize men as ever. Not a few instances, such as Mr. Schwab's rapid rise, are well known. But with 7000 men employed in this one mill,—with half of the payroll made up of unskilled men,—with the tendency at every point to reduce the number of skilled men,—with a majority of the mills in all sections of the country of the same sort practically under the one management, the prospect of rapid advancement for the rank and file becomes more and more uncertain. The sentiment frequently expressed among Homestead people that promotion is due to a pull, may be only a feeling, but it strengthens their belief that for this generation the future will hold little more than the present. The younger men are sometimes ambitious to study and work up, but the older ones feel that there is nothing ahead for them.

On the other hand, the memory of the lost fight of 1892 is still vivid, and the decisions of the corporate employer are not accepted without mental protest.

Probably no outsider can ever know just what the men do think about it all. Certain impressions, however, gathered in talks with many of them may be worth stating, as showing the lines along which Homestead men think. That the older men lack confidence in trade unions is not strange. The strike destroyed the enthusiasm that comes with success, and the hesitation about attempting to reorganize has been intensified by the growth of the Corporation and its policy of repressing any collective action. Its industrial achievements and great strength make it a foe not to be antagonized, and the men have realized its power to the full. Those who were refused re-employment because of their part in the strike, found, as I have said, that they could get no work in any mill of the Carnegie Steel Company and were in some instances unable to get it in any other steel mill. Furthermore, common report has it that anyone who proposes trade unionism in the mill is promptly discharged, and experience has gone to prove this. One phrase current in the town is: "If you want to talk in Homestead, you must talk to yourself." "What is the use?" is apparently the men's feeling. The people who determine their hours, their wages and the conditions under which they work, are to them a small group of men in New York, who know little and perhaps care less what the decision of a 10 per cent cut in his rates means to a man who has been averaging $3.00 a day; still less what it means to his wife and children. While the majority of the workers understand only vaguely the organization of a great industry, or the factors entering into its policies, they feel that their conditions of life are determined by forces too large for them to battle with.

TOPIC 42

THE IMMIGRANTS

The town and city dwellers who worked in the smoky, bustling factories and businesses of the new industrial society increasingly were new immigrants and their children. Without the labor of these new Americans the nation's economy could not have expanded so rapidly in the late nineteenth century. They also added to urban America the immense variety of personality, appearance, living style, and language of their diverse backgrounds. Their seizure of the New World's opportunities brought them both rewards and perplexing problems.

This topic is concerned largely with the so-called "new immigration" of the late nineteenth and early twentieth centuries, rather than with the "old immigration" of earlier years. The initial reading relates those two phases of population movement to American economic and social change, while the following readings deal with immigrants' reactions to their own experiences.

Reading 199

Thirty-Eight Million New Americans

The extensive migration of Europeans to the United States between 1820 and 1920 left deep imprints in American society and culture which are clearly evident today. In the following selection, historian Carl Degler describes the place of the immigrant in American life in the nineteenth and early twentieth centuries.

Excerpts from pp. 274-275, 278-283 in *Out of Our Past*, Revised Edition, by Carl N. Degler. Copyright © 1959, 1970 by Carl N. Degler. Reprinted by permission of Harper & Row, Publishers, Inc.

I

The Widening Stream

From its inception, America has been the frontier of Europe and the goal of those who were bold enough to take a second chance. All through the seventeenth, eighteenth, and nineteenth centuries, people flowed to the New World—direct responses to the economic, military, or religious troubles convulsing the Old World. During the seventeenth century, for example, the religious and economic discontent in England drove people to New England and the Chesapeake colonies; in the early eighteenth century, economic discontent in Ireland and Germany introduced the leaven of Scots-Irish and Germans into the English stock of America. But between 1820 and 1920, by far the greatest and presumably the last of the great waves of Europeans flooded to America; in that single century, 38 million came to the United States.

If one charted the annual arrivals of this last wave of immigrants, the graph would assume a pattern of peaks and valleys—but until 1914, the trend would always be upward. Along this over-all upward trend, however, two major peaks would stand out: one in the 1850's and another in the five years between 1905 and 1910.

The dates of these two peaks can serve as convenient markers for differentiating between the so-called old and new immigration. Unfortunately, these terms are somewhat misleading, since they apply to the European geographic origins of the immigrants rather than to time of arrival. But their widespread use makes them convenient nonetheless. The first peak is associated with the old immigrants—that is, those who came primarily from northern and western Europe: England, France, the Low Countries, Germany, and Scandinavia; the second with the new immigrants, the great peasant peoples of eastern and southern Europe: Italians, Greeks, Poles, Russians (including Jews), and Slavs in general. The usage "old" and "new" has some justification in that before 1880 the peoples of southern and eastern Europe were almost unknown on the immigrant ships which put in at Castle Garden in New York. As late as the decade 1881-91, in fact, these peoples constituted only a little over 18 percent of the immigrants from Europe. But in the 1890's the immigrants from northern and western Europe, though they continued to come in substantial numbers, were almost lost in the masses of people who now spilled out of the lands east of the Elbe River and south of the Alps.

77

Immigrants jammed together on the deck of an Atlantic steamship. After many hours crowded into the lower decks, or steerage quarters, of the ship, a few hours of air and sun provided one of the few pleasures of the crossing.

The actual numbers of immigrants coming into the United States in the early years of the twentieth century were almost unbelievable. In the years before 1880, the annual arrivals had never reached half a million, and only once before the end of the century did their numbers exceed three quarters of a million. After 1896, however, when the numbers of immigrants from eastern and southern Europe for the first time surpassed those from the north and the west, annual immigration frequently topped the million mark. In each of six different years before 1915, over a million new Americans arrived; in fact, between 1902 and 1914, more than half a million immigrants poured into the country every single year, and in most of the years the figure was above three quarters of a million. In the space of those twelve years, the total number of immigrants far exceeded all the new arrivals between 1820 and 1880—the peak period for the old immigration. . . .

II

Hewers of Wood and Drawers of Water

As a class, the immigrants were "hewers of wood and drawers of water" in America; moreover, in proportion to their numbers they performed more of the nation's work than did the native-born. As one friend of the immigrant pointed out in 1893, though the foreign-born population in 1870 comprised

"One-seventh of the entire population," it performed "something more than one-fifth of all the work." In 1880, this same writer went on, foreign-born workers constituted almost a third of the labor force, even though immigrants made up only 13.3 percent of the total population.

Such disproportion is not the consequence of exploitation so much as it is the result of the peculiar age distribution of the immigrant population. The great majority of the immigrants came to the United States in the prime of life—in the working years between fourteen and forty-five. For example, four-fifths of the immigrants in 1900 fell within this age range, though less than three-fifths of the native population did. Nor were Americans blind to the economic value of this age grouping. "Thus, immigration brings to us a population of working ages unhampered by unproductive mouths to feed," commented economist John R. Commons in 1906. "Their home countries have borne the expense of rearing them up to the industrial period of their lives," he thriftily pointed out, "and then America, without that heavy expense, reaps whatever profits there are on the investment." Europe was a kind of labor "farm" where workers were conveniently and cheaply raised to full size before they entered American industry.

For an America ever reaching out for more and more labor, the ratio of the sexes in the immigration which came after the 1880's was better than could have been expected. The older immigrant nationalities had often come in families, a mode of migration which tended to distribute the sexes more or less evenly. The new peoples, however, emigrated more often as single men, or married men who had left their families behind. For instance, in the decade of 1901-10, almost 70 percent of the newcomers were men; whereas in the decade 1850-60, less than 60 percent were. But it is significant that in both periods there was an excess of men, which, when taken together with the favorable age distribution, meant that immigration provided much more productive labor than was to be expected from any normal increase in population.

Though it is true that the labor of the typical immigrant, especially after 1880, was not skilled, this should not cause us to overlook the skills which the immigrant added to the wealth of America. Emigrants from industrialized and commercial northern and western Europe were noteworthy in this regard, particularly the Germans who came in the 1840's and 1850's. This nationality dominated cabinetmaking and pianomaking in New York City, for example. Even entrepreneurs in the latter industry, like Steinway, were immigrants. Germans were also prominent as skilled bakers, tailors, and shoemakers in New York. Englishmen, coming from a technically advanced society, often came, both before and after the war, as skilled workers, such as machinists, mechanics, and ship-building workers. In the years after 1865, the backbone of the American glass industry was made up of skilled Belgian workers.

The skills which these workers brought, however, comprised only a part of the immigrant's contribution to American industrial development; common, unskilled labor was the more important addition. But if important, such labor was also lowly. As an unskilled worker, the immigrant, severely limited in his choice of occupation, most often found himself in jobs at the bottom of the ladder, sometimes in occupations which no native, except perhaps a despised Negro, would accept. Before 1860, the Irish were especially conspicuous as unskilled workers. In the Boston of the 1850's, for example, they bore virtually the same relation to the culture of that city as the Negro slaves did to the contemporary South: both constituted the broad base on which rested an elegant civilization. Of all the employed Irish in Boston in 1850, 62 percent were working as laborers or as domestic servants; in 1855, the state census revealed that 98 percent of New York City's 20,000 common laborers were immigrants. After the war, the story of the unskilled is essentially the tale of the immigrant in general, so we shall save that until later.

But before 1860, the economic importance of the immigrants was not confined to industry. Many of the newcomers helped to level the forests and plow up the black earth of the western prairies. By 1860, immigrants in a new state like Minnesota constituted at least one-fifth of the inhabitants of forty-nine of the sixty-four counties; in brand-new, sparsely settled counties, the immigrants sometimes made up a majority. Even in an older state like Illinois, by then two generations in the Union, immigrants, especially Germans, comprised 20 percent or more of the population in something like one-fifth of the counties. Germans were also numerically prominent in portions of Iowa, where in eight or nine rural counties in 1860, every fifth person was an immigrant.

Wisconsin before 1860 was the most indebted to the immigrant for its agricultural growth. Immigrants comprised almost a quarter of the state's one million inhabitants at the outbreak of the war, with the Germans surpassing the total for the English, Canadian, Norwegian, and Irish. In twenty-two of the state's fifty-eight counties immigrants consti-

"Lure of American Wages" is the title of this mid-nineteenth century woodcut. John Bull, the symbol of Great Britain, attempts to restrain his people, while Uncle Sam beckons them across the Atlantic. Castle Garden was New York's immigrant depot from 1855 to 1892.

tuted a third or more of the population, and in some of those counties they were a clear majority.

Although at the end of the nineteenth century most of the immigrants were becoming industrial workers upon arrival in America, many thousands continued to push out to the new lands of the Far West and the Great Plains. Immigrants of older ethnic groups, like Germans and Scandinavians, for example, continued to be drawn to the traditional settlements of their nationalities,* but now some of the "new" nationalities were beginning to become prominent in agriculture. Italians, for instance, in 1910 were the most conspicuous

*For example, as late as 1910 both Wisconsin and Illinois still counted one fifth of their populations as foreign-born, with Germans and Scandinavians predominating. In at least nine Wisconsin counties Germans made up over a majority of the immigrants, and in each of these counties the foreign-born were more than 20 per cent of the total population.

immigrant people in thirteen of the sixteen California counties which reported 20 percent or more immigrant population. The foreign-born made up 21 percent of the population of the State of Washington in 1910; almost another quarter were second-generation immigrants. Eastern Europeans like Finns and Russians were prominent in several of the rural counties, while in others "old immigrants" like Norwegians, Germans, and Swedes were important.

On the Great Plains of Middle America in the twentieth century, the immigrant still occupied a conspicuous place in agriculture. Though Nebraska is rarely thought of as the goal of immigrants, in 1910 six counties in that state reported that the foreign-born made up one fifth or more of their population. Two agricultural counties, Colfax and Cuming, in the center of the state, counted almost three quarters of their populations as first- and second-generation immigrants, mostly from Germany and Austria.

Though by the twentieth century the immigrant played only a small part in the drama of settlement and agriculture, in some Midwestern states, like the Dakotas, he was the star. The foreign-born in South Dakota, for example, comprised 20 percent of the 1910 population in no less than seventeen counties; indeed, in three of these, one out of every three persons was an immigrant. Two thirds of the inhabitants of all but three of these seventeen counties were first- and second-generation immigrants. Even more significant insofar as influence went was the fact that individual nationalities tended to cluster together. For example, three quarters of the foreign-born in three counties were Russians (actually Germans who had emigrated from Russia). In three other counties, Norwegians made up more than half the immigrant population.

If Wisconsin in the first half of the nineteenth century was largely the creation of the European peasant, the rich state of North Dakota was the product of the immigrant at the very end of the century. In 1910 the foreign-born comprised 27 percent of the people of the state, and another 43 percent were children of immigrants. There was not a single county in which the foreign-born comprised less than 15 percent of the population, and there were twenty-eight counties in which they constituted more than a quarter. The 40,000 first-generation Norwegians were the largest ethnic group, with Russians (actually German-speaking people) running second with 32,000. The latter, in conformity with their traditional cultural exclusiveness even in Russia, were highly concentrated in five or six counties, where they often made up more than two thirds of the foreign-born population.

Important as the immigrant was in agriculture, the fact remains that the typical immigrant in the years after 1890 was a worker in a factory or mine. In 1910, only 14 percent of the foreign-born were in agriculture and forestry, but 43.5 percent were engaged in manufacturing. When the Congressional Immigration Commission of 1907 investigated the economic impact of immigration, it discovered that the labor supply in industry after industry was dominated by the foreign-born. In basic industries like iron and steel making, coal mining, construction work, copper mining and smelting, and oil refining, the foreign-born, on the average, comprised over 60 percent of the labor force. Labor in cotton-goods manufacturing, once the province of native-born farm girls, as at Lowell in the beginning of the nineteenth century, was now almost 70 percent foreign-born. By 1910, the clothing industry, even though always sprinkled with foreign workers, was drawing almost three quarters of its operatives from immigrant groups.* In terms of quantity of labor, it is evident from such figures that American industry would have expanded at a much slower pace if the muscle and brain of the immigrant had not been available.

All through our history, opponents of the immigrant have pointed to the working foreigner as the thief of the native worker's job. Undoubtedly the immigrant replaced a native-born worker, but it usually was a displacement which benefited the latter. "When the foreigner came in," observed one writer in the North American Review in 1892,

> the native engineered the jobs, the former did the shoveling. The American in every walk and condition of life . . . has been the 'boss' ever since. The foreigner plows and sows, the native reaps . . . one digs the canals, the other manages the boats; the one burrows in the mines, the other sells the product, and so on through all the various occupations.

*Certain industries, it should be noted, were conspicuous for their small percentages of foreign-born: boots and shoes counted only 27.3; collars, cuffs, and shirts, 13.3; cigars and tobacco, 32.6; and glass, 39.3.

Immigration: The View from Europe

Immigrants arrived in the United States from all areas of Europe. But, as Carl Degler made clear in the previous reading, by 1900 most of the newcomers came from eastern and southern Europe. One of those who arrived during this period was Louis Adamic (1898–1952), a native of Yugoslavia, who was fifteen when he emigrated in 1913. Adamic describes here how he first heard of America and why he and his countrymen came. This description also applies to those who came from other areas of Europe.

Excerpts from pp. 3-5, 100-101, 104-106 in *Laughing in the Jungle* by Louis Adamic. Copyright, 1932 by Louis Adamic; renewed, 1960 by Stella Adamic. Reprinted by permission of Harper & Row, Publishers, Inc.

I

Amerikanci in Carniola

As a boy of nine, and even younger, in my native village of Blato, in Carniola—then a Slovenian duchy of Austria and later a part of Yugoslavia—I experienced a thrill every time one of the men of the little community returned from America.

Five or six years before, as I heard people tell, the man had quietly left the village for the United States, a poor peasant clad in homespun, with a mustache under his nose and a bundle on his back; now, a clean-shaven *Amerikanec,* he sported a blue-serge suit, buttoned shoes very large in the toes and with india-rubber heels, a black derby, a shiny celluloid collar, and a loud necktie made even louder by a dazzling horseshoe pin, which, rumor had it, was made of gold, while his two suitcases of imitation leather, tied with straps, bulged with gifts from America for his relatives and friends in the village. In nine cases out of ten, he had left in economic desperation, on money borrowed from some relative in the United States; now there was talk in the village that he was worth anywhere from one to three thousand American dollars. And to my eyes he truly bore all the earmarks of affluence. Indeed, to say that he thrilled my boyish fancy is putting it mildly. With other boys in the village, I followed him around as he went visiting his relatives and friends and distributing presents, and hung onto his every word and gesture.

Then, on the first Sunday after his homecoming, if at all possible, I got within earshot of the nabob as he sat in the winehouse or under the linden in front of the winehouse in Blato, surrounded by village folk, ordering wine and *klobase*—Carniolan sausages—for all comers, paying for accordion-players, indulging in tall talk about America, its wealth and vastness, and his own experiences as a worker in the West Virginia or Kansas coal-mines or Pennsylvania rolling-mills, and comparing notes upon conditions in the United States with other local *Amerikanci* who had returned before him.

Under the benign influence of *cvichek*— Lower Carniolan wine—and often even when sober, the men who had been in America spoke expansively, boastfully, romantically of their ability and accomplishments as workers and of the wages they had earned in Wilkes-Barre or Carbondale, Pennsylvania, or Wheeling, West Virginia, or Pueblo, Colorado, or Butte, Montana, and generally of places and people and things and affairs in the New World. The men who returned to the village, either to stay or for a visit, were, for the most part, natural men of labor—men with sinewy arms and powerful backs—"Bohunks," or "Hunkies," so called in the United States— who derived a certain brawny joy and pride from hard toil. Besides, now that they had come home, they were no longer mere articles upon the industrial labor market, "working stiffs" or "wage slaves," as radical agitators in America referred to them, but adventurers, distant kinsmen of Marco Polo safely returned from a far country, heroes in their own eyes and the eyes of the village; and it was natural for them to expand and to exaggerate their own exploits and enlarge upon the opportunities to be found in America. Their boasting, perhaps, was never wholly without basis in fact. . . .

I remember that, listening to them, I played with the idea of going to America when I was but eight or nine.

My notion of the United States then, and for a few years after, was that it was a grand, amazing, somewhat fantastic place—the Golden Country—a sort of Paradise—the Land of Promise in more ways than one—huge beyond conception, thousands of miles across the ocean, untellably exciting, explosive, quite incomparable to the tiny, quiet, lovely Carniola; a place full of movement and turmoil, wherein things that were unimaginable and impossible in Blato happened daily as a matter of course.

In America one could make pots of money in a short time, acquire immense holdings, wear a white collar, and have polish on one's boots like a *gospod*—one of the gentry—and eat white bread, soup, and meat on weekdays as well as on Sundays, even if one were but an ordinary workman to begin with. In Blato no one ate white bread or soup and meat, except on Sundays and holidays, and very few then.

In America one did not have to remain an ordinary workman. There, it seemed, one man was as good as the next. There were dozens, perhaps scores, or even hundreds of immigrants in the United States, one-time peasants and workers from the Balkans—from Carniola, Styria, Carinthia, Croatia, Banat, Dalmatia, Bosnia, Montenegro, and Serbia—and from Poland, Slovakia, Bohemia, and elsewhere, who, in two or three years, had earned and saved enough money working in the Pennsylvania, Ohio, or Illinois coal-mines or steel-mills to go to regions called Minnesota, Wisconsin, and Nebraska, and there buy sections of land each of which was larger than the whole area owned by the peasants in Blato.... Oh, America was immense—*immense!* ...

II

Life in America

The great majority of immigrants who plunged into the turmoil of America, from the most intelligent to the least, were naturally bewildered, or numbed by the impact of the country upon their senses and their minds. Their first concern upon arrival was to find people of their own nationality, in whose midst they might orient themselves. One could seldom, if ever, get a job in one's old line. In America there was no stability, which was almost the keynote of life in the European countries before the World War. With machinery being improved from day to day, the job that one found carried with it no security. One might lose it from week to week, almost from hour to hour, and one could seldom base on its continuation any plans for the future. The more pronounced the difference in language, ways, and conditions in America and in the immigrant's own country, the more urgent it was for him to seek out his countrymen.

In the case of the Slavic immigrants eighteen or twenty years ago, at which time they came over in a steady stream, the first, although not the most important, difficulty arose in making the people here—native-born Americans and aliens of other nationalities—understand who they were and whence they hailed. The difficulty lay basically in the fact that many of them were not clear on the point themselves. If a Slovenian was asked what his nationality was, he very likely replied that he was a Kranjec or Krainer or Carniolan, from Kranjsko (German, *Krain;* English, *Carniola*). Only a few Czechs, Styrian Germans, and Italians from Trieste and Giorizia knew what he meant. It was as if a citizen from some such obscure state as Nevada, arriving in Belgrade or Lublyana, announced that his nationality was Nevadan. If he really knew what he was, he declared himself a Slovenian, but that, to the average American, Irishman, or Scandinavian, meant no more than Carniolan....

Two decades ago most of the Bohunks came to America intending to stay two or three years, four at the most, work to the limit of their endurance at whatever they might find, save every cent possible, and then, returning to the Old Country, pay the debt on the old place, buy a few additional fields and head of cattle, and start anew. But actually only a small proportion of them went back.

In the Old Country the man probably had a wife or a *punca* to whom he had sworn everlasting fidelity and promised to think of daily. But he was invariably a strong, virile he-man, and if he remained true to his vow (and as a rule he did), his womanless existence soon became intolerable. He yearned for his fair Marichka or Yova with a great yearning, and, sooner or later, he sent her a ticket to join him. She came, perhaps with two or three little Bohunks; if she was only his girl and married him here, she soon bore him a few. In either case, saving anything from his wages immediately became a difficult matter. Working conditions often changed overnight; there were strikes and lockouts; the family, which increased regularly every ten months, had to be moved from one state to another. To return to the Old Country thus became a hopeless dream.

He was caught in America and became "dung."

If he had no wife or girl to send a ticket to, he began to look about in the colony or he put a "wife-wanted" advertisement in *Narodni Glas* or some other Bohunk newspaper, which presently led to the same difficulties. And if he took to sin, he spent most of his pay on prostitutes (usually of his own nationality), and the rest—unless he was luckier than he was wise—he had to hand over to venereal-disease quacks for treatment.

In any case, he usually kept on digging coal or ore, or working in the steel-mills, or in the stockyards or forests, or on construction jobs from Portland to Portland. Gradually he abandoned all hope of returning home, even for a visit, and strove solely to make a living, watching for a chance to get out of the dirty, unhealthy, and hazardous work in the mines and mills and into something better. Perhaps he started a saloon, a grocery-store, a butcher-shop, or an undertaking-parlor, or bought a farm. If unmarried, he probably joined the army or became a hobo or a bum.

Unlike most of the other immigrants, especially the Scandinavians, the Irish, and the Germans, most of whom entered the country intending to settle, the Bohunks, with a few such exceptions as myself, had little interest in American events, institutions, and politics, even after they gave up the idea of returning home. Saturday evenings and Sunday afternoons, when they came together, the talk was largely about affairs in their native villages. Their newspapers devoted a good part of their space to clippings from the small-town sheets of southeastern Europe.

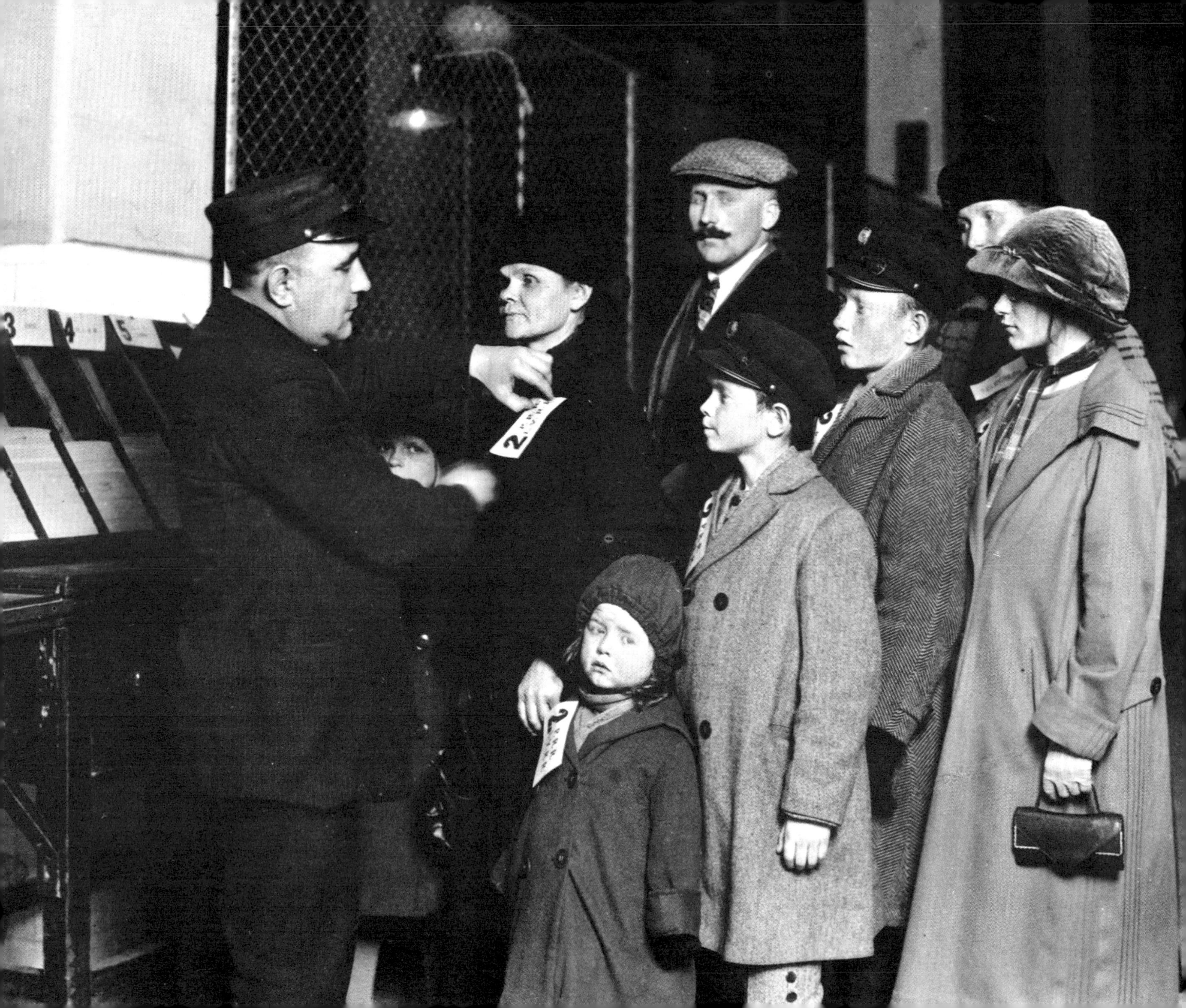

3
4
5
2

These immigrants have completed the required processes on Ellis Island, New York's immigrant depot after 1892, and are receiving "tags" allowing them to board the boat that will take them to the mainland.

Of all the Slavic groups, the Slovenians were perhaps the most assimilative, more so than the Bohemians, who, not unlike the hated Germans and Hungarians, were extremely chauvinistic, although as naturalized citizens they usually were active in civic and political affairs. This marked interest of the Bohemian Americans in the public life of their adopted country was perhaps not due so much to their cultural superiority, of which they were very conscious and proud, as to their clannishness, which surpassed even that of the Swedes and the Norwegians, and caused them to live in large, compact colonies whose leading lights were Americanized go-getters (such men as Anton Cermak, who in 1931 became mayor of Chicago).

The Immigrant's Future and His Past

Probably most immigrants came to the United States for economic reasons; many, as Louis Adamic pointed out, planned on laboring for a few years and then returning to the "Old Country." Nevertheless, many millions stayed in the United States and were deeply influenced by America's social, political, and cultural values. The following are two letters written by emigrants from Wales, in the western part of Great Britain. The first letter was written from Ohio by a David Watkins, a miner, as were many Welshmen, and the second by the Reverend D. S. Davies, a minister living in New York.

From Alan Conway, editor. *The Welsh in America*. University of Minnesota Press, Minneapolis, pp. 172-173, 322-323. © 1961 University of Minnesota.

I

The Promise of America

March 10, 1865

It is wonderful to live in a free country where the rights of men are upheld, one weighing as much as the next in the scales, with no difference between rich and poor and if you happen to meet the two on the street it would be difficult to say which was the gentleman. There is none of the pride or the inferiority of the workman here. The way to know a gentleman is by his humility and his readiness to help the poor. If he does not do that he is not considered a gentleman at all. In spite of this, there are many who are arrogant here but you can be sure that they are "greenhorns," not yet knowing the ways of the country and the respect that they get is a mockery and a cause of merriment to everyone until they come to their senses. We get trouble from some of them and we as a class, the miners, suffer most from them. Some of them are set up as bosses over us because they have just come from the Old Country and are more used to oppressing the workmen by carrying the work on at less cost. It is like this with us at the moment, as the owner of the works has sent some creature from Scotland here; but I think that he regrets it because we have had two or three strikes against him already and we will have some more to put him in his place until he leaves. If one of the bosses utters a harsh word to one of the workmen it is quite likely that there would be a strike against him the next day. There is a union of miners practically throughout the whole country and it is likely to have reached everywhere by the end of the summer. We have a weekly paper of our own which comes out regularly and belongs to no one but us. We own the press and everything belonging to it and we can convey what we are thinking to every part of the country. There's a free country for you! We ask for nothing except our rights and those we must have.

In this town there are about eight thousand souls, many of them very wealthy Welshmen, owning some of the largest trading houses in the town. There is plenty of scope here for a man to choose any kind of pleasure he wants. The general wage is four and a half dollars a day, that is eighteen shillings in your money. Everything for the sustaining of man is much dearer at the moment than in Wales.

II

The Threat of America

September 26, 1872

After coming here we could see the need for a better plan of emigration for our nation. Before we left Wales the great question was Where could we improve our worldly circumstances and where to be sure of plenty of food and clothing for one's family with less worry than there is now? As America has answered these questions, for many poor Welshmen that is the end of the argument. They emigrated to America and after coming here they found that they were losing the religious privileges of the land of their birth. They gained in the temporal things but lost in the spiritual. They found that they were in a foreign country, and in the national sense, that they had lost everything. Comfort and success are nothing when compared to the nation. It is a pity, *The Welshman* says, that the Welsh did not form a national plan of emigration fifty years ago to some new country. It is a pity that the Welsh emigration flood was not directed to the same place at that time. By now it would be a sea of Welsh. Instead, large-scale emigration has been a loss to our nation and to the Welsh language. It is believed that half a million of them have left Wales in the last hundred years and that their descendants number at least one million souls. If they were now in the same country and a million others had emigrated to them under the protection of the Welsh it would be easy to see the outcome. Unplanned emigration has meant the death of the Welsh nation and language in the United States and elsewhere. . . .

Everything here destroys our common heritage. Many of those who emigrate here from Wales join the English when they want their support and influence to uphold religion and Welsh ways. But as Welsh settlements in this strange land are weaker than the English they give their wealth, support, and intelligence to further English causes. It is always the fat horse that gets the oats and the thin horse the kicks. In addition the English have the extra strength of the children of the Welsh emigrants. The greater part of the first generation and all the second generation are American-born and lost to Wales. There are some like Stanley who are ashamed to acknowledge that they are Welsh. The result is that Welsh causes do not flourish in America.

There is not and we shall never have a Welsh college here. Those who have acquired great wealth do not become more Welsh. There is not one Welsh bookstore in the country nor a Welsh public library. The circulation of Welsh newspapers is poor so that they cannot compete with the larger newspapers in price. The people run after English things although, while doing it, they read the Welsh people and Welsh culture lower and lower. I estimate that there are no more than ten thousand who get the *Drych, Baner America,* and *Dysgedydd* (weeklies), the *Cenhadwr, Cyfaill, Glorian* and *Blodau yr Oes* (monthlies) between them. We have perhaps four hundred Welsh chapels in different states and the English pressing on them all and taking over many of them. It is true that the four Welsh denominations have twenty-two thousand members throughout the country after a hundred years of emigration but a great proportion of this number is unable to understand Welsh. The Welsh language has no prospect of success in this country and the worst thing of all is that that opinion is wholly true.

"What Do You Want of Us Poor Jews?"

Between 1890 and the outbreak of World War I in 1914, more than a million Jews came to the United States from eastern Europe and especially from Russia. Their motives were chiefly political and religious rather than economic. Between 1880 and 1906 countless Jews lost their lives in several "pogroms," or massacres, which were unofficially sanctioned by the Russian government. Even when they escaped death, Jews were restricted to an overcrowded area of western Russia, which then included Poland, and were legally banned from many types of employment. In the United States Jews faced none of these legal restrictions, though there was still prejudice. They, like other immigrant groups, settled heavily in certain sections of America's cities; these were referred to as "ghettos." In the following selection, Alfred Kazin, whose parents came from Poland, describes his family's life in the Brownsville section of Brooklyn, New York, during the 1920s.

From Alfred Kazin, *A Walker in the City* (New York, 1951), pp. 52-56, 58-61. Copyright © 1951 by Alfred Kazin. Subheadings added by the editors.

I

The Family

It was the darkness and emptiness of the streets I liked most about Friday evening, as if in preparation for that day of rest and worship which the Jews greet "as a bride"—that day when the very touch of money is prohibited, all work, all travel, all household duties, even to the turning on and off of a light—Jewry had found its way past its tormented heart to some ancient still center of itself. I waited for the streets to go dark on Friday evening as other children waited for the Christmas lights. Even Friday morning after the tests were over glowed in anticipation. When I returned home after three, the warm odor of a coffee cake baking in the oven and the sight of my mother on her hands and knees scrubbing the linoleum on the dining room floor filled me with such tenderness that I could feel my senses reaching out to embrace every single object in our household. One Friday, after a morning in school spent on the voyages of Henry Hudson, I returned with the phrase *Among the discoverers of the New World* singing in my mind as the theme of my own new-found freedom on the Sabbath.

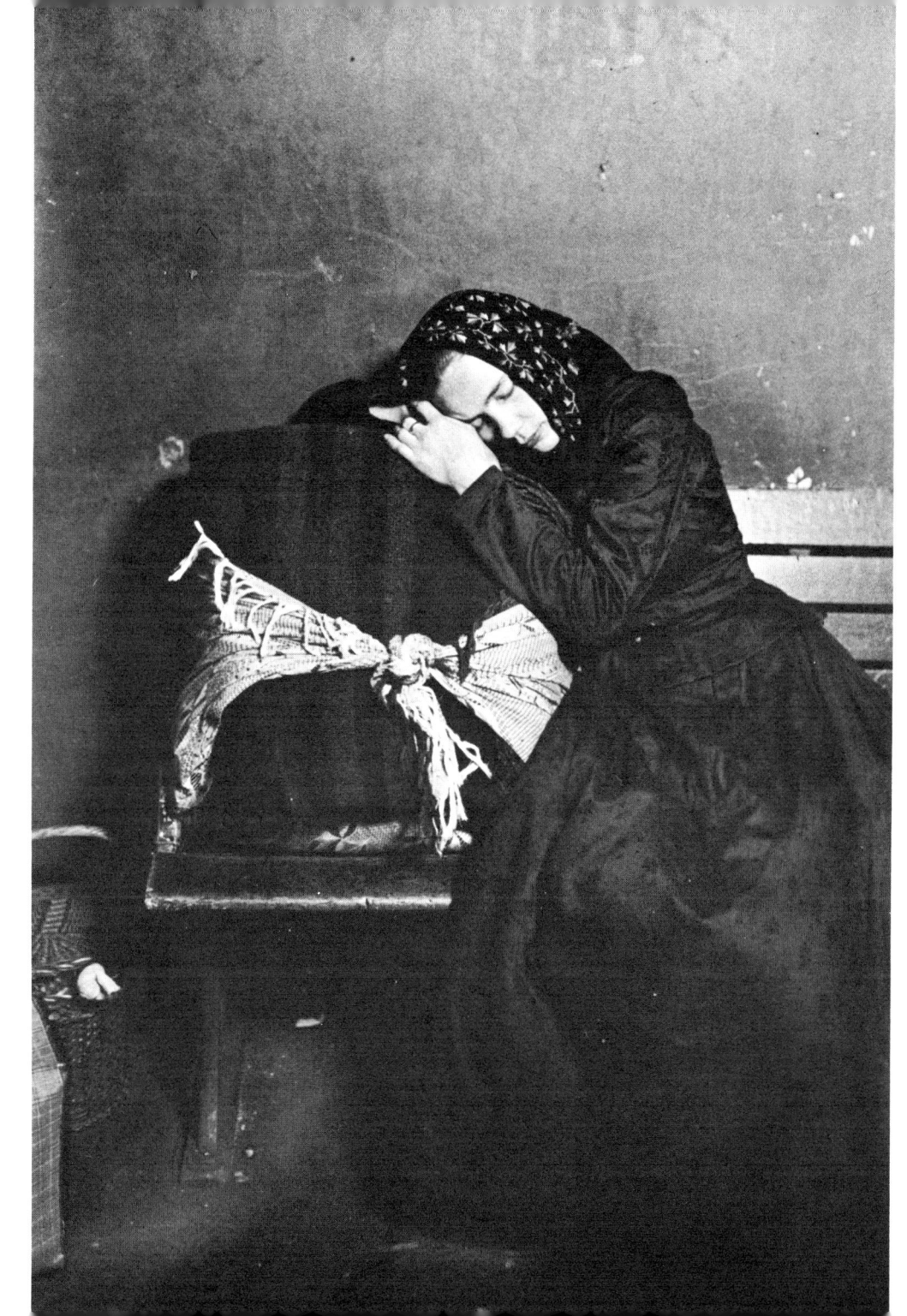

My great moment came at six, when my father returned from work, his overalls smelling faintly of turpentine and shellac, white drops of silver paint still gleaming on his chin. Hanging his overcoat in the long dark hall that led into our kitchen, he would leave in one pocket a loosely folded copy of the New York *World;* and then everything that beckoned to me from that other hemisphere of my brain beyond the East River would start up from the smell of fresh newsprint and the sight of the globe on the front page. It was a paper that carried special associations for me with Brooklyn Bridge. They published the *World* under the green dome on Park Row overlooking the bridge; the fresh salt air of New York harbor lingered for me in the smell of paint and damp newsprint in the hall. I felt that my father brought the outside straight into our house with each day's copy of the *World*. The bridge somehow stood for

An immigrant woman sleeping on her baggage in the waiting room of Ellis Island, 1905. This is another of Lewis Hine's quietly penetrating photographic studies.

freedom; the *World* for that rangy kindness and fraternalism and ease we found in Heywood Broun. My father would read aloud from "It Seems To Me" with a delighted smile on his face. "A very clear and courageous man!" he would say. "Look how he stands up for our Sacco and Vanzetti! A real social conscience, that man! Practically a Socialist!" Then, taking off his overalls, he would wash up at the kitchen sink, peeling and gnawing the paint off his nails with Gold Dust Washing Powder as I poured it into his hands, smacking his lips and grunting with pleasure as he washed himself clean of the job at last, and making me feel that I was really helping him, that I, too, was contributing to the greatness of the evening and the coming day.

By sundown the streets were empty, the curtains had been drawn, the world put to rights. Even the kitchen walls had been scrubbed and now gleamed in the Sabbath candles. On the long white tablecloth were the "company" dishes, filled for some with *gefillte* fish on lettuce leaves, ringed by red horseradish, sour and half-sour pickles, tomato salad with a light vinegar dressing; for others, with chopped liver in a bed of lettuce leaves and white radishes; the long white *khalleh*, the Sabbath loaf; chicken soup with noodles *and* dumplings; chicken, meat loaf, prunes, and sweet potatoes that had been baked all day into an open pie; compote of prunes and quince, apricots and orange rind; applesauce; a great brown nutcake filled with almonds, the traditional *lekakh;* all surrounded by glasses of port wine, seltzer bottles with their nozzles staring down at us waiting to be pressed; a samovar of Russian tea, *svetouchnee* from the little red box, always served in tall glasses, with lemon slices floating on top. My father and mother sipped it in Russian fashion, through lumps of sugar held between the teeth.

Afterwards we went into the "dining room" and, since we were not particularly orthodox, allowed ourselves little pleasures outside the Sabbath rule—an occasional game of Casino at the dining-room table where we never dined; and listening to the victrola. The evening was particularly good for me whenever the unmarried cousin who boarded with us had her two closest friends in after supper.

They were all dressmakers, like my mother; had worked with my mother in the same East Side sweatshops; were all passionately loyal members of the International Ladies Garment Workers Union; and were all unmarried. We were their only family. Despite my mother's frenzied matchmaking, she had never succeeded in pinning a husband down for any of them. As she said, they were all too *particular*—what a calamity for a Jewish woman to remain unmarried! But my cousin and her friends accepted their fate calmly, and prided themselves on their culture and their strong *progressive* interests. They felt they belonged not to the "kitchen world," like my mother, but to the enlightened tradition of the old Russian intelligentsia. Whenever my mother sighed over them, they would smile out of their greater knowledge of the world, and looking at me with a pointed appeal for recognition, would speak of novels they had read in Yiddish and Russian, of *Winesburg, Ohio,* of some article in the *Nation.*

Our cousin and her two friends were of my parents' generation, but I could never believe it—they seemed to enjoy life with such outspokenness. They were the first grown-up people I had ever met who used the word *love* without embarrassment. "*Libbe! Libbe!*" my mother would explode whenever one of them protested that she could not, after all, marry a man she did not love. "What is this love you make such a stew about? You do not like the way he holds his cigarette? Marry him first and it will all come out right in the end!" It astonished me to realize there was a world in which even unmarried women no longer young were simply individual human beings with lives of their own. *Our* parents, whatever affection might offhandedly be expressed between them, always had the look of being committed to something deeper than *mere* love. Their marriages were neither happy nor unhappy; they were arrangements. However they had met—whether in Russia or in the steerage or, like my parents, in an East Side boarding house—whatever they still thought of each other, *love* was not a word they used easily. Marriage was an institution people entered into—for all I could ever tell—only from immigrant loneliness, a need to be with one's own kind that mechanically resulted in the *family.* The *family* was a whole greater than all the individuals who made it up, yet made sense only in their untiring solidarity. I was perfectly sure that in my parents' minds *libbe* was something exotic and not wholly legitimate, reserved for "educated" people like their children, who were the sole end of their existence. My father and mother worked in a rage to put us above their level; they had married to make *us* possible. We were the only conceivable end to all their striving; we were their America. . . .

II

The Meaning of the Ghetto

Often, those Friday evenings, they spoke of *der heym,* "Home," and then it was hard for me. *Heym* was a terrible word. I saw millions of Jews lying dead under the Polish eagle with knives in their throats. I was afraid with my mother's fears, thought I should weep when she wept, lived again through every pogrom whose terrors she chanted. I associated with that old European life only pain, mud, and hopelessness, but I was of it still, through her. Whenever she would call through the roll of her many brothers and sisters and their children, remembering at each name that this one was dead, that one dead, another starving and sure soon to die—who knew *how* they were living these days in that miserable Poland?—I felt there was some supernatural Polish eagle across the sea whose face I should never see, but which sent out dark electrical rays to hold me fast.

In many ways *der heym* was entirely dim and abstract, nothing to do with me at all, alien as the skullcap and beard and frock coat of my mother's father, whom I never saw, but whose calm orthodox dignity stared up at me from an old cracked photograph at the bottom of the bureau drawer. Yet I lived each of my mother's fears from Dugschitz* to Hamburg to London to Hester Street to Brownsville through and through with such fidelity that there were times when I wished I had made that journey too, wished I could have seen Czarist Russia, since I had in any event to suffer it all over again. I often felt odd twinges of jealousy because my parents could talk about that more intense, somehow less *experimental* life than ours with so many private smiles between themselves. It was bewildering, it made me long constantly to get at some past nearer my own New York life, my having to live with all those running wounds of a world I had never seen.

*The village in Poland where his mother was from—Eds.

Then, under cover of the talk those Friday evenings, I would take up *The Boy's Life of Theodore Roosevelt* again, and moodily call out to those strangers on the summer veranda in Oyster Bay until my father spoke *his* tale of arriving in America. That was hard, too, painful in another way—yet it always made him curiously lighthearted and left me swimming in space. For he had gone off painting box cars on the Union Pacific, had been as far west as Omaha, had actually seen Sidney Hillman† toiling in Hart, Schaffner and Marx's Chicago factory, had heard his beloved Debs making fools of Bryan and Taft in the 1908 campaign,‡ had been offered a homestead in Colorado! *Omaha* was the most beautiful word I had ever heard, *homestead* almost as beautiful; but I could never forgive him for not having accepted that homestead.

"What would I have done there? I'm no farmer."

"You should have taken it! Why do we always live here!"

"It would have been too lonely. Nobody I knew."

"What a chance!"

"Don't be childish. Nobody I knew."

"Why? Why?"

"Alfred, what do you want of us poor Jews?"

So it was: we had always to be together: believers and non-believers, we were a people; I was of that people. Unthinkable to go one's own way, to doubt or to escape the fact that I was a Jew. I had heard of Jews who

†Hillman was a prominent labor leader in the garment industry—Eds.
‡Eugene Debs, Socialist candidate for President of the United States; William Jennings Bryan, Democratic candidate; William Howard Taft, Republican candidate—Eds.

pretended they were not, but could not understand them. We had all of us lived together so long that we would not have known how to separate even if we had wanted to. The most terrible word was *aleyn*, alone. I always had the same picture of a man desolately walking down a dark street, newspapers and cigarette butts contemptuously flying in his face as he tasted in the dusty grit the full measure of his strangeness. *Aleyn! Aleyn!* My father had been alone here in America as a boy. *His* father, whose name I bore, had died here at twenty-five of pneumonia caught on a garment workers' picket line, and his body flung in with thousands of other Jews who had perished those first years on the East Side. My father had never been able to find his father's grave. *Aleyn! Aleyn!*

A Question of Identity

If the first generation of immigrants struggled with the problems of getting jobs and decent places to live, their sons and daughters born in America frequently struggled to reconcile the European heritage of their parents with the American "way of life." What did it mean, they asked, to be an Italian-American, Jewish-American, or German-American? John Fante, who was born in Colorado, but whose father emigrated from Italy, describes his own experiences to show how the second generation groped for an answer to the question, Who am I?

From John Fante, "The Odyssey of a Wop," *American Mercury,* XXX (1933), pp. 89, 91–94, 96–97. Subheadings added by the editors.

I

The Second Generation

I pick up little bits of information about my grandfather. My grandmother tells me of him. She tells me that when he lived he was a good fellow whose goodness evoked not admiration but pity. He was known as a good little Wop. Of an evening he liked to sit at a table in a saloon sipping a tumbler of anisette, all by himself. He sat there like a little girl nipping an ice-cream cone. The old boy loved that green stuff, that anisette. It was his passion, and when folks saw him sitting alone it tickled them, for he was a good little Wop.

One night, my grandmother tells me, my grandfather was sitting in the saloon, he and his anisette. A drunken teamster stumbled through the swinging doors, braced himself at the bar, and bellowed:

"All right, everybody! Come an' get 'em! They're on me!"

And there sat my grandfather, not moving, his old tongue coquetting with the anisette. Everyone but he stood at the bar and drank the teamster's liquor. The teamster swung round. He saw my grandfather. He was insulted.

"You too, Wop!" said he. "Come up and drink!"

Silence. My grandfather arose. He staggered across the floor, passed the teamster, and then what did he do but go through the swinging doors and down the snowy street! He heard laughter coming after him from the saloon and his chest burned. He went home to my father.

"Mamma mia!" he blubbered. "Tummy Murray, he calla me Wopa."

"Sangue de la Madonna!"

Bareheaded, my father rushed down the street to the saloon. Tommy Murray was not there. He was in another saloon half a block away, and there my father found him. He drew the teamster aside and spoke under his breath. A fight! Immediately blood and hair began to fly. Chairs were drawn back. The customers applauded. The two men fought for an hour. They rolled over the floor, kicking cursing, biting. They were in a knot in the center of the floor, their bodies wrapped around each other. My father's head, chest and arms buried the teamster's face. The teamster screamed. My father growled. His neck was rigid and trembling. The teamster screamed again, and lay still. My father got to his feet and wiped blood from his open mouth with the back of his hand. On the floor the teamster lay with a loose ear hanging from his head. . . . This is the story my grandmother tells me.

I think about the two men, my father and the teamster, and I picture them struggling on the floor. Boy! *Can* my father fight! . . .

I enter the parochial school with an awful fear that I will be called Wop. As soon as I find out why people have such things as surnames, I match my own against such typically Italian cognomens as Bianci, Borello, Pacelli—the names of other students. I am pleasantly relieved by the comparison. After all, I think, people will say I am French. Doesn't my name sound French? Sure! So thereafter, when people ask me my nationality, I tell them I am French. A few boys begin calling me Frenchy. I like that. It feels fine.

Thus I begin to loathe my heritage. I avoid Italian boys and girls who try to be friendly. I thank God for my light skin and hair, and I choose my companions by the Anglo-Saxon ring of their names. If a boy's name is Whitney, Brown, or Smythe, then he's my pal; but I'm always a little breathless when I am with him; he may find me out. At the lunch hour I huddle over my lunch pail, for my mother doesn't wrap my sandwiches in wax paper, and she makes them too large, and the lettuce leaves protrude. Worse, the bread is homemade; not bakery bread, not "American" bread. I make a great fuss because I can't have mayonnaise and other "American" things.

The parish priest is a good friend of my father's. He comes strolling through the school grounds, watching the children at play. He calls to me and asks about my father, and then he tells me I should be proud to be studying about my great countrymen, Columbus, Vespucci, John Cabot. He speaks in a loud, humorous voice. Students gather around us, listening, and I bite my lips and wish to Jesus he'd shut up and move on.

Occasionally now I hear about a fellow named Dante. But when I find out that he was an Italian I hate him as if he were alive and walking through the classrooms, pointing a finger at me. One day I find his picture in a dictionary. I look at it and tell myself that never have I seen an uglier bastard. . . .

II

Where Are You from?

I am nervous when I bring friends to my house; the place looks so Italian. Here hangs a picture of Victor Emmanuel, and over there is one of the cathedral of Milan, and next to it, one of St. Peter's, and on the buffet stands a wine-pitcher of medieval design; it's forever brimming, forever red and brilliant with wine.

These things are heirlooms belonging to my father, and no matter who may come to our house, he likes to stand under them and brag.

So I begin to shout to him. I tell him to cut out being a Wop and be an American once in a while. Immediately he gets his razor-strop and whales hell out of me, clouting me from room to room and finally out the back door. I go into the woodshed and pull down my pants and stretch my neck to examine the blue slices across my rump. A Wop! that's what my father is! Nowhere is there an American father who beats his son this way. Well, he's not going to get away with it; some day I'll get even with him.

I begin to think that my grandmother is hopelessly a Wop. She's a small, stocky peasant who walks with her wrists crisscrossed across her belly, a simple old lady fond of boys. She comes into the room and tries to talk to my friends. She speaks English with a bad accent, her vowels rolling out like hoops. When, in her simple way, she confronts a friend of mine and says, her old eyes smiling, "You lika go the Seester scola?" my heart roars. *Mannaggia!* I'm disgraced; now they all know that I'm an Italian.

My grandmother has taught me to speak her native tongue. By seven, I know it pretty well, and I always address her in it. But when friends are with me, when I am twelve and thirteen, I pretend to ignorance of what she says, and smirk stiffly; my friends daren't know that I can speak any language but English. Sometimes this infuriates her. She bristles, the loose skin at her throat knits hard, and she blasphemes with a mighty blasphemy.

When I finish in the parochial school my people decide to send me to a Jesuit academy in another city. My father comes with me on the first day. Chiseled into the stone coping that skirts the roof of the main building of the academy is the Latin inscription: *Religioni et Bonis Artibus.* My father and I stand at a distance, and he reads it aloud and tells me what it means.

I look up at him in amazement. Is this man my father? Why, look at him! Listen to him! He reads with an Italian inflection! He's wearing an Italian mustache. I have never realized it until this moment, but he looks exactly like a Wop. His suit hangs carelessly in wrinkles upon him. Why the deuce doesn't he buy a new one? And look at his tie! It's crooked. And his shoes: they need a shine. And for the Lord's sake, will you look at his pants! They're not even buttoned in front. And oh, damn, damn, damn, you can see those dirty old suspenders that he won't throw away. Say, mister, are you really my father? you there, why, you're such a little guy, such a runt, such an old-looking fellow! You look exactly like one of those immigrants carrying a blanket. You can't be *my* father! Why, I thought, . . . I've always thought . . .

I'm crying now, the first time I've ever cried for any reason excepting a licking, and I'm glad he's not crying too. I'm glad he's as tough as he is, and we say goodbye quickly, and I go down the path quickly, and I do not turn to look back, for I know he's standing there and looking at me.

I enter the administration building and stand in line with strange boys who also wait to register for the Autumn term. Some Italian boys stand among them. I am away from home, and I sense the Italians. We look at one another and our eyes meet in an irresistible amalgamation, a suffusive consanguinity; I look away.

A burly Jesuit rises from his chair behind the desk and introduces himself to me. Such a voice for a man! There are a dozen thunderstorms in his chest. He asks my name, and writes it down on a little card.

"Nationality?" he roars.

"American."

"Your father's name?"

I whisper it, "Luigi."

"How's that? Spell it out. Talk louder."

I cough. I touch my lips with the back of my hand and spell out the name.

"Ha!" shouts the registrar. "And still they come! Another Wop! Well, young man, you'll be at home here! Yes sir! Lots of Wops here! We've even got kikes! And, you know, this place reeks with shanty Irish!"

Dio! How I hate that priest!

He continues, "Where was your father born?"

"Buenos Aires, Argentina."

"Your mother?"

At last I can shout with the gusto of truth.

"Chi-cag-oo!" Aye, just like a conductor.

Casually, by way of conversation, he asks, "You speak Italian?"

"Nah! Not a word."

"Too bad," he says.

"You're nuts," I think. . . .

III

Who Am I?

Time passes, and so do school days.

I am sitting on a wall along the plaza [in Los Angeles], watching a Mexican *fiesta* across the street. A man comes along and lifts himself to the wall beside me, and asks if I have a cigarette. I have, and lighting the cigarette, he makes conversation with me, and we talk of casual things until the *fiesta* is over. Then we get down from the wall, and still talking, go walking through the Los Angeles Tenderloin. This man needs a shave and his clothes do not fit him; it's plain that he's a bum. He tells one lie upon another, and not one is well told. But I am lonesome in this town, and a glad listener.

We step into a restaurant for coffee. Now he becomes intimate. He has bummed his way from Chicago to Los Angeles, and has come in search of his sister; he has her address, but she is not at it, and for two weeks he has been looking for her in vain. He talks on and on about this sister, seeming to gyrate like a buzzard over her, hinting to me that I should ask some questions about her. He wants me to touch off the fuse that will release his feelings.

So I ask, "Is she married?"

And then he rips into her, hammer and tongs. Even if he does find her, he will not live with her. What kind of a sister is she to let him walk these streets without a dime in his pocket, and she married to a man who has plenty of money and can give him a job? He thinks she has deliberately given him a false address so that he will not find her, and when he gets his hands on her he's going to wring her neck. In the end, after he has completely demolished her, he does exactly what I think he is going to do.

He asks, "Have *you* got a sister?"

I tell him yes, and he waits for my opinion of her; but he doesn't get it.

We meet again a week later.

He has found his sister. Now he begins to praise her. She has induced her husband to give him a job, and tomorrow he goes to work as a waiter in his brother-in-law's restaurant. He tells me the address, but I do not think more of it beyond the fact that it must be somewhere in the Italian Quarter.

And so it is, and by a strange coincidence I know his brother-in-law, Rocco Saccone, an old friend of my people and a *paesano* of my father's. I am in Rocco's place one night a fortnight later. Rocco and I are speaking in Italian when the man I have met on the plaza steps out of the kitchen, an apron over his legs. Rocco calls him and he comes over, and Rocco introduces him as his brother-in-law from Chicago. We shake hands.

"We've met before," I say, but the plaza man doesn't seem to want this known, for he lets go my hand quickly and goes behind the counter, pretending to be busy with something back there. Oh, he's bluffing; you can see that.

In a loud voice, Rocco says to me, "That man is a skunk. He's ashamed of his own flesh and blood." He turns to the plaza man.

"Ain't you?"

"Oh, yeah?" the plaza man sneers.

"How do you mean—he's ashamed? How do you mean?"

"Ashamed of being an Italian," Rocco says.

"Oh, yeah?" from the plaza man.

"That's all he knows," Rocco says. "Oh, yeah? That's all he knows. Oh, yeah? Oh, yeah? Oh, yeah? That's all he knows."

"Oh, yeah?" the plaza man says again.

"Yah," Rocco says, his face blue. *"Animale codardo!"*

The plaza man looks at me with peaked eyebrows, and he doesn't know it, he standing there with his black, liquid eyes, he doesn't know that he's as good as a god in his waiter's apron; for he is indeed a god, a miracle worker; no, he doesn't know; no one knows; just the same, he is that—he, of all people. Standing there and looking at him, I feel like my grandfather and my father and the Jesuit cook and Rocco; I seem to have come home, and I am surprised that this return, which I have somehow always expected, should come so quietly, without trumpets and thunder.

"If I were you, I'd get rid of him," I say to Rocco.

"Oh, yeah?" the plaza man says again.

I'd like to paste him. But that won't do any good. There's no sense in hammering your own corpse.

TOPIC 43

REACTIONS TO THE IMMIGRANTS

Just as immigrants themselves discovered both brighter and darker sides to their experiences in the United States, native Americans greeted the influx of foreigners with sharply differing emotions. Americans of white English Protestant derivation, who had constituted the dominant group since the early days of colonial settlement, had often disagreed over the wisdom of encouraging the immigration of those who differed from them in nationality, religion, appearance, and living style. But the economic advantages of having a constant supply of cheaper labor had always weighed heavier than concern over social divisions, as witness the arrival of hundreds of thousands of Africans, Scotch-Irish, and Germans in the colonial era and many Irish and German Catholics before the Civil War.

Immigration of diverse groups continued virtually unrestricted after the Civil War. Not until the late nineteenth and early twentieth centuries did sentiment against mass immigration grow strong enough to produce severe restrictions. The readings in this topic illuminate the significance of this mass immigration to American society, the ways older Americans felt about it, and the manner in which it came to an end in the 1920s.

Reading 204

The American and the Immigrant

The rise of the Native-American Party in the 1850s made it clear that the mass immigration of a group who were significantly different—in this case Irish Catholics—could generate considerable hostility among native-born Americans. In the following selection Maldwyn Allen Jones, a historian of American immigration, shows how this hostility developed in the late nineteenth and early twentieth centuries when the stream of immigration turned into a flood.

From Maldwyn Allen Jones, *American Immigration* (Chicago, 1960), pp. 247–248, 252–255, 260–261, 269–271, 275–277. Copyright © 1960 by the University of Chicago Press. Subheadings added by the editors.

I

The Emergence of Hostility

The dedication ceremonies for the Statue of Liberty in October, 1886, took place, ironically enough, at precisely the time that Americans were beginning seriously to doubt the wisdom of unrestricted immigration. In the prevailing atmosphere, Emma Lazarus' poetic welcome to the Old World's "huddled masses" struck an almost discordant note. Already the first barriers had been erected against the entry of undesirables. In response to public pressure Congress had suspended Chinese immigration and had taken the first tentative steps to regulate the European influx. Organized nativism, moreover, was just reviving after a lapse of a quarter of a century and would shortly be demanding restrictions

93

UNCLE SAM'S THANKSGIVING DINNER.

Thomas Nast, one of America's most famous political cartoonists, gives one interpretation of the nation's response to the great variety of immigrants in its midst. In this illustration of 1869, Uncle Sam welcomes all to his Thanksgiving dinner.

of a more drastic and general nature. This renewed agitation was no passing phase. It marked, on the contrary, the opening of a prolonged debate which was not to culminate until the 1920's, when the enactment of a restrictive code brought the era of mass immigration to a close....

The eruption of nativism which characterized the decade or so after 1885 had its origin in the social tensions of the period. The recurrence of industrial strife and of economic depression, together with the revival of interest in social reform, bred an awareness of the extent to which inequality and the hardening of class lines had resulted from the growth of an urban, industrial society. The passing of the frontier served both to heighten this realization and to induce a sense of national claustrophobia. Faced with the possibility of a reversion to European conditions, and of the disappearance of their fluid, homogeneous society, Americans began to lose confidence in the process of assimilation. The result was a nationalist outburst which stressed the need for social unity and which expressed itself in a fear-ridden and sometimes hysterical hatred of foreigners. In short, the class cleavages of the 1880's produced the same xenophobic consequences that had resulted in the 1790's from political divisions and in the 1850's from sectionalism.

Nativism came to life again for the first time since the Civil War with the Haymarket bomb outrage in Chicago in May, 1886, which aroused widespread fears of immigrant radicalism. A predisposition to associate labor discontent with foreign influence had existed even earlier, especially during the Molly Maguire riots in the Pennsylvania coalfields in the early 1870's, and again at the time of the violent railroad strikes of 1877. But it was not until the Haymarket Affair, and the conviction of a group of foreign-born anarchists for their alleged part in it, that Americans became seriously alarmed at the threat of imported revolution. Now, however, came a flood of warning against wild-eyed, foreign radicals who were alleged to be undermining the foundations of American society.

In this cartoon of 1870, Thomas Nast attacks the Catholic Church for leading what he sees as an assault on America's public schools. It is the Irish immigrant, however, whom Nast sees as giving strength to the Church and its position.

Within a month of the Haymarket Affair a new nativist political party, calling itself the American Party, came into existence in California. Here, concern at the turbulent role of the Irish in the labor movement had been growing ever since the appearance of Kearney's Workingmen's Party* a decade earlier; thus the Chicago incident simply catalyzed the existing anti-radicalism of California nativists. Arguing that immigrants were largely

*In the late 1870s Dennis Kearney, a newly naturalized Irish immigrant, led a political movement based on the often violent anti-Chinese feeling in California—Eds.

responsible for the recent nationwide wave of strikes and riots, the leaders of the American Party demanded immigration restriction, the amendment of the naturalization laws and a ban on alien ownership of real estate. But owing to the stability of the existing party structure the new organization failed to establish itself outside California, and even there its existence was short-lived.

A more broadly based phenomenon was the rapid expansion during the late eighties of patriotic, veteran, and fraternal organizations. Of these the characteristic feature was a strident nationalism which, especially

OUR PUBLIC SCHOOLS MUST AND SHALL BE PRESERVED. "FORT SUMTER." THE MAN THAT HAULS DOWN OUR PUBLIC SCHOOLS SHOOT HIM ON THE SPOT.

in the case of fraternal orders like the Order of United American Mechanics, often took the form of attacks on immigrant radicals. Significantly enough, the membership of these organizations consisted largely of just those groups—professional men, white-collar workers, small merchants, and skilled mechanics—who were suffering most from the "status revolution" of the period and who were thus most sensitive to threats to the existing order.

In older accounts the demand for immigration restriction was represented as coming largely from organized labor; business interests, conversely, were depicted as the chief defenders of an open gates policy. But this became true only after about 1905, when employers began to make great efforts to check union growth, partly through the practice of "balancing nationalities." Up to that point, however, there was no broad or clear-cut division between capital and labor upon the immigration question. Despite their demand for the prohibition of contract labor, the unions in the eighties and nineties gave only limited support to the general restriction movement. Though the declining Knights of Labor eventually declared in favor of restriction in 1892, the American Federation of Labor, with its large foreign-born membership and international outlook, could not be prevailed upon to indorse the literacy test until 1897, and even then only after bitter debate. American employers, for their part, were at first far from unanimous or consistent in their attitude to immigration. But in the last two decades of the nineteenth century many businessmen tended to be more concerned about the supposed radical tendencies of immigrants than to be appreciative of their economic value.

The re-emergence of a second nativist theme, that of anti-Catholicism, was also due basically to the nationalist anxieties of an age of crisis. But its immediate cause was the growing strength and influence of the Catholic church. The Third Plenary Council of 1884 gave a great impetus to Catholic institutional development; twenty new dioceses were established in the next decade, and the number of parochial schools so expanded that by 1890 they claimed an enrolment of 600,000 pupils. What helped make Protestants aware of these developments were the centennial celebrations of the American hierarchy in 1889, the assertion of Catholic strength which accompanied the Chicago World's Fair four years later and the appointment, also in 1893, of Cardinal Satolli as the first Apostolic Delegate to the United States. At the same time, the growing prominence of Irish politicians in American city government focused attention upon the growth of Catholic political power. And finally, the late eighties brought a revival of controversy over the public school question. The renewal of Catholic demands for a share in public school funds and the organized Catholic resistance to efforts to place parochial schools under state supervision were interpreted by many Protestants as a foreign attack upon a basic American institution, namely, "the little red schoolhouse. . . ."

II

The Beginnings of Restriction

The agitation culminated in 1896 in the passage by both houses of Congress of a literacy bill sponsored by Senator Henry Cabot Lodge of Massachusetts and providing for the exclusion of any immigrant unable to read forty words in any language. But in his last days of office President Cleveland vetoed the measure as an unworthy repudiation of America's historic role as an asylum for the oppressed.

Though restrictionists were confident that Cleveland's veto would prove to be only a minor setback, their optimism was not borne out by events. Twenty years were in fact to elapse before the campaign for a literacy test was carried to a successful conclusion. Renewed attempts to enact literacy bills in 1898, 1902, and 1906 were all defeated in Congress, and although the measure obtained congressional majorities in 1913 and 1915, it was vetoed on both occasions, first by Taft and then by Wilson.

These repeated failures are at first sight surprising. Since the restrictionists came within an ace of success in 1897, when the "new" immigrants constituted only a bare majority of the newcomers, then surely, it might be thought, they should have been able to muster enough votes to override a presidential veto in a period which saw an astonishing rise in the proportion of southern and eastern European immigrants. That they failed to do so is proof that no correlation existed between the character of immigration and the intensity of the reaction to it. Nativism rose and fell in response not to external influences but to changes in American internal conditions.

The inability of those who advocated the literacy test to achieve their objective in the period between the Spanish-American War and the outbreak of World War I was due primarily to the ebbing of the nativist impulse. The return of prosperity in the last years of the nineteenth century restored confidence in national homogeneity, and the imperialistic outburst with which it was accompanied opened new xenophobic outlets. Admittedly, national optimism received another jolt from the panic of 1907 and was therefore rather less widespread during Taft's presidency than it had been during that of McKinley. But in comparison with the early 1890's this whole period was one of buoyancy. As always, dislike of the foreigner persisted, perhaps even increased. But the air of crisis, of impending social disaster, which had characterized most of the nineties, had gone, taking with it the anxieties upon which nativism had been built....

Only on the eve of America's entry into World War I did the restrictionists manage to win enough congressional support to override a second Wilsonian veto. The Immigration Law enacted in February, 1917, was a comprehensive measure which codified existing legislation, doubled the head tax to $8.00, and added chronic alcoholics, vagrants, and "persons of constitutional psychopathic inferiority" to the list of excluded classes. The statute also established a "barred zone" in the southwest Pacific, thus excluding virtually all Asiatic immigrants not already debarred by the Chinese Exclusion Act and the Gentlemen's Agreement of 1907. Finally, the law provided for the exclusion of adult aliens unable to read a short passage in English or some other language or dialect. This requirement was not, however, to apply to aliens fleeing from religious persecution, nor was it to prevent admissible aliens from bringing in illiterate members of their immediate families.

Though the demand for the literacy test originated in pre-war conditions, its enactment in 1917 was due essentially to the added strength that restrictionism derived from the anxieties provoked by the European war. World War I was a major turning point in the history of American nativism. By making Americans aware as never before of the persistence of Old World ties, and thus of their own disunity, the conflict bred a strident demand for a type of loyalty involving complete conformity to the existing national pattern. This manifestation of the nationalist spirit, which came to be generally referred to as "100 percent Americanism," proved to be more than a mere wartime phenomenon. Persisting into the 1920's, it became an essential ingredient of the movement which carried the restrictionists to final victory.

A new insistence upon national solidarity was apparent from almost the start of the European conflict. The German-American campaign of 1914-15 for an embargo on American exports of arms to the belligerents was widely interpreted as a German-inspired attempt to overthrow American neutrality. "Germany," commented the Houston *Post* in 1915, "seems to have lost all of her foreign possessions with the exception of Milwaukee, St. Louis, and Cincinnati." Complaints of the divided loyalty of the German element developed into a widespread agitation against "hyphenated Americans," with Theodore Roosevelt and Woodrow Wilson as its leading spokesmen. Though German "tools of the Kaiser" remained the main target for criticism, Irish-Americans too incurred a great deal of hostility on account of their rabid pro-Germanism. In replying to an Irish agitator, Jeremiah O'Leary, who had protested during the 1916 election campaign against Wilson's "pro-British policies," the President wrote: "I should feel deeply mortified to have you or anybody like you vote for me. Since you have access to many disloyal Americans and I have not, I will ask you to convey this message to them...."

III

The Triumph of Restriction

Under such circumstances organized nativism experienced a notable revival in the early 1920's. Anti-Semitism increased markedly, especially in the rural regions which had learned as long ago as the Populist era to hate and fear the "International Jew." Social discrimination against Jews increased, too, though this was less indicative of the strength of nativism than was the appearance of an anti-Semitic ideology, focusing upon an alleged world conspiracy by Jews and disseminated through such publications as Henry Ford's notorious *Dearborn Independent*. Anti-Semitism was partly responsible for the astonishing growth of the Ku Klux Klan, which after 1920 spread like wildfire in the South and Middle West and which reached a membership peak of some two and a half million by 1923. Yet the heart of Klan nativism was always to be found in its virulent anti-Catholicism, the product of that same rural fundamentalism which gave the movement as a whole its characteristic evangelistic air.

While the fiery crosses of the Klan were spreading the gospel of intolerance, American nativism generally was acquiring an increasingly racial tinge. Thanks to the writings of a group of popular authors who had absorbed Madison Grant's* teachings, the racist phi-

---

*Madison Grant's *The Passing of the Great Race* (1916) emphasized the glories of the Anglo-Saxon and Teutonic races—Eds.

losophy of the intellectuals filtered down to the American masses. Especially influential in popularizing the doctrine of Nordic superiority was a series of articles in 1922 in the *Saturday Evening Post* by the novelist Kenneth Roberts, who warned that a mixture of Nordic with Alpine and Mediterranean stocks would produce only a worthless race of hybrids. About the same time, publication of the results of the United States Army's wartime psychological tests on soldiers helped still further to condition the public to race thinking. The fact that soldiers from southern and eastern Europe had markedly lower IQ scores than those from northern and western Europe and the United States was adduced as conclusive proof of Nordic intellectual superiority.

During the congressional debates on immigration restriction in 1920-21, the new racial nativism had not yet had time to develop fully. At that time the demand for restriction was based largely on the alleged need to guard against an influx of starving Europeans, whose arrival would flood an already depressed labor market. Even so, it was upon southern and eastern Europeans that criticism chiefly fell, and there was general agreement upon the need to devise some formula to exclude the "new" immigration without substantially affecting the "old." With this purpose in mind Congress enacted a provisional measure in May, 1921, which introduced the principle of numerical restriction upon the basis of nationality. The law limited the number of immigrants of each nationality during the forthcoming year to 3 percent of the number of foreign-born persons of that nationality resident in the United States at the time of the last available census, which was that of 1910.

Extended for two more years in May, 1922, this stopgap measure was superseded in 1924 by the Johnson-Reed Act, which laid down a permanent basis for admission. By now the notion that immigration policy should be based upon racial considerations was widely accepted both by the public and by Congress. Thus the purpose of the 1924 statute was avowedly to maintain the "racial preponderance [of] the basic strain on our people," and thereby to stabilize the ethnic composition of the population. The more successfully to achieve this end, the law abandoned the percentage principle for that of national origins. This involved placing an upper limit of 150,000 upon the immigration of any one year, and the assignment of quotas to each nationality in proportion to its contribution to the existing American population. But since it would take time to calculate admissions on the new basis, revised percentage quotas were to operate until 1927. These would be 2 percent quotas based upon the 1890 census, a change designed to reduce still further the proportion of south and east European entries. Countries of the Western Hemisphere were exempted from the quota system, but a complete prohibition of Japanese immigration made the pattern of Oriental exclusion almost complete.

With the enactment of this law an epoch in American history came to an end.* After three centuries of free immigration America all but completely shut her doors on newcomers. The Statue of Liberty would still stand in New York harbor, but the verses on its base would henceforth be but a tribute to a vanished ideal.

*In 1965 Congress passed a law greatly reducing the significance of the national origins system of immigration—Eds.

The "Barbarian" Invasion of America (1912)

Rapid industrialization produced changes in American society, changes which many Americans thought were for the worse. Some of these changes were blamed on the millions of immigrants from eastern and southern Europe, whose social values seemed very different from those of older Americans. One of the most hostile to the new immigrant was Prescott F. Hall (1868-1921), a founder of the Immigration Restriction League and a member of Boston's upper class.

From Prescott F. Hall, "The Future of American Ideals," *The North American Review*, CXCV (1912), pp. 94-96, 100-102. Subheadings added by the editors.

I
The Inferior Peoples

Gobineau once said, "America is likely to be, not the cradle of a new, but the grave of an old race." Is there, indeed, a danger that the race which has made our country great will pass away, and that the ideals and institutions which it has cherished will also pass?

It seems to be generally agreed that down to the period of fifteen years or so after the close of the Civil War there was a fairly definite American type, which had expressed itself, not so much in literature or art, as in politics and invention, and in certain social ideals. Washington and Lincoln, however different in some respects, both represented a certain type of English civilization, and both stood for certain political, social, and ethical points of view. The original settlers of this country were mainly Teutonic, belonging to what is now called the Baltic race, from northern Europe, which has always been distinguished for energy, initiative, and self-reliance. Impatient of much government, relying upon self-help rather than the paternalism of the State, this race was none the less firm in its allegiance to certain pretty definite religious and social standards. It insisted from the beginning on general education, and where opportunities for schooling were wanting there was nevertheless a wide training given by interchange of ideas in the home, on the farm, in the church, and in the town meeting. In town affairs every citizen was expected to take part, and usually did so, thus conferring a benefit on the community and receiving something in exchange. The result of this common racial origin and of these relatively homogeneous institutions was, as I have said, the amalgamation of the people into a fairly definite national type.

What has happened since then? To-day, less than one-half of our people are descendants of the original stock and of the early settlers. Since 1820, we have received from Europe and Asia some twenty-eight millions of people. About one-third of these came prior to 1880 and were of races kindred to those already here; in other words, they had a common heritage of institutions if not of language, and were assimilated into the general population with comparative ease. The other two-thirds, the eighteen millions who have come since 1880, have been, on the other hand, of entirely different races—of Alpine, Mediterranean, Asiatic, and African stocks. These races have an entirely different mental make-up from the Baltic race; they bring with them an inheritance of widely differing political and social ideals, and a training under social and political institutions very different from ours. The Slavic races, for example, differ from the Teutonic in temperament as much as the emotional nations of the Mediterranean. The South Italian, which constitutes the largest element in our present immigration, is one of the most mixed races in Europe and is partly African, owing to the negroid migration from Carthage to Italy. The modern Greek is by no means the Greek of the time of Pericles, either in race or temperament. The Hebrew, which constitutes the next largest element of immigration, in spite of long residence in Europe is still, as it always has been, an Asiatic race; while the Syrians, Chinese, Japanese, and Hindus are still more removed from the civilization of northern Europe and America.

This movement of peoples from the Old World to the New is on a scale unprecedented in history, and its effects cannot fail to be profound and far-reaching. What will they be?

Americans have hitherto paid very little attention to this question: first, because they have not considered the difference between hostile and peaceful invasions in history; and second, because they fail to observe that recent immigration is of an entirely different kind from that which our fathers knew. The earlier immigration having been of kindred races and having produced no profound changes, our people became used to the phenomenon and took it as a matter of course. At the present time, most of us consider that the movement now going on is similar to that which has been, and anticipate results no different from those previously observed.

If the million people coming every year came not as peaceful travelers, but as an invading hostile army, public opinion would be very different to what it is; and yet history shows that it has usually been the peaceful migrations and not the conquering armies which have undermined and changed the institutions of peoples. To take the classical error on this subject, we have been told repeatedly that, on the one hand, it was the conquering Goths and Vandals, and on the other hand, their own vice and luxury, which cost the Romans their empire. The real cause of the fall of Rome was neither of these things. It was the constant infiltration into Roman citizenship of large numbers of "barbarians"—that is, of races alien in instincts and habits of thought and action to the races which had built up the Roman Empire. For a time, indeed, the mold of political structure and social habit, though cracking, did not break; but the new-comers assimilated the Romans faster than they were themselves assimilated, and in time the mold broke in pieces. In precisely the same way some provinces of France are to-day becoming German, and others Italian, while the Germans are consciously making use of this method in their attempt to Prussianize Poland.

The "barbarians" of the present time, however, do not come from the plateaus of central Asia or from the jungles of Africa; they are the defective and delinquent classes of Europe—the individuals who have not been able to keep the pace at home and have fallen into the lower strata of its civilization. . . .

II

The Danger to America

Can we not already see certain effects of the newer immigration upon our social life? In many places the Continental Sunday, with its games and sports, its theatrical and musical performances, and its open bars, is taking the place of the Puritan Sabbath. In some of our factory towns there are many operatives living under the system of free marriage, and in at least one place the method of building tenements has been altered to correspond to this system. Professor Commons notes that we have already begun to despotize our institutions in order to deal with large masses of citizens not capable of intelligently supporting representative government. We see, also, the phenomena of political parties and groups on racial lines, with their own newspapers in foreign languages, seeking representation as racial units precisely as in Austria. These groups have already taken a conspicuous part in opposing immigration legislation, already existing or proposed, which makes it more difficult for their friends and relatives to come here; and, under our political system, these foreign-born groups already hold the balance of power in many places. This means that they often divide, not on public policy, but on some matter of racial advantage. In any case they do not and cannot combine to make parties like those of the older population.

All these changes may be good or bad, but they cannot fail to impress us; and, if these changes rise above the swirling mass of events and catch our eyes, we may be sure that more profound changes are in process beneath the surface.

We have to contend not only with alien habits and ideals, and with the fact that these differences cannot be effaced by education in one or even two generations, but also with the fact that we are getting a great many immigrants who are below the mental, moral, and physical average of both our country and their own. A recent writer in a leading German review has said: "The immigration of the last decade has increased the number of hands, but not the number of heads, in the United States." While this may be an extreme statement, there is the unanimous testimony of the Commissioner-General of Immigration, the Commissioner at the Port of New York, and the Immigration Commission, which has recently spent several years studying the matter, to the fact that for one immigrant whose defects are so marked as to put him in the classes excluded by law there are hundreds, if not thousands, who are below the average of our people, and who, as George William Curtis put it, are "watering the nation's life blood."

Recent investigations in eugenics show that heredity is a much more important factor than environment as regards social conditions—in fact, that in most cases heredity is what makes the environment. This is confirmed by the practice of the insurance companies which attach the chief importance to the hereditary characteristics of an individual. If this position is sound, education and distribution can only palliate the evils and delay fundamental changes. As Professor Karl Pearson says: "You cannot change the leopard's spots, and you cannot change bad stock to good; you may dilute it, possibly spread it over a large area, spoiling good stock, but until it ceases to multiply it will not cease to be."

America, the Melting Pot of Nations (1912)

A few months after Prescott Hall's article appeared, the same magazine printed an article putting forth a very different view of the immigrant's place in American society. The author was Percy S. Grant (1860-1927), an Episcopal minister in New York, and a man who, as he wrote, "had no admixture of blood in my own family, outside the original area of Massachusetts, for two hundred years."

From Percy S. Grant, "American Ideals and Race Mixture," *The North American Review*, CXCV (1912), pp. 513-515, 521-524. Subheadings added by the editors.

I

Why We Fear the Immigrant

The most impressive sight to be seen in America is the stream of immigrants coming off ship at Ellis Island. No waterfall or mountain holds such awesome mystery; no river or harbor, embracing the navies of the world, expresses such power; no city so puts wings to the imagination; no work of art calls with such epic beauty. But there are spectators who behold in the procession from overseas an invading army comparable to the Gothic hordes that overran Rome, who lament this meeting of Europe and America as the first act in our National Tragedy.

Undoubtedly we have a situation unknown to any other nation, past or present. In 1910 the total population of the United States was 91,972,266; of these 13,343,583 were foreign-born whites; 10,239,579 were negroes, Indians, and Asiatics. Between 1900-1910, 9,555,673 immigrants came in from over fifty races. Of the native whites forty-seven percent are the children of foreign-born parents. Of our entire population 43,972,185 were born of native white parents—that is, only forty percent.

A recent writer in *The North American Review*, Prescott F. Hall, secretary of the

League for Limiting Immigration and author of a volume on immigration, stated in the January number the case against the future of American ideals under the influence of race mixture. He began by quoting Gobineau: "America is likely to be not the cradle of a new, but the grave of an old race." Mr. Hall sought to sustain this prophecy.

I belong to no immigration league, "limiting" or "liberal"; I have had no admixture of blood in my own family, outside the original area of Massachusetts, for two hundred years, but I wish to suggest considerations that may calm the fears of Mr. Hall and his friends. In the half-dozen years since his larger study of the question a new collection of facts in the case has been made in America. A volume, *The Problem of Immigration,* just published by Professor Jenks and Professor Lauck, ought to modify considerably a pessimistic forecast. Both the authors were from the beginning connected with the United States Immigration Commission which has been studying the problem for the last four years, and they have summed up in their 484 pages the information collected in forty-two volumes of the original material published by the Commission.

Broadly speaking, our apprehension of harm to American ideals from race mixture is nothing but prejudice. Much of our dread of a deterioration of the American stock by immigration is a survival of ancient jealousy and alarm which once characterized the contact of all "natives" everywhere with all "foreigners." The sight of a foreigner meant ordinarily a raid or a war. This real dread, as it was of old, lingers in our subconsciousness. The destruction of the trait will yield only to intelligence, sympathy, and civilization.

Another element in our fear is the fetish of Teutonic superiority and the dogma of Latin degeneracy. Races that have produced in our lifetime a Cavour, a Mazzini, a Louis Pasteur, that have fought and defeated ecclesiastic and feudal enemies in their own households, have much to teach us.

In the Conference on Immigration held in New York a few years ago, there were delegates scarcely able to speak the English language who orated against later arrivals in this country than themselves and predicted our downfall if they were admitted. In short, every race considers itself superior; its diatribes against other races are sheer vanity. We Americans, in conceit of superiority, are in the same class as the Chinese. William Elliot Griffis, a writer on Asiatic people, recently declared that

> after an adult lifetime of study of the peoples of the Far East, I find few or no novelties in their history or evolution as compared with that of our own rise from savagery to civilization; nor is their human nature by a hair's breadth different from our own. What we need now to have cast in the world's melting-pot is the colossal conceit common to the white and the yellow man with more scientific comparative history.

At any rate, our free government is a standing invitation to the oppressed of other countries, and our undeveloped wealth makes a constant appeal for strong arms and hard workers. What can we do, then? We cannot shut out "foreigners" and still be true either to our own ideals or to our practical requirements. Nor can we pick and choose. There is no accepted standard of excellence except health and "literacy." Moreover, there are not enough of one foreign stock, were we to select one as the best, to do the work in the United States waiting to be done.

Why shouldn't the badly-off foreigner come here? There is no evidence that the present forms of government under which the immigrant races live at home are the best for them; many of these governments have had to meet grave popular uprisings and revolutions. We cannot say to the immigrant, "Stay where you were born, because the government there is best adapted to you." Some of our new people are even exiles—driven from their homes. Nor can we say, "Reform your government." Such a method under despotism is too uncertain for men who desire to see results.

The forms of government under which men live are not stereotyped, and, while some change slowly, others in response to the people's need change rapidly. A democracy is the most plastic form and gives freest course to evolutionary development. There is, consequently, a natural flow from rigid to plastic governments, which can only be checked by the plastic becoming set. This it cannot do without committing suicide. One of our mistakes (a most important cause, too, of our distrust of race mixture) is to suppose that our own form of government is fixed and final, only to be injured or destroyed by any change. . . .

II

Immigrants and American Ideals

The Roman Empire did not fall on account of racial degeneracy, due to the infiltration of Huns, Goths, and Vandals, but on account of the weakness of its political and industrial institutions, and the enervation of the people in the hands of the patrician class. The Roman land laws and Roman slaves, as well as the Roman system of government, which had no method of true amalgamation, but was a loose sort of confederacy, are responsible for the break-up of the Roman Empire.

The rapidity with which the democratic ideas are taken on by immigrants under the influence of our institutions is remarkable. I have personally had experiences with French-Canadians, Portuguese, Hebrews, and Italians. These races have certainly taken advantage of their opportunities among us in a fashion to promise well for their final effect upon this country. The French-Canadian has become a sufficiently good American to have given up his earlier programme of turning New England into a new France—that is, into a Catholic province or of returning to the Province of Quebec. He is seeing something better than a racial or religious ideal in the freedom of American citizenship; and on one or two occasions, when he had political power in two municipalities, he refrained from exercising it to the detriment of the public-school system. He has added a gracious manner and a new feeling for beauty to New England traits.

The Portuguese have taken up neglected or abandoned New England agricultural land and have turned it to productive and valuable use. Both the French-Canadian and the Portuguese have come to us by way of the New England textile mills.

The actual physical machinery of civilization—cotton-mills, woolen-mills, iron-mills, etc.—lock up a great deal of human energy physical and mental, just as one hundred years ago the farms did, from which later sprang most of the members of our dominant industrial class. A better organization of society, by which machinery would do still more and afford a freer play for mental and physical energy and organization, would find a response from classes that are now looked upon as not contributing to our American culture; would unlock the high potentialities in the laboring classes, now unguessed and unexpended.

The intellectual problems and the advanced thinking of the Hebrew, his fondness for study, and his freedom on the whole from wasteful forms of dissipation, sport, and mental stagnation, constitute him a more fortunate acquisition for this country than are thousands of the descendants of Colonial settlers. In short, we must reconstruct our idea of democracy—of American democracy. This done, we must construct a new picture of citizenship. If we do these things we shall welcome the rugged strength of the peasant or the subtle thought of the man of the Ghetto in our reconsidered American ideals. After all, what are these American ideals we boast so much about? Shall we say public schools, the ballot, freedom? The American stock use private schools when they can afford them; they too often leave town on Election Day; as for freedom, competent observers believe it is disappearing. The conservators and believers in American ideals seem to be our immigrants. To the Russian Jew, Abraham Lincoln is a god. If American ideals are such as pay honor to the intellectual and to the spiritual or foster human brotherhood or love culture and promote liberty, then they are safe with our new citizens who are eager for these things.

Not only do these races bring with them most desirable qualities, but they themselves are subjected to new environment and strongly influential conditions. Just here arise duties for the present masters of America. Ought they not to create an industrial, social, and educational environment of the most uplifting sort for our foreign-born citizens?

If working-people are obliged to live in unhealthful tenements situated in slums or marsh land, if the saloon is allowed to be their only social center, if they are fought by the rich in every effort to improve their condition, we may expect any misfortune to happen to them and also any fate to befall the State.

What improved *milieu* can do to improve the physique is easily seen on all sides. The increase in the height and weight of Americans in the last few decades is conspicuous. Even the size of American girls and boys has increased, and this increase in size is commonly attributed to the more comfortable conditions of life, to better food, and especially to the popularity of all forms of athletics, and the extension, as in the last twenty-five or thirty years, of the out-of-door and country life. If these factors have made so marked and visible a change in the physique of the children of native-born Americans, why may not the same conditions also contribute an improvement to the more recent immigrant stock?

Our question, then, as to the effect of race mixture is not the rather supercilious one: What are we admitting into America that may possibly injure American ideals? but, What are the old American races doing to perpetuate these ideals? And is not our future as a race, largely by our own fault, in the hands of the peasant races of Europe?

After all, for those who pin their faith to the Baltic and northern European races, there is reason for hope to be found even in current immigration. From 1899 to 1910, the Hebrew, southern Italian, Polish, and Slovak period, of the nine millions who landed in the United

States, while there were 377,527 Slovaks and 318,151 Magyars, there were 408,614 English, 586,306 Scandinavians, and 754,375 Germans, and even 136,842 Scotch, 151,774 Finnish, 439,724 Irish, and 20,752 Welsh. Two millions and a half from northern Europe—over twenty-six percent. One million seventy-four thousand are Hebrews, mostly from Russia; and the Russian Jews, according to a most distinguished German Jew, are intellectually the ablest Hebrews in America. If, on the other hand, nearly two millions of the immigrants of the last decade have been southern Italians, let us show them gratitude for their invaluable manual labor, for their willingness, their patience, their power for fast work, and their love of America. Their small stature does not argue their degeneracy. The Romans were small compared to the Goths—small, but well formed and strong. The Japanese are also small.

Indifference, prejudice, illiteracy, segregation of recent immigrants by parochial schools, by a native colonial press, bad physical and social environment, and the low American ideals of citizenship held by those the immigrant sees or hears most about, obstruct race assimilation; but all these can be changed. Yes, it is the keeping up of difference and class isolation that destroys and deteriorates. Fusion is a law of progress.

Theodore Roosevelt on the Immigrant as an American

Theodore Roosevelt (1858–1919), President of the United States from 1901 to 1909, was a wealthy American who traced his ancestry back to the original Dutch settlers of New York who had arrived in the mid-1600s. The following letters clearly reveal Roosevelt's attitude toward the immigrant's place in American society. The first two letters were written while Roosevelt was President; the last toward the end of World War I when the loyalty of some immigrants was often questioned.

Reprinted by permission of the publishers from Vol. V, pp. 296–297; Vol. VI, pp. 1042–1043; Vol. VIII, pp. 1361–1362 of Elting E. Morison, editor, *The Letters of Theodore Roosevelt.* Cambridge, Mass.: Harvard University Press, Copyright, 1952, 1954, by the President and Fellows of Harvard College.

To Frau Frederick Czermak   June 11, 1906

My dear Madam: I have received your letter and the very interesting and attractive photographs of your family and of the hunting lodge. I should not venture to advise you about coming to America. My experience has been that life in a new country is very hard for people accustomed to the social ease which comes from high position in an old country. America is an excellent place for artisans and peasants to come to, but unless you are thoroughly familiar with conditions here I should not advise you to come here for the purpose of settling as a large land owner. I certainly should not advise your coming here under any conditions until some personal representative of yours had traveled about and himself looked over the land. If your boy were old enough I should advise his doing this, but if he is not old enough then someone else should do so. I have seen so much suffering come to people of cultivation and refinement not accustomed to living hard and not accustomed to manly labor who have settled here, that I am very loath to advise such a person to come over and embark his or her little fortune in a life of a totally new type.

To Lyman Abbott   May 29, 1908

I grow extremely indignant at the attitude of coarse hostility to the immigrant taken by so many natives . . . . I have never had much chance to deal with the Slav, Magyar, or Italian; but wherever I have had the chance I have tried to do with them as with the German and the Irishman, the Catholic and the Jew, and that is, treat them so as to appeal to their self-respect and make it easy for them to become enthusiastically loyal Americans as well as good citizens. I have one Catholic in my Cabinet and have had another, and I now have a Jew in the Cabinet; and part of my object in each appointment was to implant in the minds of our fellow-Americans of Catholic or of Jewish faith, or of foreign ancestry or birth, the knowledge that they have in this country just the same rights and opportunities as everyone else, just the same chance of reward for doing the highest kind of service; and therefore just the same ideals as a standard toward which to strive. I want the Jewish young man who is born in this country to feel that Straus stands for his ideal of the successful man rather than some crooked Jew money-maker. I want the young Catholic of Irish or French descent to feel that if he acts as a good American should, he can become a Cabinet minister like Bonaparte or Wynne; a Governor of the Philippines, like Smith; a judge, like Tracey; in short, that the right chance is open to him and the right ideals before him. In my Cabinet there sit together Meyer, whose granduncle was a colonel under Blucher at Waterloo; and Bonaparte, whose great grandfather was Napoleon's brother and a king whom Meyer's granduncle helped to overthrow. That they are both good Americans and nothing else is all that we think of; ... nobody asks whether any member of my Cabinet is of English, or Scotch, or Dutch, or German, or Irish descent; whether he is Protestant, Catholic or Jew. In short, we have acted on principles of straight Americanism; and I am glad that before I end my term I shall have in my Cabinet Luke Wright, a representative of the South, a man who fought in the Confederate service, and who is just as loyal an American today as the best veterans of the Grand Army. It was the one thing which I felt was wanted to . . . emphasize the entire Americanism of the Cabinet, to give it from the national standpoint an absolutely representative character.

To Arthur Train   August 13, 1918

Dear Train: That is an admirable story of yours in the current *McClure's*. I am immensely pleased with it—it is exactly the kind of thing which ought to be written. Will you however permit me one suggestion, not in reference to this story, but to the other stories that should go with it. In this story there is a native American scoundrel, which is all right. There is also a meaner Jew scoundrel, which is also all right. But there are native American representatives of manliness and decency; and there ought also to be a Jew among them! It is very important that we shall not give the impression that we are attacking all foreigners qua foreigners. There are exceedingly bad Jews, and exceedingly bad old-stock native Americans. There are exceedingly good men who are Jews, and other exceedingly good men who are native old-stock Americans. It is the same thing with men of Irish and German extraction. I hope you will make the emphasis with all possible insistence as between all men who are good Americans, and all who are bad Americans; and that you will be careful to see that your readers clearly understand that there are Jews and Gentiles and men of old native American stock, and men of English, Irish, Scandinavian and German parentage on both sides. I agree with you that on the whole the old native stock will furnish the bulk of the leaders for Americanism; but there are any number of others also!

America: A Federation of Cultures (1916)

During the early part of this century some Americans damned the immigrant as being incapable of becoming a "real" American. Others, however, complimented the immigrant on his willingness to be "Americanized." Randolph Bourne (1886–1918), a well-known liberal journalist, took a different approach to the question. Bourne's article appeared, it should be noted, less than a year before the United States entered World War I and at a time when Americanization campaigns were common.

From Randolph Bourne, "Trans-National America," *The Atlantic Monthly*, CXVIII (1916), pp. 86–87, 89–90, 93. Subheadings added by the editors.

I

The Melting Pot

No reverberatory effect of the great war has caused American public opinion more solicitude than the failure of the "melting-pot." The discovery of diverse nationalistic feelings among our great alien population has come to most people as an intense shock. It has brought out the unpleasant inconsistencies of our traditional beliefs. We have had to watch hard-hearted old Brahmins virtuously indignant at the spectacle of the immigrant refusing to be melted, while they jeer at patriots like Mary Antin* who write about "our forefathers." We have had to listen to publicists who express themselves as stunned by the evidence of vigorous nationalistic and cultural movements in this country among Germans, Scandinavians, Bohemians, and Poles, while in the same breath they insist that the alien shall be forcibly assimilated to that Anglo-Saxon tradition which they unquestioningly label "American."

As the unpleasant truth has come upon us that assimilation in this country was pro-

---

*Mary Antin emigrated as a child from Russia. She published a number of books and articles celebrating the Americanization of the immigrant—Eds.

"Americanizing" the immigrant became a great concern during the years when millions were entering the country. Here children of recent immigrants salute the flag in New York's Mott Street Industrial School.

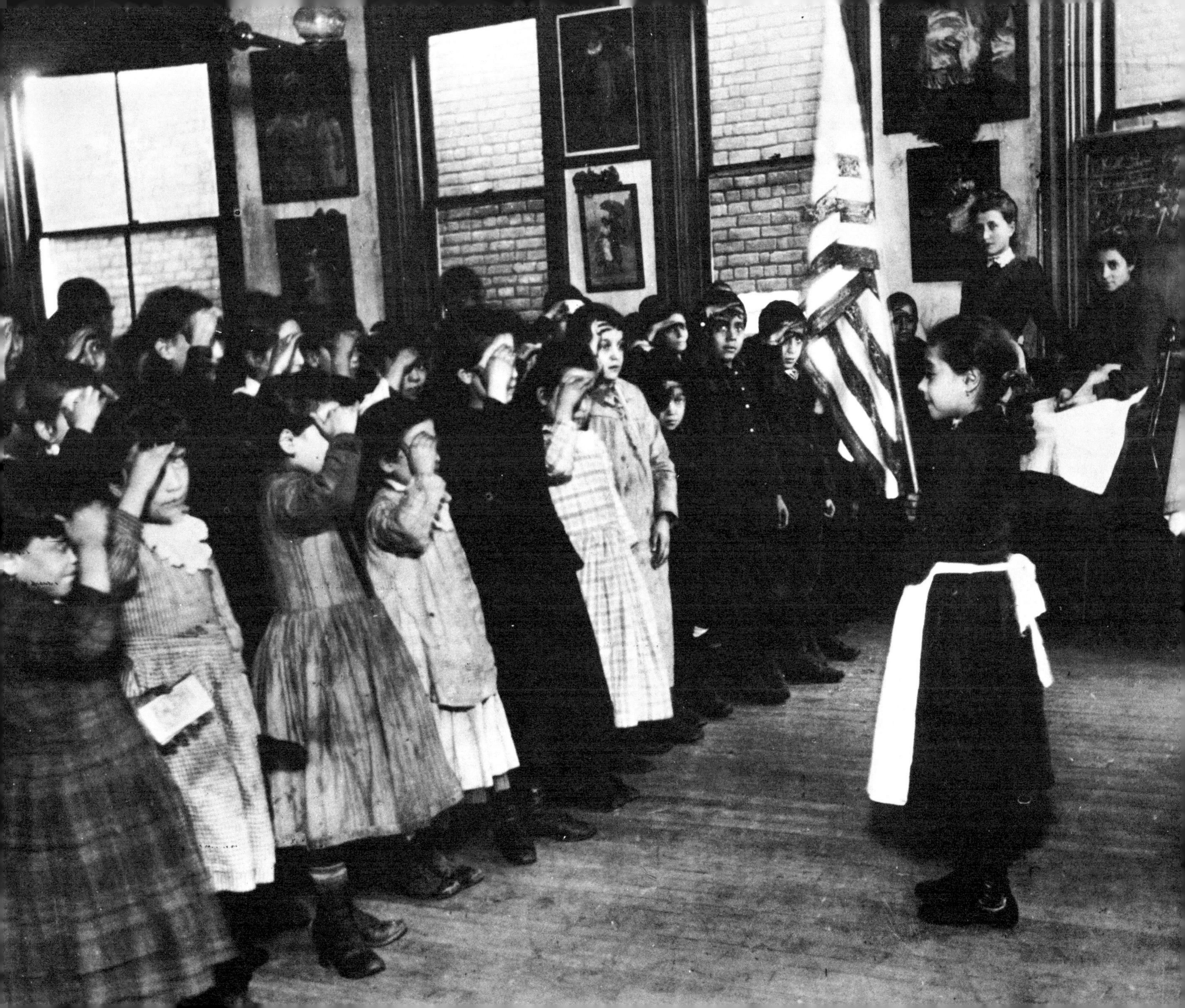

ceeding on lines very different from those we had marked out for it, we found ourselves inclined to blame those who were thwarting our prophecies. The truth became culpable. We blamed the war, we blamed the Germans. And then we discovered with a moral shock that these movements had been making great headway before the war even began. We found that the tendency, reprehensible and paradoxical as it might be, has been for the national clusters of immigrants, as they became more and more firmly established and more and more prosperous, to cultivate more and more assiduously the literatures and cultural traditions of their homelands. Assimilation, in other words, instead of washing out the memories of Europe, made them more and more intensely real. Just as these clusters became more and more objectively American, did they become more and more German or Scandinavian or Bohemian or Polish.

To face the fact that our aliens are already strong enough to take a share in the direction of their own destiny and that the strong cultural movements represented by the foreign press, schools, and colonies are a challenge to our facile attempts, is not, however, to admit the failure of Americanization. It is not to fear the failure of democracy. It is rather to urge us to an investigation of what Americanism may rightly mean. It is to ask ourselves whether our ideal has been broad or narrow—whether perhaps the time has not come to assert a higher ideal than the "melting-pot." Surely we cannot be certain of our spiritual democracy when, claiming to melt the nations within us to a comprehension of our free and democratic institutions, we fly into panic at the first sign of their own will and tendency. We act as if we wanted Americanization to take place only on our own terms, and not by the consent of the governed. All our elaborate machinery of settlement and school and union, of social and political naturalization, however, will move with friction just in so far as it neglects to take into account this strong and virile insistence that America shall be what the immigrant will have a hand in making it, and not what a ruling class, descendant of those British stocks which were the first permanent immigrants, decide that America shall be made. This is the condition which confronts us, and which demands a clear and general readjustment of our attitude and our ideal.

Mary Antin is right when she looks upon our foreign-born as the people who missed the Mayflower and came over on the first boat they could find. But she forgets that when they did come it was not upon other Mayflowers, but upon a "Maiblume," a "Fleur de Mai," a "Fior di Maggio," a "Majblomst." These people were not mere arrivals from the same family, to be welcomed as understood and long-loved, but strangers to the neighborhood, with whom a long process of settling down had to take place. For they brought with them their national and racial characters, and each new national quota had to wear slowly away the contempt with which its mere alienness got itself greeted. Each had to make its way slowly from the lowest strata of unskilled labor up to a level where it satisfied the accredited norms of social success. . . .

II

Evolving America

If freedom means the right to do pretty much as one pleases, so long as one does not interfere with others, the immigrant has found freedom, and the ruling element has been singularly liberal in its treatment of the invading hordes. But if freedom means a democratic cooperation in determining the ideals and purposes and industrial and social institutions of a country, then the immigrant has not been free, and the Anglo-Saxon element is guilty of just what every dominant race is guilty of in every European country: the imposition of its own culture upon the minority peoples. The fact that this imposition has been so mild and, indeed, semi-conscious does not alter its quality. And the war has brought out just the degree to which that purpose of "Americanizing," that is, "Anglo-Saxonizing," the immigrant has failed.

For the Anglo-Saxon now in his bitterness to turn upon the other peoples, talk about their "arrogance," scold them for not being melted in a pot which never existed, is to betray the unconscious purpose which lay at the bottom of his heart. It betrays too the possession of a racial jealousy similar to that of which he is now accusing the so-called "hyphenates." Let the Anglo-Saxon be proud enough of the heroic toil and heroic sacrifices which molded the nation. But let him ask himself, if he had had to depend on the English descendants, where he would have been living to-day. To those of us who see in the exploitation of unskilled labor the strident red *leit-motif* of our civilization, the settling of the country presents a great social drama as the waves of immigration broke over it.

Let the Anglo-Saxon ask himself where he would have been if these races had not come? Let those who feel the inferiority of the non–Anglo-Saxon immigrant contemplate that region of the States which has remained the most distinctively "American," the South. Let him ask himself whether he would really like to see the foreign hordes Americanized into such an Americanization. Let him ask himself how superior this native civilization is to the great "alien" states of Wisconsin and Minnesota, where Scandinavians, Poles, and Germans have self-consciously labored to preserve their traditional culture, while being outwardly and satisfactorily American. Let him ask himself how much more wisdom, intelligence, industry and social leadership has come out of these alien states than out of all the truly American ones. The South, in fact, while this vast Northern development has gone on, still remains an English colony, stagnant and complacent, having progressed culturally scarcely beyond the early Victorian era. It is culturally sterile because it has had no advantage of cross-fertilization like the Northern states. What has happened in states such as Wisconsin and Minnesota is that strong foreign cultures have struck root in a new and fertile soil. America has meant liberation, and German and Scandinavian political ideas and social energies have expanded to a new potency. The process has not been at all the fancied "assimilation" of the Scandinavian or Teuton. Rather has it been a process of their assimilation of us—I speak as an Anglo-Saxon. The foreign cultures have not been melted down or run together, made into some homogeneous Americanism, but have remained distinct but cooperating to the greater glory and benefit, not only of themselves but of all the native "Americanism" around them.

What we emphatically do not want is that these distinctive qualities should be washed out into a tasteless, colorless fluid of uniformity. Already we have far too much of this insipidity,—masses of people who are cultural half-breeds, neither assimilated Anglo-Saxons nor nationals of another culture. Each national colony in this country seems to retain in its foreign press, its vernacular literature, its schools, its intellectual and patriotic leaders, a central cultural nucleus. From this nucleus the colony extends out by imperceptible gradations to a fringe where national characteristics are all but lost. Our cities are filled with these half-breeds who retain their foreign names but have lost the foreign savor. This does not mean that they have actually been changed into New Englanders or Middle Westerners. It does not mean that they have been really Americanized. It means that, letting slip from them whatever native culture they had, they have substituted for it only the most rudimentary American—the American culture of the cheap newspaper, the "movies," the popular song, the ubiquitous automobile. The unthinking who survey this class call them assimilated, Americanized. The great American public school has done its work. With these people our institutions are safe. We may thrill with dread at the aggressive hyphenate, but this tame flabbiness is accepted as Americanization. The same molders of opinion whose ideal is to melt the different races into Anglo-Saxon gold hail this poor product as the satisfying result of their alchemy.

Yet a truer cultural sense would have told us that it is not the self-conscious cultural nuclei that sap at our American life, but these fringes. It is not the Jew who sticks proudly to the faith of his fathers and boasts of that venerable culture of his who is dangerous to America, but the Jew who has lost the Jewish fire and become a mere elementary, grasping animal. It is not the Bohemian who supports the Bohemian schools in Chicago whose influence is sinister, but the Bohemian who has made money and has got into ward politics. Just so surely as we tend to disintegrate these nuclei of nationalistic culture do we tend to create hordes of men and women without a spiritual country, cultural outlaws, without taste, without standards but those of the mob. . . .

III

The New America

The failure of the melting-pot, far from closing the great American democratic experiment, means that it has only just begun. Whatever American nationalism turns out to be, we see already that it will have a color richer and more exciting than our ideal has hitherto encompassed. In a world which has dreamed of internationalism, we find that we have all unawares been building up the first international nation. The voices which have cried for a tight and jealous nationalism of the European pattern are failing. From that ideal, however valiantly and disinterestedly it has been set for us, time and tendency have moved us further and further away. What we have achieved has been rather a cosmopolitan federation of national colonies, of foreign cultures, from whom the sting of devastating competition has been removed. America is already the world-federation in miniature, the continent where for the first time in history has been achieved that miracle of hope, the peaceful living side by side, with character substantially preserved, of the most heterogeneous peoples under the sun. Nowhere else has such contiguity been anything but the breeder of misery. Here, notwithstanding our tragic failures of adjustment, the outlines are already too clear not to give us a new vision and a new orientation of the American mind in the world.

THE AGRARIAN REVOLT

The industrial boom and urban growth of the late nineteenth century affected the northeastern quarter of the United States heavily but the other three-quarters only lightly. In the South and the vast stretches of the West, farming and cattle raising not only remained dominant but also grew rapidly in response to demands for food and fibre by the urban-industrial populations of the eastern United States and western Europe. However, agriculture and cattle raising were not always the dominant occupations. Products of mining and lumbering—timber, gold, silver, copper, coal, iron, and dozens of other valuable forest products and ores—also poured out of the West and South. The economic and political needs and responses of these areas, therefore, became more complicated than those where agriculture alone predominated.

As the relationships of economically developed countries with underdeveloped areas have shown in the last hundred years, the latter tend to become economic colonies of the former even when political ties are absent. In effect, nations which produce raw materials work for those which process those materials, thus producing a much greater economic advantage and more capital for further investment in the urban-industrial nation than in the rural-agricultural nation.

In the late nineteenth century the South and West occupied positions something like underdeveloped countries in relation to the Northeast and Europe, where capital and manufacturing were centered. Yet the South and West owned a weapon against undue exploitation. They were parts of a federal union, in which they could exercise political power, and hence affect economic policy through the organs of the federal government.

But use of this weapon was not easy. For twelve years, during Reconstruction, the South was dominated politically by the North, and economic colonialism proceeded even further than before the Civil War, when the South's production of cotton had depended so heavily on Northern and British financing and marketing. During the late nineteenth century, when cattlemen and farmers occupied the high, dry prairies of the West in large numbers and miners and lumbermen undertook exploitation of the West's resources on a vast scale, much of the region remained in territorial status without votes in Congress. Toward the end of the nineteenth century, however, Southern and Western influence began to assert itself more effectively, as the following readings show.

The Farmer in an Industrialized Society
(1865-1900)

Although the proportion of farmers to other workers in the United States dropped rapidly as cities and industry grew, the actual number of farmers and farms rose until 1910. Farm production rose even faster in this increasingly mechanized age, with unhappy as well as happy results.

From *American Epoch: A History of the United States Since the 1890's*, 2nd ed., by Arthur S. Link and William B. Catton. Copyright © 1963 by Arthur S. Link and William B. Catton. Reprinted by permission of Alfred A. Knopf, Inc. Pp. 7-13. Subheadings omitted or altered by the editors.

I

The Agricultural Problem, 1861-1900

Agriculture remained the principal means of livelihood for the American people even while a new industrial and urban economy was advancing with giant strides. Moreover, American agriculture went through a revolution during the last four decades of the nineteenth century as significant as the revolution that occurred in transportation and industry. Improved transportation facilities, invention of agricultural machinery, and opening of vast new farm areas all combined to hasten the shift, which had begun in the 1850's, from subsistence agriculture to commercial agriculture, from production for home and local markets to production for the world market.

American farmers generally prospered during a period of inflation and high production during the Civil War, indeed until the late 1860's. About 1869, however, they entered a quarter-century of declining prices, during many years of which they produced at an actual loss. The result was the creation of America's most serious domestic problem from 1870 to 1897.

The most obvious causes of the farmer's steady march toward economic ruin were overproduction and declining prices, as agricultural output in the United States, indeed in all the world, far outstripped demand. For example, wheat, which brought $1.11 a bushel in 1879, sold for 49 cents in 1894; corn fell from an average of 50 cents a bushel in 1879 to 21 cents in 1896, cotton from 14 cents a pound in 1873 to 4.6 cents in 1894.

The farmer's troubles were compounded by the twin burdens of excessive freight rates and high interest charges on the money that he borrowed. Railroad freight rates, fixed on the principle of charging what the traffic would bear, were in many areas exorbitant, while discriminations in rates and services, granting of secret rebates to favored shippers, pooling agreements to eliminate competition, and improper influencing of legislatures and judges were common practices of the railroad managers. As for the burden of carrying their debt load, farmers had to pay usury instead of interest in many areas. This problem was most serious in the South, where the cotton and tobacco crops were financed by outside credit and where interest charges usually consumed profits before the crops could be harvested.

The consequences of the long depression in agriculture can be read clearly in the efforts that farmers made to use political instrumentalities to extricate themselves from the slough of despair. Most of the important legislative and political battles from 1873 to 1897 revolved directly or indirectly around the agrarian campaign for relief, and a political philosophy and program that would have profound significance for twentieth-century American politics emerged out of the ferment of agrarian revolt.

The Granger movement was the farmers' first organized attempt to strike back at railroads and industrial monopolies. The Grange began in Washington in 1867 as an organization designed to ameliorate the social drabness of rural life. Spreading rapidly through the West and South, it had a national membership of over 800,000 by 1875. Farmers inevitably discussed common grievances and means of remedying them when they congregated, and it was not long before they went into politics. In the Middle West, for example, they won control of legislatures in Iowa, Illinois, Wisconsin, and Minnesota and attempted to establish fair railroad rates and practices. The Granger movement fell victim to the long depression of the 1870's, but farmers had recovered their political consciousness, and a beginning toward concerted farmer political organization had been made.

Leadership in articulating and marshaling agrarian discontent passed in the 1880's from the Grange to a new and more aggressive movement—the farmers' alliances. There were a number of alliances in the late '70's and early '80's, but they had coalesced by 1890 into three powerful groups, the Northwestern Alliance, Southern Alliance, and Colored Alliance. They plunged into politics in 1890 with a vehemence that startled and frightened the business interests, captured state after state in the South and West, and sent eloquent

In this pro-Granger cartoon of 1873, the farmer's organization tries to arouse America's farmers to the dangers of railroad corporations.

spokesmen to state legislatures and to Congress. The agrarian revolt was spectacular in its occurrence, but more significant for the future of American politics were the Alliance leaders' political philosophy and program. Economic adversity and a sense of baffling frustration had impelled farmers to abandon *laissez faire* as the right rule of political practice and to espouse a program envisaging far-reaching governmental intervention in economic affairs. The conversion of the great masses of farmers to this new philosophy, later called progressivism, made it a political force that could not long be ignored by the two major parties.

The consummation of the agrarian revolt was the organization of the Populist party in 1892 and the effort of William Jennings Bryan and his agrarian followers to win control of the federal government in 1896. Before this last campaign occurred, however, the agrarian reformers had already sounded the death knell of *laissez faire* by their efforts to solve the railroad problem and obtain an ample supply of money and credit.

The idea of public regulation of railroads was an outgrowth mainly of the Granger movement. Illinois, Wisconsin, Minnesota, and Iowa attempted in the early 1870's to prescribe equitable rates by direct legislation and established state commissions to compel nondiscriminatory services. Except for Illinois, however, these states failed to accomplish any lasting reform. The railroad interests either regained control of the legislatures and obtained repeal of the regulatory laws or else fought the railroad commissions to a standstill in state courts. A much more promising movement for reform got under way in Georgia and California in 1879, when both states established expert railroad commissions empowered to set rates.

The failure of the so-called Granger railroad laws prompted midwestern farm organizations to come out for federal regulation. This shift was occasioned in part by the general conviction that the railroad problem was beyond the competence of the individual states. It was more immediately a result of the Supreme Court's opinion, rendered in the Wabash case of 1886, that Congress alone could regulate *interstate* rates and services. This decision simply provided the final impetus for an already strong movement for federal legislation. It came to fruition in 1887 in the adoption of the Interstate Commerce Act, which decreed that rates should be fair and just, outlawed discriminatory practices, and established the Interstate Commerce Commission. It was a landmark in American political history: the first important turning away from the *laissez-faire* philosophy that had so long prevailed among federal lawmakers. As we will see later, it soon became evident that the Commerce Act conferred no real authority on the Commission; and the railroad problem was far from being settled when the agrarian revolt of the 1890's exploded in full force.

Obtaining an adequate money supply without wrecking the national financial structure was an even more perplexing problem. Yet to embattled farmers, who saw the prices of their commodities decline, the value of their properties shrink, and the burden of their debts grow heavier, this became the vital issue of the last quarter of the nineteenth century.

The money question had its origin in the federal government's issuance of some $450,000,000 in greenbacks with no gold backing during the Civil War. The greenbacks depreciated in value and contributed to the inflation of the war period, but they also helped to make money plentiful. No sooner had the war ended than the business and banking interests demanded and obtained a reduction in the greenback currency and a return to the gold standard in 1879. One result of this deflation was a decline in per capita circulation of almost 50 percent between 1865 and 1879; and commodity prices declined as money became dearer. Farmers who had incurred large mortgages during the prosperous years soon found themselves obliged to repay the same debts with commodities worth about half as much as when they had borrowed the money.

The debtor classes during the '70's and early '80's viewed the greenback as the means of their salvation. Then after 1882 they abandoned paper money and seized upon silver as the most likely instrument of inflation. The reason for this sudden shift in allegiance is not hard to find. So little silver was mined in the United States until about 1865 that the established ratio between silver and gold of 16 to 1 undervalued silver and drove it out of circulation as money. On the other hand, immense deposits of silver were discovered in the Rocky Mountain region during the 1860's and early 1870's. Production increased so rapidly that by 1879 the old ratio of 16 to 1 greatly overvalued silver and made it the perfect tool of inflationists. Silver, in contrast to greenbacks, satisfied the demand that the currency have a metallic basis, while coining silver at the ratio of 16 to 1 would ensure an expanded money supply and increased commodity prices without causing runaway inflation.

From the mid-seventies to about 1898, therefore, western and southern farmers demanded free and unlimited coinage of silver at the ratio of 16 to 1. Their representatives in Congress overrode a presidential veto to pass the Bland-Allison Act in 1878. It required the Secretary of Treasury to purchase not less than two nor more than four million dollars worth of silver monthly. Farm prices rose during the early '80's, and the silver agitation subsided. But drought and hard times in the last years of the decade stimulated renewed agitation by the Alliances for free coinage at 16 to 1. So powerful was this demand that Congress in 1890 adopted the Sherman Silver Purchase Act, which provided for the purchase by the federal government of almost the entire domestic production. As it turned out, however, the economic dislocations were too fundamental to be corrected by such a simple expedient, and the farmers' plight grew infinitely worse with the coming of the Panic of 1893.

II

The Populist Revolt, 1890-1896

The passage of the Sherman Purchase Act did not halt a sharp new downward spiral of commodity prices that began in 1891. Money was tight, credit almost inflexible, banking facilities woefully inadequate. But the national leadership of both major parties represented the industrial and banking interests, and farmers could expect little relief from either of them. In these circumstances the final revolt of the farmers developed with astonishing rapidity. The Alliances captured the Democratic party in Tennessee, Georgia, and South Carolina in 1890. By co-operating with Democrats in the midwestern and Plains states they won control of Kansas, Nebraska, South Dakota, and Minnesota as well. Next the Alliance leaders launched their own party—the People's, or Populist party—at Omaha on July 4, 1892. Thus, after nearly two decades of discontent, agrarian unrest finally took shape in political action on a national scale.

The Populist platform, the vivid preamble of which was written by Ignatius Donnelly of Minnesota, sounded the battle cry of revolt and set forth a program around which the farmers could rally. It demanded the free and unlimited coinage of silver at the ratio of 16 to 1. At the insistence of southern Alliancemen, it endorsed the so-called subtreasury plan to establish a federal commodity loan system so that farmers might borrow against their crops. It also demanded a graduated federal income tax; postal savings banks; public ownership of railroads, telegraph systems, and telephones; prohibition of alien land ownership and recovery from railroads of land illegally held; immigration restriction; the eight-hour day for industrial workers; and prohibition of the use of private armies against strikers. Finally, there were demands for measures to restore popular rule—the direct election of senators, the initiative and referendum, and the secret ballot.

The adoption of the Populist platform marked the end of an era when practically all Americans put their trust in the English Liberal ideal of a free, competitive economy, operating automatically in the general interest without decisive and planned intervention by government. The adoption of this platform heralded the coming triumph of a new progressive faith—a faith in the ability of men to overcome economic adversity and rectify social injustice by collective political action. The later progressive movement went far beyond the Populist charter in elaborating specific remedies, but the spirit, purpose, and assumptions of progressivism were inherited in large measure from the Populists, the advance guard of a new reform movement.

The Populists did not expect to win the election of 1892, but their beginning was auspicious enough. Indeed, they might well have displaced the Democratic party had the eastern, conservative element continued to dominate that party. Unforeseen events, however, wrecked the existing political alignment and destroyed Populism in the end as an independent movement.

One of the worst depressions of the nineteenth century broke out soon after the Democrat, Grover Cleveland, was inaugurated President in 1893. Cleveland was convinced that the chief cause of the depression was lack of confidence in the ability of the Treasury to maintain the gold standard, a fear induced by the Sherman Purchase Act.* He

---

*This Act required the Treasury to purchase 4,500,000 ounces of silver monthly and to pay for the silver, at the market price, with Treasury notes. The Secretary of the Treasury was authorized to redeem these Treasury notes "in gold or silver coin, at his discretion," but the Treasury Department consistently interpreted this provision to mean that the notes had to be redeemed "in gold or its equivalent."

therefore called Congress into special session in 1893 and obtained repeal of that measure. By this action, which was accomplished with the help of Republicans, the President split his own party and embittered agrarian Democrats. Cleveland next tried to get honest tariff reform and failed. He broke a railroad strike in Chicago in 1894 by using federal troops and imprisoning the strike leaders. Finally, he further antagonized farmers and debtors by his negotiations with Wall Street bankers to keep the government on the gold standard. Cleveland saved the gold standard and disrupted the Democratic party in the process. Leaders of the southern and western majority took control of proceedings when the Democrats met in national convention in Chicago in the summer of 1896 and read Cleveland and his following out of the party. The agrarians found their new leader and presidential candidate in William Jennings Bryan, a young former congressman and editor from Nebraska, who captured the convention by defying Wall Street and demanding free and unlimited coinage of silver. The toiling producers of America—the farmers and workers—he intoned, must not be crucified upon a Cross of Gold!

Although Bryan was an ardent silverite and a low-tariff advocate, he was not yet a radical of the Populist stripe. Moreover, the Democratic platform was neither as well integrated nor as advanced as the Populist platform of 1892. But the Democrats offered enough to the more radical Populists to make fusion inevitable: tariff reform, a graduated income tax, vigorous prosecution of the trusts, and, of course, free coinage of silver. Thus Populists and Democrats in the agricultural sections, the South and West, united to capture control of the federal government from the manufacturing East.

Against the young orator from Nebraska the Republicans pitted William McKinley of Ohio, a spokesman of the business interests and a reluctant champion of the gold standard. There was much at stake, and the business community rallied behind McKinley and his campaign manager, Mark Hanna. All the influence that money could buy was brought to bear against Bryan. Workers by the hundreds of thousands were told not to return to work after election day if the Democrats won. An enormous propaganda, depicting Bryan and his friends as anarchists, seditionists, and potential despoilers, was set in motion. In doubtful states like Indiana, Hanna spent money on a lavish scale.

With all the influence of organized wealth and respectable society marshaled against the Democrats, their defeat was almost inevitable. Worse still for their chances, Bryan's alleged radicalism solidified the urban middle classes and the more prosperous eastern and midwestern farmers in support of McKinley; and organized labor refused to join the proposed farmer-worker coalition. Even so, Bryan polled

Bryan and the Democrats are ridiculed in this Republican cartoon of 1896 as leading the nation into poverty by supporting monetary inflation through an increased use of silver.

6,503,000 votes, to 7,105,000 for McKinley, and carried the South and many of the states west of the Mississippi. His defeat by such a narrow margin signified that the kind of progressivism he advocated would hereafter be a major force in American politics.

The Farmer's View: "The Octopus" (1901)

Frank Norris (1870-1902), a journalist and novelist, saw an opportunity to write an epic of American life by telling the story of the impact of wheat growing, marketing, and export on people. The setting of *The Octopus*, the first of the three novels he planned to write on this theme, was California, where Norris had seen the growth of the Southern Pacific Railroad, the "octopus" of the novel. In the second novel of the trilogy, *The Pit*, he told the story of wheat marketing in the Chicago grain exchange; Norris died before writing the final novel. Norris' novels have heroes and villains, characters viewed sympathetically and unsympathetically, but above all they are shown in a context of natural and social forces that shaped their destinies. In that sense *The Octopus*, as a piece of social criticism, stood as something much more than a simple exposé of corporate greed.

From Frank Norris, *The Octopus: The Epic of the West* (New York, 1901), pp. 251-254. Copyright © 1901 by Doubleday, Page and Co.

"I'll be wanting some cars of you people before the summer is out," observed Dyke to the clerk as he folded up and put away the order that the other had handed him. He remembered perfectly well that he had arranged the matter of transporting his crop some months before, but this role of proprietor amused him and he liked to busy himself again and again with the details of his undertaking.

"I suppose," he added, "you'll be able to give 'em to me. There'll be a big wheat crop to move this year and I don't want to be caught in any car famine."

"Oh, you'll get your cars," murmured the other.

"I'll be the means of bringing business your way," Dyke went on; "I've done so well with my hops that there are a lot of others going into the business next season. Suppose," he continued, struck with an idea, "suppose we went into some sort of pool, a sort of shippers' organization, could you give us special rates, cheaper rates—say a cent and a half?"

The other looked up.

"A cent and a half! Say *four* cents and a half and maybe I'll talk business with you."

"Four cents and a half," returned Dyke, "I don't see it. Why, the regular rate is only two cents."

"No, it isn't," answered the clerk, looking him gravely in the eye, "it's five cents."

"Well, there's where you are wrong, m'son," Dyke retorted, genially. "You look it up. You'll find the freight on hops from Bonneville to 'Frisco is two cents a pound for carload lots. You told me that yourself last fall."

"That was last fall," observed the clerk. There was a silence. Dyke shot a glance of suspicion at the other. Then, reassured, he remarked:

"You look it up. You'll see I'm right."

S. Behrman came forward and shook hands politely with the ex-engineer.

"Anything I can do for you, Mr. Dyke?"

Dyke explained. When he had done speaking, the clerk turned to S. Behrman and observed, respectfully:

"Our regular rate on hops is five cents."

"Yes," answered S. Behrman, pausing to reflect; "yes, Mr. Dyke, that's right—five cents."

The clerk brought forward a folder of yellow paper and handed it to Dyke. It was inscribed at the top "Tariff Schedule No. 8," and underneath these words in brackets, was a smaller inscription, *"Supersedes No. 7 of Aug. 1."*

"See for yourself," said S. Behrman. He indicated an item under the head of "Miscellany."

"The following rates for carriage of hops in carload lots," read Dyke, "take effect June 1, and will remain in force until superseded by a later tariff. Those quoted beyond Stockton are subject to changes in traffic arrangements with carriers by water from that point."

In the list that was printed below, Dyke saw that the rate for hops between Bonneville or Guadalajara and San Francisco was five cents.

For a moment Dyke was confused. Then swiftly the matter became clear in his mind. The Railroad had raised the freight on hops from two cents to five.

All his calculations as to a profit on his little investment he had based on a freight rate of two cents a pound. He was under contract to deliver his crop. He could not draw back. The new rate ate up every cent of his gains. He stood there ruined.

"Why, what do you mean?" he burst out. "You promised me a rate of two cents and

I went ahead with my business with that understanding. What do you mean?"

S. Behrman and the clerk watched him from the other side of the counter.

"The rate is five cents," declared the clerk doggedly.

"Well, that ruins me," shouted Dyke. "Do you understand? I won't make fifty cents. *Make!* Why, I will *owe*—I'll be—be—That ruins me, do you understand?"

The other raised a shoulder.

"We don't force you to ship. You can do as you like. The rate is five cents."

"Well—but—damn you, I'm under contract to deliver. What am I going to do? Why, you told me—you promised me a two-cent rate."

"I don't remember it," said the clerk. "I don't know anything about that. But I know this; I know that hops have gone up. I know that the German crop was a failure and that the crop in New York wasn't worth the hauling. Hops have gone up to nearly a dollar. You don't suppose we don't know that, do you, Mr. Dyke?"

"What's the price of hops got to do with you?"

"It's got *this* to do with us," returned the other with a sudden aggressiveness, "that the freight rate has gone up to meet the price. We're not doing business for our health. My orders are to raise your rate to five cents, and I think you are getting off easy."

Dyke stared in blank astonishment. For the moment, the audacity of the affair was what most appealed to him. He forgot its personal application.

"Good Lord," he murmured, "good Lord! What will you people do next? Look here. What's your basis of applying freight rates, anyhow?" he suddenly vociferated with furious sarcasm. "What's your rule? What are you guided by?"

But at the words, S. Behrman, who had kept silent during the heat of the discussion, leaned abruptly forward. For the only time in his knowledge, Dyke saw his face inflamed with anger and with the enmity and contempt of all this farming element with whom he was contending.

"Yes, what's your rule? What's your basis?" demanded Dyke, turning swiftly to him.

S. Behrman emphasized each word of his reply with a tap of one forefinger on the counter before him:

"All—the—traffic—will—bear."

The ex-engineer stepped back a pace, his fingers on the ledge of the counter, to steady himself. He felt himself grow pale, his heart became a mere leaden weight in his chest, inert, refusing to beat.

In a second the whole affair, in all its bearings, went speeding before the eye of his imagination like the rapid unrolling of a panorama. Every cent of his earnings was sunk in this hop business of his. More than that, he had borrowed money to carry it on, certain of success—borrowed of S. Behrman, offering his crop and his little home as security. Once he failed to meet his obligations, S. Behrman would foreclose. Not only would the Railroad devour every morsel of his profits, but also it would take from him his home; at a blow he would be left penniless and without a home. What would then become of his mother—and what would become of the little tad? She, whom he had been planning to educate like a veritable lady. For all that year he had talked of his ambition for his little daughter to every one he met. All Bonneville knew of it. What a mark for gibes he had made of himself. The workingman turned farmer! What a target for jeers—he who had fancied he could elude the Railroad! He remembered he had once said the great Trust had overlooked his little enterprise, disdaining to plunder such small fry. He should have known better than that. How had he ever imagined the Road would permit him to make any money?

The Populist Position (1892)

Perhaps the most thorough exposition of the farmer's grievances and the proposed remedies can be found in the 1892 platform of the People's Party. The eloquent preamble was written by Ignatius Donnelly (1831–1901), a leader of the Farmer's Alliance in Minnesota. Like many of the Populist leaders, Donnelly had been active for years in such reform groups as the Grangers and the Greenback Party.

From Edward McPherson, *A Handbook of Politics for 1892* (Washington, 1892), pp. 269–271.

Assembled upon the 116th anniversary of the Declaration of Independence, the People's Party of America, in their first national convention, invoking upon their action the blessing of Almighty God, put forth in the name and on behalf of the people of this country, the following preamble and declaration of principles:

The rural and small town character of the Populist Party is suggested by this photograph of the delegates to the 1890 Nebraska state convention of the party.

I

Preamble

The conditions which surround us best justify our co-operation; we meet in the midst of a nation brought to the verge of moral, political, and material ruin. Corruption dominates the ballot-box, the Legislatures, the Congress, and touches even the ermine of the bench. The people are demoralized; most of the States have been compelled to isolate the voters at the polling places to prevent universal intimidation and bribery. The newspapers are largely subsidized or muzzled, public opinion silenced, business prostrated, homes covered with mortgages, labor impoverished, and the land concentrating in the hands of capitalists. The urban workmen are denied the right to organize for self-protection, imported pauperized labor beats down their wages, a hireling standing army, unrecognized by our laws, is established to shoot them down, and they are rapidly degenerating into European conditions. The fruits of the toil of millions are boldly stolen to build up colossal fortunes for a few, unprecedented in the history of mankind; and the possessors of these, in turn, despise the Republic and endanger liberty. From the same prolific womb of governmental injustice we breed the two great classes—tramps and millionaires.

The national power to create money is appropriated to enrich bond-holders; a vast public debt payable in legal-tender currency has been funded into gold-bearing bonds, thereby adding millions to the burdens of the people.

Silver, which has been accepted as coin since the dawn of history, has been demonetized to add to the purchasing power of gold by decreasing the value of all forms of property as well as human labor, and the supply of currency is purposely abridged to fatten usurers, bankrupt enterprise, and enslave industry. A vast conspiracy against mankind has been organized on two continents, and it is rapidly taking possession of the world. If not met and overthrown at once it forebodes terrible social convulsions, the destruction of civilization, or the establishment of an absolute despotism.

We have witnessed for more than a quarter of a century the struggles of the two great political parties for power and plunder, while grievous wrongs have been inflicted upon the suffering people. We charge that the controlling influences dominating both these parties have permitted the existing dreadful conditions to develop without serious effort to prevent or restrain them. Neither do they now promise us any substantial reform. They have agreed together to ignore, in the coming campaign, every issue but one. They propose to drown the outcries of a plundered people with the uproar of a sham battle over the tariff, so that capitalists, corporations, national banks, rings, trusts, watered stock, the demonetization of silver and the oppressions of the usurers may all be lost sight of. They propose to sacrifice our homes, lives, and children on the altar of mammon; to destroy the multitude in order to secure corruption funds from the millionaires.

Assembled on the anniversary of the birthday of the nation, and filled with the spirit of the grand general and chief who established our independence, we seek to restore the government of the Republic to the hands of the "plain people," with which class it originated. We assert our purposes to be identical with the purposes of the National Constitution; to form a more perfect union and establish justice, insure domestic tranquillity, provide for the common defense, promote the general welfare, and secure the blessings of liberty for ourselves and our posterity.

We declare that this Republic can only endure as a free government while built upon the love of the people for each other and for the nation; that it cannot be pinned together by bayonets; that the Civil War is over, and that every passion and resentment which grew out of it must die with it, and that we must be in fact, as we are in name, one united brotherhood of free men.

Our country finds itself confronted by conditions for which there is no precedent in the history of the world; our annual agricultural productions amount to billions of dollars in value, which must, within a few weeks or months, be exchanged for billions of dollars' worth of commodities consumed in their production; the existing currency supply is wholly inadequate to make this exchange; the results are falling prices, the formation of combines and rings, the impoverishment of the producing class. We pledge ourselves that if given power we will labor to correct these evils by wise and reasonable legislation, in accordance with the terms of our platform.

We believe that the power of government—in other words, of the people—should be expanded (as in the case of the postal service) as rapidly and as far as the good sense of an intelligent people and the teachings of experience shall justify, to the end that oppression, injustice, and poverty shall eventually cease in the land.

While our sympathies as a party of reform are naturally upon the side of every proposition which will tend to make men intelligent, virtuous, and temperate, we nevertheless regard these questions, important as they are, as secondary to the great issues now pressing for solution, and upon which not only our individual prosperity but the very existence of free institutions depend; and we ask all men to first help us to determine whether we are to have a republic to administer before we differ as to the conditions upon which it is to be administered, believing that the forces of reform this day organized will never cease to move forward until every wrong is righted and equal rights and equal privileges securely established for all the men and women of this country.

II

Platform

We declare, therefore—

First.—That the union of the labor forces of the United States this day consummated shall be permanent and perpetual; may its spirit enter into all hearts for the salvation of the Republic and the uplifting of mankind.

Second.—Wealth belongs to him who creates it, and every dollar taken from industry without an equivalent is robbery. "If any will not work, neither shall he eat." The interests of rural and civil labor are the same; their enemies are identical.

Third.—We believe that the time has come when the railroad corporations will either own the people or the people must own the railroads; and should the government enter upon the work of owning and managing all railroads, we should favor an amendment to the constitution by which all persons engaged in the government service shall be placed under a civil-service regulation of the most rigid character, so as to prevent the increase of the power of the national administration by the use of such additional government employes.

Finance.—We demand a national currency, safe, sound, and flexible issued by the general government only, a full legal tender for all debts, public and private, and that without the use of banking corporations; a just, equitable, and efficient means of distribution direct to the people, at a tax not to exceed 2 percent, per annum, to be provided as set forth in the sub-treasury plan of the Farmers' Alliance, or a better system; also by payments in discharge of its obligations for public improvements.

1. We demand free and unlimited coinage of silver and gold at the present legal ratio of 16 to 1.
2. We demand that the amount of circulating medium be speedily increased to not less than $50 per capita.
3. We demand a graduated income tax.
4. We believe that the money of the country should be kept as much as possible in the hands of the people, and hence we demand that all State and national revenues shall be limited to the necessary expenses of the government, economically and honestly administered.
5. We demand that postal savings banks be established by the government for the safe deposit of the earnings of the people and to facilitate exchange.

Transportation.—Transportation being a means of exchange and a public necessity, the government should own and operate the railroads in the interest of the people. The telegraph and telephone, like the post-office system, being a necessity for the transmission of news, should be owned and operated by the government in the interest of the people.

Land.—The land, including all the natural sources of wealth, is the heritage of the people, and should not be monopolized for speculative purposes, and alien ownership of land should be prohibited. All land now held by railroads and other corporations in excess of their actual needs, and all lands now owned by aliens should be reclaimed by the government and held for actual settlers only.

III

Expression of Sentiments

Your Committee on Platform and Resolutions beg leave unanimously to report the following:

Whereas, Other questions have been presented for our consideration, we hereby submit the following, not as a part of the Platform of the People's Party, but as resolutions expressive of the sentiment of this Convention.

1. Resolved, That we demand a free ballot and a fair count in all elections, and pledge ourselves to secure it to every legal voter without Federal intervention, through the adoption by the States of the unperverted Australian or secret ballot system.
2. Resolved, That the revenue derived from a graduated income tax should be applied to the reduction of the burden of taxation now levied upon the domestic industries of this country.
3. Resolved, That we pledge our support to fair and liberal pensions to ex-Union soldiers and sailors.
4. Resolved, That we condemn the fallacy of protecting American labor under

the present system, which opens our ports to the pauper and criminal classes of the world and crowds out our wage-earners; and we denounce the present ineffective laws against contract labor, and demand the further restriction of undesirable immigration.

5. Resolved, That we cordially sympathize with the efforts of organized workingmen to shorten the hours of labor, and demand a rigid enforcement of the existing eight-hour law on Government work, and ask that a penalty clause be added to the said law.
6. Resolved, That we regard the maintenance of a large standing army of mercenaries, known as the Pinkerton system, as a menace to our liberties, and we demand its abolition; and we condemn the recent invasion of the Territory of Wyoming by the hired assassins of plutocracy, assisted by Federal officers.
7. Resolved, That we commend to the favorable consideration of the people and the reform press the legislative system known as the initiative and referendum.
8. Resolved, That we favor a constitutional provision limiting the office of President and Vice-President to one term, and providing for the election of Senators of the United States by a direct vote of the people.
9. Resolved, That we oppose any subsidy or national aid to any private corporation for any purpose.
10. Resolved, That this convention sympathizes with the Knights of Labor and their righteous contest with the tyrannical combine of clothing manufacturers of Rochester, and declare it to be a duty of all who hate tyranny and oppression to refuse to purchase the goods made by the said manufacturers, or to patronize any merchants who sell such goods.

"What's the Matter with Kansas?" (1896)

The Presidential election of 1896 generated more bitter controversy than perhaps any election since that of 1860. William Jennings Bryan, the Democratic-Populist candidate, seemed to many Americans to represent the culmination of the radical political movements that had surged out of the West and South. William McKinley, the Republican nominee, stood for the status quo: that the government had no business interfering in the economic system, except to protect American industries through a high tariff. One of the most widely distributed attacks on Bryan and his Populist supporters was written by William Allen White (1868-1944), editor of the Emporia, Kansas, *Gazette* and first published in that paper in the midst of the 1896 campaign.

Reprinted with permission of The Macmillan Company from *The Autobiography of William Allen White*. Copyright © 1946 by The Macmillan Company. Pp. 280-283.

Today the Kansas Department of Agriculture sent out a statement which indicates that Kansas has gained less than two thousand people in the past year. There are about two hundred and twenty-five thousand families in this state, and there were ten thousand babies born in Kansas, and yet so many people have left the state that the natural increase is cut down to less than two thousand net.

This has been going on for eight years.

If there had been a high brick wall around the state eight years ago, and not a soul had been admitted or permitted to leave, Kansas would be a half million souls better off than she is today. And yet the nation has increased in population. In five years ten million people have been added to the national population, yet instead of gaining a share of this—say, half a million—Kansas has apparently been a plague spot and, in the very garden of the world, has lost population by ten thousands every year.

Not only has she lost population, but she has lost money. Every moneyed man in the state who could get out without loss has gone. Every month in every community sees someone who has a little money pack up and leave the state. This has been going on for eight years. Money has been drained out all the time. In towns where ten years ago there were three or four or half a dozen money-lending concerns, stimulating industry by furnishing capital, there is now none, or one or two that are looking after the interests and principal already outstanding.

No one brings any money into Kansas any more. What community knows over one or two men who have moved in with more than $5,000 in the past three years? And what community cannot count half a score of men in that time who have left, taking all the money they could scrape together?

"BLOWING" HIMSELF AROUND THE COUNTRY.

Bryan is depicted as blowing hot air at the farmers of America in this anti-Democratic cartoon of 1896.

Yet the nation has grown rich; other states have increased in population and wealth—other neighboring states. Missouri has gained over two million, while Kansas has been losing half a million. Nebraska has gained in wealth and population while Kansas has gone downhill. Colorado has gained every way, while Kansas has lost every way since 1888.

What's the matter with Kansas?

There is no substantial city in the state. Every big town save one has lost in population. Yet Kansas City, Omaha, Lincoln, St. Louis, Denver, Colorado Springs, Sedalia, the cities of the Dakotas, St. Paul and Minneapolis and Des Moines—all cities and towns in the West—have steadily grown.

Take up the government blue book and you will see that Kansas is virtually off the map. Two or three little scrubby consular places in yellow-fever-stricken communities that do not aggregate ten thousand dollars a year is all the recognition that Kansas has. Nebraska draws about one hundred thousand dollars; little old North Dakota draws about fifty thousand dollars; Oklahoma doubles Kansas; Missouri leaves her a thousand miles behind; Colorado is almost seven times greater than Kansas—the whole west is ahead of Kansas.

Take it by any standard you please, Kansas is not in it.

Go east and you hear them laugh at Kansas; go west and they sneer at her; go south and they "cuss" her; go north and they have forgotten her. Go into any crowd of intelligent people gathered anywhere on the globe, and you will find the Kansas man on the defensive. The newspaper columns and magazines once devoted to praise of her, to boastful facts and startling figures concerning her resources, are now filled with cartoons, jibes and Pefferian speeches. Kansas just naturally isn't in it. She has traded places with Arkansas and Timbuctoo.

What's the matter with Kansas?

We all know; yet here we are at it again. We have an old mossback Jacksonian who snorts and howls because there is a bathtub in the State House; we are running that old jay for Governor. We have another shabby, wild-eyed, rattle-brained fanatic who has said openly in a dozen speeches that "the rights of the user are paramount to the rights of the owner"; and we are running him for Chief Justice, so that capital will come tumbling over itself to get into the state. We have raked the old ash heap of failure in the state and found an old human hoop skirt who has failed as a businessman, who has failed as an editor, who has failed as a preacher, and we are going to run him for Congressman-at-Large. He will help the looks of the Kansas delegation at Washington. Then we have discovered a kid without a law practice and have decided to run him for Attorney General. Then, for fear some hint that the state had become respectable might percolate through the civilized portions of the nation, we have decided to send three or four harpies out lecturing, telling the people that Kansas is raising hell and letting the corn go to weed.

Oh, this is a state to be proud of! We are a people who can hold up our heads! What we need is not more money, but less capital, fewer white shirts and brains, fewer men with business judgment, and more of those fellows who boast that they are "just ordinary clodhoppers, but they know more in a minute about finance than John Sherman"; we need more men who are "posted," who can bellow about the crime of '73, who hate prosperity, and who think, because a man believes in national honor, he is a tool of Wall Street. We have had a few of them—some hundred fifty thousand—but we need more.

We need several thousand gibbering idiots to scream about the "Great Red Dragon" of Lombard Street. We don't need population, we don't need wealth, we don't need well-dressed men on the streets, we don't need cities on the fertile prairies; you bet we don't! What we are after is the money power. Because we have become poorer and ornerier and meaner than a spavined, distempered mule, we, the people of Kansas, propose to kick; we don't care to build up, we wish to tear down.

"There are two ideas of government," said our noble Bryan at Chicago. "There are those who believe that if you legislate to make the well-to-do prosperous, this prosperity will leak through on those below. The Democratic idea has been that if you legislate to make the masses prosperous their prosperity will find its way up and through every class and rest upon them."

That's the stuff! Give the prosperous man the dickens! Legislate the thriftless man into ease, whack the stuffing out of the creditors and tell the debtors who borrowed the money five years ago when money "per capita" was greater than it is now, that the contraction of currency gives him a right to repudiate.

Whoop it up for the ragged trousers; put the lazy, greasy fizzle, who can't pay his debts, on the altar, and bow down and worship him. Let the state ideal be high. What we need is not the respect of our fellow men, but the chance to get something for nothing.

Oh, yes, Kansas is a great state. Here are people fleeing from it by the score every day, capital going out of the state by the hundreds of dollars; and every industry but farming paralyzed, and that crippled, because its products have to go across the ocean before they can find a laboring man at work who can afford to buy them. Let's don't stop this year. Let's drive all the decent, self-respecting men out of the state. Let's keep the old clodhoppers who know it all. Let's encourage the man who is "posted." He can talk, and what we need is not mill hands to eat our meat, nor factory hands to eat our wheat, nor cities to oppress the farmer by consuming his butter and eggs and chickens and produce. What Kansas needs is men who can talk, who have large leisure to argue the currency question while their wives wait at home for that nickel's worth of bluing.

What's the matter with Kansas?

Nothing under the shining sun. She is losing her wealth, population and standing. She has got her statesmen, and the money power is afraid of her. Kansas is all right. She has started in to raise hell, as Mrs. Lease advised, and she seems to have an over-production. But that doesn't matter. Kansas never did believe in diversified crops. Kansas is all right. There is absolutely nothing wrong with Kansas. "Every prospect pleases and only man is vile."

The Meaning of Populism for America's Future (1896)

With the nomination of Bryan, the Democrats, the nation's oldest political party, seemed to have been captured by agrarian radicals. The rhetoric of Bryan and the Populist demands in the Democratic platform looked to conservative Eastern Democrats like a clear rejection of their wing of the party; many of them gave open or secret support to McKinley, the Republican nominee. Yet the two major parties had been so evenly balanced for so long in Congress that neither had dared to undertake significant economic or social reforms, and Populism was an attempt to force such changes. The author of the following article takes a cool look at the more fundamental meanings of Populism in that hectic election year.

From Frederick E. Haynes, "The New Sectionalism," *The Quarterly Journal of Economics*, X (1896), pp. 269-270, 288, 289-291, 294-295. Subheadings added and footnote omitted by the editors

I
East, West, and South

At the present time we are hearing a good deal of a "new sectionalism" which is said to be arraying the West and South against the East. The line of division between the sections is not definite: an area of debatable ground is claimed by both sides. The states beyond the Mississippi show most clearly the characteristics of the new sectionalism. The South has been affected by local peculiarities,—notably by the presence of a large negro population,—but its general attitude has been one of sympathy and co-operation with the West. The states between the Mississippi, the Ohio, and the Great Lakes form the debatable region. The East, which is the chief object of Western and Southern hostility, includes the New England and Middle states, with New York as a center. Kansas, Nebraska, the Dakotas, Colorado, and Nevada have been most distinctly committed to the new doctrines. These states have been strongholds of the Populists. They have furnished most of the recruits for the industrial armies. They have contributed the principal support to the demand for the free coinage of silver. In the South, Alabama and South Carolina, and more lately North Carolina, have been the chief seats of the movement. The new sectionalism, therefore, represents a cleavage among the states which divides the older and wealthier states of the East from the younger, less populous, and less wealthy states of the West and South. A line drawn from the source of the Mississippi to its junction with the Ohio, thence up the Ohio to the south-west corner of Pennsylvania, and along the southern boundary of Pennsylvania and of Maryland to the Atlantic, marks in a general way the boundary between the sections. Sixteen states, with a population of 32 millions, comprise the East, and twenty-eight states, with a population of 30 millions, the West and South,—an almost equal division of the people between the sections. Such an estimate gives to the East the debatable ground contained in the five Central states. With the threefold division we should have the following: the East with eleven states and a population of over 18 millions; the doubtful states, five in number and with over 13 million people; and the West and South with twenty-eight states and 30 millions.

The chief characteristics of this new sectionalism have been: hostility to railways; belief in an irredeemable paper money issued by the federal government; demand for the free coinage of silver at a ratio of 16 to 1; hostility to banks of all kinds; opposition to the issue of bonds; and demand for an income tax to force the holders of great wealth to contribute, according to their ability, to the needs of the government. The attitude of the West and South has been made clear in their support of the income tax, and in their defeat of all the efforts of the present administration to obtain the consent of Congress to the issue of bonds. The chaotic condition of politics during recent years is chiefly explicable as a result of the disturbing effect of the new sectionalism....

In the influence of the policy of the federal government, in the industrial relations of the East with the West and South, and in the economic changes that have come from the closer settlement of the West and the industrial transformation of the South, we have the principal influences that have produced the new sectionalism. But, in addition to these industrial and economic conditions, there are other causes that deserve attention. Among the more important of these are the corruption of the old parties, the rise of a new democracy, and the avoidance of live issues by the leading parties....

II

Rise of the Masses

The rise of a new democracy requires some further comment. It is a very general opinion that we have had a perfectly democratic government ever since 1776. During the early years of the republic the government of the country was in the hands of the aristocracies of Virginia and New England, of which Washington, Jefferson, Madison, and the Adamses were the leaders. While theoretically sovereign, the people at large were "deferential" enough (to use a phrase of Bagehot's) to allow the control of affairs to remain in the hands of their superiors in birth and position. The first serious shock to this situation came with the advent to power in 1830 of Andrew Jackson. The great middle class, so called, the people with no pretension to birth and with no inherited wealth, were gradually roused to a point where they demanded a voice in public affairs. From 1830 to 1865 large classes, before indifferent or unable to exert an influence, began to take an effective part in governmental affairs. All property qualifications, such as existed in the early days of the republic, were swept away. Legally, there was a government of the people. Nevertheless, there remained large classes who were unable to exert any real influence upon politics. The years since 1865 have witnessed the gradual coming to political consciousness of these long silent classes. Economic and industrial changes, the results of popular education, and the growth to maturity of the children of the

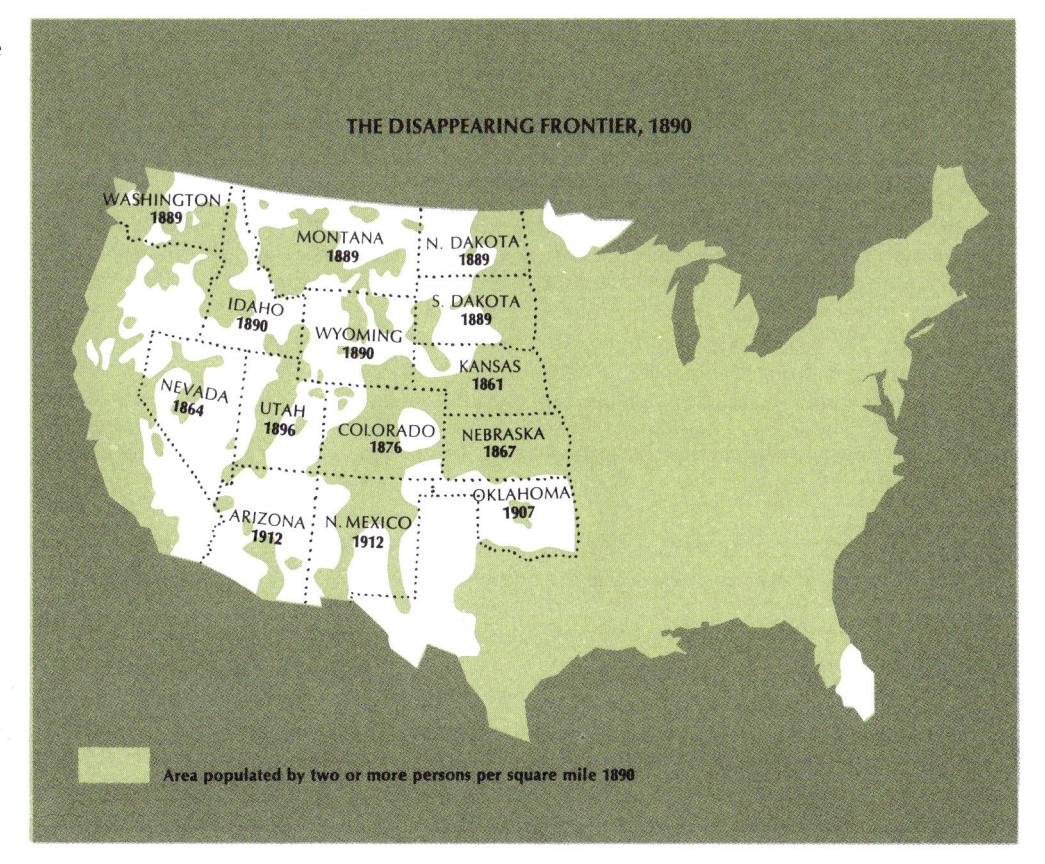

THE DISAPPEARING FRONTIER, 1890

WASHINGTON 1889
MONTANA 1889
N. DAKOTA 1889
IDAHO 1890
S. DAKOTA 1889
WYOMING 1890
KANSAS 1861
NEVADA 1864
UTAH 1896
COLORADO 1876
NEBRASKA 1867
OKLAHOMA 1907
ARIZONA 1912
N. MEXICO 1912

Area populated by two or more persons per square mile 1890

earlier immigrants from Europe, have all tended in the same direction. A similar development has been going on throughout the world. In the United States there are many indications that the great masses of the people, the working classes, are at length astir, and ready to take a real part in the control of the government. The true explanation of the so-called tidal waves of 1890, 1892, and 1894, is to be found in the participation of these classes, formerly without political influence. They show that the masses are now capable of forming opinions upon questions placed definitely before them, and have learned how to register those opinions at the polls. The passage of an unpopular tariff act was the chief cause of the tidal waves of 1890 and 1892, while in 1894 the people punished the Democrats for the disasters of 1893. The growth of labor organizations and the spread of socialistic agitation point in the same direction. The industrial armies of 1894 and the great strikes of recent years are results of the same cause. The Populist party derives its greatest strength from these very classes, hitherto unrepresented. Its rank and file are made up of the common people, and it is from their participation that it derives its great significance.

III

Avoidance of Issues

From another point of view the avoidance of live issues by the leading parties is responsible for the formation of independent movements. The great party organizations have long survived the issues they were formed to support. They have become mere machines for winning elections and keeping control of the offices. They refuse to risk anything by attempts to deal with pressing questions; and they prevent, by the very strength of their organization, the formation of new agencies. But the problems of the time become ever more insistent of attention. They will not down at the frown of party leaders. They must be dealt with, and machinery must be provided for their solution. The strength of the demand is shown by the many fruitless efforts to discover methods of solving them. In spite of great obstacles, independent organizations are formed to advocate all sorts of remedies. The refusal of the great party organizations and of well-known men to touch the problems has left the task to organizations and leaders incompetent or insufficiently equipped for the work. Because the Republicans and Democrats decline to take up the pressing industrial problems, their solution is left to the Populists. And the Populists will deserve credit if they accomplish nothing more than to lead the great parties and their leaders to face these questions. With all their faults, they have the one great merit of recognizing that industrial problems are the problems of the hour in the United States, as in the rest of the world. . . .

Our statesmen and our men of leisure and education must face these problems, and undertake their solution. The tariff must give way to questions connected with transportation, with monopolies, with the relations of employer and employed, and the reform of taxation in such manner that accumulated wealth may pay its share of the expenses of government. A proper understanding of Populism, as a movement with historical foundations and allied to similar movements in other countries, will contribute to the desired end.

Finally, the question arises as to whether the new sectionalism is to be permanent, and what is to be its influence in our national life? I trust that I have made clear that it represents something more than the mere vagary of disordered and discontented minds, that it has its roots in the past, and that it has arisen because of real grievances. The West and South have passed through a period of rapid economic development, and in the course of this development certain evils have appeared. As a result, we have complaints and recriminations. The West and South are the debtors of the East, and regard that section as grasping and avaricious. The East, having suffered frequent loss, naturally looks at the West and South as debtors anxious to avoid payment of just debts. Hence arises the Western idea of the money power, in which England and the East are represented as grasping usurers, bent on the enslavement of the world. Contrasted with this idea is the equally mistaken Eastern view of the West and South as filled with persons possessed of wild and fanatical ideas on industry and government. The hope of the future lies in a clear understanding of one section by the other, and a cordial union between them for the reform of existing abuses. Under such a union Populism will disappear, and sectionalism will cease to disturb our politics. By such a course alone can the new sectionalism pass away peacefully, leaving none of the scars and burdens still remaining to us from the great conflict by which the older sectionalism of North and South was destroyed.

The Last Days of the Frontier

The West lured emigrants by the hundreds of thousands even in the days before railroads made 2000-mile journeys comparatively easy. Here (1) a wagon train creaks slowly along the Santa Fe Trail into the Southwest. This photograph was probably taken between the Civil War and the completion of the Santa Fe Railway in 1883.

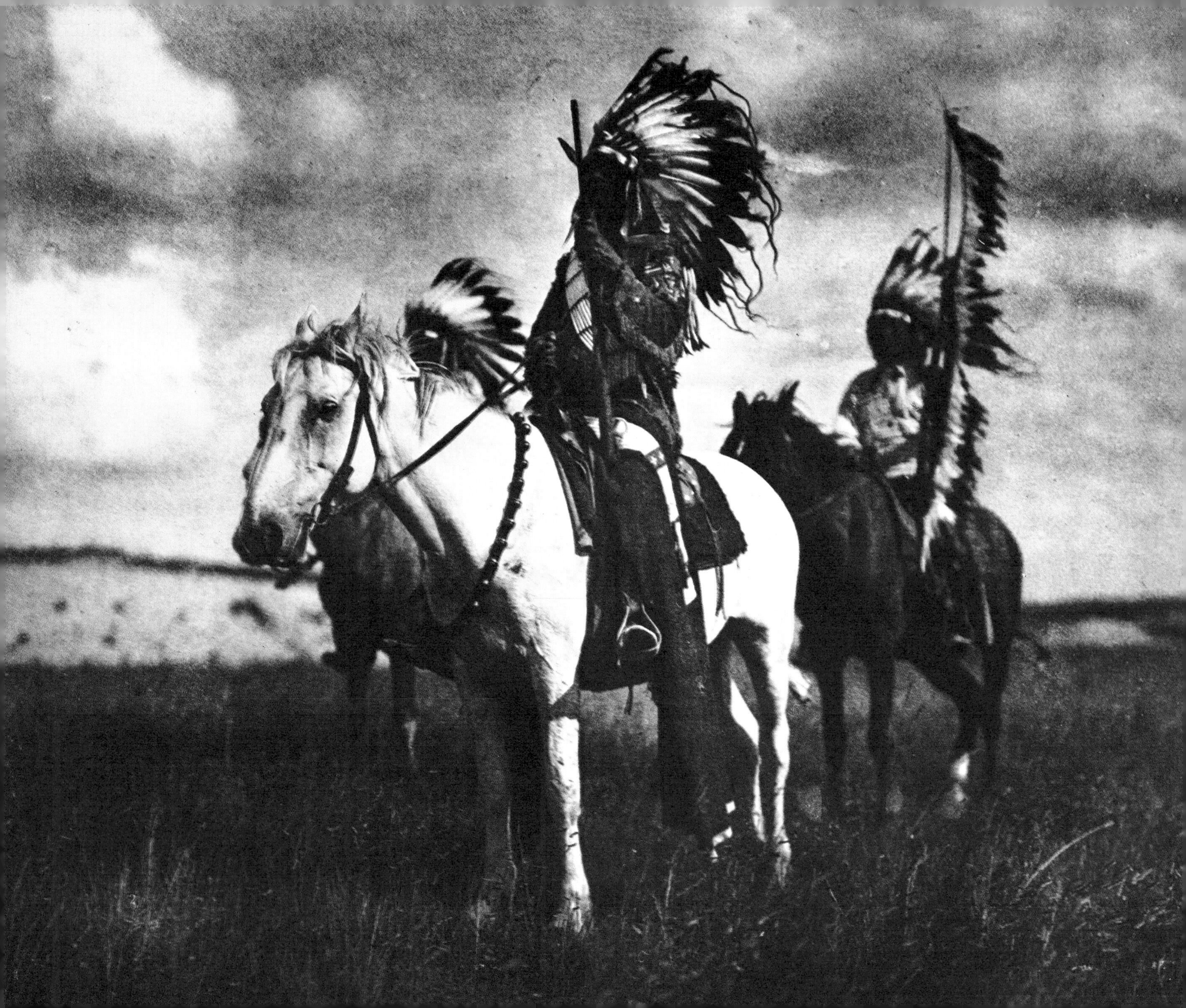

For the native inhabitants of the Western plains wagon trains spelled the end of a way of life. The seemingly endless herds of buffalo that the Indians depended on for food, clothing and shelter were doomed by encroaching civilization. By 1907 these Sioux chiefs (2) wore their regalia for photographers rather than their enemies. The way of life which overtook the Indians in a few short decades is symbolized by the wedding of Mr. and Mrs. Lew Beager (3) in Custer County, Nebraska, on August 13, 1889.

4

5

Free land in the West grew scarcer within a few decades of the passage of the Homestead Act by Congress in 1862. Occasionally a windfall came along, as with this rush for land (4) newly opened to settlers in the Oklahoma Territory. A characteristic use for the higher, drier, and westernmost plains was the herding of cattle (5), generally a hard and monotonous, rather than colorful, life for the cowboy. The raising of cattle on the open range, where they could be identified only by the brands they bore, soon came to an end, in the 1880s and 1890s, with the fencing in of the range with barbed wire, invented in 1874. In those parts of the West with enough rainfall for trees to grow, the forests disappeared at a rapid rate through the agency of such men as these (6), gathered at McDermott's Camp No. 2 somewhere in Minnesota. Where sufficient rainfall and open land existed together in the plains region, the soil's fertility produced bountiful crops, as in the view (7) of a crew threshing grain in the Roaring Fork Valley of Colorado. Where steam powered vehicles like these could move over flat land, horses and oxen were made obsolete.

8

9

130

10

On the high plains trees grew only near streams. The resulting shortage of timber and the difficulty of transporting it caused many early settlers there to make habitations by digging caves into the sides of hills, or by making walls of blocks of sod, or by combining the two (8). The windmill pumped water from a well. Civilized society, as represented by this sod school house (9) in Custer County, Nebraska, followed swiftly. The vastness of the Great Plains is seen in this view of the construction of the St. Paul, Minneapolis, and Manitoba Railroad through Montana Territory in 1887 (10); the railroad helped to open the Northwest to permanent settlement by emigrants. Discoveries of new sources of precious metals occurred at scattered locations throughout the West in the late nineteenth century. The main street of Last Chance Gulch (later Helena), Montana, in 1870 (11) reveals the boom which followed the discovery of gold there late in the Civil War.

11

The passing of time brought to the main streets of frontier towns a look of more permanence. This turn-of-the-century look at Black River Falls, Wisconsin, shows a village with a growing number of the amenities of life, such as electricity.

TOPIC 45

THE PROGRESSIVE APPROACH TO REFORM

At the turn of the twentieth century American society was ripe for a wave of reform. Since the 1870s, when the reformist urges of Reconstruction had weakened, American power, talent, and energies had been devoted largely to the settling and development of the West and the building of an industrial and urban economy. The ablest men sought the rewards of private life rather than public service; a scandalous amount of corruption occurred among local, state, and national officials; cynicism about politics became more deep-seated. At the same time, a variety of difficult economic and social problems, created by economic change and population shifts, piled up unsolved.

The emphasis on business that dominated American life made matters worse. The cult of material success, the doctrine of laissez faire in business, and the ideal of individual enterprise served well to spur economic growth, but they had little to offer in dealing with the deepening problems of effective government, economic and social justice for the less favored, and preservation of the natural environment. These tasks demanded a new philosophy of reform, new leadership, and a new generation of reformers. The men and women who responded to these challenges called themselves "Progressives," a name suggesting their confidence in producing continual improvement in American life through their reforms.

Reading 214

Reform—Progressive Style

The following reading, prepared by the editors, offers an interpretation of reform thought and action during the Progressive Era, the first fifteen years of the twentieth century.

This new cycle of reformism possessed novel aspects, but it also owed much to the past. Progressives drew heavily from the tradition of democratic and moral reform of the pre–Civil War era. Two important reform causes of the earlier period—women's rights and temperance—gained striking victories with the aid of Progressives between 1910 and 1920 when Constitutional amendments granted women the right to vote and prohibited the manufacture, sale, and use of alcoholic beverages throughout the nation. Prohibition, especially, derived much of its strength from the evangelical Protestantism that had inspired so much of pre–Civil War moral reform.

The Progressives' fight for honest government had precedents in the late nineteenth century. As early as 1872 some Republican leaders opposed their own party's corruption by forming the Liberal Republican Party. This venture, joined by some Democrats equally dissatisfied with their own party, failed but initiated a strong strain of independence among the reform-minded in both major parties. (Party regulars called them "Mugwumps.") A strong reaction to the corrupting effects of the spoils system in government resulted in a federal civil service in the Pendleton Act of 1883; this legislation owed much to the fact that President James A

133

TABLE 1 PRESIDENTIAL ELECTIONS, 1880-1900

	CANDIDATES	PARTIES	ELECTORAL VOTE	POPULAR VOTE
1880	James A. Garfield	Republican	214	4,453,295
	Winfield S. Hancock	Democratic	155	4,414,082
	James B. Weaver	Greenback-Labor		308,578
	Neal Dow	Prohibition		10,305
1884	Grover Cleveland	Democratic	219	4,879,507
	James G. Blaine	Republican	182	4,850,293
	Benjamin F. Butler	Greenback-Labor		175,370
	John P. St. John	Prohibition		150,369
1888	Benjamin Harrison	Republican	233	5,447,129
	Grover Cleveland	Democratic	168	5,537,857
	Clinton B. Fisk	Prohibition		249,506
	Anson J. Streeter	Union Labor		146,935
1892	Grover Cleveland	Democratic	277	5,555,426
	Benjamin Harrison	Republican	145	5,182,690
	James B. Weaver	People's	22	1,029,846
	John Bidwell	Prohibition		264,133
	Simon Wing	Socialist Labor		21,164
1896	William McKinley	Republican	271	7,102,246
	William J. Bryan	Democratic	176	6,492,559
	John M. Palmer	National Democratic		133,148
	Joshua Levering	Prohibition		132,007
	Charles H. Matchett	Socialist Labor		36,274
	Charles E. Bentley	Nationalist		13,969
1900	William McKinley	Republican	292	7,218,491
	William J. Bryan	Democratic	155	6,356,734
	John C. Wooley	Prohibition		208,914
	Eugene V. Debs	Socialist		87,814
	Wharton Barker	People's		50,373
	Joseph F. Malloney	Socialist Labor		39,739

Garfield had been killed by a disappointed office-seeker two years earlier. At the state and local levels reformers occasionally mounted successful purges of corrupt political machines and their leaders, like the attack on "Boss" William M. Tweed of New York City's Tammany Hall Democratic organization in the 1870s after Tweed had stolen at least eight million dollars from the city. Most political reformers during this era concentrated on preventing misuse of money or on substituting "good men" for "bad men" in office; Progressives realized the inadequacy of this approach.

Other targets of Progressive efforts were bad living and working conditions generated by the crowding of millions of new urban dwellers into areas with inadequate housing and services such as sanitation, fire and police protection, as well as the exploitation by business and industry of unprotected laborers, many of them new immigrants and women and children.

Perhaps the most novel, obvious, and difficult problem created by the new industrial growth was that of business concentration leading toward monopoly. The Progressives' approach to that problem will be dealt with in the next topic, but it should be noted that they owed much of their understanding of this problem to the attacks which Grangers, Greenbackers, Populists, labor organizations, and Socialists had been waging for some time. These early reform efforts were responsible for the Sherman Act passed by Congress in 1890; this was an attempt to keep firms which were dominant in their fields, popularly called "trusts," from achieving complete control through "unfair" practices, or from taking "unfair" advantage of the public in prices and services.

Robert M. LaFollette was one of the first and most dynamic of the progressive political reformers. Here he campaigns from the back of a wagon in his race for governor of Wisconsin in 1897. LaFollette is at the beginning of a thirty-year career as a political leader.

While Progressives gained inspiration and insight from other reform groups, they differed from Greenbackers and Populists in their interest in urban rather than rural problems (except insofar as conservation affected both city and country dwellers). They also differed from Socialists in their stout support of a reformed capitalism, and from unionists in their membership, which was drawn largely from business and professional classes.

One reason why Progressives achieved greater success in bringing about reforms on the national level than did other groups was that they acquired a significant amount of influence in the two major political parties at times when those parties were able to carry out effective legislative programs. For twenty years before 1896 neither party had had really solid control of the national government; from 1876 through 1892 no victorious candidate for President won by more than a small margin, while one or both houses of Congress usually were controlled by the opposing party. Neither party, therefore, could afford to antagonize important voting blocs by sponsoring reforms that such blocs opposed strongly. The sole major group excepted from this rule was the white South, which the Republicans alternately courted and spurned, depending on that party's sense of the political advantage to be gained by "waving the bloody shirt," that is, by recalling that most Democrats had been either Confederates or Northern opponents of the Civil War.

In 1894, however, Republicans swept both houses of Congress in a year when a Democratic administration could be blamed for a severe depression. In 1896 they retained firm control of Congress and won the Presidency, when William McKinley defeated William Jennings Bryan. The Republicans' strength, further increased in 1900 when McKinley was reelected, depended mainly on their appeal to farmers and urban dwellers in the heavily populated northeastern and north central sections of the nation. Recovery from the depression of the mid-1890s, a rise in farm prices in the late 1890s, and the temporary solution of the monetary problem after 1898 through a large increase in gold production, all enabled the Republicans to identify themselves successfully as the "party of prosperity," and to become the first party to have a clear national majority since the Democrats before the Civil War.

To use the Republican Party to effect reforms, however, Progressives needed to win recruits and make converts in Congress. Equally as important was the appearance of a national leader ready to espouse Progressive reforms. Theodore Roosevelt supplied this need for Republicans from 1901 to 1909, just as Woodrow Wilson supplied it for the Democrats when their party regained temporarily its majority position after 1912. The following readings consider various aspects of Progressivism, including some ways in which Progressives themselves differed.

Roosevelt and the Progressives

Two events of great symbolic as well as practical importance occurred in 1901: the United States Steel Corporation, the "steel trust", was created; and Theodore Roosevelt, the Progressives' hero as a trustbuster, became President. In this reading historian Henry Bamford Parkes explains the type of leader Roosevelt was.

From *The United States of America, A History*, 3rd ed., by Henry Bamford Parkes. Copyright 1953, © 1959, 1968 by Alfred A. Knopf, Inc. Reprinted by permission of the publisher. Pp. 544, 551, 552–555. Subheadings added and omitted by the editors.

I

Beliefs and Techniques

The progressive leaders believed in the traditional American ideals of democratic government, individual liberty, the rule of law, and the protection of private property, but they argued that maintenance of these ideals in the new industrial era required new political techniques. They strongly emphasized ethical, humanitarian, and religious values rather than attempting to stir up economic resentments and class hatreds. Proposals for any thoroughgoing transformation of the traditional political and economic system, such as were put forward by the Socialists, won little support. Progressivism was, in fact, a movement with predominantly middle-class objectives and viewpoint, deriving much of its support from small businessmen, farmers, and professional people. The typical progressive leader was some lawyer, journalist, or businessman who, aroused by corruption or misgovernment in his own community, started a crusade to elect better men to office, and gradually came to the realization that what was needed was a reform of the system as well as a change of men.

Like most earlier reformers in the British and American political tradition, the progressives had a pragmatic approach. Whenever they saw an evil, they attempted to deal with it, without adopting any comprehensive theory or formulating ultimate objectives. This method of piecemeal reform made for a maximum of agreement and prevented conflicts from becoming fanatical or irreconcilable. During the progressive period there was no clear-cut line of division between reformers and conservatives. Popular sentiment so strongly favored reform that most responsible political leaders recognized that it was necessary, although some of them wished to move much further than others. Party labels therefore became even more meaningless than usual. There were progressive Republicans and progressive Democrats, with no perceptible difference in their objectives. And although progressivism was probably strongest in the Middle Western farm belt, where it built on foundations laid by the Populist movement, it spread to all sections of the country. . . .

II

Theodore Roosevelt

The first of the three progressive presidents achieved power by accident. Born into a New York patrician family and educated at Harvard, Theodore Roosevelt had spent one term in the New York legislature, had ranched in Dakota, had served as a member of the United States Civil Service Commission, as head of the New York City police force, and as Assistant Secretary of the Navy, and had written extensively on American history. His activities in Cuba during the war with Spain as second-in-command of a volunteer regiment of Rough Riders made him a popular hero, and he was then elected Governor of New York. In this position he annoyed the Republican state boss, Senator Tom Platt, by showing too much independence, and Platt determined to remove him from the governorship by having him nominated for the vice-presidency. In the 1900 election Roosevelt therefore became McKinley's running mate, despite the opposition of Mark Hanna, who pointed out that there would be "only one life between that madman and the presidency." Bryan was again the Democratic candidate; and after a campaign in which imperialism was the main issue, McKinley was re-elected with a slightly larger majority than in 1896. In September 1901 McKinley was assassinated by a demented anarchist, and Roosevelt thus succeeded to the presidency. . . .

Roosevelt's trust-busting campaign began in March 1902, when he ordered the Attorney General to bring suit under the Sherman Act against the Northern Securities Company. This had been organized by two railroad magnates, James J. Hill and Edward H. Harriman, with the assistance of the House of Morgan, in order to monopolize the railroad lines of the Northwest. This was the first time that the Federal government had shown any serious intention of enforcing the Sherman Act. The Supreme Court ruled in favor of the government, and Roosevelt then went on to attack a number of other trusts, including Standard Oil. During his seven and a half years in office he was responsible for a total of forty-three cases.

Roosevelt's trust-busting crusade aroused great popular enthusiasm and equally violent indignation among the corporation magnates. Yet its economic results were not impressive. The trusts were compelled by court decisions to dissolve themselves into their component parts, but these parts could not be transferred to different ownership or compelled to compete with each other. The different sections of Standard Oil and the other trusts made informal "community of interest" agreements with each other for stabilizing prices and production, and there was no real revival of competition. The Supreme Court, moreover, gradually whittled down the Sherman Act. In the Northern Securities case it agreed, contrary to the wording of the act, that the defendants should not be held guilty of a misdemeanor and subject to criminal penalties. In the Standard Oil case (which did not reach the Court until 1911) the justices interpreted the act as prohibiting only "undue" and "unreasonable" restraint of trade. Under what circumstances a monopoly was unreasonable was for the Court to decide.

Roosevelt recognized the inadequacy of trust-busting. Declaring that he was not opposed to big business as such, but making a distinction between good and bad trusts, he said that "we draw the line against misconduct, not against wealth." As an ultimate solution he favored regulation of corporations by the Federal government instead of by the states, and prohibition of various specific forms of misconduct; but bills to this effect were rejected by Congress. But Roosevelt believed that the most important requirement was simply to assert the principle of government supremacy. "These men," he declared in his *Autobiography*, "demanded for themselves an immunity from governmental control which, if granted, would be as wicked and as foolish as immunity to the barons of the twelfth century." The absolutely vital question was whether the Government had power to control them at all.

III

Strengthening the ICC

Having made the Sherman Act more than a dead letter, Roosevelt proposed also to strengthen the other main instrument for Federal regulation of business, the Interstate Commerce Act. In 1903 Congress passed the Elkins Act requiring railroads to adhere to their published rates and forbidding them to give rebates. This act had the support of the railroad men and was directed against business corporations like Standard Oil which had obtained competitive advantages by forcing the railroads to ship their goods at preferential rates. During Roosevelt's second term several corporations were fined for securing rebates, but fully effective enforcement of the act proved to be impossible.

A much more important progressive objective was to bring about the reduction of excessive rates. Roosevelt during his second term recommended that broad powers over rates be given to the Interstate Commerce Commission; but when his more drastic proposals were blocked in the Senate, he agreed to compromise. The result was the Hepburn Act of 1906. This authorized the Commission to order a reduction of unreasonable rates; but a railroad could then appeal to the law courts, in which case the reduction could not go into effect until and unless the courts decided that it was reasonable. On the other hand, the burden of proof was now placed upon the railroad and no longer upon the Commission. Possibly the most important feature of the Hepburn Act was that the Commission was empowered to prescribe a uniform system of bookkeeping for all railroads and was thus, for the first time, able to find out what they were really doing and whether their profits were excessive.

Most progressives regarded the Hepburn Act as wholly inadequate and blamed Roosevelt for his willingness to compromise with the Senate conservatives. In view of the notorious conservatism of the courts, they were particularly disappointed by the provision for judicial review, and asked for some clear definition of what constituted a "reasonable rate," preferably one based not on the nominal capitalization of the roads but on the real physical value of the properties. Nevertheless, the Hepburn Act, in spite of its obvious weaknesses, was followed by thousands of complaints against high rates by shippers to the Commission, and prepared the way for measures in later administrations giving it full power over rates.

IV

The Coal Strike

Roosevelt's intervention in the coal strike was notable chiefly because it set a new precedent. The miners in the anthracite coal fields were one of the most exploited groups in the United States. In 1902, under the able and dynamic leadership of John Mitchell, they struck for higher wages, a nine-hour day, and union recognition. By the autumn coal was becoming scarce, and the Federal government had to intervene. But whereas previous presidents, like Hayes in 1877 and Cleveland in 1894, had intervened in labor disputes only on the side of the employers and against the workers, Roosevelt intervened in order to bring about a settlement by negotiation. The mine-owners, who had an essentially feudal attitude towards their workers, refused to negotiate with Mitchell, but were finally induced to accept arbitration by a government commission. This included a trade-union representative, who (to get around the stubborn prejudices of the owners) was officially described as an "eminent sociologist." Although union recognition was not accorded until 1916, the workers received higher wages and a nine-hour day.

V

Conservation

Probably Roosevelt's most important contribution to national welfare was his encouragement of conservation. He was the first president to realize the vital importance of this question. Public-land policies had hitherto been administered by officials in whom (as he declared) "the habit of deciding, wherever possible, in favor of private interests against the public welfare was firmly fixed." With the enthusiastic assistance of Gifford Pinchot, director of the Forest Service, Roosevelt endeavored to inculcate a different attitude. He added about 130,000,000 acres to the forest reserves (as authorized by the act of 1891) and also withdrew from entry (with doubtful legality) nearly 90,000,000 acres of land containing coal, phosphates, and water-power sites. He also helped to secure passage of the Newlands Act of 1902. Superseding the Carey Act of 1894, which had not proved very effective, this authorized the Federal government directly to establish irrigation projects on arid lands and created a Reclamation Service to supervise them. Since the passage of the act the government has constructed in the Western states a number of dams which are among the most impressive engineering projects in human history. In many other ways, most notably through the White House Conference of 1908, Roosevelt publicized the need for government action to protect and develop the country's natural resources. Thanks largely to his leadership, the American people began to realize that the time had come to establish checks on the wasteful individualism characteristic of the pioneering period.

The only other important laws passed during Roosevelt's administration were the Meat Inspection Act and the Pure Food and Drug Act, both in 1906. The former (inspired by Upton Sinclair's *The Jungle* but pushed through Congress by Roosevelt's leadership) provided for Federal inspection of factories packing meat for interstate commerce. The latter (the product of a long series of startling investigations by chemists working for the Department of Agriculture) prohibited the sale of certain harmful foods and ordered that medicines containing dangerous drugs be correctly labeled. Since few consumers understood the meaning of the labels, and since nothing was done to stop the fraudulent advertising, this measure by no means purified the drug industry. Both acts, however, marked another break with strict *laissez-faire* doctrine, according to which consumers were supposed to be capable of protecting themselves. Roosevelt urged upon Congress a number of other, and much more drastic, proposals for political and economic reforms, but was unable to overcome the opposition of the old-guard Republican leadership.

Coal was the major source of heat in turn-of-the-century America. During the nationwide coal strike of 1902, shortages quickly developed, especially in the poorest areas of the cities. Here young and old wait patiently to fill their sacks at a public distribution point.

Politics in the City—Old Style (1905)

If New York's Tammany Hall was America's best-known political machine, then Tammany's George Washington Plunkitt (1842-1924) was America's most engaging machine politician. A poor boy who made good, and the son of Irish immigrants, Plunkitt was perfectly open in telling how a city politician operated at the turn of the century. The following is from a series of newspaper interviews Plunkitt gave in 1905 to William L. Riordon, a New York newspaper man.

From the book *Plunkitt of Tammany Hall* by William L. Riordan. Intro. by Arthur Mann. Published in 1963 in a paperback edition by E. P. Dutton & Co., Inc. and used with their permission. Pp. 3, 25, 27-28. Subheadings added by the editors.

I
Honest Graft and Dishonest Graft

Everybody is talkin' these days about Tammany men growin' rich on graft, but nobody thinks of drawin' the distinction between honest graft and dishonest graft. There's all the difference in the world between the two. Yes, many of our men have grown rich in politics. I have myself. I've made a big fortune out of the game, and I'm gettin' richer every day, but I've not gone in for dishonest graft—blackmailin' gamblers, saloonkeepers, disorderly people, etc.—and neither has any of the men who have made big fortunes in politics.

There's an honest graft, and I'm an example of how it works. I might sum up the whole thing by sayin': "I seen my opportunities and I took 'em."

Just let me explain by examples. My party's in power in the city, and it's goin' to undertake a lot of public improvements. Well, I'm tipped off, say, that they're going to lay out a new park at a certain place.

I see my opportunity and I take it. I go to that place and I buy up all the land I can in the neighborhood. Then the board of this or that makes its plan public, and there is a rush to get my land, which nobody cared particular for before.

Ain't it perfectly honest to charge a good price and make a profit on my investment and foresight? Of course, it is. Well, that's honest graft. . . .

II
Running Your District

There's only one way to hold a district: you must study human nature and act accordin'. You can't study human nature in books. Books is a hindrance more than anything else. If you have been to college, so much the worse for you. You'll have to unlearn all you learned before you can get right down to human nature, and unlearnin' takes a lot of time. Some men can never forget what they learned at college. Such men may get to be district leaders by a fluke, but they never last.

To learn real human nature you have to go among the people, see them and be seen. I know every man, woman, and child in the Fifteenth District, except them that's been born this summer—and I know some of them, too. I know what they like and what they don't like, what they are strong at and what they are weak in, and I reach them by approachin' at the right side. . . .

What tells in holdin' your grip on your district is to go right down among the poor families and help them in the different ways they need help. I've got a regular system for this. If there's a fire in Ninth, Tenth, or Eleventh Avenue, for example, any hour of the day or night, I'm usually there with some of my election district captains as soon as the fire engines. If a family is burned out I don't ask whether they are Republicans or Democrats, and I don't refer them to the Charity Organization Society, which would investigate their case in a month or two and decide they were worthy of help about the time they are dead from starvation. I just get quarters for them, buy clothes for them if their clothes were burned up, and fix them up till they get things runnin' again. It's philanthropy, but it's politics, too—mighty good politics. Who can tell how many votes one of these fires bring me? The poor are the most grateful people in the world, and, let me tell you, they have more friends in their neighborhoods than the rich have in theirs.

If there's a family in my district in want I know it before the charitable societies do, and me and my men are first on the ground. I have a special corps to look up such cases. The consequence is that the poor look up to George W. Plunkitt as a father, come to him in trouble—and don't forget him on election day.

Another thing, I can always get a job for a deservin' man. I make it a point to keep on the track of jobs, and it seldom happens that I don't have a few up my sleeve ready for use. I know every big employer in the district and in the whole city, for that matter, and they ain't in the habit of sayin' no to me when I ask them for a job.

Reading 217

Politics in the City— New Style (1914)

For years middle-class reformers had been fighting the Plunkitt style of city government. They had met with little success in ending graft, whether of the honest or dishonest variety. Progressives went further than earlier "good-government" reformers by arguing not only for honest men in politics but also for the reorganization of city government. The implications of these changes were made clear by Henry Waite, the city manager of Dayton, Ohio.

From Henry M. Waite, "The City-Manager Plan—The Application of Business Methods to Municipal Government," *The American City*, XI (November, 1914), pp. 11-13. Subheadings added by the editors.

I

The Managers

The commission-manager form of government in Dayton is the application of the newest development in organization to a municipality. The commission is elected by the people on a non-partisan and short ballot. The commissioner receiving the highest number of votes is the Mayor. These five commissioners correspond to the board of directors of a corporation, and they select and appoint an executive, who is the City Manager. All the functions of the municipal government come under the City Manager, outside of the legislative functions, which are in the hands of the commission.

Under the executive in Dayton are the five operating departments. Each of these departments is headed by a director, and each of these directors is appointed by the City Manager. They are:

Director of Public Safety, covering police, fire, weights and measures

Director of Service, who has charge of the water works, engineering, the construction, repairing and cleaning of streets and sewers, the collection of garbage and ashes, and the general supervision of all public utilities

Director of Finance, who has under him the treasurer, the accountant, and the purchasing agent

Director of Welfare, having charge of all correctional institutions, hospitals, charities, parks, playgrounds, recreations, outdoor relief, and social betterment and all community and social features

Director of Law, who is the city attorney

The appointment of these directors is the first step in the application of business methods to municipal government. . . .

These directors, with the City Manager, form the staff. They meet every day for an hour and go over the important questions in each department, the same as would be done in a corporation. If there is a division of ideas in these staff meetings, a vote is taken, and while this particular function is not called for in the charter, it centralizes the entire organization. Each director is responsible for his own department. Each director makes his own appointments, subject to the approval of the City Manager, and the question of appointments is taken up at the staff meetings.

The commissioners, together with the City Manager and the Director of Finance as secretary, form the sinking fund trustees. This brings all of the finances of the government inside of the central organization.

I think everyone will agree that there has been an awakening all over the country to the inefficiency of the old forms of municipal government and to the fact that we ourselves, the voters, made the conditions what they are. We may be dissatisfied at what is being accomplished, but, as a matter of fact, we are responsible. We have allowed innumerable laws and statutes to be passed which surround municipal work with a network of red tape, making progress and efficiency impossible. We, to protect our communities and ourselves—as we thought—allowed these laws to be passed, and there we ended our interest in municipal affairs. We elected people to office and then hampered them, then condemned them. I have thought, since I have been in municipal work, that if it was possible to get one of these public jobs in the open where we could handle it as our big businesses are handled, most remarkable showings could be made. Unfortunately, however, it is impossible, due to the network of laws and the attitude of the people, to get efficiency rapidly. . . .

II

The "Boss"—Official or Unofficial

This condition of affairs has built up political machines, run by a centralized power, and we ourselves have allowed it. We have not in our governmental organizations allowed for any centralized power, and as we know in our own business that centralization is essential,

141

the political parties themselves have centralized around a boss, and we have allowed our cities to be governed by two parties—one party in power and entrenched, and the other party on the outside waiting for an opportunity to become entrenched. Our idea of municipal reform has been to throw out one party and put in the other. We have allowed these party organizations, one in and one out, to be molded under our very hands. Their strength lies in organization, and the centralized power, or boss, holds his organization together with the idea that "to the victor belong the spoils." We often hear that the city manager is nothing more than a boss, or centralized power. This may be true, but the conditions are not comparable, as under the old form of bossism the boss was unassailable—he was unofficial. Under the city-manager form the "boss" is assailable because he is official, and, under our particular charter in Dayton, the City Manager is subject to recall.

The commission-manager form of government does away with the conditions which have in the past hampered and made impossible efficiency under the old forms of government. You have a commission elected on a non-partisan ballot, which becomes the board of directors or the legislative body. They select the administrative officer who is directly responsible for the carrying out of the administrative functions. This success depends upon his fitness and general capability. He selects men who have been specially trained for the work to be done, and in this selection he is not hampered by political promises. I cannot tell you to-day the political faith of any of the men I have appointed since I have been in Dayton. "Party" and "politics" are simply left out of the reckoning. . . .

The people of a community must be educated up to a change. A few people cannot rise in their wrath and make it alone. A municipal bureau of research is absolutely necessary to our mind for three reasons: first, it compiles data which show the people the necessity of a change; second, after the change has occurred, the information and experience of the bureau are necessary for the installation of the new government; third, the information which the bureau has gathered together is necessary as a basis of comparison, after the new government has been established so that the new can be compared with the old. . . .

From this it is evident that there is considerable work necessary before any change in government is attempted. Finally, I should like to emphasize the following very important point—one I think the American people have lost sight of, but that they are now beginning to grasp: *No matter what form of government a city may have, if the people themselves are not interested in it and participate in it, that government will never be a success.*

Theodore Roosevelt on Progressive Goals

A look at the popular magazines published between 1900 and 1916, the period we label the Progressive Era, shows a tremendous surge of interest in the social ills of the country. Political corruption, economic exploitation, or the ills stemming from poverty ceased to be considered necessary evils, as reformers refused to wait for them to end "naturally." The key concept was action and few men better represented the Progressive's conception of the word than Theodore Roosevelt. Roosevelt wrote the following article, spelling out what he meant by reform, a few weeks after he left the White House in March 1909.

From Theodore Roosevelt, "Where We Can Work With Socialists," *The Outlook*, XCl (1909), pp. 662–664. Subheadings added by the editors.

I

Economic Reform and Moral Reform

It is true that the doctrines of communistic Socialism, if consistently followed, mean the ultimate annihilation of civilization. Yet the converse is also true. Ruin faces us if we decline steadily to try to reshape our whole civilization in accordance with the law of service, and if we permit ourselves to be misled by any empirical or academic consideration into refusing to exert the common power of the community where only collective action can do what individualism has left undone, or can remedy the wrongs done by an unrestricted and ill-regulated individualism. There is any amount of evil in our social and industrial conditions of to-day, and unless we recognize this fact and try resolutely to do what we can to remedy the evil, we run great risk of seeing men in their misery turn to the false teachers whose doctrines would indeed lead them to greater misery; but who do at least recognize the fact that they are now miserable. At the present time there are scores of laws in the interest of labor—laws putting a stop to child labor, decreasing the hours of labor where they are excessive, putting a stop to unsanitary crowding and living, securing employers' liability, doing away with unhealthy conditions in various trades, and the like—which should be passed by the National and the various State Legislatures; and those who wish to do effective work against Socialism would do well to turn their energies into securing the enactment of these laws. . . .

Socialism strives to remedy what is evil alike in domestic and in economic life, and its tendency is to insist that the economic remedy is all-sufficient in every case. We should all join in the effort to do away with the evil; but we should refuse to have anything to do with remedies which are either absurd or mischievous, for such, of course, would merely aggravate the present suffering. The first thing to recognize is that, while economic reform is often vital, it is never all-sufficient. The moral reform, the change of character—in which law can sometimes play a large, but never the largest, part—is the most necessary of all. In dealing with the marriage relation the Socialist attitude is one of unmixed evil. Assuredly woman should be guarded and honored in every way, her rights jealously upheld, and any wrong done her should be regarded and punished with severe judgment; but we must keep in mind the obvious fact that equality of consideration does not mean identity of function. Our effort would be to raise the level of self-respect, self-control, sense of duty in both sexes, and not to push both down to an evil equality of moral turpitude by doing away with the self-restraint and sense of obligation which have been slowly built up through the ages. We must bring them to a moral level by raising the lower standard, not by depressing the high. It is idle to prattle against the "economic dependence" of woman upon man. In the ideal household—an ideal which I believe, though very far from being universally realized, is yet now more generally realized than ever before—there is really complete economic interdependence, as well as the high spiritual and moral interdependence which is more nearly attained in happy wedlock, in a permanent partnership of love and duty, than in any other relation of life which the world has yet seen. Rights should be forfeited by neither partner; and duties should be shirked by neither partner. The duty of the woman to be the child-bearer and home-keeper is just as obvious, simple, and healthful as the duty of the man to be the breadwinner and, if necessary, the soldier. Whenever either the man or the woman loses the power or the will to perform these obvious duties, the loss is irreparable, and, whatever may be the gain in ease, amiable softness, self-indulgent pleasure, or even artistic and material achievement, the whole civilization is rotten and must fall. . . .

II
Equality of Opportunity

We should do everything that can be done, by law or otherwise, to keep the avenues of occupation, of employment, of work, of interest, so open that there shall be, so far as it is humanly possible to achieve it, a measurable equality of opportunity; an equality of opportunity for each man to show the stuff that is in him. When it comes to reward, let each man, within the limits set by a sound and farsighted morality, get what, by his energy, intelligence, thrift, courage, he is able to get, with the opportunity open. We must set our faces against privilege; just as much against the kind of privilege which would let the shiftless and lazy laborer take what his brother has earned as against the privilege which allows the huge capitalist to take toll to which he is not entitled. We stand for equality of opportunity, but not for equality of reward unless there is also equality of service. If the service is equal, let the reward be equal; but let the reward depend on the service; and, mankind being composed as it is, there will be inequality of service for a long time to come, no matter how great the equality of opportunity may be; and just as long as there is inequality of service it is eminently desirable that there should be inequality of reward.

We recognize, and are bound to war against, the evils of to-day. The remedies are partly economic and partly spiritual, partly to be obtained by laws, and in greater part to be obtained by individual and associated effort; for character is the vital matter, and character cannot be created by law. These remedies include a religious and moral teaching which shall increase the spirit of human brotherhood; an educational system which shall train men for every form of useful service—and which shall train us to prize common sense no less than morality; such a division of the profits of industry as shall tend to encourage intelligent and thrifty tool-users to become tool-owners; and a government so strong, just, wise, and democratic that, neither lagging too far behind nor pushing heedlessly in advance, it may do its full share in promoting these ends.

Another Progressive View of Morality (1909)

Many Progressives were concerned with moral, as well as political reform. To the concerned person at the turn of the century, the social stability of an earlier era seemed to be giving way to weakening family ties, independent-minded women, and sexual laxity. Theodore Roosevelt offered his definition of the problem in Reading 218. A somewhat different approach was taken by Edward A. Ross (1866-1951), a professor of sociology at the University of Wisconsin and a leading Progressive intellectual.

From Edward Alsworth Ross, "The Significance of Increasing Divorce," *The Century Magazine*, LXXVIII (1909), pp. 149-152. Subheadings added by the editors.

I

The Nature of the Problem

Twenty years ago an investigation by the Department of Labor showed that 328,716 divorces had been granted in the United States between 1867 and 1886, and that divorces were increasing two and one half times as fast as population. The recent census for 1887-1906 brings to light 945,625 divorces, and demonstrates that the movement constantly gains in velocity. At present probably one marriage in ten is broken, and in some States the proportion may be as high as one in four. Forty years ago the broad contrast was between North and South; but the divorce rates of North and South have been converging, whereas those of East and West have diverged. The Central States have two and one half times the rate of the Atlantic States, while for the Western States the proportion is three and one half.

Although the tide of divorce is rising the world over, nowhere is it so high, nowhere is it rising so fast, as in the United States. Our rate is twice that of Switzerland, thrice that of France, and five times that of Germany. . . .

In nineteen cases out of twenty the marriage purports to be shattered by some flagrant wrong, such as adultery, cruelty, drunkenness, desertion, imprisonment for crime, or neglect to provide. Nevertheless, the growth of divorce cannot be taken as a sure sign of increasing depravity on the part of husbands or wives. Often the "cause" that figures in the record is a screen for some deep-seated irritant. Physicians declare that many marital troubles have their roots in the pathology of sex, and do not argue moral fault on the part of either spouse.

Some of those who speak with utmost positiveness on the divorce problem betray a strange confusion of thought. A new legal cause for divorce is stigmatized as "an assault upon the marriage compact," as if divorce ever broke up a happy home. The clergyman who characterizes a divorce law as "a statute undermining the very substructure of society" implies that nothing but coercion holds man and wife together. One divine, with unconscious cynicism, denounces divorce as "threatening the very foundations of the home!" Another who beseeches us to "protect the poor from the evils of loose divorce statutes," evidently conceives permission to separate as a malignant entity going about rending harmonious households. One judge pictures it as "the antipodal foe of marriage," which "invades the home and defiles its sanctities," under the curious notion that there are any "sanctities" left in the home made hideous by brutality or drunkenness. Still more bizarre is the idea that by denying release to the mismated we shall "restore the purity of our homes." Evidently there is wide-spread failure to distinguish between symptom and disease. . . .

II

The Reasons

With us, thanks to woman's chance to earn, only one ninth of the girls under twenty are married. Two fifths of the girls between the ages of sixteen and twenty-four are breadwinners, and after the seven years of independence which is the lot of the average young working woman, they enter upon wedlock with a high spirit that will not brook subjection.

Nor is it to be forgotten that specialized industry in a way unfits a young woman for marriage by weaning her from the domestic arts. The girl married at eighteen directly from the parental home is more likely to make and keep a home happy than the girl who marries at twenty-five after some years in factory, store, or office. Without her old housekeeping knack, and despising the crude work of the kitchen, the latter too often fails to make home comfortable, and the couple may sink into a misery which ends in domestic shipwreck. The demoralizing reaction of home

> Women's suffrage became a leading demand during the later years of the Progressive Era. In 1913 these women paraded through the center of Washington, D.C., demanding the right to vote. The Nineteenth Amendment, granting women the suffrage, went into effect in 1920.

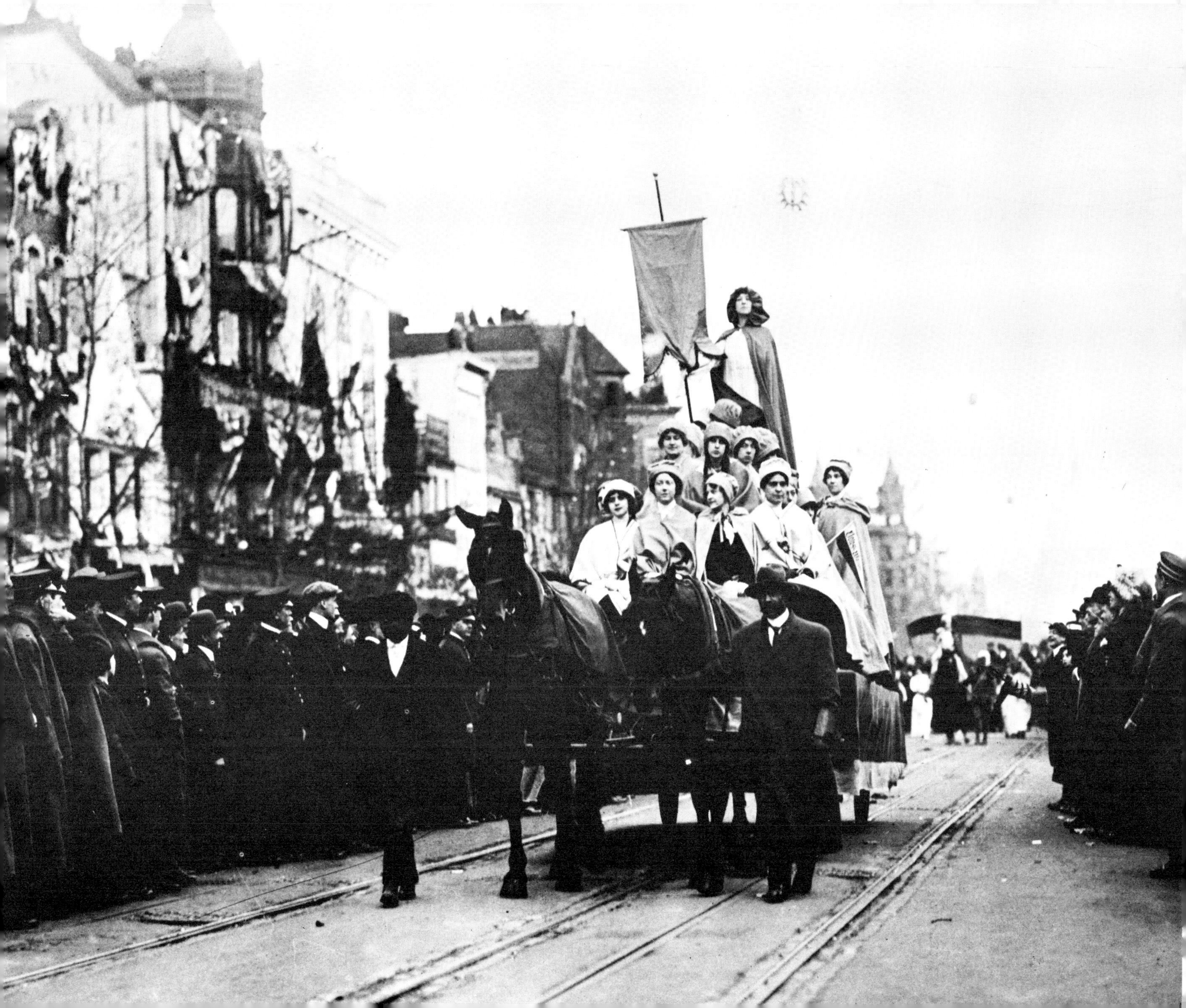

slackness is brought out by studies made by Cadbury in Birmingham. There the proportion of sober and steady men is nearly twice as great in families where the wives do not work out as in homes presided over by employed women.

Incessantly the factory planes away the economic basis of the family. In the time of our grandmothers the home was the seat of a score of productive processes, and the ideal wife was the "virtuous woman" celebrated by Solomon. She might not be a "soul-mate" to her husband, but she was a prop to the prosperity of the household. Now that the machine has captured most of the domestic processes and the middle-class home is sustained by the earnings of the husband, the wife, from a helpmate, has become a luxury. If, now, there is a rift in the lute, the husband becomes aware of carrying a burden, and resents things that are overlooked when the wife is a true yokefellow.

On the other hand, the capable, unencumbered woman, who finds herself doomed by social convention to be supported in idleness by a husband who can earn, perhaps, little more than she can, is also making a sacrifice—a sacrifice which she will chafe under in case the marriage fails to satisfy her affections.

In a word, outside of the manual-laboring class, the old economic framework of the family has largely fallen away, leaving more of the strain to come on the personal tie. Husband and wife are held together by love, conscience, and convention, but very little by that profitable co-partnership which once contributed so much to the stability of the home. . . .

It has been calculated that if the movement toward divorce retains its present velocity, in forty years one marriage in four will end by divorce and in eighty years one marriage in two. No one who understands the vital role of the family in a healthy society anticipates any such deplorable outcome. Already there are in sight certain influences that are likely to moderate the headlong movement. The industrial and intellectual emancipation of women will, of course, complete itself; but the old despotic ideal of the family will die out of men's minds and cease to be a breeder of conjugal discord. The distrust of institutions can hardly go much further. It is likely that the public, as it wins a deeper insight into the services of the family to society and to the race, will feel less sympathy with the wrongdoings, weaknesses, and whims that shatter it. Individualism, too, is probably at its zenith. In the discussion of human relations we are likely to hear less of the radical note and more of the ethical note. In proportion as the emancipated are led to an ethical view of life, they will cease to regard marriage simply as a fair-weather arrangement with personal happiness in constant view. They will recognize its inexorable demands for patience and self-control, for loyalty through sorrow and sickness, through misfortune and the aging years.

The fact that accelerated divorce is produced by the modern social situation rather than by moral decay does not make it any less the symptom of a great evil. That one marriage in ten openly fails, calls for vigorous effort to lessen the number of bad marriages. The school should instruct girls in the domestic arts which supply the material basis of the home. There should be systematic instruction of youth in the ethics and ideals of the family. The fact that the likelihood of divorce is in inverse proportion to the length of time the parties were acquainted before marriage suggests the wisdom of requiring a formal, but not public, declaration of intention to marry some weeks before a marriage license will be issued. Law or custom ought to devise some means of protecting pure women from marriage with men infected from vice. A way may be found to detect and punish the husbands who desert their families. Finally, the fact that intemperance figures in nearly a fifth of the divorces ought to invigorate the temperance movement.

The Theme of Conservation (1910)

Where earlier generations had viewed the American landscape as a threatening wilderness, unspoiled paradise, or wealth to be plundered, Progressives began to realize that the natural environment was being ravaged by uncontrolled expansion. As President, Theodore Roosevelt took the lead in setting aside forests and other reserves from exploitation. Among his ardent followers was Gifford Pinchot (1865–1946). Pinchot studied forestry in Europe and became the first professional American forester. He served as chief of the Forest Service of the Department of Agriculture from 1898 to 1910. In 1910 he was dismissed by President William H. Taft for accusing the Secretary of the Interior, Richard A. Ballinger, of undermining principles of conservation by allowing private interests to exploit natural resources belonging to the nation. Pinchot continued his career as a conservationist and as a Progressive and Republican politician, serving later as governor of Pennsylvania.

From Gifford Pinchot, *The Fight for Conservation* (New York, 1910), pp. 109-110, 111-113, 115-116, 117-119. Copyright © 1910 by Doubleday, Page, and Co. Subheadings added by the editors.

I
Conservation: For Whom?

The American people have evidently made up their minds that our natural resources must be conserved. That is good, but it settles only half the question. For whose benefit shall they be conserved—for the benefit of the many, or for the use and profit of the few? The great conflict now being fought will decide. There is no other question before us that begins to be so important, or that will be so difficult to straddle, as the great question between special interest and equal opportunity, between the privileges of the few and the rights of the many, between government by men for human welfare and government by money for profit, between the men who stand for the Roosevelt policies and the men who stand against them. This is the heart of the conservation problem to-day.

The conservation issue is a moral issue. When a few men get possession of one of the necessaries of life, either through ownership of a natural resource or through unfair business methods, and use that control to extort undue profits, as in the recent cases of the Sugar Trust and the beef-packers, they injure the average man without good reason, and they are guilty of a moral wrong. It does not matter whether the undue profit comes through stifling competition by rebates or other crooked devices, through corruption of public officials, or through seizing and monopolizing resources which belong to the people. The result is always the same—a toll levied on the cost of living through special privilege. . . .

I believe in our form of government and I believe in the Golden Rule. But we must face the truth that monopoly of the sources of production makes it impossible for vast numbers of men and women to earn a fair living. Right here the conservation question touches the daily life of the great body of our people, who pay the cost of special privilege. And the price is heavy. That price may be the chance to save the boys from the saloons and the corner gang, and the girls from worse, and to make good citizens of them instead of bad; for an appalling proportion of the tragedies of life spring directly from the lack of a little money. Thousands of daughters of the poor fall into the hands of the white-slave traders because their poverty leaves them without protection. Thousands of families, as the Pittsburgh survey has shown us, lead lives of brutalizing overwork in return for the barest living. Is it fair that these thousands of families should have less than they need in order that a few families should have swollen fortunes at their expense? Let him who dares deny that there is wickedness in grinding the faces of the poor, or assert that these are not moral questions which strike the very homes of our people. If these are not moral questions, there are no moral questions. . . .

II
The Public at Fault

We have allowed the great corporations to occupy with their own men the strategic points in business, in social, and in political life. It is our fault more than theirs. We have allowed it when we could have stopped it. Too often we have seemed to forget that a man in public life can no more serve both the special interests and the people than he can serve God and Mammon. There is no reason why the American people should not take into their hands again the full political power which is theirs by right, and which they exercised before the special interests began to nullify the will of the majority. There are many men who believe, and who will always believe, in the divine right of money to rule. With such men argument, compromise, or conciliation is useless or worse. The only thing to do with them is to fight them and beat them. It has been done, and it can be done again.

It is the honorable distinction of the Forest Service that it has been more constantly, more violently and more bitterly attacked by the representatives of the special interests in recent years than any other Government Bureau. These attacks have increased in violence and bitterness just in proportion as the Service has offered effective opposition to predatory wealth. The more successful the Forest Service has been in preventing land-grabbing and the absorption of water power by the special interests, the more ingenious, the more devious, and the more dangerous these attacks have become. . . .

Another and unusually plausible, form of attack, is to demand that all land not now bearing trees shall be thrown out of the National Forests. For centuries forest fires have burned through the Western mountains, and much land thus deforested is scattered throughout the National Forests awaiting reforestation. This land is not valuable for agriculture, and will contribute more to the general welfare under forest than in any other way. To exclude it from the National Forests would be no more reasonable than it would be in a city to remove from taxation and municipal control every building lot not now covered by a house. It would be no more reasonable than to condemn and take away from our farmers every acre of land that did not bear a crop last year, or to confiscate a man's winter overcoat because he was not wearing it in July. A generation in the life of a nation is no longer than a season in the life of a man. With a fair chance we can and will reclothe these denuded mountains with forests, and we ask for that chance.

Still another attack, nearly successful two years ago, was an attempt to prevent the Forest Service from telling the people, through the press, what it is accomplishing for them, and how much this Nation needs the forests. If the Forest Service can not tell what it is doing the time will come when there will be nothing to tell. It is just as necessary for the people to know what is being done to help them as to know what is being done to hurt them. Publicity is the essential and indispensable condition of clean and effective public service.

Since the Forest Service called public attention to the rapid absorption of the water-power sites and the threatening growth of a great water-power monopoly, the attacks upon it have increased with marked rapidity. I anticipate that they will continue to do so. Still greater opposition is promised in the near future. There is but one protection—an awakened and determined public opinion. That is why I tell the facts.

The Church and Social Reform (1907)

Throughout most of the late nineteenth century American Christian churchmen generally opposed social reform movements which involved any hint of government regulation, the one exception being the prohibition of alcoholic beverages. The Church's job was bringing individuals to Christ and not the reformation of society. The rise of industrialism and urban poverty, however, converted many clergymen to the belief that the Church had to support those movements which sought to end social misery and economic exploitation. One of the leaders in the so-called "social gospel" movement was Walter Rauschenbusch (1861–1918), a Baptist minister who spent nine years in a New York slum church before becoming a professor of theology at the Rochester Theological Seminary.

From Walter Rauschenbusch, *Christianity and the Social Order* (New York, 1907), pp. xxi–xxii, 340–342.

Western civilization is passing through a social revolution unparalleled in history for scope and power. Its coming was inevitable. The religious, political, and intellectual revolutions of the past five centuries, which together created the modern world necessarily had to culminate in an economic and social revolution such as is now upon us.

By universal consent, this social crisis is the overshadowing problem of our generation. The industrial and commercial life of the advanced nations are in the throes of it. In politics all issues and methods are undergoing upheaval and re-alignment as the social movement advances. In the world of thought all the young and serious minds are absorbed in the solution of the social problems. Even literature and art point like compass-needles to this magnetic pole of all our thought.

The social revolution has been slow in reaching our country. We have been exempt, not because we had solved the problems, but because we had not yet confronted them. We have now arrived, and all the characteristic conditions of American life will henceforth combine to make the social struggle here more intense than anywhere else. The vastness and the free sweep of our concentrated wealth on the one side, the independence, intelligence, moral vigor, and political power of the common people on the other side, promise a long-drawn grapple of contesting forces which may well make the heart of every American patriot sink within him.

It is realized by friend and foe that religion can play, and must play, a momentous part in this irrepressible conflict. . . .

The social crisis offers a great opportunity for the infusion of new life and power into the religious thought of the Church. It also offers the chance for progress in its life. When the broader social outlook widens the purpose of a Christian man beyond the increase of his church, he lifts up his eyes and sees that there are others who are at work for humanity besides his denomination. Common work for social welfare is the best common ground for the various religious bodies and the best training school for practical Christian unity. The strong movement for Christian union in our country has been largely prompted by the realization of social needs, and is led by men who have felt the attraction of the kingdom of God as something greater than any denomination and as the common object of all. Thus the divisions which were caused in the past by differences in dogma and church polity may perhaps be healed by unity of interest in social salvation.

As we have seen, the industrial and commercial life to-day is dominated by principles antagonistic to the fundamental principles of Christianity, and it is so difficult to live a Christian life in the midst of it that few men even try. If production could be organized on a basis of cooperative fraternity; if distribution could at least approximately be determined by justice; if all men could be conscious that their labor contributed to the welfare of all and that their personal well-being was dependent on the prosperity of the Commonwealth; if predatory business and parasitic wealth ceased and all men lived only by their labor; if the luxury of unearned wealth no longer made us all feverish with covetousness and a simpler life became the fashion; if our time and strength were not used up either in getting a bare living or in amassing unusable wealth and we had more leisure for the higher pursuits of the mind and the soul—then there might be a chance to live such a life of gentleness and brotherly kindness and tranquillity of heart as Jesus desired for men. It may be that the cooperative Commonwealth would give us the first chance in history to live a really Christian life without retiring from the world, and would make the Sermon on the Mount a philosophy of life feasible for all who care to try.

This is the stake of the Church in the social crisis. If society continues to disintegrate and decay, the Church will be carried down with it. If the Church can rally such moral forces that injustice will be overcome and fresh red blood will course in a sounder social organism, it will itself rise to higher liberty and life. Doing the will of God it will have new visions of God. With a new message will come a new authority. If the salt loses its saltness, it will be trodden under foot. If the Church fulfils its prophetic functions, it may bear the prophet's reproach for a time, but it will have the prophet's vindication thereafter.

The conviction has always been embedded in the heart of the Church that "the world"— society as it is—is evil and some time is to make way for a true human society in which the spirit of Jesus Christ shall rule. For fifteen hundred years those who desired to live a truly Christian life withdrew from the evil world to live a life apart. But the principle of such an ascetic departure from the world is dead in modern life. There are only two other possibilities. The Church must either condemn the world and seek to change it, or tolerate the world and conform to it. In the latter case it surrenders its holiness and its mission. The other possibility has never yet been tried with full faith on a large scale. All the leadings of God in contemporary history and all the promptings of Christ's spirit in our hearts urge us to make the trial. On this choice is staked the future of the Church.

The Supreme Court in the Progressive Era (1905)

Most Progressives wanted to legislate against what they considered immoral social, political, or economic behavior. New divorce laws, nonpartisan elections, and child labor laws were typical goals. Ultimately the Supreme Court of the United States had to decide whether these laws were constitutional, and thus enforceable, or unconstitutional, and thus null and void. The following reading contains a selection from the majority opinion in *Lochner* v. *New York*, and part of Justice Oliver Wendell Holmes' (1841–1935) dissent in that case. The case involved the power of the state government (the so-called "police power") to regulate relationships between the individual worker and his employer.

From *Lochner* vs. *New York*, 198 United States Reports, 45 (1905).

The question whether this act is valid as a labor law, pure and simple, may be dismissed in a few words. There is no reasonable ground for interfering with the liberty of person or the right of free contract, by determining the hours of labor, in the occupation of a baker.* There is no contention that bakers as a class are not equal in intelligence and capacity to men in other trades or manual occupations, or that they are not able to assert their rights and care for themselves without the protecting arm of the State, interfering with their independence of judgment and of action.

*The case involved a New York law prohibiting a baker from working more than ten hours a day—Eds.

They are in no sense wards of the State. Viewed in the light of a purely labor law, with no reference whatever to the question of health, we think that a law like the one before us involves neither the safety, the morals, nor the welfare, of the public, and that the interest of the public is not in the slightest degree affected by such an act. The law must be upheld, if at all, as a law pertaining to the health of the individual engaged in the occupation of a baker. It does not affect any other portion of the public than those who engaged in that occupation. Clean and wholesome bread does not depend upon whether the baker works but ten hours per day or only sixty hours a week. The limitation of the hours of labor does not come within the police power on that ground.

It is a question of which of two powers or rights shall prevail—the power of the State to legislate or the right of the individual to liberty of person and freedom of contract. The mere assertion that the subject relates, though but in a remote degree, to the public health, does not necessarily render the enactment valid. The act must have a more direct relation, as a means to an end, and the end itself must be appropriate and legitimate, before an act can be held to be valid which interferes with the general right of an indi-

A girl in a Carolina cotton mill, 1908, in what is perhaps Lewis Hine's most famous photograph. Reformers fought hard for state and federal laws greatly restricting the use of children in factories. Congress passed a child labor law in 1916, but the Supreme Court ruled it unconstitutional in 1918. State laws and a decline in the need for unskilled labor, however, reduced the use of child labor by the late 1920s.

vidual to be free in his person and in his power to contract in relation to his own labor. . . .

It seems to us that the real object and purpose were simply to regulate the hours of labor between the master and his employees . . . in a private business, not dangerous in any degree to morals or in any real and substantial degree, to the health of the employees. Under such circumstances the freedom of master and employee to contract with each other in relation to their employment, and in defining the same, cannot be prohibited or interfered with, without violating the Federal Constitution.

Mr. Justice Holmes, dissenting: . . . This case is decided upon an economic theory which a large part of the country does not entertain. If it were a question whether I agreed with that theory, I should desire to study it further and long before making up my mind. But I do not conceive that to be my duty, because I strongly believe that my agreement or disagreement has nothing to do with the right of a majority to embody their opinions in law. It is settled by various decisions of this court that state constitutions and state laws may regulate life in many ways which we as legislators might think as injudicious or if you like as tyrannical as this, and which equally with this, interfere with the liberty to contract. Sunday laws and usury laws are ancient examples. A more modern one is the prohibition of lotteries. The liberty of the citizen to do as he likes so long as he does not interfere with the liberty of others to do the same, which has been a shibboleth for some well-known writers, is interfered with by school laws, by the post-office, by every state or municipal institution which takes his money for purposes thought desirable, whether he likes it or not. The Fourteenth Amendment does not enact Mr. Herbert Spencer's Social Statics. . . . Some of these laws embody convictions or prejudices which judges are likely to share. Some may not. But a constitution is not intended to embody a particular economic theory, whether of paternalism and the organic relation of the citizen to the state or of *laissez faire*. It is made for people of fundamentally differing views, and the accident of our finding certain opinions natural and familiar or novel and even shocking ought not to conclude our judgment upon the question whether statutes embodying them conflict with the Constitution of the United States.

TOPIC 46

PROGRESSIVES AND THE REGULATION OF BIG BUSINESS

The mushrooming concentrations of business power that alarmed an increasing number of Americans in the late nineteenth century furnished obvious targets for Progressive reformers. Like the earlier Grangers or Populists, they felt that a corporation as large as United States Steel, with an influence on the economy ordinarily far exceeding that of the federal government itself, or railroads rich and unscrupulous enough to control state legislatures through bribery, simply could not be let alone to do as they pleased toward small businessmen or the public. Since corporations of this size sprawled across whole regions or even the continent, only the federal government seemed capable of protecting the public against the sweeping actions of such economic giants.

The readings in this topic explore the variety of responses of American businessmen to the expansion of government regulation, as well as the controversy among Progressives as to whether regulation could really control the power of giant corporations.

Reading 223

Business and Government at the Turn of the Century

The editors have prepared the following reading to give the student an account of government-business relationships as they developed just before and during the Progressive Era.

In the years following the Civil War, Congress, like society at large, was racked by the competition of diverse interests, each seeking its own ends. The Senate was especially vulnerable to influence by big business; nineteenth-century Presidents were unwilling to exert leadership in this area of public interest; the Supreme Court remained dominated by men who believed in laissez faire, the economic philosophy of letting individuals or corporations alone as long as they did not break traditional criminal or civil laws. There was trouble, too, in deciding whether the best way of dealing with giant corporations was to break them up into smaller parts or to impose more and more stringent governmental controls on them.

Earlier readings have shown how even conservative Congresses were roused by the ruthless methods and growing power of big business to adopt the Interstate Commerce Act of 1887 and the Sherman Antitrust Act of 1890. Neither type of regulation, however, had much effect at first. The Supreme Court rendered decisions that robbed both acts of much of their potential effectiveness. In the

TABLE 1 PRESIDENTIAL ELECTIONS, 1904–1920

	CANDIDATES	PARTIES	ELECTORAL VOTE	POPULAR VOTE
1904	Theodore Roosevelt	Republican	336	7,628,461
	Alton B. Parker	Democratic	140	5,084,223
	Eugene V. Debs	Socialist		402,283
	Silas C. Swallow	Prohibition		258,536
	Thomas E. Watson	People's		117,183
	Charles H. Corregan	Socialist Labor		31,249
1908	William H. Taft	Republican	321	7,675,320
	William J. Bryan	Democratic	162	6,412,294
	Eugene V. Debs	Socialist		420,793
	Eugene W. Chafin	Prohibition		253,840
	Thomas L. Hisgen	Independence		82,872
	Thomas E. Watson	People's		29,100
	August Gilhaus	Socialist Labor		14,021
1912	Woodrow Wilson	Democratic	435	6,296,547
	Theodore Roosevelt	Progressive	88	4,118,571
	William H. Taft	Republican	8	3,486,720
	Eugene V. Debs	Socialist		900,672
	Eugene W. Chafin	Prohibition		206,275
	Arthur E. Reimer	Socialist Labor		28,750
1916	Woodrow Wilson	Democratic	277	9,127,695
	Charles E. Hughes	Republican	254	8,533,507
	A. L. Benson	Socialist		585,113
	J. Frank Hanly	Prohibition		220,506
	Arthur E. Reimer	Socialist Labor		13,403
1920	Warren G. Harding	Republican	404	16,143,407
	James M. Cox	Democratic	127	9,130,328
	Eugene V. Debs	Socialist		919,799
	P. P. Christensen	Farmer-Labor		265,411
	Aaron S. Watkins	Prohibition		189,408
	James E. Ferguson	American		48,000
	W. W. Cox	Socialist Labor		31,715

landmark case of *U.S. v. E. C. Knight Co.*, in 1895, the Court ruled that an organization that controlled almost all sugar production in the country was not restraining trade because manufacturing was not trade. In the Maximum Freight Rate case in 1896 the Court found that while the Interstate Commerce Commission could object to railroad rates as unreasonably high or discriminatory, it had no power to fix new rates. The courts could set new rates, but it took a long time for decisions to be made. While the Supreme Court did uphold the government's power to prosecute businesses for conspiring to fix prices or divide up markets, in practice the Cleveland and McKinley administrations were reluctant to act against businesses. In fact, the federal government took four of its eighteen antitrust actions during these years against labor unions, targets that the authors of the Sherman Act had not intended to attack.

This climate changed during Theodore Roosevelt's administrations. As seen earlier in Reading 215, Roosevelt, while undertaking only a limited number of antitrust prosecutions and obtaining from Congress only a moderate strengthening of regulations affecting railroads and other businesses, nevertheless forced business to respect the potential power of the federal government in a way that it had not since the Civil War.

Although William Howard Taft, an Ohio Republican who succeeded Roosevelt as President in 1909, emerged as a more conservative man, his administration initiated twice as many antitrust prosecutions in four years as Roosevelt's had in seven. These included attacks on such giants as the United States Steel Corporation and the General Electric Company. Taft thus carried forward Roosevelt's policies in an even more vigorous—if quieter—way, but he lacked his patron's keen political sense. By his stout defense of an extremely high tariff passed by Congress, and by other actions, he allied himself with the Eastern-based conservative wing of the Republican Party and outraged its Progressive wing, which had most strength in the Midwest and West.

By 1911 Roosevelt, who yearned to return to the White House, grew increasingly cool toward Taft, and in the party's 1912 convention he led the Progressives in trying to displace Taft as the Presidential nominee. When the move failed, Progressive Republicans walked out of the convention and nominated Roosevelt as the candidate of the new Progressive Party. The action hurt the Republicans badly: Taft ran a poor third in the election and Roosevelt came in second to the Democratic candidate, Woodrow Wilson, former president of Princeton University and currently a reform governor of New Jersey.

In his first years in office Wilson spoke for Progressives as well as the Southern and Western forces in his party by working with Congress to adopt further restraints on big business (Clayton Act), a lower protective tariff (Underwood Tariff), and a reform of banking and currency which both gave the federal government greater power over the supply of currency and dispersed some of that power into regional banks (Federal Reserve System). In 1916 Wilson, hoping to win Progressive Republican votes in his campaign for reelection, led his party and Congress in adopting further reforms, such as a limit of eight hours of work per day for employees of interstate railways (Adamson Act), a workmen's compensation act for federal employees, and an act prohibiting employment of children under the age of fourteen in industries involved in interstate commerce (Keating-Owen Act); the last of these was found unconstitutional by the Supreme Court two years later.

To Progressives these achievements seemed impressive. Yet they failed to provide real control over the activities of big business. The Clayton Act, like its predecessor, the Sherman Act, fell into disuse during World War I when industrial production was so badly needed, and during the 1920s the Federal Trade Commission, created in 1914 as a watchdog over business practices, turned into a business-controlled friend of consolidation.

In a number of industries trends toward monopoly were checked, but less by government intervention than by the renewed development of competition in a rapidly expanding market. The fate of United States Steel symbolizes both the limitations of government regulation of big business and the effects of the growth of the market. The Supreme Court held in 1919 that the corporation had not been acting in restraint of trade before its indictment under the Sherman Act in 1911, even though it then controlled 70 per cent of steel production, because the simple fact of bigness did not constitute a violation of law. Yet this corporation, sustained in the courts and continuing to grow, yielded room to its competitors and by 1929 controlled only 40 per cent of production in a much larger market.

In the end, Progressive attempts to regulate big business succeeded to some extent in safeguarding health and safety, in such laws as the Pure Food and Drug and Meat Inspection Acts of 1906, and in penalizing unfair practices, as in the Mann-Elkins Act of 1910 which further regulated railroads. But on the whole their efforts to aid small businessmen in their fight for survival against growing giants were failures.

Reading 224

Business Concentration as a Positive Goal (1901)

Many Americans—businessmen, politicians, and the man on the street—felt that there was nothing to fear from huge business combinations. The danger, on the contrary, came from government interference. Charles Schwab, who had been one of those responsible for the creation of the United States Steel Corporation in 1901, argued for this point of view.

From Charles M. Schwab, "What May Be Expected in the Steel and Iron Industry," *The North American Review*, CLXXII (1901), pp. 655–658, 662–664. Subheadings added by the editors.

I

Nature of Progress

The larger the output, the smaller, relatively, is the cost of production. This is a trade axiom. It holds good whether the output consists of pins or of locomotives. Where the output is produced by fixed processes the rule applies with especial force. It is much more economical, proportionately, to run three machines under one roof than it is to run one. It is cheaper to run a dozen than it is to run three, and cheaper still to run a hundred. Therefore, the large plant has an undoubted advantage over the small plant, and this advantage increases almost indefinitely as the process of enlargement continues.

It is the recognition of this principle that has brought about the era of business consolidation now in full swing in the United States. Of course there are limits beyond which this cannot be carried. It is possible to conceive of an enterprise so huge that it would be unwieldy, but, thus far, the danger point in this direction is not in sight. Our enterprises have grown steadily, and at present they have reached proportions that would have been deemed impossible twenty-five years ago. The fact that they are possible now, that they run absolutely without friction, demonstrates that our economical progress is no more rapid than our enlarged knowledge warrants. We handle a hundred thousand men to-day as easily as we handled a hundred fifty years ago. This has been made possible by our superior machinery and by the development of a superb industrial system. . . .

Heretofore, it has been considered that this system could continue indefinitely along natural lines. The whole scheme of business was distinctly individual and self-formative. Competition was deemed the life of trade. The more competition, the better for all concerned. A few saw the wastefulness of this system, but there seemed apparently nothing better to take its place. Here and there, a venturesome soul tried to apply the logical solution, combination, but this was cried down on all sides. It meant, according to the popular conception, monopoly and industrial tyranny. Men who knew nothing of the science of business proclaimed the doctrine that combination meant oppression of the workingman and the domination of a plutocracy. In spite of this opposition, the system developed, though slowly, because its merit forced the most unwilling to give it a hearing. Its larger application proved that, instead of grinding the workingman and victimizing the consumer, it produced a higher standard of wages and a lower cost in the market. The effect of combination was found to be that it cut down the cost of supervision, the non-productive element of labor; that it made possible the highest development of mechanical appliances; that it displaced the middle-man who, at every step between production and consumption, was wont to take a big slice of profit, adding so much to the ultimate cost without adding anything to the value. The combination proved that the principle of economy that was found effective where a hundred machines were worked under one roof instead of ten, applied where one hundred plants were conducted under one consolidated management, instead of under one hundred separate managements. . . .

II

"Hands Off"

Supremacy in handling and transforming the raw products of the earth is to be won, not by monopolizing their production, but by handling them in such a scientific manner, in the process of manufacturing, that the cost is kept down to the lowest possible figure. A monopoly in the iron and steel business is an impossibility. No man, or set of men, could possibly bring such a thing about. No rational person would dream of attempting it. A monopoly of the wheat fields of Minnesota and the Dakotas, or of the fruit groves of California, would be simple by comparison.

No great amount of harm can be done hereafter by the men who continue to agitate against the science of business consolidation. The system is here to stay, and the people, confronted on every hand by the benefits accruing to them from it, will refuse to be seriously misled. At one time, there was danger that the development of the plan might be checked by unwise political action, but in my opinion even this danger is past. The politicians who get in the way of human progress always come to grief. The politicians who attempt to obstruct industrial development on the line along which it is moving are attempting to obstruct human progress, and the result will be inevitable. The question is really not a political one at all, and those who persist in making it political may find that they have been playing with fire. If the issue should come before the voters to-day, even though it were stated flatly as a "trust issue," it is my belief that the verdict would be, "Hands off." The country has never been so prosperous, and in a large measure this prosperity is undoubtedly due to the fact that we are managing our business affairs on an advanced basis. The most prosperous industries are those in which the consolidation idea has been carried to the greatest extent under wise management. In those industries, work is the steadiest and wages the highest. In the face of such a showing, no body of intelligent people, such as our voters are, would deliberately fly against their own interest. The chance is remote, however, that the issue will ever come up squarely at the polls, and with each succeeding day the prospect of this is bound to grow less. In spite of the politicians, who, with the fatuity often manifested by their class, misconceive public sentiment entirely upon the matter, the question will, I believe, be permitted to work itself out, as it should, in the factory and in the counting room. It is a clean-cut business proposition, and has no more place in politics than a question prescribing a general style of type in newspapers would have. Both, in a measure, are public questions; but both are of a character that hardly warrants political interference. The use of newspapers is so general that the size and style of their type has undoubtedly serious influence on the eyes of the masses, but he would be a bold politician, or a foolish one, who would agitate this question in a campaign.

The iron and steel industry of America is not apprehensive of antagonistic political action toward it either by the people or by Congress. It has done more than any other industry to make this nation great and prosperous, to give America commercial supremacy in the foreign markets. The improved processes that have come out of its pursuit have revolutionized many other industries, and made them in turn great and prosperous. The iron workers are among the most highly paid artisans in this country of high wages. The iron centres are among the wealthiest cities on earth. The consumers of iron and steel are getting the greatest value for their money known in the history of the business.

"Who Owns the United States?" (1904)

So-called "muckraking" journalism constituted one of the most striking aspects of reformism in the early twentieth century. Given their name by a Theodore Roosevelt who was sometimes irked by their itch to stir up trouble, the muckrakers sought to expose political, economic, and social evils, sometimes in sensational form but often in serious and responsible fashion. They often wrote for magazines, which were just beginning to reach a mass public, and sometimes for newspapers. By 1904 their journalistic achievements had attracted wide attention. In that year the Supreme Court handed down its landmark decision dissolving the Northern Securities Company, and in that same year Sereno Pratt, a New York financial expert, wrote a penetrating article on the extent to which the business combinations advocated by Charles Schwab (Reading 224) had become a widespread structure of big business interest.

From Sereno Pratt, "Who Owns the United States?" *The World's Work*, VII (1903–1904), pp. 4259–4260, 4262–4264, 4266. Subheadings added by the editors.

I

"A Small Group of Men"

One-twelfth of the estimated wealth of the United States is represented at the meeting of the board of directors of the United States Steel Corporation when they are all present. The twenty-four directors are:

John D. Rockefeller,	J. Pierpont Morgan,
Marshall Field,	H. H. Rogers,
E. H. Gary,	George W. Perkins,
W. H. Moore,	Norman B. Ream,
Henry C. Frick,	Charles M. Schwab,
W. E. Corey,	C. A. Griscom,
F. H. Peabody,	Daniel G. Reid,
Charles Steele,	J. D. Rockefeller, Jr.,
P. A. B. Widener,	Alford Clifford,
James H. Reid,	Robert Bacon,
William Edenborn,	Nathaniel Thayer,
E. C. Converse,	James Gayley.

They represent as influential directors more than 200 other companies. These companies operate nearly one-half of the railroad mileage of the United States. They are the great miners and carriers of coal. Among these companies are such industrial trusts as the Standard Oil, the Amalgamated Copper, the International Harvester, the Pullman, the General Electric, the International Mercantile Marine, the United States Realty and Construction, and the American Linseed. The leading telegraph system, the traction lines of New York, of Philadelphia, of Pittsburg, of Buffalo, of Chicago, and of Milwaukee, and one of the principal express companies, are represented in the board. This group includes also directors of five insurance companies, two of which have assets of $700,000,000. In the Steel board are men who speak for five banks and ten trust companies in New York City including the First National, the National City, and the Bank of Commerce, the three greatest banks in the country, and the head of important chains of financial institutions; for two banks and three trust companies in Philadelphia; for two banks and two trust companies in Chicago; for one bank and two trust companies in Boston; and for one bank and one trust company in Pittsburg, besides banking institutions in smaller cities. Telephone, electric, real estate, cable and publishing companies are represented there, and our greatest merchant sits at the board table.

What the individual wealth of these men is it would be impossible and beside the point to estimate; but one of them, Mr. John D. Rockefeller, is generally esteemed to be the richest individual in the world. But it is not the personal, but the representative, wealth of these men that makes the group extraordinary. They control corporations

THE COMING NATION

October 26, 1912 — Price 5 Cents

A JOURNAL OF THINGS DOING AND TO BE DONE

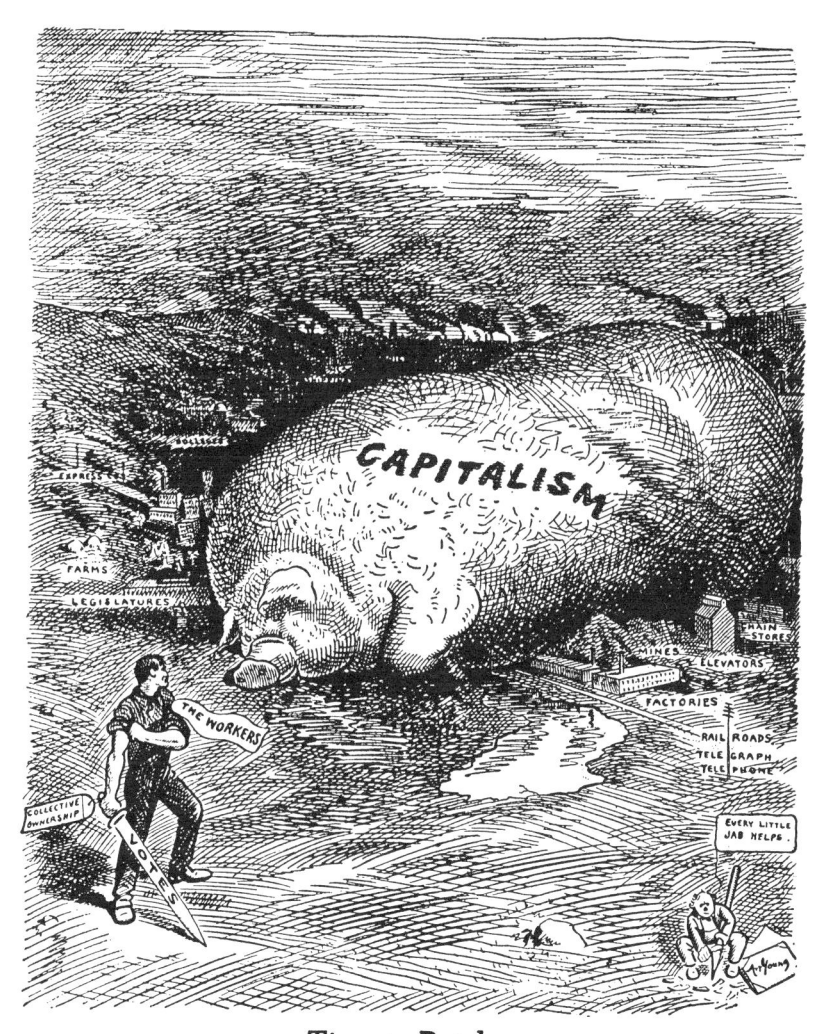

Time to Butcher
For the sake of the beast itself as well as the people

A socialist view of the American economy, 1912. Though "The Workers" are depicted as a larger-than-life hero about to slay the capitalist hog, Art Young, the cartoonist, is quick to point out that every individual even with a "little jab," can help in the fight.

whose capitalizations aggregate more than $9,000,000,000—an amount (if the capitalizations are real values) equal to about the combined public debts of Great Britain, France and the United States.

Concentration of wealth does not mean merely the amassing of vast fortunes by individuals. It is doubtful if these are much, if any, larger today in proportion to the total resources of the country than they were fifty years ago. A man worth $5,000,000 today is no richer, as related to the aggregate wealth of the United States, than a man worth $370,000 in 1850. Moreover, concentration of wealth does not necessarily mean actual ownership by groups of capitalists, for few corporations are owned outright, or even a majority of their stock, by individuals or by affiliated interests. Concentration means, rather, the control by direction or influence of great aggregations of capital.

For instance, it is not essential for the control of the Steel Corporation that the directors themselves should own a majority of the shares. Moreover, it should not be taken for granted that because these men are associated together in this company they are closely affiliated in all their interests. On the contrary, in some instances they are probably in direct antagonism. While Mr. Rockefeller and Mr. Morgan meet together in the Steel board and in other things may often join forces, they are recognized as the heads of two distinct and independent spheres of influence in

American finance. But taking into account these distinctions and limitations, it is proper to speak of this group of capitalists in the world's biggest company as a notable example of what we mean by concentration of wealth, which in its largest significance is a community of interest between individuals and corporate capital, commonly working together for the attainment of certain ends in finance and commerce.

Starting, then, from this point, it is important to consider how far this concentration has gone. In short, the question is, Who owns the United States—the 76,000,000 people who inhabit it or a small group of men, rich themselves, but mainly powerful by reason of the wealth they represent, controlling the railroads, the supplies of fuel, the output of iron and the principal trusts, able in no small measure to sway the markets, build or destroy business activity, advance or lower prices, and even dictate the policies of parties and mold legislation? . . .

II

Control of Railroad Concentration

In no other branch of business has concentration of control of wealth been so complete as in the railroads. It might be said that the very laws that have been passed to prohibit railroad monopolies have thus far served only to promote concentration. When the railroads were free to enter into pools and agreements, they were continually violating them, and the cutting of rates was a widespread evil. But when the Supreme Court of the United States decided that pooling and traffic agreements were illegal, the men in control of the competing lines deemed it necessary to consolidate them or to enter into communities of interest in order to put an end to wasteful competition.

There are 204,000 miles of railroad in the United States owned by companies having a total capitalization of more than $12,000,000,000, par value, affording livelihood to 5,000,000 persons (employees and their families), and distributing $15,685,950 in dividends to owners and $610,713,701 in wages. These railroads are nominally controlled by 2,000 corporations, of which about 1,015 are operating companies. Most of these, however, form parts of great systems. Professor Emory R. Johnson, in his recent book on "American Railway Transportation," gives a list of nineteen different railway systems whose aggregate mileage is 165,321, or nearly 81 percent of the whole. This, however, gives but a partial idea of the extent of the concentration. In reality, the consolidation is closer. These nineteen systems are practically controlled by nine men—Messrs. J. P. Morgan, J. D. Rockefeller, E. H. Harriman, George J. Gould, W. K. Vanderbilt, James J. Hill, A. J. Cassatt, William Rockefeller and W. H. Moore. . . .

III

Banking in America

Of the banking power of the United States, nearly one-half is in New York and the other eastern States. Of the aggregate of loans made by the national banks on September 15, 1902, amounting to $3,280,127,480, the amount outstanding in the banks of New York, Chicago and St. Louis, the three central reserve cities, was $877,934,942. The banks in these three cities, being the great reserve institutions of the nation, are in virtual control of the money market. In connection with the banks in Philadelphia, Boston and other large cities, they hold the key to the banking situation. Examinations show that concentration of control of these great city banks has gone so far that a comparatively small group of capitalists possesses the power to regulate the flow of credit in this country. This is said with full allowance for the keen competition for deposits that is going on between banks and trust companies.

In New York City big chains of banking institutions have been formed corresponding to the railroad systems. Moreover, the men in control of railroads and trusts have found it convenient, and indeed needful, to extend their control to banks, so that they are often closely allied to great groups of corporations.

There are seven of these chains of banks and trust companies in New York, but as there are close communities of interests between some of these, the seven groups may properly be reduced to four, and in the last analysis it is found that there are actually only two main influences, and that these are centered in Mr. Morgan and Mr. Rockefeller. There are, however, a number of independent banks not connected with any of the groups, though no doubt subject more or less to the power exerted by the groups. . . .

IV

General Conclusions

Enough has been said to establish these main facts:

1. There is a wide diffusion of wealth in this country. While it is true that the rich have been getting richer, it is not true that the poor have been getting poorer. The vast number of the steadily employed, the ease with which, as a rule, they have obtained advances of wages in the past few years, the enormous

immigration, and the immense deposits in the savings banks and building and loan associations, all testify to the higher average of prosperity among working classes.

2. This diffusion of wealth has been attended by an extraordinary concentration of capital. As a people we are rich, but we have put our wealth into a comparatively few hands to manage for us. This concentration of control is less apparent in some lines of business than in others, but it is steadily growing in all, while in railroads, banks and the leading industries it has reached a point where a few communities of interest, directed by a score or so of individuals, regulate, to a large extent, the rates of freight and of interest and in no small measure the prices of securities and commodities.

This concentration has its undoubted advantages. It is an economic evolution of tremendous power. It has, among other causes, enabled this country in the past twenty years to develop more wealth than in all the preceding years since the discovery of America. It may be argued, however, that this concentration is too high a price to pay even for benefits such as these. Concentration of the control of wealth certainly presents problems the gravity of which it is impossible to conceal or evade. How to preserve the advantages of concentration and at the same time to get rid of its evils; how to prevent the waste of competition without destroying it; how to secure stability and strength without loss of individual liberty; how to permit the railroads to combine and at the same time to provide for Government regulation of rates; how to make possible the achievement of great enterprises without resort to methods involving the violation of law and the corruption of legislatures; how to encourage promotion without the evils of overcapitalization and overspeculation; how to secure comprehensive publicity without disclosure of proper trade secrets—these form the one large problem before us that overshadows and includes all others.

Roosevelt on the Trusts (1911)

While Theodore Roosevelt gained his reputation as a defender of the public against the tyranny of big business largely through the few but heavily publicized antitrust suits of his administration, he did not attack business concentration as such. It was perfectly legal for a firm to buy out its competitors or to merge with them, as in the creation of United States Steel, and Roosevelt knew it. As he prepared to resume his political career in 1910, Roosevelt published a book setting forth his views on a variety of topics in American life. Its title, *The New Nationalism*, recalled the nationalist clubs stimulated by the Socialist vision of Edward Bellamy (Reading 185). In a magazine article the following year, Roosevelt commented on the problems produced by business concentration.

From Theodore Roosevelt, "The Trusts, The People, and The Square Deal," *The Outlook*, XCIX (1911), pp. 649, 651-653, 656. Subheadings added by the editors.

I

The Trusts

The suit against the Steel Trust by the Government has brought vividly before our people the need of reducing to order our chaotic Government policy as regards business. As President, in Messages to Congress I repeatedly called the attention of that body and of the public to the inadequacy of the [Sherman] Anti-Trust Law by itself to meet business conditions and secure justice to the people, and to the further fact that it might, if left unsupplemented by additional legislation, work mischief, with no compensating advantage; and I urged as strongly as I knew how that the policy followed with relation to railways in connection with the Inter-State Commerce Law should be followed by the National Government as regards all great business concerns; and therefore that, as a first step, the powers of the Bureau of Corporations should be greatly enlarged, or else that there should be created a Governmental board or commission, with powers somewhat similar to those of the Inter-State Commerce Commission, but covering the whole field of inter-State business, exclusive of transportation (which should, by law, be kept wholly separate from ordinary industrial business, all common ownership of the industry and the railway being forbidden). In the end I have always believed that it would also be necessary to give the National Government complete power over the organization and capitalization of all business concerns engaged in inter-State commerce....

When my Administration took office, I found, not only that there had been little real enforcement of the Anti-Trust Law and but

159

Theodore Roosevelt's reputation as a "trust-buster" and a big game hunter were combined in this very pro-TR cartoon. Note that Roosevelt has the "good trusts" firmly under control.

little more effective enforcement of the Inter-State Commerce Law, but also that the decisions were so chaotic and the laws themselves so vaguely drawn, or at least interpreted in such widely varying fashions that the biggest business men tended to treat both laws as dead letters. The series of actions by which we succeeded in making the Inter-State Commerce Law an efficient and most useful instrument in regulating the transportation of the country and exacting justice from the big railways without doing them injustice—while, indeed, on the contrary, securing them against injustice—need not here be related. The Anti-Trust Law it was also necessary to enforce as it had never hitherto been enforced, both because it was on the statute-books and because it was imperative to teach the masters of the biggest corporations in the land they were not, and would not be permitted to regard themselves as, above the law. Moreover, where the combination has really been guilty of misconduct the law serves a useful purpose, and in such cases as those of the Standard Oil and Tobacco Trusts, if effectively enforced, the law confers a real and great good.

Suits were brought against the most powerful corporations in the land, which we were convinced had clearly and beyond question violated the Anti-Trust Law. These suits were brought with great care, and only where we felt so sure of our facts that we could be fairly certain that there was a likelihood of success. As a matter of fact, in most of the important suits we were successful. It was imperative that these suits should be brought, and very real good was achieved by bringing them, for it was only these suits that made the great masters of corporate capital in America fully realize that they were the servants and not the masters of the people, that they were subject to the law, and that they would not be permitted to be a law unto themselves; and the corporations against which we proceeded had sinned, not merely by being big (which we did not regard as in itself a sin), but by being guilty of unfair practices towards their competitors, and by procuring unfair advantages from the railways. But the resulting situation has made it evident that the Anti-Trust Law is not adequate to meet the situation that has grown up because of modern business conditions and the accompanying tremendous increase in the business use of vast quantities of corporate wealth....

II

Regulation, Not Destruction

The Anti-Trust Law cannot meet the whole situation, nor can any modification of the principle of the Anti-Trust Law avail to meet the whole situation. The fact is that many of the men who have called themselves Progressives, and who certainly believe that they are Progressives, represent in reality in this matter not progress at all but a kind of sincere rural toryism. These men believe that it is possible by strengthening the Anti-Trust Law to restore business to the competitive conditions of the middle of the last century. Any such effort is foredoomed to end in failure, and, if successful, would be mischievous to the last degree. Business cannot be successfully conducted in accordance with the practices and theories of sixty years ago unless we abolish steam, electricity, big cities, and, in short, not only all modern business and modern industrial conditions, but all the modern conditions of our civilization. The effort to restore competition as it was sixty years ago, and to trust for justice solely to this proposed restoration of competition, is just as foolish as if we should go back to the flintlocks of Washington's Continentals as a substitute for modern weapons of precision. The effort to prohibit all combinations, good or bad, is bound to fail, and ought to fail; when made, it merely means that some of the worst combinations are not checked and that honest business is checked. Our purpose should be, not to strangle business as an incident of strangling combinations, but to regulate big corporations in thorough-going and effective fashion, so as to help legitimate business as an incident to thoroughly and completely safeguarding the interests of the people as a whole. Against all such increase of Government regulation the argument is raised that it would amount to a form of Socialism. This argument is familiar; it is precisely the same as that which was raised against the creation of the Inter-State Commerce Commission, and of all the different utilities commissions in the different States, as I myself saw, thirty years ago, when I was a legislator at Albany, and these questions came up in connection with our State Government. Nor can action be effectively taken by any one State. Congress alone has power under the Constitution effectively and thoroughly and at all points to deal with inter-State commerce, and where Congress, as it should do, provides laws that will give the Nation full jurisdiction over the whole field, then that jurisdiction becomes, of necessity, exclusive—although until Congress does act affirmatively and thoroughly it is idle to expect that the States will or ought to rest content with non-action on the part of both Federal and State authorities....

III

New Policy Necessary

To sum up, then. It is practically impossible, and, if possible, it would be mischievous and undesirable, to try to break up all combinations merely because they are large and successful, and to put the business of the country back into the middle of the eighteenth century conditions of intense and unregulated competition between small and weak business concerns. Such an effort represents not progressiveness but an unintelligent though doubtless entirely well-meaning toryism. Moreover, the effort to administer a law merely by lawsuits and court decisions is bound to end in signal failure, and meanwhile to be attended with delays and uncertainties, and to put a premium upon legal sharp practice. Such an effort does not adequately punish the guilty, and yet works great harm to the innocent. Moreover, it entirely fails to give the publicity which is one of the best by-products of the system of control by administrative officials; publicity, which is not only good in itself, but furnishes the data for whatever further action may be necessary. We need to formulate immediately and definitely a policy which, in dealing with big corporations that behave themselves and which contain no menace save what is necessarily potential in any corporation which is of great size and very well managed, shall aim not at their destruction but at their regulation and supervision, so that the Government shall control them in such fashion as amply to safeguard the interests of the whole public, including producers, consumers, and wage-workers. This control should, if necessary, be pushed in extreme cases to the point of exercising control over monopoly prices, as rates on railways are now controlled; although this is not a power that should be used when it is possible to avoid it. The law should be clear, unambiguous, certain, so that honest men may not find that unwittingly they have violated it. In short, our aim should be, not to destroy, but effectively and in thoroughgoing fashion to regulate and control, in the public interest, the great instrumentalities of modern business, which it is destructive of the general welfare of the community to destroy, and which nevertheless it is vitally necessary to that general welfare to regulate and control. Competition will remain as a very important factor when once we have destroyed the unfair business methods, the criminal interference with the rights of others, which alone enabled certain swollen combinations to crush out their competitors—and, incidentally, the "conservatives" will do well to remember that these unfair and iniquitous methods by great masters of corporate capital have done more to cause popular discontent with the propertied classes than all the orations of all the Socialist orators in the country put together.

Woodrow Wilson on the Trusts (1912)

Woodrow Wilson (1856–1924), a Virginian who practiced law for a short time in Georgia before entering academic life, understood the dramatic changes that industrialization and urbanization were imposing on an older and more rural way of life. It is significant that Wilson, calling for new approaches to these problems, entitled his book of 1912 *The New Freedom*. Although by that time he considered himself a Progressive, his interpretation of the place of big business differed from Theodore Roosevelt's.

From Woodrow Wilson, "The New Freedom: III, Monopoly, or Opportunity," *The World's Work*, XXV (1912–1913), pp. 540–543, 550–551. Subheadings added by the editors.

I

Monopoly, or Opportunity?

Gentlemen say, they have been saying for a long time, and therefore I assume that they believe, that trusts are inevitable. They don't say that big business is inevitable. They don't say merely that the elaboration of business upon a great cooperative scale is characteristic of our time and has come about by the natural operation of modern civilization. We would admit that. But they say that the particular kind of combinations that are now controlling our economic development came into existence naturally and were inevitable; and that, therefore, we have to accept them as unavoidable and administer our development through them. They take the analogy of the railways. The railways were clearly inevitable if we were to have transportation, but railways after they are once built stay put. You can't transfer a railroad at convenience: and you can't shut up one part of it and work another part. It is in the nature of what economists, those tedious persons, call natural monopolies; simply because the whole circumstances of their use are so stiff that you can't alter them. Such are the analogies which these gentlemen choose when they discuss the modern trust.

I admit the popularity of the theory that the trusts have come about through the natural development of business conditions in the United States; and that it is a mistake to try to oppose the processes by which they have been built up, because those processes belong to the very nature of business in our time; and that therefore the only thing we can do, and the only thing we ought to attempt to do, is to accept them as inevitable arrangements and make the best out of it that we can by regulation.

I answer, nevertheless, that this attitude rests upon a confusion of thought. Big business is no doubt to a large extent necessary and natural. The development of business upon a great scale, upon a great scale of cooperation, is inevitable, and, let me add, is probably desirable. But that is a very different matter from the development of trusts, because the trusts have not grown. They have been artificially created, they have been put together, not by natural processes, but by the will, the deliberate planning will, of men who were more powerful than their neighbors in the business world, and who wished to make their power secure against competition.

The trusts do not belong to the period of infant industries. They are not the products of the time, that old laborious time, when the great continent we live on was undeveloped, the young Nation struggling to find itself and get upon its feet amidst older and more experienced competitors. They belong to a very recent and very sophisticated age, when men knew what they wanted and knew how to get it by the favor of the Government.

Did you ever look into the way a trust is made? It is very natural, in one sense, in the same sense in which human greed is natural. If I haven't efficiency enough to beat my rivals, then the thing I am inclined to do is to get together with my rivals and say: "Don't let's cut one another's throats; let's combine and determine prices for ourselves; determine the output, and thereby determine the prices; and dominate and control the market." That is very natural. That has been done ever since freebooting was established. That has been done ever since power was used to establish control. The reason that the masters of combination have sought to shut out competition is that the basis of control under competition is brains and efficiency. I admit that any large corporation built up by the legitimate processes of business, by economy, by efficiency, is natural; and I am not afraid of it, no matter how big it grows. It can stay big only by doing its work more thoroughly than anybody else. And there is a point of bigness—as every business man in this country knows, though some of them will not admit it—where you pass the limit of efficiency and get into the region of clumsiness and unwieldiness. You can make your combine so extensive that you can't digest it into a single system; you can get so many parts that you can't assemble them as you would an effective piece of machinery. The point of efficiency is overstepped in the natural process of development, oftentimes, and it has been overstepped many times in the artificial and deliberate formation of trusts.

A trust is formed in this way: a few gentlemen "promote" it, that is to say, they get it up, being given enormous fees for their kindness, which fees are loaded on to the undertaking in the form of securities of one kind or another. The argument of the promoters is, not that every one who comes into the combination can carry on his business more efficiently than he did before; the argument is: we will assign to you as your share in the pool, twice, three times, four times, or five times what you could have sold your business for to an individual competitor who would have to run it on an economic and competitive basis. We can afford to buy it at such a figure because we are shutting out competition. We can afford to make the stock of the combination half a dozen times what it naturally would be and pay dividends on it, because there will be nobody to dispute the prices we shall fix.

Talk of that as sound business? Talk of that as inevitable? It is based upon nothing except power. It is not based upon efficiency. It is no wonder that the big trusts are not prospering in proportion to such competitors as they still have in such parts of their business as competitors have access to; they are prospering freely only in those fields to which competition has no access. Read the statistics of the Steel Trust, if you don't believe it. Read the statistics of any trust. They are constantly nervous about competition, and they are constantly buying up new competitors in order to narrow the field. The United States Steel Corporation is gaining in its supremacy in the American market only with regard to the cruder manufactures of iron and steel, but wherever, as in the field of more advanced manufactures of iron and steel, it has important competitors, its portion of the product is not increasing, but is decreasing, and its competitors, where they have a foothold, are often more efficient than it is. . . .

II

Individual Enterprise

For my part, I want the pigmy to have a chance to come out. And I foresee a time when the pigmies will be so much more athletic, so much more astute, so much more active, than the giants, that it will be a case of Jack the giant-killer. Just let some of the youngsters I know have a chance and they'll give these gentlemen points. Lend them a little money! They can't get any now. See to it that when they have got a local market they can't be squeezed out of it. Give them a chance to capture that market and then see them capture another one and another one, until these men who are carrying an intolerable load of artificial securities find that they have got to get down to hard pan to keep their foothold at all. I am willing to let Jack come into the field with the giant, and if Jack has the brains that some Jacks that I know in America have, then I should like to see the giant get the better of him, with the load that he, the giant, has to carry—the load of water! For I'll undertake to put a water-logged giant out of business any time, if you will give me a fair field and as much credit as I am entitled to, and let the law do what from time immemorial law has been expected to do—see fair play. . . .

III

Dissecting Combinations

The dominating danger in this land is not the existence of great individual combinations—that is dangerous enough in all conscience—but the combination of the combinations of the railways, the manufacturing enterprises, the great mining projects, the great enterprises for the development of the natural water-powers of the country, threaded together in the personnel of a series of boards of directors into a "community of interest" more formidable than any conceivable single combination that dare appear in the open.

The organization of business has become more centralized, vastly more centralized, than the political organization of the country itself. Corporations have come to cover greater areas than states; have come to live under a greater variety of laws than the citizen himself, have excelled states in their budgets and loomed bigger than whole commonwealths in their influence over the lives and fortunes of entire communities of men. Centralized business has built up vast structures of organization and equipment which overtop all states and seem to have no match or competitor except the federal Government itself.

What we have got to do—and it is a colossal task not to be undertaken with a light head or without judgment—what we have got to do is to disentangle this colossal "community of interest." No matter how we may purpose dealing with a single combination in restraint of trade, you will agree with me in this—that no single, avowed combination is big enough for the United States to be afraid of; but when all the combinations are combined and this final combination is not disclosed by any process of incorporation or law but is merely an identity of personnel or of interest, then there is something that even the Government of the Nation itself might come to fear—something for the law to pull apart, and gently, but firmly and persistently, dissect. . . .

I, for my part, do not want to be taken care of. I would rather starve a free man than be fed a mere thing at the caprice of those who are organizing American industry as they please to organize it. I know, and every man in his heart knows, that the only way to enrich America is to make it possible for any man who has the brains to get into the game. I am not jealous of the size of any business that has *grown* to that size. I am not jealous of any process of growth, no matter how huge the result, provided the result was indeed obtained by the processes of wholesome development, which are the processes of efficiency, of economy, of intelligence, and of invention.

The Businessman and the Progressive Movement

The question of government regulation of the economy, a question which was a central concern in the Progressive Era, directly affected businessmen, both large and small scale. For the most part Wilson, Roosevelt, and many others, both Progressive and conservative, stated their arguments so as to convince American businessmen of their validity. Robert Wiebe, a historian who has written extensively on the Progressives, analyzes the position of these businessmen as they faced the questions posed by Progressive reform.

From Robert Wiebe, "Business Disunity and the Progressive Movement, 1901–1914," *Mississippi Valley Historical Review*, XLIV (1957-1958), pp. 664-665, 679-685. Subheadings added and footnotes omitted by the editors.

I

Conventional Picture of Business

Histories of post–Civil War America, describing the rise of an industrialized society, stress businessmen's common characteristics at the expense of their differences and seldom uncover any appreciable diversity in their response to broad economic and political issues. In the standard interpretations, the businessmen appear as a united force, determined to protect group interests against all assaults. The only common exception to this treatment is to point out the antagonism between small business and big business, although even here historians tend to reunite many of these businessmen in a community of interests. In some studies the assumption of a single business outlook seems to have served primarily as a convenience to the writer. When entrepreneurs act as a group, furnishing counterpoint for other themes, their unity helps to produce a sharper, more effective narrative. In some other histories a homogeneous community develops naturally from the particular selection of business representatives—either a few prominent and verbal entrepreneurs or certain politicians, lawyers, and theorists—who presumably speak for the mass of less articulate businessmen. However valid this analysis may be for other periods of American history, an examination of businessmen's reactions to the Progressive movement indicates that far from forming a cohesive group they differed widely over the proper solution to America's problems and expended a large portion of their energies in internal conflicts.

The thirteen years between Theodore Roosevelt's ascent to the presidency and the outbreak of a general European war contained an exceptional number of public challenges to the business community's accustomed way of life. Flanked by the relative complacency of the Gilded Age and the 1920's, the Progressive era stood as a period of concentrated reform. Campaigns to make government more responsive to the voters' wishes, to allow the underprivileged a larger share of the nation's benefits, and to regulate the economic system so that it would better serve the public interest were all parts of a general movement, heavy with the accumulation of past discontent, which matured in the Progressives' reform program of the early twentieth century. To integrate the several parts of this program required guidance from the federal government, now more alert to cries for change than it had been in the nineteenth century. Thus the widespread desire for reform gained respectability and momentum during the Roosevelt administrations, grew restive in the interlude of William Howard Taft's presidency, and finally culminated in Woodrow Wilson's New Freedom. . . .

The debate among businessmen over trust control . . . suffered from hazy definition and from blurred demarcation among opponents. Part of this confusion resulted from the sudden burst of business consolidation, beginning after the election of 1896, which gave the old question of supervising industrial enterprises new dimensions of complexity and public concern. The problem of trust control became a symbol of the Progressive period's general worry over unfamiliar bigness and the decline of competition. Into this stream of unrest flowed the specific enmity of those businessmen who felt oppressed by large enterprises because of direct competition, the price of trust products, or the uncertain future of smaller entrepreneurs in an economy of giants. The exact problem was usually ill-defined, but the business conflicts were nonetheless acrimonious.

II
Sharpening of Issues

Business arguments over trust regulation remained diffuse until the Roosevelt administration dramatically placed itself in the midst of the controversy. In 1902, the government gave its basic regulatory weapon, the Sherman Antitrust Act of 1890, fresh prestige by prosecuting one of the nation's major combinations, the Northern Securities Company. Then, in the wake of this surprise, came the establishment of the Bureau of Corporations as a general investigating agency within the Department of Commerce and Labor. The smaller businessmen whose hostility toward trusts had been frustrated for lack of a satisfactory outlet now flooded the administration with pleas to champion their causes, whether they be battles with the country's great corporations or conflicts with various price-fixing retail leagues. Big-business leaders, on the other hand, concentrated upon coming to terms with this potential enemy, the federal government. Led by Elbert H. Gary, chairman of United States Steel's board of directors, the more discerning of these went directly to the source of their trouble and tried to negotiate private agreements with the administration, by which the corporations would co-operate in investigations in return for undefined but presumably lenient treatment.

These efforts to commit the government to one side or the other in trust prosecution, however, did not actively involve the majority of businessmen. Although the scandals of 1905 and 1906 concerning life insurance companies and food industries shocked many businessmen and quickened their reform impulses, most of them refused to endorse programs which might someday be turned upon them. As a result, the popular solution among mixed business organizations, such as the National Association of Manufacturers and the National Board of Trade, was a national incorporation law, elastic enough to satisfy both those desiring tighter control and those hoping for a relaxation of the Sherman Act's ban on restraint of trade.

Out of the Panic of 1907 emerged a proposal which helped to clear the lines dividing the business community. A group of powerful industrialists decided that their salvation lay in transforming the Sherman Act into an ally instead of a hovering threat. To achieve this, they formulated a plan whereby businessmen would submit their projects for expansion and communities of interest to the Bureau of Corporations which, after a thorough investigation, could immunize them from future prosecution by issuing a protective stamp of approval. With valuable help from President Roosevelt, they were able in early 1908 to bring their proposal before Congress as the Hepburn amendments to the Sherman Act. An opposition among lesser businessmen solidified immediately. While speaking most vigorously against certain peripheral labor clauses in the bill, these smaller entrepreneurs made it patently clear to congressmen that they would not tolerate any differentiation between "reasonable" and "unreasonable" restraint of trade, no matter what else the bill might contain. To these dissenters, such a law would invite a few mammoth corporations to dominate the economy with governmental assistance. The Hepburn amendments failed in an election year sensitive to big-business privileges, but its advocates did not abandon their objective.

III
The "Rule of Reason"

For a time the debate waned as the nation entered an unstable transition between Roosevelt's Square Deal and Wilson's New Freedom. Businessmen tensely watched the Supreme Court for their next guidepost. In 1911 the Court issued its long-awaited decisions on the Standard Oil and American Tobacco Company antitrust suits, ruling against the legality of each but, in its famous gloss on the Sherman Act, officially separating reasonable from unreasonable restraint of trade. Once announced, these decisions somehow seemed anticlimactic. For smaller businessmen who had opposed this distinction in 1908, the Court's interpretation naturally constituted a defeat, and even for the powerful corporations, who were theoretical victors, the decisions provided little solace. If each large enterprise had to undergo the ordeal of a judicial test in order to survive, who would be next? United States Steel received the unpleasant answer in October, 1911, in the form of an antitrust suit, and International Harvester followed it into court a few months later. These prosecutions underlined the big-business conviction that only a new, liberal law could offer permanent relief.

During the Progressive ferment of 1912, industrial leaders re-opened the campaign which had stalled with the 1908 defeat of the Hepburn amendments. They altered their advice-and-consent formula to include an interstate trade commission, similar in status to the interstate commerce commission, as well as stricter criminal liability laws, but the goal remained government sanction for business consolidation and co-operation. With this revised edition of their plan in hand, the big businessmen prepared to meet the challenge from the Wilson administration, which had been elected on a platform and in an atmosphere averse to bigness. The Democrats, too, wanted clarification of the Sherman Act, but in the Clayton bill of 1914 they chose a path opposite from the one corporation magnates followed. Instead of liberalizing the anti-trust statute, the Clayton omnibus measure promised stiffer governmental control, designating specific corporate practices as destructive of competition and henceforth illegal. Although certain sections, especially those dealing with interlocking directorates and interlacing stock ownership, appealed to many entrepreneurs whose operations were more limited in scope, the measure as a whole seemed to be "a strait-jacket upon American business" which large and small businessmen joined in denouncing.

IV
The Federal Trade Commission

The companion Democratic proposal for a Federal Trade Commission, however, contained potentially the exact solution big industrialists had sought since the days of the Hepburn amendments. Leading a far larger segment of business than before, these men concentrated their efforts upon constructing a trade commission which would serve as a business guardian. The thrust of their argument, as presented in the Chicago Association of Commerce's "Chicago Plan," by-passed the Clayton bill's approach by rejecting "further detailed definition of 'restraint of trade' or unfair practices," but at the same time embodied the contradictory complaint that "nothing hampers business like uncertainty." The reconciliation lay in a friendly Federal Trade Commission "to which we can submit business practices" and which would then "decide in advance as to the propriety, fairness and benefits of such proposed arrangements, each upon the merits of that particular case."

Smaller industrialists who had steadily fought this concept recognized their old enemy in its latest disguise. From their standpoint, none of the measures before Congress could benefit them, and therefore, with the National Association of Manufacturers in the vanguard, they organized a business drive to pressure Congress into immediate adjournment. "The Country Is Suffering from *Too Much Law*," they protested; let us "Free Business from Political Persecution." With these notes of negativism echoing throughout the debates, Congress passed a modified Clayton Act and established the Federal Trade Commission without the advisory or directive powers outlined in the "Chicago Plan." Suspicions which had persistently kept businessmen from uniting on a trust regulation program left them neutralized in 1914 while Congress enacted legislation unsatisfactory to either of the opposing forces.

The business community had split over trust control, as it had over banking and railroad legislation, into factions shaped according to the dictates of particular economic interests. Yet, beyond motives of self-interest, these specific internal contests formed a broader pattern of business conflict. Its first thread was an urban-rural rift, most clearly shown by the battle between city and country bankers over financial reform. Another thread, in some respects similar, involved a division between businessmen of the East and those of the West and South. While the urban-rural split was related to the regional division, due to a concentration of cities in the East, special sectional characteristics separated the second as a unique strand. Thus urban bankers in Chicago and New York competed during this time for financial leadership and prestige; city bankers in the Democratic South more readily accepted Wilsonian reform than did their northern—and largely Republican—counterparts; and urban businessmen in the West, where shippers predominated, fought their eastern colleagues who controlled the railroads. Cleavages according to size provided a third thread, which dominated the debate over trust regulation and which also paralleled the city-country rift among bankers. Finally, functional divisions underlay the contest between shippers and carriers over rate levels and made it difficult for bankers to rally other types of businessmen, who were their customers, behind reform programs favorable to the financiers. Interwoven in various ways depending upon the time and the issue, these four strands outlined the quarrels among businessmen over the reform programs of the period. These battles, considered as a group, give consistent testimony that conflict, not co-operation, typified the business community's reaction to crisis during the Progressive era.

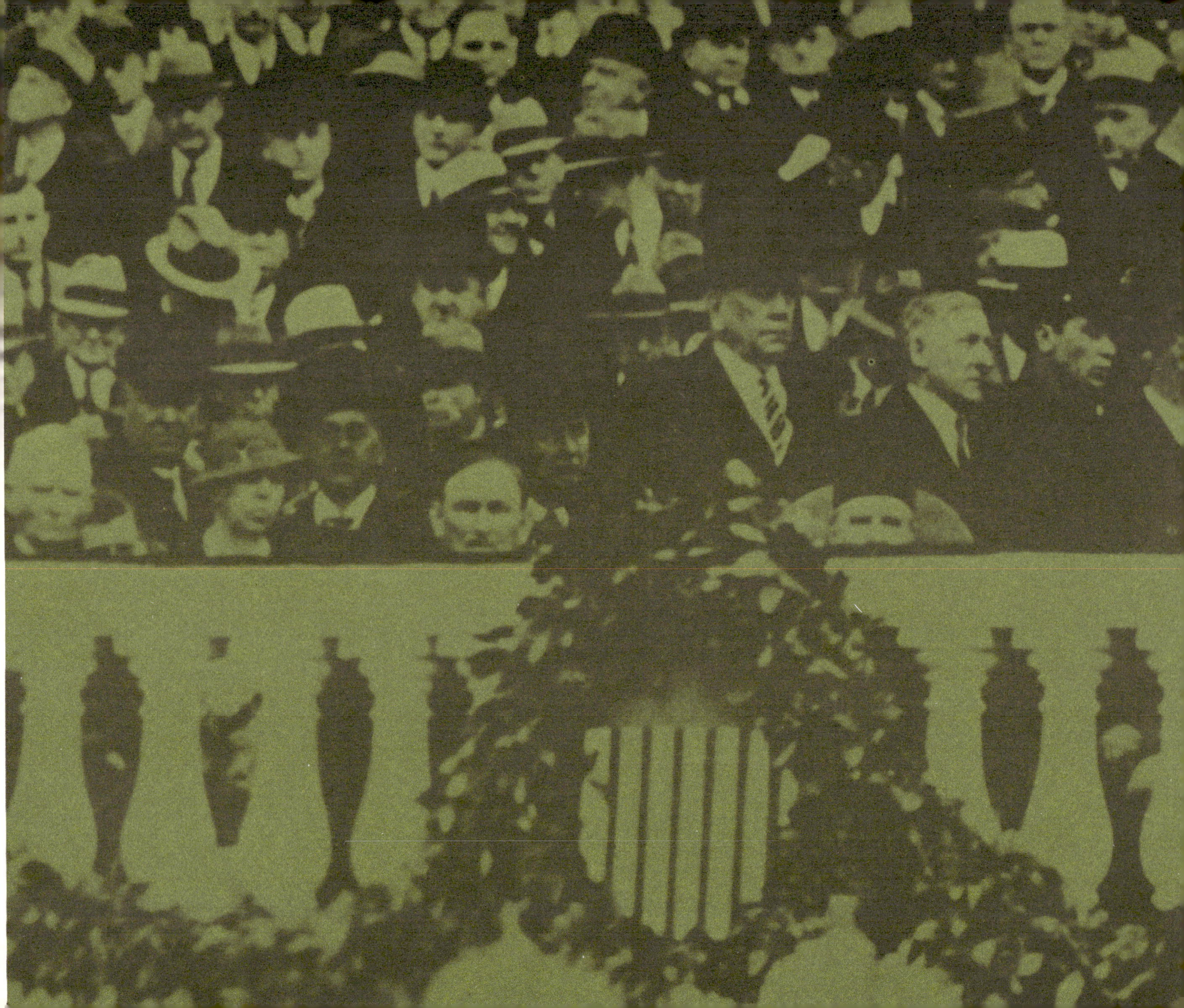

Chapter 7

Boom, Bust, Depression, Recovery: Responses to Economic Change, 1920–1945

The economic depression that began in 1929 and lasted until 1940 was the worst in American history. It made such an impression on those who endured it, and on those who have written about it, that it has come to be called the Depression, or the Great Depression. One historian, Carl Degler, has also termed it the "Third American Revolution" (the first two being the wars of 1775 and 1861) because of the ways in which it changed American actions and thinking both in the 1930s and after.

One reason why the Depression was such a shattering blow, to both the economy and to public confidence in the economy, was that the economic system as a whole had expanded to unprecedented heights in the 1920s. The resulting prosperity encouraged many Americans to believe that the nation was on the verge of eliminating poverty altogether. Then, in four years, the Depression put out of work more than twelve million persons, the principal support of (including themselves) perhaps as many as fifty million Americans.

Elsewhere in the world the Depression struck hard, even where unemployment was not so devastating as in the United States. It caused political crises and overturns of governments, notably in Germany, where popular unrest stimulated by hard times helped to establish Adolf Hitler as dictator. While American politics underwent certain striking changes, democratic government, run by conventional parties, emerged strong even after ten years of this economic challenge.

In the years between 1933 and 1945 the Democratic Party became for the first time since the Civil War the majority party in most elections. Franklin D. Roosevelt, a distant relative of Theodore Roosevelt, became the first man ever to be elected President more than twice; he was elected four times. And the New Deal, the set of programs created by Roosevelt and his party to cope with the effects of the Depression, changed American life and American politics in ways that have become permanent.

Despite its pioneer efforts to cope with economic disaster and despite heavy public support for its programs, the New Deal did not solve the problem of unemployment; probably nine million workers were still without regular jobs at the end of the 1930s. Employment finally recovered because of the production boom of World War II in 1940 and after.

The following readings trace the rise, fall, and resurgence of the economy between 1920 and 1945, as well as some of the major social and political aspects of these years.

TOPIC 47

THE NEW ERA

While World War I will be dealt with in the following chapter, its effects on the American economy must be briefly noted here. Orders for supplies from the belligerents in Europe produced a modest boom in the economy soon after the outbreak of war in August 1914. Not until the United States entered the war in 1917, however, did the war force new patterns on the economy. Then sudden and overwhelming demands by the federal government for food, fuel, transportation, and arms proved too much for a system which had had no preparation for such a crisis. Serious delays and shortages in production and bottlenecks in transportation threatened the operation of both the civilian economy and the machinery of war. In a series of laws Congress authorized temporary federal control and management of major parts of the economy. This centralized direction, aided by the cooperation of business, labor, and the public, enabled the United States to contribute the massive economic aid which was so essential to the Allied victory in 1918.

The economy reverted to private control after the war, and the 1920s witnessed the restoration of the peacetime patterns of steady growth and increasing mechanization characteristic since the mid-1800s. But these were different times. They were different partly because the application of technology, with its accompanying concentration of urban populations, produced ever more rapid and profound changes in the quality of life for a majority of the American people. The times were different also because the dynamic forces of capitalism, moving steadily toward consolidation of business into fewer and bigger units and toward the exploitation of ever-growing markets, lacked the restraining influence of Progressivism. The Progressives, while frequently wishing vainly for a return to the economy and society of an earlier and simpler day, had fought for the social responsibility of business with regulation by government as their characteristic weapon. But the resounding defeat of the Democrats in the election of 1920 and the establishment of conservative control by Republicans of both the Presidency and Congress doomed any hope Progressives had of recovering the practical and moral influence they had converted to the winning of a different kind of crusade in 1917 and 1918.

The following readings suggest some of the ways in which the economy of the 1920s significantly differed from the one before World War I.

Government and the Economy in the 1920s

In the following reading historian David Shannon considers the economic policies pursued by Republican administrations of the 1920s as well as certain developments during the decade in economic life and population shifts.

From David A. Shannon, *Between the Wars: America, 1919-1941* (Boston: Houghton Mifflin Company, 1965), pp. 31-32, 33-34, 38-39, 44-45, 85-86, 90-91. Copyright © 1965 by David A. Shannon. Subheadings and footnote added by the editors.

I

The "New Era"

In the last presidential election of the pre-depression era the Republicans pointed proudly to their record since 1921 and declared that they had inaugurated a "new era." There was much to this 1928 Republican claim. The years of Republican ascendancy had brought innovations and a new kind of relationship between the federal government and the American economy.

The men ultimately responsible for the "new era" were the two Republican presidents, Warren G. Harding and Calvin Coolidge, and the 1928 presidential candidate of the party, Herbert Hoover, who had served prominently as Secretary of Commerce since 1921. The Republicans in 1928, however, refrained from talking about President Harding. He had become embarrassing. Indeed, after he died in office in 1923 it was years before his friends and followers in his home town in Ohio were successful in getting a prominent Republican figure to give an address for the dedication of the Harding Memorial.

In retrospect at least, Harding was a tragic figure. His was simply a case of having more responsibilities and powers than his ability and character justified. He should never have been President of the United States; he should never have been nominated for the office. He was, in fact, a last-minute dark-horse choice. . . .

The corruption of the Harding administration was so spectacular that many accounts of it tend to minimize its other important features. But since Harding's policies did not differ significantly from those of his successors, they will be considered here as a unit. The Harding and Coolidge administrations and the first several months of Hoover's presidency had a strong continuity. Harding's administration was unique only in its corruption.

Much of the corruption was the work of the "Ohio gang." Harry M. Daugherty had long been a close friend of Harding's and his chief political adviser; Harding made him his Attorney General. A friend of Daugherty's, Jesse Smith, held no office of any kind but was in fact the assistant Attorney General in charge of graft. He had office space in the Department of Justice, where he arranged bribes for the Alien Property Custodian. One of the most thoroughly crooked Harding appointees was Charles R. Forbes, head of the Veterans Bureau, who required bribes before letting hospital contracts and who sold Bureau equipment to friends and then had the Bureau buy it back at a much higher price. When Harding discovered irregularities in Forbes's office in early 1923 he allowed him to resign and go to Europe. After Harding's death, when the Bureau's corruption became generally known, Forbes went to prison. The most spectacular fraud of the Harding administration involved naval oil reserves. Harding's Secretary of the Interior, former senator from New Mexico Albert B. Fall, persuaded Navy Secretary Edward Denby, a former Michigan congressman, to transfer control of the Elk Hills naval oil reserve in California and the Teapot Dome reserve in Wyoming to Fall's department. For a $100,000 "loan" delivered in a little black bag, Fall leased the Elk Hills reserve to Edward L. Doheny of the Pan American Petroleum Company; for $200,000 in Liberty bonds and $85,000 in cash, he leased the Teapot Dome oil rights to Harry F. Sinclair, who represented the Continental Trading Company. Ultimately, a jury convicted Fall for bribery.

Knowledge of at least some of the corrupt practices of his henchmen and worry about it probably contributed to Harding's death in August 1923, of pneumonia and a stroke, at the age of 58. The nation, however, did not learn of his administration's moral softness until after his death. None of the evidence about corruption in high places implicated Harding himself. Harding was the victim of his friends. But, on the other hand, he did not crack down hard on the grafters he knew about.

II

Coolidge and Hoover

Vice-President Calvin Coolidge was vacationing at his father's farm in Vermont when Harding died, and his father, a rural justice of the peace, administered the presidential oath of office. It was fitting that Coolidge took

TABLE 2 PRESIDENTIAL ELECTIONS, 1924-1928

	CANDIDATES	PARTIES	ELECTORAL VOTE	POPULAR VOTE
1924	Calvin Coolidge	Republican	382	15,718,211
	John W. Davis	Democratic	136	8,385,283
	Robert M. La Follette	Progressive	13	4,831,289
	Herman P. Faris	Prohibition		57,520
	Frank T. Johns	Socialist Labor		36,428
	William Z. Foster	Workers		36,386
	Gilbert O. Nations	American		23,967
1928	Herbert C. Hoover	Republican	444	21,391,993
	Alfred E. Smith	Democratic	87	15,016,169
	Norman Thomas	Socialist		267,835
	Verne L. Reynolds	Socialist Labor		21,603
	William Z. Foster	Workers		21,181
	William F. Varney	Prohibition		20,106

President Calvin Coolidge poses for photographers at his family's farm in Vermont. In the 1920s political figures still felt it essential to display their rural or small-town roots to the American public.

the oath in a Vermont farmhouse by the light of a kerosene lamp. A dour, unbelievably thrifty, rustic, stringy, vinegary little man, Coolidge remained always a rural New England Puritan. He was spare with his words, his emotions, and his money. So thrifty was he that he saved much of his presidential salary (he was the only modern president able to do so) and borrowed nickels from secret service men and failed to repay them. So sour was he that when Alice Roosevelt Longworth, Theodore Roosevelt's daughter and the wife of Speaker of the House Nicholas Longworth, said that Coolidge appeared to have been "weaned on a dill pickle" the whole nation could appreciate the remark. He utterly lacked color or flair. He was thoroughly honest and responsible, but he was limited in imagination.

Herbert Clark Hoover was the third president of the "new era" and quite a contrast to Harding and Coolidge. Hoover had superb qualities for business leadership and had been a highly successful engineer and executive. Vigorous, industrious, and logical, Hoover had first served in government under Democratic auspices. He was in Europe when the war began in 1914. His sense of public service prompted him first to help the American embassies at London and Paris to evacuate American citizens who wished to return to the states and then to organize relief for the overrun Belgians. He performed these tasks so ably that Wilson made him Food Administrator in 1917, an office which he directed efficiently and as effectively as the somewhat defective legislation allowed. There was some Democratic talk of nominating him for the presidency in 1920 until he announced his Republican affiliation. As Secretary of Commerce under both Harding and Coolidge with a strong voice in foreign affairs pertaining to the domestic economy, the Iowa-born Stanford University graduate was the "new era's" chief architect. But though a man of generally recognized great ability, Hoover did not have the qualities to be a popular figure. He was a little cold personally, rather formal and distant. He had been a successful engineer and business administrator, not a successful salesman. . . .

III

Republican Innovation

What was new about the "new era?" What did Hoover, who was in practice the "assistant president" for business affairs both domestic and foreign, seek to accomplish and how? How did the relations of the government with the business community during the 1920's differ from what they had been before the Progressive Era and under Presidents Roosevelt and Wilson?

In sum, Hoover envisioned a new mercantilism, both internally and externally. But this modern Richelieu stopped short of wanting to use governmental power to force business to do or not to do certain things. Quite the reverse. Hoover's plan was for government benignly to show, induce, and help business to adopt methods that would increase its efficiency and profits. Business would not only make better profits if it operated with maximum efficiency but it would also, Hoover firmly believed, help the prosperity of all and strengthen the nation generally. President Coolidge said, with his customary economy of language, "The business of America is business." Secretary Hoover certainly agreed, and had he been given to such efforts to capsule his philosophy he might have said, "The business of American government is to help business by showing it how to rationalize itself." . . .

With Secretary Hoover encouraging business cooperation on the one hand and the Department of Justice and regulatory commissions doing very little to enforce competition on the other, government provided an ideal climate for the growth of corporate concentration. Concentration of corporate wealth and power in the hands of a relatively few corporate entities—the "trusts," to use the late-nineteenth-century term—was nothing new in the 1920's. The trend had been under way ever since the Civil War; it only became accentuated during the postwar decade. Nor is it clear that the long-term trend toward monopoly or oligopoly would have been halted or reversed if Washington's attitude had been more hostile. Fundamental economic forces operated to give tremendous advantage to the integrated, rationally organized, large-scale corporation. But it is clear that the long "trustification" process hastened its pace during the 1920's and that government policies were a significant stimulus to the quicker step.

By 1929 the two hundred biggest corporations of America owned almost half the total corporate wealth and about one fifth the total national wealth. Furthermore, these powerful companies were growing far more rapidly than smaller firms; one study estimated their growth at three times the rate of all corporations. Concentration was most outstanding in industries devoted to manufacturing and mining, but other business areas had the same tendency in not quite as marked a degree. The public utilities field had a spectacular surge toward concentration in the 1920's. The number of banks in the nation declined by over five thousand during the decade, and the assets of the biggest banks became even larger than they had been early in the Wilson administration when the Pujo investigation's revelations shocked the nation. Even retailing, long thought to be a secure refuge for the small entrepreneur, gave way to big corporations establishing chains of retail outlets. By the end of the 1920's Americans bought more than one fourth of their food and clothes, about one fifth of their drugs, and almost one third of their tobacco from "chain stores." . . .

The path of the economy even during its boom years was not entirely smooth, however. Although relatively brief, the postwar depression that hit in mid-1920 was as steep and as sudden as any the American economy had ever experienced. The year 1921 was a hard one. Unemployment went up to 4,750,000, and national income was down 28 percent from the previous year. Farm prices were far too low to enable most farmers to meet their costs of production. But in 1922 the economy came back strong, and by the end of the year it was buzzing along in better shape than it had been when the depression hit. There were minor dips in the business cycle in 1924 and 1927, but they were not serious.

IV

Economic Difficulties

Besides cyclical fluctuations there were other blemishes on prosperity's record. Some economic activities did not share in the general prosperity. Agriculture never really recovered from the post-war depression, and low farm prices were the root of farmer discontent that manifested itself in McNary-Haugenism.* Some industries were in bad shape throughout the period. The world market for textiles declined when women's styles changed. A

---

*Senator Charles L. McNary of Oregon and Representative Gilbert N. Haugen attempted unsuccessfully to get the federal government to support farm prices through purchase of surplus commodities. Their third effort, in 1927, was passed by Congress but vetoed by President Coolidge—Eds.

dress in 1928 required less than one-half the material that a seamstress needed to make a dress in 1918. Furthermore, many clothes in the 1920's were made of synthetic fibers. Rayon became very popular. Consequently the textile industry was unable to pay wages consistent with the rising standard of living. The industry continued its long-range shift of operations from New England to the South, particularly to the southern Appalachians, where wage rates were lower. Coal was another sick industry. As home owners shifted gradually to other fuels for space heating and as automobiles and trucks gradually displaced the railroads, once a major market for coal, the total coal market shrank slightly. There was approximately 10 percent less coal mined at the end of the decade than there had been at the beginning. New mining technology enabled mine operators to get along with a smaller labor force. Almost one fourth of the nation's coal miners at work in 1923 were out of the pits by 1929, and since most miners lived in isolated communities where there were almost no other employment opportunities, the economic hardship in the mining towns was acute. Even employed miners worked at hourly wage rates that were 14 percent lower in 1929 than they had been in 1923. . . .

There is no question but that most industrial workers were better off materially in the 1920's than they had been earlier. Real wages (the relationship of money wages to the cost of living) in 1919 were at 105 on a scale in which 1914 was 100. By 1928 the figure stood at 132, a truly significant increase. Many an industrial worker's social ideas and assumptions earned him the unionist's contemptuous term "company man." Especially in the new industries like autos and electric appliances a large part of the labor force was composed of men who had begun their lives in small towns or on the farm, where there had been no big employers and where the terms of work were laid down by the employer on a take-it-or-leave-it basis or settled by each individual employee bargaining with the employer. Individualistic social attitudes formed in a rural society were difficult to shake, even when a man lived the anything but individualistic life of a city worker on a production line, the employee of a vast and complex corporation. It took the depression of the next decade to shock many workers from a rural background into modifying their views about the relationship of capital and labor sufficiently to join a union and make it a countervailing power to the corporation.

V

Urban Growth

There are no statistics that reveal precisely how many industrial workers in the 1920's were originally from urban areas, but the population statistics reveal a vast growth of the cities during the decade. Many rural counties continued to grow, but urban counties grew much more rapidly. The general pattern of migration was from the farm or small town to the small city of the same region and thence to a big city, often out of the region. The biggest growths were in New York City, the industrial cities on or near the Great Lakes, the San Francisco area, and Los Angeles. California tended to draw its new population from the West and the Midwest. New York's growth came from all over the nation, but the bulk of it came from the East and the Southeast. The burgeoning cities of the Midwest grew from rural-to-urban movement within the region and from migration from the South.

Great numbers of the migrants from the South were Negro. Negro migration to the North first became numerically significant during World War I. In 1910 more than 90 percent of the Negroes of the United States lived in states that had been slave areas in 1860. The census of that year showed only 850,000 Negroes living outside the South. The census of 1920 showed 1,400,000 in the North and West, most of them having migrated after 1917. The movement continued, even expanded, during the 1920's. In the 1930 census, 2,300,000 Negroes were living outside the South. The day was rapidly coming when the typical American Negro would not be a southern sharecropper but a northern or western urban wage earner.

This movement from rural to urban areas, for both Negroes and whites, came about for essentially economic reasons. Agriculture languished; industry flourished. Economic conditions pushed people off the farms and out of the small towns; better economic conditions in the cities pulled them into population clusters.

The Impact of the Automobile

The nature of the post–World War I years is impossible to understand without considering important technological and social changes which began even before the outbreak of the war. One of the key technological changes was the development and mass distribution of the automobile. The automobile is such a commonplace, even old-fashioned, means of transportation today, that it is hard to believe that there are men still alive who remember the "horseless carriage" as hardly more than a novelty. To travel short distances at the turn of the century the family either went in a carriage drawn by a horse or by electric-powered trolley cars. For long distances on land the steam-powered railroad was the only practical choice. As the following article, written by an early auto enthusiast, makes clear, the automobile changed not only the way Americans got about, but also many other aspects of their lives.

From Herbert Ladd Towle, "The Automobile and Its Mission," *Scribner's Magazine*, LIII (1913), pp. 149–152, 154. Subheadings added by the editors.

I

Triumph of the Automobile

Fifteen years ago the automobile was only a traveller's tale and the hobby of a few crackbrained experimenters. Five years ago the automobile factories of the United States produced about 100,000 cars. This year [1913] about 500,000 cars will be built, whose total value will exceed $600,000,000. One city alone will produce 300,000 cars—one factory, 200,000.

In 1905 the lowest practical price for an automobile was $900; to-day a better one costs but $600. Cars equal to those costing $1,500 and $2,000 five years ago, cost $1,200 and $1,500 to-day; and $900 buys a car better than the $1,200 car of the earlier date.

In 1908 about 300,000 of our citizens owned automobiles; before summer there will be an automobile for every 100 persons. In 1908 our export motor business was not worth mentioning. Last year it exceeded $25,000,000.

Five years ago this country had but a sprinkling of motor-trucks. They were poorly built; their advantages were doubtful; the only thing certain was the enormous latent demand. To-day there are some 40,000 motor-trucks giving satisfaction to 18,000 owners, and the percentage of growth in this business exceeds that in the pleasure-car field.

The automobile wreck was an aspect of the new invention which its advocates did not publicize. Early autos, as this photograph makes clear, offered occupants little protection in case of an accident.

To-day the invested capital in the automobile business in this country alone rivals that of the United States Steel Corporation. Most of the employees are skilled, most of them work in modern, wholesome factories, and all are well paid.

Five years ago the automobile was a transcendent plaything—thrilling, seductive, desperately expensive. Its oldest devotees could view with patience neither abstention from its charms nor the bills which followed surrender. To-day the harrowing alternative is mitigated at both ends. The bills are less and some of the excitement has worn off. Neighbor Brown, who sensibly refused to mortgage his house to buy a car in 1908, is now piling his family into a smart little black-and-red car, and is starting out on a four-day run to the Water Gap and return. And you know that he can do it now without the mortgage.

You yourself have seen the Water Gap, have explored every sunny road and leafy by-way within a hundred miles of your home, have seen the speedometer needle hang at 50 or 60, and have come unscathed through adventures which, when you think of them in cold blood, bring a creepy stirring to your spine. Your present car is good, but not showy; you keep it in a little garage behind your house and use it soberly—you and your family—nearly every day; and your motoring costs about half what it did five years ago. You seldom drive now for the mere pleasure of driving; yet your car is as much a part of your daily life as your walk to the office.

What does it all signify? This tremendous industry that has grown up almost overnight, and has made itself so necessary that a million owners of cars are giving food and roofs and clothing to another million—wage-earners and their families—for supplying them with the new means of locomotion—what does this new industry portend? How many more people are going to buy cars? Are automobiles a permanent development or a temporary fad? If permanent, how do they justify themselves—in mere pleasure, which a few can afford but more cannot, or in genuine service? Are they at bottom a liability or an asset?

Neighbor Brown, the effervescent novice, cannot teach us much. The bicycle, twenty years ago, had just as fervid votaries, but to-day the bicycle is used chiefly for getting about. How is it with you, the seasoned motorist? If you had no car, in what respect would your life and your family's be changed?

II

Automobiles and Suburbs

You and I—all of us—used to choose our homes for their nearness to train or trolley. A mile from the station, half a mile from the trolley, was our immutable limit. The gates of Paradise would not have tempted us further. Rents soared; the lucky first owners of land near a new transportation line retired from business and lived in luxury on the fruits of their good fortune; still we cheerfully paid tribute, and dotted the map with little disks and bands of high-priced real estate. Horses were expensive and a nuisance, and we did not know that we might become each his own motor-man.

But to-day your home is in a suburb, handy for the motorist but otherwise dependent on trolley service. Were it not for the automobile, your wife's need of companionship would compel removal either to the city or to a more central part of your village. Part, at least, of what you saved on the car would go out in higher rent. Then you would need some other forms of exercise and recreation—golf, weekends at the shore, or the theatre. More money! When you visit friends in the next town, you take your maid to visit *her* friends. Without the car she would have to shift for herself. And the children—you can already hear the lamentations when they learn that they have seen the last of Green Pond, and that these Saturday picnics by the babbling Wanaque River will be no more! You moved to your country home after you began motoring. Dare you say that that change was for the worse?

Perchance you have no car—as yet. But you have friends living five miles away by road. To visit them by rail, you must go half a mile to the station, ride ten miles to a junction, wait an hour, and travel a dozen miles more to a station half a mile from their home. How often do you see your friends?

Or you are a nature-lover and a busy man. The city stifles you and the daily ordeal of strap-hanging is a horror. Yet your wife declares that she will be "buried alive" if she goes where houses are more than a hundred feet apart. She has a right to her view, too. How shall yours and hers be reconciled?

Or you have children. Shall they be reduced to "tag" on the streets and in a bric-a-brac-filled apartment, or shall they have green grass, a sand-pile, trees, and a swing? Or perhaps you are a farmer, seeking means to relieve the monotony of farm life and hold your sons from the dangerous lure of the city.

For hundreds of thousands of families the automobile is at last supplying the happiest of answers. Bridging as it does the gap between rail travel and the horse, at a possible cost less than that of the latter, it has added threefold or more to the habitable areas outside of our cities. Double a certain radius and you quadruple the enclosed area. Make three miles your limit and the area becomes nine. Think what this will lead to in the course of a generation or two, and you will realize the transformation which the low-cost automobile is working. . . .

The logic of the situation points to the growth of motor colonies. It is the exceptional city family that removes outright to the farming hinterland, and in most cases distance from transportation has hitherto produced an inferior neighborhood. That latter condition is visibly giving way to the new order; already the cities have many automobile "commuters," and in every large suburb the morning and evening trains are met by scores of motor-cars. In a few years there will be hundreds.

Henry Ford and his "Tin Lizzie"

The name most closely associated with the early history of the automobile is that of Henry Ford (1863–1947). Ford did not invent the automobile nor was he the first to produce it in a factory and in substantial numbers. But he was the first to design a low-cost automobile and the first to apply successfully the principles of mass production to his model. The extent of his success can be seen by the fact that of the thirty million automobiles produced between 1909 and 1927, over fourteen million were Ford "Model T's."

Writing in 1922, Ford explained why he thought the Model T was so successful.

From Henry Ford and Samuel Crowther, *My Life and Work* (New York, 1922), pp. 68–69, 71–73, 148–149. Copyright © 1922 by Doubleday, Page and Company. Subheadings added by the editors.

I

The Model T

The design which I settled upon was called "Model T." The important feature of the new model—which, if it were accepted, as I thought it would be, I intended to make the only model and then start into real production—was its simplicity. There were but four constructional units in the car—the power plant, the frame, the front axle, and the rear axle. All of these were easily accessible and they were designed so that no special skill would be required for their repair or replacement. I believed then, although I said very little about it because of the novelty of the idea, that it ought to be possible to have parts so simple and so inexpensive that the menace of expensive hand repair work would be entirely eliminated. The parts could be made so cheaply that it would be less expensive to buy new ones than to have old ones repaired. They could be carried in hardware shops just as nails or bolts are carried. I thought that it was up to me as the designer to make the car so completely simple that no one could fail to understand it.

That works both ways and applies to everything. The less complex an article, the easier it is to make, the cheaper it may be sold, and therefore the greater number may be sold. . . .

II

Standardization

It is strange how, just as soon as an article becomes successful, somebody starts to think that it would be more successful if only it were different. There is a tendency to keep monkeying with styles and to spoil a good thing by changing it. The salesmen were insistent on increasing the line. They listened to the 5 percent., the special customers who could say what they wanted, and forgot all about the 95 percent. who just bought without making any fuss. No business can improve unless it pays the closest possible attention to complaints and suggestions. If there is any defect in service then that must be instantly and rigorously investigated, but when the suggestion is only as to style, one has to make sure whether it is not merely a personal whim that is being voiced. Salesmen always want to cater to whims instead of acquiring sufficient knowledge of their product to be able to explain to the customer with the whim that what they have will satisfy his every requirement—that is, of course, provided what they have does satisfy these requirements.

Therefore in 1909 I announced one morning, without any previous warning, that in the future we were going to build only one model, that the model was going to be "Model T," and that the chassis would be exactly the same for all cars, and I remarked:

"Any customer can have a car painted any colour that he wants so long as it is black."

I cannot say that any one agreed with me. The selling people could not of course see the advantages that a single model would bring about in production. More than that, they did not particularly care. They thought that our production was good enough as it was and there was a very decided opinion that lowering the sales price would hurt sales, that the people who wanted quality would be driven away and that there would be none to replace them. There was very little conception of the motor industry. A motor car was still regarded as something in the way of a luxury. The manufacturers did a good deal to spread this idea. Some clever persons invented the name "pleasure car" and the advertising emphasized the pleasure features. The sales people had ground for their objections and particularly when I made the following announcement:

> I will build a motor car for the great multitude. It will be large enough for the family but small enough for the individual to run and care for. It will be constructed of the best materials, by the best men to be hired, after the simplest designs that modern engineering can devise. But it will be so low in price that no man making a good salary will be unable to own one—and enjoy with his family the blessing of hours of pleasure in God's great open spaces. . . .

III

Style

It is considered good manufacturing practice, and not bad ethics, occasionally to change designs so that old models will become obsolete and new ones will have to be bought either because repair parts for the old cannot be had, or because the new model offers a new sales argument which can be used to persuade a consumer to scrap what he has and buy something new. We have been told that this is good business, that it is clever business, that the object of business ought to be to get people to buy frequently and that it is bad business to try to make anything that will last forever, because when once a man is sold he will not buy again.

Our principle of business is precisely to the contrary. We cannot conceive how to serve the consumer unless we make for him something that, as far as we can provide, will last forever. We want to construct some kind of a machine that will last forever. It does not please us to have a buyer's car wear out or become obsolete. We want the man who buys one of our products never to have to buy another. We never make an improvement that renders any previous model obsolete. The parts of a specific model are not only interchangeable with all other cars of that model, but they are interchangeable with similar parts on all the cars that we have turned out. You can take a car of ten years ago and, buying to-day's parts, make it with very little expense into a car of to-day.

The modern traffic jam was an expected part of American urban life by the 1920s. Here a stream of autos impatiently waits its chance to move along a Manhattan street. Note the double-decked buses, a common feature of mass transportation at the time.

The Impact of the Radio (1924)

The radio was perhaps the most significant breakthrough in mass communication since the invention of printing almost 500 years earlier. During the nineteenth century the telegraph and the telephone were invented, but both were dependent on wires strung between two or more points. A series of inventions around the turn of the century made possible first wireless telegraphy and then the actual wireless transmission of voices. By the early 1920s there were several broadcasting stations in operation and "radio" soon became first a national fad and then a national institution. Bruce Bliven, an editor of the liberal magazine, *The New Republic,* was one of the first Americans to try to evaluate the social significance of this advance in communications.

From Bruce Bliven, "The Future of Radio," *The New Republic,* XL (1924), pp. 135–136. Subheadings added by the editors.

I

The Future of Radio

Those who have discussed radio broadcasting as a social force have recently confined themselves to its use in political campaigns. Under the circumstances this is natural; yet it is worth remembering that after November 4 radio will still be here. To what uses which have the slightest interest for intelligent people may we expect it to be put in the three years and ten months before the voice of the politician is again heard in the land?

In the belief of those most competent to judge, radio is not a mechanical fad which will sweep the country, as bicycle riding once did, and then disappear. While its present popularity is partly attributable to novelty, it is here to stay. As improvements are added, (conceivably including radio transmission of motion pictures) it will become well nigh universal. The Department of Agriculture states that the number of receiving sets on farms has trebled in the past twelve months. Including home-made ones there are between three and four million of them in this country already, or one for each seven or eight families. It is easily within the bounds of possibility even now that a speaker may be listened to on some special occasion by a quarter or a third of the whole adult population.

It is also generally admitted that the radio is potentially a genuinely important medium of intellectual communication. Any one who will take the trouble to test it for himself may discover that (unless he is unusually visual-minded) he can follow the drift of an argument quite as well or better by hearing a speaker on the ether than by reading his remarks in next morning's paper. Despite the abnormality of listening to one whom you cannot see, it is common experience that better concentration is possible at the radio than in the public lecture hall with the distractions of a crowd. The speaker's "personal magnetism," if he has any, is enormously diminished in its power to affect the judgment of his auditors. Critical standards are preserved which are a useful assistance to independent thinking. Finally, the instant accessibility and ease of the radio are great incitements to the use of whatever intellectual opportunities it affords. Almost any owner of a receiving set will testify that at least during the first few weeks that he had it he listened to ten times as much oratorical and musical matter as during any equal period before.

But here comes the rub. In most parts of the country full 90 percent of the non-musical material on the air is sheer rubbish, not worth the attention of any one with more than an eight-year-old mind. The largest item of all on the programs is, of course, jazz music. There is likewise a quantity of somewhat better music and occasionally a performance of real importance. If its usefulness were mainly as a musical instrument, the radio would have little social value—certainly not much more than the phonograph or the self-playing piano. It is when we consider it as a device for transmitting thought that we come both to the field of greatest potential usefulness, and the worst present failure.

II

The Radio Commercial

Not only do the radio broadcasting stations give a disproportionately small amount of time to the spoken word, but the quality is in general appallingly bad. First and worst is the evil of paid advertising, most of which is not even acknowledged as such. All sorts of commercial institutions hire lecturers and "rent time on the air" for discussions almost invariably dull and vulgar and usually smeared over with the demand that the auditors shall go and buy something. Some stations, we are glad to report, refuse to permit advertising; but the tendency is the other way.

Next to paid advertising, a common feature is broadcasting after-dinner speeches. Naturally, the merit of these depends on the men who make them; but in general it is fair to say that most are made by persons not worth hearing and that even the individual who has something to say is rarely in a mood to say it.

For the rest, these ethereal speakers are a job-lot of individuals who are willing to volunteer their services without charge: the broadcasters have not yet realized that it is just as impossible for them to secure competent speakers without payment as it would be to conduct a great university with a volunteer faculty, or a leading magazine with unpaid contributors. The corps of radio volunteers includes some self-advertising would-be publicists; a few professional patriots who are trying to scare the country back into the frame of mind of the eighteen eighties; special pleaders for charity bazaars, and the like. Some good speakers who should be willing to talk at least occasionally, speakers whom the radio audience would be glad to hear, are deterred by the arbitrary supposition of the managers that the listeners can't stand more than fifteen minutes of anything. Many others don't appear because they have never been asked.

This fact brings us to the heart of the problem and helps account for the failure of broadcasting as an intellectual force today. This remarkable invention, with potential powers second only to those of the printing press and with an audience already nearly as large as that of our entire public school system, is mainly under control of men unfitted by training and personality for posts of such importance. While there are a few exceptions, such as stations maintained by universities, it is generally true that the making of programs is in the hands of underpaid individuals, picked up at haphazard, usually musicians or men whose primary interest is music. They are admirably fitted to assemble orchestras, pianists and singers; but when it comes to lectures and addresses they are about as competent as Florenz Ziegfeld is to run Columbia University.

The development of motion pictures in the United States was held back half a decade because at first it was in the control of fly-by-nights, adventurers and reformed pushcart peddlers, not one in a hundred of whom had reached the social level where one takes one's hat off indoors. Radio broadcasting seems threatened by the same fate, and for somewhat the same reason: because a remarkable new educational device has suddenly developed as a sort of by-product of industry and is therefore in the hands of business men not only ignorant of its proper use, but indifferent as to whether it is used properly or not. . . .

This new and marvelous means of transmitting ideas cannot be allowed to go largely to waste as at present; public demand will force its more intelligent use even if those in charge of it continue blind to its opportunities and responsibilities.

The Rise of a Consumer Economy

A new word became part of the average American's vocabulary in the 1920s: *consumer*. The consumer lived and worked in the city or its suburbs and produced few if any of the things he needed or wanted. Usually he did not know those who produced or even sold him the goods he used. He wore ready-made clothes to the "chain store" where he bought his food, drove home his mass-produced car, turned on the radio, and relaxed on the sofa he was purchasing on the installment plan. Near the end of the decade Paul Mazur, a New York City banker, attempted to evaluate what this emphasis on consumption meant for the American economy and society.

From *American Prosperity: Its Causes and Consequences* by Paul M. Mazur. Copyright 1928 by The Viking Press, © renewed 1956 by Paul M. Mazur. All rights reserved. Reprinted by permission of The Viking Press, Inc. Pp. 92-95, 97-98, 224-226. Subheadings added by the editors.

I

Obsolescence

But even increased advertising and more intensive selling are not sufficient in themselves entirely to explain American prosperity. The continuous extension of markets must bring the manufacturer, sooner or later, to the borders of the arid desert of low consumer purchasing power. And the appeal to an intensively cultivated market cannot maintain for long an effective effort to sell another and another duplicate of a product to the same consumer. Saturation of markets—even of American markets—is not beyond possibility for goods other than those low-priced staple items that are consumed quickly. There is tremendous or unsurmountable resistance to the sale of an item that wears out slowly if the average buyer already possesses that item with some of its useful life still intact. Wear alone made replacement too slow for the needs of American industry. And so the high-priests of business elected a new god to take its place along with—or even before—the other household gods. Obsolescence was made supreme.

Obsolescence meant being out of date. It could be created almost as fast as the turn of the calendar, certainly as rapidly as the creative power of inventive minds determined. The danger of saturation could be removed beyond the stars. If what had filled the consumer market yesterday could only be made obsolete today, that whole market would be again available tomorrow.

Consumers were intensely interested in the new. America is a rabidly progressive nation in material things, and possession of the latest this and the latest that is a favorite standard of individual progressiveness. Sales organizations besought the factory for something new. Competitors compelled the search for something new. Retailers sent legions of buyers to the corners of the world for something new. And Caesar Consumer sat upon his dais and held his thumb down for the old, and his thumb up for the new.

The staggering progress of chemical and industrial science has brought with it both the constant anticipation of new discoveries and the actual day-to-day presentation of new products to supplant kindred products already in use. Obsolescence has been to a large extent stimulated as well as made possible by the progress of science.

Each year the new crop of automobile offerings casts into obsolescence the used and unused models of the previous year. The last year's model that is mechanically perfect and has never turned a wheel all of a sudden loses twenty to thirty percent of its sales value. It has become undesirable because the consumer market is open only to this year's latest designs. The radio development made phonographs obsolete until new developments in the field of the latter created a novelty appeal. And in the radio field itself, model after model tumbles out upon the market to claim the throne and to cast into discard the rulers of yesterday that seem today only crude, dispirited pretenders. Electrical refrigeration becomes practical, and all American households become a virgin market for the product. Ice refrigeration is in consequence fighting for its existence with the assistance of a lower price basis, the limited use of electricity in homes, and national advertising of the value of using ice. But to no avail! Electric refrigeration is new and it has the benefit of American favor. Within the field of electric refrigeration itself, however, it will probably be not long before we see a series of successive models each of which is new and each of which will attempt to make its predecessors obsolete.

Another factor of importance is less operative in the case of the refrigerator, however, than, let us say, in the case of the automobile. The refrigerator, located as it is in an obscure corner of the house, is relatively unseen by neighbors. This tends in its case to extend the longevity of the old model, whereas the greater visibility of the automobile brings into play the added impetus of rivalry with neighbors and friends. The neighbors' ready recognition of new as distinguished from old models adds greatly to the factor of obsolescence of the automobile.

The automobile has, as is well known, contributed greatly to the prosperity of the country. And the auxiliary force of obsolescence has contributed tremendously to the desire which consumers have converted into the purchase of an annual production of 3,500,000 cars valued at $2,500,000,000. It was in the main Mr. Ford's failure to recognize the effectiveness of a change in models that was responsible for his poor results for the year 1927.*

II

Advertising and Instalment Buying

Clearly then, obsolescence has been a vital ingredient in American business prosperity. One step beyond, however, was still necessary in order to ensure as large a consumer demand as American business desired and, above all, needed. Generous and effective use of advertising, high pressure sales methods, and especially the replacement of wear by obsolescence would, it is true, convert consumers' sales resistance into a real desire to buy. The fact that the consumer was already exhausting a good deal of his purchasing power, however, was a serious impediment to increased sales. It was therefore necessary that increased consumer purchasing power should be created. And this was done by the extraordinary extension of instalment purchasing, the plan which enables American consumers today to satisfy many billions of dollars' worth of their needs and desires.

It is difficult to estimate the exact amount of consumer buying which is done on an instalment basis. Estimates range between five and eight billions of dollars annually out of a total annual retail volume of thirty-five to forty billion dollars. Even the most conservative estimate represents an overwhelming amount. There is cause to believe that the

---

*In 1928 Ford introduced the Model A, his first model change in twenty years—Eds.

Mass-produced consumer products appear even in this idyllic summer scene. Note that each canoe contains a phonograph; at that moment they were undoubtedly playing the latest popular songs.

total increase in retail volume which this country has experienced is almost entirely represented by sales made on the instalment plan. Undoubtedly by this measure the consumer market has been as surely extended as if five million adults had been added to the population and each of them had spent one thousand dollars per annum.

The detailed mechanics of the instalment plan vary, but the plan itself is simple in principle. It consists of the sale of an article for a small payment at the time of purchase and a promise to pay the remainder in small equal instalments over the course of the succeeding months. The length of time granted for full payment varies from ten weeks to four years; but on the whole the average instalment account runs one year. . . .

III

Prosperity Forever

As advertising has increased in the country, there has been no sign that every successful campaign garnered its entire increased sales market at the expense of some product that had been in the field before. There is likely to be, as there probably was, some encroachment, and if the product causes some other article to become obsolete, the encroachment may be serious and even fatal. But, generally, increased advertising adds both to the consumption and the production capacity of the country.

It is natural that this should be so. Advertising is an educational force. If effective, desires increase, standards of living are raised, purchases are made; purchases create production, production creates purchasing power, and the circle can be made complete if desire is at this point strong enough to convert that power into actual purchases.

Of course there exists theoretically that danger point when consumption has reached its limit. Such a breaking point is probably non-existent. Human desires seem to have no limits. Food products may some day reach a point where people's appetites are satiated or oversatiated—a day, however, far distant or at least hardly imminent. But even when that day comes, there will still be other wants and desires that are just as real—the satisfaction of which will still provide new sales opportunities. Give the world and his wife the funds with which to satisfy every need, desire, and whim, educate the world and his wife to want, and the productive capacity of the country will actually groan under the burden of the enormous demand. There may be limits to the consumption of particular products. There is no theoretical limit to general consumption possibilities.

That is what the economist means when he says that there can be no such thing as general overproduction. The world will consume all that can be produced, if only production will create the purchasing power for that consumption. There is, of course, not much solace in that principle for the industrialist who finds his capacity idle, his sales markets flooded by his competitor's goods, prices weak, and demand weaker. For him, to be sure, there is overproduction.

Nevertheless, the economist is probably right. Overproduction in a particular industry exists only because of the maladjustment between the parts of the entire economic system. To eliminate entirely such maladjustment may be impossible. But at least it is possible for most industries whose products have not passed into complete obsolescence to correct part of this maladjustment. The problem is easy to state, the answer is always difficult to find—in some cases impossible. The formula is simple—economical production, careful merchandising, consolidation, and the increased development of consumer demand.

To those, however, who feel in spite of this that there is a limit to the effective use of the industrial capacity of the country, history should relate its own reassuring story. If to the leaders of the American industry of fifty years ago some wildly romantic business prophet had suggested the possibility of the actual production figures of this year of 1928, his story would have been summarily dismissed and his sanity seriously questioned. American industry has rolled on with whirlwind speed. There is no fundamental reason to believe that such speed can be slackened either by the obstacles that may confront business or by the diminution of the energy inherent in business. Each industrial institution must of necessity forge its own way to success. But industry as a whole can plan and execute for its advancement, secure in the belief that there are no limits to the total productive capacity of the country and the resulting purchasing power, because there are no limits to the needs and desires of American consumers.

Flight from the City

When in the early days of the United States Thomas Jefferson warned against the evils of cities, he sounded a note that has had many echoes in American history. The urbanization of the Twenties provoked a ringing echo of Jefferson from one writer.

From Ralph Borsodi, *Flight From the City* (New York: Harper & Row Publishers, Inc., 1933), pp. 1-4, 5-6, 8-9. Reprinted by permission of the author.

I

Caught in the City

In 1920 the Borsodi family—my wife, my two small sons, and myself—lived in a *rented* home. We *bought* our food and clothing and furnishings from retail stores. We were *dependent* entirely upon my income from a none too certain white-collar job.

We lived in New York City—the metropolis of the country. We had the opportunity to enjoy the incredible variety of foodstuffs which pour into that great city from every corner of the continent; to live in the most luxurious apartments built to house men and women in this country; to use the speedy subways, the smart restaurants, the great office buildings, the libraries, theaters, public schools—all the thousand and one conveniences which make New York one of the most fantastic creations in the history of man. Yet in the truest sense, we could not enjoy any of them.

How could we enjoy them when we were financially insecure and never knew when we might be without a job; when we lacked the zest of living which comes from real health and suffered all the minor and sometimes major ailments which come from too much excitement, too much artificial food, too much sedentary work, and too much of the smoke and noise and dust of the city; when we had to work just as hard to get to the places in which we tried to entertain ourselves as we had to get to the places in which we worked; when our lives were barren of real beauty—the beauty which comes only from contact with nature and from the growth of the soil, from flowers and fruits, from gardens and trees, from birds and animals?

We couldn't. Even though we were able for years and years, like so many others, to forget the fact—to ignore it amid the host of distractions which make up city life.

And then in 1920, the year of the great housing shortage, the house in which we were living was sold over our heads. New York in 1920 was no place for a houseless family. Rents, owing to the shortage of buildings which dated back to the World War, were outrageously high. Evictions were epidemic—to enable rapacious landlords to secure higher rents from new tenants—and most of the renters in the city seemed to be in the courts trying to secure the protection of the Emergency Rent Laws. We had the choice of looking for an equally endurable home in the city, of reading endless numbers of classified advertisements, of visiting countless real estate agents, of walking weary miles and climbing endless flights of steps, in an effort to rent another home, or of flight from the city. And while we were trying to prepare ourselves for the struggle with this typical city problem, we were overcome with longing for the country—for the security, the health, the leisure, the beauty we felt it must be possible to achieve there. Thus we came to make the experiment in living which we had often discussed but which we had postponed time and again because it involved so radical a change in our manner of life.

Instead, therefore, of starting the irritating task of house and apartment hunting, we wrote to real estate dealers within commuting distance of the city. We asked them for a house which could be readily remodeled; a location near the railroad station because we had no automobile; five to ten acres of land with fruit trees, garden space, pasturage, a woodlot, and if possible a brook; a location where electricity was available, and last but not least, a low purchase price. Even if the place we could afford only barely complied with these specifications, we felt confident that we could achieve economic freedom on it and a degree of comfort we never enjoyed in the city. All the other essentials of the good life, not even excepting schooling for our two sons, we decided we could produce for ourselves if we were unable to buy in a neighborhood which already possessed them.

II

Escape

We finally bought a place located about an hour and three-quarters from the city. It included a small frame house, one and a half stories high, containing not a single modern improvement—there was no plumbing, no running water, no gas, no electricity, no steam heat. There were an old barn, and a chicken-house which was on the verge of collapse, and a little over seven acres of land. . . .

Before the end of the first year, the year of the depression of 1921 when millions were tramping the streets of our cities looking for work, we began to enjoy the feeling of plenty which the city-dweller never experiences. We cut our hay; gathered our fruit; made gallons and gallons of cider. We had a cow, and produced our own milk and butter, but finally gave her up. By furnishing us twenty quarts of milk a day she threatened to put us in the dairy business. So we changed to a pair of blooded Swiss goats. We equipped a poultry-yard, and had eggs, chickens, and fat roast capons. We ended the year with plenty not only for our own needs but for a generous hospitality to our friends—some of whom were out of work—a hospitality which, unlike city hospitality, did not involve purchasing everything we served our guests.

To these things which we produced in our first year, we have since added ducks, guineas, and turkeys; bees for honey; pigeons for appearance; and dogs for company. We have in the past twelve years built three houses and a barn from stones picked up on our place; we weave suiting, blankets, carpets, and draperies; we make some of our own clothing; we do all of our own laundry work; we grind flour, corn meal, and breakfast cereals; we have our own workshops, including a printing plant; and we have a swimming-pool, tennis-court, and even a billiard-room.

In certain important respects our experiment was very different from the ordinary back-to-the-land adventure. We quickly abandoned all efforts to raise anything to sell. After the first year, during which we raised some poultry for the market, this became an inviolable principle. We produced only for our own consumption. If we found it difficult to consume or give away any surplus, we cut down our production of that particular thing and devoted the time to producing something else which we were then buying. We used machinery wherever we could, and tried to apply the most approved scientific methods to small-scale production. . . .

III

The Meaning of the Experiment

What are the social, economic, political, and philosophical implications of such a type of living? What would be the consequence of a widespread transference of production from factories to the home?

If enough families were to make their homes economically productive, cash-crop farmers specializing in one crop would have to abandon farming as a business and go back to it as a way of life. The packing-houses, mills, and canneries, not to mention the railroads, wholesalers, and retailers, which now distribute agricultural products would find their business confined to the production and distribution of exotic foodstuffs. Food is our most important industry. A war of attrition, such as we have been carrying on all alone, if extended on a large enough scale, would put the food industry out of its misery, for miserable it certainly is, all the way from the farmers who produce the raw materials to the men, women, and children who toil in the canneries, mills, and packing-towns, and in addition reduce proportionately the congestion, adulteration, unemployment, and unpleasant odors to all of which the food industry contributes liberally.

If enough families were to make their homes economically productive, the textile and clothing industries, with their low wages, seasonal unemployment, cheap and shoddy products, would shrink to the production of those fabrics and those garments which it is impractical for the average family to produce for itself.

If enough families were to make their homes economically productive, undesirable and non-essential factories of all sorts would disappear and only those which would be desirable and essential because they would be making tools and machines, electric light bulbs, iron and copper pipe, wire of all kinds, and the myriad of things which can best be made in factories, would remain to furnish employment to those beweighted human beings who prefer to work in factories.

Domestic production, if enough people turned to it, would not only annihilate the undesirable and non-essential factory by depriving it of a market for its products. It would do more. It would release men and women from their present thralldom to the factory and make them masters of machines instead of servants to them; it would end the power of exploiting them which ruthless, acquisitive, and predatory men now possess; it would free them for the conquest of comfort, beauty and understanding.

TOPIC 48

SOCIAL CHANGE AND CONFLICT

Americans of the 1910s had to endure the shocks of World War I; those of the 1930s the ordeal of the Depression. Between those historical landmarks the era of the 1920s seems like a quiet interlude. Thus the following pages, which deal with social changes in that decade and the conflicts that change produced, are not intended to demonstrate that the Twenties were tumultuous. They are designed, however, to let the reader examine some new ways in which change affected society, as well as some old aspects of social conflict that broke out more intensely during the decade.

Reading 235

Tensions of the Twenties

This article, prepared by the editors, examines some of the sources of social tension among Americans in the decade of the 1920s.

I

Internal Scars

World War I, which produced a militant unity in the nation, also left some internal scars. Thousands of Americans had been persecuted, jailed, and a few even lynched because their loyalty to the nation was challenged, usually unfairly. Socialists, who included many pacifists, were especially vulnerable. The creation of the world's first Marxist socialist state, Soviet Russia, in 1917, generated additional hostility toward American socialists. When some socialists broke away to form an American communist party identified with the Russian Revolution, further hostility was directed toward them in particular.

By the 1920s several small Marxist parties existed in the nation. Each was antagonistic toward the others and none had a sizeable membership. The typical American, who had no contact with these relatively few Marxists, tended to lump them together as alien in ideology and subversive in intentions. There resulted a certain amount of public hysteria toward the Marxists, fanned by the writings of conservative publications and the speeches of politicians, apprehensive businessmen, and superpatriots. The frenzy reached a peak in 1919 and 1920 when the Department of Justice arrested thousands of persons, many of whom were not active politically, on suspicion of being revolutionaries. Despite the nationwide scope of the raids, only a few weapons were found and only a few hundred persons were discovered to be in violation of any law, usually immigration law. These were deported. The fact that the raids were directed by Attorney General A. Mitchell Palmer, a leading Progressive, suggests how reformist energies had been diverted to other purposes.

Perhaps the most celebrated episode revealing the pitch of hostility toward radicals was the case of Nicola Sacco and Bartolomeo Vanzetti. The two Italian immigrants, a shoemaker and a fish peddler, were philosophical anarchists, although there was no evidence that either was involved in an anarchist conspiracy of any kind. The two were convicted of the murder of a payroll guard in a robbery in Massachusetts in 1920 and were finally executed in 1927. The evidence against the men lacked strength, and prejudice against them by the presiding judge and others at their trial was so plain that the Sacco-Vanzetti case became the rallying point for a generation of liberals and others concerned with the preservation of civil liberties.

The involvement of radicals, some of them foreign born, as organizers in the great strike of 1919 of steel workers contributed to the workers' loss of the strike. The steel companies played heavily and successfully on the theme that radicals were trying to socialize the American economy. The loss of this strike was the first sign of a drastic decline in union strength during the 1920s. Membership in the constituent unions of the American Federation of Labor fell from about four million in 1920 to less than two million in 1930. Unemployment also weakened the attractiveness of unions by creating competition for available jobs. Industrial unemployment was higher than two million at times during the decade, largely because of technological changes that reduced industry's need for labor. But increased productivity did benefit those who held the jobs; their purchasing power rose during the decade.

The temper of Americans toward foreigners, who seemed to the wary to be contributing more problems than solutions to society, can be best illustrated by the reduction of immigration to a trickle of a mere 100,000 or so persons per year; see Reading 204 for that story.

II

Decline in Fundamentalist Religion

Another change in American attitudes had been gaining strength for some time, but it gained public attention dramatically in the 1920s. This was the gradual shift among Christians from a dogmatic, literal interpretation of the Bible toward a more liberal and flexible attitude concerning the meanings of these sacred writings. Catholics, who had always looked to the Church as the interpreter of religious doctrine, and who were aware that from time to time the Church changed its ideas about doctrine, were less affected. But many Protestant denominations split apart over questions of whether the Bible was the sole authority for human conduct and whether its words (in the King James translation of 1611) should be taken literally.

Americans of the 1970s, many of whom have had little experience with the heat of such controversies, can find no better example of it than the Scopes trial of 1926. There the forces of fundamentalism and modernism met head on in the prosecution of a young biology teacher in Dayton, Tennessee, who had violated a state law which prohibited teaching that man—as Darwin had proposed—was descended from animal ancestors rather than from an Adam and Eve created by a divine power. The trial attracted immense publicity, partly because both sides saw the dramatic possibilities of the case and partly because prominent Americans appeared as lawyers on opposite sides. William Jennings Bryan, three times a Presidential nominee, aided the prosecution, while Clarence Darrow, an agnostic who was perhaps the leading trial lawyer of the day, helped the defense. John T. Scopes' conviction by a jury was eventually reversed on a technicality by a higher court, but historians have usually viewed the episode as a victory for the modernists because of the way in which Darrow ruthlessly picked apart the logic of Bryan's defense of literalism.

In some ways the Scopes trial also symbolized the conflict between country and city, between defense of the old and the aggressiveness of change, which permeated the United States as it changed from predominantly rural to predominantly urban. In 1920 49 per cent of Americans still lived in the country and 51 per cent were living in cities and towns. By 1930 the balance had dropped to 44 per cent rural and 56 per cent urban.

The Older Generation Looks at the Jazz Age (1925)

The technological changes which occurred between 1910 and 1920 were paralleled by dramatic changes in American social values. Nineteenth-century values were under constant attack; the younger generation seemed to have different ideas about society in general, but especially about money and sex. The way the older generation, those over forty, looked at what was happening to their America is clearly revealed in the following editorial from *The Etude*, a magazine devoted to articles about classical music.

From "Is Jazz the Pilot of Disaster?" *The Etude*, XLII (1925), pp. 5-6.

I

The Danger in Jazz

The sociological significance of music at this time, when regarded from certain aspects, is horrific. The kind of music employed most by the general body of mankind must have a powerful influence upon our whole welfare. We have gone through an orgy of Jazz, a saturnalian musical revel such as the world has never known. *The Etude* has given extensive and we hope, entirely fair, consideration of the problem. The vote of our readers upon this subject is presented later in this editorial.* We conducted this discussion because we recognized in Jazz a general kind of danger in some ways too big to measure with words. We realize all the delight of sprightly, inspiriting rhythms, of fresh tone colors, introduced by Jazz instruments. On the other hand, we know that on thousands of dance floors all over America tonight, any one who cares to investigate will witness in public dances of the most wanton character, dances that would have been suppressed in a low burlesque show only a few years ago. These things are inspired by Jazz and maintained by

*Seventy-five percent of *The Etude* readers "emphatically opposed" jazz—Eds.

Jazz. Remove the music and they could not exist. Yet the whole land from coast to coast is still in the throes of this form of musical epilepsy. If you doubt this, "listen in" on the radio any night.

Tap America anywhere in the air and nine times out of ten Jazz will burst forth. A great deal of this may, of course, be a background of entirely innocent fun. It may bring great and enlivening stimulation to hard workers who need just that thing. On the other hand, we know that in its sinister aspects, Jazz is doing a vast amount of harm to young minds and bodies not yet developed to resist evil temptations. This is no mere editorial bias. Fortune has cast us into deep life channels and we have come to regard these problems in their relation to the cosmic scheme of things. We know that good music, allied with good morals and ethics, has an edifying and purifying value to the state, particularly when inculcated in the minds of children by some such plan as "The Golden Hour," which we have promoted persistently for many years.

It is a source of great and deep gratification to witness *Collier's Weekly* and other magazines inaugurating attempts to reach this goal. It is now being widely recognized as the most serious of our national aims. What our children are to-day, that will be the America of to-morrow. Nurse them solely upon the inebriated rhythms of Jazz and what may we expect for our future?

II

The Sources of Evil

How seriously this problem is regarded by scientists may be seen in the following statement made to the New York *Times* by the eminent Professor of Neuropathology at the New York Post Graduate Hospital, Dr. M. P. Schlapp, who is also the Chairman of the Medical Board of the New York Children's Courts—a court which is constantly confronted by thousands of cases resulting in part from the condition we have described. Dr. Schlapp says:

We are headed for a smash in this country, if we keep on the way we are going. There is a curve in the emotional stability of every people which is an index of their growth and power as a nation. On the upswing the nation expands and prospers and gains in power with the normal development of emotional life. Then comes a time when emotional instability sets in. When it reaches a certain point there is a collapse. We have almost reached that point. This emotional instability causes crime, feeble-mindedness, insanity. Criminal conduct is a pathological matter, just as are these other disorders.

Our emotional instability is the product of immigration, automobiles, jazz and the movies. Foreigners who have come to America have left a peaceful, orderly life without any particular emotional shock and have been plunged into a nervous maelstrom. A mere uprooting of their former lives is enough to cause considerable emotional disturbance, but this is heightened by the enormous increase in the nervous stimulation and shock of American life. It is bad enough for Americans, but far worse for those who have not grown used to it. The tremendous growth of pleasure automobiles and moving pictures in this country compared with others and the phenomenal sweep of Jazz across the country have drained off far more nervous vitality from our people than from those of other countries without putting anything in the way of energy into the reservoir of our national strength.

Perhaps this is the explanation of America's enormous crime rate at present. Perhaps this reveals why our murder rate is twice that of Italy and seven times that of England. What will it be in 1935 unless it is stopped now at the source, in childhood?

The City, the Elite, and Liquor (1923)

Perhaps the greatest social controversy of the 1920s was the issue of prohibition. For years some Americans had opposed the sale and use of alcoholic beverages, but only in the twentieth century did the movement gain nationwide power. Many social reformers active in the Progressive Era came to regard prohibition as a key measure to solve such urban problems as political corruption, poverty, and crime. In 1917 Congress banned the manufacture of intoxicating beverages to conserve grain for war use. In 1920 national prohibition was written into the Constitution through the adoption of the Eighteenth Amendment. Congress then passed the Volstead Act to enforce that amendment. But the desire for "booze" was so widespread during the 1920s that the effect was to encourage the rise of organized crime. From the beginning there was a strong movement to repeal

Keeping America dry during the era of prohibition proved a difficult, frustrating task. Cartoonist Rollin Kirby emphasizes the difficulty by showing a fleet of ships, loaded with liquor, anchored just outside the territorial waters of the United States, waiting for bootleggers to smuggle the "hooch" into a thirsty America.

the Eighteenth Amendment. Northern Democrats, led by Alfred E. Smith, governor of New York, actively supported repeal, while many Republicans felt the same way. In 1932 both the Democratic platform and the party's candidate, Franklin D. Roosevelt, called for repeal, and the Twenty-first Amendment in 1933 ended what was called the "noble experiment" of prohibition. The following article was written by a supporter of prohibition when hopes for its success were still high.

From Robert A. Woods, "Notes About Prohibition from the Background," American Academy of Political and Social Science *Annals*, CIX (September 1923), pp. 121, 123, 126, 127. Subheadings added by the editors.

I

Liquor and the True American

One of the many reasons why prohibition has seemed to me a clearly indicated cause for a settlement worker is that it strikes right up and down the strata of society. The specific evil at which it is directed is no respecter of persons. Essential indifference to it, and to all the political, economic and moral damage associated with it, has been widespread among rich and poor, educated and ignorant. It would be hard to find a more truly social evil than alcoholism. National prohibition is looked upon by disinterested foreign observers as by far the most broadly and profoundly social experiment that the world has yet seen....

It is clear enough that prohibition in a remarkably short time has achieved a very high level of success, except in a few great city centers, chiefly in the northeastern section of the country. In other words, its failure thus far, speaking broadly, lies with two elements of our population: the immigrants established in congested city colonies, and a fraction of the elite, to whom the use of alcoholic drinks has become not so much an inveterate habit as the sign and symbol of a luxurious "kultur."

Over against these stands the great representative and typical body of the American people, who already to so large an extent regard this question as closed. It is not to be conceived of that they will change their intention on account of the attitude of these two exceptional and unrepresentative groups; and it will be far worse for them to be set off in outlaw communities than to become the subjects of detailed federal coercion.

The two recalcitrant groups curiously represent the transplanted European political theories of the 18th century. The mass of the American people are combining the tradition of the Puritan commonwealth with that of modern social science. And let it be remembered that among them are a vast preponderance of the men of vision and power. To give a single instance, when the list of 1,000 signers was being made up for the petition to Congress in favor of national prohibition, so many economists from our colleges and universities sent in their names that only a fraction of them could be included without spoiling the representative character of the list....

II

The Saloon

An almost ironical aspect of the situation is that we are all of the anti-saloon contingent now. There is not even one advocate of beer and "light" wine that can tolerate the thought of the saloon's return. Remembering sadly how impossible it was before prohibition to secure among any of these advocates the slightest interest in reducing the abominations of the saloon, I cannot take very seriously their present attitude. How beer could come back and not bring the saloon is something that an impartial student of the subject can with difficulty conceive. It was carefully explained to me as a license commissioner that the saloon was a necessity. Beer, being perishable, must be kept on ice. The poor man cannot have a refrigerator. There must be the local depot where he can get it fresh for immediate consumption. The saloon was in fact one of the essential organs of democracy.

Moreover, experience showed that the beer saloon, pure and simple, was not sufficient. The five-cent drink did not pay. Whisky, the ten-cent drink, was necessary, even from the brewer's point of view if he was to collect his interest on the saloon keeper's license. Moreover, the working-man who wanted his beer, and that only, was largely a myth. The secretary of the Brewer's Association informed me that the beer saloon—which I was officially seeking to encourage—was impossible because practically everybody that went to a saloon wanted both beer and whisky. These bits of testimony are submitted in the face of the advocates of a modification of the Volstead law.

These advocates urge that we should have beer and wine sold to men and women in cafés, after the so-called "harmless" European model. Here again licensing board experience may shed light. Under the old order in Boston the majority of such places were hardly more nor less than licensed market places for prostitution. The sale of liquor was largely incidental. And, be it noted, only the lighter alcoholic drinks were current. These were not places in which young men and women got drunk. They had only such measure of alcohol as would blur the better sensibilities and spur the worse. Beer and light wine would amply suffice to bring back these open abominations in our cities. It had become increasingly common to have dancing in such places. Beer and wine would bring back this ominous combination....

An American citizen who should have said that his Government was not equal to achieving the vast untried tasks involved in entering the European war would have been considered almost in the light of a traitor. There is far less doubt that the Government will in due time, to all intents and purposes, solve the problem of prohibition enforcement.

Let us be quite specific. The federal Government will ere long solve the problem of patrolling the coasts so as very largely to prevent smuggling from the sea. All approaches from Canada can be and will be effectively guarded. The manufacture and distribution of liquor on any considerable scale can within a few years be reduced to a minimum, and in the meantime supplies held over from pre-prohibition days will be exhausted. The retail purchaser as well as the retail seller of liquor will more surely be brought within the reach of the law. The bootlegger, more and more recognized by public sentiment as the dispenser of poisoned drinks, will receive less consideration on the part of juries. Judges will more and more give jail sentences and cumulative ones. The premises used for illicit business will be closed under injunction for considerable periods. Extreme victims will pass off the scene; new ones will begin less and less to take their places—"Hooch" will not serve as the subject of bravado and endless conversation.

Reading 238

The American people are not going to be beaten in this matter. It is, above all, exceedingly unsafe for more or less powerful elements in our great cities to put those cities in an attitude of defiance to the will of the nation as a whole. Along with a strong reaction against the economic domination of the great centers, there is a rising feeling, particularly with regard to New York, that it is disseminating throughout the country a corrupting influence through many of its books, magazines, theatrical shows, moving pictures, which will not be continuously endured. To intimate to the solid, characteristically American majority of the nation, that its repudiation of alcoholic drinks must be qualified to suit a few of the large cities, and particularly in order to meet the desire of the luxurious society of those cities, is a suggestion so intolerable and so likely to bring a destructive recoil that one is amazed at the hardihood of those who offer it.

The Ku Klux Klan Interpreted (1925)

Closely allied with fear of foreigners was the rise of an organization: the Ku Klux Klan. Founded in 1915 and named after the famous secret organization of the Reconstruction Era, the KKK expanded rapidly after World War I. By the early 1920s it possessed political power not only in the South but also in the Midwest and in parts of the West as well.

Clothing itself in secrecy, preaching hatred, and practicing violence, the Klan persecuted anything that it labeled "un-American." By 1925 the organization had nearly five million members. Within a year, however, the KKK began to fall apart when some of its leaders became involved in scandals involving both women and money. The following account of an investigation of the Klan in Marion County, Ohio, home of the late President Harding, appeared when the Klan was at the height of its influence.

From Frank Bohn, "The Ku Klux Klan Interpreted," *American Journal of Sociology*, XXX, No. 4 (January 1925), pp. 385–386, 386–389. Reprinted by permission of the University of Chicago Press.

Since its organization in 1915, the Klan has probably initiated a total of between four millions and five millions of members. Much of this membership is no doubt ephemeral. Yet each soldier in this enormous army has pledged his loyalty by a most solemn oath and paid sixteen dollars for his membership card and regalia. One does not take the price of sixteen bushels of wheat away from a Missouri farmer without having produced a state of considerable excitement in the ordinarily placid and inquiring mind of that citizen. Stories about the Klan are no longer front-page news for the eastern metropolitan press. But there are several states in the Middle West and Far West where the Klan decided the presidential vote. . . .

At dinner in a small village in Marion County [Ohio], the Methodist preacher's wife held forth in tones and terms which left no doubt as to either her point of view or her conclusions. This particular preacher's wife was herself a "local preacher." That is, she was licensed to preach but not to perform the more technical duties of the regular office in the presence of her husband and hierarchical chief.

"I'll tell you what they are doing," she went on, "they're driving all the negroes into the Catholic church; and the negroes are just naturally Methodists, too. Of course we cannot take them into our congregations; but now that we are uniting again, North and South, we shall probably have a separate church just for the negroes themselves. But I shouldn't be surprised now if some of them were actually to turn Jewish. At M_____ during the last election, the Jews united with the Catholics against the Klan. It's terrible, and what is to be done? Nothing? Why, one of them told me right here in this house, sitting before our own fire that he would fight before he would let his daughter marry a negro. What nonsense! He said he would resist rule by the negroes and foreigners even if the Constitution cracked and crumbled. Oh! You should have seen his face when he said it! I waked up that night and shivered when I remembered it. But when I got my chance I had my say, you may believe that; and he hasn't been to church since."

The next day the writer left his car on the paved highway and walked up the lonely, muddy lane that led to the home of the local organizer and leader of the Klan. In appearance this cottage was a bit more humble than the average. About it lay the sixty acres that formed the farmer's patrimony. The door opened upon a decent but extremely simple interior. The farmer was in his working clothes. A cold rain beat against the windows and we sat close to a little stove in the center

The Klan of the 1920s grew strong in the South and Midwest, but also appeared elsewhere. Here a group calling itself the Women of the Ku Klux Klan makes its first public appearance on Long Island, New York.

of the livingroom. Darkness came on but no light was struck. The day and the darkness exaggerated the somber character of both the man's face and his voice. He spoke in a monotone, his lips alone moving perceptibly. His chair was tipped far back and both his hands were sunk deep into his pockets. There was no smile, no change of facial expression, during the hour of conversation. Here was a perfect representative of the Anglo-Saxon Puritan farmer in America. This face and this voice had not altered fundamentally during the three hundred years since Charles I ascended the throne of England and undertook the task of remolding the one and silencing the other. Least of all could this man be considered secretive concerning his present state of mind. He was willing, even anxious, to tell everything he knew about the Klan, excepting only the secret parts of its ritual.

The country, he said, was in the greatest danger. We were ruled by Catholics and Jews. The Jews controlled the moving-picture houses. The Catholics dominated at least 80 percent of the great newspapers. The movies were all worthless and immoral. The Jews were now upon every country cross-road taking in the money. They want nothing but money. All he wished our people to do was to let them alone. "They leave us alone, except for getting our money. The Jew knows what sort of moving pictures will pay best—those which appeal to the worst side of human nature. What happens to the army of young girls who are lost every year! From 60,000 to 75,000 of them disappear annually and are never heard of again. Why, a young girl is no longer safe on our country roads! They are picked up by men in automobiles. The Jews get them and sell them as white slaves. They have a regular price list and the business is carried on from New York to San Francisco."

He went on to say that we must take the strongest measures to protect our public schools. There are districts where the Jews would not even permit a Christmas celebration in the public schools. But the greatest danger to our school system was the Catholic influence. The Catholics and Jews together were, in his opinion, a much greater danger to the world than the Germans had ever been. He repeatedly returned to his belief that the country was in a state of terrible and unprecedented danger. It was within the "shadow of destruction." Whenever a Catholic world-war veteran died and the local post of the American Legion conducted the funeral, we were enabled to witness a strange sight at the door of the Catholic church. At that point the flag was always pulled from the coffin. The Legionaires durst not bear the flag into the church. How could the Knights of Columbus loyally support the Constitution of the United States when they had previously sworn allegiance to the Pope? "To them the Pope is Christ."

As there were no negroes at all in his vicinity, and but a few of them in Marion City, the county seat, one would hardly expect to find the race issue uppermost in the mind of this man. Yet his views on this matter were most pronounced. He accepted and stressed the Klan's position on every point. It was his belief that "when a mixture of the races occurred Providence intervenes." The children of mixed parentage, after a number of generations, were born sterile. He had no definite notion as to what might be done regarding the negroes beyond preventing them with relentless firmness from intermarrying with the whites.

In replying to the question as to what action was required in the presence of such dangers as he described, his answer emphasized the necessity of the solidarity of the native white majority at the ballot box. "There are less than 20,000,000 Catholics in America and about 3,000,000 Jews. If our 100 percent Americans are properly organized we can speedily control the country politically." Again and again he returned to his main contention—it was the sole purpose of the Klan to serve and save the country. The principles and purposes of the Klan, he was assured, contained no element inconsistent with sound patriotism, genuine Christianity, or the most spotless personal honor. His mind seemed to be obsessed by the fear that the Klan might have come too late, that the Nation might be already lost. Just before the conversation ended he let fall a sentence more significant than any other which the hour had brought forth. "We want the country ruled," he said, "by the sort of people who originally settled it; this is *our* country and we alone are responsible for its future."

Politics and Social Values in the 1928 Election

In 1928 Herbert Hoover, Secretary of Commerce in the administrations of Harding and Coolidge, won the Republican Presidential nomination easily. Hoover had a wide reputation as a humanitarian for his work in organizing relief in Europe during World War I, and as an apostle of efficiency in business. With the prosperity of the times as the chief plank in his party's platform, the chances are that no Democrat could have beaten him. Hoover faced Alfred E. "Al" Smith, four times Democratic governor of New York, who was also known as a humanitarian for his progressive legislation and who was also an economic conservative. But Hoover was a Protestant and Smith, of Irish descent, the first Catholic to be nominated for President. In the election Hoover won easily, carrying seven states in a South that had been solidly Democratic since Reconstruction, but which also was overwhelmingly Protestant. Smith, however, turned his party toward control of the nation's industrial centers by capturing the twelve largest cities, all of which had substantial numbers of recent immigrants, mostly Catholics, and all of which had given the Republican Coolidge a majority in 1924. The following article, which appeared in a leading Catholic journal, looked ahead to the election and to what seemed to the author to be a central issue.

From Charles Willis Thompson, "The Unseen Factors in Politics," *The Commonweal*, VIII (May 30, 1928), pp. 95–96. Subheadings and bracketed material added by the editors.

I

Herbert Hoover: Engineer in Politics

There is a real basis for the Republican feeling against Hoover and the Democratic feeling against Smith, and it must grind the souls of the anti-Hooverites to see their inability to convey that basis intelligibly to the public. The basis is in the nature of Hoover himself. There are many men of importance in the Republican party who feel intensely that Hoover is mentally and temperamentally unfitted to be President, but the moment they attempted to put that feeling in words they would seem to be giving voice only to childish, vindictive, splenetic prejudice. They also feel that he is unfitted to be a candidate, and that his revelation of his temperamental inadequacy will bring disaster on the party before the campaign is half over. But there is no way of getting such a feeling before the critical eyes of other men; indeed, it is pretty hard to formulate it effectively even for the purposes of soliloquy.

Hoover's supporters dwell on his superb efficiency as an administrator. His opponents are at a disadvantage in being unable to say convincingly that he would be an inefficient President. There is an intangible but real difference between being an administrator and being a President. The President ought to be a good administrator if possible, but it is essential that he should be a good handler of men. Andrew Johnson was a successful Governor of Tennessee, first in peace and then in war, because he was a good administrator, but he was not a successful President because—partly—he was not a good judge of how to handle men. . . .

II

Al Smith: City Boy Makes Good

As for Smith, the men and women who are busily marshaling impressive facts to convince the minds of his opponents are doing a necessary work, but they will never touch the principal obstacle in Smith's way, because it never becomes palpable. There are plenty who sincerely believe that a Tammany President would install vice and graft in the federal government; there are plenty who believe that a wet President would be able to change in some degree the way prohibition is "enforced" at present; there are plenty who believe that a Catholic President would take orders from the Pope about how to conduct his office. To address argument to these individuals, to present them with facts, is necessary, of course. But when all these prejudices have been argued down—supposing that they ever could be—the most serious objection to Smith would, as Walt Whitman says, "stand yet untouched, untold, altogether unreached."

It lies in the fact that to millions of Americans he not only represents, but embodies, something alien. Not something alien in race or religion, but something alien to themselves, something alien in character and outlook, something they do not understand and which they feel does not understand them and never can. Some of the perturbed Methodist clergymen in the South opposed to Smith's nomination unconsciously revealed what really moves them most profoundly, whether they themselves know it or not, when they said he was "New York minded." The phrase does not represent a mere senseless jealousy of one city; it illustrates a feeling that there are two characters growing up in this country, each of which, to the other, is foreign.

It is not only the first time the West and South have been confronted with the prospect of a President who is wet, Catholic and a member of Tammany Hall; it is the first time they have had to face a possible President who, they think, does not understand them, and whose environment and habits of thought they do not understand. Their feeling is something like what it would be if Mustapha Kemal of Turkey were, by some impossible constitutional change, to become eligible to the Presidency of the United States and to become suddenly a likely occupant of the White House.

Nor is it to be derided. There certainly is a division in aims and problems and in structural character between the great overgrown cities and the more homogeneous communities beyond them. It really is to be one of the matters the twentieth century will have to consider and deal with when it grows out of youth into middle age. There is, of course, an answer to it in this case; it is that, as small-town Presidents like McKinley and backwoods Presidents like Lincoln have been statesmanlike enough to care intelligently for the rights of the great cities, so a President from a great city might be statesmanlike enough to be the President of the whole people and not the President of Oliver Street, New York. But, though New Yorkers are certain that he would be—since as Governor he looked as carefully after the interests of Tonawanda and Lockport as for those of the East Side—the people outside New York do not know it except by hearsay, and even of hearsay they do not get as much on this subject as they do of hearsay about his religion and his opinion of Volsteadism [Prohibition].

It is the first time "the farmers," as we rather ignorantly call them, have been confronted with this dismaying situation. Roosevelt came from New York City, but the Westerners regarded him as Teddy the ranchman. [Chester] Arthur came from New York City, but in his time the split between city and country had barely begun; though even then the suspicion of the West toward the "dude President" had a considerable influence in taking votes away from him at the convention of 1884. But Smith is the terrifying metropolis incarnate.

The reporters note, without noting its significance, the comment in the South about his brown derby and his East Side speech. Why should an Oliver Street accent be any more of an argument against him than Coolidge's Yankee twang or Lincoln's Kentucky drawl? If New York can stand it to hear a Southerner pronounce the word you "yo" and "you-all," why cannot the South stand it when Smith pronounces it "yuh"? (as he does). The answer is that Smith's speech and clothes illustrate, to them, the approaching yoke for their necks of the alien cities.

The Making of a Hero (1927)

The Twenties had a tone somewhat different from the years of Progressivism and the crusade for democracy during World War I. Americans seemed generally in a mood to enjoy material prosperity, to regard bootleggers who helped the thirsty to flout prohibition as entrepreneurs not so different from those who were becoming wealthy in Wall Street, and to leave Europeans alone with their endless and hopeless squabbles. What then was the meaning of the almost hysterical acclaim Americans gave to a young aviator, Charles A. Lindbergh, who became the first man to fly the Atlantic Ocean alone? An answer was suggested by a contemporary magazine.

From *The Outlook*, Vol. 46, No. 5 (June 1, 1927), pp. 139–140. Copyright © 1927 by The Outlook Company. Subheadings added by the editors.

I

The Best of America

Charles Lindbergh, twenty-five years old, American, climbed out of his airplane on Le Bourget flying field near Paris. A score of men lifted him and let him down to the ground. A multitude, numbering thousands, encircled him.

"Well," he said, "I did it."

Did what?

He had no idea of what he had done.

He thought he had simply flown alone from New York to Paris. What he had really done was something far greater. He had fired the imagination of mankind, he had evoked all that was best in men's hearts and minds, he had erased rancor and suspicion and had lighted a flame of good will, he had started a clean breeze around the world, he had somehow imparted to his fellow-men, without respect of race or nation, a new vigor.

What this young air-mail pilot has accomplished no one could have foreseen.

He, least of all, anticipated the effect of his flight. He started out with a razor, a toothbrush, a passport, and six letters of introduction in his pocket. Apparently he thought that when he arrived he would need to clean up, have a shave, and then start out to make some acquaintances in a land of strangers. Those things that he carried in his pocket were symbols of his achievement. This fellow, who has been received in France with honors usually reserved for a ruling monarch or president, who has received an acclaim from the world like that enjoyed by few men in history, has won his greatest triumph just because he never once thought of it.

If there had been any element of braggadocio, of false pretense, of self-seeking, of vanity, in Charles Lindbergh he couldn't have done what he did. He might have flown to Paris and won the $25,000 of the Orteig prize for the first flight to that city from New York; but he could never have stirred the world into admiration. "We could have gone a thousand miles more," he said, "or—at least five hundred." "What do you mean by 'we'?" he was asked. "Well, you know," he answered, "the ship was with me." He has been nicknamed "Lucky." He deprecates the term. Luck, he declares, is not enough. Does he mention daring? or skill? or intelligence? No. It is his plane, and engine, and instruments.

Charles Lindbergh is the heir of all that we like to think is best in America. He is of the stuff out of which have been made the pioneers that opened up the wilderness, first on the Atlantic coast, and then in our great West. His are the qualities which we, as a people, must nourish. They are certainly the qualities that win, throughout the world, instant recognition and praise.

Sharing by right in the glory that is Charles Lindbergh's is his mother. She traveled from her home in Detroit to New York to bid him

"Lucky Lindy," Charles A. Lindbergh, stands beside the plane he flew from New York to Paris in May 1927. It was a characteristic pose, emphasizing his boyish mastery of the machine which he used to further his, and his nation's, destiny.

good-bye. Then, before he started, she went back to her work as an instructor in the Cass Technical High School.

She is the widow of Charles August Lindbergh, who was a Representative in Congress for ten years, was in turn a Republican, Progressive, and Farmer-Laborite, and when he died the Farmer-Labor candidate for Governor of Minnesota. It is undoubtedly to her training as well as to his Swedish and Irish inheritance that the son owes the development of those qualities which have brought him to this extraordinary triumph. She has received deserved congratulations and great honor. She has accepted them only by proxy. "The glory belongs to him," she has said, "but the boy belongs to me—and America." Evidently she has always wanted her boy to be himself. She has described his education and has made it clear that throughout her purpose had been to make it possible for him to develop and train himself. One of the councilmen of the city of Detroit has commented upon Mrs. Lindbergh's training of her son in these words: "Because we love our children we are inclined to repress them. Mrs. Lindbergh was wise enough to allow her son to shape his own destiny." . . .

II

The Flight

The flight that ended at Le Bourget began almost unheralded.

It had been known that a young air-mail pilot had entered as a competitor for the prize of $25,000 which had been offered by Raymond Orteig, a New York hotel man of French nativity. Others were preparing for the transatlantic flight. The Bellanca plane was tuning up on Long Island and was the chief

THE GROWING AIRLINE NETWORK

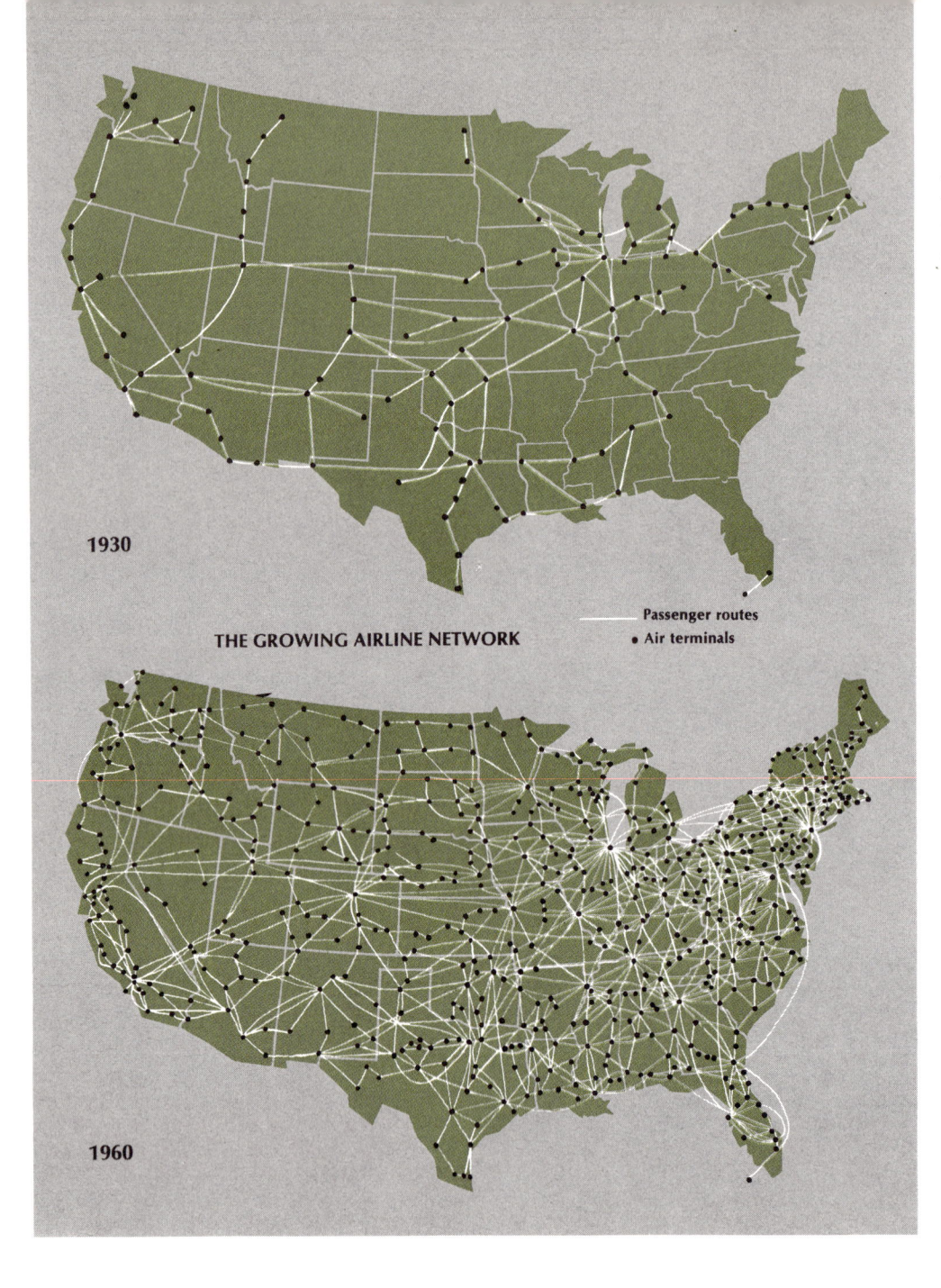

1930

1960

— Passenger routes
• Air terminals

center of interest. Almost without warning, young Lindbergh came from San Diego, California. He stopped only once on his transcontinental flight. That was at St. Louis. He had scarcely arrived in New York before he seemed ready to start again eastward. Then, early one morning, he was up, went out to his plane, and as soon as his fuel tank was filled started on his transatlantic flight.

In his cramped cockpit he faced his fuel tank and instrument board. All that he could see ahead was through a periscope. On each side of him was a window. Down below him was an opening through which he could look to learn of what is known as the drift of his machine. He had no navigator with him. He said he preferred to save the weight. Perhaps also he preferred to save possibilities of a difference of opinion on the way. At any rate, he took an inductor compass. This is an instrument, American made, which sets up an electrical field that holds an indicator in constant relationship with the magnetic lines of force on the earth. Thanks to this instrument, Lindbergh arrived over Ireland within three miles of his objective. On the way he encountered a sleet storm that threatened to cover the wings of his plane with ice and drag him down; but his skill and courage enabled him to fly out of trouble. He swept from ten feet above the water to ten thousand feet, seeking a level where the sleet was not. At last he saw the Seine, then the lights of Paris, then the flying field, and then the shouting, overwhelming multitude.

Now he wears the decoration of the Legion of Honor and is threatened with a medal from Congress. He apparently can have any job he wants from vaudeville up or down. But he says he wants to get back to the air-mail service—if they will take him.

The Younger Generation Looks at the Jazz Age (1927)

In 1926 and 1927 Vanity Fair, one of the most popular magazines of the era, published a series of articles by Elizabeth Benson, a gifted thirteen-year-old girl who was a student at Barnard College. Although the editor of Vanity Fair was a bit suspicious at first, he soon became convinced that Miss Benson had indeed written the articles, which had some enlightening things to say about youth in the 1920s.

From Elizabeth Benson, "The 'Outrageous' Younger Set," *Vanity Fair*, XXIX (1927), pp. 68, 105. Copyright © 1927, 1955 by the Condé Nast Publications, Inc. Subheadings added by the editors.

I

The Mood of Youth

There are a few understanding souls among the older generation who have pointed out, with kindly tolerance, that every younger generation has been the sorrow of its elders: that every new crop of youngsters is wild, rampageous; indecorous and rebellious at restraint. They are also generous enough to point out that it is only through the lusty protest of youngsters against the existing order of things, that social, spiritual, mechanical, industrial or political progress is recorded.

But even these tolerant defenders of the young have shaken their heads a little over us, admitting deprecatingly that we are a little bit more of a handful than the other previous crops of youthful rebels.

Many of our defenders have sought anxiously for causes of the present revolt of youth against law, society and parental authority. They have sent out ponderous questionnaires to college students, which we have answered with our tongues in our cheeks, taking an impish delight in confounding our questioners. For the truth is that we haven't particularly wanted to be understood and explained away; it has been too much fun, all this rumpus that we've been kicking up.

But we do, as a matter of fact, understand ourselves pretty well. We "psyche" ourselves with most amazing frankness. We don't mind telling *each other* just what we really are—but we hate to tell our elders. We are intensely aware of the forces which produced us, and we gloat in that awareness. It makes us feel so much wiser than our elders who can only shake their heads so helplessly and call upon heaven to witness that we are a terrible lot.

The younger American generation of which I am writing will go down to history as our post-war generation. In this article I am going to attempt to explain ourselves—the young people of today, children, let us say, of 15 to 19; to point out the forces which brought us (for I am certainly one of them, though still only 13) into being; to tell our critics what we are like, what we think of ourselves, and what forces, we believe, brought us into being....

"Oh, now we are going to have the WAR thrown at us," you say wearily. "We were expecting it!" Yes, you are going to have the WAR used as an explanation of us, the younger generation, and of *you*, too, who blamed us on the war. But I am not going to recite all the old arguments of middle-aged novelists who have been erudite enough to point out that cocktail drinking and sex freedom and wild parties were a means of forgetting and escaping the strain of the war. Those arguments are so well known, so fresh in the reader's mind, that I will make no mention of them all.

II

The Roots of Revolt

But it was not the war alone which was responsible for the wave of freedom upon which the younger generation of today is riding high, and for which it is so universally condemned. It had a much more respectable genesis than war hysteria. It was mothered by a brood of reformers such as good old, ridiculous old, crusading old Carrie Nation.* That doughty female has passed into the limbo of history, to be unearthed only as a subject of humorous analysis in the ideal-destroying pages of *The American Mercury*, and so, too, is poor Emmeline Pankhurst† now little more than a memory to be smiled at, but the forces which they and their brood helped to bring into being have been largely instrumental in moulding the character of the wild young sex radicals of today.

The Nineteenth Amendment [enfranchising women] was passed while the present younger generation was just entering adolescence. The shout of "Equality of the Sexes" mingled in our alert young ears with the rattle of broken windows and the clanging of axes upon election booths. We cut our second teeth on "Women's Rights," "The double

---

*A turn-of-the-century prohibition advocate who specialized in entering a saloon and dramatically smashing beer kegs and bottles with an axe—Eds.
†One of the leaders of the British women's rights movement—Eds.

Never was the "generation gap" so great as in the 1920s. While this "flapper" broods over Freud and his popularizers, her parents, finding little in their own Victorian, small town culture to aid them in understanding their child, are undoubtedly at a loss as to what to do. This *Life* was a humor magazine, unrelated to today's photo-essay magazine.

versus the single standard of morality," and "Birth control." Margaret Sanger* was one of our first memories. "Sex," which had been a word to whisper and blush at, was flung at us on banners carried by our crusading mothers. The wrappings were removed from the piano legs in Victorian homes and such unmentionable words as "male" and "female" mingled with "personal freedom," "sex equality," and "prohibition" in arguments between our parents around the dinner table. We didn't wholly shut our ears. . . .

And there was, of course, no restraining our joy when the delightful pastime of psychoanalysis was presented to our eager young minds. We did not invent psychoanalysis, and we can scarcely be blamed for having profited by it. We studied Freud, argued Jung, checked our dreams by Havelock Ellis, and toyed lightly with Adler.† And all these authorities warned us of the danger in repressing our normal instincts and desires. Most of us have felt very virtuous in making up our minds not to invite mental and physical ill-health by suppressing our natural tendencies, but (to

---
*Margaret Sanger was a leader of the birth control movement and an outspoken advocate of sex education—Eds.
†Sigmund Freud, Carl Jung, and Alfred Adler were leading psychoanalysts. Havelock Ellis did much to popularize psychoanalysis—Eds.

give away a secret of the sacred and honorable order of the younger generation) most of us talk big—and step pretty carefully....

We, the younger generation of today, are the children of crusaders. Our parents were always in a terrific stew over something. If it wasn't "women's rights" it was the war; if it wasn't war, it was prohibition; if it wasn't prohibition, it was a crusade against fundamentalism in religion.

The crusade for prohibition was such a worthy one! How nobly our parents fought and bled for it! And we have come along to bear the brunt of it. It is scarcely necessary to point out that the younger generation does not gaze with uplifted, adoring eyes upon the spectacle of its elders taxing themselves billions of dollars for a prohibition law which does not prohibit. We can have little respect for a law which its own makers, the older generation, show no respect for. If the older generation had only made its laws with honesty and common sense, we would not have grown up to be rebels against the law....

III

Freedom from Fundamentalism

Then those crusading parents of ours started something else which we, their children, are left to finish—and be blamed for. I refer to the crusade against fundamentalism in religion. Our parents decided that there was no hell of brimstone and forked-tailed devils, no method of frying erring souls on red-hot coals. Fine! Our elders were too set in their ways to get much good out of that happy discovery, but we, of the plastic age, have not been slow to seize upon the freedom of action which comes to people when fear of eternal damnation is removed. They can't scare us any more by telling us that we will burn in hell forever and ever, amen, if we aren't good little girls and boys, and at home and bed by ten o'clock.

So we have learned to prefer an automobile trip to the country to being bored and antagonized by the Elmer Gantrys* of our churches, or even to listening to our more enlightened preachers, I feel safe in saying that the automobile has done more to reduce the number of church-going persons of all ages than any other single factor. But it was not the younger generation which invented the automobile. That, too, we inherited from the older generation. The automobile differentiates the youth of this generation from its parents' youth by

*The Reverend Elmer Gantry was the chief character in the novel of that name by Sinclair Lewis—Eds.

many centuries, by the difference between the beast of burden age and the machine age.

Don't forget that we are not the only people living our own lives. Our parents are also having a fairly good time. They are living too much the same sort of lives as we are to cast the first stone. Hence it is left to the professional noise-makers, in the older generation, to grow alarmed about us—teachers, preachers, editorial writers....

Nature, and war, and prohibition, and feminism, and psychoanalysis, and new fashions in dress; a tottering religion, imitation of our elders, automobiles, radios and free money, the industrial era, indulgent parents, and a new physical education—these forces have had their hand in baking the pie out of which, like the four and twenty blackbirds, has sprung the younger generation of today.

It may not be a dainty dish to set before a king, or upon the altar of civilization; but the waiter has certainly set it there, and there it sits.

So, we feel justified in calling upon all those who have denounced and reviled us, and bidding them look upon us, not as individuals who have chosen their destiny, but as the inevitable products of that destiny. If we are not what we should be, we are not wholly to blame and, so far as we can see, there is very little that can be done about us.

TOPIC 49

BLACKS AND WHITES IN THE TWENTIES

Of the social changes that Americans confronted in the Twenties one of the most significant, although seldom perceived as such, was a gradual alteration in the nature of black-white relations.

Some change occurred in the South, but insofar as it affected the relative positions of the races it was slight, consisting mainly of a continuing growth in literacy of the black population as a whole and the continuing development of a black middle class in urban areas. From the outside, and from the point of view of anyone who looked for substantial changes in the generally depressed condition of American blacks, the situation in the South resembled that of the 1890s more than it differed from it.

It was in the North, and to some extent the West, that more dramatic changes appeared. There newly arrived masses of black people, in flight from the poverty and oppression of the South, hoped to find greater economic opportunity and freer expression in urban centers. As the following readings suggest, the results were both encouraging and disappointing.

Reading 242

The Struggle for Equality and Identity

The federal government abandoned its efforts to protect the civil rights of Southern blacks, and Northern whites almost universally agreed to let the (white) South solve its own problems. The years from the 1890s to the 1910s were discouraging ones for American blacks. Not until the 1910s, moreover, did black leaders agree on the best ways to carry on their struggle. From 1905 to 1909 the dogged W. E. B. Du Bois, dissatisfied with what he felt was an over-conciliatory attitude on the part of the leading black spokesman, Booker T. Washington, led a small but influential radical group known as the Niagara Movement which desired more direct action in support of black civil rights. As will be seen, the Niagara group merged with the new National Association for the Advancement of Colored People in 1910. Not until after the death of Washington in 1915 was a measure of harmony restored among black leaders, essentially on the basis of the NAACP's program. The following article summarizes subsequent important developments for American blacks from 1910 to 1930.

From David A. Shannon, *Twentieth Century America*, 2nd ed., © 1963, 1969 by Rand McNally & Company, pp. 94–95, 278–280, 281. Subheadings added by the editors.

I

New Organizations

In the summer of 1908, a race riot broke out in Springfield, Illinois, ironically within a few blocks of the home of the Great Emancipator. William English Walling, a wealthy, white, left-wing intellectual then living in New York, was in Chicago at the time and went down to Springfield to investigate the situation. Alarmed at the prospect of the racial tensions of the South growing into other parts of the nation, he wrote two magazine articles in which he described the Negro's situation and called for a revival of the old abolitionist spirit. Walling and two other white reformers, Mary White Ovington and Henry Moskowitz, a New York physician, called a series of informal meetings to discuss what should be done. In time, the Walling discussion group linked up with the Niagara movement, and in 1910 they founded together the National Association for the Advancement of Colored People to try to do with white help what the Niagara group had been unable to do alone. At first, the NAACP was a predominantly white organization. Du Bois, its salaried Director of Publicity and Research, was its only Negro officer. He also edited *The Crisis,* the NAACP magazine, which soon became popular among Negroes. Within a few years, however, Negroes had assumed most of the responsible positions in the organization which became interracial at the top level but almost altogether Negro in its mass following. In time, the NAACP was to grow to be the most effective voice of the Negro's aspirations. It did not begin with a wholesale campaign to win the Negro his full constitutional rights; it picked the objectives it thought could be won and fought militantly to achieve them.

Another interracial group that grew to prominence was the National Urban League, founded in 1911, which merged three smaller organizations concerned with social work and wider economic opportunity for Negroes. Its first president was an eminent Columbia University economics professor, F. R. A. Seligman. It came into being to help in the adjustment of Negroes when they moved to northern cities, as they began to do in a small way before 1917. By 1910, the Negro population of New York had grown to over 90,000, Philadelphia's to 84,000 and Chicago's to 44,000. As Negroes increasingly moved to northern and southern cities during and after the war, the Urban League expanded. . . .

Black homes in the rural South, Thomasville, Georgia. Blacks, who had been searching for a better life in the South since the Civil War, began leaving streets like this in large numbers early in the twentieth century, seeking a better life in the cities of the North.

II

The Negro, South and North

The most important development among American Negroes during the war and the 1920's was a huge migration out of the South. In the long run, this migration had tremendous implications. First, it enabled the Negro to receive a better formal education than he would have had in the South, and educated Negroes could give their race better leadership. Second, by moving where he could vote, the Negro in time gained political leverage in national politics that he could use to improve his position. Had there not been the big migrations of the war and postwar eras, surely the subsequent history of the Negro would have been vastly different.

Migration to the North began to become significant in 1915. It grew during the war and increased still more in the 1920's. In 1910, only about 850,000 Negroes lived outside the South; in 1920, the figure was about 1,400,000; in 1930, it was about 2,300,000. The percentage of nonsouthern Negroes to the total increased from slightly less than 10 percent in 1910 to 20 percent in 1930. Various pulls from the North and pushes from the South got the migration under way and kept it going. Prosperity created jobs in the North, although for the most part Negroes got the worst jobs available. Fewer European immigrants provided Negroes the chance to get employment that had formerly gone to "greenhorns." In the South a combination of circumstances made the Negro want to leave more than before and made it possible for him to do so. The boll weevil made cotton farming more precarious than usual, and white men increasingly moved into occupations that had traditionally been reserved for Negroes. More

A black veteran returns home (left), March 1919. Everyone is all smiles, but the summer of 1919 saw race riots in several cities in the Northern and border states and an increase in the lynching of blacks throughout the South.

widespread elementary Negro education in the South sharpened Negro aspirations and gave him the literacy necessary for most urban employment. Prosperity created jobs in southern cities as well as northern ones, and thousands of Negroes moved from their rural homes to the nearest city where they got the cash necessary to go north. Most of the northward migration was from city to city, and most of it was to the nearest northern city. Thus Negroes in the southeastern states tended to go to Washington, Baltimore, Philadelphia, and New York, and those in the central South tended to move to cities of the Midwest. Negro migration to the West Coast had not yet become significant.

The war itself wrenched thousands of Negroes from their homes and their old ways of living. Roughly four hundred thousand Negroes served in the armed forces during World War I, and about half of them served overseas. Once moved from behind a one-mule plow and shown something of the outside world (including the racial equality of France) the young Negro was not likely to return to his old life. In fact, many Negro soldiers stayed in France. Far more moved to northern cities.

The immediate disruption of traditional patterns in the South during the war and the appearance of large numbers of Negroes in the North brought an appalling outbreak of violence. In the South most interracial violence was lynching; in the North most of it was rioting. Lynching was usually rural and small-town; rioting was usually urban. Perhaps the main reason why practically all of the rioting was in the North was that only there did the Negro feel secure enough to fight back. Yet there was one serious riot at Houston, Texas, in 1917, which ended in the deaths of thirteen Negro soldiers. Another soldier riot was narrowly averted at Spartanburg, South Carolina. Negro lynchings increased from thirty-four in 1917 to sixty in

1918 and to seventy in 1919. Several of the victims were soldiers or veterans, some of them in uniform. Simultaneously in the South, the Ku Klux Klan revived and terrorized Negroes, sometimes only frightening them but often beating them.

So many riots occurred in the North in the summer of 1919—more than a score—that Negro publications referred to it as the Red Summer. The worst of the riots began in Chicago in late July when a fight began between some young Negroes and young whites at a Lake Michigan beach. The violence went on for almost two weeks before the National Guard and the police restored order. . . . When it was at last over, 15 whites had been killed and 178 injured and 23 Negroes had been killed and 342 injured. In the nation's capital a mob of white soldiers, having saved the world for democracy, roamed Negro neighborhoods to destroy property and beat up those who resisted.

Lynching and rioting were almost altogether a lower-class phenomenon. Both white and colored leaders deplored violence, and following the 1919 violence, they formed interracial commissions in both the North and the South in an effort to prevent further outbreaks. The National Association for the Advancement of Colored People undertook a campaign for the enactment of a federal law against lynching, violators of the law to be tried in federal courts. When lynchers were arrested at all, and they seldom were, their trials in state and local courts were farces. In 1921, in the face of strong public opinion, the House passed an antilynching law, but southern Senators filibustered it to death. Their stated reason for opposition was that a federal law on the subject would be an invasion of state rights.

III

The Garvey Movement

It was against this background of strife and bloodshed that millions of Negroes enlisted in the only Negro nationalist movement that had ever amounted to anything in the United States. The leader was Marcus Garvey, a remarkable Negro from Jamaica who saw himself as the Moses of his people. In 1914, Garvey founded the Universal Negro Improvement Association, but when he moved to Harlem two years later his group and idea struck little response. He went to Europe until 1918, and when he returned his organization caught on and spread quickly. It was at its height in 1920 and 1921, although it did not die out until the mid-1920's. He claimed to have six million followers; four million was a better estimate. . . .

The movement died out rather quickly, probably because it became apparent that the difficulties facing the Empire of Africa were insurmountable. The Department of Justice prosecuted him for using the mails to defraud in selling stock in the Black Star Line. Garvey foolishly conducted his own case at the trial. After a long series of legalistic holding actions, he went to prison in 1925 for a two-year term. Upon his release he was deported back to Jamaica. The Universal Negro Improvement Association collapsed. Garvey himself faded into obscurity and died in London in 1940, forgotten and broke.

Negro history for the rest of the war-to-depression period offered nothing as spectacular as the immediate postwar violence and the Garvey movement. A few Negro leaders moved into left-wing politics during the decade. A. Philip Randolph, who was later to become an outstanding and effective leader of his people, published a left-wing magazine and joined the Socialist party which was extremely weak in the 1920's. The Communists began to make a determined effort for Negro support in the late 1920's, but they met with little success. Perhaps the strongest reason for Communist failure among Negroes was the Negro's suspicion that he was being used. Nor did the Communist program of "self-determination for the Negro people in the Black Belt" make much sense to American Negroes. An attempt to transplant Joseph Stalin's theory, but not his practice, on the various nationalities in the Soviet Union, "self-determination" meant to establish an autonomous black republic in the most densely Negro-populated area of the South. This involved a kind of supersegregation, and Negroes came to call the plan "Red Crow."

Two Negro intellectual movements attracted considerable attention among American Caucasians. The "new Negro movement" among Harlem intellectuals, which produced the so-called Negro Renaissance, became a special fad among some white intellectuals. . . . White interest in the movement created a market for Negro talents, and several writers and entertainers were thereby able to work at their special crafts and make a living at it. The other movement, while not so well publicized, was more lasting. In 1915, Dr. Carter G. Woodson, a Negro historian, brought about the founding of the Association for the Study of Negro Life and History. He became editor of its chief publication, *The Journal of Negro History,* a learned quarterly. The *Journal* undoubtedly stimulated research and writing in the field. In 1926, the Association began to push an annual Negro History Week. At first the Association endeavored to reach only Negro school children during this

Reading 243

special week, and it provided teachers in dominantly Negro schools with material and lesson plans. Later, the Association enjoyed considerable success in getting special study units taught in all schools and gained the cooperation of newspapers and magazines. As a result of the Association's work, American Negroes are far better acquainted with their history than other minority groups are with their pasts.

A Black Youth in the South during the 1920s

By the 1920s a whole series of laws existed in the Southern states specifically designed to keep black Americans separate and inferior. The Jim Crow system, as exclusion or segregation by law came to be called, to some extent simply made explicit what many Americans, and most Southerners, had been customarily practicing for many years. But the very explicitness of these laws, which in effect decreed everything from separate and inferior schools to separate and inferior drinking fountains, encouraged those elements in American society whose goal was to deprive black Americans of both their rights and their self-respect. The Jim Crow South is described in great detail by the novelist Richard Wright (1909-1963) in his autobiography, *Black Boy*. Note both the physical and psychological pressures blacks felt as they lived by the code of the white South.

Excerpts from pp. 157-160, 195, 198-201, 221-223 of *Black Boy*, by Richard Wright. Copyright, 1937, 1942, 1944, 1945 by Richard Wright. Reprinted by permission of Harper & Row, Publishers, Inc. Subheadings added by the editors.

I

On Being Black

My life now depended upon my finding work, and I was so anxious that I accepted the first offer, a job as a porter in a clothing store selling cheap goods to Negroes on credit. The shop was always crowded with black men and women pawing over cheap suits and dresses. And they paid whatever price the white man asked. The boss, his son, and the clerk treated the Negroes with open contempt, pushing, kicking, or slapping them. No matter how often I witnessed it, I could not get used to it. How can they accept it? I asked myself. I kept on edge, trying to stifle my feelings and never quite succeeding, a prey to guilt and fear because I felt that the boss suspected that I resented what I saw.

One morning, while I was polishing brass out front, the boss and his son drove up in their car. A frightened black woman sat between them. They got out and half dragged and half kicked the woman into the store. White people passed and looked on without expression. A white policeman watched from the corner, twirling his night stick; but he made no move. I watched out of the corner of my eyes, but I never slackened the strokes of my chamois upon the brass. After a moment or two I heard shrill screams coming from the rear room of the store; later the woman stumbled out, bleeding, crying, holding her stomach, her clothing torn. When she reached the sidewalk, the policeman met her, grabbed her, accused her of being drunk, called a patrol wagon and carted her away.

When I went to the rear of the store, the boss and his son were washing their hands at the sink. They looked at me and laughed uneasily. The floor was bloody, strewn with wisps of hair and clothing. My face must have reflected my shock, for the boss slapped me reassuringly on the back.

"Boy, that's what we do to niggers when they don't pay their bills," he said.

His son looked at me and grinned.

"Here, hava cigarette," he said.

Not knowing what to do, I took it. He lit his and held the match for me. This was a gesture of kindness, indicating that, even if they had beaten the black woman, they would not beat me if I knew enough to keep my mouth shut.

"Yes, sir," I said.

After they had gone, I sat on the edge of a packing box and stared at the bloody floor until the cigarette went out.

The store owned a bicycle which I used in delivering purchases. One day, while returning from the suburbs, my bicycle tire was punctured. I walked along the hot, dusty road, sweating and leading the bicycle by the handle bars.

A car slowed at my side.

"What's the matter there, boy?" a white man called.

I told him that my bicycle was broken and that I was walking back to town.

"That's too bad," he said. "Hop on the running board."

He stopped the car. I clutched hard at my bicycle with one hand and clung to the side of the car with the other.

"All set?"

"Yes, sir."

The car started. It was full of young white men. They were drinking. I watched the flask pass from mouth to mouth.

"Wanna drink, boy?" one asked.

The memory of my six-year-old drinking came back and filled me with caution. But I laughed, the wind whipping my face.

"Oh, no!" I said.

The words were barely out of my mouth before I felt something hard and cold smash me between the eyes. It was an empty whisky bottle. I saw stars, and fell backwards from the speeding car into the dust of the road, my feet becoming entangled in the steel spokes of the bicycle. The car stopped and the white men piled out and stood over me.

"Nigger, ain't you learned no better sense'n that yet?" asked the man who hit me. "Ain't you learned to say *sir* to a white man yet?"

Dazed, I pulled to my feet. My elbows and legs were bleeding. Fists doubled, the white man advanced, kicking the bicycle out of the way.

"Aw, leave the bastard alone. He's got enough," said one.

They stood looking at me. I rubbed my shins, trying to stop the flow of blood. No doubt they felt a sort of contemptuous pity, for one asked:

"You wanna ride to town now, nigger? You reckon you know enough to ride now?"

"I wanna walk," I said simply.

Maybe I sounded funny. They laughed.

"Well, walk, you black sonofabitch!"

Before they got back into their car, they comforted me with:

"Nigger, you sure ought to be glad it was us you talked to that way. You're a lucky bastard, 'cause if you'd said that to some other white man, you might've been a dead nigger now."

I was learning rapidly how to watch white people, to observe their every move, every fleeting expression, how to interpret what was said and what left unsaid.

Late one Saturday night I made some deliveries in a white neighborhood. I was pedaling my bicycle back to the store as fast as I could when a police car, swerving toward me, jammed me into the curbing.

"Get down, nigger, and put up your hands!" they ordered.

I did. They climbed out of the car, guns drawn, faces set, and advanced slowly.

"Keep still!" they ordered.

I reached my hands higher. They searched my pockets and packages. They seemed dissatisfied when they could find nothing incriminating. Finally, one of them said:

"Boy, tell your boss not to send you out in white neighborhoods at this time of night."

"Yes, sir," I said.

I rode off, feeling that they might shoot at me, feeling that the pavement might disappear. It was like living in a dream, the reality of which might change at any moment.

Each day in the store I watched the brutality with growing hate, yet trying to keep my feelings from registering in my face. When the boss looked at me I would avoid his eyes. Finally the boss's son cornered me one morning.

"Say, nigger, look here," he began.

"Yes, sir."

"What's on your mind?"

"Nothing, sir," I said, trying to look amazed, trying to fool him.

"Why don't you laugh and talk like the other niggers?" he asked.

"Well, sir, there's nothing much to say or smile about," I said, smiling.

His face was hard, baffled; I knew that I had not convinced him.

He whirled from me and went to the front of the store; he came back a moment later, his face red. He tossed a few green bills at me.

"I don't like your looks, nigger. Now, get!" he snapped.

I picked up the money and did not count it. I grabbed my hat and left. . . .

II

Black Anger

While wandering aimlessly about the streets of Memphis, gaping at the tall buildings and the crowds, killing time, eating bags of popcorn, I was struck by an odd and sudden idea. If I had attempted to work for an optical company in Jackson and had failed, why should I not try to work for an optical company in Memphis? Memphis was not a small town like Jackson; it was urban and I felt that no one would hold the trivial trouble I had had in Jackson against me.

I looked for the address of a company in a directory and walked boldly into the building, rode up in the elevator with a fat, round, yellow Negro of about five feet in height. At the fifth floor I stepped into an office. A white man rose to meet me.

"Pull off your hat," he said.

"Oh, yes, sir," I said, jerking off my hat.

"What do you want?"

"I was wondering if you needed a boy," I said. "I worked for an optical company for a short while in Jackson."

"Why did you leave?" he asked.

"I had a little trouble there," I said honestly.

"Did you steal something?"

"No, sir," I said. "A white boy there didn't

want me to learn the optical trade and ran me off the job."

"Come and sit down."

I sat and recounted the story from beginning to end.

"I'll write Mr. Crane," he said. "But you won't get a chance to learn the optical trade here. That's not our policy."

I told him that I understood and accepted his policy. . . .

The most colorful of the Negro boys on the job was Shorty, the round, yellow, fat elevator operator. He had tiny, beady eyes that looked out between rolls of flesh with a hard but humorous stare. He had the complexion of a Chinese, a short forehead, and three chins. Psychologically he was the most amazing specimen of the southern Negro I had ever met. Hardheaded, sensible, a reader of magazines and books, he was proud of his race and indignant about its wrongs. But in the presence of whites he would play the role of a clown of the most debased and degraded type.

One day he needed twenty-five cents to buy his lunch.

"Just watch me get a quarter from the first white man I see," he told me as I stood in the elevator that morning.

A white man who worked in the building stepped into the elevator and waited to be lifted to his floor. Shorty sang in a low mumble, smiling, rolling his eyes, looking at the white man roguishly.

"I'm hungry, Mister White Man. I need a quarter for lunch."

The white man ignored him. Shorty, his hands on the controls of the elevator, sang again:

"I ain't gonna move this damned old elevator till I get a quarter, Mister White Man."

"The hell with you, Shorty," the white man said, ignoring him and chewing on his black cigar.

"I'm hungry, Mister White Man. I'm dying for a quarter," Shorty sang, drooling, drawling, humming his words.

"If you don't take me to my floor, you will die," the white man said, smiling a little for the first time.

"But this black sonofabitch sure needs a quarter," Shorty sang, grimacing, clowning, ignoring the white man's threat.

"Come on, you black bastard, I got to work," the white man said, intrigued by the element of sadism involved, enjoying it.

"It'll cost you twenty-five cents, Mister White Man; just a quarter, just two bits," Shorty moaned.

There was silence. Shorty threw the lever and the elevator went up and stopped about five feet shy of the floor upon which the white man worked.

"Can't go no more, Mister White Man, unless I get my quarter," he said in a tone that sounded like crying.

"What would you do for a quarter?" the white man asked, still gazing off.

"I'll do anything for a quarter," Shorty sang.

"What, for example?" the white man asked.

Shorty giggled, swung around, bent over, and poked out his broad, fleshy ass.

"You can kick me for a quarter," he sang, looking impishly at the white man out of the corners of his eyes.

The white man laughed softly, jingled some coins in his pocket, took out one and thumped it to the floor. Shorty stooped to pick it up and the white man bared his teeth and swung his foot into Shorty's rump with all the strength of his body. Shorty let out a howling laugh that echoed up and down the elevator shaft.

"Now, open this door, you goddamn black sonofabitch," the white man said, smiling with tight lips.

"Yeeeess, siiiiir," Shorty sang; but first he picked up the quarter and put it into his mouth, "This monkey's got the peanuts," he chortled.

He opened the door and the white man stepped out and looked back at Shorty as he went toward his office.

"You're all right, Shorty, you sonofabitch," he said.

"I know it!" Shorty screamed, then let his voice trail off in a gale of wild laughter.

I witnessed this scene or its variant at least a score of times and I felt no anger or hatred, only disgust and loathing. Once I asked him:

"How in God's name can you do that?"

"I needed a quarter and I got it," he said soberly, proudly.

"But a quarter can't pay you for what he did to you," I said.

"Listen, nigger," he said to me, "my ass is tough and quarters is scarce."

I never discussed the subject with him after that.

Other Negroes worked in the building: an old man whom we called Edison; his son, John; and a night janitor who answered to the name of Dave. At noon, when I was not running errands, I would join the rest of the Negroes in a little room at the front of the building, overlooking the street. Here, in this underworld pocket of the building, we munched our lunches and discussed the ways of white folks toward Negroes. When two or more of us were talking, it was impossible for this subject not to come up. Each of us hated and feared the whites, yet had a white man put in a sudden appearance we would have assumed silent, obedient smiles.

To our minds the white folks formed a kind of superworld: what was said by them during working hours was rehashed and weighed here; how they looked; what they wore; what moods they were in; who had outdistanced whom in business; who was replacing whom on the job; who was getting fired and who was getting hired. But never once did we openly say that we occupied none but subordinate positions in the building. Our talk was restricted to the petty relations which formed the core of life for us.

But under all our talk floated a latent sense of violence; the whites had drawn a line over which we dared not step and we accepted that line because our bread was at stake. But within our boundaries we, too, drew a line that included our right to bread regardless of the indignities or degradations involved in getting it. If a white man had sought to keep us from obtaining a job, or enjoying the rights of citizenship, we would have bowed silently to his power. But if he had sought to deprive us of a dime, blood might have been spilt. Hence, our daily lives were so bound up with trivial objectives that to capitulate when challenged was tantamount to surrendering the right to life itself. Our anger was like the anger of children, passing quickly from one petty grievance to another, from the memory of one slight wrong to another. . . .

III

What about the Future?

I could calculate my chances for life in the South as a Negro fairly clearly now.

I could fight the southern whites by organizing with other Negroes, as my grandfather had done. But I knew that I could never win that way; there were many whites and there were but few blacks. They were strong and we were weak. Outright black rebellion could never win. If I fought openly I would die and I did not want to die. News of lynchings were frequent.

I could submit and live the life of a genial slave, but that was impossible. All my life had shaped me to live by my own feelings and thoughts. I could make up to Bess and marry her and inherit the house. But that, too, would be the life of a slave; if I did that, I would crush to death something within me, and I would hate myself as much as I knew the whites already hated those who had submitted. Neither could I ever willingly present myself to be kicked, as Shorty had done. I would rather have died than do that.

I could drain off my restlessness by fighting with Shorty and Harrison. I had seen many Negroes solve the problem of being black by transferring their hatred of themselves to others with a black skin and fighting them. I would have to be cold to do that, and I was not cold and I could never be.

I could, of course, forget what I had read, thrust the whites out of my mind, forget them; and find release from anxiety and longing in sex and alcohol. But the memory of how my father had conducted himself made that course repugnant. If I did not want others to violate my life, how could I voluntarily violate it myself?

I had no hope whatever of being a professional man. Not only had I been so conditioned that I did not desire it, but the fulfillment of such an ambition was beyond my capabilities. Well-to-do Negroes lived in a world that was almost as alien to me as the world inhabited by whites.

What, then, was there? I held my life in my mind, in my consciousness each day, feeling at times that I would stumble and drop it, spill it forever. My reading had created a vast sense of distance between me and the world in which I lived and tried to make a living, and that sense of distance was increasing each day. My days and nights were one long, quiet, continuously contained dream of terror, tension, and anxiety. I wondered how long I could bear it.

The accidental visit of Aunt Maggie to Memphis formed a practical basis for my planning to go north. Aunt Maggie's husband, the "uncle" who had fled from Arkansas in the dead of night, had deserted her; and now she was casting about for a living. My mother, Aunt Maggie, my brother, and I held long conferences, speculating on the prospects of jobs and the cost of apartments in Chicago. And every time we conferred, we defeated ourselves. It was impossible for all four of us to go at once; we did not have enough money.

Finally sheer wish and hope prevailed over common sense and facts. We discovered that if we waited until we were prepared to go, we would never leave, we would never amass enough money to see us through. We would have to gamble. We finally decided that Aunt Maggie and I would go first, even though it was winter, and prepare a place for my mother and brother. Why wait until next week or next month? If we were going, why not go at once?

The New Emancipation: The Migration North

Richard Wright was only one of hundreds of thousands of Southern blacks who fled North between 1910 and 1930 in hopes of escaping poverty and degradation. The following account described the situation in 1916, when the northward movement was beginning to be massive, partially in response to the closing off of European immigration during World War I. Note the responses of Northern whites and Southern whites to the migration.

From *The Crisis*, XIII (1916), pp. 22, 23, 89. Subheadings added by the editors.

I

The Negro Moves North

The Negro migration from the South to the North has assumed large proportions. Definite figures are difficult to get. An estimate from Atlanta, Ga., states that at least 118,000 colored men have come North since April 1.

The Enfield Hosiery Mills Company, at Enfield, N.C., is teaching colored girls to operate in the mills. A modern mill is being erected at Rocky Mount, N.C., in which colored help only will be employed.

The Tremont Silk Mills have opened a branch factory in Harlem, in New York City, and employment has been given to 40 colored girls between the ages of 14 and 18 years. If this investment proves successful, it is planned to open other mills.

Eighty colored stevedores were used to unload the cargo from the German submarine, *Deutschland*.

The Strouse, Adler Company is fitting up a corset factory in New Haven, Conn., and will employ 100 colored girls.

As soon as 100 colored girls can be secured for employment, a factory will be opened for them in Detroit, Mich., by one of the largest wholesale drygoods and garment making concerns in that city. Clerical positions, as well as operative, will be open to colored people. A restaurant and gymnasium will be connected with the building. Operatives will average $10.00 a week.

All the slave catching machinery of the South is being put into motion to stop migration. Negroes are being arrested wholesale. Two hundred were taken from the Union Station, Savannah, Ga., and put in jail. Immigrant agents have been arrested and exorbitant license fees charged. To cap the climax, the Department of Labor has sent two colored men nosing about for evidence to keep Negroes in peonage.

Southern colored speakers, who depend upon the good will of the white South, are urging Negroes not to migrate. Richard Carroll, of South Carolina, is one. Colored people in New York will be surprised to learn from Dr. Moton, of Tuskegee, that New York Negroes find "it very difficult even now to find places to stay; they are huddled together in quarters like pigs, and many of them cannot find any place, and there is bound to be suffering this winter.

"They will take colds and develop pneumonia and consumption as well as other diseases, and either will die there or be brought home in a dying condition."

Many strikes are taking place because of this movement of labor. A number of white bricklayers in Philadelphia, Pa., struck last week because a colored bricklayer was employed. The contractor immediately paid them off and employed colored help entirely. Colored men have been employed as strike breakers among the longshoremen in the northwest. Negro workers on street cars in Panama struck, and other workmen threatened. At Marshall, Tex., 600 Negro helpers struck at the shops of the Texas and Pacific Railway. Their demands were granted and they went back to work. At Omaha, Neb., the white Musicians' Union threatened to strike if a colored band was employed in the Hughes parade. They changed their minds, however, and the Negro band marched amid great applause. At New Britain, Conn., white workers struck at the depot because 50 colored men were employed as freight handlers. . . .

II

The South's Reaction: From the Macon, Georgia *Telegraph*

"Police officers, county or city, all over the State, all over the South, should be bending every effort to apprehend and jail the labor agents now operating everywhere about us to take the best of our Negroes North to fill the rapidly widening labor breach there. This invasion of the South for Negroes isn't just a temporary raiding of our labor market, but is part of a well-thought-out and skillfully executed plan to rifle the entire South of its well-behaved, able-bodied Negro labor. Unskilled labor is at a high premium in the United States just now, a premium that will increase rather than be withdrawn. . . .

"There are those who say they'll come back quickly enough. But that isn't true. Ellis Island will not clear labor into this country again for at least one full generation, possibly two. . . .

"We must have the Negro in the South. The black man is fitted by nature, by centuries of living in it to work contentedly, effectively and healthily during the long summers of semi-tropical and tropical countries. He has been with us so long that our whole industrial, commercial and agricultural structure has been built on a black foundation. It is the only labor we have; it is the best we possibly could have—if we lose it, we go bankrupt!

"Everybody seems to be asleep about what is going on right under our noses. That is, everybody but those farmers who have wakened up of mornings recently to find every male Negro over 21 on his place gone—to Cleveland, to Pittsburgh, to Chicago, to Indianapolis. Better jobs, better treatment, higher pay—the bait held out is being swallowed by thousands of them all about us. And while our very solvency is being sucked out from underneath we go about our affairs as usual: our police officers raid poolrooms for 'loafing Negroes,' bring in twelve, keep them in the barracks all night and next morning find that ten of them have steady, regular jobs, were there merely to spend an hour in the only indoor recreation they have; our county officers hear of a disturbance at a Negro resort and bring in fifty-odd men, women and boys and girls to spend the night in the jail, to make bond at ten percent, to hire lawyers, to mortgage half of two months' wages to get back on their jobs Monday morning—although but a bare half dozen could have been guilty of the disorderly conduct. It was the week following that several Macon employers found good Negroes, men trained to their work, secure and respected in their jobs, valuable assets to their white employers, suddenly left and gone to Cleveland, 'where they don't arrest fifty niggers for what three of 'em done.' Many of these men who left haven't been replaced except with those it will take years to train to do their work as well as they did it—but at as high a cost from the start.

"It is the most pressing thing before this State today. Matters of governorships and judgeships are only bagatelle compared to the real importance of this Negro exodus going on from Georgia. There is a little lull now with winter coming on, but the spring will see it set in its full volume unless something is done at once to stop it."

A Northern Ghetto—Chicago

Richard Wright, like many others from Mississippi, Louisiana, and Alabama, headed for Chicago when he decided to go North. As in New York, Philadelphia, and Cleveland, Chicago's black population expanded rapidly: from 44,000 in 1910 to 109,000 in 1920 to 234,000 in 1930. The implications of this expansion are examined by Allan Spear in his study of Chicago's "black belt," the South Side. Note the racial attitudes prevalent just before the 1919 riot.

From Allan Spear, Black Chicago: The Making of a Negro Ghetto, 1890–1920 (Chicago, 1967), pp. 20–23, 214–217, 221–222. Copyright © 1967 by the University of Chicago. Subheadings added and footnotes omitted by the editors.

I

Development of the Ghetto

The increasing physical separation of Chicago's Negroes was but one reflection of a growing pattern of segregation and discrimination in early twentieth-century Chicago. As the Negro community grew and opportunities for interracial conflict increased, so a pattern of discrimination and segregation became ever more pervasive. And perhaps the most critical aspect of interracial conflict came as the result of Negro attempts to secure adequate housing. . . .

Negro expansion did not always mean conflict, nor did it mean that a neighborhood would shortly become exclusively black. In 1910, not more than a dozen blocks on the South Side were entirely Negro, and in many mixed areas Negroes and whites lived together harmoniously. But as Negroes became more numerous east of State and south of Fifty-first, friction increased and white hostility grew. When a Negro family moved into a previously all-white neighborhood, the neighbors frequently protested, tried to buy the property, and then, if unsuccessful, resorted to violence to drive out the interlopers.

In many cases, the residents organized to urge real estate agents and property owners to sell and rent to whites only. The whites often succeeded in keeping Negroes out, at least temporarily. When their efforts failed, they gradually moved out, leaving the neighborhood predominantly, although rarely exclusively, Negro.

Such incidents occurred with only minor variations throughout the prewar period. In 1900 three Negro families brought about "a nervous prostration epidemic" on Vernon Avenue. Five years later, an attempt to oust Negroes from a Forrestville Avenue building landed in court. In 1911, a committee of Champlain Avenue residents dealt with a Negro family in the neighborhood by the "judicious use of a wagon load of bricks"; the *Record-Herald* described the affair as "something as nearly approaching the operations of the Ku Klux Klan as Chicago has seen in many years." Englewood residents, two years later, did not have to go quite so far; the objectionable party, this time a white man with a Negro wife, agreed to sell his property to a hastily organized "neighborhood improvement association." A Negro who moved into a home on Forrestville Avenue in 1915, on the other hand, termed an offer of this type "blackmail," but after several days of intimidation, he too submitted and sold his property.

Perhaps the most serious incident, and the one which provides the most insight into the nature of the housing conflict, occurred in Hyde Park—Chicago's most persistent racial trouble spot—in 1909. A separate town until 1892, Hyde Park was still an area of pleasant, tree-shaded streets, large, comfortable homes, and a vigorous cultural life centered on the campus of the new but thriving University of Chicago. Negroes were no strangers to the community: for many years a few families, mostly house servants and hotel employees who worked in the neighborhood, had clustered on Lake Avenue near Fifty-fifth Street, on the eastern edge of Hyde Park. Now this community began to expand and Negroes occupied homes in nearby white blocks.

White Hyde Parkers responded to the Negro "invasion" with a concerted drive to keep Negroes out of white areas. The Hyde Park Improvement Protective Club was organized in the autumn of 1908; headed by a prominent attorney, Francis Harper, it soon boasted 350 members, "including some of the wealthiest dwellers on the South Side." In the summer of 1909, the Club issued a manifesto: Negro residents of Hyde Park must confine themselves to the "so-called Districts," real estate agents must refuse to sell property in white blocks to Negroes, and landlords must hire only white janitors. To implement this policy, the Club appointed a committee to purchase property owned by Negroes in white blocks and to offer bonuses to Negro renters who would surrender their leases. Moreover, the Club threatened to blacklist any real estate firm that defied its edict. "The districts which are now white," said Harper, "must remain white. There will be no compromise."

Despite the efforts of the Negro residents of Hyde Park to counter the activities with indignation meetings and boycotts, the white campaign continued. The neighborhood newspaper supported the Improvement Club, and Harper maintained that he had "received hosts of letters commending the course of the organization." When the Club was unable to persuade a Negro family to move voluntarily, the neighbors used more direct tactics: vandals broke into a Negro home on Greenwood Avenue one night and broke all the windows; the family left the next day. In September, the Club announced a boycott of merchants who sold goods to Negroes living in white neighborhoods. It urged separate playgrounds and tennis courts for Negroes in Washington Park, and, in its annual report, advocated segregation of the public schools. "It is only a question of time," a Club spokesman predicted, "when there will be separate schools for Negroes throughout Illinois." The group operated more quietly after 1909, but it had achieved its major goal. The little Negro community on Lake Avenue dwindled in size and the rest of Hyde Park remained white for forty years.

The Hyde Park episode well illustrates the intensification of anti-Negro feeling in the early twentieth century. This feeling could even create strong sentiment among whites for a return to formalized segregation—separate schools and recreation facilities. Some white Chicagoans spoke of the necessity for a residential segregation ordinance. The incident also provided an early example of techniques that were to become increasingly important as whites continually tried to stem the tide of Negro residential "invasion"; the neighborhood improvement association, the community newspaper, the boycott, and in the last resort, violence. Furthermore, the episode was significant because it occurred in a middle- and upper-class community, and its victims were middle- and upper-class Negroes attempting to find comfortable homes among people of their own economic status. The housing problem for Negroes was not restricted to the poor; even the affluent were blocked in their quest for a decent place to live. . . .

II

Race Riot

On a blisteringly hot Sunday afternoon, July 27, 1919, Eugene Williams drowned at the Twenty-ninth Street beach, touching off the calamity that had so long been feared. The rioting began on the beach when the police, ignoring Negro charges that Williams had been stoned by whites, refused to make any arrests. The Negro crowd attacked several white men, and impassioned accounts of a general racial war quickly flashed through the South Side. After dark, the white gangs west of Wentworth Avenue retaliated by beating, stabbing, or shooting thirty-eight Negroes who had accidentally wandered into white districts. Two people died the first day and over fifty were injured, but the South Side was calm on Monday morning and most Chicagoans were able to view Sunday's disorders as merely the latest in the series of minor racial outbreaks that had plagued the city all year. The *Tribune* did not even give the riot a banner headline.

But by Monday night, Chicago knew that the catastrophe had come. Rioting resumed in the late afternoon as white gangs assaulted Negro workers leaving the stockyards. Mobs pulled streetcars from their wires and dragged out Negro passengers, kicking and beating them. Negro mobs retaliated, attacking whites who worked in the black belt. As the night wore on, the white rioters became bolder: they raided Negro neighborhoods, firing shots into Negro homes from automobiles. During this night of terror—the worst period of the riot—twenty people were killed and hundreds injured....

The Chicago riot was a two-sided conflict and members of both races committed acts of wanton cruelty. Nevertheless, all objective observers agreed not only that whites were responsible for the violent incidents that led to the riot, but that they were, for the most part, the aggressors during the riot itself. Negroes, to be sure, killed and maimed innocent white men who entered the black belt. But unlike the white gangs that invaded Negro neighborhoods, Negroes rarely entered white districts to commit violence. The charges that Negroes burned the houses near the stockyards were never substantiated, and several witnesses reported having seen white men with blackened faces in the district at the time of the fire. Furthermore, Negro violence generally took the form of individual attack; there were no organized Negro gangs—comparable to the white "athletic clubs"—bent on furthering racial conflict. The final casualty figures also indicated that Negroes had been more the victims than the attackers: 23 Negroes and 15 whites died; 342 Negroes and 178 whites were injured. The grand jury that investigated the riot concluded that "the colored people suffered

The Chicago race riot of 1919 left many persons dead and injured. In the first photo a mob of whites, armed with bricks, hunts a fleeing black man. The second photo shows the aftermath of the chase—a policeman examines the scene while a reporter stares at the body.

more at the hands of the white hoodlums than the white people suffered at the hands of the black hoodlums."

Yet, many whites reacted to the riot, not by reproaching the anti-Negro elements, but by urging stricter racial segregation. The *Tribune* editorialized:

> Despite the possible justice of Negro demands, the fact is that the races are not living in harmony.... Shall there be separate bathing beaches for the white and colored?... How long will it be before segregation will be the only means of preventing murders?... How long will it be before public policy and the protection of life and property makes necessary another system of transportation?

Five days later, the *Tribune* stated that "so long as this city is dominated by whites ... there will be limitations placed on the black people.... A rebellion by Negroes against facts which exist and will persist will not help." A white minister was even more explicit: "I believe in segregating the blacks for their own good as well as the good of the whites." The Kenwood and Hyde Park Property Owners' Association responded characteristically with a demand for a conference to deal with the "promiscuous scattering of Negroes throughout white residential districts of our city." When the mayor called a special meeting of the city council to investigate the causes of the riot, one alderman immediately introduced a resolution "to consider the question of segregating the races within certain established zones." Perhaps the most irrelevant response came from the Chicago Department of the U.S. Army Intelligence Office which, in a highly confidential report,

Reading 246

blamed the riot on bolsheviks and anarchists. . . .

The riot of 1919 destroyed whatever hope remained for a peacefully integrated city. The migration had reinforced the internal pressure for a self-contained Negro community by creating new demands for services and institutions in the black belt. Now the riot and the activities of the neighborhood associations strengthened the external pressure, thwarting the expansion of the black belt and forcing it to rely more exclusively on its own resources. The black belt of 1920 had clearly delineated boundaries—Twenty-second and Fifty-fifth Streets, Wentworth and Cottage Grove Avenues. While the black belt had once included racially mixed neighborhoods, it was now becoming exclusively Negro. At the same time, the neighborhoods surrounding it remained exclusively white. Within the ghetto walls, Negroes attempted to solidify their economic and civic institutions and create a meaningful and satisfactory community life apart from White Chicago. During the next decade the black belt became the "Black Metropolis." The prosperity of the 1920's made the dream of a truly self-sufficient Negro city seem close at hand. The South Side's halcyon days had arrived.

Working for a Better Future: The NAACP

When the National Association for the Advancement of Colored People was founded in 1909, it was considered a radical organization by most whites. The white liberals and black "militants" who were active in the NAACP, however, generally took the position that what they were asking for black Americans was what most other Americans already had. By 1929, when the following statement was adopted during the twentieth annual meeting of the association, such black leaders as James Weldon Johnson, Walter White, and W. E. B. Du Bois directed the NAACP. Note the nature of the NAACP's demands.

From "Message to the American People," *The Crisis*, XXVI (1929), p. 265.

The NAACP has for twenty years worked to solve the most difficult social problem that faces America. When it was founded in 1909, Negroes were being lynched at the rate of 78 a year; the Supreme Court had never passed on the 15th Amendment. Tillman and Vardaman were the chief authorities on the race problem.* Few reputable scientists dared to assert the equality of the races. We had only 1,100 Negro college students. Physicians and sociologists predicted the inevitable extinction of American Negroes, and Negroes themselves did not believe that an organization like this could exist or function.

The Negro problem is still with us after 20 years' struggle. But it is not the same problem. We still lynch and burn at the stake, but now it's 11 a year instead of 78. A series of court decisions has laid the foundation of our real citizenship as voters, householders, travellers and workers. No reputable scientist or public speaker today denies the essential equality of all races; the physical survival of the Negro is unquestioned, we have 19,253 college students and our organization including *The Crisis* has received and expended $1,567,330 since 1909.

The NAACP did not alone and unaided bring all these results, but it was the initial and moving force, and it has proven three things: that white and black Americans can work efficiently together for human uplift; that America will furnish funds to fight race prejudice when it realizes that it is not instinctive but a deliberately fashioned weapon of hurt and gain; and thirdly and chiefly, that earnest human beings can strive for a radical and even revolutionary ideal without bloodshed and without hate.

We have still a tremendous fight before us: we face today not simply a provincial and national problem of race and color, but one that belts the world and threatens its progress. We stand here in the greatest republic of the world on fatal and strategic ground: if we prove that the most diverse races can live together here in equality, democracy and self-respect, we can lead the world to Peace, Democracy in Industry and Freedom in Art. If we fail, we turn back toward War, Poverty and Slavery.

During the past year we have suffered one grievous set-back: after our long and hitherto repeatedly successful fight against segregation, the Supreme Court has recently refused a second time to pass on the legality of private compacts to establish segregated districts, notwithstanding the fact that the court has denied this right to public law-making bodies.* Against this hideous injustice, we shall find ways still to fight on.

*Benjamin Tillman and James K. Vardaman, two white Southern politicians—Eds.

*In 1917 in *Buchanan* v. *Warley*, the Supreme Court ruled illegal a law which set up separate residential areas for blacks and whites in Louisville, Ky.—Eds.

On the other hand, our fight against Negro disfranchisement proceeds successfully: last year we established by United States Supreme Court decision the illegality of state laws disfranchising Negroes in primary elections; this year we have in Virginia a Federal District Court decision against the legality of such disfranchisement by party leaders. . . .

We welcome President Hoover's decision to clean up Southern politics and to investigate law enforcement, and we only hope that common honesty and logical consistency will not stop reform short of a full exposure of the rotten borough methods of the South, the systematic and illegal disfranchisement, lynching, segregation, injustice toward Negroes in the courts, and barbarous punishment and convict lease systems.

Especially is the crying shame of denial of common school training to Negro children a matter calling for investigation and remedy. A just share of educational funds of the United States government, of Land-Grant funds, of the Smith-Hughes and the Smith-Lever appropriations, and of other moneys, is regularly and deliberately stolen from Negro children with the knowledge and connivance of United States and State officials, and the discrimination in state educational appropriations, especially in South Carolina, Georgia, Florida, Mississippi and Alabama is notorious and often amounts to spending $16.00 for a white child and only $1.00 a year for a black child.

We still suffer the insult of the "Jim Crow" car, the discrimination of bus lines and steamships and in places of public instruction, accommodation and amusement, even when these are supported by public charter and taxation.

We still face the discrimination and exclusion of trade unions, and we hereby repeat our invitation and warning of 1924 to the American Federation of Labor:

"Is it not time that black and white labor get together? Is it not time for white unions to stop bluffing and for black laborers to stop cutting off their noses to spite their faces?

"We propose that there be formed by the National Association for the Advancement of Colored People, the American Federation of Labor, the Railway Brotherhoods and any other bodies agreed upon, an Inter-racial Labor Commission."

The present condition of colored labor is precarious; with all its advance in efficiency and variety of employment, it is meeting severe competition, especially in the South, and the traditional "Negro job" is disappearing. This hurts the Negro, but it reacts on the white for the Negro in retaliation must and will "scab" and underbid. Immediate action is called for.

And beyond this, in Africa and the colonies and the West Indies, the abolition of forced labor, the restoration of the land and political and industrial democracy and the restoring of autonomy to Haiti is not only a crying need for colored folk, but the key to the emancipation of white labor throughout the world.

We repeat today as before: the American Negroes' great weapon of offense is the ballot. We should vote. We should seek alliance with the forces which stand for honest government, the abolition of privilege, and the socialization of wealth; but whenever these liberals deny us fellowship and draw the color line, we are justified in making any political alliance which defends us from political annihilation, economic discrimination and social insult.

Finally, as just stewards, give us funds to fight. Provide cash for defense, adequate salaries and current expense. Support our organ *The Crisis;* and let us go forward to a new decade of unity and success.

Marcus Garvey and the Appeal to Black Identity

The NAACP offered one approach to solving the problems generated by racial hostilities; Marcus Garvey, a West Indian who arrived in the United States in 1916, offered another solution. In the early 1920s, Garvey secured a massive following among America's blacks. Most intellectuals, whether black or white, however, mocked him as a fraud who attracted a following by wild promises combined with elaborate costumes and banners. One of those who did take Garvey seriously was the author of the following selection, William Pickens, who at the time was field secretary for the NAACP. In 1924 Garvey was convicted in federal court for mail fraud, though it would seem that many of his associates were more dishonest than he was.

From William Pickens, "Africa for the Africans—The Garvey Movement," *The Nation,* CXIII (1921), pp. 750-751. Subheadings added by the editors.

A Black Leader

The visitor to the thriving Negro section of the Harlem district in New York any time during the month of August would have been aware that something unusual was going on. At the corners newsboys hawked the *Negro World*—"all about Marcus Garvey and the great convention." Cigar stores sold Marcus Garvey cigars. At certain hours parades drew thousands to the streets. A long one-story building, Liberty Hall, was filled all during the month with hundreds of delegates during business sessions and jammed to the doors every night. And this convention was an army with banners—red, black, and green—borne by delegates from three continents. Its leading functionaries on great occasions wore resplendent robes and at all times bore resounding titles: Potentate, Provisional President of Africa, Chaplain General, and the like. The man responsible for all this was Marcus Garvey, a West Indian Negro, not long in the United States, who asserts that in four years his Universal Negro Improvement Association has reached a membership of 4,500,000, about 45 percent from the United States, the remainder from Africa, Central and South America, the West Indies, Canada, and Europe. Reduce this high estimate as much as you like, yet it still remains an unprecedented fact that representatives of all the principal Negro groups of the world have come together in an organization which raises the cry of "Africa for the Africans!" and proposes to found a great Negro government, an African Republic, which they vow to realize if it takes five hundred years.

This is a new thing for Negroes, but in strict harmony with many a slogan old or new which white men have used. "Self-determination of all peoples," "a white Australia," "100-per cent Americanism"—how are they different in principle from Garvey's cry "Africa, the self-governing home of the Negro race"? Any phenomenon among the colored population, like the U.N.I.A., white persons at first incline to regard as a huge joke, while the better-off colored people look upon it as something which they must shun in defense of their respectability. So there are educated and conscientious colored people who live within five minutes of Liberty Hall but have never been in it, and yet believe that the whole movement is disreputable, dishonest, and disgraceful to their race, and that Garvey,

Marcus Garvey, leader of the Universal Negro Improvement Association, at the peak of his influence, 1922. Garvey claimed rightly to represent millions of black Americans. Internal weakness and external pressure soon destroyed his movement, but he left a heritage of organization of the masses which others were later to develop.

whom they have never heard, is a smart thief or a wild fanatic. But the stubborn fact remains that a man of a disadvantaged group, by his almost unsupported strength and personal magnetism, has founded so large a power in the English-speaking world as to add to the current vocabulary of that language a new word, "Garveyism...."

II
The Meaning of Color

Garvey's emphasis on racial consciousness as a bond to unite Negroes of all nations is not a retrograde movement. Possibly the idea of race may vanish in the future. But how far in the future? The comfort, convenience, and protection of hundreds of millions of Negroes cannot wait on that millennial jubilee. We might as well console a Negro who is about to be burned in Texas by prophesying to him that a thousand years from now his kind will not be burned because the constantly inflowing stream of white blood will have so lightened the skins of his group that nobody will know whom to burn. Race is now and will be for ages one of the deepest lines of human demarcation. And a race must have power and cohesion or perish. There is no such thing as the inalienable right of the individual against the established government, and when one race monopolizes the power and the functions of government, the other race or races are under the power of the governing race, even in the most advanced democracies and republics. And so interdependent are the interests of nations today that whenever any race holds power anywhere on earth the nationals and members of that race who live under the government of other races receive more respect and better treatment than the members of a race who have not the indirect backing of a racial government. That explains the queer fact that a brown-faced Japanese, who is regarded as a dangerous rival and almost feared as a potential enemy, can travel without Jim Crow in Mississippi and register at the best hotels of New York or Atlanta, while a native Negro who is a citizen and whose skin may be many shades lighter than that of the Japanese, but who has no appeal from the local white juries, will be jim-crowed in Mississippi, told that "all rooms are taken" in New York, and kicked out of the lobbies in Atlanta....

What really troubles many white observers is not the ritual but the fact that in it the Negroes are striving to express their own racial pride rather than bow down to the white man. Formerly the Negro accepted the white and straight-haired God of the white man; when the white man wrote a prayer for the health of his own king and the perpetuation of his own supremacy, the black Christian simply repeated, reinforced, and abetted the white man's supplications. But here come black Garvey and his followers praying for their own sovereignty, idealizing their own kind, pigmenting their God, and the thing sounds outrageous to some white men and ridiculous even to the Caucasianized section of the Negro race. But is not some such racial pride necessary to the strength of the race?...

III
The Right to "Self-Direction"

Whatever may be said by way of criticism, this movement of the colored masses is anything but a joke. Neither Garvey nor any other human being could ever build up such a movement among the masses if it did not answer some longing of their souls. His particular movement may fail; the new racial consciousness of the Negro will endure. The deepest instincts of the scattered scions of the Negro race, like those of every race, call for group life, group propagation, and group power. That this is a white man's country, that other races must be kept out, or if already in must be kept in their place, is the viewpoint, the belief, and the will of nine-tenths of the native white people of the United States, even the most cultured and the most religious. It is but natural that such a pervasive feeling in their environment is answered in the soul of colored folk by a striving after self-preservation and self-perpetuation. And there is a *laissez-faire* majority in both races who are always worried and anxious enough, but who are willing only to "wait on the Lord" and see what will happen from decade to decade. And, of course, "nature and time" would gradually but very slowly and very wastefully solve this problem and all other earthly problems by the creeping processes of destroying and uniformizing. But the horrors of a thousand years while waiting on nature would be a disgrace to human intellect and genius.

Out of the colored people must come their own salvation. They must be a race and a power. The preparation for it could never have started too early, and cannot start earlier than now. The earlier the start, the less waste and the fewer horrors. It may take a hundred years or five hundred, a thousand years or five thousand, but four hundred million people can never be expected either to perish or forever to renounce their right to self-direction.

Reading 248

The Young Black Speaks Out (1926)

By the 1920s, a growing number of educated, articulate blacks, many of whom now lived in the North, were deeply involved in a debate about what it meant to be a black man in America. At the same time many young whites were becoming interested in black life and black art, for this was, after all, the Jazz Age and to some whites, the black represented a freer and richer culture than what they inherited from their "Puritan" past. One of the young blacks who was most active in the debate was Langston Hughes (1902-1966), a poet who though very young was well known in the world of writing. In the following selection Hughes explains why a black ought to take pride in his own heritage.

From Langston Hughes, "The Negro Artist and the Racial Mountain," *The Nation*, CXXII (1926), pp. 692-694. Subheadings added by the editors.

I

The Negro Artist

One of the most promising of the young Negro poets said to me once, "I want to be a poet—not a Negro poet," meaning, I believe, "I want to write like a white poet"; meaning subconsciously, "I would like to be a white poet"; meaning behind that, "I would like to be a white." And I was sorry the young man said that, for no great poet has ever been afraid of being himself. And I doubted then that, with his desire to run away spiritually from his race, this boy would ever be a great poet. But this is the mountain standing in the way of any true Negro art in America—this urge within the race toward whiteness, the desire to pour racial individuality into the mold of American standardization, and to be as little Negro and as much American as possible.

But let us look at the immediate background of this young poet. His family is of what I suppose one would call the Negro middle class: people who are by no means rich yet never uncomfortable nor hungry—smug, contented, respectable folk, members of the Baptist church. The father goes to work every morning. He is a chief steward at a large white club. The mother sometimes does fancy sewing or supervises parties for the rich families of the town. The children go to a mixed school. In the home they read white papers and magazines. And the mother often says "Don't be like niggers" when the children are bad. A frequent phrase from the father is, "Look how well a white man does things." And so the word white comes to be unconsciously a symbol of all the virtues. It holds for the children beauty, morality, and money. The whisper of "I want to be white" runs silently through their minds. This young poet's home is, I believe, a fairly typical home of the colored middle class. One sees immediately how difficult it would be for an artist born in such a home to interest himself in interpreting the beauty of his own people. He is never taught to see that beauty. He is taught rather not to see it, or if he does, to be ashamed of it when it is not according to Caucasian patterns.

For racial culture the home of a self-styled "high-class" Negro has nothing better to offer. Instead there will perhaps be more aping of things white than in a less cultured or less wealthy home. The father is perhaps a doctor, lawyer, landowner, or politician. The mother may be a social worker, or a teacher, or she may do nothing and have a maid. Father is often dark but he has usually married the lightest woman he could find. The family attend a fashionable church where few really colored faces are to be found. And they themselves draw a color line. In the North they go to white theaters and white movies. And in the South they have at least two cars and a house "like white folks." Nordic manners, Nordic faces, Nordic hair, Nordic art (if any), and an Episcopal heaven. A very high mountain indeed, for the would-be racial artist to climb in order to discover himself and his people.

But then there are the low-down folks, the so-called common element, and they are the majority—may the Lord be praised! The people who have their nip of gin on Saturday nights and are not too important to themselves or the community, or too well fed, or too learned to watch the lazy world go round. They live on Seventh Street in Washington or State Street in Chicago and they do not particularly care whether they are like white folks or anybody else. Their joy runs, bang! into ecstasy. Their religion soars to a shout. Work maybe a little today, rest a little tomorrow. Play awhile. Sing awhile. O, let's dance! These common people are not afraid of spirituals, as for a long time their more intellectual brethren were, and jazz is their child. They furnish a wealth of colorful, distinctive material for any artist because they still hold their own individuality in the face of American standardizations. And perhaps these common people will give to the world its truly great Negro artist, the one who is not afraid to be himself. Whereas the better-class Negro would tell the artist what to do, the people at least let him alone when he does appear. And they are not ashamed of him—if they know he exists at all. And they accept what beauty is their own without question....

II
Black—"Without Fear or Shame"

So I am ashamed for the black poet who says, "I want to be a poet, not a Negro poet," as though his own racial world were not as interesting as any other world. I am ashamed, too, for the colored artist who runs from the painting of Negro faces to the painting of sunsets after the manner of the academicians because he fears the strange un-whiteness of his own features. An artist must be free to choose what he does, certainly, but he must also never be afraid to do what he might choose.

Let the blare of Negro jazz bands and the bellowing voice of Bessie Smith singing Blues penetrate the closed ears of the colored near-intellectuals until they listen and perhaps understand. Let Paul Robeson singing Water Boy, and Rudolph Fisher writing about the streets of Harlem, and Jean Toomer holding the heart of Georgia in his hands, and Aaron Douglas drawing strange black fantasies cause the smug Negro middle class to turn from their white, respectable, ordinary books and papers to catch a glimmer of their own beauty. We younger Negro artists who create now intend to express our individual dark-skinned selves without fear or shame. If white people are pleased we are glad. If they are not, it doesn't matter. We know we are beautiful. And ugly too. The tom-tom cries and the tom-tom laughs. If colored people are pleased we are glad. If they are not, their displeasure doesn't matter either. We build our temples for tomorrow, strong as we know how and we stand on top of the mountain, free within ourselves.

TOPIC 50

CRASH AND DEPRESSION, 1929–1933

The economic slump of the early 1930s marked the end of a long period of nearly continuous growth in the American economy, as well as in the international economy in which the United States took part. There had been many previous episodes of slowing and stalling of growth, but never one so deep and so prolonged as this; it was called the Great Depression. This ten-year period was a profound dividing point in American history. Not until 1937 did industrial production recover to its 1929 level, only to suffer from a lesser slump that lasted three more years. Not until World War II, when production of war materials began to grow and the military services drafted the young, did the pool of the unemployed, millions strong, dwindle away.

The following pages examine the nature and causes of this unprecedented economic dislocation, as well as some of its consequences, during its first few years.

Reading 249

Disaster Strikes the Economy

A dramatic fall in prices on the New York Stock Exchange between September and November 1929 signaled the beginning of the economic collapse of the early 1930s. A superficial view might lead one to suppose that the stock market crash caused the Depression, or to put it another way, that the recklessness of the gamblers who had been buying stocks on credit, expecting to sell at a higher rate, caused the breakdown of the whole economy as soon as people stopped bidding up stocks and prices fell suddenly. While unwise speculation had something to do with immediate economic losses, the Depression also had other and deeper roots, as the following article makes clear.

From Henry Bamford Parkes and Vincent P. Carosso, *Recent America, A History* (New York: Thomas Y. Crowell Company, 1963), Vol. I, pp. 470, 474–475, 476–479. Footnotes omitted by the editors.

I

The Stock Exchange

The factor immediately responsible for the stock market collapse of October, 1929, and the widespread economic depression of the 1930's which followed it was an example, in the words of John Kenneth Galbraith, of "the seminal lunacy which has always seized people who are seized in turn with the notion that they can become very rich." This desire to get rich quickly, which came to possess so many Americans in the 1920's, attracted

The Movies: Dreams and Reality for the Millions

FANTASY: Nobody is certain who first discovered that one could play tricks on the eye by running a series of still photographs, taken in sequence, before the view. Thomas A. Edison, the American inventor, is credited among others with adapting that discovery to the machine, thus creating motion pictures, or the "movies." From its first commercial venture in the United States—twenty flickering minutes of action in a nickleodeon, or five-cent show, in McKeesport, Pa., in 1905—the motion picture industry grew into a giant within twenty years. It quickly became the most powerful of the mass communications media in its influence on manners, morals, dress, speech, and the images Americans held of themselves and others. In their greatest days, between 1915 and 1950, the movies tried to do many things, but the thing they did best and most often was to provide escape from reality. *King Kong* (1933) suggests how fantasy (the giant gorilla) can intrude on reality (New York City).

2

SPECTACLE: Sometimes the movies tried to preach. David Wark Griffith, the early filmmaker, was so taken aback by the discovery that his popular *The Birth of a Nation* (1915) had strong racist themes that he committed $14 million of its profits to making partial amends. The Babylonian orgy scene at left is from his *Intolerance* (1916), a four-part Message against prejudice and hatred. He lost money. The discovery that sermons did not pay very well was not lost on Samuel Goldwyn of Metro-Goldwyn-Mayer, who is supposed to have remarked that he preferred to send messages by Western Union, and whose studio produced the unabashedly romantic musical *Rosalie* (1937). It starred Nelson Eddy, as a line-plunging baritone from West Point, and Eleanor Powell, as a dancing Balkan princess from Vassar. At right is their wedding scene. Whether producing Messages or Romances, Hollywood in its golden era agreed that lavish Spectacles would bring in the public, and they did.

4

5

HEROIC IMAGES: Bringing together the popular male actor and the role of the hero guaranteed profits for Hollywood and entertainment for the millions. Who were the idols, and which were the heroic roles fancied by Americans? Gary Cooper, at far left with Mary Brian and two horses, is the taciturn, honorable, fearless Westerner in *The Virginian* (1929); Clark Gable, next left, the epitome of the adventurer, is boss of a rubber plantation in Indo China (then merely exotic), while Jean Harlow, a lady of uncertain virtue, is his companion in *Red Dust* (1932); Henry Fonda, left, is America's greatest real-life (and mythic) hero in the nostalgic *Young Mr. Lincoln* (1939); while James Cagney, above, is both hero and villain as a cocky, ruthless gangster, not so much outwitting as overcoming the law in *Public Enemy* (1931).

8

REALISM: When Hollywood touched on actual social and personal problems, it found that adding liberal doses of romance and comedy helped to hold its audiences. Gloria Swanson, at left in the comedy *Manhandled* (1924), was one of the most popular actresses of the years when movies were still silent. Her portrayal of a department store clerk (caught here in a subway crowd) is supposed to illustrate the problems of the working girl. The movie, however, did not overwork its realism: Gloria left the department store to try the life of a rich society girl, and then gave it up for her old boy friend, who had made money in the meantime. Mechanization of the American economy, not to mention the American home, was causing sweeping changes and not a few problems. Charlie Chaplin, the great comedian, dealt with the machine age in *Modern Times* (1936), by caricaturing it. One of the closest approaches made by Hollywood to stark realism in the years before World War II came in *The Grapes of Wrath* (1940), drawn from John Steinbeck's popular novel about the hardships of farmers driven off their land by dust storms in the Plains region. Here Henry Fonda as Tom Joad, on the tailgate, and Jane Darwell as Ma Joad, beside the truck, lead the family west to California in their battered truck. The movie, like the book, made it plain that there were bitter conflicts between laborers and employers, but it ended with an optimistic note about the hopes for workers' cooperatives; the word "socialism" was taboo.

STEREOTYPES: The movies before World War II were even more segregated than American life itself. Films using black actors characteristically placed them in roles as inferiors or as entertainers kept at a safe distance from whatever real problems the plot might develop; seldom could the black role be allowed to challenge in any way the realities of discrimination. The production of a few movies with all-black casts, as in *The Green Pastures* (1936), gave black actors a much wider opportunity for leading roles. Such movies did not, however, bring them much closer to dealing with the actualities of life in America, as this scene (left) with Rex Ingram, center, as De Lawd, suggests. World War II made a difference. In *Home of the Brave* (1949) producer Stanley Kramer gambled against American prejudices in bringing out a World War II drama, starring a black actor, Douglas Dick, at center, below, containing a reasonably realistic portrayal of the psychological tensions within a group of soldiers, all white but one, on a Pacific island.

thousands to the stock market, producing the "speculative orgy" which fed the bull market of 1927, 1928, and 1929. During these years stock prices rose continuously and by leaps and bounds, with only few interruptions. The index of common stock prices (1926 = 100) was 118.3 in 1927; by 1929 it had risen by more than 50 percent to 190.3. The index price for utilities more than doubled during the same period, jumping from 116 to 234.6. Yet while it is true that by 1929 more people were directly involved in the stock market than ever before, and that a considerable number of these were engaged in speculation on a scale hitherto unprecedented, still the fact remains, as a Senate investigating committee was to disclose later, that no more than 1.5 million people were actually engaged in buying and selling stocks. This is a very small number when compared with a total population of 121.7 million. Numbers in this instance, however, are unimportant. What is significant is the extent to which the speculative psychology which characterized the Wall Street market dominated so much of American life. The stock market no longer existed primarily as a means of providing capital for productive enterprise; it had become a place where men expected to make fortunes by gambling on the prices of stocks. Billions of dollars were diverted from investment into speculation; and stock values, pushed upward by competitive bidding, ceased to bear any relation to their real capacity for earning dividends. . . .

II

Some Statistics of the Depression

The break in the stock market meant only a decline in paper values which did not directly affect the productive capacity of American industry and agriculture; the real wealth of the American people was as great in November, 1929, as it had been in September. It was therefore believed by President Hoover and by the majority of the American people that the economic system would quickly adjust itself and that prosperity would continue. Actually, however, the economy in 1929 was suffering from a number of serious weaknesses which made it impossible for the stock market to recover from the great shock it had just experienced. The result was that what had happened on Wall Street put in motion a chain of events which was to cause the greatest depression in American history.

By mid-November, paper wealth had decreased by $30 billion. (By the summer of 1932 another $45 billion would be wiped out.) The consequence was that the people who had incurred these losses—and they were the ones with most of the disposable income—began to limit their purchases of new goods, particularly of the durables which had played such an important role in sustaining the prosperity of the 1920's. Moreover, because of lack of both capital and confidence, businessmen began to invest less money than formerly in industrial expansion. The result was that production of capital goods and durable consumption goods declined, workers in these industries were laid off, and the growth of unemployment caused further contractions of purchasing power, which led in a vicious cycle to still more unemployment. After the stock market crash, the economic system could have righted itself only through a reduction in all other monetary values, including prices and debts, in proportion to the decrease in stock prices. That, however, was impossible.

The country did not feel the full effects of the crash for several years. Economic conditions slowly deteriorated during 1930 and the early months of 1931, and by the summer of that year many people believed the corner had been turned. What had happened on Wall Street had, however, caused repercussions in Europe, which reacted back upon the United States. The cessation of American loans and the decline of American foreign trade, coupled with the intrinsic weaknesses of the European economic system due to the war, led in the summer of 1931 to the collapse of central Europe—an event which was to help bring about the emergence of the Nazi dictatorship. From Austria and Germany the chain of disaster then spread to Great Britain and returned to the United States. According to President Hoover, "there came to us a concatenation of catastrophes from abroad such as we have not experienced in the whole of our economic history." The depression continued to deepen until July, 1932. Then after a slight recovery in the autumn, the trend turned downward again until March, 1933. . . .

III

Reasons for the Severity of the Depression

For more than a hundred years the American economic system had suffered from periodic depressions which had always been followed by a return to prosperity. Recovery, moreover, had been due primarily to economic causes and not to any action taken by the American government. For a number of reasons, however, the depression which began in 1929 was exceptionally acute and eventually affected almost everyone. In terms of the mass un-

Bank doors shut and locked symbolize the state of the nation's economy in the 1930s. In 1932 alone, well over 1200 banks suspended services, though many of these eventually reopened. At best, depositors were unable to withdraw their money when they needed to; at worst millions of Americans lost part or all of their savings.

employment, the extremely depressed conditions of the economy generally, and the hardships inflicted upon so many people who had never experienced economic distress before, such as the white collar salariat and professional men and women, the "great depression" was qualitatively as well as quantitatively more serious than any previous one.

Recovery was so long delayed that the American people finally insisted the government intervene. To this day, economists differ in trying to explain what brought about this extended economic crisis, which left such an impress upon the American people and gave rise to new economic, political, and social ideas and practices. The following are among the generally accepted explanations of what aggravated the instabilities in the economy and delayed recovery.

In the first place, the expansion of the capital and durable goods industries in the 1920's had been on a wholly unprecedented scale. By 1929 the supply of factories, machinery, office buildings, automobiles, and other durable goods appears to have been out of all proportion to the effective purchasing power of the nation's consumers. In the case of consumer durables, for example, many sales had been possible only by installment selling, which, by providing the means for immediate acquisition, tapped future demand. The result was that the revival of these industries was exceptionally slow. Many observers, indeed, doubted whether any revival was possible without government intervention.

In the second place, the price-fixing policies of the big corporations meant that in the capital and durable goods industries prices remained high, while production and employment were drastically reduced. In agriculture and in the more competitive consumption goods industries, on the other hand, prices were reduced while production was maintained. According to Gardiner C. Means, "the whole depression might be described as a general dropping of prices at the flexible end of the price scale and a dropping of production at the rigid end with intermediate effects between." With the exception of the railroads, most of the large corporations continued to make profits, though on a reduced scale, all through the depression. Their policy of maintaining prices, however, tended to delay any real recovery in the capital goods industries, while their drastic reduction of employment prolonged the depression by decreasing consumer purchasing power. Means illustrates his statement by . . . [table I], showing percentage decreases in prices and production between 1929 and the spring of 1933.

TABLE 1 DECREASES IN PRICES AND PRODUCTION, 1929-1933

	FALL IN PRICES	FALL IN PRODUCTION
Agricultural implements	6%	80%
Motor vehicles	16	80
Cement	18	65
Iron and steel	20	83
Textile products	45	30
Food products	49	14
Leather	50	20
Agricultural commodities	63	6

Price maintenance was particularly conspicuous in the case of certain mineral products. Throughout the depression, nickel remained at 35 cents a pound; sulfur remained at $18 a ton, its leading producer, Texas Gulf, making a 50 percent profit on every sale; aluminum sold for 24 cents a pound in 1929 and 23 cents in 1932. The effects of price fixing on a consumption goods industry are illustrated in the case of cigarettes. By maintaining prices and taking advantage of decreased costs of production, the seven leading cigarette corporations were able to increase their profits from $85 million in 1929 to $105 million in 1932.

In the third place, the depression deprived American industry of many of its foreign markets. In 1929 American exports had a total value of $5.24 billion; by 1932 the value had decreased to $1.61 billion. Recovery of these foreign outlets for American surpluses proved to be impossible. Much of the American export trade before 1929 had been financed by American loans; since, however, many of these loans went into default during the depression, American investors were unwilling to continue foreign lending. Other nations, moreover, began to raise tariff barriers, to use import quota systems, and to adopt policies of economic nationalism, partly in retaliation for the Hawley-Smoot Tariff and partly in the hope of shielding their own industries from the force of the world depression.

In the fourth place, the severity of the depression was increased by the extraordinarily intricate system of debt obligations. Interest payments which could be handled easily in 1929 were a crushing burden in the deflationary conditions of 1932, and these payments could not be scaled down except through bankruptcies. In the early stages of the depression the share of the national income going to the creditor classes was increased, which meant that the purchasing power of the remainder of the population was proportionately reduced. As one banker put it, "capital kept too much and labor did not have enough to buy its share of things." In addition to the workers who "did not have enough," he could have added most of the farmers who were always pinched for money during the 1920's. In 1930 the total amount of interest payments (though not dividend payments) were only 3.5 percent less than in 1929. The concentration of industry which had occurred in the 1920's created a complex corporate structure where in certain areas, such as public utilities and banks, one holding company was pyramided upon another. Many of these intricate holding company structures were created for no other reason than to provide opportunity to secure monopoly privileges or to issue new stocks for the insiders to manipulate to their own advantage. But once defaults and bankruptcies began on any level of these pyramids, they threatened to spread so widely and to involve so many institutions in a common ruin that even the government of President Hoover, which professed to believe in laissez-faire principles, was compelled to intervene. Rather than allow economic mechanisms to take their natural course, the government began to give support to the financial structure. Such an intervention moderated the severity of the depression; but by preventing debt obligations from being wiped out, it probably delayed any genuine recovery.

In the fifth place, there was neither the desire nor the means to regulate the banking system effectively and to curb the flow of Federal Reserve credit from going into speculative transactions on the stock market. The country's banks had encouraged borrowing on all levels. Businessmen and corporations borrowed to expand production or to speculate in securities, while individuals, in the hope of getting rich quickly and in order to satisfy their desire to acquire the many new products of the new technology, borrowed to gamble on the market and to buy on installment.

In the sixth place, the tremendous strides which had occurred in the efficiency of industry resulted in technological unemployment, fewer workers were required to produce a greater amount of goods. The new industries, like the manufacturing of automobiles and radios and those affected by them, did not take up all the workers displaced by machines in the older ones. The result was that throughout the 1920's the number of unemployed fluctuated from a low of about 464,000 in 1926 to more than 2 million in 1922 and 1924. The psychology of optimism which prevailed during the 1920's caused most people to overlook the effects of technological unemployment and the other danger signals which were undermining the prosperity. And because so many Americans had come to believe that the United States had discovered the secret of perpetual "good times," the social and human effects of the depression were even more devastating than the actual economic losses, great as they were. Facts and figures cannot begin to describe the deepening despair which gripped the American people as they passed from what had been for most of them an era of striking prosperity to one of severe depression. As the distinguished journalist Anne O'Hare McCormick wrote at the time, the depression was "the worst in the extent to which it . . . caught people unprepared."

Hoover Explains His Policies

Herbert Hoover (1874–1964), inaugurated as President only eight months before the stock market crash, became identified in the minds of many people with the Depression. Communities of shacks thrown up by bands of the homeless were called "hoovervilles," for example. Yet Hoover might more accurately be known as the first President who ever tried to use federal powers and resources on a large scale to counter the effects of a depression; in his administration the government committed hundreds of millions of dollars to those tasks. The trouble was partly that Hoover put most emphasis on saving institutions, like banks and railroads, rather than on giving direct relief to individuals in dire need. In addition, when the Depression was sinking to its depths in 1931 and 1932 he was obliged to work with unsympathetic Democratic majorities in Congress, who saw little reason why Republicans should get credit for bailing the nation out of a crisis when Republicans had so long been claiming credit for prosperity. The following excerpt from Hoover's memoirs gives some elements of his approach to the crisis. It may also suggest certain other problems which helped to block his efforts.

Reprinted with permission of The Macmillan Company from *The Memoirs of Herbert Hoover: The Great Depression, 1929–1941* by Herbert Hoover, pp. 29–32. Copyright © 1952 by Herbert Hoover. Subheadings and bracketed material added by the editors.

I

Need for Federal Action

With the October-November stock-market crash the primary question at once arose as to whether the President and the Federal government should undertake to mitigate and remedy the evils stemming from it. No President before had ever believed there was a governmental responsibility in such cases. No matter what the urging on previous occasions, Presidents steadfastly had maintained that the Federal government was apart from such eruptions; they had always been left to blow themselves out. Presidents Van Buren, Grant, Cleveland and Theodore Roosevelt had all remained aloof. A few helpful gestures, however, had been made in the past. On one such occasion it was in the form of a little currency relief; on another, the deposit of Federal money in some banks; and there was the crisis when Cleveland announced his fidelity to the gold standard to steady a panicky public.

Because of this lack of governmental experience, therefore, we had to pioneer a new field. As a matter of fact there was little economic knowledge to guide us. The previous great postwar depression of the 1870's had left almost no real economic information except as to consequences in prices, production, and employment. I may reiterate that it is not given even to Presidents to see the future. Economic storms do not develop all at once, and they change without notice. In my three years of the slump and depression they changed repeatedly for the worse—and with the speed of lightning. We could have done better—in retrospect.

The break in the stock market in late October, 1929, was followed by succeeding slumps until, by the end of November, industrial stocks had fallen to 60 percent of their high point. Even so, the business world refused, for some time after the crash, to believe that the danger was any more than that of run-of-the-mill, temporary slumps such as had occurred at three-to-seven-year intervals in the past.

However, we in the administration took a more serious view of the immediate future, partly because of our knowledge of the fearful inflation of stock-market credit, and, in the longer view, because of our fear of the situation of European economy. I perhaps knew the weaknesses of the latter better than most people from my experience in Europe during 1919 and my knowledge of the economic consequences of the Versailles Treaty.

II

Debate over Policy

Two schools of thought quickly developed within our administration discussions.

First was the "leave it alone liquidationists" headed by Secretary of the Treasury [Andrew] Mellon, who felt that government must keep its hands off and let the slump liquidate itself. Mr. Mellon had only one formula: "Liquidate labor, liquidate stocks, liquidate the farmers, liquidate real estate." He insisted that, when the people get an inflation brainstorm, the only way to get it out of their blood is to let it collapse. He held that even a panic was not altogether a bad thing. He said: "It will purge the rottenness out of the system. High costs of living and high living will come down. People will work harder, live a more moral life. Values will be adjusted, and enterprising people will pick up the wrecks from less competent people." He often used the expression, "There is a mighty lot of real estate lying around the United States which does not know who owns it," referring to excessive mortgages.

At great length, Mr. Mellon recounted to me his recollection of the great depression of the seventies which followed the Civil War. (He started in his father's bank a few years after that time.) He told of the tens of thousands of farms that had been foreclosed; of railroads that had almost wholly gone into the hands of receivers; of the few banks that had come through unscathed; of many men who were jobless and mobs that roamed the streets. He told me that his father had gone to England during that time and had cut short his visit when he received word that the orders for steel were pouring toward the closed furnaces; by the time he got back, confidence was growing on every hand; suddenly the panic had ended, and in twelve months the whole system was again working at full speed.

I, of course, reminded the Secretary that back in the seventies an untold amount of suffering did take place which might have been prevented; that our economy had been far simpler sixty years ago, when we were 75 percent an agricultural people contrasted with 30 percent now; that unemployment during the earlier crisis had been mitigated by the return of large numbers of the unemployed to relatives on the farms; and that farm economy itself had been largely self-contained. But he shook his head with the observation that human nature had not changed in sixty years.

Secretary Mellon was not hard-hearted. In fact he was generous and sympathetic with all suffering. He felt there would be less suffering if his course were pursued. The real trouble with him was that he insisted that this was just an ordinary boom-slump and would not take the European situation seriously. And he, like the rest of us, underestimated the weakness in our banking system.

But other members of the administration, also having economic responsibilities—Under Secretary of the Treasury Mills, Governor Young of the Reserve Board, Secretary of Commerce Lamont and Secretary of Agriculture Hyde—believed with me that we should use the powers of government to cushion the situation. To our minds, the prime needs were to prevent bank panics such as had marked the earlier slumps, to mitigate the privation among the unemployed and the farmers which would certainly ensue. Panic had always left a trail of unnecessary bankruptcies which injured the productive forces of the country. But, even more important, the damage from a panic would include huge losses by innocent people, in their honestly invested savings, their businesses, their homes, and their farms.

III

Decision To Act

The record will show that we went into action within ten days and were steadily organizing each week and month thereafter to meet the changing tides—mostly for the worse. In this earlier stage we determined that the Federal government should use all of its powers:

a) to avoid the bank depositors' and credit panics which had so generally accompanied previous violent slumps;
b) to cushion slowly, by various devices, the inevitable liquidation of false values so as to prevent widespread bankruptcy and the losses of homes and productive power;
c) to give aid to agriculture;
d) to mitigate unemployment and to relieve those in actual distress;
e) to prevent industrial conflict and social disorder;
f) to preserve the financial strength of the United States government, our credit and our currency, as the economic

Gibraltar of the earth—in other words, to assure that America should meet every foreign debt, and keep the dollar ringing true on every counter in the world;

g) to advance much-needed economic and social reforms as fast as could be, without such drastic action as would intensify the illness of an already sick nation;

h) to sustain the morale and courage of the people in order that their initiative should remain unimpaired, and to secure from the people themselves every effort for their own salvation;

i) to adhere rigidly to the Constitution and the fundamental liberties of the people.

The Deepening Crisis
(1932)

The following contemporary description of the Depression is taken from a magazine whose subscribers were largely businessmen.

From "No One Has Starved," Fortune, VI (September 1932), pp. 19-21, 24-27, 28. Subheadings added and footnotes deleted and added by the editors.

I

The Victims of the Depression

Dull mornings last winter the sheriff of Miami, Florida, used to fill a truck with homeless men and run them up to the county line. Where the sheriff of Fort Lauderdale used to meet them and load them into a second truck and run them up to *his* county line. Where the sheriff of Saint Lucie's would meet them and load them into a third truck and run them up to *his* county line. Where the sheriff of Brevard County would *not* meet them. And whence they would trickle back down the roads to Miami. To repeat.

It was a system. And it worked. The only trouble was that it worked too well. It kept the transients transient and it even increased the transient population in the process. But it got to be pretty expensive, one way or another, if you sat down and figured it all out—trucks and gas and time and a little coffee. . .

That was last winter.

Next winter there will be no truck. And there will be no truck, not because the transients will have disappeared from Miami: if anything, there will be more blistered Fords with North Dakota licenses and more heel-worn shoes with the Boston trade-mark rubbed out next winter than there were last. But because the sheriff of Miami, like the President of the U.S., will next winter think of transients and unemployed miners and jobless mill workers in completely different terms.

The difference will be made by the Emergency Relief Act. Or rather by the fact that the Emergency Relief Act exists. For the Act itself with its $300,000,000 for direct relief loans to the states is neither an adequate nor an impressive piece of legislation. But the passage of the Act, like the green branch which young Mr. Ringling used to lay across the forks of the Wisconsin roads for his circus to follow, marks a turning in American political history. And the beginning of a new chapter in American unemployment relief. It constitutes an open and legible acknowledgement of governmental responsibility for the welfare of the victims of industrial unemployment. And its ultimate effect must be the substitution of an ordered, realistic, and intelligent relief program for the wasteful and uneconomic methods (of which the Miami truck is an adequate symbol) employed during the first three years of the depression.

There can be no serious question of the failure of those methods. For the methods were never seriously capable of success. They were diffuse, unrelated, and unplanned. The theory was that private charitable organizations and semi-public welfare groups, established to care for the old and the sick and the indigent, were capable of caring for the casuals of a world-wide economic disaster. And the theory in application meant that social agencies manned for the service of a few hundred families, and city shelters set up to house and feed a handful of homeless men, were compelled by the brutal necessities of hunger to care for hundreds of thousands of families and whole armies of the displaced and the jobless. And to depend for their resources upon the contributions of communities no longer able to contribute, and upon the irresolution and vacillation of state Legislatures and municipal assemblies long since in the red on their annual budgets. The result was the picture now presented in city after city and state after state—heterogeneous groups of official and semi-official and unofficial relief agencies struggling under the earnest and untrained leadership of the local men of affairs against an inertia of misery and suffering and want they are powerless to overcome.

Curious bystanders look on as two long-unemployed men advertise themselves in desperation along the streets of Chicago. Scenes like this were commonplace during the Depression, as the unemployed tried every gimmick possible in their search for work.

But the psychological consequence was even worse. Since the problem was never honestly attacked as a national problem, and since the facts were never frankly faced as facts, people came to believe that American unemployment was relatively unimportant. They saw little idleness and they therefore believed there was little idleness. It is possible to drive for blocks in the usual shopping and residential districts of New York and Chicago without seeing a breadline or a food station or a hungry mob or indeed anything else much more exciting than a few casuals asleep on a park bench. And for that reason, and because their newspapers played down the subject as an additional depressant in depressing times, and because they were bored with relief measures anyway, the great American public simply ignored the whole thing. They would still ignore it today were it not that the committee hearings and the Congressional debate and the Presidential veto of relief bills this last June attracted their attention. And that the final passage of the Emergency Relief and Construction Act of 1932 has committed their government and themselves to a policy of affirmative action which compels both it and them to know definitely and precisely what the existing situation is.

II

The Facts

It should be remarked at this point that nothing the federal government has yet done or is likely to do in the near future constitutes a policy of *constructive* action. Unemployment basically is not a social disease but an industrial phenomenon. The natural and inevitable consequence of a machine civilization is a lessened demand for human labor. (An almost total elimination of human labor in plowing, for example, is not foreseeable.) And the natural and inevitable consequence of a lessened demand for human labor is an increase of idleness. Indeed the prophets of the machine age have always promised an increase of idleness, under the name of leisure, as one of the goals of industry. A constructive solution of unemployment therefore means an industrial solution—a restatement of industrialism which will treat technological displacement not as an illness to be cured but as a goal to be achieved—and achieved with the widest dispensation of benefits and the least incidental misery.

But the present relief problem as focused by the federal Act is not a problem of ultimate solutions but of immediate palliatives. One does not talk architecture while the house is on fire and the tenants are still inside. The question at this moment is the pure question of fact. Having decided at last to face reality and do something about it, what is reality? How many men are unemployed in the U.S.? How many are in want? *What are the facts?*

The following minimal statements may be accepted as true—with the certainty that they underestimate the real situation:

(1) Unemployment has steadily increased in the U.S. since the beginning of the depression and the rate of increase during the first part of 1932 was more rapid than in any other depression year.

(2) The number of persons totally unemployed is now at least 10,000,000.

(3) The number of persons totally unemployed next winter will, at the present rate of increase, be 11,000,000.

(4) Eleven millions unemployed means better than one man out of every four employable workers.

(5) This percentage is higher than the percentage of unemployed British workers registered under the compulsory insurance laws (17.1 percent in May, 1932, as against 17.3 percent in April and 18.4 percent in January) and higher than the French, the Italian, and the Canadian percentages, but lower than the German (43.9 percent of trade unionists in April, 1932) and the Norwegian.

(6) Eleven millions unemployed means 27,500,000 whose regular source of livelihood has been cut off.

(7) Twenty-seven and a half millions without regular income includes the families of totally unemployed workers alone. Taking account of the numbers of workers on part time, the total of those without adequate income becomes 34,000,000 or better than a quarter of the entire population of the country. . . .

III

Some Examples

In *Cleveland* the average of direct relief to families is $17.09 monthly. A total of 31,000 families is expected in December, rising to 38,000 next March. Income for 1932 will be about $2,000,000 short of expenditures. In *Youngstown,* due to the local optimism, no united relief was undertaken until January, 1931. Meantime homeless men slept in the garbage in the municipal incinerator to keep warm. In January an abandoned police station was made into a flophouse. Attempts of Communists to organize the flophouseholders failed and a bond issue was eventually floated. Men in desperate need get two days work a week. As Ex-Mayor Heffernan puts it: "If a man owned a small home, if a young couple possessed furniture, if a woman had a good coat or her husband a presentable suit, these things had to be sacrificed first. Not until they had drained every other resource was official charity able to do anything for them." Average relief in *Akron* has run at $14 per month with few rents being paid by the relief agencies. In *Canton* relief is down to $13.97 per family per month but there has been a slight decline in the number aided. Landlords have carried many families a year or more here as elsewhere. The Canton Community Fund Drive fell short about $102,000 of its $345,000 goal. In *Cincinnati,* of the 50,000 unemployed, at least half have not yet asked relief. About 21,000 families are now carried at an average per family of $5 per week. In *Dayton,* with 6,000 families in need, much despondency and illness due to inadequate relief is reported.

Upstate New York cities present a similar picture with relief somewhat better organized. *Pittsburgh* has 178,000 unemployed and 30,000 families on relief with expenditures for 1932 about four times 1931. Father Cox, head of the Pittsburgh hunger marchers, had purchased thirty-six acres on the outskirts of the city where a town for the unemployed will be built. In May it had shelter for 100 families. *Los Angeles* had last winter 151,000 unemployed, of whom 60,000 were heads of families, but now reports 118,000. Relief is about $23.58 per month per family, with the 1931 county poor appropriation for the 225,000 unemployed in the county smaller than the 1930 appropriation. *San Francisco* now reports 40,000 unemployed and 12,000 families on relief with an allowance for food and housing of twenty-eight cents per person a day. California has been able to give a considerable amount of work through labor camps and work relief financed from county funds and supplying in one section $24 worth of work per man every six weeks. *Birmingham* had an unemployed total of 25,000 out of its working population of 115,000 at the beginning of the year and provides an allowance of $2.50 to $4.00 per week for families averaging 4.3 persons. There were 12,000 tax delinquencies and [there] had been 6,000 tax sales and neither county nor state aid was probable. *Portland, Oregon,* has 37,500 unemployed and 13,445 families on relief. *New Orleans* has 20,000 unemployed and 2,500 families receiving aid with no more private funds in sight and completely inadequate relief. *Boston* has 103,600 unemployed with a daily food relief expenditure of seventeen cents to thirty cents and an enforced contribution system for city employees. And *Minneapolis, St. Paul,* and *Duluth* registered respectively last winter 44,000, 20,000, and 10,000 unemployed with relief in Minneapolis, at least, on a minimal basis.

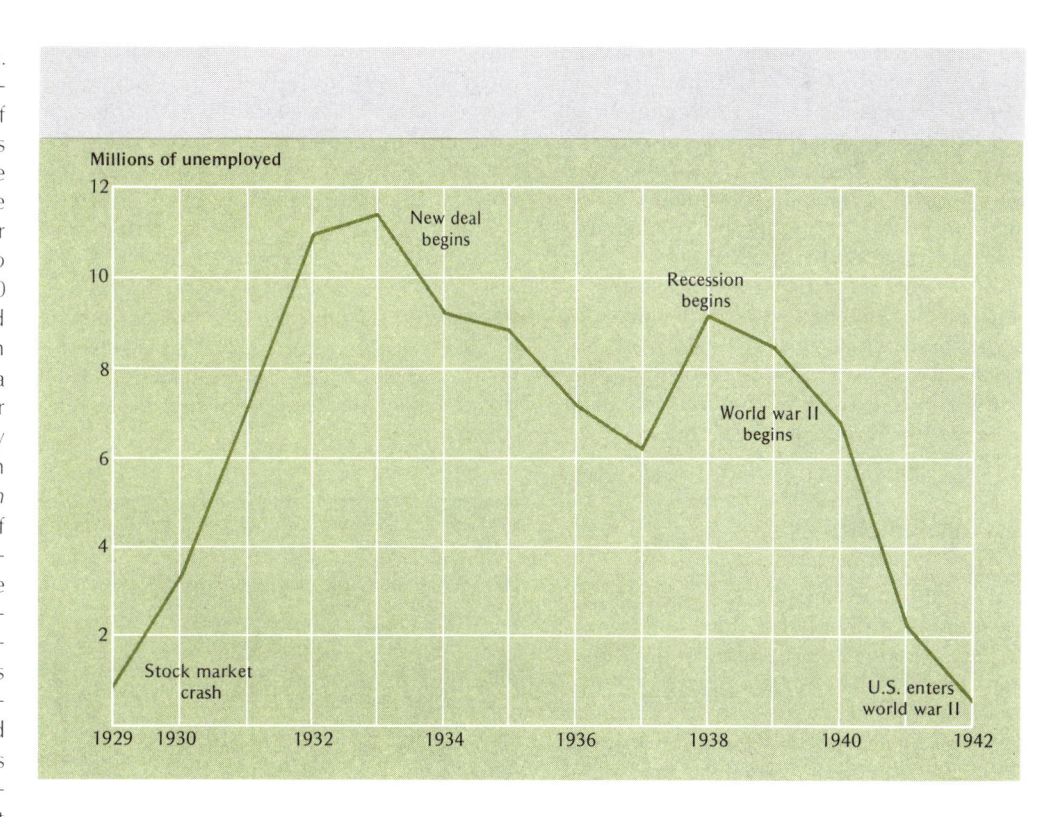

Obviously, however, urban figures give an incomplete picture of the whole industrial situation, for they do not include such areas as the industrial area of New Jersey. In Passaic County, for example, 23,749 persons, heads of families, representing 90,699 of the county's 300,000 population, have applied for relief. The authorities have been forced to pick 12,171 families, about half, and give them relief amounting to about $9 a month per family. And in Paterson 8,500 of the registered 12,000 unemployed are without relief of any kind. Moreover, the situation in the textile areas of the state is complicated by the fact that certain employers have taken advantage of the necessity of their employees to reestablish sweatshop conditions. Under such circumstances the employed as well as the unemployed become a burden upon the community. But elsewhere in the textile mill towns even the pretense of a living wage has been dropped. North Carolina has 100,000 unemployed textile workers with another 100,000 on the payrolls of closed plants, most of whom are begging on the roads, having long ago exhausted their savings from the low wage paid them before the depression. And those employed on part time are hardly better off since the full-time wage now averages about $6.50. In Georgia, in the Piedmont Mill Village of Egan Park, fifteen families have banded together to keep alive on a total weekly income of $10. And similar stories come from other towns in the region. While some of the small steel towns are almost as badly off. At Donora, Pennsylvania, there were in March 277 regular workers out of a population of 13,900 while 2,500 others performed "made work" at $3.50 per week and 2,000 others "seem to have disappeared." It is hardly necessary to add that malnutrition, undernourishment, rickets, tuberculosis, and other diseases increase under such conditions. And that relief in these areas is badly organized or nonexistent. . . .

IV
Is a Revolution Possible?

So far at least the phenomenon of migration is the only important social consequence of the depression, and the Communistic outbreaks foreseen by extremists in both directions have not taken place. The unemployed of Passaic County, New Jersey, may be and doubtless are in ugly temper. And the state of mind of the idle miners in Harlan County, Kentucky, may have been such as to justify, through fear, the otherwise unjustifiable repressive measures adopted by the local authorities. But by and large there has been extraordinarily little unrest. The two major manifestations of the year, the January hunger march of Father Cox's army to Washington and the later Bonus Expeditionary Force, were notoriously and avowedly anti-revolutionary,

> About 15,000 World War I veterans descended on Washington in the summer of 1932, demanding immediate payment of the bonus Congress had promised them. Here several thousand Bonus Marchers from California "flop" on the lawn of the Capitol to make their point as dramatically as possible.

and contrasted remarkably in number with the feeble 1,500 produced for the Communist hunger march of last December. And most of the food riots reported from various cities—or not reported—have so far been bloodless, the only fatalities having occurred in the mismanaged resistance to a job march upon the Ford factories in Dearborn in March, when four were killed and fifty wounded, the July attempt of St. Louis police to prevent a mob of 300 from rushing the City Hall where the Board of Aldermen was considering (and thereupon promptly passing) special tax bills for relief, the demonstration of 400 against the employment of non-union men on public works in Marseilles, Illinois, in the same month in which one man was killed and twenty-two wounded, and the Battle of Pennsylvania Avenue.*

*An episode in 1932 when army soldiers under General Douglas MacArthur were called out to oust a large group of veterans from unused government buildings and makeshift encampments in Washington, D.C. The veterans were vainly seeking early payment of a federal bonus for their service in World War I—Eds.

Family Life and the Depression

The effects of the Depression on families were often tragic but sometimes otherwise, as this author observes.

Excerpts from pp. 283–284, 286–287, 287–288, 292 in My America, 1928–1938, *by Louis Adamic. Copyright © 1928 by Louis Adamic. Reprinted by permission of Harper & Row, Publishers, Inc. Subheadings added by the editors.*

I

The Breadwinner

The Depression's effects upon the home or family life in the United States were as varied as they were profound; but they can be put into two general categories: On the one hand, thousands of families were broken up, some permanently, others temporarily, or were seriously disorganized. On the other hand, thousands of other families became more closely integrated than they had been before the Depression.

The reason for these different effects due to the same cause was that the economic crisis, which came upon many families in all sections of the country with the force and suddenness of a cyclone, in most cases intensified the various antagonistic and affectional attitudes or reactions of one to the other among the individuals within the family groups. Sudden economic adversity made family life more dynamic. In some cases, the so-called "hostility reactions" among the members of the family became more explosive, more damaging to the stability and harmony of the group. In other cases, conversely, the bonds of mutual affection, cooperation, and sacrifice were greatly strengthened, or even brought into full play for the first time.

These general statements apply, in greater or lesser degree, to all classes of society, except, of course, the uppermost class, in which the Depression was not felt acutely, at least not so far as family life was concerned. They apply most of all to the classes hit by unemployment.

In many working-class or white-collar homes, the man—the father and husband—was, by virtue of the dynamics of his position as breadwinner and conventional head of the family, the first to feel the impact of the unemployment situation. It was he who lost the job; in most cases, suddenly and unexpectedly. In the preceding years, what with children, illness, high-pressure salesmanship, and keeping up with the neighbors, he had been unable to save any substantial sum of money from his pay. Morally and legally he was responsible for the support of his wife and children. As soon as he lost his employment the atmosphere in his home changed. He noticed that his wife and children looked at him "funny," or at least differently. Sometimes, of course, he merely imagined that their looks were "funny" or different, but the effect upon him was the same. He became self-conscious, uneasy, resentful. This was the first hostility reaction, which often led to other sharply discordant reactions.

At the same time he began to have serious doubts about his own worth and abilities. Why had he lost his job while Bill Jones and Steve Komonski remained working? Why hadn't the boss kept him on at least upon a part-time basis? In many cases, to hide these doubts and feelings of inferiority, which usually were not new but merely intensified, he assumed a gruff, hard, or even violent manner toward everybody, including (or especially) his family. He grumbled, growled, barked back at his wife. He issued sharp commands to his children, while two or three weeks before he had never or seldom bothered them. Such behavior, of course, produced open hostility reactions on their part toward him.

This happened especially after he had come to realize that job-hunting, somehow, was a hopeless proposition and his bewilderment deepened and he was being seized by a sense of frustration. Consciously or unconsciously, he commenced to feel that forces utterly beyond his control were operating to take from him the important role of provider for the family....

In a good many cases, too, the woman, on becoming the sole or principal breadwinner, responded to the man's hostility attitude or "escape" tendencies by so conducting herself and manipulating the affairs of the home, or what was still left of it, that ultimately the man was compelled to leave. In some cases employed women took their children and literally deserted their husbands.

Of course, these latter cases, although numerous, were extreme. In most instances where hostility reactions were intense for months immediately after unemployment first hit the family, the relations of individuals within the home more or less adjusted themselves; very gradually and very painfully, of course; and the family stuck together in a loose, desperate way, fighting the battle against inimical economic forces....

II

Security and Insecurity

Also, the crisis suddenly brought out the fine characteristics of a great many people which in good times had not been apparent to other members of the family. There were cases, for instance, where husbands or wives who commanded some resources were seized by the spirit of sacrifice and helped their in-laws or their spouse's friends, although but a short while before the couple had been on the verge of separation or divorce; and later, when their own affairs were anything but looking up, the desire for breaking up the marital or family ties on the part of one or the other, or both, was less strong, with the result that they stuck it out.

The Depression also had some curious beneficial effects upon families not directly affected by it in an economic way through unemployment or otherwise. There were instances where the wife had been hostile to the husband before the crisis because she considered him economically inferior. His job was low grade and his income was small in comparison with incomes of their friends, neighbors, and acquaintances. The family's social standing was low. They had no car, no radio, which made her unhappy. She nagged him. There were emotional storms. Then, when the Depression came and *he kept his job* at a time when everybody else seemed to be losing theirs, all this suddenly changed. The woman's opinion of the man, including his economic standing, immediately improved. Her disparagement of him diminished. She ceased to nag him. He was all right. He had a job. People who formerly used to look down upon them as economically inferior now envied them; the man had work while they had none. The family's social standing improved immensely. Now the home that once was full of discord, thanks to the Depression, became a happy one. . . .

In 1931 tens of thousands of families in New York and vicinity lost their homes through foreclosures, which was true also in other cities. Most of these luckless families, of course, were working-people, but a great many of them also were families, who not so very long ago, belonged among the "better classes"—business and professional people, some of whom considered themselves wealthy in 1929. One such case was brought to my attention:

In 1929 Mr. D—— was worth over $200,000. He was a retired business man, playing the market "a little." He had a fine home in a New York suburb. His oldest son was at Harvard. Two daughters were in private schools. Mr. and Mrs. D—— had just booked a "round-the-world" passage when the Crash came. Of a sudden the world tumbled down about their heads. Hoping to save at least a part of his fortune, Mr. D—— mortgaged his home, but he no sooner got the mortgage money than it was "swallowed up by Wall Street." He was too proud to appeal to people he knew who were still wealthy. For two years the whole family struggled to save the home. During 1931 they actually starved. They sold their expensive furniture, piece by piece. The girls had to be recalled from their schools. The son quit Harvard. But it was no use. Gradually the family broke up even before the foreclosure on the home, late in 1931. The children now were scattered all over the country. One of the girls sang in a night club in Chicago. The son was a Communist who swore he would never marry or have children under the "present system." After the foreclosure Mr. and Mrs. D—— moved into a furnished room in New York City. He could get nothing to do. His mind was being affected by his plight. Finally, Mrs. D—— appealed to the charity organization they had supported in a small way for years before the Crash.

The above, again, was an extreme case. In a great many cases, of course, Depression-stricken families still hung on to their homes, which, since they had to fight to keep them, were all the more precious to them.

The Depression was having several other general effects on the home or family life of the country, and on the individuals in the home.

The number of marriages fell off during 1930 and still more during 1931. It was hard for a young man to get or keep a job. They, too, boys and girls saw the economic agony and frustration of their elders and they figured—girls more frequently than boys—that it would be sheer madness to marry. I heard boys and girls still in high school state their decision never to marry. They appeared to have an instinctive feeling that they were living in a period of uncertainty and insecurity which was apt to last a long time.

A mid-Depression view of the city dump, Marysville, California. The photographer was Dorothea Lange, one of a group who chronicled with great sensitivity the suffering endured by millions of Americans during the 1930s.

Reading 253

A Liberal Glance at Roosevelt's Plans (1932)

In 1932 the Republican National Convention renominated Herbert Hoover and glumly anticipated the worst. The Democrats nominated Franklin D. Roosevelt, who had compiled a good record in his four years as governor of New York. Roosevelt knew little about economics but a good deal about campaigning; he criticized Hoover both for spending too much and for doing too little about the Depression. Sensing victory, he spoke largely in generalities during the campaign, presenting himself as both progressive and conservative. The *New Republic,* a small but influential liberal political journal which did not think highly of either candidate, tried to assess the consequences of the probable Democratic victory.

From *New Republic,* LXXII (November 9, 1932), pp. 340–341. Subheadings added by the editors.

I

Confusing Charges and Countercharges

By this time any voters who have made an honest attempt to find out what the debate between Republicans and Democrats is all about must have become thoroughly confused. You have Roosevelt declaring that he is a progressive and wants a new deal, thus earning the support of Senators Norris, Wheeler, La Follette, Cutting and many lay citizens. You have Hoover and Mills declaring that Roosevelt is a revolutionary who wants a complete change in the "American system," and supporting that contention with the quaint argument that a Roosevelt victory means an unbalanced budget, inflation of the currency and government ownership of a few utilities. (As if there were anything revolutionary about that!) And then you have conservative supporters of Roosevelt saying that it is stupid to think he really offers the slightest menace to the established order, and contending that he will balance the budget, reject inflation and carry out the Hoover program of revival. Support for this position comes from Socialists and Communists who say that both candidates are as alike as two ball bearings at the hub of the capitalist machine. The next result is that Roosevelt's support is made up of (a) persons who don't like what the Republicans have done and want a drastic change and (b) persons who for some reason dislike Hoover, but want someone else to do about the same things.

What is the truth of the matter? Will Roosevelt be precisely the same kind of President as Hoover? If not, what will he do differently? And do these differences constitute a revolution? Only until the point is settled will those who are in favor of a significant alteration in our system, as well as those who are against such an alteration, know what to expect.

II

Effects of Roosevelt's Plans

So far as we have been able to make out, Roosevelt's idea of a new deal, when it is boiled down from generalities to concrete proposals, refers to a set of specific reforms which do embody a real difference from the Hoover policies, but which imply no change whatever in the basic characteristics of the American economic system. Let us list briefly the more important measures which we may expect, if he carries out his promises:

[1] He will apply emergency relief for the farmers by the "voluntary domestic allotment plan"—a carefully thought-out scheme to make agricultural tariffs effective. This is no more radical than the Farm Board idea, and harmonizes perfectly with the Republican doctrine of protection. But it may be more potent than Hoover "stabilization."

[2] He will extend emergency relief to the unemployed from federal funds when local funds are insufficient. This differs from the Hoover policy, if at all, only because, though Hoover has favored the policy in words, he has checked it in action.

[3] He will attempt to stimulate employment by public works. This is another case of the same.

[4] He will support a national system of labor exchanges and compulsory employment insurance, thus bringing this country up to the stage of civilization attained by European capitalist nations years ago, and giving effect to measures which Hoover himself was formerly supposed to favor.

[5] He will balance the budget by drastic economies and refrain from borrowing except for self-liquidating public works. If this differs from the Hoover policy, it will differ in performance, not in doctrine. But performance will mean that many of Roosevelt's other promises for relief and social services must be broken, because these things mean an enlargement, not a restriction, of public expenditures.

[6] He will do something to regulate the stock market and holding companies, and improve the banking system. He will refrain from stimulating bull markets with optimistic statements. If these promises are skillfully fulfilled, they will strengthen the capitalist system by curbing some of its dishonesties and excesses.

[7] He will apply federal regulations to interstate operations of public utilities and will favor the setting up of "yardsticks" under public ownership by which their performance will be measured, like Muscle Shoals*—a far smaller degree of public ownership than is already practised in most other capitalist nations. The Province of Ontario in Canada is the nearest and most dramatic example of complete public ownership of electric power.

[8] He will apply to railroads a policy which is satisfactory to unions, bosses and bondholders. *Mirabile dictu!*

[9] Though he will not cancel war debts, he will try to revive international trade by bargaining for lower tariffs. But he will not abolish protection of American workers who must compete with lower standards of living abroad.

---

*A proposed dam on the Tennessee River, a project which became part of the Tennessee Valley Authority (TVA)—Eds.

We fail to understand this policy, but whatever it is, there is one thing certain about it—it is completely compatible with capitalism.

[10] He will, in some way undefined at this writing, favor industrial planning. We are willing to bet a thousand to one that when the way is defined, it will leave economic power largely where it now resides.

The upshot of all this is not so startling as the campaign speeches would indicate. No doubt Mr. Hoover sincerely believes that such an unemployment insurance and government operation of Muscle Shoals mean the end of American individualistic capitalism. He is just about stupid enough to believe that. He does not realize that the sort of individualism which arouses his enthusiastic loyalty was really ended long ago. No doubt many of Mr. Roosevelt's progressive supporters think his program really embodies a "new deal." But it embodies nothing that reaches to the heart of the existing system, and almost nothing that has not long ago been adopted by other capitalist nations without greatly changing the distribution of income, or increasing its total amount, or providing security against economic calamity. The Socialists and Communists are no doubt exaggerating when they say that the Hoover and Roosevelt programs are exactly alike. There are discernible differences between them. How important these differences are, depends on one's estimate of the stage of social evolution which we have reached. In our eyes, they are far less important than they would have been fifteen years ago. They constitute a belated application of liberalistic meliorism to a civilization which we ought to be engaged in remodeling.

Roosevelt: Nothing To Fear but Fear Itself (1933)

Franklin D. Roosevelt (1882–1945) may not have known much about economics in 1932, but as governor of New York, which was hard-hit by the Depression, he had established the first relief agency operated by a state. In March 1933, his inaugural address as President made a strong impression upon a nation further alarmed by the widespread closing of banks in the winter of 1932–1933.

From *Nothing to Fear, The Selected Addresses of Franklin D. Roosevelt, 1932–1945*, by B. D. Zevin, ed. Copyright © 1946 by Houghton Mifflin Company. Reprinted by permission of the publisher.

I

The Problems We Face

I am certain that my fellow Americans expect that on my induction into the Presidency I will address them with a candor and a decision which the present situation of our Nation impels. This is preeminently the time to speak the truth, the whole truth, frankly and boldly. Nor need we shrink from honestly

President Franklin D. Roosevelt delivers his inaugural address, March 4, 1933. The new President spoke of himself as the leader in a "war" to be waged against the Depression, a war as demanding as any the nation had yet fought.

facing conditions in our country today. This great Nation will endure as it has endured, will revive and will prosper. So, first of all, let me assert my firm belief that the only thing we have to fear is fear itself—nameless, unreasoning, unjustified terror which paralyzes needed efforts to convert retreat into advance. In every dark hour of our national life a leadership of frankness and vigor has met with that understanding and support of the people themselves which is essential to victory. I am convinced that you will again give that support to leadership in these critical days.

In such a spirit on my part and on yours we face our common difficulties. They concern, thank God, only material things. Values have shrunken to fantastic levels; taxes have risen; our ability to pay has fallen; government of all kinds is faced by serious curtailment of income; the means of exchange are frozen in the currents of trade; the withered leaves of industrial enterprise lie on every side; farmers find no markets for their produce; the savings of many years in thousands of families are gone.

More important, a host of unemployed citizens face the grim problem of existence, and an equally great number toil with little return. Only a foolish optimist can deny the dark realities of the moment.

Yet our distress comes from no failure of substance. We are stricken by no plague of locusts. Compared with the perils which our forefathers conquered because they believed and were not afraid, we have still much to be thankful for. Nature still offers her bounty and human efforts have multiplied it. Plenty is at our doorstep, but a generous use of it languishes in the very sight of the supply. Primarily this is because rulers of the exchange of mankind's goods have failed through their own stubbornness and their own incompetence, have admitted their failure, and have abdicated. Practices of the unscrupulous money changers stand indicted in the court of public opinion, rejected by the hearts and minds of men.

True they have tried, but their efforts have been cast in the pattern of an outworn tradition. Faced by failure of credit they have proposed only the lending of more money. Stripped of the lure of profit by which to induce our people to follow their false leadership, they have resorted to exhortations, pleading tearfully for restored confidence. They know only the rules of a generation of self-seekers. They have no vision, and when there is no vision the people perish.

The money changers have fled from their high seats in the temple of our civilization. We may now restore that temple to the ancient truths. The measure of the restoration lies in the extent to which we apply social values more noble than mere monetary profit.

Happiness lies not in the mere possession of money; it lies in the joy of achievement, in the thrill of creative effort. The joy and moral stimulation of work no longer must be forgotten in the mad chase of evanescent profits. These dark days will be worth all they cost us if they teach us that our true destiny is not to be ministered unto but to minister to ourselves and to our fellow men.

Recognition of the falsity of material wealth as the standard of success goes hand in hand with the abandonment of the false belief that public office and high political position are to be valued only by the standards of pride of place and personal profit; and there must be an end to a conduct in banking and in business which too often has given to a sacred trust the likeness of callous and selfish wrongdoing. Small wonder that confidence languishes, for it thrives only on honesty, on honor, on the sacredness of obligations, on faithful protection, on unselfish performance; without them it cannot live.

Restoration calls, however, not for changes in ethics alone. This Nation asks for action, and action now.

II

The Tasks Ahead

Our greatest primary task is to put people to work. This is no unsolvable problem if we face it wisely and courageously. It can be accomplished in part by direct recruiting by the Government itself, treating the task as we would treat the emergency of a war, but at the same time, through this employment, accomplishing greatly needed projects to stimulate and reorganize the use of our natural resources.

Hand in hand with this we must frankly recognize the overbalance of population in our industrial centers and, by engaging on a national scale in a redistribution, endeavor to provide a better use of the land for those best fitted for the land. The task can be helped by definite efforts to raise the values of agricultural products and with this the power to purchase the output of our cities. It can be helped by preventing realistically the tragedy of the growing loss through foreclosure of our small homes and our farms. It can be helped by insistence that the Federal, State, and local Governments act forthwith on the demand that their cost be drastically reduced. It can be helped by the unifying of relief activities which today are often scattered, uneconomical, and unequal. It can be helped by national planning for and supervision of all forms of transportation and of communications and other utilities which have a definitely public character. There are many ways in which it can be helped, but it can never be helped merely by talking about it. We must act and act quickly.

Finally, in our progress toward a resumption of work we require two safeguards against a return of the evils of the old order: there must be a strict supervision of all banking and credits and investments, so that there will be an end to speculation with other people's money; and there must be provision for an adequate but sound currency.

These are the lines of attack. I shall presently urge upon a new Congress, in special session, detailed measures for their fulfillment, and I shall seek the immediate assistance of the several States.

Through this program of action we address ourselves to putting our own national house in order and making income balance outgo. Our international trade relations, though vastly important, are in point of time and necessity secondary to the establishment of a sound national economy. I favor as a practical policy the putting of first things first. I shall spare no effort to restore world trade by international economic readjustment, but the emergency at home cannot wait on that accomplishment. . . .

Action in this image and to this end is feasible under the form of government which we have inherited from our ancestors. Our Constitution is so simple and practical that it is possible always to meet extraordinary needs by changes in emphasis and arrangement without loss of essential form. That is why our constitutional system has proved itself the most superbly enduring political mechanism the modern world has produced. It has met every stress of vast expansion of territory, of foreign wars, of bitter internal strife, of world relations.

It is to be hoped that the normal balance of Executive and legislative authority may be wholly adequate to meet the unprecedented task before us. But it may be that an unprecedented demand and need for undelayed action may call for temporary departure from that normal balance of public procedure.

I am prepared under my constitutional duty to recommend the measures that a stricken Nation in the midst of a stricken world may require. These measures, or such other measures as the Congress may build out of its experience and wisdom, I shall seek, within my constitutional authority, to bring to speedy adoption.

But in the event that the Congress shall fail to take one of these two courses, and in the event that the national emergency is still critical, I shall not evade the clear course of duty that will then confront me. I shall ask the Congress for the one remaining instrument to meet the crisis—broad Executive power to wage a war against the emergency, as great as the power that would be given to me if we were in fact invaded by a foreign foe.

For the trust reposed in me I will return the courage and the devotion that befit the time. I can do no less.

We face the arduous days that lie before us in the warm courage of national unity; with the clear consciousness of seeking old and precious moral values; with the clean satisfaction that comes from the stern performance of duty by old and young alike. We aim at the assurance of a rounded and permanent national life.

We do not distrust the future of essential democracy. The people of the United States have not failed. In their need they have registered a mandate that they want direct, vigorous action. They have asked for discipline and direction under leadership. They have made me the present instrument of their wishes. In the spirit of the gift I take it.

In this dedication of a Nation we humbly ask the blessing of God. May He protect each and every one of us. May He guide me in the days to come.

TOPIC 51

THE CREATION OF THE NEW DEAL

The Great Depression resembled a time of social revolution because the enormous economic problems and distresses were accompanied by real possibilities for turning government and society in new directions. The economic crisis of the early 1930s generated a variety of solutions, ranging from military rule to technocracy (in which society would be run by engineers) to socialism. The possibility of genuine change in American society and politics appeared more likely than at any time since Lincoln's assumption of near-dictatorial powers at times during the Civil War.

Nearly all proposals for dealing with the Depression contained the assumption that the federal government should assume far greater responsibility for national economic and social well-being. The so-called New Deal, the Democratic Party's answer to the crisis after it swept Congress and the Presidency in 1932, created vast new federal powers at the expense of the states and private business, and the change became one of the New Deal's enduring legacies. Other dimensions of the New Deal will appear in the following pages.

These readings suggest some of the pressures under which President Franklin D. Roosevelt and his party worked from the early 1930s until 1935, when they began to realize that despite their many plans and programs, and despite the renewed authority given them by smashing victories in the Congressional elections of 1934, the economy continued to stagnate without real signs of recovery.

Reading 255

A Plea for a Planned Economy (1932)

Socialists and other critics of the American system of private enterprise had long argued that it caused booms by ruthless competition and depressions by overproduction. They also charged that its profit motive, its tendencies toward monopoly, and the strong influence of capitalists on government resulted in price and wage policies that put too much wealth in the hands of too few people and too little purchasing power in the hands of the masses of farmers and workers. The events of 1929 to 1932 seemed to offer considerable justification for their critique. The critics looked abroad with great interest at Soviet Russia, which had brought its factory production and many other aspects of economic life under state control. Similarly, the Fascist government in Italy, which was organizing private business into giant corporations to be controlled by the state, also attracted attention. George Soule, an economist and an editor of the *New Republic* (see Reading 253), argued in 1932 for an American version of planning but without the totalitarian features of Russia and Italy.

Reprinted with permission of The Macmillan Company from *A Planned Society* by George Soule, pp. 232-233, 252-254, 262-263. Copyright © 1932 by George Soule. Subheadings added by the editors.

I

Plentiful Resources

The fundamental observation which points to most of the faults and disparities of our economy is that it might produce many more goods, and much more human welfare, than it does. We have the natural resources, the engineering skill, the plants and machinery, the labor supply, to increase the average standard of living steadily and fairly rapidly. It is now commonplace to speak of the absurd contrast between "overproduction," or over-equipment to produce, almost every necessity and luxury of life, and the fact that many persons are in want. This fact sets the stage for our effort.

Our late "new era" of supposedly endless prosperity had two pretensions which, though they were far from being realities under an unplanned order, may be taken as natural starting points for a plan. Their desirability has gained wide acceptance. One is the "economy of high wages"; the other, the stabilization of industry and employment. The failure to effectuate them has caused surprise among the strongest adherents of an unplanned economy. Among the general population it has caused breadlines, broken families, suicides, rickety children, scurvy, tuberculosis, hopeless and disordered minds. It is worth while to challenge the business order to get down to brass tacks about these pretensions. Either it should abandon them or else seriously set to work to make them good. . . .

II

Planning Agency

There is needed a National Economic Board at the top, representing the whole public. This would correlate the plans and practices of the various industries with one another. It would bring together the relevant statistical material from all sources and fill in the gaps. It would work out a general plan for raising the lowest incomes and regulating the flow of investment and credit. It would turn its attention, like a searchlight, on those areas and industries which were causing trouble and obstructing the general program. It would advise government as to its responsibilities in the carrying out of the program.

This Board should be composed, not of bargaining representatives of various interests, but of qualified experts representing the nation as a whole. It should, of course, have an adequate staff of economists, statisticians, engineers and accountants. As a representative of the general interest, it ought to be established by law, with certain duties and powers. It should be supported by governmental appropriation, and appointed by the President, with the advice and consent of the Senate.

One of the first duties of a Board like this would be to help in working out the best form of organization for each industry, and represent the public in the drafting of that organization. It would, for instance, call together representatives of the soft coal mine owners, the consumers of coal, the coal technicians and the organizations of labor in coal. It would say to them:

> Your industry is, and has been for years, one of the chief obstacles to a genuine prosperity for the nation. It must be organized to pay higher wages without charging unduly high prices, give steady employment, and offer efficient service. What needs to be done to control your industry and make it a sound unit in a national economy? We are instructed by Congress to aid you and your experts in formulating a plan of organization for these purposes. We are delegating our own experts to advise you at every stage of your researches and deliberations. We will give you two years to produce a proposal, though we should like one as soon as possible. When your proposal is ready, we will either approve it or disapprove it, having in mind the objectives to be sought. If you do not produce a plan, or do not produce one which we can approve, we are instructed by Congress to make one of our own. If legislation is required, we shall recommend to Congress the measures we approve. After the coal organization is set up, we shall continue to keep in close touch with it, in order to see that the objectives are approached, and in order to correlate your annual plans for wages, employment, production, prices, profits and investment with those of other industries.

In tackling an organizing job of this kind, the Board would have in mind the possibility, not merely of a trade association or cartel, but of large consolidations under some form of public regulation, and of complete public ownership, by such a device as a publicly owned corporation which would buy out the existing individual owners with debentures. The Board should not be limited in its ultimate choice by any bias in favor of "private enterprise" on the one hand or in favor of "socialism" on the other. It should choose the form which, after thorough examination, seemed best suited to the ends in view. My own opinion is that in this case, public ownership would be found most desirable, as in other basic industries.

III
Goals of Planning

The Board would, in the same manner, put up to the construction industry and its chief customers the task of organizing to prevent the wide swings of activity which now do much to shove us to heights of inflation and then plunge us down again. It would put experts to work in order to see what would have to be done to provide good housing, in healthful and pleasant surroundings, for the majority of the population which now cannot afford it. This is one of the greatest unused opportunities to provide a better standard of life and, at the same time, furnish a large amount of employment in the building industry and those which supply its materials. It is a magnificent way to use surplus savings, instead of pouring them into unneeded and unused equipment.

So the problems of each productive industry would be approached, industry by industry....

The planning activity here sketched would, if it succeeded, fulfill the requirements learned from our war experience in planning. It begins with an objective capable of arousing enthusiasm—a war against poverty, unemployment, insecurity, an expansion of the standard of living, a great national effort toward a finer civilization, a desire to do a good job and use properly the tools we have. By its devices to increase purchasing power and predict consumer demand, and its control of expenditures for new investment, it builds up the economic equivalent for political police power. It can decide questions as to how much we need to produce and in what order. It can point out to industry the necessities inherent in the situation—the facts which, in the end, exert authority. For the very essence of planning is not just someone's capricious desire to plan, but conscious adjustment to the situation created by modern technology.

The Need for Public Investment (1932)

Few people in 1932 had any new ideas about coping with the Depression short of the adoption of a planned economy (Reading 255). One man with a new idea was the distinguished British economist John Maynard Keynes. Keynes' ideas on monetary policy were adopted in modified form—much too timidly, Keynes thought—by the New Dealers. Though denounced by conservatives, Keynesian policies were eventually adopted by both major political parties in the 1960s and 1970s. In 1932 Stuart Chase, a writer, lecturer, and consultant on economics, outlined Keynes' ideas in a book.

Reprinted with permission of The Macmillan Company from *A New Deal* by Stuart Chase, pp. 1–2, 142, 143–145. Copyright © 1932 by Stuart Chase. Subheadings added by the editors.

I
The Purpose of an Economic System

John Maynard Keynes tells us that in one hundred years there will be no economic problem. He is probably right. We have already largely solved the problem of production, in the sense that the nations of America and Western Europe are equipped to produce more than enough to go around. In a few years Russia will undoubtedly join them. We have left the economy of scarcity behind and entered the economy of abundance—though very few of us realize this, and most of our thinking is still in terms of scarcity economics, a cultural lag which we shall presently discuss. A billion and a half horses of mechanical energy, added to the time-honored stock of man and animal power, have at last put us in the position where, if we care to concentrate our energy, we can raise more food than we can eat, build more houses than we can inhabit, fabricate more clothing than we can wear out. Only by wasting and even deliberate destruction—such as the burning of cotton, corn, and coffee—can we dispose of the present output under the prevailing price system.

Distribution, the other wing of the economic problem, is *not* solved, as the present depression bears eloquent testimony. We can pile up the goods in the warehouse with an efficiency hitherto unknown to homo sapiens, but there they stick. We cannot get them out in sufficient volume either to keep the productive plant functioning steadily, and thus economically, or to keep the general population adequately fed, sheltered, and clothed. At times—as in America from 1922 to 1929—the flow, while far below capacity, leaving many millions on the ragged edge, is relatively better. At other times—as in 1921, and from 1930 to the present date—it is totally inadequate. Warehouses bulge and children cry for food....

If the government borrowed or inflated for a bold program of public works which absorbed two or three million of the unemployed directly—thus feeding a huge new stream into the river bed of purchasing power—thus stimulating industry—thus causing more of the unemployed to be absorbed as food and clothing workers—thus adding to purchasing power again—thus checking the domestic price fall—thus strengthening the banks.... We should come close to a recurring decimal upward. The budget, left to go hang today, would be balanced out of the taxes of a revived nation tomorrow. "The idea," says Keynes, "that a public works program represents a desperate risk to cure a moderate evil is the reverse of truth. It is a negligible risk to cure a monstrous anomaly." And again: "To bring up the bogy of inflation as an objection to capital expenditure [by the state] is like warning a patient who is wasting away from emaciation of the dangers of excessive corpulence." And again: "It is not the miser who gets rich; but he who lays out his money in fruitful investment." ...

II

Role of the State

To repeat and emphasize again: The state can do what no individual or private group can do. As Czar of the nation's money, it can expand or shrink the supply, rising above the limitations of the individual who must live within the rules. Governments make the rules. If the state desires to check deflation it can check it; to create employment on useful and worthy projects, it can create it; to augment purchasing power, it can augment it. Nobody else can do it. Fire engines are for conflagrations too great for the householder to extinguish. The bankers and their friends want to keep the fire horses safe in their stalls while the world burns down. A difficulty with this proposal is that the engine house may burn down too. If we carry "economy" of every kind to its logical conclusion, we shall find that we have balanced the budget at nought on both sides, with all of us flat on our backs starving to death from a refusal, for reasons of economy, to buy one another's services. Economy is only useful from the national point of view in so far as it diminishes our consumption of imported goods. For the rest its fruits are entirely wasted in unemployment, business losses and reduced savings.

One parting shot, before we leave this monstrous animism. The witch doctors say that the state should embark on no extensive public works because it takes capital away from private business, and the state—according to the doctrine of laissez-faire—is notoriously inefficient. This assumption is packed with nonsense. To begin with, it presupposes a fixed loan fund; the more the state gets, the less for private enterprise. There is no such fixity; the credit pyramid, as we have seen, can shrink and expand within wide limits, even on a gold apex. Secondly, it assumes that private capital *wants* to expand. If there is one thing which private capital will not do in a depression it is extend its facilities. It would rather take a red-hot poker than a new bank loan. The incentive is all in the direction of getting out of debt, rather than borrowing more. If there is expansion to be done, the state must do it, for nobody else in his senses can afford to. Thirdly, whether the state is more or less efficient than private enterprise is an excellent subject for college debating teams, but has nothing to do with this particular emergency. "Even if half the public works program were wasted we would still be better off." Why? Because in the end, it is either public works or the dole, and with the former, you at least secure something for your money. Think of the useful and necessary things which the state can do—and which private enterprise, even under "normal" conditions, will not do—highways, grade crossings, water ways, parks, playgrounds, afforestation, slum clearance, education, research, regional planning. Every day the government postpones such measures makes the problem of halting deflation more difficult. By the time this book is in print it may be too late for salvation by public works alone.

The New Deal Attacks the Crisis (1933)

Once in office Roosevelt and his advisers moved quickly with a legislative program to give motion to the nearly idle economy. The following reading recounts some of the major elements of the early New Deal.

From The Urban Nation, 1920–1960 *by George E. Mowry. Copyright © 1965 by George E. Mowry. Reprinted by permission of Hill and Wang, Inc. Pp. 93–95, 95–96, 96–98, 98–99. Subheadings, footnote, and bracketed material added by the editors.*

I

The First Measures

On March 4 Roosevelt boldly told the country that he expected unusual speed and action

TABLE 1 PRESIDENTIAL ELECTIONS, 1932–1944

	CANDIDATES	PARTIES	ELECTORAL VOTE	POPULAR VOTE
1932	Franklin D. Roosevelt	Democratic	472	22,809,638
	Herbert C. Hoover	Republican	59	15,758,901
	Norman Thomas	Socialist		881,951
	William Z. Foster	Communist		102,785
	William D. Upshaw	Prohibition		81,869
	Verne L. Reynolds	Socialist Labor		33,276
	William H. Harvey	Liberty		53,425
1936	Franklin D. Roosevelt	Democratic	523	27,752,869
	Alfred M. Landon	Republican	8	16,674,665
	William Lemke	Union		882,479
	Norman Thomas	Socialist		187,720
	Earl Browder	Communist		80,159
	D. Leigh Colvin	Prohibition		37,847
	John W. Aiken	Socialist Labor		12,777
1940	Franklin D. Roosevelt	Democratic	449	27,307,819
	Wendell L. Willkie	Republican	82	22,321,018
	Norman Thomas	Socialist		99,557
	Roger Q. Babson	Prohibition		57,812
	Earl Browder	Communist		46,251
	John W. Aiken	Socialist Labor		14,892
1944	Franklin D. Roosevelt	Democratic	432	25,606,585
	Thomas E. Dewey	Republican	99	22,014,745
	Norman Thomas	Socialist		80,518
	Claude A. Watson	Prohibition		74,758
	Edward A. Teichert	Socialist Labor		45,336

from Congress, but that if Congress should fail, he was prepared to seek extraordinary emergency powers of a wartime nature to confront the desperate situation. On his first day in office the President closed all the nation's banks without grant of authority.* Five

*A number of governors had already closed banks in their states to prevent frightened depositors from withdrawing their savings—Eds.

days later he presented to Congress a draft banking bill which, when passed in a few hours, went far to preserve banking assets and to restore public confidence in the financial structure. Observing on the following day that many liberal governments had been "wrecked on rocks of loose fiscal policy," he asked for and obtained wide powers to economize on veterans' pensions and to slash pay rates to Federal employees. But within the next six weeks he secured the passage of a spate of measures involving the expenditure of billions of dollars. Half a billion was made available to the states for direct unemployment relief. Three billion was appropriated for a gigantic public works program. The creation of the Civilian Conservation Corps and the farm and home loan policy to rescue distressed mortgages obligated the government for billions more.

The gigantic New Deal relief program, which in its entirety and over an eight-year span touched almost one-third of the nation's workers, was at once the most controversial and the most popular of the Administration's efforts. The conservative and parochial-minded objected, of course, as much to Roosevelt's assumption that to every man was due the opportunity to work as to the Federal government's direct efforts to provide the jobs. They denounced the New Deal reasoning that by such "pump priming" the economy might be restored to something near the normal level, and they even opposed the extensive public works program which Hoover had accepted in a much less generously financed version. The insistence of Secretary of Interior Harold Ickes, director of the Public Works Administration, that the public buildings, dams, schools, and highways to be built be of palpable use and initiated locally and that many be susceptible of self-amortization did little to soften the more conservative criticism, even though the extent to which private contractors and the building industry would profit was obvious.

II

Hopkins as Administrator

But far more opposition arose to the many relief projects headed by Harry Hopkins, the former director of social work in New York State, who rapidly became for many Republicans the New Deal bête noire, perhaps because of his single-minded devotion to Roosevelt but perhaps also because his ruthless energy and amazing efficiency were wedded to a bundle of intensely held social convictions. He was, observed a colleague, "a high-minded holy roller in a semi-religious frenzy."

At the very start of the relief program Hopkins became public champion of the "immediate work instead of dole" approach for the unemployed, even though many of the projects amounted only to leaf sweeping and grass cutting. The public ridicule of the relief worker on the Federal Emergency Relief Administration's payroll as a man leaning on a shovel and of the project as "boondoggling" deterred Hopkins not at all from combining a deep concern for human dignity with the administration of public relief....

The New Deal's legislative program during the hundred days was just as paradoxical as its actions on economy and spending. Although the President had spoken of driving the money changers from the temple and of substituting "social values" for that of "monetary profit," his financial proposals were characteristically far more temperate than his language. The financial acts of 1933 prohibited commercial banks from trading in securities. They gave the Federal Reserve banks far more power over their members in regulating the rate of interest charged and the volume of loans made. They transferred many decision-making powers from the twelve regional banks to the national Federal Reserve Board, and made the latter more responsive to the President. The Securities Act provided for rigorous regulation over what had been a self-governing free market. But though these acts signalized a radical shift of power away from private enterprisers to the government and made possible for the first time a managed currency, they abolished neither private ownership of the nation's basic financial institutions nor monetary gain as the impelling force of the economy.

III
Novel Farm and Business Programs

The Administration's programs for agriculture and business were also radical, when measured by historic standards.... The essential idea behind the AAA [Agricultural Adjustment Act] was to pay farmers for curtailing production of major crops to achieve a balance between supply and demand. Under the scheme production of important staples was to be limited until their prices reached "parity" with non-agricultural prices, "parity" being defined as the price ratio existing during the years 1909–1914. This "ordered harvest," it was hoped, could be secured by an elaborate plan of setting marketing quotas for individual farmers, who would be paid for their reduced output by a tax on the processers of farm goods. The necessity for approval by two-thirds of the farmers involved gave the plan a democratic aura. The AAA abolished neither private holdings nor the profit motive in farming. But it did emphasize group ends and objectives at the expense of the individual. As violations of both the spirit and the letter of the Act grew, so did the necessity for increasing restrictive and coercive measures. Eventually production quotas for some crops were assigned to particular acreage plots, and the right to grow and sell specific produce at the going market price without penalties was frozen to the ownership of particular land parcels. Agricultural planning thus introduced a host of regulations which substantially curtailed the freedom of the individual husbandman.

The New Deal's major hopes for recovery lay in the National Industrial Recovery Act, the essential ideas for which came from organized business. Arguing that unfair and unregulated competition had in part destroyed prosperity, Gerard Swope, President of the General Electric Company, proposed a vast scheme for the self-regulation of business, which he hoped would "stabilize production and prices" and lead to recovery. This idea, supported by the United States Chamber of Commerce, appealed to the planning-minded Administration, which also saw it as a way to stabilize wages and spread existing work among more men, and at the same time as a vehicle to kill off much more radical labor legislation being proposed in Congress. At a press conference on April 12, Roosevelt said the NIRA's aims were to spread employment over a large number of people, to prevent any individual from working too many hours, and to stop the drift toward concentration of industrial production. The President described it as a national scheme for "the regulation of production." To achieve these diverse and contradictory ends, the Congressional Act set aside the antitrust laws and provided for the adoption of industry-wide codes of business conduct. A national code prohibited the employment of anyone under sixteen years of age, established a minimum wage scale of forty cents an hour and a maximum work week of thirty-five hours.

Hurriedly 557 separate industrial codes were adopted by representatives of various industries, in the making of which small

The Blue Eagle, symbol of the NRA, is depicted rescuing Uncle Sam from the clutches of the Depression. The eagle here wears an academic mortar board, suggesting that the idea for a National Recovery Administration originated among the so-called "Brain Trust," a group of Roosevelt's advisers containing several university professors.

business had some voice, labor had little, and the consumer almost none. Some of the codes, such as in cotton textiles, for example, sought to curtail production by limiting the use of machines, in this case spinning machines, to a maximum number of hours a week. Others sought to establish minimum prices for industrial products by a complicated system of computing production costs. Practically all of them sought to abolish "unfair competition" by regulating the branding of products, the granting of credit terms, rebates for volume buyers, and other discriminatory sales practices. Inherent in the codes was the obvious desire to apportion markets, limit production, and to a degree eliminate price competition. Although the revolutionary scheme was described as one of self-government by industry, it was apparent that the codes were essentially made by the large industries and favorable to them. Hailing the advent of the codes, one Wall Street publication stated that in the long run the "large aggregates of finance capital" stood to benefit from the new regime. But even large business had to pay something for its new freedom from competition and antitrust laws. As will be noted later, Section 7a of the NIRA gave labor the legal right to organize unions, the exploitation of which subsequently resulted in a measurable transfer of power from industry to labor. . . .

IV
Creation of the TVA

During the hundred days, the business community had to submit to another great incursion of governmental power into what had been considered an essentially private domain. The Tennessee Valley Authority Act instituted not only regulation but out right government competition in the production and sale of electric power. The rise of the interstate electric power industry had been one of the amazing business phenomena of the twenties. Technically American industry led the world, and the spread of electrical lighting and appliances throughout cities and farmsteads effected a virtual revolution in American life. The electrical industry had much to its credit in creating artificial daylight out of the night and in decreasing immeasurably the amount of human toil. But the industry, essentially unregulated during the twenties, had become the plaything of corporate manipulators, who, piling holding company upon holding company, contributed little to efficiency and much to the public cost and the profit for the few. Led by Senator George W. Norris of Nebraska, a small band of Congressional reformers sought unsuccessfully in the twenties to bring the interstate aspects of industry under effective public control. They did manage to defeat the efforts of Presidents Coolidge and Hoover to sell the publicly constructed Wilson Dam on the Tennessee River to private interests. Norris' long struggle was partially successful in April 1933, when Roosevelt proposed and Congress passed an act creating the Tennessee Valley Authority, a public corporation with wide powers to plan for the full development of the natural resources of the Tennessee River valley, comprising most of the upper South. Ostensibly the TVA was established to engage in flood control and to further navigation of the river, tasks in which it succeeded admirably. But a subsidiary clause in the Act empowered it to sell power, and within a few years the manufacture, transport, and sale of electric current from its twenty newly constructed dams became its major concern.

Frances Perkins: The Roosevelt I Knew

As governor of New York Roosevelt named as his commissioner of labor Frances Perkins (1882–1965), a former settlement house worker expert in social problems. As President he appointed her Secretary of Labor, the first woman to hold a Cabinet post. Historians have praised her memoirs of the New Deal era as among the most candid and objective of those who served with Roosevelt.

From *The Roosevelt I Knew* by Frances Perkins. Copyright 1946 by Frances Perkins. All rights reserved. Reprinted by permission of The Viking Press, Inc. Pp. 328–331, 331–332. Subheadings added by the editors.

I
Believed in Private Ownership

I knew Roosevelt long enough and under enough circumstances to be quite sure that he was no political or economic radical. I take it that the essence of economic radicalism is to believe that the best system is the one in which private ownership of the means of production is abolished in favor of public ownership. But Roosevelt took the status quo in our economic system as much for granted as his family. They were a part of his life, and so was our system; he was content with it. He felt that it ought to be humane, fair, and honest, and that adjustments ought to be made so that the people would not suffer from poverty and neglect, and so that all would share.

He thought business could be a fine art and could be conducted on moral principles. He thought the test ought to be whether or not business is conducted partly for the welfare of the community. He could not accept the idea that the sole purpose of business was to make more and more money. He thought business should make and distribute goods with enough profit to give the owners a comfortable living and enable them to save something to invest in other productive enterprises. Yes, he felt that stockholders had a place and right and that a business ought to be conducted so that they would earn modest interest, while the workers got good wages and the community profited by low prices and steady work.

But he couldn't see why a man making enough money should want to go on scheming and plotting, sacrificing and living under nervous tension, just to make more money. That, of course, made him unable to sympathize with the ambitions and drive of much of the American business fraternity. But he liked and got along well with those businessmen who shared, as many did, the point of view that business is conducted partly for the

255

welfare of the country as well as to make money. They liked and trusted him and understood his objectives. Gerard Swope of the General Electric Company, Thomas J. Watson of the International Business Machines Company, Ernest Draper of the Hills Brothers Company, Donald and Hugh Comer, southern textile manufacturers, who had a humane if not a trade union conception of the rights of their workers and of the employers' duty in relation to them, were all comprehensible to the President. He liked Walter Chrysler, although I am not sure that Chrysler fully embraced the idea that enough is enough, particularly if his rivals were making more. But he did have some of the attitude that there was nothing remarkable in itself about making money.

It is true that Roosevelt never met a payroll, and many businessmen took it into their heads that he could not possibly comprehend business unless he had had that experience. This, of course, is part of the limitation of the business fraternity itself.

II

Willing To Experiment

Roosevelt was entirely willing to try experiments. He had no theoretical or ideological objections to public ownership when that was necessary, but it was his belief that it would greatly complicate the administrative system if we had too much. He recognized, however, that certain enterprises could best be carried on under public control. He recognized that we probably would never have enough cheap electric power to supply the needs of the people if the Government did not undertake vast programs in the Tennessee and Missouri valleys, and he believed that plenty of power at low rates was necessary for the development of a high standard of living and for business progress. Just as the need for production in wartime is so great that the Government must take a hand in it, so he was able to accept the idea that in peacetime too the Government must sometimes carry on enterprises because of the enormous amount of capital expenditure required or the preponderance of the experimental element. He was willing to concede that there were some fields in which such Government participation might be required permanently. But he always resisted the frequent suggestion of the Government's taking over railroads, mines, etc., on the ground that it was unnecessary and would be a clumsy way to get the service needed.

A superficial young reporter once said to Roosevelt in my presence, "Mr. President, are you a Communist?"

"No."

"Are you a capitalist?"

"No."

"Are you a Socialist?"

"No," he said, with a look of surprise as if he were wondering what he was being cross examined about.

The young man said, "Well, what is your philosophy then?"

"Philosophy?" asked the President, puzzled. "Philosophy? I am a Christian and a Democrat—that's all."

Those two words expressed, I think, just about what he was. They expressed the extent of his political and economic radicalism. He was willing to do experimentally whatever was necessary to promote the Golden Rule and other ideals he considered to be Christian, and whatever could be done under the Constitution of the United States and under the principles which have guided the Democratic party.

The young reporter, or his editor, did not think the answer had any news value, and nothing was printed about it. I suppose if the President had answered that he thought there was something remarkable in Communism or capitalism, it would have been a headline story.

III

Views of Government

I am certain that he had no dream of great changes in the economic or political patterns of our life. I never heard him express any preference for any form of government other than the representative republic and state-federal system which have become the pattern of political organization in the United States under the Constitution. At the beginning of his administration, and also, I think, at the end, he would have said that the states and their administrative systems should be strengthened and maintained. Nevertheless, federal legislation and administration must occur in some fields. If there could be greater co-operation among the states, that would be fine. But they should permit federal intervention on behalf of certain things that could not be done by them alone.

He believed in leadership from the office of the President, a leadership based upon the immense sources of information and analysis which the Executive Department had and which were available to the President. He fully recognized, however, the importance of Congress and the desirability of maintaining the strength of our congressional system. For that reason he wished at times that the people of the country would be more careful about whom they sent to Congress, to be sure that the congressman elected would not only represent his constituents but take part, in-

Reading 259

telligently and constructively, in making laws for all the people....

Roosevelt was not very familiar with economic theory. He thought of wealth in terms of the basic wealth in agriculture, transportation, and services which were the familiar pattern of his youth. He recognized or took for granted the changes that had come about in our economy in his own lifetime: the shift in emphasis from agriculture to industry and distribution, the importance of the financial elements. Honorable methods in all business matters seemed to him imperative and to be insisted upon, by changes in the law if necessary. And under "honorable" he instinctively included wages and working conditions of the best, together with friendly, fair industrial relations. But, he had, I am sure, no thought or desire to impose any overall economic or political change on the United States. Some of the high-strung people who advised him from time to time did, I think, have ideas of this sort, but he always laughed them off and used their brilliant analyses for some project that would do some immediate good to people in distress.

Did the New Deal represent a sharp break with American traditions? Most New Dealers felt that it did not, that Roosevelt's policies had evolved out of the nation's reform tradition, although some of them felt that these policies were not evolving fast enough. Cartoonist Clifford Berryman shows the New Deal tree, characteristically in academic garb to show its "Brain Trust" roots, blossoming into a profusion of "alphabet" agencies.

Hoover Denounces the New Deal (1935)

As the New Deal entered its third year Herbert Hoover, who had predicted disaster if Roosevelt were elected, felt that events were proving him right. This excerpt comes from a speech he gave to Republicans in Sacramento, California, on March 22, 1935.

Reprinted by permission of Charles Scribner's Sons from Addresses Upon the American Road, 1933-1938. *Copyright 1938 by Edgar Rickard. Pp. 40-43. Subheadings added by the editors.*

I
Republican Responsibility

The Republican Party today has the greatest responsibility that has come to it since the days of Abraham Lincoln. That responsibility is to raise the standard in defense of fundamental American principles. It must furnish the rallying point for all those who believe in these principles and are determined to defeat those who are responsible for their daily jeopardy.

1. The American people have directly before them the issue of maintaining and perfecting our system of orderly individual liberty under constitutionally conducted government, or of rejecting it in favor of the newly created system of regimentation and bureaucratic domination in which men and women are not masters of government but are the pawns or dependents of a centralized and potentially self-perpetuating government. That is, shall we as a nation stand on the foundations of Americanism, gaining the great powers of progress inherent in it, correcting abuses which arise within it, widening the security and opportunities that can alone be built upon it?

Before us is the sink into which first one great nation after another abroad is falling. America must look today, as in the past, to the creative impulses of free men and women, born of the most enterprising and self-reliant stock in the world, for productive genius, for expansion of enterprise, for economic recovery, for restoration of normal jobs, for increased standards of living, for reform of abuse of governmental or economic powers, and for advance from outworn modes of thought. The freedom of men to think, to act, to achieve, is now being hampered.

2. The American people have a right to determine for themselves this fundamental issue, and it is solely through the Republican Party that it can be presented for determination at the ballot box. To accomplish this the country is in need of a rejuvenated and vigorous Republican organization. That rebirth of the Republican Party transcends any personal interest or the selfish interest of any group. That organization will be the stronger if, like your own sessions, it springs from the people who believe in these principles.

3. It is well that the young men and women of the Republican Party should meet and give attention to this drift from national moorings. Some of the concrete results of these policies are already apparent. The most solemn government obligations have been repudiated. The nation is faced with the greatest debt ever known to our country. The currency has been rendered uncertain. The government has been centralized under an enormous bureaucracy in Washington which has dictated and limited the production of our industries, increasing the costs and prices of their products with inevitable decreased consumption. Monopolistic practices have been organized on a gigantic scale. Small business men have been disabled and crushed. Class conflicts have been created and embittered. The government has gone into business in competition with its citizens. Citizens have been coerced, threatened and penalized for offenses unknown to all our concepts of liberty. The courts are proclaiming repeated violations of the Constitution.

Because of food destruction and restraint on farm production, foreign food is pouring into our ports, purchase of which should have been made from our farmers. The cost of living is steadily advancing. More people are dependent upon the government for relief than ever before. Recovery is still delayed. The productive genius of our people, which is the sole road to recovery and to increased standards of living, is being stifled, the nation impoverished instead of enriched. The theories of this Administration do not work. They are no longer a propagandized millennium; they are self-exposed.

4. The people have a right to an opportunity to change these policies. It is the duty of the Republican Party to offer that opportunity. And beyond insistence upon American foundations of government, it is the duty of the Party to insist upon realistic methods of recovery, real jobs for labor and real markets for the farmer. Those methods lie in removing the shackles and uncertainties from enterprise. After nearly six years of depression, liquidation, restriction of all manner of purchases and improvements, we stand on the threshold of a great forward, economic movement, if only the paralyzing effects of mistaken governmental policies and activities may be removed.

II
Need for More Production

The present conception of a national economy based upon scarcity must in all common sense be reversed to an economy based upon production, or workman, farmer, and business man alike are defeated. Surely economic life advances only through increasing production by use of every instrument science gave to us, through lowering of costs and prices with consequent increase in consumption, and through higher real wages to the worker and real return to the farmer. Effective reform of abuses in business and finance must be undertaken through regulation and not through bureaucratic dictation or government operation. Protection to individual enterprise from monopolies must be re-established whereby the smaller businesses may live. Stifling uncertainties of currency manipulation must be removed. Government expenditures which, if continued on the present scale, can create only bankruptcy or calamitous inflation, must be curtailed. The effective participation of the States and local governments in relief under non-partisan administrators must be re-established so that waste, extravagance, and politics may be eliminated and the people better served.... Better safeguards to the individual against the dislocations of advancing industry, national calamity and old age must be discovered. But these problems of business, agriculture, and labor become much easier with a restoration of economic common sense. Indeed, a score of economic and social questions must be solved, and in their answers are locked the real advancement of life and the attainment of security and contentment in the American home—for that is the ultimate expression of American life. But their solution will not be found in violation of the foundations of human liberty.

An Attack on Capitalism (1935)

To American socialists the failure of Roosevelt to restore the economy to normal operation by 1935 was proof that the New Deal in reality served the interests of big business. This Marxist critique indicates the unhappiness of at least parts of the left.

From *The Economic Consequences of the New Deal*, copyright 1935 by Benjamin Stolberg and Warren Jay Vinton. Reprinted by permission of Harcourt Brace Jovanovich, Inc. Pp. 64–67, 81–82, 85. Subheadings added by the editors.

I

New Deal Inconsistencies

In its attempt to evade the fundamental contradictions of our economy the New Deal was bound to rely on panaceas. Its whole program is in essence nothing but a well-intentioned synthesis of errors. What it accomplishes in one direction it undoes in another. It is like the Russian peasant who cut some cloth from the front of his pants to patch the hole in the seat; and then cut from the leg of his pants to patch the front. After repeating this operation a dozen times he wound up, very much like the New Deal, with his pants all in patches and the migratory hole still there. (Of course the Moujik finally got himself a new pair of pants, but that is another story.)

The strangest of all the New Deal illusions is its dream of making Big Ownership accept an economy of abundance. But, unfortunately for this Utopian vision, capitalism is an economy of measured scarcity. Business is successful to the extent to which it gauges correctly that optimum point of profit at which a maximum price coincides with a maximum demand. And the more nearly it succeeds in curtailing production at that point, the better business it is. The vital concern of Big Industry is to prevent an abundance of goods from flooding the market.

In boom times production is tempted into abundance and scarcity gets out of hand. Capitalist recovery from the ensuing depression lies in the reorganization of scarcity. During the New Era Big Industry blundered into a disastrous abundance. And its potential productivity is now so great that it cannot get out of the depression under its own power. It needed the aid of government to reestablish scarcity and to enforce recovery; and that is exactly what the National Recovery Administration is all about. The codes, avowedly written for the "regulation of competition," are obviously an apparatus for industrial scarcity-mongering.

In order to protect Big Ownership in its scarcity program, the New Deal had to integrate agriculture into the same program. For agriculture during the World War had so increased its production that the collapse of its price structure became a permanent threat to manufacturing prices. And the organization of agricultural scarcity is exactly what the Agricultural Adjustment Administration is all about.

II

Repression of Labor

The inner drive of labor, however, is always for greater abundance, for more goods for less money, for shops running at full speed. And so, to integrate labor into this program of anti-social scarcity, the New Deal has been forced, for all its liberal pretensions, to liquidate every expression of labor unrest. And that is exactly why the President insists on a truce between capital and labor, which it is the function of the National Labor Relations Board to achieve.

In short, the first and foremost of the New Deal panaceas, the N.R.A. and the A.A.A., have only served to render more explicit, through an enormous administrative apparatus, what has always been implicit in the nature of Big Ownership. Under capitalism scarcity is the life of trade.

But since it is in the nature of panaceas to mistake their objectives, the New Deal goes right on believing that it is socially planning towards a more abundant life. And to reassure itself it has set up the National Consumers Board, under the chairmanship of the daughter of the Harriman millions, to attempt to undo exactly what the N.R.A. and the A.A.A. were set up to do. The purely academic function of this Board is to organize the notoriously unorganized consumer to brave the massed power of Big Industry in its drive toward scarcity....

The economic consequences of the New Deal have been exactly what might have been foreseen by a competent Brain Trust. Capitalist recovery, on the classic lines of laissez-faire, has not only been impeded but arrested. And its only economic alternative, social planning on socialist lines, has been sedulously avoided.

III

Promotes Big Ownership

The New Deal is trying to right the unbalance of our economic life by strengthening all its contradictions. For Big Ownership it tries to safeguard profits and to keep intact the instruments of its financial domination. For the middle classes it tries to safeguard their small investments, which only serves to reintrench Big Ownership. For labor it tries to raise wages, increase employment, and assure some minimum of economic safety, while at the same time it opposes labor's real interests through its scarcity program. In trying to move in every direction at once the New Deal betrays the fact that it has no policy.

And it has no policy because as a liberal democracy it must ignore the overwhelming fact of our epoch, the irreconcilable conflict between capital and labor. The result is that we are today neither an economy of balanced scarcity, nor an economy of progressive abundance, nor in transit from one to the other. We are today in an economy of stalemate....

When profits rise while wages lag it means but one thing. It means that behind the vivid confusion of the New Deal, the redistribution of the national income is stealthily and fatally progressing *upwards*, and that the power of Big Ownership is steadily enlarging. And unless the government succeeds in reversing this disastrous process, Big Ownership is bound to intensify the crisis in the long run.

There is nothing the New Deal has so far done that could not have been done better by an earthquake. A first-rate earthquake, from coast to coast, could have reestablished scarcity much more effectively, and put all the survivors to work for the greater glory of Big Business—with far more speed and far less noise than the New Deal.

Huey Long: Share Our Wealth (1935)

Huey P. Long (1893–1935) was a poor boy who created an invincible political machine in Louisiana and went from its governorship to the U.S. Senate. His success in his native state resulted from his policy of a new Populism which brought higher taxes to big businesses and new social and economic benefits to the poor, as well as from his ruthlessness in controlling elections and the legislature, which some people called dictatorship. In Washington, Long saw an opportunity to challenge Roosevelt and the New Deal from a different direction, one that seemed to have more promise for a would-be presidential candidate than either the conservatism of a Hoover or the socialism of a Benjamin Stolberg. On March 7, 1935, Long delivered the following radio broadcast. It was in part a reply to an attack on him by General Hugh S. Johnson, an ardent New Dealer and former head of the National Recovery Administration.

From *Vital Speeches of the Day* (March 25, 1935), pp. 394, 395, 396, 397. Published by the City News Publishing Co., Inc. Subheadings added by the editors.

I

Confiscation of Fortunes

So now, ladies and gentlemen, I introduce again, for fear that there are some who have just tuned in and do not know who is talking. This is Huey P. Long, United States Senator from Louisiana, talking over a National Broadcasting Company hookup, from Washington, D. C....

I propose, first, that every big fortune will be cut down immediately. We will cut that down by a capital levy tax to where no one will own more than a few millions of dollars. As a matter of fact, no one can own a fortune in excess of three to four millions of dollars, just between you and me, and I think that is too much. But we figure we can allow that size of a fortune and give prosperity to all the people, even though it is done....

So America would start again with millionaires, but with no multi-millionaires or billionaires; we would start with some poor, but they wouldn't be so poor that they wouldn't have the comforts of life. The lowest a man could go would not take away his home and the home comforts from him.

America, however, would still have a $65,000,000,000 balance after providing these homes. Now what do we do with that? Wait a minute and I will tell you.

Second: We propose that after homes and comforts of homes have been set up for the families of the country, that we will turn our attention to the children and the youth of the land, providing first for their education and training.

We would not have to worry about the problem of child labor, because the very first thing which we would place in front of every child would be not only a comfortable home during his early years, but the opportunity for education and training, not only through the grammar school and the high school, but through college and to include vocational and professional training for every child.

If necessary, that would include the living cost of that child while he attended college, if one should be too distant for him to live at home and conveniently attend, as would be the case with many of those living in the rural areas....

II

Labor and Production

Now, when we have landed at the place where homes and comfort are provided for all families and complete education and

SPRING SONGS

The Share Our Wealth plan of Louisiana Senator Huey Long and the National Union for Social Justice of Father Charles Coughlin, Detroit's "radio priest," drew a great deal of support in the mid-1930s, causing the President considerable alarm. Both Long and Coughlin drew mass followings from America's working class, men and women who still could not find steady work after several years of the New Deal.

training for all young men and women, the next problem is, what about our income to sustain our people thereafter. How shall that be arranged to guarantee all the fair share of what soul and body need to sustain them conveniently. That brings us to our next point.

We propose:

Third: We will shorten the hours of labor by law so much as may be necessary that none will be worked too long and none unemployed. We will cut hours of toil to thirty hours per week, maybe less; we may cut the working year to eleven months' work and one month vacation, maybe less.

If our great improvement programs show we need more labor than we may have, we will lengthen the hours as convenience requires. At all events, the hours for production will be gauged to meet the market for consumption.

We will need all our machinery for many years because we have much public improvement to do. And further, the more use that we may make of them the less toil will be required for all of us to survive in splendor.

Now, a minimum earning would be established for any person with a family to support. It would be such an earning, on which one, already owning a home, could maintain a family in comfort, of not less than $2,500 per year to every family. . . .

No. 4. That agricultural production will be cared for in the manner specified in the Bible. We would plow under no crops; we would burn no corn; we would spill no milk into the river; we would shoot no hogs; we would slaughter no cattle to be rotted. What we would do is this:

We would raise all the cotton that we could raise, all the corn that we could raise, and everything else that we could raise. Let us say, for example, that we raised more cotton than we could use.

But here again I wish to surprise you when I say that if every one could buy all the towels, all the sheets, all the bedding, all the clothing, all the carpets, all the window curtains, all of everything else they reasonably need, America would consume 20,000,000 bales of cotton per year without having to sell a bale to the foreign countries.

The same would be true of the wheat crop, and of the corn crop, and of the meat crop. Whenever every one could buy the things they desire to eat, there would be no great excess in any of those food supplies.

III
How To Deal with Surpluses

But for the sake of argument, let us say, however, that there would be a surplus. And I hope there will be, because it will do the country good to have a big surplus. Let us take cotton as an example.

Let us say that the United States will have a market for 10,000,000 bales of cotton, and that we raise 15,000,000 bales of cotton. We will store 5,000,000 bales in warehouses provided by the government. If the next year we raise 15,000,000 bales of cotton and only need 10,000,000, we will store another 5,000,000 bales of cotton, and the government will care for that.

When we reach the year when we have enough cotton to last for twelve or eighteen months we will plant no more cotton for that next year. The people will have their certificates of the government, which they can cash in for that year for the surplus, or if necessary, the government can pay for the whole 15,000,000 bales of cotton as it is produced every year, and when the year comes that we will raise no cotton we will not leave the people idle and with nothing to do. . . .

No. 5. We will provide for old age pensions for those who reach the age of 60, and pay it to all those who have an income of less than $1,000 per year, or less than $10,000 in property or money.

This would relieve from the ranks of labor those persons who press down the price for the use of their flesh and blood.

Now, the person who reaches the age of 60 would already have the comforts of home as well as something else guaranteed by reason of the redistribution that had been made of things. They would be given enough more to give them a reasonably comfortable existence in their declining days.

However, such would not come from a sales tax or taxes placed upon the common run of people. It would be supported from the taxes levied on those with big incomes and the yearly tax that would be levied on big fortunes so that they would always be kept down to a few million dollars to any one person.

No. 6. We propose that the obligations which this country owes to the veterans of its wars, including the soldiers' bonus, and to care for those who have been either incapacitated or disabled, would be discharged without stint or unreasonable limit.

I have always supported each and every bill that has had to do with the payment of the bonus due to the ex-service men. I have always opposed reducing the allowances which they have been granted. It is an unfair thing for a country to begin its economy while big fortunes exist, by inflicting misery on those who have borne the burden of national defense.

Now, ladies and gentlemen, such is the share our wealth movement. What I have here stated to you will be found to be approved by the law or our Divine Maker. You will find it in the Book of Deuteronomy, from the twenty-fifth to the twenty-seventh chapters. You will find it in the writings of King Solomon. You will find it in the teachings of Christ. You will find it in the words of our great teachers and statesmen of all countries and of all times. If you care to write to me for such proof, I shall be glad to furnish it to you free of expense by mail.

Will you not organize a share our wealth society in your community tonight or tomorrow to place this plan into law? You need it; your people need it. Write me, wire to me; get into this work with us if you believe we are right.

Help to save humanity. Help to save this country. If you wish a copy of this speech or a copy of any other speech I have made, write me and it will be forwarded to you. You can reach me always in Washington, D.C.

THE SEARCH FOR SECURITY

Because the nation was still bogged down in the Depression, President Roosevelt and his party realized that new plans would have to be devised if they were to win the 1936 elections. By 1935 the New Deal leaders had abandoned attempts at overall planning, as embodied in the NIRA and to a lesser extent the AAA, and concentrated on more immediate relief and reform measures.

Most meaningful to the millions of unemployed was the Relief Act of 1935, which in the next eight years led to the spending of eleven billion dollars and the employment of more than eight million persons, ranging from laborers to artists and actors. A variety of other legislation followed. For example, the Resettlement Administration aided impoverished farmers to settle where they could make a living, while the National Youth Administration gave part-time jobs to young people, thus enabling many of them to continue their education.

The New Dealers also pressed for a second kind of legislation designed to restructure big business. The Banking Act of 1935 strengthened greatly the federal influence over the nation's banking system. The Public Utility Holding Company Act gave the federal government sweeping regulatory power over public utilities, while the Revenue Act of 1935 raised taxes steeply for both corporations and individuals with high incomes.

Ironically, two of the New Deal reforms which had the most profound effect on American life were pressed on F. D. R. by those outside his administration. The two, which are dealt with in the following pages, were the Social Security Act and the National Labor Relations Act, both passed in 1935. The first provided a national system of old age and unemployment insurance; the second, also called the Wagner Act, gave a measure of federal protection to those who attempted to organize unions among American industrial workers.

Politically, the combination of relief and reform which made up the "second New Deal" ensured Roosevelt's overwhelming reelection in 1936 over Governor Alfred Landon of Kansas, his Republican opponent. What was equally significant was the fact that Roosevelt easily defeated the radical parties of the right and left despite his continuing struggle with the Depression. The Populist-like Union party—which combined elements of the supporters of such people as Huey Long (who was assassinated by a political enemy in 1935), Father Charles Coughlin, an anti-Semitic free-silverite with a wide following from his radio broadcasts, and Dr. Francis Townsend, author of a liberal pension plan for the elderly—ran a distant third, while radical parties of the left were snowed under completely. Democrats also increased their already large majorities in both houses of Congress.

During the late 1930s, however, Congress enacted little additional reform legislation. A severe financial recession in 1937 forced F. D. R. to expand relief measures rapidly. At the same time Roosevelt attacked the Supreme Court, which earlier had declared unconstitutional the AAA, the NIRA, and a number of other New Deal measures. The President urged Congress to enlarge the membership of the "over-worked" Court by appointing additional sympathetic judges. After a bitter fight, Congress refused to tamper with so revered an institution, while the Court itself showed much discretion by quickly declaring constitutional such recent New Deal measures as the National Labor Relations Act and the Social Security Act.

The Court fight and the recession kept the Roosevelt administration busy until the elections in late 1938, when the Republicans made strong gains in Congress. This fact, coupled with the start of war in Europe in September 1939, ended New Deal efforts at domestic reform.

In this typical WPA project men work on highway construction in Missouri. The Works Progress Administration, created by the Relief Act of 1935, employed an average of about two million men and women a month at an average monthly wage in 1936 of $52.14. That was not much money, even by Depression standards, but a WPA job was eagerly sought as better than no job at all.

Reading 262

Roosevelt: The Goal of Social Justice (1935)

With millions out of work and millions more in daily fear of losing their jobs, the quest for security, both physical and social, became the central issue of American life. The Roosevelt administration realized that it needed a program of some kind to reduce the increasing support being given such panaceas as Huey Long's "Share Our Wealth" clubs (Reading 261), Father Coughlin's Social Justice movement, and the Townsend Clubs' demand for $200 monthly pensions for the elderly unemployed.

In late 1934 Roosevelt began to consider several proposals for federal old-age insurance as well as a national system of unemployment insurance. Such plans had already been submitted in Congress, modeled on systems that had been operating in Western Europe for decades. On January 4, 1935, the President offered his social security plan to Congress.

From *The New York Times,* January 5, 1935.

I

Social Justice

Throughout the world change is the order of the day. In every nation economic problems, long in the making, have brought crises of many kinds for which the masters of old practice and theory were unprepared. In most nations social justice, no longer a distant ideal, has become a definite goal, and ancient governments are beginning to heed the call. . . .

It is important to recognize that while we seek to outlaw specific abuses, the American objective of today has an infinitely deeper, finer and more lasting purpose than mere repression. Thinking people in almost every country of the world have come to realize certain fundamental difficulties with which civilization must reckon. Rapid changes—the machine age, the advent of universal and rapid-communication and many other new factors have brought new problems. Succeeding generations have attempted to keep pace by reforming in piecemeal fashion this or that attendant abuse. As a result, evils overlapped and reform becomes confused and frustrated. We lose sight, from time to time, of our ultimate human objectives. . . .

I recall to your attention my message to the Congress last June in which I said: "Among our objectives I place the security of the men, women, and children of the nation first." That remains our first and continuing task; and in a very real sense every major legislative enactment of this Congress should be a component part of it.

In defining immediate factors which enter into our quest, I have spoken to the Congress and the people of three great divisions:

1. The security of a livelihood through the better use of the national resources of the land in which we live.
2. The security against the major hazards and vicissitudes of life.
3. The security of decent homes.

I am ready to submit to the Congress a broad program designed ultimately to establish all three of these factors of security—a program which because of many lost years will take many future years to fulfill.

A study of our national resources, more comprehensive than any previously made, shows the vast amount of necessary and practicable work which needs to be done for the development and preservation of our natural wealth for the enjoyment and advantage of our people in generations to come. The sound use of land and water is far more comprehensive than the mere planting of trees, building of dams, distributing of electricity or retirement of submarginal land. It recognizes that stranded populations, either in the country or the city, cannot have security under the conditions that now surround them.

To this end we are ready to begin to meet this problem—the intelligent care of population throughout our nation, in accordance with an intelligent distribution of the means of livelihood for that population. A definite program for putting people to work, of which I shall speak in a moment, is a component part of this greater program of security of livelihood through the better use of our national resources.

Closely related to the broad problem of livelihood is that of security against the major hazards of life. Here also a comprehensive survey of what has been attempted or accomplished in many nations and in many States proves to me that the time has come for action by the national government. I shall send to you, in a few days, definite recommendations based on these studies. These recommendations will cover the broad subjects of unemployment insurance and old-age insurance, of benefits for children, for mothers, for the handicapped, for maternity care and for other aspects of dependency and illness where a beginning can now be made.

The third factor—better homes for our people—has also been the subject of experimentation and study. Here, too, the first practical steps can be made through the proposals which I shall suggest in relation to giving work to the unemployed....

II

The Best Way

I am not willing that the vitality of our people be further sapped by the giving of cash, of market baskets, of a few hours of weekly work cutting grass, raking leaves or picking up papers in the public parks. We must preserve not only the bodies of the unemployed from destitution, but also their self-respect, their self-reliance and courage and determination. This decision brings me to the problem of what the government should do with approximately five million unemployed now on the relief rolls.

About one million and a half of these, belong to the group which in the past was dependent upon local welfare efforts. Most of them are unable for one reason or another to maintain themselves independently—for the most part through no fault of their own. Such people, in the days before the great depression, were cared for by local efforts—by States, by counties, by towns, by cities, by churches and by private welfare agencies. It is my thought that in the future they must be cared for as they were before. I stand ready through my own personal efforts, and through the public influence of the office that I hold, to help these local agencies to get the means necessary to assume this burden.

The security legislation which I shall propose to the Congress will, I am confident, be of assistance to local effort in the care of this type of cases. Local responsibility can and will be resumed, for, after all, common sense tells us that the wealth necessary for this task existed and still exists in the local community, and the dictates of sound administration require that this responsibility be in the first instance a local one.

There are, however, an additional 3,500,000 employable people who are on relief. With them the problem is different and the responsibility is different. This group was the victim of a nationwide depression caused by conditions which were not local, but national. The Federal Government is the only governmental agency with sufficient power and credit to meet this situation. We have assumed this task and we shall not shrink from it in the future. It is a duty dictated by every intelligent consideration of national policy to ask you to make it possible for the United States to give employment to all of these 3,500,000 employable people now on relief, pending their absorption in a rising tide of private employment.

Social Security for All (1935)

Congress passed the Social Security Act in August 1935 after considerable discussion but little organized opposition. *Newsweek*, a national news magazine, described the act soon after its passage. Almost four decades later the sums involved seem pitifully small, but for millions of Americans even a few dollars a month guaranteed to them in their old age or at times of unemployment offered an important measure of security. Note, however, the immediate consequences of paying for the system through taxes on employers and employees.

From "Social Security," *Newsweek*, VI (August 17, 1935), pp. 5–6. Subheadings added by the editors.

I

How the System Works

Money thus spent is well invested; it is used to ward off a revolution.

Otto von Bismarck wrote that to a friend in 1887. A Socialist uprising once had cost the Iron Chancellor "another sleepless night." To silence radical foes of his reactionary policy, he instituted the world's first governmental health insurance–old age pension system.

Franklin D. Roosevelt sleeps soundly. But his repeated promise to give the United States a More Abundant Life has kept legislators awake. Last week Congress ended one of its many long wrangles. To Mr. Roosevelt it dished up for signature the Wagner-Lewis Social Security Bill—and put America on the trail a German statesman had broken almost a century ago.

Security: The President's signature will put social security machinery into immediate motion. The bill provides:

A Old Age Pensions: This dole system by Federal subsidy becomes effective at once and remains operative until rendered needless by—

B Old Age Insurance: Taxation will supply premiums, starting in 1937; benefit payments begin in 1942. In theory accumulations of premiums will ultimately supersede the dole subsidy and protect from indigence all citizens 65 or older.

C Unemployment Insurance: To protect workers from poverty and ill health if they lose their jobs. Premiums (by taxation) begin next Jan. 1.

General: The bill sets aside Federal funds to help States, 1—care for needy women and children; 2—help blind and otherwise disabled children and adults; 3—maintain public health services.

Case A: Last month Mary Blank celebrated her 64th birthday by drawing her weekly $2 from New York's Relief Bureau. This pittance merely supplements the few dollars her daughter, Alice, sends her every month from California, where the girl has held a job since 1930. That year Mrs. Blank, aging and alone, lost her place as a seamstress. She hasn't worked since.

This time next year, at 65, she won't need her daughter's help. The nation's taxpayers will mail Mrs. Blank a gift of $30 a month. Under the new Law, New York State will give her $15 and the Federal Government a like amount drawn from a subsidy of some $50,000,000 for old age pensions.

Old people like Mrs. Blank will get varying benefits, depending on the States they reside in and the measure of help they need to live "in decency and health." Whatever they get, the Federal Government will pay half of it, up to $15 a month.

Case B: Mrs. Blank's daughter is 23. Unlike her mother, Alice will be able to protect herself against penniless old age—under the old age insurance plan. Her Los Angeles employer pays her $25 a week. In 1937, if she still has her job, she will begin giving her employer $1 a month; this he will turn over to the United States Treasury with a dollar of his own. Alice's payments—and her employer's—will graduate up to $3 a month each in 1949 and remain level thereafter, in 1977 Alice should be able to mark her 65th birthday by retiring with a $51.25 monthly pension.

President Franklin D. Roosevelt signs the Social Security Act, August 14, 1935. Two of the measure's strongest backers stand directly behind the President. They are Senator Robert F. Wagner of New York and Secretary of Labor Frances Perkins.

Less fortunate is her uncle, Henry Jones, 58—too old to profit by years of insurance premiums, too young not to work. He makes the same salary as Alice, which means he will pay $1 a month until 1940 and $1.50 a month until 1942. Then he will be 65. If his employer decided to retire him, Jones will get a pension of $17.50 a month—an irksome drop from $25 a week.

Case C: Alice isn't thinking much about old age now; what worries her is that she might lose her job. The Social Security Bill provides for her—although it does not protect many of her contemporaries: domestic servants, farmhands, "casual workers," and others.

In 1936—one year before Alice and her employer begin the old age premiums—the boss will start paying $1 a month to protect her against the hazards of unemployment. By 1937 he will pay $2, plus the $1 old age excise. On this basis the government by 1949 will be collecting from the firm $9 a month for Alice's social security: $3 from her and $6 from the boss. Uncle Sam will consider the employer's $6 an excise and allow deduction from Federal duties up to $90 an employe. But the girl's levy the government regards as straight income tax.

Uncle Sam forgets Alice on another count: the Security Bill says nothing of compensation standards. Each State will fix its own schedule; if Alice gets fired she will take whatever the Sacramento legislators think fit to give her. To date, Wisconsin alone provides its residents with unemployment relief. New York puts a system into effect next year. California, Washington, New Hampshire, and Utah last Spring promised to put such laws in operation after passage of the Federal Bill.

Administration supporters call the bill the most ambitious piece of social legislation ever undertaken by any government. It covers as wide a field as its prototype, the British system, but promises far greater benefits. By 1950, taxes will annually raise $2,800,000,000 to protect 27,000,000 or more Americans against poverty and unemployment. . . .

II
The Court and the Cost

The bill's passage brought Administration cheers. But some Washington critics mumbled "He who laughs last—" thinking of the Supreme Court of the United States. That body, they pointed out, might be able to blast the Great Social Experiment with two charges:

I   In its Railroad Retirement Act decision last Spring the highest court ruled that the Federal Government cannot raise money for specific social ends. The Constitution says taxes may be used only to "provide for the general welfare."

II The tribunal has held the Federal Government must not interfere with the States' legislative prerogatives: the Social Security Bill would put pressure on States to pass laws in its support.

Radicals, who howled the measure didn't go far enough, thought the States got too much power. They wanted the plan to remain on a national basis, subsidized by higher inheritance and income taxes. They voiced a third complaint: The law makes no provisions for 2,000,000-odd nomads—the hordes turned loose by the depression to seek whatever work they could get along the nation's highways.

Critical economists reasoned:

Fundamentals: The government, embarking on its colossal venture, ignores the first principle of the insurance business—starting with sufficient capital to meet potential claims. For social security Britain spends some $450,000,000 a year. Mr. Roosevelt proposes ultimately to distribute $2,800,000,000.

Investment Query: The bill sets up a Social Security Board of three. This body must invest the tax monies in rigidly safe bonds. Danger: The government in time of stress might finance expenditures with the immense funds thus ultimately built up: disguised inflation.

Purchasing Power: Most employers can't afford the 6 percent insurance levies. This means they will cut wages, or raise prices, or both. The 3 percent employe tax will act as a pay cut anyhow. Result: increase in living costs, decrease in public confidence.

Sum total of criticism: Recovery retarded.

A Critique of Social Security (1937)

Would the Social Security Act lead to the end of financial insecurity for most Americans? This question was hotly argued in the late 1930s. The act is analyzed in the following reading by Abraham Epstein, an expert on social security systems, who for many years had been fighting for an effective system in the United States.

From Abraham Epstein, "The Future of Social Security," *The New Republic*, (January 27, 1937), pp. 373, 375. Subheadings added by the editors.

I

Insurance as Cure-all

Reversing a generation of condemnation and taboo, the American people now fancy social insurance as a cure-all for their economic ills. . . .

Of the many comprehensive social-insurance systems abroad the British plan has proved most successful. This is due chiefly to the fact that from the start it stressed the *social* rather than the *insurance* phase of the problem. Instead of following the principles of private insurance, the English aimed primarily to guarantee a modest basic income for all workers in need. Rejecting high contributions from workers and their employers to build reserves for the future—which reduce immediate purchasing power—the British government sought to augment the purchasing power of the masses by distributing the security costs among all classes of the population. Through this wise use of social insurance Britain not only maintained wage rates but kept its index of unemployment at a lower level than any other nation throughout its prolonged depression. It was also enabled to emerge from the depression earlier and on a sounder basis than any other country, with the national economy in better balance.

The insurance provisions of our Social Security Act have little in common with the English program. First, the British system covers practically all the industrial emergencies. The Social Security Act confines itself mainly to only two of the major risks—old age and unemployment—with some provision for the needy orphans and blind. The grave problem of sickness, which in normal times constitutes the chief cause of poverty, is not touched. Second, instead of distributing the insurance costs among all elements of society, the Act places the burden entirely upon the wage-earners and consumers of the nation. Its insurance provisions actually relieve the wealthy from their share of the social burden which, through the poor laws, they have helped to carry for over 300 years. Its regressive payroll taxes merely oblige the poor to share their poverty in order to sustain the impoverished, thereby aggravating the existing maldistribution of income. Moreover, the heavy direct withdrawals from workers' wages and the taxes on employer payrolls—which will be passed on to workers as consumers in the form of increased prices—can only tend to reduce further the present inadequate purchasing power. The wage taxes may also intensify employer's efforts to install labor-saving machinery in order to reduce payrolls.

Because the payroll and wage taxes cannot supply sufficient revenue, the Act establishes scant security. It not only ignores the problem of the 10,000,000 unemployed, but offers little protection to the future unemployed as well as to the aged for a generation to come. Under the existing laws only a few of the future unemployed will be able to obtain $15 a week for more than ten weeks. For the next twenty years at least, most aged workers will be fortunate to draw a pension of $20 or $25 a month. An insured worker must earn $100 per month uninterruptedly for twenty years and retire from all work before he can get a pension of $32.50 per month. Not a penny is provided for his wife if he lives. Few men or women working today will live to receive the maximum pension of $85 monthly, attainable only by those who earn $3,000 every single year for forty-three years. . . .

II

The Weakness of the New System

Obviously, no government can shift the cost of the accumulated burden of old-age dependency to the younger workers without incalculable social harm. The tax is levied on earnings, not incomes. Younger persons striving to raise families need every dollar they earn. The United States, like all other countries, must realize that this burden can be carried only as a community responsibility, shared equitably by all classes of the population. Provision for the older group can be made only through an adequate system of non-contributory pensions or by government supplements to the old-age-insurance system. . . .

While the sound national administration of the old-age-insurance plan enables the attainment of its social objectives without altering its basic structure, much greater difficulty is encountered in reconstructing the present cumbersome tax-credit plan for unemployment insurance, which, from the start, was opposed by every student of the problem. This plan suffers not only from the same anti-social concepts found in the old-age-insurance program but, in addition, employs such a topheavy administrative mechanism that improvement through mere amendment is impossible. Like the old-age-insurance plan, it cannot achieve its objectives—to provide protection for the unemployed and enhance the security of the nation. It offers little security for the unemployed because: (a) It completely ignores the huge basin of existing unemployed: (b) it fails to provide benefits after the short insurance period has been passed; (c) it fails to consider the dependents of the insured.

Reading 265

Moreover, unlike the unified national old-age-insurance plan, the unemployment-insurance system requires the creation of forty-eight additional state tax systems and duplicating bookkeeping systems for employers. Discouraging uniformity, it frustrates any hope of establishing an adequate system of unemployment insurance throughout the United States. It permits of all kinds of state systems regardless of their efficacy. At best, it can bring only a miscellany of forty-eight divergent state plans creating endless confusion, great inequality among states as well as among workers and employers in the states, and bad feeling on the part of the unemployed.

The Unionization of Big Steel (1937)

The Depression spurred the growth and formation of unions throughout American industry. Membership in unions was at a low point in the 1920s, but their promise of job security increased their attractiveness considerably in the 1930s. The union movement itself was slow to take advantage of the situation. The dominant national organization, the American Federation of Labor (AFL), tried only reluctantly to organize such major industries as steel and automobile manufacturing. Led by John L. Lewis of the United Mine Workers, a number of labor leaders broke away from the AFL and organized the Committee on Industrial Organizations, whose major goal was to organize all workers in a given industry into a single union, as opposed to the craft-union approach of the AFL. CIO organizers immediately turned to the steel industry. The passage of the National

THE GREAT DIVIDE

The CIO, with its industrial union philosophy, split off from the AFL, an organization dominated by craft unions, in the struggle to organize the giant steel industry. The CIO's success in organizing both the steel and the auto industries made it a dynamic force in the economic and political life of the nation.

Labor Relations Act (the Wagner Act) in 1935 gave unions a potentially powerful weapon, for it forced industries to hold elections among workers to see if they wished to be represented by a union. The activities of the Steel Workers Organizing Committee (SWOC) in the Pittsburgh area are described in the following excerpt from testimony before a Congressional committee.

From U.S. Senate, Committee on Education and Labor, 76th Congress, Third Session, *Hearings . . . on . . . Bills to Amend the National Labor Relations Act*, Part 24 (February 6 and 7, 1940), pp. 4657–4660, 4638–4639. Subheadings added by the editors.

I

Steel Workers in the 1930s

Little Siberia they called it, and with good reason. The A.F. of L. organizers were not even permitted to enter Aliquippa (then called Woodlawn) during the great steel strike in 1919. Friends or relatives of its inhabitants were not allowed to stop for an unauthorized visit. Roads were barred and every stranger alighting from the train was questioned, and, if he could not render a good account of himself and his business, hustled into jail overnight and then back to whence he came. When the great steel strike was called in September 1919 the cordon sanitaire proved its effectiveness; not a man walked out of the Jones & Laughlin Aliquippa mills.

This control was not limited to emergency occasions. It was ever-present, all pervasive. Of the 30,000 people living in the town, 12,000 were employed in the Jones & Laughlin mills, thus leaving only a very small percentage of the adults to carry on the necessary activities in the town. The corporation owned the street railway system (now abolished), the motor-coach system, the water supply system, and approximately 700 homes occupied by its workers. It dominated the municipal government and financial institutions of the town. In short, it was the undisputed overlord.

The town was built on hills and forests. The streets were crooked and badly paved. The only level stretch of ground was the main street of the town which followed the course of a feeder stream and the mill which was situated on the stream's delta. The town was divided into sections—plans—which completely segregated one district from another. The "hunkies" lived in one plan; the Negroes in another; the foreman and supervisory staff, highly skilled whites, and company favorites in a third, etc. Under this arrangement a sharp exclusiveness developed. People lived, married and died within their own group, scarcely realizing except for contact in the mill that any other nationality or race existed there. West Aliquippa was more of an appendage to the mill itself. It stretched beyond the north end of the plant; was completely owned by the company and had only one means of communication with the outside—a single road which led under the railroad tracks. All other streets led either to the river, the slag heap, or to the mill.

But time wrought changes, and 1933 brought forth the New Deal, the National Industrial Recovery Act, and section 7a thereof. That section ostensibly guaranteed the right freely to organize for purposes of collective bargaining. In order to forestall genuine organization, Jones & Laughlin, along with hundreds of other companies, set up an employee representation plan in June 1933. The plan, usually referred to as the E.R.P., provided for the election of officers by the employees, and machinery for the settlement of grievances. It was never submitted to the employees for approval; they were simply told to elect representatives. . . .

II

Enter the Steel Workers Organizing Committee

On June 17, 1936, Joseph Timko was sent into Beaver Valley with a staff of organizers. Timko was an international representative of the United Mine Workers, fresh from a year in Bloody Harlan County, Ky. Before that he had been president of district 11, U.M.W.A., Indiana. Timko was a rugged, hard-working, powerful, aggressive personality. He was a worker himself, and inspired confidence in other workers. He was a believer in unionism because he had seen what the union had done for him and his father. He had no theoretical training or knowledge, and was interested in none. A pious Catholic, he was denounced as a Communist. He was still young, having just turned forty when he arrived at Aliquippa.

Timko was instructed to take over Beaver Valley Lodge 200 on behalf of the S.W.O.C. He held his first meeting on June 19, 1936, at the Democratic headquarters in Aliquippa. Members of the J. & L. police were in the vicinity, obtaining the names of all the men who attended the meeting. Of the 18 men present at the first meeting, 13 were discharged within a week. These men were in such widely scattered departments as open hearth, seamless, boiler room, welded tube, electrical, wire and nail mill, and blast furnace. The 18 men who attended this meeting were the most active in the organization. About 1 month later another purge was ordered—this time 12 active union men were discharged within a similar period of 7 days. . . .

Captains Mauk and Harris, of the J. & L. police, considered the Aliquippa police department merely as an adjunct of the mill police. The [Aliquippa] borough police were given specific duties to perform and, according to sworn testimony, they more than carried out their orders. In cooperating with the company in its effort to stamp out unionism in Aliquippa, the city police acted with the fury of the Inquisition. Statements like the following can be multiplied many times:

> In 1934 I was arrested for some kind of disturbance that went on at plan 11, extended. My landlord, Ignuts Ianacich, told me that while I was away a city cop and Kelley of the J. & L. police broke into my room and searched it. They went through the trunk and found my union cards and took them away with them. Later in the same day two city police called at my home and said that Burgess Sohn wanted to see me. At headquarters, Chief Ambrose had me searched and took the union cards which were in my coat pocket.
>
> The next day I was again called into the police headquarters by Chief Ambrose. He showed me my union cards and asked me what they were. I said that they were union pledge cards and then he slapped me twice on my face.
>
> The following day I was again taken to the office of Chief Ambrose and was handcuffed. A minute or two later, Kelley and Captain Harris, of the J. & L. police, forced me into the room. Ambrose looked at my handcuffs and said, "Not tight enough. We better squeeze them a little more." He did so, causing me great pain. The pain caused me to shake, and Captain Harris looked at me and said, "What's the matter? Got a cold?" Then he said, "How do you like the union now?" I was then put back in my cell. When my case came up in Beaver I was acquitted of assault and was freed. . . .

III

Collective Bargaining

By May 1937 a distinct majority of Aliquippa's steel workers had become members of the S.W.O.C. In addition, a majority of the Jones & Laughlin Steel Corporation's twelve-thousand-odd employees in its Pittsburgh Works had also become members of the S.W.O.C. On behalf of these members the S.W.O.C. requested a conference with the corporation's officials early in May. The United States Steel Corporation had already recognized S.W.O.C. and signed a collective-bargaining contract with it. The same form of recognition was requested from Jones and Laughlin, which hesitated to grant it. Instead, Jones & Laughlin rushed plans to convert its company union, or employee representative plan, into a so-called independent union to compete with the S.W.O.C. This brought negotiations to a head, and in self-defense the Jones & Laughlin workers went on strike. The strike, at once, was successful; in fact, it was 100 percent. When the Jones & Laughlin officials saw their works completely closed down for the first time in their history, they reentered negotiations with the S.W.O.C. The corporation officials told me and my associates that they would sign a contract similar to the one between the S.W.O.C. and U.S. Steel, provided we could show that a majority of Jones & Laughlin's workers were S.W.O.C. members. Unlike the case of Judge Elbert Gary in 1919, these Jones & Laughlin officials were sincere. The real question in dispute was not the right of the union to exist, as was the case in 1919, but merely whether the union actually represented a majority of the workers.

Happily for the workers and the corporation, the National Labor Relations Board was in existence. Because of the existence of the Board, the Jones & Laughlin strike was one of the shortest on record, involving approximately 25,000 workers. It lasted just 36 hours.

In the past there would have been no other way out than a long-drawn-out battle, but here under the Wagner Act there was a definite, sane, constitutional, and democratic way of settling our differences. The company said we did not really represent its men. S.W.O.C. insisted that it did. The obvious way to settle it, therefore, was to hold an election.

The National Labor Relations Board provided the machinery for this, and the strike was settled with an agreement that the terms of the U.S. Steel contract would be in effect until an election was held by the National Labor Relations Board within 10 days to determine whether or not the Steel Workers Organizing Committee represented a majority of the Jones & Laughlin employees. The result was a smashing victory—17,208 for the union and 7,207 against the union.

The Jones & Laughlin Steel Corporation thereupon signed a collective-bargaining contract with the S.W.O.C. recognizing it as the sole bargaining agency for all of its production and maintenance workers.

Reading 266

Jones & Laughlin Steel Corporation Basic Contract (1937)

The following reading, taken from the contract SWOC negotiated with the Jones & Laughlin Steel Corporation, reveals clearly what unions were concerned about at the time.

From U.S. Senate, Committee on Education and Labor, 76th Congress, Third Session, Hearings . . . on . . . Bills to Amend the National Labor Relations Act, Part 24 (February 6 and 7, 1940), pp. 4667-4668.

"This agreement, dated May 25, 1937, between Jones & Laughlin Steel Corporation (hereinafter referred to as the 'corporation') and the Steel Workers Organizing Committee, or its successor (hereinafter referred to as the 'union') on behalf of all of the employees of the corporation in its Pittsburgh and Aliquippa works and at the Pittsburgh warehouse.

"Section 1. It is the intent and purpose of the parties hereto that this agreement will promote and improve industrial and economic relationships between the union and the corporation, and to set forth herein the basic agreement covering rates of pay, hours of work, and conditions of employment to be observed between the parties hereto.

"The term 'employee,' as used in this agreement, shall not include foremen or assistant foremen in charge of any classes of labor, watchmen, or any salaried employees.

"Sec. 2. *Recognition.*—The corporation recognizes the union as the exclusive collective-bargaining agency for all of its employees. The corporation recognizes and will not interfere with the right of its employees to become members of the union. There shall be no discrimination, interference, restraint, or coercion by the corporation or any of its agents against any members because of membership in the union. The union, its members and agents, agrees not to intimidate or coerce employees into membership and also not to solicit membership on corporation time or plant property.

"Sec. 3. *Wages.*—Effective March 16, 1937, there was an increase in wages of 10 cents an hour on all rates which were formerly $4.20 a day, or a minimum for this classification of $5 a day of 8 hours. Such classifications formerly receiving less than $4.20 a day or less than $52\frac{1}{2}$ cents per hour, were increased 10 cents per hour. There was an increase of 10 cents per hour in all other hourly rates, and an equivalent increase in all tonnage and piecework rates which will net under normal expected earnings an increase of not less than 80 cents per day of 8 hours. These wages as increased shall continue in effect during the life of this agreement.

"Sec. 4. *Hours of work.*—Effective March 16, 1937, there was established an 8-hour day and a 40-hour week. Time and one-half has been paid and will be paid during the life of this agreement for all overtime in excess of 8 hours in any one day or for all overtime in excess of 40 hours in any 1 week.

"A day may be a calendar day or any 24-hour period, and a week may be a calendar week or any five regular 8-hour turns on consecutive days, followed by a 48-hour rest period, at the option of the corporation, except that where necessary in any department the work shall be divided in accordance with a schedule to be prepared, mutually satisfactory to the corporation and the union.

"An employee shall not be paid both daily and weekly overtime for the same hours so worked.

"Sec. 5. *Vacations.*—Each employee who, prior to May 1, 1937, was continuously in the service of the corporation 5 years or more (continuity of service to be based on Jones & Laughlin Steel Corporation Pension Fund Rules for service continuity) shall receive 1 week's vacation with pay, such vacation to be taken in a single period. Those who are granted vacations will be paid 40 hours of wages at their average rate of earnings per hours which was paid for during the month of May 1937.

"Vacations will, so far as possible, be granted at times most desired by employees, but the final right to allotment of vacation period is exclusively reserved to the corporation in order to insure the orderly operation of the works.

"Sec. 6. *Seniority.*—It is understood and agreed that in all cases of promotion or increase, or decrease of forces, the following factors shall be considered, and where factors (b), (c), (d), and (e) are relatively equal, length of continuous service shall govern.

"(a) Length of continuous service.
"(b) Knowledge, training, ability, skill, and efficiency.
"(c) Physical fitness.
"(d) Family status, number of dependents, etc.
"(e) Place of residence.

"Sec. 7. *Adjustment of grievances.*—Should any difference arise between the corporation and the union or any employee of the corporation as to the meaning and application of the provisions of this agreement, or should any local trouble of any kind arise in any plant, there shall be no suspension of work on account of such differences but an earnest effort shall be made to settle such differences immediately in the following manner:

"First, between the aggrieved employee and the foreman of the department involved;

"Second, between a member or members of the grievance committee, designated by the union, and the foreman and superintendent of the department;

"Third, between a member or members of the grievance committee, designated by the union, and the general superintendent or manager of the works or his designated assistant;

"Fourth, between the representatives of the national organization of the union and the representatives of the executives of the corporation; and

"Fifth, in the event the dispute shall not have been satisfactorily settled, the matter shall then be appealed to an impartial umpire to be appointed by mutual agreement of the parties hereto. The decision of the umpire shall be final. The expense and salary incident to the services of the umpire shall be paid jointly by the corporation and the union.

Specified periods shall be agreed upon between the grievance committee and the general superintendent or manager of each works or his designated assistant, for the presentation of grievances hereunder. Provided, however, that matters pertaining to discharges or other matters that cannot reasonably be delayed until the time of the next regular meeting may be presented at any time in accordance with the foregoing provisions.

"The grievance committees for the Pittsburgh works, including Pittsburgh warehouse, and for the Aliquippa works shall consist each of not less than three employees of that works, and not more than 10 such employees, designated by the union, who will be afforded such time off, without pay, as may be required.

"First, to attend regularly scheduled committee meetings, and

"Second, to attend meetings pertaining to discharges, or other matters which cannot reasonably be delayed until the time of the next regular meeting.

"Third, any member of the grievance committees shall have the right to visit departments other than his own in his own works at all reasonable times for the purpose of transacting the legitimate business of the grievance committee, after notice to and permission from his department superintendent or his designated representative.

"The actual number of members of the grievance committee at each works shall be mutually agreed upon between the general superintendent or manager of the works and the union, and in no case shall there be more than one member in any department.

"The union reserves the right to refuse to take up a grievance on behalf of any employee who is not a member of the union, in which event such employee shall have to present and take up his grievances directly with the corporation.

"Sec. 8. *Management.*—The management of the works and the direction of the working forces, including the right to hire, suspend, or discharge for proper cause, or transfer, and the right to relieve employees from duty because of lack of work, or for other legitimate reason, is vested exclusively in the corporation: *Provided,* That this will not be used for purposes of discrimination against any member of the union."

Aliquippa Celebrates
(1937)

The National Labor Relations Act (Wagner Act) was only partly successful as a union organizing weapon. Until 1937 no one knew whether or not the courts would rule the act unconstitutional. In 1937, at the height of President Roosevelt's attempt to add Justices to the Supreme Court, that body declared the act constitutional. The impact of the decision in Aliquippa, a steel town near Pittsburgh (see reading 265), was vividly portrayed in a contemporary magazine report.

From Rose M. Stein, "Aliquippa Celebrates," *The Nation,* CLXXVII (April 24, 1937), p. 466.

"When I hear Wagner bill went constitutional I happy like anything. I say, good, now Aliquippa become part of United States." The speaker, Pete C———, was fired from his job in the Jones and Laughlin steel mill in Aliquippa last June. Pete figured there was something un-American about his dismissal after twenty-six years of steady and apparently satisfactory service. He thought it un-American, too, when stool pigeons turned his wife and son against him, and when company police threatened him with bodily harm if he did not quit signing up the "hunkies" for the union. He did not quit. "Hell, no!" He flashed a bunch of signed application cards in proof as he climbed into an automobile to join the parade in celebration of the Supreme Court's decision in the Jones and Laughlin case. "Joke on stool pigeon all right. Even Supreme Court say to workingman, go ahead and organize, ho, ho, ho." He laughed till the tears came.

A line of cars covered with bright signs and blowing their horns moved along Franklin Avenue, the main street of Aliquippa, whose 30,000 inhabitants are solely dependent for their livelihood upon the Jones and Laughlin mills. The traffic police gave them right of way; company police were nowhere to be seen. The first two cars bore signs reading, "We Are the Ten Men Fired for Union Activity by J. & L. We Are Ordered Back to Work by the Supreme Court." Aliquippa's business community poked heads out of doors and windows, looked, smiled, occasionally waved. There was obvious restraint. Even a phenomenal court decision cannot overnight instil courage and enthusiasm into a community accustomed to walking the chalk line. But when the cars began their climb up to the hills where the 12,000 steel workers live, they were greeted with cheers and applause. No sign of fear there, no hesitancy, no restraint. All welcomed Aliquippa's ten heroes, all greeted with enthusiasm the sign on one of the cars, "The Workers of Aliquippa Are Now Free Men."

The heroes of Aliquippa, and the number of years they worked for Jones and Laughlin before they were fired, are Royal Boyer, eleven years; Eli Bozich, eight years; Domenic Brandy, twenty-five years; Ronald Cox, fifteen years; Martin Dunn, five years; Martin Gerstner, fourteen years; George Marell, fourteen years; Harry Phillips had worked for the company off and on since before the war and had been steadily employed for three years; Angelo Razanno, eight years; Angelo Volpe, twenty-one years. All were members of the Amalgamated Association of Iron, Steel, and Tin Workers at the time of their dismissal. All joined that union as soon as it was organized in the fall of 1934. Phillips, Volpe, and Gerstner were officers. The others were active in recruiting members, especially Domenic Brandy among Italians, Eli Bozich among Serbians, Royal Boyer among Negroes. All defied the management's request to vote in the 1935 company-union election. All were warned that the company "would close the plant and throw the key in the river before it would recognize an outside union," that the union was "no damned good," and that the active unionists were "on the spot." All were shadowed twenty-four hours a day. All had their homes watched. Some were beaten up. . . .

The restoration of each job gives labor a sense of power, dignity, and self-importance. With but few exceptions the fired men became the most active union workers. Twenty-five became full-time organizers. Most of the fired men will go back to their mill jobs if given the opportunity. They will go back with a great deal of experience in labor organization, and it is safe to predict that before long they will become union officers and grievance-committee representatives. Unwittingly industry helped the union drive by sending some of the best workers into it.

Managers and straw bosses who did the firing will find it very difficult to negotiate grievances with these men, and since promiscuous firing is now forbidden, some of the bosses will have to go. Something in the nature of an exodus has already begun, and bosses of a more liberal turn of mind are being installed. One of Jones and Laughlin's vice-presidents in charge of the terroristic activities in Aliquippa has lost his job. He did not make good. Rumor has it that others will follow, including the heads of the company's private police force. All this was brought about by the Wagner bill, mused Pete as he settled himself in the back seat of the car. "Wagner bill sure gonna do lots for workingman. Maybe you can send me Wagner bill?" he asked. "I wanna see what him like."

An Evaluation of the New Deal

The New Deal, with its many programs and many approaches, is not an easy part of American history to comprehend. In the years since the 1930s historians have shifted from a generally uncritical admiration to a more balanced view of the accomplishments and failures of Franklin D. Roosevelt and his administration. George Mowry, a historian of twentieth-century America, offers one evaluation of the era.

From *The Urban Nation, 1920–1960* by George E. Mowry, Copyright © 1965 by George E. Mowry. Reprinted by permission of Hill and Wang, Inc. Pp. 123–127. Subheadings added by the editors.

I

Economic and Social Changes

What had the New Deal accomplished? While it made few, if any, really revolutionary changes, it so accelerated existing trends that the years 1933–1937 can be considered the most eventful in domestic politics since the days of the Civil War. Among its many achievements, perhaps the most noteworthy was saving the nation from chaos in March 1933. Its success in inspiring confidence in the financial structure was a critical act in the history of the country. Only slightly less important was its recognition of the necessity for feeding the needy, supplying work for the jobless, and protecting the owners of homes, farms, and small business from loss of their establishments. For all such relief work the New Deal spent some $8 to $10 billion in nonrecoverable funds, an expenditure which despite the accompanying inefficiency and corruption was one of the best the nation ever made. Had deflation been permitted to run its course, as Secretary of the Treasury Andrew Mellon proposed, much of the middle class might have been wiped out. The New Deal attained what few democratic governments have been able to achieve in such periods of acute social stress. It was creative enough to retain the loyalties of the majority without forcing either the left or the right into violent opposition. Except on the labor-capital front, where the action was often local and almost never pointed toward government, there was less violence from marching men after 1933 than before that date.

By its economic and labor reforms the New Deal shifted power somewhat from the reigning business classes, some of it to the newly inspirited labor unions, but most to the government itself. The prestige of big business took a severe beating during the Depression and New Deal years, a pummelling that accounted for much of its choleric attitude toward the Roosevelt Administration. To a slight degree, the owning classes may have lost a fraction of their inheritance. One study of the gross national product showed that between 1929 and 1939 the proportion going into interests, rents, and corporate dividends decreased by about 3 percent, while a similar figure appeared as an increase in the sum of wages and salaries. But the most palpable loss of the business classes was the power to make decisions vital to the economy. Previous to 1933 the setting of interest rates, the methods by which securities were sold, the determination of wage and salary scales and the choice of individuals for employment, the prices at which electric power, coal, oil, and even farm goods should be sold, the number of dwelling units to be built in a community, and a host of other questions had been decided either by millions of enterprisers or by an industrial and financial elite. After 1933 such decisions were invariably influenced and sometimes controlled by the Federal government. In many instances, the decisions of the new regime were not made on the grounds of profit and loss, nor were profit and loss the only guiding determinants for others. Often political considerations bulked larger than economic ones. The new state of affairs was summed up by a business periodical, in 1937, as one in which economic life was "arrogantly" dominated by politics, resulting in a system in which the "law of supply and demand" was in shambles, production was "artificially restricted or stimulated," and a horde of unproductive politicians were dominating the banking system and setting prices and wages at "false levels." A more friendly analysis summarized the change in the economy as one in which the front page of the daily newspaper had become "more important to the business man than the market page, and the White House press conference of vaster import than the closing prices on the New York Stock Exchange."

Economically and socially, the most significant failure of the New Deal was its inability to achieve recovery and a reasonably efficient economy. After six years of reform and spending, 8 to 10 million workers were still unemployed in 1939. Per capita income was still considerably below the 1929 figure. The economy did not recover its 1929 productiveness and did not absorb all the stagnant labor power until the government primed the pumps with billions for preparedness and war. But since the process of achieving prosperity by allocating an increasing amount of the total national energy to producing nonuseful goods was to be the normal one for the next quarter century, perhaps the New Deal should not be judged too harshly for not obtaining what two postwar Administrations failed at.

II

Political Changes

The New Deal made almost as many substantial changes in the political system of the 1920's as it did in economic life. During its first four years practically all important legislation originated not in Congress but in the executive branch of the government, the Wagner Labor Act constituting the principal exception. Throughout the hundred days, Congress virtually abstained from changing important features in the draft legislation presented to it. Often during this hectic period newly created administrative agencies were empowered to issue their own regulations, which would have the same legality as if enacted by Congress. This tendency to delegate substantial legislative power to executive agencies was somewhat curtailed by the NIRA decision. But by the end of the New

Deal, Congress had almost ceased to be a legislation-initiating body in important matters and had become a reviewing, modifying, and negating agency.

Although Roosevelt's contest with the Supreme Court diminished his personal prestige, it also resulted in a substantial loss of power both for the Court and for the several states. By radically broadening the Federal power over interstate commerce, the Court seriously limited its own power to declare Federal economic regulation unconstitutional, as well as that of the state to intervene in economic matters. The residual powers of the states were also steadily reduced by the numerous New Deal subsidies, for along with each subsidy ran the mandate of the Federal government. To help pay the mounting bills the Federal government invaded the traditional sources for state taxes, notably such consumer items as gasoline and automobile tires. But probably the most potent force in the erosion of state power lay in the proliferation of direct beneficial relations between the Federal government and the individual. Before 1933 only a few citizens had had direct beneficial relations with Washington. By 1939 the Federal government and its agencies were making money payments to farmers, to men on relief and Federal works projects, to college and high school students, to the aged, to the unemployed, to widows, to dependent children, and to the needy blind. It was also making loans directly, or guaranteeing them at low interest rates, to home owners, farmers, sharecroppers, and small businessmen. Hundreds of thousands of citizens took advantage of government-financed housing projects, school and college buildings, parks and playgrounds. As these ties became more numerous, and as the national pattern of movement from state to state in search of climatic or

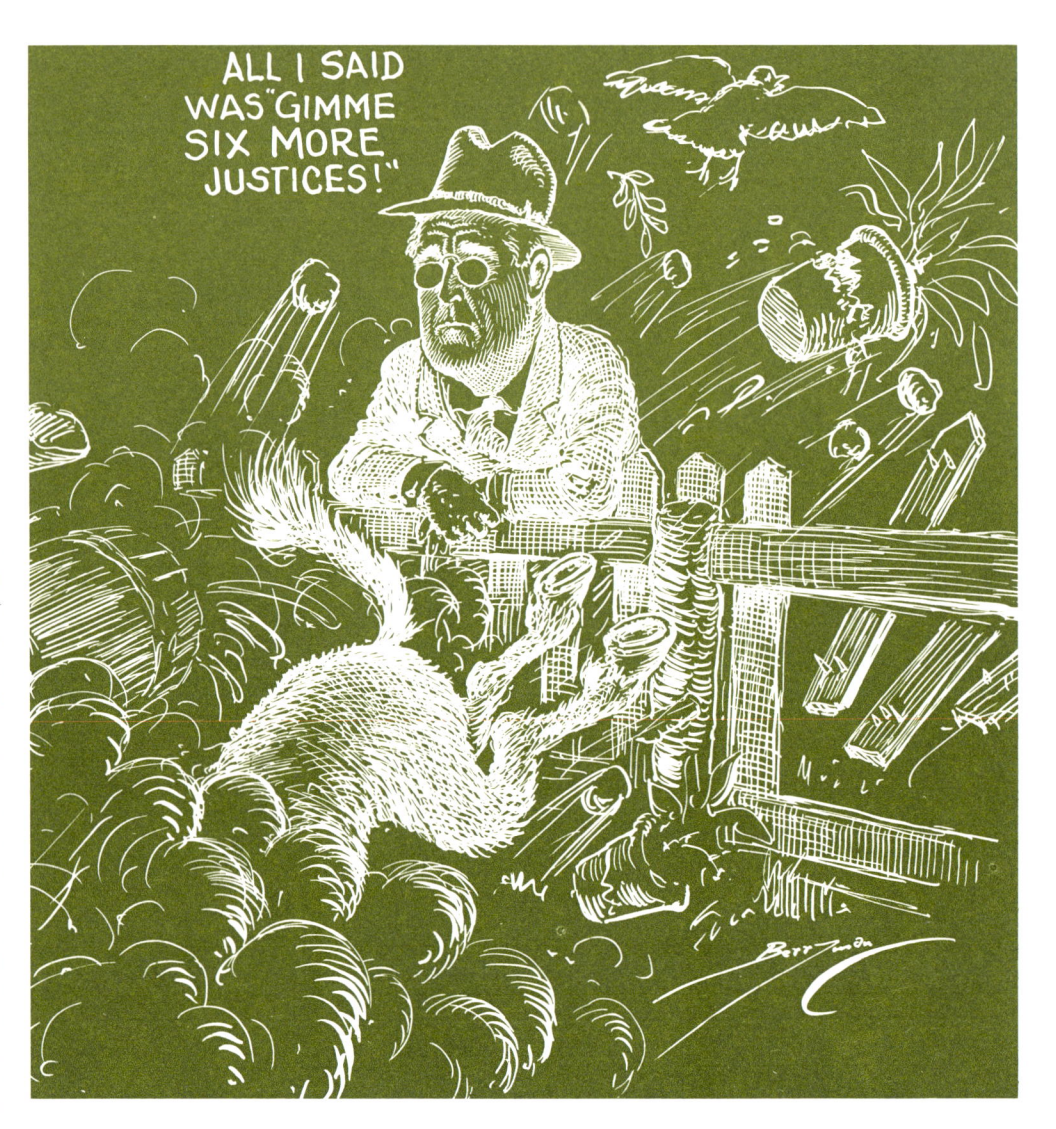

The Democratic mule kicks out in protest against President Roosevelt's proposal to add additional Justices to the United States Supreme Court. Roosevelt had hoped his plan would enable him to nominate several Justices sympathetic to the New Deal. He succeeded instead in giving Republicans and conservative Democratics a political weapon which they used to stall the New Deal for crucial months in 1937.

economic opportunity was accelerated, state and parochial loyalties withered and Americans became more and more national-minded.

In the realm of pure politics the New Deal scored perhaps its most astounding success. From 1894 to 1930 the Democratic party had been distinctly a minority one, winning only three Congressional elections in the thirty-six years, with two of those occurring in 1912 and 1914, when Theodore Roosevelt had split Republican unity. But after 1932 the New Deal fashioned a coalition of urban voters, composed largely of the underprivileged classes and minority ethnic groups, which, when tied to the South and other distressed rural areas, produced a majority in six successive Congressional elections and in seven of the following nine. The new majority was, of course, a disparate one, full of conflicting and anomalous elements. By 1937, despite the Administration's extensive aid to agriculture, rural America was obviously alienated by the urban parts of the New Deal program. This was especially true of the South, whose attitude toward the racial and immigrant minorities in the northern cities was intensely colored by its own racial history. But so strong was the people's memory of the Depression, and so vivid the remembered contrast between Republican passivity and New Deal action, that the victorious coalition held together long after its reason for being had disappeared. To that extent post–World War II politics was based upon past memories instead of current issues.

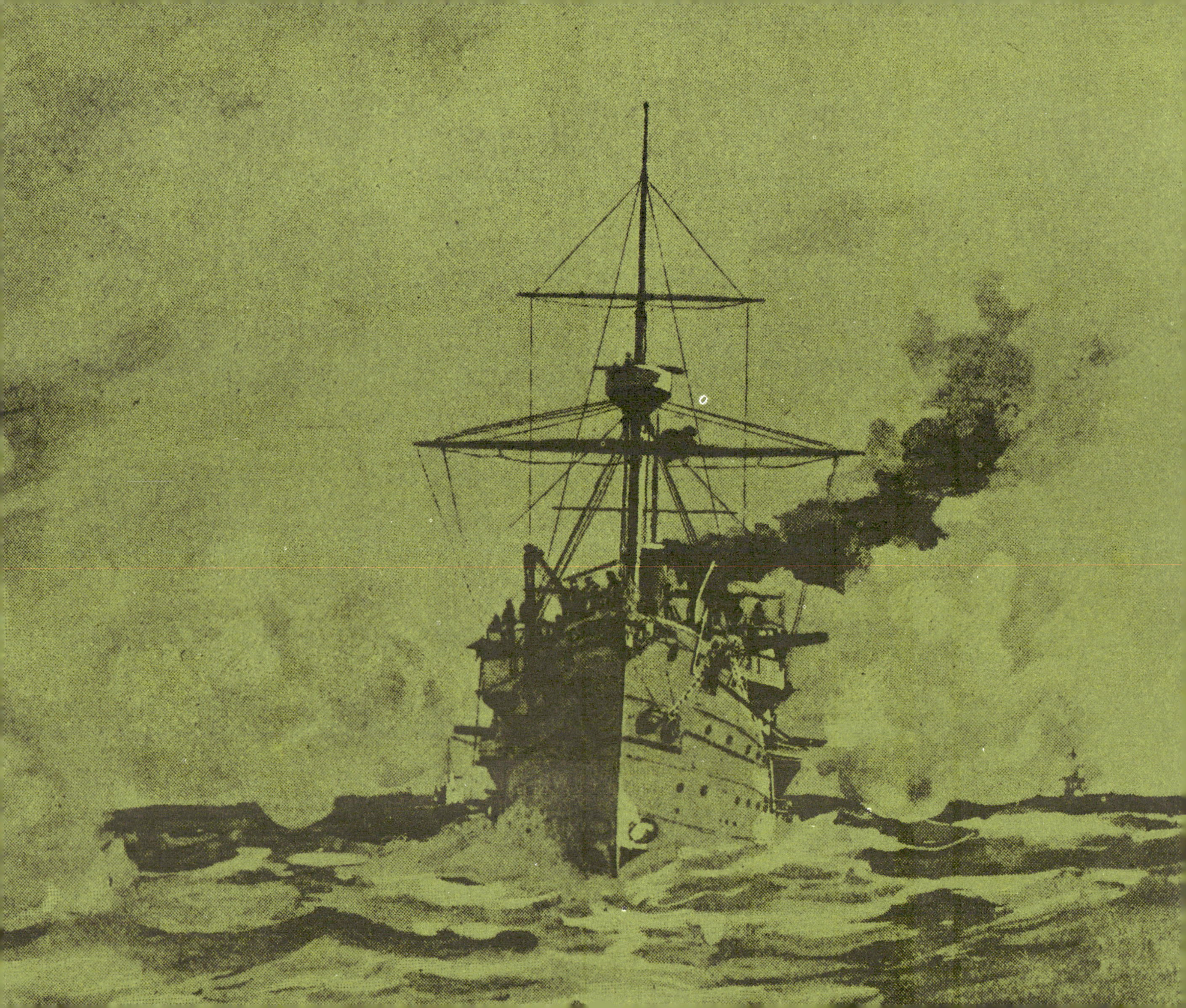

Chapter 8

The United States Becomes a World Power

During the nineteenth century Americans directed most of their energies toward the expansion and development of their continental empire. This process stirred conflict: expansion generated the war with Mexico and many battles with displaced Indian tribes. Even the Civil War arose partly out of the question of whether slavery should be allowed to move westward with migrant Americans.

In contrast, the United States enjoyed peaceful relationships with the great powers of the world. This happy circumstance came about partly because none of the major European powers had both the ability and the desire to block American expansion, partly because the British, whose navy effectively controlled the Atlantic, shared the American desire that European powers refrain from further colonial ventures in Latin America, and partly because Europe itself experienced a remarkable period of freedom from major international wars. Such conflicts as the Crimean War in the 1850s and the Franco-Prussian War of 1870–1871 were either too distant or too limited to threaten American interests. Significantly, neither war impaired American seaborne commerce.

In the late nineteenth century, however, a new wave of European colonizing activities in Africa and Asia, the rise of three newly unified or emergent powers—Germany, Italy, and Japan—and a number of other important factors served to increase sharply the competition of the great powers. A war might quickly involve many of these great powers.

For reasons which are complex, Americans joined in the expansion of Western (and Japanese) control over what we now call "underdeveloped" areas and their peoples. As the United States rapidly expanded its interests and influence, it found itself faced with new responsibilities for safeguarding them. One problem confronting the student is why the United States, seemingly secure in its continental domain and powerful enough to defeat any potential invader, chose this new role.

Of the areas where this expansion of interests and influence took place, Latin America was the most important. The fact that the nation had at last acquired enough economic strength and potential military power to enforce the Monroe Doctrine played a part here, but changing circumstances, in both Latin America and Europe, were also responsible.

When the outbreak of war between Austria-Hungary and Serbia in 1914 finally activated the system of alliances among the great powers of Europe, a world war resulted. The United States, having remained aloof from the alliance system by traditional policy, tried to remain neutral and to bring about a negotiated settlement of the war. Both efforts failed. The United States helped to bring an end to the war only by taking part in the defeat of the Central Powers, led by Germany.

Could the victorious Allies create a settlement which would preserve the peace of the world against aggressive nations and prevent a recurrence of a war that had cost twenty million lives? President Woodrow Wilson of the United States thought so and joined in writing a peace treaty which aimed, however imperfectly, at those ends. Many of his fellow Americans, however, disagreed about the extent of their responsibility for enforcing such a peace. In the end the United States Senate, which has power under the Constitution to ratify or reject treaties, rejected the Versailles Treaty and with it American participation in the League of Nations. How effective as an agent of peace the League might have been with American membership remains a matter of debate. What is certain is that the United States, by decision or by default, avoided an important opportunity to influence world affairs.

The United States, however, could not isolate itself from the world in the 1920s and 1930s. No matter what the wishes of some of its citizens, the nation's economic and political influence was so great that its actions caused reverberations throughout the world. When in the 1930s a revived Germany began to assert itself in Europe, and in Asia Japan began to act similarly, the United States again faced the question of what to do with its enormous power. In examining the half century between 1890 and 1940 this chapter will consider the central questions of why American expansion took place when it did, why the United States manifested certain attitudes toward involvement in international politics, and what significance expansion, neutrality, withdrawal, and intervention had for Americans and for others.

Ivan and Brother Jonathan glare at each other across the Pacific Ocean. In the late 1870s Russia was exerting pressure against both China and India. At the same time, the United States was extending its influence into the Pacific by concluding a commercial treaty with the Kingdom of Hawaii (the Sandwich Isles).

TOPIC 53

AMERICAN DESTINY AND OVERSEAS EXPANSION

By the late nineteenth century the United States effectively dominated the North American continent. Some Americans argued that their territorial destiny had been fulfilled and that the nation's energies should be turned to internal social and economic development. Others, while not denying the need for internal development, nevertheless felt America's economic and political destiny would not be fulfilled until the nation had made its influence felt beyond the oceans. The following readings examine this conflict over America's future through a study of the proposed annexation of the Hawaiian Islands in 1893.

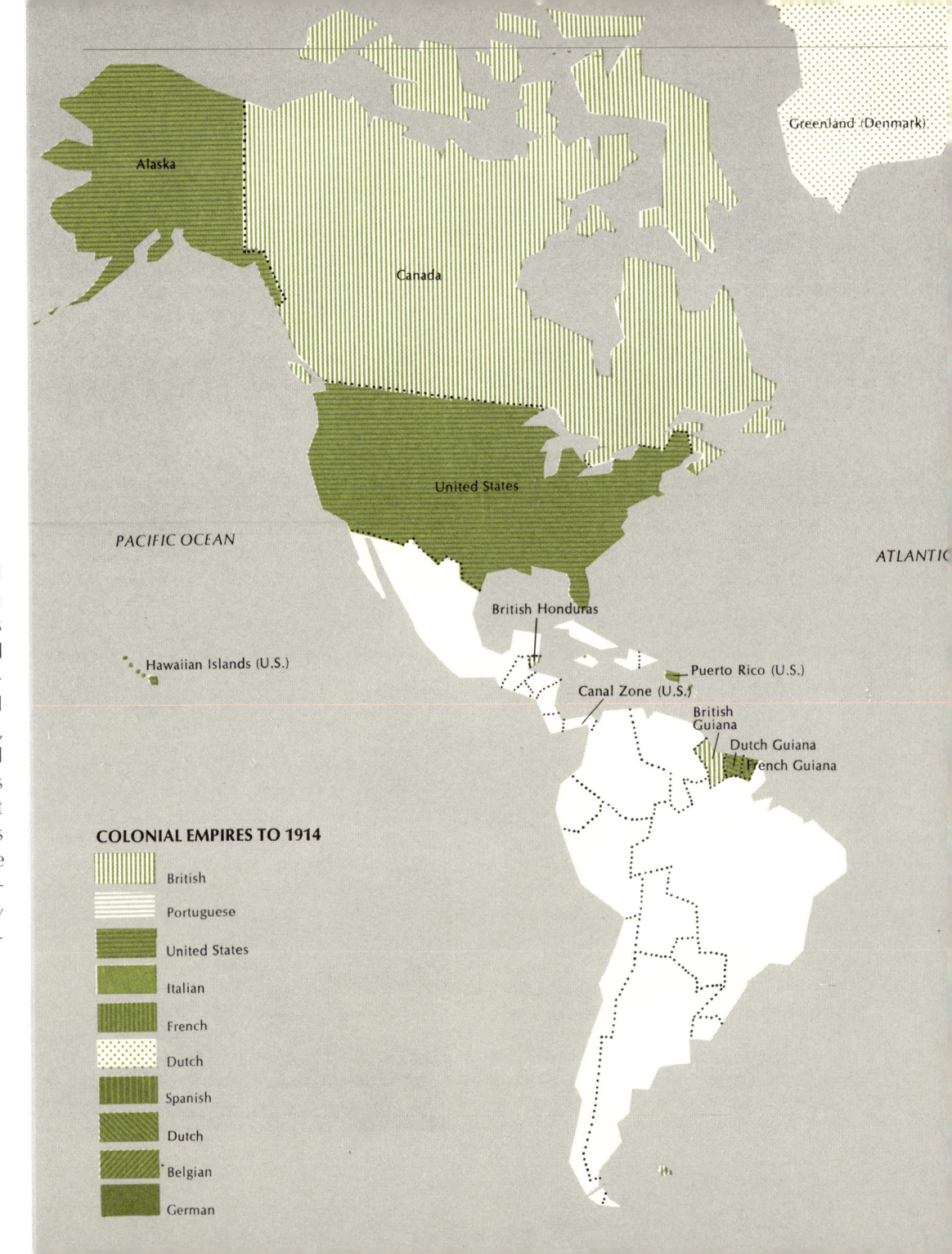

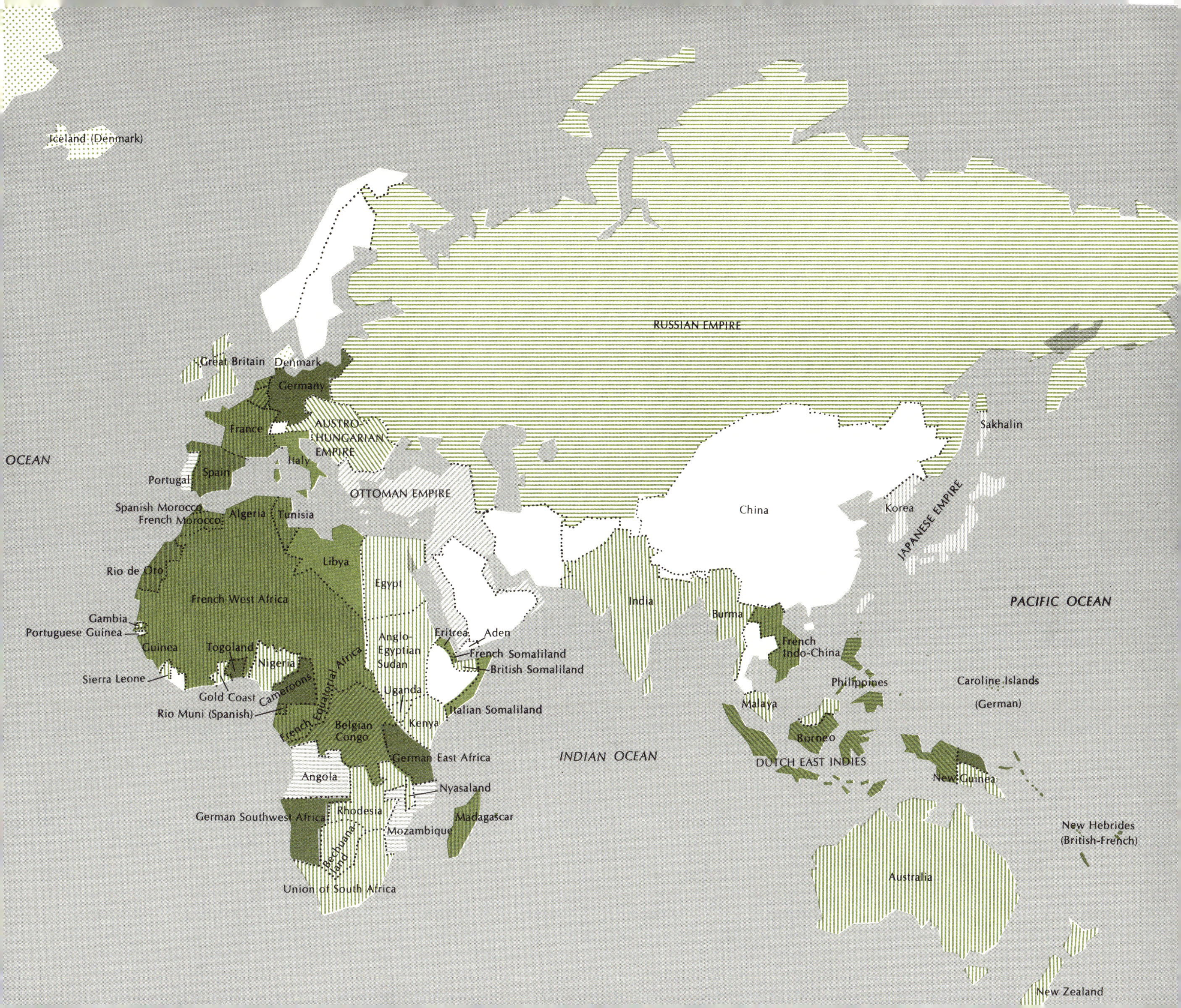

Iceland (Denmark)
OCEAN
Great Britain
Denmark
Germany
France
AUSTRO-HUNGARIAN EMPIRE
Italy
Spain
Portugal
OTTOMAN EMPIRE
RUSSIAN EMPIRE
Sakhalin
China
Korea
JAPANESE EMPIRE
PACIFIC OCEAN
Spanish Morocco
French Morocco
Algeria
Tunisia
Libya
Egypt
Rio de Oro
French West Africa
Gambia
Portuguese Guinea
Guinea
Togoland
Nigeria
Sierra Leone
Gold Coast
Cameroons
Rio Muni (Spanish)
French Equatorial Africa
Anglo-Egyptian Sudan
Eritrea
Aden
French Somaliland
British Somaliland
Uganda
Italian Somaliland
Kenya
Belgian Congo
German East Africa
Angola
Nyasaland
Rhodesia
German Southwest Africa
Mozambique
Madagascar
Bechuana-land
Union of South Africa
INDIAN OCEAN
India
Burma
French Indo-China
Philippines
Caroline Islands (German)
Malaya
Borneo
DUTCH EAST INDIES
New Guinea
New Hebrides (British-French)
Australia
New Zealand

Reading 269

The Force of Nationalism

Earlier readings have revealed how a strong sense of national identity arose among Americans in the eighteenth and nineteenth centuries, as well as how deep feelings of nationality worked to unite the North during the Civil War and then to reunite the South with the North after the war. Even as these events occurred, forces were at work to intensify national identities and feelings throughout the whole Western world. In the following selection, historian Boyd C. Shafer analyzes the ways in which nationalism grew in many countries, including the United States.

From *Nationalism: Myth and Reality*, copyright, 1955, by Boyd C. Shafer. Reprinted by permission of Harcourt Brace Jovanovich, Inc. Pp. 182–184, 185, 186, 187–189, 190–195, 197, 201–202, 204, 206–207. Subheadings added and footnotes omitted by the editors.

I

Indoctrination of Children

There is no evidence that the child is born with inherent love of nation; indeed until the age of eight or nine he scarcely understands what the "homeland" is. The Swiss psychologist, J. Piaget, in his meticulous study of two hundred children was "struck by the fact, that . . . children the initial stages of their development, did not appear to display any marked inclination towards nationalism." He found that a "slow and laborious process was necessary before children attained an awareness of their own homeland and that of others."

From his family, nevertheless, the child at an early age learns respect for the law, awe for the policemen, and love of national heroes. Very likely in his early family life he is conditioned to respond to the words and symbols representing the homeland, his reflexes being conditioned to automatic reaction in favorable patterns when he hears or sees them. A great many parents came to feel as Clemenceau, the French war leader, did about France: if there was a country which had a right to the love of its children and to obtain their first smile it was theirs. In the nineteenth and twentieth centuries, then, as most parents became more aware of and loyal to their nations, the children, born into the parents' cultural outlook, absorbed patriotic attitudes which would remain with them through their own adult lives. If as members of the human race they were already gregarious in tendencies, the home environments in which they grew shaped these tendencies toward their national group.

What family life began in this respect, the schools continued and shaped further in the direction of nationalism. Possibly the most distinctive quality of man, compared to other species, is his "teachability." Governments and patriots everywhere employed the schools to teach national patriotism. If the school systems varied in detail from country to country, in every nation the trend was toward making education universal, secular, compulsory, and patriotic. By the twentieth century such education existed everywhere in western Europe and the United States and almost all individuals in these areas were affected by it.

From at least the time of the French Revolution rulers have realized the value of formal education in the inculcation of loyalty. All during the century and a half since then universities and colleges have often been centers of nationalist education. In time of war especially, the professors, like those, for example, at Berlin during the Napoleonic wars, at Paris in 1870, and at American universities in World War I, have pleaded and propagandized for the national cause. As early as 1827 the American states of Massachusetts and Vermont required the teaching of American history in the lower schools. From a study of over eight hundred American textbooks of the period 1776–1865 one recent American authority concluded that the elementary schools "operated as a primary instrument for the inculcation of nationalism in the United States," a nationalism that "not only taught the child hatred and contempt for other nations but exalted a conservative brand of nationalism for domestic use." After the 1870's, with the rise of universal public education, efforts intensified to make all the schools centers of patriotic inspiration. . . .

Text and teacher alike, with few notable exceptions, taught the student that his own country was high-minded, great, and glorious. If his nation went to war it was for defense, while the foe was the aggressor. If his nation won its wars, that was because his countrymen were braver and God was on their side. If his nation was defeated that was due only to the enemy's overwhelmingly superior forces and treachery. If his country lost territory, as the French lost Alsace-Lorraine in 1870, that was a crime; whatever it gained was for the good of humanity and but its rightful due. The enemy was "harsh," "cruel," "backward." His own people, "kind," "civilized," "progressive."

Again and again the student learned, "My country, right or wrong, but always my country." Again and again he was instructed that he should be "prepared to endure hunger, thirst and cold for the sake of the Fatherland," and "be ready to die rather than abandon" his post. In the United States from the 1890's more and more school children were forced by law or social pressure to "pledge allegiance" to their flag. In the schools everywhere they were taught to be good citizens which meant in practice that they were to love their own country, always put it first in their affections, have no other idol before them. . . .

And the teaching was apparently effective. When in 1897 in France, examiners asked candidates for the modern baccalaureate, "What purpose does the teaching of history serve?", 80 percent answered, "To promote patriotism." When in the late 1920's Professor Bessie Pierce questioned 1,125 students in the public secondary schools of Pennsylvania and Iowa, she found that the great majority regarded defense of country as the highest form of patriotism and only four admitted that the United States "has carried on some enterprises which we can't be proud of." . . .

II

The Images of Nationalism

Everywhere men turned, their cultures influenced them to become national minded. Within each group symbols and stereotypes arose to stir their imaginations, to arouse their loyalties. Each national group had its own national holidays, its own symbolic animal, flower, or tree, its own saint, and its own mythical half-human character which somehow personified it. John Bull, Marianne, Uncle Sam, and Michel equaled England, France, the United States, and Germany. A shamrock was Ireland, a bear Russia. These symbols somehow took on mystical qualities. For each people their own flag, its colors and its designs came to represent all that was heroic and good, beautiful and true, what was highest in civilization, something never to be desecrated, something always to be worshiped.

At different times peoples attributed different meanings to these symbols as did the French to Marianne. Usually they incorporated for each group what each thought were its finest characteristics: John Bull is dogged and Uncle Sam honest. By so doing individuals within each group could "appropriate the complimentary adjectives" for their "own countrymen," and by "reflection of virtue" for themselves. Thus they could describe themselves as hard-working, intelligent, generous, brave, and peace-loving. On the other hand each people tended to see other national groups through stereotypes given quite opposite meanings. "John Bull, for Germany, becomes a caddish, insolent ogre-like figure: Uncle Sam, for Europe, a desiccated, heartless Shylock, and German Michel, for France, a sly double-crossing fool; in the same way Marianne is all too easily transformed into a flighty harum-scarum." Reinforced by literature, history, and the movies these stereotypes for each people, both the "good" for themselves and the "bad" for other nationalities, tended to become fixed. After Hollywood had portrayed and twentieth-century American children had viewed Americans as handsome heroes and German, Japanese, and Russians as brutal beasts for years, it would be difficult for most Americans to see them as individuals who, like Americans, varied widely both physically and mentally.

III

Patriotic Groups

To be certain that individuals were shaped by the nationalist pattern, patriots in each nation formed societies to bring pressure upon governments and to propagandize for "right ideals." Early in the nineteenth century these societies, like the *Hetairia Philike* in Greece, the Carbonari and "Young Italy" in the Italies, the *Burschenschaft* in the Germanies, the *Selspabet for Norges vel* in Norway, and the Philomathians in Poland strove to create national consciousness, to unify their peoples and to obtain national independence. Once these objectives were obtained, similar if less conspiratorial societies were formed to intensify national loyalty, to strengthen the national military forces, and to guard and to extend (particularly in the case of the British and Germans) the nation's possessions. From the 1880's these patriotic organizations sprang up rapidly. Composed usually of respectable, middle-class, and conservative citizens, many of them with some military background, they had a stake in the established order, liked it, and wanted to keep "superior" people like themselves on top. To do so as well as to stimulate patriotism they prodded governments to indoctrinate national ideals through the schools, to push national interests exclusively by whatever methods seemed necessary, and to nationalize (or eliminate) the "alien" groups within the nation.

To attempt to list all these patriotic societies would take too much space. In a brief examination of the American records the present writer found fifty-odd such groups established in the United States before 1917, and one count revealed eighty-four in Germany in 1914. Among the most prominent

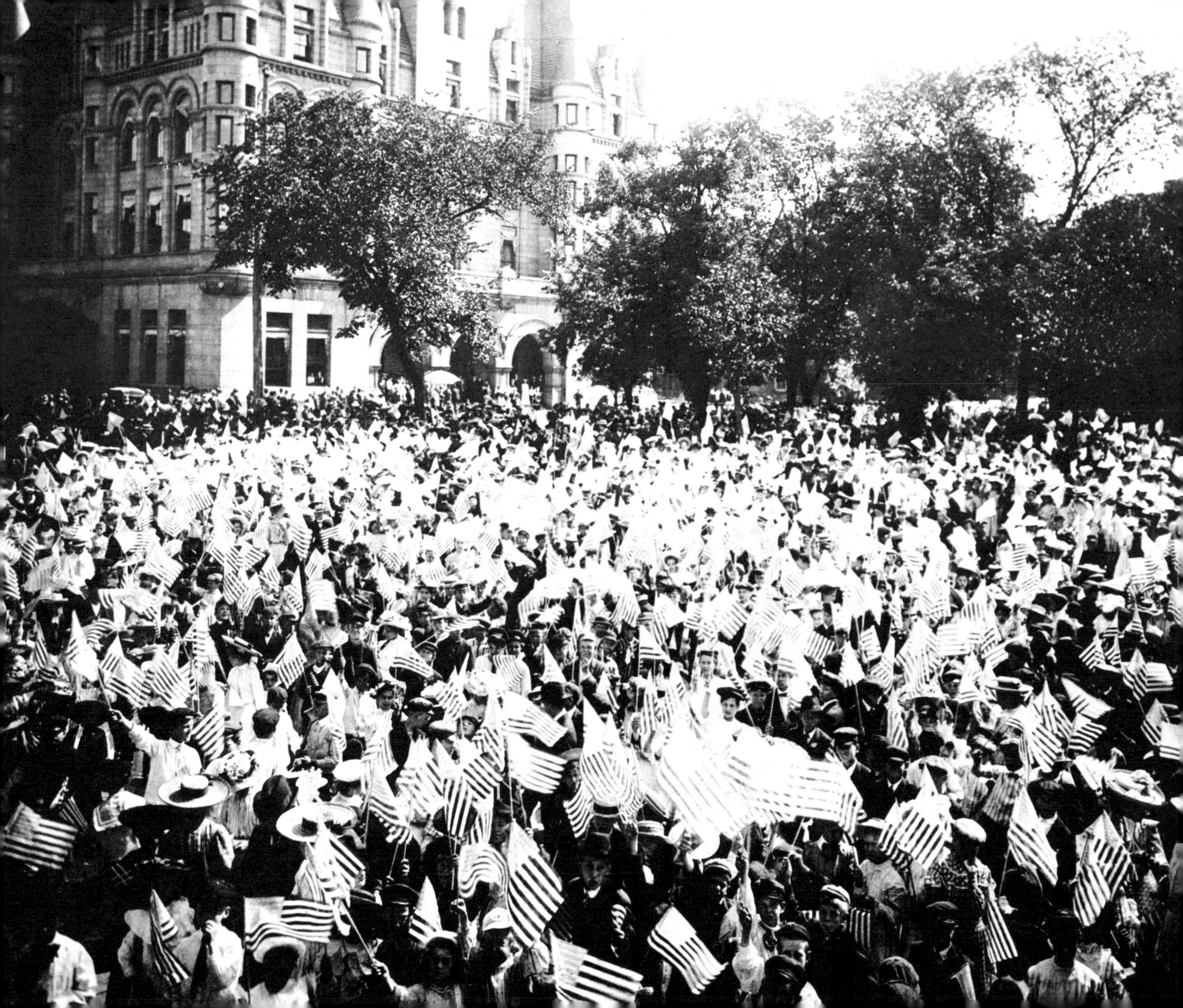

The symbols of nationalism. Hundreds of school children in St. Paul, Minnesota, vigorously wave American flags on the Fourth of July, 1905.

societies were the Royal Empire Society and the Primrose League of Britain, the Daughters of the American Revolution and the Grand Army of the Republic in the United States, the League of Patriots and the National Alliance for the Increase of French Population in France, and the Pan-German League and the Navy League in Germany.

These groups and the many like them held meetings to hear inspirational patriotic talks. They published magazines, occasionally newspapers, and handed out propaganda in pamphlets and news stories. They brought pressure upon their governments to increase military appropriations and adopt "strong" foreign policies. They demanded the teaching of patriotism and tried to weed out unpatriotic teachers and teachings. They exhibited the national flags and relics and publicly celebrated national holidays. They attempted to "Americanize" or "Germanize" the foreigners within their gates, and to "purify" the national languages. They were vociferously for any and all policies which in their view enhanced the prestige of their nation. They were just as vociferously against anything they thought foreign or international.

Their memberships were usually not large, the better-known organizations numbering 40,000 to 300,000 and only occassionally, like the American GAR and the British Primrose League, exceeding a million. But they spoke loudly and with self-assurance. While a few, like the Pan-German League, would be unpopular with their governments, while most of them were filled with old gentlemen and ladies, they served to make national patriotism respectable. Not infrequently as in the case of the various Navy and Security Leagues they influenced political leaders who wished to be re-elected, and thereby were successful in increasing the size of the military establishments. If they were not effective in any other way, they spread fear of other nations, caused many of their compatriots to "view with alarm," hence accentuated distrust of foreigners and sharpened feelings of national exclusiveness.

While there was no society that might be termed "typical" among them, the early activities of one, the Daughters of the American Revolution, is not unrepresentative. The Daughters held patriotic assemblies to inspire themselves and their communities. They presented copies of national songs and documents to schools, convinced boards of education and legislatures that the American flag should be flown on every school, decried any "misuse" of the flag, and asked that men (not women) doff their hats when it passed. They reviewed the national history, especially its glorious moments, made pilgrimages to historical spots, gave entertainments in historical costumes, and erected national monuments. They gave prizes to children for patriotic essays and made certain that the "right" books were in the libraries. "In every way" the Daughters desired to "cherish, maintain and extend the institutions of American freedom, to foster true patriotism and love of country," which, of course, meant they wanted other Americans to be loyal to their kind of nation. While like most of the patriotic societies they shunned politics (on paper), they were always on the side of the national authorities, particularly the conservative ones. They were always fearful of the "foreigner"; they were always against any "radical" doctrines like socialism; and they were always for "adequate" defense which in practice meant the biggest army and navy the country could afford without heavy taxes upon the well-to-do.

With all these social pressures upon them, few men could be anything but national patriots. As David Hume observed in the eighteenth century, "the human mind is of a very imitative nature; nor is it possible for any set of men to converse often together, without acquiring a similitude of manners, and communicating to each other their vices as well as virtues...." Men were forced into national molds by their cultures....

IV

National Rivalries

The national governments... turned the eyes of more and more of their citizens toward the nation. At the same time forces encroaching upon the nation-state from without had a similar effect. As each state grew stronger, it, with the prevailing conditions of international anarchy, seemed to threaten every other nation. For its own security each national government believed it must create a solid and strong national front against every other nation. Each nation in consequence had to build its military forces, make alliances, expand its trade and its colonial empire. That this solution ultimately brought disaster, not security, proved nothing. No nation could afford to stop building land forces, sea forces, air forces, no nation could withdraw from its colonies and tear down its trade walls—unless all the others did. All felt obligated, on the contrary, to build, build, build. When a committee of three British admirals in 1888 gave it as their opinion that the British navy should be larger than "that of any two powers," they were simply leading the way to a tremendous naval race in which all the great powers had to take part. The Germans led by Admiral von Tirpitz and their Navy League and the Americans under the influence of Admiral Mahan, President Theodore Roosevelt, and their steel manufacturers indulged in the same kind of fantasy—to be safe each nation had to have a navy capable of "defending" (expanding) the national interests against all possible opponents anywhere at any time. The result could not be anything but fear and eventual war and these in turn accentuated nationalism. Each national official felt bound to forward his nation's military might, to assume an aggressive foreign policy. If he did not he was a traitor who criminally betrayed his country....

In the system of power relationships that characterized international politics each nation believed that to survive it had to follow this pattern, to form an independent national government, weld itself together into an ever more uniform, integrated, coherent whole. Here a kind of social Darwinism, a competitive struggle among nations, seemed to operate. If the "survival of the fittest" did not really apply to the national struggles, patriots thought that it did and what they thought was more significant than the truth or falsity of the doctrine. What was believed about group survival, was equally applicable if the nation was to forward what its members considered their interests, the national interests.

Josiah Strong: The Anglo-Saxon Mission (1885)

In the nineteenth century, Christians in many Western countries increased their efforts to convert peoples in non-Christian parts of the world to their faith. The missionary movement grew rapidly, especially among American Protestants. A leader in the movement was the Reverend Josiah Strong (1847-1916), a Congregationalist minister. Strong's version of the Christian message was colored by both national and racial ideas. In his widely sold book, *Our Country*, published in 1885, he offered his fellow Americans his vision of their future.

Reprinted by permission of the publishers from pp. 200, 201-202, 205-206, 210-211, 212-214, 215-216 of Josiah Strong, *Our Country*, edited by Jurgen Herbst. Cambridge, Mass.: Harvard University Press, Copyright, 1963, by the President and Fellows of Harvard College.

I

The Two Great Ideas

Every race which has deeply impressed itself on the human family has been the representative of some great idea—one or more—which has given direction to the nation's life and form to its civilization. Among the Egyptians this seminal idea was life, among the Persians it was light, among the Hebrews it was purity, among the Greeks it was beauty, among the Romans it was law. The Anglo-Saxon is the representative of two great ideas, which are closely related. One of them is that of civil liberty. Nearly all of the civil liberty of the world is enjoyed by Anglo-Saxons: the English, the British colonists, and the people of the United States....

The other great idea of which the Anglo-Saxon is the exponent is that of a pure *spiritual* Christianity. It was no accident that the great reformation of the sixteenth century originated among a Teutonic, rather than a Latin people. It was the fire of liberty burning in the Saxon heart that flamed up against the absolutism of the Pope. Speaking roughly, the peoples of Europe which are Celtic are Roman Catholic, and those which are Teutonic are Protestant; and where the Teutonic race was purest, there Protestantism spread with the greatest rapidity. But, with beautiful exceptions, Protestantism on the continent has degenerated into mere formalism.... That means that most of the spiritual Christianity in the world is found among Anglo-Saxons and their converts; for this is the great missionary race....

II

The Battle of Numbers

It is not necessary to argue to those for whom I write that the two great needs of mankind, that all men may be lifted up into the light of the highest Christian civilization, are, first, a pure, spiritual Christianity, and second, civil liberty. Without controversy, these are the forces which, in the past, have contributed most to the elevation of the human race, and they must continue to be, in the future, the most efficient ministers to its progress. It follows, then, that the Anglo-Saxon, as the great representative of these two ideas, the depositary of these two greatest blessings, sustains peculiar relations to the world's future, is divinely commissioned to be, in a peculiar sense, his brother's keeper. Add to this the fact of his rapidly increasing strength in modern times, and we have well-nigh a demonstration of his destiny. In 1700 this race numbered less than 6,000,000 souls. In 1800, Anglo-Saxons (I use the term somewhat broadly to include all English-speaking peoples) had increased to about 20,500,000, and now, in 1890, they number more than 120,000,000, having multiplied almost six-fold in ninety years. At the end of the reign of Charles II. the English colonists in America numbered 200,000. During these two hundred years, our population has increased two hundred and fifty-fold. And the expansion of this race has been no less remarkable than its multiplication. In one century the United States has increased its territory ten-fold, while the enormous acquisition of foreign territory by Great Britain—and chiefly within the last hundred years—is wholly unparalleled in history. This mighty Anglo-Saxon race, though comprising only one-thirteenth part of mankind, now rules more than one-third of the earth's surface, and more than one-fourth of its people. And if this race, while growing from 6,000,000 to 120,000,000, thus gained possession of a third portion of the earth, is it to be supposed that when it numbers 1,000,000,000, it will lose the disposition, or lack the power to extend its sway? . . .

We may be reasonably confident that a hundred years hence this one race will outnumber all the peoples of continental Europe. And it is possible that, by the close of the next century, the Anglo-Saxons will outnumber all the other civilized races of the world. Does it not look as if God were not only preparing in our Anglo-Saxon civilization the die with which to stamp the peoples of the earth, but as if he were also massing behind that die the mighty power with which to press it? My confidence that this race is eventually to give its civilization to mankind is not based on mere numbers—China forbid! I look forward to what the world has never yet seen united in the same race; viz., the greatest numbers, *and* the highest civilization.

III

American Leadership

There can be no reasonable doubt that North America is to be the great home of the Anglo-Saxon, the principal seat of his power, the center of his life and influence. Not only does it constitute seven-elevenths of his possessions, but here his empire is unsevered, while the remaining four-elevenths are fragmentary and scattered over the earth. Australia will have a great population; but its disadvantages, as compared with North America, are too manifest to need mention. Our continent has room and resources and climate, it lies in the pathway of the nations, it belongs to the zone of power, and already, among Anglo-Saxons, do we lead in population and wealth. Of England, Franklin once wrote: "That pretty island which, compared to America, is but a stepping-stone in a brook, scarce enough of it above water to keep one's shoes dry." England can hardly hope to maintain her relative importance among Anglo-Saxon peoples when her "pretty island" is the home of only one-twentieth part of that race. With the wider distribution of wealth, and increasing facilities of intercourse, intelligence and influence are less centralized, and peoples become more homogeneous; and the more nearly homogeneous peoples are, the more do *numbers tell.* . . .

IV

The Purpose of God

What is the significance of such facts? These tendencies infold the future; they are the mighty alphabet with which God writes his prophecies. May we not, by a careful laying together of the letters, spell out something of his meaning? It seems to me that God, with infinite wisdom and skill, is training the Anglo-Saxon race for an hour sure to come in the world's future. Heretofore there has always been in the history of the world a comparatively unoccupied land westward, into which the crowded countries of the East have poured their surplus populations. But the widening waves of migration, which millenniums ago rolled east and west from the valley of the Euphrates, meet to-day on our Pacific coast. There are no more new worlds. The unoccupied arable lands of the earth are limited, and will soon be taken. The time is coming when the pressure of population on the means of subsistence will be felt here as it is now felt in Europe and Asia. Then will the world enter upon a new stage of its history—*the final competition of races, for which the Anglo-Saxon is being schooled.* Long before the thousand millions are here, the mighty *centrifugal* tendency, inherent in this stock and strengthened in the United States, will assert itself. Then this race of unequaled energy, with all the majesty of numbers and the might of wealth behind it—the representative, let us hope, of the largest liberty, the purest Christianity, the highest civilization—having developed peculiarly aggressive traits calculated to impress its insti-

Reading 271

Nationalism, Expansion, and Hawaii (1893)

Expansion of the United States from the Mississippi River to the Pacific Coast and the Rio Grande provided rich rewards for American energies and enormous satisfaction for American pride. Until the late nineteenth century, however, there seemed to be little interest among Americans for an expansion of their domain beyond these limits. They were indifferent to the purchase of Alaska in 1867 and a variety of efforts, both official and unofficial, to acquire territory in the Caribbean area came to nothing. A rapid increase in schemes to obtain colonies by European countries in the late nineteenth century, however, aroused the uneasy feeling among some Americans that they too ought to join the colonial race. In 1878 the United States took a tentative step in this direction by establishing a joint protectorate (with Britain and Germany) over the Samoan Islands in the South Pacific Ocean. A much more striking test of American interest in acquiring overseas possessions came in 1893. The Hawaiian Islands were already commercially dependent on the United States, since the latter bought nearly all Hawaii's exports (at that time largely sugar), and had recently obtained the right to maintain a naval base at Pearl Harbor. Although a native monarch ruled Hawaii, sugar planters and businessmen, mostly American, British, and German by birth, controlled its economy. When Queen Liliuokalani (1838–1917) showed signs of wanting to exercise more authority, the planters and

ACCORDING TO THE IDEAS OF OUR MISSIONARY MANIACS.
The Chinaman must be converted, even if it takes the whole military and naval forces of the two greatest nations of the world to do it.

Missionaries did more than carry Christianity abroad. Often they also provided an entering wedge for European expansion into Asia and Africa. "Saving the heathen" was popular in both Europe and America, but there were also those who opposed the idea that the American flag, and the military force it represented, should necessarily follow on the heels of the missionaries.

tutions upon mankind, will spread itself over the earth. If I read not amiss, this powerful race will move down upon Mexico, down upon Central and South America, out upon the islands of the sea, over upon Africa and beyond. And can any one doubt that the result of this competition of races will be the "survival of the fittest"?

292

Queen Liliuokalani, the last native ruler of Hawaii.

businessmen staged a bloodless revolution, overthrew her, established a provisional government on January 17, 1893, and invited the United States to annex Hawaii. All this took place with the knowledge, approval, and assistance of the American minister to Hawaii, John L. Stevens. The following five excerpts reveal the varied reactions of American newspapers to the events of 1893.

From *Public Opinion*, XIV, (February 4, 11, 1893), pp. 415, 416, 439.

DENVER *NEWS* (DEMOCRATIC), JANUARY 29

There can be little doubt of the great importance which the acquisition of these islands will prove to the Pacific coast cities. Their ownership would at once give strength to the naval force of this Government and a most commanding position in the event of a naval war between the United States and France, England or Germany. There can be no question about the right of an independent nation, great or small, unbound by treaty, to annex itself to any other country. About the only question that can arise to defeat the efforts of the provisional Hawaiian government for annexation is as to the legality and stability of the Government that seeks it. If it becomes stable and recognized by other nations the right of annexation is beyond question. This step by the Hawaiians has precipitated a most interesting situation. What will the United States do? What will European governments say? We must wait and see.

BOSTON *HERALD* (INDEPENDENT), JANUARY 30

One can easily understand the wish of the white citizens and many of the foreign residents of the Hawaiian Islands to have the ex-kingdom annexed to the United States. Nine-tenths of their trade is with this country; the future of Hawaii as an independent State is uncertain, in view of the disposition of the great nations of Europe to seize and absorb such territory as they can lay their hands upon; the disproportionate number of relatively ignorant natives and Chinese upon the islands, and the recent falling off of the official income. Annexation to the United States and the change to a territory, governed by officials appointed by the authorities at Washington, would solve at once a number of doubtful problems. But it does not follow that the advantages would be reciprocal. We should not wish to have one of the great powers of Europe seize the Hawaiian group and occupy it as a naval station, or by special laws exclude us from the trade we now have; but with these exceptions, it would be very much to our advantage to have the Hawaiian people independent of us. In a trade way we could not gain by annexation anything we do not now possess, while politically the union would bring with it new problems of difference in race and conditions to add to those which we now have. But even more than this is the international burden we should then assume. Hawaii would be our one weak point, liable to assault in a foreign war by the navy of the enemy, and rendering it necessary that we should maintain a much larger naval force than is now needed; that we should spend great sums of money in fortifications, and be prepared to send a large force of soldiers to Honolulu. So far as England is concerned, although she would doubtless protest, under our treaty arrangements with her, to annexation, if it were made, she would have us at a disadvantage, for the distant islands would be the one place in our National domain where she could assail us under conditions signally in her favor.

WASHINGTON *POST* (INDEPENDENT), FEBRUARY 1

The Hawaiian question is a National question. It is one of patriotic feeling and plain common sense. Shall we take Hawaii, and thereby prosper and magnify ourselves, or shall we let England take it, and thereby enfeeble and humiliate us? If we be a great nation, with pride and purpose and intelligence, we shall seize the opportunity. If we are inert, cowardly and stupid we'll keep quiet and let England complete the chain of her hostile environment. Lord Rosebery is reported as having said to a representative of the late Hawaiian Monarchy that England, France and Germany would hardly consent to our occupation of the islands. That points, of course, to England's favorite policy of intimidation in the first place and, failing in that, to her traditional expedient of getting somebody else to do her fighting. But intimidations will not work in this case. France and Germany have no terrors for us, even in the highly improbable event of their becoming cat's paws for England, and the expedient will fail because neither France nor Germany can afford to go to war away from home.

This is an affair for us to settle for ourselves. Hawaii is the natural and logical outpost of the United States in the Pacific. Its possession would mean the saving of incalculable millions in coast defense and the control of the commercial pathways of more than half the salt water on the globe. The Hawaiians have come to us for protection and help, and in responding to their petition we shall immeasurably strengthen and enrich ourselves. Shall we do it? That is the only question. England's protests are not to be considered. We do not need Great Britain's approval in our National affairs, and, even if we did, that is the last thing we should get where our advantage lay. Leave England out of the question, and let us consider only what is our profit and honor in the case. If England ventures to interfere or to throw obstacles in the way of our will and pleasure, let England look to herself. This country has grown since 1776.

SAN FRANCISCO *CHRONICLE* (REPUBLICAN), FEBRUARY 1

The English, with that stupidity which is well called insular, and with a conceit begotten of conquest of naked and half-starved savages in various obscure portions of the globe, have undertaken to throw doubt upon the right of the people of Hawaii to dispose of themselves and their future as might seem best to them, and to say, with a true John Bullish hum and haw, that they do not know that they can consent to a transfer of the Hawaiian Islands to the American flag. It is not believed that the English will do anything more than grumble, but if they should manage to make a combination with every power in Europe to prevent the annexation of Hawaii to the United States their victory would contain the seeds of an ultimate defeat which would prove their ruin. In the present unsettled conditions of affairs in Europe the United States would be received with open arms as an ally by any combination of powers that could be suggested. If England has any regard for her own welfare she will let Hawaii and the United States settle their affairs without any interference on her part.

MINNEAPOLIS *TIMES* (DEMOCRATIC), FEBRUARY 2

It is quite probable that England will enter a protest against any attempt by the United States to arbitrarily annex the Sandwich Islands,* but that she has the slightest disposition to go to war with us over Claus Spreckles' sugar plantation, there is absolutely no ground for asserting. Nor is there any more reason to believe that the people of this country will ever consent to a war with England over our right to confer the dignity and privileges of American citizenship upon the leprous descendents of the Sandwich Island cannibals. War with England over such a petty matter is simply an impossibility; for such a war would be not merely a moral evil, but a social and commercial disaster. It would

*Another term for the Hawaiian Islands—Eds.

affect, if it did not interrupt the manufacturing interests of both countries. The loss of life which might ensue is a comparatively small matter, but the inevitable stagnation of business and the measureless suffering and wretchedness it would occasion are of deep concern to all. But from the purely commercial standpoint a rupture between the United States and England would be a calamity to appall the imagination.

The Question of Conspiracy

As further details of the little revolution of January 1893 became known in the United States, Americans began to realize that an American official had played a leading role. Minister John L. Stevens, in response to a plea by the conspirators that American lives and property were being threatened, requested that marines from the naval vessel *Boston* be landed. The marines, about 150 in number, took along two artillery pieces. There was no sign of violence on shore. Next day the revolutionary businessmen proclaimed the overthrow of Queen Liliuokalani from the steps of the capitol building with the marines and the artillery pieces in attendance. The queen yielded under protest and appealed to the United States government in Washington. As the following newspaper editorials reveal, Americans differed in their reactions to this coup.

From *Public Opinion*, XIV, (February 18, 1893), p. 467.

CHICAGO *NEWS RECORD* (INDEPENDENT), FEBRUARY 11

Minister Stevens' action in flying the Stars and Stripes of the United States over the government house in Honolulu and proclaiming Hawaii under an American protectorate may yet prove to have been very timely. Had he waited until the British Minister there had gained the moral support of a cruiser full of British marines, now on their way thither, it is possible that a flag of different colors would have been flying where he has placed our own. There can be no differences of opinion over the main question. The United States Government must have the first voice in the affairs and control of Hawaii. No power has any right to take precedence in this. As to the question of annexation or a protectorate there will be time now to decide that without fear of interference. Good sense and the best interests of the country counsel the establishment of a permanent protectorate and the adoption of annexation only after such protectorate shall be determined to be inexpedient. In any event our supremacy in Hawaii is quite certain. We shall probably assume a guiding hand over the destinies of that important archipelago for all time.

CHICAGO *HERALD* (DEMOCRATIC), FEBRUARY 11

The sugar ring is clearly behind the pretended revolution. No revolution, in fact, has taken place. A corrupt intrigue aiming only at the bounty which the sugar ring hopes to get has found a co-operator in an American Minister who has used an American gunboat and American marines to intimidate and dethrone a constitutional sovereign and to inflict upon a community entirely able to take care of themselves a revolutionary junta pretending to be a provisional government. The President and Secretary of State have restrained from act or word making the American people *particeps criminis* in the conspiracy of Claus Spreckels, aided and abetted by Minister Stevens. The American people are not going to be tricked by spurious cries of continental supremacy. We want no supremacy that is not ours by right. We are supreme at Hawaii in the only way we desire to be supreme; we control its trade and we will not suffer any other foreign power to invade or absorb the islands, as we do not need to absorb and shall not invade them ourselves. No jingoism!

American marines from the warship *Boston* conducted an artillery drill at their camp in Honolulu, while thousands of miles away in Washington the United States Congress debated whether to annex the islands.

Further Thoughts on Annexation

As the following examples of newspaper reactions reveal, the problem of the annexation of Hawaii contained a variety of issues in addition to the one of American connivance in the January revolution.

From *Public Opinion*, XIV, (February 18, 25, 1893), pp. 466, 467, 488; XV, (May 2, 1893), p. 169.

PITTSBURGH *DISPATCH* (INDEPENDENT), FEBRUARY 12

The talk of defending our Pacific coast by a naval station 2,000 miles away is worse than absurd. The United States has attained its greatness simply by staying at home and minding its own business. By that means we are not put to the expense of maintaining a great military and naval establishment, and our growth and prosperity, by keeping our Government within our borders, have been the marvel of the world. If we wish to scatter our resources all over the world, the Hawaiian and Nicaraguan schemes afford eligible opportunities. But do we wish to throw to the winds the policy which has made this country powerful and prosperous? It will be well to think twice before answering that question in the affirmative.

BOSTON *TRAVELLER* (REPUBLICAN), FEBRUARY 13

Is Hawaii worth annexing, or should the United States abandon it to itself and leave it to work out its own destiny? There are facts and figures worthy [of] consideration. In the fiscal year ending June 30, 1892, the United States alone received Hawaiian products, chiefly sugar, to the value of $8,075,881. That is an astonishing amount of merchandise for 85,000 people, many of them hampered by the indolence common to natives of tropical countries, to be able to sell for export in a single year, and, of course, the surplus products of Hawaii were not all marketed in the United States. The total exports were about $9,000,000, or over $100 for every man, woman or child in the Hawaiian Islands. A similar export trade in proportion to the population of the United States would make the annual shipments of merchandise from this country about $6,500,000,000, or about six times as much as they have ever been in the history of the nation. Such a foreign commerce, maintained by a country with only a semi-civilized system of government, is at once a proof of almost phenomenal natural resources. In this case figures and statistics tell the story.

SAN FRANCISCO *EXAMINER* (DEMOCRATIC), FEBRUARY 15

It is natural that the Administration and Congress should look to California for an expression of public sentiment on the Hawaiian question, and should be guided to a large extent by what they hear from the Western shores. California is the nearest State to Hawaii. Californian interests are most closely bound up in the Hawaiian trade and Californians will be affected by the annexation more than any other of the American people. The opinion of California should be given plainly. California wants Hawaii annexed. It is recognized here that the islands cannot maintain an independent existence. It is recognized here how fatal it would be to American control in the Pacific to allow the islands to pass to British control. And for these reasons California, through her newspapers, her legislature, her commercial bodies, demands that the request of the Hawaiians be granted, and that the American flag float over the island territory. It is to be understood, however, that California demands conditions. The thousands of Chinese and other contract laborers on the islands must not be allowed to come here. They must be kept to the islands, and when their term of service is up they must be returned to their homes without acquiring any privileges as American residents. There is no difficulty in accomplishing this. If the annexation treaty contains this provision in its terms it will be sufficient to keep out the Chinese. It is stated in the Washington dispatches that such a clause is in the agreement that is offered to the United States. No privileges of citizenship are to be conferred by annexation and no privileges of residence given the contract laborers in any other part of the United States. This will be satisfactory to California. Every possible objection from this quarter is met by it. Hawaii must belong to the United States. The islands are necessary to the political and commercial control of the Pacific and they must be ours.

NEW YORK *COMMERCIAL ADVERTISER* (INDEPENDENT), FEBRUARY 18

In dealing with a partly barbarous country, the United States is not amenable to the same demands of justice which a civilized country might properly make of us. The native population is entitled to humane treatment, but the underlying principle in the negotiations is that law and order must be insisted upon by the nations of the earth. When a people proves itself unable to maintain a stable government, it is the province of a higher civilized nation to step in and supply the need. The Hawaiians are to be treated kindly, firmly as children. The time has passed for seriously regarding them as competent to govern themselves, or to tell others how to govern them. President Harrison has more wisely taken his counsel from superior, trustworthy Anglo-Saxons. Then, his duty clear, he ceased to talk, and acted. The Anglo-Saxons are the nation builders of the world. To lavish sympathy on the poor, dying contingent of an aboriginal race is permissible, but to prate of the "justice" of temporizing with them, when decisive action is called for, is to forget the history of nations in all times under the grim but beneficent law which confers on highly civilized States the prerogatives of government.

THE REVEREND WILLIAM B. OLESON, HONOLULU, IN *NEW YORK INDEPENDENT*, MAY 11

It will be of interest to know that there is a movement on foot to organize the Japanese

Reading 274

into a league to agitate the question of suffrage rights for all the subjects of Japan resident in the Hawaiian Islands. This movement does not wear any signs of spontaneity, and is apparently being conducted by agents of the Japanese Government. There is some unwritten history in connection with the relations of the two countries in recent years that strongly re-enforces the belief current among the most intelligent citizens of Honolulu that Japan has been gradually developing a policy with reference to Hawaii that would in a few years have brought this country under the domination of Asiatic rather than American civilization. This is not yet out of the range of possibility. Should America decide not to absorb Hawaii, then it alone assumes the responsibility of saying to Anglo-Saxon civilization, in this essentially American outpost, "Retreat to the American continent; thus far shalt thou go, but no farther."

Triumph of Liberty or Insult to the Flag?

President Grover Cleveland (1837-1908), a Democrat, began his second term of office on March 4, 1893, succeeding Benjamin Harrison, the Republican who had defeated him four years earlier. A treaty for the annexation of Hawaii had been drawn up hastily by the Harrison administration in its last days and was still before the Senate. Cleveland, aware that the revolution had had American co-operation, withdrew the treaty from the Senate and dispatched Congressman James H. Blount, a Georgia Democrat with long experience on the House Committee on Foreign Affairs, to investigate the events in Hawaii. On his arrival Blount found that Minister Stevens had declared Hawaii a temporary American protectorate, pending action by the United States government. Blount ordered that the protectorate be ended and that the flag be lowered. Again newspapers differed sharply in their reactions to the event.

From *Public Opinion*, XV, (April 22, 1893), p. 70.

ST. LOUIS *REPUBLIC* (DEMOCRATIC), APRIL 15

The action of the Cleveland Administration in Hawaii will be indorsed by all who have not repudiated the principles of liberty and justice. Mr. Cleveland has refused to believe the transparent lie that Spreckels and his associates in Honolulu are the people of Hawaii. He has refused to allow them the further use of the American flag in their schemes of fraud and usurpation. Nothing less was to have been expected from an honest man and a patriotic American. Mr. Cleveland has justified the expectations of those who looked to him as the guardian of our Democratic traditions, as the friend of liberty—of the liberty of weaker peoples as well as of our own. We could have seized these islands without difficulty. The people have few arms, and even if well armed they could do nothing against our immense resources. Germany and England would have been glad to see us commit such a crime, as they could then expect our countenance in similar crimes that they are contemplating. Nothing stood in the way of this robbery as nothing stood in the way of the dismemberment of Poland.

Reading 275

NEW YORK *PRESS* (REPUBLICAN), APRIL 17

Every enemy of American ideas and republican institutions, every foe of the American name, every upholder of the divine right of monarchs to misrule by brute force, will rejoice at the deliberate insult offered by Grover Cleveland to the American flag at Hawaii. Nothing was omitted on the part of the Administration to make the insult complete. All possible publicity was given to the act. Notice has been given of the hour at which it was to be performed in order to secure a multitude of witnesses of the formal humiliation of the symbol of the Republic. The gallant marines of the Boston were drawn up to see the disgraceful lowering of the flag that no foeman has ever been able to conquer or to dishonor. The one man selected from a great nation by the President to order the hauling down of the Stars and Stripes at Honolulu was a Bourbon ex-Confederate, who had fought to tear down the American flag and trample it under foot, and whose hostility to American ideas and interests has apparently not abated since he bore arms against the Nation.

Carl Schurz: Big Navies and Aggression

Among the Republicans who resisted the attraction of expansion was Carl Schurz (1829-1906), a German immigrant who became a political leader, Civil War diplomat and general, United States Senator, and journalist. Schurz was a member of the so-called "Mugwump" faction of the Republican Party and often differed with party regulars. In late 1893 Schurz wrote a magazine article which summed up many of the anti-annexationist positions shown in the previous readings. To it he added some thoughts about the meaning of naval expansion.

From Carl Schurz, "Manifest Destiny," *Harper's New Monthly Magazine*, LXXXVII, (October 1893), pp. 744, 745.

It will not be denied that in case of war with a strong naval power the defence of Hawaii would require very strong military and naval establishments there, and a fighting fleet as large and efficient as that of the enemy; and in case of a war with a combination of great naval powers, it might require a fleet much larger than that of any of them. Attempts of the enemy to gain an important advantage by a sudden stroke, which would be entirely harmless if made on our continental stronghold, might have an excellent chance of success if made on our distant insular possession, and then the whole war could be made to turn upon that point, where the enemy might concentrate his forces as easily as we, or even more easily, and be our superior on the decisive field of operations. It is evident that thus the immense advantage we now enjoy of a substantially unassailable defensive position would be lost. We would no longer possess the inestimable privilege of being stronger and more secure than any other nation without a large and costly armament. Hawaii, or whatever other outlying domain, would be our Achilles' heel. Other nations would observe it, and regard us no longer as invulnerable. If we acquire Hawaii, we acquire not an addition to our strength, but a dangerous element of weakness.

It is said that we need a large navy in any case for the protection of our commerce, and that if we have it for this purpose it may at the same time serve for the protection of outlying national domains without much extra expense. The premise is false. We need no large navy for the protection of our commerce. Since the extinction of the Barbary pirates and of the Western buccaneers, the sea is the safest public highway in the world, except, perhaps, in the Chinese waters. Our commerce is not threatened by anybody or anything, unless it be the competition of other nations and the errors of our own commercial policy; and against these influences war-ships avail nothing. . . .

In another respect a large navy might prove to the American people a most undesirable luxury. It would be a dangerous plaything. Its possession might excite an impatient desire to use it, and lead us into strong temptations to precipitate a conflict of arms in case of any difference with a foreign government, which otherwise might easily be settled by amicable adjustment. The little new navy we have has already perceptibly stimulated such a spirit among some of our navy officers and civilian navy enthusiasts, who are spoiling for an opportunity to try the new guns. We remember their attitude during the late Chilian difficulty, when it was absolutely certain to any candid mind that our little sister republic would, after a little bluster, ultimately make every apology demanded. And there is no project of territorial acquisition or of "vigorous foreign policy" ever so extravagant that does not find hot advocates in navy circles. Every new war-ship we build will be apt further to encourage this tendency; and nothing will be wanting but the growth of the belief among navy officers that they can make themselves heroes of a new era by using their opportunities for carrying on some vigorous foreign policy on their own motion to render the navy the more dangerous to the peace and dignity of this republic the more ships we have. No great power can do so much among the nations of the world for the cause of international peace by the moral force of its example as the United States. The United States will better fulfil their mission and more exalt their position in the family of nations by indoctrinating their navy officers in the teachings of Washington's farewell address than by flaunting in the face of the world the destructive power of rams and artillery.

Nothing could be more foolish than the notion we hear frequently expressed that so big a country should have a big navy. Instead of taking pride in the possession of a big navy, the American people ought to be proud of not needing one. This is their distinguishing privilege, and it is their true glory.

Grover Cleveland: "An Armed Invasion"

In a special message to Congress on December 18, 1893, President Cleveland put an official end to the attempt to annex Hawaii. Agitation for annexation continued, however, since the revolutionaries succeeded in staying in power and keeping Queen Liliuokalani in retirement. (She subsequently wrote "Aloha

Oe," the official song of the islands.) In 1898, when awareness of naval strategy was at a high pitch because of the events of the Spanish-American War, annexation of Hawaii was easily accomplished. But in 1893 Cleveland's strong statement against taking advantage of the revolution won wide approval.

From James D. Richardson, comp., *Messages and Papers of the Presidents* (New York, 1897), XIII, pp. 5901-5902.

I believe that a candid and thorough examination of the facts will force the conviction that the Provisional Government owes its existence to an armed invasion by the United States. Fair-minded people, with the evidence before them, will hardly claim that the Hawaiian Government was overthrown by the people of the islands or that the Provisional Government had ever existed with their consent. I do not understand that any member of this Government claims that the people would uphold it by their suffrages if they were allowed to vote on the question.

While naturally sympathizing with every effort to establish a republican form of government, it has been the settled policy of the United States to concede to people of foreign countries the same freedom and independence in the management of their domestic affairs that we have always claimed for ourselves, and it has been our practice to recognize revolutionary governments as soon as it became apparent that they were supported by the people. For illustration of this rule I need only to refer to the revolution in Brazil in 1889, when our minister was instructed to recognize the Republic "so soon as a majority of the people of Brazil should have signified their assent to its establishment and maintenance"; to the revolution in Chile in 1891, when our minister was directed to recognize the new Government "if it was accepted by the people," and to the revolution in Venezuela in 1892, when our recognition was accorded on condition that the new Government was "fully established, in possession of the power of the nation, and accepted by the people."

As I apprehend the situation, we are brought face to face with the following conditions:

The lawful Government of Hawaii was overthrown without the drawing of a sword or the firing of a shot by a process every step of which, it may safely be asserted, is directly traceable to and dependent for its success upon the agency of the United States acting through its diplomatic and naval representatives.

But for the notorious predilections of the United States minister for annexation the committee of safety, which should be called the committee of annexation, would never have existed.

But for the landing of the United States forces upon false pretexts respecting the danger to life and property the committee would never have exposed themselves to the pains and penalties of treason by undertaking the subversion of the Queen's Government.

But for the presence of the United States forces in the immediate vicinity and in position to afford all needed protection and support the committee would not have proclaimed the Provisional Government from the steps of the Government building.

And finally, but for the lawless occupation of Honolulu under false pretexts by the United States forces, and but for Minister Stevens's recognition of the Provisional Government when the United States forces were its sole support and constituted its only military strength, the Queen and her Government would never have yielded to the Provisional Government, even for a time and for the sole purpose of submitting her case to the enlightened justice of the United States.

Believing, therefore, that the United States could not, under the circumstances disclosed, annex the islands without justly incurring the imputation of acquiring them by unjustifiable methods, I shall not again submit the treaty of annexation to the Senate for its consideration, and in the instructions to Minister Willis, a copy of which accompanies this message, I have directed him to so inform the Provisional Government.

TOPIC 54

POWER IN THE CARIBBEAN AND PACIFIC

American interest in the Hawaiian Islands was a prelude to an expansion of political, economic, and military influence, not only in the Pacific, but in the Caribbean as well. The American nation seemed, in fact, to be deliberately testing its strength in those areas just beyond the shores of the continent. The United States demonstrated in the Spanish-American War that it considered itself a great power like such European nations as Great Britain, France, and Germany. And, like all great powers of the era, it sought to demonstrate its strength by dominating areas outside its national boundaries.

Reading 277

Sea Power and American Strategy

Americans committed to the idea of the United States as a world power directed their attention increasingly to the need for a strong navy. The fleet served the same function at the turn of the century as nuclear weapons did a half century later. Alfred Thayer Mahan (1840–1914), the author of the following selection, was a United States naval officer who became a noted historian and a theorist of the role of sea power in a nation's rise and fall. Many politicians, such as Theodore Roosevelt, were greatly influenced by his argument for a powerful fleet. In addition, Mahan's views affected policy in Europe, especially in Germany.

From Alfred Thayer Mahan, "The United States Looking Outward," *The Atlantic Monthly*, LXVI (1890), pp. 821–824. Subheadings added by the editors.

I

The End of Isolation

Our self-imposed isolation in the matter of markets, and the decline of our shipping interest in the last thirty years, have coincided singularly with an actual remoteness of this continent from the life of the rest of the world. . . .*

When the Isthmus is pierced this isolation will pass away, and with it the indifference of foreign nations. From wheresoever they

*Mahan is here referring to the proposed canal connecting the Atlantic and Pacific across the Isthmus of Panama—Eds.

come and whithersoever they afterward go, all ships that use the canal will pass through the Caribbean. Whatever the effect produced upon the prosperity of the adjacent continent and islands by the thousand wants attendant upon maritime activity, around such a focus of trade will center large commercial and political interests. To protect and develop its own, each nation will seek points of support and means of influence in a quarter where the United States has always been jealously sensitive to the intrusion of European powers. The precise value of the Monroe doctrine is very loosely understood by most Americans, but the effect of the familiar phrase has been to develop a national sensitiveness, which is a more frequent cause of war than material interests; and over disputes caused by such feelings there will preside none of the calming influence due to the moral authority of international law, with its recognized principles, for the points in dispute will be of policy, of interest, not of conceded right. Already France and England are giving to ports held by them a degree of artificial strength uncalled for by their present importance. They look to the near future. Among the islands and on the mainland there are many positions of great importance, held now by weak or unstable states. Is the United States willing to see them sold to a powerful rival? But what right will she invoke against the transfer? She can allege but one,—that of her reasonable policy supported by her might.

Whether they will or no, Americans must now begin to look outward. The growing production of the country demands it. An increasing volume of public sentiment demands it. The position of the United States, between the two Old Worlds and the two great oceans, makes the same claim, which

A modern navy, many Americans came to believe in the 1890s, would be a crucial factor in the nation's rise as a world power. Here steel-clad, steam-powered American warships fire at targets while on maneuvers in the Atlantic.

will soon be strengthened by the creation of the new link joining the Atlantic and Pacific. The tendency will be maintained and increased by the growth of the European colonies in the Pacific, by the advancing civilization of Japan, and by the rapid peopling of our Pacific States with men who have all the aggressive spirit of the advanced line of national progress. Nowhere does a vigorous foreign policy find more favor than among the people west of the Rocky Mountains....

II

Defense and Policy

The military needs of the Pacific States, as well as their supreme importance to the whole country, are yet a matter of the future, but of a future so near that provision should immediately begin....

To provide this, three things are needful: First, protection of the chief harbors by fortifications and coast-defense ships, which gives defensive strength, provides security to the community within, and supplies the bases necessary to all military operations. Secondly, naval force, the arm of offensive power, which alone enables a country to extend its influence outward. Thirdly, it should be an inviolable resolution of our national policy that no European state should henceforth acquire a coaling position within three thousand miles of San Francisco,—a distance which includes the Sandwich and Galápagos islands and the coast of Central America. For fuel is the life of modern naval war; it is the food of the ship; without it the modern monsters of the deep die of inanition. Around it, therefore, cluster some of the most important considerations of naval strategy. In the Caribbean and the Atlantic we are confronted with many a foreign coal depot, and perhaps it is not an unmitigated misfortune that we, like Rome, find Carthage at our gates bidding us stand to our arms; but let us not acquiesce in an addition to our dangers, a further diversion of our strength, by being forestalled in the North Pacific.

In conclusion, while Great Britain is undoubtedly the most formidable of our possible enemies, both by her great navy and the strong positions she holds near our coasts, it must be added that a cordial understanding with that country is one of the first of our external interests. Both nations, doubtless, and properly, seek their own advantage; but both, also, are controlled by a sense of law and justice drawn from the same sources, and deep-rooted in their instincts. Whatever temporary aberration may occur, a return to mutual standards of right will certainly follow. Formal alliance between the two is out of the question, but a cordial recognition of the similarity of character and ideas will give birth to sympathy, which in turn will facilitate a cooperation beneficial to both; for, if sentimentality is weak, sentiment is strong.

American Policy in Two Hemispheres

In the following selection, historian Samuel Hays narrates the series of events which, in the few years surrounding the turn of the twentieth century, made the world aware of the growing power of the United States.

From Samuel P. Hays, *The Response to Industrialism, 1885-1914* (Chicago, 1957), pp. 169-171, 173-175, 178-182. Copyright © 1957 by the University of Chicago Press. Subheadings added by the editors.

I

The Caribbean Area

United States interest in a more positive policy in the Caribbean quickened with the Venezuelan crisis of 1895. The dispute involved a long-standing disagreement between Great Britain and Venezuela over the boundary between British Guiana and Venezuela and aroused the American public to denounce England bitterly. President Cleveland, responding to this pressure, dispatched a sharp note to England demanding arbitration of the controversy. When the British Foreign Office replied in an equally caustic manner, even denying the validity of the Monroe Doctrine, Cleveland recommended to Congress that the United States itself take steps to establish the correct boundary and to enforce it. The two countries appeared perilously close to war over a seemingly trivial incident. But England, diplomatically isolated in Europe and in need of friendship in the Western Hemisphere, soon agreed to arbitrate, and the incident was amicably settled.

The Cuban revolt against Spain riveted the attention of the United States even more firmly on the Caribbean. In striking contrast to their lack of interest in the Cuban insurrection of 1868-78, Americans expressed warm approval of the revolutionaries of 1895-98. Brutal methods which the Spanish used to suppress the revolt—differing little from their opponents' techniques, but more widely publicized—aroused much sympathy for the Cubans. The American "yellow press," especially William Randolph Hearst's *Journal* and Joseph Pulitzer's *World*, bitter rivals in New York City, eagerly played up Cuban atrocity stories. The American people avidly consumed this sensationalism; during 1898 the *Journal*'s daily circulation rose from 800,000 to 1,500,000. The popular demand for intervention in Cuba increased in February, 1898, when the battleship "Maine" exploded in Havana Harbor with a loss of over 250 men. Although its cause was never established, Americans immediately blamed Spain for this tragedy. The administration, though peaceful in intent and bearing, could not withstand such public sentiment. The American people rapidly brushed aside Spanish overtures to settle the matter on terms close to American demands, and Congress eagerly approved McKinley's request for war. In a brief en-

A civil war among the various factions in Cuba is seen in this American cartoon of 1898 as an even worse fate than Spanish misrule. The implication is that the United States must intervene in force to save Cuba from the fires of "anarchy."

counter, remembered by most Americans as the war in which Theodore Roosevelt led his Rough Riders in a well-publicized charge up San Juan Hill, the American forces rapidly overwhelmed the weaker Spaniards; at the Paris Peace Conference in 1898 Cuba became independent, and the United States acquired the Philippines, Guam, and Puerto Rico.

Caribbean diplomacy after the Spanish-American War centered around the construction and defense of an isthmian canal. Dramatic illustration of the need for such a project came during the Spanish-American War when the battleship "Oregon" steamed from Puget Sound around Cape Horn—three times the distance had a canal been available—to join the main squadron off Cuba. In central American diplomacy prior to the 1880's, the United States had concentrated on preventing other nations from building a canal without American co-operation. In 1850, for example, the Clayton-Bulwer Treaty with England had provided that neither nation would carry out the project alone. As the American eagle spread its wings wider in the post–Civil War era, interest arose in an "American canal under American control." The commitment to joint construction, however, blocked the movement. Efforts to annul the Clayton-Bulwer Treaty, initiated as early as 1881, did not succeed until 1901; in the second Hay-Pauncefote Treaty of that year, England freed the United States from its obligation.

II

Acquisition of the Panama Canal

The canal project also had to clear a maze of Latin-American diplomacy and intrigue. In the Spooner Act of 1902 Congress approved the Panama instead of the Nicaragua route, and the following year Hay signed the Hay-Herran Convention in which Colombia, owner of Panama, granted the United States the right to construct the canal. The Colombian Congress rejected the Hay-Herran pact, despite a virtual United States ultimatum that Colombia would "regret" it if she did not ratify the convention without modification. Colombians objected that it provided only slender compensation and seriously compromised their nation's sovereignty. Thereupon the Panamanians revolted from Colombia on November 3, 1903. The U.S.S. "Nashville" conveniently appeared on the scene to prevent Colombia from suppressing the revolt, and Secretary John Hay (1838-1905) warned that the United States would not tolerate Colombian steps to restore authority over the area. The administration knew of the impending event, hoped that it would succeed, and, as Hay put it, was "not to be caught napping." Roosevelt later boasted, "I took the Canal Zone," an exaggeration but close to the truth. One hour after receiving news of the revolt, Roosevelt authorized that the new government be recognized, and on November 18 the two countries signed the Hay-Bunau-Varilla Treaty granting the United States the desired canal rights. By 1914 the Panama Canal was open for traffic. In 1916 the United States completed its canal diplomacy when in the Bryan-Chamorro Treaty it secured from Nicaragua a perpetual right to construct a waterway through that country.

The entire Caribbean area now became crucial to the national defense of the United States. As one commentator observed, "No matter how strongly the isthmian canal may be fortified it would, in war, serve us no purpose . . . if our fleet could not control its approaches." The United States quickly established naval bases in the Caribbean and secured greater political control over its bordering countries to guarantee influence in the area "at least to the extent deemed necessary to prevent its domination by any other strong power." In effect the Caribbean became a dependency of a United States which would not tolerate basic decisions contrary to its interests and would use force to guarantee that end. During the first three decades of the twentieth century the United States repeatedly intervened in Caribbean countries and established a number of protectorates there.

After the Spanish-American War, Cuba was in form independent; in fact, she became a satellite in the United States orbit. The Platt Amendment to the army appropriation bill of March 2, 1901, guaranteed this. Passed when it appeared that the Cuban constitutional convention would ignore Cuban–United States relations, the Platt Amendment provided that Cuba could not permit a foreign power to secure even partial control there, that she could not incur an indebtedness that might result in foreign intervention, that the United States could step in to preserve order and maintain Cuban independence, and that Cuba would sell or lease naval and coaling stations to the United States. The Cubans reluctantly incorporated the Platt Amendment into their constitution in June, 1901, after they had been told, in effect, that the United States would not otherwise withdraw its army from Cuba. To prevent Cuba from eliminating the agreement by constitutional amendment after departure of the military government, the United States in 1903 successfully insisted that it be incorporated into a treaty between the two nations.

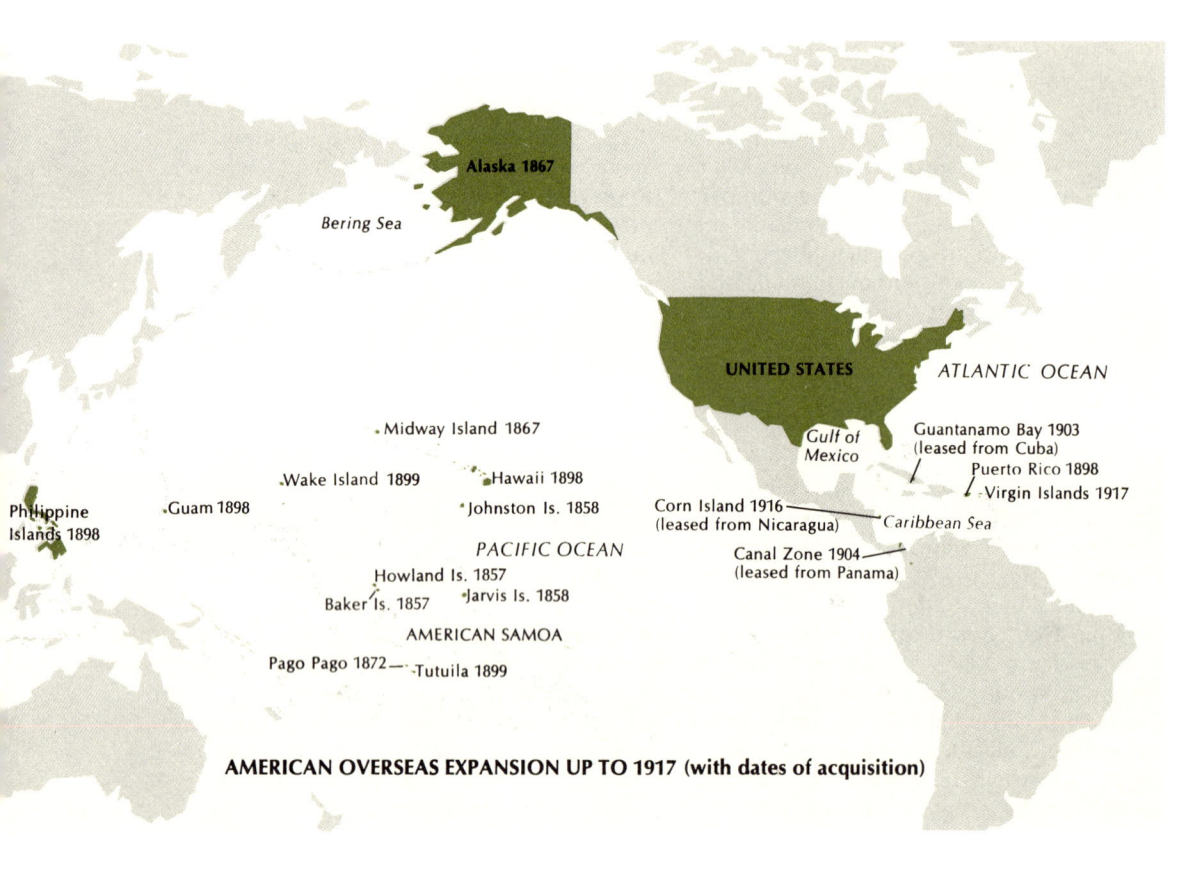

AMERICAN OVERSEAS EXPANSION UP TO 1917 (with dates of acquisition)

Alaska 1867
Bering Sea
UNITED STATES
ATLANTIC OCEAN
Gulf of Mexico
Guantanamo Bay 1903 (leased from Cuba)
Puerto Rico 1898
Virgin Islands 1917
Corn Island 1916 (leased from Nicaragua)
Caribbean Sea
Canal Zone 1904 (leased from Panama)
Midway Island 1867
Wake Island 1899
Hawaii 1898
Johnston Is. 1858
Guam 1898
Philippine Islands 1898
PACIFIC OCEAN
Howland Is. 1857
Baker Is. 1857
Jarvis Is. 1858
AMERICAN SAMOA
Pago Pago 1872
Tutuila 1899

III

Growth of Protectorates

Other protectorates followed in rapid order. In the Hay-Bunau-Varilla Treaty, for example, the United States permanently guaranteed the territorial integrity and independence of Panama. Protectorates stemmed most frequently from a fear that European nations might attempt forcibly to collect debts owed them by Caribbean governments. Creditors had rarely been pleased with the repayment records of shaky Latin-American regimes. In exasperation, England, Germany, and Italy in 1902 forcibly sought to persuade the Venezuelan dictator Cipriano Castro to come to terms. In settling this incident the World Court two years later ruled that those creditors who had used force had claims prior to those who had not. This decision greatly alarmed the State Department, for it seemed to place a premium on armed intervention to collect Western Hemisphere debts. In 1904 a similar situation seemed on the point of erupting in Santo Domingo. This time the Roosevelt administration worked out an agreement with the Dominican government in which the United States assumed control of the customs service and apportioned 55 percent of its receipts to repay European creditors.

On this occasion the President enunciated the "Roosevelt Corollary" to the Monroe Doctrine: henceforth when the internal affairs of nations of the Western Hemisphere might be such as to encourage European intervention, the United States itself would intervene to forestall such action. As Roosevelt announced in his message to Congress on December 6, 1904, "Chronic wrongdoing . . . may force the United States, however reluctantly . . . to the exercise of an international police power." The implications of the Roosevelt Corollary soon became clear. The original financial protectorate in the Dominican Republic had been established in co-operation with Dominican political leaders. By 1916, however, no candidate for the Dominican presidency could be found who would agree to the absolute authority of the United States on the island. From 1916 to 1922, accordingly, the United States Department of the Navy governed that republic.

The State Department soon came to look upon the United States business interests in the Caribbean as allies in political control; they could drive out European businessmen, establish closer economic ties between Caribbean countries and the United States, and aid in promoting political stability in an area torn with frequent strife. American businessmen were not averse to such a policy; they often wanted to go even further and secure outright annexation of areas in which their investments were at stake. Throughout

Filipinos at first welcomed American troops, believing they had come to liberate them from Spanish rule. When it became clear, however, that the United States intended to retain the Philippines, the insurgents, led by Emilio Aguinaldo, began a guerrilla war which was not fully suppressed until 1902. Here captured, wounded insurgents await transportation to a hospital. American soldiers relax in the background.

the nineteenth century economic and strategic expansion had been closely intertwined; in the twentieth century the United States took up a more self-conscious encouragement and protection of economic ties with Caribbean countries to undergird political strategy.

Roosevelt carried out this policy, soon known popularly as "Dollar Diplomacy," in Cuba, Ecuador, and Bolivia; President Taft and his Secretary of State, Philander C. Knox, used it more extensively to establish protectorates in Central America. In 1909, for example, Secretary Knox prevented the Nicaraguan government from quelling a revolt and then demanded control of the customs from the new government and persuaded it to transfer the public debt from European to United States creditors. President Wilson continued Caribbean "Dollar Diplomacy"; in 1915 American troops occupied Haiti, and the Senate approved a treaty which granted control of the Haitian customs to the United States, established an American financial adviser, and secured from Haiti an agreement never to lease or sell territory to a third power. . . .

IV

Expansion in the Pacific

Acquisition of the Philippines stemmed not from long-standing substantial interests but from timely action by one man, Theodore Roosevelt. As Assistant Secretary of the Navy during the McKinley administration Roosevelt had dispatched Admiral George Dewey

(1837-1917) to the Pacific to pounce upon Manila once the United States had opened war against Spain in Cuba. Until Dewey easily defeated the Spanish fleet in Manila Harbor, the people of the United States had known little about the Philippines; in entering the war they had thought of a Cuban crusade rather than a venture into Asian affairs. Roosevelt's action, however, forced the Philippines and the entire Far East into the diplomacy and strategy of the United States. After the war, President McKinley at first hesitated to retain the islands; when it became clear that self-denial would only render them ripe for picking by another power and that Manila might play an important role in Far Eastern trade and politics, the administration abandoned independence for the Philippines in favor of annexation. The Senate, moreover, in approving this action, defeated a proposal to grant independence in the immediate future....

The new interests of the United States in the Far East inevitably drew the nation into the tangled web of imperial rivalries in China. In the late nineteenth century Great Britain, Germany, Russia, France, and Japan competed for concessions, spheres of influence, naval bases, and territory in the weak and tottering Chinese empire. To protect its interests in the Far East, the United States in turn sought to prevent the dismemberment of China and to counteract the demand for exclusive concessions by a plea for an "open door" for commercial enterprise in the empire. Such views dovetailed nicely with those of American missionaries and businessmen in eastern Asia. Textile manufacturers who dominated the North China textile trade, capitalists who sought railroad concessions in China, and steel manufacturers who hoped to capture the new market for steel when the railroads were constructed all became worried lest economic opportunities in the Orient be lost.

With such problems in mind, Secretary of State Hay in 1899 dispatched to six major world powers the first two Open Door notes, a plea for equal commercial opportunity in China. In their replies the six powers indicated many reservations to such a viewpoint, but the Secretary blithely announced that they had agreed to uphold the principle. The following year, during the antiforeign Boxer revolt in Peking, Hay bestirred himself again. Much to the relief of American businessmen and missionaries in the Far East, he sent 2,500 marines to join the armed forces of other powers to relieve the foreign embassies from their Boxer besiegers. But Hay also feared that intervention might lead to infringement of Chinese sovereignty; to forestall such an event he dispatched a second Open Door note, declaring that the United States intended to support not only commercial opportunity but the territorial integrity of China as well. President McKinley revealed the tentativeness of American activity in the Far East when, much to the dismay of Americans in China, he ordered the marines home; the President had a fall election on his hands.

V

Russia and Japan

At the turn of the century Russian expansion into Manchuria constituted the major disturbing influence in the Orient. Running athwart Japanese ambitions in the same area, Russian advances touched off the Russo-Japanese War of 1904-05. Winning this conflict, the Japanese displaced Russia as the rising power of East Asia. Foreign policies of the United States shifted in accordance with the changing Asiatic scene. Prior to the Russo-Japanese War Americans had feared Russia more, and upon the outbreak of that conflict our sympathies had been with Japan. When Japan won the war, however, such leaders as President Roosevelt began to look upon that nation as the major threat to our interests in the Far East. When Japan invited Roosevelt to mediate in the war, the President accepted, hoping to prevent the victors from gaining too much at the peace settlement. At the Portsmouth, New Hampshire, peace conference Japan abandoned both a large indemnity claim and a demand for the northern half of the island of Sakhalin....

Japanese-American relations, however, remained discordant. The Japanese blamed the United States for failure to gain more at Portsmouth; they became even more aroused over treatment of their fellow countrymen in the Pacific Coast states. Californians took up an energetic anti-Japanese campaign after the Russo-Japanese War. In October, 1906, the San Francisco Board of Education ordered Orientals to attend segregated public schools. To allay anti-American feeling which this incident aroused in Japan, President Roosevelt persuaded the San Francisco authorities to permit Japanese children to attend school with whites in return for an end to Japanese immigration. In the Gentlemen's Agreement of 1907-08 (a series of diplomatic notes, not a treaty), Japan agreed not to permit immigration of coolies directly to the United States mainland. But this settlement only temporarily quieted feelings on both sides. Californians continued to inflame Japanese-American relations; in 1913 the state legislature effectively barred Japanese from owning land in that state, an action which greatly embarrassed the Wilson administration.

The Nation Denounces the Panama Affair (1903)

As Samuel Hays pointed out in his account of United States foreign policy (Reading 278), the so-called "Panama Affair" focused the attention of Americans, both North and South, on the penetration of Latin America by the United States. *The Nation*, a leading liberal journal, had some strong words to say about President Roosevelt's action in helping to "liberate" Panama from Colombia.

From *The Nation*, LXXII (November 12, 1903), p. 371; (November 19, 1903), p. 395.

I

November 12, 1903

President Roosevelt has now ordered acts of war against Colombia. No other interpretation can be put upon his instructions to our naval commanders to prevent Colombian troops from embarking at Buenaventura, or any other national port. This goes far beyond the preliminary affront to Colombia in recognizing the twenty-minute republic of Panama, as Senator Teller aptly calls it. That was bad enough. It was an act which Professor Woolsey of the chair of international law in Yale University declares to be without justification in correct principles. To notify a Government that a seceding State has "accomplished" its independence, almost before the central authorities had heard that there was even a revolution, was a step which would, of course, have led to an instant declaration of war if the offended nation had not been as an infant to a prize-fighter. But now the President has outdone even that act of aggression, and has put us technically in a state of war with Colombia. Almost more amazing is the reason which he assigns for it. "The Washington Government," says the official dispatch, "holds that this policy is in the interest of the general good." But the President of the United States is a creature of law. Warrant for his public acts he must seek, not in his own magnanimous though possibly fallible impulses, but in the law of the land—in treaties, in the Constitution, in the statutes of the United States. It is safe to say, however, that in none of these can Mr. Roosevelt find the shred of a sanction for his hostile course towards Colombia. He sends his vessels of war to Colombian waters and asserts jurisdiction there. He threatens to sink any transport which may put to sea with troops of a country with which we are at peace. And when we ask *quo warranto?* the answer is "the general good"—that is, Mr. Roosevelt's own notion of what the general good requires. It is the stereotyped plea of irresponsible tyrants in all ages.

II

November 19, 1903

To show how scrupulously correct was our own conduct throughout, we need to read only the telegrams laid before Congress. Why, we did not recognize the revolution a minute before it occurred! In our supreme desire to follow the right course in stealing a canal, we telegraphed our consul at Panama on November 3 to find out if there was a revolution for us to recognize. He promptly replied that there was none yet, but hoped there would be in the course of the night. So, with great forbearance, our Government waited—with some impatience, it is true, but still it waited. Then note also how absolutely proper we were in paying no attention to Colombia's protest against our shearing off her best province. That protest did not arrive in Washington, Secretary Hay carefully observes, until two hours and fifteen minutes after we had recognized the independence of Panama. Of course, it was then too late to do anything. Justice might have required us to act, but think of the bad form! Seriously, the official dispatches sent in to Congress, meagre as they are, and far from telling the whole story as they are, make it certain that our Government knew all about the Panama revolution in advance, and had arranged to give aid and comfort to the insurrectionists. How else can we interpret the orders sent to Admiral Glass on November 2, *two days before the revolution*, "Prevent landing of any armed force, either Government or insurgent, with hostile intent, at *any point within fifty miles of Panama*"? There could not be a plainer guarantee to the rebels of immunity from attack by Colombian troops.

A Poet Celebrates the Panama Affair (1904)

Unlike the editor of *The Nation* (Reading 279), many Americans were enthusiastic over the prospect of a canal linking the Caribbean to the Pacific, a canal controlled by the United States. At times this enthusiasm was expressed poetically.

From James Jeffrey Roche, "Panama," *Scribner's Magazine*, XXXV (1904), p. 423.

Reading 281

Latin Americans Consider the Panama Affair (1904)

So far these readings have focused on the reaction in the United States to expansion southward. The Panama Affair, however, made Latin Americans increasingly aware of the power of their North American neighbor. As the following reading makes clear, there was considerable uneasiness among Latin Americans about the intentions of their neighbor to the north.

From Louis E. Van Norman, "Latin-American Views of Panama and the Canal," *The American Monthly Review of Reviews*, XXIX (1904), pp. 335–337. Subheadings added by the editors.

I

A Colombian Opinion

The press of Colombia itself even is by no means as bitter or unanimous in its opposition to the independence of Panama as one might be led to expect. Early in December last, one of the influential papers of Bogotá, the *Relator*, contained a trenchant article arraigning the Colombian Government for its injustice and treachery to the Isthmus. This paper declared that the movement for independence in Panama was general and unanimous, and that there will be no reaction. It pointed out that Colombia has betrayed the confidence of the Isthmus by "its work of iniquity and spoliation.". . .

PANAMA

By James Jeffrey Roche

Here the oceans twain have waited
All the ages to be mated,—
Waited long and waited vainly,
Though the script was written plainly:
"This, the portal of the sea,
Opes for him who holds the key;
Here the empire of the earth
Waits in patience for its birth."
But the Spanish monarch, dimly
Seeing little, answered grimly:
"North and South the land is Spain's;
As God gave it, it remains.
He who seeks to break the tie,
By mine honor, he shall die!"

So the centuries rolled on,
And the gift of great Colón,
Like a spendthrift's heritage,
Dwindled slowly, age by age,
Till the flag of red and gold
Fell from hands unnerved and old,
And the granite-pillared gate
Waited still the key of fate.

Who shall hold that magic key
But the child of destiny,
In whose veins has mingled long
All the best blood of the strong?
He who takes his place by grace
Of no single tribe or race,
But by many a rich bequest
From the bravest and the best.
Sentinel of duty, here
Must he guard a hemisphere.

Let the old world keep its ways;
Naught to him its blame or praise;
Naught its greed, or hate, or fear;
For all swords be sheathéd here.

Yea, the gateway shall be free
Unto all, from sea to sea;
And no fratricidal slaughter
Shall defile its sacred water;
But—the hand that oped the gate
  shall forever hold the key!

II

What Pacific Coast South America Thinks

The countries on the west coast of the continent, Ecuador, Peru, and Chile, are certain to benefit greatly by the canal. The most influential journals of Ecuador, such as the *Grito del Pueblo,* the *Nacion,* the *Telegrafo,* and the *Tiempo,* of Guayaquil, and the *Tiempo,* the *Derecho,* and others of Quito, however, are unanimous in condemning the conduct of the United States Government in this affair. The *Grito del Pueblo* accuses President Roosevelt of having "not only encouraged, but actually forced, the people of Panama to separate from Colombia." These journals know that the canal will benefit their country, but do not approve of the means employed, and urge "a union, or confederation, of all Latin-American republics to protect themselves against the spoliatory tendencies of the United States." The *Nacion,* of Guayaquil, which is the commercial capital of the country, however, is certain that the canal will be of incalculable benefit to South America. . . .

The *Comercia,* the daily newspaper of Lima, ridicules the Colombian appeal to the South American nations to take up arms against the people on the north. According to this journal, Peruvians "are certain that the United States is responsible for the success of the revolution in Panama." But, at the same time, "opinion generally favors the step taken by the people of the Isthmus,—so far, at least, as it tends to the completion of the canal.". . .

Chile would also largely benefit by the canal; and the daily newspapers of that country admit the fact. The *Mercurio* (Santiago) declares that "the only thing to take into account is the canal itself, and that the canal will revolutionize commercial conditions. Let us look northward." The *Ley* (Santiago) is much alarmed, and declares that "if it be shown that the United States actually interfered in the Isthmus to bring on the revolution, we have here a portent of the utmost gravity to South America," and the *Imparcial* (Santiago) declares, "Let us be on guard everywhere, in order that the South American continent may be preserved for the South Americans." The *Porvenir* (Valparaiso) can see no evidence of interference by the United States. But the *Chilian Times,* the British paper published in Valparaiso, declares that the promptitude with which the new republic was recognized by the United States "lends color to the supposition that the separatist movement has been engineered by the great republic, with the object of facilitating the termination of the canal across the Isthmus. If this be the object of the movement, the change is to be welcomed, no matter how it has been brought about.". . .

III

Venezuelan Opinion

The Venezuelan newspapers, generally, remember the aid received from the United States against Europe, and for the most part limit their comment to counseling Colombia to let well enough alone, and to get what benefit she herself can out of the canal. The *Colaborador Andino* (Merida) declares that the canal is an absolute national necessity. It advises Colombia to submit gracefully to the loss of Panama. The *Combaté* (Caracas) believes in the integrity of the United States, and cannot forget the aid against Europe; but the *Pregonero* (Caracas) clamors for a South American alliance for mutual protection.

IV

Mexico and Central America

The Liberal Press of Mexico blames the government of Colombia for what has happened in Panama. The *Imparcial,* of Mexico City, known as a semi-official newspaper, the *Patria,* of the same city; the *Libertad,* of Guadalajara City, and the *Correo de la Tarde,* of Mazatlán, Sinaloa, say that "the misgovernment of Colombia and the rejection of the Hay-Herran treaty were the causes of the intervention of the United States in Panama, a necessary but deplorable fact, as it tends to the aggrandizement of Uncle Sam and his permanent establishment at the south of our country." The influential Catholic newspapers, such as the *Tiempo,* the *Pais,* and the *Voz de Mexico,* published in the capital, declare that "no justification can be found for the conduct of the United States, the government of which has betrayed the confidence of the Latin-American peoples, has committed a dishonorable act, and has violated the law of nations and the public faith guaranteed by public treaties." The *Tiempo* also says that "the future integrity of Mexico and Central America is put in jeopardy, especially that of Mexico, which, from now on, has been put inside of an iron circle."

Some of the most influential newspapers of Central America, such as the *Diario del Salvador,* the *Latino Americano,* the *Comercio,* of Managua, Nicaragua, and the *Republica,* of San José, Costa Rica, consider the part taken by the government of the United States in Panama "as a plain robbery, a manifestation of its new imperialistic policy, and

Roosevelt Defends His Actions in Panama

Theodore Roosevelt, President of the United States, was either the hero or the villain of the Panama Affair, depending on one's view of the wisdom or folly of his actions. Roosevelt, however, had no doubts about both the short and long-range benefits of United States control of a canal linking Europe and Asia via the Americas. The following selection gives Roosevelt's views after he had had a decade to reflect on his actions.

Reprinted by permission of Charles Scribner's Sons from *Theodore Roosevelt: An Autobiography.* Copyright 1913 Charles Scribner's Sons; renewal copyright 1941 Edith K. Carow Roosevelt. Pp. 512-513, 516-517, 520-523. Subheadings added by the editors.

I

Use of Authority

By far the most important action I took in foreign affairs during the time I was President related to the Panama Canal. Here again there was much accusation about my having acted in an "unconstitutional" manner—a position a menace to the integrity of the weaker republics on this continent." They know, and confess, that the building of the inter-oceanic canal is a public necessity; but, they say, "such an end could have been accomplished by means more honorable and just."

which can be upheld only if Jefferson's action in acquiring Louisiana be also treated as unconstitutional; and at different stages of the affair believers in a do-nothing policy denounced me as having "usurped authority"—which meant, that when nobody else could or would exercise efficient authority, I exercised it....

Ever since 1846 we had had a treaty with the power then in control of the Isthmus, the Republic of New Granada, the predecessor of the Republic of Colombia and of the present Republic of Panama, by which treaty the United States was guaranteed free and open right of way across the Isthmus of Panama by any mode of communication that might be constructed, while in return our Government guaranteed the perfect neutrality of the Isthmus with a view to the preservation of free transit....

The experience of over half a century had shown Colombia to be utterly incapable of keeping order on the Isthmus. Only the active interference of the United States had enabled her to preserve so much as a semblance of sovereignty. Had it not been for the exercise by the United States of the police power in her interest, her connection with the Isthmus would have been sundered long before it was. In 1856, in 1860, in 1873, in 1885, and 1901, and again in 1902, sailors and marines from United States warships were forced to land in order to patrol the Isthmus, to protect life and property, and to see that the transit across the Isthmus was kept open. In 1861, in 1862, in 1885, and in 1900, the Colombian Government asked that the United States Government would land troops to protect Colombian interests and maintain order on the Isthmus. The people of Panama during the preceding twenty years had three times sought to establish their independence by revolution or secession—in 1885, in 1895, and in 1899....

II

Hay-Herran Treaty

President Maroquin, through his Minister, had agreed to the Hay-Herran Treaty in January, 1903. He had the absolute power of an unconstitutional dictator to keep his promise or break it. He determined to break it. To furnish himself an excuse for breaking it he devised the plan of summoning a Congress especially called to reject the canal treaty. This the Congress—a Congress of mere puppets—did, without a dissenting vote; and the puppets adjourned forthwith without legislating on any other subject. The fact that this was a mere sham, and that the President had entire power to confirm his own treaty and act on it if he desired, was shown as soon as the revolution took place, for on November 6 General Reyes, of Colombia, addressed the American Minister at Bogotá, on behalf of President Maroquin, saying that "if the Government of the United States would land troops and restore the Colombian sovereignty" the Colombian President would "declare martial law; and, by virtue of vested constitutional authority, when public order is disturbed, would approve by decree the ratification of the canal treaty as signed; or, if

> The military advantage the Panama Canal gave to the United States was perhaps the most attractive feature of the project for many Americans, including President Theodore Roosevelt. For the first time the nation's growing navy could steam quickly from ocean to ocean. Here the battleships *Missouri* and *Ohio* are seen passing through the Miraflores Locks in 1915.

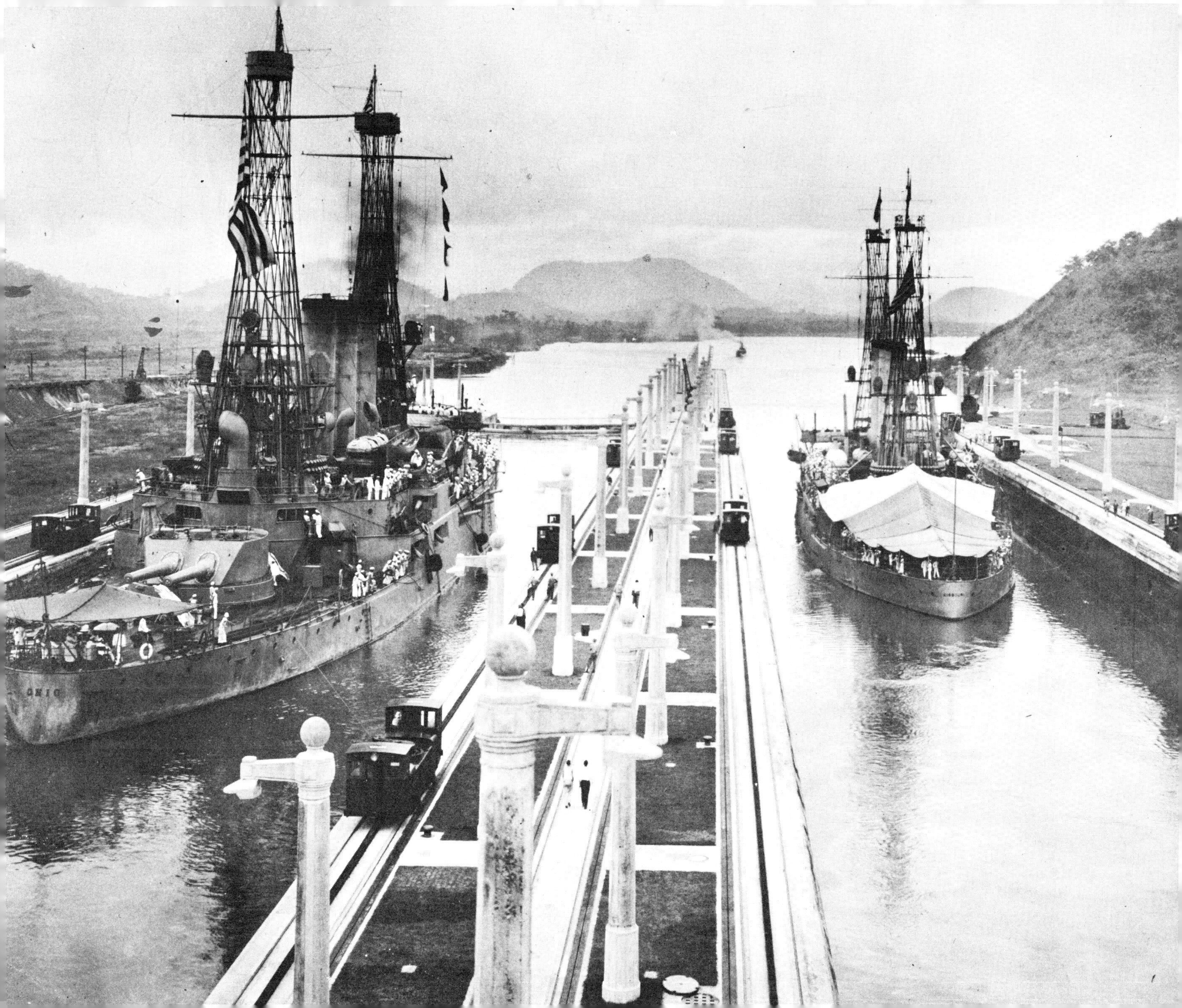

the Government of the United States prefers, would call an extra session of the Congress—with new and friendly members—next May to approve the treaty." This, of course, is proof positive that the Colombian dictator had used his Congress as a mere shield, and a sham shield at that, and it shows how utterly useless it would have been further to trust his good faith in the matter.

When, in August, 1903, I became convinced that Colombia intended to repudiate the treaty made the preceding January, under cover of securing its rejection by the Colombian Legislature, I began carefully to consider what should be done. By my direction, Secretary Hay, personally and through the Minister at Bogotá, repeatedly warned Colombia that grave consequences might follow her rejection of the treaty. The possibility of ratification did not wholly pass away until the close of the session of the Colombian Congress on the last day of October. There would then be two possibilities. One was that Panama would remain quiet. In that case I was prepared to recommend to Congress that we should at once occupy the Isthmus anyhow, and proceed to dig the canal; and I had drawn out a draft of my message to this effect. But from the information I received, I deemed it likely that there would be a revolution in Panama as soon as the Colombian Congress adjourned without ratifying the treaty, for the entire population of Panama felt that the immediate building of the canal was of vital concern to their well-being. Correspondents of the different newspapers on the Isthmus had sent to their respective papers widely published forecasts indicating that there would be a revolution in such event.

Moreover, on October 16, at the request of Lieutenant-General Young, Captain Humphrey and Lieutenant Murphy, two army officers who had returned from the Isthmus, saw me and told me that there would unquestionably be a revolution on the Isthmus, that the people were unanimous in their criticism of the Bogotá Government and their disgust over the failure of that Government to ratify the treaty; and that the revolution would probably take place immediately after the adjournment of the Colombian Congress. They did not believe that it would be before October 20, but they were confident that it would certainly come at the end of October

THE BIG STICK IN THE CARIBBEAN SEA

President Roosevelt's view of the Caribbean as an American pond emerges clearly in this none too friendly caricature of 1904. The President had just sent the fleet on a "goodwill" tour of the Caribbean, letting it be known that it would be the United States, rather than any European power, which would deal with trouble in the area.

or immediately afterwards, when the Colombian Congress had adjourned. Accordingly I directed the Navy Department to station various ships within easy reach of the Isthmus, to be ready to act in the event of need arising.

These ships were barely in time. On November 3 the revolution occurred. Practically everybody on the Isthmus, including all the Colombian troops that were already stationed there, joined in the revolution, and there was no bloodshed. But on that same day four hundred new Colombian troops were landed at Colón. Fortunately, the gunboat *Nashville*, under Commander Hubbard, reached Colón almost immediately afterwards, and when the commander of the Colombian forces threatened the lives and property of the American citizens, including women and children, in Colón, Commander Hubbard landed a few score sailors and marines to protect them. By a mixture of firmness and tact he not only prevented any assault on our citizens, but persuaded the Colombian commander to re-embark his troops for Cartagena. On the Pacific side a Colombian gunboat shelled the City of Panama, with the result of killing one Chinaman—the only life lost in the whole affair.

No one connected with the American Government had any part in preparing, inciting, or encouraging the revolution, and except for the reports of our military and naval officers, which I forwarded to Congress, no one connected with the Government had any previous knowledge concerning the proposed revolution, except such as was accessible to any person who read the newspapers and kept abreast of current questions and current affairs. By the unanimous action of its people, and without the firing of a shot, the state of Panama declared themselves an independent republic. The time for hesitation on our part had passed.

My belief then was, and the events that have occurred since have more than justified it, that from the standpoint of the United States it was imperative, not only for civil but for military reasons, that there should be the immediate establishment of easy and speedy communication by sea between the Atlantic and the Pacific. These reasons were not of convenience only, but of vital necessity, and did not admit of indefinite delay.

The Realities of Power in the Pacific (1905)

By the first decade of the twentieth century two new powers were making their strength felt in Asia. A few years earlier the United States had destroyed the Spanish fleet and seized the Philippines. At about the same time Japan had established itself on the Asian mainland by extending its control over Korea. The hopes and fears of these two growing powers are made clear in the following reading.

From Tyler Dennett, *Roosevelt and the Russo-Japanese War* (New York, 1925), pp. 112–115. Copyright © 1925 by Doubleday, Page and Co. Subheadings added and footnotes omitted by the editors.

On July 29, 1905, Count Katsura, Japanese Premier and Minister for Foreign Affairs, had what is known in diplomatic parlance as a "conversation" with a personal representative of President Roosevelt, not a member of the Department of State.* An agreed memorandum of this conversation was drawn up and is to be found among the Roosevelt Papers of that date. The views expressed on behalf of President Roosevelt were confirmed in a telegram on July 31, 1905. The memorandum is of peculiar interest because (1) it was a full statement of a policy to which President Roosevelt had freely committed himself at least six months earlier; (2) it shows how the acquisition of the Philippines had brought the American Government into the realm of world politics; and (3) it records a very definite and official commitment of the Japanese Government as to its policy toward the Philippines. The memorandum reads as follows:

First, in speaking of some pro-Russians in America who would have the public believe that the victory of Japan would be a certain prelude to her aggression in the direction of the Philippine Islands,——[the American] observed that Japan's only interest in the Philippines would be, in his opinion, to have these islands governed by a strong and friendly nation like the United States, and not to have them placed either under the misrule of the natives, yet unfit for self-government, or in the hands of some unfriendly European Power. Count Katsura confirmed in the strongest terms the correctness of his views on the point and positively stated that Japan does not harbour any aggressive designs whatever on the Philippines; adding that all the insinuations of the yellow peril type are nothing more or less than malicious and clumsy slanders calculated to do mischief to Japan.

Second, Count Katsura observed that the maintenance of general peace in the extreme East forms the fundamental principle of Japan's international policy. Such being the case, he was very anxious to exchange views with——[the American] as to the most effective means for insuring this principle. In his own opinion the best, in fact the only, means for accomplishing the above object would be to form good understanding between the three governments of Japan, the United States, and

*The personal representative of the President was Secretary of War William Howard Taft.

Great Britain which have common interests in upholding the principle of eminence [sic]. The Count well understands the traditional policy of the United States in this respect and perceives fully the impossibility of their entering into a formal alliance of such nature with foreign nations, but in view of our common interests he could [not] see why some good understanding or an alliance in practice if not in name, should not be made between these three nations, in so far as respects the affairs in the Far East. With such understanding firmly formed, general peace in these regions would be easily maintained to the great benefit of all Powers concerned.

———[The American] said that it was difficult, indeed impossible, for the President of the United States of America to enter even to any understanding amounting in effect to a confidential informal agreement, without the consent of the Senate, but that he felt sure that without any agreement at all the people of the United States was [sic] so fully in accord with the people of Japan and Great Britain in the maintenance of peace in the Far East that whatever occasion arose appropriate action of the Government of the United States, in conjunction with Japan and Great Britain, for such a purpose could be counted on by them quite as confidently as if the United States were under treaty obligations to take [it].

Third, in regard to the Korean question, Count Katsura observed that Korea being the direct cause of our war with Russia, it is a matter of absolute importance to Japan that a complete solution of the peninsula question should be made as the logical consequence of the war. If left to herself after the war Korea will certainly draw back to her habit of entering into any agreements or treaties with other Powers, thus resuscitating the same international complications as existed before the war. In view of the foregoing circumstances Japan feels absolutely constrained to take some definite step with a view to precluding the possibility of Korea falling back into her former condition and of placing us again under the necessity of entering upon another foreign war.

———[The American] fully admitted the justness of the Count's observations and remarked to the effect that, in his personal opinion, the establishment by Japanese troops of a suzerainty over Korea to the extent of requiring that Korea enter into no foreign treaties without the consent of Japan was the logical result of the present war and would directly contribute to permanent peace in the East. His judgment was that the President would concur in his views in this regard, although he had no authority to give assurance of this; indeed,———[the American] added that he felt much delicacy in advancing the views he did for he had no mandate for the purpose from the President. . . . He could not, however, in view of Count Katsura's courteous desire to discuss the question, decline to express his opinions. . . .

Such a diplomatic *coup* was too much for the Japanese Government to keep entirely secret. On October 4, 1905, the *Kokumin* published an allusion to the conversation which reveals how much they had misunderstood its purpose and character:

> In fact, it is a Japanese Anglo-American alliance. We may be sure that when once England became our ally America also became a party to the agreement. Owing to peculiar national conditions America cannot make any open alliance, but we should bear in mind that America is our ally though bound by no formal treaty: we firmly believe that America, under the leadership of the world statesman, President Roosevelt, will deal with her Oriental problems in cooperation with Japan and Great Britain.

In judging this remarkable document it is of the utmost importance to keep in mind that it was not a sacrifice of Korea for the sake of the Philippines. On the contrary, in return for a statement of American policy toward Korea which had been fixed for more than six months, and which was consistent with the policy of more than twenty years, the American Government had secured from Japan a most official and explicit disclaimer of any aggressive designs on the Philippines.

Roosevelt Explains His Policy toward Japan

Theodore Roosevelt took great pride in his Asian policy, which he viewed as a vital element in America's rise as a world power. He was, however, deeply aware of the potential threat Japan posed to his vision of America's role in Asia. Roosevelt left office in March 1909, but he did not cease his attempts to influence foreign policy under President William Howard Taft, his hand-picked successor.

Reprinted by permission of the publishers from Vol. VI, pp. 1510-1511, 1513-1514; Vol. VII, pp. 189-190 of Elting Morison, et al., eds., *The Letters of Theodore Roosevelt.* Cambridge, Mass.: Harvard University Press, Copyright, 1952, 1954, by the President and Fellows of Harvard College. Footnotes omitted by the editors.

Washington, February 8, 1909

My dear Senator Knox: You are soon to become Secretary of State under Mr. Taft. At the outset both he and you will be overwhelmed with every kind of work; but there is one matter of foreign policy of such great and permanent importance that I wish to lay it before the President-to-be and yourself. I speak of the relations of the United States and Japan. . . .

[Japan] is a most formidable military power. Her people have peculiar fighting capacity. They are very proud, very warlike, very sensitive, and are influenced by two contradictory feelings, namely, a great self-confidence, both ferocious and conceited, due to their victory over the mighty empire of Russia; and a great touchiness because they would like to be considered as on a full equality with, as one of the brotherhood of, Occidental nations, and have been bitterly humiliated to find that even their allies, the English, and their friends, the Americans, won't admit them to association and citizenship, as they admit the least advanced or most decadent European peoples. Moreover, Japan's population is increasing rapidly and demands an outlet, and the Japanese laborers, small farmers, and petty traders would, if permitted, flock by the hundred thousand into the United States, Canada, and Australia. . . .

As regards the [Asian] mainland, our policy should have three sides, and should be shaped not to meet the exigencies of this year or next, but to meet what may occur for the next few decades. Japan is poor and is therefore reluctant to go to war. Moreover, Japan is vitally interested in China and on the Asiatic mainland and her wiser statesmen will if possible prevent her getting entangled in a war with us, because whatever its result it would hamper and possibly ruin Japan when she came to deal again with affairs in China. But with so proud and sensitive a people neither lack of money nor possible future complications will prevent a war if once they get sufficiently hurt and angry; and there is always danger of a mob outbreak there just as there is danger of a mob outbreak here. Our task therefore is on the one hand to meet the demands which our own people make and which cannot permanently be resisted and on the other to treat Japan so courteously that she will not be offended more than is necessary; and at the same time to prepare our fleet in such shape that she will feel very cautious about attacking us. Disturbances like those going on at present are certain to occur unless the Japanese immigration, so far as it is an immigration for settlement, stops. For the last six months under our agreement with Japan it has been stopped to the extent that more Japanese have left the country than have come into it. But the Japanese should be made clearly to understand that this process must continue and if there is relaxation it will be impossible to prevent our people from enacting drastic exclusion laws; and that in such case all of us would favor such drastic legislation. Hand in hand with insistence on the stopping of Japanese immigration should go insistence as regards our own people that they be courteous and considerate, that they treat the Japanese who are here well; and above all that they go on with the building of the navy, keep it at the highest point of efficiency, securing not merely battleships but an ample supply of colliers and other auxiliary vessels of every kind. Much of the necessary expense would be met by closing the useless navy yards. By the way, the fighting navy should not be divided; it should be kept either in the Pacific or in the Atlantic, merely a squadron being left in the other ocean and this in such shape that in the event of war it could avoid attack and at once join the main body of fighting ships.

All this is so obvious that it ought not to be necessary to dwell upon it. But our people are shortsighted and have short memories—I suppose all peoples are shortsighted and have short memories. The minute we arrange matters so that for the moment everything is smooth and pleasant, the more foolish peace societies, led by men like ex-Secretary of State Foster and ex-Secretary of the Navy Long, clamor for a stoppage in the building up of the navy. On the other hand, at the very moment when we are actually keeping out the Japanese and reducing the number of Japanese here, demagogs and agitators like those who have recently appeared in the California and Nevada Legislatures work for the passage of laws which are humiliating and irritating to the Japanese and yet of no avail so far as keeping out immigrants is concerned; for this can be done effectively only by the National Government. The defenselessness of the coast, the fact that we have no army to hold or reconquer the Philippines and Hawaii, the fact that we have not enough battleships nor enough auxiliaries in the navy—all these facts are ignored and forgotten. On the other hand, the Japanese, if we do not keep pressure upon them will let up in their effort to control the emigration from Japan to this country, and they must be continually reminded that unless they themselves stop it, in the end this country is certain to stop it, and ought to stop it, no matter what the consequences may be.

Private   New York, December 22, 1910

Dear Mr. President: In the first place, I wish a merry Christmas and a happy New Year to you and yours.

Now as to your letter of December 20th. . . . Our vital interest is to keep the Japanese out of our country, and at the same time to preserve the good will of Japan. The vital interest of the Japanese, on the other hand, is in Manchuria and Korea. It is therefore peculiarly our interest not to take any steps as regards Manchuria which will give the Japanese cause to feel, with or without reason, that we are hostile to them, or a menace—in however slight a degree—to their interests. Alliance with China, in view of China's absolute military helplessness, means of course not an additional strength to us, but an additional obligation which we assume; and as I utterly disbelieve in the policy of bluff, in national and international no less than in private affairs, or in any violation of the old frontier maxim, "Never draw unless you mean to shoot," I do not believe in our taking any position anywhere unless we can make good; and as regards Manchuria, if the Japanese choose to follow a course of conduct to which we are adverse, we cannot stop it unless we are prepared to go to war, and a successful war about Manchuria would require a fleet as good as that of England, plus an army as good as that of Germany. The "open-door" policy in China was an excellent thing, and will I hope be a good thing in the future, so far as it can be maintained by general diplomatic agreement; but as has been proved by the whole history of Manchuria, alike under Russia and under Japan, the "open-door" policy, as a matter of fact, completely disappears as soon as a powerful nation determines to disregard it, and is willing to run the risk of war rather than forego its intention. How vital Manchuria is to Japan, and how impossible that she should submit to much outside interference therein, may be gathered from the fact—which I learned from Kitchener in England last year—that she is laying down triple lines of track from her coast bases to Mukden, as an answer to the double tracking of the Siberian Railway by the Russians. However friendly the superficial relations of Russia and Japan may at any given time become, both nations are accustomed to measure their foreign policy in sections of centuries; and Japan knows perfectly well that sometime in the future, if a good occasion offers, Russia will wish to play a return game of bowls for the prize she lost in their last contest.

TOPIC 55

THE FAILURE OF NEUTRALITY

The first targets for American overseas expansion offered little political or military opposition. Spain was one of the weakest of European nations, while no Caribbean country could resist American demands for long. Restraint in these ventures came largely from opposition to expansion within the United States. In August 1914, however, war broke out in Europe, a war which shortly involved all the world's major powers, except the United States. The reaction of the United States to World War I, before it entered the war in April 1917, revealed how Americans responded to an international situation fraught with far more danger than that encountered in their "splendid little war" with Spain.

Though the United States' first ventures in overseas expansion and its growing navy placed it among the world's important powers, most Americans still thought of their nation as a disinterested neutral. Since the nation remained outside the rival networks of military alliances, the other great powers continued to regard the United States as relatively separate from their immediate interests. World War I put an end to this illusion, but not without an agonizing struggle involving the desire of Americans to keep their precious neutrality.

Reading 285

The Origins of World War I

The following selection, by European historian James M. Powell, provides a background for the events leading to World War I. As Professor Powell points out, the fighting did not begin as the result of a *direct* confrontation between the major European powers: Great Britain, France, Germany, and Russia. It began as a local confrontation in south-central Europe between Austria-Hungary, a monarchy large in area but weak in national identity, and Serbia, a small Balkan state, which became part of the new nation of Yugoslavia in 1919.

From James M. Powell, *The Civilization of the West* (New York, 1967), pp. 437–439, 440–441. Copyright © 1967 by James M. Powell. Subheadings altered by the editors.

I

Tensions within Europe

Historians who have concentrated on the period prior to World War I and who have studied the causes of that war have almost all pointed to the developing tensions between the leading nations of Europe in the period from 1890 to 1914. Certainly, in comparison with the preceding decades, this period was one of tremendous diplomatic activity and one which saw numerous threats to the peace of the world. The rivalries of the powers in their quest for colonies led to frequent crises, some of a serious nature. Yet not all of the tensions within the European state-system are traceable to imperialistic factors.

National honor and prestige were also at stake. Indeed, the future of man could depend on popular reaction to some insult to the nation. Moreover, underlying the entire climate of international affairs was the transformation of European society by the growth of industry and the accompanying social tensions. The great calm that had marked so much of nineteenth-century foreign affairs was drawing to a close.

On the surface, Europe was enjoying an almost unprecedented prosperity in the years just before the war. Even the working classes had more than at any other period in the past. The growth of social welfare programs, though far from universal, went a long way toward alleviating some of the more urgent ills of industrial society. But what was more important, there was promise of more to come. The future did not look so bleak as the past. Yet hope, which should inspire patience, has very often been the instrument of unrest. Although some progress had come and more was on its way, the ugliness of present reality pressed against the workers and their leaders to cause them to ask for that "more" immediately. Agitation increased in most of Europe in this period. England weathered the budget crisis and the reform of the House of Lords in 1911. France attempted to divert its workers with large doses of nationalism. In Germany, the Kaiser ignored his parliament and the signs of increasing social unrest while he pursued the imperial will-o'-the-wisp. In Austria-Hungary, the old regime held on for dear life in hope that some better future might suddenly dawn. Southeastern Europe smoldered with unrestrained nationalistic feeling that threatened the peace of the area. Finally, the fearsome government of the Russian autocracy, shaken by internal revolution and the Russo-Japanese War of 1905, propped itself up with severely repressive measures and dreams of its invincibility. Under these circumstances, while it is correct to say that there was no real desire for war in any of these countries, it is even more correct to say that the leaders of the European powers were not unalterably opposed to war either. In fact, some even saw advantages that might accrue from war.

If internal social and political pressures created a climate favorable to the outbreak of war, these had significant help from the growth of nationalistic sentiments among the masses. The popular press, which had come into its own in the late nineteenth century with the spread of literacy, caught up the jingos and slogans of national honor and made these too often a substitute for responsible journalism. But the masses were receptive. The spread of universal military conscription created the idea of the citizen soldier. Pride in uniform and even some remains of medieval chivalric conceptions of warfare became part of the popular image of the army. Military parades became expressions of popular national feelings. There were few critics of militarism. Once the mighty behemoth of the popular will turned its hatred against another power and the whole machinery of nationalistic propaganda began to crank out messages exaggerating the insults to national honor and the dangers to national sovereignty, it traveled forward under its own power, grinding under all opposition and ignoring all messages of caution. In this sense, the democratic will became a dangerous instrument of nationalistic aggrandizement.

Before 1890, Bismarck had worked to preserve peace through an alliance of the powers of Eastern and Central Europe. England had remained aloof and France was therefore isolated. However, the diplomatic relations of the powers shifted dramatically following the dismissal of the "Iron Chancellor" by Kaiser William II. Germany moved closer to Austria-Hungary at the expense of her Russian ally; France took advantage of Germany's lapse to enter an alliance with Russia. When England and France settled their colonial differences in North Africa, these two powers found it expedient to work more closely together. Thus, the Franco-Russian alliance took on a new coloring as the British moved closer to France. Behind these shifts lay the story of the changing balance of power in Europe.

The idea of the balance of power was not new; England had worked to secure allies on the continent in the seventeenth and eighteenth centuries to counterbalance the French superiority. But through most of the nineteenth century, the English had held themselves aloof from continental affairs. Secure on their island with the most powerful navy in the world, they had not felt the need of continental allies. However, the unification of Germany and Italy materially changed the situation in Europe. Under Bismarck, Germany had emerged as the leading military power on the continent. However, as we have noted, his cultivation of peace, which had included a policy of friendship with England, combined with Franco-British rivalries elsewhere in the world to discourage the English from entering into any European alliances against the Germans. What altered this picture and persuaded England to change her stance was primarily the increasing threat of Germany under the aggressive leadership of Kaiser William II and the growing conflicts between England and other industrial powers, especially Germany. . . .

II

War and Peace, July–August 1914

The assassination of Francis Ferdinand [heir to the throne of Austria-Hungary] was an act of terrorism by a Serbian nationalist. Suitably enough, therefore, the act that precipitated the crisis that led to war sprang from the spirit of nationalism. This fact was even more fitting than appearances might first suggest, for World War I was the first test of the national state, a war in which huge armies of conscripts struggled to defend the principle of nationhood. Behind all the slogans lurked the spirit of nationalism.

There was no immediate necessity for the war. Austria blamed the Serbs for the murder of Ferdinand and demanded satisfaction. The Austrian demands amounted to a surrender of sovereignty by the Serbs. Russia, from her position as the mother of all the Slavs, announced her support for the Serbs. Germany hesitated briefly before pledging aid to Austria. Yet the decision for war was not clear-cut. To enforce her demands, Austria mobilized. Russia also mobilized, though her leaders wanted only a partial mobilization to support their diplomacy. Germany responded with a demand for demobilization of Russia and, failing to receive assurances that her request would be heeded, declared war on Russia on August 1, 1914. The attack on Russia immediately brought France into the war. England remained neutral until August 4, when it was clear that she had no alternative. Then she announced that she was joining France because the Germans had invaded neutral Belgium in violation of international treaties guaranteeing Belgian neutrality. Italy remained outside the war until 1915, then declared war on Austria and Germany. Japan joined England and used the war as a pretext for taking over the German concessions on the Shantung Peninsula. The United States stayed neutral until 1917, then maintained that German submarine warfare was its reason for going to war. The Ottoman Empire, the Balkan countries, and many smaller countries chose sides in the contest. It was a world war.

Wilson: The Choice Is Ours (1914)

A few weeks after the outbreak of fighting in Europe, President Woodrow Wilson sought to define the role of both the United States and of the American people in the rapidly expanding conflict.

From U.S. Department of State, Papers Relating to the Foreign Relations of the United States, 1914 Supplement, The World War (Washington, D.C., 1928), pp. 551–552.

My Fellow Countrymen: I suppose that every thoughtful man in America has asked himself, during these last troubled weeks, what influence the European war may exert upon the United States, and I take the liberty of addressing a few words to you in order to point out that it is entirely within our own choice what its effects upon us will be and to urge very earnestly upon you the sort of speech and conduct which will best safeguard the nation against distress and disaster.

The effect of the war upon the United States will depend upon what American citizens say and do. Every man who really loves America will act and speak in the true spirit of neutrality, which is the spirit of impartiality and fairness and friendliness to all concerned. The spirit of the nation in this critical matter will be determined largely by what individuals and society and those gathered in public meetings do and say, upon what newspapers and magazines contain, upon what ministers utter in their pulpits, and men proclaim as their opinions on the street.

The people of the United States are drawn from many nations, and chiefly from the nations now at war. It is natural and inevitable that there should be the utmost variety of sympathy and desire among them with regard to the issues and circumstances of the conflict. Some will wish one nation, others another, to succeed in the momentous struggle. It will be easy to excite passion and difficult to allay it. Those responsible for exciting it will assume a heavy responsibility, responsibility for no less a thing than that the people of the United States, whose love of their country and whose loyalty to its Government should unite them as Americans all, bound in honor and affection to think first of her and her interests, may be divided in camps of hostile opinion, hot against each other, involved in the war itself in impulse and opinion if not in action.

Such divisions among us would be fatal to our peace of mind and might seriously stand in the way of the proper performance of our duty as the one great nation at peace, the one people holding itself ready to play a part of impartial mediation and speak the counsels of peace and accommodation, not as a partisan, but as a friend.

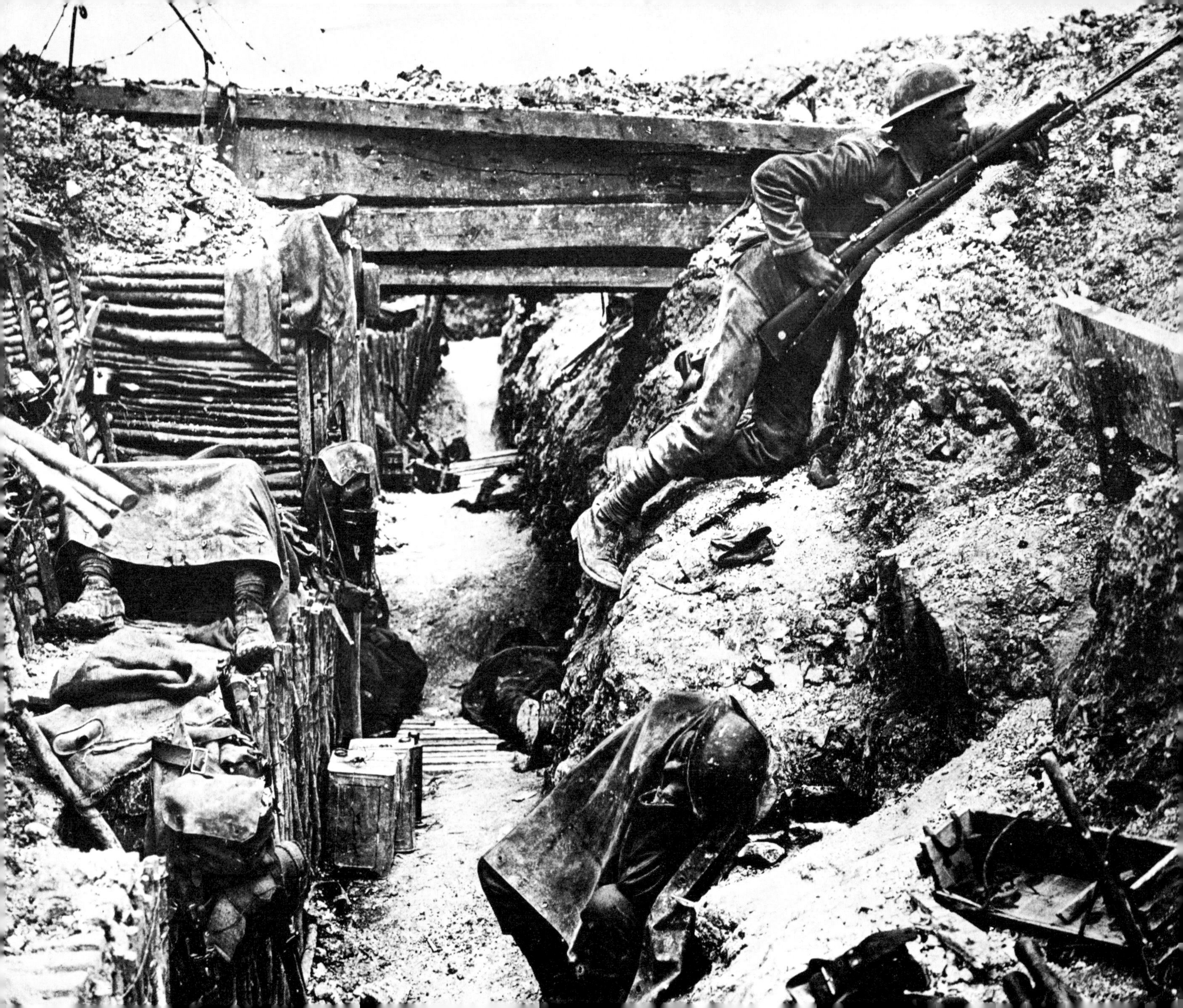

Reading 287

A British soldier crouches on the edge of a front-line trench in northern France, July 1916. For nearly four years the Allies and the Germans fought a war of attrition from hundreds of miles of opposing trenches such as this one.

I venture, therefore, my fellow countrymen, to speak a solemn word of warning to you against that deepest, most subtle, most essential breach of neutrality which may spring out of partisanship, out of passionately taking sides. The United States must be neutral in fact as well as in name during these days that are to try men's souls. We must be impartial in thought as well as in action, must put a curb upon our sentiments as well as upon every transaction that might be construed as a preference of one party to the struggle before another.

Roosevelt: Morality and Self-Preservation

Italy, a member of the Triple Alliance (Central Powers) did not enter until 1915 and then it did so on the side of the Allies. Belgium, although neutral at the outset of the War, was invaded by Germany and joined the Allied Powers.

THE EUROPEAN NATIONS DIVIDE FOR WAR
- Allied Powers
- Central Powers

Americans quickly began to make moral judgments about the actions of the nations involved in World War I. The German invasion of neutral Belgium in the first days of the war caused many Americans to condemn Germany for its immorality in conquering a small, defenseless nation. Former President Theodore Roosevelt tried to evaluate the reasons for German military policy in an article written soon after the event.

From Theodore Roosevelt, "The World War: Its Tragedies and Its Lessons," *The Outlook*, CVIII (September 23, 1914), pp. 171–172, 175.

When a great nation is struggling for its existence it can no more consider the rights of neutral powers than it can consider the rights of its own citizens as these rights are construed in times of peace, and . . . everything must bend before the supreme law of national self-preservation. Whatever we may think of the morality of this plea, it is certain that almost all great nations have in time past again and again acted in accordance with it. . . . I wish it explicitly understood that I am not at this time passing judgment one way or the other upon Germany for what she did to Belgium. But I do wish to point out just what was done, and to emphasize Belgium's absolute innocence and the horrible suffering and disaster that have overwhelmed her in spite of such innocence. And I wish to do this so that we as a nation may learn aright the lessons taught by the dreadful Belgian tragedy.

Germany's attack on Belgium was not due to any sudden impulse. It had been carefully planned for a score of years, on the assumption that the treaty of neutrality was, as Herr von Bethmann-Hollweg observed, nothing but "paper," and that the question of breaking or keeping it was to be considered solely from the standpoint of Germany's interest....

The Belgians, when invaded, valiantly defended themselves. They acted precisely as Andreas Hofer and his Tyrolese, and Koerner and the leaders of the North German Tugenbund, acted in their day; and their fate has been the fate of Andreas Hofer, who was shot after his capture, and of Koerner, who was shot in battle. They fought valiantly, and they were overcome. They were then stamped under foot. Probably it is physically impossible for our people, living softly and at ease, to visualize to themselves the dreadful woe that has come upon the people of Belgium, and especially upon the poor people. Let each man think of his neighbors—of the carpenter, the station-agent, the day laborer, the farmer, the grocer—who are round about him, and think of these men deprived of their all, their homes destroyed, their sons dead or prisoners, their wives and children half starved, overcome with fatigue and horror, stumbling their way to some city of refuge, and when they have reached it, finding air-ships wrecking the houses with bombs and destroying women and children....

The prime fact as regards Belgium is that Belgium was an entirely peaceful and genuinely neutral power which had been guilty of no offense whatever. What has befallen her is due to the further fact that a great, highly civilized military power deemed that its own vital interests rendered imperative the infliction of this suffering on an inoffensive although valiant and patriotic little nation.

I think, at any rate I hope, I have rendered it plain that I am not now criticizing, that I am not passing judgment one way or the other, upon Germany's action. I admire and respect the German people. I am proud of the German blood in my veins. When a nation feels that the issue of a contest in which, from whatever reason, it finds itself engaged will be national life or death, it is inevitable that it should act so as to save itself from death and to perpetuate its life. What has occurred to Belgium is precisely what would occur under similar conditions to us, unless we were able to show that the action would be dangerous. If any Old World military power, European or Asiatic, were engaged in war, and deemed such action necessary *and safe*, it would at once seize the Panama Canal, or the Danish or Dutch West Indies, or Magdalena Bay, exactly as Belgium and Luxembourg have been overrun by Germany, as Korea has been seized by Japan. They would certainly so act if they thought we would in any real crisis pay heed to the political theories resulting in the all-inclusive arbitration treaties that have just been negotiated in Washington. They would refrain from so acting only if they knew we would instantly and resolutely act ourselves in such manner as to forestall and defeat their action....

One of the main lessons to learn from this war is embodied in the homely proverb, "Speak softly and carry a big stick." Persistently only half of this proverb has been quoted in deriding the men who wish to safeguard our National interest and honor. Persistently the effort has been made to insist that those who advocate keeping our country able to defend its rights are merely adopting "the policy of the big stick." In reality, we lay equal emphasis on the fact that it is necessary to speak softly; in other words, that it is necessary to be respectful toward all people and scrupulously to refrain from wronging them, while at the same time keeping ourselves in condition to prevent wrong being done to us.

Early Challenges to Neutrality

The United States soon was one of the few industrial nations not directly involved in the fighting. Despite President Wilson's plea for neutrality "in thought as well as in action," it was not long before American emotions as well as the nation's agricultural and industrial output became deeply involved in the European war. The following narrative traces that process of involvement.

From William E. Leuchtenburg, *The Perils of Prosperity, 1914-1932* (Chicago, 1958), pp. 13-17. Copyright © 1958 by the University of Chicago Press.

Through the summer of 1914, Americans watched the growing war crisis almost with indifference. When, after weeks of gestures and countergestures, Britain sent her ultimatum to Germany, Secretary of Agriculture Houston recorded, "I had a feeling that the end of things had come. . . . I stopped in my tracks, dazed and horror-stricken." To the very last hour, war seemed unbelievable; when it came, it struck with a stunning sense of finality.

The only reasonable explanation was that Europe had gone berserk. The European powers, declared the New York Times, "have reverted to the condition of savage tribes roaming the forests and falling upon each other in a fury of blood and carnage to achieve the ambitious designs of chieftains clad in skins and drunk with mead." If the war had any rational cause at all, Americans thought, it could be found in the imperialist lust for markets. "Do you want to know the cause of the war?" asked Henry Ford. "It is capitalism, greed, the dirty hunger for dollars." "Take away the capitalist," Ford asserted, "and you will sweep war from the earth."* Americans rejoiced in their isolation from Old World lunacy; and, after the initial sense of horror, their chief feeling was one of gratitude that they were not involved. "We never appreciated so keenly as now," wrote an Indiana editor, "the foresight exercised by our forefathers in emigrating from Europe."

President Woodrow Wilson urged a course of complete neutrality: he even asked movie audiences not to cheer or to hiss either side. The war, he said, was one "with which we have nothing to do, whose causes cannot touch us." Wilson cautioned the American people to be "impartial in thought as well as in action," but the impossibility of this soon became obvious. German-Americans and Irish-American Anglo-phobes cheered on the German cause. To many of the progressives, Britain suggested monarchy, privileged classes, and their ancient enemy Lombard Street (seat of international financiers). Germany (the Wisconsin reformers' model for a generation) suggested social insurance, the university scientist, and municipal reform. But sympathy for the Central Powers was on the whole a minority feeling. Overwhelmingly, American sentiment went out to the Allies.

Men who as schoolboys had read Gray and Tennyson, who knew Wordsworth's lake country as though they had tramped it themselves, who had been stirred by stories of Sir Francis Drake and Lord Nelson, could not be indifferent to the English cause. Nor did any nation evoke a greater sentimental attachment than France, the country of Lafayette, the land which had come to the aid of the Colonists in their struggle for independence.

At the same time, Americans had nervously eyed German militarism ever since the accession of Kaiser Wilhelm II in 1888. When Germany invaded Belgium in the early days of the war, Americans were outraged not only by the invasion of a neutral nation but by Chancellor Bethmann-Hollweg's tactless remark that the treaty with Belgium was "just a scrap of paper." The Machiavellianism, the glorification of brute force by the Germans, seemed amply proven by events like the sack of Louvain and, although in later years their influence was greatly exaggerated, by atrocity tales like those of the crucified Canadian and the Belgian babies with their hands severed. The execution of Nurse Edith Cavell, the destruction of the Cathedral of Rheims, and the mass deportation of French and Belgian civilians to forced labor completed the picture of a Prussian militarism which in its deliberate *schrecklichkeit* menaced Western civilization. Nevertheless, despite the indignation over Belgium, the United States had no thought of intervening. Even the bellicose Theodore Roosevelt, who would soon be the leader of the war hawks in America, wrote: "Of course it would be folly to jump into the gulf ourselves to no good purpose; and very probably nothing that we could have done would have helped Belgium."

As the struggle in Europe settled down to a war of attrition between great land armies, it quickly became clear that victory would go to the nation which could maintain control of the seas. Britain, the great naval power of the world, lost no time in taking advantage of its strategic position. In November, 1914, England mined the North Sea, seized American vessels carrying noncontraband goods to neutral nations, and forced all merchant ships to thread a narrow channel under British control. The Allies attempted nothing less than a gigantic blockade of the Central Powers; if they could prevent neutral merchantmen, in particular American ships, from carrying vital materials to Germany, they could force the Central Powers to sue for peace.

The United States could have taken a strong line with Britain, for Britain did not dare provoke a serious quarrel with her chief source of supply while she was involved in a desperate war. President Wilson, however, was unwilling, at a time when the Germans had overrun Belgium, to deprive Britain of her naval superiority. With England under such pressure, he felt a strong stand by the United States against Britain would be an unneutral act. Moreover, Wilson could not help but be

---

*In speaking of "capitalists" Ford was attacking 'the' bankers of the Eastern United States and Europe. As a wealthy and powerful industrialist Ford believed in private enterprise independent of bank control—Eds.

influenced in his definition of "neutrality" by his own sympathies for the British cause, however much he tried to control them. Wilson had modeled his career on the example of English statesmen, he was an extravagant admirer of British government, and he actually courted his second wife by reading passages from Bagehot and Burke.

Wilson's closest advisers were firmly committed to the Allies. Robert Lansing, first Counselor and then Secretary of State, deliberately delayed the resolution of disputes in order to avoid a showdown with Britain. By May, 1915, Lansing was convinced that American democracy could not survive in a world dominated by German power. Wilson's alter ego, Colonel Edward House, was scarcely less pro-Ally, while, whenever notes of protest were sent to London, the strongly pro-British ambassador Walter Hines Page watered them down. On one occasion, Page took an American protest to Sir Edward Grey and said: "I have now read the despatch, but I do not agree with it; let us consider how it should be answered!" The result was the same as if the United States itself had embargoed all trade with Germany. Commerce with Germany and Austria fell from $169 million in 1914 to $1 million in 1916.

The outbreak of war in Europe at first produced a serious economic recession in this country, but by the spring of 1915 Allied war orders were stoking American industry and opening up new markets for farm products. Boom times came to the United States as trade with the Allies jumped from $825 million in 1914 to $3,214 million in 1916. Before the war was many months old, the Allied cause and American prosperity became inextricably intertwined. When Allied funds quickly became exhausted, the United States

A Matter of Routine
President Wilson—"This calls for a note—Mr. Secretary, just bring me in a copy of our usual No. 1 Note to Germany—'Humanity' Series."

In November 1915 an Austrian submarine torpedoed without warning the *Ancona*, an Italian passenger liner. Nine Americans were among the several hundred who died. Though President Wilson sent a strong protest to the Austrian government, he refused either to break diplomatic relations or to threaten Austria with war. Wilson's moderation prompted this British cartoon, which laid the ultimate blame for the sinking on Germany, Austria's ally in World War I.

An American Diplomat Views the British (1914)

The views of American ambassadors to the warring nations significantly influenced American policy as shaped by President Wilson and the Department of State. Walter Hines Page (1855-1918), a highly respected journalist, was America's representative in Great Britain. As William Leuchtenburg pointed out in the previous reading, Ambassador Page had very definite views about the virtues and defects of the nations at war.

From *Papers Relating to the Foreign Relations of the United States: The Lansing Papers* (Washington, D.C., 1939), Vol. I, pp. 259-261.

confronted the alternatives of permitting the Allies to borrow funds from American bankers or of allowing purchases to fall off sharply, with the probable consequence of a serious depression. At the outset of the war, Secretary of State William Jennings Bryan had warned that money was "the worst of all contrabands because it commands everything else," and Wilson, anxious about the country's gold reserve, had banned American loans and let it appear that he shared Bryan's concern. In March, 1915, however, Wilson and even Bryan relented and permitted the House of Morgan to extend a large credit to France. By the time the United States entered the war, the Allies had borrowed over $2 billion.

The Ambassador in Great Britain (Page) to the Secretary of State

London, December 28, 1914
(Received January 11, 1915)

We have made the mistake sometimes to accuse them [the British]—or to seem to insinuate—that they are giving us trouble in order to increase their own trade or their profit from trade. However keen they may be in this way in peaceful times (and they surely are good tradesmen!) they are not using the war to gain any such advantage. They are playing the game fairly. But they are playing it very hard now (hard-pressed as they are) and they are guilty of having no fixed policy. About trade-restrictions, they are as they are about the censorship—they don't know how to do it. I think that this perfectly fair protest will hasten them to learn.

I have been somewhat afraid of this sort of misunderstanding between the two Governments. On our side, you have seemed at times to think that the British were using their sea-power to gain commercial advantage. I am persuaded that this is not true. They have but one thought now—to starve out the enemy. In this process they are starving out also many of their own business people. This Government has more protests from its own shippers and merchants than it has from all the neutral countries combined. . . .

I try to look far ahead: where shall we stand when it ends? We shall have the hatred of the Germans whatever we do because of the preponderance of American opinion against Germany. We shall have the esteem of a lessened number of the English because we keep our strict neutrality. I feel that constantly and am constantly criticized for the care I give the Germans and the German interests. I have a drawer full of letters (all unanswered) full of criticism even of our Government for having anything to do with the Germans and for refraining from protests about the German conduct of the war. To keep a long look ahead seems wise. When it ends we want first the approval of our own consciences and then the approval, as far as we can get it, of all nations—of this nation in particular because it is worth more to us than any other. We shall win their approval by standing up stoutly for our rights, but not by seeming to accuse them of motives that they have not. You may be sure they go and will go the whole length to keep our good will, provided we credit them with wishing to do the fair thing. They do not wish to do us an unfair turn—only to starve out their enemy; and that they are going to do at all costs. Of course the heaviest cost falls on them. They are not now thinking about their trade—or anybody else's—I mean the Government isn't. You'll find the cue to their actions in their determination to win.

An American Diplomat Views the Germans (1915)

James Gerard (1867-1951), American ambassador in Berlin, like his counterpart in London, freely supplied opinions as well as information to Washington. The following dispatches should be compared to that sent by Page (see Reading 289).

From *Papers Relating to the Foreign Relations of the United States: The Lansing Papers* (Washington, D.C., 1939), Vol. I, pp. 664–665.

I

The Ambassador in Germany (Gerard) to the Secretary of State

Berlin, October 15 [1915]

I had a long interview (over one hour) today with the Kaiser alone. I am supposed by rule here not to inform anyone of what he said—otherwise he will not receive me again or talk confidentially. The audience took place at Potsdam—had a special car going down and Royal carriage at station. Several ministers went down also to present their letters of credence. . . .

Having much trouble now to get British prisoners clothed in German camps. It is a delicate matter to handle. Visited one camp myself and had all prisoners about 1800 lined up with all the clothes and blankets they possessed for my inspection. . . .

The Germans are very bitter against our Embassy in Petrograd. Also at the loan in America—and especially at the attendant banquets to the loan commissioners—must say these banquets are not very neutral.

I hope we are getting ready for defence—If these people win we are next on the list—in some part of South or Central America which is the same thing.

II

The Ambassador in Germany (Gerard) to the Secretary of State

Berlin [November 1, 1915?]

My Dear Mr. Secretary: I and the staff are much obliged for your telegram permitting us to take vacations and allowing me to go home—I am afraid that unless the President or you wish particularly to see me that I had better stick here—we have very heavy work and the English would not understand it if I left. I am having a hard fight now to get the British prisoners clothed for the winter.

I think before the winter is out that we shall be on meat and butter cards as well as bread—already on two days a week meat cannot be sold and on three days pork cannot be sold. . . .

They are not yet taking men over 45 here and claim that they have plenty of men left. The actual losses to date are about 850,000 killed and three hundred and fifty thousand crippled. I have known cases of men being wounded and going back four and even five times. There is still absolute confidence in the result and I cannot see, myself, how Germany can be beaten. . . .

I am afraid that after this war the Navy party will be all for attacking the U.S.A. in order to show the Navy is worth something—get revenge for the loans and export of arms, a slice of Mexico or S. America and money. And if Germany is successful in the war the country and army will agree to this raid.

Submarine Warfare Results in an American Warning (1916)

By 1916 American feelings and government policy focused increasingly on one issue: Germany's use of a new weapon, the submarine. Other weapons—the machine gun, the airplane, poison gas and the tank—were introduced on a large scale during the war, but the submarine was the only weapon which directly affected Americans during the period of neutrality, 1914–1917. Though the German government often limited its submarines to attacks on warships and armed merchant ships, the new weapon was at its most destructive when it could strike suddenly at any ship which might be carrying supplies to Germany's foes. The first dramatic evidence of the submarine's awesome power occurred in May 1915, with the war less than a year old, when the U-20 sank the British passenger liner *Lusitania* with the loss of over a thousand lives, including more than a hundred Americans. Another incident occurred in March 1916 when the French passenger ship *Sussex* was torpedoed. After much discussion, Robert Lansing (1864–1928), American Secretary of State, sent the following note to the German government.

From *Papers Relating to the Foreign Relations of the United States, 1916 Supplement* (Washington, D.C., 1929), pp. 232–234.

Vessels of neutral ownership, even vessels of neutral ownership bound from neutral port to neutral port, have been destroyed along with vessels of belligerent ownership in constantly increasing numbers. Sometimes the merchantmen attacked have been warned and summoned to surrender before being fired on or torpedoed; sometimes their passengers and crews have been vouchsafed the poor security of being allowed to take to the ship's boats before the ship was sent to the bottom. But again and again no warning has been given, no escape even to the ship's boats allowed to those on board. Great liners like the *Lusitania* and *Arabic* and mere passenger boats like the *Sussex* have been attacked without a moment's warning, often before they have even become aware that they were in the presence of an armed ship of the enemy, and the lives of non-combatants, passengers, and crew have been destroyed wholesale and in a manner which the Government of the United States can not but regard as wanton and without the slightest color of justification. No limit of any kind has in fact been set to their indiscriminate pursuit and destruction of merchantmen of all kinds and nationalities within the waters which the Imperial Government has chosen to designate as lying within the seat of war. The roll of Americans who have lost their lives upon ships thus attacked and destroyed has grown month by month until the ominous toll has mounted into the hundreds.

The Government of the United States has been very patient. At every stage of this distressing experience of tragedy after tragedy it has sought to be governed by the most thoughtful consideration of the extraordinary circumstances of an unprecedented war and to be guided by sentiments of very genuine friendship for the people and Government of Germany. It has accepted the successive explanations and assurances of the Imperial Government as, of course, given in entire sincerity and good faith, and has hoped, even against hope, that it would prove to be possible for the Imperial Government so to order and control the acts of its naval commanders as to square its policy with the recognized principles of humanity as embodied in the law of nations. It has made every allowance for unprecedented conditions and has been willing to wait until the facts became unmistakable and were susceptible of only one interpretation.

It now owes it to a just regard for its own rights to say to the Imperial Government that that time has come. It has become painfully evident to it that the position which it took at the very outset is inevitable, namely, the use of submarines for the destruction of an enemy's commerce is, of necessity, because of the very character of the vessels employed and the very methods of attack which their employment of course involves, utterly incompatible with the principles of humanity, the long-established and incontrovertible rights of neutrals, and the sacred immunities of noncombatants.

The torpedoing of the British passenger ship *Sussex* in March 1916 caused the deaths of several Americans, among many of other nationalities. President Wilson then issued a virtual ultimatum to Germany to cease unrestricted submarine warfare. Germany did in fact yield to American demands for the remainder of 1916.

Stop!

If it is still the purpose of the Imperial Government to prosecute relentless and indiscriminate warfare against vessels of commerce by the use of submarines without regard to what the Government of the United States must consider the sacred and indisputable rules of international law and the universally recognized dictates of humanity, the Government of the United States is at last forced to the conclusion that there is but one course it can pursue. Unless the Imperial Government should now immediately declare and effect an abandonment of its present methods of submarine warfare against passenger and freight-carrying vessels, the Government of the United States can have no choice but to sever diplomatic relations with the German Empire altogether. This action the Government of the United States contemplates with the greatest reluctance but feels constrained to take in behalf of humanity and the rights of neutral nations.

Lansing

Germany Attempts an Alliance with Mexico (1917)

The German government backed down in 1916 and agreed to restrict its use of the submarine in the face of Lansing's threat to break diplomatic relations. But the stalemated war was causing terrible losses to Germany as well as to her enemies. Because it seemed to be their last hope to cripple the Allies' power to resist, German military leaders in late 1916 demanded and received permission to unleash their one effective sea weapon against all ships bringing supplies to Great Britain and France, even though such a policy would probably bring war with the United States. A German official initiated the following plan to counter American hostile efforts in case the United States did enter the war. The details of the plan were intercepted and decoded by the British and then passed along to Ambassador Page in London. The sender of the coded telegram, Zimmermann, was an official of the German foreign office.

From *Papers Relating to the Foreign Relations of the United States, 1917, Supplement 1* (Washington, D.C., 1931), p. 147.

The Ambassador in Great Britain (Page) to the Secretary of State

(Telegram)
London, February 24, 1917, 1 P.M.
(Received 8:30 P.M.)

For the President and the Secretary of State. Balfour has handed me the text of a cipher telegram from Zimmermann, German Secretary of State for Foreign Affairs, to the German Minister to Mexico, which was sent via Washington and relayed by Bernstorff on January 19. You can probably obtain a copy of the text relayed by Bernstorff from the cable office in Washington. The first group is the number of the telegram, 130, and the second is 13042, indicating the number of the code used. The last group but two is 97556, which is Zimmermann's signature. I shall send you by mail a copy of the cipher text and of the decode into German and meanwhile I give you the English translation as follows:

We intend to begin on the 1st of February unrestricted submarine warfare. We shall endeavor in spite of this to keep the United States of America neutral. In the event of this not succeeding, we make Mexico a proposal of alliance on the following basis: make war together, make peace together, generous financial support and an understanding on our part that Mexico is to reconquer the lost territory in Texas, New Mexico, and Arizona. The settlement in detail is left to you. You will inform the President of the above most secretly as soon as the outbreak of war with the United States of America is certain and add the suggestion that he should, on his own initiative, invite Japan to immediate adherence and at the same time mediate between Japan and ourselves. Please call the President's attention to the fact that the ruthless employment of our submarines now offers the prospect of compelling England in a few months to make peace. Signed, Zimmermann.

A Senator Pleads for Peace (1917)

By early 1917 few public officials continued to oppose war openly. One who did was Senator William Stone (1848–1918) of Missouri, chairman of the Foreign Relations Committee. He gave his reasons in a Senate speech on March 3, 1917.

From Congressional Record, 64th Congress, 2nd Session (Washington, D.C., 1917), pp. 4888, 4890, 4892, 4893.

Whole pages of Lord Northcliffe's American newspapers are devoted to stories and protests about the submarine war zone established by Germany around Great Britain and along the coast of France. This action of the German Government is denounced in unmeasured terms, as no doubt it should be. But, Mr. President, there is another side to this about which little is said in these Northcliffe publications, but to which I shall allude. While Germany has declared her submarine zone as a blockade, England has at the same time covered a still larger area of the high seas, and planted that area with submerged contact mines. Germany notified the President of her act, defining the area to be covered by her operations, and England notified the President of the area within which she had made it impossible for ships to pass without incurring almost certain destruction from submerged mines. Undoubtedly both of these things are violative of the rules of maritime warfare observed and practiced by all nations of the world before the inauguration of this unspeakable conflict. My mind is not sufficiently analytical to draw a line of differentiation between a paper blockade by submarines and a paper blockade by submerged contact mines. Only two or three days ago I saw a table printed in a Washington paper giving a list by names of American vessels destroyed by both submarines and by mines. Six had been sunk by submarines and five by mines. I had as soon be killed by a torpedo as by a mine....

The one thing we hear very much about just now is the "freedom of the seas." Freedom of the seas! That is an old doctrine and a good one. I stand for it steadfastly and loyally, and would fight for it whenever I believed that any other nation sought, out of any kind of antagonism to the real spirit of that doctrine, to drive us from the seas. As a fundamental proposition I would defend our right to rove the seas unhindered, and would strike with all the power of the Nation in resentment against any nation interfering with us with the purpose and intent of arbitrarily and insolently limiting our right to the use of the seas. There can be no division of sentiment in this country as to that. But at this time we are facing a peculiar, unusual, abnormal situation. A great war is raging. One of the belligerents assumes to establish what they call a blockade through the instrumentality of submarines; another belligerent assumes to establish a blockade through the instrumentality of submerged mines. If we wish to be very technical and hard-fisted we can break in upon this situation and dive headlong into the turbulence seething in these narrow areas of the sea. That is with us altogether a matter of common sense and public policy. Senators frothing with a fine frenzy may ask, "Who shall dare to deprive an American citizen of his unrestricted right to go upon the seas when and where he pleases?" Possibly no one should dare to do that terrible thing; nevertheless I venture to say that the American citizen who would with glaring foolhardiness deliberately go into the very mouth of this maritime hell, where war is raging in its most ruthless form, wrapping the American flag about him and shouting defiance to the world, would be rendering a very poor service to his country. Sometime ago the Senate determined against issuing an official warning to American citizens not to embark on vessels loaded with war munitions, and there that matter had stood ever since. Not so, however, with other countries. While we are seemingly encouraging American citizens to incur these hazards, Canada, Australia, New Zealand, South Africa, the great colonial dependencies of Great Britain, have, with the approval of the London Government, undertaken to prevent their noncombatant people from embarking on ships bound through the zones of danger to European ports....

Then we are told that our shipping is being congested and our commerce desperately injured by this submarine blockade. We are told that American ships engaged in European traffic are tied up; that they can not obtain insurance; that cargoes are being piled up in the North Atlantic ports unable to secure adequate transportation. All this may be true; I do not know. But I venture to say that the great bulk of these waiting cargoes is composed of war contraband. I venture to believe that there are enough of these delayed cargoes to freight many vessels composed almost wholly of war munitions and supplies intended for the armed forces of one or more of the belligerents. Shall we go to war to insure the transportation of these death-dealing commodities? Would you arm one of J. P. Morgan's ships and send it forth, leaving the issue of peace or war with Germany to the discretion of the captain of that vessel? It would be just as well to arm a British merchantman and send her forth in the "peaceful pursuit" of commerce....

British papers and the Northcliffe American papers, representing a powerful syndicate, have sought to alarm the American public with the notion that if German arms should come out of the war victoriously the next hostile step Germany would take would be against the United States; that if Germany should be victorious over France and England, she would then seek to conquer the United States and subject this great people to her dominion. Even books to that effect have been written and gratuitously circulated in America, and moving pictures displaying the horrors of a German invasion of the United States have been exhibited in Washington and other cities. This is so ludicrous that it is almost impossible to treat it seriously. It is even more foolish than the alleged intrigue of Zimmermann with Carranza, by and through which Germany would back Mexico in overrunning the United States and reannexing Texas, New Mexico, and Arizona. Why, sir, if we should turn the people of these three border States loose and tell them to "go to it," within three months they would lift the American flag once more above the halls of the Montezumas. Is it not really diverting to be told that Germany at her best could overrun the United States, and especially now, when, in the most favorable aspects of the situation, she must come out of this war broken in purse and in martial strength? When did it come to pass that Uncle Sam must lay his head on the palpitating breast of Uncle Johnny Bull with a timid sense of dependence? We are not dependent upon any of these nations, nor all of them together.

Wilson Calls for War (1917)

The United States responded to Germany's declaration of unlimited submarine warfare by breaking off diplomatic relations and making it clear that German action could become a cause for war. When German U-boats began to carry out their nation's declared policy, President Wilson, on April 2, 1917, asked Congress for a declaration of war.

From *Papers Relating to the Foreign Relations of the United States, 1917, Supplement 1* (Washington, D.C., 1931), pp. 195-203.

I

German Submarine Policy

Gentlemen of the Congress: I have called the Congress into extraordinary session because there are serious, very serious, choices of policy to be made, and made immediately, which it was neither right nor constitutionally permissible that I should assume the responsibility of making.

On the 3rd of February last I officially laid before you the extraordinary announcement of the Imperial German Government that on and after the 1st day of February it was its purpose to put aside all restraints of law or of humanity and use its submarines to sink every vessel that sought to approach either the ports of Great Britain and Ireland or the western coasts of Europe or any of the ports controlled by the enemies of Germany within the Mediterranean. That had seemed to be the object of the German submarine warfare earlier in the war, but since April of last year the Imperial Government had somewhat restrained the commanders of its undersea craft in conformity with its promise then given to us that passenger boats should not be sunk and that due warning would be given to all other vessels which its submarines might seek to destroy, when no resistance was offered or escape attempted, and care taken that their crews were given at least a fair chance to save their lives in their open boats. The precautions taken were meagre and haphazard enough, as was proved in distressing instance after instance in the progress of the cruel and unmanly business, but a certain degree of restraint was observed. The new policy has swept every restriction aside. Vessels of every kind, whatever their flag, their character, their cargo, their destination, their errand, have been ruthlessly sent to the bottom without warning and without thought of help or mercy for those on board, the vessels of friendly neutrals along with those of belligerents. Even hospital ships and ships carrying relief to the sorely bereaved and stricken people of Belgium, though the latter were provided with safe-conduct through the proscribed areas by the German Government itself and were distinguished by unmistakable marks of identity, have been sunk with the same reckless lack of compassion or of principle....

I an not now thinking of the loss of property involved, immense and serious as that is, but only of the wanton and wholesale destruction of the lives of noncombatants, men, women, and children, engaged in pursuits which have always, even in the darkest periods of modern history, been deemed innocent and legitimate. Property can be paid for; the lives of peaceful and innocent people can not be. The present German submarine warfare against commerce is a warfare against mankind.

It is a war against all nations. American ships have been sunk, American lives taken, in ways which it has stirred us very deeply to learn of, but the ships and people of other neutral and friendly nations have been sunk and overwhelmed in the waters in the same way. There has been no discrimination. The challenge is to all mankind. . . .

With a profound sense of the solemn and even tragical character of the step I am taking and of the grave responsibilities which it involves, but in unhesitating obedience to what I deem my constitutional duty, I advise that the Congress declare the recent course of the Imperial German Government to be in fact nothing less than war against the Government and people of the United States; that it formally accept the status of belligerent which has thus been thrust upon it; and that it take immediate steps not only to put the country in a more thorough state of defense but also to exert all its power and employ all its resources to bring the Government of the German Empire to terms and end the war. . . .

II

American Motives Defined

While we do these things, these deeply momentous things, let us be very clear, and make very clear to all the world what our motives and our objects are. . . . Our object . . . is to vindicate the principles of peace and justice in the life of the world as against selfish and autocratic power and to set up amongst the really free and self-governed peoples of the world such a concert of purpose and of action as will henceforth ensure the observance of those principles. Neutrality is no longer feasible or desirable where the peace of the world is involved and the freedom of its peoples, and the menace to that peace and freedom lies in the existence of autocratic governments backed by organized force which is controlled wholly by their will, not by the will of their people. We have seen the last of neutrality in such circumstances. We are at the beginning of an age in which it will be insisted that the same standards of conduct and of responsibility for wrong done shall be observed among nations and their governments that are observed among the individual citizens of civilized states.

We have no quarrel with the German people. We have no feeling towards them but one of sympathy and friendship. It was not upon their impulse that their Government acted in entering this war. It was not with their previous knowledge or approval. It was a war determined upon as wars used to be determined upon in the old, unhappy days when peoples were nowhere consulted by their rulers and wars were provoked and waged in the interest of dynasties or of little groups of ambitious men who were accustomed to use their fellow men as pawns and tools. Self-governed nations do not fill their neighbour states with spies or set the course of intrigue to bring about some critical posture of affairs which will give them an opportunity to strike and make conquest. Such designs can be successfully worked out only under cover and where no one has the right to ask questions. Cunningly contrived plans of deception or aggression, carried, it may be, from generation to generation, can be worked out and kept from the light only within the privacy of courts or behind the carefully guarded confidences of a narrow and privileged class. They are happily impossible where public opinion commands and insists upon full information concerning all the nation's affairs.

A steadfast concert for peace can never be maintained except by a partnership of democratic nations. No autocratic government could be trusted to keep faith within it or observe its covenants. It must be a league of honour, a partnership of opinion. Intrigue would eat its vitals away; the plottings of inner circles who could plan what they would and render account to no one would be a corruption seated at its very heart. Only free peoples can hold their purpose and their honour steady to a common end and prefer the interests of mankind to any narrow interest of their own. . . .

III

German Hostility

One of the things that has served to convince us that the Prussian autocracy was not and could never be our friend is that from the very outset of the present war it has filled our unsuspecting communities and even our offices of government with spies and set criminal intrigues everywhere afoot against our national unity of counsel, our peace within and without, our industries and our commerce. Indeed it is now evident that its spies were here even before the war began; and it is unhappily not a matter of conjecture but a fact proved in our courts of justice that the intrigues which have more than once come perilously near to disturbing the peace and dislocating the industries of the country have been carried on at the instigation, with the support, and even under the personal direction of official agents of the Imperial Government accredited to the Government of the United States. Even in checking these things and trying to extirpate them we have sought to put the most generous interpretation possible upon them because we knew that their source lay, not in any hostile feeling or purpose of the German people towards us (who were, no doubt, as ignorant of them as we ourselves were), but only in the selfish designs of a Government that did what it pleased and told its people nothing. But they have played their part in serving to convince us at last that that Government entertains no real friendship for us and means to act against our peace and security at its convenience. That it means to stir up enemies against us at our very doors the intercepted note to the German Minister at Mexico City is eloquent evidence.

We are accepting this challenge of hostile purpose because we know that in such a government, following such methods, we can never have a friend; and that in the presence of its organized power, always lying in wait to accomplish we know not what purpose, there can be no assured security for the democratic governments of the world. We are now about to accept gage of battle with this natural foe to liberty and shall, if necessary, spend the whole force of the nation to check and nullify its pretensions and its power. We are glad, now that we see the facts with no vile or false pretence about them, to fight thus for the ultimate peace of the world and for the liberation of its peoples, the German peoples included: for the rights of nations great and small and the privilege of men everywhere to choose their way of life and of obedience. The world must be made safe for democracy. Its peace must be planted upon the tested foundations of political liberty. We have no selfish ends to serve. We desire no conquest, no dominion. We seek no indemnities for ourselves, no material compensation for the sacrifices we shall freely make. We are but one of the champions of the rights of mankind. We shall be satisfied when those rights have been made as secure as the faith and the freedom of nations can make them. . . .

It is a distressing and oppressive duty, gentlemen of the Congress, which I have performed in thus addressing you. There are, it may be, many months of fiery trial and sacrifice ahead of us. It is a fearful thing to lead this great peaceful people into war, into the most terrible and disastrous of all wars, civilization itself seeming to be in the balance. But the right is more precious than peace, and we shall fight for the things which we have always carried nearest our hearts—for democracy, for the right of those who submit to authority to have a voice in their own governments, for the rights and liberties of small nations, for a universal dominion of right by such a concert of free peoples as shall bring peace and safety to all nations and make the world itself at last free. To such a task we can dedicate our lives and our fortunes, everything that we are and everything that we have, with the pride of those who know that the day has come when America is privileged to spend her blood and her might for the principles that gave her birth and happiness and the peace which she has treasured. God helping her, she can do no other.

TOPIC 56

VERSAILLES: THE PROSPECT OF COLLECTIVE SECURITY

The declaration of an armistice and the triumph of the Allied armies on November 11, 1918, ended the war but did not end conflict over why the United States fought. Woodrow Wilson went to the peace talks, held at Versailles, near Paris, in January 1919, with the avowed purpose of including American war aims in the eventual treaty. One of these aims, or at least an aim of Wilson and many other Americans, was the creation of an international organization, involving all nations, which would establish procedures for resolving conflicts to avoid war. Though Wilson had to compromise, even forsake, some of the aims the United States had claimed to be fighting for, he did achieve his goal of helping to create a League of Nations. Wilson felt the League would provide security for the United States in the postwar world, but many Americans disagreed. Security, some argued, could come only through isolation from the troubles of the world. Others agreed that the United States, as a great power, could no longer avoid involvement, but insisted that it remain free to take completely independent action. The ensuing conflict between Wilson and those who opposed him is the theme of this topic.

Reading 295

Victory and the Making of Peace (1918-1920)

Once committed to war the United States government and the American people committed themselves to victory with great enthusiasm, if not always with great wisdom. Despite the war fever, President Wilson, as well as many other Americans, felt strongly that a world dedicated to peace ought to emerge out of wartime destruction. In the following selection historian William Miller narrates the events of the war and the hopes expressed for the future.

From *A History of the United States* by William Miller. Copyright © 1958, 1962, 1968 by William Miller. Reprinted by permission of the publisher, Dell Publishing Co., Inc. Pp. 333-336. Subheadings added by the editors.

I

American Aid Arrives

When the United States entered the war, Britain and France were in much worse shape than most Americans, including the President, realized. But the United States, for all the growing spirit of "preparedness" was in even worse shape to help. On June 5, 1917, almost ten million Americans between the ages of twenty-one and thirty-one registered for the recently enacted draft; but almost a year passed before any sizable numbers of trained American troops were available to their commanding General, John J. Pershing. It took even longer for the United States to equip its forces with anything besides hand arms, and in fact most of the artillery used by them

BOYS and GIRLS!
You can help your Uncle Sam Win the War

Save your Quarters Buy War Savings Stamps

The United States, like other warring nations, exerted great pressure on its citizens to support the war effort. Posters were widely used during World War I, most of them urging specific actions, such as helping to raise the billions of dollars necessary to wage a modern war. The grim realities of trench warfare, however, rarely appeared in such posters.

was of British and French manufacture. American tanks and planes also were late in coming and not as numerous as had been hoped. In the meantime the Germans were chewing up French and British manpower and shipping, and these nations were verging on collapse. The fiercest blow of all was the November Revolution in Russia which saw the Bolsheviks overthrow the moderate Kerensky government and make a separate peace with the Germans. This released German troops from the Eastern front and permitted the Central Powers to build up their forces for their great assault in the West in the spring of 1918.

During most of the period General Pershing had resisted Allied demands for the use of American troops to bolster French and British lines. His policy was to build up, train, and equip a huge American Army which, independently, would "draw the best German divisions to our front and... consume them." Before this Army was ready, thousands of American troops were made available to Marshal Foch, who was in command of all Allied military activities. The American Sec-

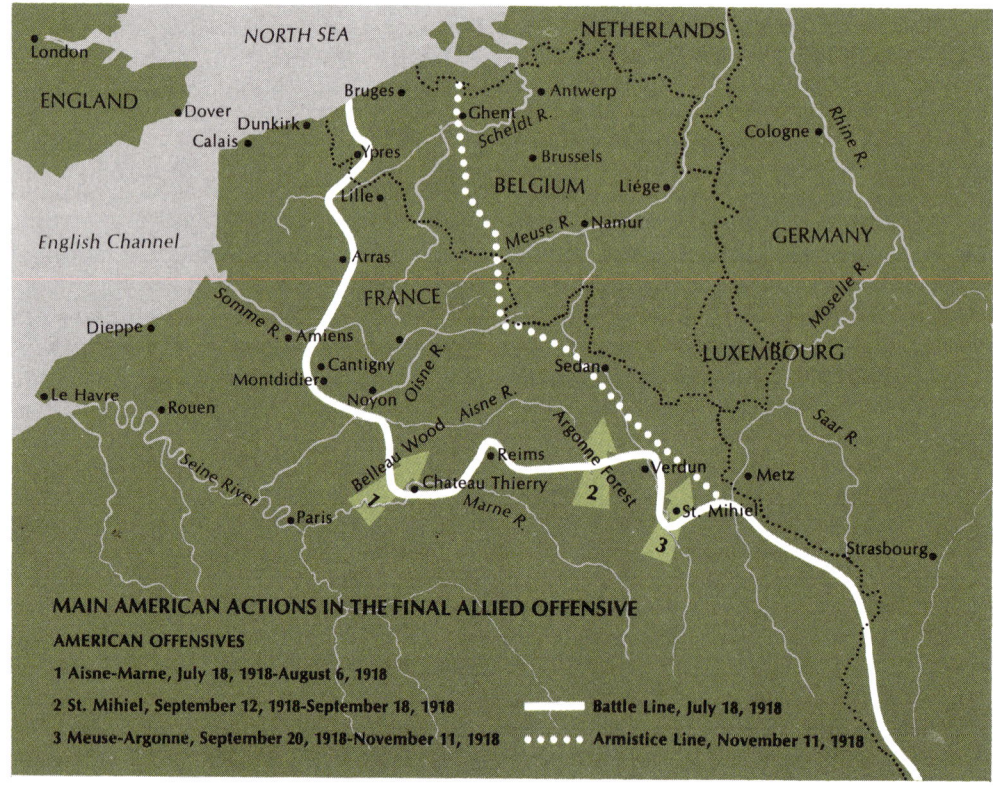

MAIN AMERICAN ACTIONS IN THE FINAL ALLIED OFFENSIVE

AMERICAN OFFENSIVES
1 Aisne-Marne, July 18, 1918-August 6, 1918
2 St. Mihiel, September 12, 1918-September 18, 1918
3 Meuse-Argonne, September 20, 1918-November 11, 1918

— Battle Line, July 18, 1918
⋯ Armistice Line, November 11, 1918

ond Division, starting on May 31, 1918, contributed greatly to halting the Germans at Château-Thierry on the Marne, just fifty miles from Paris. This Division then helped clear the enemy out of Belleau Wood. In July 85,000 Americans helped the British and French blunt the German offensive in the Rheims-Soissons theatre; and in August they took part in the Allied counter-offensive which continued right to the end of the war in November.

On August 10 the American First Army, 550,000 strong, took the offensive and wiped the Germans from St. Mihiel. In September Pershing's entire force of over a million played the major role in the Meuse-Argonne offensive which two months later crumbled the last of German resistance on land. By then the American Navy and Merchant Marine, employing the new technique of convoying, had begun to check the German U-boat offensive. Coming as it did so soon after the Russian defection, American aid to the Allied forces in the actual fighting clinched the victory over the Germans. But it is well to remember that America was a late entry and that her war dead numbered slightly more than 100,000. The allied Russians, French, and English had lost four million men.

II

The Statement of War Aims

One of Wilson's wartime innovations was the establishment in 1917 of the Committee on Public Information under the leadership of George Creel. This Committee was charged with "selling" the war to the American people, and the theme it stressed most frequently was that this war would make the world safe for democracy; that it was a war to end war. By the time the United States entered the fighting, Wilson himself had a well-developed peace plan which he hoped would implement the theme of his propaganda office.

The Allied powers, however, had long since made secret treaties looking toward the dismemberment of Germany, the exaction of heavy indemnities from her, the dismantling of her overseas empire and her navy. Russia was a party to these treaties, and after assuming power in November 1917, the Bolsheviks threatened to make a mockery of Allied claims to be fighting for "civilization" against the barbaric "Hun," and especially of American claims to be fighting for justice and humanity, by publishing the terms of the secret treaties. Wilson determined to forestall them. When Britain and France refused to cooperate, Wilson moved independently on January 5, 1918, to announce before a joint session of Congress the famous "Fourteen Points" in which he defined his war aims. Among these were demands for open diplomacy, freedom of the seas, the removal of trade barriers, and the adjustment of international boundaries on the principle of self-determination by the peoples involved. In point fourteen Wilson made his plea for a League of Nations "affording mutual guarantees of political independence and territorial integrity to great and small states alike."

Wilson's determination to prevent the utter destruction of Germany appealed to her war-weary people, and as their military fortunes declined in 1918, the Germans' morale fell even faster. By October 20, Germany acknowledged a readiness to accept Wilson's surrender terms; on November 8 her delegates capitulated to Marshal Foch; and three days later the war ended.

Already the discord which was to mar the peace conference had become apparent among the Allied powers. They were also aware of the likelihood of American rejection of the projected conference's work. In elections in England and France in 1918, vindictiveness against Germany paid great political dividends; hardly a word dared be spoken for a humane peace. In the American Congressional elections that year, the Republicans gained control of Congress. Wilson's partisanship during the campaign virtually insured that no "Democratic" peace could win approval in the Senate; his failure to include senators of either party among his associates at the peace conference itself only sealed the doom of that conference's work as far as American confirmation was concerned.

III

Results of the Peace Conference

The peace conference at Versailles began officially on January 18, 1919. By late March little had been accomplished and on March 24 Wilson, Clemenceau of France, Lloyd George of Britain, and Orlando of Italy—the famous "Big Four"—took matters in hand. By the end of April they were ready to present Germany with their peace terms, and these were formally accepted by the new German Republic—the Kaiser having abdicated the previous November—on June 23.

The Versailles Treaty did include much of Wilson's program for redrawing the map of Europe and imposing democratic forms of government on the new nations. In achieving this much Wilson made many damaging concessions as far as self-determination of nationality was concerned. His major concession, however, was most disastrous. This was his acquiescence in imposing on the new German state the crushing financial repara-

Through the addition of more than a million fresh American troops in the summer of 1918, the war-weary, battle-decimated Allied armies obtained a crucial key to victory. Here American infantry soldiers advance through the shattered remains of a French forest in the final Allied offensive in the fall of 1918.

tions demanded by the Allied European powers. If Wilson understood the hatred reparations would evoke in the German people who had known little but starvation for years, he also planned to forestall any violent expression of it by creating the League of Nations, the keystone of his entire program.

Ultimately, the Versailles Treaty did create a League of Nations, but one with no independent force of its own and dependent for effectiveness on United States participation. The rejection of the League and the entire Versailles Treaty by the vindictive United States Senate in 1920 literally killed the Messianic president and the whole justification for his adventure into the political and military maelstrom of Europe. The overwhelming victory of a nonentity like the Republican Warren G. Harding in the presidential elections of 1920 disclosed the country's fatigue with foreign involvements. Harding promised the people little but a return to "normalcy." Whatever they understood by that, the people embraced it.

Two British soldiers, an American sailor, and a Red Cross nurse celebrate the Allied victory in Paris.

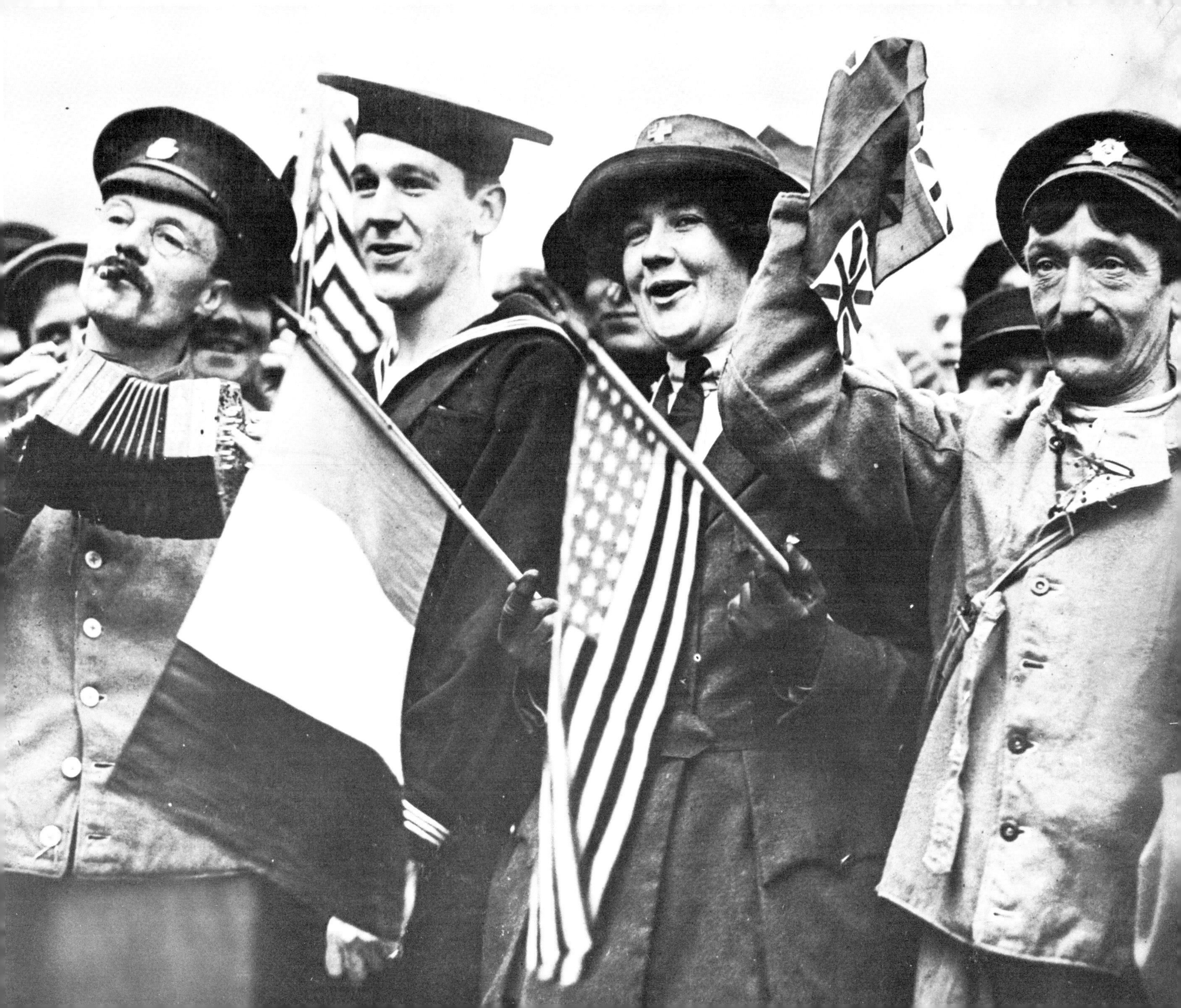

Reading 296

The Versailles Treaty and Collective Security

A proposed international organization, called the League of Nations, was only a part of the Versailles Treaty, but the proposed League became a focus of bitter controversy in the United States. President Wilson felt strongly that the League would provide an alternative to war; his opponents, led by Senators Henry Cabot Lodge of Massachusetts and William Borah of Idaho, saw it as a threat to national sovereignty. Two relevant articles from the Versailles Treaty are reprinted below.

From *Papers Relating to the Foreign Relations of the United States, the Paris Peace Conference, 1919* (Washington, D.C., 1947), Vol. XIII, pp. 83–84.

THE PEACE SETTLEMENT: Europe In 1920

Nations newly created or reestablished by the peace treaties after World War I

I

Article 10

The Members of the League undertake to respect and preserve as against external aggression the territorial integrity and existing political independence of all Members of the League. In case of any such aggression or in case of any threat or danger of such aggression the Council shall advise upon the means by which this obligation shall be fulfilled.

II

Article 11

1. Any war or threat of war, whether immediately affecting any of the Members of the League or not, is hereby declared a matter of concern to the whole League, and the League shall take any action that may be deemed wise and effectual to safeguard the peace of nations. In case any such emergency should arise the Secretary General shall on the request of any Member of the League forthwith summon a meeting of the Council.

2. It is also declared to be the friendly right of each Member of the League to bring to the attention of the Assembly or of the Council any circumstance whatever affecting international relations which threatens to disturb international peace or the good understanding between nations upon which peace depends.

Irish Nationalism and the Treaty (1919)

Attacks on a League of Nations, as embodied in Articles Ten and Eleven of the Versailles Treaty, came from many sources. One such petition, or memorial, was presented to the Committee on Foreign Relations of the United States Senate on November 3, 1919.

From *Congressional Record*, 66th Congress, 1st Session, Part 5 (Washington, D.C., 1919), pp. 4653–4654.

The Chairman [Lodge] Are you ready to go on?

Judge Cohalan. I am going to call upon Mr. Patrick J. Lynch, of the Supreme Court of Indiana, to read the memorial on the behalf of those who have come here. They have come from practically every State in the Union, from all walks in life, and from all over the country. We wish that it were possible to get people from the different parts of the country to be heard, but we have prepared a general memorial, and then later we will hand in the names of those who have signed.

The following memorial was read by Mr. Patrick J. Lynch:

Memorial to the Senate of the United States

"Senators: We, citizens of the United States, of Irish blood, but attached above all things to this Republic and its Constitution, respectfully pray that the proposed treaty now before you be rejected as a direct violation of the principles on which this war was fought as they were defined by President Wilson in these words, addressed to Congress:

"'National aspirations must be respected; peoples may now be dominated and governed only by their own consent. "Self-determination" is not a mere phrase. It is an imperative principle of action, which statesmen will henceforth ignore at their peril. . . .'

"Ireland has been asserting continuously her claim to independence for eight centuries. America is bound to her by close ties of friendship and of obligation for manifold services in peace and war. One-fifth of this entire population is of Irish extraction. In every war which America has fought Irishmen have shed their blood in a measure far in excess of their proportion to population. We ask that Ireland be not the only nation excluded from the benefit of the glorious principles enunciated by Mr. Wilson, as those which the Great War was fought to establish.

"We especially denounce article 10 of the proposed league of nations as a device to stifle the conscience of civilization and render it impotent to condemn, and, by condemning, to end the oppression of weak nations enslaved by powerful neighbors. It impeaches the most creditable page in our history and discredits the circumstances and conditions in which our Republic was born and our liberty achieved. . . .

"Under article 11 it becomes the right of the council of the league to prevent an assembly of American citizens to petition their Government to afford relief to an oppressed nation. On this point article 11 specifically says:

"'It is also declared to be the friendly right of each member of the league to bring to the attention of the assembly or of the council any circumstance whatever affecting international relations which threatens to disturb international peace or the good understanding between nations on which peace depends.'

"Under that clause our Congress could not express in the future, as it did in the past, our sympathy with countries like Greece, seeking freedom from the Turk;

the South American Republics, seeking liberty from Spain; or tender a welcome to Kossuth, of stricken Hungary; or Parnell, pleading for a self-governing Ireland. . . .

"Through long centuries of oppression Ireland has maintained her national spirit largely because she has always hitherto been able to cherish a hope that she might receive from some well-disposed foreign power the assistance which would insure her independence. She looked to Spain for this aid at the close of the sixteenth century; to France in the seventeenth, eighteenth, and nineteenth centuries. She looks for it now in the twentieth century to America, and we confidently hope and pray that the Senate will not allow that light of hope to be extinguished."

Senator Lodge Attacks the League of Nations
(1919)

Senator Henry Cabot Lodge (1850–1924), a close friend of former President Theodore Roosevelt, had long supported American expansion in the Caribbean and the Pacific, as well as the idea of a strong army and navy. Though he believed the United States must inevitably be deeply involved in world affairs, he nevertheless bitterly opposed a League of Nations, for reasons he stated in the Senate on August 12, 1919.

From *Congressional Record*, 66th Congress, 1st Session, Part 4 (Washington, D.C., 1919), pp. 3669–3780.

I

Involvement in Civil Wars

I object in the strongest possible way to having the United States agree, directly or indirectly, to be controlled by a league which may at any time, and perfectly lawfully and in accordance with the terms of the covenant, be drawn in to deal with internal conflicts in other countries, no matter what those conflicts may be. We should never permit the United States to be involved in any internal conflict in another country, except by the will of her people expressed through the Congress which represents them.

With regard to wars of external aggression on a member of the league, the case is perfectly clear. There can be no genuine dispute whatever about the meaning of the first clause of article 10. In the first place, it dif-

TEACHING HIM WHAT TO SAY

This pro-Wilson cartoon of February 1920 has Republican newspapers parroting Senator Henry Cabot Lodge, a bitter political enemy of the President and leader in the fight to modify the Versailles Treaty extensively, with "reservations," before Senate ratifications.

fers from every other obligation in being individual and placed upon each nation without the intervention of the league. Each nation for itself promises to respect and preserve as against external aggression the boundaires and the political independence of every member of the league. Of the right of the United States to give such a guaranty I have never had the slightest doubt. . . . The point I wish to make is that the pledge is an invididual pledge. We have, for example, given guaranties to Panama and for obvious and sufficient reasons. The application of that guaranty would not be in the slightest degree affected by ten or twenty other nations giving the same pledge, if Panama, when in danger, appealed to us to fulfill our obligation. We should be bound to do so without the slightest reference to the other guarantors. In article 10 the United States is bound on the appeal of any member of the league not only to respect but to preserve its independence and its boundaries, and that pledge, if we give it, must be fulfilled.

II

Legal and Moral Obligations

There is to me no distinction whatever in a treaty between what some persons are pleased to call legal and moral obligations. A treaty rests and must rest, except where it is imposed under duress and securities and hostages are taken for its fulfillment, upon moral obligations. No doubt a great power impossible of coercion can cast aside a moral obligation if it sees fit and escape from the performance of the duty which it promises. The pathway of dishonor is always open. I for one, however, can not conceive of voting for a clause of which I disapprove because I know it can be escaped in that way. Whatever the United States agrees to, by that agreement she must abide. Nothing could so surely destroy all prospects of the world's peace as to have any powerful nation refuse to carry out an obligation, direct or indirect, because it rests only on moral grounds. Whatever we promise we must carry out to the full, "without mental reservation or purpose of evasion." To me any other attitude is inconceivable. Without the most absolute and minute good faith in carrying out a treaty to which we have agreed, without ever resorting to doubtful interpretations or to the plea that it is only a moral obligation, treaties are worthless. The greatest foundation of peace is the scrupulous observance of every promise, express or implied, of every pledge, whether it can be described as legal or moral. No vote should be given to any clause in any treaty or to any treaty except in this spirit and with this understanding.

I return, then, to the first clause of article 10. It is, I repeat, an individual obligation. It requires no action on the part of the league, except that in the second sentence the authorities of the league are to have the power to advise as to the means to be employed in order to fulfill the purpose of the first sentence. But that is a detail of execution, and I consider that we are morally and in honor bound to except and act upon that advice. The broad fact remains that if any member of the league suffering from external aggression should appeal directly to the United States for support the United States would be bound to give that support in its own capacity and without reference to the action of other powers, because the United States itself is bound, and I hope the day will never come when the United States will not carry out its promises. If that day should come, and the United States or any other great country should refuse, no matter how specious the reasons, to fulfill both in letter and spirit every obligation in this covenant, the United States would be dishonored and the league would crumble into dust, leaving behind it a legacy of wars. If China should rise up and attack Japan in an effort to undo the great wrong of the cession of the control of Shantung to that power, we should be bound under the terms of article 10 to sustain Japan against China, and a guaranty of that sort is never invoked except when the question has passed beyond the stage of negotiation and has become a question for the application of force. I do not like the prospect. It shall not come into existence by any vote of mine. Article 11 carries this danger still further, for it says:

> Any war or threat of war, whether immediately affecting any of the members of the league or not, is hereby declared a matter of concern to the whole league and the league shall take any action that shall be deemed wise and effectual to safeguard the peace of nations.

"Any war or threat of war" means both external aggression and internal disturbance, as I have already pointed out in dealing with article 3. "Any action" covers military action, because it covers action of any sort or kind. Let me take an example, not an imaginary case, but one which may have been overlooked, because most people have not the slightest idea where or what a King of the Hejaz is. The following dispatch appeared recently in the newspapers:

> *Hejaz against Bedouins*
>
> The forces of Emir Abdullah recently suffered a grave defeat, the Wahabis

attacking and capturing Kurma, east of Mecca. Ibn Savond is believed to be working in harmony with the Wahabis. A squadron of the royal air force was ordered recently to go to the assistance of King Hussein.

Hussein I take to be the Sultan of Hejaz. He is being attacked by the Bedouins, as they are known to us, although I fancy the general knowledge about the Wahabis and Ibn Savond and Emir Abdullah is slight and the names mean but little to the American people. Nevertheless, here is a case of a member of the league—for the King of the Hejaz is such a member in good and regular standing and signed the treaty by his representatives, Mr. Rustem Haidar and Mr. Abdul Havi Aouni. Under article 10, if King Hussein appealed to us for aid and protection against external aggression affecting his independence and the boundaries of his kingdom, we should be bound to give that aid and protection and to send American soldiers to Arabia. It is not relevant to say that this is unlikely to occur; that Great Britain is quite able to take care of King Hussein, who is her fair creation, reminding one a little of the Mosquito King, a monarch once developed by Great Britain on the Mosquito Coast of Central America. The fact that we should not be called upon does not alter the right which the King of Hejaz possesses to demand the sending of American troops to Arabia in order to preserve his independence against the assaults of the Wahabis or Bedouins. I am unwilling to give that right to King Hussein, and this illustrates the point which is to me the most objectionable in the league as it stands—the right of other powers to call out American troops and American ships to go to any part of the world, an obligation we are bound to fulfill under the terms of this treaty. I know the answer well—that of course they could not be sent without action by Congress. Congress would have no choice if acting in good faith, and if under article 10 any member of the league summoned us, or if under article 11 the league itself summoned us, we should be bound in honor and morally to obey. There would be no escape except by a breach of faith, and legislation by Congress under those circumstances would be a mockery of independent action. Is it too much to ask that provision should be made that American troops and American ships should never be sent anywhere or ordered to take part in any conflict except after the deliberate action of the American people, expressed according to the Constitution through their chosen representatives in Congress?

Wilson Defends the League of Nations (1919)

The burden of defending the League of Nations fell largely on President Wilson. Forced to be on the defensive in the fall of 1919 when the Senate appeared to be ready to accept a series of amendments authored by Lodge that would have weakened the League, Wilson undertook a speaking tour by railroad across the country despite his poor health. In a key speech, given at Pueblo, Colorado, on September 25, 1919, the President sought to explain how the League would insure peace in the future without limiting the freedom of the United States to act in its own interests. Wilson suffered a severe stroke after the speech and was taken back to Washington incapable of further action. While he recovered slowly over the winter, the nature of his illness probably helped to keep him from reaching the compromise with his foes which would have permitted the ratification of the treaty. The Senate failed again to ratify the amended treaty in a final vote of forty-nine to thirty-five on March 19, 1920. The votes which would have provided the two-thirds majority needed for ratification were held by Democrats who favored it but who were forbidden by Wilson to accept Lodge's amendments.

From *Congressional Record*, 66th Congress, 1st Session, Part 7 (Washington, D.C., 1919), pp. 6425–6426.

I

The Heart of the Covenant

When you come to the heart of the covenant, my fellow citizens, you will find it in article 10, and I am very much interested to know that the other things have been blown away like bubbles. There is nothing in the other contentions with regard to the league of nations, but there is something in article 10 that you ought to realize and ought to accept or reject. Article 10 is the heart of the whole matter. What is article 10? I never am certain that I can from memory give a literal repetition of its language, but I am sure that I can give an exact interpretation of its meaning. Article 10 provides that every member of the league covenants to respect and preserve the territorial integrity and existing political independence of every other member of the league as against external aggression. Not against internal disturbance. There was not a man at that table who did not admit the sacredness of the right of self-determination, the sacredness of the right of any body of people to say that they would not continue to live under the Government they were then living under, and under article 11 of the covenant they are given a place to say whether they will live under it or not. For following article 10 is article 11, which makes it the right of any member of the league at any time to call attention to anything, anywhere, that is likely to disturb the peace of the world or the good understanding between nations upon which the peace of the world depends. I want to give you an illustration of what that would mean.

II

Morals and International Law

You have heard a great deal—something that was true and a great deal that was false—about that provision of the treaty which hands over to Japan the rights which Germany enjoyed in the Province of Shantung in China. In the first place, Germany did not enjoy any rights there that other nations had not already claimed. For my part, my judgment, my moral judgment, is against the whole set of concessions. They were all of them unjust to China, they ought never to have been exacted; they were all exacted by duress from a great body of thoughtful and ancient and helpless people. There never was any right in any of them. Thank God, America never asked for any, never dreamed of asking for any. But when Germany got this concession in 1898, the Government of the United States made no protest whatever. That was not because the Government of the United States was not in the hands of high-minded and conscientious men. It was. William McKinley was President and John Hay was Secretary of State—as safe hands to leave the honor of the United States in as any that you can cite. They made no protest because the state of international law at that time was that it was none of their business unless they could show that the interests of the United States were affected, and the only thing that they could show with regard to the interests of the United States was that Germany might close the doors of Shantung Province against the trade of the United States. They, therefore, demanded and obtained promises that we could continue to sell merchandise in Shantung. Immediately following that concession to Germany there was a concession to Russia of the same sort, of Port Arthur, and Port Arthur was handed over subsequently to Japan on the very territory of the United States. Don't you remember that when Russia and Japan got into war with one another the war was brought to a conclusion by a treaty written at Portsmouth, N.H., and in that treaty, without the slightest intimation from any authoritative sources in America that the Government of the United States had any objection, Port Arthur, Chinese territory, was turned over to Japan? I want you distinctly to understand that there is no thought of criticism in my mind. I am expounding to you a state of international law. Now, read articles 10 and 11. You will see that international law is revolutionized by putting morals into it. Article 10 says that no member of the league, and that includes all these nations that have demanded these things unjustly of China, shall impair the territorial integrity or the political independence of any other member of the league. China is going to be a member of the league. Article 11 says that any member of the league can call attention to anything that is likely to disturb the peace of the world or the good understanding between nations, and China is for the first time in the history of mankind afforded a standing before the jury of the world. I, for my part, have a profound sympathy for China, and I am proud to have taken part in an arrangement which promises the protection of the world to the rights of China. The whole atmosphere of the world is changed by a thing like that, my fellow citizens. The whole international practice of the world is revolutionized.

But you will say, 'What is the second sentence of article 10? That is what gives very disturbing thoughts.' The second sentence is that the council of the league shall advise what steps, if any, are necessary to carry out the guaranty of the first sentence, namely, that the members will respect and preserve the territorial integrity and political independence of the other members. I do not know any other meaning for the word 'advise' except 'advise.' The council advises, and it can not advise without the vote of the United States. Why gentlemen should fear that the Congress of the United States would be advised to do something that it did not want to do I frankly can not imagine, because they cannot even be advised to do anything unless

The scene in December 1918, as President Wilson arrives in Dover, England, on his way to the Paris Peace Conference. Harmony and affection prevail here, but in Paris Wilson found the conference saturated with suspicion and distrust. Those emotions helped to shape the final peace treaty with Germany, a fact which disturbed and confused many Americans.

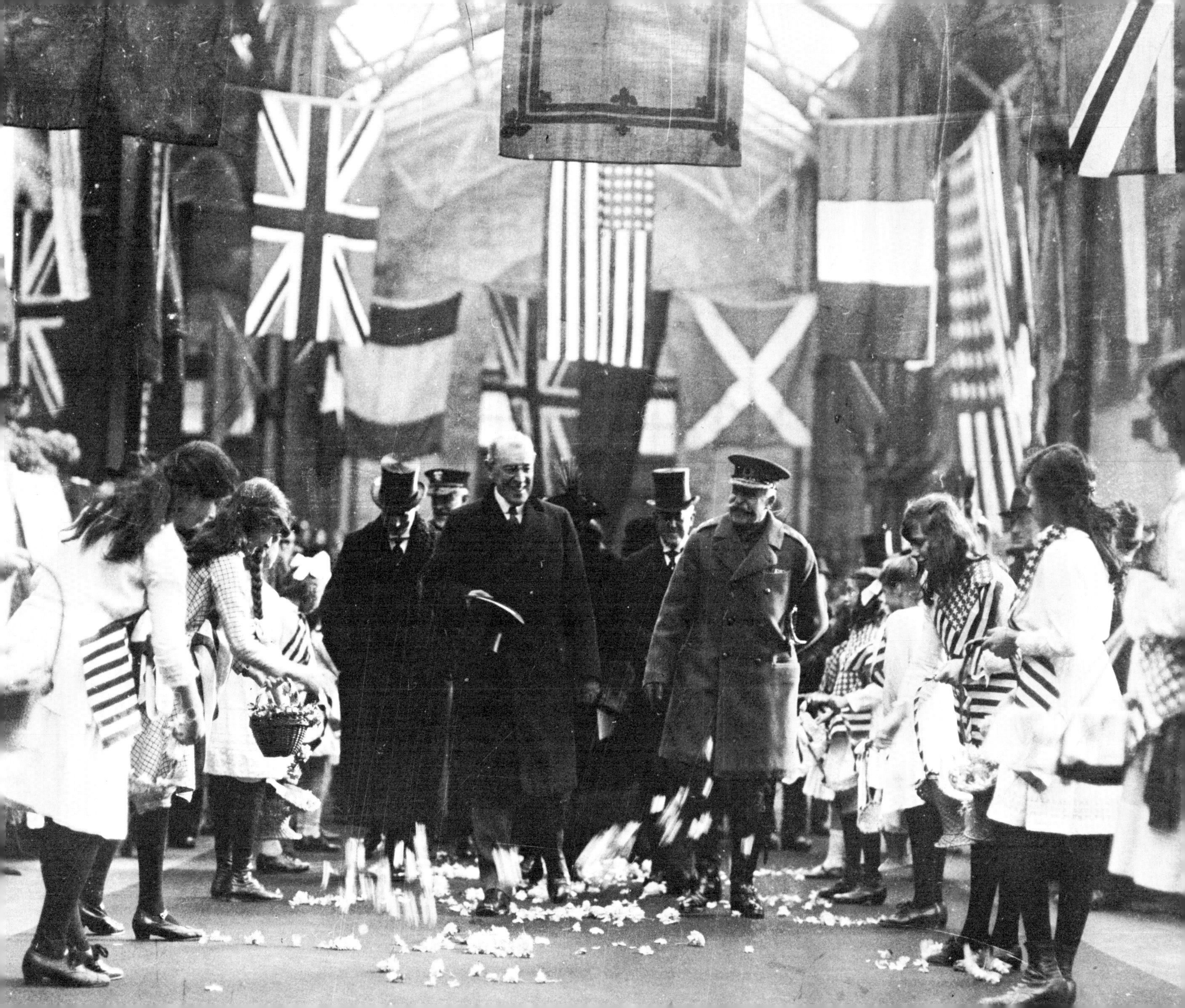

their own representative has participated in the advice. It may be that will impair somewhat the vigor of the league, but nevertheless, the fact is so, that we are not obliged to take any advice except our own, which to any man who wants to go his own course is a very satisfactory state of affairs. Every man regards his own advice as best, and I dare say every man mixes his own advice with some thought of his own interest. Whether we use it wisely or unwisely, we can use the vote of the United States to make impossible drawing the United States into any enterprise that she does not care to be drawn into.

Woodrow Wilson: A Prophet Ahead of His Time

For almost fifty years historians have grappled with the significance of Woodrow Wilson's policies after World War I. Some have found Wilson appealing, some appalling, but all have felt that the controversy he was so much a part of in 1919 revealed a great deal about both the man and the nation he led. Writing at the end of World War II, diplomatic historian Thomas A. Bailey offers one view of Wilson and his policies in the following reading.

From Thomas A. Bailey, *Woodrow Wilson and the Great Betrayal* (New York, 1945), pp. 367–369. Copyright © 1945 by Thomas A. Bailey.

Should the United States have ratified the treaty and joined the League? In the face of the evidence herein presented, there can be only one answer. We had very little if anything to lose—perhaps the trivial expenses of the League; and everything to gain—possibly a preventing of so-called World War II. No nation was ever trapped in the League, as our isolationists feared: Japan got out, Germany got out, Russia was thrown out. Where the possible losses were so negligible, and the probable gains so tremendous, the United States, as Wilson repeatedly pointed out, was more than justified in taking the chance.

Would the results have been essentially different if we had joined the League?

The conclusions here must of course be more speculative. But it seems clear that some kind of "slump in idealism" would have come sooner or later, and it may legitimately be doubted whether, when the pinch came, the United States would have provided adequate support for the League of Nations. The events of the 1930's would seem to support such a view, but we must remember that the set of circumstances then encountered might not have come into being if we had joined the League in the first instance.

General Jan C. Smuts said that not Wilson but "humanity" failed at Paris. This is a striking statement that has little meaning, in part because the real failure came after Paris. If a horseman spurs his mount at a twelve-foot brick wall, who is responsible for the ensuing accident: the horse that fails to make the jump, or the rider who has attempted an impossible feat?

A horseman must know his horse and its limitations; a statesman must know his people and their limitations, as well as the limitations of foreign peoples. Otherwise he is not a statesman. He must not set for his people impossible goals, however desirable they may be in the abstract. He must train public opinion by gradations for the new tasks—not try to shoot Niagara all at once. He must educate the people in advance for the responsibility which he is asking them to shoulder. Otherwise, even though they may temporarily take on the burden, they are likely to find it too wearisome and cast it aside.

Wilson engineered a revolution in our foreign policy when he undertook to lead the American people out of the path of isolationism into that of effective world cooperation. Yet the isolationists, aided by the circumstances set forth, were able to effect a counterrevolution, and take us back into the old paths. But it is possible that this counterrevolution would have come within a few years anyhow; the people were not yet fully ready for a major departure.

The great Covenanter was eternally right in recognizing that isolationism was but a mirage, and that the next war would surely drag us in, and that the new organization for peace had to be based upon justice for all. The stakes were enormous; they were worth giving one's life for. He failed in part because he seems not to have realized that his was a dual task: making a peace and changing a national—perhaps a world—psychology.

Wilson was the greatest of the neutral statesmen, the greatest mediator, the greatest war leader, the greatest peacemaker, the greatest tragedy, and the greatest disappointment. Reaching for the stars, he crashed to earth.

But his was a magnificent failure, and in some ways a successful failure. Wilson once said, "Ideas live; men die." His ideas have lived. The Wilsonian tradition has been kept alive, and countless thousands of men and women have vowed that we shall not make the same mistakes again.

Reading 301

Wilson's Goals: Tragic and Unachievable

Norman Graebner, like Thomas A. Bailey (Reading 300), is a historian of American foreign policy. Graebner, however, views Wilson in the light of the "inescapable reality of a state system" and comes to a conclusion about Wilson's goals quite different from that of Professor Bailey.

From *Ideas and Diplomacy: Readings in the Intellectual Tradition of American Foreign Policy* by Norman A. Graebner. Copyright © 1964 by Oxford University Press, Inc. Reprinted by permission. Pp. 416–417.

Wilson's designation of America's proper role in international affairs, enunciated with deep conviction and appealing phraseology, gave American idealism a new birth and fastened it unshakably to the nation's attitudes and expectations in the realm of foreign relations. Wilson's speeches more than his actions carried the intent and had the effect of undermining completely an established diplomatic tradition that had, through much of the

The men who saw themselves as determining the future of the world—the Big Four at the beginning of the Paris Peace Conference. Seated, from left to right, are Orlando of Italy, Lloyd George of Great Britain, Clemenceau of France, and Wilson of the United States.

nation's history, taken its strength, consciously or unconsciously, from the words and policies of all American statesmen from Washington to Lincoln. What was tragic in Wilson's leadership was not that he warred on the finest traditions of the Founding Fathers, but that he warred with such remarkable success. Wilson had attached the nation's diplomacy to the unachievable. Thus his idealism, in assigning to the United States a revolutionary role in world affairs, carried the seeds of vanity and disappointment. In divorcing the country from its load of original sin and placing it morally above all others, Wilson incurred the resentment of much of the world's leadership. Despite his impressive rhetoric, he could never demonstrate how one nation's foreign policies could achieve such transcendent goals as the establishment and maintenance of freedom and justice for all mankind. Such purposes not only separated the nation's objectives from the limited means of politics and diplomacy, but also undermined its capacity to render humanity some genuine, if limited, service. It would have been no betrayal of American idealism or American moral purpose to have accepted the established rules of European diplomacy as had all the nation's early diplomatists.

Wilson eventually committed the errors of all leaders who ignore the limits of politics. He proposed a body of thought which had little or no relationship to the political realities with which he was forced to contend. At Versailles he became the embodiment of his self-created problem. Even while proclaiming the virtues of open diplomacy and self-determination he was forced to engage in deliberations of profound secrecy week after week. Like all idealists in power, Wilson eventually over-promised every group that attributed some precise meaning to his words—the Germans, the Allies, and the American people. . . .

Ironically, Wilson's failure to fasten his concepts of world politics to the continuing existence of the old diplomacy in no way shattered the attachment of his followers to the views he had proclaimed. Perhaps the reason is clear. Wilson, whether purposefully or not, had devised an international system which, if accepted by all the major powers of the world, would have fastened the *status quo* on the international order of power, thus assuring the United States and the victorious democracies their predominant position in world affairs at little or no cost to themselves. Wilson's principles, tragically, were less concerned with justice than with the prevention of change. Their virtue flowed from that morality which he and other Allied leaders assigned to the Versailles system itself. Any attack on that system would be by definition immoral and a defiance of the principles embodied in Wilsonian thought. Had the President defended the Versailles Treaty as a proper definition of the interests of the United States around the world and thus an arrangement to be protected by force if necessary, he might have established the foundations of a viable national response to post-war world politics. But by defending his system as an expression of the sentiments of mankind, to be guaranteed by the universal acceptance of his principles of justice and self-determination, he led his followers to reject as either immoral or nonexistent the inescapable reality of a state system operating through the traditional means of power politics and the balance of power.

TOPIC 57

THE SECOND FAILURE OF NEUTRALITY: WORLD WAR II

Before World War I the United States' relative isolation in the New World simplified the conduct of American foreign relations. After the war many Americans looked back nostalgically to the days when they had been able to ignore events in Europe and Asia. Yet after the Spanish-American War the United States had control of the Philippines and thus was directly involved in Asian affairs. After World War I every major European nation, with the exception of the Soviet Union, was deeply in debt to the United States. However it might desire isolation, the United States was deeply involved—politically, economically, and culturally—in Europe and Asia. During the Depression of the 1930s Americans were enmeshed in their internal troubles, but the expansion of German power under Adolf Hitler and Japan's invasion of China forced American attention outward across the Atlantic and the Pacific.

Reading 302

The Coming of the Second World War (1919-1939)

The United States was not directly involved in the events leading up to the outbreak of war in September 1939. Because of isolationist sentiment and the economic depression of the 1930s, most Americans were overwhelmingly concerned with domestic problems. Nevertheless, as tensions rapidly increased both in Europe and Asia, the United States had to face the reality of a world heading for another massive conflict. The following reading gives the necessary background for understanding the world situation Americans faced in 1939.

From Crane Brinton, John Christopher, and Robert Lee Wolff, *Civilization in the West* © 1964. Reprinted by permission of Prentice-Hall, Inc., Englewood Cliffs, New Jersey. Pp. 627-628, 634, 636-639. Subheadings added by the editors.

I

The United States in the 1920s

With a population three times that of France, the United States in World War I lost fewer than one-tenth as many men as the French. In material terms the United States gained from the war: Allied war orders stimulated heavy industry; New York was outstripping London as the financial center of the world; the dollar had begun to dethrone the pound. Some interest on the war debts of the Allies came in until 1933, and the stimulation of American industry exceeded the losses when the debts were finally repudiated in the early 1930s. Despite American victory and prosper-

349

ity, however, the national revulsion against the war in 1919 and the years following was as great as that in Europe. In the presidential election of 1920, the Republicans ousted the Democrats, who had been in control since 1913; and the Republican victory was repeated in 1924 and 1928. This was the era of the Republican presidents, Harding (1921–1923), Coolidge (1923–1929), and Hoover (1929–1933).

In American public opinion there was a strong wave of isolationist sentiment, the wish to withdraw from international politics, reflected in the Senate's repudiation of the Treaty of Versailles and of the League of Nations. Yet isolationism was by no means universal, and it may be that a few concessions to the Republicans by President Wilson would have produced the necessary two-thirds majority in the Senate required by the Constitution for treaties; or that a commanding figure on the Republican side might have put through the idea of a bipartisan foreign policy. Many Americans, however, felt that they had done all that was necessary by beating the Germans, and were reluctant to involve American innocence and virtue any further with European sophistication and vice.

Isolationism was reflected in the high tariff policies of the period: the Fordney-McCumber Tariff of 1922 and the Smoot-Hawley Tariff of 1930 set increasingly high duties on foreign goods. These laws, designed to protect American high wage scales against competition from cheaper foreign labor, made it impossible for the European debtor nations to earn dollars in the American markets and so to repay their debts. Although Congress acquiesced in a general scaling-down of the obligations of defeated Germany, it tended to reduce the complexities of the debts owed us by our Allies to President Coolidge's simple dictum: "They hired the money, didn't they?" Isolationism expressed itself also in a reversal of the traditional American policies of free immigration. In 1924 an annual quota limit was established for all countries as 2 percent of the number of nationals of that country resident in the United States in 1890. Since the heavy immigration from eastern and southern Europe had come mainly after 1890, the selection of that year was designed to reduce the flow from those areas to a trickle.

But of course isolationism was only relative. In 1928, Frank B. Kellogg, the Secretary of State, submitted a proposal for the renunciation of war to the European powers. Similar proposals came from the French Foreign Minister, Aristide Briand. Together they were incorporated as the Pact of Paris (Kellogg-Briand Pact, August, 1928), eventually signed by 23 nations including the United States. The obvious fact that the Pact did not prevent World War II should not obscure the deep concern of the United States with the peace of the world. American businessmen, American money, and American goods were everywhere in the world. In the Far East as early as 1922 the United States took the lead in the Nine-Power Treaty, committing them all, including Japan, to respect the sovereignty and integrity of China. Thus, even in the period of isolationism the United States was committed to certain foreign obligations that it would later honor....

II

The Rise of European Fascism

In many ways the period we have been considering was hardly more than a 20-years' truce. The Western democracies, Britain and France, generally (though often ineffectually) supported by the United States, proved unable to prevent the rise of the fascist and communist powers. In the end Germany, allied with two of its enemies in the First World War, Italy and Japan, took the lead in new aggressions. The Nazis claimed that Versailles—with its war-guilt clause, its reparations, its provisions taking Germany's colonies and denying her the right to rearm—had made a new war a necessity....

Step by step during the 1930s, while the League in general proved powerless to stop them, Japan, Italy, and Germany upset the peace of the world. The Japanese seizure of Manchuria in 1931 was the first step. Henry L. Stimson, the American Secretary of State, declared that the United States would recognize no gains made by armed force; but the other democracies failed to follow his lead. The Lytton report to the League of Nations branded the Japanese as aggressors, but no nation seemed interested; Japan withdrew from the League (March, 1933).

In October, 1933, Hitler withdrew Germany from the League, serving notice on the world of his own aggressive intentions. On March 16, 1935, he denounced the Versailles limitations on German armaments and openly began to rebuild the German armies. In April the League condemned this action, but Hitler went on rearming. In May France hastily concluded a treaty of alliance with the USSR against German aggression; Hitler continued rearming. In June the British signed a naval agreement with Germany, limiting the German navy to one-third the size of the British and their submarine force to 60 percent of the British. Though this may have been realistic, it seemed to the French like British treachery. In March, 1936, Hitler sent German troops into the Rhineland, the zone demilitarized by the Treaty of Versailles. Once again, he met with nothing but verbal protests. It is altogether probable that a united British-French show of force against the violation of Germany's obligations would have ended Hitler's career then and there.

Having witnessed the Japanese and German success through illegal violence, Mussolini took advantage of a frontier incident to demand Ethiopia for Italy (1934). Though the British and the French tried to appease him by offering great economic and political concessions in Ethiopia, they did insist that its nominal independence be preserved, for it was a member of the League. But Mussolini invaded Ethiopia in October, 1935, avenging with planes, tanks, and poison gas the humiliating defeat inflicted on Italy by the Ethiopians in 1896. While the King of Italy became Emperor of Ethiopia, the rightful Emperor, Haile Selassie, denounced the aggression before the League, most of whose members voted to invoke Article 16 of the Covenant to impose economic sanctions against a member that had gone to war in violation of its pledges. But sanctions failed: Oil was not included among the forbidden articles, and it continued to be sold to Italy. Britain and France did nothing to check the movement of Italian troops and munitions through the Suez Canal. The failure of the sanctions against Italy finished the League as an instrument in international politics. Italy withdrew in 1937. The trained international civil servants that had dealt with the drug traffic, prostitution, and other problems continued to function until the United Nations absorbed them after World War II.

In July, 1936, came the Franco *coup* against the Spanish Republic and the start of the Spanish Civil War in which Hitler, Mussolini, and Stalin all intervened. The Western democracies failed to follow the usual practice in international law of sending arms to the legal government. The success of the fascists' intervention in Spain increased their appetites as well as their boldness. In October, 1936, Mussolini signed with Hitler the pact formally establishing a Rome-Berlin "Axis." Early in 1938 Hitler began a violent newspaper and radio propaganda campaign against the Austrian government; he summoned Chancellor Schuschnigg to his Bavarian retreat in Berchtesgaden, unloosed a bullying tirade against him, and then moved the German armies into Vienna. The *Anschluss* of Austria to Germany, favored by Pan-Germans and

Adolf Hitler's compelling power as a speaker emerges in this photograph of the German leader addressing a Nazi Party rally in the mid-1930s.

Nazis and opposed by the victors of the First World War, was an accomplished fact.

III

Munich, The Final Straw

Hitler's next target was the Czechoslovak republic, the only Central or Eastern European state where parliamentary democracy had succeeded, thanks to the rich and well-balanced economy and to the enlightened policies of the first President, Thomas Masaryk. But Czechoslovakia also included a minority of 3.4 million Germans, who felt contempt for the Slavs and tried to sabotage the republic. Hitler supported the agitation of these "Sudeten" Germans and demanded autonomy for them in the spring of 1938. The Czechs counted on their alliance with France to protect them against the dismemberment of their country, but neither the French nor the British were willing to run the risk of a military show-down with Hitler. By September, 1938, Hitler was in full cry against alleged Czech misdeeds, and a full-fledged European crisis had broken out. Twice the British Prime Minister, Neville Chamberlain, personally pleaded with Hitler to moderate his demands. Then, at Munich (September 29, 1938), Hitler and Mussolini met with Chamberlain and the French Premier, Daladier. Though allied with the French, the Soviet Union was not invited to Munich; the rebuff helped persuade Stalin that the Western powers were interested only in turning Hitler's armies east against him, and that he had better make what terms he could.

At Munich, Hitler won the consent of the democracies to the dismemberment of Czechoslovakia; the Czechs were forced to acquiesce as the West let them down. The Germans took over the Sudeten lands along with the mountain defenses of the Czech border, Poland received small border areas, while the agricultural area of Slovakia was given autonomy, and Hitler guaranteed the remainder of the state. But, after a six-months' lull, Hitler violated his last agreement with the Czechs and marched his forces into Prague (March, 1939) after bullying the President of Czechoslovakia, Hacha, as he had bullied Schuschnigg. Somehow, this was at last the last straw. Chamberlain seems finally to have been convinced that Hitler could never be counted on to keep his word. The "peace with honor" that Chamberlain had proudly announced he had won at Munich proved to have been neither. The British followed the march into Prague with a guarantee of assistance to Poland (April, 1939), next on Hitler's calendar. And Mussolini, who had been vainly trying to bully France into ceding Nice and Savoy, Corsica, and Tunisia, found an enemy he could intimidate and attacked the backward little Balkan state of Albania (April, 1939).

We now know that appeasement of Hitler was hopeless from the first; he had all along intended to destroy Czechoslovakia and move against Poland. Contemptuous of the French and British, he was prepared to fight them if he could avoid a two-front war. To this end he opened negotiations with a Stalin already convinced that the Soviet Union could never depend on Britain and France. On August 23, 1939, to the horror of the West, Germany and Russia reached a nonaggression pact; they agreed secretly on a new partition of Poland. When the Germans invaded Poland a week later, the British and French honored their obligations and declared war on Germany. The victorious Allies of the First World War had with extreme reluctance abandoned their defensive position; World War II was under way.

A Guarded Plea for Neutrality (1939)

A few days after Germany invaded Poland, President Franklin D. Roosevelt spoke to the American people by radio. Both the President and the people were well aware of the process by which the United States had entered World War I, some twenty years before. With this earlier experience in mind, Roosevelt outlined what he would and would not do in reaction to the new European war.

From *U.S. Department of State Bulletin*, I (1939), p. 201.

Tonight my single duty is to speak to the whole of America.

Until 4:30 this morning I had hoped against hope that some miracle would prevent a devastating war in Europe and bring to an end the invasion of Poland by Germany.

For 4 long years a succession of actual wars and constant crises have shaken the entire world and have threatened in each case to bring on the gigantic conflict which is today unhappily a fact. . . .

It is easy for you and me to shrug our shoulders and say that conflicts taking place thousands of miles from the continental United States, and, indeed, the whole American hemisphere, do not seriously affect the Americas—and that all the United States has to do is to ignore them and go about our own business. Passionately though we may desire detachment, we are forced to realize that every word that comes through the air, every ship that sails the sea, every battle that is fought does affect the American future.

Let no man or woman thoughtlessly or falsely talk of America sending its armies to European fields. At this moment there is being prepared a proclamation of American neutrality. This would have been done even if there had been no neutrality statute on the books, for this proclamation is in accordance with international law and with American policy.

This will be followed by a proclamation required by the existing Neutrality Act. I trust that in the days to come our neutrality can be made a true neutrality. . . .

We have certain ideas and ideals of national safety, and we must act to preserve that safety today and to preserve the safety of our children in future years.

That safety is and will be bound up with the safety of the Western Hemisphere and of the seas adjacent thereto. We seek to keep war from our firesides by keeping war from coming to the Americas. For that we have historic precedent that goes back to the days of the administration of President George Washington. It is serious enough and tragic enough to every American family in every State in the Union to live in a world that is torn by wars on other continents. Today they affect every American home. It is our national duty to use every effort to keep them out of the Americas.

And at this time let me make the simple plea that partisanship and selfishness be adjourned, and that national unity be the thought that underlies all others.

This Nation will remain a neutral nation, but I cannot ask that every American remain neutral in thought as well. Even a neutral has a right to take account of facts. Even a neutral cannot be asked to close his mind or his conscience.

I have said not once but many times that

Reading 304

I have seen war and that I hate war. I say that again and again.

I hope the United States will keep out of this war. I believe that it will. And I give you assurances that every effort of your Government will be directed toward that end.

As long as it remains within my power to prevent, there will be no blackout of peace in the United States.

American Response to Nazi Victories: "The Arsenal of Democracy" (1940)

After quickly conquering Poland, Germany made no further moves against its declared foes, France and Great Britain. Then, in the spring of 1940, the German army launched a second *blitzkrieg*. By June it had conquered much of Western Europe, including France. The German air force soon began large-scale bombing raids on British cities, hoping to beat Germany's one remaining declared enemy into submission. Americans watched these events nervously, some urging massive aid to Great Britain, but most resisting entering any armed conflict. To cap Germany's military victories, Hitler signed an agreement with Italy and Japan, the so-called Tripartite Pact, pledging each nation to come to the aid of the others in event of future attacks on them. President Roosevelt reacted to this pact publicly in a radio address on December 29, 1940.

From *U.S. Department of State Bulletin*, IV (1940), pp. 3-4, 6-7.

I

Threat of the Axis Pact

Never before since Jamestown and Plymouth Rock has our American civilization been in such danger as now.

For, on September 27, 1940, by an agreement signed in Berlin, three powerful nations, two in Europe and one in Asia, joined themselves together in the threat that if the United States interfered with or blocked the expansion program of these three nations—a program aimed at world control—they would unite in ultimate action against the United States.

The Nazi masters of Germany have made it clear that they intend not only to dominate all life and thought in their own country, but also to enslave the whole of Europe, and then to use the resources of Europe to dominate the rest of the world.

Three weeks ago their leader stated, "There are two worlds that stand opposed to each other." Then in defiant reply to his opponents, he said this: "Others are correct when they say: 'With this world we cannot ever reconcile ourselves.'... I can beat any other power in the world." So said the leader of the Nazis.

In other words, the Axis not merely admits but proclaims that there can be no ultimate peace between their philosophy of government and our philosophy of government.

In view of the nature of this undeniable threat, it can be asserted, properly and categorically, that the United States has no right or reason to encourage talk of peace until the day shall come when there is a clear intention on the part of the aggressor nations to abandon all thought of dominating or conquering the world.

At this moment, the forces of the states that are leagued against all peoples who live in freedom are being held away from our shores. The Germans and Italians are being blocked on the other side of the Atlantic by the British, and by the Greeks, and by thousands of soldiers and sailors who were able to escape from subjugated countries. The Japanese are being engaged in Asia by the Chinese in another great defense.

In the Pacific is our fleet.

Some of our people like to believe that wars in Europe and Asia are of no concern to us. But it is a matter of most vital concern to us that European and Asiatic war-makers should not gain control of the oceans which lead to this hemisphere.

One hundred and seventeen years ago the Monroe Doctrine was conceived by our Government as a measure of defense in the face of a threat against this hemisphere by an alliance in continental Europe. Thereafter, we stood on guard in the Atlantic, with the British as neighbors. There was no treaty. There was no "unwritten agreement."

Yet, there was the feeling, proven correct by history, that we as neighbors could settle any disputes in peaceful fashion. The fact is that during the whole of this time the Western Hemisphere has remained free from aggression from Europe or from Asia.

Does anyone seriously believe that we need to fear attack while a free Britain remains our most powerful naval neighbor in the Atlantic? Does any one seriously believe, on the other hand, that we could rest easy if the Axis powers were our neighbor there?

If Great Britain goes down, the Axis powers will control the continents of Europe, Asia, Africa, Australasia, and the high seas—and

354

they will be in a position to bring enormous military and naval resources against this hemisphere. It is no exaggeration to say that all of us in the Americas would be living at the point of a gun—a gun loaded with explosive bullets, economic as well as military.

We should enter upon a new and terrible era in which the whole world, our hemisphere included, would be run by threats of brute force. To survive in such a world, we would have to convert ourselves permanently into a militaristic power on the basis of [a] war economy.

Some of us like to believe that even if Great Britain falls, we are still safe, because of the broad expanse of the Atlantic and of the Pacific.

But the width of these oceans is not what it was in the days of clipper ships. At one point between Africa and Brazil the distance is less than from Washington to Denver—five hours for the latest type of bomber. And at the north of the Pacific Ocean, America and Asia almost touch each other.

Even today we have planes which could fly from the British Isles to New England and back without refueling. And the range of the modern bomber is ever being increased. . . .

II

No Escape from Danger

Frankly and definitely there is danger ahead—danger against which we must prepare. But we well know that we cannot escape danger, or the fear of it, by crawling into bed and pulling the covers over our heads.

Some nations of Europe were bound by solemn non-intervention pacts with Germany. Other nations were assured by Germany that they need never fear invasion. Non-intervention pact or not, the fact remains that they were attacked, overrun, and thrown into the modern form of slavery at an hour's notice or even without any notice at all. As an exiled leader of one of these nations said to me the other day: "The notice was a minus quantity. It was given to my government two hours after German troops had poured into my country in a hundred places."

The fate of these nations tells us what it means to live at the point of a Nazi gun.

The Nazis have justified such actions by various pious frauds. One of these frauds is the claim that they are occupying a nation for the purpose of "restoring order." Another is that they are occupying or controlling a nation on the excuse that they are "protecting it" against the aggression of somebody else.

For example, Germany has said that she was occupying Belgium to save the Belgians from the British. Would she hesitate to say to any South American country, "We are occupying you to protect you from aggression by the United States"?

Belgium today is being used as an invasion base against Britain, now fighting for its life. Any South American country, in Nazi hands, would always constitute a jumping-off place for German attack on any one of the other republics of this hemisphere.

Analyze for yourselves the future of two other places even nearer to Germany if the Nazis won. Could Ireland hold out? Would Irish freedom be permitted as an amazing exception in an unfree world? Or the islands of the Azores which still fly the flag of Portugal after five centuries? We think of Hawaii as an outpost of defense in the Pacific. Yet, the Azores are closer to our shores in the Atlantic than Hawaii is on the other side. . . .

The experience of the past two years has proven beyond doubt that no nation can appease the Nazis. No man can tame a tiger into a kitten by stroking it. There can be no appeasement with ruthlessness. There can be no reasoning with an incendiary bomb. We know now that a nation can have peace with the Nazis only at the price of total surrender.

Oswald Garrison Villard, pacifist and publisher of the liberal magazine *The Nation*, urges American neutrality in European disputes at an early anti-war rally in April 1935.

Even the people of Italy have been forced to become accomplices of the Nazis; but at this moment they do not know how soon they will be embraced to death by their allies.

The American appeasers ignore the warning to be found in the fate of Austria, Czechoslovakia, Poland, Norway, Belgium, the Netherlands, Denmark, and France. They tell you that the Axis powers are going to win anyway; that all this bloodshed in the world could be saved; and that the United States might just as well throw its influence into the scale of a dictated peace, and get the best out of it that we can.

They call it a "negotiated peace." Nonsense! Is it a negotiated peace if a gang of outlaws surrounds your community and on threat of extermination makes you pay tribute to save your own skins?

Such a dictated peace would be no peace at all. It would be only another armistice, leading to the most gigantic armament race and the most devastating trade wars in history. And in these contests the Americas would offer the only real resistance to the Axis powers.

With all their vaunted efficiency and parade of pious purpose in this war, there are still in their background the concentration camp and the servants of God in chains.

The history of recent years proves that shootings and chains and concentration camps are not simply the transient tools but the very altars of modern dictatorships. They may talk of a "new order" in the world, but what they have in mind is but a revival of the oldest and the worst tyranny. In that there is no liberty, no religion, no hope.

The proposed "new order" is the very opposite of a United States of Europe or a United States of Asia. It is not a government based upon the consent of the governed. It is not a union of ordinary, self-respecting men and women to protect themselves and their freedom and their dignity from oppression. It is an unholy alliance of power and pelf to dominate and enslave the human race.

The British people are conducting an active war against this unholy alliance. Our own future security is greatly dependent on the outcome of that fight. Our ability to "keep out of war" is going to be affected by that outcome.

III

Avoid War through Aid

Thinking in terms of today and tomorrow, I make the direct statement to the American people that there is far less chance of the United States getting into war if we do all we can now to support the nations defending themselves against attack by the Axis than if we acquiesce in their defeat, submit tamely to an Axis victory, and wait our turn to be the object of attack in another war later on.

If we are to be completely honest with ourselves, we must admit there is risk in *any* course we may take. But I deeply believe that the great majority of our people agree that the course that I advocate involves the least risk now and the greatest hope for world peace in the future.

The people of Europe who are defending themselves do not ask us to do their fighting. They ask us for the implements of war, the planes, the tanks, the guns, the freighters, which will enable them to fight for their liberty and our security. Emphatically we must get these weapons to them in sufficient volume and quickly enough, so that we and our children will be saved the agony and suffering of war which others have had to endure.

Let not defeatists tell us that it is too late. It will never be earlier. Tomorrow will be later than today.

Certain facts are self-evident.

In a military sense Great Britain and the British Empire are today the spearhead of resistance to world conquest. They are putting up a fight which will live forever in the story of human gallantry.

There is no demand for sending an American Expeditionary Force outside our own borders. There is no intention by any member of your Government to send such a force. You can, therefore, nail any talk about sending armies to Europe as deliberate untruth.

Our national policy is not directed toward war. Its sole purpose is to keep war away from our country and our people.

Democracy's fight against world conquest is being greatly aided, and must be more greatly aided, by the rearmament of the United States and by sending every ounce and every ton of munitions and supplies that we can possibly spare to help the defenders who are in the front lines. It is no more unneutral for us to do that than it is for Sweden, Russia, and other nations near Germany to send steel and ore and oil and other war materials into Germany every day.

We are planning our own defense with the utmost urgency; and in its vast scale we must integrate the war needs of Britain and the other free nations resisting aggression.

This is not a matter of sentiment or of controversial personal opinion. It is a matter of realistic military policy, based on the advice of our military experts who are in close touch with existing warfare. These military and naval experts and the members of the Congress and the administration have a single-minded purpose—the defense of the United States. . . .

IV
Organizing Production Efforts

Nine days ago I announced the setting up of a more effective organization to direct our gigantic efforts to increase the production of munitions. The appropriation of vast sums of money and a well-coordinated executive direction of our defense efforts are not in themselves enough. Guns, planes, and ships have to be built in the factories and arsenals of America. They have to be produced by workers and managers and engineers with the aid of machines, which in turn have to be built by hundreds of thousands of workers throughout the land.

In this great work there has been splendid cooperation between the Government and industry and labor.

American industrial genius, unmatched throughout the world in the solution of production problems, has been called upon to bring its resources and talents into action. Manufacturers of watches, of farm implements, linotypes, cash registers, automobiles, sewing machines, lawn mowers, and locomotives are now making fuses, bomb-packing crates, telescope mounts, shells, pistols, and tanks.

But all our present efforts are not enough. We must have more ships, more guns, more planes—more of everything. This can only be accomplished if we discard the notion of "business as usual." This job cannot be done merely by superimposing on the existing productive facilities the added requirements for defense.

Our defense efforts must not be blocked by those who fear the future consequences of surplus plant capacity. The possible consequences of failure of our defense efforts now are much more to be feared.

After the present needs of our defense are past, a proper handling of the country's peacetime needs will require all of the new productive capacity—if not more.

No pessimistic policy about the future of America shall delay the immediate expansion of those industries essential to defense.

I want to make it clear that it is the purpose of the Nation to build now with all possible speed every machine and arsenal and factory that we need to manufacture our defense material. We have the men, the skill, the wealth, and above all, the will.

I am confident that if and when production of consumer or luxury goods in certain industries requires the use of machines and raw materials essential for defense purposes, then such production must yield to our primary and compelling purpose.

I appeal to the owners of plants, to the managers, to the workers, to our own Government employees, to put every ounce of effort into producing these munitions swiftly and without stint. And with this appeal I give you the pledge that all of us who are officers of your Government will devote ourselves to the same wholehearted extent to the great task which lies ahead.

As planes and ships and guns and shells are produced, your Government, with its defense experts, can then determine how best to use them to defend this hemisphere. The decision as to how much shall be sent abroad and how much shall remain at home must be made on the basis of our over-all military necessities.

We must be the great arsenal of democracy. For us this is an emergency as serious as war itself. We must apply ourselves to our task with the same resolution, the same sense of urgency, the same spirit of patriotism and sacrifice, as we should show were we at war.

Lindbergh: Avoid Defeat through True Neutrality (1941)

President Roosevelt's reactions to continued German successes caused many Americans to believe the United States was moving toward an open alliance with Great Britain. One of those who protested most vehemently against any American involvement in a European war was Charles Lindbergh, who in 1927 became the first person to fly the Atlantic Ocean alone (see Reading 240). Lindbergh spoke for the American First Committee, the most influential of several antiwar groups.

From New York Times, *April 24, 1941. © 1941 by the New York Times Company. Reprinted by permission. Subheadings added by the editors.*

I
The United States and Great Britain

I know I will be severely criticized by the interventionists in America when I say we should not enter a war unless we have a reasonable chance of winning. That, they will claim, is far too materialistic a viewpoint. They will advance again the same arguments that were used to persuade France to declare war against Germany in 1939. But I do not believe that our American ideals, and our way of life, will gain through an unsuccessful war. And I know that the United States is not prepared to wage war in Europe successfully at this time. We are no better prepared today than France was when the interventionists in Europe persuaded her to attack the Siegfried Line.

APPEASING A POLECAT

The America First Committee, a leading antiwar group, and its leaders, Colonel Charles Lindbergh and Senator Burton Wheeler, are ridiculed in this cartoon, first published in the pro-Allied Philadelphia *Record* in August 1941.

I have said before, and I will say again, that I believe it will be a tragedy to the entire world if the British Empire collapses. That is one of the main reasons why I opposed this war before it was declared, and why I have constantly advocated a negotiated peace. I did not feel that England and France had a reasonable chance of winning. France has now been defeated; and, despite the propaganda and confusion of recent months, it is now obvious that England is losing the war. I believe this is realized even by the British Government. But they have one last desperate plan remaining. They hope that they may be able to persuade us to send another American Expeditionary Force to Europe, and to share with England militarily, as well as financially, the fiasco of this war.

I do not blame England for this hope, or for asking for our assistance. But we now know that she declared a war under circumstances which led to the defeat of every nation that sided with her from Poland to Greece. We know that in the desperation of war England promised to all those nations armed assistance that she could not send. We know that she misinformed them, as she has misinformed us, concerning her state of preparation, her military strength, and the progress of the war.

In time of war, truth is always replaced by propaganda. I do not believe we should be too quick to criticize the actions of a belligerent nation. There is always the question whether we, ourselves, would do better under similar circumstances. But we in this country have a right to think of the welfare of America first, just as the people in England thought first of their own country when they encouraged the smaller nations of Europe to fight against hopeless odds. When England asks us to enter this war, she is considering her own future, and that of her empire. In making our reply, I believe we should consider the future of the United States and that of the Western Hemisphere.

It is not only our right, but is our obligation as American citizens to look at this war objectively and to weigh our chances for success if we should enter it. I have attempted to do this, especially from the standpoint of aviation; and I have been forced to the conclusion that we cannot win this war for England, regardless of how much assistance we extend.

I ask you to look at the map of Europe today and see if you can suggest any way in which we could win this war if we entered it. Suppose we had a large army in America, trained and equipped. Where would we send it to fight? The campaigns of the war show only too clearly how difficult it is to force a landing, or to maintain any army, on a hostile coast.

Suppose we took our Navy from the Pacific, and used it to convoy British shipping. That would not win the war for England. It would at best permit her to exist under the constant bombing of the German air fleet. Suppose we had an air force that we could send to Europe. Where could it operate? Some of our squadrons might be based in the British Isles; but it is physically impossible to base enough aircraft in the British Isles alone to equal in strength the aircraft that can be based on the Continent of Europe.

I have asked these questions on the supposition that we had in existence an Army and an air force large enough and well enough equipped to send to Europe; and that we would dare to remove our Navy from the Pacific. Even on this basis, I do not see how we could invade the Continent of Europe successfully as long as all of the Continent and most of Asia is under Axis domination. But the fact is that none of these suppositions are correct. We have only a one-ocean Navy. Our Army is still untrained and inadequately equipped for foreign war. Our air force is deplorably lacking in modern fighting planes.

When these facts are cited, the interventionists shout that we are defeatists, that we are undermining the principles of democracy, and that we are giving comfort to Germany by talking about our military weakness. But everything I mention here has been published in our newspapers, and in the reports of congressional hearings in Washington. Our military position is well known to the governments of Europe and Asia. Why, then, should it not be brought to the attention of our own people?

I say it is the interventionist in America, as it was in England and in France, who gives comfort to the enemy. I say it is they who are undermining the principles of democracy when they demand that we take a course to which more than 80 percent of our citizens are opposed. I charge them with being the real defeatists, for their policy has led to the defeat of every country that followed their advice since this war began. There is no better way to give comfort to an enemy than to divide the people of a nation over the issue of foreign war. There is no shorter road to defeat than by entering a war with inadequate preparation. Every nation that has adopted the interventionist policy of depending on some one else for its own defense has met with nothing but defeat and failure.

When history is written, the responsibility for the downfall of the democracies of Europe will rest squarely upon the shoulders of the interventionists who led their nations into war uninformed and unprepared. With their shouts of defeatism, and their disdain of reality, they have already sent countless thousands of young men to death in Europe. From the campaign of Poland to that of Greece, their prophecies have been false and their policies have failed. Yet these are the people who are calling us defeatists in America today. And they have led this country, too, to the verge of war.

II

Why We Should Not Intervene

There are many such interventionists in America, but there are more people among us of a different type. That is why you and I are assembled here tonight. There is a policy open to this nation that will lead to success—a policy that leaves us free to follow our own way of life, and to develop our own way of life, and to develop our own civilization. It is not a new and untried idea. It was advocated by Washington. It was incorporated in the Monroe Doctrine. Under its guidance, the United States became the greatest nation in the world.

It is based upon the belief that the security of a nation lies in the strength and character of its own people. It recommends the maintenance of armed forces sufficient to defend this hemisphere from attack by any combination of foreign powers. It demands faith in an independent American destiny. This is the policy of the America First Committee today. It is a policy not of isolation, but of independence; not of defeat, but of courage. It is a policy that led this nation to success during the most trying years of our history, and it is a policy that will lead us to success again.

We have weakened ourselves for many months, and still worse, we have divided our own people by this dabbling in Europe's wars. While we should have been concentrating on American defense we have been forced to argue over foreign quarrels. We must turn our eyes and our faith back to our own country before it is too late. And when we do this, a different vista opens before us. Practically every difficulty we would face in invading Europe becomes an asset to us in defending America. Our enemy, and not we, would then have the problem of transporting millions of troops across the ocean and landing them on a hostile shore. They, and not we, would have to furnish the convoys to transport guns and trucks and munitions and fuel across three thousand miles of water. Our battleships and submarines would then be fighting close to their home bases. We would then do the bombing from the air and the torpedoing at sea. And if any part of an enemy convoy should ever pass our Navy and our air force, they would still be faced with the guns of our coast artillery and behind them the divisions of our Army.

The United States is better situated from a military standpoint than any other nation in the world. Even in our present condition of unpreparedness no foreign power is in a position to invade us today. If we concentrate on our own defenses and build the strength that this nation should maintain, no foreign army will ever attempt to land on American shores.

War is not inevitable for this country. Such a claim is defeatism in the true sense. No one can make us fight abroad unless we ourselves are willing to do so. No one will attempt to fight us here if we arm ourselves as a great nation should be armed. Over a hundred million people in this nation are opposed to entering the war. If the principles of democracy mean anything at all, that is reason enough for us to stay out. If we are forced into a war against the wishes of an overwhelming majority of our people, we will have proved democracy such a failure at home that there will be little use of fighting for it abroad.

The time has come when those of us who believe in an independent American destiny must band together and organize for strength. We have been led toward war by a minority of our people. This minority has power. It has influence. It has a loud voice. But it does not represent the American people. During the last several years I have traveled over this country from one end to the other. I have talked to many hundreds of men and women, and I have letters from tens of thousands more, who feel the same way as you and I.

Most of these people have no influence or power. Most of them have no means of expressing their convictions, except by their vote which has always been against this war. They are the citizens who have had to work too hard at their daily jobs to organize political meetings. Hitherto, they have relied upon their vote to express their feelings; but now they find that it is hardly remembered except in the oratory of a political campaign. These people—the majority of hardworking American citizens, are with us. They are the true strength of our country. And they are beginning to realize, as you and I, that there are times when we must sacrifice our normal interests in life in order to insure the safety and the welfare of our nation.

Such a time has come. Such a crisis is here. That is why the America First Committee has been formed—to give voice to the people who have no newspaper, or newsreel, or radio station at their command; to the people who must do the paying, and the fighting, and the dying if this country enters the war.

Whether or not we do enter the war rests upon the shoulders of you in this audience, upon us here on this platform, upon meetings of this kind that are being held by Americans in every section of the United States today. It depends upon the action we take, and the courage we show at this time. If you believe in an independent destiny for America, if you believe that this country should not enter the war in Europe, we ask you to join the America First Committee in its stand. We ask you to share our faith in the ability of this nation to defend itself, to develop its own civilization, and to contribute to the progress of mankind in a more constructive and intelligent way than has yet been found by the warring nations of Europe. We need your support, and we need it now. The time to act is here.

Beginning of an Undeclared Naval War
(1941)

World War II had been going on for two years when President Roosevelt made the following radio address on September 11, 1941. A few months earlier Nazi Germany had taken on a major new foe when it invaded the Soviet Union. Even before the latest German move the United States had begun to prepare militarily. In September 1940 Congress approved the Selective Service Act, America's first peacetime program of compulsory military service. In March 1941 Congress, at the President's urgent request, approved the so-called Lend-Lease Act, in which the United States in effect agreed to furnish a financially bankrupt Great Britain the war supplies needed to continue fighting. In June 1941 Roosevelt promised Lend-Lease aid to the hard-pressed Russians. At about the same time American warships extended patrols as far as Iceland, thus protecting merchant ships carrying supplies across the Atlantic. This was done on the grounds that American responsibility for keeping war away from the Western Hemisphere entitled the United States to protect shipping that far. The result was not surprising: a German submarine attacked an American destroyer. In this report on the event, President Roosevelt did not mention that the destroyer had been tracking the submarine and reporting its position to British warships. The Navy Department announced this fact five weeks later.

From *U.S. Department of State Bulletin*, V (1941), pp. 193–194, 196.

The Navy Department of the United States has reported to me that on the morning of September fourth the United States destroyer *Greer*, proceeding in full daylight towards Iceland, had reached a point southeast of Greenland. She was carrying American mail to Iceland. She was flying the American flag. Her identity as an American ship was unmistakable.

She was then and there attacked by a submarine. Germany admits that it was a German submarine. The submarine deliberately fired a torpedo at the *Greer,* followed later by another torpedo attack. In spite of what Hitler's propaganda bureau has invented, and in spite of what any American obstructionist organization may prefer to believe, I tell you the blunt fact that the German submarine fired first upon this American destroyer without warning, and with deliberate design to sink her.

Our destroyer, at the time, was in waters which the Government of the United States had declared to be waters of self-defense—surrounding outposts of American protection in the Atlantic.

In the north, outposts have been established by us in Iceland, Greenland, Labrador, and Newfoundland. Through these waters there pass many ships of many flags. They bear food and other supplies to civilians; and they bear matériel of war, for which the people of the United States are spending billions of dollars, and which, by congressional action, they have declared to be essential for the defense of their own land.

The United States destroyer, when attacked, was proceeding on a legitimate mission. . . .

A few months ago an American-flag merchant ship, the *Robin Moor,* was sunk by a Nazi submarine in the middle of the South Atlantic, under circumstances violating long-established international law and every principle of humanity. The passengers and the crew were forced into open boats hundreds of miles from land, in direct violation of international agreements signed by the Government of Germany. No apology, no allegation of mistake, no offer of reparations has come from the Nazi Government.

In July 1941, an American battleship in North American waters was followed by a submarine which for a long time sought to maneuver itself into a position of attack. The periscope of the submarine was clearly seen. No British or American submarines were within hundreds of miles of this spot at the time, so the nationality of the submarine is clear.

Five days ago a United States Navy ship on patrol picked up three survivors of an American-owned ship operating under the flag of our sister Republic of Panama—the S.S. *Sessa.* On August seventeenth, she had been first torpedoed without warning and then shelled, near Greenland, while carrying civilian supplies to Iceland. It is feared that the other members of her crew have been drowned. In view of the established presence of German submarines in this vicinity, there can be no reasonable doubt as to the identity of the attacker.

Five days ago, another United States merchant ship, the *Steel Seafarer,* was sunk by a German aircraft in the Red Sea two hundred and twenty miles south of Suez. She was bound for an Egyptian port.

Four of the vessels sunk or attacked flew the American flag and were clearly identifiable. Two of these ships were warships of the American Navy. In the fifth case, the vessel sunk clearly carried the flag of Panama. . . .

These Nazi submarines and raiders are the rattlesnakes of the Atlantic. They are a menace to the free pathways of the high seas. They are a challenge to our sovereignty. They hammer at our most precious rights when they attack ships of the American flag—symbols of our independence, our freedom, our very life.

It is clear to all Americans that the time has come when the Americas themselves must now be defended. A continuation of attacks in our own waters, or in waters which could be used for further and greater attacks on us, will inevitably weaken American ability to repel Hitlerism.

Do not let us split hairs. Let us not ask ourselves whether the Americas should begin to defend themselves after the fifth attack, or the tenth attack, or the twentieth attack.

The time for active defense is now. . . .

My obligation as President is historic; it is clear; it is inescapable.

It is no act of war on our part when we decide to protect the seas which are vital to American defense. The aggression is not ours. Ours is solely defense.

But let this warning be clear. From now on, if German or Italian vessels of war enter the waters the protection of which is necessary for American defense they do so at their own peril.

The orders which I have given as Commander-in-Chief to the United States Army and Navy are to carry out that policy—at once.

The sole responsibility rests upon Germany. There will be no shooting unless Germany continues to seek it.

That is my obvious duty in this crisis. That is the clear right of this sovereign nation. That is the only step possible, if we would keep tight the wall of defense which we are pledged to maintain around this Western Hemisphere.

Reading 307

Public Sentiment: Anti-Nazi but Anti-War
(1940–1941)

Americans had ample time to react to the war in Europe before being forced into it by the effects of the Japanese attack on Pearl Harbor on December 7, 1941. The following public opinion polls reveal American sentiments in the last months of peace.

From Gallup and Fortune polls, *The Public Opinion Quarterly*, VI (1942), pp. 149–151, 161–164.

I

U.S. Participation

Do you think the U.S. will go into the war in Europe sometime before it is over, or do you think we will stay out of the war? (Dec. 17, '41—AIPO)*

TREND:	MAY 1940	NOVEMBER 1941
Would go to war sooner or later with Germany	62%	85%
Would not or undecided	38	15

*This poll was taken before the outbreak of war on December 7, 1941.—Eds.

> Hollywood attacked Hitler's Germany in *The Mortal Storm* (1940), a movie the reviewer of the *New York Times* described as "blistering anti-Nazi propaganda." In this scene, a Nazi storm trooper (played by Ward Bond) threatens two members (played by Maria Ouspenskaya and Margaret Sullavan) of the family of a German-Jewish professor who had opposed Nazi efforts to take control of his university.

Which one of the following statements most nearly represents your attitude toward the present war? (Dec. '41—FOR.)

	OCTOBER SURVEY	DECEMBER SURVEY
Those who think this is our war are wrong, and the people of this country should resist to the last ditch any move that would lead us any further toward war	17.4% ⎫	12.7% ⎫
A lot of mistakes have brought us close to a war that isn't ours, but now that it's done we should support in full the government's program	23.1 ⎭ 40.5%	27.5 ⎭ 40.2%
While at first it looked as though this was not our war, it now looks as though we should back England until Hitler is beaten	40.7% ⎫	39.0% ⎫
It is our war as well as England's, and we should have been in there fighting with her before this	10.7 ⎭ 51.4%	15.0 ⎭ 54.0%
Don't know	8.1	5.8

Would you be willing to see our navy used if necessary? Our air force? Our army? (Dec. '41—FOR.)

Trend: Asked of the 27.5% who think the government program should be supported even if the war is not ours and the 39% who think we should now back England to beat Hitler.

	NAVY		AIR FORCE		ARMY	
	OCTOBER	DECEMBER	OCTOBER	DECEMBER	OCTOBER	DECEMBER
Yes	81.4%	90.8%	79.2%	89.5%	67.6%	78.4%
No	11.1	5.8	12.6	7.0	22.4	16.9
Don't know	7.5	3.4	8.2	3.5	10.0	4.7

Which of these two things do you think is the more important, that this country keep out of war, or that Germany be defeated? (Oct. 4, '41—AIPO)

Of those expressing an opinion		
That Germany be defeated	70%	
That U.S. stay out	30	
By parties	THAT GERMANY BE DEFEATED	THAT U.S. STAY OUT
Democrats	77%	23%
Republicans	64	36
By sections		
New England and Middle Atlantic	70%	30%
East Central	63	37
West Central	64	36
South	88	12
West	69	31
By income		
Upper income	76%	24%
Middle income	74	26
Lower income	65	35

Which of these two things do you think is the more important—that this country keep out of war, or that Germany be defeated? (Nov. 2, '41—AIPO)

	LABOR UNION MEMBERS	ENTIRE NATION
Keep out of war	34%	32%
Defeat Germany	66	68

Which of these two things do you think is more important—that Germany be defeated or that this country keep out of war? (Nov. 8, '41—AIPO)

	N.Y. CITY	15TH PENNSYLVANIA CONG. DIST.	ENTIRE NATION
Germany be defeated	54%	61%	68%
Stay out of war	46	39	32

Which of these two things do you think is the more important—that this country keep out of war, or that Germany be defeated? (Dec. 17, '41—AIPO)

TREND	DEFEAT GERMANY	STAY OUT
Dec. 1940	60%	40%
Jan. 1941	68	32
April	67	33
May	62	38
Oct.	70	30
Nov.	68	32
Dec. (before war)	68	32

II

Threat to United States

Which country is the greater threat to America's future—Germany or Japan? (Dec. 23, '41—AIPO)

Believe Germany the greater threat	64%
Believe Japan the greater threat	15

III

Aid to Britain

So far as you personally are concerned, do you think President Roosevelt has gone too far in his policies of helping Britain, or not far enough? (Oct. 8, '41—AIPO)

Too far	About right	Not far enough
27%	57%	16%

SECTIONAL ANALYSIS	TOO FAR	ABOUT RIGHT	NOT FAR ENOUGH
New England and Middle Atlantic	27%	55%	18%
East Central	34	51	15
West Central	31	59	10
South	14	61	25
Far West	24	62	14

TREND	TOO FAR	ABOUT RIGHT	NOT FAR ENOUGH
Today	27%	57%	16%
June	23	55	22
May	21	59	20

So far as you personally are concerned, do you think President Roosevelt has gone too far or not far enough in his policy of aiding Britain? (Nov. 2, '41—AIPO)

	LABOR UNION MEMBERS	ENTIRE NATION
Too far	27%	27%
About right	55	57
Not far enough	18	16

Should the Neutrality Act be changed to permit American merchant ships with American crews to carry war materials to Britain? (Nov. 5, '41—AIPO)

TREND	YES	NO	UNDECIDED
April	30%	61%	9%
Sept.	46	40	14
Early-Oct.	46	40	14
Mid-Oct.	54	37	9
Today	61	31	8

BY PARTIES	REPUBLICAN VOTERS		
	YES	NO	UNDECIDED
Mid-Oct.	49%	44%	7%
Today	59	34	7

	DEMOCRATIC VOTERS		
	YES	NO	UNDECIDED
Mid-Oct.	62%	28%	10%
Today	66	27	7

VOTE IN LEADING STATES			
	YES	NO	UNDECIDED
New York	61%	33%	6%
Penna.	62	32	6
Ill.	50	44	6
Ohio	50	38	12
Cal.	67	26	7

IV

Shooting on Sight

In general do you approve or disapprove of having the United States navy shoot at German submarines or warships on sight? (Oct. 2, '41—AIPO)

Approve 62% Disapprove 28% No opinion 10%

SECTIONAL VOTE	APPROVE SHOOT ON SIGHT	DISAPPROVE	UNDECIDED
New England and Mid Atlantic	61%	29%	10%
East Central	56	35	9
West Central	56	31	13
South	78	15	7
Far West	64	27	9

BY PARTIES	REPUBLICAN VOTERS	DEMOCRATIC VOTERS
Yes	56%	68%
No	36	22
Undecided	8	10

V

U.S. Participation

Should the United States enter the war now? (Oct. 4, '41—AIPO)

Of those expressing an opinion	
U.S. should enter war now	21%
U.S. should not enter war now	79

TOPIC 58

WAR WITH JAPAN: INEVITABLE RESULT OR DIPLOMATIC FAILURE?

The outbreak of any war opens the question of why it started. World War II is no exception. Since Japan chose to attack the United States in 1941, the question frequently is reduced to why the Japanese felt they had to do so. Did the United States constitute a serious threat to Japanese independence? Could Japan have achieved her foreign policy goals without active intervention by the United States? Did the United States misunderstand Japan's position or intentions? Did the United States provoke Japan? Historians are frequently faced with questions like these, and to answer them they must sift through both evidence and opinions. This topic explores both the rise of Japan as the leading military-industrial power of East Asia and the response of Americans to Japanese expansion. In the final two readings two students of the subject offer conflicting interpretations as to why disagreement between Japan and the United States turned into open warfare.

Reading 308

Japan: The First Modern Power in Asia

Historian James M. Powell narrates the rise of modern Japan, giving the necessary background for an understanding of Japanese-American relations in 1940 and 1941. It must be remembered that until the mid-nineteenth century Japan had been a feudal state isolated from the West. In 1905, its army and navy defeated Russian forces and displaced that nation as the dominant power in Northeast Asia.

From James M. Powell, *The Civilization of the West: A Brief Interpretation* (New York, 1967), pp. 490-492. Copyright © 1967 by James M. Powell. Subheadings added by the editors.

I

The New Japan, 1868-1931

Modernization had brought Japan the respect of the Western powers. Victory in the Russo-Japanese War [1904-1905] had taught them that Japan had ambitions of her own for the development of Asia not necessarily in agreement with those of the Europeans. Japanese entry into World War I had not received the enthusiastic support of England, who would have preferred to see Japan remain neutral in order to stabilize the political situation. England realized the nature of Japan's ambitions and had no desire to aid them. However, she was in too weak a position to prevent the Japanese from carrying out their decision.

The entry of Japan into World War I on the side of the allies was more than an opening toward possible imperial expansion. By this

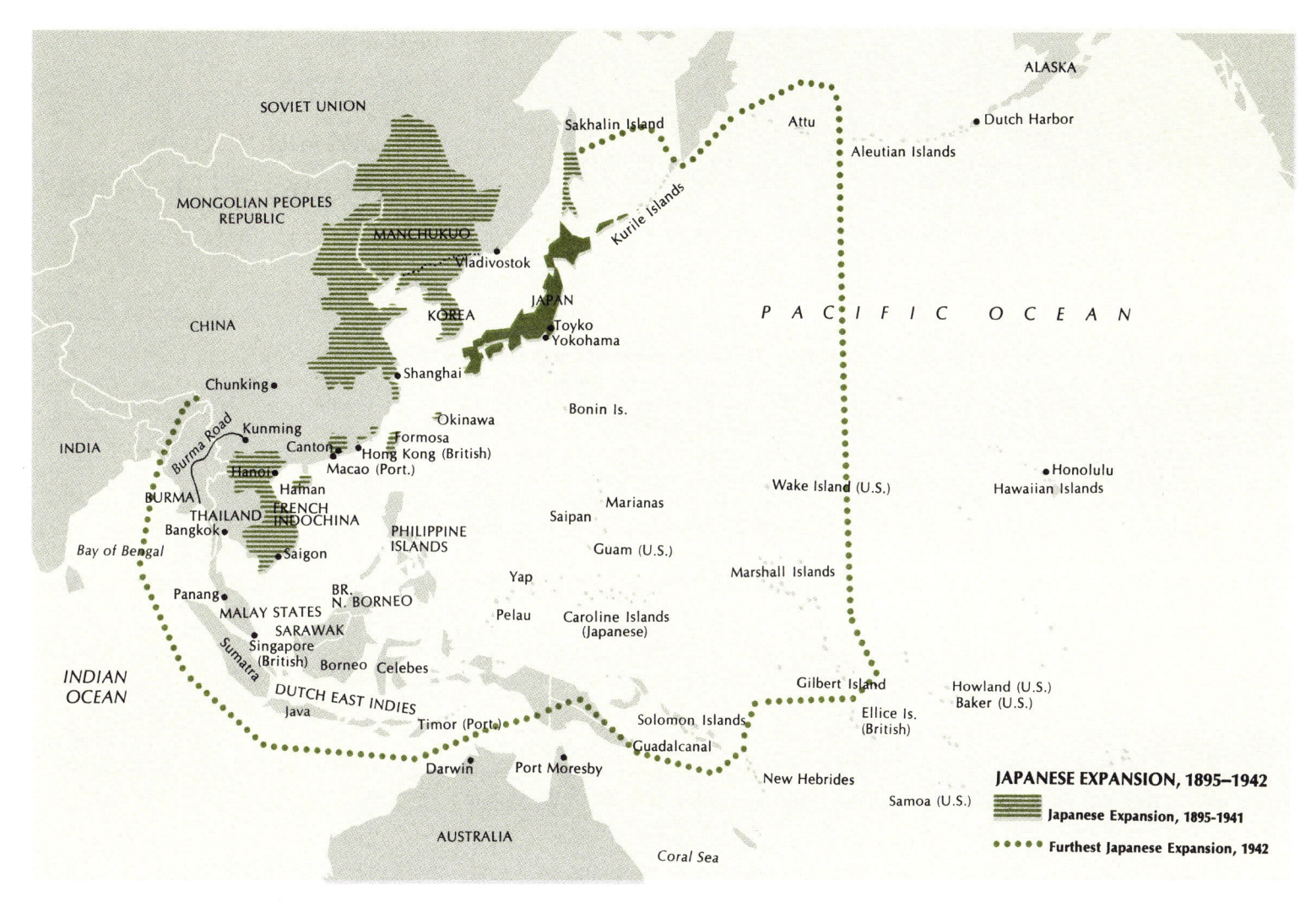

JAPANESE EXPANSION, 1895–1942

▨▨▨ Japanese Expansion, 1895-1941
••••• Furthest Japanese Expansion, 1942

avenue, the Japanese secured further recognition of their position as a major power, indeed the only major power in Asia. She had gone far toward achieving equality to the Western powers in foreign relations. But the war also offered a safe opportunity for expansion in China at German expense. As a result of the war, Japan secured Germany's former sphere of influence on the Shantung Peninsula, a very significant key to the control of north China.

During most of the twenties, Japan pressed its advantage against China with economic rather than political weapons. Her government was dominated by the conservative interests of "big business," who had no desire to fight a war that might interrupt the lucrative Chinese trade. However, reluctance to fight did not mean relaxation of the tactics of harassment that had characterized the Japanese policy toward the Republic of China since its founding. The Twenty-One Demands presented to General Yuan during World War I still formed the basic text for Japanese policy toward China; the main features of this plan were economic domination and political subservience.

Democracy had made no progress in Japan before World War II. The Japanese Parliament had no real control over the ministers of the government. The emperor had been reduced, after 1931, to the position of a mere figurehead, with the real power in the hands of a group of top-level generals and admirals. In the process of industrialization, Japan had followed the continental European model and allowed the development of huge cartels or monopolies. As a result great wealth was concentrated in the hands of Japan's leading industrialists. With their emphasis on the growth of industry, the Japanese had permitted the industrialists a major voice in all phases of government policy. True, industry had prospered, but Japan remained a tightly controlled society ruled by a relatively small group of individuals. Under these circumstances, parliamentary government in Japan had never been anything but a façade. With the rise to power of the military, that façade remained.

II

Japan Expands

The increasing militarism of the Japanese during the thirties paralleled the "tough" policy adopted by Hitler in Germany. It is hardly surprising, therefore, to find these two powers drawn closer during the years after 1935. The mounting criticism of Japan in Europe and America promoted the alliance of Germany and Japan.

The first big outbreak of Japanese aggression during the thirties occurred in Manchuria. This outer province of China lay along the Russia border and was only loosely controlled by the republican government. Japan took advantage of several minor incidents in 1931 to take over the area. In all probability, the Japanese had manufactured most of the incidents that led to their invasion. In place of the Chinese warlord who had ruled the region for China, the Japanese established a puppet Manchu emperor in Manchuria, now called Manchukuo. This puppet regime hung over the Chinese as a threat of impending doom at the hands of Japan. The attack on Manchuria lasted but a few months. It aroused considerable public opinion against Japan in the West, but brought no sanctions. Neither the United States nor England pressed hard for effective measures to force Japan to return the territory to China. The League of Nations debated a resolution to condemn Japan for more than two years before finally voting to condemn the action. By that time, the League itself was in its death agony. Japan simply helped to hasten the demise of that unfortunate body by her withdrawal. Failure to censure Japanese invasion of Manchuria and effectively to control aggression there was a prelude to later failures in Ethiopia and in the withdrawal of Nazi Germany. The League, which the American Senate had steadfastly rejected, had once promised the hope of world peace. By the mid-thirties, this slim reed was proving how poorly the victors of World War I had worked in their effort to create an institution for peace.

Japanese success in Manchuria opened the door to further incidents on Chinese soil. During most of the thirties, when the Chiang government was trying to build a modern Chinese state, it had to cope with continued Japanese harassment. In 1937, the Japanese gave up all pretence and invaded China. The first act of World War II had begun in Asia, though few at the time were willing to see the Chinese-Japanese War other than as a distant struggle between alien peoples.

Ambassador Grew Advocates a Hard Line
(1940)

When European control of Southeast Asia was noticeably weakened because of Germany's military victories over France and The Netherlands in 1940, the United States government began to eye Japan nervously. Japanese industry, and thus its military might, was totally dependent on natural resources imported from abroad. The oil-rich Netherlands East Indies, French Indo-China, with its large output of rubber and rice, and British Malaya, with its tin mines, seemed ripe for conquest by Japanese armed forces, now the most powerful in Asia. In September 1940 Joseph C. Grew (1880–1965), United States Ambassador to Japan, offered an evaluation of Japanese actions and possible American reactions for his superiors in Washington.

From U.S. Department of State, *Peace and War: United States Foreign Policy, 1931–1941* (Washington, D. C., 1943), pp. 569–572.

I

Avenues Open to Japan

Whatever the intentions of the present Japanese Government may be there cannot be any doubt that the military and other elements in Japan see in the present world situation a "golden opportunity" to carry their dreams of expansion into effect; the German victories, like strong wine, have gone to their heads; they have believed implicitly until recently in Great Britain's defeat; they have argued that the war will probably be ended

Chinese troops crouch behind makeshift barricades thrown up across a Shanghai street in a futile attempt to prevent the Japanese conquest of the city in 1937. By 1941 the Japanese army had occupied the entire coastal region of China and driven deep into the interior. Yet after four years of war Japan was still unable to destroy effective Chinese resistance, partly because of British and American support of Generalissimo Chiang Kai-shek and his government.

in a quick German victory and that Japan's position in Greater East Asia should be consolidated while Germany is still agreeable and before Japan might be robbed of her far-flung control in the Far East by the eventual hypothetical strengthening of the German naval power; although carefully watching the attitude of the United States they have discounted effective opposition on our part. It has been and is doubtful that the saner heads in and out of the government will be able to control these elements.

However, now a gradual change can be sensed in the outburst of exhilaration which greeted the inception of the new government. It is beginning to be seen by the Japanese Government, the army, the navy, and the public, that Germany may not defeat Great Britain after all, a possibility which I have constantly emphasized in the plainest language to my Japanese contacts and now, in addition to that dawning realization, they see that Britain and the United States are steadily drawing closer together in mutual defense measures with the American support of the British fleet by the transfer of fifty destroyers and with our acquisition of naval bases in British Atlantic possessions. Reports are being heard of our rapid construction of a two-ocean Navy and of our consideration of strengthening our Pacific naval bases and they even hear rumors that we will eventually use Singapore. Japanese consciousness is logically being affected by these rumors and developments. They tend on the one hand to emphasize the potential danger facing Japan from the United States and Great Britain eventually acting together in positive action (Japan has long appreciated the danger of combined Anglo-American measures as evidenced by the efforts to avoid the simultaneous irritation of these two countries) or from the United States acting alone. They furnish cogent arguments on the other hand for those Japanese elements who seek political and economic security by securing raw material sources and markets entirely within Japanese control. In regard to Germany, it is beginning to be questioned by the Japanese whether even a victorious Germany would not furnish a new hazard to their program of expansion both in China and in their advance to the south. Meanwhile, an uncertain factor in their calculations is always the future attitude and position of Russia. They are beginning to be concerned by these various considerations. High-powered diplomacy, particularly in the Dutch East Indies, will continue. But the fact that the Japanese military forces could be restrained even temporarily by the government from their plans for a headlong invasion of Indo-China denotes a degree of caution which I have no doubt was influenced partially at least by the American attitude. Until the world situation, particularly the position of the United States, becomes clearer the "nibbling policy" appears likely to continue.

I have expressed the opinion in previous communications that American-Japanese relations would be set on a downward curve if sanctions were applied by the United States. It is true that measures are now justified by our new program of national preparedness which need not fall within the category of outright sanctions. On the other hand, the probability must be contemplated that drastic embargoes on such important products as oil, of which a super-abundance is known to be possessed by the United States, would be interpreted by the people and government of Japan as actual sanctions and some form of retaliation might and probably would follow. The risks would depend not so much upon the careful calculations of the Japanese Government as upon the uncalculating "do or die" temper of the army and navy should they impute to the United States the responsibility for the failure of their plans for expansion. It may be that such retaliation would take the form of counter-measures by the government but it would be more likely that it would be some sudden stroke by the navy or army without the prior authorization or knowledge of the government. These dangers constitute an imponderable element which cannot be weighed with assurance at any given moment. However, it would be short sighted to deny their existence or to formulate policy and adopt measures without fully considering these potential risks and determining the wisdom of facing them squarely.

II

The Status Quo

In the following observations I am giving careful consideration to both fundamental purposes of my mission, namely the advancement and protection of American interests and the maintenance of good relations between Japan and the United States. Should these two fundamental purposes conflict the preponderant emphasis to be placed on either one is a matter of high policy which is not within my competency. My object is only to set before the Washington administration the outstanding factors in the situation as viewed from the standpoint of this embassy. Since I have set forth carefully the inevitable hazards which a strong policy involves, I now turn respectfully to the hazards involved in the policy of *laissez faire*.

It is impossible in a discussion of the specific question of relations between the United States and Japan to view that problem in its proper perspective unless it is considered part and parcel of the world problem which presents in brief the following aspects: (a) Britain and America are the leaders of a large world-wide group of English-speaking peoples which stand for a "way of life" which today is being threatened appallingly by Italy, Germany, and Japan. . . . The avowed purpose of these powers is the imposition of their will upon conquered peoples by force of arms. In general, the uses of diplomacy are bankrupt in attempting to deal with such powers. Occasionally diplomacy may retard, but it cannot stem the tide effectively. Only by force or the display of force can these powers be prevented from attaining their objectives. Japan is today one of the predatory powers; having submerged all ethical and moral sense she has become unashamedly and frankly opportunist, at every turn seeking to profit through the weakness of others. American interests in the Pacific are definitely threatened by her policy of southward expansion, which is a thrust at the British Empire in the east. (b) Admittedly America's security has depended in a measure upon the British fleet, which has been in turn and could only have been supported by the British Empire. (c) If the support of the British Empire in this her hour of travail is conceived to be in our interest, and most emphatically do I so conceive it, we must strive by every means to preserve the status quo in the Pacific, at least until the war in Europe has been won or lost. This cannot be done, in my opinion, nor can we further protect our interests properly and adequately merely by the expression of disapproval and carefully keeping a record thereof. Clearly, Japan has been deterred from the taking of greater liberties with American interests only because she respects our potential power; equally is it (clear) that she has trampled upon our rights to an extent in exact ratio to the strength of her conviction that the people of the United States would not permit that power to be used. It is possible that once that conviction is shaken the uses of diplomacy may again become accepted. (d) Therefore, if by firmness we can preserve the status quo in the Pacific until and if Great Britain is successful in the European war, a situation will be faced by Japan which will render it impossible for the present opportunist philosophy to keep the upper hand. Then it might be possible at a moment to undertake a readjustment of the whole problem of the Pacific on a frank, fair, and equitable basis which will be to the lasting benefit of both Japan and America. Until there is in Japan a complete regeneration of thought, a show of force, coupled with the determination that it will be used if necessary, alone can effectively contribute to such an outcome and to our own future security.

... I believe that in the present outlook and situation we have come to the time when the continuance of restraint and patience by the United States may and will probably lead to developments which will make progressively precarious relations between the United States and Japan. I hope that if the people and the Government of Japan can be led to believe that they are overplaying their hand, eventually there will come about a reverse swing of the pendulum in which it will be possible to reconstruct good relations between the United States and Japan. I consider the alternative to be hopeless.

Grew Suggests Easing Pressure on Japan (1941)

In 1941 the United States government used a variety of pressures on Japan in an attempt to block Japanese penetration of Southeast Asia, as well as to persuade her to give up trying to conquer China. American moves included an almost complete halt on shipments of scrap metal, needed for Japan's steel industry, and the threat to have the Dutch drastically reduce shipments to Japan from their East Indian oil fields. Ambassador Grew interpreted the effectiveness of American pressure in a message to Washington dated November 3, 1941.

From U.S. Department of State, *Peace and War: United States Foreign Policy, 1931–1941* (Washington, D. C., 1943), pp. 772–775.

(1) I refer [to] a leading article from the Tokyo *Nichi Nichi* of November 1 (reported in my telegram No. 1729 of that date), with a banner headline declaring "Empire Approaches Its Greatest Crisis" and introducing a despatch from New York with a summary of a statement the Japanese Embassy reportedly gave to the *New York Times* regarding the need of ending the United States–Japanese economic war. Both the article and the *Nichi Nichi* editorial (see my telegram of November 1, 7 P.M.) are believed to be close reflections of Japanese sentiments at present.

(2) I also refer to my various telegraphic reports during several months past analyzing the factors affecting policy in Japan and I have nothing to add thereto nor any substantial revision to make thereof. A conclusive estimate may be had of Japan's position through the application to the existing situation and the immediate future of the following points:

(a) It is not possible for Japan to dissociate either Japan or the conflict with China from the war in Europe and its fluctuations.

(b) In Japan political thought ranges from medieval to liberal ideas and public opinion is thus a variable quantity. The impact of events and conditions beyond Japan may determine at any given time which school of thought shall predominate. (In the democracies, on the other hand, owing to a homogeneous body of principles which influence and direct foreign policy and because methods instead of principles are more likely to cause differences of opinion, public opinion is formed differently.) For example, in Japan the pro-Axis elements gained power following last year's German victories in Western Europe; then Japanese doubt of ultimate German victory was created by Germany's failure to invade the British Isles, this factor helping to reinforce the moderate elements; and finally Germany's attack on the Soviet Union upset the expectation of continued Russo-German peace and made the Japanese realize that those who took Japan into the Tripartite Alliance had misled Japan.

(c) An attempt to correct the error of 1940 may be found in the efforts to adjust Japanese relations with the United States and thereby to lead the way to conclusion of peace with China, made by Prince Konoye and promised by the Tojo Cabinet. If this attempt fails, and if success continues to favor German arms, a final, closer Axis alinement may be expected.

(d) I and my staff have never been convinced by the theory that Japan's collapse as a militaristic power would shortly result from the depletion and the eventual exhaustion of Japan's financial and economic resources, as propounded by many leading American economists. Such forecasts were unconsciously based upon the assumption that a dominant consideration would be Japan's retention of the capitalistic system. The outcome they predicted has not transpired, although it is true that the greater part of Japan's commerce has been lost, Japanese industrial production has been drastically curtailed, and Japan's national resources have been depleted. Instead, there has been a drastic prosecution of the process to integrate Japan's national economy, lacking which there might well have occurred the predicted collapse of Japan. What has happened to date therefore does not support the view that continuation of trade embargoes and imposition of a blockade (proposed by some) can best avert war in the Far East.

(3) I call your attention, in this regard, to my telegram No. 827, September 12, 1940 (which reported the "golden opportunity" seen by Japanese army circles for expansion as a consequence of German triumphs in Europe). I sent this telegram under circumstances and at a time when it appeared unwise and futile for the United States to adopt conciliatory measures. The strong policy recommended in that telegram was subsequently adopted by the United States. This policy, together with the impact of world political events upon Japan brought the Japanese Government to the point of seeking conciliation with the United States. If these efforts fail, I foresee a probable swing of the pendulum in Japan once more back to the former Japanese position or even farther. This would lead to what I have described as an all-out, do-or-die attempt, actually risking national hara-kiri, to make Japan impervious to economic embargoes abroad rather than to yield to foreign pressure. It is realized by observers who feel Japanese national temper and psychology from day to day that, beyond peradventure, this contingency not only is possible but is probable.

(4) If the fiber and temper of the Japanese people are kept in mind, the view that war probably would be averted, though there might be some risk of war, by progressively imposing drastic economic measures is an uncertain and dangerous hypothesis upon which to base considered United States policy and measures. War would not be averted by such a course, if it is taken, is our own view. However, each view is only opinion, and, accordingly, to postulate the correctness of either one and to erect a definitive policy thereon would, in the belief of the Embassy, be contrary to American national interests. It would mean putting the cart before the horse. The primary point to be decided apparently involves the question whether war with Japan is justified by American national objectives, policies, and needs in the case of failure of the first line of national defense, namely, diplomacy, since it would be possible only on the basis of such a decision for the Roosevelt administration to follow a course which would be divested as much as possible of elements of uncertainty, speculation, and opinion. I doubt not that such a decision, irrevocable as it might well prove to be, already has been debated fully and adopted, because the sands are running fast.

(5) You will realize that, in the above discussion of this grave, momentous subject, I am not in touch with the intentions and thoughts of the Administration thereon, and I do not at all mean to imply that Washington is pursuing an undeliberated policy. Nor do I intend to advocate for a single moment any "appeasement" of Japan by the United States or recession in the slightest degree by the United States Government from the fundamental principles laid down as a basis for the conduct and adjustment of international relations, American relations with Japan included. There should be no compromise with principles, though methods may be flexible. My purpose is only to ensure against the United States becoming involved in war with Japan because of any possible misconception of Japan's capacity to rush headlong into a suicidal struggle with the United States. While national sanity dictates against such action, Japanese sanity cannot be measured by American standards of logic. We have no need to be over concerned respecting the bellicose tone and substance at present of the Japanese press (which in the past several years has attacked the United States intensely in recurrent waves), but underestimating Japan's obvious preparations to implement a program in the event the alternative peace program fails, would be short-sighted. Similarly it would be short-sighted for American policy to be based upon the belief that Japanese preparations are no more than saber rattling, merely intended to give moral support to the high pressure diplomacy of Japan. Japan may resort with dangerous and dramatic suddenness to measures which might make inevitable war with the United States.

Public Sentiment Increasingly Opposes Japanese Expansion (1941)

Throughout 1941 Americans became increasingly aware of two possible foes: Japan to the west and Germany to the east. Public opinion polls (see also Reading 307) reveal the extent of that awareness.

From Gallup and Fortune polls, *Public Opinion Quarterly,* VI (1942), pp. 149-151, 163.

I

U.S. Participation

Do you think the U.S. will go to war against Japan sometime in the near future? (Dec. 7, '41—AIPO)

Yes 52%   No 27%   Unready to guess 21%

Which one of these statements comes closest to expressing your feelings about Japan? (Oct. '41—FOR.)

Japan has proved her right to grow and we should not interfere with her	3.5%
While Japan may be a threat in the future, we should not get excited about her until she attacks some of our territory or interferes with our supplies	43.0
	46.5%
Japan has already gone far enough and we should place our fleet across her path and tell her another step means war	33.8
Japan has already gone too far and we should immediately declare war on her	3.4
	37.2
Don't know	16.3

II

Threat to U.S.

Which country is the greater threat to America's future—Germany or Japan? (Dec. 23, '41—AIPO)

Believe Germany the greater threat   64%
Believe Japan the greater threat   15

III

Aid to China

Do you think we should send China all the military supplies we can spare? (Oct. '41—FOR.)

Yes 59.5%   No 21.2%   Don't know 19.3%

IV

Policy toward Japan

Should the United States take steps now to prevent Japan from becoming more powerful, even if this means risking war with Japan? (Nov. 14, '41—AIPO)

TREND

	YES	NO	UNDECIDED
July	51%	31%	18%
Sept.	70	18	12
Today	64	25	11

Yes 69%   No 20%   Undecided 11%

Same question (Dec. 7, '41—AIPO)

Yes 69%   No 20%   Undecided 11%

Reading 312

Breakdown of Negotiations: A Diplomatic Failure?

The Japanese attack on Pearl Harbor on December 7, 1941, made meaningless Ambassador Grew's advice to ease pressure on Japan (see Reading 310). Germany and Italy declared war on the United States on December 11. Thus within a few days the United States went to war with the powers it had been fencing with, short of open conflict, for more than two years. Historians, in viewing the events leading up to American entry into the war, have disagreed widely on both facts and interpretations. One influential view was presented shortly after the war's end by William Henry Chamberlin, a well-known journalist and writer.

From William Henry Chamberlin, *America's Second Crusade* (Chicago, 1950), pp. 158-168. Copyright © 1950 by Henry Regnery Company. Subheadings added and some footnotes omitted by the editors.

I

Inability to Act

What is perhaps most surprising, as one reviews the tangled course of events in the last months before Pearl Harbor, is the inability of the Roosevelt Administration either to make a constructive move toward peace or to take effective precautions against war. The able and experienced American Ambassador to Japan, Joseph C. Grew, cabled to the State Department on January 27, 1941, a warning

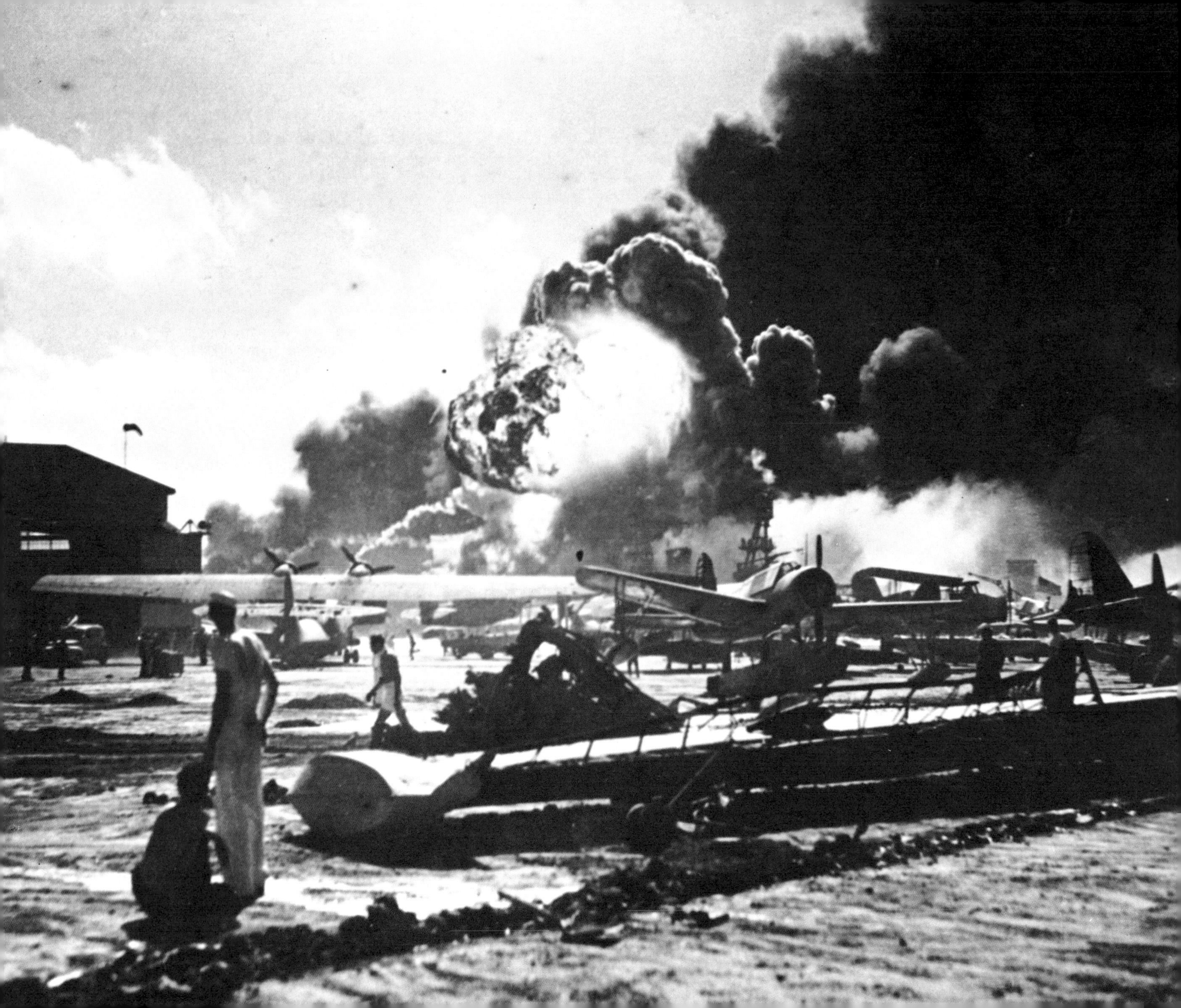

of a possible attack on Pearl Harbor. This was based on information from the Peruvian Minister, who stated he had heard from many sources, including a Japanese one, "that a surprise mass attack on Pearl Harbor was planned by the Japanese in the event of 'trouble' between Japan and the United States, that the attack would involve the use of all the Japanese military facilities." The State Department passed on this information to the War and Navy Departments.

Given a Japanese decision to risk war with the United States, a surprise blow at the American Pacific fleet, concentrated at the great Hawaiian base, was a very probable development. Japanese military and naval teaching had always emphasized the importance of secrecy and surprise. The experience of the war in Europe showed that certain operations which would not have been technically feasible in World War I could be carried out because of the increased range of air power.

But the orders and information sent by the higher military authorities in Washington to General Walter C. Short and Admiral Husband E. Kimmel, respectively commanders of the military and naval forces at Pearl Harbor, were notably lacking in precision and urgency. The commanders on the spot were encouraged to maintain a normal, "business as usual" attitude until the attack actually took place.

This was all the stranger and less excusable because United States cryptoanalysts, through an operation known as MAGIC, had cracked the code used in communications from Tokyo to members of the Japanese diplomatic corps throughout the world. This created a situation suggestive of playing poker while watching your opponent's cards in a mirror....

With MAGIC supplementing other sources of intelligence, the State, War, and Navy Departments were kept in close and prompt touch with important Japanese Government decisions. The German invasion of Russia placed before the Japanese Cabinet the necessity of such a decision. Von Ribbentrop was urging the Japanese Government to invade Siberia and take advantage of the promised Soviet military collapse.

But the Japanese Cabinet decided otherwise. There was no oil in Siberia. The United States, with a tender solicitude for Soviet interests that seems strange in the retrospect of 1950, was almost threatening war in the event of a Japanese move hostile to Russia.

II

Decides To Move South

So the Japanese Cabinet resolution, confirmed by a solemn Imperial Council* on July 2, was against the Siberian adventure and in favor of a move to the south. The Army was authorized to occupy the southern part of French Indo-China. From this vantage point there was a triple threat, to the Philippines, to Malaya and Siam, and to the Netherlands East Indies. However, Prime Minister Konoye still hoped that war with the West could be avoided. As he says in the memoir which he

*These Councils, held in the presence of the Emperor with the participation of the highest military and naval officers and civilian officials, were a familiar and regular mark of important Japanese state decisions.

wrote before committing suicide, following the end of the war:

"There was a good prospect that we might use the advance of the Japanese troops in Indo-China as the basis of a compromise in the Japanese-American talks then under way. I am confident I will be able to prevent a war."

Konoye made a desperate effort, a sincere effort, in the judgment of Ambassador Grew, to reach a settlement with the United States in August and September 1941. His desire was for a personal meeting with Roosevelt, and he was willing to make the important concession of taking the initiative and going to American soil, to Alaska or Honolulu, for the conference.

There had been an informal proposal for a Konoye-Roosevelt meeting in April. Admiral Toyoda, who had succeeded the bellicose and garrulous Matsuoka as Foreign Minister after the German attack on Russia, developed this suggestion in a talk with Grew on August 18. Toyoda intimated that Japan would be willing to withdraw from Indo-China as soon as the China affair was settled and suggested that Konoye should go to Honolulu to meet Roosevelt. Admiral Nomura repeated the invitation to Roosevelt on August 23.

Roosevelt at first was favorably impressed by the prospect of the meeting. He indicated a preference for Juneau, Alaska, over Honolulu. However, he accepted Hull's suggestion that there should be no talk until there had been a preliminary agreement about the points at issue.

It was on this obstacle that the proposed meeting, which might have staved off the Pacific war, foundered. There was no willingness on Hull's part to leave any room for give-and-take, to allow some scope for negotiation after the meeting began.

As two sailors look on, a fuel dump explodes at the wreckage-strewn Naval Air Station at Pearl Harbor on December 7, 1941. Why the Japanese were able to carry out a surprise attack so successfully has been the subject of controversy for three decades.

III

Proposal for Meeting Fails

As a consequence, although the Japanese proposal was never flatly rejected, it was allowed to perish from long neglect. That Konoye was eager for the meeting and was willing to take considerable risks, political and personal,* in order to bring it about is evident from Grew's account of his experience in the preliminary talks in Tokyo. The United States at that time had an excellent diplomatic team in Tokyo. Grew was a veteran career diplomat of seasoned judgment and long experience. His counselor, Eugene Dooman, possessed an unusual and remarkable mastery of the difficult and complex Japanese language.

On September 6, Konoye and his secretary, Ushiba, invited Grew and Dooman to dinner at the home of a Japanese friend under circumstances of extreme privacy. Konoye professed willingness to accept Hull's four principles and said the Ministers of War and the Navy had given complete agreement to his plan. A full general and a full admiral would accompany him, so that the services would be committed to accept the results of the conference. The Vice-Chiefs of Staff of the Army and Navy would also take part.

The Japanese Prime Minister emphasized the importance of the time factor. He could not guarantee a settlement six months or a year in the future. Now he was confident of success. When Grew raised the point that Japanese words in the past had not always corresponded with Japanese actions, Konoye assured him that any commitments he (Konoye) would undertake would bear no resemblance to the irresponsible assurances of the past. The Premier added that, if President Roosevelt would desire to communicate suggestions personally and confidentially, he would be glad to arrange subsequent secret meetings with Grew. Konoye expressed his earnest hope that "in view of the present internal situation in Japan the projected meeting with the President could be arranged with the least possible delay."

There were later talks between Ushiba and Dooman and between Toyoda and Grew. The Japanese proposals, as set forth by Toyoda, were in substance those which Nomura had presented in the spring.

Grew strongly recommended the meeting in a report to the Secretary of State on September 29. This report may be summarized as follows:

> The Ambassador, while admitting that risks will inevitably be involved, no matter what course is pursued toward Japan, offers his carefully studied belief that there would be substantial hope at the very least of preventing the Far Eastern situation from becoming worse and perhaps of insuring definitely constructive results, if an agreement along the lines of the preliminary discussions were brought to a head by the proposed meeting of the heads of the two governments.... He raises the questions whether the United States is not now given the opportunity to halt Japan's program without war, or an immediate risk of war, and further whether through failure to use the present opportunity the United States will not face a greatly increased risk of war. The Ambassador states his firm belief in an affirmative answer to these two questions.
>
> The Ambassador does not consider unlikely the possibility of Prince Konoye's being in a position to give President Roosevelt a more explicit and satisfactory engagement than has already been vouchsafed in the course of the preliminary conversations.

Grew further warned of the possibility of serious Japanese reaction if the preliminary discussion should drag on in the hope of obtaining clear-cut commitments. He predicted:

> The logical outcome of this will be the downfall of the Konoye Cabinet and the formation of a military dictatorship which will lack either the disposition or the temperament to avoid colliding head-on with the United States.

Grew notes on October 1 that a Japanese friend of high standing informed him that political circles now know of Konoye's intention, and that the proposal is generally approved, even among the military, because of the economic necessity of reaching a settlement with the United States. About the same time the Ambassador made the following comment in his diary:

> For a Prime Minister of Japan thus to shatter all precedent and tradition in this land of subservience to precedent and tradition, to wish to come hat in hand, so to speak, to meet the President of the United States on American soil, is a gauge of the determination of the Government to undo the vast harm already accomplished in alienating our powerful and progressively angry country.... Prince Konoye's warship is

---

*Assassination had been the fate of many Japanese statesmen who opposed the extreme militarists.

ready waiting to take him to Honolulu or Alaska or any other place designated by the President, and his staff of the highest military, naval and civilian officers is chosen and rarin' to go.

IV

Konoye Resigns

But Hull was unmoved and immovable. He sometimes expressed the view that the maintenance in power of the Konoye Cabinet afforded the best prospect of keeping the peace. But he refused to give this Cabinet any diplomatic encouragement. Konoye resigned on October 16 and was succeeded by General Hideki Tojo.

From this time events began to move at a swifter pace. The blockade of Japan by America, Great Britain, and the Netherlands Indies was beginning to pinch. It became increasingly clear from the public statements of Japan's leaders and from the private messages intercepted by MAGIC that the sands of peace were running out, that the United States must choose between some kind of compromise and a strong probability of war. The suggestion of a time limit began to appear in the Japanese secret communications. So the new Japanese Foreign Minister, Shigenori Togo, sent this message to Nomura:

> Because of various circumstances, it is absolutely necessary that all arrangements for the signing of this agreement be completed by the 25th of this month. I realize that this is a difficult order, but under the circumstances it is an unavoidable one. Please understand this thoroughly and tackle the problem of saving the Japanese-American relations from falling into a chaotic condition.

Another Japanese envoy, Saburo Kurusu, a career diplomat with an American wife, was rushed to Washington in mid-November, the transpacific Clipper being held for him at Hong Kong. Kurusu arrived in Washington on November 17 and was received by Roosevelt and Hull. It was later suggested that Kurusu possessed advance knowledge of the blow that was being prepared against Pearl Harbor. But it seems more probable that his coming to Washington was merely in line with the familiar Japanese practice of having more than one man responsible for action in a moment of grave crisis.

Nomura's desire to avoid war was unquestionably genuine, as indicated by his intercepted message of November 19:

> After exhausting our strength by four years of the China Incident, following right upon the Manchurian Incident, the present is hardly an opportune time for venturing upon another long-drawn-out war on a large scale. I think it would be better to fix up a temporary "truce" now in the spirit of "give-and-take" and make this the prelude to greater achievements later.

V

Deadline Delayed to November 29

Tokyo offered Nomura and Kurusu a slight relaxation of the original time limit on November 22. The envoys were informed that it would be satisfactory if an agreement were reached by the twenty-ninth. This communication, which, of course, was available to high American officials, ended on this ominous note:

> "This time we mean it, that the deadline absolutely cannot be changed. After that things are automatically going to happen."

The background of this warning was that on November 25 a Japanese task force under the command of Admiral Isoruku Yamamoto was to take off, with Pearl Harbor as its objective. The advancement of the time limit was apparently because it was realized in Tokyo that this force could be turned back without committing any act of aggression if an agreement were reached while the expedition was in its early stages.

The Japanese Government had worked out for discussion a Plan A and a Plan B, the latter the limit of concessions. Plan B, submitted to Hull by Nomura and Kurusu on November 20, was worded as follows:

> Japan and the United States to make no armed advance in any region in Southeast Asia and the Southwest Pacific area.
>
> Japan to withdraw her troops from Indo-China when peace is restored between Japan and China or when an equitable peace is established in the Pacific area.
>
> Japan and the United States to cooperate toward acquiring goods and commodities which the two countries need in the Netherlands East Indies.
>
> Japan and the United States to restore their commercial relations to those prevailing prior to the freezing of assets, and the United States to supply Japan a required quantity of oil.
>
> The United States to refrain from such measures and actions as would prejudice endeavors for the restoration of peace between Japan and China.

377

VI

Stopgap Plan Proposed

These proposals met with no favor in the eyes of Secretary Hull. He did not believe the Japanese offer to withdraw from southern Indo-China was adequate compensation for the lifting of the American blockade. However, he seriously considered a counter-proposal, aimed at creating a three months' *modus vivendi*. This was the only conciliatory move the American Government seems to have thought of making during the protracted negotiations with Japan in 1941, and this move was not made.

An undated memorandum in Roosevelt's handwriting seems to have contained the germ of the *modus vivendi* idea:

"US to resume economic relations . . . some oil and rice now—more later. Japan to send no more troops . . . US to introduce Japanese to Chinese, but . . . to take no part in their conversations."

Henry Morgenthau, Secretary of the Treasury, who liked to have a finger in every diplomatic pie, set his staff to work preparing a detailed blueprint of a temporary economic truce. Some features of the Treasury plan were incorporated in the scheme which was finally approved by Hull after being worked over by State Department experts.

This scheme provided for mutual American and Japanese pledges against aggressive moves in the Pacific, for Japanese withdrawal from southern Indo-China and limitation of Japanese forces in northern Indo-China to 25,000 men. The *quid pro quo* was to be a relaxation of the blockade, permitting Japan to export freely and to import limited supplies of cotton, oil, food, and medical supplies.

No one can say whether the influence of the Japanese moderates would have been strong enough to stop the planned attack in return for these restricted American concessions. But the offer was never made. Hull dropped his one experiment in conciliation under pressure from China and Great Britain.

Eden and Churchill, Chiang Kai-shek and his brother-in-law, T. V. Soong, Owen Lattimore, American adviser to Chiang, all eagerly took a hand in blocking this tentative move toward peace. The *modus vivendi* had been cautiously framed with a view to offering minimum concessions. But Eden, in a message of November 25, wanted to make stiffer demands on the Japanese: complete withdrawal from Indo-China and suspension of military activities in China.

Lattimore reported from Chungking that any *modus vivendi* now arrived at with Japan would be disastrous to Chinese belief in America. Chiang Kai-shek, according to Lattimore, questioned his ability to hold the situation together "if the Chinese national trust in America is undermined by reports of Japan's escaping military defeat by diplomatic victory."

The idea that Japan faced military defeat as a result of any past, present, or prospective action by China was unrealistic, if not downright ludicrous. But in the fevered atmosphere of the time it was a good propaganda line. Hull later declared that "Chiang has sent numerous hysterical cable messages to different Cabinet officers and high officials in the Government—other than the State Department."

As a climax Churchill introduced himself into the situation with a special message which reached Roosevelt on November 26:

Of course it is for you to handle this business and we certainly do not want an additional war. There is only one point that disquiets us. What about Chiang? Is he not having a very thin diet? Our anxiety is about China. If they collapse our joint danger would enormously increase. We are sure that the regard of the United States for the Chinese cause will govern your action. We feel that the Japanese are most unsure of themselves.

Under this barrage of foreign criticism Hull's impulse to offer the truce arrangement wilted. As Secretary of War Stimson records in his diary for November 26: "Hull told me over the telephone this morning that he had about made up his mind not to give the proposition that Knox and I had passed on the other day to the Japanese, but to kick the whole thing over, to tell them he had no proposition at all."

On the previous day, November 25, there had been an important council at the White House, with the President, Hull, Stimson, Knox, Marshall, and Stark present. The spirit of this meeting is reflected in Stimson's comment in his diary:

"The question was how we should maneuver them [the Japanese] into firing the first shot without allowing too much danger to ourselves."

Here, perhaps, is a clue both to the abandonment of the truce proposal and to the curious absence of concern for normal precautionary measures at Pearl Harbor.

VII

Hull Makes Ten-Point Proposal

Secretary Hull certainly made a notable contribution to the end suggested by Stimson when, after discarding his compromise proposal, he handed the Japanese envoys what amounted to a demand for unconditional

Reading 313

surrender in a set of ten proposals presented to them on November 26. One of these proposals was that Japan should withdraw its forces from Indo-China and from China. Another demanded that there should be no support of any government in China other than the National Government (Chiang Kai-shek).

There was a suggestion for a multilateral nonaggression pact among the governments principally concerned in the Pacific. Only on these terms, which amounted to relinquishment by Japan of everything it had gained on the mainland during the preceding ten years, would the United States consent to restore normal economic relations. After reading these proposals Kurusu remarked that when they were communicated to Tokyo the Government would be likely to throw up its hands.

Technically Hull's ten points did not constitute an ultimatum. No time limit was set and counterproposals were not excluded. But when one considers the circumstances under which they were presented, and their completely uncompromising character, one may feel that the Army Board which investigated the Pearl Harbor attack was justified in describing Hull's communication as "the document that touched the button that started the war."

Breakdown of Negotiations: An Inevitable Result?

Not all historians agree with the viewpoint of Chamberlin (Reading 312). Joseph W. Ballantine arrives at a different conclusion by studying the history of Japanese-American relations during the 1930s.

From Joseph W. Ballantine, "Mukden to Pearl Harbor: The Foreign Policies of Japan." Excerpted by permission from *Foreign Affairs*, XXVII (1948-1949), pp. 651-652, 658-664. Copyright by the Council on Foreign Relations, Inc., New York. Subheadings added by the editors.

I

Army Urges Expansion

During the decade and more preceding Pearl Harbor a conflict went on within the Japanese Government between a dominant group in the Army, which insisted upon plunging the country into a course of forcible expansion, and civilian and Navy leaders, who were either opposed to such a course or perceived grave risks in it. Each successive step toward the fulfillment of expansionist aims was taken on the initiative of the Army, often in defiance of constituted authority, until finally the moderates lost control of the situation altogether and an Army-dictated Cabinet under Prince Konoye came into office in July 1940. The complete story of this struggle and of the victory of the Army was revealed for the first time by the International Military Tribunal for the Far East, which on November 12, 1948, completed the reading of its judgment in the trial of the 25 major Japanese war criminals, on which the Tribunal had sat for over two years. Many of the essential facts are still little known, and the full significance of the revelations seems scarcely to have been appreciated in the United States.

It is an amazing record of how a reckless, determined and ruthless military group succeeded in imposing its will upon an irresolute nation; of how that group relied upon an extraordinary abuse of power in order to gain its ends, and resorted freely to intrigue, duplicity, terrorism and assassination. It shows that the opposing majority, apprehensive lest the military, if crossed, be aroused to take extreme measures, supinely tried to placate and appease the warmakers. A review of the record suggests that the sequence of events that carried Japan inexorably one step at a time toward the fateful decision to go to war against the western Powers falls into three stages. The first reached from 1928 until February 1936, when expansionist moves were made by the Army on its own initiative without awaiting, and often in defiance of, government orders. The second was from March 1936 until September 1940, when the Japanese Government itself adopted a policy of expansion but with substantial reservations. And September 1940, when the Japanese Government decided to proceed with expansion even at the risk of war, marked the beginning of the final stage. . . .

II

Axis Alliance Quickens Action

The conclusion of the Tripartite Alliance [with Germany and Italy] marked Japan's transit from the second to the final stage of a course of unreserved expansion, and war with the western Powers, if necessary. The plans for action as drawn up by the Foreign Office and approved by the Cabinet early in October called for: 1, the early successful settlement of the China affair; 2, the negotiation of a non-aggression pact with the Soviet Union; 3, the incorporation of the countries of Southeast Asia and the islands of the Malay Archipelago in the so-called "Co-Prosperity

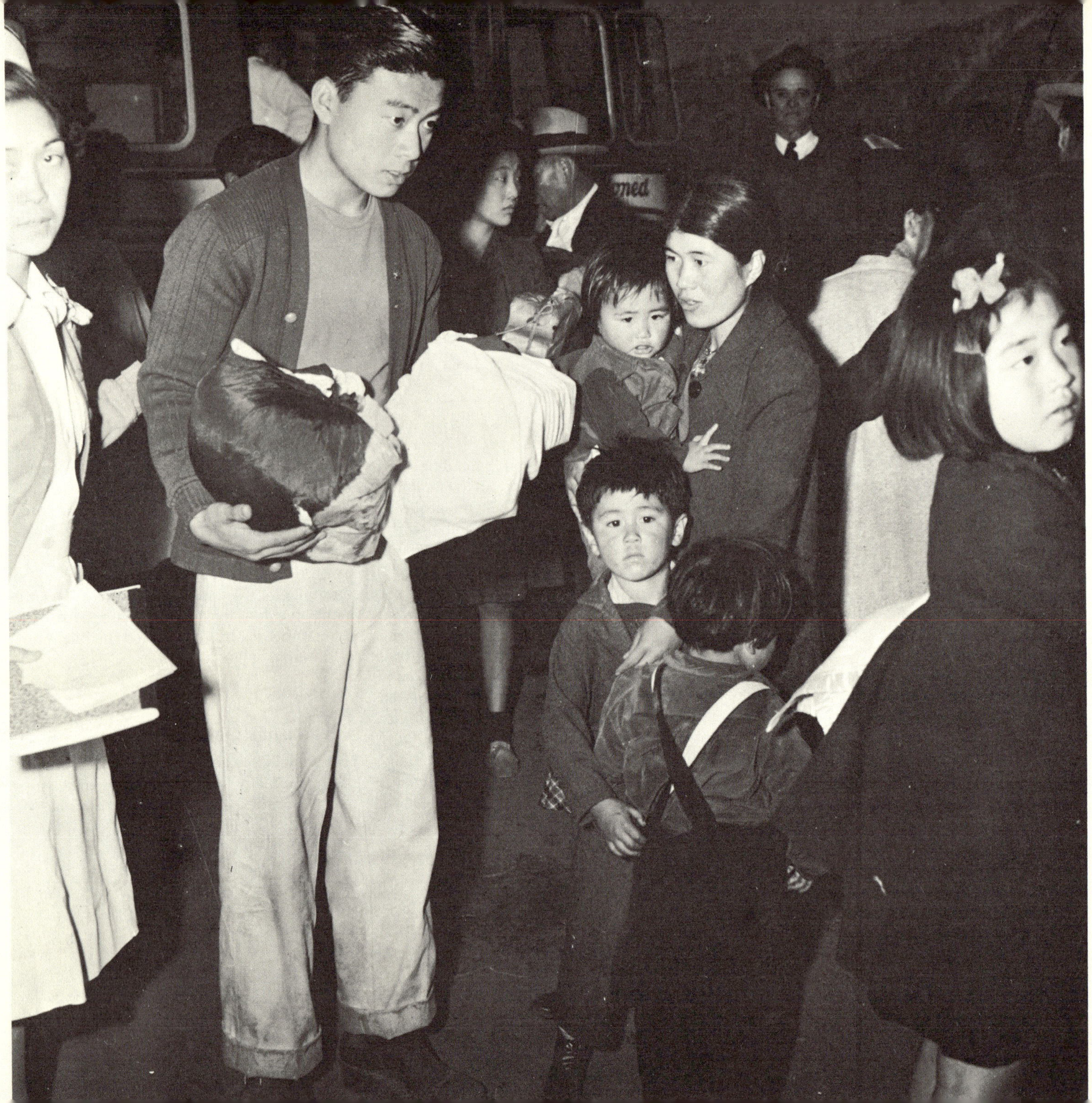

Japanese advances in the Pacific in the early months of the war produced a sense of panic on the West Coast of the United States. This fear, coupled with long-held hostility toward Japanese and Americans of Japanese descent, in turn produced in February 1942 a federal order requiring everyone of Japanese descent to be removed to internment camps in the interior of the country. About 112,000 persons were eventually forced into these camps. Many of them suffered both loss of their property and considerable physical hardship.

Sphere" (*i.e.* the establishment of domination or control there). At a Four Ministers' Conference held on September 4, even India, Australia and New Zealand had been marked for inclusion in Japan's sphere of influence.

All possibility of a settlement with Chiang Kai-shek was destroyed by the conclusion two months later by Japan of a "treaty" with the puppet régime of Wang Ching-wei at Nanking. And in April of the following year a neutrality pact, rather than a non-aggression pact, was concluded with the Soviet Union.

For the realization of the expanded Co-Prosperity Sphere two plans were worked out, to be pursued along parallel lines or alternatively, according to exigencies. One plan called for reliance upon "diplomacy" (if that term can be rightfully applied to the tactics of chicanery and intimidation contemplated and attempted), and the other upon military action. Each of the two plans focused upon Singapore and the Philippines, presumably because it was believed that the rest of the area coveted would fall like a ripe plum into Japan's hands. The diplomatic plan, fantastic as it may sound, was to make an offer to Great Britain to mediate the European conflict in return for British recognition of the Co-Prosperity Sphere (including surrender of Singapore), and to propose to the United States that Japan would recognize Philippine independence in return for United States recognition of the Co-Prosperity Sphere. Japan intended to occupy Singapore and Malaya in any case, along with the Netherlands Indies, but not the Philippines or Guam unless war broke out with the United States.

The military plan for taking Singapore contemplated first the securing of advance bases in Indo-China and Siam by means of concluding protective treaties with those countries. The next step would await a settlement in China or a German invasion of Britain—whichever occurred first—or, failing either, some substantial German military successes. In January 1941, Japanese and German military experts agreed that attack on Singapore should follow occupation of Saigon and a landing on the Malay peninsula. Aerial photography was undertaken in the latter area to collect data for a landing. Military currency was printed for use in the countries along the line of advance. On February 10, 1941, Matsuoka informed the German Ambassador that an attack on Singapore had been planned; three days later he instructed the Japanese Ambassador at London to inform Foreign Minister Eden that a report communicated to him by the British Ambassador at Tokyo of impending Japanese action was a ridiculous fantasy. On February 22, the Japanese Ambassador at Berlin told von Ribbentrop that preparation for attack on Singapore would be completed by May, and that for safety's sake preparations had also been made for war against the United States and Great Britain.

The preparations for war against the United States envisaged a plan for the destruction of the Pacific fleet at Pearl Harbor. The Japanese relied on seizing all points in the western Pacific and Indian Oceans before the United States could prepare a counterattack. They expected that the United States would weary of a prolonged war and negotiate a peace settlement on the basis of recognition of Japanese supremacy in the territories that had been seized. In January 1941, the Commander of the Combined Fleets approved and transmitted to Imperial General Headquarters a plan for a surprise attack at Pearl Harbor while the two countries were at peace. In late May the Japanese Navy began training for the attack, and dive-bombing was practised at Kagoshima.

III

Japan Encounters Setbacks

By June 1941, Japan had received a number of setbacks to her hope of achieving southward expansion through diplomacy. A settlement in China had failed to materialize. Negotiations with the Dutch to obtain large quantities of oil and other materials from the East Indies had broken down, and Japan's reserves of war supplies were in danger of depletion. Germany had failed to invade Britain, and the British had rebuffed a Japanese approach looking to the mediation of the European conflict. Although the United States had expressed a willingness to explore the possibilities of a comprehensive Pacific settlement for which the Japanese had asked, Secretary Hull had made it clear that this Government would not enter into any agreement that disregarded the rights and interests of other countries. This meant that there was little hope that the United States would recognize the program of annexations politely called the Co-Prosperity Sphere.

These discouragements failed to divert Japan from her fixed purposes. When Germany attacked Russia on June 22, some Japanese leaders proposed postponing the southern project in favor of an onset on the Russian Far East, but they were overruled at an Imperial Conference on July 2. Here it was decided to continue diplomatic negotiations while completing final preparations for military action. The troops that later made landings in Malaya and the Philippines began practising along the China coast and in Hainan and Formosa. Attention was devoted to experimenting with and perfecting a shallow water torpedo, and refueling at sea was practised so that the more secluded northern route could be used for sneaking up on Pearl Harbor.

Japan's occupation of southern Indo-China was declared by Japan's Foreign Minister on July 26 to be for the purpose of winding up the China affair. He alleged that Japan had reports of an intended encirclement of Indo-China that would interfere with that purpose. The Tribunal found no evidence of any such intended encirclement, but did find conclusive evidence that Japan's reason for advancing into southern Indo-China was to secure bases for attacking Singapore and the Netherlands Indies. Such bases would also threaten the Philippines. The conclusion coincides with that reached at the time by the United States Government, prompting it to freeze Japanese assets on July 26. In a memorandum of the Department of State of May 19, 1942, it was explained that

> by this further expansion in southern Indo-China Japan virtually completed the encirclement of the Philippine Islands and placed its armed forces within striking distance of vital trade routes. This constituted an overt act directly menacing the security of the United States and other Powers that were at peace with Japan. It created a situation in which the risk of war became so great that the United States and other countries concerned were confronted no longer with the question of avoiding such risk but from then on with the problem of preventing a complete undermining of their security.... Under those circumstances and in the light of those considerations, the Government of the United States decided at that point, as did certain other governments especially concerned, that discontinuance of trade with Japan had become an appropriate, warranted and necessary step—as an open warning to Japan and as a measure of self-defense.

The British and Netherlands Governments also froze Japanese assets.

IV

Conference Defines "Minimum Demands"

On September 6 the Imperial Conference decided that Japan should endeavor to gain acceptance of certain "minimum" demands incidental to achieving the purpose of southern expansion through negotiations with the United States and Great Britain, and, in the event of the failure of the negotiations by October, a decision on the opening of hostilities should be made. Japan's "minimum" demands were as follows:

1. Noninterference with Japan's efforts to settle the China affair, including discontinuance of assistance to Chiang Kai-shek and the closing of the Burma Road.
2. Abstention from action in the Far East to threaten Japan's national defense; from establishing any military "interests" in Siam, China, the Netherlands Indies and the Soviet Far East, from strengthening armaments in the Far East; and the recognition of Japan's special relationship with Indo-China.
3. Cooperation with Japan in obtaining supplies of materials and the restoration of commercial relations.

In return, Japan would engage to make no military advance beyond Indo-China except toward China, to withdraw her troops from Indo-China after an equitable peace had been effected with China, and to guarantee the neutrality of the Philippines.

This proposed basis of a settlement, with minor variations, formed the essence of the terms put forward by Japan to the United States on successive occasions, including the final set of terms delivered on November 20, which the Japanese Foreign Minister described in his instructions to Ambassador Nomura as an "ultimatum." They called upon the United States and Great Britain to abandon China to Japan, and provide Japan with the materials for a Japanese advance into American, British and Dutch territories in the Far East. The reciprocal commitments that Japan offered to make, even if the Japanese Government had been one that could be trusted, were valueless, since Japan proposed to determine unilaterally what constituted an "equitable" peace with China and expected British and American recognition of Japan's "special relationship" with Indo-China. With such American, British and Dutch demilitarization in the Far East as Japan demanded, there would have been no need of moving Japanese troops beyond Indo-China. Acceptance of the Japanese demands would have meant that Japan gained all that she sought without fighting. . . .

It seems quite clear from the facts brought out in the trial and judgment of the Tribunal that at no time during the period after Japan's occupation of Manchuria would it have been possible to have brought Japan to abandon her policy of territorial and political expansion through measures short of the application of superior force. After 1932, Japan was determined to hold her grip on Manchuria. After 1937, it became Japan's fixed policy to subjugate all the rest of China as well, and, after 1940, to dominate the whole of the Far East and the western Pacific region. It is also abundantly clear that after the summer of 1941 Japan's leaders, with their reserves of oil running lower and with the golden opportunity to realize the dreams of a rich empire slipping by, would brook no delay, and that the United States could not have gained more time by further exploration of the issues and the possibilities. The Japanese were not offering to negotiate a reasonable settlement by process of agreement; they were presenting demands, to be accepted or rejected. The United States had only two choices: either to yield to the Japanese demands and sacrifice principles and security, or to decline to yield and take the consequences.

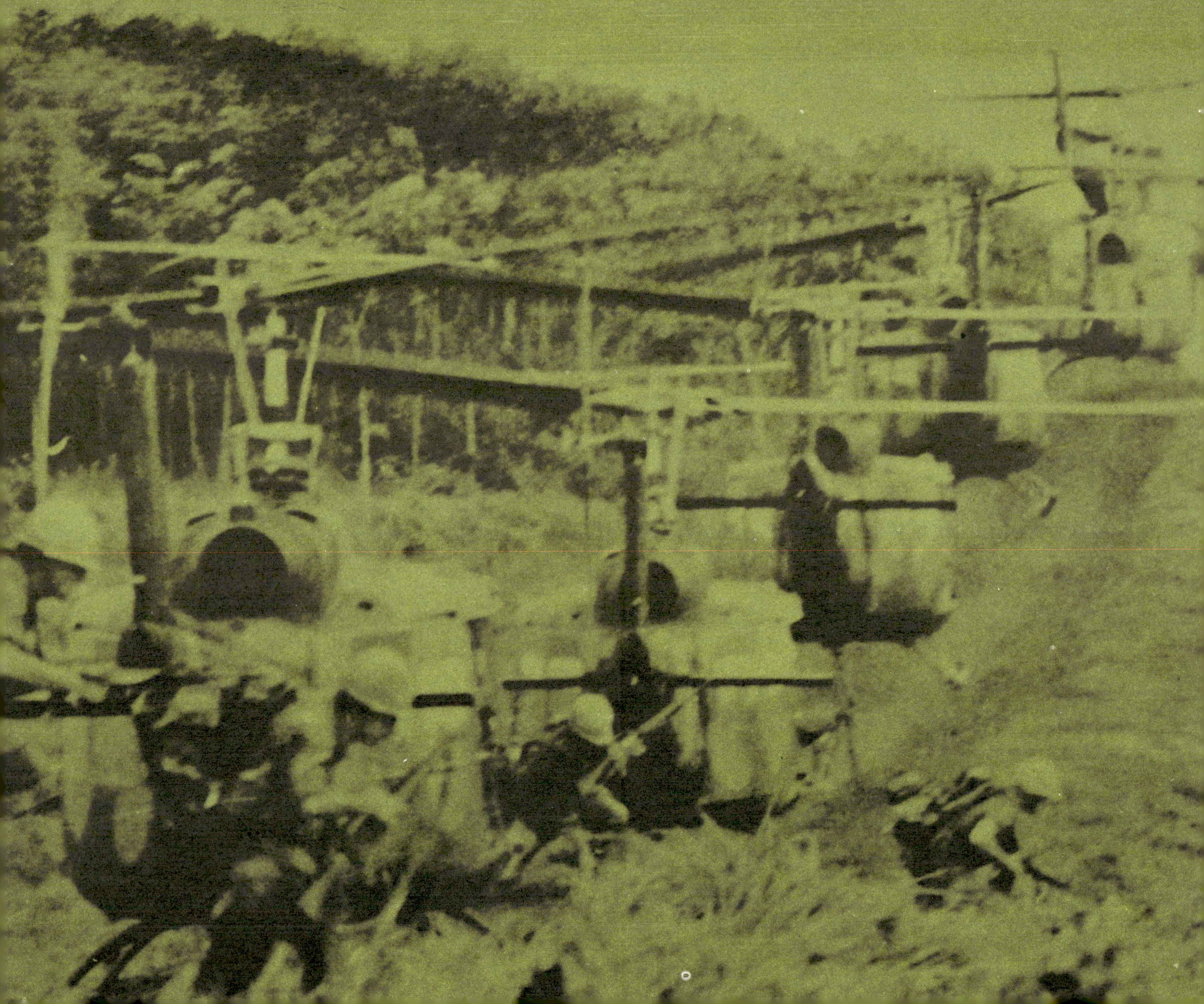

Chapter 9

The Reconstruction of World Politics, 1941–1971

In the years immediately before United States entrance into World War II, Americans vigorously argued the merits of deeper involvement in the Allied cause. One can only guess what the United States would ultimately have done, in both Europe and Asia, if Japan had not resolved the debate by attacking Pearl Harbor on December 7, 1941. Germany and Italy ended all uncertainty a few days later by declaring war on the United States. Americans angrily entered a war which seemed as clear a case of good versus evil as could be found in the history of the modern world.

The United States in 1945 emerged from the war as the only combatant nation economically and politically strong. Germany and Japan, of course, were devastated, but only somewhat more than many of America's allies. The nations of Europe suffered extensively from both the German conquest and the Anglo-American and Russian sweeps across the continent. China went through much the same experience. Even the Soviet Union, whose armies were the largest in the world in 1945, was in poor shape, for its chief industrial and agricultural regions had been ravaged by four years of warfare.

Twenty-five years later West Germany and Japan had risen from the ashes to become two of the most prosperous nations in the world. China had gone through a revolution following the defeat of the Japanese and had emerged in 1949 with a Communist government. Great Britain and France had lost the colonial possessions they had acquired laboriously over the previous century. The peoples of Asia and Africa, for many years scarcely more than pawns in European power politics, had by the 1960s begun to assert an independence of spirit and action which gave them a voice in determining their futures. And, pervading every aspect of world affairs since 1945, the United States and the Soviet Union, allies for four years against Germany, glared at each other as they competed for power and influence throughout the world.

The emergence of the United States as one of the two greatest powers, the interaction of the great powers in the nuclear age, and their involvement with the new nations of Asia, Africa, and Latin America provide the underlying themes for the topics in this chapter. This and the following chapter are open-ended, since these trends are still evolving rapidly.

TOPIC 59

THE WAR AND THE NUCLEAR AGE

The defeat of Germany in May 1945 and the surrender of Japan the following August ended one phase of a thirty-year conflict which is still going on. The Allies had already begun to quarrel among themselves; even before the last shot had been fired there were fears that the United States and the Soviet Union would come into conflict over the shaping of the peace.

The dropping of atomic bombs on Hiroshima and Nagasaki ended World War II, though whether their use was *necessary* to end the war remains an extremely controversial question. In 1945 the United States alone possessed atomic weapons, a hard fact which impressed both friend and foe. The massive destructiveness of a single atomic bomb made it both a fearful military weapon and a potent diplomatic threat. After exploring the course of World War II, the readings in this topic focus on the significance of atomic weapons both in ending the war and in shaping the relationship between the United States and the Soviet Union immediately after the war.

Reading 314

The United States in World War II (1941-1945)

Just as in World War I, the United States became the last of the great military-industrial powers to join in World War II. Once involved, however, the United States prepared itself like the other warring nations for total war and demanded of its enemies unconditional surrender. The course of the war from 1941 to 1945 is described in the following selection.

From Chester G. Starr *et al., A History of the World,* © 1960 by Rand McNally & Company, Vol. II, pp. 539-543.

The American attitude had been sympathetic to the democratic cause from the beginning of hostilities, although at first Washington would not go beyond moral encouragement to England and France. After the great German victories in western Europe, however, it began to extend military and economic aid to the British. Indeed, in order to insure the uninterrupted flow of supplies across the Atlantic, it sent troops to Greenland, Iceland, and Ireland and provided merchantmen with naval protection against submarines. The difference between antifascist neutrality and antifascist belligerency was rapidly melting away when developments in the Far East created the immediate occasion for the final transition from one to the other.

Japan, engaged since 1937 in military operations against China, had taken advantage of the defeat of France to win control over Indo-China. Its war machine, however, depended heavily on imports from the New

An American Army Air Force B-17 in a bombing run over Germany, 1944. By the end of World War II, thousand-bomber raids were ordinary occurrences over both Germany and Japan. Such raids caused widespread devastation and death, but failed to achieve the expected goal of many advocates of air power: destruction of civilian morale and the will to continue the war.

World of strategic materials, mainly oil, steel, scrap iron, copper, and lead. In the summer of 1941 President Roosevelt cut off the shipment of goods to the Japanese in order to curb their imperialistic ambitions, leaving them no choice but to abandon their colonial conquests or to acquire new economic resources. Their answer came on December 7, "a date which will live in infamy," when a surprise air raid on the Hawaiian Islands crippled the United States navy and exposed the western Pacific to the attack of the expansionists in Tokyo. Four days later Germany and Italy declared war on America, and the campaign in eastern Europe, in the Mediterranean, and in Asia merged in one great global conflict.

The spring and summer of 1942 were the high-water mark of Axis success. In the Soviet Union a new offensive was swiftly carrying the Germans toward the rich oil fields of

Caucasia; in North Africa General Erwin Rommel, "the desert fox," was leading the fascist forces deep into Egypt to within seventy miles of Alexandria; in the Far East the Japanese were seizing the Netherlands East Indies, the Philippines, Hong Kong, Malaya, and Burma. Then the tide began to turn. The Red Army succeeded in pushing back the Wehrmacht in a series of savage battles, of which the most important took place at Stalingrad. In the Pacific the mikado's warships were stopped in the Coral Sea and at Midway Island, while his troops got their first taste of defeat when the United States marines landed on Guadalcanal in the Solomon Islands. And in the Mediterranean theater of operations a concerted advance by the British from the east and the Americans from the west closed in on the German Afrika Korps, capturing its last strongholds of Tunis and Bizerte in May, 1943.

The next campaign against the Axis was an invasion of Italy, designed to topple the shaky régime of Mussolini. The swift conquest of Sicily did lead to the resignation of the Duce, but Hitler rushed enough troops south to gain control of most of the peninsula. For nearly another two years hard fighting continued amid the Apennines. By the beginning of 1944, however, the grand coalition against fascism was winning the upper hand on all fronts. In eastern Europe the Russians were crossing their pre-war frontiers, carrying the war to the enemy. In the Italian boot the Allied armies were slowly advancing northward toward Rome. In the Far East the forces of General Douglas MacArthur, having occupied strategic points in the Gilbert and the Marshall islands, were sending their bombers closer and closer to the Japanese homeland. Everywhere the struggle was financed by

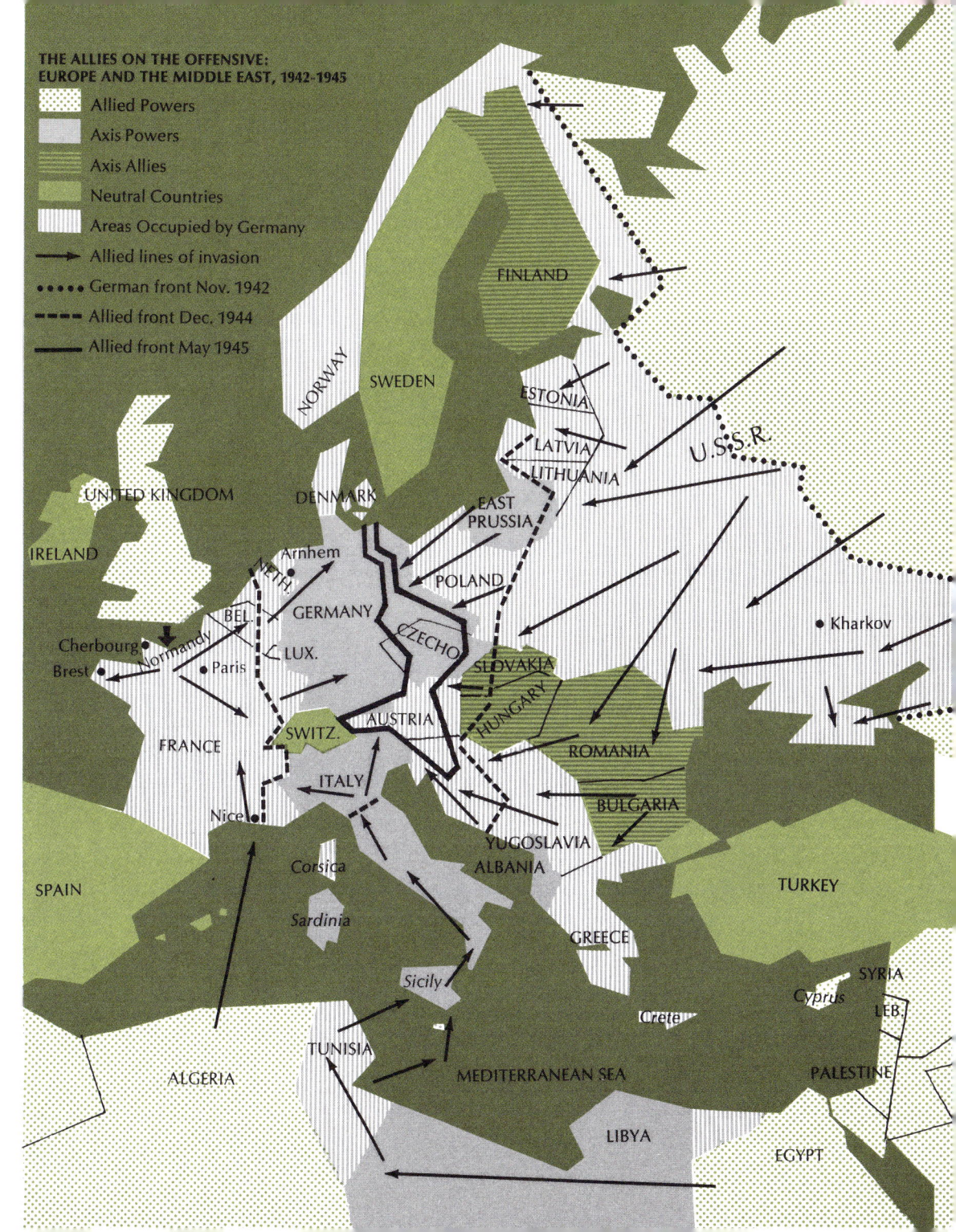

America, which was producing vast quantities of war materials and shipping them to the four corners of the earth. The New World, protected by its oceans against air attack and military invasion, had become the arsenal of democracy.

The last phase of the war opened on June 6, 1944, with the invasion of western Europe by Allied troops under General Dwight D. Eisenhower. They succeeded by the end of the summer in driving the enemy out of France and Belgium, while the Red Army was making itself master of eastern Europe and approaching the frontiers of East Prussia. Recognizing the hopelessness of the military situation, a group of German officers attempted to assassinate Hitler in order to facilitate peace negotiations. But their effort failed, and the struggle went on to the bitter end. Late in 1944 the Wehrmacht launched a last desperate offensive against the western Allies in the Forest of Ardennes. When that failed, the Third Reich was left incapable of further effective resistance.

In the spring of 1945 a co-ordinated attack by the Russians in the east and the Americans in the west culminated in the meeting of their forces along the Elbe on April 25. Five days later, as his capital was falling to the troops of the Soviet Union, the Führer committed suicide, and on May 7 in Reims General Alfred Jodl accepted the instrument of unconditional surrender for Germany. Japan continued to fight alone for another few months, although the Allies had in the meantime retaken the Philippines and were now in a position to raid Japanese cities from air bases on Iwo Jima and Okinawa only a thousand miles from Yokohama and Nagasaki. What finally forced the mikado's government to agree to lay down its arms was first the destruction of the city of Hiroshima by an atomic bomb on August 6, and then two days later the entry of Russia into the conflict in the Far East. In the middle of the month Japan announced its readiness to meet the demands of the grand coalition, and on September 2 its civilian and military leaders signed the terms of capitulation on board the U.S.S. *Missouri*. Hostilities which had begun in the summer of 1939 on the road to Danzig came to an end six years later on the other side of the world in Tokyo Bay.

THE ALLIES ON THE OFFENSIVE: Asia And The Pacific, 1942-1945

American soldiers make their way through a badly damaged French town in their drive to the German border in the fall of 1944. The Allied invasion of France, the so-called Second Front (the first being in Russia) began on the sixth of June 1944. By early September well over two million soldiers, mostly American and British, had been landed in France.

The agony of total conflict made familiar by the First World War recurred on an even more tragic scale in the Second World War. Those killed on the battlefield numbered some fifteen million men, while civilian losses were at least equally great. One out of every twenty-two Russians, one out of every twenty-five Germans, one out of every forty-six Japanese was dead or missing. The bitter quip that during hostilities the safest place is the front proved to be almost literally true. In England 20 per cent of all homes were damaged or destroyed; in Germany close to 25 per cent of the buildings were reduced to rubble; entire cities like Stalingrad, Warsaw, Kassel, and Rotterdam were desolate ruins; in Hiroshima a single atomic explosion took the lives of fifty thousand people and leveled four square miles. The financial costs of the conflict were estimated at from two to four trillion dollars, but what currency could express human suffering and sorrow? The Axis treated conquered countries with a ruthless brutality. It even organized a systematic,

Reading 315

Planning the Peace

In many ways, fighting the war was the simpler aspect of the struggle for the Allies. They knew, at least, that the enemies, Germany, Italy, and Japan, were to be defeated by the most effective weapons available. But planning the peace brought to the surface conflicts between the United States, Great Britain, the Soviet Union, China, and France. Each sought to impose its own interests on the reshaping of the world following the defeat of their common foes. Historians John Stipp, Allen Dirrim, and C. Warren Hollister offer a view of this debate among the Allies, especially as it affected the creation of the United Nations.

cold-blooded extermination of ethnic minorities which brought death to six million Jews. Yet the democracies were not entirely above reproach either. Their mass bombing of enemy countries drew no distinction between the good and the bad, the innocent and the guilty. How many Americans felt uneasy in March, 1945, about the great air raid on Tokyo which caused 185,000 civilian casualties? How many Britons protested two months later against the sack of Berlin by the Red Army? Amid the hatred and cruelty which had become instruments of modern warfare there was little room for such unpatriotic sentiments as compassion for the other side.

From John L. Stipp, Allen W. Dirrim and C. Warren Hollister, *The Rise and Development of Western Civilization, 1660 to the Present* (New York, 1967), pp. 611-613. Copyright © 1967 by John Wiley and Sons, Inc.

Even before the war's end, plans were made for the creation of a world organization that would prevent the coming of another great conflict. The basic motivation, of course, derived from man's growing realization that civilization and modern war are incompatible. Tactically the planning for a new world organization was made considerably easier by the habit formed during the war by the Big Three's leaders of holding face-to-face meetings to discuss mutual concerns. From 1943 to 1945 no less than five of these conferences brought the Allied heads of state together. Because the meetings dramatized the emergence of an incipient one-worldism (as well as produced decisions we need to note), we may give brief notice to them.

The first conference was set up by Roosevelt and Churchill at Casablanca (1943) to decide upon general matters of strategy and policy. Out of it came the decision to land troops in Africa . . . in preparation for the invasion of Europe, and the policy of unconditional surrender eventually applied to Italy, Germany, and Japan. Later that year Roosevelt, Churchill, and Chiang Kai-shek conferred in Cairo, and Roosevelt and Churchill moved on to Tehran in Persia. This afforded Roosevelt his first opportunity to meet Stalin who, understandably, urged the immediate opening of a Second Front; he also demanded the ultimate breaking up of Germany into a number of small states. In February 1945, as the ring was closing around Germany, the three leaders met again, this time in the Crimea at Yalta. In this meeting certain major decisions were reached: a defeated Germany was to be disarmed, demilitarized, and dismembered, as the Allies "might deem requisite for future peace and security"; Russia promised to declare war against Japan soon after Germany's defeat; certain territories in Asia were to be given to Russia; a new world organization would take the place of the discredited League of Nations. Following Germany's surrender in May 1945, Allied leaders—this time Attlee, who replaced Churchill after a Labour electoral victory, Truman, who became President in April 1945 upon the death of Roosevelt, and Stalin—met at Potsdam, a suburb of Berlin. To the three d's of the German policy outlined at Yalta, two others were added: denazification and democratization; and dismemberment was toned down to decentralization. It was also decided to divide Germany into four occupation zones until a general peace conference could meet and draw up a definite settlement. Berlin, deep in the Russian assigned area, was also divided into four spheres of occupation, one for each of the Big Three, and one for France.

Plans for peace as well as war brought representatives of the great powers to the conference table from time to time during the war period. In 1941 Roosevelt and Churchill met in Canada to formulate a statement of war aims. To a later generation harassed by seemingly endless crises, the Atlantic Charter, as it came to be called, may seem highly idealistic. Both America and Britain foreswore any intention to annex foreign territories, promised to honor the wishes of the people concerned in whatever territorial changes were to be effected, unequivocally supported the principle of self-determination for every people, and declared their faith in the possibility of creating a world free from fear and want. In January 1943, representatives of twenty-six countries signed a pact embodying these principles. Later in the year the United Nations Relief and Rehabilitation Administration (U.N.R.R.A.) was created to provide food, clothing, and medical supplies to nations ravaged by the war.

When it became apparent in late 1944 that the war was drawing to an end, representatives of Britain, Russia, China, and the United States held a series of meetings in Dumbarton Oaks (in Washington, D.C.) to lay the groundwork for the creation of the new international organization. Early the next year (April to June 1945) representatives from fifty nations met in San Francisco to draw up a constitution for the new organization, to be called the United Nations. To carry out its purposes—to maintain world peace, to "develop friendly relations among nations," and to "encourage respect for human rights" and freedoms—three main bodies were created. One, the General Assembly, was commissioned to consider world problems of almost any kind and to make recommendations about what should be done. Every member was given one vote; all resolutions required a majority vote for passage. The size of the second body, the Security Council, was limited to eleven members (now fifteen), including five permanent members: the United States, Britain, France, the Soviet Union, and "Nationalist" China. Both the United States and the U.S.S.R. insisted upon the right of each Council member to exercise an absolute veto whenever its national interests indicated the need for it. Thus, although the Council was given the right to sanction the use of military force to oppose aggression, the negative vote of any one of the Council's members could stop U.N. action. None of the great states would have agreed to become working members of the organization if this provision had not been included. Otherwise, they stood the chance of being outvoted on a sanctions measure by small states that could not assume the power responsibility for making the decision effective. The third branch, the General Secretariat, was set up to exercise executive functions much in the manner of the American presidency. Finally, like the old League, the U.N. also was given the authority to set up a number of auxiliary organizations dealing, for example, with labor and health conditions, the world's food supply, and the problem of coordinating international civil aviation activities. It should be emphasized that despite the panoply of powers given to the new world body it was intended to be, and remains, a loose confederation of sovereign states.

A U.S. Marine Corps mortar crew in action on the island of Iwo Jima, February 1945. The marines suffered about 20,000 casualties in a month's fighting to secure this barren volcanic island in the Western Pacific. Iwo Jima quickly became a U.S. air base, one in a string of island bases used to carry out massive air raids on the Japanese home islands.

Reading 316

The Bomb That Changed the World

The atomic bomb was the single most destructive weapon used in World War II. After the war its existence generated one of the most controversial issues involved in planning the peace. Yet the dropping of an atomic bomb on Hiroshima was not an isolated act of destruction, but part of a philosophy of war which was shared in large measure by both Allied powers and Axis powers. Fred Cook, a journalist, examines the broader implications of this philosophy in a study of what he calls "the warfare state."

Reprinted with permission of The Macmillan Company from *The Warfare State* by Fred J. Cook, pp. 115-116, 118-120. © 1962 by Fred J. Cook. Footnotes omitted by the editors.

The atomic bomb that fell on Hiroshima exploded with only slightly less impact among America's civilian institutions. Yet only a small minority at the time appreciated its implications. The public at large, the Military and the statesmen united in a mood of patriotic awe and pride at the immensity of our achievement, and few persons, in high place or low, had the vision to recognize its true significance. Plainly, however, such superdestructive power rendered all the old criteria of power obsolete; clearly, the ruthless employment of that power to obliterate 80,000 men, women and children in one blinding flash meant that all considerations of morality, all moral restraint, had now become archaic concepts; and this combination—the possession of the limitlessly lethal weapon, the demise of morality—signified that naked force had been enthroned over the world as never before. This stark fact carried with it inevitable corollaries. The final enthronement of force spelled inevitably the beginning of the world's most awesome arms race in which each nation would seek to possess that force; and it virtually insured the complete dominance of the Military since only the Military would be supposed to know all the answers in the realm of force. . . .

Both the moral and strategic dilemmas of the coming atomic age had been foreseen by the more perceptive men, and they were to be argued to their pre-ordained wrong turnings. If World War I had undermined the fibre of western man and led to the depravity of Hitler, World War II had marked the virtual death of western morality. The fascist dictators began it, and democracy, giving only lip service to the principles of Christianity, had aped the ways of the dictators. Hitler had ordered the mass-bombing extermination of Rotterdam; the Allies replied, as soon as they had the power, with the indiscriminate bombing of German cities. War, a barbarity that for generations had been waged under strict rules of conduct for the protection of the homes and the civilization of a nation, now lost the justification of this purpose, for mass slaughter became one of its primary objectives. No longer were women and children to be protected by the armies; they were to be one of the prime targets of armies everywhere under the Fascist-Nazi theory that such sub-human horrors would break the national will to resist. No longer was there even the pretext that high-flying bombers were seeking out military targets. In night bombing raids such as the one in which the R.A.F. destroyed Hamburg by blast and fire storm, total destruction of an entire population became the goal. As Lewis Mumford has written, the "democratic governments sanctioned the dehumanized techniques of fascism. This was Nazidom's firmest victory and democracy's most servile surrender."

Once the surrender had been made, there is considerable evidence that the war lords of the Allies came to relish the slaughter. The dedicated fanatics of air power had to prove, at whatever cost, the validity of their thesis that bombing alone could bring a great nation to its knees, and so the raids over Germany were mounted in ever greater fury against centers of civilian population in which the military targets were minimal. In the closing days of the war in Europe, with the Nazi system obviously doomed, crushing area attacks were launched against the cities of Augsberg, Bochum, Leipzig, Hagen, Dortmund, Oberhausen, Schweinfurt and Bremen. These cities, as the U.S. Strategic Bombing Survey later acknowledged, contributed only minute percentages to over-all German production. In all of them, there were just three big war plants, the steel works at Dortmund and the aircraft plants at Bremen and Leipzig. Each was a specific target that could have been bombed separately, but in each case the city, not the installation, became the objective.

"On what basis was the death of these eight cities decided upon?" Professor Fleming has asked with reason.

> We have elaborate precautions to prevent the execution of one innocent individual. He must be clearly guilty, beyond peradventure of doubt, but when we are engaged in mass destruction the death of cities will be decided

by a few military men, doubtless estimable men, who write down the names of the doomed cities on a piece of paper.

Does a board of generals gravely decide that ten more cities must die? Or does a single man condemn ten cities to death by putting their names on a list of the doomed?

The destruction wrought by conventional bombs and shells: a street in Berlin shortly after the end of World War II.

The destruction wrought by an atomic bomb: a residential area of Nagasaki, Japan. Here an American plane dropped an A-bomb on August 9, 1945, three days after the first one was dropped on Hiroshima.

This was war, World War II style. Armies no longer fought armies alone; they sought the death and destruction of an entire population. Yet we had not become, in the early stages at least, so callous as not to recognize that this changed concept *did* pose a moral issue. This, naturally, we recognize no longer. We calmly discuss obliterating people by the millions as if such a deed were nothing more than an exercise in semantics. The inhumanity implicit in our calm acceptance of the concept marks in itself the illimitable horizon of the barbarous once it has become the acknowledged norm. Under the pressures of war, without as yet the active presence of the A-bomb, the moral issue could hardly have been expected to be perceived in the terms of the ultimate crisis it has become; but it is at least significant that its implications were foreseen in higher military circles and were for a time quite seriously debated.

"As late as the spring of 1942," Lewis Mumford has written,

> as I know by personal observation, a memorandum was circulated among military advisers in Washington propounding this dilemma: If by fighting the war against Japan by orthodox methods it might require five or ten years to conquer the enemy, while with incendiary air attacks on Japanese cities Japan's resistance might be broken down in a year or two, would it be morally justifiable to use the second means? Now it is hard to say which is more astonishing, that the morality of total extermination was then seriously debated in military circles or that today its morality is taken for granted, as outside debate, even among a large part of the clergy.

More than any other event that has taken place in modern times this sudden radical change-over from war to collective extermination reversed the whole course of human history.

By 1945 the vital decision had been made, the generals calmly chalked off the cities that were to die, and only the most wild-eyed idealists had any qualms about the inhuman process. We devised napalm bombs and built 1,000-bomber air fleets to fry the Japanese in their homeland. One fire raid on Tokyo incinerated an estimated 125,000 persons; another, nearly 100,000. So a precedent was established. When mass slaughter on such horrifying scale once was accepted as a fact of war, why be squeamish about whether the deed was to be done with napalm bombs in long, flaming, agonizing hours, or by the demoniac energy of the atom in a few blinding minutes? The mind of man had already been conditioned to accept, even to welcome and cheer, the most fiendish slaughter that the mind of man was capable of devising.

Why the United States Dropped the Bomb

The use of the atomic bomb ended the war with Japan, the final phase of World War II. Yet there remains a controversy among historians as to why the bomb was used. Were Hiroshima and Nagasaki destroyed to end the war or to frighten the Soviet Union? One answer to this question is offered by Gar Alperovitz, a historian of America's foreign relations.

From Gar Alperovitz, "Why We Dropped the Bomb," *The Progressive*, XXIX (August, 1965), pp. 11–13. Copyright © 1965 by *The Progressive*. Subheadings added by the editors.

I

Axis and Allies

Dear Mr. President, I think it is very important that I should have a talk with you as soon as possible on a highly secret matter. I mentioned it to you shortly after you took office, but have not urged it since on account of the pressure you have been under. It, however, has such a bearing on our present foreign relations and has such an important effect upon all my thinking in this field that I think you ought to know about it without much further delay.

> Secretary of War Henry L. Stimson
> to President Truman, April 24, 1945

This note was written twelve days after Franklin Delano Roosevelt's death and two weeks before World War II ended in Europe. The following day Secretary Stimson advised President Truman that the "highly secret matter" would have a "decisive" effect upon America's postwar foreign policy. Stimson then outlined the role the atomic bomb would play in America's relations with other countries. In diplomacy, he confided to his diary, the weapon would be a "master card."

In the spring of 1945, postwar problems unfolded as rapidly as the Allied armies converged in Central Europe. During the fighting which preceded Nazi surrender the Red Army conquered a great belt of territory bordering the Soviet Union. Debating the consequences of this fact, American policy-makers defined a series of interrelated problems: What political and economic pattern was likely to emerge in Eastern and Central Europe? Would Soviet influence predominate? Most important, what power—if any—did the United States have to effect the ultimate settlement on the very borders of Russia?

Roosevelt, Churchill, and Stalin had attempted to resolve these issues of East-West influence at the February, 1945, Yalta Conference. With the Red Army clearly in control of Eastern Europe, the West was in a weak bargaining position. It was important to reach an understanding with Stalin before American troops began their planned withdrawal from the European continent. Poland, the first major country intensely discussed by the Big Three, took on unusual significance; the balance of influence struck between Soviet-oriented and Western-oriented politicians in the government of this one country could set a pattern for big-power relationships in the rest of Eastern Europe.

Although the Yalta Conference ended with a signed accord covering Poland, within a few weeks it was clear that Allied understanding was more apparent than real. None of the heads of government interpreted the somewhat vague agreement in the same way. Churchill began to press for more Western influence; Stalin urged less. True to his well-known policy of cooperation and conciliation, Roosevelt attempted to achieve a more definite understanding for Poland and a pattern for East-West relations in Europe. Caught for much of the last of his life between the determination of Churchill and the stubbornness of Stalin, Roosevelt at times fired off angry cables to Moscow, and at others warned London against an "attempt to evade the fact that we placed, as clearly shown in the agreement, somewhat more emphasis . . . [on Soviet-oriented Polish politicians in the government]."

President Roosevelt died on April 12, 1945, only two months after Yalta. When President Truman met with Secretary Stimson to discuss the "bearing" of the atomic bomb upon foreign relations, the powers were deeply ensnarled in a tense public struggle over the meaning of the Yalta agreement. Poland had come to symbolize *all* East-West relations. Truman was forced to pick up the tangled threads of policy with little knowledge of the broader, more complex issues involved.

Herbert Feis, a noted expert on the period, has written that "Truman made up his mind that he would not depart from Roosevelt's course or renounce his ways." Others have argued that "we tried to work out the problems of the peace in close cooperation with the Russians." It is often believed that American policy followed a conciliatory course, changing—in reaction to Soviet intransigence—only in 1947 with the Truman Doctrine and the Marshall Plan. My own belief is somewhat different. It derives from the comment of Mr. Truman's Secretary of State, James F. Byrnes, that by early autumn of 1945 it was "understandable" that Soviet leaders should feel American policy had shifted radically after Roosevelt's death. It is now evident that, far from following his predecessor's policy of cooperation, shortly after taking office President Truman launched a powerful foreign policy initiative aimed at reducing or eliminating Soviet influence in Europe.

II

A Change of Policy

The ultimate point of this study is not, however, that America's approach to Russia changed after Roosevelt. Rather it is that the atomic bomb played a role in the formulation of policy, particularly in connection with President Truman's only meeting with Stalin, the Potsdam Conference of late July and early August, 1945. Again, my judgment differs from Feis's conclusion that "the light of the explosion 'brighter than a thousand suns' filtered into the conference rooms at Potsdam only as a distant gleam." I believe new evidence proves not only that the atomic bomb influenced diplomacy, but that it determined much of Mr. Truman's shift to a tough policy aimed at forcing Soviet acquiescence to American plans for Eastern and Central Europe.

The weapon "gave him an entirely new feeling of confidence," the President told his Secretary of War, Henry L. Stimson. By the time of Potsdam, Mr. Truman had been advised on the role of the atomic bomb by both Secretary Stimson and Secretary of State Byrnes. Though the two men differed as to tactics, each urged a tough line. Part of my study attempts to define how closely Truman followed a subtle policy outlined by Stimson, and to what extent he followed the straightforward advice of Byrnes that the bomb (in Mr. Truman's words) "put us in a position to dictate our own terms at the end of the war."

Stalin's approach seems to have been cautiously moderate during the brief few months here described. It is perhaps symbolized by the Soviet-sponsored free elections which routed the Communist Party in Hungary in the autumn of 1945. I do not attempt to interpret this moderation, nor to explain how or why Soviet policy changed to the harsh totalitarian controls characteristic of the period after 1946.

The judgment that Truman radically altered Roosevelt's policy in mid-1945 nevertheless obviously suggests a new point of departure for interpretations of the cold war. In late 1945, General Dwight D. Eisenhower observed in Moscow that "before the atom bomb was used, I would have said, yes, I was sure that we could keep the peace with Russia. Now I don't know . . . People are frightened and disturbed all over. Everyone feels insecure again." To what extent did postwar Soviet policies derive from insecurity based upon a fear of America's atom bomb and changed policy? I stop short of this fundamental question, concluding that further research is needed to test Secretary Stimson's judgment that "the problem of our satisfactory relations with Russia [was] not merely connected with but [was] virtually dominated by the problem of the atomic bomb."

Similarly, I believe more research and more information are needed to reach a conclusive understanding of why the atomic bomb was used. The common belief is that the question is closed, and that President Truman's explanation is correct: "The dropping of the bombs stopped the war, saved millions of lives." My own view is that available evidence shows the atomic bomb was not needed to end the war or to save lives—and that this was understood by American leaders at the time.

General Eisenhower recently recalled that in mid-1945 he expressed a similar opinion to the Secretary of War: "I told him I was against it on two counts. First, the Japanese were ready to surrender and it wasn't necessary to hit them with that awful thing. Second, I hated to see our country be the first to use such a weapon . . ." To go beyond the limited conclusion that the bomb was unnecessary is not possible at present.

Perhaps the most remarkable aspect of the decision to use the atomic bomb is that the President and his senior political advisers do not seem ever to have shared Eisenhower's "grave misgivings." They simply assumed that they would use the bomb, never really giving serious consideration to not using it. Hence, to state in a precise way the question, "Why was the atomic bomb used?" is to ask why senior political officials did *not* seriously question its use, as General Eisenhower did.

The first point to note is that the decision to use the weapon did not derive from overriding military considerations. Despite Mr. Truman's subsequent statement that the weapon "saved millions of lives," Eisenhower's judgment that it was "completely unnecessary" as a measure to save lives was almost certainly correct. This is not a matter of hindsight; *before the atomic bomb was dropped each of the Joint Chiefs of Staff advised that it was highly likely that Japan could be forced to surrender "unconditionally" without use of the bomb and without an invasion.* Indeed, this characterization of the position taken by the senior military advisers is a conservative one.

General George C. Marshall's June 18 appraisal was the most cautiously phrased advice offered by any of the Joint Chiefs: "The impact of Russian entry on the already hopeless Japanese may well be the decisive action levering them into capitulation . . ." Admiral William D. Leahy was absolutely certain there was no need for the bombing to obviate the necessity of an invasion. His judgment after the fact was the same as his view before the bombing: "It is my opinion that the use of this barbarous weapon at Hiroshima and Nagasaki was of no material assistance in our war against Japan. The Japanese were already defeated and ready to surrender . . ." Similarly, through most of 1945, Admiral Ernest J. King believed the bomb unnecessary, and Generals Henry H. Arnold and Curtis E. LeMay defined the official Air Force position in this way: Whether or not the atomic bomb should be dropped was not for the Air Force to decide, but explosion of the bomb was not necessary to win the war or make an invasion unnecessary.

Similar views prevailed in Britain long before the bombs were used. General Hastings Ismay recalls that by the time of Potsdam, "for some time past it had been firmly fixed in my mind that the Japanese were tottering." Ismay's reaction to the suggestion of the bombing was, like Eisenhower's and Leahy's, one of "revulsion." And Churchill, who as early as September, 1944, felt that Russian entry into the war with Japan was likely to force capitulation, has written: "It would be a mistake to suppose that the fate of Japan was settled by the atomic bomb. Her defeat was certain before the first bomb fell . . ."

The military appraisals made before the weapons were used have been confirmed by numerous post-surrender studies. The best known is that of the United States Strategic Bombing Survey. The Survey's conclusion is unequivocal: "Japan would have surrendered even if the atomic bombs had not been dropped, even if Russia had not entered the war, and even if no invasion had been planned or contemplated."

That military considerations were not decisive is confirmed—and illuminated—by the fact that the President did not even ask the opinion of the military adviser most directly concerned. General Douglas MacArthur, Supreme Commander of Allied Forces in the Pacific, was simply informed of the weapon shortly before it was used at Hiroshima. Before his death he stated on numerous occasions that, like Eisenhower, he believed the atomic bomb was completely unnecessary from a military point of view.

III
The Role of Politics

Although military considerations were not primary, unquestionably political considerations related to Russia played a major role in the decision; from at least mid-May in 1945, American policy-makers hoped to end the hostilities before the Red Army entered Manchuria. For this reason they had no wish to test whether Russian entry into the war would force capitulation—as most thought likely—long before the scheduled November Allied invasion of Japan. Indeed, they actively attempted to delay Stalin's declaration of war.

Nevertheless, it would be wrong to conclude that the atomic bomb was used simply to keep the Red Army out of Manchuria. Given the desperate efforts of the Japanese to surrender, and President Truman's willingness to offer assurances to the Emperor, it is entirely possible that the war could have been ended by negotiation before the Red Army had begun its attack. But after history's first atomic explosion at Alamogordo neither the President nor his senior political advisers were interested in exploring this possibility.

One reason may have been their fear that if time-consuming negotiations were once initiated, the Red Army might attack in order to seize Manchurian objectives. But, if this explanation is accepted, once more one must conclude that the bomb was used primarily because it was felt to be politically important to prevent Soviet domination of the area.

Such a conclusion is difficult to accept, for American interests in Manchuria, although historically important to the State Department, were not of great significance. The further question therefore arises: Were there other political reasons for using the atomic bomb? In approaching this question, it is important to note that most of the men involved at the time who since have made their views public always mention *two* considerations which dominated discussions. The first was the desire to end the Japanese war quickly, which was not primarily a military consideration, but a political one. The second is always referred to indirectly.

In June, for example, a leading member of President Truman's Advisory Interim Committee's scientific panel, A. H. Compton, advised against the Franck report's suggestion of a technical demonstration of the new weapon: Not only was there a possibility that this might not end the war promptly, but failure to make a combat demonstration would mean the "loss of the opportunity to impress the world with the national sacrifices that enduring security demanded." The general phrasing that the bomb was needed to "impress the world" has been made more specific by J. Robert Oppenheimer. Testifying on this matter some years later he stated that the second of the two "overriding considerations" in discussions regarding the bomb was "the effect of our actions on the stability, on our strength, and the stability of the postwar world." And the problem of postwar stability was inevitably the problem of Russia. Oppenheimer has put it this way: "Much of the discussion revolved around the question raised by Secretary Stimson as to whether there was any hope at all of using this development to get less barbarous relations with the Russians."

Vannevar Bush, Stimson's chief aide for atomic matters, has been quite explicit: "That bomb was developed on time . . ." Not only did it mean a quick end to the Japanese war, but "it was also delivered on time so that there was no necessity for any concessions to Russia at the end of the war."

Alternatives to the Bomb

Gar Alperovitz (see Reading 317) explained why American policy makers decided to use the atomic bomb, an explanation that emphasized their concern over future Soviet-American relations. Other students of the subject have arrived at more complex explanations, taking into consideration the emotions and ideas generated by four years of total war.

Reprinted by permission of Coward, McCann & Geoghegan, Inc. from *The Decision to Drop the Bomb* by Fred Freed and Len Giovannitti. Copyright © 1965 by Fred Freed and Len Giovannitti. Pp. 307–316. Subheadings added by the editors.

I
The Choices before the United States

In August 1945, with the approval of the President, the Smyth report was made public.

Written by Professor Henry D. Smyth, chairman of the Department of Physics at Princeton and a consultant to the Manhattan District, it was a history of the development of the bomb written before the test at Alamogordo.

"The end of June," Smyth wrote, "finds us expecting from day to day to hear of the explosion of the first atomic bomb devised by man." But Smyth had no doubt about what had been created:

> A weapon ... that is potentially destructive beyond the wildest nightmare of the imagination; a weapon so ideally suited to sudden unannounced attack that a country's major cities might be destroyed overnight by an ostensibly friendly power.

This weapon, Smyth went on to say, had not been devised "by the devilish inspiration of some warped genius but by the arduous labor of thousands of normal men and women working for the safety of their country."

The energy released in uranium fission, he said, was "only about one tenth of one percent of its mass." If scientists should discover a means of releasing even a small percentage of the mass of "some common material, civilization would have the means to commit suicide at will."

The impact of this new fact in the world, its effect on war, diplomacy, life itself, Smyth said, "raises many questions that must be answered in the near future.... These questions are not technical questions; they are political and social questions and the answers given to them may affect all mankind for generations."

By the time the report was made public the atomic age had already begun: Three atomic weapons had been exploded, two Japanese cities had been destroyed, over a hundred thousand Japanese had died. Of wartime necessity, the decisions that led to this introduction to the new age had been made by a few men in secret. Right or wrong they had set a direction and a tone. The world would not be the same. The steps they had taken could not be retraced.

Did they have a choice?

Was the choice they made justified?

Would the world have been a better place if they had made a different choice?

In answer to the first question, they did have a choice. It was not *necessary* to drop an atomic bomb on Japan to *win* the war. The war was already almost won in the summer of 1945. It was a matter of time and bloodshed until Japan would be forced to surrender.

The surrender might have been brought about in several ways. Both Japanese and American military testimony indicates the Allied victory could have been accomplished by an invasion. But all agree that against the suicidal resistance the Japanese were prepared to mount, at least for a brief time, losses on both sides would have been enormous.

But there were other alternatives that might have ended the war without an invasion and without the use of the atomic bomb. One was the fire raids. On this subject, General LeMay has said:

> General Arnold made a visit to our headquarters in the late spring of 1945 and he asked that question: When is the war going to end? ... We went back to some of the charts we had been showing him showing the rate of activity, the targets we were hitting, and it was completely evident that we were running out of targets along in September and by October there wouldn't really be much to work on, except probably railroads or something of that sort. So we felt that if there were no targets left in Japan, certainly there probably wouldn't be much war left.

Such a strategy, the burning of the remaining Japanese cities, between August 6 and September or October, might well have ended the war. Loss of American life would have been inconsiderable, although the number of American dead would probably have been raised by several thousand.

What seems clear is that many more Japanese than died at Hiroshima and Nagasaki would have died in the two or three months of fire raids that LeMay estimated would be needed to end the war, and that Japanese suffering and privation would have been considerably increased.

Another alternative was the Navy's proposal to starve Japan into surrender. This process would obviously have been slower, perhaps more painful than the fire assault.

II

New Factors

But in the summer of 1945 the United States suddenly had in its hands a weapon that made quick victory seem certain and, by that time,

---

The characteristic mushroom-shaped cloud created by a nuclear explosion, in this case the atomic test staged by the United States at Bikini atoll in the Central Pacific in July 1946. Such tests by the United States and Russia, and later by Great Britain, France, and China, kept the world's peoples aware of the ever-increasing destructiveness of nuclear weapons.

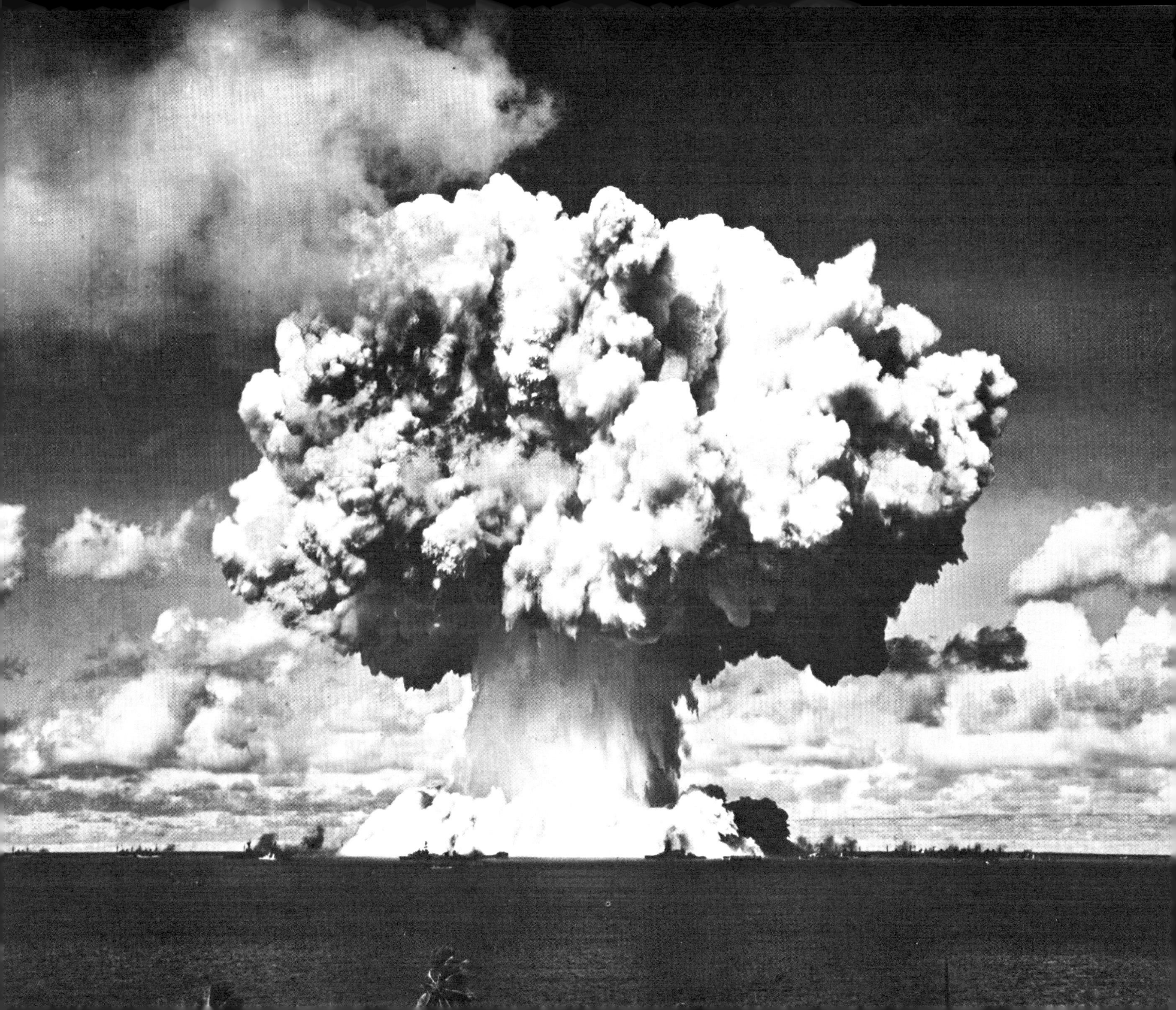

the reasons that made such a quick victory desirable had multiplied. No longer was it the *sole* aim of the United States policy to win the war with the minimum loss of life. Now there were new factors.

One was Europe, since the end of the war in a chaotic state, with the danger of economic breakdown threatening France and England, as well as the war-ravaged nations to the east. Without United States money and resources there would be hunger in Europe in the winter of 1945–46. Beyond the humanitarian desire to feed hungry people, there was among some of the American leaders recognition of the practical fact that in this season of anarchy "half and maybe all of Europe might be communistic by the end of next winter." To almost all of the United States policy makers it was now clear that in the immediate postwar world the Soviet Union would no longer be an ally but, at the least, a rival, and possibly an outright enemy.

By mid-August the Soviet Union would be in the war against Japan. Stalin had already made it clear that he wanted to share in the occupation of the home islands. He had indicated his feeling that the Emperor should be removed. He plainly favored a Japan that would be politically and economically weak, that would afford no "counterweight" to the Soviet Union in the Far East. But Byrnes, Grew, Forrestal and Stimson all agreed that a viable Japan was desirable. All, to a greater or lesser degree, foresaw a possible showdown in the Far East with the Soviet Union.

Thus, to the wartime goal of ending the war as quickly as possible with a minimum loss of life, were now added strong, practical, political reasons why, in the view of the policy makers, that goal would be desirable.

Even more practically there was this fact: Opinion was now divided among American policy makers, and between American and British policy makers, on the terms to end the war. "Unconditional surrender" was a catch phrase. In Japan it required redefinition and there was growing disagreement as to what it meant. But if the war could be ended quickly, in Churchill's words, "at the cost of a few explosions," this disagreement would not have to be worked out. It could simply be ignored.

The atomic bomb, then, was ready for use at a moment when it would not only end the war, but when it seemed to solve for Allied policy makers many of the internal and external problems that were beginning to pressure them.

P.M.S. Blackett, the British physicist and Nobel laureate, and others argue that the dropping of the atomic bombs was actually not the final military operation of the Second World War but the first diplomatic move in the Cold War. In other words, that its main target was not Japan but the Soviet Union.

It can be argued persuasively that the Soviet Union was, in the final days before Hiroshima, much on the minds of Truman, Byrnes and Stimson. It is equally clear that until he knew the results of the Trinity test on the evening of July 16, Truman saw as his main purpose at Potsdam to bring the Red Army into the war against Japan. In the twenty-one days that followed, he and his advisers seemed, despite the President's later denials, completely to change their minds. This does not, however, mean that their sole, or even primary, reason for using the bomb was as a political weapon against the Russians. This political consideration was an *additional* reason.

Was the Bomb Necessary?

To the question: Would the world have been a better place if they had made a different choice?—there is no answer. The bomb would not have remained a secret. The Soviet Union would have acquired it. Bigger bombs and more efficient delivery systems would have followed. That the great powers of the world were ready to or capable of giving up control of such enormous leverage in the arena of international politics seems unlikely. Some have suggested that the destruction of Hiroshima and Nagasaki had a salutary effect: That the people of the world now knew what this new weapon would do, had seen its power, and so were more disposed than they might have been to fear it and the danger of a new war. In this view, the dead of Hiroshima and Nagasaki are martyrs to the survival of the rest of civilization. No one can say whether this is true or nonsense. One would like to believe that rational man can understand the bomb's capacity to destroy without requiring physical evidence of it against human life. In any case, the nuclear age was born. It exists. It cannot be returned to the laboratory.

If the answer to the first question is that there was a choice, the answer to the third is that, having made the choice, it is useless to speculate on what might have been. What does seem useful is to ask whether the use of the atomic bomb, which was not *necessary*, was in fact *justified*.

To put it another way: Could the bomb have been used to end the war and save lives without dropping it on Japanese cities?

Since 1945 the most frequent charge against those who made the decision is that there ought to have been a *demonstration* first. But the word has been used so imprecisely that there has been much confusion about what kind of demonstration is meant and how it might have been held. Some suggested a technical demonstration on a desert island. Dr. Edward Teller wanted to see a bomb exploded high in the air at night over Tokyo Bay. Admiral Lewis Strauss thought a forest outside Tokyo would be a suitable target. Dr. Rudolph Peierls' conception of a demonstration was the bombing of an area with a smaller population than Hiroshima's, "probably destroying some houses, probably killing some people, because an abstract test wouldn't have been so impressive." Dr. Teller felt that an explosion over Tokyo Bay "would have impressed the Emperor" and "in all probability it would have ended the war." Dr. Robert Oppenheimer spoke of such a demonstration as "an enormous nuclear firecracker detonated at great height doing little damage" and was unsure that it would have had any profound effect. Dr. James B. Conant expressed doubt that the Japanese, if they had been invited to Alamogordo, would have been impressed by the test there. Clearly the scientists were divided as to the usefulness of *any* kind of demonstration, and those closest to the policy makers, including the four members of the Scientific Advisory Panel, were not able to recommend one that they felt was "likely to induce surrender."

If some of the scientists could later complain that they had not known the political and military situation at the time Hiroshima was bombed, they had known better than anyone else the scientific situation. Yet none of the key scientists—Oppenheimer, Compton, Fermi, Lawrence, Conant or Bush—proposed a demonstration even after witnessing the bomb test at Alamogordo.

IV
Other Possibilities

Was there any other possibility?

There was at least one other: A specific early warning to Japan concerning the nature of the new weapon combined with a strong inducement to the Japanese leaders to end the war.

Such a warning and such inducement were proposed at various times in the months before the Potsdam Declaration. At the June 18 meeting of the Joint Chiefs with Truman, McCloy proposed a specific warning. In May, Grew urged telling the Japanese that the Emperor could be retained and that Japan would not be destroyed as a nation. Yet in the end no warning of the existence of the bomb was issued, and the hint that the Emperor might remain on his throne was so obscure that hardly any Americans, much less Japanese, understood it.

Why did the warning omit any reference to the bomb, or to the Emperor? Had the Americans who drafted and issued the Declaration at Potsdam already made up their minds to drop the bomb, regardless of the Japanese answer? Were they no longer receptive to the possibility of surrender until at least one bomb had been dropped on a Japanese city?

Whatever the merits of a specific warning as to the nature of the new weapon, the idea was quickly discarded. Byrnes, Stimson and Marshall all opposed it. When McCloy suggested it in June at a meeting of the President and the Joint Chiefs, no one supported him. There was an often-expressed fear that if there were such a specific warning and then the bomb failed to live up to its promise, the blow to United States morale and the encouragement to the Japanese military to fight "to the bitter end" would be enormously damaging. Behind this thinking may have been a fear of the political repercussions within the United States to such a failure. The military also had doubts about the success of a mission about which the Japanese had been warned. On this point, however, the authors find themselves in agreement with Herbert Feis, who argues

> that the risk [of warning Japan] should have been taken and the cost endured, for by doing this we might have been spared the need to use it [the bomb]. In the more likely event that the Japanese would not have heeded even the most explicit and ample warning, we as a people would be freer of any remorse. . . .

When the subject of an ultimatum first came up, Stimson agreed with Grew about retaining the Emperor but he opposed delivering the ultimatum until the bomb had been tested because he saw the bomb as the "shock" that would cause the Japanese to end the war if the ultimatum failed. Once the test was successful he urged that the ultimatum be issued immediately, although without specific mention of the bomb. But by then his influence with the President had waned. Byrnes' advice now carried greater weight. And Byrnes was deeply sensitive to the probable outcry from Congress, the liberals and the public if he seemed to lessen the unconditional surrender terms Roosevelt had laid down. In the minds of many Americans the Emperor was the symbol and core of Japanese militarism. It would be appeasement of the militarists to allow him to remain.

Byrnes was also aware that the Soviet Union did not want to retain the Emperor. He was prepared to issue the ultimatum without consulting Stalin but not to change the conditions of surrender. This, it was felt, might lead Stalin to believe, as he had regarding Italy, that the Allies were trying to sign a separate peace with Japan. This kind of breach could not, before Hiroshima, be risked.

The result was that Byrnes' ultimatum was a compromise. As he said, "the very purpose of it was to assure them [the Japanese] that they could have the decision and at the same time not start a controversy among ourselves about the position of the Emperor."

The ultimatum was delayed for ten days, from the 16th of July, when the news of the successful test reached Potsdam, until the 26th. During that period the Hiroshima bomb arrived at Tinian and the orders for its delivery were cut. Whatever the reason for the delay in issuing the ultimatum, it would seem to have made little difference. The Japanese military forced its rejection and there is no indication that ten days more would have changed their minds.

Another possibility remains: Could the Allies have exploited the Japanese peace feelers?

Probably there was nothing that could have been done about those which were carried out by various individuals in Switzerland, Sweden and Germany in the spring of 1945. None of these Japanese diplomats had a clear mandate from those in power in Tokyo. None could negotiate authoritatively. But Ambassador Sato's efforts in Moscow were on a different level. The Army approved of his mission and the Foreign Minister urged him day after day to find a way out of the war for Japan.

The situation was complicated, however, by the fact that Stalin was the one leader who was committed to avoiding peace before August when his armies would enter the war and assure the concessions he had won at Yalta as the price of this entry.

The United States, however, knew about Sato's efforts. Could anything have been done to utilize this knowledge? Probably not. If the United States had asked the Soviet Union to open negotiations, the Soviets would surely have insisted on deposing the Emperor, sharing the occupation of the home islands and neutralizing Japan as a viable economic and political entity. Such terms would not have been acceptable to Japan, nor were they any longer satisfactory to the United States or Great Britain. Could negotiations have been carried out directly with Japan? Not without risking an open break with the Soviet Union. With Soviet armies poised in Eastern Europe and in Manchuria, such a move would certainly have been impractical as well as immoral. After Hiroshima and Nagasaki the United States might be able to dictate the terms of the Japanese surrender on the home islands. Certainly it would be foolish and dangerous before.

Beyond this, assuming the possibility of negotiations, Japan was not, in the peace feelers it extended to the Soviet Union, thinking of unconditional surrender. Nor was there any guarantee that the military would permit the surrender even if the government leaders agreed. And the effect of prolonged negotiations on the American public, conditioned by four years of bitter anti-Japanese propaganda, unconditional surrender, the memory of Pearl Harbor and the desire to see Japanese militarism wiped out, was incalculable. No American politician was prepared to risk the repercussions.

In the summer of 1945 Japan was on the brink of defeat. The civilian leaders were looking for a way out of the war. The military was pledged to one final bloody battle. The Soviet Union did not want to negotiate on any terms; the United States could not negotiate on the only terms the Japanese might find acceptable. An ultimatum was delivered that, largely for political reasons, failed to make the one point that might have provoked an interested response. However, in light of the struggle that went on within the Japanese government even after two atomic bombs and the Russian invasion of Manchuria and Korea, it is far from certain that an earlier ultimatum of any kind would have led to a quick surrender.

On the other hand, it is on this question of the timing of the ultimatum, with the assurance to Japan that she could retain her Emperor, that Stimson felt the United States may have failed to grasp the opportunity for an earlier surrender, possibly before the bomb was used. After the war he wrote:

> Only on the question of the Emperor did Stimson take, in 1945, a conciliatory view; only on this question did he later believe that history might find that the United States, by its delay in stating its position, had prolonged the war.

V

Unanswered Questions

Finally, it must be asked: Did the atomic bombs, in fact, end the war? The argument persists that Japan was ready to surrender anyway. This is reasonable, if no time limit is set on how soon the surrender would take place or how long Japan would hold out for better terms than those that were finally accepted. It has been said that Japan was ready in the spring to accept the terms agreed to in August; that is, retention of the Emperor and preservation of Japan as a nation. But the Emperor who was allowed to remain in August was not the Emperor Japan hoped to preserve before the atomic attack. The Emperor in August was subordinate to the Allied Supreme Commander. The Emperor was no longer divine. He had no promise of tenure He was to become a constitutional monarch in the democratic style of Europe. This clearly was not what the military had in mind when it spoke of preserving the "prerogatives" of the Emperor. What Japan was prepared to accept in the spring was a reduction of status but a retention of political, social and economic structure with the military caste still the core of power. To accept the destruction of the military society required the "shock" Stimson had foreseen.

Was this shock the bomb, or was it the Soviet entry into the war? The Japanese military were seeking a last suicidal battle on Japanese soil and for this it did not matter whether the Red Army was in Manchuria or not. Only one thing could prevent this last battle. If the enemy had a weapon that could destroy the power of the Japanese military *without an invasion,* the cause of the "last battle" fanatics was lost. The atomic bomb was that unique weapon.

It was in Churchill's words "almost supernatural." As soldiers the Japanese military could be excused for not being able to cope with it. They could surrender and still save face. As Cabinet Secretary Sakomizu said, the atomic bomb "provided an excuse" or in the words of Marquis Kido, "The presence of the atomic bomb made it easier for us politicians to negotiate peace."

Was the decision to use the bomb justified?

In the end the decision was made because a decision not to use it could *not* be justified. At the most pragmatic level, if it were not used Congress and the public would ask angry questions about the expenditure of two billion dollars for a weapon that was then withheld from combat. American soldiers would die and their families would ask if they could have been saved had the weapon been used. The Japanese might surrender if they were told they could keep their Emperor, if they were sufficiently warned, if the Red Army came into the war. But then again they might not. The fire raids might finish Japan. But that would take longer and kill more Japanese. The invasion force was forming, the veterans of Guadalcanal, Tarawa, Iwo Jima and Okinawa. The invasion might never have to be launched, but who could be certain? The Soviets were threatening Europe and making demands in the Far East. The United States wanted to avoid conflict but wouldn't it be better if the war against Japan could be ended before the Soviet Union got into it? Wasn't it finally the duty of the government to use any weapon that would save American lives? The momentum for this decision had been building since the project began. The tentative date had been talked about in 1944. Without an overriding reason to reverse its thrust, neither Stimson nor Truman nor any other leader could or wanted to stop it.

As Stimson wrote:

> If victory could be speeded by using the bomb, it should be used. If victory must be delayed in order to use the bomb, it should not be used. . . . The bomb was thus not treated as a separate subject, except to determine whether it should be used at all; once that decision had been made, the timing and the method of the use of the bomb were wholly subordinated to the objective of victory.

A generation later the pressure for victory seems less urgent. The death of a few more soldiers, the question of unconditional surrender, even the confrontation of the Soviet Union in the Far East, seem less immediate. The horror of the destruction of two cities, the deaths of more than a hundred thousand people, by two bombs, remains. A burden of moral guilt cannot be shaken.

TOPIC 60

THE COLD WAR

The war left two great military-industrial powers, the United States and the Soviet Union. Though large areas of the latter had been physically devastated by the war, the United States remained untouched by bomb or bullet. Since the Bolshevik Revolution of 1917 relationships between the two countries had ranged from hostile through the 1920s, to cool in the 1930s, to friendly during their common struggle against Nazi Germany. Despite cooperation between the Soviets and the Americans, a cooperation which began with the extension of lend-lease aid to Russia in the fall of 1941, mutual suspicion remained latent. The end of the war brought this suspicion to the surface. Each feared the power of the other and each consequently tried to consolidate or extend its influence. This topic considers the evidence for the fears underlying the "Cold War" and goes on to explore the nature of the American foreign policy which emerged in the late 1940s to cope with the perceived Russian threat.

Reading 319

The Cold War (1945-1949)

The hot war of 1939 to 1945 was almost immediately replaced by the Cold War which, in various forms, continues to the present. The nature and course of the conflict in the years following Hiroshima is presented in the following reading.

From John L. Stipp, Allen W. Dirrim and C. Warren Hollister, *The Rise and Development of Western Civilization, 1660 to the Present* (New York, 1967), Vol. II, pp. 659-661. Copyright © 1967 by John Wiley and Sons, Inc. Subheadings added and footnotes omitted by the editors.

I

Causes of the Cold War

Were he alive, Hitler could point with some gloating to a statement that he made just before his suicide in 1945: "With the defeat of the Reich . . . there will remain in the world only two powers capable of confronting each other—the United States and Soviet Russia. The laws of both history and geography will compel these two Powers to a trial of strength. . . ." Although we may seek comfort from the fact that one of the age's greatest liars spoke these lines, we cannot deny that the first of the two theses proved itself, at least until the advent of Communist China partially invalidated the Führer's arithmetic.

After the war collaboration between the capitalist and Communist worlds came to an abrupt end. It is idle to deny, although some have attempted to, that ideology was a basic cause of the cold war. In 1848 the bourgeois world was horrified at the pronouncements of the Communist Manifesto. A hundred years later it had much more reason to be apprehensive. Even though, as we have seen, Soviet Russia had lost over twenty million of its people in the war and had suffered a scarring of its earth beyond the comprehension of any who did not live there, it emerged from the long "Years of the Gun" with a greater strength than this ancient land had ever known. Its leaders believed that its Marxist way of life had saved it from destruction. Available evidence plainly indicates that its masses, although weary of Stalin, were not of a mind to turn the clock back to pre-Soviet capitalism. For millions in Russia and in other lands, Communism had come to stay. But Communists believed that staying meant encountering, battling, and eventually overcoming the non-Communist world. For their part, many among the capitalist ruling elites believed that the world would never know either peace or prosperity so long as the "Communist menace" existed.

But more than ideology was involved in the renewed struggle. Soviet leaders remembered that after World War I the Western powers had ringed Russia with a tight "cordon sanitaire."* This time they were determined to forestall a repetition of this by doing some ringing of their own. Before the war had ended they had annexed Estonia, Latvia, Lithuania, and a portion of Poland. By 1948 they had set up Communist regimes in Czechoslovakia, Albania, Bulgaria, Rumania, and Hungary. The eastern provinces of Germany,

---
*Before 1939 the nations of eastern Europe were generally hostile to the Soviet Union—Eds.

occupied by Russian troops since early 1945, were also consolidated into the German Democratic Republic (1949), under Russian domination. Thus the Russian push westward was motivated by a mixture of ideological concerns, determination to revenge the sealing-off strategy of the Western powers after World War I, and plain, old-fashioned imperial aggrandizement.

II
A Series of Crises

The first serious crisis in the renewed capitalist-communist struggle occurred in the Balkans in early 1947. For several years Communist insurrectionists had tried to overthrow the reactionary monarchical regime in Greece, but had been thwarted by military and economic aid supplied by Britain. In 1947 the British Labour government . . . frankly admitted that Britain's own pressing needs necessitated the abandonment of this policy. To prevent an otherwise certain Communist take-over, President Truman ordered American intervention. Thereafter American money, arms, and military advisers were sent to Greece in an ever-increasing volume. With this aid the Greek government was finally able to put down the insurrection and consolidate its position (1949). Because Soviet Russia had put similar pressure on Turkey, aid under the "Truman Doctrine" was extended to that nation.

Simultaneously, United States Secretary of State George Marshall urged Congress to legislate a gigantic economic-recovery program for Europe. Originally the program was designed to stimulate the economic recovery of all of Europe by extending unusually generous loans to countries applying for them. However, between Marshall's formulation of the plan in 1947 and Congressional enactment of it into law in 1948 the occurrence of two events substantially changed its original purpose. One was the American intervention just noted; the other was Soviet Russia's adamant stand against any Communist country accepting American aid. Both events gave the President and his advisers the opportunity they wanted to use the Marshall Plan to forestall the advance of Communism in Western Europe. In short, the European Economic Program became a weapon in the cold war.

To counteract Western pressures the Soviet Union, in late 1947, revived the Third International* . . . under a new name—Cominform. Ostensibly an agency to facilitate the exchange of information among Communist states, it actually functioned as a political propaganda instrument supporting anticapitalist solidarity around the world. Its influence was soon felt in important developments in France, Czechoslovakia, Italy, and Germany. In November of 1947, French Communist leaders called for a general strike. Because both economic and political conditions in the Fourth Republic were in anything but a healthy condition, the call posed a real threat to the government. For several weeks it appeared that spreading violence and sabotage might actually destroy the democratic system. Strong government action gradually wore down the insurrectionists, however, so that by mid-December the strike was given up. In February of 1948, events took a different turn in Czechoslovakia. For several years democratic leaders there had been able to keep Soviet influence within moderate bounds.

*An international organization of Communist parties—Eds.

Premier Joseph Stalin, at right, dictator of the Soviet Union throughout the early years of the Cold War, talks with Foreign Secretary Vyacheslav Molotov, one of his chief advisers. The scene is the Yalta Conference in February 1945, a meeting of Roosevelt, Churchill, and Stalin at which the issues underlying the Cold War began to emerge.

Now Moscow gave the signal for a showdown with which the little country, surrounded by Communist satellite states, was unable to cope. Thereafter it followed a strict Stalinist line. The Communist take-over deeply shocked the Western world and, of course, intensified the cold war.

Soon Italian Communists began a gigantic rally to win mass support for their candidates in the general elections of 1948. Because a majority of Italy's Socialists, under Pietro Nenni, joined with the Communists in what was called the People's Bloc, and because Italy's politico-economic situation was even more unstable than France's, it appeared possible, even likely, that another capitalist regime would fall. But the recent example of Czechoslovakia, combined with American pressure and the Pope's strong support of anti-Bloc efforts, gave the Christian Democrats and their allies a substantial victory.

Much more threatening to the precarious peace of the world was the Berlin crisis of June 1948 to May 1949. To deter the Western powers from creating a West German state, Russia cut off land access to their sectors of divided Berlin, deep within the Soviet zone. Because the city had become a symbol of Western power vis-à-vis Soviet designs in Europe, Western statesmen felt that their sectors of the city had to be supplied at all costs. They therefore organized a gigantic airlift to bring in food, fuel, and other necessities. For a while during the winter months of 1948 and 1949, the city's demands for coal alone almost caused the project to collapse. Somehow enough planes and skilled airmen to fly them were found to carry it off, and in May the Russians admitted defeat by lifting the blockade. The residue of resentment and heightened tension on both sides, however, further widened the gap between them.

III

The Creation of NATO

One rather logical result of this crisis was the creation of the North Atlantic Treaty Organization (1949). It was essentially a military alliance, and its basic purpose was to secure the non-Communist states of Europe against Soviet aggression. The signatories agreed that "an armed attack against one or more of them in Europe or North America shall be considered an attack against them all." Although made up of some fifteen states, the United States, Britain, and France in practice bore the chief responsibility for making the organization strong enough to discharge its principal obligations. Headquarters were established outside of Paris where weekly meetings of the NATO Council were held. General Dwight Eisenhower was appointed supreme commander of NATO's military forces, which were made up of contingents contributed by member states. Eventually, Russia and the Communist states of Eastern Europe formed a similar organization under the terms of the Warsaw Pact (1954). Thus, within ten years after the destruction of Nazi Germany, the major powers, and many of the minor ones, were grouped into two opposing camps, each armed and bitter in its denunciations of the machinations of the other.

Where Are We Headed?
(1946)

A few months after the end of World War II historian Henry Steele Commager looked at the unsettled world situation and asked a question which concerned many Americans: Is our national policy leading us toward war or toward peace?

From Henry Steele Commager, "Where Are We Headed?" *The Atlantic Monthly,* CLXXVII (February 1946), pp. 54, 55, 57–58. Subheadings added by the editors.

I

What Is American Policy?

The major issue confronting the American people today is not whether we should share the atomic bomb, or establish a Scientific Foundation under government auspices, or adopt conscription, or merge the Army and the Navy, or retain control of islands in the Pacific, or any one of the other particular problems that agitate our Congressmen and inspire our editorial writers. It is rather the great issue that underlies and controls all these particular issues: What kind of policy are we to have? Are we to have a war policy or a peace policy? Or are we to have a patch-quilt miscellany of policies without coherence or purpose? . . .

It is always difficult for a people to look at themselves objectively, to see themselves through the eyes of others. If we are to allay the suspicions and enlist the cooperation of other peoples, however, we must try to understand how our conduct appears to them.

An objective observer would find the United States not only the greatest military power but one of the most ambitious. He would note that while we possess the strongest navy in the world, we plan to build one even stronger; that while we have the most powerful air force, we plan to create one even more powerful. He would point out that though we maintain the Monroe Doctrine as a hemispheric policy, we expect to make our voice heard in the affairs of Poland, Yugoslavia, Greece, Palestine, Iran, China, Siam, and Java as well as in Germany and Japan.

He would add that our power is economic as well as military—that we are not only the best-armed and best-equipped of nations, but the richest and soundest. Alone of the major powers we emerged from the war physically unscathed, and in a position to devote all our energies to normal peacetime pursuits. With the largest and most modern industrial plant, we are prepared to capture the markets of the world. With the largest merchant marine, we are in a position to dominate world trade. With the largest gold reserves and the strongest financial system in the world, we are going to be the world's bankers.

However innocent our motives, however logical our conduct, however imperative our program may appear to ourselves, they do not necessarily appear innocent or logical or imperative to other peoples. And if we start an armament race, we cannot blame other nations if they choose to enter that race. If we continue to make atom bombs, we cannot be surprised if other nations undertake to make bigger and more effective bombs. If we try to seize the markets of the world, or dominate its airways, we must expect a trade war and an air war. However pure our motives or irreproachable our purposes, we cannot maintain a double standard of international morality for ourselves and other countries.

Such, to be sure, is not our intention. Our policy is not one of aggression. We are not planning permanent possession of atomic secrets. We do not propose to use our newly acquired island bases for imperialistic purposes. We are not really prepared to enter an armaments race. We do not wish to ruin the trade or steal the markets of our former allies. Any such program might fairly be interpreted as a conspiracy. And there is no conspiracy. There is not even a policy. And that, in fact, is the heart of the difficulty. . . .

II

The UN and the Arms Race

What does all this mean—our effort to keep the atomic secret and to organize scientific research for military purposes, our agitation for universal military service, our rearmament program, our retention of a perimeter of air and naval bases in the Atlantic and Pacific, our psychological conditioning for war? It means that though we have abandoned isolationism intellectually, we have not yet abandoned it emotionally, or adjusted ourselves to the reality of One World. It means that though we know an atomic war would be fatal to every country involved in it, we still prefer to act as if our first duty were to prepare for war rather than to prevent war. It means that though we have formally committed ourselves to the United Nations Organization and are active in its deliberations, we prefer to conduct our security policy as if that organization did not exist or were condemned in advance to impotence. It means that we are using our position as the leading nation in the world to inspire fear rather than confidence. And this mischievous course of conduct has not even the dignity of an official program. It is one to which we are committing ourselves haphazardly and almost absent-mindedly.

Perhaps the worst thing about this program is that even on its own terms it is foredoomed to failure. In the first place the American people are not, and should not be, willing to pay the price for its implementation. It is not merely that an armaments race would impose an intolerable burden upon a nation already heavily in debt. Money is, after all, an expendable factor in the search for national security. It is rather that such a race would require, to be effective, the rigorous control of every feature of the scientific and industrial life of the nation for military purposes. It would require the subordination of all those values which we cherish to the values which we have heretofore held hateful. It would set us on the road which, as Germany and Japan have proved, leads to social, economic, and moral ruin.

In the second place, even if we were prepared to pay this price, the program would still give us no consoling assurance of security. Even with the atomic bomb, with controlled scientific research, with conscription, with an Air Force and a Navy built to the specifications of our military advisers, with island bases ringing us east and west, we should still be vulnerable. It is doubtful whether, with all our wealth and ingenuity, we could win an armaments race. . . .

It seems clear, then, that we are in danger of following not so much a misguided as an unguided policy. At best that policy may commit us to a program of militarism which we have not approved, which is uncongenial to the American character, and which will not in any event assure us the kind of security we want and need. At worst it may lead to a futile armaments race, impair national and world economy, exacerbate our relations with our former allies, and frustrate the grand purposes of the United Nations Organization.

The Russian Menace (1947)

Henry Steele Commager (see Reading 320) saw uncertainty in America's attitude toward the rest of the world. He had hopes, however, for a policy based on international cooperation, rather than one based on military confrontation. William C. Bullitt (1891-1967), United States ambassador to the Soviet Union from 1933 to 1936 and to France from 1936 to 1941, offers a different view of the era.

From William C. Bullitt, "Can Truman Avoid World War III?" *The American Mercury,* LXIV (1947), pp. 645, 647–649, 654–655. Subheadings added by the editors.

I

The Truman Doctrine

> The foreign policy and the national security of this country are involved.... Totalitarian régimes imposed on free peoples, by direct or indirect aggression, undermine ... the security of the United States.... It must be the policy of the United States to support free peoples who are resisting attempted subjugation by armed minorities or by outside pressures.... This is a serious course upon which we embark. I would not recommend it except that the alternative is much more serious.
>
> *President Truman, March 12, 1947*

At times in human history there are words which are acts. President Truman's words of March 12, 1947, constitute such an act—an act of great service to the American people. For by his words he ended our disastrous policy of drift, and set a course that may bring us not only to security but also to peace....

The United States today has the world's largest navy and mightiest air force and exclusive possession of the atomic bomb. But in this same world with us is a totalitarian dictator who is just as determined to crush us and make the world his world as Hitler was to crush France. And time is running against us as time ran against France after March 1936. Each day that passes brings us closer to the day when the Soviet Union will have the atomic bomb. Each day brings increased strength to Stalin's army and air force; for the major productive energies of the Soviet Union are still being turned into production for war. Each day Stalin's domination of Eastern and Central Europe becomes more effective, and even now he could employ all the resources of that vast area containing more than a hundred million souls for war against us. He has annexed Estonia, Latvia, Lithuania, and parts of Finland, Poland, Czechoslovakia and Rumania; and has brought under his domination all Poland, all Rumania, Bulgaria, Yugoslavia, Albania, and the Red Army zones in Germany and Austria. He is relentlessly closing his iron grip on Hungary, Czechoslovakia and Finland.

He is bringing pressure on Greece and Turkey too great for them to resist by their own unaided strength. His fifth columns are attempting to Communize all Germany, and his agents have become so powerful in France and Italy that they have been able to compel acceptance of their leaders as members of the governments of those great states.

II

The Danger in Asia

At the eastern end of Stalin's vast empire, which now contains more than a sixth of the surface of the earth, the agents of the Communist dictator have been equally active. The Chinese Communist Army, fighting with arms delivered to it by the Soviet government, has been able to prevent the Chinese government from establishing its authority in large areas of North China, and is attempting to overthrow the government. The Soviet government controls fully the northern zone of Korea, and by propaganda and the activities of its agents is attempting to Communize the southern, American zone. In Indo-China, Communists trained in Moscow have captured leadership of the independence movement.

Even within the inner bastion of the United States—the Western Hemisphere—Stalin's agents are moving from success to success. Three Communists sit today as members of the government of Chile. In Cuba and Venezuela the Communists are already a potential threat to democratic government. Brazil awoke recently to find that the Communists had become the largest party in the city council of its capital, Rio de Janeiro. In nearly all of Latin America the Communists are gaining increased control of the trade unions.

Moreover, each day the situation of the states of Europe and Asia which remain outside Stalin's control grows worse. Great Britain is in the grip of the most dangerous economic crisis that has confronted any great state in modern times, and her financial resources no longer permit her to carry the burdens of her empire. She has announced that she will quit India definitely and permanently in 1948; she is withdrawing her troops from Egypt; and has decided to hand her mandate over Palestine to the United Nations. Faced by the imminent problem of earning enough to feed, house and clothe her people, Great Britain can no longer afford to protect other peoples from Soviet aggression. France is living from hand to mouth under the threat of a Communist-contrived general strike. The sweep of the Communists in Italy is still restrained by the presence of American and British troops, but these forces will soon be withdrawn, and the Communists will be free to strike for power. The economic and financial crisis in China is so grave that the advance of the Chinese army against the Communists is threatened by economic collapse behind its lines. Throughout the entire earth Stalin's forces are on the offensive and the democracies are in retreat. To prevent Stalin from uniting the strength of Europe, Asia and Africa for a final assault on the Western Hemisphere is today a vital interest of the United States. . . .

III

What America Needs To Do

Greece, Turkey, France, China—how many more nations will need our help? There may be many more, and within the limits of our abilities, for our own self-defense, we must help them to resist Soviet aggression. They are our allies in Stalin's undeclared war against us. And let us not imagine that even Stalin's death would stop that war. As long as the Soviet Union remains a totalitarian dictatorship, controlled by men who, of their own volition, deliberately and consciously, have chosen to declare themselves the enemies of all peoples who live in freedom, Soviet forces, armed and secret, will continue to strive to seize strategic positions from which to attack us, Soviet spies and agents will be active in all the great centers of our country, in our labor unions, in our government. There will be no true peace on earth but only an armistice as long as a privileged and persecuting caste of Communists controls the peoples of the Soviet Union. Their objective is the conquest of the world for Communism and peace to them is merely a period in which to prepare for new aggressions.

How then is it possible to say honestly that President Truman's policy of supporting "free peoples who are resisting attempted subjugation by armed minorities or by outside pressures" may bring us to peace? War is not inevitable. But our only chance to avoid war with the Soviet Union lies in the possibility that now, when we are far stronger than the USSR, we shall have the foresight, energy and courage to prevent Stalin from dominating new strategic areas and more peoples, and shall ourselves organize the free peoples of the world to resist Soviet imperialism, so that the present inferiority of the Soviet Union will become permanent. We can build up such moral and physical force against the totalitarian dictatorship of the Soviet Union, that when it has succeeded in manufacturing the atomic bomb it will not dare to use it. But until the day when the Soviet peoples control their own government, they will not be permitted by their masters to live with us as fellow citizens of a united world. Until that day we can preserve our independence and peace only by keeping the Soviet dictator constantly confronted by superior force.

That force must be not merely military, economic, and financial but also the force of ideas. We have had freedom for so many years, we have lived so long under a Bill of Rights honestly enforced, that we are apt to forget that the idea of freedom is the most explosive force in the world of politics. All men hate to live under the eye and hand of an omnipotent secret police. Tyranny, whether it be called by the name of Communism or fascism, or by any other name, is loathed by all normal men and women. There is nothing new in the issue which the Communists have raised. It is the old, old issue between freedom and slavery. The world of western democracy today confronts the same menace of Asiatic tyranny which 2500 years ago confronted the democracy of Athens.

The United States inaugurated the European Recovery (Marshall) Plan to aid the nations of Western Europe to rebuild their war-shattered economies. An economically strong West, it was felt, would be better able to resist Soviet pressure. Here a British cartoonist depicts Stalin raging behind his "iron curtain," while Marshal Tito of Yugoslavia, who later broke with Stalin to become neutral, peers longingly at the material wealth available to those who would cooperate with the United States.

The Sources of Soviet Conduct (1947)

As the United States and the Soviet Union maneuvered for position in the late 1940s (see Reading 319), experts differed in their interpretations of Soviet policy. One of the most influential interpretations appeared in July 1947, under the title "The Sources of Soviet Conduct." Though the article was signed "X" it soon became known that the author was George F. Kennan, a foreign policy adviser in the State Department.

From George F. Kennan, "The Sources of Soviet Conduct." Excerpted by permission from *Foreign Affairs*, XXV (1947), pp. 566, 571–573, 580–582. Copyright by the Council on Foreign Relations, Inc., New York. Subheadings added by the editors.

I

The Background of Soviet Action

The political personality of Soviet power as we know it today is the product of ideology and circumstances: ideology inherited by the present Soviet leaders from the movement in which they had their political origin, and circumstances of the power which they now have exercised for nearly three decades in Russia. There can be few tasks of psychological analysis more difficult than to try to trace the interaction of these two forces and the relative rôle of each in the determination of official Soviet conduct. Yet the attempt must be made if that conduct is to be understood and effectively countered.

It is difficult to summarize the set of ideological concepts with which the Soviet leaders came into power. Marxian ideology, in its Russian-Communist projection, has always been in process of subtle evolution. The materials on which it bases itself are extensive and complex. But the outstanding features of Communist thought as it existed in 1916 may perhaps be summarized as follows: (a) that the central factor in the life of man, the factor which determines the character of public life and the "physiognomy of society," is the system by which material goods are produced and exchanged; (b) that the capitalist system of production is a nefarious one which inevitably leads to the exploitation of the working class by the capital-owning class and is incapable of developing adequately the economic resources of society or of distributing fairly the material goods produced by human labor; (c) that capitalism contains the seeds of its own destruction and must, in view of the inability of the capital-owning class to adjust itself to economic change, result eventually and inescapably in a revolutionary transfer of power to the working class; and (d) that imperialism, the final phase of capitalism, leads directly to war and revolution. . . .

Of the original ideology, nothing has been officially junked. Belief is maintained in the basic badness of capitalism, in the inevitability of its destruction, in the obligation of the proletariat to assist in that destruction and to take power into its own hands. But stress has come to be laid primarily on those concepts which relate most specifically to the Soviet régime itself: to its position as the sole truly Socialist régime in a dark and misguided world, and to the relationships of power within it.

The first of these concepts is that of the innate antagonism between capitalism and Socialism. We have seen how deeply that concept has become imbedded in foundations of Soviet power. It has profound implications for Russia's conduct as a member of international society. It means that there can never be on Moscow's side any sincere assumption of a community of aims between the Soviet Union and powers which are regarded as capitalist. It must invariably be assumed in Moscow that the aims of the capitalist world are antagonistic to the Soviet régime, and therefore to the interests of the peoples it controls. If the Soviet Government occasionally sets its signature to documents which would indicate the contrary, this is to be regarded as a tactical manoeuvre permissible in dealing with the enemy (who is without honor) and should be taken in the spirit of *caveat emptor*. Basically, the antagonism remains. It is postulated. And from it flow many of the phenomena which we find disturbing in the Kremlin's conduct of foreign policy: the secretiveness, the lack of frankness, the duplicity, the wary suspiciousness, and the basic unfriendliness of purpose. These phenomena are there to stay, for the foreseeable future. There can be variations of degree and of emphasis. When there is something the Russians want from us, one or the other of these features of their policy may be thrust temporarily into the background; and when that happens there will always be Americans who will leap forward with gleeful announcements that "the Russians have changed," and some who will even try to take credit for having brought about such "changes." But we should not be misled by tactical manoeuvres. These characteristics of Soviet policy, like the postulate from which they flow, are basic to the internal nature of Soviet power, and will be with us, whether in the foreground or the background, until the internal nature of Soviet power is changed.

This means that we are going to continue for a long time to find the Russians difficult to deal with. It does not mean that they should be considered as embarked upon a do-or-die program to overthrow our society by a given date. The theory of the inevitability of the eventual fall of capitalism has the fortunate connotation that there is no hurry about it. The forces of progress can take their time in preparing the final *coup de grâce*. Meanwhile, what is vital is that the "Socialist fatherland"—that oasis of power which has been already won for Socialism in the person of the Soviet Union—should be cherished and defended by all good Communists at home and abroad, its fortunes promoted, its enemies badgered and confounded. The promotion of premature, "adventuristic" revolutionary projects abroad which might embarrass Soviet power in any way would be an inexcusable, even a counter-revolutionary act. The cause of Socialism is the support and promotion of Soviet power, as defined in Moscow. . . .

II

A Rival, Not a Partner

It is clear that the United States cannot expect in the foreseeable future to enjoy political intimacy with the Soviet régime. It must continue to regard the Soviet Union as a rival, not a partner, in the political arena. It must continue to expect that Soviet policies will reflect no abstract love of peace and stability, no real faith in the possibility of a permanent happy coexistence of the Socialist and capitalist worlds, but rather a cautious, persistent pressure toward the disruption and weakening of all rival influence and rival power.

Balanced against this are the facts that Russia, as opposed to the western world in general, is still by far the weaker party, that Soviet policy is highly flexible, and that Soviet society may well contain deficiencies which will eventually weaken its own total potential. This would of itself warrant the United States entering with reasonable confidence upon a policy of firm containment, designed to confront the Russians with unalterable counterforce at every point where they show signs of encroaching upon the interests of a peaceful and stable world.

But in actuality the possibilities for American policy are by no means limited to holding the line and hoping for the best. It is entirely possible for the United States to influence by its actions the internal developments, both within Russia and throughout the international Communist movement, by which Russian policy is largely determined. This is not only a question of the modest measure of informational activity which this government can conduct in the Soviet Union and elsewhere, although that, too, is important. It is rather a question of the degree to which the United States can create among the peoples of the world generally the impression of a country which knows what it wants, which is coping successfully with the problems of its internal life and with the responsibilities of a World Power, and which has a spiritual vitality capable of holding its own among the major ideological currents of the time. To the extent that such an impression can be created and maintained, the aims of Russian Communism must appear sterile and quixotic, the hopes and enthusiasm of Moscow's supporters must wane, and added strain must be imposed on the Kremlin's foreign policies. For the palsied decrepitude of the capitalist world is the keystone of Communist philosophy. Even the failure of the United States to experience the early economic depression which the ravens of the Red Square have been predicting with such complacent confidence since hostilities ceased would have deep and important repercussions throughout the Communist world.

By the same token, exhibitions of indecision, disunity, and internal disintegration within this country have an exhilarating effect on the whole Communist movement. At each evidence of these tendencies, a thrill of hope and excitement goes through the Communist world; a new jauntiness can be noted in the Moscow tread; new groups of foreign supporters climb on to what they can only view as the band wagon of international politics; and Russian pressure increases all along the line in international affairs.

It would be an exaggeration to say that American behavior unassisted and alone could exercise a power of life and death over the Communist movement and bring about the early fall of Soviet power in Russia. But the United States has it in its power to increase enormously the strains under which Soviet policy must operate, to force upon the Kremlin a far greater degree of moderation and circumspection than it has had to observe in recent years, and in this way to promote tendencies which must eventually find their outlet in either the break-up or the gradual mellowing of Soviet power. For no mystical, Messianic movement—and particularly not that of the Kremlin—can face frustration indefinitely without eventually adjusting itself in one way or another to the logic of that state of affairs.

Thus the decision will really fall in large measure in this country itself. The issue of Soviet-American relations is in essence a test of the over-all worth of the United States as a nation among nations. To avoid destruction the United States need only measure up to its own best traditions and prove itself worthy of preservation as a great nation.

Surely, there was never a fairer test of national quality than this. In the light of these circumstances, the thoughtful observer of Russian-American relations will find no cause for complaint in the Kremlin's challenge to American society. He will rather experience a certain gratitude to a Providence which, by providing the American people with this implacable challenge, has made their entire security as a nation dependent on their pulling themselves together and accepting the responsibilities of moral and political leadership that history plainly intended them to bear.

A Dissent on Containment (1947)

Many of the arguments offered by George Kennan (see Reading 322) served to justify the action President Truman took to frustrate the possibilities of Soviet control of Greece and Turkey. The concept of containment became the basis for a political and military policy of encircling the Soviet Union with military bases and unfriendly nations. Walter Lippmann, one of America's most widely respected political commentators, promptly disagreed with the evolving policy of containment, at least as it seemed to be practiced by the United States Government.

Excerpts from pp. 21-23, 35, 38-39, 52-54, 58-59 in *The Cold War* by Walter Lippmann. Copyright, 1947 by Walter Lippmann. Reprinted by permission of Harper & Row, Publishers, Inc. Subheadings added by the editors.

I

The Dangers of Containment

The policy of containment, which Mr. X recommends, demands the employment of American economic, political, and in the last analysis, American military power at "sectors" in the interior of Europe and Asia. This requires, as I have pointed out, ground forces, that is to say reserves of infantry, which we do not possess.

The United States cannot by its own military power contain the expansive pressure of the Russians "at every point where they show signs of encroaching." The United States cannot have ready "unalterable counterforce" consisting of American troops. Therefore, the counterforces which Mr. X requires have to be composed of Chinese, Afghans, Iranians, Turks, Kurds, Arabs, Greeks, Italians, Austrians, of anti-Soviet Poles, Czechoslovaks, Bulgars, Yugoslavs, Albanians, Hungarians, Finns and Germans.

The policy can be implemented only by recruiting, subsidizing and supporting a heterogeneous array of satellites, clients, dependents and puppets. The instrument of the policy of containment is therefore a coalition of disorganized, disunited, feeble or disorderly nations, tribes and factions around the perimeter of the Soviet Union.

To organize a coalition among powerful modern states is, even in time of war and under dire necessity, an enormously difficult thing to do well. To organize a coalition of disunited, feeble and immature states, and to hold it together for a prolonged diplomatic siege, which might last for ten or fifteen years, is, I submit, impossibly difficult.

It would require, however much the real name for it were disavowed, continual and complicated intervention by the United States in the affairs of all the members of the coalition which we were proposing to organize, to protect, to lead and to use. Our diplomatic agents abroad would have to have an almost unerring capacity to judge correctly and quickly which men and which parties were reliable containers. Here at home Congress and the people would have to stand ready to back their judgments as to who should be nominated, who should be subsidized, who should be whitewashed, who should be seen through rose-colored spectacles, who should be made our clients and our allies.

Mr. X offers us the prospect of maintaining such a coalition indefinitely until—eventually—the Soviet power breaks up or mellows because it has been frustrated. It is not a good prospect. Even if we assume, which we ought not, that our diplomatic agents will know how to intervene shrewdly and skillfully all over Asia, the Middle East, and Europe, and even if we assume, which the Department of State cannot, that the American people will back them with a drawing account of blank checks both in money and in military power, still it is not a good prospect. For we must not forget that the Soviet Union, against which this coalition will be directed, will resist and react.

In the complicated contest over this great

"Well, boys, Monroe wanted to prevent Europeans from interfering with American affairs. We've got to prevent them from interfering with European affairs."

Verdens Gang (Oslo)

Many Europeans, even those from countries friendly to the United States, showed uneasiness at the rapid expansion of American influence in Western Europe during the late 1940s. A Norwegian newspaper in 1947 offered this comment on what was seen as the desire of the United States to determine Europe's future. Caricatured, left to right, are Republican Senators Arthur W. Vandenberg and Robert A. Taft, President Harry Truman, and retired General George C. Marshall, who had become Secretary of State.

heterogeneous array of unstable states, the odds are heavily in favor of the Soviets. For if we are to succeed, we must organize our satellites as unified, orderly and reasonably contented nations. The Russians can defeat us by disorganizing states that are already disorganized, by disuniting peoples that are torn with civil strife, and by inciting their discontent which is already very great.

As a matter of fact this borderland in Europe and Asia around the perimeter of the Soviet Union is not a place where Mr. X's "unassailable barriers" can be erected. Satellite states and puppet governments are not good material out of which to construct unassailable barriers. A diplomatic war conducted as this policy demands, that is to say conducted indirectly, means that we must stake our own security and the peace of the world upon satellites, puppets, clients, agents about whom we can know very little. Frequently they will act for their own reasons, and on their own judgments, presenting us with accomplished facts that we did not intend, and with crises for which we are unready. The "unassailable barriers" will present us with an unending series of insoluble dilemmas. We shall have either to disown our puppets, which would be tantamount to appeasement and defeat and the loss of face, or must support them at an incalculable cost on an unintended, unforeseen and perhaps undesirable issue....

II
An Alternate Policy

I am contending that the American diplomatic effort should be concentrated on the problem created by the armistice—which is on how the continent of Europe can be evacuated by the three non-European armies which are now inside Europe. This is the problem which will have to be solved if the independence of the European nations is to be restored. Without that there is no possibility of a tolerable peace. But if these armies withdraw, there will be a very different balance of power in the world than there is today, and one which cannot easily be upset. For the nations of Europe, separately and in groups, perhaps even in unity, will then, and then only, cease to be the stakes and the pawns of the Russian-American conflict....

For if, and only if, we can bring about the withdrawal of the Red Army from the Yalta line to the new frontier of the Soviet Union —and simultaneously, of course, the withdrawal of the British and American armies from continental Europe—can a balance of power be established which can then be maintained. For after the withdrawal, an attempt to return would be an invasion—an open, unmistakable act of military aggression. Against such an aggression, the power of the United States to strike the vital centers of Russia by air and by amphibious assault would stand as the opposing and deterrent force. And until treaties are agreed to which bring about the withdrawal of the Red Army, the power of the United States to strike these vital centers would be built up for the express purpose of giving weight to our policy of ending the military occupation of Europe.

All the other pressures of the Soviet Union at the "constantly shifting geographical and political points," which Mr. X is so concerned about—in the Middle East and in Asia—are, I contend, secondary and subsidiary to the fact that its armed forces are in the heart of Europe. It is to the Red Army in Europe, therefore, and not to ideologies, elections, forms of government, to socialism, to communism, to free enterprise, that a correctly conceived and soundly planned policy should be directed.

III
Truman and Marshall

In the introduction to this essay, I said that Mr. X's article on "The Sources of Soviet Conduct" was "a document of primary importance on the sources of American foreign policy" in that it disclosed to the world the estimates, the calculations, and the conclusions on which is based *that part* of American foreign policy which is known as the Truman Doctrine. Fortunately, it seems to me, the Truman Doctrine does not have a monopoly. Though it is a powerful contender for the control of our foreign policy, there are at least two serious competitors in the field. One we may call the Marshall line, and the other is the American commitment to support the United Nations.

The contest between the Truman Doctrine on the one hand, the Marshall line and the support of U.N. on the other is the central drama within the State Department, within the Administration, within the government as a whole. The outcome is still undecided.

The real issue is hidden because the Truman Doctrine was promulgated shortly after General Marshall became Secretary of State, and because he made the decision to go to the support of Greece and Turkey, which was a concrete application of the Truman Doctrine. The issue is confused by the fact that Mr. Molotov and the Soviet propaganda abroad and many publicists here at home are representing the Marshall proposals to Europe as an application of the Truman Doctrine. The confusion is compounded still more because the Director of Secretary Marshall's Planning Staff is now known, through the publication of Mr. X's article, to have been the leading expert upon whose observations, predictions, and hypotheses the Truman Doctrine is based.

Nevertheless, if we look at the two main theaters of American diplomatic interest—at China and at Europe—and if we fix our attention on Secretary Marshall's approach, we can see a line of policy developing which is altogether different from the line of the Truman Doctrine. General Marshall's report on China, which has now been reviewed and confirmed by General Wedemeyer, made it quite clear that in his judgment we could not, and should not, attempt the kind of intervention in China which we are carrying on in Greece. The Marshall and Wedemeyer reports do not argue that we can contain the Soviet Union and erect unassailable barriers in its path by participating in the Chinese civil war, as we are in the Greek civil war, and by underwriting Chiang Kai-shek's government as we are underwriting the Athens government. The Marshall line in China is not an application of the Truman Doctrine, but of an older American doctrine that we must not become entangled all over the world in disputes that we alone cannot settle.

Yet the Marshall line in China is not isolationist. It would not end in our ceasing to interest ourselves in China and in giving Russia a free hand. But it is emphatically not the line of the Truman Doctrine which would involve us as partisans in the Chinese conflict and as patrons of one faction.

The line of the Marshall policy in China is to disentangle the United States, to reduce, not to extend, our commitments in Asia, to give up the attempt to control events which we do not have the power, the influence, the means, and the knowledge to control.

The proposal which Secretary Marshall addressed to Europe in his Harvard speech last June was animated by the same fundamental conception—as China's problem has to be dealt with primarily by the Chinese, so European problems have to be dealt with primarily by Europeans. Thus there was no "Marshall Plan" for Europe: the essence of his proposal was that only a European plan for Europe could save Europe, or provide a basis on which the American people could prudently and fairly be asked to help Europe save itself. The Marshall proposal was not, as Mr. Molotov and many Americans who do not understand it have tried to make out, an extension to Europe as a whole of the experiment in Greece. Quite the contrary. In Greece we made an American plan, appropriated the money, entered Greece and are now trying to induce the Greek government to carry out our plan. In the Harvard speech Secretary Marshall reversed this procedure. He told the European governments to plan their own rehabilitation, and that then he would go to Congress for funds, and that then the European governments would have to carry out their plans as best they could with the funds he could persuade Congress to appropriate.

The difference is fundamental. The Truman Doctrine treats those who are supposed to benefit by it as dependencies of the United States, as instruments of the American policy for "containing" Russia. The Marshall speech at Harvard treats the European governments as independent powers, whom we must help but cannot presume to govern, or to use as instruments of an American policy....

IV
The UN

We may now consider how we are to relate our role in the United Nations to our policy in the conflict with Russia. Mr. X does not deal with this question. But the State Department, in its attempt to operate under the Truman Doctrine, has shown where that doctrine would take us. It would take us to the destruction of the U.N.

The Charter and the organization of the United Nations are designed to maintain peace *after* a settlement of the Second World War has been arrived at. Until there is a settlement of that war, the United Nations does not come of age: it is growing up, it is at school, it is learning and practicing, it is testing its procedure, gaining experience. During this period, which will not come to an end until the great powers have agreed on peace treaties, the United Nations cannot deal with disputes that involve the balance of power in the world. The balance of power has to be redressed and settled in the peace treaties by the great powers themselves, principally, as I have tried to show, by the withdrawal of their armies from the continent of Europe.

Until such a settlement is reached, the United Nations has to be protected by its supporters from the strains, the burdens, the discredit, of having to deal with issues that it is not designed to deal with.

The true friends of the United Nations will, therefore, be opposed to entangling the world organization in the Soviet-American conflict. No good and nothing but harm can come of using the Security Council and the Assembly as an arena of the great dispute, or of acting as if we did not realize the inherent limitations of the Charter and thought that somehow we could by main force and awkwardness use the United Nations organization to overawe and compel the Russians. All that can come of that is to discredit the United Nations on issues that it cannot settle and thus to foreclose the future of the U.N., which can begin only if and when these issues have been settled.

Judging by the speeches on the Greek affair of the British and the American delegates, Sir Alexander Cadogan and Mr. Herschel Johnson appear to be acting on instructions which treat the U.N. as expendable in our conflict with Russia. It is a great pity. Nothing is being accomplished to win the conflict, to assuage it, or to settle it. But the U.N., which should be preserved as the last best hope of mankind that the conflict can be settled and a peace achieved, is being chewed up. The seed corn is being devoured.

Why? Because the policy of containment, as Mr. X has exposed it to the world, does not have as its objective a settlement of the conflict with Russia. It is therefore implicit in the policy that the U.N. has no future as a universal society, and that either the U.N. will be cast aside like the League of Nations, or it will be transformed into an anti-Soviet coalition. In either event the U.N. will have been destroyed.

Reading 324

The North Atlantic Treaty (1949)

By 1949 the American government stood firmly committed to the policy of containment. This policy was best expressed in a series of regional military treaties, the most elaborate of which was the North Atlantic Treaty. On March 18, 1949, Secretary of State Dean Acheson delivered a radio address explaining the treaty and defending American dominance of a European alliance designed to contain the Soviet Union.

From *Department of State Bulletin*, XX (March 27, 1949), pp. 385, 386–387.

The Atlantic pact is a collective self-defense arrangement among the countries of the North Atlantic area. It is aimed at coordinating the exercise of the right of self-defense specifically recognized in article 51 of the United Nations Charter. It is designed to fit precisely into the framework of the United Nations and to assure practical measures for maintaining peace and security in harmony with the Charter. . . .

What are the principal provisions of the North Atlantic pact? I should like to summarize them.

First, the pact is carefully and conscientiously designed to conform in every particular with the Charter of the United Nations. This is made clear in the first article of the pact, which reiterates and reaffirms the basic principle of the Charter. The participating countries at the very outset of their association state again that they will settle all their international disputes, not only among

TO WHOM IT MAY CONCERN.

The Atlantic Pact, out of which grew the North Atlantic Treaty Organization (NATO), emerged in 1949 as an alliance of the United States and most Western European nations against what was seen as an expanding Soviet Union. The image of the Atlantic Pact barbed wire parallels the popular view of the "iron curtain" as the boundary marking the Russian sphere of influence in Europe.

themselves but with any nation, by peaceful means in accordance with the provisions of the Charter. This declaration sets the whole tone and purpose of this treaty.

The second article is equally fundamental. The associated countries assert that they will preserve and strengthen their free institutions and will see to it that the fundamental principles upon which free institutions are founded are better understood everywhere. They also agree to eliminate conflicts in their economic life and to promote economic cooperation among themselves. Here is the ethical essence of the treaty—the common resolve to preserve, strengthen, and make understood the very basis of tolerance, restraint, and freedom—the really vital things with which we are concerned.

This purpose is extended further in article 3, in which the participating countries pledge themselves to self-help and mutual aid. In addition to strengthening their free institutions, they will take practical steps to maintain and develop their own capacity and that of their partners to resist aggression. They also agree to consult together when the integrity or security of any of them is threatened. The treaty sets up a council, consisting of all the members, and other machinery for consultation and for carrying out the provisions of the pact.

Successful resistance to aggression in the modern world requires modern arms and trained military forces. As a result of the recent war, the European countries joining in the pact are generally deficient in both requirements. The treaty does not bind the United States to any arms program. But we all know that the United States is now the only democratic nation with the resources and the productive capacity to help the free nations of Europe to recover their military strength.

Therefore, we expect to ask the Congress to supply our European partners some of the weapons and equipment they need to be able to resist aggression. We also expect to recommend military supplies for other free nations which will cooperate with us in safeguarding peace and security.

In the compact world of today, the security of the United States cannot be defined in terms of boundaries and frontiers. A serious threat to international peace and security anywhere in the world is of direct concern to this country. Therefore it is our policy to help free peoples to maintain their integrity and independence, not only in Western Europe or in the Americas, but wherever the aid we are able to provide can be effective. Our actions in supporting the integrity and independence of Greece, Turkey, and Iran are expressions of that determination. Our interest in the security of these countries has been made clear, and we shall continue to pursue that policy.

In providing military assistance to other countries, both inside and outside the North Atlantic pact, we will give clear priority to the requirements for economic recovery. We will carefully balance the military assistance program with the capacity and requirements of the total economy, both at home and abroad.

But to return to the treaty, article 5 deals with the possibility, which unhappily cannot be excluded, that the nations joining together in the pact may have to face the eventuality of an armed attack. In this article, they agree that an armed attack on any of them, in Europe or North America, will be considered an attack on all of them. In the event of such an attack, each of them will take, individually and in concert with the other parties, whatever action it deems necessary to restore and maintain the security of the North Atlantic area, including the use of armed force.

This does not mean that the United States would be automatically at war if one of the nations covered by the pact is subjected to armed attack. Under our Constitution, the Congress alone has the power to declare war. We would be bound to take promptly the action which we deemed necessary to restore and maintain the security of the North Atlantic area. That decision would be taken in accordance with our constitutional procedures. The factors which would have to be considered would be, on the one side, the gravity of the armed attack, on the other, the action which we believed necessary to restore and maintain the security of the North Atlantic area. . . .

Any one with the most elementary knowledge of the processes of democratic government knows that democracies do not and cannot plan aggressive wars. But for those from whom such knowledge may have been withheld I must make the following categoric and unequivocal statement, for which I stand with the full measure of my responsibility in the office I hold: This country is not planning to make war against anyone. It is not seeking war. It abhors war. It does not hold war to be inevitable. Its policies are devised with the specific aim of bridging by peaceful means the tremendous differences which beset international society at the present time.

TOPIC 61

TROUBLE IN EAST ASIA, 1950–1954

The Korean War of 1950 to 1953 was the first major military involvement of the United States on the Asian mainland. In that sense, if no other, President Truman's decision to commit American ground troops to aid South Korea was a crucial moment in American history. When, on June 25, 1950, North Korean troops crossed the 38th parallel, the boundary between the two Koreas, American foreign policy makers could have viewed it in several ways. They might have seen it as a civil war, as a Moscow-directed "limited" war designed to extend Soviet Russia's influence in Asia, or as the first step by the Soviet Union to execute a carefully directed world-wide plan, the next move of which could come in Europe or the Middle East. The entry of Chinese "volunteers" into the war on the side of the North Koreans in late 1950 was similarly open to several interpretations. The interpretations of President Truman and his advisers of these actions by North Koreans and Chinese helped to shape the actions, both military and political, the United States took in Korea and the rest of Asia in 1950 and in the next two decades as well.

Reading 325

China, Korea, and the Cold War

As the United States developed a system of military alliances in Europe (see Reading 324), events in Asia compelled American leaders to redefine foreign policy in that area of the world. The great new factor which forced this redefinition was the victory of the Chinese Communists in 1949, ending a civil war which had lasted more than twenty years. President Harry Truman and Secretary of State Dean Acheson were still in the process of working out a policy toward Communist China when in June of 1950 another civil war broke out in Korea, a peninsula jutting from the north Asian mainland into the Sea of Japan. Historian L. S. Stavrianos details the rise of Communist China and the course of the Korean War in the following reading.

From L. S. Stavrianos, *The World Since 1500: A Global History*, © 1966. Reprinted by permission of Prentice-Hall, Inc., Englewood Cliffs, New Jersey. Pp. 590–591, 591–592, 592–594. Subheadings added by the editors.

I

The Emergence of Red China

In 1950, the focus of the Cold War shifted from Europe to the Far East. By this time a balance had been reached in Europe between East and West. But in the Far East the balance was upset by a momentous development—the triumph of the Communists in China. Just as the Bolshevik Revolution was the outstanding by-product of World War I,

The conquest of China by communist armies had become almost a parade by the time Shanghai, the largest seaport in the nation, was occupied in late 1949. The armored vehicles moving along this Shanghai street are of Japanese manufacture. They were taken by the Russian army during their occupation of Manchuria at the end of World War II and later turned over to the People's Liberation (Chinese Communist) Army.

so the Chinese Communist Revolution was the outstanding by-product of World War II.

Chiang Kai-shek had become the master of China in 1928, but from the outset his Kuomintang regime was threatened by two mortal enemies, the Communists within and the Japanese without. During World War II his position became particularly difficult. The country was divided into three sections: the east, controlled by the Japanese and administered through a puppet government at Nanking; the northwest, controlled by the Communists operating from their capital at Yenan; and the west and southwest, ruled by Chiang's Nationalist government from its capital in Chungking.

It was during the war years that Chiang's regime was irretrievably undermined. Chiang traditionally had depended on the support of the conservative landlord class and of the relatively enlightened big businessmen. The latter were largely eliminated when the Japanese overran the east coast, and Chiang was left with the self-centered and short-sighted landlords of the interior. His government became increasingly corrupt and unresponsive to the needs of a peasantry wracked and aroused by years of war. In contrast to the decaying Kuomintang, the Communists carried out land reforms in their territories, thereby winning the support of the peasant masses. They also had a disciplined and efficient organization that brought order out of political and economic chaos in the areas under their control. They were more successful than the Nationalists, moreover, in portraying themselves as patriots dedicated to ridding the country of foreign invaders and restoring China's unity, pride, and greatness.

Such was the situation when Japan's surrender in August, 1945, set off a wild scramble by the Nationalists and Communists to take over the Japanese-occupied parts of China. The Communists issued orders to their troops to take over the areas held by the Japanese. Chiang Kai-shek promptly cancelled these orders and insisted that the Communists make no move without instructions from him. He was ignored, and clashes occurred between Communist and Kuomintang forces. With civil war imminent, the United States sent a mission under General George Marshall to attempt to negotiate a settlement. But neither side could overcome its fear and suspicion of the other, and Marshall's mediation proved abortive. By 1947 the final showdown was at hand.

The Communists occupied the countryside around the major cities, being helped by the Russians, who turned over to them the arms the Japanese had surrendered in Manchuria. The Nationalists, aided by the transportation services of the United States Navy and Air Force, won all the main cities, including Nanking, and also rushed troops north to Manchuria. The latter move was a strategic blunder. The Kuomintang forces found themselves in indefensible positions and were forced in the fall of 1948 to surrender to the Chinese Red Army. A chain of comparable military disasters followed in quick succession. The Communist armies swept down from Manchuria through the major cities of North China. By April, 1949, they were crossing the Yangtze and fanning out over South China. The American ambassador in Nanking reported at the time to Washington: "The ridiculously easy Communist crossing of the Yangtze was made possible by defections at key points, disagreements in the High Command, and the failure of the Air Force to give effective support."

The Communist steamroller advanced even more rapidly in the south than in the north. By the end of 1949 it had overrun all of mainland China. Chiang fled to the island of Taiwan (Formosa), while in Peking the Communist leader, Mao Tse-tung, proclaimed the People's Republic of China on October 1, 1949, and brought about a turning point in the history of China, and indeed of the entire world. . . .

The victory of communism in China was a serious setback for the United States. In Japan, however, the postwar occupation was dominated by the United States. Japan, in contrast to Germany, was governed by a single Supreme Command of the Allied powers, which included Allied representatives. The Supreme Commander (General Douglas MacArthur) and the bulk of the occupation forces were American.

MacArthur's instructions were to disarm and demilitarize the country, develop democratic institutions, and create a viable economy. Accordingly, he disbanded the imperial army and navy, banned patriotic organizations, stripped Emperor Hirohito of the divinity attributed to him, and purged education of its militaristic elements. In 1947 he proclaimed a democratic constitution that transferred sovereignty from the emperor to the people, guaranteed individual rights, and granted women equal status with men. In the economic field the most important measure was wholesale redistribution of land. By 1952, 90 percent of the arable acreage was owned by former tenants. Less successful was the attempt to break up the large family corporations, or *zaibatsu,* that had dominated the prewar industry, finance, and foreign trade. The initial measures against the *zaibatsu* were dropped because it was felt that they hampered economic recovery.

Although far less revolutionary than the Communist upheaval in China, the occupation of Japan nevertheless had a profound impact on that country. The Japanese always had been receptive to foreign ways, but never to the degree in which they were since World War II. The cataclysmic defeat suffered in that struggle discredited the old order. The younger generation in particular sought new models and leaders, and was persuasively encouraged to do so. . . .

II

Hot War in Korea

The tragedy of Korea is that its location has made it a natural bridge between China and Japan. Repeatedly it has been fought over by the two countries, and occasionally by Russia also. Since 1895—and formally since 1910—Korea had passed under Japanese rule. Thereafter it was in effect a colony, though unique in that it was under Asian rather than European domination. During World War II, at the 1943 Cairo Conference, the United States, Britain, and China declared that, "in due course" Korea should once more be free and independent. But a generation of Japanese rule had left Korea without the necessary experience for self-government. The victorious Allies decided, therefore, that for a period of not more than five years Korea, though independent, should be under the trusteeship of the United States, Russia, Britain, and China.

With the surrender of Japan, American and Russian troops poured into Korea. For purposes of military convenience the 38th parallel was set as the dividing line in their operations. The coming of the Cold War froze this temporary division in Korea as it did in Germany. The Russians set up in their zone a regime dominated by the Communist New People's Party. In the south, the Americans leaned on English-speaking Koreans, who usually were members of the conservative upper class. In August, 1948, a Republic of Korea was proclaimed in the south, with Dr. Syngman Rhee as president. A month later the North Koreans formed their People's Democratic Republic under Kim Il-sung.

These two leaders symbolized in their persons the basic differences between the two zones. Kim Il-sung, still in his thirties, was Moscow-trained, secretary of the Korean Communist Party, and since 1931 an underground resistance fighter against the Japanese. Syngman Rhee, an elder statesman of over seventy, had fought the Japanese since the turn of the century. A graduate of Harvard and Princeton, a student and admirer of Woodrow Wilson, and a Methodist missionary, he had lived for decades in China and the United States as head of the Korean government-in-exile. A UN commission attempted without success to mediate between the regimes headed by these two men. So strong were the feelings that the commission warned in September, 1949, of the danger of civil war.

On June 24, 1950, civil war did begin, when North Korean troops suddenly crossed the 38th parallel in order to "liberate" South Korea. Within a few hours the UN commission reported that South Korea was the victim of aggression. The next day the UN Security

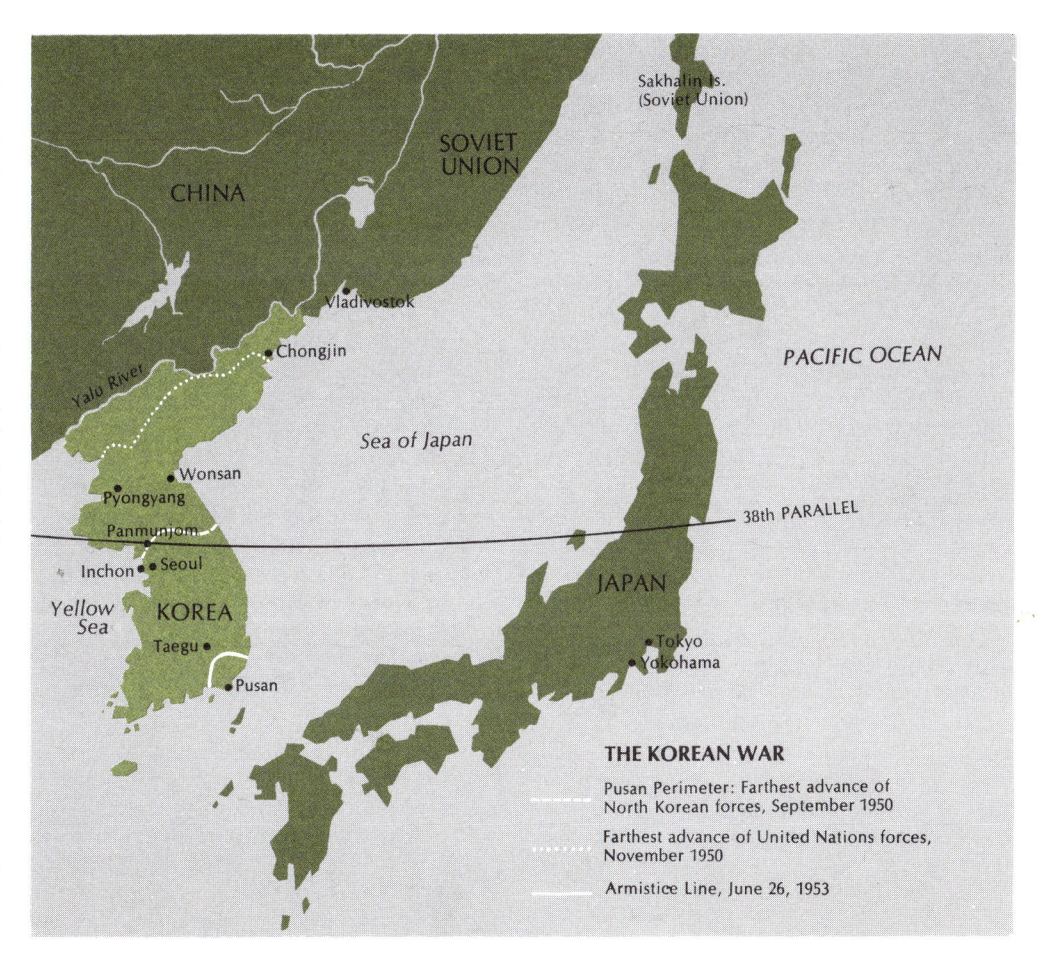

THE KOREAN WAR

Pusan Perimeter: Farthest advance of North Korean forces, September 1950

Farthest advance of United Nations forces, November 1950

Armistice Line, June 26, 1953

Council adopted an American resolution calling for an immediate cease-fire and the withdrawal of the North Koreans to the 38th parallel. The same afternoon and on the following day President Truman conferred with his advisors and decided to give full military support to South Korea. On June 27 the Security Council asked UN members to "furnish such assistance to the Republic of Korea as may be necessary to repel the armed attack and to restore international peace and security in the area." Thus the United Nations for the first time in its brief history had decided to use force. The Security Council's decision was made possible only because of Russia's temporary boycott of its meetings in protest against the refusal to admit Communist China in place of Nationalist China.

Forty UN member states responded to the Security Council's appeal and provided supplies, transport, hospital units, and, in some cases, combat forces. But the main contribution, aside from that of South Korea, came from the United States, and General MacArthur served as commander in chief. The course of the Korean War fell into two phases—the first before, and the second after, the Chinese intervention. The first phase began with the headlong rush of the North Korean forces down the length of the peninsula to within fifty miles of the port of Pusan at the southern tip. Then on September 14, 1950, an American army landed at Inchon, far up the coast near the 38th parallel, and in twelve days retook the South Korean capital, Seoul. The North Koreans, their communications severed, fell back as precipitously as they had advanced. By the end of September the UN forces had reached the 38th parallel.

The question now was whether to cross or not to cross. The issue was transferred to the General Assembly, because the Soviet Union, with its veto power, had returned to the Security Council. On October 7, 1950, the Assembly resolved that "all constituent acts be taken . . . for the establishment of a unified, independent, and democratic government in the sovereign state of Korea." The next day American forces crossed the 38th parallel and quickly occupied Pyongyang, the North Korean capital. By November 22 they reached the Yalu River, the boundary line between Korea and the Chinese province of Manchuria.

At this point the second phase of the Korean War began with a massive attack by Chinese "volunteers" supported by Russian-made jets. The Chinese drove southward rapidly in what looked like a repetition of the first phase of the war. Early in January, 1951, they retook Seoul, but the UN forces now recovered and held their ground. In March, Seoul once more changed hands, and by June the battleline ran roughly along the 38th parallel. The most significant feature of this second phase of the war is that it was kept strictly localized despite the involvement of both China and the United States. This occurred because neither regarded the future of Korea as a matter of really vital national interest. Hence the United States did not use the atomic bomb, and the Soviet Union sent no troops. The war was kept at the level of an "incident," despite the scale of the fighting.

By mid-1951 it was apparent that a stalemate prevailed at the front. Large-scale fighting petered out, and armistice negotiations started. After two years of stormy and often-interrupted negotiations, an armistice agreement was concluded on July 27, 1953. The terms reflected the military stalemate. The line of partition between North and South Korea remained roughly where it had been before the war. The Western powers had successfully contained communism in Korea and had vindicated the authority of the United Nations. The Chinese had secured North Korea as a Communist buffer-state between Manchuria and Western influences. And meanwhile, most of the Korean countryside had been laid waste and about 10 percent of the Korean people had been killed.

The United States Acts To Defend South Korea (1950)

The North Korean invasion of South Korea drew an immediate American response. On the request of the United States, the Security Council of the United Nations called on UN-member nations to join in giving military and other aid to South Korea; the Soviet Russian delegate to the Security Council, being temporarily absent, failed to cast a veto of this resolution. President Harry S Truman issued a statement to the American people, given below, in which he argued the case for collective opposition to North Korea. Following the President's message is part of some testimony given by Secretary of State Dean G. Acheson at hearings conducted by the U. S. Senate the following year, in which Acheson offered an interpretation of the meaning of the North Korean invasion.

From Department of State *Bulletin*, XXIII (July 3, 1950), 5; and from U. S. Senate Armed Forces and Foreign Relations Committees,

Hearings, 82d Congress, 1st session, Part 3, pp. 1714–1717. Subheadings added and omitted by the editors.

I

President Truman, June 27, 1950

In Korea, the Government forces, which were armed to prevent border raids and to preserve internal security, were attacked by invading forces from North Korea. The Security Council of the United Nations called upon the invading troops to cease hostilities and to withdraw to the 38th Parallel. This they have not done but, on the contrary, have pressed the attack. The Security Council called upon all members of the United Nations to render every assistance to the United Nations in the execution of this resolution. In these circumstances, I have ordered United States air and sea forces to give the Korean Government troops cover and support.

The attack upon Korea makes it plain beyond all doubt that communism has passed beyond the use of subversion to conquer independent nations and will now use armed invasion and war. It has defied the orders of the Security Council of the United Nations issued to preserve international peace and security. In these circumstances, the occupation of Formosa by Communist forces would be a direct threat to the security of the Pacific area and to United States forces performing their lawful and necessary functions in that area.

Accordingly, I have ordered the Seventh Fleet to prevent any attack on Formosa. As a corollary of this action, I am calling upon the Chinese Government on Formosa to cease all air and sea operations against the mainland. The Seventh Fleet will see that this is done. The determination of the future status of Formosa must await the restoration of security in the Pacific, a peace settlement with Japan, or consideration by the United Nations.

I have also directed that United States forces in the Philippines be strengthened and that military assistance to the Philippine Government be accelerated.

I have similarly directed acceleration in the furnishing of military assistance to the forces of France and the Associated States in Indochina and the dispatch of a military mission to provide close working relations with those forces.

I know that all members of the United Nations will consider carefully the consequences of this latest aggression in Korea in defiance of the Charter of the United Nations. A return to the rule of force in international affairs would have far-reaching effects. The United States will continue to uphold the rule of law.

I have instructed Ambassador Austin, as the representative of the United States to the Security Council, to report these steps to the Council.

II

Secretary Acheson, 1951

Mr. Chairman and gentlemen, the real issues in the discussion before us are peace or war, and the survival of human freedom. . . .

The Four Freedoms, the Atlantic Charter, the United Nations—these were not cynical slogans. They represented the idea which our people felt in their hearts was worth fighting for.

It has been the purpose of our foreign policy to keep faith with that idea.

The attempt to build a collective-security system on the basis of the cooperation of all the great powers broke down because of the policies of the Soviet Union. But Soviet ambitions have not been able to obstruct our determined efforts.

Within the framework of the Charter of the United Nations we have been building a collective-security system based on the cooperation of those nations who are dedicated to peace.

The united and determined effort of our people to build effective instruments for keeping the peace is recorded in a series of vigorous and farsighted actions: the United Nations Charter itself, the Rio Treaty, the Greek-Turkish aid program, the Marshall plan, the North Atlantic Treaty, and the mutual defense assistance program.

We have been building our strength, together with our allies. We must be strong enough to keep the peace.

Side by side with these programs there is another basic element in our foreign policy—to assist the hundreds of millions of people who were acquiring their independence after the war, so that they might be free to develop in their own way, and to join in an international system for preserving the peace.

Our hopes for peace required us to understand the changes which were in motion among vast populations of the Middle East and Asia, and to help peoples who had just gained their independence from losing it again to the new imperialism of the Soviet Union.

Those are the big central ideas that express what we have been trying to do in the world.

The attack on Korea was a blow at the foundation of this whole program. It was a challenge to the whole system of collective security, not only in the Far East, but everywhere in the world. It was a threat to all nations newly arrived at independence. This dagger thrust pinned a warning notice to the wall which said: "Give up or be conquered."

This was a test which would decide whether our collective-security system would survive or would crumble. It would determine whether other nations would be intimidated by this show of force.

The decision to meet force with force in Korea was essential. It was the unanimous view of the political and military advisers of the President that this was the right thing to do. This decision had the full support of the American people because it accorded with the principles by which Americans live.

As a people we condemn aggression of any kind. We reject appeasement of any kind. If we stood with our arms folded while Korea was swallowed up, it would have meant abandoning our principles, and it would have meant the defeat of the collective security system on which our own safety ultimately depends.

What I want to stress here is that it was not only a crucial decision whether or not to meet this aggression; it was no less important how this aggression was to be dealt with.

In the first place, the attack on Korea has been met by collective action. The United States brought the aggression in Korea before the United Nations, not only because the Charter requires it, but also because the authority and even the survival of that organization was directly involved.

The response of some members of the United Nations, in terms of their capacities and their other security responsibilities, has been generous and wholehearted.

The total action is admittedly an imperfect one, as might be expected of beginning steps in a collective-security system. But the development of this system requires us to take into consideration the dangers and interests of those associated with us, just as we want them to take into consideration our dangers and interests.

In the second place, our response to the aggression against Korea required a careful estimate of the risks involved in the light of the total world situation.

There was the risk that the conflict might spread into a general war in Asia, a risk that the Chinese Communists might intervene, a risk that the Soviet Union might declare itself in.

We take it for granted that risk of some sort is implicit in any positive policy, and that there is also a risk in doing nothing.

The elements of risk and the means of reducing that risk to us and to the rest of the free world quite properly influenced our policy in Korea.

It has been our purpose to turn back this Communist thrust, and to do it in such a way as to prevent a third world war if we can. This is in accord with one of the most fundamental tenets of our policy—to prevent, insofar as we can do so, another world war.

It is against this basic purpose that the operation in Korea, and the plans for carrying it to a conclusion, need to be considered....

The alluring prospect for the Communist conspiracy in June 1950—the prospect of a quick and easy success which would not only win Korea for the Kremlin but shake the free nations of Asia and paralyze the defense of Europe—all this has evaporated.

Instead of weakening the rest of the world, they have solidified it. They have given a powerful impetus to the military preparations of this country and its associates in and out of the North Atlantic Treaty Organization.

We have doubled the number of our men under arms, and the production of matériel has been boosted to a point where it can begin to have a profound effect on the maintenance of the peace.

The idea of collective security has been put to the test, and has been sustained. The nations who believe in collective security have shown that they can stick together and fight together.

New urgency has been given to the negotiation of a peace treaty with Japan, and of initial security arrangements to build strength in the Pacific area.

These are some of the results of the attack on Korea, unexpected by—and I am sure most unwelcome to—the Kremlin.

American marines move along the beach at Inchon, South Korea, in September 1950. During the previous three months the North Koreans had pushed the South Korean and American forces into a small area around the port of Pusan in southeast Korea, where they managed to hold a line of defense. The amphibious invasion at Inchon, on the west coast of central Korea, together with a strong thrust northward from the Pusan area, caught the North Koreans by surprise and sent them fleeing north in disarray.

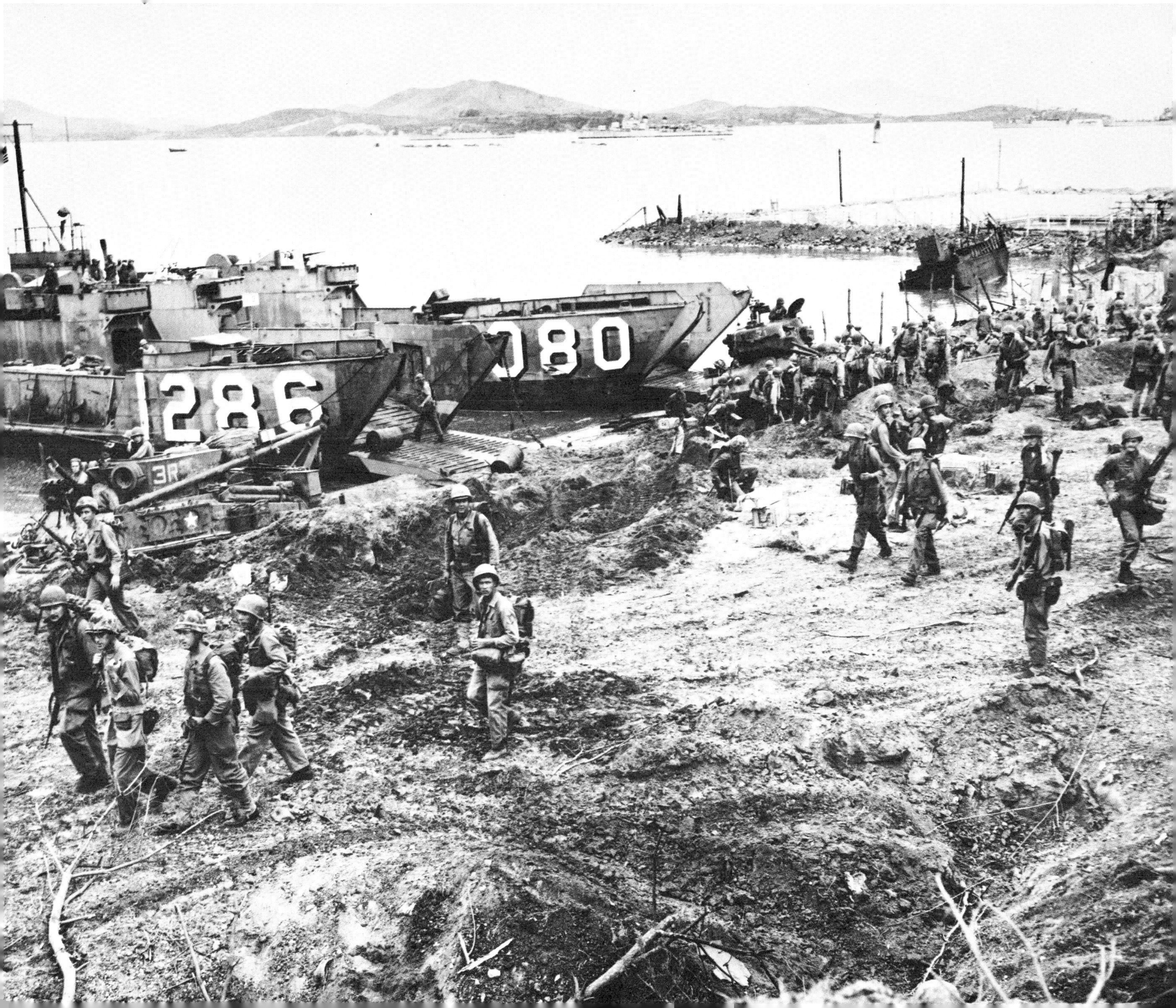
286
080
3R

Conference at Wake Island (1950)

On October 15, 1951, President Truman and his staff journeyed to the mid-Pacific to meet General Douglas MacArthur on Wake Island. MacArthur, named head of United Nations forces in Korea, had recently directed a breakthrough of American troops which in a few weeks had driven the North Koreans out of South Korea. A few days earlier MacArthur had ordered UN forces across the 38th parallel, a move which made some American leaders increasingly nervous about Chinese or Soviet intervention.

From Omar N. Bradley, compiler, Substance of Statements Made at Wake Island Conference on October 15, 1950 (Washington, D. C., 1951), pp. 1, 5, 7.

The following were at the table: The President; General of the Army Douglas MacArthur; Admiral Arthur W. Radford, commander in chief, United States Pacific Fleet; Ambassador John Muccio; Secretary of the Army Frank Pace; Col. A. L. Hamblen; Ambassador at Large Philip C. Jessup; General of the Army Omar N. Bradley; Assistant Secretary of State Dean Rusk; Mr. W. Averell Harriman.

The conference opened at 0736 [on October 15, 1950].

The President asked General MacArthur to state the rehabilitation situation with reference to Korea.

[General MacArthur] It cannot occur until the military operations have ended. I believe that formal resistance will end throughout North and South Korea by Thanksgiving. There is little resistance left in South Korea—only about 15,000 men—and those we do not destroy, the winter will. We now have about 60,000 prisoners in compounds.

In North Korea, unfortunately, they are pursuing a forlorn hope. They have about 100,000 men who were trained as replacements. They are poorly trained, led, and equipped, but they are obstinate and it goes against my grain to have to destroy them. They are only fighting to save face. Orientals prefer to die rather than to lose face. . . .

[The President] What are the chances for Chinese or Soviet interference?

[General MacArthur] Very little. Had they interfered in the first or second months it would have been decisive. We are no longer fearful of their intervention. We no longer stand hat in hand. The Chinese have 300,000 men in Manchuria. Of these probably not more than 100,000 to 125,000 are distributed along the Yalu River. Only 50,000 to 60,000 could be gotten across the Yalu River. They have no Air Force. Now that we have bases for our Air Force in Korea, if the Chinese tried to get down to Pyongyang there would be the greatest slaughter.

With the Russians it is a little different. They have an air force in Siberia and a fairly good one, with excellent pilots equipped with some jets and B-25 and B-29 planes. They can put 1,000 planes in the air with some 200 to 300 more from the Fifth and Seventh Soviet Fleets. They are probably no match for our Air Force. The Russians have no ground troops available for North Korea. They would have difficulty in putting troops into the field. It would take 6 weeks to get a division across and 6 weeks brings the winter. The only other combination would be Russian air support of Chinese ground troops. Russian air is deployed in a semicircle through Mukden and Harbin, but the coordination between the Russian air and the Chinese ground would be so flimsy that I believe Russian air would bomb the Chinese as often as they would bomb us. Ground support is a very difficult thing to do. Our marines do it perfectly. They

American successes in Korea brought a meeting between President Harry Truman, right, and General Douglas MacArthur, left, at Wake Island in the Pacific to resolve differences over strategy. The outcome of the conference, in mid-October 1950, was to allow MacArthur's forces to continue their advance in North Korea toward the Chinese border. At that point the commanders entertained little suspicion that the Chinese Communists would intervene in the war. Major Gen. Courtney Whitney, MacArthur's aide, is at center.

have been trained for it. Our own Air and Ground Forces are not as good as the marines but they are effective. Between untrained air and ground forces an air umbrella is impossible without a lot of joint training. I believe it just wouldn't work with Chinese Communist ground and Russian air. We are the best. . . .

[The President] I would like to hear your views, General, on a possible Pacific pact or some other arrangements similar to that in the Atlantic.

[General MacArthur] A Pacific pact would be tremendous, but due to the lack of homogeneity of the Pacific nations, it would be very difficult to put into effect. If the President would make an announcement like the Truman doctrine, which would be a warning to the predatory nations, it would have a great effect. It is not possible to get a pact, since they are so nonhomogeneous. They have no military forces. Only the United States has the forces. All they want is the assurance of security from the United States. The President should follow up this conference with a ringing pronouncement. I believe that at this time, after the military successes and the President's trip, it would have more success than a Pacific pact.

[Admiral Radford] I was in Manila last May during the conference Quirino called. I didn't attend the meetings but I spoke to a number of delegates. There was generally the same feeling that General MacArthur brought out. They didn't feel they could get together but they would like to know in advance of any announcement. I am sure they would heartily agree but would like to be consulted. I believe such a pronouncement could be included in the UN speech and if they could be consulted, they would feel they were in on the ground floor. The peace will be upset again in 6 months if you do not take steps to stop it. We just have to face the facts of life. We must continue the policy followed in Korea to maintain the peace. The situation in Indochina is the most puzzling of all as to what we can do or what we should do.

[Mr. Harriman]. When you speak of the Truman doctrine, do you mean direct external aggression or do you mean the type of thing that has been going on in Indochina and has previously occurred in Greece to which the Truman doctrine was directed?

[General MacArthur] I am referring to direct aggression.

American Intervention: The Chinese View

L. S. Stavrianos made clear (Reading 325) that from an American viewpoint the Korean War had two phases: before and after Chinese intervention in December 1950. From the Chinese viewpoint, however, the nature of the war changed when American forces crossed into North Korea in late September. A rare view of the workings of Red Chinese foreign policy was provided by K. M. Panikkar, Indian ambassador to Peking. In Part I of the following selection Panikkar describes Chinese reaction when American troops moved across the 38th parallel. In Part II, Panikkar reports the situation in December 1950 when Chinese Communist armies were in the process of driving American and South Korean troops out of North Korea.

From K. M. Panikkar, *In Two Chinas* (London: George Allen & Unwin Ltd., 1955), pp. 117-118. Subheadings added by the editors.

I

China Reacts: October 1950

The situation in Korea [was] changed all of a sudden by the American landings at Inchon. There were great rejoicings in the western camp in China, and if the Chinese on their part were bitterly disappointed they showed no signs of it. When the northern lines began to be rolled up and the Americans and their allies were shouting of victory, my thoughts were all on Taiwan, for I felt that if the Americans were able to carry everything before them in Korea they might be tempted to encourage Chiang to attack the mainland and thus precipitate a world war. The situation seemed altogether confused. There were rumours of large-scale troop movements from the Peking area to the north, and a western Military Attaché told me that he had information that a continuous stream of troop trains was passing Tientsin. It was when things were in this state of uncertainty that General Nieh Yen-jung, the acting Chief of Staff who was also the Military Governor of Peking, with the inoffensive title of mayor, came to dine with me on the 25th of September. General Nieh, with his round face and shaven head, gives one the impression of a Prussian officer. But he is a pleasant-spoken man, friendly and ready to discuss matters with an air of frankness. After the dinner the conversation turned to Korea. General Nieh told me in a quiet and unexcited manner that the Chinese did not intend to sit back with folded hands and let the Americans come up to their border. This was the first indication I had that the Chinese proposed to intervene in the war. I was taken aback a little by this statement, all the more impressive because it was said in a quiet and pleasant tone, as if he were telling me that he intended to go shooting the next day. I asked him whether he realized in full the implications of such an action. He replied: "We know what we are in for, but at all costs American aggression has to be stopped. The Americans can bomb us, they can destroy our industries, but they cannot defeat us on land."

I tried to impress on him how destructive a war with America would be; how the Americans would be able to destroy systematically all the industries of Manchuria and put China back by half a century, how China's coastal towns would be exposed to bombardment and how even the interior could be bombed. He only laughed. "We have calculated all that," he said. "They may even drop atom bombs on us. What then? They may kill a few million people. Without sacrifice a nation's independence cannot be upheld." He gave some calculations of the effectiveness of atom bombs and said: "After all, China lives on the farms. What can atom bombs do there? Yes, our economic development will be put back. We may have to wait for it.". . .

At midnight on the 2nd of October, after I had been asleep for an hour and a half, I was awakened by my steward with the news that Chen Chia-kang, the Director of the Asian Affairs of the Foreign Ministry, was waiting for me in the drawing-room. I hastily put on my dressing-gown and went downstairs, not knowing what it could be which had brought so important an officer at midnight to my house. Chen was very apologetic about the lateness of the hour but added that the matter was most important and that the Prime Minister desired to see me immediately at his residence. . . . At 12:30 I was with Premier Chou En-lai at his official residence.

Though the occasion was the most serious I could imagine, a midnight interview on questions affecting the peace of the world, Chou En-lai was as courteous and charming as ever and did not give the least impression of worry or nervousness or indeed of being in any particular hurry. He had the usual tea served and the first two minutes were spent in normal courtesies, apology for disturbing me at an unusual hour, etc. Then he came to the point. He thanked Pandit Nehru for what he had been doing in the cause of peace, and said no country's need for peace was greater than that of China, but there were occasions when peace could only be defended by determination to resist aggression. If the Americans crossed the 38th parallel China would be forced to intervene in Korea. Otherwise he was most anxious for a peaceful settlement, and generally accepted Pandit Nehru's approach to the question. I asked him whether he had already news of the Americans having crossed the borders. He replied in the affirmative but added that he did not know where they had crossed. I asked him whether China intended to intervene, if only the South Koreans crossed the parallel. He was emphatic: "The South Koreans did not matter but American intrusion into North Korea would encounter Chinese resistance."

I returned home at 1:30 where my first secretary and cypher assistant were waiting. A telegram conveying the gist of the conversation with my own appreciation of the situation went the same night to New Delhi. . . .

II

China on the Offensive: December 1950

When the extent of American defeat became known I became very worried. My fear was that though the Americans might be dissuaded from dropping atom bombs, they might in desperation attack Manchuria and thereby extend the war. I was aware of the growing strength of China in the air: and the Chinese were certain that if Manchuria were attacked the Soviets would intervene. So with the authority of the Prime Minister, I approached the Chinese Government again (on the 8th of December) with the request that they should make a declaration that their forces would not move beyond the 38th parallel; that they would not move into South Korea. The line I took was that such a declaration would help to mobilize neutral opinion in China's favour and that they stood to lose nothing, as unless America agreed to respect that line China would also not be bound by her declaration. I also tried hard to prove to Chang Han-fu that it was foolish to think that a military decision was possible, for though the Americans might be forced back they could hold selected points on the coast as long as they had naval and air superiority. So the settlement had to be by negotiation, and now, as China had already shown her military strength, would it not be better, I argued, to offer to negotiate. . . .

On the 11th of December Chou En-lai sent for me. We had an hour's conversation. The refrain of his talk was: "What do the Americans want? Do they want peace as we do, or are they going to persist in aggression? The Attlee-Truman communiqué clearly shows that what they want is war not peace." I replied that Government policies should not be judged from communiqués but I was sure that Britain at least wanted peace and a Chinese declaration about the 38th parallel would help Britain and others who were trying to restrain the U.S.A. Chou En-lai replied, "So far as the 38th parallel is concerned, it is we, China and India, who wanted to uphold it. But MacArthur has demolished it and it exists no longer." I was altogether depressed after the interview for it was clear to me that the Chinese would not stop at the 38th parallel and the allies of America would be forced to trail behind in any action the U.S. proposed.

Chinese Intervention: The American View

Though driven out of North Korea, United Nations forces managed by the spring of 1951 to stabilize the war front at or near the 38th parallel, the old boundary between the two Koreas. There were vocal groups in the United States, however, that urged an all-out war for victory, including attacks on China itself. General MacArthur openly supported such demands, despite orders from President Truman to remain silent. In April 1951 Truman relieved MacArthur of his command. This was initially a highly unpopular move, which generated much political controversy in the United States. In defense of both his removal of MacArthur and his Asian policy, President Truman offered the following explanation to the American people.

From Harry S Truman, "Preventing a New World War," *Department of State Bulletin,* XXIV (April 16, 1951), pp. 603–605. Subheadings added by the editors.

I

The Lessons Learned in Korea

I want to talk plainly to you tonight about what we are doing in Korea and about our policy in the Far East.

In the simplest terms, what we are doing in Korea is this: We are trying to prevent a third world war.

I think most people in this country recognized that fact last June. And they warmly supported the decision of the Government to help the Republic of Korea against the

Communist aggressors. Now, many persons, even some who applauded our decision to defend Korea, have forgotten the basic reason for our action.

It is right for us to be in Korea. It was right last June. It is right today.

I want to remind you why this is true.

The Communists in the Kremlin are engaged in a monstrous conspiracy to stamp out freedom all over the world. If they were to succeed, the United States would be numbered among their principal victims. It must be clear to everyone that the United States cannot—and will not—sit idly by and await foreign conquest. The only question is: When is the best time to meet the threat and how?

The best time to meet the threat is in the beginning. It is easier to put out a fire in the beginning when it is small than after it has become a roaring blaze.

And the best way to meet the threat of aggression is for the peace-loving nations to act together. If they don't act together, they are likely to be picked off, one by one.

If they had followed the right policies in the 1930's—if the free countries had acted together, to crush the aggression of the dictators, and if they had acted in the beginning, when the aggression was small—there probably would have been no World War II.

If history has taught us anything, it is that aggression anywhere in the world is a threat to peace everywhere in the world. When that aggression is supported by the cruel and selfish rulers of a powerful nation who are bent on conquest, it becomes a clear and present danger to the security and independence of every free nation.

This is a lesson that most people in this country have learned thoroughly. This is the

Fighting in Korea became a war of position, as suggested by this photograph of American marines taking cover from enemy bombardment. After the United Nations forces halted the sweep southward of Chinese Communist "volunteer" armies, the front became stabilized somewhat north of the 38th parallel. For more than two years the antagonists fought bloody battles for small amounts of territory. The vast American superiority in air power helped the allies to stop Chinese and North Korean attacks but, in the hilly Korean countryside, could not break the military stalemate.

basic reason why we joined in creating the United Nations. And since the end of World War II we have been putting that lesson into practice—we have been working with other free nations to check the aggressive designs of the Soviet Union before they can result in a third world war.

That is what we did in Greece, when that nation was threatened by the aggression of international communism.

The attack against Greece could have led to general war. But this country came to the aid of Greece. The United Nations supported Greek resistance. With our help, the determination and efforts of the Greek people defeated the attack on the spot.

Another big Communist threat to peace was the Berlin blockade. That too could have led to war. But again it was settled because free men would not back down in an emergency.

The aggression against Korea is the boldest and most dangerous move the Communists have yet made.

The attack on Korea was part of a greater plan for conquering all of Asia.

I would like to read to you from a secret intelligence report which came to us after the attack. It is a report of a speech a Communist army officer in North Korea gave to a group of spies and saboteurs last May, one month before South Korea was invaded. The report shows in great detail how this invasion was part of a carefully prepared plot. Here is part of what the Communist officer, who had been trained in Moscow, told his men: "Our forces," he said, "are scheduled to attack South Korean forces about the middle of June. . . . The coming attack on South Korea marks the first step toward the liberation of Asia."

Notice that he used the word "liberation." That is Communist double-talk meaning "conquest."

I have another secret intelligence report here. This one tells what another Communist officer in the Far East told his men several months before the invasion of Korea. Here is what he said:

> In order to successfully undertake the long awaited world revolution, we must first unify Asia. . . . Java, Indochina, Malaya, India, Tibet, Thailand, Philippines, and Japan are our ultimate targets. . . . The United States is the only obstacle on our road for the liberation of all countries in southeast Asia. In other words, we must unify the people of Asia and crush the United States.

That is what the Communist leaders are telling their people, and that is what they have been trying to do.

They want to control all Asia from the Kremlin.

This plan of conquest is in flat contradiction to what we believe. We believe that Korea belongs to the Koreans, that India belongs to the Indians—that all the nations of Asia should be free to work out their affairs in their own way. This is the basis of peace in the Far East and everywhere else.

The whole Communist imperialism is back of the attack on peace in the Far East. It was the Soviet Union that trained and equipped the North Koreans for aggression. The Chinese Communists massed 44 well-trained and well-equipped divisions on the Korean frontier. These were the troops they threw into battle when the North Korean Communists were beaten.

The question we have had to face is whether the Communist plan of conquest can be stopped without general war. Our Government and other countries associated with us in the United Nations believe that the best chance of stopping it without general war is to meet the attack in Korea and defeat it there.

That is what we have been doing. It is a difficult and bitter task.

But so far it has been successful.

So far, we have prevented World War III.

So far, by fighting a limited war in Korea, we have prevented aggression from succeeding and bringing on a general war. And the ability of the whole free world to resist Communist aggression has been greatly improved. . . .

II

The Best Course To Follow

But you may ask: Why can't we take other steps to punish the aggressor? Why don't we bomb Manchuria and China itself? Why don't we assist Chinese Nationalist troops to land on the mainland of China?

If we were to do these things we would be running a very grave risk of starting a general war. If that were to happen, we would have brought about the exact situation we are trying to prevent.

If we were to do these things, we would become entangled in a vast conflict on the continent of Asia and our task would become immeasurably more difficult all over the world.

What would suit the ambitions of the Kremlin better than for our military forces to be committed to a full-scale war with Red China?

It may well be that, in spite of our best efforts, the Communists may spread the war. But it would be wrong—tragically wrong—for us to take the initiative in extending the war.

The dangers are great. Make no mistake about it. Behind the North Koreans and Chinese Communists in the front lines stand additional millions of Chinese soldiers. And behind the Chinese stand the tanks, the planes, the submarines, the soldiers, and the scheming rulers of the Soviet Union.

Our aim is to avoid the spread of the conflict.

The course we have been following is the one best calculated to avoid an all-out war. It is the course consistent with our obligation to do all we can to maintain international peace and security. Our experience in Greece and Berlin shows that it is the most effective course of action we can follow.

First of all, it is clear that our efforts in Korea can blunt the will of the Chinese Communists to continue the struggle. The United Nations forces have put up a tremendous fight in Korea and have inflicted very heavy casualties on the enemy. Our forces are stronger now than they have been before. These are plain facts which may discourage the Chinese Communists from continuing their attack.

Second, the free world as a whole is growing in military strength every day. In the United States, in Western Europe, and throughout the world, free men are alert to the Soviet threat and are building their defenses. This may discourage the Communist rulers from continuing the war in Korea—and from undertaking new acts of aggression elsewhere.

If the Communist authorities realize that they cannot defeat us in Korea, if they realize it would be foolhardy to widen the hostilities beyond Korea, then they may recognize the folly of continuing their aggression. A peaceful settlement may then be possible. The door is always open.

Then we may achieve a settlement in Korea which will not compromise the principles and purposes of the United Nations.

I have thought long and hard about this question of extending the war in Asia. I have discussed it many times with the ablest military advisers in the country. I believe with all my heart that the course we are following is the best course.

I believe that we must try to limit the war to Korea for these vital reasons: to make sure that the precious lives of our fighting men are not wasted; to see that the security of our country and the free world is not needlessly jeopardized; and to prevent a third world war.

A number of events have made it evident that General MacArthur did not agree with that policy. I have therefore considered it essential to relieve General MacArthur so that there would be no doubt or confusion as to the real purpose and aim of our policy.

It was with the deepest personal regret that I found myself compelled to take this action. General MacArthur is one of our greatest military commanders. But the cause of world peace is more important than any individual.

The change in commands in the Far East means no change whatever in the policy of the United States. We will carry on the fight in Korea with vigor and determination in an effort to bring the war to a speedy and successful conclusion.

Reading 330

Decision on Vietnam (1954)

Fighting did not end in Korea until the spring of 1953. In November 1952, Dwight Eisenhower, military hero of World War II, had been elected President, defeating Democrat Adlai Stevenson. Though Eisenhower did negotiate a settlement in Korea, there remained the question of American policy toward change by revolution and civil war in Asia. There had been a combination of both in Indochina, a French colony, since 1945. The French, however, were on the verge of total defeat by the spring of 1954, having committed their best troops and equipment to the defense of Dienbienphu, a town in northern Vietnam now encircled by the Communist-led Vietminh. Chalmers Roberts, a journalist with sources of inside information, revealed what happened when President Eisenhower and John Foster Dulles, his Secretary of State, were confronted by this new Asian crisis.

From Chalmers M. Roberts, "The Day We Didn't Go To War," *The Reporter,* XI (September 14, 1954), pp. 31–32, 34, 35. Subheadings and footnotes added by the editors.

I

A Conference in the State Department

Saturday, April 3, 1954, was a raw, windy day in Washington, but the weather didn't prevent a hundred thousand Americans from milling around the Jefferson Memorial to see the cherry blossoms—or twenty thousand of them from watching the crowning of the 1954 Cherry Blossom Queen.

President Eisenhower drove off to his Maryland mountain retreat called Camp David. There he worked on his coming Monday speech, designed, so the White House said, to quiet America's fears of Russia, the H-bomb, domestic Communists, a depression. But that Saturday morning eight members of Congress, five Senators and three Representatives, got the scare of their lives. They had been called to a secret conference with John Foster Dulles. They entered one of the State Department's fifth-floor conference rooms to find not only Dulles but Admiral Arthur W. Radford, chairman of the Joint Chiefs of Staff, Under Secretary of Defense Roger Kyes, Navy Secretary Robert B. Anderson, and Thruston B. Morton, Dulles's assistant for Congressional Relations. A large map of the world hung behind Dulles's seat, and Radford stood by with several others. "The President has asked me to call this meeting," Dulles began.

The atmosphere became serious at once. What was wanted, Dulles said, was a joint resolution by Congress to permit the President to use air and naval power in Indo-China. Dulles hinted that perhaps the mere passage of such a resolution would in itself make its use unnecessary. But the President had asked for its consideration, and, Dulles added, Mr. Eisenhower felt that it was indispensable at this juncture that the leaders of Congress feel as the Administration did on the Indo-China crisis.

Then Radford took over. He said the Administration was deeply concerned over the rapidly deteriorating situation. He used a map of the Pacific to point out the importance of Indo-China. He spoke about the French Union forces then already under siege for three weeks in the fortress of Dienbienphu.

The admiral explained the urgency of American action by declaring that he was not even sure, because of poor communications, whether, in fact, Dienbienphu was still holding out. (The fortress held out for five weeks more.)

Dulles backed up Radford. If Indo-China fell and if its fall led to the loss of all of Southeast Asia, he declared, then the United States might eventually be forced back to Hawaii, as it was before the Second World War. And Dulles was not complimentary about the French. He said he feared they might use some disguised means of getting out of Indo-China if they did not receive help soon.

The eight legislators were silent: Senate Majority Leader Knowland and his G.O.P. colleague Eugene Millikin, Senate Minority Leader Lyndon B. Johnson and his Democratic colleagues Richard B. Russell and Earle C. Clements, House G.O.P. Speaker Joseph Martin and two Democratic House leaders, John W. McCormack and J. Percy Priest.

What to do? Radford offered the plan he had in mind once Congress passed the joint resolution.

Some two hundred planes from the thirty-one-thousand-ton U.S. Navy carriers *Essex* and *Boxer,* then in the South China Sea ostensibly for "training," plus land-based U.S. Air Force planes from bases a thousand miles away in the Philippines, would be used for a single strike to save Dienbienphu.

The legislators stirred, and the questions began.

Radford was asked whether such action would be war. He replied that we would be in the war.

If the strike did not succeed in relieving the fortress, would we follow up? "Yes," said the Chairman of the Joint Chiefs of Staff.

Would land forces then also have to be used? Radford did not give a definite answer.

In the early part of the questioning, Knowland showed enthusiasm for the venture, consistent with his public statements that something must be done or Southeast Asia would be lost.

But as the questions kept flowing, largely from Democrats, Knowland lapsed into silence.

Clements asked Radford the first of the two key questions: "Does this plan have the approval of the other members of the Joint Chiefs of Staff?"

"No," replied Radford.

"How many of the three agree with you?"

"None."

"How do you account for that?"

"I have spent more time in the Far East than any of them and I understand the situation better."

Lyndon Johnson put the other key question in the form of a little speech. He said that Knowland had been saying publicly that in Korea up to ninety percent of the men and the money came from the United States. The United States had become sold on the idea that that was bad. Hence in any operation in Indo-China we ought to know first who would put up the men. And so he asked Dulles whether he had consulted nations who might be our allies in intervention.

Dulles said he had not.

The Secretary was asked why he didn't go to the United Nations as in the Korean case. He replied that it would take too long, that this was an immediate problem.

There were other questions. Would Red China and the Soviet Union come into the war if the United States took military action? The China question appears to have been sidestepped, though Dulles said he felt the

American sailors, aiding refugees from North Vietnam, spray them with insecticide before transporting them to new homes in South Vietnam in August 1954. The transfer took place as part of the agreements reached shortly before in Geneva, Switzerland, where the French conceded independence to North Vietnam, South Vietnam, Laos, and Cambodia, parts of its former empire in Indochina. The nationalist-communist Vietminh forces, in control in North Vietnam, agreed to permit an exchange of peoples who wanted to move from North Vietnam to South Vietnam, or vice versa. The U.S. helped to carry out the exchange.

Soviets could handle the Chinese and the United States did not think that Moscow wanted a general war now. Further, he added, if the Communists feel that we mean business, they won't go "any further down there," pointing to the map of Southeast Asia.

John W. McCormack, the House Minority Leader, couldn't resist temptation. He was surprised, he said, that Dulles would look to the "party of treason," as the Democrats had been called by Joe McCarthy in his Lincoln's Birthday speech under G.O.P. auspices, to take the lead in a situation that might end up in a general shooting war. Dulles did not reply.

In the end, all eight members of Congress, Republicans and Democrats alike, were agreed that Dulles had better first go shopping for allies. Some people who should know say that Dulles was carrying, but did not produce, a draft of the joint resolution the President wanted Congress to consider.

The whole meeting had lasted two hours and ten minutes. As they left, the Hill Delegation told waiting reporters they had been briefed on Indo-China. Nothing more.

II
Searching for a Policy

This approach to Congress by Dulles and Radford on behalf of the President was the beginning of three weeks of intensive effort by the Administration to head off disaster in Indo-China. Some of those at the meeting came away with the feeling that if they had agreed that Saturday to the resolution, planes would have been winging toward Dienbienphu without waiting for a vote of Congress—or without a word in advance to the American people.

For some months now, I have tried to put together the bits and pieces of the American part in the Indo-China debacle. But before relating the sequel, it is necessary here to go back to two events that underlay the meeting just described—though neither of them was mentioned at that meeting.

On March 20, just two weeks earlier, General Paul Ely, then French Chief of Staff and later commander in Indo-China, had arrived in Washington from the Far East to tell the President, Dulles, Radford, and others that unless the United States intervened, Indo-China would be lost. This was a shock of earthquake proportions to leaders who had been taken in by their own talk of the Navarre Plan to win the war.

In his meetings at the Pentagon, Ely was flabbergasted to find that Radford proposed American intervention without being asked. Ely said he would have to consult his government. He carried back to Paris the word that when France gave the signal, the United States would respond.

The second event of importance is the most difficult to determine accurately. But it is clear that Ely's remarks started a mighty struggle within the National Security Council [NSC], that inner core of the government where our most vital decisions are worked out for the President's final O.K. The argument advanced by Radford and supported by Vice-President Nixon and by Dulles was that Indo-China must not be allowed to fall into Communist hands lest such a fate set in motion a falling row of dominoes.

Eisenhower himself used the "row-of-dominoes" phrase at a press conference on April 7. On April 15, Radford said in a speech that Indo-China's loss "would be the prelude to the loss of all Southeast Asia and a threat to a far wider area." On April 16 Nixon, in his well-publicized "off-the-record" talk to the newspaper editors' convention, said that if the United States could not otherwise prevent the loss of Indo-China, then the Administration must face the situation and dispatch troops. And the President in his press conference of March 24 had declared that Southeast Asia was of the "most transcendent importance." All these remarks reflected a basic policy decision. . . .

On Friday, April 23, Bidault* showed Dulles a telegram from General Henri-Eugène Navarre, then the Indo-China commander, saying that only a massive air attack could save Dienbienphu, by now under siege for six weeks. Dulles said the United States could not intervene.

But on Saturday Admiral Radford arrived and met with Dulles. Then Dulles and Radford saw Eden.† Dulles told Eden that the French were asking for military help at once. An allied air strike at the Vietminh positions

*Georges Bidault, French premier—Eds.
†Anthony Eden, Great Britain's foreign secretary—Eds.

around Dienbienphu was discussed. The discussion centered on using the same two U.S. Navy carriers and Phillippine-based Air Force planes Radford had talked about to the Congressional leaders. . . .

Eden said forcefully that he could not agree to any such scheme of intervention, that he personally opposed it. He added his conviction that within forty-eight hours after an air strike, ground troops would be called for, as had been the case at the beginning of the Korean War. . . .

American intervention collapsed on that Saturday, April 24. On Sunday Eden arrived in Geneva with word of the "No" from the specially convened British Cabinet meeting. And on Monday, the day the Geneva Conference began, Eisenhower said in a speech that what was being sought at Geneva was a "modus vivendi" with the Communists. . . .

This mixture of improvisation and panic is the story of how close the United States came to entering the Indo-China war. Would Congress have approved intervention if the President had dared to ask it? This point is worth a final word.

On returning from Geneva in mid-May, I asked that question of numerous Senators and Representatives. Their replies made clear that Congress would, in the end, have done what Eisenhower asked, provided he had asked for it forcefully and explained the facts and their relation to the national interest of the United States.

Whether action or inaction better served the American interest at that late stage of the Indo-China war is for the historian, not for the reporter, to say. But the fact emerges that President Eisenhower never did lay the intervention question on the line. In spite of the NSC decision, April 3, 1954, was the day we *didn't* go to war.

TOPIC 62

EISENHOWER, DULLES, AND AMERICAN POWER

In the 1950s the conduct of American foreign policy was determined by two beliefs. One was that fear of American nuclear retaliation was the chief factor preventing the Russian army from sweeping across Western Europe. The second belief was that sudden social change, especially by means of revolution, anywhere in the world was potentially dangerous to the United States. President Dwight D. Eisenhower, elected in 1952, and John Foster Dulles, his Secretary of State, had the task of devising policies based on these beliefs, which would show that the frustrations of the Korean War had not weakened American power, yet which would also convince the world of America's peaceful intentions. This topic considers the nature, effectiveness, and future implications of the Eisenhower-Dulles policies.

Reading 331

The Eisenhower Era
(1953–1960)

The years of the Eisenhower administration, 1953 through 1960, can be best understood through a study of the series of world-wide "incidents" which characterized America's foreign relations. In the following selection historian Stewart Easton offers a narrative of the events which tested the beliefs underlying the Eisenhower-Dulles foreign policy.

From *The Western Heritage, from 1500 to the Present* by Stewart C. Easton. Copyright © 1966 by Holt, Rinehart and Winston, Inc. Reprinted by permission of the publisher. Pp. 533–548. Subheadings added by the editors.

I

The New Men in Washington and Moscow

The Truman-Acheson policy of containment was continued without major change in the Eisenhower-Dulles era. Secretary Dulles remained in office from the beginning of the Eisenhower administration until April 1959, when illness compelled his retirement, and the President all these years allowed him virtually a free hand, using his incomparable prestige and genial personality only rarely to assuage wounded feelings and express publicly unquestioned personal desire for peace and improved relations with Russia. But on the whole neither Secretary Dulles nor Congress was willing to make any significant or lasting concessions on the American side, nor was Premier Khrushchev on the Russian. The era was dominated by an ever intensifying arms race, the production and testing of ever more powerful bombs, the development of new delivery systems, especially the intercontinental missiles powered by rockets. Neither side was willing to allow the other to keep any momentary advantage that appeared. Progress in the intermittent disarmament negotiations was virtually impossible, and it was clear enough that no true basis for negotiation existed; and not all the pressure attempted by allies and neutrals could do more than bring the principals to the conference table, where they continued to adopt the rigid positions which mutual suspicion dictated....

Within the USSR there had been numerous changes since the death of Stalin.* After a short period during which Georgi Malenkov held power conjointly with Molotov and Nikita Khrushchev, the latter emerged as the most powerful of the trio as secretary of the Communist party. His colleagues were given other jobs and Marshal Bulganin became prime minister. The new leaders quickly became reconciled with "deviationist" Yugoslavia, and decided to sign a peace treaty with Austria, the latter being one of the demands put forward by the West as a preliminary condition for improved relations. After the treaty had been signed, both American and Russian troops withdrew from the country. A naval base in Finnish territory was also restored to Finland later in the year. As a result of this generally improved climate a "summit" meeting of leaders was held in Geneva in July 1955. No concrete results emerged from the meeting (except for the agreement to admit some satellite and pro-Western states into the United Nations as a package deal), but for

*Stalin died in March 1953—Eds.

438

The general turns to politics. Dwight D. Eisenhower, supreme commander of the Western allies in Europe during World War II, resigned as commander of NATO forces in 1952 to run for the Republican Party nomination for President. He won both the nomination and the election. Here he strikes a typical pose while campaigning.

the first time in many years there was an atmosphere of cordiality and some slight relaxing of suspicions. . . .

Early in 1956 the Twentieth Soviet Party Congress was held in which Khrushchev repudiated Stalinism and attacked Stalinist tyranny as it had existed in Russia, making clear that he himself was in favor of relaxing tensions, not only at home but abroad. This revelation of Stalin's misdeeds created confusion in the parties abroad, which had grown accustomed to regarding the Soviet Union and Stalin as the fountainhead of true Marxian wisdom. Partly as a result of being taken seriously in the satellite countries, Khrushchev was faced with serious revolts against Stalinist leadership in both Poland and Hungary.

In Poland the new leader Gomulka, recently released from prison, stood his ground against Khrushchev, and as a result the Soviet Union acquiesced in a moderate liberalization of the regime under Gomulka, who was after all still a Communist. It was far otherwise in Hungary, where an uprising brought Imre Nagy, a "deviationist," back to power as the head of a government from which he had been expelled a few years before by a Stalinist. Nagy, though also nominally a Communist, was unable to control the direction of the uprising, and agreed to the "neutrality" of his country and its withdrawal from the Warsaw Pact. After a few futile efforts to handle the situation without the use of force, Khrushchev found that he had no alternative but to crush the rebellion with the aid of Russian troops and heavy equipment or stand by and see the break-up of the satellite empire. Hungary without doubt would have been sucked into the Western orbit, and this could no more be permitted than the unification of Germany by free elections without guarantees of West German neutrality. The insurgents fought valiantly, but the position was hopeless, and more than 200,000 Hungarians escaped to Austria and Yugoslavia and exiled themselves, many of them to America. The episode showed clearly both that the Soviet Union was unwilling to relinquish her hold on eastern Europe and that the "liberation of the captive nations," so often promised by American speakers and by the United States-controlled Radio Free Europe, was not to be achieved except by force, which the United States was not prepared to furnish in that cause. Under the leadership of a more acceptable Communist, liberalization in Hungary was soon permitted, demonstrating that internal reforms could be permitted in the post-Stalin era. But there could be no escape from the Soviet security system, and only Communists acceptable to Moscow would be permitted to govern the satellite states.

II

Trouble in the Middle East

As it happened, the revolt in Hungary coincided in time with the Anglo-Franco-Israeli invasion of Egypt.... In this episode Secretary Dulles was so furious with the British and French for not informing him in advance of their intentions (which, of course, he would have violently opposed) that he and the Russian delegate at the United Nations teamed up to condemn the expedition both in the Security Council, where the resolution was vetoed by Britain and France, and in the General Assembly where it was passed. The Soviet Union, for her part, threatened Britain and France directly with dire consequences—Israel had already halted her invasion at Anglo-French insistence—if they did not desist, and stated that she was determined to "crush the aggressors and restore peace in the Middle East." Whether it was American or Russian pressure that proved efficacious, the British and French submitted and ordered a cease-fire. At all events, it was the Soviet Union which received most credit for bringing the invasion to its humiliating end, and relations of the United States with her allies were—perhaps permanently—embittered....

As a result of the apparent intention of the Soviet Union to play an important role in the Middle East, from which she had hitherto refrained, President Eisenhower went before Congress and requested authorization to use American armed forces against "overt aggression from any nation controlled by international Communism," stating that the Soviet Union had long sought to dominate the Middle East. It may be remarked that this was a somewhat unlikely prospect in view of the tight ring of bases sealed only the year before in the Baghdad Pact, to whose military committee the United States now agreed to belong, thus acquiring the right to station her air force in these lands. This was, indeed the position taken by some Senators, nineteen of whom voted against giving the President the right he sought. The Senate also lessened the impact of what came to be called the Eisenhower Doctrine by making the use of force dependent on the request by the aggrieved nation in danger from "international Communism."...

In the summer of 1958 there was a bloody revolution in Iraq, during which the king and the pro-Western premier were atrociously murdered. This determined the United States government to take a step that had been contemplated for several months, ever since an intermittent civil war had broken out in the tiny state of Lebanon over an attempt by President Chamoun to rig elections in his favor. He had already appealed for help under the Eisenhower Doctrine, which did not seem applicable. But the revolution in Iraq decided the issue, and marines landed in Lebanon in force in battle dress, but found nothing to do, though their presence may have served as a warning to the Iraqis that nothing should be done to offend the Americans, such as, for example, playing oil politics. It was more difficult to remove the marines than to land them, as nothing changed in the situation except that President Chamoun was peacefully replaced. In November they were evacuated.

With the United States deploying power in the eastern Mediterranean and completing the encirclement of the Soviet Union by land by adhering to the Baghdad Pact, Khrushchev's position at home became difficult. His proclaimed policy of coexistence had paid no dividends, as the Chinese unkindly pointed out, accusing him of lack of enterprise and enthusiasm for revolution. In return Khrushchev criticized some features of the Chinese economic program (the Great Leap Forward) and explained that the establishment of communes was incorrect. This was one of the first clear signs of a cooling of the relationship between China and the Soviet Union, which gave no support, even verbal, to the crushing of the Tibetan rebellion by the Chinese the following year, nor did the Soviet Union take the side of China in the dispute with India over frontiers. Within his own party, however, Khrushchev won a considerable victory, and before the end of the year he had ousted his opponents from their positions of power and become the unquestioned leader and spokesman for the Soviet Union, a position he held until his fall in 1964. In relation to the United States all he could do was to proclaim as loudly as possible that the Soviet Union would retaliate with rocket-borne nuclear weapons if she were attacked.

"You Sure Everything's All Right, Foster?"

III

The Space Race

Verisimilitude was given to this threat when late in 1957 the Russians sent up the first man-made satellite, known as Sputnik, demonstrating in a spectacular manner the capabilities of Russian scientists and engineers, and the technical efficiency of her rocketry. As much as anything else, this achievement brought home to Americans the probability that the Soviet Union could indeed retaliate and deliver her nuclear weapons by rocket, and that there was in truth a nuclear stalemate. This actual superiority in the thrust of Soviet rockets . . . caused a minor revolution in American education, leading to the establishment of special scholarships for budding scientists and a great increase in the quantity of technical education offered in the schools and colleges. The unthinkable had happened. The United States in a crucial field of scientific endeavor had been overtaken and surpassed by the backward Russians, whose abilities in this field of expertise had always been much underrated. . . .

But there was no letup in the costly arms race. For a few years there was an informal agreement to stop nuclear testing in the atmosphere in order to lessen hazards from radiation, but in time this was brought to an end by the Russian desire to test some huge

A frequent and biting critic of American political leadership in the post-World War II years has been Herbert Block (Herblock) of the *Washington Post*. Here, in 1954, Herblock satirizes President Eisenhower's willingness to let Secretary of State John Foster Dulles direct American foreign policy in turbulent times.

new multimegaton bombs, and the United States in turn resumed her own testing. It was not until 1963 that a treaty banning testing in the atmosphere was finally signed by all important nations except France and Communist China, which were both in the process of manufacturing nuclear weapons and needed to test them. Underground testing, however, continued, but at least this did not, except in the case of accident, contribute significantly to the radiation in the atmosphere.

Meanwhile in 1958 Khrushchev had again tested the nerves of the West by precipitating a new crisis over Berlin. When the West showed no signs of making any concessions, he let the matter lapse for the time being. In 1959, after the retirement and death of Secretary Dulles, President Eisenhower took over the direction of foreign policy himself for the first time in his administration, and another thaw ensued. Khrushchev was invited to the United States, where he apparently enjoyed himself and had a *tête-à-tête* conversation with the President at Camp David. Numerous cultural exchanges between the United States and the Soviet Union were arranged. But the following year, after another summit meeting had been arranged, this time for Paris, Khrushchev evidently had second thoughts about its possible utility. Instead of meeting with the President, he staged a violent scene because a United States high-flying reconnaissance plane had been shot down over Russia. President Eisenhower, clearly insufficiently briefed, issued contradictory explanations, but would not apologize or admit that the United States had had no right to make such flights. Official explanations indeed were by turns misleading and boastful. The flights had been going on for a long time, it was said, and this was the first plane that had been shot down. Though the President called off future flights over Russia, the summit meeting never took place. The Berlin struggle was renewed in 1961 during the regime of President Kennedy, when the East Germans, with Soviet troops watching, erected a concrete wall to separate East Berlin from West Berlin, thereby sealing off the constant loss of Germans to the West. The Wall still stands today at the time of writing.

The United States Backs a Revolution (1954)

While the United States and the Soviet Union glared at each other, political unrest increased rapidly throughout the world. Revolutions and suppression of revolutions occurred more and more often. The United States, the Soviet Union, and later Communist China each tried to manipulate outbreaks to its own advantage. One such revolt, in an area very sensitive to the United States, occurred in Guatemala in 1954. At the very time President Eisenhower (1890–1969) and his advisers considered intervening in Vietnam (see Reading 330) they faced the problem of a seemingly Communist-dominated government in Central America, a relatively short distance away.

From Dwight D. Eisenhower, *Mandate for Change, 1953–1956* (New York, 1963), pp. 504, 505, 507–510. Copyright © 1963 by Dwight D. Eisenhower. Subheadings added and footnotes omitted by the editors.

I

A Latin American Menace

The first of these problems was waiting for me when I entered the White House. It involved Guatemala, a beautiful land of Central America whose mountains and moderate climate make it one of the garden spots of the hemisphere. The troubles had been long-standing, reaching back nine years to the Guatemalan revolution of 1944, which had resulted in the overthrow of the dictator General Jorge Ubico. Thereafter, the Communists busied themselves with agitating and with infiltrating labor unions, peasant organizations, and the press and radio. In 1950 a military officer, Jacobo Arbenz Guzman, came to power and by his actions soon created the strong suspicion that he was merely a puppet manipulated by Communists. . . .

Arbenz denied that his government was Communist, a denial that was issued in a speech at a May Day celebration featuring seventy thousand marchers. But by the middle of October 1953, the Assistant Secretary of State for Inter-American Affairs, John Moors Cabot, said publicly that Guatemala was "openly playing the Communist game"; for example, it accepted the ridiculous Communist contention that the United States had conducted bacteriological warfare in Korea. . . .

In the two months from March to May, 1954, the agents of international Communism in Guatemala continued their efforts to penetrate and subvert their neighboring Central American states, using consular agents for their political purposes and fomenting political assassinations and strikes. In Guatemala itself the government answered protests by suspending constitutional rights, conducting mass arrests, and killing leaders in the political opposition.

In May things came to a head. On the 17th of that month Foster Dulles reported to the press that the United States had reliable information on a shipment of arms from behind the Iron Curtain. The arms had been loaded on the *Alfhem,* a Swedish ship chartered by a British company, at the East German Baltic port of Stettin. The ship was at that moment being unloaded at Puerto Barrios in Guatemala. The ship had mysteriously changed its announced destination and its course three times en route, apparently in an effort to confuse observers. We learned that the cargo contained two thousand tons of small arms, ammunition, and light artillery pieces manufactured in the Skoda arms factory in Czechoslovakia. This quantity far exceeded any legitimate, normal requirements for the Guatemalan armed forces.

On May 19 Nicaragua broke diplomatic ties with Guatemala. Five days later we announced that the United States was airlifting arms to Honduras and Nicaragua to help counter the danger created by the Czech shipment to Guatemala. Our initial shipment comprised only fifty tons of rifles, pistols, machine guns, and ammunition, hardly enough to create apprehension in neighboring states.

On May 24, 1954, I informed the Legislative leaders of measures we were planning to take. Honduras and Nicaragua had asked for help. Among other things, we would (1) prevent any further Communist arms build-up in Central America by stopping suspicious foreign-flag vessels on the high seas off Guatemala to examine cargo (an action conforming to the United Nations Charter and Caracas resolution*) and (2) convene another meeting of the Organization of American States to consider next steps. We would, of course, advise Mexico and other friendly countries of our plans.

Our quarantine measures soon ran into trouble. We were able to hold up at Hamburg some six tons of 20-mm. anti-aircraft shells in transit to Guatemala from Switzerland. Action on the high seas, however, was a different matter. While well within the capabilities of the Navy, such measures would require at least the tacit cooperation of our allies, principally Britain, to avoid placing an almost fatal strain on our relations. At first such cooperation was difficult to obtain, at least completely, from the British. Foster communicated with Anthony Eden on the matter, and the latter finally, with misgivings, issued a statement which we considered adequate.

II

A Question of Intervention

Meanwhile, in Guatemala, Arbenz had declared a state of siege and launched a reign of terror. Then on June 18 armed forces under Carlos Castillo Armas, an exiled former colonel in the Guatemalan Army, crossed the border from Honduras into Guatemala, initially with a mere handful of men—reportedly about two hundred. As he progressed he picked up recruits. Simultaneously three obsolete bombers, presumably under his direction, buzzed Guatemala City and bombed the ordnance depot. Things seemed to be going well for Castillo's small band until June 22.

*The Tenth Inter-American Conference, held in March 1954, approved a resolution condemning the spread of communism in the Americas—Eds.

On that date Allen Dulles reported to me that Castillo had lost two of the three old bombers with which he was supporting his "invasion."

A meeting was arranged that afternoon with Foster Dulles, Allen Dulles, and Henry F. Holland, who had succeeded John Cabot as Assistant Secretary of State for Inter-American Affairs. The point at issue was whether the United States should cooperate in replacing the bombers. The country which had originally supplied this equipment to Castillo was willing now to supply him two P-51 fighter-bombers if the United States would agree to replace them. The sense of our meeting was far from unanimous. Henry, a sincere and dedicated public servant and a real expert in Latin American affairs, made no secret of his conviction that the United States should keep hands off, insisting that other Latin American republics would, if our action became known, interpret our shipment of planes as intervention in Guatemala's internal affairs. Others, however, felt that our agreeing to replace the bombers was the only hope for Castillo Armas, who was obviously the only hope of restoring freedom to Guatemala.

"What do you think Castillo's chances would be," I asked Allen Dulles, "without the aircraft?"

His answer was unequivocal: "About zero."

"Suppose we supply the aircraft. What would the chances be then?"

Again the CIA chief did not hesitate: "About 20 percent."

I considered the matter carefully. I realized full well that United States intervention in Central America and Caribbean affairs earlier in the century had greatly injured our standing in all of Latin America. On the other hand, it seemed to me that to refuse to cooperate in providing indirect support to a strictly anti-Communist faction in this struggle would be contrary to the letter and spirit of the Caracas resolution. I had faith in the strength of the inter-American resolve therein set forth. On the actual value of a shipment of planes, I knew from experience the important psychological impact of even a small amount of air support. In any event, our proper course of action—indeed my duty—was clear to me. We would replace the airplanes.

As my visitors prepared to leave the office, I walked to the door with Allen Dulles and, smiling to break the tension, said, "Allen, that figure of 20 percent was persuasive. It showed me that you had thought this matter through realistically. If you had told me that the chances would be 90 percent, I would have had a much more difficult decision."

Allen was equal to the situation. "Mr. President," he said, a grin on his face, "when I saw Henry walking into your office with three large law books under his arm, I knew he had lost his case already."

Delivery of the planes was prompt and Castillo successfully resumed his progress. After five days, during which the Guatemalan Army announced its refusal to support Arbenz, he announced that he was relinquishing power to a Colonel Diaz as the head of a new provisional government. Two days later a second change deposed Diaz and brought the anti-Communist Colonel Elfego Monzón to power. Thereafter, further negotiations, with Ambassador Peurifoy and President Oscar Osorio of El Salvador as mediators, brought Colonel Castillo Armas into Monzón's new ruling junta, eventually as its head.

Meanwhile the United Nations Security Council had deferred action on the Guatemala matter during an investigation by the Inter-American Peace Committee of the Organization of American States, but the change of government had made further action unnecessary.

Guatemala's Tragedy

It was relatively easy for the United States to impose its will in Guatemala. President Eisenhower made clear (see Reading 332) his belief that indirect intervention was for the benefit of both nations, but not all Americans agreed. One who disagreed was Bernard Rosen, an American who had taught history and economics in Guatemala for several years.

From Bernard Rosen, "Counter Revolution: Guatemala's Tragedy," *The Nation* (July 24, 1954), pp. 87, 88–89.

I

The Sources of Revolution

To the people of the United States the overthrow of the Arbenz regime was merely another incident in the West's anti-Communist crusade. For Guatemala, however, the event had far different implications, and the issue of communism was involved only because the United States injected it. The real issues antedate the anti-Communist crusade; indeed, they antedate communism.

Throughout the nineteenth century two main forces struggled for supremacy on the Guatemalan scene—the anti-clerical liberals, who were the partisans of the ideas of the French revolution, and the conservatives, who upheld the status quo and the traditionalism which stemmed from Spanish colonialism. Except for brief interludes the conservatives held the power, and Guatemala remained a backward, semi-feudal country, controlled by landholders and clericals who kept a landless peasantry in a state of abysmal ignorance and poverty. A strong middle class, the necessary base for a flourishing liberal movement anywhere, was virtually non-existent.

In the 1870's the liberals came to power and under the leadership of the dynamic Justo Rufino Barrios separated church and state, expropriated church properties, and established a secular public-school system. In order to further the country's economic development they invited the American capitalists to supply the necessary funds. Rufino Barrios was particularly interested in the construction of railroads, believing that they would contribute more than any other single factor to the modernization of Guatemala. . . .

From 1900 on successive dictatorships kept the masses in their place and guaranteed that the foreign enterprises and the native landholders should enjoy the fruits of their labor. Social pressures, however, have a way of building up, and in 1944 a virtually spontaneous popular upheaval overthrew the thirteen-year-old Ubico government.

II

Middle-Class Reform

Historically the 1944 revolution belonged to the liberal current which brought Mariano Galvez and Rufino Barrios to power in the nineteenth century. It was a belated bourgeois revolution, not, as its enemies asserted, a "red" revolution. Middle-class intellectuals, supported by the masses, became the new rulers of Guatemala and inaugurated policies calculated to lead the country along the path of bourgeois development.

Under Arévalo, and later Arbenz, Guatemala moved rapidly into a period of bourgeois reform. A new constitution gave the people the civil rights enjoyed in advanced Western nations. Labor and peasant organizations were legalized. Steps were taken to diversify the agriculture of the country and get away from a one-crop coffee economy. A government-sponsored institute was established, headed by an agronomist lent to Guatemala by President Perón of Argentina, to aid capitalists who wished to expand their enterprises or start new ones. Construction of a new highway from Guatemala City to Puerto Thomás on the Atlantic was begun, with the object of breaking the transportation monopoly of the International Railway of Central America, which is controlled by the United Fruit Company. Finally, an agrarian law was adopted, designed to break up the estates and create a class of independent farmers.

None of the reforms of Arévalo and Arbenz can possibly be considered Communist. Even the controversial agrarian law of Arbenz, which the troglodyte opponents of the 1944 revolution revile as "communism," is no more than a mild middle-class reform. The propaganda against it reminds one of the campaigns of slander directed against "bolshevik" Mexico in the twenties and early thirties. The law itself states that its purpose was to "liquidate feudal property . . . in order to develop . . . capitalist methods of production in agriculture and prepare the road for the industrialization of Guatemala."

Hampered by the non-existence of a strong bourgeoisie and the dearth of capital, Avévalo and Arbenz resorted to the expedient made use of by other bourgeois states in the past—namely, direct state intervention to obtain funds for promoting industrial development. Perón and the recent middle-class governments of Mexico have done the same thing. The new constitution sanctioned such state intervention. Article 88 says that "the state will orient the national economy" and that the "primary function of the state is to promote agriculture and industry in general." Article 90 goes on to say that "the state recognizes the existence of private property and guarantees it as a feature of society." This Latin American version of Keynesian economics is certainly not communism.

However, the middle-class reformers were much weaker than their control of the state apparatus made them appear to be. Hemmed in by the foreign enterprises and native landholders on one side and by the mass of peasants and workers on the other, they could not by themselves reshape Guatemalan society. Hence the political tactics of Arévalo and Arbenz. *The workers and peasants were to be used as a means to an end*—namely, the creation of a bourgeois society. But the labor and peasant movements were run by the Communists, and the bourgeois leaders were too weak to oppose the infiltration of Communists into the government, particularly in the education, propaganda, and agrarian departments. In consequence Marxist and socialist terminology came to be used in the official *Diario de Centro America* and in government propaganda in general.

The Guatemalan middle-class reformers were not the first in Latin America to resort to "radicalism" to win over the masses. Their Mexican predecessors went even farther. I have in my possession textbooks used in Mexican public schools during the Cárdenas administration which expound primitive communism and celebrate the victory of the Third International. And I also recall that Mexican Cabinet ministers spoke in the name of "dialectic materialism" and the "classless society." The Cárdenas government was not Communist; why try to pin the label on the Arévalo and Arbenz governments?

The shortcomings of those administrations and their game of give and take with the Communists must not blind us to the fact that Arbenz was overthrown by a combination of reactionary forces united around a negative "anti-communism." The middle-class reformers furthered, in a small way, economic and social progress; the reactionary "anti-Communist" combination can only hold it back. The "anti-Communists" are not likely to do away overnight with all the innovations introduced by Arévalo and Arbenz, but a brake will be put on new reforms, and those that cannot be undone will be kept within bounds.

To say that the only interest of the new government is to block communism in Guatemala and destroy a "Soviet beachhead" in the Americas is nonsense. Its chief target is the reforms mentioned above, particularly the agrarian reform which was expected to undermine the power of the landholders and the foreign enterprises. Admittedly the Communist infiltration was a factor in the Guatemalan equation and made the United States apprehensive. But the conflict was not primarily caused by the issue of communism.

I have no way of knowing in detail what role the United States played in the recent uprising. But one thing is certain. By harping on the threat of the "Soviet beachhead" and keeping silent about the real meaning of the 1944 revolution, the United States showed itself to be opposed not only to communism in Guatemala but also to the industrial development of the country. Apparently the United States opposes not only "red" but also bourgeois revolutions in backward countries.

The Soviet Union Suppresses a Revolution (1956)

Revolution and counterrevolution were not exclusive problems of the United States. As historian Stewart Easton pointed out (see Reading 331), in 1956 anti-Soviet socialist groups overthrew the Russian-dominated communist regime in Hungary. The Soviet government reacted by sending troops to restore the pro-Russian government. Mikhail Suslov, a leader of the Soviet Communist Party, defended his government's actions in a speech soon after the event.

From the *New York Times*, November 7, 1956. © 1956 by the New York Times Company. Reprinted by permission.

The former Hungarian leadership, which was permitted in the past no small measure of crude mistakes, has not understood the requirements of the moment. It acted with extreme delays, as a result of which it has evoked the discontent of the masses.

Reactionary anti-Socialist elements, directed by international reaction, have immediately taken advantage of this to open an assault on the people's democratic order. With false slogans, they succeeded for a certain time in misguiding considerable masses of people and, in particular, young people.

Counter-revolutionary forces at one time set up an extremely dangerous position for the fate of socialism in Hungary.

The Government of Imre Nagy, which was formed in these circumstances, was giving reactionary forces one concession after another and, having cleared the way to counter-revolution, it disintegrated. Counter-revolutionary bands unleashed terror, they savagely murdered prominent public leaders, they strung up or shot Communists and prominent workers.

An intensified movement of arms and of numerous officers and soldiers who had served in Hitlerite forces and in Horthy's Fascist Army took place across the Western frontier of Hungary. Hungary was in complete chaos and arbitrariness.

The direct danger of the restoration of capitalist and landowner's orders became imminent as well as that of revival of fascism. A victory of reaction and fascism in Hungary would not only have meant the loss by the Hungarian workers of all conquests gained by them in struggle against landowners and capitalists, but it would create a danger to other Socialist countries by bringing their frontiers closer to imperialist bases.

At this moment of responsibility in the life of the Hungarian people, Socialist forces of the country took the only correct decision: to create [a] revolutionary workers' and peasants' Government able to bar the road to reaction and fascism.

In the interests of the people of the Hungarian working class, of its motherland, the revolutionary workers' and peasants' Government addressed a request to the command of the Soviet troops to help the Hungarian people crush the black forces of reaction and counter-revolution, to restore the people's Socialist order, to restore order and tranquillity in the country.

At present the Socialist forces of the people's Hungary, together with units of the Soviet Army, have crushed the forces of reaction and counter-revolution. They did not allow counter-revolution to trample underfoot the gains of socialism.

The Soviet people, working people of all Socialist countries, all progressive forces of the world, which were seriously troubled these last days by the course of events in Hungary, are rejoicing at the victory achieved by the Hungarian working people over the counter-revolution.

Hungary was, and will continue to be, in the family of Socialist countries a free, independent Socialist state with equal rights.

The Soviet Union is full of determination to achieve improvement in relation with the great power of the West, the United States.

We, of course, know that some elements in the United States are still attempting to meddle in international difficulties, fanning Soviet-American differences. However, such policy is detrimental to the United States itself.

The sooner an end is put to it, the greater will be the gain for universal peace and security of all peoples, including the American people.

The Suez Crisis (1956)

At the same time the Soviets were suppressing the Hungarian Revolution, long-simmering tensions in the Middle East erupted into open battle, with a combined Israeli-British-French effort to take control of the Suez Canal from Egypt (see Reading 331). As with Guatemala, President Eisenhower attempted to fit this

British bitterness at the outcome of the Suez crisis of 1956 is reflected in this cartoon from *Punch*. Russian and American pressure, both inside and outside the United Nations, had forced the British, French, and Israelis to halt their invasion of Egypt over the latter's seizure of the Suez Canal, at a time when the Russians themselves were repressing by force a revolution in Hungary. Here UN Secretary Dag Hammarskjold reproves Israeli, French, and British leaders while ignoring Russian hypocrisy and brutality. President Gamal Abdel Nasser of Egypt, rescued by events, smirks at left.

conflict with Egypt into the broader context of American-Soviet tensions. What follows is the text of a letter Eisenhower wrote to his good friend, former British Prime Minister Winston Churchill.

Dwight D. Eisenhower, *Waging Peace, 1956–1961* (New York, 1965), pp. 680–681. Copyright © 1965 by Dwight D. Eisenhower.

November 27, 1956

Dear Winston: I agree fully with the implication of your letter that . . . back of the difficulties that the free world is now experiencing lies one principal fact that none of us can afford to forget. The Soviets are the real enemy of the Western World, implacably hostile and seeking our destruction.

Many months ago it became clear that the Soviets were convinced that the mere building of mighty military machines would not necessarily accomplish their purposes, while at the same time their military effort was severely limiting their capacity for conquering the world by other means, especially economic. Unquestionably the greatest factor in turning their minds away from general war as a means of world conquest was their knowledge of America's and Britain's large and growing strength in nuclear and fission weapons.

Starting almost at the instant that Nasser took his high-handed action with respect to the Canal, I tried earnestly to keep Anthony [Eden] informed of public opinion in this country and of the course that we would feel compelled to follow if there was any attempt to solve by force the problem presented to the free world through Nasser's action. I told him that we were committed to the United Nations and I particularly urged him, in a letter of July thirty-first, to avoid the use of

A BRITISH COMMENT ON THE U.N.'S ACTIONS

Illingworth, copyright by Punch, 1956

force, at least until it had been proved to the world that the United Nations was incapable of handling the problem. My point was that since the struggle with Russia had obviously taken on a new tactical form, we had to be especially careful that any course of action we adopted should by its logic and justice command world respect, if not sympathy. I argued that to invade Egypt merely because that country had chosen to nationalize a company would be interpreted by the world as power politics and would raise a storm of resentment that, within the Arab States, would result in a long and dreary guerrilla warfare; something on the order that the French are now experiencing in Algeria.

I have tried to make it clear that we share the opinion of the British . . . [and] others that . . . we would have to concert our actions in making certain that he [Nasser] did not grow to be a danger to our welfare. But for the reasons I have given above, I urged that the nationalization of the Canal Company was not the vehicle to choose for bringing about correction in this matter.

Sometime in the early part of October, all communication between ourselves on the one hand and the British and the French on the other suddenly ceased. Our intelligence showed the gradual buildup of Israeli military strength, finally reaching such a state of completion that I felt compelled on two successive days to warn that country that the United States would honor its part in the Tri-Partite Declaration of May, 1950—in short, that we would oppose clear aggression by any power in the Mid-East.

But so far as Britain and France were concerned, we felt that they had deliberately excluded us from their thinking; we had no choice but to do our best to be prepared for whatever might happen.

The first news we had of the attack and of British-French plans was gained from the newspapers and we had no recourse except to assert our readiness to support the United Nations, before which body, incidentally, the British Government had itself placed the whole Suez controversy.

Now I still believe that we must keep several facts clearly before us, the first one always being that the Soviets are the real enemy and all else must be viewed against the background of that truth. The second fact is that nothing would please this country more nor, in fact, could help us more, than to see British prestige and strength renewed and rejuvenated in the Mid-East. We want those countries to trust and lean toward the Western World, not Russia. A third fact is that we want to help Britain right now, particularly in its difficult fuel and financial situation, daily growing more serious.

All we have asked in order to come out openly has been a British statement that it would conform to the resolutions of the United Nations. The United Nations troops do not, in our opinion, have to be as strong as those of an invading force because any attack upon them will be an attack upon the whole United Nations and if such an act of folly were committed, I think that we could quickly settle the whole affair.

. . . I continue to believe that the safety of the Western World depends in the final analysis upon the closest possible ties between Western Europe, the American hemisphere, and as many allies as we can induce to stand with us. If this incident has proved nothing else, it must have forcefully brought this truth home to us again. A chief factor in the union of the free world must be indestructible ties between the British Commonwealth and ourselves.

The only difficulty I have had in the particular instance is the fact that to me it seemed the action of the British Government was not only in violation of the basic principles by which this great combination of nations can be held together, but that even by the doctrine of expediency the invasion could not be judged as soundly conceived and skillfully executed.

So I hope that this one may be washed off the slate as soon as possible and that we can then together adopt other means of achieving our legitimate objectives in the Mid-East. Nothing saddens me more than the thought that I and my old friends of years have met a problem concerning which we do not see eye to eye. I shall never be happy until our old time closeness has been restored.

With warm regard and best wishes for your continued health.

As ever, Ike E.

Applying the Eisenhower Doctrine: Lebanon (1958)

In mid-July 1958 President Eisenhower ordered United States marines into Lebanon, a small nation on the eastern shore of the Mediterranean Sea. At the same time he issued a statement justifying his actions. This statement should be compared to earlier American reactions to events in Guatemala, Hungary, and Egypt.

From *Department of State Bulletin*, XXXIX (August 4, 1958), pp. 183–185.

I

Intervention

Yesterday was a day of grave developments in the Middle East. In Iraq a highly organized military blow struck down the duly constituted Government and attempted to put in its place a committee of Army officers. The attack was conducted with great brutality. Many of the leading personalities were beaten to death or hanged and their bodies dragged through the streets.

At about the same time there was discovered a highly organized plot to overthrow the lawful Government of Jordan.

Warned and alarmed by these developments, President Chamoun of Lebanon sent me an urgent plea that the United States station some military units in Lebanon to evidence our concern for the independence of Lebanon, that little country which itself has for about 2 months been subjected to civil strife. This has been actively fomented by Soviet and Cairo broadcasts and abetted and aided by substantial amounts of arms, money, and personnel infiltrated into Lebanon across the Syrian border.

President Chamoun stated that without an immediate show of United States support the Government of Lebanon would be unable to survive against the forces which had been set loose in the area.

The plea of President Chamoun was supported by the unanimous action of the Lebanese Cabinet.

After giving this plea earnest thought and after taking advice from leaders of both the executive and congressional branches of the Government, I decided to comply with the plea of the Government of Lebanon. A few hours ago a battalion of United States Marines landed and took up stations in and about the city of Beirut. . . .

II

Indirect Aggression

When the attacks on the Government of Lebanon began to occur, it took the matter to the United Nations Security Council, pointing out that Lebanon was the victim of indirect aggression from without. As a result, the Security Council sent observers to Lebanon in the hope of thereby insuring that hostile intervention would cease. Secretary-General Hammarskjöld undertook a mission to the area to reinforce the work of the observers.

We believe that his efforts and those of the United Nations observers were helpful. They could not eliminate arms or ammunition or remove persons already sent into Lebanon. But we believe they did reduce such aid from across the border. It seemed, last week, that the situation was moving toward a peaceful solution which would preserve the integrity of Lebanon and end indirect aggression from without.

Those hopes were, however, dashed by the events of yesterday in Iraq and Jordan. These events demonstrate a scope of aggressive purpose which tiny Lebanon could not combat without further evidence of support. That is why Lebanon's request for troops from the United States was made. That is why we have responded to that request.

Some will ask, does the stationing of some United States troops in Lebanon involve any interference in the internal affairs of Lebanon? The clear answer is "no."

First of all, we have acted at the urgent plea of the Government of Lebanon, a Government which has been freely elected by the people only a little over a year ago. It is entitled, as we are, to join in measures of collective security for self-defense. Such action, the United Nations Charter recognizes, is an "inherent right."

In the second place what we now see in the Middle East is the same pattern of conquest with which we became familiar during the period of 1945 to 1950. This involves taking over a nation by means of indirect aggression; that is, under the cover of a fomented civil strife the purpose is to put into domestic control those whose real loyalty is to the aggressor.

It was by such means that the Communists attempted to take over Greece in 1947. That effort was thwarted by the Truman Doctrine.

It was by such means that the Communists took over Czechoslovakia in 1948.

It was by such means that the Communists took over the mainland of China in 1949.

It was by such means that the Communists attempted to take over Korea and Indochina, beginning in 1950.

You will remember at the time of the Korean war that the Soviet Government claimed that this was merely a civil war, because the only attack was by north Koreans upon south Koreans. But all the world knew that the north Koreans were armed, equipped, and directed from without for the purpose of aggression.

This means of conquest was denounced by the United Nations General Assembly when it adopted in November 1950 its resolution entitled "Peace Through Deeds." It thereby called upon every nation to refrain from "fomenting civil strife in the interest of a foreign power" and denounced such action as "the gravest of all crimes against peace and security throughout the world."

We had hoped that these threats to the peace and to the independence and integrity of small nations had come to an end. Unhappily, now they reappear. Lebanon was selected to become a victim.

Last year the Congress of the United States joined with the President to declare that "the United States regards as vital to the national interest and world peace the preservation of the independence and integrity of the nations of the Middle East."

I believe that the presence of the United States forces now being sent to Lebanon will have a stabilizing effect which will preserve the independence and integrity of Lebanon. It will also afford an increased measure of security to the thousands of Americans who reside in Lebanon.

We know that stability and well-being cannot be achieved purely by military measures. The economy of Lebanon has been gravely strained by civil strife. Foreign trade and tourist traffic have almost come to a standstill. The United States stands ready, under its mutual security program, to cooperate with the Government of Lebanon to find ways to restore its shattered economy. Thus we shall help to bring back to Lebanon a peace which is not merely the absence of fighting but the well-being of the people.

Cold War and the Necessity of Peace (1958)

At the end of the 1950s, Walter Millis, an author who had written much on war and American foreign policy, tried to make some sense out of the series of conflicts, large and small, in which the United States had been involved since the end of World War II. What can we learn from the recent past, he asked, which will guide us in the 1960s?

From Walter Millis, "How to Compete with the Russians, "*New York Times Magazine*, February 2, 1958, pp. 12, 53–54. © 1958 by the New York Times Company. Reprinted by permission.

I

The Dilemma before Us

Since the early post-war years Americans have been asking themselves an increasingly grim question: In a world of rapidly developing nuclear weapons, and a world polarized between the non-Communist West and a mighty and aggressive Soviet power, is it possible to defend the American free society without destroying its essential freedoms in the process? Can we meet effectively the Communist challenge without ourselves becoming so militarized and "communized" that we lose all resemblance to the democratic, free-enterprise social system that we have known?

In varying forms, the question has been with us since Hiroshima, but in the intense debate over the appropriate American response to the newly dramatized power of Soviet communism, it has been raised again and with a deeper urgency. Unfortunately, there has been little to show that we have faced up to the problem of how to retain our freedoms in the process of defending them; much to suggest that these freedoms may be irretrievably lost unless we can bring a good deal sounder analysis than anyone has yet employed to the large issues of defense, war and power policy in the nuclear age. . . .

Can a military society, organized primarily around great bombs and rockets, remain a free society—free in thought, belief and debate, free in the power of the ballot or in the right to strike, free in its access to the information on which its policy-makers arrive at their decisions and free to apply its intelligence and creative powers to the production of better decisions? It seems improbable.

If, under the courses we are now following, the free society is not destroyed in the nuclear fires; if it is not corrupted from within by the illiberal and immoral implications of its basic foreign policy, it will still face a third peril. Simply stated, this is that the Russian Communist empire will win the world from us by those non-military means which our own policies and attitudes have done so much to facilitate.

Only recently has the Pentagon come to a serious realization of the extent to which, by staking everything on the threat of instant thermonuclear retaliation, it has paralyzed *any* use of military force as an instrument for the regulation and control of contemporary international relations. The suggested exits from the dilemma are not promising. In one concept, military power can be restored to its historic role in international policy, without touching off the megaton holocaust, by providing small but highly expert and powerfully weaponed forces to fight "brush-fire" wars. But it is increasingly difficult—especially after our refusal to intervene in the Dienbienphu crisis in Indochina and our stern suppression of the Anglo-French police action at Suez—to picture any situation to which this "brush-fire" concept would be applicable.

In another concept, military power can again be made usable through "limited war."

The thought here is that the great "strategic" weapons of mass extermination can be tacitly immobilized by both sides, each understanding that the only function of such weapons is to prevent their use by the other side. Beneath this tremendous double threat, war could still be waged by limited means—even for quite large objectives, such as the hegemony of Western Europe—using no more than "tactical" nuclear weapons and hurling them only at such genuinely military objectives as would not invite reprisals of mass extermination.

But today even "tactical" nuclear weapons are frequently as powerful as the bombs which at Hiroshima and Nagasaki seemed "absolute"; how such things could be thrown indiscriminately around a continental battlefield like Western Europe without ending in a universal war of extermination is not easy to see. The idea of limited nuclear warfare seems of dubious value.

The conclusion is that war has become obsolete in international relations. But if war is unavailable as an instrument of policy, how are we to prevent the spread of Soviet influence through the Middle East, into Africa, to the ultimate erosion of free Europe and, at last, the extinction of our own free society? We certainly cannot do so by insisting upon regarding our whole relationship with Russia in terms of a war that it is no longer possible to fight. Many close students of Soviet policy are convinced that, far from contemplating military attack upon the United States or its allies, Russia's major aim is the avoidance of any risk of actual war, if only because peace alone provides the dictatorship with the shield under which it can successfully operate at home as well as abroad. . . .

II

The Real Meaning of Coexistence

If the American people will both recognize and accept the plain actualities of contemporary international relations—rather than fear-engendered myths, largely of our own creation—we can call off the "cold war" tomorrow and apply ourselves genuinely to a solution of the problems of "competitive coexistence." We can, as C. L. Sulzberger put it in a recent column in The Times, forget the war on "international communism" and "stick to self-defense, life, liberty and the pursuit of happiness."

To do so we must recognize that "coexistence" means the continued existence of both of the two great systems of social and political organization, and that the "competition" is, in the words of George F. Kennan, internal rather than external. "The real competition is to see who moves most successfully to the solution of his own peculiar problems," not in forms of military power which are unusable as instruments of policy.

The establishment of Communist regimes in China, North Korea, North Vietnam and in Central Europe is the result of historic processes which, whether good or ill, cannot be undone by any form of power available to the West; we should accept the situation and learn to live with and deal with it rather than indulge in counter-revolutionary hopes and propaganda which are futile to begin with and ill become the greatest of the conservative and status quo powers.

Until some genuine communication has been re-established between the Western and Communist worlds, we cannot abandon the arms race—and it is useless to suppose that further "disarmament" discussions will magically provide some formula that will permit us to do so but we can pitch it at its lowest rather than at the highest suggested by the most extreme and unrealistic of fears. If we really believe, as President Eisenhower said, that "there is no substitute for peace": if, in fact, our policy excludes war as an instrument, we can plainly say so. We can lay our nuclear cards upon the table, thus putting a real rather than a fictitious pressure upon the Russians to do the same and declare their own intentions.

Specific issues, like those of Germany or the Middle East, where Communist and Western national interests clash, will then become susceptible to negotiation. We can and should negotiate with the Russians, but it must be—as it has never been since 1945—a genuine negotiation in which we are no longer looking for the ultimate destruction of an enemy but for accommodation with a rival in a situation in which the survival of both is actually more to the advantage of each than the destruction of either would be.

TOPIC 63

McCARTHY AND COMMUNISM: LOYALTY OR CONFORMITY?

The preceding readings have been concerned with the world-wide implications of post-World War II American foreign policy. Yet the Cold War also had dramatic effects on life within the United States. To the reality of spying on the part of the Soviet Union was added the much more general fear of subversion. This was the pervasive belief that traitors were "undermining" domestic social and political institutions on "orders" from Moscow. This fear, combined with a long-standing fear of foreign radicalism, produced the post-World War II Red Scare which has been labeled "McCarthyism." The following readings analyze this phenomenon, in terms of its effect on individuals, on foreign policy, and on the willingness of Americans to dissent from the status quo.

Reading 338

The Rise and Fall of Senator McCarthy

The saga of Joseph McCarthy (1908-1957) provided some of the most dramatic moments in domestic politics of the 1950s, a scene dominated by the genial but bland character of President Dwight Eisenhower. The search for security by both the United States and the Soviet Union produced the Cold War. The anger generated by the fear that the United States was being betrayed by "disloyal" Americans created what historian Forrest McDonald calls the "Great Witch Hunt".

Forrest McDonald, *The Torch is Passed: The United States in the 20th Century,* 1968, Addison-Wesley, Reading, Mass. Pp. 371-372, 373, 374, 385-387. Subheadings added and footnotes omitted by the editors.

I

The Red Scare, 1950-1952

The irrational side of the general protest, the Great Witch Hunt of 1950 to 1954, was closely linked with the phenomenon of McCarthyism and with the war, but it actually started six months before the attack in Korea and a month before Senator Joseph McCarthy discovered the Communist menace.

The real beginning was the Hiss case. In January, 1950, Alger Hiss—a former New Dealer, a secondary advisor at Yalta, and one of the organizers of the San Francisco conference to establish the United Nations—was convicted of perjury for denying before a congressional investigating committee that he had passed government secrets to the Russians in the 1930's. The Hiss trial had unfolded dramatically. A self-avowed former Communist agent, Whittaker Chambers, who was then an editor of *Time* magazine, confronted Hiss face to face at a hearing of the House Un-American Activities Committee in New York, and accused Hiss of participating in a Communist ring in the 1930's. Hiss, the only one of Chambers's many alleged spies and Communists who voluntarily appeared, denied the charge. Chambers persisted. Eventually Hiss walked over to Chambers and even examined his teeth. Yes, Hiss said, he had known Chambers, by another name, but he knew nothing of any Communist activities. Chambers again contradicted Hiss, and produced from a hollowed pumpkin on his farm a number of State Department documents that he said Hiss had copied in 1938. Thanks in large measure to the energetic sleuthing of Congressman Richard Nixon, Hiss was indicted for perjury, found guilty, and sent to the penitentiary—still protesting his innocence.

The conviction of Hiss raised widespread suspicion that espionage permeated the entire national government—especially since Secretary of State Acheson came to Hiss's defense, and a number of prominent American liberals, including Justice Felix Frankfurter and Illinois' Governor Adlai E. Stevenson, testified as to Hiss's good character at his trial. The New Deal itself, as Alistair Cooke commented, seemed to be on trial. The conviction of Julius and Ethel Rosenberg and British scientist Klaus Fuchs for passing filched atomic secrets to the Russians added to the din. "In the name of Heaven," cried Senator Homer Capehart, "is this the best America can do?" and Americans by the millions demanded that somebody be found to "clean up the mess in Washington."

The man who moved most spectacularly—and most damagingly—to capitalize on the "mess" was the junior senator from Wisconsin, Joseph R. McCarthy. McCarthy launched a demagogic crusade that was focused almost exclusively on his charge that the government was infested, "top to bottom," with Communists, but his popularity and his strength rested elsewhere: on the general frustration with the deliberately stalemated war in Korea, on the massive social changes that were taking place and the attendant longing for a return to a bygone state of "normalcy," on the widespread tension produced by the Cold War and the nuclear arms race, on the deep-rooted American habit of looking for a scapegoat on whom to blame all things that go wrong.

Equally important, the old nativists and isolationists emerged from under the rocks where they had been hiding since Pearl Harbor: the same places that had produced (and in many instances the same persons who had been) negative-style progressives in the teens, the Ku Klux Klansmen and progressive-isolationists in the twenties, and America Firsters in the thirties, provided the overwhelming bulk of McCarthy's support. The psychology, too, was the same as it had been before: the hysterical crusade against the "international Communist conspiracy" was, in its psychological essence, the same as the earlier crusades against immigrants, city-dwellers, and Wall Street capitalists (1901–1917), German warmongers (1917–1918), Jewish and Italian radicals (1919–1925), bankers and utility holding company operators (1927–1934), and the kaleidoscopic succession of groups who served as master villains in the 1930's.

II
McCarthy Attacks

McCarthy initiated his campaign a month after Hiss was convicted. Speaking before the Republican Women of West Virginia in February, 1950, he charged that the State Department was "thoroughly infested" with Communists. He had in his hand, he said, a list of the names of 205 State Department employees who were or had been Communists. The traitors, said McCarthy, were not mainly people from the working or farming classes, but eastern Anglophiles and intellectuals and rich people, Ivy Leaguers and Wall Streeters and old Yankees—the very groups who, in different guises, had been the heads of all the earlier alleged conspiracies. The worst traitor of all, McCarthy added, was Dean Acheson himself—"a pompous diplomat in striped pants, with a phony British accent."

When McCarthy was later asked about the list, the magic number changed. Now there were only 87 Communists in the State Department, then 83. When McCarthy was asked to name names, the list decreased to nine, six of whom had never worked in the State Department; the other three occupied positions that could not influence policy. . . .

State governments, businesses, universities, and small-town vigilante groups joined in the crusade to purge the nation of Communists and their sympathizers. On the floor of the Texas legislature one member proposed that the wearing of six-shooters be legalized as a means of cleaning out the Communists and "pinkos"; but the legislature settled for requiring every man, woman, and child who was in any way connected with a publicly supported school or other institution to sign an oath testifying to his loyalty and swearing that he had never been a Communist. Many states required loyalty oaths of public employees, and so did a considerable number of colleges and universities; the entertainment industry developed blacklists, prohibiting employment to persons suspected of past or present Communist associations; other businesses, even the least sensitive industries, developed security and loyalty systems more strict than those of the federal government.

Not everyone was caught up in the craze; some held to time-tested values. Justice Hugo Black, for example, in dissenting from the Court's opinion in the case of *Dennis v. United States* (1951), said that "there is hope that in calmer times, when the present pressures, passions, and fears subside, this or some later court will restore the First Amendment liberties to the high preferred place where they belong in a free society." In vetoing the McCarran Act President Truman wrote: "In a free country we punish men for the crimes they commit, but never for the opinions they have." The bill, the president added, struck "blows at our own liberties"; "let us not," he said, "in cowering and foolish fear, throw away the ideals which are the fundamental basis of our free society." The Chancellor of the University of Chicago, Robert M. Hutchins, also spoke out: "We are busily engaged in adopting the most stupid and unjust of the ideas prevalent in Russia and are doing so in the name of Americanism." But few major politicians except Truman bucked McCarthy and McCarthyism consistently and openly, and very few newspapers joined the Madison *Capital Times*, of McCarthy's home state, in daring to attack him with any regularity. Instead, most politicians kept silent or got on his bandwagon, and the press so publicized his hit-and-run charges as to

Senator Joseph R. McCarthy of Wisconsin, chairman of a Senate investigating subcommittee, holds a press conference in New York City in October 1953. Two of the subcommittee's investigators, Roy Cohn, left, and G. David Schine, right, were prominent figures in the hearing by another Senate committee into the affairs of the subcommittee the following year.

Eisenhower "numbers game." They wanted to know how many employees were dismissed for being disloyal and how many were let go for other reasons. The case of Dr. J. Robert Oppenheimer, who had directed the manufacture of the first atomic bombs, was of particular interest. Though the famous scientist had associated with Communists in his earlier life, the Atomic Energy Commission ruled that he had not been disloyal. The Commission did, however, say that he had other "fundamental defects," and hence recommended that his security clearance be revoked.

McCarthy was heard from next. Basking in the warmth of the publicity that his witch-hunting gave him, McCarthy was not at all disposed to surrender his position to the president. With adroit political maneuvering, McCarthy secured the chairmanship of the Government Operations Committee and its strategic Permanent Subcommittee on Investigations. Operating from that base, McCarthy renewed his red-hunting in earnest. He began his campaign with attacks on the Voice of America, on American libraries in foreign countries, and on the Central Intelligence Agency, all of which he saw as infiltrated by Communists.

make him the most known and most powerful figure in the country, with the possible exception of Truman himself. . . .

III

Eisenhower and McCarthy

Shortly after he entered office . . . [President Eisenhower] attempted to silence McCarthy and other red-baiters by ordering a full-scale revision of the loyalty system. Employees were to be dismissed not only for disloyalty, but for alcoholism, drug addiction, and immoral conduct. In all, 6926 "separations" from government service were made between May of 1953 and October of 1954. These doings, however, did not bring peace. The Democrats were the first to criticize. They disliked the

Then McCarthy took on the United States Army, and that was the beginning of his downfall. It started when he asked why Major Irving Peress, an obscure dentist, had been given an honorable discharge though he was suspected of having Communist sympathies. McCarthy put the question to General Ralph Zwicker, a much decorated World War II hero. Acting on orders from his superiors, Zwicker refused to answer. Enraged, McCarthy charged that the general did not have the brains of a five-year-old, and that he was unfit to wear an American uniform. At this point, the investigations became tragically comic. First, Secretary of the Army Robert Stevens ordered Zwicker not to answer; then he reversed himself, directing Zwicker to give McCarthy the information that he sought. Disturbed by its decrease of prestige, the Army countered by issuing sensational charges against McCarthy and his two chief assistants, committee counsel Roy Cohn and executive director Francis Carr. The Army charged that the trio had used the threat of investigation to obtain special privileges for Cohn's close friend, Private David Schine, the son of a wealthy hotel magnate and a former consultant to the investigating committee. Never one to let the last word escape him, McCarthy countered the Army's claim. The Army was holding Schine as a "hostage," he said, in order to compel the committee to halt its probe, but the committee would not be so intimidated.

Placing Senator Karl Mundt in the chair temporarily, McCarthy launched off into his investigation of his 46 charges against the Army. The colorful hearings stirred the nation's interest; televised daily, they outdrew the soap operas. For 36 days during the spring of 1954, millions watched as McCarthy lambasted the Army, as Republicans and Democrats on the committee wrangled, and as the benign, soft-spoken Army counselor Joseph Welch, an elderly, balding Boston lawyer, grilled the elusive, shrewd, brash young attorney Ray Cohn. The outcome could have been predicted: the Republican majority on the committee exonerated McCarthy, the Democrats condemned McCarthy for condoning Cohn's improper activities in behalf of Schine, and both sides were severely critical of Stevens's vacillation. Soon after the hearings, Cohn resigned, Welch went back to resume his Boston practice, and Stevens, after holding on for a decent period of time, retired to private life.

The Senate, however, was not as kind to McCarthy as the committee had been. He had gone too far, and Senators Ralph Flanders, a Vermont Republican, William Fulbright, an Arkansas Democrat, and Wayne Morse, an Oregon Independent, brought formal charges of misconduct against him. A special committee of three Republicans and three Democrats, headed by a conservative Utah Republican, Senator Arthur Watkins, conducted an orderly investigation and recommended Senate censure of McCarthy. The Senate complied, 67 to 22, and the president discreetly added his "vote" by praising Watkins for a "splendid job." Again McCarthy sought the last word. He called Watkins cowardly and stupid; he termed the Senate trial a "lynch party," and he sarcastically apologized to the American people for recommending Eisenhower's election. These indeed were the last of McCarthy's words that received attention. When the Democrats took control of the Senate in 1957, McCarthy lost his committee chairmanships; later in the year he died, a bitter and frustrated man of 48.

McCarthy: The Conspiracy against America

It is impossible to understand the full fury of Senator Joseph McCarthy's anger unless one reads or hears the Senator's own words. In the following speech, made on the floor of the Senate in 1951, McCarthy mercilessly attacks two of his favorite targets: Secretary of Defense George Marshall and Secretary of State Dean Acheson.

From Major Speeches and Debates of Senator Joe McCarthy *(Washington, D.C., 1951), pp. 218–219, 305, 307. Subheadings added by the editors.*

I

America's Failure in Korea

This administration, which has given us this caricature of a war, is now bent on an even worse horror—a phony and fraudulent peace. It is planned by Secretary Marshall and the elegant and alien Acheson—Russian as to heart, British as to manner. We even hear cries for a fraudulent peace within this Chamber. In support of their campaign for a fraudulent peace, its advocates wage a campaign of fear.

The President threatens us with the destruction of our cities by Russian bombs unless we continue to pursue his empty, defeatist strategy in the Far East. The President's only answer to the splendid counsel of General MacArthur is that we must on no account offend the Soviet Union. One of the administration's two principal spokesmen on this matter seeks to frighten us with the admonition that unless we mind our P's and Q's in Korea, "This very Capitol Building, this very Senate Chamber may be blown to smithereens next week or the week after." Mr. President, that is not the great heart of America speaking.

I do not think we need fear too much about the Communists dropping atomic bombs on Washington. They would kill too many of their friends that way.

I never thought that I would live to see the day that Senators representing sovereign States would rise on the floor of the Senate and actually debate and argue to the effect that we should not protect the lives of our young men, whom we ourselves have sent into battle, merely because, if we were to fight back, we might make someone angry.

In my boyhood in Wisconsin, we had a deep pride in our country, in its strength as well as its wealth, in its high destiny as a great free society as well as in its opportunities for individual riches or position. We were simple, uncomplicated Americans, not above dying, if need be, for the land we love. We had self-assurance, too, and we assumed that whenever our security, our way of life, and our ideals were threatened by a hostile force, we would have the physical strength, and also the strength of character, to defend those values by force of arms, and to the utmost, regardless of consequences. We were not misled and enfeebled by abstractions such as collective security and by the tortured, twisted reasoning of men of little minds and less morals who for the first time in the history of this Nation argue that we should not vigorously fight back when attacked and in every way possible protect the lives of our men for fear of making an enemy or potential enemy mad, and that we dare not win a war.

We hear the President in a Nation-wide broadcast saying, "Even if we win," Mr. President, listen to those words—"even"—"even if we win." When before in the history of this Nation has a President been so craven? Imagine George Washington, when he was leading this small, physically weak Nation against mighty and powerful England, saying to his troops, "Even if we win." Imagine Lincoln, in even the darkest days of the Civil War, saying, "Even if we win." Imagine Churchill, in England's darkest days during World War II when invasion was imminent, saying, "Even if we win." Imagine what might well have happened to England if those had been his words instead of his immortal words, "We shall fight on the beaches, we shall fight on the landing grounds, we shall fight in the fields and in the streets, we shall fight in the hills; we shall never surrender." Imagine Roosevelt, when he addressed the Congress on that fateful December 8, saying, "Even if we win."

As I listen to the debates in this Chamber and hear the testimony of the President's spokesmen, it makes me sick down deep inside. But when I get out of Washington into the United States, it is a healthy feeling—for then is answered the question: Where stand the people? Not with the Gospel of fear which is being preached to us. Not with the craven fears of the President and his spokesmen but rather with the wholesome American view regarding the integrity and self-reliance of America. . . .

II

The Gospel of Fear

What is the purpose of such craven actions and utterances? Is it to condition us to defeat in the Far East, to soften us up so that we shall accept a peace upon the Soviet empire's terms in Korea; a peace which would put the enemy one step nearer to Alaska? And how, may I ask, did Russia acquire the technical secrets, the blue-prints, the know-how to make the bombs with which the administration seeks to terrify us? I have yet to hear a single administration spokesman raise his voice against the policy of suppression, deceit, and false witness with which this administration has protected the Soviet agents who have abstracted those secrets from us.

The people, Mr. President, recognize the weakness with which the administration has replaced what was so recently our great strength. They are troubled by it. And they do not think it accidental. They do not believe that the decline in our strength from 1945 to 1951 just happened. They are coming to believe that it was brought about, step by step, by will and intention. They are beginning to believe that the surrender of China to Russia, the administration's indecently hasty desire to turn Formosa over to the enemy and arrive at a cease-fire in Korea instead of following the manly, American course prescribed by MacArthur, point to something more than ineptitude and folly. They witness the conviction of Hiss, which would not have happened had he not brought a private suit for damages against Whittaker Chambers; they followed the revelations in the Remington case, the Marzani case, and the others which have disclosed at the heart of Government active Soviet agents influencing policy and pilfering secrets; they note the policy of retreat before Soviet assertion from Yalta to this day, and they say: This is not because these men are imcompetents; there is a deeper reason.

How can we account for our present situation unless we believe that men high in this Government are concerting to deliver us to disaster? This must be the product of a great conspiracy, a conspiracy on a scale so immense as to dwarf any previous such venture in the history of man. A conspiracy of infamy so black that, when it is finally exposed, its principals shall be forever deserving of the maledictions of all honest men. . . .

III

The Great Conspiracy

What is the objective of the great conspiracy? I think it is clear from what has occurred and is now occurring; to diminish the United States in world affairs, to weaken us militarily, to confuse our spirit with talk of surrender in the Far East, and to impair our will to resist evil. To what end? To the end that we shall be contained, frustrated and finally fall victim to Soviet intrigue from within and Russian military might from without. Is that far-fetched? There have been many examples in history of rich and powerful states which have been corrupted from within, enfeebled and deceived until they were unable to resist aggression.

The United States first ventured into world affairs a bare half century ago. Its rise to world leadership was almost unprecedentedly sudden. We call this a young country. It is in terms of the tenure of the settlement by Europeans on these lands. It is also in terms of the spirit and daring of its people. Yet the United States belongs to, is the last great example of, the farthest projection of an old culture. The vast and complicated culture of the west, which bloomed with the spread of the Gothic cathedrals and the universities which has carried science and technology and art and the human values to lengths nowhere else dreamed of and whose sway covered the earth only a few years ago, is in manifest decay. We see the symptoms of decay in Western Europe. We find evidences of it here.

There is a rising power, not yet a culture; a power barbarous to us which has attracted many followers and devotees in the heart of the west. Why these men and women of the west are so attracted lies outside our interest at this moment. We know that these enemies of the west are here, we know they are at work among us, burrowing, mining, sapping ceaselessly; seeking to destroy our civilization. We know principally because we see the results of their work. We cannot always detect them at it. That is not an easy task as we have seen with the notorious case of Alger Hiss.

The enemies of our civilization, whether alien or native, whether of high or low degree, work in the dark. They are that way more effective. It is easy to single out, identify, and isolate a frank and open Communist. The Communists openly among us are scarcely a problem at all. They have the aversion and contempt of all honest Americans. It is the clandestine enemy which taxes our ingenuity.

It is the great crime of the Truman administration that it has refused to undertake the job of ferreting the enemy from its ranks. I once puzzled over that refusal. The President, I said, is a loyal American; why does he not lead in this enterprise? I think that I know why he does not. The President is not master in our own house. Those who are master there not only have a desire to protect the sappers and miners—they could not do otherwise. They themselves are not free. They belong to a larger conspiracy, the world-wide web of which has been spun from Moscow. It was Moscow, for example, which decreed that the United States should execute its loyal friend, the Republic of China. The executioners were that well-identified group headed by Acheson and George Catlett Marshall.

Reading 340

A Defense of Conformity (1954)

The most able defense of McCarthy came not from the Senator, who was always attacking someone, but from the pens of two young conservative intellectuals, William F. Buckley, Jr. and L. Brent Bozell. In the following selection the authors detail what they see as the deeper social goals behind the slashing attacks of the Wisconsin Senator.

From William F. Buckley, Jr. and L. Brent Bozell, *McCarthy and His Enemies* (Chicago, 1954), pp. 331, 332–334. Copyright © 1954 by Henry Regnery Company. Subheadings added and footnotes omitted by the editors.

I

McCarthyism's Conformity

McCarthyism, on the record, is not in any sense an attempt to prevent the airing of new ideas. It is directed not at *new* ideas but at *Communist* ideas, of which the last thing that can be said is that they are new or untried. The McCarthyites are doing their resourceful best to make our society inhospitable to Communists, fellow-travelers, and security risks in the government. To this end, they are conducting operations on two fronts: (1) they seek to vitalize existing legal sanctions, and (2) they seek to harden existing anti-Communist prejudices and channel them into effective social sanctions. . . .

The conformity attendant upon McCarthyism, then, adds up to something like this: (1) *persons who conspire to overthrow the government by force* are subject to legal sanctions (the Smith Act, for example), primarily

457

that of imprisonment; (2) *persons in public service about whose loyalty or security there is a "reasonable doubt"* are subject to legal sanctions (the various security regulations), primarily that of exclusion from government employment; (3) *persons other than government employees about whom there exist reasonable grounds for believing they are "pro-Communist,"* are to some extent subject to legal sanctions (possibly the McCarran Act or the Attorney General's list of subversive organizations), primarily that of having their activities officially labeled as "Communist" or "subversive" or (as with the Feinberg Law or the statutory loyalty oath requirements) that of being excluded from certain jobs; they are furthermore subject, increasingly, to social sanctions, primarily of the type that have been aimed at Lattimore and Schuman and Shapley.

These sanctions are not the same all over the country. In some localities, in sections of the Midwest for example, the sanctions hit people who might escape them elsewhere. In the rare instance, a single Communist-front affiliation may endanger public hostility and bring down severe social sanctions on a man's head. In the academic arena of the East, by contrast, the level of enforced conformity is decidedly lower, and sometimes descends nearly to zero. Southern Baptist College X fires Jones when there are apparently no reasonable grounds for believing him to be a pro-Communist. But Harvard, Williams and Johns Hopkins retain Shapley, Schuman and Lattimore on their faculties when reasonable grounds abound for believing them to be pro-Communist.

II

McCarthy and the Liberals

The claim is often made that McCarthyism has as its ultimate objective the exclusion of Liberals from positions of power, prestige and influence in the American community; and that the present campaign against Communists and fellow-travelers is merely the thin edge of the wedge. It is therefore curious that the one instance which lent a modicum of factual support to this fear received little or no attention from Liberal publicists.

In October of 1952, Senator McCarthy delivered his widely heralded attack on Adlai Stevenson, which people generally expected would turn into an attempt to connect the Democratic candidate with Communism. With millions of listeners glued to radio and TV, McCarthy reached, not for a red paint brush, but for a list of some of Stevenson's top advisors: Archibald MacLeish, Bernard De Voto, Arthur Schlesinger, Jr. Was his point that these men were *Communists?* No, that was not McCarthy's point. His objection to these men was not that they were Communists, or even pro-Communists, but that they were Liberals—atheistic, soft-headed, anti-anti-Communist, ADA Liberals. . . .

Whether the speech was a conscious effort to narrow the limits of tolerable opinion so as to exclude left-wing Liberals, only McCarthy can say. The fact that he has not reiterated the point suggests that, if this was his intent, he was not very serious about it. It is far more likely that he intended to deliver a traditional political campaign speech highlighting the disqualifications of his Party's opponents. But it may well be we have not heard the last of this idea. Some day, the patience of America may at last be exhausted, and we will strike out against Liberals. Not because they are treacherous like Communists, but because, with James Burnham, we will conclude "that they are mistaken in their predictions, false in their analyses, wrong in their advice, and through the results of their actions injurious to the interests of the nation. That is reason enough to strive to free the conduct of the country's affairs from the influence of them and their works." But the real point, for our purposes, is that the mainstream of McCarthyism flows past the Liberals as gently as the Afton; and the MacLeishs, De Votos and Schlesingers have no grounds for arguing that any sustained effort is being made to read *them* out of the community.

It is still only *Communist* ideas that are beyond the pale. And the evidence is convincing that the function of Senator McCarthy and his colleagues is not that of defining or creating a new orthodoxy with which individuals are being called upon to conform. The American community affirmed anti-Communism long before McCarthy started in. McCarthy's function has been to harden the *existing* conformity.

We are left with the final question: whether the conformity urged by McCarthyism is doing a service to America and, therefore, whether we should view it with approval. Certainly the vast majority of the American people have already given *their* answer to the question; for, after all, the approaching conformity is of their own making, and they must be presumed to approve what they are doing. Most Americans, the available evidence seems to say, favor anti-Communism, and tight security in the civil service. But we are asking, of course, whether the majority is *right;* and therefore we must take account of the misgivings of the intelligentsia. What should be said of their resolute and impassioned opposition to McCarthyism?

Simply this. They are confused, they have misread history, and they fail to understand social processes. What is more, they do not feel the faith they so often and so ardently express in democracy. There is only one alternative to this explanation: that they are opposed to the decline of Communist influence at home. The determination of the American people to curb Communism cannot be dismissed as a capricious, ignorant, or impetuous decision. There is, we contend, a great deal of difference between a society's harassing the exponents of an idea that has been thoroughly examined and found objectionable, and its harassing the exponents of an idea simply because it hurls a novel challenge at traditional notions. Our Schumans, Shapleys and Lattimores have become unacceptable not because they are known to hold ideas and values at variance with those of the majority of Americans, but because they expound a *particular* set of ideas and values which Americans have explored and emphatically rejected, and because the propagation of these ideas fortifies an implacable foreign power bent on the destruction of American independence.

The Long Trial of John Paton Davies

Fears generated by the Red scare of the 1950s permeated American society, as Forrest McDonald pointed out in Reading 338. How these fears influenced American policy makers, and the consequent effects on both domestic affairs and foreign policy, are well illustrated by the experiences of John Paton Davies, a Foreign Service officer whose career was wrecked by McCarthy.

From John W. Finney, "The Long Trial of John Paton Davies," *New York Times Magazine*, August 31, 1969, pp. 7–9, 23. © 1969 by the New York Times Company. Reprinted by permission. Subheadings added by the editors.

I

The Pitfalls in Making Policy

Fifteen years after Senator Joseph R. McCarthy began to fade from the scene following his censure by the Senate, it is an accepted and somewhat consoling dictum that McCarthyism was only an aberration—one of those inquisitions that periodically plague American society, but which our leaders, in their wisdom and courage, are able to suppress. The case of John Paton Davies Jr., however, provides a disturbing demonstration that McCarthyism is not completely dead, and that it still casts an inhibiting pall over the Federal Government.

Davies was one of McCarthy's principal targets, charged, along with other Foreign Service officers, with the "loss of China" to the Communists. Every time McCarthy mentioned his name it was enough to intimidate a Secretary of State, provoke a Congressional investigation or bring a new round of harassment for one of the more promising diplomats of the day.

In retrospect, it is evident that Davies's only crime was that he was too honest and foresighted in describing developments in China during 1943 and 1944 while serving as political adviser to Gen. Joseph W. Stilwell, the chief of staff in the China theater. For his outspoken but accurate reports—including negative assessments of Chiang Kai-shek and his deteriorating regime—he was made a political scapegoat. In November, 1954, in an act of abject obeisance to McCarthyism, Secretary of State John Foster Dulles stripped the 46-year-old Davies of his security clearance and fired him from the Foreign Service.

In many ways, Davies was as much a victim of the Eastern establishment as he was of Joseph McCarthy. The establishment never tires of preaching individual liberties, but it was too timid in the Davies case to protect those of one man, even though he was one of its talented members. To that extent, it was just as guilty as McCarthy—perhaps more so, for long after the Senator had died the establishment was still reluctant to correct one of the grave personal injustices of our time.

It was not until the evening of Jan. 13, 1969, that Davies's long ordeal came to an end: he was 60 years old and seated in the study of his northwest Washington home, when he received a telephone call from his lawyer, Walter S. Surrey, telling him that the State Department had at long last granted him security clearance.

It would be reassuring to record this as a proper epilogue to an ignoble saga. But the protracted process of John Davies's vindication is far from reassuring. It is, rather, a disillusioning commentary on our times—a profile in political cowardice in which the Kennedy Administration declined to right a wrong because it feared political repercussions, and a story of personal indifference by a Secretary of State who turned his back on a friend and former colleague. It is a story of Kafkaesque dimensions in which a State Department bureaucracy, having committed an error, decided to protect itself rather than correct it.

In another sense, it is a story linked to the tragedy of Vietnam. For, in the normal course of events—as was recently pointed out by John K. Fairbank of Harvard, a leading Asian scholar—Davies would have risen to become an Assistant Secretary of State. He was born and reared in China and has a strong knowledge of guerrilla warfare, and Fairbank wonders whether the State Department would have been quite so ready to get involved in Vietnam if he had been in a position of policy-making authority.

That, perhaps, is only speculation. But there is no question about the direct relationship between the Davies case and Asian policy in general. McCarthy's personal vendetta against the "men who lost China" succeeded in driving out of the Foreign Service the few diplomats who had any direct knowledge of that country. It also had the effect, as has been noted by O. Edmund Clubb, another expert on Asia forced out of the State Department during the McCarthy era, of freezing American policy toward the region in "an inflexible mold best described as a simplistic anti-Communism aiming at the military containment of China."

The injustice done to Davies goes back to Nov. 5, 1954, when he was summoned to Dulles's office and curtly told he had been fired as a security risk because, as Dulles was to explain later in a press release, he had shown "lack of judgment, discretion and reliability." In a sense, that day was the climax to a case that had been developing since November, 1945, when Maj. Gen. Patrick J. Hurley, in a long, intemperate letter of resignation as Ambassador to China, charged that American policy—which he construed as unqualified support of the Chiang Kai-shek regime—had been sabotaged by "professional Foreign Service men." A few days later, in testimony before the Senate Foreign Relations Committee, he identified Davies as one of them.

To Davies, by then assigned to the embassy in Moscow, "this was the first little ominous sign" of what was to turn into a nightmarish inquisition. Seven times in seven years he was to be called before State Department loyalty-security boards, and once before a Civil Service Commission board. Each time he was cleared. But, with the inexorability of a Greek tragedy, he was slowly drawn down in a maelstrom of political events that terrified politicians and ruined individual lives.

II

Enter McCarthy

The principal villain in this tragedy was, of course, Senator McCarthy, who, in August, 1951, listed Davies among 26 past or present State Department employes "suspected" of disloyalty. But Lyle H. Munson, a one-time member of the Central Intelligence Agency, also played a dark role in the Davies's undoing. He did this by circumventing regulations and telling the Senate Internal Security Subcommittee about the so-called "Tawny Pipit Case."

To this day that case remains a tantalizing mystery—a rare glimpse into the obscure operations of the intelligence world. The way Munson described it to Congressional witch-hunters, Tawny Pipit (an English bird akin to the lark) was the code name for a project Davies conceived in 1949, while a member of the State Department's Policy Planning Staff. It involved having the C.I.A. hire a mixed group experienced in China affairs, some of whose members were alleged to be Communists, for a psychological warfare operation against Communist China.

Davies still refuses to discuss the case, just as he did when he told the Senators that it was only "slightly less sensitive than atomic energy." From the subsequent testimony of Gen. Walter Bedell Smith, at that time Director of Central Intelligence, it became apparent that Davies was proposing a highly involved operation that is now the norm in the intelligence community but which the C.I.A., then a fledgling agency, could not fully understand, let alone implement.

The project was never carried out. Nor, as General Smith emphasized to a Davies security board in 1952 and again to the Senate Foreign Relations Committee in 1953, was the proposal any reason to question Davies's loyalty. By then, however, the damage had been done. The McCarthyites no longer could blame Davies for "the loss of China" since events had borne out his estimates of 1943–44 that the Chiang government was "politically bankrupt," but now they had a post-China example of his "pro-Communist sympathies."

Such was the prevailing hysteria of the moment that it did not matter that Tawny Pipit was conceived as an anti-Communist operation, apparently aimed at diverting the energies and military forces of the still insecure Chinese Communist Government. But then, one of the underlying ironies of the whole case is that Davies was then and still is a conservative traditionalist who became, by current standards, a hardliner toward the Soviet Union. For example, in 1950, some months after the first Soviet atomic explosion, he recommended a "preventive showdown with the Soviet Union" through the assumption of a firm position toward Moscow.

Davies might still have survived the inquisition if the Eisenhower Administration, in one of its most complete capitulations to

McCarthyism, had not changed the rules governing security clearance. In fact, one of its first acts was to institute the new procedures under which clearance would be dependent, not only upon an individual's loyalty, but also upon his "reliability and trustworthiness."

By those vague standards there would be many a politician not entitled to clearance, but this did not concern the new Administration. Intimidated by Senator McCarthy, the State Department, in December, 1953, decided to press the Davies case. It was probably not a coincidence that a month earlier the Senator had complained that, while the Administration had "gotten rid of 1,456 Truman holdovers who were all security risks," it had "struck out" in not firing Davies, whom he described as "part and parcel of the old Acheson-Lattimore-Vincent-White-Hiss group which did so much toward delivering our Chinese friends into Communist hands."

At the direction of Secretary Dulles, the case was handed to a five-man board headed by Lieut. Gen. Daniel Noce, the Inspector General of the Army, for Davies's ninth security hearing. Although it was to pass judgment on the charge that Davies "actually opposed and sought to circumvent United States policy toward China," none of the board's members had any background in foreign affairs. It is little wonder, then, that they arrived at a decision as contradictory as it was confusing. They found, on the one hand, that Davies was not "disloyal in the sense of having any Communist affinity or consciously aiding or abetting any alien elements hostile to the United States or performing his duties or otherwise acting so as intentionally to serve the interests of another government in preference to the interests of the United States." But, on the other hand, they said Davies's "observation and evaluation of the facts, his policy recommendations, his attitude with respect to existing policy, and his disregard of proper forbearance and caution in making known his dissents outside privileged boundaries were not in accordance with the standard required of Foreign Service officers and show a definite lack of judgment, discretion and reliability."

III

"I Spoke Out"

The principal charge, therefore, was that Davies did not stay within proper boundaries while serving in China. Admittedly, he was a freewheeler during that period, but that was inherent in his dual and frequently conflicting assignments. As a Foreign Service officer he was listed as a second secretary at the United States Embassy in Chungking. But he had gone to China at the request of the Army to serve as political adviser to General Stilwell.

Ambassador Hurley never appreciated the way Davies would file reports or talk with reporters—in his Stilwell advisory capacity—without clearing his actions with the embassy. In addition, the two men disagreed on fundamental policy. Davies dissented from Hurley's unqualified support of Chiang Kai-shek, concluding that the Chiang regime was collapsing from its own decadence and corruption. He believed that the long-term American interest lay in assuring that the Communist government that emerged was friendly to the United States, and, more important, independent of the Soviet Union. In two of his many articulate, foresighted reports, he cabled in November, 1944:

Chiang's feudal China cannot long co-exist alongside a modern dynamic popular government in North China.

The Communists are in China to stay. And China's destiny is not Chiang's but theirs.

We should not abandon Chiang Kai-shek. To do so at this juncture would be to lose more than we would gain. We must for the time being continue recognition of Chiang's Government.

But we must be realistic. We must not indefinitely underwrite a politically bankrupt regime. And, if the Russians are going to enter the Pacific war, we must make a determined effort to capture politically the Chinese Communists rather than allow them to go by default wholly to the Russians . . . If the Russians enter North China and Manchuria, we obviously cannot hope to win the Communists entirely over to us, but we can through control of supplies and post-war aid expect to exert considerable influence in the direction of Chinese nationalism and independence from Soviet control.

Davies's difficulty was that he was foresighted to the point of being prophetic. As he was to explain to the Noce board:

"If in our struggle with the Soviet world we are to win out without resort to war, a split in the Soviet-Chinese bloc would seem to be an essential prerequisite. Short of the overthrow of the Soviet regime, the most devastating political defeat that the U.S.S.R. could suffer would be Peking's defection from Moscow's camp."

Davies was ahead, not only of events, but of American political thought as well. The concept of the separability of Moscow and Peking, widely accepted today, was considered heretical to the point of disloyalty in that era, when Communism was viewed as a monolithic threat and any criticism of the Chiang Government incurred the wrath of the powerful China lobby.

In the emotionalism and fear of the moment, few apparently stopped to think that the Noce board was striking, not just at Davies and his recommendations, but at the very foundations of the Foreign Service. For Davies was accused of nonconformity rather than disloyalty—nonconformity to what the board misconstrued to be the standards of the service. In an organization with a tradition of factual reporting and independence of judgment, the new standard was thus to be conformity. The message of the Davies decision was clear: henceforth, any Foreign Service officer who dared to question policy, who sent back reports that did not support policy or who associated with individuals deemed questionable by the security office, ran the danger of being declared unreliable.

Prophetically, Davies described the dilemma facing a Foreign Service officer in a letter to General Noce shortly before his dismissal:

> When a Foreign Service officer concludes that a policy is likely to betray national interests, he can reason to himself that, as ultimate responsibility for policy rests with the top officials of the Department, he need feel no responsibility for the course upon which we are embarked; furthermore, his opinions might be in error or misunderstood or misrepresented—and so the safest thing for a bureaucrat to do in such a situation is to remain silent. Or, a Foreign Service officer can speak out about his misgivings and suggest alternative policies, knowing that he runs serious personal risks in so doing. I spoke out.

Curiously, the letter provided the conclusive evidence in the biased predetermined proceedings.

The Legacy of McCarthyism (1961)

Previous readings have made clear the effect of the Red Scare on both individuals and foreign policy. In this reading historian H. Stuart Hughes evaluates the influence of McCarthy on the generation of the 1950s, both as to its political attitudes and its willingness to act upon its beliefs.

From H. Stuart Hughes, "Why We Had No Dreyfus Case," The American Scholar, XXX (1961), pp. 473–479. Subheadings added by the editors.

I

How We Failed

The "McCarthy Era" of American history officially ended with the censure of the Wisconsin Senator by his colleagues in the autumn of 1954. His death two and a half years later only seemed to confirm what the verdict of his fellow Senators had already announced: that the influence he had wielded over American life had vanished even more swiftly and inexplicably than it had appeared. Soon people began to speak in the past tense of the methods that had been associated with his name. The implication was that informing on others—and the subtle but tormenting fears that went along with it—had ceased to be a feature of the American scene. Those citizens (mostly intellectuals) whom revulsion from McCarthy's way had aroused to militance relaxed their previous sense of urgency. The battle for freedom, they thought, had been triumphantly concluded.

A moment's reflection might have shown them that this was far from true. McCarthy had not succumbed to the righteous indignation of the American intellectual community. He had been condemned by his peers on narrow grounds—for little more than a breach of senatorial courtesy—and the wider issue of what he stood for had never been settled. President Eisenhower and his immediate subordinates never admitted that they had done wrong during the year when they had tried to "appease" the demagogue from Wisconsin; Secretary of State Dulles continued to wrap himself in the garb of a moralist, and the public forgot how he had sacrificed experienced and devoted diplomats to McCarthy's wrath. It is symptomatic of the extremely limited nature of the anti-McCarthy victory that of the two Presidential candidates chosen six years later, [Richard Nixon and John Kennedy] one was thought to have opposed the senatorial resolution of censure, while the other had abstained from voting.

A few individual injustices were rectified after McCarthy's fall. But there was no wholesale rehabilitation of the innocent nor punishment of the guilty. Where a liberaliza-

"I Have Here In My Hand —"

This cartoon by Herblock of the *Washington Post,* one of Senator Joseph McCarthy's sharpest critics, appeared during a Senate committee's hearings into charges by McCarthy, chairman of the Senate subcommittee on governmental operations, and countercharges by officials of the Department of the Army. The legend "I have here in my hand" refers to previous McCarthy assertions of knowledge of the identity of substantial numbers of Communists in the federal government. The Senator never documented those charges. The "doctored photo" and "faked letter" were items submitted by the subcommittee's staff whose genuineness was challenged at the hearings.

tion of policy occurred, as in the matter of passports, it was not President Eisenhower himself who acted, but the courts which forced a reluctant Administration to correct the abuses that had become established as public policy. Only a minority among the citizenry called for the abolition of McCarthy's forum, the Senate Internal Security subcommittee. And after the Democrats gained control of the Senate and took over the subcommittee's chairmanship, it continued to coerce witnesses into "naming names" by pressures that were quieter than McCarthy's, but closely resembled them. The questioning of Linus Pauling in the summer of 1960 was a particularly notorious example of procedure that recalled the grim years from 1950 to 1954. While Senator Eastland of Mississippi was in charge, this might be explained away as a regrettable example of backwoods behavior. After Senator Dodd of Connecticut took over, it became difficult to find excuses for the conduct of a man who bore the marks of respectability and who represented one of the best educated constituencies in the country.

It is only when one talks to the very young that one realizes how devastating the legacy of the McCarthy years has been. The college generation of today has quite literally had to learn its political and ideological vocabulary from scratch. For the better part of a decade the motto "Don't sign or join anything" recommended itself to ambitious youth; almost no fundamental issue was publicly discussed. Not until 1957 was the post-McCarthy slumber broken with the launching of the first important nonconformist effort, the Committee for a Sane Nuclear Policy. Meantime the young people and students accepted as normal the detailed scrutiny of their opinions (and even sexual attitudes) by an army of government sleuths. And we, their professors, mostly submitted to being questioned about our students, choosing the lesser evil for fear that if we refused to answer we would jeopardize their chances for public service.

Yet this seemed a sorry return for the splendid fashion in which the students themselves had not told on *us* when the going was rough in the period between Eisenhower's inauguration and McCarthy's fall.

The record is not a pretty one. Very few people have anything to be proud of—no more than a distinguished minority of American intellectuals and certainly not the Democratic party. Although Adlai Stevenson made a number of noble statements during the campaign of 1952, and although many of the nonprofessional enthusiasts whom that campaign mobilized into service thought of it as a battle more against McCarthy than against Eisenhower, the majority of organization Democrats—including, of course, the young paladin who was to lead them to victory in 1960—treated the whole issue as merely peripheral and embarrassing.

Here Truman bears a heavy responsibility. No doubt he was outraged by McCarthy's methods. But he failed to do the one thing that might have cleared the air and substituted historical fact for murky suspicion. By his original gesture of dismissing the issue of Communists in government as a "red herring," he tied his party's hands for an effective defense or counterattack against such a charge in the years that followed. By refusing to admit the Communists had in fact "penetrated" the federal service during the New Deal and war years, he made it impossible to discuss honestly in public the extent of that penetration and how much it had actually accomplished.

How many Communists succeeded in entering federal service? Estimates vary, but the number cannot be higher than a few hundred, mostly in the newer war agencies. How much influence did they exert on policy? Only three or four possible Communists were ever identified in positions of high responsibility. Did the majority of Communists in government profit from their positions to engage in conspiratorial or treasonous activities? Here the answer is an emphatic no. From my own experience as a State Department official during a period when Communists were still in government service, I can vouch for the fact that most of them honestly tried to do the job assigned, with their peculiar ideology deflecting their judgment only now and then, but most of the time simply adding a certain zeal and seriousness to the performance of their duties. When and how did they leave the Federal Government? Here my memories check with the fragmentary official statements emanating from the Truman Administration. Nearly all the Communists resigned during the year and a half immediately following the war. Most left of their own volition, having concluded that the atmosphere in Washington was no longer propitious. Others were eased out through forced resignations or intimations that their usefulness had come to an end. Some of the procedures employed in removing them were extremely harsh, and a number of non-Communists also found themselves obliged to resign, but at least the thing was done in private, the fiction of resignation was preserved, and individuals dropped from federal service did not experience as severe difficulties in finding private employment as were encountered subsequently by those purged in the McCarthy era.

These are the approximate facts. I should add a summary statement of the conclusions that historians have reached on the three areas of war and postwar policy in which Communist influence was supposed to have been most important: Yalta, China and Germany. On Yalta the evidence is conclusive. The publication of the private records of the conference in the mid-1950's proved disappointing to those Republicans who had hoped to draw political profit from them. Far from documenting any sort of treason, these papers failed to show that Alger Hiss (whose case, by the way, must be regarded as still open) had played an influential role, and further demonstrated that on one of the few occasions when he was consulted Hiss advised resistance to Soviet demands. In short, the Yalta documents contained none of the sensational revelations that Roosevelt's enemies had promised.

On China, the evidence is more tangled. But from the mass of controversy and recrimination, three central facts emerge. First, the advisers on China policy who were later pilloried and hounded from government service were guilty of nothing worse than an honest error of judgment: they underestimated the Marxist ruthlessness of the Communist leaders. Secondly, these diplomats were not Communists themselves. Third, their advice did not decisively alter the course of events. I know of no qualified expert on China who denies that Mao Tse-tung and his associates would have come to power in any case; the only remote possibility of preventing it lay in a massive American military effort which stood no chance of popular acceptance in the prevailing postwar mood of "get the boys home" as fast as possible.

On German policy alone, I think, some case

for Communist influence can be made. My own impression during service as an OSS officer in Germany during the summer and autumn of 1945 was that two or three American Communists with high positions in the economic branches of military government were urging a punitive policy that was consciously intended to favor Soviet aims. But this type of assertion is extremely hard to document. At the close of the war a punitive attitude toward Germany was by no means restricted to Communists; many American Jews, for example, were understandably anxious to revenge the murder of six million of their coreligionists. Here, as in the China case, pro-Communist attitudes were not decisive in altering American actions. After a few months of confusion, our Government settled into a reasonably coherent and constructive policy of rebuilding the German economy and German democratic institutions.

Such is the defense that President Truman might have made of the first year and a half of his Administration. He might have stated quite frankly that in the "Popular Front" atmosphere of the decade 1935–1945 some Communists did indeed enter the federal service. He might have added that in the very different ideological climate of the opening phases of the cold war these Communists were quietly eased out—indeed, that virtually all of them had departed *more than two years* before McCarthy blew his opening trumpet with his famous speech detailing the number of "subversives" in the Department of State. The President might have concluded that during their brief stay in Washington the Communists had accomplished very little indeed. Truman said none of these things—or at least said none of them completely and unequivocally. This is one reason why America in the early 1950's never had its Dreyfus Case.*

I mean that we did not have our Dreyfus Affair in the sense that there emerged no single test case that could serve as a symbol and a battle cry to all who felt themselves threatened or whom a more abstract indignation had aroused to champion the cause of justice. Unlike France at the turn of the century, the United States in the 1950's did not find the human being whose plight could dramatize the whole issue and whose triumphal acquittal by the courts could serve as a stinging rebuke to the Administration and a precedent for rehabilitating all the others who had suffered from the arbitrary acts of public officials.

There were two possible contenders for the role of test case. One, of course, was Alger Hiss, and initially many liberals rallied to his support. But as the evidence presented in Hiss's two trials became increasingly damning, most of those who had at first been ready to spring to his defense concluded that he might well be guilty—or at the very least that the case was insufficiently clear to serve as a general test. A minority of men of good will stuck with Hiss to the last and have never stopped asserting his innocence. A great many more, and I count myself among them, remained unconvinced of his guilt, or at least

*In 1894 Captain Alfred Dreyfus of the French Army was sentenced to life imprisonment for having betrayed military secrets to Germany. It was later shown that Dreyfus, a Jew, probably had been framed to protect an army major who was a member of the French aristocracy. Subsequent efforts to free Dreyfus found the French political left supporting his release, while conservative political groups urged his continued imprisonment—Eds.

of his guilt *as charged by Whittaker Chambers*. In the case of Captain Dreyfus, the innocence of the accused eventually became clear to everyone not irremediably prejudiced against him. In the case of Alger Hiss, this was far from true. To this day, doubt has persisted: the overwhelming suspicion remains that for reasons that have still to be explained both the prosecution and the defense tried to conceal relevant information; the full context of the events in question has never emerged.

The case of Owen Lattimore at first sight appeared more promising. For he had been merely a government consultant rather than a public official like Hiss. (Most liberal-minded people, I think, were willing to grant, as I would, the right of the Federal Government to protect itself against spies and saboteurs by removing Communists from the truly "sensitive" positions in the foreign and defense establishments.) Moreover, in the case of Lattimore, the charge of Communist affiliation rested on nothing but innuendo; it never came remotely close to being proved. When all the deceptive verbiage of his accusers had been stripped away, the worst that could be said against him was that he had made pro-Soviet statements and given bad advice on China policy.

Surely these were insufficient reasons for pillorying him in public and suspending him from his university post. The injustice was patent. Still the American intellectual community held back: only a minority rallied to Lattimore's defense. People found all sorts of reasons for reluctance, besides the fear for their own jobs which was mostly unadmitted. Particularly, they found a lack of total candor in Lattimore's replies to Senator McCarthy. Here they forgot a simple psychological fact: it is hard to keep clearheaded and consistent in facing a bully. Beyond that, most American liberals were seeking the impossible; they were looking for a perfect test case. They forgot—if they ever knew—that Captain Dreyfus had been far from an ideal witness in his own defense, and that from the personal standpoint he left much to be desired. In the great imperfection of human affairs, ideal test cases seldom appear. We have to take our issues where we find them. We have to fight our ideological and moral battles not on ground of our own choosing, but on the foggy and swampy terrain that our enemies have selected.

II

The New Generation

But this was not all:

American liberals and radicals were uneasy in their consciences. They could not spring to the defense of others because they were unsure of their own innocence.

This was McCarthy's greatest triumph. This was the abiding poison he left with us. He succeeded in creating a sense of guilt among thousands of intelligent and public-spirited people—a large part of the intellectual and moral elite of the nation. Not only did he deprive the Government of their service and counsel during a decade when these were badly needed. He crippled their own thought by stirring within them the demon of self-doubt. McCarthy and his aides had never made a systematic study of psychoanalytic theory. But their infernal intuition had revealed to them one of its essential discoveries: that it is precisely the most conscientious and scrupulous people who suffer from the heaviest burden of unconscious guilt.

Thus each man who felt even remotely threatened by the wave of "security" discharges and sanctions began to scrutinize his own conscience and to assess exactly how guilty he himself had been. There grew up a cult of fine distinctions and careful gradations of guilt. People forgot that when large moral issues are in play, fine distinctions are useless, or worse than useless. When spiritual and intellectual survival is at stake, as was quite literally true in this country from 1950 to 1954, it is a simple question of "we" against "they." The barricades are up, and we cannot afford to be choosy about those who are fighting beside us. Rather than splitting hairs over whether or not a Communist should be fired from a university teaching post—a common-sense answer was that he should not, since the psychological havoc on the campus that would result from his discharge far outbalanced any presumed gain in protecting the minds of the young—the liberal intellectuals would have done better to close ranks and to proclaim their solidarity with the vast majority of the accused. Nor would they have had to make an explicit exception for the tiny minority of spies and saboteurs whom millions of man-hours of government sleuthing every so often unearthed. For these did not fall into the category of the ideologically persecuted. They came rather under the jurisdiction of the ordinary criminal procedure by which any government—even the most tolerant, like that of Great Britain—has traditionally tried to protect itself from harm.

What exactly did liberals find themselves guilty of when they scrutinized their own consciences? "Softness" toward Russia? Illusions about Communist China? A nostalgia for the Soviet-American solidarity that had won the struggle against fascism? A failure to detect the Communist inspiration of their acquaintances who had involved them in fine-sounding "front" activities? That was about all. What it added up to was a rather vague and blundering protest against the dissolution of the anti-fascist solidarity of wartime and the drift toward the division of the world into two armed camps in the years after 1945.

More concretely, the ideological attitude of many liberals in the later 1940's betrayed two serious weaknesses. It indulged in "wave of the future" reasoning, assuming the eventual victory of communism without inquiring sufficiently what could be done to deflect its triumphant course, and softening the outlines of communism itself to make that victory more palatable. It also inclined toward overcompensation. Suspecting that the anti-Communists exaggerated the abuses of Soviet despotism, a large number of generous-minded Americans jumped to the conclusion that the reverse must be true. They found it difficult to believe in the reality of the Russian forced-labor camps. They refused to plumb the depths of evil in Stalin's soul: they had vented the one great hatred of their lives on the person of Hitler, and they could not summon up the same unforgiving wrath against a second tyrant. For tens of thousands of articulate Americans over the age of thirty, the struggle against fascism had been the central moral experience of their youth; they did not have the heart to remobilize their energies for another such combat.

The chief sin of this type of thinking was what came to be called "anti-anti-communism." To balance its lack of realism, we may recall certain of its other aspects which seemed utopian at the time but which ten years later have a much more sensible look: a refusal to consider the world as irrevocably split and a concern for keeping open bridges across the great ideological divide, more particularly to those nations (like India) or groups (like European neutralists) that were trying to remain uncommitted in the cold war. Such were the constructive features of the "anti-anti-Communist" position. Along with them went a prophetic understanding of the moral debasement that the anti-Communist crusade would inflict on the American people.

For all their faults, Americans of this variety did far less harm than their adversaries. They also did less harm than the other kind of liberals who aided in the early stages of the anti-Communist drive from 1945 to 1950. After McCarthy himself went into action and pushed the campaign against "subversives" far beyond their original intention, many of the anti-Communist liberals regretted what they had done—as one, I remember, was honest enough to tell me at the high point of the Senator's power in 1953. But by then it was too late. He and his fellow Sorcerers' Apprentices had helped to unleash forces over which they had totally lost control.

A moral debasement—that was the ultimate legacy of the McCarthy era. Or rather, a moral numbness. Most people were not corrupted by what they went through or what they saw going on around them. They were simply stunned by it. Better still, they were confirmed in a habit of mental dissociation and compartmentalized thinking that the conclusion of the war itself had made a psychological necessity.

When the atomic bomb dropped over Hiroshima in August 1945, I recall sensing that the world had suddenly stood still and that life would never be the same again. I suspect a great many of my countrymen felt the same way. The experience was not exactly one of personal or national guilt. It was that something so awful (in both senses of the term) had happened that the usual criteria for judging men and events would no longer serve. It was an *impersonal* experience—a shock from outside so enormous that the only way one felt able to deal with it was by dissociating oneself and refusing to think about it. More than a decade was to pass before I could bear to concentrate my mind on the question of nuclear warfare.

The shock of Hiroshima confirmed a national tendency that had begun to manifest itself with the terror bombing of German cities in the two years preceding. It marked a further, and perhaps decisive, stage in an erosion of moral responses. Our ruthless obliteration of German dwellings and cultural landmarks—far beyond any clear military necessity—had evoked almost no protest at home; the same lack of moral indignation was apparent a half decade later when the American public accepted as quite natural the napalm bombing of Korean villages. Those rare individuals who did object usually did so in the privacy of their own consciences. Public protest seemed futile: a pall of dull acceptance settled over the American soul.

It would be tempting to investigate how much this change in attitude had to do with the vogue of a fatalistic neoreligiosity that became apparent at the same time. Certainly the young people who in these years took so kindly to Kierkegaard and Dostoevski found in such authors' bleak acceptance of the evils of the human condition a reflection of their own sense of moral impotence. It was the same with *one kind* of Existentialism. Americans were not attracted by the activist, ethically strenuous and socially conscious emphasis in the writings of Jean-Paul Sartre. They found congenial, rather, Existentialism's analysis of the absurdities of life and the impossibility of unambiguous moral choices.

If we add to this religious and philosophical fatalism, two further elements—the lack of major public debate on crucial issues, and the substantial reconciliation of intellectuals to the *status quo* (through comfortable jobs, research contracts and the like)—we can begin to assess the full dimensions of the post-Hiroshima and post-McCarthy transformation. First came a deadening of sensibility. On this followed bewilderment and a feeling that problems had become too big and complex for the mere individual citizen to grasp (with both the national Administration and the intellectuals aiding the process by insisting that only "experts" were qualified to express opinions). Finally ensued a *privatization* of life, a tendency on the part of each man to retreat to the cultivation of his own suburban garden. The vast majority of the accused in the McCarthy era had not the slightest desire to see their own woes made into test cases or matters of public concern. They ran for cover instead. Most cases of injustice never came to light and were correspondingly difficult to rectify after McCarthy's fall. This was still another reason why we had no Dreyfus Case.

In some moral dilemmas it is worse to be pettily right than nobly in error. Such could be said of countless Americans who in the course of becoming properly "sophisticated" about communism lost their capacity for honest indignation. They forgot that every ideological commitment involves the risk of making a mistake, and that people who always play it safe make no contribution to awakening or enlightening their countrymen. Nor did the harm stop here. For a whole decade, school teachers and college professors denied their students the long-sanctioned right of the young to seek their own path and learn from their own errors. Most of the men and women who came of age in the decade 1948–1957, and who are now in their late twenties and early thirties, never knew what they were missing. Only a few of them were aware of their loss, and these I remember as bemused students, nostalgic for the ideological experiences that had passed them by.

Suddenly in the spring of 1960 I realized with a shock that a new student generation had sprung into life. In the widespread demonstrations against racial segregation a new age group had won its political spurs. The picketings and meetings of that spring involved only a minority of college students. But this minority was soon recognizable as the intellectually active and devoted which in each generation takes the moral lead. And the fact that its energies subsequently turned toward activities on behalf of peace suggested that its concern for racial equality formed part of a wider protest against inhuman behavior at home and abroad.

To those of us who had grown discouraged by a lack of response among our immediate juniors, the discovery of this new student generation has been immensely heartening. It has given us a chance to leap over a ten-year span and take up again where we left off when the ideological blight descended upon America. In my own intellectual community of Greater Boston, such efforts as the review *Dissent* and the neoradical Committee of Correspondence have been notably reinforced by support from the very young.

Yet this support comes to us with a difference. We who regard ourselves as stimulators of a New Left realize that our student allies do not think exactly as we do. To them, we seem talky and old-fashioned. They are impatient with words and with theories; they dislike the vocabulary of leftist democracy that to my age group is second nature. They prefer factual analysis—and direct action where possible. Impatient with ideological rhetoric, they find almost incomprehensible polemics that shook the American Left in the decades from 1917 to 1948.

Basically, I think this is a good thing. I find it healthy that the students of today are starting off afresh with so little concern for old ideological battles; in this sense—as having wiped the slate clean—our country's ten-year slumber has been of positive benefit. I shall be quite happy to see the young people take leadership from us and direct the new radicalism of America into courses we would never have imagined. I agree that most of the traditional phraseology of the Left has become worn and stale. I should welcome being treated as an old fogey if it should mean a new vigor and inspiration on the part of the young.

Yet in another sense it is too early for us to abdicate. The political virginity of today's students is wonderful—but it is also disconcerting. It is a curious experience for a person like myself who has been accused of "softness" toward Soviet Russia to find himself obliged to explain in the most elementary terms the differences between Communism and a free society. The experience of recent history is still relevant. The student generation of today can learn from the record of a yesterday that is fast sinking into legend or forgetfulness. It is for them primarily that I have dredged up the slime of an era that no one can recall without shame—in the hope that when *they* are confronted with their Dreyfus Case they will rise to the challenge better than we did in the years of our country's supreme moral crisis.

TOPIC 64

CUBA AND REVOLUTION IN THE AMERICAS

For fifteen years the principal events of the Cold War took place far from the United States, as the nation remained deeply involved in political controversy and military actions in Europe, the Middle East, and Asia. In 1959, however, fears were multiplied many times over in Washington by the triumph of Fidel Castro in Cuba. By 1960 many believed that communism had finally gained a foothold in the Americas.

For many years Americans had taken a proprietary attitude toward Latin America. The United States had displaced Great Britain as the principal economic influence in the region by the early twentieth century. Combined political and economic interests led to what was called "dollar diplomacy," in which the United States intervened in the internal affairs of a number of Latin American nations (see Reading 278). In the 1930s Presidents Hoover and Roosevelt substituted for dollar diplomacy a "Good Neighbor" policy which abandoned overt American political intervention in Latin America, but left undisturbed the domination of large parts of the economies of many Latin American countries by American corporations.

Cuba was one of the nations most thoroughly dominated by American interests. In many ways Cuba prospered. Its large sugar and tobacco crops sold at high prices on a protected market in the United States. Havana was the major city in the Caribbean region, and Cuba had one of the largest middle classes in Latin America. Nevertheless, North American influence was ever present, much of the wealth from agriculture and the newer industries flowed to the United States, and most of the people, as in the rest of Latin America, were poor agricultural or urban laborers. There were periods of political democracy in Cuba, but for most of the twenty-five years before 1959 the country had been ruled by Fulgencio Batista, a frequently ruthless military dictator. One of Batista's chief opponents in the 1950s was Fidel Castro, a young lawyer who led a mountain-based guerrilla band. Though Castro won few military victories, he waged a highly successful propaganda war which, along with the withdrawal of American aid, severely weakened Batista's regime. In January 1959 Batista fled and Fidel Castro entered Havana. The rise of a leftist revolutionary regime next door to the world's foremost capitalist nation soon generated consequences alarming to the United States government, and the further consequences of confrontation washed the shores of many Latin American nations, beginning with the Dominican Republic, in the succeeding years.

Nuclear Confrontation in the Americas

With each change of administration in Washington the same question recurred: would the Cold War be handled in quite the same way as before? The Cuban crisis of 1961 to 1962 offered John F. Kennedy, who took office as President in January 1961, an opportunity to define a new approach to American foreign policy. Historian Stewart Easton provides the history of recent Cuban-American relations in the following selection.

From *The Western Heritage, from 1500 to the Present* by Stewart C. Easton. Copyright © 1966 by Holt, Rinehart and Winston, Inc. Reprinted by permission of the publisher. Pp. 538-541. Subheadings added by the editors.

I

Ike and Cuba, 1959-1960

In the last year of the Eisenhower administration a new bone of contention arose in which the Soviet Union became involved. Prime Minister Fidel Castro of Cuba, a revolutionary who had come to power by ousting an American-backed dictator in 1959, had been turning increasingly to the left and antagonizing the middle class in his small island. A very large number of this group had been admitted as refugees to the United States, where they plotted to return to Cuba and overthrow the Castro government. Relations between the United States and Cuba deteriorated rapidly from early in the revolutionary regime, in part because of the nationalization of large estates and sugar industries, including many that belonged to Americans. In February 1960 Cuba negotiated a $100 million loan with the USSR, and it became clear that Castro intended to make his country as far as possible economically independent of the United States, which had virtually controlled the economy for the whole period of Cuba's national existence. But from the Cuban point of view, the greatest danger was the possibility that the United States would sponsor an invasion by Cuban exiles and that she herself would intervene directly. President Eisenhower gave instructions as early as March 1960 that a select group of exiles should be trained by the Central Intelligence Agency in Guatemala, so that they might be able to "act at the proper time." In May, Cuba established formal diplomatic relations with the USSR, and further trade agreements were signed with Soviet satellite countries. When Castro demanded that United States oil companies process Soviet oil, they refused. This was followed by their nationalization without compensation. Similar incidents followed. The United States cut Cuba's sugar quota and finally placed an embargo on Cuban sugar imports. In December 1960 Cuba signed a new trade agreement with the Soviet Union by which the latter agreed to send technicians to Cuba and build a large number of industrial plants. President Eisenhower, who had warned the other Latin American nations of the dangers to be expected from this entry of "international Communism" into the hemisphere and had prevented Britain from selling jet planes to Cuba, at last gave the formal indication that relations between the United States and Cuba no longer had any meaning, and he severed diplomatic relations on January 3, a few days before his successor, John F. Kennedy, was to be inaugurated.

II

Kennedy and Cuba, 1961-1963

The most urgent task that met President Kennedy on his taking office was to decide what to do about Cuba. The general thinking of his advisers was that Cuba was becoming a Communist country if it was not one already; and though Castro himself might not be a Communist, many of his closest associates, and probably his brother, were. There was already a virtually complete embargo on trade between the United States and Cuba, and the CIA-trained armies of exiles were expecting to be unleashed against their homeland at any moment. Castro evidently had fairly precise information about the planned invasion, and he constantly accused the United States of planning aggression, while at the same time suggesting almost as frequently that he was ready to negotiate differences with the new President. In the end the President decided that the invasion should go forward, but he continued to try to prevent the United States from intervening openly. The result was that she intervened also ineffectively, and had the worst of both worlds. The Bay of Pigs invasion by exiles failed for lack of air support by the United States, which the exiles had counted on, and most of the invaders were taken prisoner. Eventually an indemnity (or ransom, according to the point of view) in the form of medical supplies was paid in exchange for the return of the prisoners. Thereafter the United States not only maintained her own embargo, but tried to prevent other nations from trading with Cuba in the hope that her economy would collapse.

It was this aspect of the struggle between the Great Power and the small island that brought about the ever increasing activity of the Soviet Union in Cuba, so that the island, whose leader, Castro, was later to claim that he was and had always been a Marxist-Leninist, became a virtual satellite of the Soviet Union. However unwilling Khrushchev may have been to help Cuba with enormous loans, some of them unlikely to be paid off within the foreseeable future, he was not left much option, especially not with China also giving aid and constantly urging Khrushchev on in his struggle with the "imperialists." Cuba could not get oil from any sources other than Russia because of the American embargo, and oil was a necessity. It was also far from certain that the United States would not sponsor, and perhaps take part in, another invasion. Castro therefore demanded arms and modern artillery from his good friend, and these too were supplied, as it was now so well established that Cuba was a Russian responsibility that it would have been extremely damaging to Russia's prestige if Cuba had been abandoned and forced to submit to American pressure.

Toward the end of 1962 there were persistent rumors that the Soviet Union was installing in Cuba rockets capable of destroying the cities in the eastern United States (IBM's, Intermediate Ballistic Missiles) if they had nuclear warheads. When the CIA confirmed this through overflights which kept the United States at all times informed of all that photographs could convey, the deadliest crisis of the nuclear age followed.

Cuban rebel leader Fidel Castro poses with followers at their base in the Sierra Maestra mountains in eastern Cuba in September 1957. In January 1959 Castro's forces won control of the country, forcing dictator Fulgencio Batista into exile.

It may never be established why Khrushchev sent missiles to Cuba. Obviously, from the Cuban point of view, only weapons of this kind could halt another invasion, in which this time Cuban exiles might be supported by United States ground troops and air cover. The possibility of Cuban retaliation against American cities might give the United States government pause, whereas Cuba could not for long defend herself against overwhelming land and air forces. But even though the Soviet Union herself is threatened by rockets installed on United States-controlled bases close to the Russian borders, this was the first time that any Russian leader attempted such an obviously provocative and dangerous reply, made even more hazardous by the presence of the United States base of Guantánamo on the island, from which her troops could be deployed.

Although the idea was widely accepted in the United States that the Russians hoped to add weight to their nuclear threat against the United States by placing intermediate-range missiles in their advanced outpost of Cuba so close to the American coastline, such weapons in fact would add almost nothing to Russian nuclear capability that rocket-carrying submarines and intercontinental missiles did not already give her. Khrushchev cannot have been unaware of the risk, and it scarcely seems possible that he can have imagined that the United States, with her military forces deployed so powerfully around the world, would have permitted this nuclear build-up so close to home. Just possibly he may have hoped to compel the United States to face the dangers to herself from the ever intensifying arms race. But though in this he did prove partly successful, the stunning diplomatic defeat he suffered and the poor figure he was forced to cut, especially in the eyes of the Chinese, when he withdrew the missiles, were surely too high a price to pay.

President Kennedy handled the emergency with masterly aplomb, threatening only as much force as was sufficient to attain his ends. The United States Navy patrolled the sea lanes, prepared to turn back by force the Russian missile-carrying convoys that were on the way to the island, and the ships duly turned back. Khrushchev quickly agreed to remove the missiles and to accept the good offices of the United Nations secretary-general in arriving at an agreement. Although Khrushchev was not able to win firm agreement to his terms, namely that the United States promise not to invade Cuba and that some bases close to the Soviet Union be abandoned, the island in fact has not been invaded, and the United States has apparently agreed to accept an uneasy coexistence; some bases have also been abandoned, as the United States had already intended before the confrontation. In removing his missiles Khrushchev also made it clear that Cuba was still under Soviet protection and that retaliation would follow an invasion—a threat which may or may not be a binding one on his successors.

III

Developing Coexistence

The Cuban incident led to a year in which there was a marked decrease in tension between the United States and the USSR, much of it the result of President Kennedy's evident desire to lessen it and the conciliatory speeches he continued to make, as well as the Test-Ban Treaty.... It was also noteworthy that some strong support in this endeavor came from the Vatican, where the aged Pope John XXIII in a striking encyclical *Pacem in Terris* (Peace on Earth) made it clear that in his view the Communists were misguided rather than necessarily wicked, that they should not be regarded as outcasts from humanity, that all men, Christians, members of other religions, and "atheistic" Communists, were all equally the children of God. The greatest need for humanity was therefore to lay a basis for conciliation and bring an end to the Cold War (April 1963). President Kennedy, indeed, became so widely regarded as a man who himself sincerely desired a reconciliation with the Soviet Union—even though he stepped up action against the Communists in Vietnam and showed no signs of wishing to come to an accommodation with the Chinese Communists—that when he was so tragically assassinated on November 22, 1963, the first reaction of many persons throughout the world was that it must have been the American chauvinists and professional anti-Communists who were behind it, since they could not endure that any gestures should be made toward conciliation with the unchanging Russian "enemy." For them there was no alternative to the Cold War except a hot one, and there should be no relaxation until "victory" had been achieved.

President Johnson, however, continued the policy of his predecessor, both in the Far East, where the struggle was intensified, and elsewhere, where the détente continued. The replacement of Khrushchev by Kosygin and Brezhnev in October 1964 made no apparent difference in relations between the two nations. The increasing evidence for the existence of a real quarrel between the Russians and Chinese, which was not abated by the fall of Khrushchev, led to serious consideration of what this might mean for the future of the Cold War in Europe and whether the time might have come for a fundamental reappraisal of United States–USSR relations.

Reading 344

Kennedy and Cuba (1962)

The decision of the Soviet Union to support the Cuban government by placing medium-range missiles on the island, as Stewart Easton pointed out, generated a crisis in Washington. We are fortunate to have several accounts by "insiders" as to how decisions were made by President Kennedy and his advisers. What follows is the story told by Theodore Sorensen, the President's aide and friend.

Excerpts from pp. 682-683, 716-717, 724-725 in *Kennedy* by Theodore C. Sorensen. Copyright © 1965 by Theodore C. Sorensen. Reprinted by permission of Harper & Row, Publishers, Inc.

I

Kennedy's Choices

The bulk of our time Tuesday through Friday was spent in George Ball's* conference room cavassing all the possible courses as the President had requested, and preparing the back-up material for them: suggested time schedules or scenarios, draft messages, military estimates and predictions of Soviet and Cuban responses. Initially the possibilities seemed to divide into six categories, some of which could be combined:

1. Do nothing.
2. Bring diplomatic pressures and warnings to bear upon the Soviets. Possible forms included an appeal to the UN or OAS for an inspection team, or a direct approach to Khrushchev, possibly at a summit conference. The removal of our missile bases in Turkey in exchange for the removal of the Cuban missiles was also listed in our later discussions

*George Ball, Undersecretary of State—Eds.

as a possibility which Khrushchev was likely to suggest if we didn't.

3. Undertake a secret approach to Castro, to use this means of splitting him off from the Soviets, to warn him that the alternative was his island's downfall and that the Soviets were selling him out.
4. Initiate indirect military action by means of a blockade, possibly accompanied by increased aerial surveillance and warnings. Many types of blockades were considered.
5. Conduct an air strike—pinpointed against the missiles only or against other military targets, with or without advance warning. (Other military means of directly removing the missiles were raised—bombarding them with pellets that would cause their malfunctioning without fatalities, or suddenly landing paratroopers or guerrillas—but none of these was deemed feasible.)
6. Launch an invasion—or, as one chief advocate of this course put it: "Go in there and take Cuba away from Castro."

Other related moves were considered—such as declaring a national emergency, sending a special envoy to Khrushchev or asking Congress for a declaration of war against Cuba (suggested as a means of building both Allied support and a legal basis for blockade, but deemed not essential to either). But these six choices were the center of our deliberations.

Choice No. 1—doing nothing—and choice No. 2.—limiting our response to diplomatic action only—were both seriously considered. As some (but not all) Pentagon advisers pointed out to the President, we had long lived within range of Soviet missiles, we expected Khrushchev to live with our missiles nearby, and by taking this addition calmly we could prevent him from inflating its importance. All the other courses raised so many risks and drawbacks that choice No. 2 had its appeal. All of us came back to it at one discouraged moment or another; and it was advocated to the President as a preferable alternative to blockade by one of the regular members of our group in the key Thursday night meeting....

But the President had rejected this course from the outset. He was concerned less about the missiles' military implications than with their effect on the global political balance. The Soviet move had been undertaken so swiftly, so secretly and with so much deliberate deception—it was so sudden a departure from Soviet practice—that it represented a provocative change in the delicate status quo. Missiles on Soviet territory or submarines were very different from missiles in the Western Hemisphere, particularly in their political and psychological effect on Latin America. The history of Soviet intentions toward smaller nations was very different from our own. Such a step, if accepted, would be followed by more; and the President's September pledges of action clearly called this step unacceptable. While he desired to combine diplomatic moves with military action, he was not willing to let the UN debate and Khrushchev equivocate while the missiles became operational.

Various approaches to Castro (choice No. 3) —either instead of or as well as to Khrushchev—were also considered many times during the week. This course was set aside rather than dropped. The President increasingly felt that we should not avoid the fact that this was a confrontation of the great powers—that the missiles had been placed there by the Soviets, were manned and guarded by the Soviets, and would have to be removed by the Soviets in response to direct American action.

The invasion course (choice No. 6) had surprisingly few supporters. One leader outside our group whose views were conveyed to us felt that the missiles could not be tolerated, that the Soviet motivation was baffling, that a limited military action such as a blockade would seem indecisive and irritating to the world, and that an American airborne seizure of Havana and the government was the best bet. But with one possible exception, the conferees shared the President's view that invasion was a last step, not the first; that it should be prepared but held back; that an invasion—more than any other course—risked a world war, a Soviet retaliation at Berlin or elsewhere, a wreckage of our Latin-American policy and the indictment of history for our aggression.

Thus our attention soon centered on two alternatives—an air strike and a blockade. . . .

II

Success

Upon awakening Sunday morning, October 28, I turned on the news on my bedside radio, as I had each morning during the week. In the course of the 9 A.M. newscast a special bulletin came in from Moscow. It was a new letter from Khrushchev, his fifth since Tuesday, sent publicly in the interest of speed. Kennedy's terms were being accepted. The missiles were being withdrawn. Inspection would be permitted. The confrontation was over.

Hardly able to believe it, I reached Bundy* at the White House. It was true. He had just called the President, who took the news with "tremendous satisfaction" and asked to see

*McGeorge Bundy, Special Assistant for National Security Affairs—Eds.

the message on his way to Mass. Our meeting was postponed from 10 to 11 A.M. It was a beautiful sunday morning in Washington in every way.

With deep feelings of relief and exhilaration, we gathered in the Cabinet Room at eleven, our thirteenth consecutive day of close collaboration. Just as missiles are incomparably faster than all their predecessors, so this world-wide crisis had ended incredibly faster than all its predecessors. The talk preceding the meeting was boisterous. "What is Castro saying now?" chortled someone. Robert McNamara* said he had risen early that morning to draw up a list of "steps to take short of invasion." When he heard the news, said John McCone,* "I could hardly believe my ears." Waiting for the President to come in, we speculated about what would have happened

1. if Kennedy had chosen the air strike over the blockade . . .
2. if the OAS and other Allies had not supported us . . .
3. if both our conventional and our nuclear forces had not been strengthened over the past twenty-one months . . .
4. if it were not for the combined genius and courage that produced U-2 photographs and their interpretations . . .
5. if a blockade had been instituted before we could prove Soviet duplicity and offensive weapons . . .
6. if Kennedy and Khrushchev had not been accustomed to communicating directly with each other and had not left that channel open . . .

*McNamara was Secretary of Defense—Eds.
*McCone was Director of the Central Intelligence Agency—Eds.

7. if the President's speech of October 22 had not taken Khrushchev by surprise . . .
8. if John F. Kennedy had not been President of the United States.

John F. Kennedy entered and we all stood up. He had, as Harold Macmillan would later say, earned his place in history by this one act alone. He had been engaged in a personal as well as national contest for world leadership and he had won. He had reassured those nations fearing we would use too much strength and those fearing we would use none at all. Cuba had been the site of his greatest failure and now of his greatest success. The hard lessons of the first Cuban crisis were applied in his steady handling of the second with a carefully measured combination of defense, diplomacy, and dialogue. Yet he walked in and began the meeting without a trace of excitement or even exultation. . . .

Displaying the same caution and precision with which he had determined for thirteen days exactly how much pressure to apply, he quickly and quietly organized the machinery to work for a UN inspection and reconnaissance effort. He called off the Sunday overflights and ordered the Navy to avoid halting any ships on that day. (The one ship previously approaching had stopped.) He asked that precautions be taken to prevent Cuban exile units from upsetting the agreement through one of their publicity-seeking raids. He laid down the line we were all to follow—no boasting, no gloating, not even a claim of victory. We had won by enabling Khrushchev to avoid complete humiliation—we should not humiliate him now. If Khrushchev wanted to boast that he had won a major concession and proved his peaceful manner, that was the loser's prerogative. Major problems of implementing the agreement still faced us. Other danger spots in the world remained. Soviet treachery was too fresh in our memory to relax our vigil now....

III

Significance of Kennedy's Triumph

The fate of Cuba, however, was the least of the consequences of the Cuban missile crisis. That confrontation has aptly been called "the Gettysburg of the Cold War." For the first time in history, two major nuclear powers faced each other in a direct military challenge in which the prospects of a nuclear exchange were realistically assessed. Berlin, had its access been cut off, and even Laos, had there been no cease-fire, made a total of three potentially "major clashes with the Communists . . . in twenty-four months which could have escalated," said the President, adding "That is rather unhealthy in a nuclear age."

Khrushchev, it appeared, had reached the same conclusion. He had looked down the gun barrel of nuclear war and decided that that course was suicidal.

He had tried the ultimate in nuclear blackmail—dispatching not the usual missile threats, which had been issued over a hundred times since Sputnik, but the missiles themselves. The move having failed, nuclear blackmail was no longer an effective weapon in Berlin or anywhere else.

He had tested his premise that the United States lacked the will to risk all-out war in defense of its vital interests. That premise having proved wrong, he was less likely to underestimate our will again.

He had attempted a quick, easy step to catch up on the Americans in deliverable nuclear power. That step having been forced back, he implicitly accepted the superiority of our strategic forces as a fact with which he must and could live.

He had accepted—although only in Cuba, not in the Soviet Union—both a measure of inspection and an acknowledgment that the aerial camera was rapidly ending total secrecy. And he had learned, finally, that the American President was willing to exercise his strength with restraint, to seek communication and to reach accommodations that did not force upon his adversary total humiliation.

The result of all these lessons was apparently an agonizing reappraisal of policy within the Communist camp. The Soviet-Chinese split had been further widened when the Chinese—who had simultaneously and successfully attacked Russia's friend India—openly assailed Khrushchev for his weakness in Cuba. Throughout the winter of 1962-1963 the Kremlin appeared to flounder. Reports of a new power struggle were widespread. But the change which finally emerged was one not of personnel but of policy—a change not of basic purposes but of methods and manner. The taunts and threats to his leadership from the Red Chinese caused Khrushchev to reshuffle his priorities, removing conflict with the West from the top of his agenda. They also required him to prove concretely the value of coexistence and to isolate the more reckless Chinese position.

In the aftermath of the Cuban missile crisis a Soviet freighter carries home parts for bombing planes. The fuselages for three planes are visible at right center. This photograph was taken by the Navy in December 1962.

Fidel Castro: "A Grave Threat to the United States"

Theodore Sorensen (Reading 344) felt Kennedy's Cuban policy was based on a wise interpretation of the situation. Richard Nixon, on the other hand, viewed the results of the crisis as a near-disaster. Nixon had been a Senator, then Vice President from 1953 through 1960 under Eisenhower. He had been active in foreign policy matters in both positions. In 1960 he ran for President but lost to Kennedy. In 1964 Nixon looked back on the Cuban affair and offered his judgment.

From Richard M. Nixon, "Cuba, Castro, and John F. Kennedy," *Reader's Digest*, LXXXV (November, 1964), pp. 283, 295–297, 300.

On April 19, 1959, I met for the first and only time the man who was to be the major foreign-policy issue of the 1960 Presidential campaign; who was destined to be a hero in the warped mind of Lee Harvey Oswald, President Kennedy's assassin; and who in 1964 is still a major campaign issue.

The man, of course, was Fidel Castro. It is safe to say that no other individual in the world has created such a conflict of opinion in the United States. Many foreign-policy experts strongly support Sen. J. William Fulbright's view that Castro is merely "a nuisance but not a grave threat to the United States." The opposing view, which I share, is that Castro is a dangerous threat to our peace and security—and that we cannot tolerate the presence of his communist regime 90 miles from our shores. . . .

By October 16, 1962, there was no longer any doubt. The CIA laid on the President's desk photographs of Soviet missiles in place in Cuba. The photos had been taken by the CIA's U-2 planes, and the evidence could not be brushed aside.

On October 22, 1962, President Kennedy made his dramatic announcement that the Soviet Union had secretly moved medium-range ballistic missiles and jet bombers into Cuba. He ordered a blockade, and demanded the removal of existing missiles, with on-site inspection to make certain that the job was done.

This was the finest hour of his Presidency. People, not only in this country but throughout the free world, applauded this forceful commitment of American strength to the defense of freedom and the cause of peace. By finally calling Khrushchev's bluff, President Kennedy assured his own place in history as the man who made nuclear blackmail an obsolete form of diplomacy.

But, again, the tragic history of American indecisiveness repeated itself. The persistent clique of advisers who had stayed Kennedy's hand at the Bay of Pigs began at once to nibble away at the new strong policy. They insisted that the whole dispute be turned over to the United Nations for negotiation and settlement. By convincing the President that he should back away from the strong course of action he had initially outlined, they enabled the United States to pull defeat out of the jaws of victory. These were the results of following their incredibly bad advice:

There was no insistence on onsite inspection. "Offensive" missiles were apparently removed, but "defensive" missiles were allowed to remain.

Not only were the Cuban exiles prohibited from engaging in further harassing actions against Castro, but the United States became committed to a no-invasion policy.

This weak-kneed foreign policy encouraged the enemy to bolder and bolder action. Shiploads of Soviet arms have continued to pour into Cuba—until today, except for the United States and Canada, the island is the strongest military power in the Western Hemisphere.

Khrushchev's gamble in putting missiles into Cuba was merely another application of the time-tested communist doctrine—"Two steps forward, one step backward." The operation turned out to be a net gain for the Kremlin. . . .

While the danger of destruction by total war has gone down, the danger of defeat without total war has gone up. Those who urge that we seek an "accommodation" with the communists fail to realize that when the communist leaders talk softly they are increasing their subversive and revolutionary activities. This is the situation with which the United States is presently confronted. It is a situation which calls for realistic thinking about communist strategy and tactics, and for a new policy to meet the threat that faces us.

We must understand that the communist threat is worldwide, and if communism takes over in one country the tremors are felt clear around the world. We need, therefore, a worldwide approach. I completely reject the idea that there are so-called peripheral areas, collateral areas—like Cuba and Vietnam—that are not important.

For world communist leaders the battle for Cuba is not about Cuba. It is about Latin America. And the eventual target is the United States. Cuba, for example, is at our very doorstep. All the world looks on and sees that we do nothing to help our neighbors who are enslaved by a communist dictator. Is it any wonder that they are doubtful that we mean to resist communism in other parts of the world?

At this critical period, we must make up our minds that there cannot be one further retreat any place in the free world. We must have the military strength, the economic programs and the political-action programs to resist any further retreat. Rather than a policy of flexibility, of softening, of conciliation, we must have a strong and determined policy. We must let those in the target nations know that the non-communist world has had enough of this continued encroachment, and that we are now going to stand firm.

Teetering on the Brink

I. F. Stone, a well-known editor and political commentator, offers his evaluation of the actions of the United States, the Soviet Union, and Cuba during the days of crisis. Readers should carefully compare Stone's views to those of Sorensen and Nixon (Readings 344 and 345).

From I. F. Stone, "The Brink," *The New York Review of Books*, VI (April 14, 1966), pp. 12, 13-14, 15-16. Subheadings added and footnotes omitted by the editors.

I

A Game of Chicken?

The essential, the terrifying, question about the missile crisis is what would have happened if Khrushchev had not backed down. It is extraordinary, in the welter of magazine articles and books dealing with the missile crisis, how rarely this question is raised. The story is told and retold as a test and triumph of the Kennedy brothers. But the deeper reaches of the story are avoided, as if we feared to look too closely into the larger implications of this sucessful first foray into nuclear brinkmanship. We may not be so lucky next time.

The public impression created by the government when the presence of the missiles in Cuba was verified is that they represented a direct threat to America's cities. For those a little more sophisticated it was said that they threatened the balance of power. But Elie Abel's new book on *The Missile Crisis*, like the earlier accounts by [Theodore] Sorensen and [Arthur] Schlesinger, shows that this was not the dominant view in the inner councils of the White House. Abel quotes McNamara [the Secretary of Defense] as saying, "A missile is a missile. It makes no great difference whether you are killed by a missile fired from the Soviet Union or from Cuba." But in the week of argument, Abel relates, McNamara came to concede that even if the effect on the strategic balance was relatively small, "the political effect in Latin America and elsewhere would be large." As Sorensen wrote in his *Kennedy*,

> To be sure, these Cuban missiles alone, in view of all the other megatonnage the Soviets were capable of unleashing upon us, did not substantially alter the strategic balance *in fact*.... But that balance would have been substantially altered *in appearance* [italics in original]; and in matters of national will and world leadership, as the President said later, such appearances contribute to reality.

The real stake was prestige.

The question was whether, with the whole world looking on, Kennedy would let Khrushchev get away with it. The world's first thermonuclear confrontation turned out to be a kind of ordeal by combat between two men to see which one would back down first. Schlesinger relates that in the earlier Berlin crisis, he wrote a memorandum to Kennedy protesting the tendency to define the issue as "Are you chicken or not?" But inescapably that's what the issue came around to....

In the eyeball to eyeball confrontation, it was Khrushchev who was forced to blink first. This was magnificent as drama. It was the best of therapies for Kennedy's nagging inferiority complex. Like any other showdown between the leaders of two contending hordes or tribes, it was also not without wider political significance. Certainly the fright it gave Khrushchev and the new sense of confidence it gave Kennedy were factors in the *détente* which followed. The look into the abyss made both men really feel in their bones the need for coexistence. But one may wonder how many Americans, consulted in a swift electronic plebiscite, would have cared to risk destruction to let John F. Kennedy prove himself.

II

The Role of Domestic Politics

A curious aspect of all three accounts, Sorensen's, Schlesinger's, and Abel's, is how they slide over Kennedy's immediate political situation. There might have been dispute as to whether those missiles in Cuba really represented any change in balance of terror, any substantial new threat to the United States. There could have been no dispute that to face the November elections with these missiles intact would have been disastrous for Kennedy and the Democrats. The first alarms about missiles in Cuba, whether justified or not at the time, had been raised by the Republican Senator Keating. President Kennedy had assured the country on September 4 that the only missiles in Cuba were anti-aircraft with a 25-mile range and on September 13 that new Soviet shipments to Cuba were not a "serious threat." The election was only three weeks off when the presence of nuclear missiles on the island were confirmed on October 15 by aerial photographs. There was no time for prolonged negotiations, summit conferences, or U.N. debates if the damage was to be undone before the election. Kennedy could not afford to wait. This gamble paid off when he was able on October 28 to "welcome" Khrushchev's "statesmanlike decision" to dismantle the missiles, and on November 2, four days before the election, to announce that they were being crated for removal. But what if the gamble had failed? What if Khrushchev, instead of backing down when he did, had engaged in a delaying action, offering to abide by the outcome of a United Nations debate? The Republicans would have accused Kennedy of gullibility and weakness; the nuclear menace from Cuba would certainly have cost the Democrats control of the House of Representatives. After the Bay of Pigs fiasco, the damage to Kennedy's reputation might have been irreparable even if ultimately some peaceful deal to get the missiles out of Cuba were achieved. Kennedy could not wait. But the country and the world could. Negotiations, however prolonged, would have been better than the risk of World War III. This is how the survivors would have felt. Here Kennedy's political interests and the country's safety diverged. . . .

III

The Role of Our Allies

There was fear in the inner circle that our Western allies might share this cool estimate. Perhaps this was one reason we did not consult them before deciding on a showdown. As Sorensen writes, "Most West Europeans cared nothing about Cuba and thought we were over-anxious about it. Would they support our risking a world war, or an attack on NATO member Turkey, or a move on West Berlin, because we now had a few dozen hostile missiles nearby?" Similarly Schlesinger reveals that Macmillan,* when informed of Kennedy's plans, was troubled "because Europeans had grown so accustomed to living under the nuclear gun that they might wonder what all the fuss was about."

To consult was to invite advice we did not wish to hear. Abel reveals that when Acheson arrived as the President's special emissary to let De Gaulle* know what was afoot, "De Gaulle raised his hand in a delaying gesture that the long departed kings of France might have envied," and asked, "Are you consulting or informing me?" When Acheson confessed that he was there to inform not consult, De Gaulle said dryly, "I am in favor of independent decisions." But three years later De Gaulle was to make an independent decision of his own and ask NATO to remove its bases in France. One reason for this was the Cuban missile crisis. As De Gaulle said at his last press conference February 21:

> . . . while the prospects of a world war breaking out on account of Europe are dissipating, conflicts in which America engages in other parts of the world—as the day before yesterday in Korea, yesterday in Cuba, today in Vietnam—risk, by virtue of that famous escalation, being extended so that the result would be a general conflagration. In that case Europe—whose strategy is, within NATO, that of America—would be automatically involved in the struggle, even when it would not have so desired . . . France's determination to dispose of herself . . . is incompatible with a defense organization in which she finds herself subordinate.

Had the Cuban missile crisis erupted into a thermonuclear exchange, NATO bases in France would automatically have been involved: They would have joined in the attack and been targets for the Russians. France, like the other NATO countries, might have been destroyed without ever being consulted. It is not difficult to understand De Gaulle's distrust of an alliance in which the strongest member can plunge all the others into war without consulting them.

IV

The Dangers Involved

Kennedy no more consulted NATO before deciding to risk World War over Cuba than Khrushchev consulted the Warsaw Pact satellites before taking the risky step of placing missiles on the island. The objection to Khrushchev's course, as to Kennedy's, was primarily political rather than military. There is general agreement now that the Russians may have been tempted to put missiles in Cuba to redress in some small part the enormous missile gap against them which McNamara disclosed after Kennedy took office; for this view we can cite, among other studies, a Rand

---
*Harold Macmillan, British Prime Minister—Eds.
*Charles De Gaulle, at that time President of France—Eds.

Corporation memorandum written for the Air Force by Arnold L. Horelick. In retrospect the Air Force turned out to be the victim of its own ingenuity in developing the U-2. So long as the U.S. had to depend on surmise and normal intelligence, it was possible to inflate the estimates of Russian missile strength to support the demand for larger Air Force appropriations: hence first a bomber gap and then a missile gap, both of which turned out to be non-existent. But when the U-2's began to bring back precise information, the nightmarish missile computations hawked by such Air Force mouthpieces as [Senator] Stuart Symington and Joseph Alsop began to be deflated. Despite the sober warnings of Eisenhower and Allen Dulles* that there was no missile gap, the Democrats used it in the 1960 campaign only to find on taking office that the gap was the other way. Militarily the missiles on Cuba didn't make too much difference. Even the Horelick study for the Air Force admits that these missiles "would presumably have been highly vulnerable to a U.S. first strike, even with conventional bombs," and their number was too small for a Soviet first strike. "Moreover," Horelick writes, "there would have been a problem, though perhaps not an insurmountable one, of coordinating salvoes from close-in and distant bases so as to avoid a ragged attack." (If missiles were fired at the same time from Cuba and Russia, the ones from nearby Cuba would have landed so far in advance as to give additional warning time.) Their deployment in Cuba bears all the earmarks of one of those febrile improvisations to which the impulsive Khrushchev was given, as in his proposals for a "troika" control of the United Nations.

*Director of the Central Intelligence Agency—Eds.

Khrushchev was guilty of a foolish duplicity. Gromyko* gave Kennedy a message from Khrushchev that he would suspend any action about Berlin until after the November election so as not to embarrass Kennedy. This and a Tass communique of September 11 made Kennedy and his advisers feel certain that the Russians would not upset the situation by secretly placing nuclear missiles in Cuba. Tass said the Soviet Union's nuclear weapons were so powerful and its rockets so wide-ranging "that there is no need to search for sites for them beyond the boundaries of the Soviet Union." How could Khrushchev hope to negotiate with Kennedy when the President discovered that he had been so grossly gulled? By first installing the missiles and then telling an easily detected lie about so serious a matter, Khrushchev shares responsibility with Kennedy for bringing the world to its first thermonuclear brink.

Because Kennedy succeeded and Khrushchev surrendered, the missile crisis is being held up as a model of how to run a confrontation in the thermonuclear age. In his February 17 statement advocating negotiations with the Vietcong, and offering them a place in a future government, Senator Robert F. Kennedy said Hanoi "must be given to understand as well that their present public demands are in fact for us to surrender a vital national interest—but that, as a far larger and more powerful nation learned in October of 1962, surrender of a vital interest of the United States is an objective which cannot be achieved." In the missile crisis the Kennedys played their dangerous game skillfully. They kept their means and aims sharply limited, resisting pressures to bomb the island and to demand the removal of Castro as well

*Soviet Foreign Minister Andrei Gromyko—Eds.

as the missiles. For this restraint we are indebted to the Kennedys. But all their skill would have been to no avail if in the end he [Khrushchev] had preferred his prestige, as they preferred theirs, to the danger of a world war. In this respect we are all indebted to Khrushchev.

The missile crisis is a model of what to avoid. This is the lesson John F. Kennedy learned. "His feelings," Schlesinger writes in the finest passage of his *A Thousand Days*,

> underwent a qualitative change after Cuba: A world in which nations threatened each other with nuclear weapons now seemed to him not just an irrational but an intolerable and impossible world. Cuba thus made vivid the sense that all humanity had a common interest in the prevention of nuclear war—an interest far above those national and ideological interests which had once seemed ultimate.

This, and not the saga of a lucky hairbreadth balancing act on an abyss, is what most needs to be remembered about the missile crisis, if we are to avoid another.

The Future of Democracy in the Americas

After the failure of the American-backed invasion of Cuba in April 1961, President Kennedy sought to counter the influence of Latin American communism by proposing an economic aid program for Latin America modeled on the Marshall Plan, an aid program which had enabled Western Europe to regain its strength a decade earlier. The billions of dollars the Alliance for Progress pumped into Latin America provided some marginal economic benefits, such as 140,000 new houses, 8200 classrooms, and 700 community water systems, but did little to produce more democratic governments, a goal which had been part of President Kennedy's original proposal. The nervousness of the United States toward left-wing movements in Latin America was illustrated in 1965. In April President Lyndon Johnson ordered about 22,000 American troops into the Dominican Republic to prevent a feared communist seizure of power. The fears, however, proved to be much exaggerated. In the following selection Dan Kurzman, a journalist who traveled widely in Latin America, discusses the implications of American policy in the area.

Reprinted by permission of G. P. Putnam's Sons from *Santo Domingo: Revolt of the Damned* by Dan Kurzman. Copyright © 1965 by Dan Kurzman. Pp. 297-299, 307-309. Subheadings and footnote added by the editors.

I

The Core of a Dilemma

The United States role in the Dominican crisis pointed up the dilemma in which Washington finds itself entrapped in Latin America. The Johnson Administration has been accused, particularly since its Dominican intervention, of reverting to the days of "gunboat diplomacy" when force was commonly used to impose the will of the United States on the Latin-American countries. On the surface, this might seem true. Marines were, after all, sent into the Dominican Republic in 1965 just as they were sent into hemispheric countries, including the Dominican Republic, in the days of Theodore Roosevelt.

But there is a big difference. In the past, the marines, and other instruments of force, were used primarily for the purpose of furthering U.S. economic and strategic interests. Washington, in fact, rationalized that it had a moral right to do this, since where U.S. capital went local living standards rose. It did not seem to occur to U.S. leaders that this big-stick policy of casual intervention was a form of colonialism alien to the U.S. tradition. Nor did they appear to realize, especially before President Franklin D. Roosevelt instituted far-reaching social reforms in the United States itself, that the economic advantages of U.S. "imperialism" benefited only the ruling classes to the exclusion of the suppressed lower classes.

A gradual change in the U.S. attitude began on a substantial basis with F.D.R.'s Good Neighbor policy, with the accent on nonintervention by the United States in the internal affairs of its Latin-American neighbors. This process crystallized into a truly revolutionary shift in thinking with the inauguration of President Kennedy's Alliance for Progress, which was intended to foster large-scale social and economic development within a democratic framework.

In a sense, the Alliance was a negation of the Good Neighbor policy. For whereas the latter gave the United States an excuse to recognize and accept any rightist or militarist who might come to power in a Latin-American country, since the United States was bound not to interfere, the Alliance, in calling for democratic reforms, gave the United States an excuse to exert pressure for the establishment of democratic regimes. And this excuse, as indicated earlier, was used to the maximum degree when Kennedy sent warships to the Dominican Republic in 1962 to save the country for democracy. In other words, he reintroduced the policy of intervention, but in the service of the people rather than of the dictators as had been the case in the pre-F.D.R. decades.

How does the Dominican intervention differ from the "gunboat diplomacy" of those decades? The guiding purpose of the latter was basically colonial in nature, but this was not true of the former. The Johnson Administration sent troops to Santo Domingo as the result of a genuine fear, whether justified or not, that a second Cuba was about to materialize. These troops were sent with the greatest reluctance and not with the casualness that characterized "big stick" thinking. Collaboration with rightist, nondemocratic forces was pursued as a temporary tactical need in the face of an emergency, not as a matter of policy.

The Johnson Administration is still basically committed to the principles of the Alliance for Progress as espoused by President Kennedy, and the Dominican adventure appears to have been an individual diversion from the main track of policy.

But the fact that this diversion was considered necessary is the core of the American dilemma. On the one hand, Washington wants to promote democratic development as an essential alternative to Castro communism among the oppressed masses. But on the other, it fears such development, particularly in the less-developed countries, since inexperienced democratic regimes, it feels, in many cases subconsciously, will prove less resistant to Communist infiltration than the rightist military regimes with which U.S. diplomats have for so long dealt. It was true that many of these regimes often cozied up to the Communists for their own tactical ends, but there was always a residual confidence that the militarists, with their penchant for the use of force when necessary, would know how to handle the Reds. . . .

II

The Role of Democracy in Latin America

The Administration's distrust in hemispheric democracy reflects a lack of understanding not only of the basic forces at work in Latin America, but of the unique problem posed by that area in relation to other underdeveloped regions. President Kennedy did seem to have appreciated this distinction. He thus emphasized the need for democracy in Latin America, but, in general, did not do so in the Afro-Asian world. A coup in Thailand or in Afghanistan, for example, elicited no White House statements about the importance of constitutionality.

The difference lies basically in the social and cultural backgrounds of Latin America on the one hand, and the Afro-Asian world on the other. The Afro-Asian nations settled their most important social problems when they ousted the European colonialists who had both exploited and helped them for many decades. These colonialists had, in a sense, played the role of the upper ruling class of society. Their physical departure left in charge, in most cases, indigenous nationalists with at least some roots in the people. Many of these nationalist leaders have become dictators, and many are corrupt, but they have also displayed varying degrees of social consciousness. If they haven't given their people political freedom—and in many cases, the Afro-Asians are too underdeveloped to understand the modern state, much less democracy, which, in general, is completely alien to their clan, tribal, and village cultures—they have given them a feeling of being equal with their fellows, and they have instituted many social reforms, often too many in relation to the available resources. Democracy in some of these countries, therefore, is not necessarily an essential prerequisite for social and economic progress, and in some cases is not even desired by the people.

The contrary is true, however, in Latin America. For one thing, it is not easy there to throw out exploiting colonialists. They are not foreigners, but part of the country; built-in colonialists whose Spanish ancestors (Portuguese in the case of Brazil) ruled the continent with an iron hand. These ancestors left a legacy of feudal authoritarianism with those sons who decided not to return to Spain and Portugal when the Latin-American nations won independence. That legacy is today at the root of the region's troubles. As reflected in the case of the Dominican Republic, the independent oligarchies that developed allied themselves with ambitious middle-class military officers who discovered that profitable business opportunities, social prestige, and important privileges could flow from such arrangements.

Thus, no Atatürks* have ruled in Latin America. The dictators there have seldom had roots in the people, nor any inclination to promote social reform, or even economic progress beyond that which has been beneficial to themselves and their relatives and friends. Under these circumstances, real social and economic advances can only be made if the people have a direct say in the government. And this means, in the Latin-American context, either democracy or the twisted equality of communism.

*Kemal Atatürk was a popular leader who ruled Turkey from 1922 to 1938—Eds.

TOPIC 65

THE DECISION TO INTERVENE IN VIETNAM

In 1954 the United States had refused to become directly involved in rescuing the French as they faced military defeat in Indochina (see Reading 330). Ten years later American military forces were directly and openly committed in those parts of Indochina now known as South Vietnam and North Vietnam. In August 1964 American planes bombed several North Vietnamese naval bases. Six months later, in February 1965, the United States initiated massive bombing raids against North Vietnamese supply routes and anything else defined as a military target. In this topic we seek the reasons behind these decisions, the reasons offered by both the United States government and those who opposed its policies.

Reading 348

Vietnam: Central Issue of the 1960s

The involvement of the United States in Vietnam is rooted not only in the Cold War, but in the struggle to end overt European domination of the non-western world. Both aspects of the situation are considered in the following reading. The reader should also look again at Reading 330, which describes American reaction to the Vietnamese situation in 1954.

From *A History of the Western World* by R. R. Palmer and Joel Colton. Copyright © 1971 by Alfred A. Knopf, Inc. Reprinted by permission of the publisher. Pp. 956–957, 997–999.

European domination ended in 1954 in the former French colonial union of French Indochina but not until after seven and a half years of full-scale fighting between French armies and communist-led nationalist forces. The leader of the nationalist forces in Vietnam was the Paris-educated, Moscow-trained communist, Ho Chi Minh who, after waging guerrilla warfare against the Japanese during the war, proclaimed an independent republic at the war's end. The Japanese, as they withdrew, also proclaimed Indochinese independence under an emperor. The French in Paris were willing to concede a large measure of self-rule to the peoples of Indochina, but negotiations broke down and fighting began at the end of 1946. Because the leadership of the independence movement soon fell into the hands of Ho Chi Minh and the communists, the French could claim that they were bent not on preserving nineteenth-century colonial privileges but on stemming the tide of world communism. Yet the advance of communism in Asia, as distinct from its advance in eastern Europe, was closely linked to nationalism and to genuine native discontent.

The United States, anticolonialist but ready to champion anticommunist movements, gave considerable financial aid to the French but after its own involvement in the Korean War shrank from open intervention. The war severely drained the morale and resources of the French Republic. In the end the French forces suffered a disastrous defeat at the battle of Dien Bien Phu in 1954 and shortly thereafter negotiated a truce. At an international conference at Geneva an armistice was arranged and the independence of Vietnam, Laos, and Cambodia recognized. . . .

The agreement at Geneva in 1954 partitioned Vietnam at the seventeenth parallel into a communist North Vietnam with its capital at Hanoi and presided over by Ho Chi Minh and a noncommunist South Vietnam established at Saigon. The partition was to last only until a referendum was held, but the referendum did not take place. Communist guerrilla activities, supported by North Vietnam, and with the backing of the Chinese People's Republic, harassed the republic in South Vietnam. A communist-sponsored National Liberation Front, the Vietcong, operating in the south, grew in strength, terrorizing and coercing the South Vietnamese peasantry but more often than not winning their support.

The United States, under Republican and Democratic administrations, from President Eisenhower on, took the position that it was necessary to check communist aggression in South Vietnam in order to prevent the other states in Asia from being toppled one by one—like a set of dominoes, the theory went. Accordingly, the United States bolstered the South Vietnam regime in Saigon with military advisers, financial backing, and arms and at the same time sought to democratize the regime whose undemocratic practices and widespread corruption it found embarrassing.

American involvement became deeper. In 1960 a few hundred military advisers were present; in 1962, 4,000 soldiers were in combat and the first battle deaths reported. In 1964, on the ground that North Vietnamese torpedo boats had attacked United States ships in the Gulf of Tonkin, President Johnson authorized heavy bombing raids on supply bases in the north in retaliation. The bombing raids mounted in intensity. In searching for the elusive Vietcong in the south, napalm was used to burn and destroy entire villages; the result was the defoliation of hundreds of thousands of acres of land; the survivors became homeless refugees. The commitment of American ground troops and the number of casualties rose steadily. By the end of the 1960s the United States had over 500,000 troops committed; by 1970 American battle deaths, exceeding those in Korea and surpassed only by casualties in the two world wars, rose above 40,000. More tons of explosives had been dropped than had been used against all the Axis powers in the Second World War. The Vietnamese death toll, counting both sides, was estimated at 750,000.

The other Western powers were unenthusiastic and gave little support. Domestic dissatisfaction in the United States swelled; the war in Vietnam became a root cause of riots and disorders in American universities and cities. The question was widely debated whether the United States had the responsibility or capability, despite its enormous

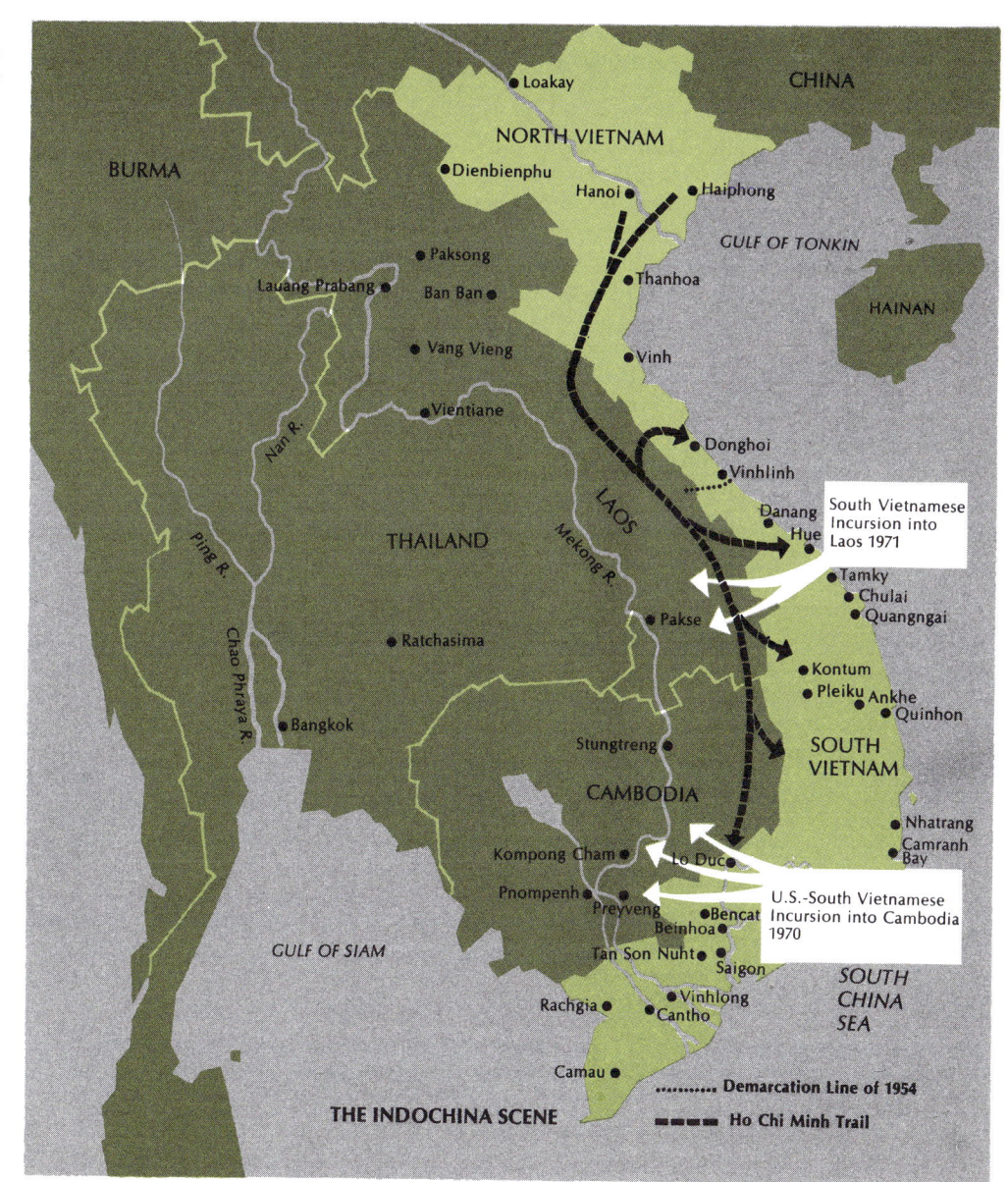

THE INDOCHINA SCENE

strength, to police the world against communist aggression, whether the American presence in Vietnam was an unwanted foreign presence reminiscent of Western intrusion in the age of imperialism, whether bombing raids that reached to within ten miles of the Chinese border might not provoke Chinese direct intervention and provoke a third world war, whether the South Vietnam regime could be stabilized and democratized to make the sacrifices worthwhile, and whether the continued hostilities might not end in the utter destruction of the entire hapless country. Critics with a knowledge of Asian history argued, too, that the Vietnamese had a long record of self-protection from their Chinese neighbors and that even a Vietnam united under communist preponderance would not necessarily mean complete subjugation by the Chinese. Although many continued to believe in the necessity of the American intervention in order to halt communist aggression, by the end of the 1960s the United States took steps to cease its bombing operations, to begin a scheduled withdrawal of troops, and to encourage peace negotiations.

Retaliation in the Gulf of Tonkin (1964)

A highly significant incident in the United States' relationship with Vietnam occurred in August 1964, a few miles off the coast of North Vietnam in the Gulf of Tonkin. Two American destroyers reported having been attacked by North Vietnamese torpedo boats, and in retaliation President Johnson ordered American carrier planes to bomb North Vietnamese naval bases. The incident began a major escalation of the Vietnamese War, or at least of American involvement in that war. In Part I of this reading President Johnson announces his decision. In Part II his Secretary of Defense, Robert McNamara, gives the official American version of the incident in a press conference held shortly after the President's address to the nation.

From the *New York Times*, August 6, 1964. © 1964 by the New York Times Company. Reprinted by permission.

I

The President Announces a Decision

My fellow Americans:

As President and Commander in Chief, it is my duty to the American people to report that renewed hostile actions against United States ships on the high seas in the Gulf of Tonkin have today required me to order the military forces of the United States to take action in reply.

The initial attack on the destroyer Maddox on Aug. 2 was repeated today by a number of hostile vessels attacking two U.S. destroyers with torpedoes.

The destroyers and supporting aircraft acted at once on the orders I gave after the initial act of aggression.

We believe at least two of the attacking boats were sunk. There were no U.S. losses.

The performance of commanders and crews in this engagement is in the highest tradition of the United States Navy.

But repeated acts of violence against the armed forces of the United States must be met not only with alert defense but with positive reply.

That reply is being given, as I speak to you tonight. Air action is now in execution against gunboats and certain supporting facilities in North Vietnam which have been used in these hostile operations.

In the larger sense, this new act of aggression aimed directly at our own forces again brings home to all of us in the United States the importance of the struggle for peace and security in Southeast Asia.

Aggression by terror against the peaceful villages of South Vietnam has now been joined by open aggression on the high seas against the United States of America.

The determination of all Americans to carry out our full commitment to the people and to the Government of South Vietnam will be redoubled by this outrage. Yet our response for the present will be limited and fitting.

II

McNamara: Attacks Were Unprovoked

Secretary McNamara: As you know on August 2 and again on August 4, North Vietnamese surface vessels attacked U.S. destroyers operating on routine patrol in international waters in the Gulf of Tonkin.

In retaliation for this unprovoked attack on the high seas, our forces have struck the bases used by the North Vietnamese patrol craft. During the night, 64 attack sorties were launched from the U.S. carriers Ticonderoga and Constellation against the four North Vietnamese patrol bases and certain support facilities associated with those bases....

The oil storage depot, which contains 14 tanks, approximately 10 percent of the total petroleum storage capacity of North Vietnam, was 90 percent destroyed. Smoke was observed rising to 14,000 feet. In addition

I. F. Stone: Brainwashing the Public

The President's version of the action which took place in the Gulf of Tonkin raised a number of serious doubts in the minds of some critics of American foreign policy. I. F. Stone, the prominent Washington journalist who was also critical of American action in the Cuban missile crisis, launched the attack on the official version by raising a number of penetrating questions.

From I. F. Stone, "What Few Know About the Tonkin Bay Incidents," *I. F. Stone's Weekly*, XII (August 24, 1964), pp. 1-4. Subheadings added by the editors.

I

Concealing the Truth

The American government and the American press have kept the full truth about the Tonkin Bay incidents from the American public. Let us begin with the retaliatory bombing raids on North Vietnam. When I went to New York to cover the UN Security Council debate on the affair, UN correspondents at lunch recalled cynically that four months earlier Adlai Stevenson told the Security Council the U.S. had "repeatedly expressed" its emphatic disapproval "of retaliatory raids, wherever they occur and by whomever they are committed." But none mentioned this in their dispatches....

Even in wartime, reprisals are supposed to be kept within narrow limits. Hackworth's *Digest*, the State Department's huge Talmud of international law, quotes an old War Department manual, *Rules of Land Warfare*, as authoritative on the subject. This says reprisals are never to be taken "merely for revenge" but "only as an unavoidable last resort" to "enforce the recognized rules of civilized warfare." Even then reprisals "should not be excessive or exceed the degree of violence committed by the enemy." These were the principles we applied at the Nuremberg trials. Our reprisal raids on North Vietnam hardly conformed to these standards. By our own account, in self-defense, we had already sunk three or four attacking torpedo boats in two incidents. In neither were our ships damaged nor any of our men hurt; indeed, one bullet imbedded in one destroyer hull is the only proof we have been able to muster that the second of the attacks even took place. To fly 64 bombing sorties in reprisal over four North Vietnamese bases and an oil depot, destroying or damaging 25 North Vietnamese PT boats, a major part of that tiny navy, was hardly punishment to fit the crime. What was our hurry? Why did we have to shoot from the hip and then go to the Security Council? Who was Johnson trying to impress? Ho Chi-minh? Or Barry Goldwater?

This is how it looks on the basis of our own public accounts. It looks worse if one probes behind them. Here we come to the questions raised by Morse of Oregon on the Senate floor Aug. 5 and 6 during debate on the resolution giving Johnson a pre-dated declaration of war in Southeast Asia. Morse was speaking on the basis of information given in executive session by Secretaries Rusk and McNamara to a joint session of the Senate Committee on Foreign Relations and Armed Services. Morse said he was not justifying the attacks on U.S. ships in the Bay of Tonkin but "as in domestic criminal law," he added, "crimes are some-

---

to the damage to the torpedo boat bases and their support facilities, approximately 25 of the boats were damaged or destroyed.

Two of our aircraft were lost, two of our aircraft were damaged, all others have been recovered safely on the carriers. The destroyers Maddox and Turner Joy, which have been operating on routine patrol in the Gulf of Tonkin, have resumed their patrol operations in international waters.

Last night I announced that moves were under way to reinforce our forces in the Pacific area. These moves include the following actions: First, an attack carrier group has been transferred from the First Fleet on the Pacific coast to the Western Pacific. Secondly, interceptor and fighter bomber aircraft have been moved into South Vietnam. Thirdly, fighter bomber aircraft have been moved into Thailand. Fourthly, interceptor and fighter bomber squadrons have been transferred from the United States into advance bases in the Pacific. Fifthly, an antisubmarine task force group has been moved into the South China Sea. And finally, selected army and marine forces have been erted and readied for movement....

Q. Mr. Secretary, how do you explain these attacks?

A. I can't explain them. They were unprovoked. As I told you last night, our vessels were clearly in international waters. Our vessels, when attacked, were operating in this area, roughly 60 miles off of the North Vietnamese coast.

Q. There have been reports that South Vietnamese vessels were showing or taking some sort of action against North Vietnam approximately at this time.

A. No, to the best of my knowledge, there were no operations during the period I was describing last night.

times committed under provocation" and this "is taken into account by a wise judge in imposing sentence."

II

How Close Were the Patrols?

Morse revealed that U.S. warships were on patrol in Tonkin Bay nearby during the shelling of two islands off the North Vietnamese coast on Friday, July 31, by South Vietnamese vessels. Morse said our warships were within 3 to 11 miles of North Vietnamese territory, at the time, although North Vietnam claims a 12-mile limit. Morse declared that the U.S. "knew that the bombing was going to take place." He noted that General Khanh had been demanding escalation of the war to the North and said that with this shelling of the islands it was escalated. Morse declared the attack was made "by South Vietnamese naval vessels—not by junks but by armed vessels of the PT boat type" given to South Vietnam as part of U.S. military aid. Morse said it was not just another attempt to infiltrate agents but "a well thought-out military operation." Morse charged that the presence of our warships in the proximity "where they could have given protection, if it became necessary" was "bound to be looked upon by our enemies as an act of provocation." The press, which dropped an Iron Curtain weeks ago on the anti-war speeches of Morse and Gruening, ignored this one, too.

Yet a reading of the debate will show that Fulbright and Russell, the chairmen of the two committees Rusk and McNamara had briefed in secret session, did not deny Morse's facts in their defense of the Administration and did not meet the issue he raised. Fulbright's replies to questions were hardly a model of

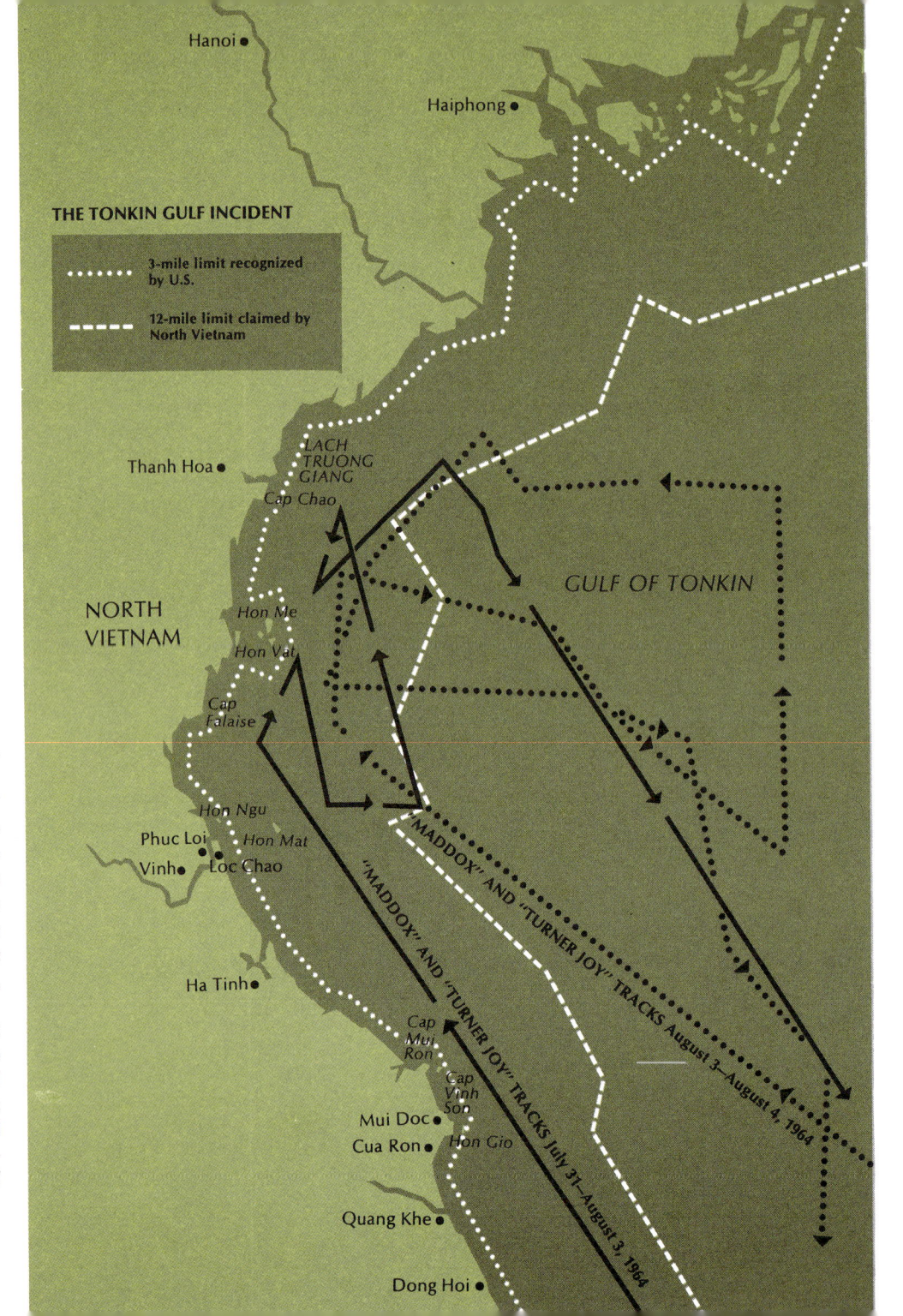

THE TONKIN GULF INCIDENT

· · · · · 3-mile limit recognized by U.S.

- - - - - 12-mile limit claimed by North Vietnam

frankness. When Ellender of Louisiana asked him at whose request we were patrolling in the Bay of Tonkin, Fulbright replied: "These are international waters. Our assistance to South Vietnam is at the request of the South Vietnamese government. The particular measures we may take in connection with that request is our own responsibility."

Senator Nelson of Wisconsin wanted to know how close to the shore our ships had been patrolling:

Mr. Fulbright: "It was testified that they went in at least 11 miles in order to show that we do not recognize a 12-mile limit, which I believe North Vietnam has asserted."

Mr. Nelson: "The patrolling was for the purpose of demonstrating to the North Vietnamese that we did not recognize a 12-mile limit?"

Mr. Fulbright: "That was one reason given...."

Mr. Nelson: "It would be mighty risky if Cuban PT boats were firing on Florida, for Russian armed ships or destroyers to be patrolling between us and Cuba, 11 miles out."

When Ellender asked whether our warships were there to protect the South Vietnamese vessels shelling the islands, Fulbright replied:

> The ships were not assigned to protect anyone. They were conducting patrol duty. The question was asked specifically of the highest authorities, the Secretary of Defense and the Secretary of State. They stated without equivocation that these ships, the Maddox and the C. Turner Joy, were not on convoy duty. They had no connection whatever with any Vietnamese ships that might have been operating in the same general area.

Fulbright did not deny that both destroyers were in the area at the time of the July 31 shelling and inside the territorial limits claimed by North Vietnam. He did not deny Morse's charge that the U.S. knew about the shelling of the islands before it took place. He merely denied that the warships were there to cover the operation in any way. Our warships, according to the official account, just happened to be hanging around. Morse's point—which neither Fulbright nor Russell challenged—was that they had no business to be in an area where an attack was about to take place, that this was bound to appear provocative. Indeed the only rational explanation for their presence at the time was that the Navy was looking for trouble, daring the North Vietnamese to do something about it.

III

Why Our Ships Moved Out to Sea

Morse made another disclosure. "I think I violate no privilege or secrecy," he declared, "if I say that subsequent to the bombing, and apparently because there was some concern about the intelligence that we were getting, our ships took out to sea." Was this intelligence that the ships were about to be attacked within the territorial waters claimed by North Vietnam? Morse said our warships went out to sea and "finally, on Sunday, the PT boats were close enough for the first engagement to take place." This dovetails with a curious answer given by Senator Russell at another point in the debate to Senator Scott of Pennsylvania when the latter asked whether Communist China had not published a series of warnings (as required by international law) against violations of the 12-mile limit. Russell confirmed this but said, "I might add that our vessels had turned away from the North Vietnamese shore and were making for the middle of the gulf, *where there could be no question,* at the time they were attacked."

The italics are ours and call attention to an evident uneasiness about our legal position. The uneasiness is justified. A great many questions of international law are raised by the presence of our warships within an area claimed by another country as its territorial waters while its shores were being shelled by ships we supplied to a satellite power. There is, first of all, some doubt as to whether warships have a right of "innocent passage" through territorial waters even under peaceful circumstances. There is, secondly, the whole question of territorial limits. The 3-mile limit was set some centuries ago by the range of a cannon shot. It has long been obsolete but is favored by nations with large navies. We make the 3-mile limit the norm when it suits our purposes but widen it when we need to. We claim another 9 miles as "contiguous waters" in which we can enforce our laws on foreign ships. While our planes on reconnaissance operate three miles off other people's shores, we enforce an Air Defense Identification Zone on our own coasts, requiring all planes to identify themselves when two hours out. In any case, defense actions may be taken beyond territorial limits. The law as cited in the U.S. Naval Academy's handbook, *International Law for Sea-Going Officers,* is that "the right of a nation to protect itself from injury" is "not restrained to territorial limits... It may watch its coast and seize ships that are approaching it with an intention to violate its laws. It is not obliged to wait until the offense is consummated before it can act."

More important in this case is the doctrine of "hot pursuit." The North Vietnamese radio claims that in the first attack it chased the U.S. warships away from its shores. "The right of hot pursuit," says Schwarzenberger's *Manual of International Law*, "is the right to continue the pursuit of a ship from the territorial sea into the high sea." The logic of this, our Naval Academy handbook explains, is that "the offender should not go free simply because of the proximity of the high seas." It is easy to imagine how fully these questions would be aired if we spotted Russian ships hanging around in our waters while Cuban PT boats shelled Key West....

IV
How the Public Is Brainwashed

These circumstances cast a very different light on the Maddox affair, but very few Americans are aware of them. The process of brainwashing the public starts with off-the-record briefings for newspapermen in which all sorts of far-fetched theories are suggested to explain why the tiny North Vietnamese navy would be mad enough to venture an attack on the Seventh fleet, one of the world's most powerful. Everything is discussed except the possibility that the attack might have been provoked. In this case the "information agencies," i.e., the propaganda apparatus of the government, handed out two versions, one for domestic, the other for foreign consumption. The image created at home was that the U.S. had manfully hit back at an unprovoked attack—no paper tiger we. On the other hand, friendly foreign diplomats were told that the South Vietnamese had pulled a raid on the coast and we had been forced to back them up. As some of the truth began to trickle out, the information agencies fell back on the theory that maybe the North Vietnamese had "miscalculated." That our warships may have been providing cover for an escalation in raiding activities never got through to public consciousness at all.

The two attacks themselves are still shrouded in mystery. The Maddox claims to have fired three warning shots across the bow of her pursuers; three warning shots are used to make a merchantman heave-to for inspection. A warship would take this as the opening of fire, not as a warning signal. The North Vietnamese radio admitted the first encounter but claimed its patrol boats chased the Maddox out of territorial waters. The second alleged attack North Vietnam calls a fabrication. It is strange that though we claim three boats sunk, we picked up no flotsam and jetsam as proof from the wreckage. Nor have any pictures been provided. Whatever the true story, the second incident seems to have triggered off a long planned attack of our own.

Further Light on the Gulf of Tonkin Episode

Shortly after the incidents in the Gulf of Tonkin and the American bombings that followed, the United States Congress responded to the urging of President Johnson and passed the so-called Tonkin Gulf Resolution of August 1964. The resolution authorized the President to take any action he felt necessary to protect American security in Vietnam. Over the next three years the Tonkin Gulf Resolution was used as a justification for large-scale commitment of American military forces. By 1968 the frustrations of the war had generated a great deal of dissent in the United States, dissent reflected in hearings held by the Senate Foreign Relations Committee. The committee closely questioned government officials, such as Secretary of Defense Robert McNamara, about what had happened in the Gulf of Tonkin in August 1964.

From I. F. Stone, "McNamara and Tonkin Bay: The Unanswered Questions," *New York Review of Books*, X (March 28, 1968), p. 11.

In his prepared statement [of Feb. 20, 1968] McNamara made an admission which must have cost his pride a good deal. It shows that he was not in full control of his own Department at a crucial moment. The fact that he disclosed it himself would lead a trained lawyer to believe that he knew or feared that documents in the hands of the Committee's staff had already disclosed this, and that he thought it best to slip the fact into his statement to protect himself under interrogation. This is what the Secretary said: "I learned subsequent to my testimony of August 6, 1964, that another South Vietnamese bombardment took place on the night of August 3–4." And at page 90 of the printed record, under interrogation by Senator Cooper, McNamara added a supplementary revelation. "At the time of the specific incidents of August 4," he admitted to Cooper, "I did not know of the attack by the South Vietnamese, but we knew of the operations, and some senior commanders above the level of the commanders of the task force did know the specific dates of the operations." This seems to mean that certain senior commanders knew something McNamara still did not know three days later when he appeared before the Senate committees on the Tonkin Gulf resolution four years ago.

To appreciate the import of this revelation one must turn to the Morse speeches, and to the classified messages and information he courageously made public in them. If we look at Morse's speech of February 29 we will see that the patrols on which the Maddox was engaged were far from "routine," not only in the sense that they were electronic espionage missions, but that, when the first attack occurred on the Maddox August 2, 1964, it was only the third occasion since 1962—or within two and a half years—on which an American naval ship had approached the North Vietnamese coast. "The appearance of an American destroyer," Morse disclosed on the basis of the Pentagon documents obtained by the committee but still classified, "the appearance of an American destroyer along the Vietnam coast was highly unusual." The next point to be noted is that the first attack on the Maddox followed by 40 hours the first coastal bombardment of North Vietnam by the raiding vessels we had supplied the South Vietnamese.

Now we can understand the significance of McNamara's revelation. On August 2 the Maddox was attacked for the first time. On August 3 the President warned of serious consequences if that attack were repeated and announced that we were not only sending the Maddox back into those waters but a second destroyer, the Turner Joy, with it. That night, the night of August 3–4, there was a second coastal bombardment, the knowledge of which—so McNamara says—was kept from him though it was known to certain higher naval commanders and presumably arranged by the joint South Vietnamese and MACV headquarters in Saigon, which we now know from this new hearing directed these naval attacks. It was the night after this second bombardment—the night of August 4–5—that the alleged second attack on the Maddox and the new destroyer accompanying it took place. Whether the second attack actually took place or not—and this is still unclear—that new coastal bombardment was a provocation likely to make a second clash more probable, and therefore to trigger the retaliation Johnson had already threatened.

State Department: Aggressive War from the North (1965)

In February 1965 the United States began large-scale bombing raids on North Vietnamese targets. Recognizing the action as a major escalation of the war, the Department of State issued a so-called "White Paper," which explained and justified the bombing policy as a logical result of communist aggression.

From United States Department of State, *Aggression From the North: The Record of North Viet-Nam's Campaign to Conquer South Viet-Nam* (Washington, D. C., 1965), pp. 3–5, 11, 22–24, 28–29. Subheadings added by the editors.

I

Armed Aggression against South Vietnam

The hard core of the Communist forces attacking South Viet-Nam are men trained in North Viet-Nam. They are ordered into the South and remain under the military discipline of the Military High Command in Hanoi. Special training camps operated by the North Vietnamese army give political and military training to the infiltrators. Increasingly the forces sent into the South are native North Vietnamese who have never seen South Viet-Nam. A special infiltration unit, the 70th Transportation Group, is responsible for moving men from North Viet-Nam into the South via infiltration trails through Laos. Another special unit, the maritime infiltration group, sends weapons and supplies and agents by sea into the South.

The infiltration rate has been increasing. From 1959 to 1960, when Hanoi was establishing its infiltration pipeline, at least 1,800 men, and possibly 2,700 more, moved into South Viet-Nam from the North. The flow increased to a minimum of 3,700 in 1961 and at least 5,400 in 1962. There was a modest decrease in 1963 to 4,200 confirmed infiltrators, though later evidence is likely to raise this figure.

For 1964 the evidence is still incomplete. However, it already shows that a minimum of 4,400 infiltrators entered the South, and it is estimated more than 3,000 others were sent in.

There is usually a time lag between the entry of infiltrating troops and the discovery of clear evidence they have entered. This fact, plus collateral evidence of increased use of the infiltration routes, suggests strongly that

1964 was probably the year of greatest infiltration so far.

Thus, since 1959, nearly 20,000 VC officers, soldiers, and technicians are known to have entered South Viet-Nam under orders from Hanoi. Additional information indicates that an estimated 17,000 more infiltrators were dispatched to the South by the regime in Hanoi during the past 6 years. It can reasonably be assumed that still other infiltration groups have entered the South for which there is no evidence yet available.

To some the level of infiltration from the North may seem modest in comparison with the total size of the Armed Forces of the Republic of Viet-Nam. But one-for-one calculations are totally misleading in the kind of warfare going on in Viet-Nam. First, a high proportion of infiltrators from the North are well-trained officers, cadres, and specialists. Second, it has long been realized that in guerrilla combat the burdens of defense are vastly heavier than those of attack. In Malaya, the Philippines, and elsewhere a ratio of at least 10-to-1 in favor of the forces of order was required to meet successfully the threat of the guerrillas' hit-and-run tactics.

In the calculus of guerrilla warfare the scale of North Vietnamese infiltration into the South takes on a very different meaning. For the infiltration of 5,000 guerrilla fighters in a given year is the equivalent of marching perhaps 50,000 regular troops across the border, in terms of the burden placed on the defenders.

Above all, the number of proved and probable infiltrators from the North should be seen in relation to the size of the VC forces. It is now estimated that the Viet Cong number approximately 35,000 so-called hard-core forces, and another 60,000–80,000 local forces. It is thus apparent that infiltrators from the North—allowing for casualties—make up the majority of the so-called hard-core Viet Cong. Personnel from the North, in short, are now and have always been the backbone of the entire VC operation.

It is true that many of the lower level elements of the VC forces are recruited within South Viet-Nam. However, the thousands of reported cases of VC kidnapings and terrorism make it abundantly clear that threats and other pressures by the Viet Cong play a major part in such recruitment....

II

Infiltration by Native North Vietnamese

The Communist authorities in Hanoi are now assigning native North Vietnamese in increasing numbers to join the VC forces in South Viet-Nam. Heretofore, those in charge of the infiltration effort have sought to fill their quotas with soldiers and others born in the South. The 90,000 troops that moved from South Viet-Nam to the North when the Geneva accords ended the Indochina War have provided an invaluable reservoir for this purpose. Now, apparently, that source is running dry. The casualty rate has been high, and obviously many of those who were in fighting trim 10 years ago are no longer up to the rigors of guerrilla war.

In any case, reports of infiltration by native North Vietnamese in significant numbers have been received in Saigon for several months. It is estimated that as many as 75 percent of the more than 4,400 Viet Cong who are known to have entered the South in the first 8 months of 1964 were natives of North Viet-Nam....

III

Organization—Centered in Hanoi

The VC military and political apparatus in South Viet-Nam is an extension of an elaborate military and political structure in North Viet-Nam which directs and supplies it with the tools for conquest. The Ho Chi Minh regime has shown that it is ready to allocate every resource that can be spared—whether it be personnel, funds, or equipment—to the cause of overthrowing the legitimate Government in South Viet-Nam and of bringing all Viet-Nam under Communist rule.

Political direction and control of the Viet Cong is supplied by the Lao Dong Party, i.e. the Communist Party, led by Ho Chi Minh. Party agents are responsible for indoctrination, recruitment, political training, propaganda, anti-Government demonstrations, and other activities of a political nature. The considerable intelligence-gathering facilities of the party are also at the disposal of the Viet Cong.

Overall direction of the VC movement is the responsibility of the Central Committee of the Lao Dong Party. Within the Central Committee a special Reunification Department has been established. This has replaced the "Committee for Supervision of the South" mentioned in intelligence reports 2 years ago. It lays down broad strategy for the movement to conquer South Viet-Nam....

The National Front for the Liberation of South Viet-Nam is the screen behind which the Communists carry out their program of conquest. It is the creature of the Communist Government in Hanoi. As noted above the Communist Party in the North demanded establishment of such a "front" three months before its formation was actually announced in December 1960. It was designed to create the illusion that the Viet Cong campaign of subversion was truly indigenous to South Viet-Nam rather than an externally directed Communist plan.

The front has won support primarily from the Communist world. Its radio faithfully repeats the propaganda themes of Hanoi and Peiping. When its representatives travel abroad, they do so with North Vietnamese passports and sponsorship. The front's program copies that of the Lao Dong Party in North Viet-Nam. . . .

IV

Military Organization

Military affairs of the Viet Cong are the responsibility of High Command of the People's Army of North Viet-Nam and the Ministry of

The lightning speed of attack in modern war appears in this assault by American airborne troops against a suspected Vietcong position in South Vietnam in 1966.

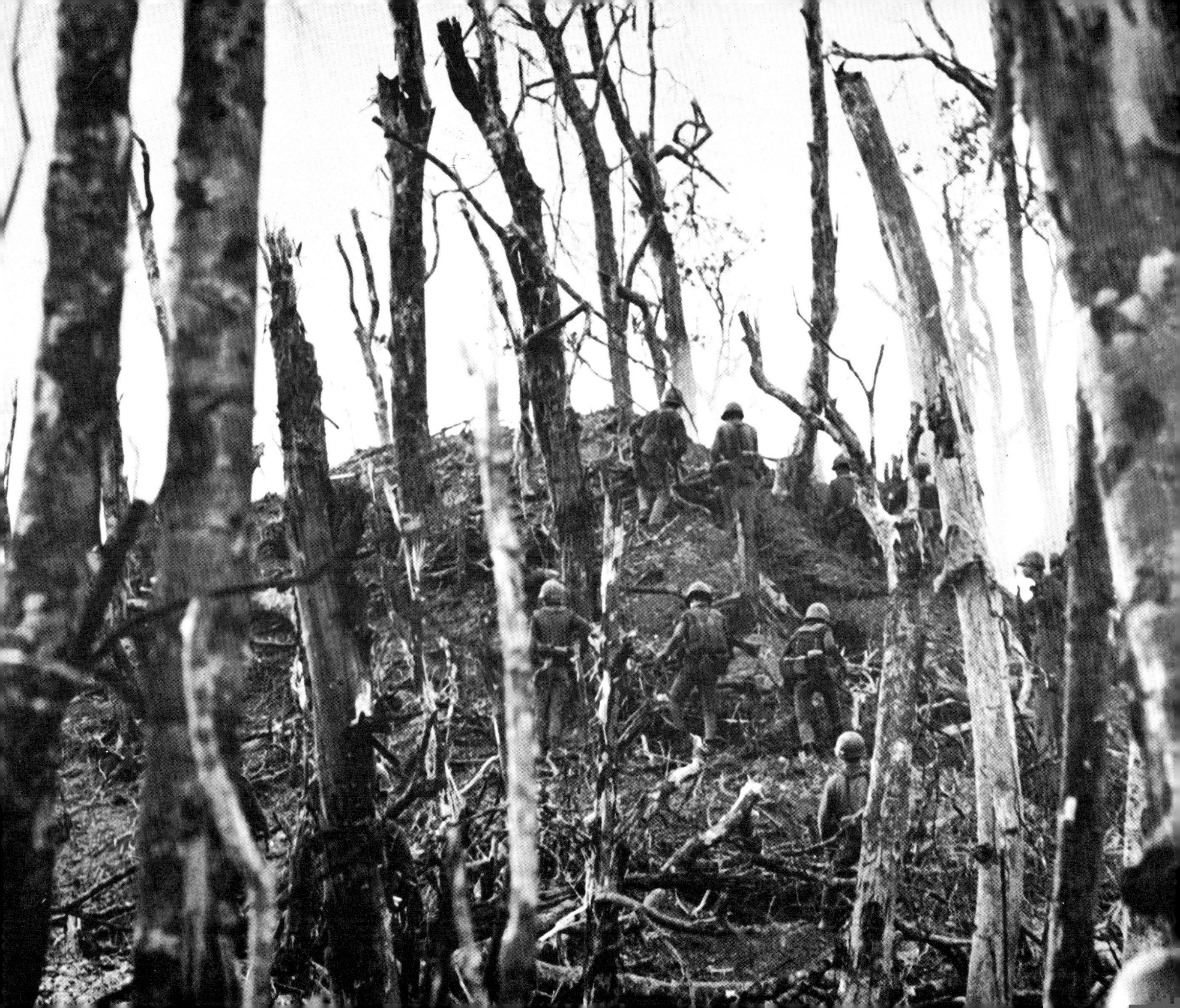

The weary grind of defense continues in modern warfare despite new communications and weapons; men under attack must still dig in, fight back, and wait for help. Here South Vietnamese soldiers seek out enemy mortar gunners who had been dropping shells on their firebase in 1966. American helicopter gunships came to their aid in helping to destroy the mortar position.

Defense, under close supervision from the Lao Dong Party. These responsibilities include operational plans, assignments of individuals and regular units, training programs, infiltration of military personnel and supplies, military communications, tactical intelligence, supplies, and the like. The six military regions are the same as those of the VC political organization.

The military structure of the Viet Cong is an integral part of the political machinery that controls every facet of VC activity in South Viet-Nam under Hanoi's overall direction. Each political headquarters from the Central Office down to the village has a military component which controls day-to-day military operations. Similarly, each military headquarters has a political element, an individual or a small staff. This meshing of political and military activity is designed to insure the closest cooperation in support of the total Communist mission. It also gives assurance of political control over the military. . . .

The hard core of the VC military organization is the full-time regular unit usually based on a province or region. These are well-trained and highly disciplined guerrilla fighters. They follow a rigid training schedule that is roughly two-thirds military and one-third political in content. This compares with the 50–50 proportion for district units and the 70 percent political and 30 percent military content of the village guerrilla's training.

The size of the Viet Cong regular forces has grown steadily in recent years. For example, the Viet Cong have five regimental headquarters compared with two in 1961. And the main VC force is composed of 50 battalions, 50 percent more than before. There are an estimated 139 VC companies. Hard-core VC strength now is estimated at about 35,000, whereas it was less than 20,000 in 1961.

The main force battalions are well armed with a variety of effective weapons including 75-mm. recoilless rifles and 81–82-mm. mortars. The companies and smaller units are equally well equipped and have 57-mm. recoilless rifles and 60-mm. mortars in their inventory. It is estimated that the Viet Cong have at least 130 81-mm. mortars and 300 60-mm. mortars. There is no precise estimate for the number of recoilless rifles in their hands, but it is believed that most main force units are equipped with them. In at least one recent action the Viet Cong employed a 75-mm. pack howitzer. This mobile weapon, which has a range of 8,500 yards, will increase the Viet Cong capabilities to launch long-range attacks against many stationary targets in the country.

Supporting the main force units of the Viet Cong are an estimated 60,000–80,000 part-time guerrillas. They are generally organized at the district level where there are likely to be several companies of 50 or more men each. These troops receive only half pay, which means they must work at least part of the time to eke out a living.

Below the irregular guerrilla forces of the district are the part-time, village-based guerrillas. They are available for assignment by higher headquarters and are used for harassment and sabotage. They are expected to warn nearby VC units of the approach of any force of the legal government. They provide a pool for recruitment into the VC district forces.

The record shows that many of the village guerrillas are dragooned into service with the Viet Cong. Some are kidnaped; others are threatened; still others join to prevent their families from being harmed. Once in the Viet Cong net, many are reluctant to leave for fear of punishment by the authorities or reprisal by the Communists. . . .

V

The Reason for Air Strikes

Though it has been apparent for years that the regime in Hanoi was conducting a campaign of conquest against South Viet-Nam, the Government in Saigon and the Government of the United States both hoped that the danger could be met within South Viet-Nam itself. The hope that any widening of the conflict might be avoided was stated frequently.

The leaders in Hanoi chose to respond with greater violence. They apparently interpreted restraint as indicating lack of will. Their efforts were pressed with greater vigor and armed attacks and incidents of terror multiplied.

Clearly the restraint of the past was not providing adequately for the defense of South Viet-Nam against Hanoi's open aggression. It was mutually agreed between the Governments of the Republic of Viet-Nam and the United States that further means for providing for South Viet-Nam's defense were required. Therefore, air strikes have been made against some of the military assembly points and supply bases from which North Viet-Nam is

Reading 353

conducting its aggression against the South. These strikes constitute a limited response fitted to the aggression that produced them.

Until the regime in Hanoi decides to halt its intervention in the South, or until effective steps are taken to maintain peace and security in the area, the Governments of South Viet-Nam and the United States will continue necessary measures of defense against the Communist armed aggression coming from North Viet-Nam.

I. F. Stone: Civil War in the South (1965)

When the United States began to bomb North Vietnam, it seemed evident to many persons that the United States had moved closer to a major commitment of American forces in Southeast Asia. I. F. Stone, one of the most persistent critics of American foreign policy, takes a hard look at the State Department's White Paper (Reading 352) and offers an analysis of both the White Paper and United States policy in general.

From I. F. Stone, "A Reply To The White Paper," *I. F. Stone's Weekly*, March 8, 1965. Subheadings added by the editors.

I

How Many Northern Guerrillas?

That North Viet-Nam supports the guerrillas in South Viet-Nam is no more a secret than that the United States supports the South

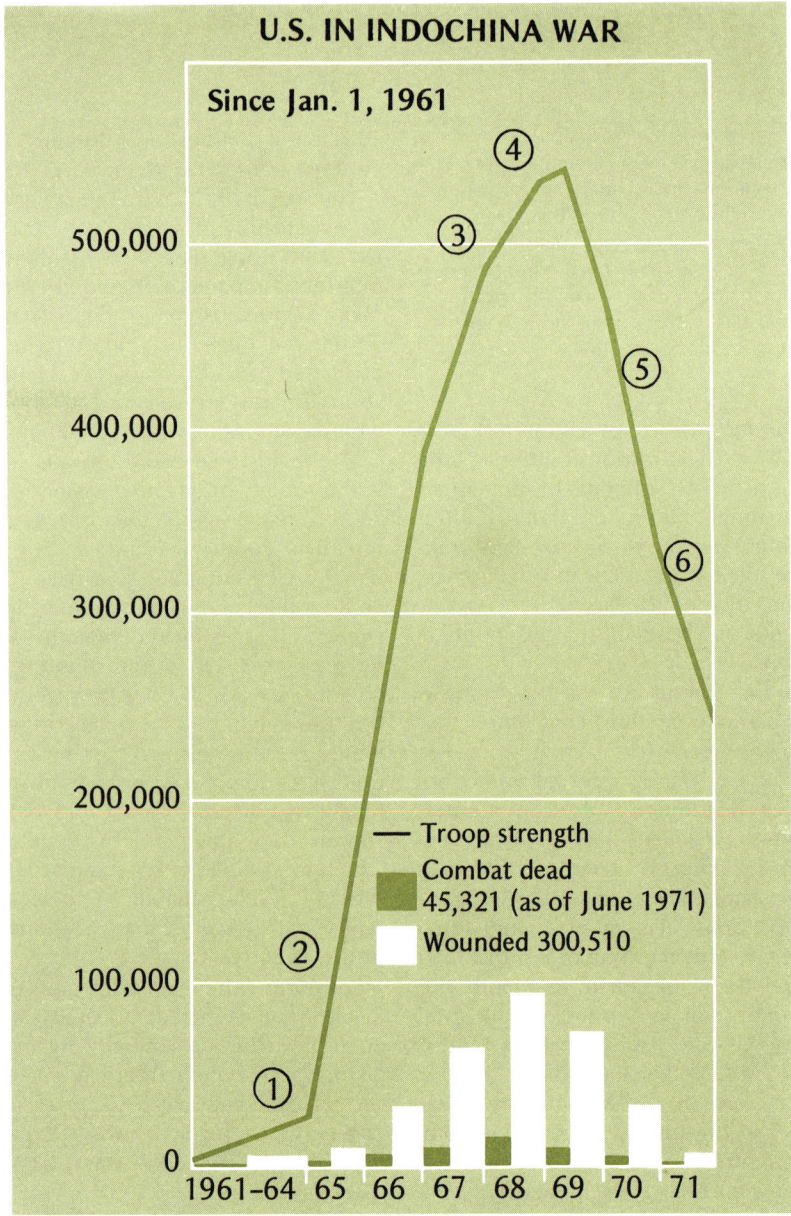

U.S. IN INDOCHINA WAR

Since Jan. 1, 1961

— Troop strength
■ Combat dead 45,321 (as of June 1971)
□ Wounded 300,510

1. Gulf of Tonkin Incident and Congressional resolution.
2. Widespread bombing of North Viet-Nam begins.
3. Viet Cong Tet Offensive.
4. Paris peace talks begin.
5. Invasion of Cambodia.
6. Invasion of Laos.

Vietnamese government against them. The striking thing about the State Department's new White Paper is how little support it can prove. . . .

The White Paper's story on the influx of men from the North . . . deserves a closer analysis than the newspapers have given it. Appendix C provides an elaborate table from 1959–60 to 1964 inclusive, showing the number of "confirmed" military infiltrees per year from the North. The total is given as 19,550. One way to measure this number is against that of the military we have assigned to South Viet-Nam in the same years. These now total 23,500, or 25 percent more, and 1,000 are to be added in the near future. The number of North Vietnamese infiltrees is "based on information . . . from at least two independent sources." *Nowhere are we told how many men who infiltrated from the North have actually been captured.* There is reason to wonder whether the count of infiltrees may be as bloated as the count of Viet-Cong dead; in both cases the numbers used are estimates rather than actual bodies.

The White Paper calls the war an invasion and claims "that as many as 75 percent of the more than 4,400 Viet-Cong who are known to have entered the South in the first eight months of 1964 were natives of North Viet-Nam." But a careful reading of the text and the appendices turns up the names of only six North Vietnamese infiltrees. In Part I of the White Paper, Section B gives "individual case histories of North Vietnamese soldiers" sent South by Hanoi but all nine of these are of South Vietnamese origin. The next Section, C, is headed "Infiltration of Native North Vietnamese." It names five infiltrees but one of these is also from the South. That leaves four North Vietnamese natives. Then, in Appendix C, we are given the case histories and photographs of nine other Viet-Cong sent south by Hanoi. The report does not explain which ones were originally from the South but it does give the names of the provinces in which they were born. When these are checked, it turns out that only two of the nine were born in North Viet-Nam. This gives us a total of six northern infiltrees. It is strange that after five years of fighting, the White Paper can cite so few.

II

A Rebellion in the South

None of this is discussed frankly in the White Paper. To do so would be to bring the war into focus as a rebellion in the South, which may owe some men and materiel to the North but is largely dependent on popular indigenous support for its manpower, as it is on captured U.S. weapons for its supply. The White Paper withholds all evidence which points to a civil war. It also fails to tell the full story of the July, 1962, Special Report by the International Control Commission. Appendix A quotes that portion in which the Commission 2-to-1 (Poland dissenting) declared that the North had in specific instances sent men and materiel south in violation of the Geneva Accords. But nowhere does the State Department mention that the same report also condemned South Viet-Nam and the U.S., declaring that they had entered into a military alliance in violation of the Geneva Agreements. The U.S. was criticized because it then had about 5,000 military advisers in South Viet-Nam. The Geneva Accords limited the U.S. military mission to the 684 in Viet-Nam at the time of the 1954 cease fire. The U.S. and South Viet-Nam were also criticized by the I.C.C. for hamstringing the Commission's efforts to check on imports of arms in violation of the Geneva Accords.

The reader would never guess from the White Paper that the Geneva Accords promised that elections would be held in 1956 to reunify the country. The 1961 Blue Book at least mentioned the elections, though somehow, managing to make them seem a plot. "It was the Communists' calculation," the Blue Book put it, "that nationwide elections scheduled in the accords for 1956 would turn all of South Viet-Nam over to them. . . . The authorities in South Viet-Nam refused to fall into this well-laid trap." The White Paper omits mention of the elections altogether and says, "South Viet-Nam's refusal to fall in with Hanoi's scheme for peaceful takeover came as a heavy blow to the Communists." This is not the most candid and objective presentation. From the Viet-Minh point of view, the failure to hold the elections promised them when they laid down their arms was the second broken promise of the West. The earlier one was in 1946 when they made an agreement to accept limited autonomy within the French union, and welcomed the returning French troops as comrades of the liberation. Most of the French military did not want to recognize even this limited form of independence, and chose instead the road which led after eight years of war to Dien Bien Phu.

III

That "Economic Miracle" Again

The most disingenuous part of the White Paper is that in which it discusses the origins of the present war. It pictures the war as an attack from the North, launched in desperation because the "economic miracle" in the

South under Diem had destroyed Communist hopes of a peaceful takeover from within. Even the strategic hamlets are described as "designed to improve the peasant's livelihood" and we are asked to believe that for the first time in history a guerrilla war spread not because the people were discontented but because their lot was improving!

The true story is a story of lost opportunities. The Communist countries acquiesced in the failure to hold elections. Diem had a chance to make his part of the country a democratic showcase. The year 1956 was a bad one in the North. There was a peasant uprising and widespread resentment among the intellectuals over the Communist Party's heavy-handed thought control. But Diem on the other side of the 17th Parallel was busy erecting a dictatorship of his own. In 1956 he abolished elections even for village councils. In 1957 his mobs smashed the press of the one legal opposition party, the Democratic Bloc, when it dared criticize the government. That was the beginning of a campaign to wipe out every form of opposition. It was this campaign and the oppressive exactions imposed on the peasantry, the fake land reform and the concentration camps Diem set up for political opponents of all kinds, which stirred ever wider rebellion from 1958 onward in the grass roots *before* North Viet-Nam gave support. It was this which drove oppositionists of all kinds into alliance with the Communists in the National Liberation Front.

Long before the North was accused of interference, its government was complaining to the Control Commission of "border and airspace violations by the south and infringements of the Geneva Agreement by the introduction of arms and U.S. servicemen." For four years after Geneva, both North Viet-Nam and China followed the "peaceful coexistence" policy while the U.S. turned South Viet-Nam into a military base and a military dictatorship. It is in this story the White Paper does not tell, and the popular discontent it does not mention, that the rebellion and the aid from the North had their origins.

TOPIC 66

AMERICAN RESPONSIBILITIES IN THE 1970S

Previous topics in this chapter have examined America's evolving relationship with the rest of the world during the past thirty years. In the following readings a United States Senator, a historian, and two respected journalists offer their views as to the significance for the 1970s of recent American involvement in Asia, Europe, and elsewhere. Although there are as many points of disagreement as agreement among the authors, each essay will help the reader to use what he has learned from the past to shape his own views about future American foreign policy.

Reading 354

Senator Fulbright: The Arrogance of Power

Senator J. William Fulbright of Arkansas has for many years participated actively in the making of American foreign policy. As chairman of the Senate Foreign Relations Committee he had initially supported American retaliation after the Gulf of Tonkin incident in August 1964. He had, however, also shown extreme caution over becoming involved in a land war on the Asian continent. As the war escalated and hundreds of thousands of American troops poured into Vietnam, Senator Fulbright openly questioned not only the expansion of the war, but the entire nature of American foreign policy.

From J. William Fulbright, *The Arrogance of Power* (New York, 1966), pp. 245–247, 255–257. Copyright © 1966 by J. William Fulbright. Subheadings added by the editors.

I

The Two Americas

There are two Americas. One is the America of Lincoln and Adlai Stevenson [Democratic candidate for President in 1952 and 1956]; the other is the America of Teddy Roosevelt and the modern superpatriots. One is generous and humane, the other narrowly egotistical; one is self-critical, the other self-righteous; one is sensible, the other romantic; one is good-humored, the other solemn; one is inquiring, the other pontificating; one is moderate, the other filled with passionate intensity; one is judicious and the other arrogant in the use of great power.

We have tended in the years of our great power to puzzle the world by presenting to it now the one face of America, now the other, and sometimes both at once. Many people all over the world have come to regard America as being capable of magnanimity and farsightedness but no less capable of pettiness and spite. The result is an inability to anticipate American actions which in turn makes for apprehension and a lack of confidence in American aims.

The inconstancy of American foreign policy is not an accident but an expression of two distinct sides of the American character. Both are characterized by a kind of moralism, but one is the morality of decent instincts tempered by the knowledge of human imperfection and the other is the morality of absolute self-assurance fired by the crusading spirit. The one is exemplified by Lincoln, who found it strange, in the words of his second Inaugural Address, "that any man should dare to ask for a just God's assistance in wringing their bread from the sweat of other men's faces," but then added: "let us judge not, that we be not judged." The other is exemplified by Theodore Roosevelt, who in his December 6, 1904, Annual Message to Congress, without question or doubt as to his own and his country's capacity to judge right and wrong, proclaimed the duty of the United States to exercise an "internal police power" in the hemisphere on the ground that "Chronic wrongdoing, or an impotence which results in a general loosening of the ties of civilized society, may in America . . . ultimately require intervention by some civilized nation. . . ." Roosevelt of course never questioned that the "wrongdoing" would be done by our Latin neighbors and we of course were the "civilized nation" with the duty to set things right.

After twenty-five years of world power the United States must decide which of the two sides of its national character is to predominate—the humanism of Lincoln or the arrogance of those who would make America the world's policeman. One or the other will help shape the spirit of the age—unless of course we refuse to choose, in which case America may come to play a less important role in the world, leaving the great decisions to others.

The current tendency is toward a more strident and aggressive American foreign policy, which is to say, toward a policy closer to the spirit of Theodore Roosevelt than of Lincoln. We are still trying to build bridges to the communist countries and we are still, in a small way, helping the poorer nations to make a better life for their people; but we are also involved in a growing war against Asian communism, a war which began and might have ended as a civil war if American intervention had not turned it into a contest of ideologies, a war whose fallout is disrupting our internal life and complicating our relations with most of the world.

Our national vocabulary has changed with our policies. A few years ago we were talking of détente and building bridges, of five-year plans in India and Pakistan, or agricultural cooperatives in the Dominican Republic, and land and tax reform all over Latin America. Today these subjects are still discussed in a half-hearted and desultory way but the focus of power and interest has shifted to the politics of war. Diplomacy has become largely image-making, and instead of emphasizing plans for social change, the policy-planners and political scientists are conjuring up "scenarios" of escalation and nuclear confrontation and "models" of insurgency and counter-insurgency.

The change in words and values is no less important than the change in policy, because words *are* deeds and style *is* substance insofar as they influence men's minds and behavior. What seems to be happening, as Archibald MacLeish has put it, is that "the feel of America in the world's mind" has begun to change and faith in "the idea of America" has been shaken for the world and, what is more important, for our own people. MacLeish is suggesting—and I think he is right—that much of the idealism and inspiration is disappearing from American policy, but he also points out that they are not yet gone and by no means are they irretrievable:

> . . . if you look closely and listen well, there is a human warmth, a human meaning which nothing has killed in almost twenty years and which nothing is likely to kill. . . . What has always held this country together is an idea—a dream if you will—a large and abstract thought of the sort the realistic and the sophisticated may reject but mankind can hold to.

The foremost need of American foreign policy is a renewal of dedication to an "idea that mankind can hold to"—not a missionary idea full of pretensions about being the world's policemen but a Lincolnian idea expressing that powerful strand of decency and humanity which is the true source of America's greatness. . . .

II

An Idea Mankind Can Grasp

Favored as it is, by history, by wealth, and by the vitality and basic decency of its diverse population, it is conceivable, though hardly likely, that America will do something that no other great nation has ever tried to do—to effect a fundamental change in the nature of international relations. It has been my purpose in this book to suggest some ways in which we might proceed with this great work. All that I have proposed in these pages—that we make ourselves the friend of social revolution, that we make our own society an example of human happiness, that we go beyond simple reciprocity in the effort to reconcile hostile worlds—has been based on two major premises: first, that, at this moment in history at which the human race has become capable of destroying itself, it is not merely desirable but essential that the competitive instinct of nations be brought under control; and second, that America, as the most powerful nation, is the only nation equipped to lead the world in an effort to change the nature of its politics.

If we accept this leadership, we will have contributed to the world "an idea mankind can hold to." Perhaps that idea can be defined as the proposition that the nation performs its essential function not in its capacity as a *power,* but in its capacity as a *society,* or, to put it simply, that the primary business of the nation is not itself but its people.

Obviously, to bring about fundamental changes in the world we would have to take certain chances: we would have to take the chance that other countries could not so misinterpret a generous initiative on our part as to bring about a calamity; we would have to take a chance that later if not sooner, nations which have been hostile to us would respond to reason and decency with reason and decency. The risks involved are great but they are far less than the risks of traditional methods of international relations in the nuclear age.

Robert Wolfe: American Capitalism and Imperialism

If we are interested in bringing about fundamental changes in the world, we must start by resolving some critical questions of our foreign relations: Are we to be the friend or the enemy of the social revolutions of Asia, Africa, and Latin America? Are we to regard the communist countries as more or less normal states with whom we can have more or less normal relations, or are we to regard them indiscriminately as purveyors of an evil ideology with whom we can never reconcile? And finally, are we to regard ourselves as a friend, counselor, and example for those around the world who seek freedom and who also want our help, or are we to play the role of God's avenging angel, the appointed missionary of freedom in a benighted world?

The answers to these questions depend on which of the two Americas is speaking. There are no inevitable or predetermined answers because our past has prepared us to be either tolerant or puritanical, generous or selfish, sensible or romantic, humanly concerned or morally obsessed, in our relations with the outside world.

Historian Robert Wolfe was as disturbed as William Fulbright over the implications of recent American foreign policy, but he perceived different reasons for this policy. Wolfe felt there were certain basic structural factors in American economic and political life that drove the nation toward worldwide military involvement. In the following essay he warns of possible future dangers if the logic of American imperialism is followed through.

From Robert Wolfe, "American Imperialism and the Peace Movement," *Studies on the Left*, VI (May–June, 1966), pp. 33–38, 39. Copyright © 1966 by Studies on the Left, Inc. Subheadings added by the editors.

I

Military Spending and Foreign Policy

Whatever the need to protect foreign investments by military means, there is certainly an intimate connection between American foreign policy and military spending. It was the American commitment to the "defense" of Western Europe which provided the original rationale for the creation of a vast nuclear arsenal; and it was the American commitment to the "defense" of Southeast Asia which led to the massive build-up of our conventional military forces as well. At the same time as it has served to justify military spending, moreover, American imperialism has also had important political repercussions on the domestic scene. The link between the Korean War and the rise of McCarthyism is well known; but it is sometimes forgotten that despite the demise of McCarthy the continuation of the Cold War has made it possible to transform McCarthyism into a permanent feature of the American political landscape. The elimination of the Communist Party as an active factor in American politics, the emasculation of the liberal and socialist left, the domestication of the trade union movement, all this and more can be traced in large part to the combined economic and political impact of American imperialism upon American society. In brief, there can be no doubt that imperialism has played an absolutely central role in assuring the survival and continued growth of capitalism in the United States.

To state the position in this form, it seems to me, is inevitably to raise the question: to what extent are military spending and domestic reaction not only the consequence but also the cause of imperialism abroad? The mere existence of the military establishment and the political attitudes associated with it tends to militate against the adoption of a foreign policy which might result in a lessening of international tensions and hence a reduction in military spending. As everyone knows, those who have the greatest vested interest in the military establishment are also ardent advocates of a hard line in foreign affairs. What ought to be remembered, however, is that the demands of the war hawks in the Pentagon are hardly more extreme than the actual policies followed during the last twenty years. After all, John F. Kennedy, the architect of the so-called détente with the Soviet Union, took office on a pledge to increase military spending and promptly discovered a Berlin crisis which justified that increase. And Lyndon Johnson, everybody's peace candidate in 1964, finds it so essential to defend freedom in Vietnam that he must ask Congress for an additional $13 billion in military appropriations. Is it not possible that the determination with which Kennedy and Johnson confront the foe in Berlin and Vietnam is related to the immense economic and political advantages to be gained from such a course?

II

The Myths of Foreign Aggression

In approaching the problem from this angle I do not mean to ascribe any deep Machiavellian cunning to the policy makers in Washington. To the contrary, there is every reason to believe that these men do in fact see themselves faced with a world-wide Communist conspiracy which must be resisted at every turn if the American way of life is to be preserved. The source of this perception is to be found in the actual spread of socialism since 1917; and the source of their opposition to that trend is to be found in the very real economic interests which social revolution abroad endangers. But while Washington seeks to defend real interests, it seeks to do so on the basis of a mythological view of the world, a view which derives from a total inability to understand the spread of socialism except in terms of foreign aggression, mysterious subversion and Great Power intervention. Precisely because Washington itself pursues its goals by no other means, it believes its own propaganda which attributes the same techniques to the other side. Precisely because the United States is an imperialist nation, it finds no difficulty in accepting the myth of Soviet and Chinese imperialism. Were this mythological perception of no value to the system or even a positive hindrance, it would have long since been corrected. What perpetuates and gives substance to the myth is the massive military spending and atmosphere of political reaction which it endangers. The ultimate proof of the existence of the Communist conspiracy is that it is so profitable to combat. Just as the mythology of anti-Communism serves to justify military spending and domestic reaction, so military spending and domestic reaction serve to reinforce and preserve the mythology of anti-Communism and the foreign policies which derive from it.

It is, in the final analysis, this continuing interaction between imperialism abroad and its repercussions at home which give rise to that element of over-protection in American foreign policy noted earlier. Because it is now virtually an economic and political necessity to perceive the world through the categories of the myth, American imperialism has become increasingly incapable of distinguishing between real and unreal threats. Despite all the evidence to the contrary, it continues to behave as if by isolating and encircling the Soviet Union and China, it could halt the course of revolution in the Third World. Despite all the evidence to the contrary, it continues to act as if the socialist world were a monolithic bloc and the triumph of socialism in Vietnam a victory for Chinese imperialism. Despite all the evidence to the contrary, it continues to believe that if it does not intervene everywhere in the world, socialism must be everywhere victorious tomorrow. The final irony, of course, is that by pursuing such policies the United States ends by transforming its phantasies into realities. By treating the Cuban regime as a Soviet outpost in the Western Hemisphere, it compels the Soviet Union to place missiles in Cuba. The mythology of anti-Communism not only justifies military spending and domestic reaction; it also provides the necessary confirmation for its own distorted perceptions. In this sense one might almost argue that the real goal of American imperialism today is not so much to preserve capitalist holdings abroad as it is to preserve and give substance to the myth upon which capitalism at home now rests.

III

Vietnam and the Loss of Influence

In no case has this mythological function of American imperialism been of more decisive significance than in Vietnam. The main reason why the war has aroused so much opposition within the ranks of the Cold War Establishment itself is that it is justified by neither economic nor strategic considerations commensurate with the grave risks involved. Not only are American investments in Vietnam of negligible significance, but American holdings in the entire Far East (as of 1963) totalled only $1.5 billion, of which the greater part was invested in Japan and the Philippines, two countries which are not even part of the Asian mainland. Even if the economic stake in the rest of the Far East were greater than it is, moreover, there is little reason to believe that the triumph of socialism in South Vietnam would endanger it to any significant degree. Ironically enough, some radical critics of the war have been compelled to accept the Administration's own rationale, the "domino theory," because they are rightly unwilling to attribute American policies to Johnson's personal caprice. All the same, the evidence that the United States is fighting in Vietnam in order to defend its interests in Southeast Asia is no stronger when presented by the left than by the right. The victory of the Viet-Minh in 1954 had no major international repercussions; and there is no country in Southeast Asia today, with the possible exception of Laos, where revolutionary forces are strong enough to derive a real impetus from an NLF victory in South Vietnam. As Johnson's liberal critics have not failed to point out, the actual effect of the war has been rather to undermine American influence in the area, most notably in Cambodia. Of course one might still insist that even if an NLF victory did not immediately alter the balance of forces in Southeast Asia, the knowledge that the United States could be forced to withdraw would provide a source of tremendous encouragement to other revolutionary movements throughout the world. It is likely that the Administration believes this; but what it ignores is that the desperate conditions which produce revolutions do not permit revolutionaries to pause and consider whether or not they will offend the United States. The lesson of Vietnam—if it is intended as a lesson—is no lesson at all.

In order to understand American policy in Vietnam, it seems to me, one must have reference to the self-justifying logic of anti-Communism and military spending described above. Not only does the war provide a suitable occasion for an increase in military appropriations and a series of repressive measures—such as the attempt to register the Du Bois Clubs—directed against the left; it also serves to bolster that anti-Communist mythology without which even the normal rate of military spending could not be sustained. Both Kennedy and Johnson (prior to 1965) could easily have withdrawn from Vietnam without the slightest damage to American prestige or their own political standing. They had only to blame the whole thing on the perfidy of the South Vietnamese ruling class, whose belief in its own capacity to retain power had declined in direct proportion to the increase in its deposits in Swiss banks. They chose to remain because to have withdrawn would have been to give the lie to the whole myth of "aggression from the North" which they had so assiduously propagated. They chose to remain because to have withdrawn would have been an admission that there was no real reason for being there in the first place. They chose to remain because to have withdrawn would have dealt a serious blow to that whole doctrine of global resistance to Communist aggression which American capitalism no longer knows how to dispense with. Unwilling to expose the American people to such a rude awakening, and fortified by the economic and political advantages to be derived from such a course, first Kennedy and then Johnson determined to stay in Vietnam; and in order to stay, in the face of a rapidly deteriorating military situation, they were compelled to become ever more deeply involved.

The point at which American policy passed entirely into a phantasy world of its own creation was in February of 1965, when Johnson embarked upon the bombing of North Vietnam. It is quite possible that Johnson believed that by bombing the North he could compel Ho Chi Minh to call off the war in the South. Such a notion, although totally mistaken, would be consistent with Washington's conception of what revolution is all about. But even this theory does not suffice to explain why Johnson continues the bombings long after their military and political futility has become entirely obvious. In the final analysis, Johnson is bombing North Vietnam because he wants to prove to himself, to his critics and to the American people that the United States is in fact confronted with a clear case of Communist aggression in the South. By devastating the North, Johnson declares: here is the proof of your complicity, for why else would we attack you? . . .

IV
The Threat to World Survival

What follows from the above is that the monstrous irrationality which characterizes American policy in Vietnam also causes American imperialism to pose a very real threat to world survival itself. British and French imperialism, for all of its barbarous atrocities, was at least compelled to preserve the peoples which it sought to exploit; and when it could no longer maintain its domination through military means, it found ways of accommodating itself to the changing situation. American imperialism, insofar as it derives from the implacable need to justify its own myths, can make no such accommodation. Mythical interests, unlike real ones, cannot be compromised or negotiated; they must stand or fall as an integral whole. Already during the Cuban missile crisis Kennedy proved that the United States government was perfectly capable of threatening nuclear war in order to preserve its own mythological universe intact. In Vietnam today only the incredible forbearance of the Soviet Union and China has prevented another major confrontation with the United States. Almost fifty years ago Lenin noted that imperialism, from the political standpoint, was more than a striving after foreign conquest, that it was "in general, a striving towards violence and reaction." It is this amorphous "striving towards violence and reaction" which has come to constitute the most dangerous feature of American imperialism today. Unless a way is found to wake the United States from that phantasy world in which it now acts, there is good reason to believe that the ultimate nightmare of nuclear war may also be played out on the stage of the real world.

Reading 356

Irving Kristol: We Must Remain a Policeman

Irving Kristol, prominent journalist and editor, offers another view of the significance for the future of American actions during the 1960s, in Vietnam and elsewhere. Kristol, it should be noted, was a strong advocate of the containment policies of the 1950s.

From Irving Kristol, "We Can't Resign as 'Policeman of the World'," *New York Times Magazine*, May 12, 1968, pp. 26-27, 105-106, 109, 112-113. © 1968 by the New York Times Company, Inc. Reprinted by permission.

I

The Implications of Vietnam

I pretend to no greater foresight than the next man on how the present negotiations over Vietnam will proceed. But whether they move swiftly or not, or smoothly or not, it is nevertheless not too early for us to contemplate the meaning of the Vietnam experience for American foreign policy. Moreover, it is extremely important that we do so in the least polemical and most judicious of tempers. For the implications of this experience are nothing less than momentous.

Everyone is to some extent aware that American foreign policy, after this trauma, will never again be the same. But too many people seem to be content to leave it at this, under the impression that, the recent past having been so awful, the future—whatever its shape or form—can only represent an improvement. There is, it seems to me, a shocking lack of recognition of the fact that the debacle in Vietnam initiates a major crisis in American foreign policy—and perhaps in world history too.

Thus, there are many people who have concluded rather smugly that, from now on, a chastened United States will be more reluctant to exercise a roving commission as "policeman of the world." The conclusion itself is indisputable: any future Administration will be most hesitant about entering into a new military commitment overseas, and will even think twice before moving to honor an old one.

Still, the fact remains that the moving force behind American foreign policy in these last two decades has been something more than mere presumption or "arrogance of power." For the world *needs* a measure of policing—the world *does* rely on American power, does count on American power, does look to American power for the preservation of a decent level of international law and order. It wasn't arrogance on our part that cast us in the role of mediator and arbitrator in the Cyprus dispute. Nor was it any kind of narrow self-interest: The nations of Western Europe have far more at stake in avoiding a war between Greece and Turkey than we do, and we certainly could not care less about Cyprus itself, where we have neither bases nor investments. Nevertheless, when that dispute flared up, it was to the United States that both Greece and Turkey naturally turned. Had we decided to keep hands off, a Greco-Turkish war would have been inevitable and the entire Middle East would have been thrown into bloody turmoil, with consequences that pass imagining.

Along these same lines, one can only wonder what the situation in Central Africa would be today if we had not helped establish stability of a kind in the Belgian Congo, an area of no direct concern—economic or military—to us. We intervened there because most of the world thought it was our responsibility to do so—we had the ships, the planes, the men and the money, too.

Power breeds responsibilities, in international affairs as in domestic—or even private. To dodge or disclaim these responsibilities is one form of the abuse of power. If, after Vietnam, the nations of the world become persuaded that we cannot be counted upon to do the kind of "policeman's" work the world's foremost power has hitherto performed, throughout most of history, we shall unquestionably witness an alarming upsurge in national delinquency and international disorder everywhere. Nor shall we remain unaffected, in our chrome-plated American fortress. Let me propose an example of how drastically we might indeed be affected—one which has received surprisingly little attention.

I happen to think that the Administration's "domino theory" is a perfectly correct description of what an American defeat (as against a settlement that falls short of victory for either side) will lead to. But let us assume that I'm wrong and that the nations of Southeast Asia will remain uncoerced, unintimidated and unsubverted by a Communist Vietnam, allied or not with a Communist China. There still remains the question of how India is going to react to a situation in which the sole and unrivaled Great Power in Asia is a nuclear-armed China. Can anyone doubt that—dominoes or no dominoes—the immediate consequence of an American withdrawal from Asia will be India's arming itself with nuclear weapons?

Even now, the Indian Government is balking at signing the nonproliferation agreement, so laboriously negotiated by the United States and Russia, because it is skeptical of the willingness or ability of these two powers to protect her from nuclear blackmail on the part of China. Should the United States cease being an Asian military power—as is now being urged by so many—this skepticism will turn into certitude. India will then start arming itself with nuclear weapons—it has had the technical capacity to do so for some time now. And if India proceeds, can Pakistan be far behind? How do we contemplate a world in which India and Pakistan glower at each other, their fingers curled around nuclear triggers? *That* is the kind of thing which has been at stake in Vietnam.

Or take another example, in another part of the world. If Israel becomes convinced that the United States, after its bitter experience in Vietnam, is unable or unwilling to use its military power in the Middle East to assure Israel's survival as a nation—if this power is all symbol and no substance—it will inevitably start constructing nuclear weapons. Egypt, of course, will do likewise, with or without Russian assistance. How do we contemplate such a confrontation? That, too, has been at stake in Vietnam.

It is exceedingly strange that so many people who have a sincere and passionate concern over the Bomb should be oblivious to the fact that we live in a nuclear age. To listen to self-appointed leaders of the "peace movement," one would think that the only danger posed by the Bomb is that some crazy general in the Pentagon will abruptly decide to use it. Unfortunately, it is extremely difficult for official United States spokesmen to discuss this matter in public. How can the State Department or the White House talk bluntly of the dangers of a lot of kooky little (or not so little) nations playing around with nuclear weapons? How can Dean Rusk publicly assert that we don't *trust* India, or Pakistan, or Egypt, or Brazil, or whomever with nuclear arms?

Protocol quite properly forbids such candor. But protocol does not affect the basic realities, which are available to inspection by anyone who is willing to look at this world with eyes unclouded by ideology. It is a world which, without "policing," will almost certainly blow itself to bits. . . .

II
Rules of the Nuclear Age
In the nuclear age, there have emerged certain ground rules governing the *modus operandi* and the *modus vivendi* of Great Powers. The keystone of this system of rules is the assumption that no Great Power will attempt to revise the status quo by the use of force and violence—either directly or through a surrogate. It can use money, propaganda or various means of persuasion and intimidation, covert and overt, to tilt the balance of power in its favor. But it cannot use force—for such use of force brings with it the prospect of a military confrontation between Great Powers, and such a confrontation in turn immediately raises the possibility of a nuclear holocaust.

This is what the doctrine of "containment" has come to mean. It is not a peculiarly American doctrine, and certainly not an intrinsically anti-Communist one, since the Soviet Union in practice also subscribes to it. It is, to be sure, a relatively conservative doctrine, since it insists that the pattern of world power change gradually, subtly, as unobtrusively as possible. But when a world walks on explosive eggshells, as ours has been doing for nearly two decades now, there is no alternative to such conservatism.

It is in defense of this version of "containment" that the United States intervened in South Vietnam. The exact historical circumstances of our intervention, over which there is now so much controversy, are not terribly significant. The involvement in Vietnam—an involvement that was sustained by three very different Administrations—derives ineluctably from the fundamental principle of American foreign policy in the nuclear age. We did not intervene in Indonesia, when that nation (so much more important than Vietnam) was apparently slipping into Communist domination, because this fundamental principle was not being challenged. We intervened in Vietnam because it was.

To be sure, there are all sorts of novel aspects to the Vietnam situation. Unlike the war in Korea, it is part civil war, part nationalist rebellion against Western influence, part military aggression by Hanoi. But then, it is the doctrine of Mao (echoed, with variations, by Ho and Castro) that exactly such "wars of national liberation" are the most productive methods of violently upsetting the prevailing international equilibrium. The war in Vietnam is no accident; it is not the consequence of any failure of "mutual understanding"; it is a war set in motion by a policy. It is a policy clearly and unequivocally announced by leaders of "Left Communism" throughout the world. It is, moreover, a policy directed as much against the Soviet Union as against the United States—and which the Soviet Union repudiates as vigorously as does the United States. . . .

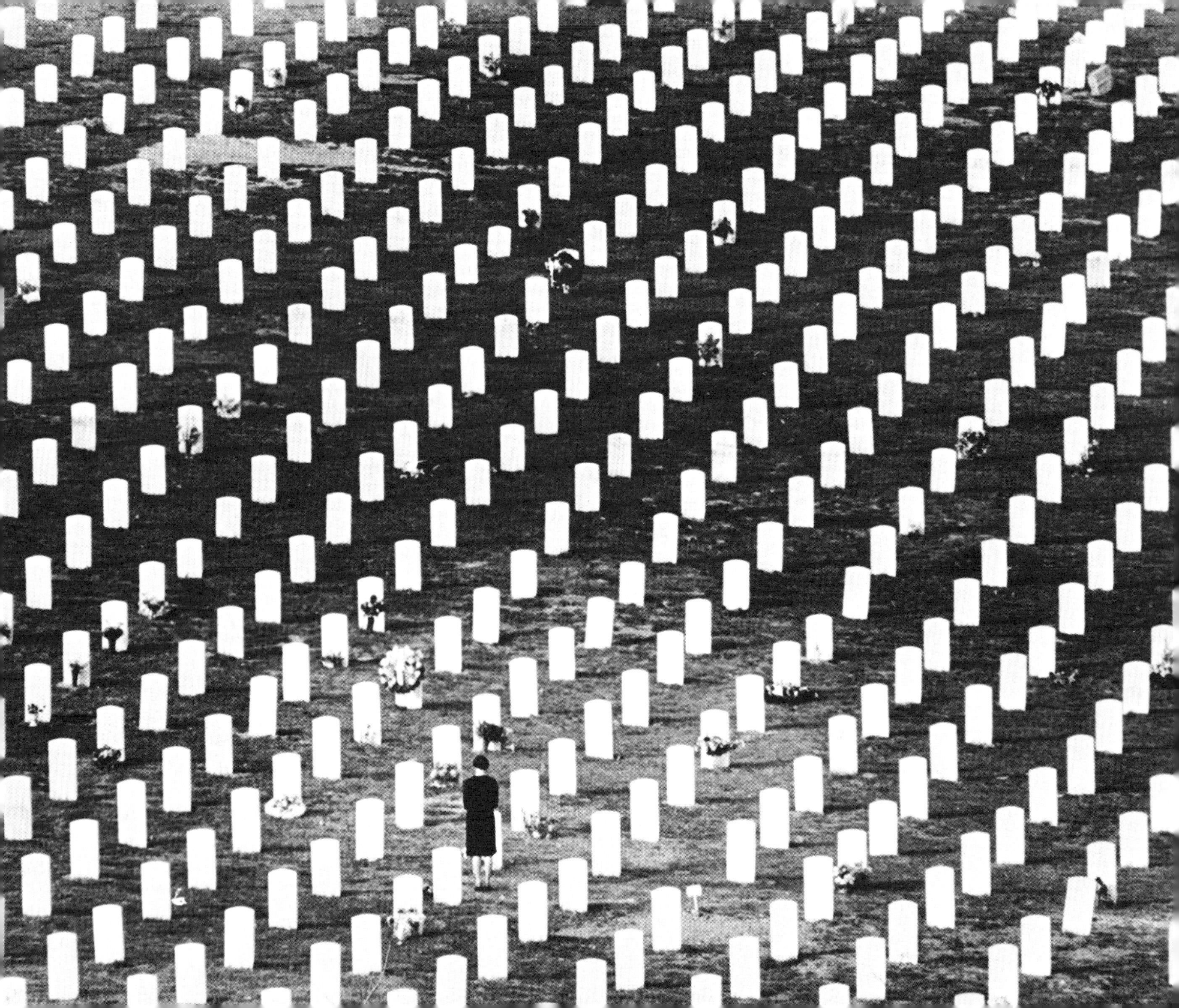

III

The Position of "Colonialism"

The framework within which our foreign policy must operate is reasonably flexible, but there are limits. And in Vietnam, we ran up against one of these limits and have had to fall back in disarray. It is now clear that, in practicing the policy of "containment," we cannot intervene in a situation where such intervention might put us, for any length of time, in a "colonialist" position. We started out, in Vietnam, with what seemed to be a traditional "intervention"—limited in scope, intention and time. We found ourselves involved in a minor (if bloody) war which we could not win, since in order even to have a chance to win we would, in effect, have had to transform South Vietnam into an American colony. We should have had to appoint American officers to give South Vietnamese troops the leadership they have been lacking, American proconsuls to govern Vietnam provinces and institute overdue reforms, American educators to overhaul the absurdly antiquated educational system that the French left behind them, etc., etc. We just were not—and are not—going to do that: it goes too abrasively against the American grain. And not having done it in Vietnam, we are not going to do it elsewhere. There is not going to be any American colonial empire, acquired in some fit of "absent-mindedness."

But it is more than the anticolonialist heritage of the American republic that, as we can now see, sets limits to our policy of "containment." There is also the very structure of American society today.

The policy of "containment" has assumed—and must assume—a democratic citizenry prepared to fight an interminable series of "frontier wars." This assumption was gravely shaken during the Korean war, at the end of which a great many people solemnly said, "Never again." But memories fade quickly in politics, especially when they are inconvenient. And it would have been highly inconvenient, to put it mildly, for the makers of our foreign policy to believe that they could not really rely on "limited wars" to prevent the world from moving into grave disequilibrium. So they decided to think otherwise; and, for a while, they seemed to be correct in doing so. Up until only a few years ago, one could listen to Administration officials speaking enthusiastically of the "firm resolve and temperate mood" of the American people, prepared to "shoulder their responsibilities" as a world power. No one in Washington is singing that kind of song today.

It is now as clear as can be that a modern social democracy—whether it be the United States, Britain or France—cannot do what most thoughtful students of foreign policy agree it ought to do, in its own interest and the world's. It cannot engage, for any long period of time, in those "limited wars" that are necessary to preserve international law and order. The Great Powers of the 19th century could do so because they relied on tightly knit professional armies; because their small, homogeneous educated classes (the makers, to all intents and purposes, of "public opinion") identified themselves with national *grandeur*; because economic growth and social welfare were not then thought to be the overriding obligation of Government; because the mass of the people was imbued with a kind of unthinking chauvinism that made it deferential to any official definition of foreign policy. In other words, because they were not 20th-century social democracies.

Today, it is quite otherwise. Our educated classes are providing the social base for a new left which, like the old, regards foreign policy as a sinister distraction from the urgent need of social transformation at home. Our working class, still highly patriotic and not at all left in its ideology, nevertheless is resentful of any overseas commitments that require it to forgo those annual advances in its material comfort it now regards as "natural." Our middle class is politically belligerent and is impatient with any foreign policy that burdens it with new taxes. In addition, we have our "underclass"—largely Negro—that can understandably imagine a set of national priorities very different from that of the State Department's. . . .

As I see it, therefore, the end of the Vietnam war will not conclude our "time of troubles," as so many now assume, but rather inaugurate a new era of even greater turbulence in international affairs—and with domestic repercussions that are bound to be massive, if for the moment unpredictable. The major threat is not that certain areas will now fall under some kind of Communist control—though, if this should happen in Latin America, it will be of no little concern to us. The truly frightening possibility is that, with an American foreign policy that forsakes sustained and limited military commitments—

The assumption of responsibility and power in world affairs has had many meanings to Americans. One of the meanings is simply that men by the hundreds of thousands have given their lives to make possible that assumption of power and responsibility. These rows of the graves of servicemen and ex-servicemen at Arlington National Cemetery suggest the dimensions of that sacrifice.

that abandons the policeman's role most of the world has come to expect of us even while bitterly resenting it (who likes policemen?)—those nations which feel their security threatened will have no alternative but to rely on their own nuclear arsenals. It is even conceivable that United States foreign policy will wander erratically between extremes: neoisolationist up to a point, and then—when the pressure of events becomes unendurable—reliance on (at least tactical) nuclear weapons.

It may yet turn out to be one of the great ironies of world history that the United States and the Soviet Union should have succeeded in negotiating a nonproliferation agreement at the very moment when such an agreement could only be another scrap of paper.

Reading 357

Walter Lippmann: Beyond Our Natural Limits

On the eve of the 1970s Henry Brandon, a British newspaperman, interviewed Walter Lippmann, the dean of American journalists, whose long career nearly spanned the twentieth century. Though Lippmann, at 80, mused, "I am bored with the past, I am only interested in the future," he nevertheless drew many lessons from the past which he felt would be of use in the future.

From Henry Brandon, "A Talk with Walter Lippmann, at 80, about this 'Minor Dark Age'," *New York Times Magazine*, September 14, 1969, pp. 25-27, 134-136. © 1969 by the New York Times Company, Inc. Reprinted by permission. Subheadings added by the editors.

I

Lessons of the Past

When we settled down in Lippmann's study to discuss the world, I suggested that he also reminisce a little, for after all he had a lot to look back to; no living newspaperman has seen as many of the great as he has. "I am bored with the past, I am only interested in the future," he replied a little grumpily, but he mellowed as we talked.

[Brandon] The U.S. finds itself engulfed in a deep social crisis. Do you see it as a consequence of a failure of your generation and of its ruling élite because they did not pay enough attention to such problems as poverty and hunger?

[Lippmann] It's quite clear from the results that we see about us that there has been a failure. It hasn't been due to paying too little attention to poverty and hunger. I ascribe the essence of the failure to miscalculation, to misunderstanding our post–World War II position in the world. That has turned our energies away from our real problems. The error is not merely the trouble in Vietnam, but the error lies in the illusion that the position occupied in the world by the United States at the end of the war was a permanent arrangement of power in the world. It wasn't. The United States was victorious; but by then all the imperial structures which set the bounds of American power had been destroyed: the German Reich, the Japanese empire. The result is that we flowed forward beyond our natural limits and the cold war is the result of our meeting the Russians with no buffers between us. That miscalculation, which was made by my generation, has falsified all our other calculations—what our power was, what we could afford to do, what influence we had to exert in the world.

[Brandon] But don't you think that if the United States had not preserved after World War II its then boundaries, Western Europe would have been in serious danger of going Communist?

[Lippmann] I always have believed in holding Western Europe and we certainly had to defend it, but I don't think Western Europe would have gone Communist. I think there were natural limits to the extension of the Soviet—or, in a more realistic sense, of Russian—power. They had reached the limits of their power or well beyond them when the armistice came in World War II.

[Brandon] Well, how do you explain, for instance, the Communist thrust into South Korea?

[Lippmann] I think it was a miscalculation on their part. We miscalculated and so did they. They tried to do more than they could do. They thought the opportunities were greater than they were and they ran into not merely American opposition but the opposition of 16 nations united against them.

[Brandon] It has often been said that the U.S. could afford guns and butter. It now seems that the U.S. can't afford both.

[Lippmann] The United States could and can afford guns and butter, but it can't afford a military position with infantry across both oceans. There are limits to the reach of American military power, and those were transgressed during the cold-war period.

[Brandon] So you see the failure of your generation not as due to a lack of attention and funds to alleviate social ills, but to the wrong world philosophy, am I correct?

[Lippmann] Yes, that's correct.

[Brandon] Do you then feel that the present generation is justified in its protests?

[Lippmann] I think it's justified in its protests and I include in the present generation not only the young people but a very large part of the population. The overexpansion which President Nixon has used as a keynote of his foreign policy is now increasingly evident to all the young, middle-aged and old people. That overexpansion in the nineteen-fifties—beginning before the Korean War, beginning really with the Truman Doctrine—has been the cause of the distortion of our whole way of political life.

II

The Situation Today

[Brandon] How do you then see the role of American leadership in the world?

[Lippmann] The United States should basically accept the fact that its sphere of effective military influence is what is often called the blue-water strategy. What happens on the land—on the surface—in the Eurasian Continent is something we can negotiate about but not something which we can direct and govern.

[Brandon] What is your bargaining position then based on?

[Lippmann] On our economic influence and our wealth and the fact that we are more or less invulnerable to attack from the Eurasian mainland. We have, of course, air and sea supremacy in both oceans.

[Brandon] Well, where would you draw the borders?

[Lippmann] Roughly at the blue water.

[Brandon] Would you explain what you mean by the blue water?

[Lippmann] Blue water excludes inshore positions and shore positions, on the eastern rim of Asia particularly. That leaves a very large area of the Pacific and Pacific islands and even continents like Australia within the sphere which we have a vital interest in defending. We can't govern beyond that. We have to strike a balance of forces with the masters of the Eurasian Continent, whoever they are. But we cannot govern or police the Eurasian Continent.

[Brandon] On the European side where would be the boundary?

[Lippmann] The boundary as left by World War II was the line down the middle of Germany. That will have to disappear in a reasonably short time, because after a generation we cannot any longer say that this is the line that divides Europe. Europe will have to find its own balance and equilibrium and unity without the presence of American infantry.

[Brandon] And what will maintain the balance between the Soviet Union and Western Europe?

[Lippmann] Whatever maintains the balance between two great powers: possession of power.

[Brandon] But Western Europe has nothing compared to the power of the Soviet Union.

[Lippmann] Well, they'll have to develop it.

[Brandon] Do you think the Europeans are capable of doing this today?

[Lippmann] I think so. I'll put it another way. I think the Russians are equally incapable of holding as much as they acquired as a result of World War II. They'll have to pull back just as we are pulling back. One thing we've learned in the last generation is that big powers, big in numbers and territorial size, are no longer great powers. They can be defied. The smaller powers with the use of technology can stand us off. Even in Vietnam, we haven't been defeated, but we have failed because of the resistance of the North Vietnamese.

[Brandon] Yes, but isn't the advent of the nuclear strategic talks—which will be conducted without the smaller powers present, and I am not critical of that—symbolic of the continued dominance of the superpowers?

[Lippmann] I think what we know now about nuclear power is that it's good only to balance nuclear power. It cannot be used against anybody else because our nuclear power is good only as a balance and deterrent to the nuclear power of the Soviet Union. Theirs vice versa. We can't use nuclear power in Vietnam; they can't use it in Czechoslovakia, they can't use it in Rumania, they can't use it anywhere where they're in trouble.

[Brandon] Not even against China?

[Lippmann] It is quite conceivable that the Soviet Union might make a pre-emptive strike at China's nuclear power. But it won't be total war. Neither China nor the Soviet Union can invade the other seriously. It will remain a border war, and I don't think theirs will be a pacified border as far ahead as we can see.

[Brandon] How do you foresee, then, the relationship between the United States and the Soviet Union on one side and China on the other?

[Lippmann] Believing as I do' that we're in the age—I'm not talking about the next six months—of the decline of very great, very large powers in influence, I expect to see the breakup of the Soviet empire in Asia and possibly the breakup of the Chinese empire. They're too big to govern. I think those will go along with the deflation of the American ambition—not ambition because I don't think the people had the ambition—but the American theory that we are the guardians of the world.

[Brandon] When you talk of breakup of the Soviet Union or China, do you mean that some of the republics now part of the Soviet Union would become independent?

[Lippmann] They will break down along the edges, with that long, 5,000-mile frontier which is neither Russian nor Chinese.

[Brandon] And on the Chinese side. . . .

[Lippmann] I don't know enough about Asia, but I think China is obviously too big to be governed as one central state.

III

Looking Ahead

[Brandon] What kind of policy should the United States pursue with the Soviet Union? There is a controversy as to whether the U.S., for instance, should side with the Soviet Union to help contain China, or should she play an even hand between the two?

[Lippmann] First of all we must make perfectly sure that the nuclear power is really balanced, that there is no question about the impossibility of waging nuclear war, using nuclear weapons as an instrument of diplomacy. After that, I think our best policy is one of absolute neutrality or hands off, and let nature take its course. I wouldn't align myself with anybody.

[Brandon] Do you think that this balance of the nuclear field is best maintained by the status quo or through disarmament talks?

[Lippmann] I don't have very great hopes for the disarmament talks. I think the reality is the fact that nuclear war is made impossible for both the nuclear powers by the facts of life, and as long as that's maintained that is the essence of it. . . .

[Brandon] Are you surprised that there are virtually no representatives of the so-called Establishment in the Nixon Administration?

[Lippmann] I look on Nixon himself and his administration as engaged in deflating, not merely the financial inflation, but deflating the political inflation which was built up in the course of generations, built up really from the time that Wilson promised to make "the world safe for democracy"; then by Franklin Roosevelt promising "to save the world from fear" and by Kennedy trying to save it from revolutionary wars, and finally Johnson trying to make a Great Society everywhere, not merely in the United States. Those were inflated promises, and we're now in the process of unrolling or deflating that inflation. In the course of time an Establishment grew up which had vested interests in these inflated promises and programs. It's perfectly natural that they shouldn't be active or shouldn't be enthusiastic about the deflationary process which we're now living in. Deflation is always uninspiring. You always feel, "My God, I wish something exciting would happen!"

The country is fed up with what I'm calling now inflationary promises. I think they're tired of high prices, they're tired of having wars, of having responsibilities all over the place.

[Brandon] Do you think that this attitude will lead to a new isolationism?

[Lippmann] If you measure the opposite of isolationism by the extreme expansion which we suffered (as I've said before) as a result of the military consequences of the Second World War—yes, of course, it is. Any drawing back is more isolationist than going forward, but in the sense that the United States will be isolationist as it was when World War I came along, I certainly don't.

[Brandon] Well, that's a very poor yardstick . . .

[Lippmann] That's the opposite extreme.

[Brandon] But where do you think is really the borderline today between the U.S. maintaining a role of leadership in the world and new isolationism?

[Lippmann] The borderline, as I said, strategically and for the use of infantry, is in the two oceans in the blue-water areas.

[Brandon] But doesn't it go further in Europe?

[Lippmann] Western Europe, of course, has a very fuzzy frontier, but Western Europe and North America and Central America are the common homeland of Western civilization and they must be defended. Beyond that our military power does not really effectively reach.

[Brandon] Let's take another comparative yardstick. The "America First" idea before World War II. How would that compare to the situation today?

[Lippmann] The "America First" idea before World War II was an attempt to go back to the isolation of pre–World War I. First, they said our influence should be the three-mile limit outside the continental United States. Then they gradually agreed that we'd probably defend Hawaii and Alaska and a little belt of water around South America.

I think the difficulty for you, Henry, if I may say so, being English, is that you are haunted by the notion that the United States is going to fill the role in the 20th century that Britain thinks it filled in the 19th century. I mean after the Napoleonic War the theory was that there was a *Pax Britannica* in the world. After World War II, Britain having exhausted itself and America becoming very strong, the theory was propagated—foremost of all by Churchill himself after World War II—that from now we would have a *Pax Americana* in the world. Now, that proved to be an illusion. We're living in the aftermath of that. There is no such thing as a *Pax Americana*. There won't be a *Pax Sovietica* or anything like it, because the world is too big to be governed by anybody. There will be no central place—not London, not Washington, not the United Nations—to which you can go and resolve every conflict.

[Brandon] So the world will rest on an unwritten constitution.

[Lippmann] And on the balance of forces. The world, I think, has lost its appetite for big wars. Small wars, such as we see now in Ulster and along the borders of Israel—that people will continue to fight about.

[Brandon] But couldn't the big powers be dragged into a fight like Israel?

[Lippmann] They could be, nobody can say they can't be or won't be, but they will increasingly try to avoid it as long as the balance of nuclear power is maintained because it's too absolutely, devastatingly suicidal for everybody concerned and there could be no winner in a nuclear war.

[Brandon] Let me turn to a more immediate problem. What sort of outcome do you foresee in Vietnam?

[Lippmann] I think that the United States will withdraw, is withdrawing. I don't think we are doing it as neatly as the formula expounded by the Administration. I think if this withdrawal and gradual pulling at it continues, the Government in Saigon will collapse. When it collapses, a new Government will take its place which will be acceptable as a negotiator, both with the Vietcong and with Hanoi. I don't think that's very glorious. I think it could be done very much more neatly and with less loss of the moral and spiritual realities of that conflict by announcing (I think we should have announced when President Nixon took office) that the object of the negotiations in Paris was to negotiate the withdrawal of the American forces from the continent of Asia over a period of two or three years, subject to terms of amnesty and whatnot, which would make the thing humane if not glorious. In other words, we should have admitted, not that we were defeated—because we haven't been defeated—but that we have failed in the attempt to extend our influence through the kind of government we think we believe in, for whenever we go, that influence will evaporate anyway.

[Brandon] What do you think will be the consequences of such an outcome?

[Lippmann] I think that Hanoi will become the dominant part of Vietnam, North Vietnam will dominate South Vietnam. It's the stronger part of it, and it will be Communist, probably more or less like Yugoslavia is Communist, relatively speaking, and it won't make very much of a difference.

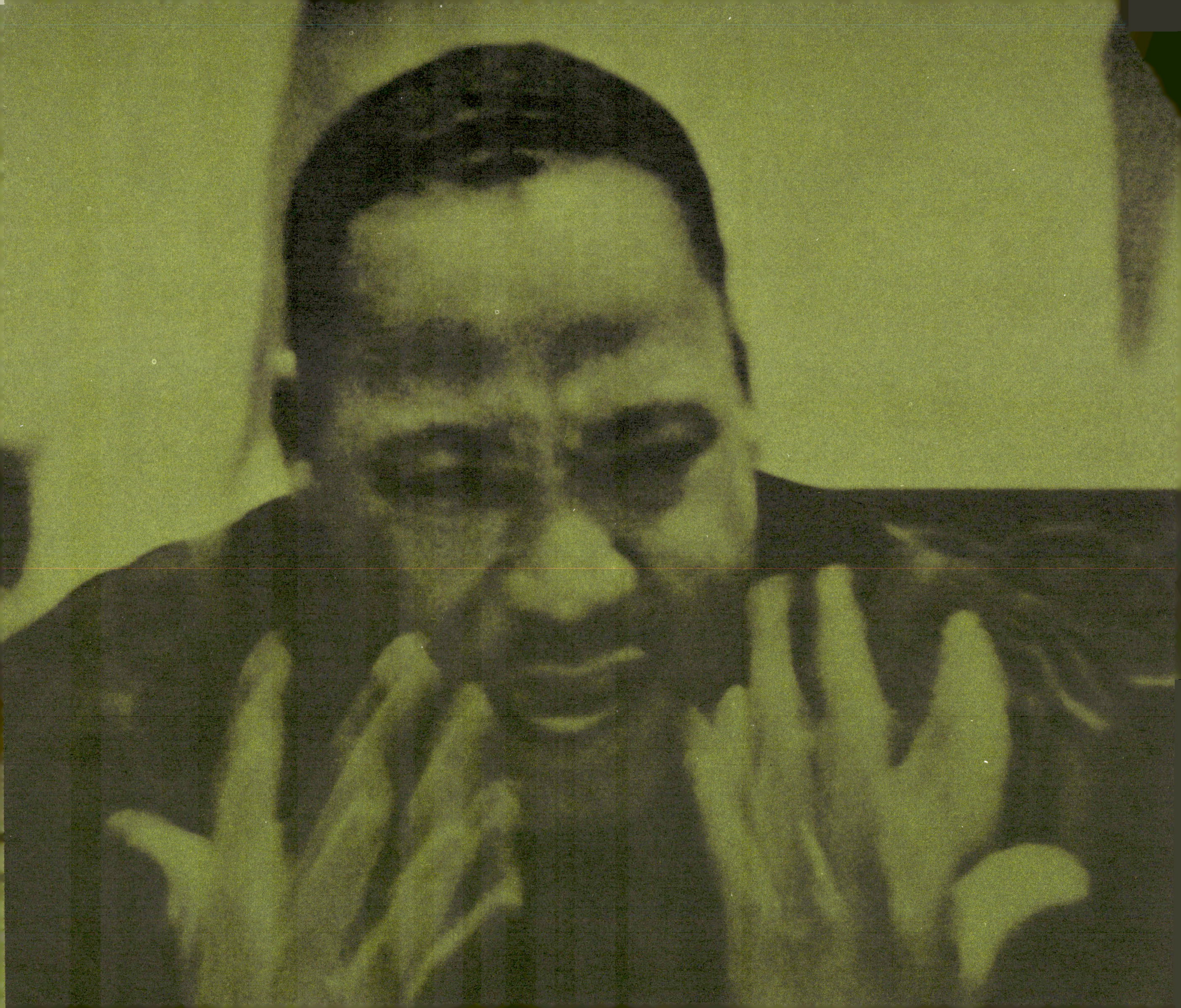

Chapter 10

A Troubled Society, 1945–1972

For many years after 1945 the memories of the Great Depression and of World War II shadowed Americans' thoughts, influencing strongly their private behavior and their public policies. In Chapter 9 the strong influence of the past on foreign policy has been suggested; most Americans came to believe that the weakness of the Western democracies, especially their "appeasement" of Nazi Germany, had led to World War II. It followed logically, they thought, that maintaining a strong military posture and demonstrating the willingness to use force was the best policy to adopt toward possible foes, Soviet Russia and later Communist China, to prevent World War III.

The harshness of the Depression created social and economic insecurities which continued to shape private actions and public decisions well into the 1950s. When Harry Truman became President after Roosevelt's death in April 1945, he understood the importance of maintaining the full employment of wartime to avoid a severe economic decline after the war.

As fears of another depression lessened in the early 1950s, other issues arose. One of the most dramatic grew in part out of the fervent espousal of democratic ideals during the war. One of the deepest sins of the Nazis, most Americans felt, was their racism, as expressed in their slaughter of Jews, Slavs, and other "inferior" peoples. Yet of course white Americans had long practiced a system of racial oppression toward Afro-Americans. Black agitation and white guilt combined to produce the Civil Rights Movement, the final consequences of which are yet to be seen.

Finally, the growth of a new generation, bred not on depression and total war, but on prosperity and Cold War, generated new social interests which led in turn to agitation for economic and social changes. The discovery—or rediscovery—of poverty in America, the rise of a so-called youth culture, and a sweeping loss of faith in the righteousness of national means and ends, led to a divisiveness, in intensity, like the conflict preceding the Civil War.

The readings which follow explore the search for security after World War II and the social conflicts of the 1960s. The events still to come in the 1970s will give the reader additional insight on these problems, but one can only speculate about what those events will be.

TOPIC 67

FROM RAGS TO RICHES, 1945–1960

To Americans in 1945 economic realities meant the Depression of the 1930s and the war-induced prosperity of the early 1940s. Above all, the nation hoped to maintain prosperity in peacetime while dreading the possibility that it could not be done. Thus, as Henry Bamford Parkes points out in Reading 358, the most significant law passed by Congress during the early postwar years was the Maximum Employment Act of 1946. Yet, as the debates over the act made clear, few persons were confident that the federal government could actually ensure "full employment" in peacetime. The struggle to escape the insecurities generated by the Depression thus became the dominant domestic theme of the late 1940s and 1950s.

Reading 358

Coping with Prosperity

The United States emerged from World War II hungry for the prosperity denied it in the 1930s. The war economy of the early 1940s gave the American people money to spend but few things to spend it on. One of the principal tasks facing Harry Truman, President from 1945 through 1952, and his successor Dwight D. Eisenhower, was to ensure economic security for the nation. While Truman and later Eisenhower struggled with domestic problems, it should be remembered that the strains of the Cold War forced them to devote much of their time to matters of foreign policy. American historian Henry Bamford Parkes provides a narrative of the post–World War II era in the following reading.

From *The United States of America: A History*, by Henry Bamford Parkes. Copyright © 1968 by Alfred A. Knopf, Inc. Reprinted by permission of the publisher. Pp. 675–677, 678–680, 692–694, 697–698. Subheadings added and footnotes omitted by the editors.

I

America after the War

The Americans faced their post-war problems under an inexperienced chief executive. Roosevelt had been re-elected in 1944, his Republican opponent being Thomas E. Dewey, Governor of New York. But his fourth term lasted for only four months. He died suddenly on April 12, 1945, and the presidency passed to Vice-President Harry S. Truman. Like many of his predecessors, Truman owed his nomination mainly to his political availability.

In the Democratic convention of 1944 the traditional conflicts between Southerners and Northerners, conservatives and progressives, had again come into the open. After Southern and conservative groups had prevented the nomination of Henry Wallace, who had served as vice-president since 1941, Truman, from the border state of Missouri, had been chosen as the most acceptable compromise candidate.

Senator from Missouri since 1934, Truman had done valuable work as head of a committee investigating waste and inefficiency in war production. But he seemed hardly qualified to lead the world's most powerful nation at one of the most critical periods in human history. Until his election to the Senate at the age of fifty, he had been a farmer, a small businessman, and a holder of minor political offices, and had had substantially the same experiences and way of life as millions of other middle-class Americans. Of all the presidents of the United States, in fact, it was perhaps Harry Truman who came closest to being an average citizen, with all his characteristic virtues and limitations. His record in office proved, on the whole, to be a reassuring demonstration of the vitality of American ideals. He made serious errors. When led astray by explosive emotions, he could be stubbornly wrong-headed, and was sometimes much too loyal to unworthy friends. But on major issues, especially in foreign affairs, he rose to the responsibilities of his high office and provided by no means ineffectual leadership.

Although Truman declared that he would continue Roosevelt's policies, his direction during his early years in office was very uncertain, with a number of abrupt shifts between conservatism and progressivism. In the end he settled to a definitely progressive course, advocating a Fair Deal as a sequel to the New Deal, appealing (like Roosevelt) to organized labor, the farmers, and the middle-class liberals, and fighting the Southern conservatives in the Democratic Party. But during the first eighteen months of his presidency almost all the surviving New Dealers left the government and were replaced by men of a different type, many of them being machine politicians or small-town lawyers and businessmen with little experience of national affairs.

Truman made some of his worst mistakes in his appointments to departments concerned with domestic administration. Given responsible positions in a government which had immense powers over the national economy and which was spending between thirty and forty billion dollars a year, a catastrophically large number of officials took advantage of their opportunities. Within a few years standards of honesty in the lower brackets of some departments, especially the Bureau of Internal Revenue, declined to levels perhaps as low as during the Grant administration. Probably the most disturbing trend was not so much the amount of actual bribery and theft but the spread of lax ethical attitudes. Many officials, while technically honest, saw nothing wrong in doing favors for friends. In consequence, Washington was soon swarming with unsavory characters, known as "five-per-centers," who made fortunes by cultivating influence in government circles and fixing contacts for businessmen who wanted special privileges. The personal integrity and good intentions of Harry Truman were unquestionable; but the sprawling Federal bureaucracy was soon in need of drastic purification.

For about two years after the surrender of the Axis, domestic affairs were dominated by the gradual removal of controls and the return to peacetime ways of living. Industry reconverted to production for civilian use; and the government, fearing that the process would be accompanied by large-scale unemployment, made every effort to ease the transition. Taxes were reduced, loans were made to business through RFC [Reconstruction Finance Corporation], money remained plentiful and interest rates low, and billions of dollars' worth of government-owned war plants and surplus war material were sold off at bargain rates. Actually all the fears of a depression proved to be baseless, and the country soon entered upon the most remarkable prosperity period in its entire history.

As soon as the war ended, men in the services and their relatives at home put pressure on the authorities for rapid demobilization, and the dissolution of American armed forces proceeded so rapidly that the country had difficulty in meeting its occupation obligations in Germany and Japan. This made it necessary for Congress to continue selective service until 1947. By January of that year the country had a total of only about 1,000,000 men in the army and navy. Thus the United States rapidly ceased to be a first-class military power—a change which had potentially catastrophic effects in world politics. Discharged veterans were given educational opportunities and some economic assistance under the G.I. Bill of Rights, which had become law in 1944.

As after World War I, reconversion was accompanied by widespread labor disputes. Labor had been able to maintain its standards of living during the war through overtime pay. The unions now demanded increases in regular wage rates in order to compensate for the expected loss of overtime, and during the eighteen months following VJ-Day there were a series of strikes in major industries—automobiles, steel, coal, and railroads. In most instances, the unions gained substantial wage increases, while the government authorized the industries involved to pass on the costs to the consumer through higher prices. . . .

II

Legislation

The only significant law dealing with domestic affairs was the Maximum Employment Act of February 1946. The administration had wanted a measure based on Keynesian principles which would establish government responsibility for maintaining "full employment" and provide, when necessary, for Federal spending on a sufficient scale to prevent depression. The bill as finally passed fell far short of these hopes, though it represented a significant innovation in Federal policy. It set a goal of "maximum" rather than "full" employment, and provided for a board of three economists who were to prepare annual reports on the state of the national economy and make recommendations to the President.

The administration's surrender on price-control was followed by defeat at the polls, and in 1946, when the 80th Congress was elected, the Republicans won control of both houses for the first time since 1930. Under the leadership of Senator Taft of Ohio, their chief spokesman on internal policy, they set out to revise the Wagner Act and limit the powers of labor unions. The Taft-Hartley Act, passed over Truman's veto, became law in June 1947. According to its sponsors, its purpose was to bring about legal equality between employers and employees and to safeguard the community against abuses of power on the part of labor unions. Labor leaders, on the other hand, bitterly denounced it as an attempt to destroy collective bargaining. The act declared that unions could be sued if they violated contracts, outlawed the closed shop, declared illegal a long list of practices in which unions had frequently engaged, and authorized the government to obtain an eighty-day injunction against any strike that would endanger national safety. The NLRB, which had been set up by the Wagner Act to protect the rights of labor, was now to be reorganized as a court for the enforcement of collective bargaining rules upon both employers and unions.

Apart from the Taft-Hartley Act, the 80th Congress made no drastic revisions in New Deal legislation. The Republican majority, supported by many conservative Democrats, paid no attention to Truman's recommendations for further reforms; but, on the other hand, they showed no serious desire to return to the 1920's. Much was heard about the dangers of the "welfare state" and the virtues of unrestricted free enterprise. But such basic New Deal measures as social security and support for farm prices underwent only minor changes, and the government continued to exercise broad powers over the economy through its currency and credit policies.

III

The Election of 1948

The year 1948 seemed like a Republican year. Governor Dewey* won the nomination for the second time; and apparently anticipating an

*Thomas E. Dewey, governor of New York—Eds.

easy victory if he avoided damaging mistakes, he largely restricted himself to generalities in his speeches. Truman was renominated by the Democrats in spite of opposition from both the right and the left wing of the party, after which two splinter groups broke away and chose candidates of their own. Southern "Dixiecrats," hostile to Truman's demands for Federal legislation to protect the rights of Negroes, nominated Governor J. Strom Thurmond of South Carolina, while Northern radicals who were not yet convinced that the Soviet Union was a threat to peace and who disliked the administration's foreign policies nominated Henry Wallace and assumed the name "Progressive."

Virtually everybody but Truman himself assumed that his defeat was inevitable. But the President conducted a fighting campaign, making speeches at every whistle stop on cross-country tours and lambasting the 80th Congress for its refusal to accept his Fair Deal program. As a result of the Progressive and Dixiecrat secessions, he won slightly less than half the popular vote, but he had a popular majority over Dewey of more than 2,000,000, with a substantial lead in the electoral college. Even with the loss of part of the South, the combination of groups won to the Democratic Party by the New Deal was still unbeatable. In fact, a number of liberals campaigning in state elections ran well ahead of the President.

Truman's remarkable triumph had few political results. The 81st Congress, though controlled by the Democrats, was not much more receptive to his recommendations than the 80th. It extended the social-security system to cover more groups of citizens, raised minimum-wage scales, and voted money for low-cost housing. But it refused to enact laws for national health insurance, Federal enforcement of civil rights for Negroes, Federal subsidies for education, and the rest of the Fair Deal program. Meanwhile, international tensions were increasing, and the growing Soviet threat soon brought a return to war production. In actuality, in spite of the popularity of the Fair Deal with a large part of the electorate, there was no strong popular pressure for further reform legislation. Production was booming, jobs were easy to find, and almost everybody in the country was earning far more than ever before. . . .

IV

President Dwight Eisenhower

The Far Eastern policy of the Truman administration and its alleged softness with Communists at home were vigorously debated throughout the presidential campaign of 1952. The Republican Party, however, was again deeply divided, along much the same lines as in 1940. The more liberal and internationalist wing of the party, with a mainly European orientation in foreign policy, picked General Eisenhower as its candidate. In June, Eisenhower turned over his European command to General Ridgway (who was replaced in the Far East by Mark Clark), and came home to campaign for the nomination. More conservative Republicans, with a greater interest in the Far East, supported Senator Taft. After a bitter fight the Eisenhower forces won control of the Republican convention, and nominated their candidate by a narrow margin. The Democrats, substantially in agreement about foreign policy but violently divided about domestic issues, found a leader whom almost all groups in the party were willing to support in Adlai Stevenson, Governor of Illinois since 1948.

In his campaign speeches Stevenson displayed a comprehension of the issues and a moral idealism unequaled by any previous presidential candidate since Woodrow Wilson, and even many of his opponents admitted that he spoke with the accents of greatness. But he could not counteract the immense personal prestige of General Eisenhower or the accumulated popular resentment against the corruption of the Truman administration, its failure to prevent high prices, and its inability to end the Korean war. Running far ahead of the rest of the Republican ticket in nearly every state, Eisenhower was swept into office by a record-breaking popular vote of 33,936,252 as against 27,314,992 for Stevenson. By much smaller margins the Republicans also won control of both houses of Congress.

Thus twenty years of Democratic ascendancy had come to an end. But even though the American people had decided that it was time for a change in Washington, they had not voted to put the clock back to the 1920's. During the campaign Eisenhower had pledged himself to maintain, and even extend, all the major reforms of the New Deal; and he had won the Republican nomination as the spokesman of an internationalist foreign policy. The victorious party had been asked to purify the Federal administration and to bring more vigor and efficiency to the execution of its programs; it had not been given a mandate for any fundamental change of objectives, either at home or abroad.

In spite of his long army career, the new president was by temperament a man of peace, his most conspicuous qualification for leadership being his capacity for smoothing discords and evoking cooperation. Conciliation was therefore the keynote of the Eisenhower administration, in both its domestic and its foreign programs. Although its critics complained that some essential issues were being evaded rather than solved, there can be no doubt that it was remarkably successful in reducing the political tensions that had characterized the Roosevelt and Truman periods. Eisenhower's middle-of-the-road policies won the support of moderate men in each political party and decreased the strength of both the right-wing Republicans and the left-wing Democrats.

It was, of course, to be expected that the new administration would be more friendly to business than its Democratic predecessors. Big business was strongly represented in the

The demand for suburban housing in the decade following World War II produced many real estate developments such as this one, located near Washington, D.C. By the middle 1950s the suburbs had become the characteristic place of residence of the American middle class. As a result of this population shift, the "shopping center" emerged to serve buying needs of suburbanites. Meanwhile, an increasing number of industries, whose workers commuted largely by automobile, began operations in outlying areas. Thus the old central city, dominant in the earlier twentieth century, faced a fight for survival as the century waned.

cabinet, its outstanding spokesmen being George M. Humphrey, Secretary of the Treasury, and Charles E. Wilson, Secretary of Defense. Most of the price-control regulations that had been imposed during the Korean war were quickly removed, while the administration's inclination to promote private rather than public ownership of power and natural resources soon began to cause liberals to complain of a "give-away program." The most obvious changes from the Truman period, however, were in fiscal policy. As soon as it assumed office, the new administration began to make deep cuts in government spending, especially on defense and foreign aid, with the ultimate intention of both reducing taxes and balancing the budget. These objectives were achieved by the fiscal year 1955–56; spendings were down to 64 billion dollars (nearly 60 percent of which was for defense), as contrasted with 73 billion in the last Truman year, while revenues slightly exceeded this figure although there were considerable tax reductions.

Yet in spite of the administration's firm belief in the superiority of private enterprise, its spokesmen made it plain that, in the event of an economic recession, they would make use of all the methods of controlling the economy which had been worked out under the New Deal. Nor did they propose to repeal any of the basic measures of the previous twenty years. Although the hopes of union leaders for a revision of the Taft-Hartley Act were not fulfilled, there was no attempt to diminish further the rights and powers of organized labor. In 1954 the social-security system was expanded to cover ten million additional workers, and the scale of payments was increased; further extensions were voted by Congress in 1956. Eisenhower advocated legislation calling for new government spending on public health, housing, education, and other needs, especially notable being a sixteen-year 33-billion-dollar highway program, which was accepted by Congress in 1956. After 1955, expenditures again began to rise, reaching almost 72 billion dollars in the fiscal year 1957–58. . . .

V

The Eisenhower Administration— The Final Years

Party labels during the Eisenhower period were even more meaningless than usual, since each party was still sharply divided. Eisenhower was unable to reunite the Republicans and his program consistently encountered more vigorous opposition from the right wing of his own party than from the official leaders of the Democratic opposition. The former supporters of Senator Taft (who died in July 1955) continued to display a deep nostalgia for the lost simplicities of the nineteenth century, remaining suspicious of government paternalism at home and internationalism abroad. Eisenhower endeavored to work with the party organization, supporting all Republican candidates for election, but in private conversations he even considered breaking with the right wing and forming a new centrist political party. Meanwhile the Democrats were still split between Northern progressives and Southern conservatives, the question of civil rights for Negroes being the most acute cause of dissension. A majority of the electorate, however, were plainly in favor of continued moderation, and showed it by combining support for Eisenhower with a preference for Democratic control of Congress.

The Republicans lost control of both houses of Congress in the elections of 1954. This made relatively little difference in the functioning of the government, since the Democratic leaders eschewed partisan politics, maintained a middle-of-the-road attitude, and in some ways gave more effective support to Eisenhower's program than the Republicans had done. But this indication that the Democrats were still the majority party meant that the Republicans could have little hope of winning the next presidential election unless Eisenhower could be persuaded to run again. This seemed improbable when he suffered a coronary thrombosis in September, 1955, but he made a remarkable recovery from this attack and also from an abdominal operation for ileitis in June, 1956. After his doctors had pronounced him fit for a second term, his renomination became a certainty. The Republican convention also retained Richard Nixon as his running mate, despite some suggestions that he lacked the experience and personal qualities needed for possible succession to the highest office.

Adlai Stevenson was again chosen by the Democrats, after some bitter primary contests with Senator Estes Kefauver of Tennessee. The campaign was unexciting and there was never any serious doubt about the outcome. Stevenson was unable to find any election issues that aroused much popular interest, and his speeches failed to arouse as much enthusiasm among liberals as in 1952. Eisenhower and Nixon were re-elected by overwhelming majorities, winning 33,212,325 popular votes and 457 electoral votes, as against 24,192,953 and 74 for Stevenson. The Democrats, however, retained their lead in both houses of Congress.

After this remarkable political triumph the administration no longer had such smooth sailing. The national economy went into a tailspin in the later months of 1957. There was a sharp increase in unemployment, and the federal budget for 1957-58 incurred a deficit of nearly three billion dollars; but in marked contrast with its attitude four years earlier, the administration preferred to deal with the recession by conservative methods. At the same time it was facing new difficulties at home in the field of race relations, while its foreign policies were impeded by an apparent growth of anti-American sentiment in various parts of the world. In consequence, there was a marked increase in public criticism and congressional opposition. As had happened during the later years of many previous administrations, it seemed likely that political conflicts would prevent the adoption of any important new measures until after the next presidential election.

Back to 1929?

The editor of The Christian Century, a liberal Protestant journal, makes it clear that concern for economic stability in 1946 could not be separated from the concern generated by the early struggles of the Cold War.

From "Back to 1929?" Copyright 1946 Christian Century Foundation. Reprinted by permission from the August 21, 1946, issue of The Christian Century. Pp. 1006-1007.

One of the most important questions now being discussed behind the scenes at Paris* is how far the Russian economic system is to be extended westward in Europe. In our justifiable concern that totalitarianism shall not be forced, by reparations and other means, on nations which prefer to maintain free institutions, we dare not ignore the part that the successful and uninterrupted functioning of our own economic order inevitably plays in that decision. If the economic basis of American democracy proves itself able to withstand the strains of the next decade, there can be little doubt that western and a considerable proportion of central Europe will choose democracy. But if our economy collapses again as it did in 1929, no political agreement can possibly prevent the extension of the Russian system to the Atlantic.

Because the American economy dominates the non-communist world, stabilization of our economic processes is an obligation we owe not only to our own people but also to humanity. More than half the productive capacity in the world is concentrated in American industry. So the authoritative Economist, leading British publication in this field, is not speaking in figures of speech when it declares in its issue of July 6: "While the political future of the world is being decided in Paris, its economic future is being decided in Washington." It is being decided not only by America's action in the international field, but even more effectively by our policy at home. The fact that we are "having a boom and enjoying it" is therefore a matter of global significance.

*A conference at which representatives of the major powers were attempting to write peace treaties officially ending World War II—Eds.

"The lesson of recorded economic history," says the Economist, "would be that there never has been a boom of the strength and extravagance that this one is acquiring without a corrective action of greater or lesser intensity." It notes with alarm that the only proposals being discussed in America to ease the tension when the inevitable slump begins involve the great extension of foreign trade to the point where, the British journal fears, we will "wreck the export markets of the world." Recognizing that the British loan irrevocably links their economy with ours, the editorial concludes that Britain has "the right to ask the Americans for some tangible proof that they are not leading us back to 1929."

We may as well admit that we are not providing that proof. Indeed, most of the evidence points in the opposite direction. This British observer notes that "one of the remarkable features of the present time in America is the universal belief in the inevitability of a slump in 1950 or thereabouts." It is true that belief in the inevitability of a crash is universal here. The only difference of opinion relates to the time of the collapse. What we fail to see is the very great peril in which general acceptance of this belief places us and all the nations which are linked to our own in an interdependent world economy.

Universal acceptance of the "boom-bust" cycle as a sort of natural law of economics makes it impossible for anybody to take effective action to prevent a crash, or to reduce the violence of the shift from one extreme to the other. It makes the citizen unwilling to take such steps as lie within his power to head off disaster. It renders him cynical of efforts which are made by others in the public interest. It inoculates the whole economic system with a gambling fever. Manager and

The Changing Distribution of Wealth

laborer, farmer and manufacturer, merchant and processor, each carries on in a rising frenzy of self-seeking, hoping he will not be "caught short" but willing to take a chance before the bubble bursts.

This state of affairs also gravely imperils our relations with other nations as the strongest democratic power. Sweden and other countries which are in position to do so are trying to insulate themselves against violent instability in the American business cycle. Instead of seeking closer relations with us, they are forced to hedge against our expected collapse by seeking closer relations with Russia. And Russia is encouraged in her efforts to present the Soviet system as the stable, full-employment alternative to the wild and catastrophic fluctuations which she says are inherent in all economies not completely controlled by the state. . . .

In this situation, nothing is more important than that the citizens of this country realize the global perils inherent in an American collapse. If we are not to lead the world back to 1929, it is necessary that we take immediate steps to stabilize our economy. The first step should be a clear statement of public policy, backed by a pledge entered into by industry, labor, business, agriculture and consumers, to stop the inflationary spiral. The establishment and maintenance of a new price-wage line is a necessary second step. All-out cooperation, like that achieved during the war, can bring stabilization. Prices and wages can be controlled, and largely by voluntary means, if all concerned realize how important control is to the survival of democracy in the world. Additional steps necessary include a sharp reduction by government of its huge payroll and its inflationary spending and larger efforts to feed the hungry and to restore the shattered production of war-devastated countries.

During the 1950s Americans regained enough faith in their economy to shift emphasis from stability, based on the fear of another depression, to expansion, based on the belief that an expanding economy was a healthy one. Fortune, *one of the country's leading business magazines, analyzed the situation in the middle 1950s.*

From the Editors of Fortune, *The Changing American Market* (New York, 1955), pp. 13–14, 16–17, 24–28. Copyright © 1955 by Time, Inc. Reprinted by permission. Subheadings added by the editors.

I

The Prosperity of the 1950s

All history can show no more portentous economic phenomenon than today's American market. It is colossal, soaking up half the world's steel and oil, and three-fourths of its cars and appliances. The whole world fears it and is baffled by it. Let U.S. industry slip 5 percent, and waves of apprehension sweep through foreign chancelleries. Let U.S. consumer spending lag even half as much, and the most eminent economists anxiously read the omens. The whole world also marvels at and envies this market. It is enabling Americans to raise their standard of living every year while other countries have trouble in maintaining theirs. And of course the whole world wants to get in on it. For it still can punish the incompetent and inefficient, and still reward handsomely the skillful, efficient, and daring.

The American market is all this mainly because it is a changed and always changing market. The underlying reason for the American market's growth and changeability is the nation's rising productivity, or output per man-hour—that cachet of efficiency without which no nation today is civilized or even modern. American productivity is of course the world's highest. For years it has been increasing unevenly but incessantly at an average rate of about 2 percent a year, and it has done even better since 1947. And because productivity is rising so swiftly, the market is expanding much faster than the population. For rising productivity, in the long run, ends up as rising purchasing power, and the standard of living rises, palpably if not uniformly. People who could buy x amount of goods five years ago may buy x plus 8 or 10 or 15 percent today, and x plus 16 or 20 or 30 percent five years from now. Such is the dynamism that gives the American Dream its economic substance. . . .

There were in 1953 in the U.S., *Fortune* estimates, a total of 51 million family units, 42 percent more than in 1929, who got $222 billion, or 87 percent more than in 1929. Plainly, the nation as a whole had gained enormously. But look at how this has pushed families above the $4,000 level, where, economists agree, "discretionary" buying power becomes significant:

The $4,000-to-$7,500 group in 1953 contained 18 million family units or 35 percent of the total. *And they got $93 billion or 42 percent of total income.* Since 1929, in other words, this group has more than trebled in both numbers and income.

Furthermore, this new middle market has enjoyed its greatest growth since 1947. Between 1941 and 1947, *Fortune* estimates, the number of family units in it increased by only 13 percent, and their total income by 14 percent. But since 1947 the number of family units in it has increased by *40 percent*, and their total income by *36 percent*. The last few years obviously have made the new middle market.

The last few years have also expanded the hitherto narrow upper groups. In 1947 there were two million family units in the $7,500-to-$10,000 group, and they got a total of $17 billion; in 1953 there were nearly three million family units in the group, and they got a total of $24 billion. Even the $10,000-and-over group, since 1947, grew from two million to 2,200,000 family units, and its total income from $32 billion to $41 billion. But this top group is much different from the corresponding group in 1929. Although it is now slightly more than twice the size it was in 1929, it had in 1953 only 73 percent more income than in 1929. This reflects the great decline in the top income shares detailed by Simon Kuznets in his definitive study, *Shares of Upper Income Groups in Income and Savings*. The top 1 percent, he showed, got (after taxes) 19 percent of the total income in 1929, but only 8 percent in 1946. What has happened is that the extremely high incomes have been slashed by taxes, and more of the group is closer to the average than in 1929. The $10,000-and-over market, in other words, is a much more homogeneous and much less "classy" market than it was in 1929. It furnishes few if any customers for Spanish castles like those Addison Mizner built for the Palm Beach crowd in the early 1920s, but it furnishes thousands of potential customers for Cadillacs, and year-round air-conditioning systems.

Now look at the bottom group. In 1929, remember, 80 percent of the family units got less than $4,000, and together they got less than half of the total income. Today, by contrast, about half the family units get less than $4,000, and they account for a little more than a quarter of the income. The $4,000-and-under group, moreover, is now much better off, with a much smaller percentage of family units under $1,000 and $2,000:

Fewer than 10 percent of family units got less than $1,000 in 1953—against 16 percent in 1929.

Only 23 percent got less than $2,000—against 43 percent in 1929.

Only 38 percent got less than $3,000—against nearly 66 percent in 1929.

And now 17 percent get $3,000 to $4,000, against 11 percent in 1929. Many of these, of course, are farmers or live in small towns or suburbs and have their gardens and other equivalents of income. They probably enjoy a *real* standard of living equal to or better than that of many in higher income groups. And the chances are good that many will soon move to a higher level.

All in all, 58 percent of family units today have a real income of $3,000 to $10,000, against 31 percent in 1929....

II

The Reasons for the Prosperity

At all events, population changes have transformed the American market. There were in 1953, for example, 61 percent more children under five than there were in 1941, and 45 percent more between five and ten. Makers of children's goods have been feeling the hot wave of demand. And the increase in births is a major factor in the continuing demand for new and bigger houses.

There are more people sixty and over, and fewer ten-to-thirty-year-old people than there were in 1941, and the ten-to-nineteen age group shows a slight decline, too. This will mean a smaller market in the twenty-to-forty age group for years to come. Since this group will be supporting more young and old people, it may have to spend relatively less on personal items such as clothes and jewelry and more on housing and household goods.

As for the growing number of older people—the sixty-and-over group is more than 41 percent bigger than it was in 1941 and 20 percent bigger than in 1947—it means more sales not only for vitamin pills, drugs, and medical services, but also for back-saving household appliances and a whole range of products for leisure, such as garden tools, cameras, games, do-it-yourself tools, and TV sets.

How long and how fast will the U.S. continue to grow? A few amateurs see a nation of 180 million by 1960. Many demographers, adamant in their reasoning that births will decline again, believe that the most we can look forward to is about 165 million or 170 million by 1960. *Fortune* projects roundly 175 million....

And the population is not only rising, it is distributing itself and its income more evenly around the country. This growing homogeneity can be observed everywhere. What any traveler can see but may not always notice is that most towns and cities are, commercially speaking, almost exactly alike. They boast the same chain stores, liquor stores, candy stores, department stores, shoe stores, and the same prices.

During the industrial shifts of wartime, which accelerated departures from the farm, more people moved around than ever moved before. The movement has kept up. In nearly every year since 1947 some 30 million have moved—eight to ten million to different counties or states. This contributed largely to the growth of the West—to the fact that California and Arizona have grown more than 50 percent since 1940.

At the same time—at least until 1947—regional differences in income diminished remarkably. Back in 1929, per capita disposable income of the Southwest was 50 percent below the national average, while that of the industrialized Middle Atlantic states was 42 percent above it. Today per capita disposable income of the Middle Atlantic states, though it has increased 75 percent since 1929, is only 15 percent above the national average, while per capita income in the Southwest, showing the largest regional gain (more than 270 percent) is only 18 percent below the national average. The Great Lakes is also 15 percent above the national average. The New England and Far West regions are a bit above average, and the Plains states and the Southeast are below. But much less change has occurred since 1947.

The distinctive feature of the regional trend since 1947 is what has happened *within* regions. Today more than half the population lives in 168 metropolitan areas, which account for almost two-thirds of the retail volume and about nine-tenths of the wholesale volume of the nation. And this shift seems essentially the result of the colossal migration to the suburbs.

The suburbs, moreover, seem a major factor in today's high birth rate. Nobody knows (yet) whether people move to the suburbs because they have children, or whether they have children because they live in the suburbs. But the fact remains that rising income has enabled millions who never could live in the suburbs to live there; and suburbanites not only want children but have them.

Suburbia is becoming the most important single market in the country. No longer does the city dweller, male or female, set the styles. It is the suburbanite who starts the mass fashion—for children, hard-tops, culottes, dungarees, vodka martinis, outdoor barbecues, functional furniture, picture windows, and costume jewelry. Not all suburbs are alike, but they are more alike than different. And within themselves they are remarkably homogeneous markets. Just how much more homogeneous than the old central city, with its three or four broad income classes, is revealed in *Fortune's* series on "The Transients" and their way station, Park Forest, Illinois (May–August, 1953).

Yet homogeneity is not the whole story of the new All-American market. Thirty years ago, in one of his early editions of *The American Language,* H. L. Mencken made the point that the American speech, despite or because of its rough vigor and inventiveness, was strikingly uniform, and, compared to other languages, lacking in true regional dialects. Since then it has become even more uniform. At the same time, however, it has expanded and grown richer and more expressive, developing new variations, pungencies, subtleties. So it is with the market. It has become and is still growing more homogeneous. But the wealth of its resources is at the same time endowing it with more depth and variety— and more opportunities for the businessman who looks for them.

The $4,000-and-over consumer is one with a certain "discretionary" buying power. He is also one with more sophisticated tastes. For one thing, he is rapidly becoming better educated. Two-fifths of the adult population today has had a high-school education or better, against a fourth back in 1940. And the proportion is rising as each year's graduating class includes nearly three-fourths of today's youngsters. Moreover, the consumer is getting ideas from fashion, home, and "consumer" magazines, whose circulation has boomed.

The growing wealth and improved taste of the new middle market, in other words, are creating special needs and markets within itself. They fall roughly into two groups: (1) the new mass market for the special or novel product, and (2) the market for the elaborated, frilled-up variety of what is essentially the standard, mass-produced item.

Years ago many a manufacturer couldn't afford to make specialties in quantity; the market for them was simply too small. Today, however, the new middle-income market has created a mass demand for them. There is now a big tall-gal market, a big little-woman market, a big baby-furniture market.

So with the frilled-up variety of the standard item. Back in the "class" and "mass" days [before 1929] manufacturers tended to make several wholly different models or varieties of everything. Today they make a standard bare shell and provide the variations afterward. All Chevrolets are essentially alike. But you can spend anywhere from $1,500 to $2,500 on a Chevrolet, depending on whether you buy extra chrome work, rear-view mirrors, and bumpers to protect your bumpers. Refrigerators of any given make are essentially alike, but you can pay more than twice as much for one if you want a cold wall, self-defroster, a fifty-pound freezing chest, butter trays, and twin crispers.

The Capitalism of the Proletariat?

During the late nineteenth and early twentieth centuries there were repeated struggles to establish labor unions as legitimate institutions in industrial America. During the 1930s and 1940s this was accomplished. Daniel Bell, a sociologist, offers his view of what this meant for the unions themselves as well as its effect on American political and economic life.

From Daniel Bell, "The Capitalism of the Proletariat?" *Encounter*, X (February, 1958), pp. 17, 20, 21-23. Subheadings added by the editors.

I

Unions in Postwar America

Trade unionism, said George Bernard Shaw, is the capitalism of the proletariat. Like all such epigrams, it is a half-truth, calculated to irritate the people who believe in the other half. American trade unionism would seem to embody Shaw's description, but in fact it only half-embodies it—at most. True, the American labour leader will mock socialism and uphold capitalism; yet he has built the most aggressive trade union movement in the world—and one, moreover, that has larger interests than mere economic gain. Abroad, the European Marxist hears the labour leader praise the free enterprise system as the most successful method yet devised for a worker to obtain a fair, and rising share, of the country's wealth; within the U.S., the American businessman listens to the labour leader denouncing him in wild and often reckless rhetoric as a greedy profiteer, monopolist, and exploiter. How reconcile these contradictions? One U.S. labour leader sought to do so in these terms: *to* your wife, he said, you talk one way; *about* your wife, you talk another. Very clever; but, one might add, another half-truth—at most.

William James once said that whenever you meet a contradiction you must make a distinction, for people use the same words but mean two different things. One way out of this seeming contradiction, therefore, is to see American trade unionism as existing in two contexts, as a *social movement* and as an economic force (*market unionism*), and accordingly playing a different rôle in each. . . .

In effect, then, the logic of market unionism leads to a limited, uneasy partnership of union and company, or union and industry. Uneasy because in many cases employers would still prefer to exercise sole power, although the more sophisticated employers know the value of such powerful allies as the union in safeguarding their interests. Uneasy, too, because there is still the historic tendency of labour, acting as a social movement, to oppose the employers as a class. This tendency derives from the ideological conception of labour as the "underdog." More specifically, it has been reinforced by the political alliances, forged in the early days of the New Deal, which enabled labour to obtain legislative protection for its organising activities. These political alliances lead necessarily to wider areas of group or class conflict; tax policy, subsidising housing, medical insurance, and the whole range of welfare measures which add up to a more or less coherent philosophy of liberal politics.

To-day, all unions are, willy-nilly, forced into politics. The problem is what sort of politics will be played. Will the A.F.L.-C.I.O. simply be a political arm for market unionism, protecting the various interest groups that are its members, or will it become an integral part of a genuine social movement? . . .

II

The Problems Ahead

Where U.S. labour goes from here is a difficult question, for the trade union movement is now at an impasse. The source of its difficulty lies deep in the facts of present-day American life.

1. *Union membership has reached its upper limit.* In the last five years U.S. unions have ceased to grow. In fact, the proportion of the unionised in the work force has actually declined.

To-day there are roughly 16 million workers (plus another 850,000 members of Canadian affiliates) belonging to American trade unions as against two million a quarter of a century ago. Measured against a labour force of 65 million persons, this is slightly under 25 per cent.; seen more realistically as a proportion of the wage and salaried persons (i.e., excluding farmers, self-employed professionals, and small businessmen) the unions have organised about 30 percent. of the employee group of the society. But in organising this 30 percent., they have reached a saturation mark; they have organised as much of their potential as they can.

If one distinguishes between blue-collar and white-collar workers, then it is likely that about 75 percent. of the blue-collar force—factory workers, miners, railway men, building craftsmen, and labourers—belong to unions.

In coal and metal-mining, in railroad and construction, in public utilities, unions have organised between 80 and 90 percent. of the blue-collar force. In basic manufacturing—auto, aircraft, steel, rubber, ship, glass, paper, electrical equipment, transportation equipment—about 80 percent. of plant and production workers are organised. The remaining obstacle in the unorganised units is their small size. A U.A.W. survey, for example, showed that 97 percent. of the unorganised plants within the union's "jurisdiction" have less than fifty workers. These plants are extremely difficult to organise. The social relations within a small firm are very different from those in a large one—the identification with an employer is greater; employer counter-pressure is easier; the cost to the union of reaching and servicing these places is very high and often "uneconomic," since unions, as business organisations, have their cost and efficiency problems as well. The only unorganised *industries* are oil, chemicals, and textiles. In oil and chemicals, wages are extraordinarily high because labor costs are only a slight element in total costs, and workers are organised in independent unions. In textiles, the old paternalistic and southern mill-village pattern has been strong enough to resist unionisation.

What then of the other fields? In the trade and service fields, employing about fifteen million workers, unions have only a slight foothold—in restaurants, hotels, laundries—but usually only in the metropolitan centres where other unions have been able to help organisation. Most of these units are small, and thus difficult to organise.

In the white-collar and office field (banks, real estate, insurance, as well as the office forces of the large industrial companies), unions have failed signally. In plants where the blue-collar force is organised, the firm usually follows the practice of granting tandem wage increases to the office workers, so that the latter have no need or incentive to join a union. In the insurance companies and in white-collar employment generally, there is a high turnover. Jobs are held by young girls, recruited directly from school, who leave for marriage after five or six years, and who are reluctant to join a union. In general, white-collar workers in the U.S. shrink, for status reasons, from identifying themselves with the dirty-handed blue-collar workers. In European and Asian countries, teachers and civil service employees may consider themselves the leaders of the working class. In the U.S. these groups seek to emphasise the differences between them.

2. *Unions have reached the limits of collective bargaining*. This may be a startling statement, but yet it is one of the most important facts tending to reshape the American labour movement. By the "limits of collective bargaining" I mean simply the growing awareness by unions that they can obtain wage and welfare increases equal only to the increases in the productivity of the country. Such a story may be an old one to unions in Europe, who are sensitive to the trade positions of their countries, but it is new in the U.S. . . .

3. *The rise of the salariat*. A third crucial change in the nature of the American labour movement arises from the shifting composition of the work force. Briefly put, the *proletariat* is being replaced by a *salariat,* with a consequent change in the psychology of the workers. The trend arises in part from the fact, as Colin Clark long ago noted, that with increasing productivity, greater output is being achieved with a smaller industrial work force, while the demand for new services, entertainment, education, recreation, and research means the spread of more and new middle-class occupations. But we have appreciated less the changes in the work force *within* the giant manufacturing firms themselves. For with the increases in production have come increases in research, merchandising, sales and office force, etc. In the chemical industry, for example, from 1947 to 1952, production increased 50 percent.; the blue-collar force increased 3 percent.; the white-collar force by 50 percent. In the fifteen largest corporations in the country, the salaried work force is already one-third to one-half of the hourly-paid production force. For example:

	HOURLY WORKERS	SALARIED WORKERS
du Pont	52,000	31,000
Standard Oil	30,000	27,500
Westinghouse	70,000	40,000
Ford	135,000	40,000
G.M.	360,000	130,000

These salaried groups do not speak the old language of labour. Nor can they be appealed to in the old class-conscious terms. Their rise poses a difficult problem for the leadership of the American labour movement.

4. *The loss of élan and the disfavor of the public*. The labour movement, in its present form, is less than twenty-five years old, and the men on top are the men who built it. But they are no longer young—the average age of the A.F.L.-C.I.O. executive council is in the middle sixties—and they have lost their élan. The organising staffs, too, are old, and there is no longer the reservoir of young radicals to rely on for passing out leaflets at the plant gates.

Reading 362

But more than this, there is a crisis in union morality and public confidence. It is not simply a problem of racketeering. Racketeering is shaped by the market. It has always had a hold in the small-unit construction trades, the long-shoremen, and the teamsters, where the chief cost to an employer is "waiting time," and where one can therefore easily exact a toll from employers. And one finds no racketeering in the mass-production industries. Even in the fields where "shake-downs" are common, racketeering is on a considerably smaller scale to-day than twenty-five years ago when the industrial gangster flourished in the U.S. The real sickness lies in the decline of unionism as a moral vocation, the fact that so many union leaders have become money-hungry, taking on the grossest features of business society, despoiling the union treasuries for private gain. And where there has not been outright spoliation—typical of the teamster, bakery, textile, and laundry unions—one finds among union leaders an appalling arrogance and high-handedness in their relation to the rank-and-file, which derives from the corruption of power. Such gross manifestations of power have alienated a middle-class public which, for twenty years, was tolerant of, if not sympathetic to, unionism.

The Organization Man
(1956)

One of the most powerful images of a particular type of American created in the postwar era was the "man in the gray flannel suit." In Sloan Wilson's novel of that name, the conservatively dressed hero was a talented, well-educated individual who fought to advance himself by being an efficient member of a powerful organization. The effect of this image on college youth drew the attention of William H. Whyte, Jr.; he wrote about it in one of the most widely read books of the 1950s.

From William H. Whyte, Jr., *The Organization Man* (New York, 1956), pp. 69–71, 77–79. Copyright © 1956 by William H. Whyte, Jr. Subheadings added and footnotes omitted by the editors.

The "insider" of the youth culture of the 1950s. In this scene from *Bernadine* (1957), Pat Boone does his best to cheer up classmate Dean Jagger, despondent after an argument with his girl friend. Their lives and "crushes" were offered by Hollywood as typical of American high school youth, youth who broke into clean-cut songs at the drop of a clean-cut hat.

A Generation of Bureaucrats

When I was a college senior in 1939, we used to sing a plaintive song about going out into the "cold, cold world." It wasn't really so very cold then, but we did enjoy meditating on the fraughtness of it all. It was a big break we were facing, we told ourselves, and those of us who were going to try our luck in the commercial world could be patronizing toward those who were going on to graduate work or academic life. We were taking the leap.

The "outsider" of the youth culture of the 1950s. The motorcycle gang crowds around its leader, Marlon Brando, in *The Wild One* (1953). This movie shocked many Americans with its portrayal of rootless, aimless youths who first took over and then terrorized a small town. Despised and powerless as individuals, they found identity and strength in the cult-like existence of the motorcycle gang.

Seniors still sing the song, but somehow the old note of portent is gone. There is no leap left to take. The union between the world of organization and the college has been so cemented that today's seniors can see a continuity between the college and the life thereafter that we never did. Come graduation, they do not go outside to a hostile world; they transfer.

For the senior who is headed for the corporation it is almost as if it were part of one master scheme. The locale shifts; the training continues, for at the same time that the colleges have been changing their curriculum to suit the corporation, the corporation has responded by setting up its own campuses and classrooms. By now the two have been so well molded that it's difficult to tell where one leaves off and the other begins.

The descent, every spring, of the corporations' recruiters has now become a built-in feature of campus life. If the college is large and its placement director efficient, the processing operation is visibly impressive. I have never been able to erase from my mind the memory of an ordinary day at Purdue's placement center. It is probably the largest and most effective placement operation in the country, yet, much as in a well-run group clinic, there seemed hardly any activity. In the main room some students were quietly studying company literature arranged on the tables for them; others were checking the interview timetables to find what recruiter they would see and to which cubicle he was assigned; at the central filing desk college employees were sorting the hundreds of names of men who had registered for placement. Except for a murmur from the row of cubicles there was little to indicate that scores of young men were, every hour on the half hour, making the decisions that would determine their whole future life.

Someone from a less organized era might conclude that the standardization of this machinery—and the standardized future it portends—would repel students. It does not. For the median senior this is the optimum future; it meshes so closely with his own aspirations that it is almost as if the corporation was planned in response to an attitude poll.

Because they are the largest single group, the corporation-bound seniors are the most visible manifestation of their generation's values. But in essentials their contemporaries headed for other occupations respond to the same urges. The lawyers, the doctors, the scientists—their occupations are also subject to the same centralization, the same trend to group work and to bureaucratization. And so are the young men who will enter them. Whatever their many differences, in one great respect they are all of a piece; more than any generation in memory, theirs will be a generation of bureaucrats.

They are, above all, conservative. Their inclination to accept the status quo does not necessarily mean that in the historic sweep of ideas they are conservative—in the more classical sense of conservatism, it could be argued that the seniors will be, in effect if not by design, agents of revolution. But this is a matter we must leave to later historians. For the immediate present, at any rate, what ideological ferment college men exhibit is not in the direction of basic change.

This shows most clearly in their attitude toward politics. It used to be axiomatic that young men moved to the left end of the spectrum in revolt against their fathers and then, as the years went on, moved slowly to the right. A lot of people still believe this is true, and many businessmen fear that twenty years of the New Deal hopelessly corrupted our youth into radicalism. After the election of 1952 businessmen became somewhat more cheerful, but many are still apprehensive, and whenever a poll indicates that students don't realize that business makes only about 6 percent profit, there is a flurry of demands for some new crusade to rescue our youth from socialistic tendencies.

If the seniors do any moving, however, it will be from dead center. Liberal groups have almost disappeared from the campus, and what few remain are anemic. There has been no noticeable activity at the other end of the spectrum either. When William Buckley, Jr., produced *God and Man at Yale,* some people thought this signaled the emergence of a strong right-wing movement among the young men. The militancy, however, has not proved particularly contagious; when the McCarthy issue roused and divided their elders, undergraduates seemed somewhat bored with it all.

Their conservatism is passive. No cause seizes them, and nothing so exuberant or willfully iconoclastic as the Veterans of Future Wars has reappeared. There are Democrats and Republicans, and at election time there is the usual flurry of rallies, but in comparison with the agitation of the thirties no one seems to care too much one way or the other. There has been personal unrest—the suspense over the prospect of military service assures this—but it rarely gets resolved into a thought-out protest. Come spring and students may start whacking each other over the head or roughing up the townees and thereby cause a rush of concern over the wild younger generation. But there is no real revolution in them, and the next day they likely as not will be found with their feet firmly on the ground in the recruiters' cubicles. . . .

II
Security and Opportunity

When seniors are put to speculating how much money they would like to make twenty or thirty years hence, they cite what they feel are modest figures. Back in forty-nine it was $10,000. Since then the rising cost of living has taken it up higher, but the median doesn't usually surpass $15,000. For the most part seniors do not like to talk of the future in terms of the dollar—on several occasions I have been politely lectured by someone for so much as bringing the point up.

In popular fiction, as I will take up later, heroes aren't any less materialistic than they used to be, but they are decidedly more sanctimonious about it. So with seniors. While they talk little about money, they talk a great deal about the good life. This life is, first of all, calm and ordered. Many a senior confesses that he's thought of a career in teaching, but as he talks it appears that it is not so much that he likes teaching itself as the sort of life he associates with it—there is a touch of elms and quiet streets in the picture. For the good life is equable; it is a nice place out in the suburbs, a wife and three children, one, maybe two cars (you know, a little knock-about for the wife to run down to the station in), and a summer place up at the lake or out on the Cape, and, later, a good college education for the children. It is not, seniors explain, the money that counts.

They have been getting more and more relaxed on the matter each year. In the immediate postwar years they were somewhat

Reading 363

nervous about the chances for the good life. They seemed almost psychotic on the subject of a depression, and when they explained a preference for the big corporation, they did so largely on the grounds of security. When I talked to students in 1949, on almost every campus I heard one recurring theme: adventure was all very well, but it was smarter to make a compromise in order to get a depression-proof sanctuary. "I don't think AT & T is very exciting," one senior put it, "but that's the company I'd like to join. If a depression comes there will always be an AT & T." (Another favorite was the food industry; people always have to eat.) Corporation recruiters were unsettled to find that seniors seemed primarily interested in such things as pension benefits and retirement programs.

Seven years of continuing prosperity have made a great difference. Students are still interested in security but they no longer see it as a matter of security *versus* opportunity. Now, when they explain their choice, it is that the corporation is security *and* opportunity both.

Facts and Fictions of U.S. Capitalism (1959)

The postwar era began with the fear that another depression was just around the corner; by 1960 Americans had much stronger faith in their economic future. But their confidence had been largely transferred from the ability of the individual to shape his destiny to the power of institutions to shape it for him. Big government, big labor, big business, emerged as the institutions which most affected American lives. Yet the character of these institutions, and especially their relationships to each other, remained unclear. Economist David Bazelon clarifies one important aspect of the question when he asks who actually runs the American economic machine.

From David T. Bazelon, "Facts and Fictions of U.S. Capitalism," *The Reporter*, XXI (September 17, 1959), pp. 43-44, 47-48. Subheadings added by the editors.

I

Capitalism and Corporations

We seem, as a nation, to be committed equally to increasing production and deceiving ourselves about our productive system. The realities of the American economy are massive and dominant in our way of life; and they are extraordinarily dynamic and original in their evolving nature. But the rhetoric we employ to describe this core activity of ours is overwhelmingly obscurantist: reality and image are hardly within hailing distance. To put it simply, we suffer from an astonishing amount of downright mythical thinking about money and property and basic economic organization. While we all know that America manufactures as much as all the rest of the world, the words, images, and ideological structures we use to represent to ourselves what we are and what we do tend to be a quarter, a half, or even a full century old. Old, irrelevant, and misleading.

This stricture applies to liberals and socialists as well as to N.A.M.* publicists and their businessmen backers. Indeed, to be fair, one should credit many of the centrally placed executives and managers with a distinctly superior though unshared comprehension of our economic system. As for the rest of us, we seem to have been too busy enjoying its beneficence to have bothered to examine its realities. It is about time we began.

The falsification of economic reality, buttressed by the laziness (or something) of the educated, is becoming a highly organized, even essential instrument of policy—and that is always dangerous, politically, morally, and intellectually. To obscure, as a matter of policy, the existence and nature of the dominant power in a society is to undermine the basic creative sources of social life. This falsification presents America in the classic image of free enterprise and private-property capitalism; its consequence is to conceal the incontestable fact that we are dominated by great faceless corporations "owned" by no one and run by self-designated "managers."

There is a great deal of talk on Madison Avenue these days about the "corporate image," which means giving a humanized face to these impersonal structures. And the New York Stock Exchange publicists are pushing hard the idea of a "People's Capitalism," which has as much to do with capitalism proper as "People's Democracy" has to do with democracy proper. The purpose of these maneuvers is to plug some of the more gaping holes in the traditional web of justifications which, before the New Deal, was deemed sufficient in itself.

What is being simultaneously justified and obscured is the revolutionary emergence of a new American property system—and the fact that the men in control of it, the managers, occupy unexampled positions of power

*National Association of Manufacturers—Eds.

529

and privilege which are not based on entrepreneurial accumulation or private ownership, to which they were "elected" only by their peers, and for which they have been answerable only to history.

The managers of corporate industrial wealth and the big-money funds—along with their expert advisers—are the ones who are creating the new system; they run it, and they also best understand it. They know everything worth knowing in a practical way about money, property, and basic economic organization—because that's what they manage. They milk the pre-tax dollar and thread their way through government regulation on behalf of all sizable funds or forms of wealth. They are personally intimate with the intricacies of the fragmentation of property ownership and the alienation of capital because their very existence derives from those crucial changes in our property system.

What are some of the things the managers "know" that the rest have not gotten around to learning? We had better—because of their elaborate nature—avoid the subjects of the tax-torn dollar and other government regulation. But we might take a straight look at property as such. And here the invitation to understanding reads: *Nothing is very private in a mass society, including property.*

Advanced or even adequate thinking about property by the people who manage it requires what might be called a nonpossessory or non-owning frame of mind. As any good manager knows, ownership is irrelevant—the main thing is control. And frequently control is created or ensured by means of *giving up* ownership or by having certain others own the property. Management control of big corporations, for instance, is based on a dispersal of stock ownership among as large a public as possible: AT & T has 1,600,000 stockholders, no one of whom owns more than one-thirtieth of one percent. The Ford family retained control over Henry Ford's creation only by giving its stock in the company to a foundation; if it had held on to ownership, it would have lost control. Sears, Roebuck is controlled by company stock held in the company's pension trust: here the management consolidated its position by "giving away" huge sums of money. Managers manage, they don't own. . . .

II
The End of Capitalism

The problem of bigness has been with us since the building of the railroads a century ago, and of course it was a great political issue in the trust-busting era around the turn of the century. From that day till this, the liberal view has been to prevent or disperse the concentration of economic power, rather than to accept it and control it. This has been the impulse behind a considerable amount of fundamental legislation—the Sherman and Clayton Acts, the Robinson-Patman Act, resale price maintenance, the setting up of the Federal Trade Commission, etc. Whatever else may be said of this great effort to preserve capitalism in its classic image, it must at least be pointed out that it has failed. It may have slowed down or in some cases deflected the basic trend, and it certainly made a lot of lawyers rich; but after fifty years of this sort of thing our economy is more than ever dominated by big corporations. If the program is justified as a form of public subsidy to free enterprise in the form of small business, similar to our approach to the farmers, then it is perhaps acceptable. But as a comprehensive program or theory, it is mostly irrelevant to U.S. society.

This liberal attitude is based as solidly on the atavistic myths—of free enterprise and private property—as any N.A.M. speech is. Each group is working a different side of a street that runs through a ghost town.

[Karl] Marx and [Thorstein] Veblen among others were quite right after all in one fundamental insight; industrialism was bound eventually to burst out of the strait jacket of early capitalist forms of property—if not into socialism, then into "Americanism." An industrial system, as distinct from an ideology or way of doing business, has a dynamic of its own, which is simply to be itself, to produce efficiently. As long as a society can afford not to produce—is able to deny the industrial dynamic—it can join any property system and any economic ideology it may whimsically desire with the actual system of industry. But when production becomes imperative, any form of property and any ideological element may be required to give way. Give way in fact, of course, not necessarily in name. Which accounts for many of the misnamed facts in our industrial picture.

The end of capitalism in America as a recognizable entity results from three major historical events—the Great Depression, the Second World War, and this endless cold war involving continuous competition in production with the Soviet Union. Many good Democrats feel that the New Deal saved capitalism, but that is putting things wrong end up: corporate concentration saved (and imperceptibly transcended) capitalism, while the New Deal merely saved the corporations, by making it possible for them to produce again. That remains one of the primary functions of our Federal government—to keep saving the corporations. It is unnecessary to refer in detail to the numerous means the government has used to bolster purchasing power, or to help organize corporations among themselves. To indicate the scope of the latter, Mr. Berle* asserts that "Roughly two-thirds of American industry and much of American finance is controlled by a formal or informal Federal industrial plan."

Not only do corporations regulate themselves through government agencies and similar devices, but it is a fact—to be obscured only by conventional thinking—that the very existence of an AT & T or a GM or an RCA is in itself a form of economic planning on a national industrial scale. True, such planning has no broad or socially debated purpose, and is subject to no exterior responsibility other than the brute verdict of events—but still it *is* that rationalized economic planning so dear to the hearts of older socialists. (It seems an amusing irony that the creepiest part of creeping socialism should be its daily augmentation by the corporate managers.)

So, among other things, the imperatives of production result in an accelerated corporate rationalization of the economy. Let us state these imperatives seriatim, so as to recognize their overwhelming force:

Thou shalt not allow another Great Depression.

Thou shalt produce fully and efficiently.

Thou shalt compete globally with the Soviet Union—a competition whose key terms are not merely tons of steel and numbers of automobiles but the purposeful organization of production and the rate of industrial growth.

Finally, thou shalt raise and spread the American standard of living.

Almost everything unique about our system results from the action of these imperatives. Since they cannot be expected to diminish, it is fair to assume that we will continue to change in the direction already marked out. We may all see the day again (as with the NRA) when the president of, say, General Motors insists on more "socialist" control over industry. After all, what's good for the country may also be good for General Motors—at least for the *people* of General Motors, if not for the Thing Itself.

So that's our unnamed property system, still woodenly or deceitfully miscalled "private." But is all this a word game? No. The issue is, first, to recognize the existence of this crucial power now held by corporate and other managers, and then to request them to justify it to us. Power must be legitimated, otherwise any talk of law itself, much less democratic citizenship, becomes absurdly irrelevant. There are two somewhat contradictory "legitimations" of corporate power current today, one obscurely explicit and the other largely implied: (1) it doesn't exist, and (2) it "works."

The claim that it doesn't exist derives entirely from the word "private": corporations are private property, and thus are assimilated to an older system of justifications. This view leads one to the truly remarkable proposition that the personality of a young executive (and that of his fiancée) is *not* private, but the multibillion-dollar telephone system *is!*

The legitimation of corporate power because it "works" amounts to what is probably the lowest level of ideology yet reached by man in his brief but painful rise from the prelingual slime. To coin a lawyer-like phrase, it is unanswerable, contemptible, and irrelevant—and is to be understood as meaning nothing more than *You got yours, Jack.* As long as Jack accepts the statement, it is indeed unanswerable—and we are well on our way to accepting unlegitimated power at the very center of our civilization. The worst effect of the lack of legitimation is, as C. Wright Mills* screamingly asserts, that ideology and then ideas and finally mind itself become irrelevant to national life. And this is profoundly frightening.

The subject of politics is power. Probably the main reason there is no longer anything recognizably like significant political activity in the United States is that those who would engage in it have failed or refused to confront the facts of national power. They don't or won't see where it is. Let us hope that this situation is transitory, that like the genteel poor we were temporarily embarrassed by insufficient ideological funds.

The most deeply disturbing aspect of our situation is that nobody is holding a gun to our head: we are *free* to engage in politics—and indeed we were as a nation created free in order to do so. But to pick up our birthright requires at least a significant number of us to indicate with reasonable frankness and accuracy *what* the basic national power is, *where* it is, and *who* the stewards of it are. If the subject of politics is power, the means is ideological discussion, argument, and conflict. Now in this grand activity many things and many qualities are useful, but one is absolutely indispensable—namely, vital ideology itself. And that's our problem: our ideologies have become so irrelevant to the facts of life that it is all the ordinary citizen can do to stay awake while the great debate about our father's world goes on.

---

*Adolph A. Berle, economist and former Assistant Secretary of State—Eds.

*C. Wright Mills [1916-1962], sociologist—Eds.

TOPIC 68

THE ATTACK ON JIM CROW

This topic and the following two explore the changing relationships of blacks and whites in mid-twentieth-century America. The continuing crisis in racial relations recalls earlier struggles in American life. Much of the nation's history a hundred years earlier had centered on the issue of slavery and the allied question of the role of blacks in a "free" society. While in the pre–Civil War era the argument took place largely among whites about what to do with blacks, a hundred years later blacks themselves took a far more active and influential role in determining the course of events. In their attempts to become masters of their own fate, large numbers of black Americans confronted whites more directly and more persistently than ever before in American history.

Reading 364

Black and White in America (1930-1954)

Two historians of black-white relations in America offer in the following reading a narrative of the rising tide of protest that strongly influenced the Supreme Court decision of 1954 which ended school segregation by law. To later generations these decades might appear tame, but a careful study of the events justifies calling them, as the authors do, "revolutionary."

From Chapter 11, "The Negro in a Time of Democratic Crisis," taken from *The Negro American: A Documentary History* by Leslie H. Fishel, Jr., and Benjamin Quarles. Copyright © 1967 by Scott, Foresman and Company. Reprinted by permission. Pp. 447, 449-453. Subheadings added by the editors.

I

The New Deal Era

President Franklin D. Roosevelt's consummate ability to personalize his understanding of human exploitation and underprivilege made him the most attractive President, for Negro citizens, since the Civil War. Robert Vann, publisher of the Negro weekly Pittsburgh *Courier*, who was brought into the 1932 campaign by some of Roosevelt's lieutenants, advised his race to "go home and turn Lincoln's picture to the wall. The debt has been paid in full." Yet, like Lincoln, Roosevelt's actual commitments to the American Negro were slim. He was more a symbol than an activist in his own right. His compassion, though real, was tempered by his own background, by the enormity of the decisions which came up to him, and by political considerations. An enthusiastic politician, he used political weights and measures on a political scale to judge the evidence, and the Negro was often found wanting. When Walter White, the executive secretary of the NAACP, obtained an audience through the good graces of Mrs. Eleanor Roosevelt to plead for the President's public support of the anti-lynching bill, FDR demurred because he needed southern votes in Congress on other matters.

Roosevelt did not publicly associate himself with Negro projects or Negro leaders before 1935, but his programs and some of his associates were more aggressive. Early in 1933, he approved of a suggestion that someone in his administration assume the responsibility for fair treatment of the Negroes, and he asked Harold Ickes to make the appointment. A young white Georgian, Clark Foreman, came to Washington at Ickes' request to handle the task, and brought in as his assistant an even younger Negro of great promise, Robert C. Weaver. Foreman successfully made his way through the burgeoning maze of new agencies which were springing up and did a respectable job of calling to the attention of agency heads and their assistants an awareness of the special problems of Negroes. Along with Ickes, Daniel Roper, the Secretary of Commerce; Harry Hopkins, FDR's relief administrator; and Aubrey Williams, a Hopkins deputy, were sympathetic to committing the New Deal to work more generously with and for Negroes.

From the first, the various New Deal agencies carried the major burden of this emphasis, since they translated words into bread and butter, shelter, and schooling. For the Negro, the most significant were the Federal Employment Relief Administration (FERA), the National Recovery Administration (NRA), the Works Progress Administration, later called the Work Projects Administration (WPA), the Agricultural Adjustment Administration (AAA), the Tennessee Valley Authority (TVA), the National Youth Administration (NYA), the Civilian Conservation Corps (CCC), and the public housing efforts of several agencies. There were others in the alphabetical jungle which assisted Negroes, as whites, in more specialized ways, such as the Federal Writers' Project, and the Office of Education studies. The very number of agencies added credence to the emergent fact that, for the first time, the federal government had engaged and was grappling with some of the fundamental barriers to race progress. . . .

The labor movement, strengthened by New Deal legislation and internal reorganization, confronted, as one of its problems, the question of Negro members. Older unions such as the United Mine Workers and the International Ladies Garment Workers Union welcomed Negroes without distinction. When the CIO broke from the A.F.L., its nucleus of unions including the new and somewhat fragile organizations in the automobile, rubber, and steel industries accepted Negroes on an equal basis, except in those localities where race friction was high. The United Textile Workers attempted to do the same, but the existence of textile plants in southern states made this task more onerous. It was not enough for a union to resolve, as the CIO did, to accept members without regard to race, creed, or color, or even, as the UAW and the organizing committees of the steelworkers did, to offer Negro workers a chance to join up. Negroes still hung back, alternately tempted and frightened by management's offers and threats. The wave of the future was with the industrial unions, and *Opportunity's* declaration to Negro steelworkers that it would be "the apotheosis of stupidity" for them to stay out of the union battling for recognizance in 1937, was prophetic. The success of the Brotherhood of Sleeping Car Porters, under the leadership of A. Philip Randolph, in gaining recognition as the bargaining agent with the Pullman Company after a twelve-year struggle, marked the beginning of the race's influence in national labor circles and on national labor policy. After his union was recognized, Randolph prodded the A.F.L. to grant it an international charter, making it an equal with other member unions, and he never eased up his fight to liberalize the A.F.L.'s racial policies. Even though he was not persuasive enough to break down these craft and railway-union prejudices, Randolph emerged before World War II as a dominant voice in Negro circles and a power to be reckoned with in American unionism.

II

Protest in the 1940s

With the exception of the church, the major Negro organizations felt the sting of mass apathy. "We recognize our lack of skill at mass appeal," NAACP's Roy Wilkins admitted in 1941. The national office of NAACP attracted men and women of an intellectual bent whose convictions on race matters had not changed with the seasons, since the organization was still dedicated to the abolition of segregation and discrimination. But the spark which had sent John Shillady, Walter White, and James Weldon Johnson into race-hatred areas, North and South, burned low. On the national level, the NAACP fought its battles in court, in Congress, and in the press, but not in communities where racism flourished. At local levels, it depended upon its branches, many of which were woefully weak in finances and leadership, to seek out and rectify racial problems of every description. Its base was too narrow for its superstructure, and its bones creaked from inaction at the community level; yet it thrived because it learned to speak the language of influence in political circles and because it chose wisely the cases of discrimination and segregation which it pursued through the courts. Indeed, the road to the 1954 desegregation decisions was charted, bulldozed, paved, and landscaped by the NAACP.

The National Urban League was tested during the depression and not found wanting. Its leadership was similar to that of the NAACP, except that to the extent that its goals were more specific, framed in terms of employment, family welfare, health, and education, it was accused of being more timid, dominated by white liberals, and hostile to trade unionism. Its chief executive, E. K. Jones, replied to these criticisms in a private memo in 1941. The League, he said, was not a Negro but "truly an interracial movement. . . . Any movement of this character which advocates understanding through conference and discussion must necessarily refrain from advocating mass action of one race calculated to force the other group to make concessions." Gunnar Myrdal, the Swedish sociologist whose monumental study of the Negro in America was published during World War II, found that the League worked actively with unions and held "the lead as a pro-union force among the Negro people." Urban League branches were beginning to receive local

Walter White, executive secretary of the NAACP, addresses an outdoor rally held during the Association's 1947 convention in Washington, D.C. At this time the NAACP was in the midst of a long series of court cases attacking segregation by law (the Jim Crow system). Seated to the left of Walter White are President Harry S. Truman and Eleanor Roosevelt, wife of the late President, both of whom addressed the rally in support of the Association's views.

support from Community Funds, which gave them greater strength and a source for independent leadership.

The sudden shock of the surprise attack which drew the United States into World War II served more to expose sore spots than to blanket them in loyalty. In the First World War, the protests against unequal treatment were slow to develop and not widely heard, but the Second World War was different. Even before Pearl Harbor, clamors arose from the South warning that the Negro was not going to "come out of this war on top of the heap as he did in the last one." However distorted the comparison, the attitude was clear, and it influenced the government's decision to extend pre–Pearl Harbor patterns into the war period.

The Negro soldier remained separate in the armed services, and not always welcome. Judge William L. Hastie resigned as civilian aide to the Secretary of War in protest against the dissembling tactics of the Army Air Corps to keep the Negro on the ground. *The Crisis*, returning to a World War I cry, criticized the appointment of southern white officers for Negro troops and the explanation that they could handle them better. When FDR queried Walter White about the carelessness of the Negro press and the consistency of its attack on the war effort, White replied that better treatment for Negroes in the armed services and the invitation of Negro editors to presidential press conferences and top briefings would clear the problem.

The prosperity of war industry and the proscriptive southern mores once again attracted thousands of Negroes to northern cities. The consequent overcrowding and war tension heated racism to the boiling point, as the riots in New York, Detroit, and Los Angeles demonstrated. For the Negro, racism was the same wherever it appeared. In Roy Wilkins' words, "it sounds pretty foolish to be *against* park benches marked 'Jude' in

Berlin, but to be *for* park benches marked 'Colored' in Tallahassee, Florida." Negroes could not understand why whites drew distinctions between the Nazi ideology of Aryan supremacy and the American ideology of white supremacy.

The death of Roosevelt and the end of the war in 1945 terminated an era. The office of the Presidency now symbolized a concern for justice and equality for all Americans, including Negroes. The White House had taken a stand in favor of the principle of equal rights, although the practice had lagged. The new President, Harry S. Truman, a man of lesser parts, was to take the next practical step and declare in specifics his belief in the equality of men of whatever race under the law. Where Roosevelt concealed the particular in the general principle, Truman spoke out without check. Where Roosevelt used the excuse of war to delay integration, Truman used the excuse of peace to accelerate it. Where Roosevelt used the federal government to increase economic opportunities for all, Truman used the federal government to increase economic opportunities for Negroes. While the Truman Fair Deal never approximated the energy and the excitement of the Roosevelt New Deal, it was the former which capitalized on the Negro's readiness to take an equal place in American democracy.

III

Civil Rights Becomes a Political Issue

Three major strands marked the period between the end of the war and the Supreme Court's 1954 desegregation decision. One related to the improving economic condition of the Negro, a second to the reports of the three Presidential committees, and the third to the increasingly significant role of the United States Supreme Court in racial matters. The Negro's improving economic condition stemmed from a variety of causes. In microcosm, the successful introduction of Jackie Robinson into baseball's National League in 1947 is exemplary, since his breakthrough eventually opened the gates in almost every professional sport. In like manner, the appointment of Ira DeA. Reid to the faculty of New York University was a breakthrough in higher education of lesser quantity but equal quality. Other major universities and colleges eventually followed suit. The forceful policy of the CIO, led by the United Auto Workers, brought the A.F.L. into line. The Negro, Walter Reuther warned in late 1945, "should not allow his painful experiences with many of the old craft unions of the American Federation of Labor to embitter him against all labor unions." Both the Negro and the A.F.L. took the hint. Some craft unions still held out, generally by subterfuge, but the weight of the major unions and their two national federations swung unequivocally to the side of equal opportunity without regard to race.

The *Report* of the President's Civil Rights Committee in 1947 had immediate and far-reaching repercussions. The President's Executive Order 9980 established a fair employment procedure within the government structure. Executive Order 9981 was even more significant since it, in effect, abolished discrimination in the armed services. The committee established by this order to study the situation and make recommendations published its report, *Freedom to Serve,* in 1950, by which time all three of the service branches had abolished the quota system of enlistment and segregation in any form, including separate units and limited opportunities. The Navy was first in its implementation, having started even before the President's order, and although the Army dragged its feet, the committee was satisfied that the order and its execution were effective. A year later, a third Executive Order, 10308, established a President's Committee to insure compliance by government contractors with contractual regulations prohibiting discrimination because of race, creed, color, or national origin. The Committee's report was filed early in 1953.

The political reverberations to these dramatic steps by President Truman echoed in the halls of Congress and almost split the Democratic party asunder. In 1948, the Dixiecrats walked out of the Democratic convention in protest to the strong civil rights plank which the young junior Senator from Minnesota, Hubert Humphrey, had pushed through. Truman's election victory that year, in the face of the walkout and the left-wing Progressive Party, was convincing evidence that civil rights had attracted voter support. In Congress, this message from the electorate went unheeded; southern Democrats and conservative Republicans, whose constituencies sent different messages to them, blocked all efforts to write civil rights into statute.

Negroes in general and the NAACP in particular could take some satisfaction in knowing that the Supreme Court was slowly opening basic rights, but in the area of education the progress was even more marked. The NAACP invested heavily of its time and funds in widening educational opportunities by court action. The University of Maryland in 1935 had capitulated at the graduate-school level without taking the case to the Supreme Court. Three years later Missouri was instructed to educate a Negro law student, but its subterfuge worked so well that it tried it again in 1942 by establishing a two-room graduate school in journalism for one qualified Negro graduate student. The University of Oklahoma followed suit when the Supreme Court allowed Missouri's effort to stand, but the end was in sight. In 1950 Texas was told by the Court that its Negro law school had to be equal to that of the white University of Texas Law School, and the doors of the latter were duly opened to Negroes. In a paralled case, Oklahoma was rebuked for permitting a Negro student to be segregated within its state university, and the practice ceased. With a Supreme Court which read the Constitution as a document protecting the rights of all citizens and with the opening of universities at the graduate level, the time was ripe for an all-inclusive appeal for educational opportunities.

The twenty years between the inauguration of Franklin D. Roosevelt and the eve of the Supreme Court desegregation decision were the most revolutionary two decades in the history of the American Negro up to that time. In part, the elemental movements had little to do with race matters; depression, war, prosperity—these were not issues of black and white. Yet they determined a basic posture change: that whites and Negroes would work closely together on matters of national and international importance which had nothing to do with race. Perhaps the most startling development to emerge from these decades was that prominent Negroes began to assume responsibilities in government, business, labor, athletics, education, and the social services which had no connection with race. Negroes, finally, were working in critical jobs because they were needed, and not simply because they were Negroes.

Brown v. Board of Education (1954)

The United States Supreme Court's decision in the case of *Oliver Brown, et al. v. Board of Education of Topeka, Kansas,* was not an isolated event in the development of black-white relations in America. It reflected both the elaborate legal preparations of the NAACP and significant social changes among both blacks and whites. Chief Justice Earl Warren delivered the unanimous opinion of the Court on May 17, 1954.

From 347 U.S. 483.

I

The Facts of the Case

These cases come to us from the States of Kansas, South Carolina, Virginia, and Delaware. They are premised on different facts and different local conditions, but a common legal question justifies their consideration together in this consolidated opinion.

In each of the cases, minors of the Negro race, through their legal representatives, seek the aid of the courts in obtaining admission to the public schools of their community on a nonsegregated basis. In each instance, they had been denied admission to schools attended by white children under laws requiring or permitting segregation according to race. This segregation was alleged to deprive the plaintiffs of the equal protection of the laws under the Fourteenth Amendment. In each of the cases other than the Delaware case, a three-judge federal district court denied relief to the plaintiffs on the so-called "separate but equal" doctrine announced by this Court in *Plessy* v. *Ferguson,* 163 U.S. 537. Under that doctrine, equality of treatment is accorded when the races are provided substantially equal facilities, even though these facilities be separate. In the Delaware case, the Supreme Court of Delaware adhered to that doctrine, but ordered that the plaintiffs be admitted to the white schools because of their superiority to the Negro schools.

The plaintiffs contend that segregated public schools are not "equal" and cannot be made "equal," and that hence they are deprived of the equal protection of the laws. Because of the obvious importance of the question presented, the Court took jurisdiction. Argument was heard in the 1952 Term, and reargument was heard this Term on certain questions propounded by the Court.

Reargument was largely devoted to the circumstances surrounding the adoption of the Fourteenth Amendment in 1868. It covered exhaustively consideration of the Amendment in Congress, ratification by the states, then existing practices in racial segregation, and the views of proponents and opponents of the Amendment. This discussion and our own investigation convince us that, although these sources cast some light, it is not enough to resolve the problem with which we are faced. At best, they are inconclusive. The most avid proponents of the post-War Amendments undoubtedly intended them to remove all legal distinctions among "all persons born or naturalized in the United States." Their opponents, just as certainly, were antagonistic to both the letter and the spirit of the Amendments and wished them to have the most limited effect. What others in Congress and the state legislatures had in mind cannot be determined with any degree of certainty.

An additional reason for the inconclusive nature of the Amendment's history, with respect to segregated schools, is the status of public education at that time. In the South, the movement toward free common schools, supported by general taxation, had not yet taken hold. Education of white children was largely in the hands of private groups. Education of Negroes was almost nonexistent, and practically all of the race were illiterate. In fact, any education of Negroes was forbidden by law in some states. Today, in contrast, many Negroes have achieved outstanding success in the arts and sciences as well as in the business and professional world. It is true that public education had already advanced further in the North, but the effect of the Amendment on Northern States was generally ignored in the congressional debates. Even in the North, the conditions of public education did not approximate those existing today. The curriculum was usually rudimentary; ungraded schools were common in rural areas; the school term was but three months a year in many states; and compulsory school attendance was virtually unknown. As a consequence, it is not surprising that there should be so little in the history of the Fourteenth Amendment relating to its intended effect on public education.

In the first cases in this Court construing the Fourteenth Amendment, decided shortly after its adoption, the Court interpreted it as proscribing all state-imposed discriminations against the Negro race. The doctrine of "separate but equal" did not make its appearance in this Court until 1896 in the case of *Plessy* v. *Ferguson, supra,* involving not education but transportation. American courts have since labored with the doctrine for over half a century. In this Court, there have been six cases involving the "separate but equal" doctrine in the field of public education. In *Cumming* v. *County Board of Education,* 175 U.S. 528 and *Gong Lum* v. *Rice,* 275 U.S. 78, the validity of the doctrine itself was not challenged. In more recent cases, all on the graduate school level, inequality was found in that specific benefits enjoyed by white students were denied to Negro students of the same educational qualifications. *Missouri ex rel. Gaines* v. *Canada,* 305 U.S. 337; *Sipuel* v. *Oklahoma,* 332 U.S. 631; *Sweatt* v. *Painter,* 339 U.S. 629; *McLaurin* v. *Oklahoma State Regents,* 339 U.S. 637. In none of these cases was it necessary to reexamine the doctrine to grant relief to the Negro plaintiff. And in *Sweatt* v. *Painter, supra,* the Court expressly reserved decision on the question whether *Plessy* v. *Ferguson* should be held inapplicable to public education.

In the instant cases, that question is directly presented. Here, unlike *Sweatt* v. *Painter,* there are findings below that the Negro and white schools involved have been equalized, or are being equalized, with respect to buildings, curricula, qualifications and salaries of teachers, and other "tangible" factors. Our decision, therefore, cannot turn on merely a comparison of these tangible factors in the Negro and white schools involved in each of the cases. We must look instead to the effect of segregation itself on public education.

II

The Present and the Future

In approaching this problem, we cannot turn the clock back to 1868 when the Amendment was adopted, or even to 1896 when *Plessy* v. *Ferguson* was written. We must consider public education in the light of its full development and its present place in American life throughout the Nation. Only in this way can it be determined if segregation in public schools deprives these plaintiffs of the equal protection of the laws.

Today, education is perhaps the most important function of state and local governments. Compulsory school attendance laws and the great expenditures for education both demonstrate our recognition of the importance of education to our democratic society. It is required in the performance of our most basic public responsibilities, even service in the armed forces. It is the very foundation of good citizenship. Today it is a principal instrument in awakening the child to cultural values, in preparing him for later professional training, and in helping him to adjust normally to his environment. In these days, it is doubtful that any child may reasonably be expected to succeed in life if he is denied the opportunity of an education. Such an opportunity, where the state has undertaken to provide it, is a right which must be made available to all on equal terms.

We come then to the question presented: Does segregation of children in public schools solely on the basis of race, even though the physical facilities and other "tangible" factors may be equal, deprive the children of the minority group of equal education opportunities? We believe that it does.

In *Sweatt* v. *Painter, supra,* in finding that a segregated law school for Negroes could not provide them equal educational opportunities, this Court replied in large part on "those qualities which are incapable of objective measurement but which make for greatness in a law school." In *McLaurin* v. *Oklahoma State Regents, supra,* the Court, in requiring that a Negro admitted to a white graduate school be treated like all other students, again resorted to intangible considerations: "... his ability to study, to engage in discussions and exchange views with other students, and, in general, to learn his profession." Such considerations apply with added force to children in grade and high schools. To separate them from others of similar age and qualifications solely because of their race generates a feeling of inferiority as to their status in the community that may affect their hearts and minds in a way unlikely ever to be undone. The effect of this separation on their educational opportunities was well stated by a finding in the Kansas case by a court which nevertheless felt compelled to rule against the Negro plaintiffs:

> Segregation of white and colored children in public schools has a detrimental effect upon the colored children. The impact is greater when it has the sanction of the law; for the policy of separating the races is usually interpreted as denoting the inferiority of the Negro group. A sense of inferiority affects the motivation of a child to learn. Segregation with the sanction of law, therefore, has a tendency to retard the educational and mental development of Negro children and to deprive them of some of the benefits they would receive in a racially integrated school system.

Whatever may have been the extent of psychological knowledge at the time of *Plessy v. Ferguson*, this finding is amply supported by modern authority. Any language in *Plessy v. Ferguson* contrary to this finding is rejected.

We conclude that in the field of public education the doctrine of "separate but equal" has no place. Separate educational facilities are inherently unequal. Therefore, we hold that the plaintiffs and others similarly situated for whom the actions have been brought are, by reason of the segregation complained of, deprived of the equal protection of the laws guaranteed by the Fourteenth Amendment. This disposition makes unnecessary any discussion whether such segregation also violates the Due Process Clause of the Fourteenth Amendment.

The Significance of the Supreme Court Decision

The Supreme Court's school desegregation decision focused the nation's attention sharply on the South. While the 1954 decision met with cheers and boos, both supporter and opponent agreed that a new era of the black-white struggle had dawned. In 1955 the Court issued a decree specifying some general principles for carrying out school desegregation. In response to that opinion Robert Carter and Thurgood Marshall, two of the black lawyers who had presented the NAACP's case in both 1954 and 1955, offered their views as to what actions should follow from the Court's rulings.

From Robert L. Carter and Thurgood Marshall, "The Meaning and Significance of the Supreme Court Decree," *The Journal of Negro Education*, XXIV (1955), pp. 397, 402–404. Subheadings added by the editors.

I

A Ticket to Desegregation

On May 31st, 1955, the long-awaited decision of the Supreme Court, on how to implement its opinion declaring segregation in public education unconstitutional, was handed down. Like the decision of May 17, 1954, it was read by the Chief Justice of the United States for a unanimous Court, and its language was simple, direct and non-technical. After the 1954 opinion, it seemed anti-climatic, but nothing world shaking should have been expected. Utterance of a practical formula pursuant to which a great constitutional and moral abstraction may become a part of our daily lives sometimes seems to have far less impact than the initial statement of the principle itself. And that seemed to be the situation in this case.

While the Court's solution differed from that proposed by counsel for the Negro litigants, chiefly in regard to the fixing of a deadline for compliance, the formula devised is about as effective as one could have expected. The net result should be to unite the country behind a nationwide desegregation program, and if this takes place, the Court must be credited with having performed its job brilliantly....

The decision has opened the door for Negroes to secure unsegregated educational facilities if they so desire. There has been some disappointment among anti-segregationists that no time limit was set. Certainly, on the surface at least, a time limit would have afforded a sense of security that segregation would end within a specific number of years. We fear, however, that such security would have been fed on false hopes.

Signs like "colored waiting room" offered visible evidence of the Jim Crow system of segregation by law in the South. Here blacks wait at the Durham, North Carolina, bus station in 1940. Once on the bus they would by law have to sit in the rear seats.

Some states—Missouri, Maryland, West Virginia and Kentucky seem to fall in this category—would have taken official steps to comply with whatever formula the Court devised. Pressure skillfully applied in a few other states would have resulted in the adoption of a similar policy. While desegregation could be successfully undertaken in many areas of the deep South tomorrow, little will be done for the most part unless Negroes demand and insist upon desegregation. In states such as Georgia and Mississippi, it looks as if desegregation will be accomplished only after a long and bitter fight, the brunt of which will have to be borne by Negroes. In short, we must face the fact that in the deep South, with rare exceptions, desegregation will become a reality only if Negroes exhibit real militancy and press unrelentingly for their rights. And this would have been the situation no matter what kind of decision the Court had handed down.

A Second Reconstruction

1   Between 1877, when Reconstruction of the post-Civil War South ended, and the 1950s most efforts by American blacks to achieve fair and equal treatment under law could have been symbolized by the recent quiet plea for racial justice shown at right. Through those years changes in racial relations were characteristically slow, and the largely-segregated racial system in the United States was maintained in part by sporadic violence by whites in many areas. Beginning in the 1950s, however, the pace of racial change accelerated and the tone of black protests became more and more assertive. The largest volume of protest, found at first in the South, where legal discrimination against blacks was still widespread, shifted gradually to the North, Midwest, and West. In those regions the largest black ghettoes—producers of de facto segregation and large pools of black unemployment—were located. The pictures on the following pages reveal aspects of what can be fairly described as a second Reconstruction, one which continued into the 1970s.

A boycott of the city bus system in Montgomery, Alabama, in December 1955 was touched off when Mrs. Rosa Parks defied a city ordinance by refusing to give up her seat in a crowded bus so that a white passenger might be seated. She was immediately arrested by the city police. At left, Mrs. Parks, between an officer and her attorney, arrives for a court hearing. Montgomery blacks eventually won when the Supreme Court declared such segregation unconstitutional. A previous Supreme Court decision (1954) prohibiting segregation by race in public schools came to a test of strength in 1957, when federal troops escorted the first black pupils into Little Rock Central School (below) after vain resistance by Governor Orval Faubus of Arkansas and mobs of whites.

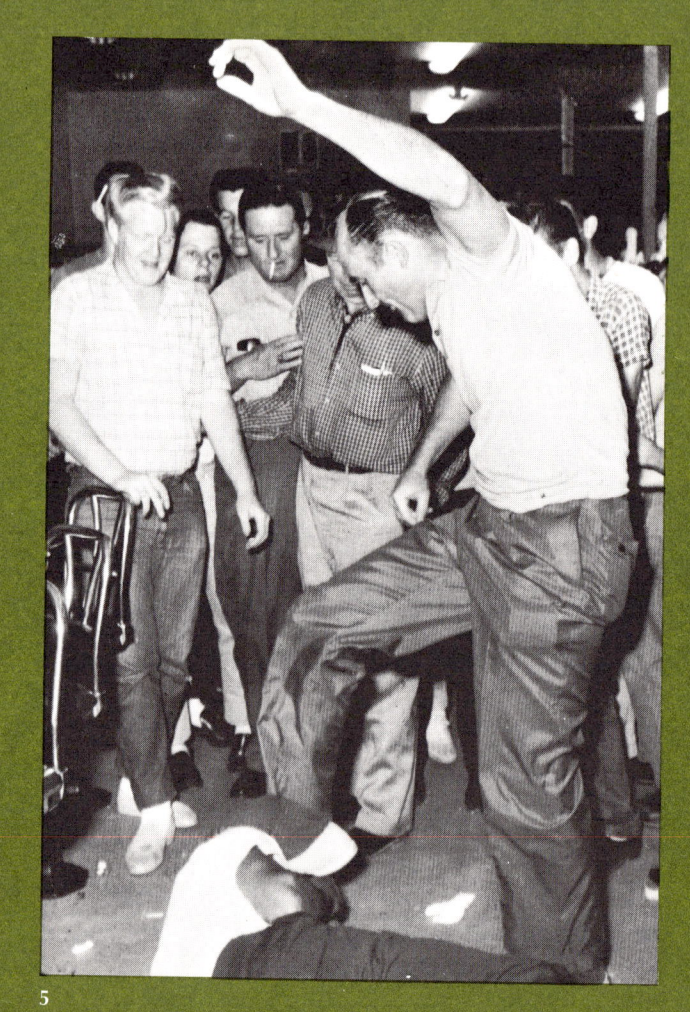

In city after city, sometimes aided by court actions but often triumphing by sheer persistence, bravery, and economic pressure, blacks brought an end to the segregation of many public and quasi-public facilities. At left, students in Chattanooga, Tenn., integrate a lunch counter in 1960. Such episodes were often accompanied by violent reactions by opponents. Above, in an incident in Jackson, Miss., in 1963, a white bystander kicks a demonstrator who has just been dragged from a lunch counter stool.

For many years there had been no effective way for black Americans to obtain legal enforcement of certain civil rights, such as the right to vote and the right to equality in public accommodations, in places where state and local officials obstructed enforcement. In August 1963 several hundred thousand civil rights supporters, both black and white, staged a "March on Washington" to publicize their demands for federal action to enforce civil rights. It was the largest rally ever seen in the nation's capital. Above, the demonstrators mass between the Lincoln Memorial (from where the photograph was taken) and the Washington Monument. At right, President John F. Kennedy meets leaders of the March at the White House. From left: Whitney Young of the National Urban League, Dr. Martin Luther King of the Southern Christian Leadership Conference, Rabbi Joachim Prinz of the American Jewish Congress, A Philip Randolph, labor leader and director of the March, President Kennedy, Walter Reuther of the AFL-CIO, and Roy Wilkins of the NAACP.

In 1964, for the first time since Reconstruction, blacks in Mississippi organized a statewide effort to gain political participation through their Freedom Democratic Party, of which the convention headquarters is shown above. They sent their own delegates to the national Democratic Party nominating convention in that year, but they were refused seats in the Mississippi delegation. In the following year Congress, urged on by President Lyndon B. Johnson, passed a Voting Rights Act which sent federal officials into parts of the South to register voters. At left, a federal registrar fills out a form for a prospective black voter in Canton, Miss., in January 1966.

10

11

The breaking down of established patterns of segregation in the 1950s and 1960s came as a shock to many American whites, as with the woman demonstrator above. Among those joining the fight to preserve segregation were members of the tiny American Nazi Party, a few of whom are shown demonstrating in Grant Park, Chicago, in 1969.

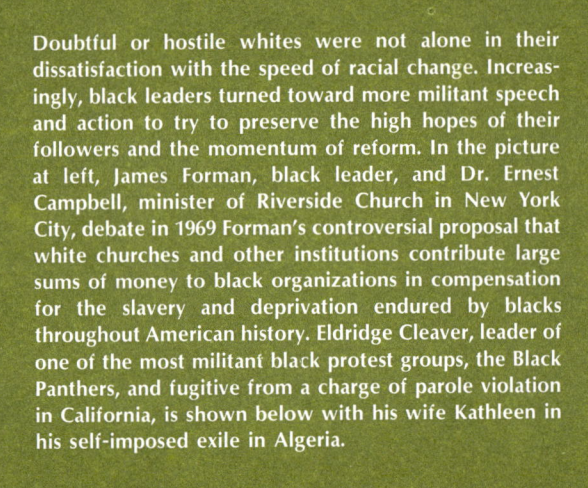

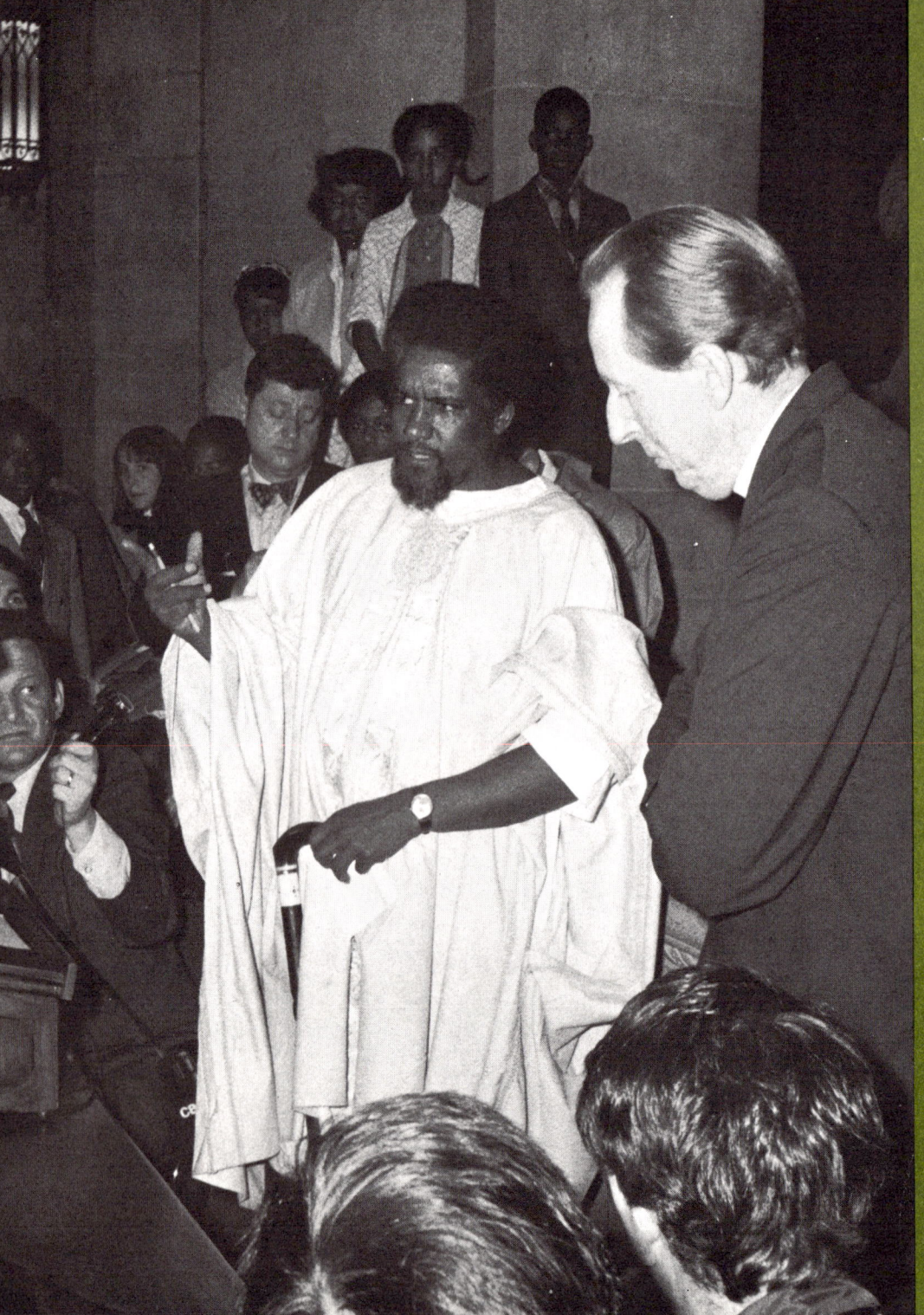

Doubtful or hostile whites were not alone in their dissatisfaction with the speed of racial change. Increasingly, black leaders turned toward more militant speech and action to try to preserve the high hopes of their followers and the momentum of reform. In the picture at left, James Forman, black leader, and Dr. Ernest Campbell, minister of Riverside Church in New York City, debate in 1969 Forman's controversial proposal that white churches and other institutions contribute large sums of money to black organizations in compensation for the slavery and deprivation endured by blacks throughout American history. Eldridge Cleaver, leader of one of the most militant black protest groups, the Black Panthers, and fugitive from a charge of parole violation in California, is shown below with his wife Kathleen in his self-imposed exile in Algeria.

14

The Black Panther organization became in the 1960s a symbol of the desire of many American blacks, especially those living in the ghettoes of the nation's large cities, to achieve pride in their identity and power to relieve the frustrations of poverty and unemployment. In a number of cities the Panthers undertook constructive community action programs. But their militance and possession of weapons brought local police down on them repeatedly, sometimes justifiably, sometimes not. The results included several gun battles and the deaths of both Panthers and policemen. In the picture above, Black Panthers demonstrate in April 1969 against participation in the war in Vietnam.

If a deadline had been fixed, it would have been open to attack as being arbitrary, unrealistic and unfair to the South, and this would have given the demagogues a great opportunity to secure support for an attitude of open defiance. Perhaps with this in mind, and with the realization that deadline or not Negroes would have to make desegregation a reality, the Court avoided setting a time limit. Now with no deadline set, and local judges with an understanding of local problems empowered to administer and supervise the desegregation process, what more could the South realistically ask for except repudiation of the May 17th decision? As a result, it is likely that the attitude will be one of resignation to living within the law, once Negroes make it clear that they will insist that their community desegregate its schools. Now deadlines will be fixed by local federal courts. The cry that the local judge is unfamiliar with local problems cannot be sustained, and the possibility of defying the authority of the respected and on the scene symbol of law and order, even aside from the power to punish for contempt, is remote indeed. Great responsibility has been placed at the local level where it belongs, and where it would have been exercised in any event.

There will be, of course, federal judges whose views on the wisdom of segregation are so deep seated that they will seek to use their equitable discretion to frustrate and delay litigation aimed at forcing compliance. In these instances, lawyers will have to use their knowledge of legal procedure to make the judge render justice. By and large, however, events will disclose that the local federal judges will not be disposed to wink at efforts to avoid full compliance with the Supreme Court's ruling. All in all, the net result should be that more widespread voluntary desegregation is now possible than might have occurred had a more stringent order been issued.

The decision was a good one. The Court has reaffirmed its pronouncement that segregation is unconstitutional and throughout the opinion stress is placed upon the necessity for full compliance at the earliest practicable date. Delays may be occasioned by various devices. This would result in any case. We can be sure that desegregation will take place throughout the United States—tomorrow in some places, the day after in others and many, many moons, hence in some, but it will come eventually to all. We look upon the May 31st decision as a ticket to desegregation which is now available to every parent and child who needs it and wants to use it.

II

What about the Future?

As for the next steps, at present the most important thing to do is to get a copy of the opinion, read it and explain its implications to others. Segregationists were at first jubilant, but much of the jubilation has died. Anti-segregationists have no cause for disappointment. Rather, theirs should be an attitude of quiet confidence.

Efforts should be made to secure the support for voluntary desegregation from among individuals and organizations, and with that support, pressure should be brought on school boards to get them to voluntarily desegregate their schools. Each local NAACP Branch will be engaged in an effort to secure voluntary compliance in many areas in the South and will need and welcome all the assistance it can get.

While the immediate problem is to secure desegregation in the public schools in the Southern and border states, it should be remembered that segregation and other forms of racial prejudices present a national, not a regional problem. Northerners need to take a long look at their school systems and bend their efforts to eliminating segregation in their own public schools. One recognizes that here the defense is residential segregation, but that is really no answer. Surely we must have the ingenuity and skill to alleviate racial segregation in our schools without being required to await the long range levelling of racial barriers with respect to housing occupancy. If segregation in public schools is bad for our children in Atlanta, Georgia, it ought to be equally bad for them in New York City, Chicago, Philadelphia or Boston.

Finally, it is important that the strongest pressures against the continuation of segregation, North or South, be continually and constantly manifested. Probably, as much as anything else, this is the key to the elimination of discrimination in the United States.

Mixed Schools and Mixed Blood

Not all Americans saw the desegregation decisions of 1954 and 1955 as opportunities for progress and an ending of white oppression of blacks. In the following selection Herbert Ravenel Sass, author, journalist, and native South Carolinian, offers a series of arguments defending white supremacy in the South and in the nation.

From Herbert Ravenel Sass, "Mixed Schools and Mixed Blood," *The Atlantic Monthly*, CXCVIII (November, 1956), pp. 45, 48–49. Subheadings added by the editors.

I

The Meaning of Race

What may well be the most important physical fact in the story of the United States is one which is seldom emphasized in our history books. It is the fact that throughout the three and a half centuries of our existence we have kept our several races biologically distinct and separate. Though we have encouraged the mixing of many different strains in what has been called the American "melting pot," we have confined this mixing to the white peoples of European ancestry, excluding from our "melting pot" all other races. The result is that the United States today is overwhelmingly a pure white nation, with a smaller but considerable Negro population in which there is some white blood, and a much smaller American Indian population.

The fact that the United States is overwhelmingly pure white is not only important; it is also the most distinctive fact about this country when considered in relation to the rest of the New World. Except Canada, Argentina, and Uruguay, none of the approximately twenty-five other countries of this hemisphere has kept its races pure. Instead (though each contains some pure-blooded individuals) all these countries are products of an amalgamation of races—American Indian and white or American Indian, Negro, and white. In general the pure-blooded white nations have outstripped the far more numerous American mixed-blood nations in most of the achievements which constitute progress as commonly defined.

These facts are well known. But now there lurks in ambush, as it were, another fact: we have suddenly begun to move toward abandonment of our 350-year-old system of keeping our races pure and are preparing to adopt instead a method of racial amalgamation similar to that which has created the mixed-blood nations of this hemisphere; except that the amalgamation being prepared for this country is not Indian and white but Negro and white. It is the deep conviction of nearly all white Southerners in the states which have large Negro populations that the mingling or integration of white and Negro children in the South's primary schools would open the gates to miscegenation and widespread racial amalgamation....

For the elementary public school is the most critical of those areas of activity where the South must and will at all costs maintain separateness of the races. The South must do this because, although it is a nearly universal instinct, race preference is not active in the very young. Race preference (which the propagandists miscall race prejudice or hate) is one of those instincts which develop gradually as the mind develops and which, if taken in hand early enough, can be prevented from developing at all.

Hence if the small children of the two races in approximately equal numbers—as would be the case in a great many of the South's schools—were brought together intimately and constantly and grew up in close association in integrated schools under teachers necessarily committed to the gospel of racial integration, there would be many in whom race preference would not develop. This would not be, as superficial thinkers might suppose, a good thing, the happy solution of the race problem in America. It might be a solution of a sort, but not one that the American people would desire. It would inevitably result, beginning with the least desirable elements of both races, in a great increase of racial amalgamation, the very process which throughout our history we have most sternly rejected. For although to most persons today the idea of mixed mating is disagreeable or even repugnant, this would not be true of the new generations brought up in mixed schools with the desirability of racial integration as a basic premise. Among those new generations mixed matings would become commonplace, and a greatly enlarged mixed-blood population would result.

That is the compelling reason, though by no means the only reason, why the South will resist, with all its resources of mind and body, the mixing of the races in its public schools. It is a reason which, when its validity is generally recognized, will quickly enlist millions of non-Southerners in support of the South's position. The people of the North and West do not favor the transformation of the United States into a nation composed in considerable part of mixed bloods any more than the people of the South do. Northern support of school integration in the South is due to the failure to realize its inevitable biological effect in regions of large Negro population. If Northerners did realize this, their enthusiasm for mixed schools in the South would evaporate at once.

II

What about the Future?

There are other cogent reasons for the white South's stand: the urgent necessity of restoring the Constitution and our federal form of government before they are permanently destroyed by the Court's usurpation of power; the equally urgent necessity of re-establishing law and precedent instead of sociological and psychological theory as the basis of the Court's decisions; the terrible damage which racial integration would do to the South's whole educational system, black as well as white. These and other aspects have been fully and effectively explored and need not be touched upon here.

But the underlying and compelling reason for the South's refusal to operate mixed schools—its belief that mixed schools will result in ultimate racial amalgamation—has been held virtually taboo and if mentioned in the North is not examined at all but is summarily dismissed as not worthy of consideration. The amalgamation "bogey," it is said, is not really believed by intelligent Southerners but is a smoke screen used to hide the South's real motives, which are variously described, ranging from plain sadism to a shrewd determination to deprive the Negro of education so that he can never displace the Southern white man. Besides, it is confidently alleged, the Negro does not wish to destroy the identity of his race by merging it with the white race.

Both those statements are incorrect. As already pointed out, the fear that mixed schools in the South would open the way to racial amalgamation is not a bogey or a smoke screen or a pretense of any kind but the basic animating motive of the white South in resisting the drive of the N.A.A.C.P. and its supporters. The second statement is as erroneous as the first. The Negro leaders do want racial amalgamation; they not only want the right to amalgamate through legal intermarriage but they want that right to be exercised widely and frequently.

It is only natural and human that they should feel this way. The truth is that these ambitious, intelligent, often amalgamated, and often genuinely dedicated Negro men and women feel about this matter exactly as white men and women would feel if they were similarly constituted and circumstanced—fusion of the two races would solve the Negro's problem at once. How much of the Negro rank and file consciously seeks amalgamation is a question; to the Southern Negro in particular the thought of intermarriage is still new and strange. As for the Northern leaders of the movement, some of them make no bones about it, and when they do evade the question they do so only for reasons of strategy.

But actually it does not matter much whether or not intermarriage is the admitted aim of the N.A.A.C.P. strategists. To suppose that, proclaiming the virtual identity of the races, we can promote all other degrees of race mixing but stop short of interracial mating is—if I may use an overworked but vivid simile—like going over Niagara Falls in a barrel in the expectation of stopping three fourths of the way down. The South is now the great bulwark against intermarriage. A very few years of thoroughly integrated schools would produce large numbers of indoctrinated young Southerners free from all "prejudice" against mixed matings.

It is because there the adolescent and "unprejudiced" mind can be reached that the integrationists have chosen the Southern schools as their primary target; and it is precisely because the adolescent and therefore defenseless mind would there be exposed to brain-washing which it would not know how to refute that the white South will not operate integrated public schools. If the South fails to defend its young children who are not yet capable of defending themselves, if it permits their wholesale impregnation by a propaganda persuasive and by them unanswerable, the salutary instinct of race preference which keeps the races separate, as in Nature, will be destroyed before it develops and the barriers against racial amalgamation will go down.

This is the new and ominous fact which, as was said at the beginning of this article, lurks in ambush, concealed like a viper in the school integration crusade. Success of that crusade would mean that after three and a half centuries of magnificent achievement under a system of racial separateness and purity, we would tacitly abandon that system and instead would begin the creation of a mixed American race by the fusion of the two races which, as H. G. Wells expressed it, are at opposite extremes of the human species.

Many well-meaning persons have suddenly discovered that the tenets of the Christian religion and the professions of our democratic faith compel us to accept the risks of this hybridization. No one who will face up to the biological facts and really think the problem through can believe any such thing or see the partial suicide of the white race in America (and of the Negro race also) as anything other than a crime against both religion and civilization.

I have tried to show here the basic and compelling reason why the Southern people, who know the facts of life in the South better than any doctrinaire sociologist viewing the scene from his ivory tower, see no possible course save to stand firm in their resistance to school integration no matter what may be the consequences of their resistance. When a people believes that something even dearer than its life is threatened, there isn't much use in pointing out its duty to obey the law which threatens it, especially when it is almost unanimously of the opinion that the law is a perversion. And the South has ample precedent for resistance. In a much firmer sense the Prohibition Amendment was the law of the land, and the North even more than the South made a mockery of it. So too was the federal fugitive slave act the law of the land, yet many Northern states nullified and openly violated it.

Moreover, fortifying the South for its ordeal is the conviction that it is defending something far greater than itself: that integrity of race and that pride of race which all great peoples have—the Chinese, the Japanese, the Arabs, the Jews, for instance—and without which no people is worth its salt. There is good hope that before too long this will begin to be recognized outside the South. The current pseudoscientific buncombe about racial identity is at last being questioned openly. It will be exploded completely with the ending of the leftist-liberal taboo which has practically sealed the lips of geneticists able and willing to discuss racial realities, and our Lysenko-like excursion in the realm of race will come to an end. Then it will be seen that the South, in maintaining the actuality and the great significance of racial differences, has not been "racist" in any evil sense but has been the defender of something permanently important to the whole American people; and that the Supreme Court, in launching the Negro on an offensive which cannot and should not succeed, has dealt a terrible blow to his advancement and his happiness.

The Little Rock Crisis
(1957)

Confrontation followed confrontation as black Southerners began to act to end school segregation. Throughout the South blacks organized and began court action to have state and local laws enforcing segregation declared unconstitutional. In some border areas, such as Kansas, Missouri, and Washington, D.C., school segregation by law ended quickly, although in many areas residential living patterns kept schools all black and all white, or predominantly black and predominantly white. In much of the South, however, conflict and violence followed attempts to end the racial status quo. One of the most striking episodes occurred in 1957 in Little Rock, Arkansas, where the violence involved not only local citizens but also the state and federal governments

Reprinted from "Step By Step . . . The Build-Up To A Crisis," *U.S. News & World Report* (October 4, 1957), pp. 55–57. Copyright 1957 *U.S. News & World Report.*

I

A Plan for Gradual Integration

The chain of events that led to the sending of federal troops to Little Rock started more than two years ago.

In May, 1955, the Little Rock school board prepared a plan for gradual integration, to begin at Central High School in September, 1957.

Early in 1956, attorneys for the National Association for the Advancement of Colored People (NAACP) asked the U.S. District Court to order an end to segregation in Little Rock.

The school board presented its plan for gradual integration to the court. The plan was approved by Judge John E. Miller, and was upheld by the U.S. Eighth Circuit Court of Appeals.

Late in August, 1957, trouble started. In what follows, you get the step-by-step developments.

August 29—Chancellor Murray O. Reed, of State Chancery Court, granted the petition of a white parent and ordered the school board not to proceed with integration. Governor Orval E. Faubus testified at the hearing that "violence, bloodshed and riots" would result if the integration plan were carried out. He said revolvers had been found on Negro and white students.

August 30—U.S. District Judge Ronald N. Davies, a North Dakotan serving temporarily in Arkansas, issued a temporary injunction prohibiting use of the Chancery Court's order.

The school board announced that it would go ahead with its plan to admit Negro students to Central High School on September 3.

September 2—Governor Faubus ordered Maj. Gen. Sherman T. Clinger, State Adjutant General, to mobilize certain units of the Arkansas National Guard. The Governor's order stated: "You are directed to place off limits to white students those schools for colored students and to place off limits to colored students those schools heretofore operated and recently set up for white students. This order will remain in effect until the demobilization of the Guard or until further orders."

September 3—President Eisenhower told his news conference that he was in touch with the office of Attorney General Herbert Brownell, Jr., which was "taking a look" at the Little Rock situation, and that "the next decision will have to be by the lawyers and jurists."

At a special hearing, Judge Davies directed the school board to disregard the troops and to permit Negroes to attend classes.

September 4—National Guardsmen and State troopers surrounding Central High School turned back nine Negro students who attempted to enter.

Governor Faubus declared that he had placed the troops there "to preserve peace and order" and that he was not defying federal court orders.

Judge Davies ordered U.S. District Attorney Osro Cobb to begin a complete investigation "to determine the responsibility for interference with the integration order . . . and to report your findings to me with the least practicable delay."

Attorney General Brownell announced in Washington that the U.S. district attorney, the U.S. marshal and the Federal Bureau of Investigation would take part in the investigation ordered by Judge Davies.

Governor Faubus sent President Eisenhower a telegram stating that the issue in Little Rock "is whether or not the head of a sovereign State can exercise his constitutional powers and discretion in maintaining peace and good order within his jurisdiction." The Governor's telegram continued:

> I have strong reasons to believe that the telephone lines to the Arkansas executive mansion have been tapped—I suspect the federal agents.
>
> The situation in Little Rock grows more explosive by the hour. This is caused for the most part by the misunderstanding of our problems by a federal judge who decreed "immediate" integration of the public schools of Little Rock without hearing any evidence whatsoever as to the conditions now existing in this community.
>
> The situation is further aggravated by the impending unwarranted interference of federal agents. If these actions continue, or if my executive authority as Governor to maintain the peace is breached, then I can no longer be responsible for the results.

The Governor added that "the blood that may be shed will be on the hands of the Federal Government and its agents" and requested the President's "understanding and co-operation."

September 5—The President, answering the Governor's telegram, declared: "The only assurance I can give you is that the Federal Constitution will be upheld by me by every legal means at my command." He said also: "There is no basis of fact to the statements you make in your telegram that federal authorities have been considering taking you into custody or that telephone lines to your executive mansion have been tapped by any agency of the Federal Government." . . .

II

The Governor Meets the President

September 10—Appearing on a television program, the Governor denied that he had called out the National Guard in order to block integration and said he would be willing to meet the President or "with anyone" in an attempt to resolve the problem. He charged that Judge Davies had been sent to Arkansas to force integration.

An Assistant Attorney General and the district attorney reported to Judge Davies on the investigation that he had ordered. They declared that the Governor, General Clinger and Colonel Johnson "obstruct and interfere with the carrying out" of the court's integration orders, and requested that these three officials be enjoined from continuing to do so.

Judge Davies ordered that the three officials appear in court September 20 for a hearing on the issuance of a preliminary injunction against them.

The President told a group of Republican leaders that he favored "patience" in handling the Little Rock situation.

September 11—Governor Faubus telegraphed the President, pointing out that "we jointly share great responsibility under the Federal Constitution" and requesting a conference with him "to counsel together in determining my course of action."

The President's answering telegram suggested that the Governor see him at Newport on September 13 or 14.

September 14—The President and the Governor conferred at Newport.

The President then issued a statement saying they had held "a constructive discussion" and that the Governor had stated his intention to respect the court's decisions.

Governor Faubus issued a statement a little later saying that he accepted the Supreme Court's 1954 decision on integration as "the law of the land" that "must be obeyed," but declaring that "changes necessitated by court orders cannot be accomplished overnight." . . .

III

Police Replace National Guard

September 21—A statement by the President called the Governor's withdrawal of troops "a necessary step in the right direction" and expressed confidence that "the citizens of Little Rock and the State of Arkansas will welcome this opportunity to demonstrate that in their city and in their State proper orders of a United States court will be executed promptly and without disorder."

In a second statement, the President called attention to the withdrawal of the National Guard, the decision of the school board to carry out its integration plan and the word of local authorities that they were prepared to maintain law and order. He said: "The sincere and conscientious efforts of the citizens of Little Rock prior to September 2 show that they are persons of good will and feel a responsibility to preserve and respect the law—whether or not they personally agree with it. I am confident that they will vigorously oppose any violence by extremists."

September 22—Governor Faubus declared at Sea Island, Ga., that he was "somewhat apprehensive" about what might happen if Negro students attempted to enter Central High School immediately. He said the President "has shown great patience and understanding in one of the most difficult problems facing this nation," but that "some of those in the palace guard have agitated the situation and caused trouble. They were motivated politically, they saw an opportunity." In this connection he mentioned Attorney General Brownell, "who was rather adamant, and it was his Justice Department that came into the case improperly, we thought."

Little Rock's Mayor Mann issued this statement:

A strong police detail will be on hand at Little Rock Central High School to deal with any effort by mob leaders to breach the peace of this community. Arrangements have been made for additional assistance if that becomes necessary.

Violations of city ordinances and State laws will be dealt with firmly. I have advised that violations of the pending federal injunctions will meet the full weight of the U.S. Government. I feel confident that city authorities have the complete support of this community on the issue of mob rule as opposed to law and order.

Mrs. Margaret Jackson, vice president of the League of Central High Mothers, told newsmen: "We hope to have a big demonstration to show that the people of Little Rock are still against integration. I hope that they [the Negroes] won't get in.

IV

The Fighting Starts

September 23—Nine Negro students entered Central High School by a side door. When a waiting crowd of about 1,000 persons heard about it, fighting broke out, and the heavy guard of city and State police was unable to control the situation. Several persons were injured. Police escorted the Negro students safely from the building.

Mayor Mann charged that the violence was the result of a plan and that it "bore all the marks of the professional agitators."

A few hours later, the President issued this statement:

I want to make several things very clear about the disgraceful occurrences of today at Central High School in the City of Little Rock, Ark. They are:

1. The federal law and orders of a United States District Court, implementing that law, cannot be flouted with impunity by any individual, or any mob of extremists.

2. I will use the full power of the United States, including whatever force may be necessary, to prevent any obstruction of the law and to carry out the orders of the federal court.

3. Of course, every right-thinking citizen will hope that the American sense of justice and fair play will prevail in this case. It will be a sad day for this country—both at home and abroad—if school children can safely attend their classes only under the protection of armed guards.

4. I repeat my expressed confidence that the citizens of Little Rock and of Arkansas will respect the law and will not countenance violations of law and order by extremists.

The President also issued a proclamation citing the day's developments at Little Rock and commanding "all persons engaged in such obstruction of justice to cease and desist therefrom, and to disperse forthwith."

September 24—On orders of the President, Regular Army troops were flown to Little Rock from Fort Campbell, Ky., and the entire Arkansas National Guard was placed in federal service.

The President explained his actions in a nation-wide broadcast.

Reading 369

How Long, How Long . . . ?

In 1962 Mrs. Daisy Bates, a black newspaper editor who was one of the leaders in the Little Rock struggle, offered her view as to the significance of the event for black and white Americans.

Copyright © 1962 by Daisy Bates. From the book *The Long Shadow of Little Rock*, published by David McKay Company, Inc. Reprinted by permission of the publishers. Pp. 219-220, 222-225. Subheadings added by the editors.

I

The Significance of Little Rock

In the great struggle of the colored peoples of the world for equality and independence—the struggle that is one of the truly crucial events of the twentieth century—the episode of the children in Little Rock is a landmark of historic significance.

The epic fight that was necessary for a few Negro children to gain admittance to a "white" school had a dramatic effect on America and the whole world. Only through the unbelievable outrage at Little Rock was the world brought to a sharp realization of the shameful discrimination that the world's greatest democracy directs even against young children—in the country that boasts of being the leader of the "free world" and prides itself upon having given mankind a Constitution based upon individual dignity and liberty. . . .

Tremendous changes have taken place in the field of civil rights since the Little Rock crisis. However, the United States Government, one hundred years after the Emancipation Proclamation, still finds itself grappling with the so-called "Negro problem." We are still faced with the grim fact that twenty million American Negro citizens suffer discrimination in citizenship ninety-odd years after the adoption of the Thirteenth, Fourteenth, and Fifteenth Amendments to the Constitution.

Most Americans seem to be blind to the signs of the times, which point clearly to

Integration, even token integration, proceeded slowly and with considerable violence in the years after the Little Rock crisis. Here Carolyn King (second from left) walks the six blocks from her home to integrate a previously all-white high school in Birmingham, Ala., in the fall of 1964. White youths heckled her along the route to the school. A year earlier Birmingham had been rent by confrontations, some of them violent, between blacks and whites. The tension culminated in the deaths of four children when white extremists bombed a black church.

first-class citizenship for American Negro citizens as a prime ingredient of a democratic world of liberty and equality. Even if most Americans are unseeing, the rest of the world is not. Dr. Heinrich Hellstern, head of the relief organization of the Swiss Evangelical Church, has observed fittingly:

> Little Rock is now the most famous American city besides New York and Chicago. Every boy in our country knows the name of Little Rock. Events such as you had in Little Rock and like those in New Orleans have repercussions all over the world. Your people must understand that the world has changed. They must understand that it is not just a local event—it has a world aspect. If your people will realize this, they will understand better their own federal government. I know that it is difficult and there are many tensions, but it is the task for all who are responsible for international relations.

II

What about the Future?

What has happened in the five years since President Eisenhower ordered the troops into Little Rock to desegregate Central High School? Only seventy-eight Negro children have been assigned by the school board to formerly all-white junior and senior high schools!

What else has happened in these five years? The Little Rock story has been supplanted by stirring demonstrations of another kind, yet part of the same struggle for human dignity. There were the lunch counter sit-ins and the Freedom Rides that have produced memorable and heart-rending episodes.

In one such episode, a mother sat in a southern courtroom and heard a judge sentence her two sons to prison, along with their college classmates, for trying to purchase a cup of coffee at a lunch counter marked "For White Only." Tears were flowing from her eyes as she watched the police herd her sons off to jail. A white reporter leaving the courtroom paused beside her, touched her shoulder, and said, "I'm sorry." She looked at him and said: "Don't feel sorry for me. I have never been so proud of my sons as I am today."

What else has happened? There was held an election in which the two great political parties entered candidates pledged to sponsor legislative action in the field of civil rights. Since then, the President has taken affirmative executive action on a few isolated civil rights matters, but the positive leadership on broader, more meaningful measures that was promised in pre-election speeches has seemingly been forgotten. Millions of Negroes, along with many white citizens, have been left disillusioned.

What else? In 1962 a combination of southern legislators and northern Republicans threw the United States Senate into parliamentary paralysis in a maneuver to prevent civil rights legislation on the issue of voting privileges for southern Negroes who had finished the sixth grade of elementary school. Civil rights legislation has thus been postponed. Again, millions of Americans were left disillusioned. The promise of first-class citizenship to southern Negroes remains but a promise.

What else? There are stirrings among Negro Americans that the politicians ignore at the peril not only to themselves but to any government that turns its back on the lessons of history. Disillusionment breeds contempt and hostility. It fosters ugliness and undermines the democratic spirit from which our nation draws its strength.

Meanwhile, a large portion of the Negro masses is losing faith in American democracy. This is demonstrated by the growing influence on the American Negro of the nationalist organizations that have sprung up during recent years. The strongest and most widely known of these is the "Black Muslims." Whites are barred from membership. The Muslims stress the dignity of the black man. They are passive only as long as they are treated by the white man with dignity and respect. Many have joined because of a desire to belong. For the most part they have been denied a right to participate in the political and cultural development of this nation. With few exceptions, millions of Negroes live and die feeling unwanted in this country.

The leaders of these organizations claim well over two hundred thousand members. Most want no part of the white world. One Muslim told me: "We are organized for peace, but we are prepared for war." Will there one day be a bloody war on American soil—between Americans—because of the lack of forthrightness on the part of our Government to eradicate the inhuman practice of brutality and degradation now being perpetrated against American Negroes? Only America can answer this question.

And so the battle for civil rights continues. The actors on the 1957 Little Rock stage have faded from the national scene. Their places have been filled by thousands of Negro and white Americans in the crusade for equality—at the ballot box and at the lunch counter, at work and in school, in the churches and in the neighborhood, in the buses and on the beaches.

Reading 370

Black Activism (1955-1965)

Sociologist Alphonso Pickney analyzes the expansion of protest beyond the realm of school segregation in the following reading. He begins the story with an account of the Montgomery, Alabama, bus boycott, an example of direct nonviolent action, which made Martin Luther King a national leader.

Alphonso Pickney, *Black Americans* © 1969. Reprinted by permission of Prentice-Hall, Inc., Englewood Cliffs, New Jersey. Pp. 185-186, 187-189, 190-193. Subheadings added and footnotes omitted by the editors.

I

Martin Luther King and Nonviolence

On December 1, 1955, a Negro seamstress, Mrs. Rosa Parks, boarded a public bus in Montgomery, Alabama. She took a seat in the section set aside for Negroes. Shortly thereafter she was ordered to vacate her seat so a white man could occupy it. She refused and was arrested. When word of the arrest spread through the black community, the Montgomery Bus Boycott was organized. The bus boycott lasted for more than a year, ending in December 1956, when the Supreme Court upheld a lower court ruling outlawing racial segregation on buses in Montgomery.

This massive demonstration of solidarity among Negroes in opposition to long-standing practices of segregation and discrimination can be considered the first major act of resistance by Negroes in modern times and signals the birth of what might be called the Negro Revolt. The story of the Montgomery Bus Boycott spread throughout black communities in the United States and served as an impetus for similar acts in other cities. Tallahassee, Florida, and Birmingham, Alabama, followed with bus boycotts. Nonviolent resistance to what was considered an "evil" system composed of "unjust" laws became the official means of dealing with the caste system of the South. The philosophy of nonviolence, according to its principal spokesman [Martin Luther King], contains the following elements: (1) active resistance to "evil," (2) attempts to win one's opponent through understanding, (3) directing one's attack against forces of "evil," rather than against persons performing such acts, (4) willingness to accept suffering without retaliation, (5) refusal to hate one's opponent, and (6) the conviction that the universe is on the side of justice.

As the nonviolent resistance movement spread, massive opposition to social change in the realm of race relations was intensified by white Southerners. One hundred Southern members of Congress signed the Southern Manifesto, opposing the Supreme Court decision of 1954. They vowed "to use all lawful means to bring about a reversal of this decision which is contrary to the Constitution." Accordingly, laws implementing massive resistance to desegregation were enacted in Alabama, Georgia, Louisiana, Mississippi, South Carolina, and Virginia. While the Southern Manifesto did not explicitly call for the use of violence as a means of preventing Negro pupils from attending schools with white pupils, its impact served to generate violence. . . .

Little Rock was not alone in its policy of massive resistance to integration through the

TOPIC 69

DIRECT ACTION AND CIVIL RIGHTS

The Supreme Court decision of 1954 and the resulting efforts to desegregate schools touched off a wave of activism. In response to the decision, black Americans and like-minded whites quickened their attacks on other forms of segregation. For a decade after 1954 incident followed incident as blacks combined direct action with law suits in an attempt to destroy the social, economic, and political barriers to equal treatment they had long confronted. The following readings tell the story of the events of that decade and reveal the variety of tactics employed, the role of sympathetic whites, the opposition of other whites, and the sense of frustration which paralleled pride in achievements.

closing of public schools. When desegregation was ordered for the Virginia cities of Norfolk, Charlottesville, and Front Royal, the governor responded by closing the schools involved. In Prince Edward County, Virginia, resistance to desegregation was so strong that the county's public schools were closed from 1959 to 1964.

In the years immediately following 1954, little desegregation of public schools was accomplished. Every September, at the beginning of the school year, one could expect the news releases to carry stories of violence directed toward Negro pupils. These pupils were frequently required to walk through racist mobs to get to class, and, once in the classroom, they experienced a variety of insults and physical abuse from younger racists.

On the college level desegregation was not achieved without violence. At both the University of Mississippi and the University of Alabama the admittance of Negroes triggered violence from white students. In fact, the admission of one black student to the University of Mississippi in 1962 triggered violence which ended in two deaths and 100 injuries. It was finally necessary to station 12,000 federal troops on the campus to assure the attendance of this student in classes.

The Rev. Dr. Martin Luther King, Jr., depicted at a particularly dynamic moment, was the best known leader of the Civil Rights Movement in the decade following 1954. King and his Southern Christian Leadership Council (SCLC) were the most articulate exponents of non-violent opposition to the segregation and oppression of black Americans. He was assassinated in Memphis, Tennessee, in April 1968.

Federalized National Guardsmen were required to escort two black students to classes at the University of Alabama in 1963.

II

The Civil Rights Movement

By 1960 desegregation of public education was proceding at a slow pace, and in the Deep South massive resistance remained an effective answer to the Supreme Court's ruling and to the demands of Negroes. Feelings of despair over the school segregation issue were widespread in the black community. The federal government assumed no responsibility for assuring enforcement of Negroes' declared constitutional rights. The responsibility for desegregating schools rested with Negroes themselves, and when they sought admission for their children to desegregated schools, it was frequently a long, costly, and complicated court procedure. Segregation and discrimination were still the social norms throughout the South, and all-white Southern juries continued to refuse to convict white persons responsible for lynching black people.

In February 1960 four black college students in North Carolina sought service at a lunch counter in a five-and-dime store. When they were denied service, they remained seated. The manager ordered the lunch counter closed, but they remained seated, reading their textbooks. The news of their actions quickly spread throughout the country, and within a few days the "sit-in" movement had spread to 15 cities in five Southern states. Whenever a group of black people appeared at a lunch counter, a mob of Southern whites appeared to heckle and jeer them. But the actions of the students inspired many others, black and white, to support them. Because of the determined resistance to desegregation of Southern white persons, and because of the strong determination of Negroes for social change in race relations, thousands of white Americans joined forces with the Negroes to give birth to the civil rights movement. Black college students organized the Student Nonviolent Coordinating Committee (SNCC) to coordinate activities aimed at desegregating places of public accommodation in the South. Peaceful demonstrations, led by college students, occurred in every major city where racial segregation was practiced openly. Thousands of Negroes and their white supporters were jailed for violating local segregation laws. The lunch counter demonstrations were accompanied by nationwide economic boycotts of the stores which maintained practices of segregation. Within a period of one and a half years it is reported that at least 70,000 black and white persons participated in the sit-in movement. More than 3,600 were arrested, and some 141 students and 58 faculty members were expelled by college authorities for their activities. Altogether, one or more establishments in each of 108 Southern and border cities had been desegregated because of the sit-ins. . . .

III

Behind the Civil Rights Acts

The civil rights movement appealed to increasingly large numbers of white Americans. Demonstrations protesting all forms of segregation and discrimination were conducted throughout the United States, especially in the South. There were attacks on legally imposed segregation in the South and *de facto* segregation elsewhere and on discriminatory practices throughout the country. There were demonstrations at public libraries, swimming pools, public parks, and at seats of municipal government throughout the Deep South and Border South. Discrimination against black people in voting became a special target for civil rights activists, based on the assumption that, once armed with the franchise, Negroes would be in a position to elect public officials sympathetic to their demands. The Civil Rights Act of 1960 provided for the appointment of federal voting referees to receive applications to qualify voters if it could be proved that a person had been denied the right to vote because of race. Throughout the South voter registration schools were set up in churches. The response of many white Southerners was characteristic of their resistance to change in existing practices. Negro churches were bombed and burned. Churches had traditionally been exempt from the tyranny which Southern Negroes encountered daily, and now it appeared that they were not even safe in their houses of worship. Appeals to federal officials were in vain, and the reign of terror continued unabated. Arrests for these activities were rare, for local policemen often supported such activities. Black people and their white supporters remained nonviolent despite daily provocations and beatings.

On occasion one city was selected to be a major target of civil rights demonstrations. SNCC selected Greenwood, Mississippi, as the site of its emancipation centennial campaign in response to an attempt to assassinate one of its field workers. They organized a massive voter registration campaign and were met by heavily armed policemen with police dogs. When they attempted to escort local Mississippi Negroes to register to vote, they were attacked by the police and their dogs. The late Martin Luther King, Jr., selected Birmingham, Alabama, as SCLC's* major site of anti-segregation demonstrations during the centennial year. Birmingham was one of the most rigidly segregated larger cities in the South, and it was felt that if segregation barriers there could be penetrated, it would make for less difficulty elsewhere. The demonstrators were met in Birmingham by a force of policemen and firemen led by a well-known segregationist. Police and firemen were ordered to use a variety of techniques to curb the demonstrations, including fire hoses, cattle prods, and police dogs. For several days the demonstrators met greater brutality from law enforcement personnel than they had ever encountered previously, and the policemen and firemen were supported in their acts by an injunction from a local judge prohibiting protest marches. When the demonstrators defied this injunction, hundreds of them were jailed. The constitutional right of citizens to petition peacefully for redress of grievances was violated, and the Department of Justice issued a statement that it was watching the situation but that it was powerless to act. It was decided by the leaders of the demonstrations that schoolchildren should participate along with adults. They, too, were met by police clubs, dogs, and fire hoses. The pictures of the repressive measures used by the police and firemen served to alert the nation and the world to the extremes which segregationists would resort to in order to maintain white supremacy.

A turning point was reached in Birmingham when, following a meeting of the Ku Klux Klan, the home of the brother of the late

*Southern Christian Leadership Council, the civil rights organization headed by Martin Luther King, Jr.—Eds.

Martin Luther King, Jr., and the motel which had served as King's headquarters and residence were bombed. Thousands of Negro demonstrators abandoned the philosophy of nonviolence and took to the streets with bottles and stones. They burned houses and stores and stoned policemen and passing cars. Before the uprising ended, they had burned a nine-block area of the city. When the demonstrators had requested federal protection from police dogs, fire hoses, and police clubs, the President announced that no federal agency could act. However, when the Negroes stoned white policemen and other citizens, federal troops were dispatched to Alabama within hours. Apparently the latter constituted acts of violence, while the former did not.

Demonstrations in many other Southern and border cities followed those in Birmingham. Danville, Virginia, and Cambridge, Maryland, were among the most prominent. During the summer of 1963 some 35 homes and churches were bombed or burned, at least ten people were killed, and more than 20,000 demonstrators were arrested. Thousands of others were shocked by cattle prods, set upon with high-pressure fire hoses, bitten by police dogs, and beaten by policemen. The summer demonstrations culminated in August, when some 250,000 Negroes and their white supporters participated in the March on Washington, the largest civil rights demonstration in history. As a direct outgrowth of these demonstrations Congress enacted the Civil Rights Act of 1964. The major provisions of this act are: (1) sixth-grade education was established as a presumption of literacy for voting purposes; (2) segregation and discrimination in places of public accommodation were outlawed; (3) public facilities (parks, playgrounds, libraries, etc.) were desegregated; (4) the Attorney General was authorized to file school desegregation suits; (5) discrimination was outlawed in all federally assisted activities; (6) discrimination by employers or unions with 100 or more employees or members was outlawed; (7) the Attorney General was authorized to intervene in private suits in which persons alleged denial of equal protection of the laws under the Fourteenth Amendment.

IV

Turning to the Ballot

The leaders of several civil rights organizations, after achieving the victory which this act signaled, decided to concentrate their activities on voter registration and education. They had been urged by the Department of Justice to concentrate on these activities instead of street demonstrations. Consequently, in 1964 the Mississippi Summer Project was organized. Thousands of black and white activists journeyed to Mississippi to engage in activities aimed at improving the status of that state's nearly one million Negroes. They concentrated on voter education and registration and on "freedom schools." The activists were subjected to a serious initial setback when three of their volunteers were abducted and murdered by a mob of local racists. Throughout the summer they were subjected to a variety of harassments and abuse. The casualty list was high: by October 21 at least three persons had been killed, 80 were beaten, three were wounded by gunfire in 35 shootings, more than 35 churches were burned, 35 homes and other buildings were bombed, and more than 1,000 persons had been arrested. In addition, several unsolved murders of local Negroes were recorded.

The Civil Rights Act of 1964 contained a provision ensuring Negroes the right to vote in all elections. However, when they attempted to register, a variety of techniques, especially intimidation, served to keep them from exercising this right. Consequently the major effort for 1965 was the campaign to ensure the right to vote. Resistance to Negro voting rights was strong. Several civil rights organizations decided to focus their attention on Alabama, which had been one of the most intransigent in this regard. Attempts to register Negroes failed, and a march from Selma to Montgomery was planned to dramatize the plight of that state's black citizens. Thousands of black activists and their white supporters gathered in Selma for the march. Several attempts to march were thwarted by the police, under orders from a local sheriff. Acts of excessive use of force by police were widespread, and these acts served to motivate additional thousands of citizens, including many clergymen, from all over the United States to join the activists in Selma. The march finally materialized but not without violence. Two white activists and one Negro were killed and scores of others were injured.

The Selma to Montgomery march served as a stimulus for the Voting Rights Act of 1965, which made it possible for Southern Negroes to register and vote with little difficulty. It was also the last mass demonstration of the civil rights movement. During the years of peak activity the civil rights movement enlisted the support of thousands of Americans, both black and white. Its nonviolent, direct action approach is responsible for many of the changes affecting the status of Southern Negroes. But its goals and methods were hardly applicable to the problems facing the many Negroes in urban slums throughout the country. Thousands of Negroes and their white supporters had combined for what was felt to be the most significant movement for social change in the United States. The issues were clear, and, although there were differences on means toward achieving the goals, a coalition of many groups had united to work for a common end: the eradication of segregation and discrimination in American life. To a significant degree they were successful in achieving greater civil rights for Negroes, but black Americans remained a basically oppressed underclass of citizens.

The Sit-in Movement

Contemporary organized student protests did not begin with young whites in the mid-1960s but with young blacks several years earlier. The sit-in movement, as Professor Pickney pointed out, started in February 1960, in Greensboro, North Carolina, when black college students decided they had had enough of segregation in public places. Within a few years the Movement, as it came to be called, spread to the deepest parts of the Deep South. Anne Moody, a black student at Tougaloo College, near Jackson, Mississippi, describes the efforts to integrate that city's lunch counters in the spring of 1963.

From *Coming of Age in Mississippi* by Anne Moody. Copyright © 1968 by Anne Moody. Reprinted by permission of the publisher, The Dial Press. Pp. 263-267. Subheadings added by the editors.

I

The Sit-in

I had become very friendly with my social science professor, John Salter, who was in charge of NAACP activities on campus. All during the year, while the NAACP conducted a boycott of the downtown stores in Jackson, I had been one of Salter's most faithful canvassers and church speakers. During the last week of school, he told me that sit-in demonstrations were about to start in Jackson and that he wanted me to be the spokesman for a team that would sit-in at Woolworth's lunch counter. The two other demonstrators would be classmates of mine, Memphis and Pearlena. Pearlena was a dedicated NAACP worker, but Memphis had not been very involved in the Movement on campus. It seemed that the organization had had a rough time finding students who were in a position to go to jail. I had nothing to lose one way or the other. Around ten o'clock the morning of the demonstrations, NAACP headquarters alerted the news services. As a result, the police department was also informed, but neither the policemen nor the newsmen knew exactly where or when the demonstrations would start. They stationed themselves along Capitol Street and waited.

To divert attention from the sit-in at Woolworth's, the picketing started at J. C. Penney's a good fifteen minutes before. The pickets were allowed to walk up and down in front of the store three or four times before they were arrested. At exactly 11 A.M., Pearlena, Memphis, and I entered Woolworth's from the rear entrance. We separated as soon as we stepped into the store, and made small purchases from various counters. Pearlena had given Memphis her watch. He was to let us know when it was 11:14. At 11:14 we were to join him near the lunch counter and at exactly 11:15 we were to take seats at it.

Seconds before 11:15 we were occupying three seats at the previously segregated Woolworth's lunch counter. In the beginning the waitresses seemed to ignore us, as if they really didn't know what was going on. Our waitress walked past us a couple of times before she noticed we had started to write our own orders down and realized we wanted service. She asked us what we wanted. We began to read to her from our order slips. She told us that we would be served at the back counter, which was for Negroes.

"We would like to be served here," I said.

The waitress started to repeat what she had said, then stopped in the middle of the sentence. She turned the lights out behind the counter, and she and the other waitresses almost ran to the back of the store, deserting all their white customers. I guess they thought that violence would start immediately after the whites at the counter realized what was going on. There were five or six other people at the counter. A couple of them just got up and walked away. A girl sitting next to me finished her banana split before leaving. A middle-aged white woman who had not yet been served rose from her seat and came over to us. "I'd like to stay here with you," she said, "but my husband is waiting."

The newsmen came in just as she was leaving. They must have discovered what was going on shortly after some of the people began to leave the store. One of the newsmen ran behind the woman who spoke to us and asked her to identify herself. She refused to give her name, but said she was a native of Vicksburg and a former resident of California. When asked why she had said what she had said to us, she replied, "I am in sympathy with the Negro movement." By this time a crowd of cameramen and reporters had gathered around us taking pictures and asking questions, such as Where were we from? Why did we sit-in? What organization sponsored it? Were we students? From what school? How were we classified?

I told them that we were all students at Tougaloo College, that we were represented by no particular organization, and that we planned to stay there even after the store closed. "All we want is service," was my reply to one of them. After they had finished probing for about twenty minutes, they were almost ready to leave.

At noon, students from a nearby white high school started pouring in to Woolworth's. When they first saw us they were sort of surprised. They didn't know how to react. A few started to heckle and the newsmen became interested again. Then the white students started chanting all kinds of anti-Negro slogans. We were called a little bit of everything. The rest of the seats except the three we were occupying had been roped off to prevent others from sitting down. A couple of the boys took one end of the rope and made it into a hangman's noose. Several attempts were made to put it around our necks. The crowds grew as more students and adults came in for lunch.

II

Violence

We kept our eyes straight forward and did not look at the crowd except for occasional glances to see what was going on. All of a sudden I saw a face I remembered—the drunkard from the bus station sit-in. My eyes lingered on him just long enough for us to recognize each other. Today he was drunk too, so I don't think he remembered where he had seen me before. He took out a knife, opened it, put it in his pocket, and then began to pace the floor. At this point, I told Memphis and Pearlena what was going on. Memphis suggested that we pray. We bowed our heads, and all hell broke loose. A man rushed forward, threw Memphis from his seat, and slapped my face. Then another man who worked in the store threw me against an adjoining counter.

Down on my knees on the floor, I saw Memphis lying near the lunch counter with blood running out of the corners of his mouth. As he tried to protect his face, the man who'd thrown him down kept kicking him against the head. If he had worn hard-soled shoes instead of sneakers, the first kick probably would have killed Memphis. Finally a man dressed in plain clothes identified himself as a police officer and arrested Memphis and his attacker.

Pearlena had been thrown to the floor. She and I got back on our stools after Memphis was arrested. There were some white Tougaloo teachers in the crowd. They asked Pearlena and me if we wanted to leave. They said that things were getting too rough. We didn't know what to do. While we were trying to make up our minds, we were joined by Joan Trumpauer. Now there were three of us and we were integrated. The crowd began to chant, "Communists, Communists, Communists." Some old man in the crowd ordered the students to take us off the stools.

"Which one should I get first?" a big husky boy said.

"That white nigger," the old man said.

The boy lifted Joan from the counter by her waist and carried her out of the store. Simultaneously, I was snatched from my stool by two high school students. I was dragged about thirty feet toward the door by my hair when someone made them turn me loose. As I was getting up off the floor, I saw Joan coming back inside. We started back to the center of the counter to join Pearlena. Lois Chaffee, a white Tougaloo faculty member, was now sitting next to her. So Joan and I just climbed across the rope at the front end of the counter and sat down. There were now four of us, two whites and two Negroes, all women. The mob started smearing us with ketchup, mustard, sugar, pies, and everything on the counter. Soon Joan and I were joined by John Salter, but the moment he sat down he was hit on the jaw with what appeared to be brass knuckles. Blood gushed from his face and someone threw salt into the open wound. Ed King, Tougaloo's chaplain, rushed to him.

At the other end of the counter, Lois and Pearlena were joined by George Raymond, a CORE* field worker and a student from Jackson State College. Then a Negro high school boy sat down next to me. The mob took spray paint from the counter and sprayed it on the new demonstrators. The high school student had on a white shirt; the word "nigger" was written on his back with red spray paint.

We sat there for three hours taking a beating when the manager decided to close the store because the mob had begun to go wild with stuff from other counters. He begged and begged everyone to leave. But even after fifteen minutes of begging, no one budged.

*Congress of Racial Equality, a leading civil rights organization—Eds.

They would not leave until we did. Then Dr. Beittel, the president of Tougaloo College, came running in. He said he had just heard what was happening.

About ninety policemen were standing outside the store; they had been watching the whole thing through the windows, but had not come in to stop the mob or do anything. President Beittel went outside and asked Captain Ray to come and escort us out. The captain refused, stating the manager had to invite him in before he could enter the premises, so Dr. Beittel himself brought us out. He had told the police that they had better protect us after we were outside the store. When we got outside, the policemen formed a single line that blocked the mob from us. However, they were allowed to throw at us everything they had collected. Within ten minutes, we were picked up by Reverend King in his station wagon and taken to the NAACP headquarters on Lynch Street.

After the sit-in, all I could think of was how sick Mississippi whites were. They believed so much in the segregated Southern way of life, they would kill to preserve it. I sat there in the NAACP office and thought of how many times they had killed when this way of life was threatened. I knew that the killing had just begun. "Many more will die before it is over with," I thought. Before the sit-in, I had always hated the whites in Mississippi. Now I knew it was impossible for me to hate sickness. The whites had a disease, an incurable disease in its final stage. What were our chances against such a disease? I thought of the students, the young Negroes who had just begun to protest, as young interns. When these young interns got older, I thought, they would be the best doctors in the world for social problems.

Reading 372

"Negroes with Guns"

Though the doctrine of nonviolent resistance on the part of blacks dominated the period, not everyone subscribed to it. Whites frequently resisted the changing of racial relations with great violence. The tradition of physical resistance on the part of blacks was an old one. In the post-1954 era one of the most dramatic examples of the revival of that tradition took place in Monroe, North Carolina, where Robert F. Williams, head of the local NAACP chapter, defended the black man's right of self-defense in the face of white attacks.

From Robert F. Williams, *Negroes With Guns* (New York, 1962), pp. 42, 45–48. Copyright © 1962 by Marzani and Munsell, Inc. Subheadings added by the editors.

I

White People Only

In June of 1961 the NAACP Chapter of Monroe, North Carolina, decided to picket the town's swimming pool. This pool, built by WPA money, was forbidden to Negroes although we formed one quarter of the population of the town. In 1957 we had asked not for integration but for the use of the pool one day a week. This was denied and for four years we were put off with vague suggestions that someday another pool would be built. Two small Negro children had meantime drowned swimming in creeks. Now, in 1961, the City of Monroe announced it had surplus funds, but there was no indication of a pool, no indication of even an intention to have a pool. So we decided to start a picket line. We started the picket line and the picket line closed the pool. When the pool closed the racists decided to handle the matter in traditional Southern style. They turned to violence, unlawful violence.

We had been picketing for two days when we started taking lunch breaks in a picnic area reserved for "White People Only." Across from the picnic area, on the other side of a stream of water, a group of white people started firing rifles and we could hear the bullets strike the trees over our heads. The chief of police was on duty at the pool and I appealed to him to stop the firing into the picnic area. The chief of police said, "Oh, I don't hear anything. I don't hear anything at all." They continued shooting all that day. The following day these people drifted toward the picket line firing their pistols and we kept appealing to the chief of police to stop them from shooting near us. He would always say, "Well, I don't hear anything . . ."

II

"God Damn, The Niggers Have Got Guns!"

The picket line continued. On Sunday, on our way to the swimming pool, we had to pass through the same intersection (U.S. 74 and U.S. 601). There were about two or three thousand people lined along the highway. Two or three policemen were standing at the intersection directing traffic and there were two policemen who had been following us from my home. An old stock car without windows was parked by a restaurant at the intersection. As soon as we drew near, this car started backing out as fast as possible. The driver hoped to hit us in the side and flip us over. But I turned my wheel sharply and the junk car struck the front of my car and both cars went into a ditch.

Then the crowd started screaming. They said that a nigger had hit a white man. They were referring to me. They were screaming, "Kill the niggers! Kill the niggers! Pour gasoline on the niggers! Burn the niggers!"

We were still sitting in the car. The man who was driving the stock car got out of the car with a baseball bat and started walking toward us and he was saying, "Nigger, what did you hit me for?" I didn't say anything to him. We just sat there looking at him. He came up close to our car, within arm's length with the baseball bat, but I still hadn't said anything and we didn't move in the car. What they didn't know was that we were armed. Under North Carolina state law it is legal to carry firearms in your automobile so long as these firearms are not concealed.

I had two pistols and a rifle in the car. When this fellow started to draw back his baseball bat, I put an Army .45 up in the window of the car and pointed it right into his face and I didn't say a word. He looked at the pistol and he didn't say anything. He started backing away from the car.

Somebody in the crowd fired a pistol and the people again started to scream hysterically, "Kill the niggers! Kill the niggers! Pour gasoline on the niggers!" The mob started to throw stones on top of my car. So I opened the door of the car and I put one foot on the ground and stood up in the door holding an Italian carbine.

All this time three policemen had been standing about fifty feet away from us while we kept waiting in the car for them to come and rescue us. Then when they saw that we were armed and the mob couldn't take us, two of the policemen started running. One ran straight to me and he grabbed me on the shoulder and said, "Surrender your weapon! Surrender your weapon!" I struck him in the face and knocked him back away from the car and put my carbine in his face and I told him we were not going to surrender to a mob. I told him that we didn't intend to be lynched. The other policeman who had run around the side of the car started to draw his revolver out of the holster. He was hoping to shoot me in the back. They didn't know that we had more than one gun. One of the students (who was seventeen years old) put a .45 in the policeman's face and told him that if he pulled out his pistol he would kill him. The policeman started putting his gun back into the holster and backing away from the car, and he fell into the ditch.

There was a very old man, an old white man out in the crowd, and he started screaming and crying like a baby and he kept crying, and he said, "God damn, God damn, what is this God damn country coming to that the niggers have got guns, the niggers are armed and the police can't even arrest them!" He kept crying and somebody led him away through the crowd.

Steve Presson, who is a member of the Monroe City Council, came along and he told the chief of police to open the highway and get us out of there. The chief of police told the City Councilman, "But they've got guns!" Presson said, "That's OK. Open the highway up and get them out of here!" They opened the highway and the man from the City Council led us through. All along the highway for almost a third of a mile people were lined on both sides of the road. And they were screaming "Kill the niggers! Kill the niggers! We aren't having any integration here! We're not going to swim with niggers!"

By the time we got to the pool, the other students who had gone on had already started the picket line. There were three or four thousand white people milling around the pool. All the city officials were there including the Mayor of Monroe. They had dark glasses on and they were standing in the crowd. And the crowd kept screaming. Then the chief of police came up to me and he said, "Surrender your gun." And I told him that I was not going to surrender any gun. That those guns were legal and that was a mob, and if he wanted those guns he could come to my house and get them after I got away from there. And then he said, "Well, if you hurt any of these white people here, God damn it, I'm going to kill you!" I don't know what made him think that I was going to let him live long enough to shoot me. He kept saying, "Surrender the gun!" while the white people kept screaming.

The City Councilman reappeared and said that the tension was bad and that there was a chance that somebody would be hurt. He conceded that I had a right to picket and he said that if I were willing to go home he would see that I was escorted. I asked him who was going to escort us home. He said "the police." I told him that I might as well go with the Ku Klux Klan as go with them. I said I would go with the police department under one condition. He asked what that was. I told him I would take one of the students out of my car and let them put a policeman in there and then I could rest assured that they would protect us. And the police said they couldn't do that. They couldn't do that because they realized that this policeman would get hurt if they joined in with the mob.

The officials kept repeating how the crowd was getting out of hand; somebody would get hurt. I told them that I wasn't going to leave until they cleared the highway. I also told them that if necessary we would make our stand right there. Finally they asked me what did I suggest they do, and I recommended they contact the state police. So they contacted the state police and an old corporal and a young man came; just two state patrolmen. Three or four thousand people were out there, and the city had twenty-one policemen present who claimed they couldn't keep order.

The old man started cursing and told the people to move back, to spread out and to move out of there. And he started swinging a stick. Some of the mob started cursing and he said, "God damn it, I mean it. Move out." They got the message and suddenly the crowd was broken up and dispersed. The officials and state police knew that if they allowed the mob to attack us a lot of people were going to be killed, and some of those people would be white.

Two police cars escorted us out; one in front and one behind. This was the first time this had ever been done. And some of the white people started screaming "Look how they are protecting niggers! Look how they are taking niggers out of here!"

As a result of our stand, and our willingness to fight, the state of North Carolina had enforced law and order. Just two state troopers did the job, and no one got hurt in a situation where normally (in the South) a lot of Negro blood would have flowed. The city closed the pool for the rest of the year and we withdrew our picket line.

Malcolm X

When the Black Muslims emerged into the public limelight in 1960 they both fascinated and frightened white Americans. Here was a well-organized group of black people who frankly admitted they hated whites, who preached separation, not integration, and who condemned Christianity and preached Islam, the religion, they believed, of the world's colored peoples. Led by Elijah Muhammad, the Muslims had been active for several decades and by the late 1950s claimed a membership of over 100,000. But it was Malcolm X, born Malcolm Little, whose dramatic presentation of the Muslim cause spurred international interest. In 1964 Malcolm X broke with Elijah Muhammad, though Malcolm remained a follower of Islam. He was assassinated in 1965. The following reading is taken from an interview Malcolm had with the editors of Playboy magazine in 1963.

From "Playboy Interview: Malcolm X," *Playboy*, X (May, 1963), pp. 53-54, 60, 62-63. Subheadings added by the editors.

I

The Goals of the Muslims

[Playboy] What is the ambition of the Black Muslims?

[Malcolm X] Freedom, justice and equality are our principal ambitions. And to faithfully serve and follow the Honorable Elijah Muhammad is the guiding goal of every Muslim. Mr. Muhammad teaches us the knowledge of our own selves, and of our own people. He cleans us up—morally, mentally and spiritually—and he reforms us of the vices that have blinded us here in the Western society. He stops black men from getting drunk, stops their dope addiction if they had it, stops nicotine, gambling, stealing, lying, cheating, fornication, adultery, prostitution, juvenile delinquency. I think of this whenever somebody talks about someone investigating us. Why investigate the Honorable Elijah Muhammad? They should subsidize him. He's cleaning up the mess that white men have made. He's saving the Government millions of dollars, taking black men off of welfare, showing them how to do something for themselves. And Mr. Muhammad teaches us love for our own kind. The white man has taught the black people in this country to hate themselves as inferior, to hate each other, to be divided against each other. Messenger Muhammad restores our love for our own kind, which enables us to work together in unity and harmony. He shows us how to pool our financial resources and our talents, then to work together toward a common objective. Among other things, we have small businesses in most major cities in this country, and we want to create many more. We are taught by Mr. Muhammad that it is very important to improve the black man's economy, and his thrift. But to do this, we must have land of our own. The brainwashed black man can never learn to stand on his own two feet until he is on his own. We must learn to become our own producers, manufacturers and traders; we must have industry of our own, to employ our own. The white man resists this because he wants to keep the black man under his thumb and jurisdiction in white society. He wants to keep the black man always dependent and begging—for jobs, food, clothes, shelter, education. The white man doesn't want to lose somebody to be supreme over. He wants to keep the black man where he can be watched and retarded. Mr. Muhammad teaches that as soon as we separate from the white man, we will learn that we can do without the white man just as he can do without us.

The white man knows that once black men get off to themselves and learn they can do for themselves, the black man's full potential will explode and he will *surpass* the white man. . . .

II

Malcolm's Story

[Playboy] Could you give us a brief review of the early life that led to your own "salvation"?

[Malcolm X] Gladly. I was born in Omaha on May 19,1925. My light color is the result of my mother's mother having been raped by a white man. I hate every drop of white blood in me. Before I am indicted for hate again, sir—is it wrong to hate the blood of a rapist? But to continue: My father was a militant follower of Marcus Garvey's "Back to Africa" movement. The Lansing, Michigan, equivalent of the Ku Klux Klan warned him to stop preaching Garvey's message, but he kept on and one of my earliest memories is of being snatched awake one night with a lot of screaming going on because our home was afire. But my father got louder about Garvey, and the next time he was found bludgeoned in the head, lying across streetcar tracks. He died soon and our family was in a bad way. We were so hungry we were dizzy and we had nowhere to turn. Finally the authorities came in and we children were scattered about in different places as public wards. I happened to become the ward of a white couple who ran a correctional school for white boys. This family liked me in the way they liked their house pets. They got me enrolled in an all-white school. I was popular, I played sports and everything, and studied hard, and I stayed at the head of my class through the eighth grade. That summer I was 14, but I was big enough and looked old enough to get away with telling a lie that I was 21, so I got a job working in the dining car of a train that ran between Boston and New York City.

On my layovers in New York, I'd go to Harlem. That's where I saw in the bars all these men and women with what looked like the easiest life in the world. Plenty of money, big cars, all of it. I could tell they were in the rackets and vice. I hung around those bars whenever I came in town, and I kept my ears and eyes open and my mouth shut. And they kept their eyes on me, too. Finally, one day a numbers man told me that he needed a runner, and I never caught the night train back to Boston. Right there was when I started my life in crime. I was in all of it that the white police and the gangsters left open to the black criminal, sir. I was in numbers, bootleg liquor, "hot" goods, women. I sold the bodies of black women to white men, and white women to black men. I was in dope, I was in everything evil you could name. The only thing I could say good for myself, sir, was that I did not indulge in hitting anybody over the head.

[Playboy] By the time you were 16, according to the record, you had several men working for you in these various enterprises. Right?

[Malcolm X] Yes, sir. I turned the things I mentioned to you over to them. And I had a good working system of paying off policemen. It was here that I learned that vice and crime can only exist, at least the kind and level that I was in, to the degree that the police cooperate with it. I had several men working and I was a steerer myself. I steered white people with money from downtown to whatever kind of sin they wanted in Harlem. I didn't care what they wanted, I knew where to take them to it. And I tell you what I noticed here—that my best customers always were the officials, the top police people, businessmen, politicians and clergymen. I never forgot that. I met all levels of these white people, supplied them with everything they wanted, and I saw that they were just a filthy race of devils. But despite the fact that my own father was murdered by whites, and I had seen my people all my life brutalized by whites, I was still blind enough to mix with them and socialize with them. I thought they were gods and goddesses—until Mr. Muhammad's powerful spiritual message opened my eyes and enabled me to see them as a race of devils. Nothing had made me see the white man as he is until one word from the Honorable Elijah Muhammad opened my eyes overnight.

[Playboy] When did this happen?

[Malcolm X] In prison. I was finally caught and spent 77 months in three different prisons. But it was the greatest thing that ever happened to me, because it was in prison that I first heard the teachings of the Honorable Elijah Muhammad. His teachings were what turned me around. The first time I heard the Honorable Elijah Muhammad's statement, "The white man is the devil," it just clicked. I am a good example of why Islam is spreading so rapidly across the land. I was nothing but another convict, a semi-illiterate criminal. Mr. Muhammad's teachings were able to reach into prison, which is the level where people are considered to have fallen as low as they can go. His teachings brought me from behind prison walls and placed me on the podiums of some of the leading colleges and universities in the

The intensity with which Malcolm X expressed his views is caught by this portrait of the Black Muslim leader. Malcolm became the leading spokesman of the Muslims in the early 1960s. Television coverage made white Americans uncomfortably aware of the existence of a group who expressed hatred of whites for their long-standing oppression of blacks. He was assassinated in New York in February 1965.

country. I often think, sir, that in 1946, I was sentenced to 8 to 10 years in Cambridge, Massachusetts, as a common thief who had never passed the eighth grade. And the next time I went back to Cambridge was in March 1961, as a guest speaker at the Harvard Law School Forum. This is the best example of Mr. Muhammad's ability to take nothing and make something, to take nobody and make somebody. . . .

III

What Can Whites Do?

[Playboy] Is there anything then, in your opinion, that could be done—by either whites or blacks—to expedite the social and economic progress of the Negro in America?

[Malcolm X] First of all, the white man must finally realize that *he's* the one who has committed the crimes that have produced the miserable condition that our people are in. He can't hide this guilt by reviling us today because we answer his criminal acts—past and present—with extreme and uncompromising resentment. He cannot hide his guilt by accusing us, his victims, of being racists, extremists and black supremacists. The white man must realize that the sins of the fathers are about to be visited upon the heads of the children who have continued those sins, only in more sophisticated ways. Mr. Elijah Muhammad is warning this generation of white people that they, too, are also facing a time of harvest in which they will have to pay for the crime committed when their grandfathers made slaves out of us.

But there *is* something the white man can do to avert this fate. He must atone—and this can only be done by allowing black men, those who choose, to leave this land of bondage and go to a land of our own. But if he doesn't want a mass movement of our people away from this house of bondage, then he should separate this country. He should give us several states here on American soil, where those of us who wish to can go and set up our own government, our own economic system, our own civilization. Since we have given over 300 years of our slave labor to the white man's America, helped to build it up for him, it's only right that white America should give us everything *we* need in finance and materials for the next 25 years, until our own nation is able to stand on its feet. Then, if the Western Hemisphere is attacked by outside enemies, we would have both the capability and the motivation to join in defending the hemisphere, in which we would then have a sovereign stake.

The Honorable Elijah Muhammad says that the black man has served under the rule of all the other peoples of the earth at one time or another in the past. He teaches that it is now God's intention to put the black man back at the top of civilization, where he was in the beginning—before Adam, the white man, was created. The world since Adam has been white—and corrupt. The world of tomorrow will be black—and righteous. In the white world there has been nothing but slavery, suffering, death and colonialism. In the black world of tomorrow, there will be *true* freedom, justice and equality for all. And that day is coming—sooner than you think.

Reading 374

Mississippi Summer (1964)

With the Mississippi Summer Project of 1964 the Civil Rights Movement of the previous decade reached a peak. In that summer a coalition of civil rights groups (labeled COFO) brought to Mississippi about 650 young black and white activists. Their intention was to educate in a few short weeks black Mississippians, young and old, about their rights as Americans, especially their political rights. In the midst of their efforts three of them, James Chaney, Michael Schwerner, and Andrew Goodman, were murdered. What follows are excerpts from letters of Mississippi Summer participants written both before and after the murders of their three co-workers.

From Elizabeth Sutherland, ed., *Letters from Mississippi* (New York: McGraw-Hill Book Co., 1965). Used with permission of McGraw-Hill Book Co. Pp. 101-102, 174-175, 189-190, 191-194. Subheadings added by the editors.

I

School for Freedom

Hattiesburg, August 1

The Summer Project has two Freedom Schools in Palmer's Crossing, a rural community about two miles outside of Hattiesburg. The two schools have nine teachers, five of them (including myself) professionals. It has been rough. Much of what we know about teaching must be unlearned or relearned here. The standard academic approach has not worked at all well, even when material has been simplified . . . The kids we are dealing with are not trained to listen to and absorb information presented in an organized, "logical," manner . . . The students do not seem to be able to follow a point-by-point presentation at all, whether simple or complex. They learn by talking, by conversation, by rambling around and beating the nearby bushes. And they learn by acting things out.

We have rather small children (aged 8 and up), and these are our worst problems. Once when it was my turn to babysit I tried to hold a lesson on politics. None of the little kids knew what politics or government were, so I asked them if they knew what the mayor is. Someone volunteered that the mayor is sort of like a horse. (This led to a spelling lesson on "mayor" and "mare"). In order to get down to real basics, I asked if anyone had ever seen a street or road. Yes, they had. How, I asked, did they think streets and roads got there? Who made them? Here the civics lesson came to an end. "God," a little girl replied. A lengthy theological discussion followed. "Does God make trees?" "Yes." "Do people make trees?" "No." "Does God make houses?" "Yes." "Do people make houses?" "No. God makes everything." This position seemed unassailable by logic alone, so, thinking that something massive must be done at once, I asked a few of the more sober-minded boys if they had ever seen someone build a house. Indeed they had, and I launched them on a long description of how this is done, making sure that real people figured prominently in the description. It was not without interest, but it wasn't a civics lesson.

One day we listened to the recording of "In White America" . . . The kids were struck by the incident in the Little Rock integration riots, in which a small Negro girl describes movingly how she was spit on and cursed as she tried to go to the previously all white school. Our discussion soon came to examine the purposes of school integration. All the kids were totally convinced that integration will mean that they would get schooling as good as the whites. It was, for them, a very simple point: Negro schools, in hundreds of little ways, are not as good as white schools.

I tried to make the question more theoretical. Suppose Mississippi should decide to spend as much money on Negro education as it does on white, so that the two schools would really be equal. Would they still favor integrated schools? For some of the kids this possibility was too incredible to accept seriously. They could not imagine Mississippi making Negro schools equal. But others saw that the point of the question was whether integration has a value in itself, apart from the equality it would bring. Few kids seemed ever to have thought of it just that way, but a little prompting gave them an idea. Did they think that Negroes and whites in Mississippi really understood each other? There was a chorus of deeply felt Noes. They quite frankly admitted not understanding white people any better than white people understood them. Did they think this would be true if whites and Negroes had been going to school together all their lives? Probably not. I was then able to get in a philosophic point about education. Education, I said, is supposed to give people an understanding of what the world is really like. A school system that closes students off to half the people in their world cannot do this. And so segregation deprives whites equally with Negroes. . . .

One Man—One Vote

July 17

Here is the Freedom Day special issue....

Wednesday nite Stokely [Carmichael] spoke at a very large mass meeting. He had been stopped by a well-known highway patrol goon some miles north of here, and told the folks about his interview. The cop asked him how come some niggers always laugh and smile so much, hoping to make Stokely mad How come niggers sit on the porch, how come they drink so much and cut each other up. Stokely said "that's right—niggers drink too much—but they learned it from the white man. Niggers are lazy, and they learned that from the white man,—haven't you seen white folks sitting up on their porches?" With Stokely talking about niggers all the time, the cop couldn't get him by using the word. And Stokely said, "Now we're learning from the white man about how to vote, baby, so they'd better watch out."

In the morning, I helped coordinate the transportation to the courthouse, and went around the neighborhood trying to get people to go down to register. Went down with one car, arrived just in time to see the first group of about 30 pickets going off to jail. They had been piled into a big bus with bars across the windows. They were banging on the windows and screaming FREEDOM at the top of their lungs. Later in the morning, I got word that a cattle prod had been used, and that a 7-months pregnant woman had been dragged down the sidewalk with a billy stick under her nose....

Mourners attend the burial of James Chaney who, with two fellow civil rights workers, was murdered by Klan members because of his activities in the Mississippi Summer Project of 1964. The deaths of Chaney, a black, and Michael Schwerner and Andrew Goodman, who were whites, embittered many young civil rights activists, who now felt that their non-violent attitudes and practices during the previous decade had done little to mitigate the virulent hatred of white racists.

III

Three Murders

Meridian, August 4

Last night Pete Seeger was giving a concert in Meridian. We sang a lot of freedom songs, and every time a verse like "No more lynchings" was sung, or "before I'd be a slave I'd be buried in my grave," I had the flash of understanding that sometimes comes when you suddenly think about the meaning of a familiar song . . . I wanted to stand up and shout to them, "Think about what you are singing—people really have died to keep us all from being slaves." Most of the people there still did not know that the bodies had been found. Finally just before the singing of "We Shall Overcome," Pete Seeger made the announcement. "We must sing 'We Shall Overcome' now," said Seeger. "The three boys would not have wanted us to weep now, but to sing and understand this song." That seems to me the best way to explain the greatness of this project—that death can have this meaning. Dying is not an ever-present possibility in Meridian, the way some reports may suggest. Nor do any of us want to die. Yet in a moment like last night, we can feel that anyone who did die for the Project would wish to be remembered not by tributes or grief but by understanding and continuation of what he was doing. . . .

As we left the church, we heard on the radio the end of President Johnson's speech announcing the air attacks on Vietnam . . . I could only think "This must not be the beginning of a war. There is still a freedom fight, and we are winning. We must have time to live and help Mississippi to be alive." Half an hour before, I had understood death in a new way. Now I realized that Mississippi, in spite of itself, has given real meaning to life. In Mississippi you never ask, "What is the meaning of life?" or "Is there any point to it all?" but only that we may have enough life to do all that there is to be done. . . .

Laurel, August 11

Dear Folks, . . . The memorial service began around 7:30 with over 120 people filling the small, wooden-pew lined church. David Dennis of CORE, the Assistant Director for the Mississippi Summer Project, spoke for COFO. He talked to the Negro people of Meridian—it was a speech to move people, to end the lethargy, to make people stand up. It went something like this:

> I am not here to memorialize James Chaney, I am not here to pay tribute—I

Deputy Sheriff Cecil Price (left) and Sheriff Lawrence Rainey (right), both of Neshoba County, Mississippi, two of seventeen KKK members arraigned in December 1964 on federal charges of conspiring against the three civil rights workers whose bodies were found the previous August. The federal government filed conspiracy charges because the state had failed to bring murder charges against the suspects. In October 1967 a jury found Deputy Sheriff Price and six others guilty of conspiracy. Price received a six-year jail sentence. Sheriff Rainey was among those acquitted.

am too sick and tired. Do YOU hear me, I am S-I-C-K and T-I-R-E-D. I have attended too many memorials, too many funerals. This has got to stop. Mack Parker, Medgar Evers, Herbert Lee, Lewis Allen, Emmett Till, four little girls in Birmingham, a 13-year old boy in Birmingham, and the list goes on and on. I have attended these funerals and memorials and I am SICK and TIRED. But the trouble is that YOU are NOT sick and tired and for that reason YOU, yes YOU, are to blame. Everyone of your damn souls. And if you are going to let this continue now then you are to blame, yes YOU. Just as much as the monsters of hate who pulled the trigger or brought down the club; just as much to blame as the sheriff and the chief of police, as the governor in Jackson who said that he "did not have time" for Mrs. Schwerner when she went to see him, and just as much to blame as the President and Attorney General in Washington who wouldn't provide protection for Chaney, Goodman and Schwerner when we told them that protection was necessary in Neshoba County . . . Yes, I am angry, I AM. And it's high time that you got angry too, angry enough to go up to the courthouse Monday and register—everyone of you. Angry enough to take five and ten other people with you. Then and only then can these brutal killings be stopped. Remember it is your sons and your daughters who have been killed all these years and you have done nothing about it, and if you don't do nothing NOW baby, I say God Damn Your Souls. . . .

Mileston, August 9

Dear Blake, . . . Dave finally broke down and couldn't finish and the Chaney family was moaning and much of the audience and I were also crying. It's such an impossible thing to describe but suddenly again, as I'd first realized when I heard the three men were missing when we were still training up at Oxford, I felt the sacrifice the Negroes have been making for so long. How the Negro people are able to accept all the abuses of the whites—all the insults and injustices which make me ashamed to be white—and then turn around and say they want to love us, is beyond me. There are Negroes who want to kill whites and many Negroes have much bitterness but still the majority seem to have the quality of being able to look for a future in which whites will love the Negroes. Our kids talk very critically of all the whites around here and still they have a dream of freedom in which both races understand and accept each other. There is such an overpowering task ahead of these kids that sometimes I can't do anything but cry for them. I hope they are up to the task, I'm not sure I would be if I were a Mississippi Negro. As a white northerner I can get involved whenever I feel like it and run home whenever I get bored or frustrated or scared. I hate the attitude and position of the Northern whites and despise myself when I think that way. Lately I've been feeling homesick and longing for pleasant old Westport and sailing and swimming and my friends. I don't quite know what to do because I can't ignore my desire to go home and yet I feel I am a much weaker person than I like to think I am because I do have these emotions. I've always tried to avoid situations which aren't so nice, like arguments and dirty houses and now maybe Mississippi. I asked my father if I could stay down here for a whole year and I was almost glad when he said "no" that we couldn't afford it because it would mean supporting me this year in addition to three more years of college. I have a desire to go home and to read a lot and go to Quaker meetings and be by myself so I can think about all this rather than being in the middle of it all the time. But I know if my emotions run like they have in the past, that I can only take that pacific sort of life for a little while and then I get the desire to be active again and get involved with knowing other people. I guess this all sounds crazy and I seem to always think out my problems as I write to you. I am angry because I have a choice as to whether or not to work in the Movement and I am playing upon that choice and leaving here. I wish I could talk with you 'cause I'd like to know if you ever felt this way about anything. I mean have you ever despised yourself for your weak conviction or something. And what is making it worse is that all those damn northerners are thinking of me as a brave hero. . . .

Martha

TOPIC 70

INTEGRATION, SEPARATION, AND BLACK POWER

The late 1960s saw increasing disillusionment among both blacks and whites. The relatively straightforward goal of desegregation of the 1950s and early 1960s no longer satisfied those who desired change. Although "Jim Crow," that is, segregation by law, had been badly crippled there was intense disagreement over its replacement. Some argued for de facto segregation, that is, segregation by custom, such as existed in residential patterns in Northern cities. Others, both black and white, urged total integration, ending all forms of legal and customary exclusion. The number of blacks who began to feel that the situation was hopeless increased. Many added their voices to calls for separation, whether in the United States or through a return to Africa. Still other blacks urged the race to draw together and to use its political and economic power to push for greater influence within the system. Finally, an increasing number of blacks joined white radicals to urge a drastic restructuring of society as the only way to end racism.

Reading 375

The New Mood of Black Americans

The events of the mid-1960s demonstrated that blacks could no longer be kept quiet with the promise of equality but the reality of inequality. Verbal and physical violence, which had always been characteristic behavior of whites against blacks, were now being expressed by blacks toward whites. The urban riots of the late 1960s were only dramatic expressions of this desire to strike back.

From David Shannon, *Twentieth Century America* (Chicago, 1969), pp. 651–654. Copyright © 1963, 1969 by Rand McNally and Company. Subheadings added by the editors.

I

Black Power

Just as rivers have a way of overflowing their banks and cutting new channels so did the stream of revolt of American Negroes; the movement that had gained unprecedented momentum since the mid-1950's experienced basic changes in the years Johnson was President. Where the main focus of black struggle had been in the South, the center of primary attention was shifting to northern and western cities. (By the late 1960's, only a minority of Negroes lived in the former Confederate states, and most of the northern and western majority lived in big cities.) Where the main thrust of the movement has been for voting and other political rights, it was beginning to veer off in other directions, largely economic. Where the movement had once been almost unanimously behind the goal of racial inte-

573

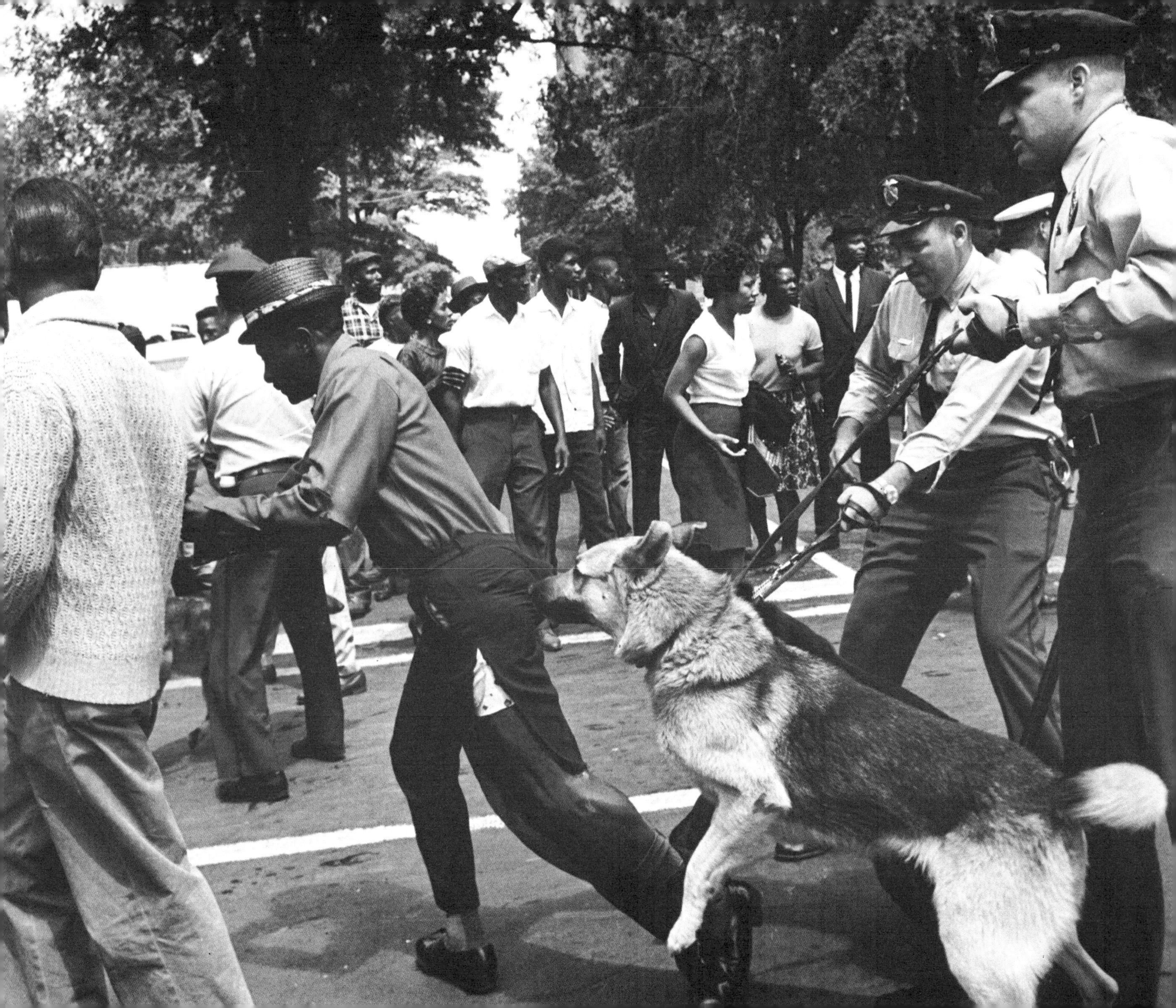

gration, there were increasing doubts about the possibility and even the desirability of integration and an increasing interest in black separatism. Where the main effort of the movement, unconsciously or not, had been to gain access to white-dominated traditional institutions (in the pattern of earlier groups, both economic and ethnic, who strived to gain a place at the nation's table) there now was a growing tendency to say that institutions such as government, unions, and schools were hopeless even if Negroes shared their direction and that what really was needed was a fundamental economic and social reconstruction. Where only a few had dissented from the view that only non-violent tactics should be used, now there were increasing numbers who rejected non-violence as a philosophy, at least doubted its effectiveness as a tactic, or who advocated violence, or the threat of it, as a means toward the goal. There was rapidly developing a new mood, more impatient, angrier, more desperate.

The new mood and attitudes could be seen in what was happening in the main Negro organizations. The biggest and oldest of them, the NAACP and the Urban League, continued to grow, but whites became less prominent in them, there was more internal bickering, and they became generally more militant and radical. Established leaders had to run fast to stay ahead of their followers. In 1968 the remarks to a group of young black militants by the highly able but unmistakably middle class director of the Urban League, Whitney M. Young, Jr., were applauded and welcomed with shouts of "Amen, the brother has returned." CORE (Congress of Racial Equality), which was predominantly white from its founding in 1942 until the mid-1960's, suffered a split in 1968. The large Brooklyn and Bronx chapters announced their departure, charging CORE leadership was a "civil rights aristocracy" and asserting it was not working hard enough for "the destruction of white capitalism in black communities." The Student Nonviolent Coordinating Committee (SNCC, "Snick") underwent an upheaval in the summer of 1966 when non-students who were not advocates of non-violence gained control. The Southern Christian Leadership Conference seemed to flounder after the death of its leader, Dr. King, in April, 1968.

Behind these developments in the main Negro organizations were several matters that were bringing about a shift in the whole movement. One clear factor was the "generation gap." Most of the leaders had been in their forties or older—as are the leaders in most stable institutions—and the young people, those who were most active in demonstrations and most likely to be beaten or jailed or both, were impatient and rebellious. Many of the young militants had been in the movement from childhood, and they could not see that their activities had got the results they wanted. Another factor was that the frustrations of the black militants were real ones: gains in civil rights as such, in the right to vote primarily, had not significantly improved their lives. Perhaps even there had been a retrogression. In any case, expectations had exceeded reality, and disappointment and disillusion triggered bitter impulses of retribution. Still another factor were outbreaks of violent rioting in the Negro quarters of large cities, especially in 1965 and thereafter. In sum, the Negro temper was changing from a demand for full political participation in a democracy, irrespective of region but with a primarily southern focus, to a bristling, short-tempered revolt against conditions in the ghettos. The movement was becoming increasingly involved in old-fashioned class conflict, such as had existed in densely populated cities in America and abroad since the seventeenth and eighteenth centuries. It was class conflict, but it had the significant difference of race.

The slogan of "black power," which became popular in 1966, both excited and confused the Negro movement. The slogan symbolized different things to different people, both black and white. To some it meant simply immediate victory or fight; a resort to violence. This was the way frightened whites frequently understood it. To others it meant Negro control of the ghetto and the various institutions there, with whites being completely out of policy matters. To still others it meant what could be called black capitalism: Negro businesses of all kinds, with Negro capital, workers, managers, and customers. Late in the decade there seemed to be a sketchy consensus developing toward the latter two positions, but there was little agreement about how it could be reached. One matter on which there was a wide consensus was Negro "cultural nationalism": black art, "soul" music, Negro literature, "black is beautiful."

In trying to suppress demonstrations by suddenly assertive blacks in the South, local police often used such devices as fire hoses, electrified cattle prods, and dogs. Here police deal with demonstrators trying to organize a protest march from Selma to Montgomery, Ala., in the spring of 1965. Eventually, through federal court order and under the protection of federal troops, the march took place. Thousands of supporters came from all parts of the country to join in the final day of the March.

II
Long, Hot Summers

Many ghetto problems, it was clear, would remain if there were no racial prejudice and if political democracy were perfect, even though in fact they were enormously complicated by prejudice and democratic imperfections. The black ghetto's problems were similar in many ways to those of white slums, particularly in an earlier day. Rural people without urban and industrial skills, ill-prepared for the complexities of densely populated society, present special problems, and government generally failed to meet them satisfactorily. Housing in ghettos was deplorable beyond the imagination of more fortunate people. Lack of adequate sanitation facilities and insufficient public sanitation, combined with poverty and inadequate private health services, created and perpetuated fearful health problems. (Nationally, the Negro infant mortality rate was twice as high as the white.) Poor public education reduced the chances of children to break out of the ghetto or gain the powers and skills to improve it. Crime (and fear of crime among the law-abiding) was worse in the slums than elsewhere. Transportation was poor, which made it difficult to get to jobs far from home. Because of poor education, formal and informal, slum-dwellers were vulnerable to sharp business practices and other ways of exploiting the ignorant and socially weak.

Situations like this were not new in America. They had existed, for example, in Irish slums in Boston and in Italian and Jewish poor neighborhoods in New York recently enough to be remembered by thousands. But this is not to say that the black ghetto was just a latter-day version of the immigrant slum. Color identified the black ghetto inhabitant more immediately and permanently than those who lived in South Boston or the Lower East Side. European immigrants had no background of slavery. And while there certainly was prejudice against the Irish, Italians, and Jews, it was not so virulent or pervasive as anti-black feelings. America would be foolish to look to the historical record of immigrant slum-dwellers and their rise in a few generations and assume that the future holds a parallel development for the residents of black ghettos. There are many differences other than race and a background of severe oppression. The number of unskilled workers needed is smaller today. The pattern of inner-city ghetto surrounded by white suburbs—a white doughnut surrounding a black hole—is different from the nineteenth- and early twentieth-century pattern, where industry and other employment existed close to the slums. Historical analogies are tricky; the history of the European migrants may or may not be repeated by the migrants from the rural South. Historical situations may recur, but history does not necessarily repeat itself.

There had been many uprisings in nineteenth-century America, particularly where the Irish were the largest immigrant group, but they had not attracted as much attention nationally as the Negro ghetto riots of the 1960's. The first really big black riot, the first one to shake the nation deeply, was in the Watts section of Los Angeles in 1965, although there had been lesser disturbances the two previous years in several other cities. In 1966 there were more riots than ever before, but none was as serious as the Watts upheaval. Then in 1967 came worse ones; the biggest riots were in Newark and Detroit, but matters were serious in Tampa, Cincinnati, Atlanta, and several cities near Newark. In the spring of 1968 there was much looting and burning in the nation's capital.* The usual pattern was an "incident" between young men of the ghetto and white policemen, followed by angry reaction to the real or imagined injustice, bricks through store windows, looting, arson, police reinforcement with national guardsmen, and the gradual restoration of order. Particularly in 1967, the police and guardsmen behaved with a disdain for law and prudence that rivalled the rioters'. President Johnson in 1967 appointed a special panel on riots with Governor Otto Kerner of Illinois as chairman, and this group's *Report of the National Advisory Commission on Civil Disorders* described the disturbances and analyzed their causes cogently.

The evidence does not suggest that the riots were started by black militant organizations—although some of the farthest-out leaders tried to exploit them for ideological advantage—or that the rioting was other than spontaneous. But the riots had a profound effect upon Negro organizations even though they did not arise directly from the movement. Black revolutionists could point to the outbreaks as evidence of a revolutionary spirit in the ghetto, or at least a violent one in some circumstances, and they could argue that the excessively violent reaction of the police and guardsmen indicated that "whitey" was not susceptible to reasoned appeal and would not consent peacefully to a basic change in racial matters. The riots also appeared to move Negro moderate leaders to a more militant position.

*Riots in Washington and many other cities were triggered by the assassination of Martin Luther King in Memphis, Tennessee, in April 1968—Eds.

Reading 376

Riots in the Cities (1967)

Urban riots after 1965 made people realize that black frustration and anger existed in every region of the country and not the South alone. The motivations, dimensions, and significance of these outbreaks emerged in the following study of Plainfield, New Jersey, taken from the report of the Presidential commission, headed by Illinois Governor Otto Kerner, created to investigate the riots.

From "Plainfield," *Report of the National Advisory Commission on Civil Disorders* (Washington, D.C., 1968), pp. 41–45. Subheadings added by the editors.

Stores in the business section of Watts, a predominantly black district in Los Angeles, burn out of control after being firebombed during the second of six nights of rioting in August 1965. In the next few years blacks released their anger and frustration in major riots in cities throughout the nation.

Quite clearly, the riots polarized black and white attitudes. The "white backlash" was strong, and there were conservative demagogues ready to take advantage of it. White liberals, sensitive to being cursed with that label because they had thought it an honorable one, rarely defended the riots; they only urged that such violence be understood and that the roots of it be attacked. Those whose sense of justice and morality had been outraged by Alabama police chiefs, Mississippi sheriffs, and Ku Klux murderers were less prone to give aid and sympathy. Among both Negroes and whites was a growing tendency to lump together all in the other population except for the people one knew personally. Few who yearned for justice, harmony, and peaceful relations could see grounds for optimism.

I

A Nice, Quiet Town

New Jersey's worst violence outside of Newark was experienced by Plainfield, a pleasant, tree-shaded city of 45,000. A "bedroom community," more than a third of whose residents work outside the city, Plainfield had had relatively few Negroes until 1950. By 1967, the Negro population had risen to an estimated 30 percent of the total. As in Englewood, there was a division between the Negro middle class, which lived in the East side "gilded ghetto," and the unskilled, unemployed and underemployed poor on the West side.

Geared to the needs of a suburban middle class, the part-time and fragmented city government had failed to realize the change in character which the city had undergone, and was unprepared to cope with the problems of a growing disadvantaged population. There was no full-time administrator or city manager. Boards, with independent jurisdiction over such areas as education, welfare and health, were appointed by the part-time mayor, whose own position was largely honorary.

Accustomed to viewing politics as a gentleman's pastime, city officials were startled and upset by the intensity with which demands issued from the ghetto. Usually such demands were met obliquely, rather than head-on.

In the summer of 1966, trouble was narrowly averted over the issue of a swimming pool for Negro youngsters. In the summer of 1967, instead of having built the pool, the city began busing the children to the county pool a half-hour's ride distant. The fare was 25 cents per person, and the children had to provide their own lunch, a considerable strain on a frequent basis for a poor family with several children.

The bus operated only on 3 days in midweek. On weekends the county pool was too crowded to accommodate children from the Plainfield ghetto.

Pressure increased upon the school system to adapt itself to the changing social and ethnic backgrounds of its pupils. There were strikes and boycotts. The track system created *de facto* segregation within a supposedly integrated school system. Most of the youngsters from white middle-class districts were in the higher track, most from the Negro poverty areas in the lower. Relations were strained between some white teachers and Negro pupils. Two-thirds of school dropouts were estimated to be Negro.

In February 1967 the NAACP, out of a growing sense of frustration with the municipal government, tacked a list of 19 demands and complaints to the door of the city hall. Most dealt with discrimination in housing, employment and in the public schools. By summer, the city's common council had not responded. Although two of the 11 council members were Negro, both represented the East side ghetto. The poverty area was represented by two white women, one of whom had been appointed by the council after the elected representative, a Negro, had moved away.

Relations between the police and the Negro community, tenuous at best, had been further troubled the week prior to the Newark outbreak. After being handcuffed during a routine arrest in a housing project, a woman had fallen down a flight of stairs. The officer said she had slipped. Negro residents claimed he had pushed her.

When a delegation went to city hall to file a complaint, they were told by the city clerk that he was not empowered to accept it. Believing that they were being given the run-around, the delegation, angry and frustrated, departed. . . .

On one of the quiet city streets, two young Negroes, D. H. and L. C., had been neighbors. D. H. had graduated from high school, attended Fairleigh Dickinson University and, after receiving a degree in psychology, had obtained a job as a reporter on the Plainfield *Courier-News*.

L. C. had dropped out of high school, become a worker in a chemical plant, and, although still in his twenties, had married and fathered seven children. A man with a strong sense of family, he liked sports and played in the local baseball league. Active in civil rights, he had, like the civil rights organizations, over the years, become more militant. For a period of time he had been a Muslim.

The outbreak of vandalism aroused concern among the police. Shortly after midnight, in an attempt to decrease tensions, D. H. and the two Negro councilmen met with the youths in the housing project. The focal point of the youths' bitterness was the attitude of the police—until 1966 police had used the word "nigger" over the police radio and one officer had worn a Confederate belt buckle and had flown a Confederate pennant on his car. Their complaints, however, ranged over local and national issues. There was an overriding cynicism and disbelief that government would, of its own accord, make meaningful changes to improve the lot of the lower-class Negro. There was an overriding belief that there were two sets of policies by the people in power, whether law enforcement officers, newspaper editors, or government officials: one for white, and one for black.

There was little confidence that the two councilmen could exercise any influence. One youth said: "You came down here last year. We were throwing stones at some passing cars, and you said to us that this was not the way to do it. You got us to talk with the man. We talked to him. We talked with him, and we talked all year long. We ain't got nothing yet!"

However, on the promise that meetings would be arranged with the editor of the newspaper and with the mayor later that same day, the youths agreed to disperse.

At the first of these meetings, the youths were, apparently, satisfied by the explanation that the newspaper's coverage was not deliberately discriminatory. The meeting with the mayor, however, proceeded badly. Negroes present felt that the mayor was complacent and apathetic, and that they were simply being given the usual lip service, from which nothing would develop.

The mayor, on the other hand, told Commission investigators that he recognized that "citizens are frustrated by the political organization of the city," because he, himself, has no real power and "each of the councilmen says that he is just one of the 11 and therefore can't do anything."

After approximately 2 hours, a dozen of the youths walked out, indicating an impasse and signaling the breakup of the meeting. Shortly thereafter, window smashing began. A Molotov cocktail was set afire in a tree. One fire engine, in which a white and Negro fireman were sitting side by side, had a Molotov cocktail thrown at it. The white fireman was burned.

As window smashing continued, liquor stores and taverns were especially hard hit. Some of the youths believed that there was an excess concentration of bars in the Negro section, and that these were an unhealthy influence in the community.

Because the police department had mobilized its full force, the situation, although serious, never appeared to get out of hand. Officers made many arrests. The chief of the fire department told Commission investigators that it was his conclusion that "individuals making fire bombs did not know what they were doing, or they could have burned the city."

At 3 o'clock Sunday morning, a heavy rain began, scattering whatever groups remained on the streets.

II

The Riot

In the morning, police made no effort to cordon off the area. As white sightseers and churchgoers drove by the housing project there was sporadic rock throwing. During the early afternoon, such incidents increased.

At the housing project, a meeting was convened by L. C. to draw up a formal petition of grievances. As the youths gathered it became apparent that some of them had been drinking. A few kept drifting away from the parking lot where the meeting was being held to throw rocks at passing cars. It was decided to move the meeting to a county park several blocks away.

Between 150 and 200 persons, including almost all of the rock throwers, piled into a caravan of cars and headed for the park. At approximately 3:30 P.M., the chief of the Union County park police arrived to find the group being addressed by David Sullivan, executive director of the human relations commission. He "informed Mr. Sullivan he was in violation of our park ordinance and to disperse the group."

Sullivan and L. C. attempted to explain that they were in the process of drawing up a list of grievances, but the chief remained adamant. They could not meet in the park without a permit, and they did not have a permit.

After permitting the group 10 to 15 minutes grace, the chief decided to disperse them. "Their mood was very excitable," he reported, and "in my estimation no one could appease them so we moved them out without too much trouble. They left in a caravan of about 40 cars, horns blowing and yelling and headed south on West End Avenue to Plainfield."

Within the hour, looting became widespread. Cars were overturned, a white man was snatched off a motorcycle, and the fire department stopped responding to alarms because the police were unable to provide protection. After having been on alert until midday, the Plainfield Police Department was caught unprepared. At 6 P.M., only 18 men were on the streets. Checkpoints were established at crucial intersections in an effort to isolate the area.

Officer John Gleason, together with two reserve officers, had been posted at one of the intersections, three blocks from the housing project. Gleason was a veteran officer, the son of a former lieutenant on the police department. Shortly after 8 P.M., two white youths, chased by a 22-year-old Negro, Bobby Williams, came running from the direction of the ghetto toward Gleason's post.

As he came in sight of the police officers, Williams stopped. Accounts vary of what happened next, or why Officer Gleason took the action he did. What is known is that when D. H., the newspaper reporter, caught sight of him a minute or two later, Officer Gleason was two blocks from his post. Striding after Williams directly into the ghetto area, Gleason already had passed one housing project. Small groups were milling about. In D. H.'s words: "There was a kind of shock and amazement," to see the officer walking by himself so deep in the ghetto.

Suddenly, there was a confrontation between Williams and Gleason. Some witnesses report Williams had a hammer in his hand. Others say he did not. When D. H., whose attention momentarily had been distracted, next saw Gleason he had drawn his gun and was firing at Williams. As Williams, critically injured, fell to the ground, Gleason turned and ran back toward his post.

Negro youths chased him. Gleason stumbled, regained his balance, then had his feet knocked out from under him. A score of youths began to beat him and kick him. Some residents of the apartment house attempted to intervene, but they were brushed aside. D. H. believes that, under the circumstances and in the atmosphere that prevailed at that moment, any police officer, black or white, would have been killed.

After they had beaten Gleason to death, the youths took D. H.'s camera from him and smashed it.

Fear swept over the ghetto. Many residents—both lawless and law-abiding—were convinced, on the basis of what had occurred in Newark, that law enforcement officers, bent on vengeance, would come into the ghetto shooting.

People began actively to prepare to defend themselves. There was no lack of weapons. Forty-six carbines were stolen from a nearby arms manufacturing plant and passed out in the street by a young Negro, a former newspaper boy. Most of the weapons fell into the hands of youths, who began firing them wildly. A fire station was peppered with shots.

Law enforcement officers continued their cordon about the area, but made no attempt to enter it except, occasionally, to rescue someone. National Guardsmen arrived shortly after midnight. Their armored personnel carriers were used to carry troops to the fire station, which had been besieged for five hours. During this period only one fire had been reported in the city. . . .

Michigan National Guardsmen with fixed bayonets move down a rubble-strewn, fire-swept street on Detroit's West Side during the height of that city's riot of July 1967. In addition to millions of dollars in property damage, forty-three persons were killed and over six hundred injured, some by police and guardsmen, some by rioters, in the few days of violence.

III

Cooling It

At 8 P.M., the New Jersey attorney general, human relations director, and commander of the state police, accompanied by the mayor, went to the housing project and spoke to several hundred Negroes. Some members of the crowd were hostile. Others were anxious to establish a dialogue. There were demands that officials give concrete evidence that they were prepared to deal with Negro grievances. Again, the meeting was inconclusive. The officials returned to City Hall.

At 9:15 P.M., L. C. rushed in claiming that—as a result of the failure to resolve any of the outstanding problems, and reports that people who had been arrested by the police were being beaten—violence was about to explode anew. The key demand of the militant faction was that those who had been arrested during the riot should be released. State officials decided to arrange for the release on bail of 12 arrestees charged with minor violations. L. C., in turn, agreed to try to induce return of the stolen carbines by Wednesday noon.

As state officials were scanning the list of arrestees to determine which of them should be released, a message was brought to Colonel Kelly of the state police that general firing had broken out around the perimeter.

The report testified to the tension: an investigation disclosed that one shot of unexplained origin had been heard. In response, security forces had shot out street lights, thus initiating the "general firing."

At 4:00 o'clock Tuesday morning, a dozen prisoners were released from jail. Plainfield police officers considered this a "sellout."

When, by noon on Wednesday, the stolen carbines had not been returned, the governor decided to authorize a mass search. At 2:00 P.M., a convoy of state police and National Guard troops prepared to enter the area. In order to direct the search as to likely locations, a handful of Plainfield police officers were spotted throughout the 28 vehicles of the convoy.

As the convoy prepared to depart, the state community relations director, believing himself to be carrying out the decision of the governor not to permit Plainfield officers to participate in the search, ordered their removal from the vehicles. The basis for his order was that their participation might ignite a clash between them and the Negro citizens.

As the search for carbines in the community progressed, tension increased rapidly. According to witnesses and newspaper reports, some men in the search force left apartments in shambles.

The search was called off an hour and a half after it was begun. No stolen weapons were discovered. For the Plainfield police, the removal of the officers from the convoy had been a humiliating experience. A half hour after the conclusion of the search, in a meeting charged with emotion, the entire department threatened to resign unless the state community relations director left the city. He bowed to the demand.

On Friday, seven days after the first outbreak, the city began returning to normal.

The White Backlash

In the mid-1960s the word *polarization* came into popular use as the national scope of racial conflict became evident. It was not that many blacks and whites were suddenly hostile toward each other; that had been the case for many years. Rather, it meant the growing demands of blacks, both in the North and in the South, for all forms of social, economic, and political advancement, were forcing the indifferent, most of whom were whites, to support actively or to oppose changes in the racial status quo. The phrase "white backlash" was coined to identify those who vigorously opposed change. The following reading describes an example of white backlash in a school-busing struggle in a residential area of New York City.

From Peggy Streit, "Why They Fight for the P. A. T.," *New York Times Magazine*, September 20, 1964, pp. 20–21, 122. © 1964 by the New York Times Company. Reprinted by permission. Subheadings added by the editors.

I

Integration Up North

"The way I see it, it's like this," said the taxi driver. "If I had kids of school age I'd join P.A.T.* And I'd keep the kids out of school just as long as we white people didn't get our rights. Now don't get me wrong. I ain't got nothing against colored people. If they want good schools, they ought to have good schools. But they ought to go to schools in *their* neighborhood—just like white kids ought to go to school in *their* neighborhood."

The taxi stopped at a red light. The traffic on Van Wyck Boulevard rumbled by the drab, squat commercial buildings—a bar, a hardware store, a beauty parlor, a real-estate office advertising a six-room two-story, one-family house for $15,000.

"You know Queens?" he asked. "South Richmond Hill? South Ozone Park? No? I was born and raised here," he said proudly. "Just like my folks. There's a lot of second- and third-generation families out here. It's a real neighborly place—not like New York City where nobody cares who lives next door and nobody owns their own home."

Leaving behind the pounding commercial traffic, the taxi turned off abruptly into a more tranquil world of narrow residential streets lined by modest homes—house after identical house, like rows of ditto marks. But they shared the sedate dignity of a clean, orderly neighborhood, their aging ungracious architecture softened by the sycamore trees.

"Like I was saying," continued the taxi driver, "you buy a house because you want your kid to go to a school nearby and the church is just around the corner. And then, here comes the government or school board and what do they say? They say, 'Mister, you can't send your kid to school near you. You got to bus him to school in a Negro neigh-

---
*Parents and Taxpayers, an antibusing organization—Eds.

borhood, 20 blocks away, that's been—what do they call it—*paired* with a white school because of racial imbalance.' Now I ask you, is that right? And I say to you, no—that ain't right. We're losing our freedoms in this country. Next thing you know, they'll be telling you where to go to church."

The taxi slowed to a halt outside the home of P.A.T. official June Reynolds. "I'm sure glad I'm not that school-board guy, Gross," he chuckled, with wry satisfaction. "You know how women's voices go up when they get mad? Tell the ladies: 'God bless them.'"

"Now," said Mrs. Reynolds, "what would you like to know about our group?" Her cluttered desk was the only disorder in a living room like countless others in the neighborhood—wall-to-wall carpets, meticulously vacuumed; modern furniture gleaming with polish; earthenware lamps, their orange shades still protected by plastic wrappers; a large-screen television set; reproductions of oriental art on the walls . . . a picture of modest but proud possession.

Size? "There are about 2,700 of us," she replied, "with 300 hard-core members doing most of the work—the executive board, the telephone girls who call about P.A.T. meetings and poll members, and the block captains who ring doorbells for new members."

Membership? "Mostly parents with elementary-school kids, of course, but some people without children. This is a moral issue, too, not just an educational one."

Purpose? "To protect our children, preserve our neighborhood-school system, and keep our children from being bused into strange districts."

Activities? "Well, we organize protests against pairing and busing, and we've been urging members to write to their newspapers and councilmen. Things like that."

The racial issue? She paused irresolutely. "The racial issue doesn't have anything to do with what we want," she said, "We believe in open enrollment. If Negroes want to go to white schools where there's room, they should be allowed to. And we believe in the improvement of Negro schools. It's not true what people say—that we don't like Negroes and we don't want them in our schools. If they live in our neighborhood they have a right here. But nobody has a right to send our children *away* from our neighborhood.". . .

II
"We're Not Bad People"

June Reynolds, a young, fresh-faced, bright-eyed, dedicated dynamo, doesn't have anything against Negroes either. "I went to school with Negroes when I was a girl," she said, "If I were a Negro, how would I see to it that my kids got a better education and a chance in the world?" She answered herself without hesitation. "I'd move into an interracial neighborhood. I wouldn't live in Harlem for anything in the world. I'd scrub floors. I'd take in laundry. I'd get any kind of job to get out of Harlem—and I know I'd succeed because I believe that in the United States anybody can do anything if he tries hard enough.

"Look at my father: Negroes can at least speak English, but when my father came here from Italy he had to learn the language, so he went to night school. Then he got a job as a wrapper in a bakery. He worked there 47 years and was a supervisor when he retired. The way I see it," she added with finality, "if a Negro lives in Harlem, it's because he likes it there and because he doesn't want to work hard enough to get out of that environment."

Hannah Edell, a round, small, blond woman with soft pink cheeks and a troubled voice, was a little less dogmatic.

"Yes, I think the Negro has been discriminated against," she said, "and I think they should be helped along. But I don't think their problem is educational. It's social. I know that some Negroes think, 'Why should I bother to get an education if I can't get a job afterwards?'—and that's what I mean by a social problem. It's up to large corporations to give them jobs."

She acknowledged the obvious question with a long, hard sigh. "Yes, I know," she said. "Why *shouldn't* large corporations give their jobs to the best-educated—and they are usually white."

She paused then reflected sadly: "It's a vicious circle, isn't it? One hardly knows where to begin. But one thing I *do* know," she went on, gaining assurance. "They shouldn't begin with our children. Integration isn't a problem for children to solve—or their parents. It's up to the politicians, big corporations—other people. And the Board of Education. This problem has existed for a long time. Why didn't the board do something to improve Negro education a long time ago, so things wouldn't have got to this state?"

Joe Lamanna, project manager for a contractor, saw the problem differently. A large young man, dark-eyed, handsome, well-turned-out and the possessor of a college degree earned after five and a half years of night school, he is proud of his Italian ancestry, of his home in one of Ozone Park's more affluent districts and of a gigantic new car, which he won in a church raffle.

"This is most of all a moral issue," he said. "What right does anybody—*anybody*—have to tell me what to do? Where does it all end? I worked with Negroes on a construction job

Controversy over integration of schools swept the North in the late 1960s and continued into the 1970s. These controversies sometimes turned into open conflict and revealed the nationwide scope of black-white tensions. Here members of the Queens, New York City, chapter of the Congress of Racial Equality picket a local high school, urging a city-wide policy of school integration.

for seven years. They don't work hard or help their children in school or care about their families or keep their homes clean. But that's not the issue. I just won't tolerate anybody telling me I've got to send my son into another neighborhood to school."

His small, chic wife agreed. "I don't think I have a moral obligation to anyone—to my family, my husband and child maybe, but no one else. If Negroes have been deprived of some rights it's because they haven't worked for them. They don't deserve them. And the only way they're finally going to get them is through hard work—not by having our children bused into their schools." Her voice rose in distress.

"People just aren't psychologically ready for all this—this mixing," she complained. "We're not bad people out here in Ozone Park. We don't want to hurt anybody. We are decent, hard-working, church-going, law-abiding people—but we're bewildered. Bewildered by this bombshell of racial integration. Why do things have to change overnight? Why can't it be gradual?"

Though differently expressed, the views of P.A.T. members coincide on most questions.

> Slavery? Sure Negroes were slaves once and that was terrible. But they haven't been slaves for 100 years. How could they use that anymore as an excuse for not getting ahead?

Color? It wasn't their color that was holding them back. It was the kind of people they were and the things they did and things they didn't do.

Discriminated against? Not really. In the South, maybe, but there was no segregation in New York City. They could go into any restaurant. Look at the Jews. They lived in ghettos once. They couldn't get certain kinds of jobs once. They had been discriminated against much longer than the Negroes, and look how well they had done.

Substandard schools? But why hadn't they *done* something about their schools before now? White mothers would have. Why had they been so apathetic all these years?

"If I were God, what would I do to improve the lot of the Negro?" echoed a P.A.T. supporter. "If I were God, I'd make everybody white."

The Black Manifesto (1969)

The white backlash created a black backlash. The level of frustration among blacks, always high and especially so among the young, increased in the 1960s as change seemed to come at an agonizingly slow pace. At times only mass violence, as in the urban riots, seemed to move whites to positive action. At the same time, of course, the riots accelerated the white backlash. An increasing number of black militant organizations, such as the Black Panthers, appeared in response to what was seen as a worsening situation. In the spring of 1969 James Forman, a former head of SNCC, spoke before another black power group where he presented a "Black Manifesto." Couched in revolutionary rhetoric, Forman's analysis offered his solution to the problem. In the next year Forman interrupted a number of church and synagogue services to read the manifesto to white congregations.

From James Forman, "Black Manifesto," *Renewal*, IX (June, 1969), pp. 9–11.

Brothers and Sisters:

We have come from all over the country, burning with anger and despair not only with the miserable economic plight of our people, but fully aware that the racism on which the Western world was built dominates our lives. There can be no separation of the problems of racism from the problems of our economic, political, and cultural degradation. To any black man, this is clear.

But there are still some of our people who are clinging to the rhetoric of the Negro and we must separate ourselves from those Negroes who go around the country promoting all types of schemes for Black Capitalism.

Ironically, some of the most militant Black Nationalists, as they call themselves, have been the first to jump on the bandwagon of black capitalism. They are pimps; Black Power Pimps and fraudulent leaders and the people must be educated to understand that any black man or Negro who is advocating a perpetuation of capitalism inside the United States is in fact seeking not only his ultimate destruction and death, but is contributing to the continuous exploitation of black people all around the world. For it is the power of the United States Government, this racist, imperialist government, that is choking the life of all people around the world. . . .

Where do we begin? We have already started. We started the moment we were brought to this country. In fact, we started on the shores of Africa, for we have always resisted attempts to make us slaves and now we must resist the attempts to make us capitalists. It is the financial interest of the U.S. to make us capitalists, for this will be the same line as that of integration into the mainstream of American life. Therefore, brothers and sisters, there is no need to fall into the trap that we have to get an ideology. We HAVE an ideology. Our fight is against racism, capitalism and imperialism and we are dedicated to building a socialist society inside the United States where the total means of production and distribution are in the hands of the State and that must be led by black people, by revolutionary blacks who are concerned about the total humanity of this world. And, therefore, we obviously are different from some of those who seek a black nation in the United States, for there is no way for that nation to be viable if in fact the United States remains in the hands of white racists. Then too, let us deal with some arguments that we should share power with whites. We say that there must be a revolutionary black Vanguard and that white people in this country must be willing to accept black leadership, for that is the only protection that black people have to protect ourselves from racism rising again in this country.

Racism in the U.S. is so pervasive in the mentality of whites that only an armed, well-disciplined, black-controlled government can insure the stamping out of racism in this country. And that is why we plead with black people not to be talking about a few crumbs, a few thousand dollars for this cooperative, or a thousand dollars which splits black people into fighting over the dollar. That is the intention of the government. We say . . . think in terms of total control of the U.S. Prepare ourselves to seize state power. Do not hedge, for time is short and all around the world, the forces of liberation are directing their attacks against the U.S. It is a powerful country, but that power is not greater than that of black people. We work the chief industries in this country and we could cripple the economy while the brothers fought guerrilla warfare in the streets. This will take some long-range planning, but whether it happens in a thousand years is of no consequence. It cannot happen unless we start. How then is all of this related to this conference?

First of all, this conference is called by a set of religious people, Christians, who have been involved in the exploitation and rape of black people since the country was founded. The missionary goes hand in hand with the power of the states. We must begin seizing power wherever we are and we must say to the planners of this conference that you are no longer in charge. We the people who have assembled here, thank you for getting us here, but we are going to assume power over the conference and determine from this moment on the direction in which we want it to go. We are not saying that the conference was planned badly. The staff of the conference have worked hard and have done a magnificent job in bringing all of us together and we must include them in the new membership which must surface from this point on. The conference is now the property of the people who are assembled here. This we proclaim as fact and not rhetoric and there are demands that we are going to make and we insist that the planners of this conference help us implement them.

We maintain we have the revolutionary right to do this. We have the same rights, if you will, as the Christians had in going into Africa and raping our Motherland and bringing us away from our continent of peace and into this hostile and alien environment where we have been living in perpetual warfare since 1619.

Our seizure of power at this conference is based on a program and our program is contained in the following *Manifesto:*

TO THE WHITE CHRISTIAN CHURCHES
AND THE JEWISH SYNAGOGUES
IN THE UNITED STATES OF AMERICA
AND ALL OTHER RACIST INSTITUTIONS

Black Manifesto

We the black people assembled in Detroit, Michigan, for the National Black Economic Development Conference are fully aware that we have been forced to come together because racist white America has exploited our resources, our minds, our bodies, our labor. For centuries we have been forced to live as colonized people inside the United States, victimized by the most vicious, racist system in the world. We have helped to build the most industrial country in the world.

We are therefore demanding of the white Christian churches and Jewish synagogues which are part and parcel of the system of capitalism, that they begin to pay reparations to black people in this country. We are demanding $500,000,000 from the Christian white churches and the Jewish synagogues. This total comes to 15 dollars per nigger. This is a low estimate for we maintain there are probably more than 30,000,000 black people in this country. $15 a nigger is not a large sum of money and we know that the churches and synagogues have a tremendous wealth and its membership, white America, has profited from and still exploits black people. We are also not unaware that the exploitation of colored peoples around the world is aided and abetted by the white Christian churches and synagogues. This demand for $500,000,000 is not an idle resolution or empty words. Fifteen dollars for every black brother and sister in the United States is only a beginning of the reparations due us as people who have been exploited and degraded, brutalized, killed and persecuted. Underneath all of this exploitation, the racism of this country has produced a psychological effect upon us that we are beginning to shake off. We are no longer afraid to demand our full rights as a people in this decadent society.

Towards Integration as a Goal

Civil rights activist Bayard Rustin, an early worker in the Congress of Racial Equality and the main organizer of the 1963 March on

Washington, attempts in the following reading to interpret the concept of integration for the racial scene of the 1970s.

From Bayard Rustin, "Towards Integration as a Goal," *The American Federationist*, LXXVI (January, 1969), pp. 5-7. Subheadings added by the editors.

I

Separatism and Despair

The proposition that separation may be the best solution of America's racial problems has been recurrent in American Negro history. Let us look at the syndrome that has given rise to it.

Separation, in one form or another, has been proposed and widely discussed among American Negroes in three different periods. Each time, it was put forward in response to an identical combination of economic and social factors that induced despair among Negroes. The syndrome consists of three elements: great expectations, followed by dashed hopes, followed by despair and discussion of separation.

The first serious suggestion that Negroes should separate came in the aftermath of the Civil War. During that war many Negroes had not only been strongly in favor of freedom but had fought for the Union. It was a period of tremendous expectations. Great numbers of Negroes left the farms and followed the Union Army as General Sherman marched across Georgia to the sea; they believed that when he got to the sea they would be not only free but also given land—"forty acres and a mule." However, the compromise of 1876 and the withdrawal of the Union Army from the South dashed those expectations. Instead of forty acres and a mule, all they got was a new form of slavery.

Out of the ruins of those hopes emerged Booker T. Washington, saying in essence to Negroes: "There is no hope in your attempting to vote, no hope in attempting to play any part in the political or social processes of the nation. Separate yourself from all that and give your attention to your innards: that you are men, that you maintain dignity, that you drop your buckets where they are, that you become excellent of character."

Of course, it did not work. It could not work. Because human beings have stomachs, as well as minds and hearts, and equate dignity, first of all, not with caste but with class. I preached the dignity of black skin color and wore my hair Afro style long before it became popular: 'I taught Negro history in the old Benjamin Franklin High School, where I first got my teaching experience, long before it became popular.

But in spite of all that, it is my conviction that there are three fundamental ways in which a group of people can maintain their dignity: one, by gradual advancement in the economic order; two, by being a participating element of the democratic process; and three, through the sense of dignity that emerges from their struggle. For instance, Negroes never had more dignity than when Martin Luther King won the boycott in Montgomery or at the bridge in Selma.

This is not to say that all the values of self-image and identification are not important and should not be stimulated; but they should be given secondary or tertiary emphasis for, unless they rest on a sound economic and social base, they are likely only to create more frustration by raising expectations or hopes with no ability truly to follow through.

The second period of frustration and the call for separation came after World War I. During that war, 300,000 Negro troops went to France—not for the reason Mr. Wilson thought he was sending them, but because they felt that if they fought for their country they would be able to return and say: "We have fought and fought well. Now give us at home what we fought for abroad."

Again, this great expectation collapsed in total despair as a result of postwar developments: Lynchings in the United States reached their height in the early twenties; the Palmer raids did not affect Negroes directly but had such a terrifying effect on civil liberties that no one paid any attention to what was happening to Negroes; Ku Klux Klan moved its headquarters from Georgia to Indianapolis, the heart of the so-called North; and unemployment among Negroes was higher at that period than it had ever been before. It was at that time, too, that Negroes began their great migration to the North, not from choice but because they were being driven off the land in the South by changed economic conditions.

The war having created great expectations, and the conditions following the war having shattered them, a really great movement for separation ensued—a much more significant movement than the current one. Marcus Garvey organized over 2 million Negroes, four times the number the NAACP has ever organized, to pay dues to buy ships to return to Africa.

Today, we are experiencing the familiar syndrome again. The Civil Rights Acts of 1964 and 1965 and the Supreme Court decisions all led people seriously to believe that progress was forthcoming, as they believed the day Martin Luther King said, "I have a dream." What made the March on Washington in 1963 great was the fact that it was the culmination of a period of great hope and anticipation.

But what has happened since? The ghettos are fuller than they have ever been, with 500,000 people moving into them each year and only some 40,000 moving out. They are the same old Bedford-Stuyvesant, Harlem, Detroit and Watts, only they are much bigger, with more rats, more roaches and more despair.

There are more Negro youngsters in segregated schoolrooms than there were in 1954—not all due to segregation or discrimination, perhaps, but a fact. The number of youngsters who have fallen back in their reading, writing and arithmetic since 1954 has increased, not decreased, and unemployment for Negro young women is up to 35, 40 and 50 percent in the ghettos. For young men in the ghettos, it is up to 20 percent and this is a conservative figure. For family men, the unemployment is twice that of whites. Having built up hopes, and suffered the despair which followed, we are again in a period where separation is being discussed.

I maintain that, in all three periods, the turn to separation has been a frustration reaction to objective political, social and economic circumstances. I believe that it is fully justified, for it would be the most egregious wishful thinking to suppose that people can be subjected to deep frustration and yet not act in a frustrated manner. . . .

II

Maximum Feasible Participation

There is an aspect of the present thrust toward black nationalism that I call reverse-ism. This is dangerous. Black people now want to argue that their hair is beautiful. All right. It is truthful and useful. But, to the degree that the nationalist movement takes concepts of reaction and turns them upside down and paints them glorious for no other reason than that they are black, we're in trouble—morally and politically. The Ku Klux Klan used to say: "If you're white, you're right; if you're black, no matter who you are, you're no good." And there are those among us who are now saying the opposite of the Ku Klux Klan: "He's a whitey, he's no good."

The Ku Klux Klan said: "You know, we can't have black people teaching" and they put up a big fight when the first Negro was hired in a white school in North Carolina. Now, for all kinds of "glorious" reasons, we're turning that old idea upside down and saying: "Well, somehow or other, there's soul involved and only black teachers can teach black children." But it is not true. Good teachers can teach children. The Ku Klux Klan said: "We don't want you in our community; get out." Now there are blacks saying: "We don't want any whites in our community for business or anything; get out." The Ku Klux Klan said: "We will be violent as a means of impressing our will on the situation." And now, in conference after conference, a small number of black people use violence and threats to attempt to obstruct the democratic process.

What is essential and what we must not lose sight of is that true self-respect and a true sense of image are the results of a social process and not merely a psychological state of mind.

It is utterly unrealistic to expect the Negro middle class to behave on the basis alone of color. They will behave, first of all, as middle-class people. The minute Jews got enough money to move off Allen Street, they went to West End Avenue. As soon as the Irish could get out of Hell's Kitchen, they beat it to what is now Harlem. Who thinks the Negro middle classes are going to stay in Harlem? I believe that the fundamental mistake of the nationalist movement is that it does not comprehend that class ultimately is a more driving force than color and that any effort to build a society for American Negroes that is based on color alone is doomed to failure.

Now, there are several possibilities. One possibility is that we can stay here and continue the struggle; sometimes things will be better, sometimes they will be worse. Another is to separate ourselves into our own state in America. But I reject that because I do not believe that the American government will ever accept it. Thirdly, there is a possibility of going back to Africa and that is out for me, because I've had enough experience with the Africans to know that they will not accept that.

There is a kind of in-between position—stay here and try to separate and yet not separate. I tend to believe that both have to go on simultaneously. That is to say, there has to be a move on the part of Negroes to develop black institutions and a black image, and all this has to go on while they are going downtown into integrated work situations, while they are trying to get into the suburbs, if they can, while they are doing what all other Americans do in their economic and social grasshopping. That is precisely what the Jew has done. He has held on to that which is Jewish, and nobody has made a better effort at integrating out there and making sure that he's out there where the action is. It makes for tensions, but I don't believe there's any other viable reality.

Furthermore, I believe that the most important thing for those of us in the trade union movement, in the religious communities and in the universities is not to be taken in by methods that appeal to people's viscera but do not in fact solve the problems that stimulated their viscera.

We must fight and work for a social and economic program which will lift America's poor, whereby the Negro who is most grievously poor will be lifted to that position where he will be able to have dignity.

Secondly, we must fight vigorously for Negroes to engage in the political process, since there is only one way to have maximum feasible participation—and that is not by silly little committees deciding what they're going to do with a half million dollars, but by getting out into the real world of politics and making their weight felt. The most important thing that we have to do is to restore a sense of dignity to the Negro people.

If that can happen, the intense frustration around the problem of separation will decrease as equal opportunities—economic, political and social—increase. And that is the choice before us.

Blacks In the United States (1969)

In the following tables the reader is given some of the statistical evidence used to evaluate the mobility, both physical and economic, of blacks in the United States in the recent past.

Tables I-VII from U.S. Bureau of Labor Statistics, *Current Population Reports*, Series P. 23, No. 29. Chart I from U.S. Bureau of Labor Statistics, *Employment and Earnings*, XVI (April, 1970), p. 33.

TABLE 1 NEGROES AS A PERCENT OF THE TOTAL POPULATION IN THE UNITED STATES AND IN EACH REGION, 1940, 1950, 1960 AND 1969

	1940*	1950*	1960	1969
United States	10	10	11	11
South	24	22	21	19
North	4	5	7	9
Northeast	4	5	7	9
North Central	4	5	7	8
West	1	3	4	5

*Data exclude Alaska and Hawaii.

TABLE 2 PERCENTAGE OF POPULATION INSIDE AND OUTSIDE METROPOLITAN AREAS, 1950, 1960, AND 1969

	NEGRO			WHITE		
	1950	1960	1969	1950	1960	1969
United States	100	100	100	100	100	100
Metropolitan areas	56	65	70	60	63	64
Central cities	43	52	55	34	30	26
Suburbs	13	13	15	26	33	38
Outside metropolitan areas	44	35	30	40	37	36

TABLE 3 PROPORTION OF NEGROES IN EACH OF THE 30 LARGEST CITIES, 1950, 1960, AND ESTIMATED 1967

	1950	1960	1967 (ESTIMATE)		1950	1960	1967 (ESTIMATE)
New York, N.Y.	10	14	19	New Orleans, La.	32	37	41
Chicago, Ill.	14	23	30	Pittsburgh, Pa.	12	17	21
Los Angeles, Calif.	9	14	18	San Antonio, Tex.	7	7	8
				San Diego, Calif.	5	6	7
Philadelphia, Pa.	18	26	33	Seattle, Wash.	3	5	7
Detroit, Mich.	16	29	39	Buffalo, N.Y.	6	13	17
Baltimore, Md.	24	35	41	Cincinnati, Ohio	16	22	24
Houston, Tex.	21	23	22	Memphis, Tenn.	37	37	40
Cleveland, Ohio	16	29	34	Denver, Colo.	4	6	9
Washington, D.C.	35	54	69	Atlanta, Ga.	37	38	44
St. Louis, Mo.	18	29	37	Minneapolis, Minn.	1	2	4
Milwaukee, Wis.	3	8	14	Indianapolis, Ind.	15	21	24
San Francisco, Calif.	6	10	14	Kansas City, Mo.	12	18	22
				Columbus, Ohio	12	16	19
Boston, Mass.	5	9	15	Phoenix, Ariz.	5	5	5
Dallas, Tex.	13	19	22	Newark, N.J.	17	34	49

TABLE 4 NEGRO AND OTHER RACES AS A PERCENT OF ALL WORKERS IN SELECTED OCCUPATIONS, 1960 AND 1969

(Annual averages for 1960 and January-November averages for 1969)

	1960	1969
Total, employed	11	11
Professional and technical	4	6
Medical and other health	4	8
Teachers, except college	7	10
Managers, officials, and proprietors	2	3
Clerical	5	8
Sales	3	4
Craftsmen and foremen	5	7
Construction craftsmen	6	8
Machinists, jobsetters, and other metal craftsmen	4	6
Foremen	2	4
Operatives	12	14
Durable goods	10	14
Nondurable goods	9	14
Nonfarm laborers	27	24
Private household workers	46	44
Other service workers	20	19
Protective services	5	8
Waiters, cooks, and bartenders	15	14
Farmers and farm workers	16	11

TABLE 5 NEGRO AND WHITE MEDIAN FAMILY INCOME BY REGION IN 1968; AND NEGRO FAMILY INCOME AS A PERCENT OF WHITE, BY REGION FROM 1965 TO 1968

	MEDIAN FAMILY INCOME, 1968		NEGRO INCOME AS A PERCENT OF WHITE			
	NEGRO	WHITE	1965	1966	1967	1968
United States	$5,359	$8,936	54	58	59	60
Northeast	6,460	9,318	64	68	66	69
North Central	6,910	9,259	74	74	78	75
South	4,278	7,963	49	50	54	54
West	7,506	9,462	69	72	74	80

TABLE 6 MEDIAN INCOME OF NEGRO AND WHITE MEN 25 TO 54 YEARS OLD BY EDUCATIONAL ATTAINMENT, 1968; NEGRO INCOME AS A PERCENTAGE OF WHITE

		MEDIAN INCOME 1968		NEGRO INCOME AS A PERCENT OF WHITE
		NEGRO	WHITE	
Elementary:	Total	$3,900	$5,844	67
	Less than 8 years	3,558	5,131	69
	8 years	4,499	6,452	70
High school:	Total	5,580	7,852	71
	1 to 3 years	5,255	7,229	73
	4 years	5,801	8,154	71
College:	1 or more years	7,481	10,149	74

TABLE 7 PERCENTAGE OF NEGRO AND WHITE ENROLLED IN SCHOOL, BY AGE, 1960, 1966, AND 1968

	NEGRO			WHITE		
	1960†	1966	1968	1960	1966	1968
3 and 4 years	—*	14†	19	—*	12	15
5 years	51	65	69	66	74	78
6 to 15 years	98	99	99	99	99	99
16 and 17 years	77	85	86	83	89	91
18 and 19 years	35	38	45	39	48	51
20 to 24 years	8	8	12	14	21	22

*— Represents zero.
†Negro and other races.

Chart 1

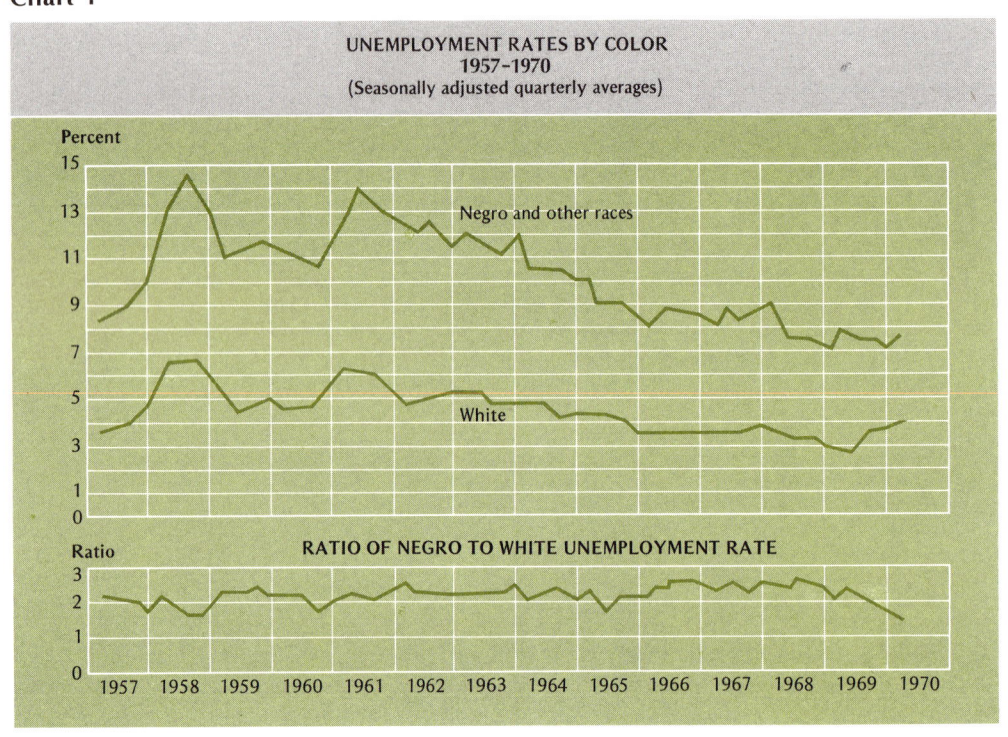

UNEMPLOYMENT RATES BY COLOR
1957-1970
(Seasonally adjusted quarterly averages)

Negro and other races

White

RATIO OF NEGRO TO WHITE UNEMPLOYMENT RATE

TOPIC 71

THE PROBLEM OF POVERTY

Changing times and ideas allow us to see more clearly major aspects of society, even though those aspects have always been there. In the 1950s white Americans "discovered" the oppression of black Americans although such oppression had been going on for several hundred years. Then in the 1960s middle-class Americans realized that others of their countrymen, both black and white, were living in dire poverty. There was nothing new about poverty in America. What was new, however, was the widening economic gap between the upper two-thirds of Americans and the lower third. After World War II prosperous conditions enabled many Americans to become materially well-off, but millions of others remained poor. The discovery of these millions, after two decades of economic expansion, shocked many Americans, especially the young who had benefited most from their nation's affluence.

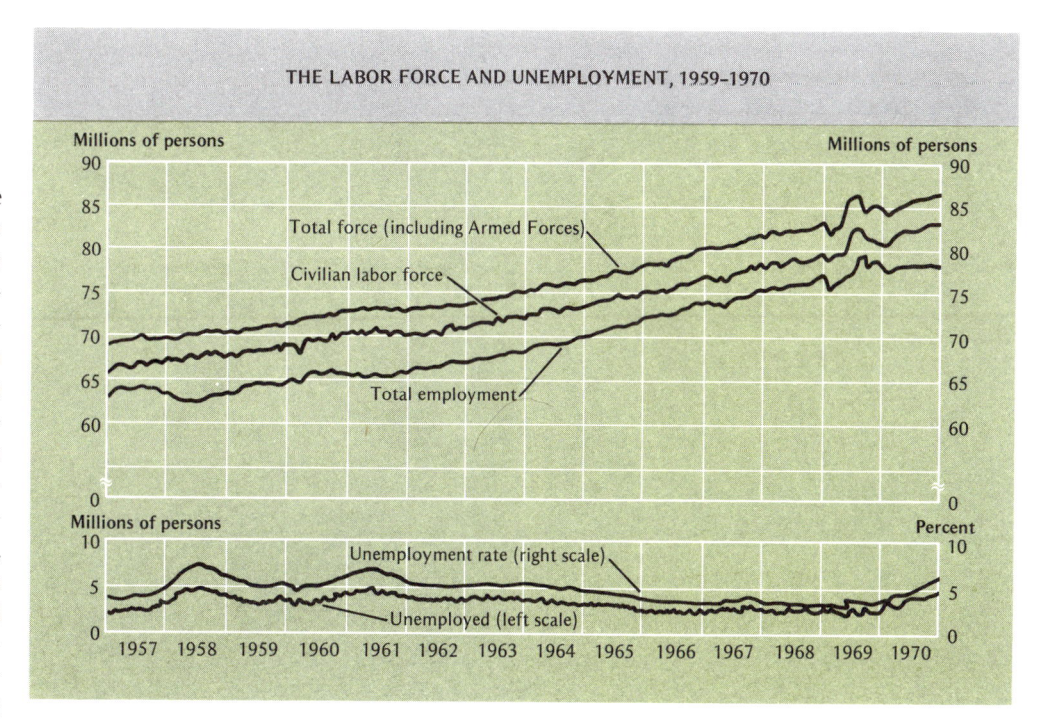

THE LABOR FORCE AND UNEMPLOYMENT, 1959–1970

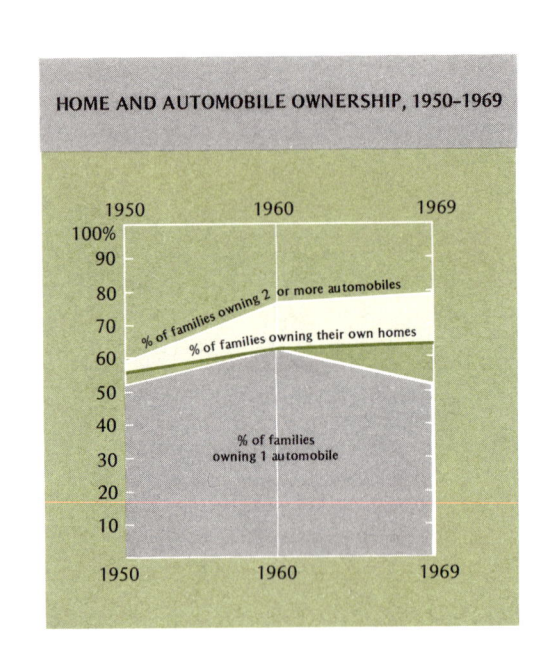

HOME AND AUTOMOBILE OWNERSHIP, 1950-1969

% of families owning 2 or more automobiles
% of families owning their own homes
% of families owning 1 automobile

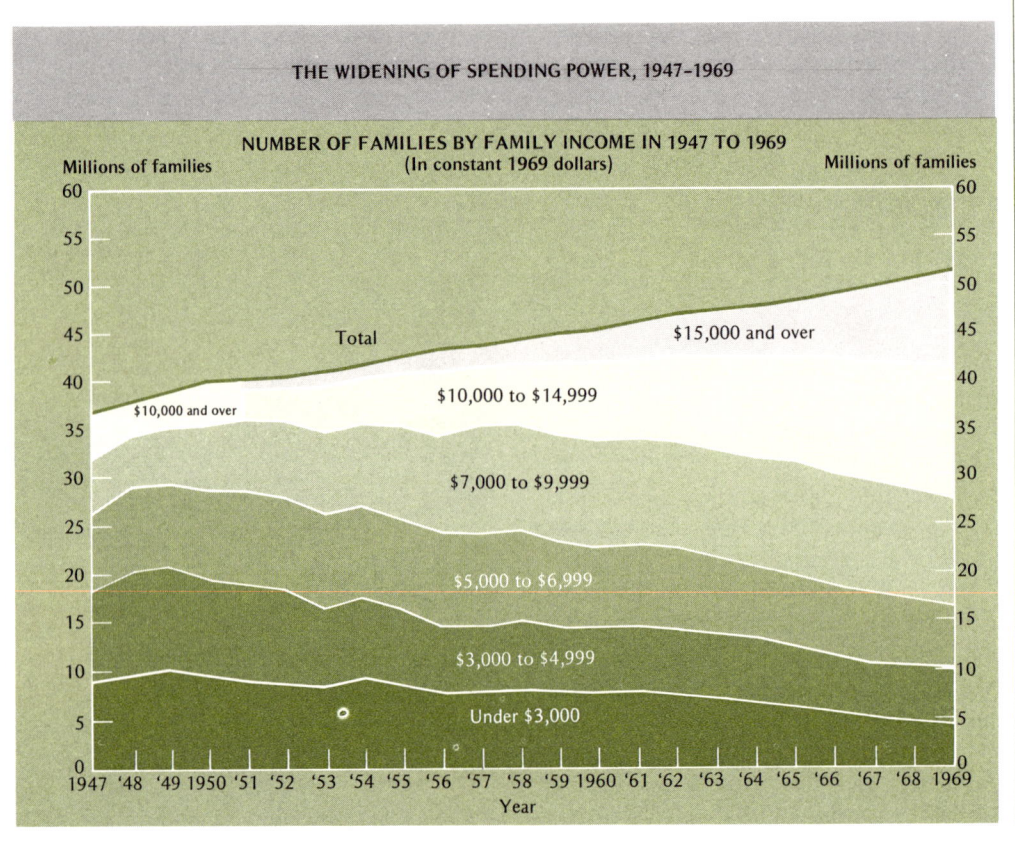

THE WIDENING OF SPENDING POWER, 1947-1969

NUMBER OF FAMILIES BY FAMILY INCOME IN 1947 TO 1969
(In constant 1969 dollars)

- Total
- $10,000 and over
- $15,000 and over
- $10,000 to $14,999
- $7,000 to $9,999
- $5,000 to $6,999
- $3,000 to $4,999
- Under $3,000

Reading 381

The Emergence of the "Great Society" (1961-1968)

The political record of the 1960s began on a note of youthful enthusiasm as two men in their forties, John F. Kennedy and Richard Nixon, contended for the Presidency. Both had been young naval lieutenants during World War II, and thus, unlike Eisenhower, far from the center of power. Both began their national political careers shortly after the war. By a narrow margin Kennedy was elected and became President in January 1961. Kennedy thus became the first Roman Catholic to be elected to the Presidency. His vigor and enthusiasm promised new, if unspecified, goals for Americans. In the following reading historian Henry Bamford Parkes offers an overview of the decade, tracing the shift from hope and optimism to anger and cynicism.

From *The United States of America: A History*, by Henry Bamford Parkes. Copyright © 1968 by Alfred A. Knopf, Inc. Reprinted by permission of the publisher. Pp. 750, 754, 756-757, 764-765. Subheadings added by the editors.

I

The Kennedy Record

The legislative record of the Kennedy administration was disappointing to liberals. The President advocated a long list of reforms, designed to bring about faster progress in raising living standards, increasing production, improving education, making medical care more widely available, promoting civil rights for the protection of the Negro population, and dealing with city slums and the appalling wastage of natural resources. With this kind of program, Kennedy could ask for

The medium of television became a central part of American political campaigns with the 1960 Presidential campaign. For the first (and so far, only) time the two principal candidates confronted each other directly in a series of televised debates. They are Democrat John F. Kennedy (left) and Republican Richard M. Nixon (right). Both men were as much concerned in these debates with projecting an "image" as with presenting opinions on domestic and international issues. Kennedy clearly dominated the television debates, but nevertheless barely edged out Nixon in the November election.

support from all major groups in American society without arousing class struggles, though it could be roughly described as liberal and as a logical sequel to the New Deal. Congress voted some money for several of these programs but was unwilling to complete them. Despite Kennedy's personal popularity, he was unable to persuade that recalcitrant body of the need for broader legislative action. The country appeared to be prosperous (scarcely anybody noticed the continuing phenomenon of mass poverty for about one fifth of the population), and Congress could see no urgency in the kind of problems that were then becoming important and chose to take its time about dealing with them. The only legislative success that caught the public imagination was one of the smallest and least political. This was the establishment of the Peace Corps, which dispatched young people to backward countries to engage in teaching and other needed activities. Thus the record of 1961 was meager, and that of 1962 and 1963 was even emptier, apart from the Trade Expansion Act of 1962, which provided for the negotiation of further mutual reductions of tariff duties. In domestic affairs the most dramatic event was Kennedy's rebuke to United States Steel in April 1962, for raising its prices and thereby endangering the administration's attempts to check inflation. Kennedy's moderate political attitudes did not make him subservient to business when he thought that businessmen misbehaved. . . .

II

The Assassination

By the autumn of 1963 there can be little doubt that Kennedy had made substantial gains in popular approval and support. He had his own style of leadership which the American people had come to recognize and like. Though congressional dilatoriness had prevented his administration from becoming associated with any particular kind of legislation, the personalities of Kennedy himself and his most favored collaborators had become distinctive additions to the image of the American character. Not representing the father figure of President Eisenhower, Kennedy stood for a youthful adventurousness and for the pursuit of excellence in all areas of American life.

Most of the Kennedy program was still awaiting legislative action when, on November 22, 1963, the course of history was abruptly and unpredictably changed by the murder of the President. Kennedy was visiting Dallas, Texas at the request of Vice-president Johnson in the hope that his presence would help to unify the divisions in the Texan Democratic party. While his motorcade was passing through the streets of Dallas, he was killed by shots fired from the upper window in an office building. It was established by the Dallas police with a reasonable degree of certainty that the murderer was Lee Harvey Oswald, that he was motivated by leftist political convictions, and that he had acted by himself, without connections to any group or organization, leftist or otherwise. Oswald was quickly apprehended, but further investigation was hampered by the shooting of Oswald by Jack Ruby, a Dallas night-club operator, who had a pathological devotion to the dead President. . . .

III

Lyndon Johnson Succeeds Kennedy

The Johnson administration during its first two years in office was perhaps more fruitful in liberal legislation than any of its predecessors except that of Franklin Roosevelt. Much credit was owing to Lyndon Johnson himself, who managed to combine liberal legislative proposals with successful appeals to middle-of-the-road sentiment. That he was a southerner who had many western qualities, and that he had the confidence of American businessmen and also labor gave him unusual political strength. To use one of his favorite words, he was able to create a consensus.

Amid a mass of Federal legislation, most of which differed from that of previous presidencies chiefly in the lack of effective opposition, two acts of Congress seemed especially notable. The Civil Rights Act of June 1964, passed after the unprecedented defeat of a filibuster by southern senators, guaranteed protection by the Federal government of Negroes' political and economic rights. Meanwhile Americans living below decent levels, white as well as Negro, were to receive direct assistance through the Office of Economic Opportunity set up under the Anti-Poverty Act. According to the President, one fifth of all Americans needed assistance to reach what should be regarded as adequate living standards, the most obvious examples being the inhabitants of Appalachia and the urban slums. Numerous other measures along lines that had begun to win general acceptance—such as a cut in taxes to stimulate production, an increase in minimum wages, medical insurance for persons above the age of 65 (medicare) and continued foreign aid—attested further to the popularity of the President.

As the elections of 1964 approached, it was increasingly obvious that a Johnson victory could be prevented only by a miracle. This was perhaps the main cause for the lack of qualified Republican candidates. Why should any promising aspirant accept the nomination when it was certain to end in defeat? This situation, however, offered an opportunity for Republican right-wingers.

So-called conservatism had been slowly increasing, or perhaps only attracting more publicity, ever since World War II. It believed in the abolition of the welfare state and a return to laissez-faire principles at home and in the destruction of Communism abroad. It received lavish financial aid from conservative-minded businessmen, and it claimed to have the support of a majority of the people. According to its advocates, it had failed hitherto to win elections because the Republican party had been controlled by eastern liberal groups who had not appealed to conservative-minded voters. Actually its program was quite unrealistic; its economic policy meant a return to nineteenth-century individualism, which could not be reconciled with the economics of big corporations; and its foreign policy could lead only to World War III. It can perhaps be best defined as a nostalgia for the lost simplicities of the early nineteenth century.

In the Republican convention of 1964 it became apparent that men of conservative inclinations had captured the party machinery and were determined to control both the drafting of the platform and the choice of the candidate. "Me-tooism" was to be repudiated; and the nomination went to Barry Goldwater, senator from Arizona, who had been preaching conservatism on platforms and in books for the previous decade. The Democratic convention was clearly controlled by Johnson, who was personally responsible for the vice-presidential nomination of Hubert Humphrey, the liberal senator from Minnesota. Goldwater never looked even remotely like a winner, and it was difficult for voters to take his candidature seriously. He rarely made a speech without being guilty of a political faux pas. Perhaps the most damaging of his utterances were those dealing with atomic warfare, in which he showed no awareness of its destructive potentialities. But his proposals to abolish most of the New Deal were almost equally effective in alienating voters. The result of the election was a sweeping Democratic victory. Johnson received more than 43 million of the popular vote as against 27 million for Goldwater. . . .

IV

The American Dilemma, 1968

The American people of 1968 presented a somewhat paradoxical spectacle. They had enjoyed economic prosperity for a number of years, and there seemed to be no valid reason why it should not continue indefinitely. The average young American could count on getting a job and acquiring a reasonably fair share of the goods of this world. The economic problems that had been so serious during the 1930s no longer invited much attention. Acute poverty still existed more than was generally recognized, but government intervention could gradually reduce it. It is true that the prosperity depended partly on heavy government spending for defense, but if it ever became possible to reduce defense spending there were numerous other needs awaiting government investment.

There was also a growing feeling of security in international relations. The Soviet Union, though still frequently guilty of diplomatic bad manners, no longer seemed to be expecting a world war; and with more reservations the same could probably be said of China. The war in Vietnam was a major cause of anxiety, but it did not seem likely to spread into a larger conflict.

The Peace Corps was one program of the Kennedy Administration that appealed to both the emotions and the intellects of many young Americans. Thousands of them spent years in Africa, Asia, or South America working in a variety of projects. Here a Peace Corps worker teaches in a small school he built of bamboo matting in Chimboto, a city on the coast of Peru.

Poverty in America

The Other America: Poverty in the United States was one of the most influential books to appear in the 1960s. Michael Harrington's study generated profound feelings of guilt among middle-class Americans, who sensed that the prosperity they were so proud of had, in part, been based on the suffering of others. Harrington, a young democratic socialist, offered his view of "the other America" in hopes it would stir the society into making fundamental changes in the way it distributed its enormous wealth.

Reprinted with permission of The Macmillan Company from *The Other America: Poverty in the United States* by Michael Harrington. Copyright © 1962 by Michael Harrington. Pp. 10–12, 19–20, 185–186. Subheadings added by the editors.

I

Where Are the Poor?

The millions who are poor in the United States tend to become increasingly invisible. Here is a great mass of people, yet it takes an effort of the intellect and will even to see them.

I discovered this personally in a curious way. After I wrote my first article on poverty in America, I had all the statistics down on paper. I had proved to my satisfaction that there were around 50,000,000 poor in this country. Yet, I realized I did not believe my own figures. The poor existed in the Government reports; they were percentages and numbers in long, close columns, but they were not part of my experience. I could prove that the other America existed, but I had never been there.

My response was not accidental. It was typical of what is happening to an entire society, and it reflects profound social changes in this nation. The other America, the America of poverty, is hidden today in a way that it never was before. Its millions are socially invisible to the rest of us. No wonder that so many misinterpreted Galbraith's title and assumed that "the affluent society" meant that everyone had a decent standard of life. The misinterpretation was true as far as the actual day-to-day lives of two-thirds of the nation were concerned. Thus, one must begin a description of the other America by understanding why we do not see it.

There are perennial reasons that make the other America an invisible land.

Poverty is often off the beaten track. It always has been. The ordinary tourist never left the main highway, and today he rides interstate turnpikes. He does not go into the valleys of Pennsylvania where the towns look like movie sets of Wales in the thirties. He does not see the company houses in rows, the rutted roads (the poor always have bad roads whether they live in the city, in towns, or on farms), and everything is black and dirty. And even if he were to pass through such a place by accident, the tourist would not meet the unemployed men in the bar or the women coming home from a runaway sweatshop.

Then, too, beauty and myths are perennial masks of poverty. The traveler comes to the Appalachians in the lovely season. He sees the hills, the streams, the foliage—but not the poor. Or perhaps he looks at a run-down mountain house and, remembering Rousseau rather than seeing with his eyes, decides that "those people" are truly fortunate to be living the way they are and that they are lucky to

---

Yet, in spite of these reasons for security, the more sensitive and cultivated members of the younger generation displayed a loss of faith in the ideals and institutions of American society which was probably more profound than any comparable rebellion in an earlier generation. Every new generation has its own way of rebelling and its own way of conforming, and both of them are necessary. Rebellion in the 1930s had been largely political and economic in motivation and objective. In the 1950s and 1960s it was mainly cultural and led to a total repudiation of accepted contemporary values. Obviously only a small group actually participated in the rebellion, but this included many of the more gifted members of the new generation.

Starting with the "beat" generation and borrowing their vocabulary mainly from Negro jazz musicians, a series of student groups developed a new view of life, the main ingredients being pacifism, Zen Buddhism, fast automobile driving, sexual experiences which were likely to be somewhat mechanical and promiscuous, and (in the 1960s) psychedelic drugs. But after rejecting American society, they were drawn back into it by their desire to make effective protest against the Vietnam war and against the denial of Negro rights. More than any other issue for several generations, these aroused the most bitter feelings, and both issues could be understood only by a deep examination of American values. The United States had entered the Vietnam war with the best intentions, yet the results seemed wholly destructive. What had caused this tragic misjudgment? As for the struggle for civil rights, much could be said on both sides, but what was plain was that this generation was required to begin paying the price for several hundred years of denial of the rights of Negroes.

be exempt from the strains and tensions of the middle class. The only problem is that "those people," the quaint inhabitants of those hills, are undereducated, underprivileged, lack medical care, and are in the process of being forced from the land into a life in the cities, where they are misfits.

These are normal and obvious causes of the invisibility of the poor. They operated a generation ago; they will be functioning a generation hence. It is more important to understand that the very development of American society is creating a new kind of blindness about poverty. The poor are increasingly slipping out of the very experience and consciousness of the nation.

If the middle class never did like ugliness and poverty, it was at least aware of them. "Across the tracks" was not a very long way to go. There were forays into the slums at Christmas time; there were charitable organizations that brought contact with the poor. Occasionally, almost everyone passed through the Negro ghetto or the blocks of tenements, if only to get downtown to work or to entertainment.

Now the American city has been transformed. The poor still inhabit the miserable housing in the central area, but they are increasingly isolated from contact with, or sight of, anybody else. Middle-class women coming in from Suburbia on a rare trip may catch the merest glimpse of the other America on the way to an evening at the theater, but their children are segregated in suburban schools. The business or professional man may drive along the fringes of slums in a car or bus, but it is not an important experience to him. The failures, the unskilled, the disabled, the aged, and the minorities are right there, across the tracks, where they have always been. But hardly anyone else is.

In short, the very development of the American city has removed poverty from the living, emotional experience of millions upon millions of middle-class Americans. Living out in the suburbs, it is easy to assume that ours is, indeed, an affluent society. . . .

II

The New Poor

Finally, one might summarize the newness of contemporary poverty by saying: These are the people who are immune to progress. But then the facts are even more cruel. The other Americans are the victims of the very inventions and machines that have provided a higher living standard for the rest of the society. They are upside-down in the economy, and for them greater productivity often means worse jobs; agricultural advance becomes hunger.

In the optimistic theory, technology is an undisguised blessing. A general increase in productivity, the argument goes, generates a higher standard of living for the whole people. And indeed, this has been true for the middle and upper thirds of American society, the people who made such striking gains in the last two decades. It tends to overstate the automatic character of the process, to omit the role of human struggle. (The CIO was organized by men in conflict, not by economic trends.) Yet it states a certain truth—for those who are lucky enough to participate in it.

But the poor, if they were given to theory, might argue the exact opposite. They might say: Progress is misery.

As the society becomes more technological, more skilled, those who learn to work the machines, who get the expanding education, move up. Those who miss out at the very start find themselves at a new disadvantage. A generation ago in American life, the majority of the working people did not have high-school educations. But at that time industry was organized on a lower level of skill and competence. And there was a sort of continuum in the shop: the youth who left school at sixteen could begin as a laborer, and gradually pick up skill as he went along.

Today the situation is quite different. The good jobs require much more academic preparation, much more skill from the very outset. Those who lack a high-school education tend to be condemned to the economic underworld—to low-paying service industries, to backward factories, to sweeping and janitorial duties. If the fathers and mothers of the contemporary poor were penalized a generation ago for their lack of schooling, their children will suffer all the more. The very rise in productivity that created more money and better working conditions for the rest of the society can be a menace to the poor. . . .

In conclusion, one can draw a summary statistical picture of the other America.

The poor in America constitute about 25 percent of the total population. They number somewhere between 40,000,000 and 50,000,000, depending on the criterion of low income that is adopted.

The majority of the poor in America are white, although the nonwhite minorities suffer from the most intense and concentrated impoverishment of any single group.

A declining number and percentage of the poor are involved in farm work, and although rural poverty is one of the most important components of the culture of poverty, it does not form its mass base.

In addition to the nonwhite minorities, the groups at a particular disadvantage are: the aged, the migrant workers, the industrial rejects, children, families with a female head,

The rural South still contains a large segment of the nation's poor, despite the migration of both blacks and whites to Southern and Northern cities. A black girl stares into the camera's lens, perhaps trying to fathom what lies beyond the view from her Mississippi farm cabin.

people of low education. These various characteristics of the culture of poverty tend to cluster together. (The large families have had the least gain of all family groups in recent years, and hence more children among the poor.)

The people who are in this plight are at an enormous physical disadvantage, suffering more from chronic diseases and having less possibility of treatment.

The citizens of the culture of poverty also suffer from more mental and emotional problems than any group in American society.

These figures do not confirm any of the complacent theories that poverty is now in "pockets," that it is nonwhite and rural, and so on. Rather, they indicate a massive problem, and one that is serious precisely because it concerns people who are immunized from progress and who view technological advance upside-down.

Is There Really a New Poor?

Many writers depict poverty in America as if there were little connection between poverty in the past and in the present. Historian Stephan Thernstrom contradicts this opinion by analyzing what Americans have defined as "the poor" in the course of the last hundred years.

From Stephan Thernstrom, "Is There Really a New Poor?" in Jeremy Larner and Irving Howe, *Poverty: Views from the Left* (New York, 1968), pp. 83–85, 87–89, 93. Reprinted by permission of William Morrow and Company, Inc. Copyright © 1967 by Dissent Publishing Assn. Subheadings added by the editors.

I

The "Old" Poor and the "New" Poor

A specter is haunting the imaginations of commentators upon the contemporary scene, the specter of the "new poor." In days of old (precise time conveniently unspecified), the cliché goes, "the immigrant saw poverty as a *temporary state* and looked forward to the day when he or his children could gain greater access to opportunity and financial resources. The poor of today are more inclined to regard poverty as a *permanent way of life* with little hope for themselves or their children. This change in the outlook of the poor can be explained by changes in the opportunity structure." (From Louis Furman's *Poverty in America*.) You can fill in the rest for yourself easily enough: the poor of old had aspirations; the poor today do not. The poor of old had a culture; the poor today have only a culture of poverty. The poor once had political machines which protected them; now they have only social workers who spy upon them. And the crucial contrast, from which so much else follows: the poor were once on the lowest rungs of a ladder most of them could climb; the poor today are a fixed underclass, a permanent proletariat.

A compelling, dramatic image, this, but is there any evidence that it is *true*? This is not the place for an exhaustive analysis of the data, but I suggest that the answer is negative. Much depends, of course, upon just whom we have in mind when we refer to "the poor"—the semantic hazards here are even larger than in most issues of social policy. If, for instance, we insist that the authentically poor are the kinds of people Oscar Lewis describes in his studies of "the culture of poverty," it is difficult to say anything at all about whether there are more or fewer of them and whether their lot is better or worse than it used to be, because the historical record provides few clues by which to make a judgment. But such simple operational definitions as income, concentration in unskilled or semi-skilled jobs, etc., yield relatively straightforward conclusions. These conclusions will not be palatable to the kind of mindless radical who reasons "things are terrible. Q.e.d: they are getting worse," though they certainly do not, I will argue, dictate a complacent view of the fate of the other America.

First, a word on the poor considered as an income class. There has been a good deal of heated argument about precisely where to draw the poverty line, but little attention to what seem the two points of greatest significance. One is that wherever the line is drawn—$3000, $4000, or whatever—an ever-smaller fraction of the American population falls below that line. The long-term trend of per capita income in this country is dramatically upward, and the way in which that income is distributed has not shifted abruptly in a direction unfavorable to those on the lower end of the scale. The rich have been getting richer, all right, but the poor have been getting richer at much the same rate. There has been no major increase in the proportion of the national income going to those on the bottom in recent decades—a fact American liberals have been pathetically slow to recognize. But the unpleasant truth that there is no pronounced trend toward more equal distribution of income in this country should not obscure the elementary fact that the disadvantaged are now receiving the same fraction of a pie which has grown substantially larger. Admittedly they *expect* more; in some ways it can be said that they *need* more, but that it *is* more is of considerable consequence, however it might seem to those of us who do not have to worry about the grocery bills.

A second observation is that it is very important to know whether the poverty line currently in favor in Washington, or some other (presumably higher) figure preferred by those of us on the left, marks off an *entity* with more or less stable membership, or whether it is a mere category into which Americans fall and out of which they climb in rapid succession. If we can assume that some fixed figure represents a minimal decent income for a family of a certain size, and that all those below it are living in poverty, it is obviously important to know if it is pretty much the same families who fall below that line year after year, as is commonly assumed

599

by proponents of the "new poverty" thesis, or if there is a great deal of annual turnover in the composition of the group. Some people with desperately low incomes, after all, are graduate students. Are many of the poor temporary victims? No one has any idea about the extent of continuity in the lowest income categories in the American past—say, in the nineteenth and early twentieth centuries—though there is a common and highly questionable assumption that there was little continuity then. What is more remarkable is that hardly anything is known about the continuity of low income in present-day America. . . .

II
Assumptions about Poverty

If we turn to another aspect of the new poverty thesis—the assumption that it is now far more difficult for a low-skilled manual laborer to work his way up the occupational ladder than it once was—there is again a startling lack of evidence to buttress the claim. For all of the facile talk we hear about the barriers against mobility growing ever higher, the fragmentary knowledge we have about the American class structure in the past and the extensive literature on current occupational mobility patterns suggests that changes in the opportunity structure over the past century have been minimal, and that those minimal changes are in the direction of greater upward mobility today. It is clear that the educational requirements for many desired jobs have been going up steadily, but it also appears that, on the whole, the expansion of educational opportunities has kept pace with, if not outrun, this development. It may be that decisive career choices are being made earlier than they once were—that now people permanently drop out of the race for certain attractive positions when they drop out of school, positions for which there were once fewer formal requirements; but I am very doubtful that this has resulted in less recruitment from below. To some extent, it has had the opposite effect, in that the change has been part of an increasingly universalistic process of selection.

It is doubtful indeed that a new poverty has recently been created in this country because of creeping arteriosclerosis of the occupational structure. Unskilled and semi-skilled laborers still do rise to a higher occupation during their lifetimes, in at least a minority of cases; their sons still make the jump more frequently than their fathers.

Impressive though it is, the evidence on rates and patterns of occupational mobility does not entirely dispose of the arguments of the pessimists. They would emphasize that the demand for unskilled labor, the capacity of the economy to absorb raw newcomers and assure them steady wages, is not what it was when the Golden Door was open to all. That could be true without lowering the rates of occupational mobility, of course. This has become a received truth in discussions of contemporary poverty without the benefit of the slightest critical examination, it seems to me. It is indubitable that the demand for unskilled labor is not what it used to be, if we take as our measure the proportion of jobs that are classified as unskilled; and indeed, discussions of this point often allude to the shrinking of the unskilled category in this century and the mushrooming of the white-collar group, as if that proves something. But what about the demand relative to the supply? To say that this relationship has changed in a way unfavorable to the unskilled is to assert that the pool of unemployed laborers—the marxian industrial reserve army—is characteristically larger now than it was in the past; and that wage differentials between unskilled and other types of work are now larger. Neither of these propositions can be substantiated.

As to the first, we have a decent time series on average annual unemployment only back to 1900, and one broken down for specific occupational groups—which is really what we want—only since 1940. But you needn't dig at all deeply into historical data to arrive at the conclusion that, however hard it may be for many people to find steady employment in our society today, it was often still harder in the past. Robert Hunter's 1904 study *Poverty* pulls together a few chilling fragments we might profitably recall. In the year 1900, 44.3 percent of the unskilled laborers in the United States were unemployed at some time; of a sample of Italian workers in Chicago, for example, 57 percent had been out of a job some time during the previous year, with the average time unemployed running over seven months! The fact that horror stories like this become increasingly difficult to duplicate as we approach the present, plus the mild but distinct downward trend in the overall unemployment time series since 1900 makes me feel very skeptical about the common assumption that things are getting worse for those on the bottom. . . .

I do not, in sum, see any grounds for believing that this country is now threatened by a mass of "new poor" whose objective situations, especially their opportunities to rise out of poverty, are much worse than those of earlier generations. The real changes I see are generally encouraging, or at least mixed. Some families are worse off today because they can't reap the benefits of child labor; but in the long run, presumably, their children are better off.

I think that one can be clear-headed about what is happening without being complacent about the status quo. I have never understood why so many Americans believe that to assert that things are bad you must insist that they are getting worse. I would argue that they could well be getting a little better—as the situation of the poor in America is, on the whole—and still be intolerably bad. A little less unemployment can still be too damned much unemployment, in a culture where people have become civilized enough to understand that recurrent unemployment is due not to the will of God but to the inaction of man. To conjure up a Golden Age from which to judge the present and find it wanting is quite unnecessary, and as de Tocqueville pointed out long ago, it is even slightly un-American, for the American way is to reject the achievements of the past as a standard for the present or future; Americans, he said, use the past only as a means of information, and existing facts only as a lesson used in doing otherwise and doing better.

The Poor: A Conservative View

Growing interest in the economically deprived produced a demand for government action either to aid the poor to move up the economic ladder or at least to eliminate the harsher aspects of poverty. But there were those who argued that this approach would do harm by fostering dependence on government programs. The *National Review,* one of the nation's leading conservative journals, presented this viewpoint in 1963.

From Robert J. Dwyer, "I Know About the Negroes and the Poor," *National Review*, XV (December 17, 1963), pp. 517, 521. Reprinted by permission of National Review, 150 East 35th Street, New York, New York 10016.

There is a sign which hangs behind the bar in quite a few neighborhood taverns in Milwaukee. It says, "It is better to be rich and healthy than poor and sick." Now you would not think this simple axiom would have to be spelled out for the leading intellectuals of our time, not even those who write for the *New Yorker.* Two notable articles published in that magazine—"Letter from a Region of my Mind" by James Baldwin and "Our Invisible Poor" by Dwight Macdonald—undertake to engage our emotions on the side of the underdog. Certainly, both Negroes and poor people can use our sympathetic understanding, and we can be grateful for what Baldwin and Macdonald have done to arouse it. But what cries out for our understanding is precisely the opposite of what Baldwin and Macdonald call our attention to. Both insist that we must *give* something to the poor and to the colored people. They even say that what we must give is justice. Equality must be recognized, says Baldwin; the poor must be subsidized, says Macdonald.

Not so, I submit. And, further, I submit that most poor people in America today are poor because they want to be. They make themselves the way they are by being lazy, uneducated, sick, undependable. They are all handicapped in the sense that they cannot or *will not* compete in the not very competitive society of modern America.

Perhaps not many readers see the picture from my vantage point. I live with both the so-called invisible poor of Macdonald and the Negro of Baldwin. In 1905, my grandfather bought a house around the corner from where I now live, when the neighborhood was solid, respectable, middle class. For reasons which probably have something to do with my writing this piece, I am raising my six children here. The tone of the block has, of course, deteriorated. It has been, for a generation now, a blighted neighborhood. ("Blighted neighborhood" is effete talk for the more plebeian expression, "Negroes live there.") The unusual thing about it is that the ratio of colored people to white people has remained constant for over ten years now. My barber said today, "The thing about this neighborhood is that the whites and the colored work it out all right when they live next door to each other.". . .

What America needs, then, is some tough optimism. This is what I ask James Baldwin to believe. This is what I ask Dwight Macdonald to demand of his poor people. And the way to recapture this faith for America, I solemnly believe, is to make it rotten for the poor. We must again, as in times past, attach a terrible stigma to being poor. We must make it very unpleasant, disgraceful, in fact, to be poor, to be dependent on welfare. FDR was never more inspired than when he warned us that continuous relief saps the moral fiber of a nation. We have all been shocked by stories in the press of second and third generations, of 27 or 35 persons, all descendants of one woman, all illegitimate, and all having been supported all of the days of their life by ADC.* These people have drunk deep of the narcotic spring of welfarism. They are an example of what can happen if we do not reverse the trend. We cannot afford, morally, economically, or psychically, to continue to encourage this kind of civil irresponsibility. We cannot, of course, let people starve. Western civilization, Christian culture, has always suffered fools gladly, has for centuries fed the village bum. We must continue to do so. But we must stop paying him to teach his children his irresponsible, drunken ways. We must go back to the Victorian concept that it is respectable to earn your own way in the world. One of the places to start is in our schools, by installing a strict performance basis for promotion from one grade to another. This will serve as an antidote to the influence of non-competitive parents. Another obvious step is to stop making welfare payments by check, through the mail. If you had four children, and could receive by mail a check for $298 tax free each month for doing nothing, would you be interested in working 40 hours a week in order to bring home a net pay check of $84.50? (This would mean that you would be working 40 hours a week for a monthly increase in income of $40.69.) The only possible way of making the average man think this pittance worthwhile is to make the welfare payment demeaning, degrading, disgraceful, so that even if the parents are willing to accept it, the children will rebel, and bend every effort to live a respectable life on their own initiative.

In short, let us make it rotten for the poor, whether they be white or colored—without any discrimination at all. Let us provide them with an incentive to stop being poor. They will, in a generation or two, conform to the minimum standards of education and self-discipline necessary for self-support. They will conform to our society. Then, if society is worth conforming to, we will have it made.

The War on Poverty (1964)

Poverty soon became a potent political issue. Shortly after Lyndon Johnson became President he urged Congress to enact legislation to enable the federal government to wage a "war" on poverty. After much debate Congress passed the Economic Opportunity Act, which is described in the following reading.

Reprinted from "900 Millions to Start—Who'll Get the Poverty Dollars," U.S. News and World Report (August 24, 1964), pp. 36, 37–38. Copyright 1964 U.S. News and World Report.

The Johnson Administration, armed now with a broad grant of authority from Congress, is set to launch a massive attack on poverty in this country.

It's to be an attack that will affect vast numbers of people in cities, towns and farming areas all across the United States.

Cost to the Federal Treasury: more than 900 million dollars in the next 12 months, probably more than a billion a year in the future.

Congress gave the go-ahead by passing the Economic Opportunity Act of 1964. The bill went to the White House on August 11.

Under provisions of this law, the Federal Government is committed to a whole batch of new social-welfare programs, supervised by a brand-new Government agency.

The long-range aim: to try to eliminate some of the causes of poverty, and to boost the incomes of poor people.

The Administration has officially defined as "poor" those having family incomes of $3,000 a year or less, or individual incomes of $1,500 a year or less. . . .

In what follows you get an idea of how the antipoverty dollars are to be allocated and how the specific programs are intended to work.

Job Corps. The idea for this program harks back to the Civilian Conservation Corps of depression days. But there are two major differences:

Training centers are to be established in both urban and rural areas, and women as well as men may enroll. Women and men will have separate camps.

The Corps will be open to youths between the ages of 16 and 21 who may or may not have finished high school.

An antipoverty official says it is hoped the first enrollees can be accepted "early in October."

Each enrollee must take an oath of loyalty to the U.S. Training centers will be racially integrated.

Job Corps members will serve up to two years. Besides room, board and medical care, they are to be paid $50 a month. They will get this in a lump sum when their service ends, or they may have $25 of that allocated monthly to their families. In the latter case the families would also get another $25 a month from the Government.

Rural conservation camps will have from 100 to 200 youths each. They will engage in soil and water development, timber con-

---

*Aid to Dependent Children, a federally-supported welfare program—Eds.

Growing concern about poverty and its effects jolted a number of large corporations into creating programs to aid at least a few of the poor. A major life insurance company invested about $250,000 in this black-owned, black-operated supermarket in North Dorchester, Massachusetts. The supermarket created sixty jobs for residents of this low-income neighborhood.

servation, wildlife projects and similar work. Urban centers will concentrate on teaching skills most in demand by employers. These might include classes in auto repair, carpentry, and machinery operation and maintenance.

About 100,000 or more young people are expected to be enrolled in the Job Corps eventually.

Work-training program. This is aimed at providing part-time jobs for youngsters of high-school age—to keep them in school, or to help them get back if they left for lack of money.

Jobs will be arranged in State and local public-service agencies and nonprofit organizations.

Suppose, for instance, a teen-ager is under pressure to quit high school in his junior year to get a job and supplement the family's income.

Under this program, he will be assigned a job after school hours and on Saturday—perhaps as an assistant in a child-care center, as a library worker or as a file clerk in a municipal office.

About 200,000 young people are to be covered by this program.

Jobs for college students. This is aimed at helping needy youths get a college education. Assistance will be offered to both undergraduates and graduate students.

Most of the money will come from the Government. It will be supplemented by funds put up by universities, colleges and community agencies. Jobs will be offered both on and off campus.

For example, a student may be given part-time work in a college dormitory, dining hall, professor's office, laboratory or library. Or he may be a helper in a recreation center, playground, park or elementary school.

All told, as many as half a million collegians are to be aided when the project gets rolling. In the first year, it will apply to some 140,000 students.

Funds for farmers. Farm families whose incomes are barely above the subsistence level will be helped by this program, slated to cost 50 millions in the first year.

Loans up to $2,500 for as long as 15 years will be available to low-income farm families. The money can be used to buy and improve real estate, reduce debt, or to improve farm income.

Fighting Poverty in the 1970s

In 1970, Michael Harrington, whose book *The Other America* had done so much to create interest in the issue of poverty, published an article entitled "The Betrayal of the Poor." Six years of a war on poverty, Harrington felt, had helped some individuals, but had done little to change the conditions which were continuing to generate new poor.

From Michael Harrington, "The Betrayal of the Poor," *The Atlantic Monthly*, CCXXV (January, 1970), pp. 71–72, 73–74. Subheadings added by the editors.

I

The Situation Today

In the seventies the poor may become invisible again. And even if that tragedy does not occur, there will still be tens of millions living in the other America when the country celebrates its two-hundredth anniversary in 1976.

This prediction should be improbable. Lyndon B. Johnson declared an "unconditional war" on poverty in 1964. Congress agreed, and for the next four years the White House recited awesome statistics on the billions which were being spent on social betterment. The sixties was a time of marches and militancy, of students and churches committing themselves to abolish want, and of documentary presentations of the nation's domestic shame by all the mass media. Indeed, the impression of frenetic government activity was so widespread that Richard Nixon campaigned in 1968 with a promise to slow

---

A farmer might borrow $2,000, for instance, to buy a flock of chickens and build hen houses so he can get into the business of producing eggs and broilers.

Or, a farmer may decide a fishing or hunting camp would bring in rental income. He can get a loan to build and equip a small lodge or cabin.

Loans will be offered to farm co-operatives that serve predominantly low-income families. There will also be money for improving the living conditions of migrant farm workers and for helping to educate their children.

Business loans. Suppose you are a small businessman who wants to expand or improve your operation so you can hire someone who is now out of work. You may qualify for a loan of up to $25,000, repayable over 15 years.

Under this program, a man who owns a gasoline station might borrow money to add auto-repair facilities so he could hire an unemployed auto mechanic.

Perhaps a man sees an opportunity to open a lunch counter and carry-out food shop in a busy downtown area. A loan will be available if he can show that he can successfully operate such a business.

The Small Business Administration, which will administer this program, has indicated that it particularly wants to help small retail and service establishments run by Negroes.

Average loans are expected to be well under $25,000. Drugstores, barber shops, tailoring shops and other service facilities are likely to benefit.

Work-experience projects. These ventures are described as primarily pilot programs to show States how to set up facilities to educate and give jobs to breadwinners now getting some form of public assistance.

Federal funds can be used, for example, to set up a class for training relief recipients in furniture repair, janitorial work or practical nursing.

The aim will be to try to get people off relief.

Domestic Peace Corps. This volunteer group will enroll people age 18 and over who can help in social-service projects.

A retired schoolteacher, for instance, might offer to teach children on an Indian reservation; or a housewife with training as a social worker might work with children in a mental hospital.

Volunteers will be paid $50 a month plus room and board. As many as 5,000 volunteers may be taken the first year, but enrollment will not start until several months from now.

Community-action plans. This part of the antipoverty effort is one of the broadest and, up to now, one of the most vaguely defined.

Under its terms, almost any program run by a community or private nonprofit organization that promises to aid illiterates or to offer jobs to needy people could qualify for federal aid.

Initial projects will center around community houses, playgrounds, adult-education facilities, health clinics.

The Federal Government will put up 90 percent of the money for such projects in the first two years of the program, and 50 percent thereafter.

Congress wrote two major restrictions into the new antipoverty law before sending it to the White House. One permits a Governor to veto any project for his State under the youth programs and the community-action sections of the law. A second is intended to prevent the law from benefiting any political party, or the Job Corps from being used for political purposes.

down the pace of innovation. So how, then, argue that poverty will persist in the seventies and perhaps once again drop out of the society's conscience and consciousness?

The fact is that society has failed to redeem the pledges of the sixties and has taken to celebrating paper triumphs over poverty. Thus in August of 1969 the Department of Commerce announced that the number of the poverty-stricken had dropped from 39.5 million to 25.4 million in a matter of nine years (1959-1968). The only problem, as will be seen, is that the numbers prettied up the reality.

When Lyndon Johnson declared his social war in the State of the Union message of 1964, the Council of Economic Advisers defined poverty as a family income of less than $3000 a year. This was a rough measure, since it didn't take into account family size or geographic location, yet it was extremely useful in identifying the groups which were particularly afflicted.

In the next few years the criteria were made much more sophisticated. In a brilliant attempt to define poverty objectively, the Social Security Administration took the Department of Agriculture's Economy Food Plan as a base figure for the poverty level. This was about 80 percent of the Low Cost Plan which many welfare agencies had used to estimate budgets; it consisted in a temporary emergency diet. In 1964, the Economy Plan had provided $4.60 per person a week, or 22 cents a meal, and the poverty income "line" was $3100 a year. In 1969, it was $4.90 a week, and a four-member family was said to be poor if its income was below $3553 a year.

These definitions were drawn up by concerned public servants, some of them with a deep personal commitment to abolish the outrage they were defining. But note an extraordinary fact. Between 1961 and 1969, the poverty level was raised by only $453 a year, or about 14 percent for the five years. Yet during this same period, union workers, with an average increase in wage settlements in 1968 of 6.6 percent, were not making any substantial gains in purchasing power. In other words, the statistics enormously underestimate the disastrous impact of inflation upon the poor. And this problem was not simply a matter of personal income, for some of the most dramatic inflationary increases took place in the area of medical services and thereby canceled out all of the increases in Medicare benefits and forced some people out of Medicaid.

But there was another optimistic assumption in the official definition. When the Economy Food Plan was taken as the base figure, it was assumed that all other needs would cost twice the amount of the grocery bill. But, to keep up with changes in the economy and society since then, one should compute the other items at three times the price of food, not two. By using the erroneous assumptions of the Eisenhower fifties, the government abolished the poverty of 12 million Americans who were still poor.

If it seems extreme to suggest that honest, and even concerned, experts could thus overlook the anguish of 12 million of their fellow citizens, consider the famous Census undercount in 1960: almost 6 million Americans, mainly black adults living in Northern cities, were not enumerated. Their lives were so marginal—no permanent address, no mail, no phone number, no regular job—that they did not even achieve the dignity of being a statistic. Again the extent of misery was underestimated.

In 1967 there were roughly 12 million citizens whom the Council of Economic Advisers called the "near poor" (with incomes between $3335 and $4345 for families of four). If these numbers were underestimated in the same way as were the poor, there are 16 million Americans who are but one illness, one accident, one recession away from being poor again. If, as now seems so possible, America in the seventies should reduce its social efforts, this group will lose almost as much as the poor.

And there is another, and even larger, segment of the population whose destiny is related to that of the other Americans. In late 1966, the Bureau of Labor Statistics figured that it would take $9191 for a "moderate standard of living"—you could buy a two-year-old used car and a new suit every four years. It should be remembered that raising the minimum wage for the lowest paid workers tends to help raise the take of those who are organized and much better off, but turning our back on the poor creates a political and social atmosphere in which the needs of an increasing number of people can be overlooked.

Perhaps the simplest way to get a summary view of the dangerous trends is to examine one generation of broken promises in the area of housing.

The government promised every citizen a decent dwelling in 1949. Under the leadership of a conservative Republican, Senator Robert A. Taft, the Congress agreed that the private housing market was not serving the needs of the poor. They therefore pledged to build 810,000 units of low-cost housing by 1955. In 1970, one generation later, that target has not yet been achieved. But the problem is not what the government did not do, but what it did instead. For while Washington was providing cheap money and princely tax deductions for more than 10 million affluent home builders in suburbia, it was taking housing away from the poor. As the President's National Commission on Urban Problems, chaired by former Senator Paul Douglass, reported in January, 1969, "Government action through urban renewal, highway programs, demolition on public housing sites, code enforcement and other programs has destroyed more housing for the poor than government at all levels has built for them." In 1968 a law was passed pledging the United States to do in the seventies what it had pledged to do in the fifties. Within a year it became clear that it was unlikely that the nation would redeem this second promise. To build 26 million new housing units in ten years, 6 million of them low-cost, would require speeding up the production of dwellings for the poor to twenty times the present rate. And as George Romney, the Secretary of Housing and Urban Development, admitted in 1969, it is quite possible that we will fall 10 million units behind the goal.

What this means for the seventies is the further decay of the central cities of America, an increase in the already massive level of housing poverty which afflicts a third of the people—and the emergence of ghost towns in the middle of metropolis. . . .

II

Planning for the Future

First of all there must be planning. There should be an Office of the Future attached to the presidency and a Joint Congressional Committee on the Future which would receive, debate, and adopt or modify annual reports from the White House.

Suburban home builders, automobile manufacturers, and trucking companies all pick up their huge federal subsidies without a thought of pollution. And now—not simply if poverty is to be abolished, but if the quality of life in America is to be kept from deteriorating—we must consider the "side effects" of new technologies even more scrupulously than we do those of new drugs. A year before his death, Dwight Eisenhower urged the building of new cities, racially and socially integrated and with new jobs. Mr. Nixon apparently agrees. But the enormously complex planning needed to accomplish such a task is not going to be done by the invisible hand of "Adam Smith."

Second, there must be billions of dollars in social investments. President Nixon, like President Johnson before him, hopes that private enterprise can do the job. His first version of this philosophy was called "black capitalism," and he ordered the concept extended to all the impoverished minorities when he took office. But the blunt economic facts of life are that costs in the slums are twice as high as in the suburbs, congestion much more serious, the labor market relatively untrained, and the neighborhoods unprofitable for big business. Minority enterprises can, of course, make a contribution to their areas and should be helped generously, but for the vast majority they offer no real hope.

As the sixties were ending, there did seem to be one area in which the cooperation of the public and private sector worked: employment. The National Association of Businessmen, with strong federal help, is trying to put poverty-stricken and minority workers into good jobs, and the measurable gains have been highly publicized. However, a 1969 analysis by the *Wall Street Journal* was not so sanguine. The main reason for the hirings, Alan Otten wrote, was the tight labor market, and any increase in unemployment—which is inevitable given the Nixon strategy against inflation—would turn these people back out on the streets. Yet when the Automobile Workers Union proposed to the Ford Corporation that its older members be permitted to take a voluntary layoff so that the new men could stay on, the company refused. The reason was simple: the supplementary unemployment compensation for a veteran is costlier than for a new worker. The profit motive was stronger than social conscience.

Early in the seventies the gross national product of the United States will pass the $1 trillion mark. As an article in *Fortune* calculated this trend, there would be a fiscal "dividend"—the automatic increase in government income without any rise in taxes which takes place when the GNP becomes larger—of $38 billion in 1974 and around $80 billion by 1980. The problem under these circumstances is not finding the resources but being intelligent enough to use them democratically and creatively.

In his 1969 welfare message, President Nixon made a sharp attack on the unevenness of the present states' rights welfare system. But in his proposals he urged Congress to delegate even more power to the very local administrations which had previously abused it, and he came out for a federal minimum which would leave people well below the poverty line. In the Nixon program, Washington would provide the funds to bring family payments up to $1600 a year, and the twenty states which now pay less than that would be required to contribute only half of their present welfare spending up to the total.

Instead of thus institutionalizing a federal

minimum which is less than 50 percent of the way to the poverty line, the United States should adopt the principle that all of its citizens are legally entitled to a decent income. Lyndon Johnson's outgoing Cabinet computed that one version of such a social involvement, a negative income tax, would cost between $15 and $20 billion a year. Given the *Fortune* prediction of an $80 billion dividend by 1980, that amount is clearly within the country's means.

Such a program should have a work incentive. Instead of the typical American practice of taxing the earnings of the welfare recipient 100 percent (by reducing his benefits by the amount of his wages), the individual should be allowed to keep a decreasing proportion of his income supplement as his pay goes up. But this also means that there must be a vast increase in the number of decent jobs. In New York City, where Aid to Dependent Children payments approximate the level of menial jobs in the economy, there is no motive for the mothers to look for work, and they haven't. So a guaranteed income with a work incentive means a commitment to genuine full employment.

And that is where the notion of a guaranteed income ties in with the right to work. It was Franklin Roosevelt who first urged, in the campaign of 1944, that if the private economy does not provide jobs for the people, then the public economy must. If the promises of the Housing Acts of 1949 and 1968 were carried out, there would be a labor shortage and the country would discover that it really needs the unused work potential of the poor and the near poor. The effect of such a program would not be inflationary because workers would be producing valuable goods and services for their wages.

As the seventies begin, the nation needs planned long-range social investments to provide a decent home for every citizen and to guarantee either a living income or a good job for all. If the cities continue to sprawl and technology revolutionizes the land in a casual, thoughtless way, polluting our natural resources, it is the poor who will be the most cruelly used, but the entire nation will suffer as well.

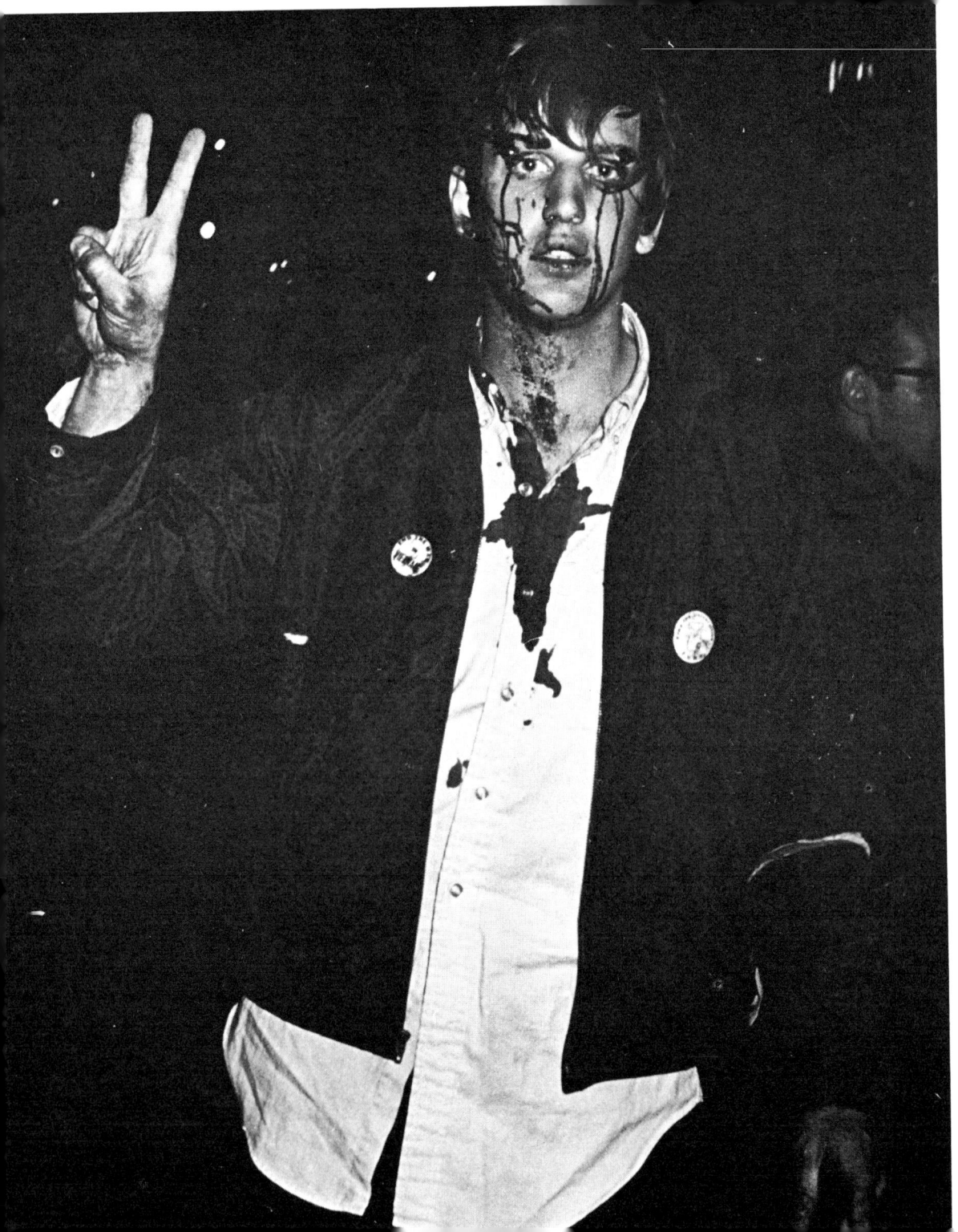

TOPIC 72

YOUTH AND THE NEW POLITICS

In the 1960s a new generation came of age. This generation had no significant direct contact with either the Depression or World War II. Consequently many young people disagreed with their elders over both domestic social standards, which emphasized economic security, and foreign policy, with its fear of communist aggression. The impact of the members of the new generation was even greater, because there were so many of them. As the accompanying population chart makes clear, the generation which came of age in the 1960s increasingly reflected the post–World War II "baby boom." In 1969, those aged ten to twenty-nine made up almost 35 percent of the American population, because the birth rate decreased during the Depression and in the 1960s. The young adults of the 1960s and early 1970s will be influential for decades to come.

The following pages concentrate on the political implications of the rise of this new generation. Though political activity is only one aspect of the so-called youth culture, it is an aspect central to present-day concerns.

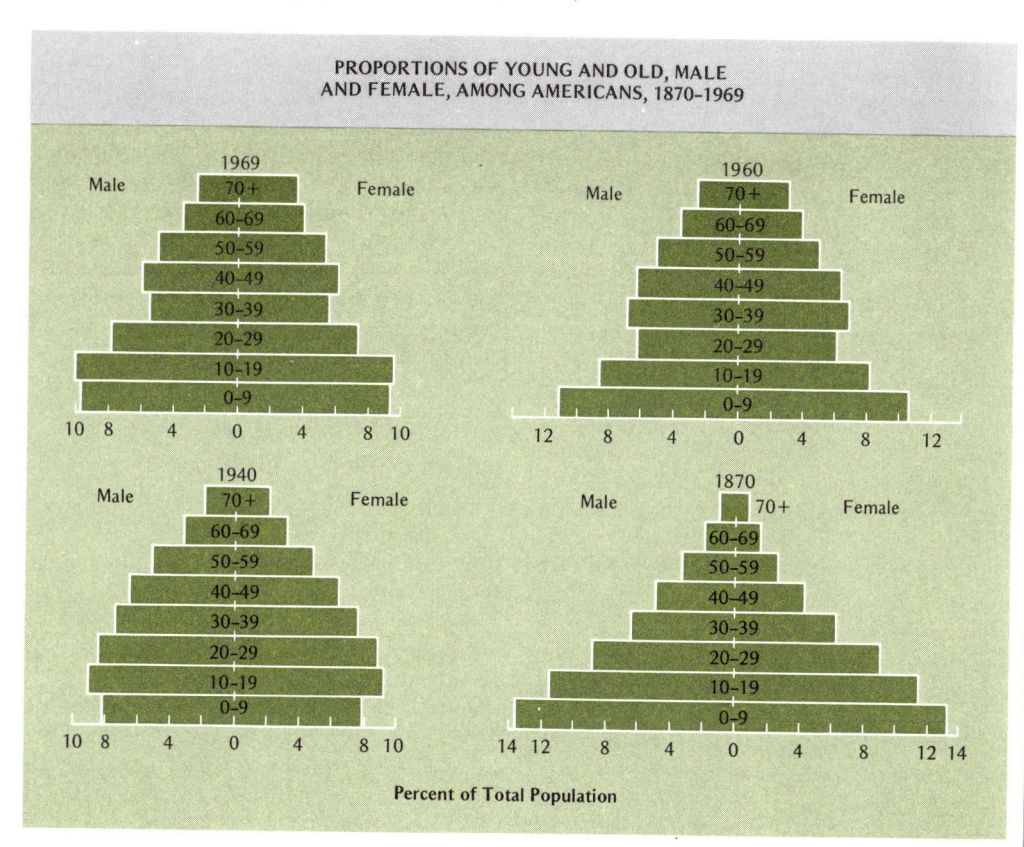

PROPORTIONS OF YOUNG AND OLD, MALE AND FEMALE, AMONG AMERICANS, 1870–1969

Percent of Total Population

Reading 387

The New Radicals

Youthful radicalism seemed very new in the 1960s. The fears generated by McCarthyism, the desire to forget the Depression-linked radicalism of the 1930s, and the seeming necessity to present to the rest of the world an image of a united America, worked together to make both extreme right and extreme left politically unpopular. The revival of left-wing radicalism is narrated here by two sociologists.

From Paul Jacobs and Saul Landau, *The New Radicals* (New York, 1966), pp. 8–10, 11–14. Copyright © 1966 by Paul Jacobs and Saul Landau. Subheadings added by the editors.

I

The Movement's Origins

The Movement's origins are elusive and have many strands. In the 1930s and 1940s the radical movement encompassed a broad spectrum of organizations and political beliefs: the Communists and their front groups; the socialists, Trotskyists, and other anti-Stalinist organizations; sections of the CIO and a few other unions. The Communist groups, drawing worldwide support, dominated American radicalism, since their size and prestige were greater than any of the other political tendencies. And although the American Communist Party was shaken in 1939 by the Stalin-Hitler nonaggression pact, the Nazi attack on the Soviet Union returned them to political acceptability.

But by the mid-fifties the old movement was nearly dead. The Communist Party had declined badly in the postwar period, because of government persecution and its own internal weaknesses. The trade unions were no longer crusading, many once radical anti-Communists had become supporters of the Establishment, and the socialists were barely distinguishable from the liberal democrats.

Then, when today's young radicals were still in junior high school, the entire Communist world was shaken by the revelations about Stalin made at the 20th Party Congress. The Communist movement soon suffered further blows from the uprisings in Hungary and Poland. The Labor Youth League (LYL), the Communist Party youth group, was disbanded shortly after the shock of 1956, but it would have declined from internal stress anyway. At the very time the American Marxists were being disillusioned by the actions of Soviet socialism, England, France, and Israel joined in an invasion of Egypt. A few intellectuals, faced with Western imperialism and brutal Soviet Marxism, began seeking a fresh way out of the crisis, developing what C. Wright Mills described as The New Left.

It started in England, where in 1957 a group of university intellectuals published two new journals, *Universities and Left Review* and *The New Reasoner*. In 1959 they merged into the *New Left Review*. Many of the editors had been members of or had been close to the Communist Party at Oxford. For them the failure of Marxism was more a failure of the vulgar Communist Marxists than of the theory. In the new journals the ideals of socialism were rediscovered, and the kind of humanist analysis that had been forgotten through purges, war, and Cold War was revived. Often, too, *New Left Review* debated ideas that could not comfortably be talked about within the framework of Soviet Marxism: alienation and humanism.

New Left political clubs of college and working-class youth followed the magazine's formation, and through 1959 this small group lit a new spark under dormant English radicalism—Aldermaston marches* in support of peace and against nuclear testing grew larger each year, and the Labour Party swung to the New Left position on nuclear weapons, for one year.

By the end of the fifties concern for racial justice was developing among American students. A strong reaction to the indignities of fear and anxiety heaped on the country by McCarthy and a general rejection of the symbols of American affluence were growing. Some youth responded with the "beat" mood; others developed an interest in the new British intellectual radicalism; still others rejected the style of life practiced by J. D. Salinger's characters.

Simultaneously, a group in the American pacifist movement, strongly influenced by pacifist leader A. J. Muste, was developing a "third camp" position, which rejected both the American and Soviet Cold War positions, concentrating instead on attempting to create a third force to resist all militarism. Many "third camp" pacifists had been involved in the civil rights struggle, to which they had brought the nonviolent techniques that they had been studying and practicing since the outbreak of World War II. And although their original interest and commitment had an informal religious base, they moved over easily to politics.

As McCarthyism waned in the late fifties a group of university intellectuals, much like the British New Left although less vigorous

*Protests against the basing of American submarines, equipped with nuclear weapons, at Aldermaston, England—Eds.

and certain, began to develop around the universities of Wisconsin, California at Berkeley, and Chicago. At Wisconsin the Socialist Club was formed by ex-LYLers and younger undergraduates who had never experienced Communist Party schooling; at Berkeley a similar group called SLATE formed a student political party; at Chicago a student political party founded in the early fifties was revived.

At Wisconsin the success of the Socialist Club and the inspiration of the British New Left were combined with the teaching of William Appleman Williams, the historian, who attempted to use Marxism creatively to understand American history. The result was the publication of *Studies on the Left*, "a journal of research, social theory and review." Several months later at the University of Chicago a group of graduate students began to publish *New University Thought*. . . .

II

The Movement in the 1960s

Another generation graduated from high school, and the colleges and universities became breeding grounds for campus political activity and the civil rights drive. Some of the young people in The Movement began to exhibit an inclination for activism and a spirit of anti-intellectualism, in part a rejection of the very university system in which they were involved. "The University" came to be regarded as part of the Establishment, and as the point of immediate contact, the most oppressive part.

Unlike their immediate predecessors, who had published magazines like *Studies* and *New University Thought*, this new group of youth activists knew little about the debates of the thirties. They learned about Stalinism,

Trotskyism, and Social Democracy only in an academic context. Outside the classroom they referred with a sneer to the "old days"—the thirties, forties, and now the fifties. Like the rest of American society, the old left, they believed, had in some way "betrayed" them: They had "sold out" or else were "hung up" on old and dead battles. To most of these young people Marx, Lenin, and Trotsky had little relevance for what they understood to be America's problems. They simultaneously refused to identify with the Soviet Union or to be greatly concerned about injustice in any of the Communist societies. Their enemy was the American society and its Establishment.

Many of the young people in this activist generation were the children of parents who had been the radicals and left liberals of the thirties and the forties. At home they had heard the discussions about civil rights, and they knew of the political pall that hung over the country during the McCarthy era. They had learned a set of ideals from their parents and now, much to their parents' discomfiture, they were trying to put those ideals into practice.

And so by 1960 this new generation was throwing itself against American society, literally and figuratively. They found a new hero in Castro, the man of action, the man without an ideology, whose only interest seemed to be bettering the life of the Cuban people. They responded to the youthful Castro with enthusiasm and demanded "fair play" for the Cuban Revolution.

In May 1960 they were ready for an action of their own, and the opportunity was provided by the House Un-American Activities Committee. Hundreds of students from the campuses of the University of California at Berkeley and San Francisco State College, joined by some of the people who were moving away from the inactivity of the "beat" coffee houses, demonstrated physically against the Committee's San Francisco hearing. And after the demonstration, which received enormous publicity, they scorned the allegation that they had been led or inspired by the Communists. That charge, which they knew to be untrue, only reinforced their feelings of distrust for the celebrants of American society.

They identified, too, with the Freedom Riders who went South in 1960 and 1961; for this again meant taking direct action with their own bodies against segregation. They were not interested in theory, and so the long historical articles even in such left journals as *Studies* were not seen by them as being relevant.

III

The Emergence of Radical Activism

This new activist Movement influenced even those who thought of themselves as being outside of society. As the apolitical "beats"—almost alone as symbols of protest in the fifties—turned their concern to concrete issues of racial equality and peace, their style, dress, and decor affected the activists. Arguments about politics began to include discussions of sexual freedom and marijuana. The language of the Negro poet-hipster permeated analyses of the Cuban Revolution. Protests over the execution of Caryl Chessman* ultimately brought together students and some Bohemians—the loose and overlapping segments of what was to become known as The Movement.

---

*Chessman's execution in California's gas chamber was followed by widespread anti-death penalty protests—Eds.

President Kennedy gauged accurately the need of many youth to participate in programs for justice, and a few of the new activists were attracted to the Peace Corps. The Peace Corps stressed, at least in its appeal, a non-paternalistic, activist program in which people would be helped to help themselves, but most activists rejected the Peace Corps or any other government program. They felt American society supported rascism, oppressive institutions, capital punishment, and wars against popular movements in underdeveloped countries. "Alienation" was used to describe the society's effects on its citizens, and American society was seen as the source of injustice and suffering everywhere. While opposed to injustice and suppression of liberty in general, the activists did not feel the same outrage against Castro or Mao or Khrushchev that they could against their own rulers. It was "our" fault. Brought up and nurtured on the United Nations and liberal political values, hearing them articulated so well by President Kennedy and Adlai Stevenson, they demanded purity at home first, and when it was not forthcoming, quickly became convinced that it was impossible, that there was something rotten at the core of American society.

This dashing of hopes, the feeling that they had succumbed to what turned out to be only rhetoric on the part of Kennedy and Stevenson, was an important part of their turning so bitterly against the Establishment.

And while the older ones among them had been able to articulate their views in a speech or a pamphlet, some of the younger ones, those who came into The Movement later and rejected politics—a small but growing number of middle-class youth—made a virtue of their inability to articulate and analyze coherently. They talked "from the gut,"

Reading 388

Another View of America (1956)

stumblingly, haltingly, using the language of the new folksingers, deliberately adopting a style that was the antithesis of that they had heard from their professors.

In their revulsion against the liberal intellectuals who were celebrating America and the end of ideology, the young activists rejected all ideology and traditional party politics, turning instead to where the action was, to SNCC, formed in 1960 by Negroes and whites, Southern and Northern. SNCC wasn't political; it was concerned with right and wrong, with people. The SNCC ideal of morality in action also provided the spur for the Students for a Democratic Society (SDS) and its community and campus programs: the decision to act was reinforced by the role of the liberal intellectuals in the 1961 Bay of Pigs episode and the 1962 missile crisis.

What began perhaps as a rebellion against affluence and liberal hypocrisy grew in a few years into a radical activism that protested injustice at the very core of the society. But when even this was tolerated by the structures that were under attack, some of the young radicals began to think about something beyond rebellion or radical protest. The Movement now is struggling to develop an ideology that will guide them toward building an organization that can compete for political power.

Allen Ginsberg became well known as one of the so-called "beat" writers of the late 1950s. His writings, especially his poem "Howl," and his lectures have continued to influence contemporary literary activities. The irrepressible, irreverent, and eccentric Ginsberg became a respected and symbolic figure to many persons in the anti-Establishment youth culture of the 1960s.

Americans in the 1950s were generally still caught up in their search for material prosperity and, they thought, security. Political dissent, as H. Stuart Hughes pointed out (see Reading 342), was at a low ebb. In the late 1950s, however, a small group of young poets and novelists, including Jack Kerouac, Allen Ginsberg, and Gregory Corso, jolted conventional society. The so-called "Beat" writers were more bohemian than political in their orientation, but their desire for new life styles was clear enough. Allen Ginsberg, perhaps the most enduring of the Beats, gives his view of the nation's life style and politics in the poem, "America."

From Allen Ginsberg, "America" in *Howl and Other Poems* (San Francisco, 1956), pp. 31–33, 34. Copyright © 1956, 1959 by Allen Ginsberg. Reprinted by permission of City Light Books.

AMERICA

America I've given you all and now I'm
   nothing.
America two dollars and twentyseven cents
   January 17, 1956.
I can't stand on my own mind.
America when will we end the human war?
Go fuck yourself with your atom bomb.
I don't feel good don't bother me.
I won't write my poem till I'm in my right
   mind.
America when will you be angelic?
When will you take off your clothes?
When will you look at yourself through the
   grave?
When will you be worthy of your million
   Trotskyites?
America why are your libraries full of tears?
America when will you send your eggs to
   India?
I'm sick of your insane demands.
When can I go into the supermarket and
   buy what I need with my good looks?
America after all it is you and I who are
   perfect not the next world.

Your machinery is too much for me.
You made me want to be a saint.
There must be some other way to settle this argument.
Burroughs is in Tangiers I don't think he'll come back it's sinister.
Are you being sinister or is this some form of practical joke?
I'm trying to come to the point.
I refuse to give up my obsession.
America stop pushing I know what I'm doing.
America the plum blossoms are falling.
I haven't read the newspapers for months, everyday somebody goes on trial for murder.
America I feel sentimental about the Wobblies.
America I used to be a communist when I was a kid I'm not sorry.
I smoke marijuana every chance I get.
I sit in my house for days on end and stare at the roses in the closet.
When I go to Chinatown I get drunk and never get laid.
My mind is made up there's going to be trouble.
You should have seen me reading Marx.
My psychoanalyst thinks I'm perfectly right.
I won't say the Lord's Prayer.
I have mystical visions and cosmic vibrations.
America I still haven't told you what you did to Uncle Max after he came over from Russia.

I'm addressing you.
Are you going to let your emotional life be run by Time Magazine?
I'm obsessed by Time Magazine.
I read it every week.
Its cover stares at me every time I slink past the corner candystore.
I read it in the basement of the Berkeley Public Library.
It's always telling me about responsibility. Businessmen are serious. Movie producers are serious. Everybody's serious but me.
It occurs to me that I am America.
I am talking to myself again.

Asia is rising against me.
I haven't got a chinaman's chance.
I'd better consider my national resources.
My national resources consist of two joints of marijuana millions of genitals an unpublishable private literature that goes 1400 miles an hour and twentyfive-thousand mental institutions.
I say nothing about my prisons nor the millions of underprivileged who live in my flowerpots under the light of five hundred suns.
I have abolished the whorehouses of France, Tangiers is the next to go.
My ambition is to be President despite the fact that I'm a Catholic. . . .

America this is quite serious.
America this is the impression I get from looking in the television set.
America is this correct?
I'd better get right down to the job.
It's true I don't want to join the Army or turn lathes in precision parts factories, I'm nearsighted and psychopathic anyway.
America I'm putting my queer shoulder to the wheel.

Revolt at Berkeley (1964)

The Beat poets generally inclined toward withdrawal from the competitive materialism they saw as disfiguring America. By the early 1960s, however, a new breed of young radicals appeared, demanding a direct confrontation with middle-class America and its institutions, even if it led to violence. One of the first manifestations of this movement occurred on the Berkeley campus of the University of California in 1964. The issue was the right to make political speeches on campus, a practice generally forbidden on California state campuses. Mario Savio, a student in his early twenties, was one of the most articulate of the radical student leaders. The following reading is taken from a speech he made at the height of the controversy.

From Mario Savio, "An End to History," *Humanity*, December, 1964, pp. 3–4, 6. Subheadings added by the editors.

I

The Meaning of Free Speech

Last summer I went to Mississippi to join the struggle there for civil rights. This fall I am engaged in another phase of the same struggle, this time in Berkeley. The two battlefields may seem quite different to some observers, but this is not the case. The same rights are at stake in both places—the right to participate as citizens in democratic society and the right to due process of law. Further, it is a struggle against the same enemy. In Mississippi an autocratic and powerful minority rules, through organized violence, to suppress the vast, virtually powerless, majority. In California, the privileged minority manipulates the University bureaucracy to suppress the students' political expression. That "respectable" bureaucracy masks the financial plutocrats; that impersonal bureaucracy is the efficient enemy in a "Brave New World."

In our free speech fight at the University of California, we have come up against what may emerge as the greatest problem of our nation—depersonalized, unresponsive bureaucracy. We have encountered the organized status quo in Mississippi, but it is the same in Berkeley. Here we find it impossible usually to meet with anyone but secretaries. Beyond that, we find functionaries who cannot make policy but can only hide behind the rules. We have discovered total lack of response on the part of the policy makers. To grasp a situation which is truly Kafkaesque, it is necessary to understand the bureaucratic mentality. And we have learned quite a bit about it this fall, more outside the classroom than in.

As bureaucrat, an administrator believes that nothing new happens. He occupies an ahistorical point of view. In September, to get the attention of this bureaucracy which had issued arbitrary edicts suppressing student political expression and refused to discuss its action, we held a sit-in on the campus. We sat around a police car and kept it immobilized for over thirty-two hours. At last, the administrative bureaucracy agreed to negotiate. But instead, on the following Monday, we discovered that a committee had been appointed, in accordance with usual regulations, to resolve the dispute. Our attempt to convince any of the administrators that an event had occurred, that something new had happened, failed. They saw this simply as something to be handled by normal University procedures.

The same is true of all bureaucracies. They begin as tools, means to certain legitimate goals, and they end up feeding their own existence. The conception that bureaucrats have is that history has in fact come to an end. No events can occur now that the Second World War is over which can change American society substantially. We proceed by standard procedures as we are.

The most crucial problems facing the United States today are the problem of automation and the problem of racial injustice. Most people who will be put out of jobs by machines will not accept an end to events, this historical plateau, as the point beyond which no change occurs. Negroes will not accept an end to history here. All of us must refuse to accept history's final judgment that in America there is no place in society for people whose skins are dark. On campus students are not about to accept it as fact that the university has ceased evolving and is in its final state of perfection, that students and faculty are respectively raw material and employees, or that the university is to be autocratically run by unresponsive bureaucrats.

Here is the real contradiction: the bureaucrats hold history as ended. As a result significant parts of the population both on campus and off are dispossessed, and these dispossessed are not about to accept this ahistorical point of view. It is out of this that the conflict has occurred with the university bureaucracy and will continue to occur until that bureaucracy becomes responsive or until it is clear the university can not function.

The things we are asking for in our civil rights protests have a deceptively quaint ring. We are asking for the due process of law. We are asking for our actions to be judged by committees of our peers. We are asking that regulations ought to be considered as arrived at legitimately only from the consensus of the governed. These phrases are all pretty old, but they are not being taken seriously in America today, nor are they being taken seriously on the Berkeley campus. . . .

II

Search for a Meaningful Future

Many students here at the University, many people in society, are wandering aimlessly about. Strangers in their own lives, there is no place for them. They are people who have not learned to compromise, who for example have come to the University to learn to question, to grow, to learn—all the standard things that sound like clichés because no one takes them seriously. And they find at one point or other that for them to become part of society, to become lawyers, ministers, businessmen, people in government, that very often they must compromise those principles which were most dear to them. They must suppress the most creative impulses that they have; this is a prior condition for being part of the system. The University is well structured, well tooled, to turn out people with all the sharp edges worn off, the well-rounded person. The University is well equipped to produce that sort of person, and this means that the best among the people who enter must for four years wander aimlessly much of the time questioning why they are on campus at all, doubting whether there is any point in what they are doing, and looking toward a very bleak existence afterward in a game in which all of the rules have been made up, which one cannot really amend.

It is a bleak scene, but it is all a lot of us have to look forward to. Society provides no challenge. American society in the standard conception it has of itself is simply no longer exciting. The most exciting things going on in America today are movements to change America. America is becoming ever more the Utopia of sterilized, automated contentment. The "futures" and "careers" for which American students now prepare are for the most part intellectual and moral wastelands. This chrome-plated consumers paradise would have us grow up to be well-behaved children. But an important minority of men and women coming to the front today have shown that they will die rather than be standardized, replaceable and irrelevant.

You Don't Need a Weatherman to Know Which Way the Wind Blows

The youth movement had a distinctive political cast by the late 1960s. The Students for a Democratic Society (SDS), a group which had its origins in the Civil Rights Movement, became the center of much radical political activity. How much is unclear, due largely to the secrecy which soon surrounded the organization's activities. The "Weatherman" faction of the SDS, led by Mark Rudd, a student activist from Columbia University, was perhaps the most outspoken element in SDS. What follows are excerpts from the policy statement the Weathermen submitted to the 1969 SDS convention.

From Karen Ashley, et al., "You Don't Need a Weatherman to Know Which Way the Wind Blows," *New Left Notes*, June 18, 1969, pp. 3, 5, 7–8.

I
International Revolution

The contradiction between the revolutionary peoples of Asia, Africa and Latin America and the imperialists headed by the United States is the principal contradiction in the contemporary world. The development of this contradiction is promoting the struggle of the people of the whole world against US imperialism and its lackeys.

Lin Piao,
Long Live the Victory of People's War!

People ask, what is the nature of the revolution that we talk about? Who will it be made by, and for, and what are its goals and strategy?

The overriding consideration in answering these questions is that the main struggle going on in the world today is between US imperialism and the national liberation struggles against it. This is essential in defining political matters in the whole world: because it is by far the most powerful, every other empire and petty dictator is in the long run dependent on US imperialism, which has unified, allied with, and defended all of the reactionary forces of the whole world. Thus, in considering every other force or phenomenon, from Soviet imperialism or Israeli imperialism to "workers struggle" in France or Czechoslovakia, we determine who are our friends and who are our enemies according to whether they help US imperialism or fight to defeat it.

So the very first question people in this country must ask in considering the question of revolution is where they stand in relation to the United States as an oppressor nation, and where they stand in relation to the masses of people throughout the world whom US imperialism is oppressing.

The primary task of revolutionary struggle is to solve this principal contradiction on the side of the people of the world. It is the oppressed peoples of the world who have created the wealth of this empire and it is to them that it belongs; the goal of the revolutionary struggle must be the control and use of this wealth in the interests of the oppressed peoples of the world.

It is in this context that we must examine the revolutionary struggles in the United States. We are within the heartland of a world-wide monster, a country so rich from its world-wide plunder that even the crumbs doled out to the enslaved masses within its borders provide for material existence very much above the conditions of the masses of people of the world. The US empire, as a world-wide system, channels wealth, based upon the labor and resources of the rest of the world, into the United States. The relative affluence existing in the United States is directly dependent upon the labor and natural resources of the Vietnamese, the Angolans, the Bolivians and the rest of the peoples of the Third World. All of the United Airlines Astrojets, all of the Holiday Inns, all of Hertz's automobiles, your television set, car and wardrobe already belong, to a large degree, to the people of the rest of the world.

The Students for a Democratic Society (SDS) came into being in the early 1960s as part of the Civil Rights Movement. By the end of the decade SDS had broadened its attack to include the entire political-economic structure of the United States, urging that only radical change could cure the grave ills of the nation. Here SDS members march along a Chicago street as part of demonstrations there in October 1969.

Therefore, any conception of "socialist revolution" simply in terms of the working people of the United States, failing to recognize the full scope of interests of the most oppressed peoples of the world, is a conception of a fight for a particular privileged interest, and is a very dangerous ideology. While the control and use of the wealth of the Empire for the people of the whole world is also in the interests of the vast majority of the people in this country, if the goal is not clear from the start we will further the preservation of class society, oppression, war, genocide, and the complete emiseration of everyone, including the people of the US.

The goal is the destruction of US imperialism and the achievement of a classless world: world communism. Winning state power in the US will occur as a result of the military forces of the US overextending themselves around the world and being defeated piecemeal; struggle within the US will be a vital part of this process, but when the revolution triumphs in the US it will have been made by the people of the whole world. For socialism to be defined in national terms within so extreme and historical an oppressor nation as this is only imperialist national chauvinism on the part of the "movement.". . .

II
A Revolutionary Movement of Young People

In terms of the above analysis, most young people in the US are part of the working class. Although not yet employed, young people whose parents sell their labor power for wages, and more important who themselves expect to do the same in the future—or go into the army or be unemployed—are undeniably members of the working class. Most kids are well aware of what class they are in, even though they may not be very scientific about it. So our analysis assumes from the beginning that youth struggles are, by and large, working class struggles. But why the focus now on the struggles of working class youth rather than on the working class as a whole?

The potential for revolutionary consciousness does not always correspond to ultimate class interest, particularly when imperialism is relatively prosperous and the movement is in an early stage. At this stage, we see working class youth as those most open to a revolutionary movement which sides with the struggles of Third World people: the following is an attempt to explain a strategic focus on youth for SDS.

In general, young people have less stake in a society (no family, fewer debts, etc.), are more open to new ideas (they have not been brainwashed for so long or so well), and are therefore more able and willing to move in a revolutionary direction. Specifically in America, young people have grown up experiencing the crises in imperialism. They have grown up along with a developing black liberation movement, with the liberation of Cuba, the fights for independence in Africa, and the war in Vietnam. Older people grew up during the fight against Fascism, during the cold war, the smashing of the trade unions, McCarthy, and a period during which real wages consistently rose—since 1965 disposable real income has decreased slightly, particularly in urban areas where inflation and increased taxation have bitten heavily into wages. This crisis in imperialism affects all parts of the society. America has had to militarize to protect and expand its Empire; hence the high draft calls and the creation of a standing army of three and a half million, an army which still has been unable to win in Vietnam. Further, the huge defense expenditures—required for the defense of the Empire and at the same time a way of making increasing profits for the defense industries—have gone hand in hand with the urban crisis around welfare, the hospitals, the schools, housing, air, and water pollution. The State cannot provide the services it has been forced to assume responsibility for, and needs to increase taxes and to pay its growing debts while it cuts services and uses the pigs to repress protest. The private sector of the economy can't provide jobs, particularly unskilled jobs. The expansion of the defense and education industries by the State since World War II is in part an attempt to pick up the slack, though the inability to provide decent wages and working conditions for "public" jobs is more and more a problem.

As imperialism struggles to hold together this decaying social fabric, it inevitably resorts to brute force and authoritarian ideology. People, especially young people, more and more find themselves in the iron grip of authoritarian institutions. Reaction against the pigs or teachers in the schools, welfare pigs or the army is generalizable and extends beyond the particular repressive institution to the society and the State as a whole. The legitimacy of the State is called into question for the first time in at least 30 years, and the anti-authoritarianism which characterizes the youth rebellion turns into rejection of the State, a refusal to be socialized into American society. Kids used to try to beat the system from inside the army or from inside the schools; now they desert from the army and burn down the schools. . . .

III
Repression and Revolution

As institutional fights and anti-pig self-defense of them intensify, so will the ruling class's repression. Their escalation of repression will inevitably continue according to how threatening the movement is to their power. Our task is not to avoid or end repression; that can always be done by pulling back, so we're not dangerous enough to require crushing. Sometimes it is correct to do that as a tactical retreat, to survive to fight again.

To defeat repression, however, is not to stop it but to go on building the movement to be more dangerous to them; in which case, defeated at one level, repression will escalate even more. To succeed in defending the movement, and not just ourselves at its expense, we will have to successively meet and overcome these greater and greater levels of repression.

To be winning will thus necessarily, as imperialism's lesser efforts fail, bring about a phase of all-out military repression. To survive and grow in the face of that will require more than a larger base of supporters; it will require the invincible strength of a mass base at a high level of active participation and consciousness, and can only come from mobilizing the self-conscious creativity, will and determination of the people.

Each new escalation of the struggle in response to new levels of repression, each protracted struggle around self-defense which becomes a material fighting force, are part of the international strategy of solidarity with Vietnam and the blacks, through opening up other fronts. They are anti-war, anti-imperialist and pro-black liberation. If they involve fighting the enemy, then these struggles are part of the revolution.

Therefore, clearly the organization and active conscious participating mass base needed to survive repression are also the same needed for winning the revolution. The Revolutionary Youth Movement speaks to the need for this kind of active mass-based movement by tying city-wide motion back to community youth bases, because this brings us close enough to kids in their day-to-day lives to organize their "maximum active participation" around enough different kinds of fights to push the "highest level of consciousness" about imperialism, the black vanguard, the state and the need for armed struggle.

On Madness and Violence (1970)

The growth of violence, and even more the rhetoric of violence as exemplified by the speeches and literature of the Weathermen, produced a widespread reaction in middle-class America. A 1970 editorial in the *National Review*, a conservative journal, sums up much of this reaction.

From "Radicals: Ilse Koch Section," *National Review*, XXII (April 21, 1970), pp. 394–397. Reprinted by permission of National Review, 150 East 35th Street, New York, New York 10016. Subheadings added by the editors.

I

The Extent of Violence

In his *Recollections* of the Revolution of 1848, Alexis de Tocqueville observes that as the political and social crisis approached, large numbers of unfamiliar but obviously demented individuals became prominent in the streets and cafés of Paris. There existed, Tocqueville implies, some deep connection between the approaching crisis and the appearance of madmen in public places. Were Tocqueville alive in the United States today he could make the same sort of observation, but he would see much more clearly just why this phenomenon occurs.

> On the night of October 27, 1967, in the wee hours of that darkness, guns blazed in the heart of Black Oakland, on Seventh and Willow Streets. The quiet of the night was shattered by the minor thunder of the guns. Death stalking a circle around warring men, and the shadow of death was created by the blaze leaping from the barrel of a gun. A pig white lay dead, deep fried in the fat of his own b——. Another pig white lay there, similar to the dead one in every respect except that he did not die.

So writes Eldridge Cleaver, campus hero, lion of the paperbacks and of black studies courses.

"Dig it," cooed Bernardine Dohrn, speaking about the Sharon Tate murders. "First they killed those pigs, then they ate dinner in the same room with them, then they even shoved a fork into a victim's stomach! Wild!" Bernadine Dohrn is a leader of the SDS Weatherman faction. Susan Atkins, after holding Sharon Tate so that "Tex" could stab her to death, wonders whether she should slice open the corpse to save the unborn child: "I flashed [argot for "suddenly thought"], wow, there's a living being in there." Susan Atkins, at least so far, is nonpolitical—an Aquarian Age Bonnie to Manson's spooky Clyde: but among Cleaver, Dohrn and the Manson "family" there exist stylistic and emotional continuities. Manson, for example, dreamed like Cleaver of a great race war; he desired to precipitate it by carrying out raids on the police using armed dune buggies, annihilating every pig from the Mojave to Los Angeles.

On West 11th Street in New York City, Diana Oughton, blue-blood, and Theodore Gold, Weatherman, blew themselves to bits in a secret bomb factory. The explosives were to be used to destroy Columbia University. Abbie Hoffman, whose *Woodstock Nation* is a great campus favorite, lo, even at Columbia,

> American college campuses became the scene of numerous, often violent, demonstrations in the late 1960s. Though the protests usually centered on the Vietnam War, many of them, including bitter confrontations at Columbia University, San Francisco State, Berkeley, Jackson State, and Cornell, involved racial issues or the power of students in campus affairs. The confrontation at San Francisco State College in 1969 produced this scene of police massing to disperse student demonstrators.

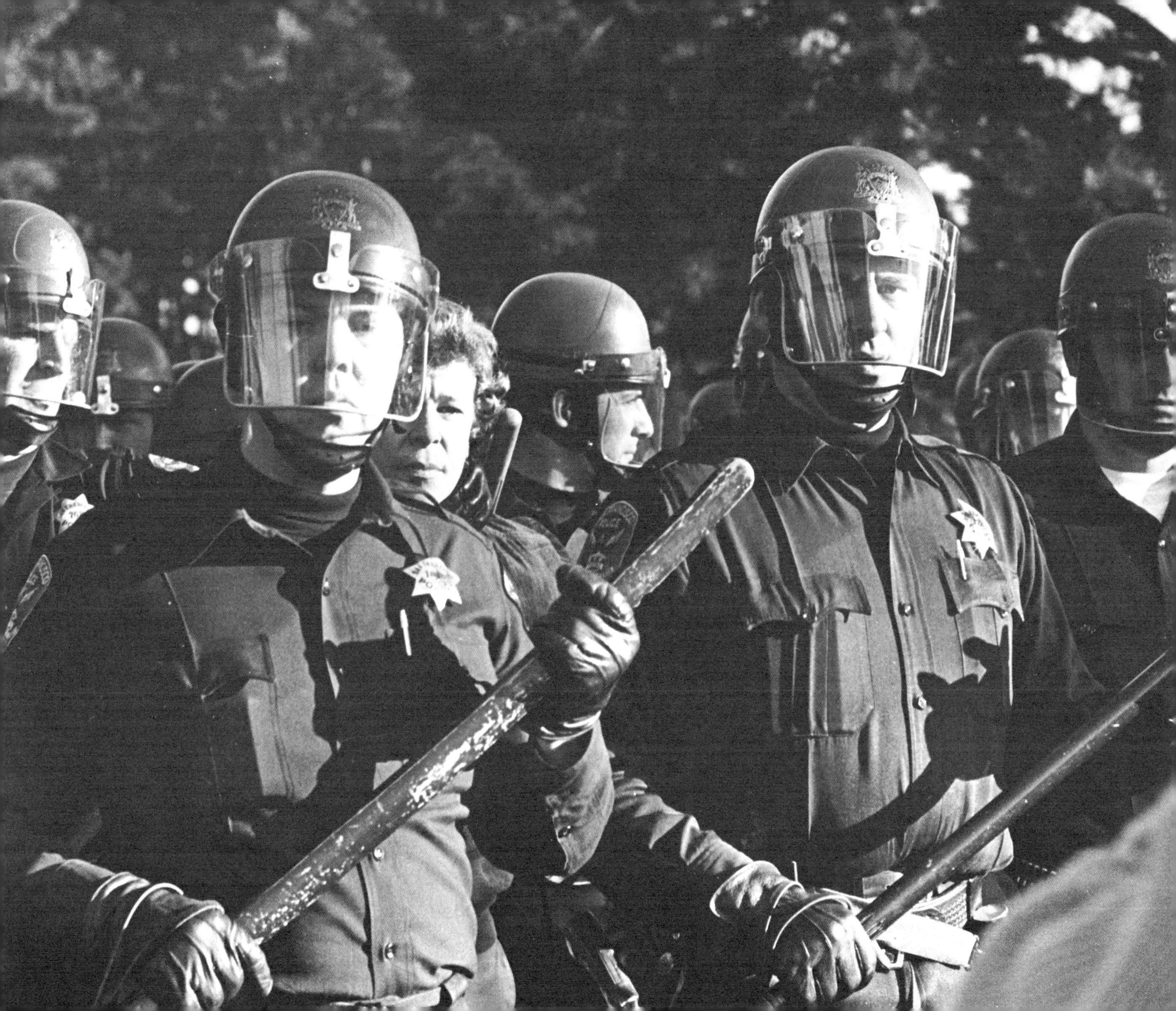

visited that campus and outlined its future: "BOOM, BOOM, BOOM." Enthusiastic applause.

In the April *Ramparts* there appears a guardedly sympathetic piece on Manson. The March *Esquire* devotes most of that issue to satanist cults in California and the point of view of the magazine toward these is highly ambiguous. The chic-Left *New York* Magazine, April issue, runs a sympathetic interview with a non-student who hangs around on the fringes of Columbia: "Marc" is deeply involved in the spreading bomb-culture, and predicts that during the coming summer New York will be paralyzed by the bombing of tunnels, bridges and subways.

The police and the FBI are hunting for Kathryn Wilkerson, a Weatherman who is also the stepdaughter of the speaker of the New Hampshire state legislature. She had been in the 11th Street bomb factory.

In his new book *Do It!*, just published by Simon and Schuster, Jerry Rubin, a campus hero like Cleaver and Hoffman, and a wall-poster presence in avant-garde circles, delivers to us his vision of the desirable American future:

> Every high school and college in the country will close with riots and sabotage and cops will circle the campuses, standing shoulder to shoulder. The schools belong to the pigs. Millions of young people will surge into the streets of every city, dancing, singing, smoking pot, f—— in the streets, tripping, burning draft cards, stopping traffic. . . .

Two unmistakable hallmarks of decadence are the inability to recognize blatant evil and a reluctance to call it by its name. As the evidence touched upon here suggests, evil has become a felt, nay a celebrated presence in American life. To be sure, one or more of these individuals may be mad in the clinical sense; but when you examine their words and their behavior it becomes clear that, mad or sane, they are moved by a common impulse. They do not mistakenly perceive the good as evil, and, acting on the mistaken perception, try to destroy the supposed evil. Bernadine Dohrn does not perceive sticking a fork into a murder victim's stomach as good; she perceives it precisely as evil and as such affirms it. Eldridge Cleaver does not intend his statements about killing white pigs and frying them in b—— to be perceived as good; he intends them to be perceived as evil, because he knows that evil has its own kind of power—it frightens and menaces.

Even aesthetically there are give-aways. Hoffman and Rubin, all hair, coarse features and freaky clothes, do not expect to be perceived as beautiful; they expect to be perceived as ugly. The affirmation of ugliness, which they personally epitomize, is the aesthetic version of the moral affirmation of evil. Their rote obscenity is intended, exactly, as obscenity. Their language is the analogue not of the logos but of the anti-logos. They deliberately and icily intend a defacement of the idea of the human being as that idea has been affirmed not only in Western civilization but in all the higher civilizations.

II

What Must Be Done

No doubt there have existed in all places and at all times people who hate beauty merely because it is beautiful, who hate power merely because it is powerful, and who hate goodness merely because it is good: for they know that *they* are not good, or beautiful, or powerful. As Iago says of Cassio, "He has a daily beauty in his life,/ That makes me ugly." But any healthy society possesses both formal and informal ways of very strictly containing such perverted impulses.

We, instead, have cynical publishing houses like Simon and Schuster, who have just published Rubin and celebrated him this way in their jacket blurb: "*Do It!* is to be danced to. Read aloud. Studied. Memorized. Burned. Swallowed. Eaten. But most important, after living through the experience of this book, take its final advice: Do It!" Would there be—mixed blessing!—a Simon and Schuster in a Rubin world? No doubt such publishers as Simon and Schuster would have outbid each other for the privilege of publishing *Mein Kampf*—in comparison with Rubin, a lucid and gentle work.

We also have cynical and cowardly faculties, like the one at Buffalo, where the operative committee has announced that it will tolerate a substantial degree of disruption and destruction of university property.

And we have cynical and deluded politicians like John Lindsay—a Weimar liberal if there ever was one—traveling out to Berkeley, even as bombs go off in his own city, and telling students that the Nixon Administration is an instrument of repression and a danger to freedom, and advising that very special student audience that *they*—Free Speech Movement, Che and Mao posters, People's Park, Vietnam Commencement, and all the rest of it—that *they* are the last best hope of free men. It is only too characteristic that Lindsay, when asked about the spread of bombing in New York, replied: "The use of explosives in order to tear down the system is self-defeating." A bit of tactical advice from

Reading 392

the Coach? If the SDS were engaged, in the manner of Ilse Koch,* in turning "pig" skins into lampshades, Lindsay no doubt would shake his head and observe that it was counter-productive.

If Tocqueville were writing his reflections on the current condition of American society he would certainly observe that madness and violence are spreading because they receive "respectable" sanction and support from institutions and men who are, precisely, responsible; and who must be called to account.

Thoughts on a Troubled El Dorado (1970)

What is the deeper significance of the re-emergence of political protest, especially protest coming from the younger generation? In the following essay Henry Grunwald managing editor of the news magazine Time, searches for that meaning and its implications for the future.

From Henry Grunwald, "Thoughts on a Troubled El Dorado," *Time*, June 22, 1970, pp. 18-19, 20-21. Reprinted by permission from TIME, The Weekly Newsmagazine. Copyright Time, Inc., 1970.

---

*Ilse Koch was the wife of a Nazi concentration camp official. It was learned after World War II that she had ordered some dead victims of the camp skinned and their skin used for lampshades—Eds.

I

A Divided America

As one moves through today's America, a set of terms from South Africa comes to mind: *verkrampte*, meaning literally "the cramped ones," or "the closed-minded," and *verligte*, literally "the enlightened ones," or "the open-minded." Perhaps those terms define the most significant division in our deeply divided country....

Obviously, these terms originate in a totally different context. Obviously, it would be utterly false to present the conflict in America today as a contest between the children of light and the children of darkness. But within every state, within every community—and within many individuals—there is a conflict between impulses: merely to condemn or somehow to understand, merely to shut out change or somehow to move with it.

Therefore the real polarization, the crucial struggle, is not between Middle America and all the rest. It is everywhere, it is within Middle America—it is within America's own heart.

In earlier times of crisis, there always were certain very American talismans to which one could turn for reassurance. Now the magic does not seem to work any more. One source of comfort used to be the sheer size of the land: the vastness of America, surprising again and again no matter how often one had glimpsed it from plane or train, always promised that there was enough room for everyone, enough space to dwarf all factions and conflicts. Now the huge stretches seem oddly empty, even useless despite the abundance they produce, and one is all too conscious of the fact that our fate is being decided in the crowded cities. For them, the wide spaces have little meaning except at times by way of mocking the urban claustrophobia.

Another source of comfort used to be the countless signs of American inventiveness and ingenuity, a tradition stretching from colonial tinker to modern technocrat, asserting not only mastery over nature but also a sly, triumphant outwitting of every kind of adversity. It was the frontier spirit mechanized. Despite the triumph of the moon voyages, that spirit now seems suddenly unequal to mundane problems: they are beyond the powers of technological or scientific tinkering.

Perhaps the greatest source of comfort used to be the plain common sense and decency of most Americans, the more or less good-humored willingness to see the other side of a dispute. Possibly that tolerance has always been a bit more illusion than fact. Today, at any rate, you find people everywhere whose common sense is consumed by anger, whose decency is limited to their own kind, whose tolerance is only for those who substantially agree with them, and whose openness to change lasts only as long as change does not seriously unsettle them. There seems to be developing a kind of American tribalism that is not wholly new, but is taking more virulent forms than ever before.

II

The View from Middle America

A few scenes:

EL DORADO, KANS. It's pronounced El Do-*ray*-do, but the symbolic significance of the name is hard to escape. A town of 13,000 people, solid houses, well-kept lawns and quiet streets on which Andy Hardy might be expected to appear at any minute. A town with a junior college of truly distinguished architecture, sitting like a graceful fortress-shrine in the windy Kansas plain. A town with a gleaming computerized newspaper plant to keep up with the outside world. Except that the town doesn't really want to keep up. Says the paper's publisher: "If we had our way, we'd build a fence around this town. We don't want your Mickey Mouse problems. We don't need them." The real "new isolationists" do not want to withdraw from foreign countries: the publisher and his like-minded fellow townsmen are, if anything, interventionists. But they do want to withdraw from New York; Lindsay-land and the other big U.S. cities are more alarming now than the jungles of Indochina or the wiles of Europe. The world overseas represents almost an escape from America.

In the country club with its placid hilltop view, a group of El Dorado's most solid citizens reflects the town's bitter confusion about the war. As elsewhere, there is the danger of turning the conflict into a morality play. Honor, freedom, the future of America, say those who echo the President; crime and shame, say the radicals, quoted daily on TV and in the press. Those in the middle who cannot live with either version are increasingly beleaguered. Most people still talk about making a stand against Communism, though they are increasingly unsure whether Viet Nam represents the right place or the right method. Here, as elsewhere, even the fiercest hawks tend to say that getting into the war was a mistake in the first place. It is not so much that El Dorado's people support the war as that they are angered by radical attacks on the country, the President, the armed forces. The President, they argue, must know what he is doing. One gets the distinct impression that if he changed his stance—for instance, if he were to call the war a mistake and announce a much faster exit—El Dorado would go along with him. Most people instinctively stand with the President. Richard Nixon himself, apparently a passionless man, provokes a passionless, no-alternative kind of support; but the President of the U.S. remains a strong focus of loyalty and hope. More than a "pause" from crisis, El Dorado rather desperately wants leadership.

One line is heard almost as often as the one about Viet Nam having been a mistake: even the angriest critics of the young concede that "they have a point, they have some valid criticisms." The Methodist minister in the group speaks up for the young, for their idealism, for the need to hear them. So does the Republican state representative. Yet tolerance of radical youth is distinctly a minority position. One civic leader observes: "Well, maybe we do need something of the police state; maybe we do need a little repression." The young radicals, in the words of a woman member of the school board, "are traitors and they should be treated as traitors."

Later that night some of the local radicals assemble in a rickety frame house by the railroad tracks, amid scented candles and tequila. They do not seem especially traitorous: a dozen people in their 20s, a young minister, some teachers, some Vista and other OEO workers. The stories about trouble in El Dorado spill out: kids busted for selling an underground paper, a teacher dismissed for his unorthodox ways, poor people and blacks (El Dorado has only a few) deprived of their rightful unemployment benefits. The complaints are utterly earnest, sincere, not negligible—yet not major, either. One feels that much of the confrontation in this community is still symbolic—repression still more verbal than actual, dissent still token and vague. It is perhaps significant that most of these dissenters have come to El Dorado—in a rather touching desire to help—from other communities. El Dorado has to import its rebels. But this does not mean that it fails to be troubled, indeed tortured, by the same fears as the rest of the country, for no fence can keep them out. . . .

III

The View from the Campus

Another scene:

UNIVERSITY OF MINNESOTA, MINNEAPOLIS. A student strike is in progress. In front of the student union, a rock band is playing and a crowd lounges on the grass in a holiday mood. But the atmosphere is even more festive and more exciting inside. For here, the unique heady sense of joint action has taken hold, the camaraderie of the common cause. Tables where coeds sell pamphlets—Marx, Marcuse, Che. Other tables with various buttons and badges of dissent. Posters, Proclamations—demands addressed to the President of the United States, to the Governor of the state, the spelling a trifle erratic. Everywhere, the calls to specific action: organize transport, line up pickets, circulate petitions. It has often been noted that in times of grief or stress, doing concrete things, even small things, brings a sense of relief. So it is here. To a great extent, the purpose of such strikes is action quite divorced from ultimate accomplishment, a desperate desire to shake off a sense of impotence, the need to *do* something, anything.

In a room near by, a group of strike leaders and other students are gathered to discuss the situation. There is much talk of revolution—the word is repeated endlessly, like an incantation. The students are confused about whether they are using the word as program or merely as prediction, whether revolution must be organized and made to happen (as some insist) or whether it will happen inevitably (as most claim). It is somehow odd that Marxism's hoary theoretical dilemma about the inevitability of revolution reappears in this young, eager group in Minneapolis. There is some confusion not only about the eschatology of revolution, but also about its very meaning. When pressed, most admit that what they mean by revolution is really radical reform; they are impatient with such distinctions, perhaps because they fail to understand that what seems to be merely a semantic difference has often decided the fate of political movements (and sometimes of nations).

As so often with youth, a sense of revelation surrounds some very old, familiar ideas—as if the world and good and evil had just been discovered yesterday. "Human rights, not property rights"—the phrase is a rallying cry, without any apparent realization that the concept would not seem exactly revolutionary to the U.S. Supreme Court.

And yet there is some justice in their sense of discovery. The principles you praise as part of the existing order are too often mere clichés, vitiated by countless exceptions, delays, chicanery, corruption or plain indifference. You may try to tell the students that the regimes that emblazon human rights on their banners—from the French Revolution onward—in fact almost invariably result in bloody repression; while the bourgeois, capitalist regimes, for all their mundane emphasis on profit and property, in fact allow people wider freedoms and a greater scope than any other political system. But you know that this argument simply isn't good enough. For the point about these young people is that their approach is not comparative but absolute, not historical but utopian (and as Americans, we dare not use the word utopian as synonymous with "impossible" or "silly"). They don't care whether America is better than other countries; they care only that it is not as good as it should be, as it once promised to be.

IV
"How Are We Doing?"

They are probably no more ignorant of history than any other generation; if anything, they probably know more. The difference is that they lack a *sense* of history, a respect for it, that they refuse to draw certain lessons from it. They are told, for instance, that in their passionate condemnation of the Viet Nam War, they may well be in the minority among the American people. Are they ready to impose their will on the majority? And don't they know what has happened as a result of such attempts in the past? They refuse to be cowed by this. "What is the majority?" they ask. "How can you speak of majority will when that will is shaped by the Government information machine or by the media? If the majority knew the real facts, they would feel differently." Sophistry? Agnewism? Sure. But containing elements of truth.

Most of these students would argue that if driven far enough, they would favor violence. But by and large, they are against it, not necessarily on principle but because they consider it a self-defeating tactic. It is odd to find, by the way, how grateful one is these days to anyone who announces that he eschews violence. It used to be a minimal attitude, it almost went without saying that one opposed violent methods. Now, on hearing that assurance, we are inclined to rush up to the speaker, shake his hand and embrace him as a brother moderate.

At any rate, some of these young people do have a rather special attitude about violence. There is some talk about "trashing," breaking windows or setting fires. One of them argues quite seriously: "But that isn't really violence. That's only destroying property. Violence is hurting *people*." For "hurting people," read "the war in Viet Nam." The argument bespeaks a sincerely felt humanism. But surely it also suggests that these sons of affluence have little regard for material property, little understanding that for many people its acquisition and preservation represent a very human right indeed.

The radical youth care nothing about the recession that worries their elders. They have a deep revulsion from capitalism, though they seem to understand little about its true nature—and above all, about the true nature of the alternatives to capitalism. And yet one wonders with a pang: Do they know something we don't know? Have they got hold of an insight that we have not yet quite faced ourselves—that acquisitive, Faustian man may be dying? The notion is not limited to youth. Isn't one extraordinary, still-echoing piece of evidence the fact that even a Republican President in a State of the Union speech cast doubt on the gospel of growth?

How to cope with these students in Minneapolis or with other dissenters and radicals? One imperative is to make distinctions between them, to recognize that—like the Middle Americans—they are not a single-minded bloc, that they include *verkrampte* and *verligte* in their ranks. But the most important thing of all is to be responsive without letting the radicals dictate the terms of discussion. Many of them ask for unreasonable and impossible things. It is utterly wrong to conclude from this, as many people do, that therefore it is useless to do reasonable and possible things. But we will have to stretch our definition of what is reasonable and possible. When reform of U.S. institutions is mentioned, most Americans still think of a few cosmetic and very gradual changes. The radicals force us to think about more than that: not instant utopia, but a convincing commitment to reform and convincing proof that things are moving. Yes, radicals must be told that violence is wrong, that the rights of others must be protected, that the left can be as fascist as the right. Of course. But to say all these things, while necessary, is not sufficient.

The job of building America has only just begun—or so one feels, traveling across a country that still conveys a haunting sense of tentativeness. Other nations, in Europe and Asia, *are*. Even in times of extreme crisis, a Frenchman cannot imagine Europe or the world existing without France. Perhaps an American cannot quite imagine the world existing without the U.S. either. But he knows that only a short time ago the U.S. was not there; he knows, vaguely perhaps, that the U.S. is as much an idea as it is a country, an experiment unique in history. That is why the U.S. has this constant passion for examining itself, to judge itself and be judged. "How are we doing?" is the big American question—not how is the economy doing, or the President, or the parties, or education, or traffic—but the whole thing, the whole enterprise. It is for this reason that we tend to be manic-depressive in our view of ourselves: one moment the greatest, strongest country on earth, the hope of the world; the next moment on the brink of decay and disaster. That is why American patriotism can be so strident, so naive, so defensive. The fiercest insistence that this is God's country, the most devout treatment of the flag as an icon, suggest an inner doubt, a sense of impermanence and vulnerability. The trouble is not excessive nationalism but, on the contrary, inadequate nationalism—if we define the term not as aggressive superiority but a sure sense of self.

TOPIC 73

THE FUTURE OF THE NATIONAL COMMUNITY

The social issues raised in the late 1950s and 1960s—black-white relations, poverty amid affluence, the nature of America's place in the world, and the role to be played by the younger generation in national decision making—remain key issues in the 1970s. The deep concern about the quality of the environment must, of course, be added to this list.

The election of Richard Nixon to the Presidency in November 1968 produced in the next few years some modifications in approaches to these social problems. No new ones emerged, however, nor did Nixon offer radically different solutions. Perhaps the most significant development within the United States involved the economic system. In the mid-1960s President Lyndon Johnson promised both "guns and butter." That is, billions of dollars to fight a war in Vietnam and billions of dollars to satisfy the needs and desires of the American people. Such a policy by 1968 had produced a rapidly expanding economy but an even more rapidly expanding inflation. In 1969 President Nixon initiated a conservative policy involving a contraction of federal spending, the theory being that a "cooling" of the economy would lessen the rate of inflation even though, unfortunately, it would also increase unemployment. However, only half of Nixon's economic policy worked. Unemployment increased to some 6 per cent of the labor force, but the rate of inflation did not decrease. In August 1971 Nixon, influenced by mounting apprehension in and out of Congress about this strange and trying combination of economic recession and high rate of inflation, abruptly abandoned his long-standing opposition to drastic federal intervention. He announced a temporary freeze on the levels of wages and prices as well as a 10 per cent added duty on imported goods, intended to make American products competitive with more cheaply produced foreign goods on the domestic market. Both steps had previously been authorized by congress.

The Nixon administration also attempted the difficult task of trying to extricate the United States from Vietnam without losing the Vietnamese War. The President committed the nation to a limited withdrawal in Vietnam (310,000 American troops in South Vietnam in mid-1970 and 130,000 in early 1972) while at the same time the government extended United States involvement in Laos and Cambodia.

The coexistence of contraction and expansion, both at home and abroad, contributed greatly to the sense of uncertainty and tension among Americans. But, of course, such short-range policies were subject to major change in a short period. In the following and final reading of this volume four prominent American historians use the past to clarify the present, in order to gain an understanding of the future.

The Lessons of the Past: Historians View America in the 1970s

Historians spend most of their time attempting to understand the past, but underlying much of their efforts is a desire to use their knowledge to comprehend the present and, in a small way, perhaps influence the future. In the following series of essays, four well-known American historians take up the task of using their deep knowledge of the past to analyze the present and consider possibilities for the future. There are as many areas of disagreement as agreement among Eugene Genovese, Daniel Boorstin, Staughton Lynd, and Arthur M. Schlesinger, Jr. The value of their essays lies not in the extent of their agreement, but in the ways they use historical perspective to attack contemporary problems.

From "The Spirit of '70," *Newsweek*, LXXVI (July 6, 1970), pp. 25-34. Copyright Newsweek, Inc., 1970.

I

Eugene Genovese, "A Massive Breakdown"

When a growing portion of the nation's youth loudly proclaims its defection from everything; when even the most traditional and conservative campuses seethe with perpetual turmoil; when two successive Presidents worry about a credibility gap (a polite way of saying that a significant number of Americans consider their President a liar); when black people find themselves trapped between failure of a promised integration and white resistance to black control of black communities; when white people generally split between those who feel guilty about the blacks and those who unashamedly hate them—two variations, although not to be equated, of old-fashioned white racism; when the richest nation in world history cannot keep its water and air clean, much less eliminate poverty; when great cities are acknowledged to be ungovernable, not to mention unlivable; when the country is racked with fear, foreboding, and hopelessness—then we had better declare a state of spiritual crisis, for the alternative would be to declare that irrationality, decadence, and disorder constitute our normal and preferred national condition.

The United States has gone through rough times before, but the present crisis has no genuine predecessors. The spiritual crises of the mid-nineteenth century, highlighted by a long and bloody sectional war, are certainly not to be minimized. But today, for the first time, the country faces a massive breakdown, manifested in every section, class and stratum, in faith in its ideals, institutions and prospects.

Today, a large number of Americans publicly proclaim that their country is fighting an unjust and immoral war and is committing acts that qualify as war crimes. These Americans are, of course, a minority even of the antiwar public, and their existence as a sizable group is not unprecedented—consider, for example, the hostile reaction at home to the Mexican War. But the steady augmentation of their numbers warns of a deeper malaise.

Perhaps even more striking is the vast number who oppose the war on other than moral grounds and who may very well already constitute a majority of the nation. At first glance these people direct only strategic and tactical criticisms and wish simply to admit a particular miscarriage of foreign policy; on the surface no great moral issue arises from their dissent. But Americans have never before admitted that our country could be beaten, much less beaten by a ragged army of non-white guerrillas. The demand to recognize defeat and stop playing God could and should be interpreted as a healthy national awakening to the limits of power—an inevitable and welcome stage in the maturation of a great world power. But Americans have never believed that we could be beaten in anything; that some problems might not be immediately soluble or indeed soluble at all; that a national cause as just as ours could ever be abandoned by God.

It is no accident that so many who begin by urging a tactical reconsideration in Vietnam end by denouncing the war as a crime. Americans have always believed that we are invincible precisely because we are God's chosen and the bearers of His morality to the world. For those infected with two centuries or more of self-righteous chauvinism, our debacle in Vietnam must call into question our national cause and—even in this secular age—seem like God's abandonment of His people in the wake of their succumbing to the sins of pride and avarice. Thus, even those who speak for Realpolitik, including the most cynical and opportunist, have unwittingly contributed to the breakdown of an increasingly brittle and shoddy spiritual façade.

The disillusionment with the war could not, however, by itself have caused our celebrated sense of national virtue and omnipotence to crumble so quickly. Had it not intersected with the racial crisis, the decay of our cities, the rising tide of official and popular violence, and the other manifestations of our having to contend with a ruling class (how else should we describe the handful who have a stranglehold on the nation's wealth and access to power?) that has neither the will nor ability to rule effectively, its effects would surely have been muted and protracted. When, for example, we think of our spiritual condition, we usually think first of the defection, political and cultural, of our youth. But our youth, in turning their backs on the values of their parents, schools and communities, respond to much more than the war, and it is difficult to believe that an end to the war will bring an end to their defection.

Both young and old, in different and sometimes opposing ways, have been shaken by the exposure of an enormous gap between our national pretensions and our national practice: an egalitarian society cannot keep its pledge of racial integration after more than fifteen years of sustained efforts; a democratic society suffers one President after another who is elected on a platform of ending a war each immediately proceeds to escalate; a constitutional political order sees nothing wrong with having Presidents Truman, Eisenhower, Kennedy, Johnson and Nixon wage

Ethnic groups which previously had been present but unheard on the American scene, now are articulating their needs to the rest of the nation. Here a group of militant Mexican-Americans (Chicanos) accents a pride in their past by celebrating Mexican Independence Day on the steps of the Colorado State Capitol in Denver.

war without the Congressional declaration required by the Constitution; a peace-loving society creates the greatest military machine in world history and permits its requirements to take priority over all others and indeed to crush all hopes of adequate response to pressing social ills; an idealistic and affluent society (in fact, a society that has historically identified its idealism with its affluence) is unable to demonstrate that any of its ideals are compatible with an affluence based on a commitment to the ethos and economic practice of the marketplace.

Young people respond, as do their elders, to the inability of so rich and powerful a country to solve its deepest problems. Their elders, having fought their way through depression and world war to a decent standard of living, which they once considered proof of their own moral virtue, respond with fear and confusion. Young people, who have little or no investment of their own lives in the material conditions on which they have been raised, are psychologically in much better condition to take a hard and sometimes brutal view of the quality of life their parents' struggle has purchased.

The simultaneous disasters in Asia and at home have exposed several decades of systematic deception, which the self-deception of the 1950s cult of affluence and suburbia has come to symbolize. From Truman to Nixon we have been told of the splendors and achievements of our capitalist economy, which ostensibly has cured the inherent ills revealed during the Great Depression. Only one or two small details were left out. Even the much-revered John F. Kennedy never thought it necessary to mention that this splendor has rested on the creation of an enormous war machine that has effectively blocked commitments to housing, education, safety, transportation, health and other requirements of human welfare. Nor has anyone in the government bothered to point out that the same Keynesian controls on which the prevention of a major depression depend have a few small side effects, such as a severe inflationary burden on large portions of the working and middle classes.

The deception in foreign policy has been much worse, but it was not until the 1960s that we had a generation sufficiently removed from the happy days of Harry Truman and Joseph McCarthy to laugh when they were told that America was leading something called the free world against a monolithic Communist empire that was somehow on the verge of fratricidal war. In the past, it had been easy enough to convince the American public that Thieus and Kys were defending the freedom of their own people and ours; that periodic interventions from Guatemala to Iran to the Congo were altogether altruistic, in contradistinction to such nasty Soviet interventions as those in Hungary and Czechoslovakia; that the wanton murder of 500,000 "Communists" by a pro-Western government in Indonesia was none of our business, but that we should all be outraged and ready to protect against the Soviet Union's unwillingness to permit free emigration of Jews; or that Chiang Kai-shek rightfully represented China in the United Nations. Indeed, so anesthetized had Americans become, so accustomed to believing in sheer lying as some Orwellian truth, that the country was stunned when young people started laughing.

The crisis is indeed spiritual, but its root lies in the palpable failure of our vaunted capitalist social system. It should not be necessary, even in these crazy times, to defend the genuine achievements of our national culture, among which we may find a profound commitment to personal freedom, political participation and social justice. But so long as the defense of capitalism in its corporate and oligopolistic phase and its political and military priorities takes precedence over those values and simultaneously remains confused with them, no solution will be possible. The spiritual crisis can only be resolved through the creation of a political movement capable of realizing our national ideals by the reordering of our economic and social priorities through the restructuring of our economy.

The decline and fall of the Roman Empire took 400 years or so; in the interim a great civilization slipped further and further into decadence, degradation and despair. Perhaps a benevolent God will grant our civilization as much time, but no one should count on it. If we fail to generate a political movement of national reconstruction, the existing order may last in this country for a long time, but it is now clear that it will never be able to quench the revolutionary flames now engulfing the earth.

The great political and moral problem for the world as a whole is the reconciliation of socialism, which has increasingly become the banner of the oppressed peoples of Asia, Africa and Latin America, with personal freedom and the tradition of free and rational criticism that have been the glories of Western civilization. Only the West can effect that reconciliation, and the West can do nothing without the United States. If, therefore, we fail here, we shall guarantee the death of the most precious parts of our hard-won heritage and—ironically—contribute to the victory of a totalitarian socialism everywhere.

II

Daniel Boorstin, "A Case of Hypochondria"

Our inventive, up-to-the-minute, wealthy democracy makes new tests of the human spirit. Our very instruments of education, of information and of "progress" make it harder every day for us to keep our bearings in the larger universe, in the stream of history and the whole world of peoples who feel strong ties to their past. A new price of our American standard of living is our imprisonment in the present.

That imprisonment tempts us to a morbid preoccupation with ourselves, and so induces hypochondria. That, the dictionary tells us, is "an abnormal condition characterized by a depressed emotional state and imaginary ill health; excessive worry or talk about one's health." We think we are the beginning and the end of the world. And as a result we get our nation and our lives, our strengths and our ailments, quite out of focus.

We will not be on the way to curing our national hypochondria unless we first accept the unfashionable possibility that many of our national ills are imaginary and that others may not be as serious as we imagine. Unless we begin to believe that we won't be dead before morning, we may not be up to the daily tasks of a healthy life.

We are overwhelmed by the instant moment—headlined in this morning's newspaper and flashed on this hour's newscast. As a result we can't see the whole real world around us. We don't see the actual condition of our long-lived body-national. And so we can't see clearly whatever may be the real ailments from which we actually suffer.

In a word, we have lost our sense of history. In our schools, the story of our nation has been displaced by "social studies"—which is the study of what ails *us*. In our churches the effort to see man *sub specie aeternitatis* has been displaced by the "social gospel"—which is the polemic against the supposed special evils of our time. Our book publishers and literary reviewers no longer seek the timeless and the durable, but spend most of their efforts in fruitless search for *à la mode* "social commentary"—which they pray won't be out of date when the issue goes to press in two weeks or when the manuscript becomes a book in six months. Our merchandizers frantically devise their 1970½ models (when will the 1970¾'s arrive?) which will cease to be voguish when their sequels appear three months hence. Neither our classroom lessons nor our sermons nor our books nor the things we live with nor the houses we live in are any longer strong ties to our past. We have become a nation of short-term doomsayers.

Without the materials of historical comparison, having lost our traditional respect for the wisdom of ancestors and the culture of kindred nations, we are left with nothing but abstractions, nothing but baseless utopias to compare ourselves with. No wonder, then, that so many of our distraught citizens libel us as the worst nation in the world, or the bane of human history (as some of our noisiest young people and a few disoriented Negroes tell us). For we have wandered out of history. And all in the name of virtue and social conscience!

We have lost interest in the real examples from the human past which alone can help us shape standards of the humanly possible. So we compare ours with a mythical Trouble-Free World, where all mankind was at peace. We talk about the War in Vietnam as if it were the first war in American history—or at least the first to which many Americans were opposed. We condemn our nation for not yet having attained perfect justice, and we forget that ours is the most motley and miscellaneous great nation of history—the first to use the full force of law and constitutions and to enlist the vast majority of its citizens in a strenuous quest for justice for all races and ages and religions.

We flagellate ourselves as "poverty ridden"—by comparison only with some mythical time when there was no bottom 20 percent in the economic scale. We sputter against The Polluted Environment—as if it was invented in the age of the automobile. We compare our smoggy air not with the odor of horsedung and the plague of flies and the smells of garbage and human excrement which filled cities in the past, but with the honeysuckle perfumes of some nonexistent City Beautiful. We forget that even if the water in many cities today is not as spring-pure nor as palatable as we would like, for most of history the water of cities (and of the countryside) was undrinkable. We reproach ourselves for the ills of disease and malnourishment, and forget that until recently enteritis and measles and whooping cough, diphtheria and typhoid, were killing diseases of childhood, puerperal fever plagued mothers in childbirth, polio was a summer monster.

Flooded by screaming headlines and hourly televised "news" melodramas of dissent and "revolution," we haunt ourselves with the illusory ideal of some "whole nation" which had a deep and outspoken "faith" in its "values."

We become so obsessed by where we are that we forget where we came from and how we got here. No wonder that we begin to lack the courage to confront the normal ills of modern history's most diverse, growing, burbling Nation of Nations.

Our national hypochondria is compounded by distinctively American characteristics. The American belief in speed, which led us to build railroads farther and faster than any other nation, to invent "quick-lunch" and self-service to save that terrible ten-minute wait, to build automobiles and highways so we can commute at 70 miles an hour, which made us a nation of instant cities, instant coffee, TV-dinners, and instant everything, has bred in us a colossal impatience. Any social problem that can't be solved instantly by money and legislation seems fatal. Our appliances and our buildings and our very lives seem out of date even before they are ready for occupancy. What can't be done right now seems hardly worth doing at all.

Some of these current attitudes are themselves the late-twentieth-century perversions of the old American Booster Spirit, which has had no precise parallel anywhere else. Totalitarian nations have been marked by their obsession with "planning"—with five-year plans and ten-year plans. But planning expresses willingness to accept a sharp distinction between present and future, between the way things are and the way they might be. And that distinction has never been too popular in the U.S.A. The nineteenth-century Boosters of Western cities defended their extravagant boasts by saying there was no reason to wait, if you were actually bragging only about things that were certain to happen. To them the beauties of Oleopolis or Gopher City were none the less real simply because "they had not yet gone through the formality of taking place."

This Booster-Vagueness has always made Americans wonderfully unpedantic about the distinction between the present and the future. The amiable vagueness, which once gave an optimistic nineteenth-century America the energy and the hope to go on, still survives. But in a hypochondriac twentieth-century America its effects can be disastrous. Now that very same extravagant vagueness leads some Americans to believe that every battle is Armageddon—and that the battle is already lost. And that the nation is none the less dead simply because the national demise "has not yet gone through the formality of taking place."

An immigrant nation, without an established religion and without political dogma, had to depend heavily on its sense of a shared past (and a shared future). American history itself was an antidote to dogmatism and utopianism. It proved that a nation did not need to be altogether one thing or another. Federalism was a way of combining local control with national government. Ethnic pluralism was a way of allowing people to keep as much as they wanted of their Old World language, religion and cuisine—to live among themselves as much as they wished. The immigrant was not compelled either to keep or to abandon his Old World identity. Free public schools, and the American innovations of the free high school and the public college, tried to have standards and yet give everybody the same commodity. The nation aimed to preserve "free private enterprise" (freer and on a larger scale than anywhere else) and yet to provide social security, farm price supports and other insurances against the free market. On a priori grounds, each of these would have seemed impossible, and they were all messy, philosophically speaking.

The best antidote, then, against ruthless absolutes and simple-minded utopias has been American history itself. But that history becomes more and more inaccessible when the technology and institutions of our time imprison us in the present. How can we escape the prison?

First, we must awaken our desire to escape. To do this we must abandon the prevalent belief in the superior wisdom of the ignorant. Unless we give up the voguish reverence for youth and for the "culturally deprived," unless we cease to look to the vulgar community as arbiters of our schools, of our art and literature, and of all our culture, we will never have the will to de-provincialize our minds. We must make every effort to reverse the trend in our schools and colleges—to move away from the "relevant" and toward the cosmopolitanizing, the humanizing and the unfamiliar. Education is learning what you didn't even know you didn't know. The last thing the able young Negro needs is "black studies"—which simply re-enforces the unfortunate narrowness of his experience and confines him in *his* provincial present. We all need more ancient history, more medieval history, more of the history and culture of Asia and Africa.

Then, we must enlarge and widen and deepen what we mean by our history. The preoccupation with politics which has been the bane of the history classroom fosters the unreasonable notions that today governments are the root of all good and evil. The self-righteous effort by self-styled prophets of self-vaunted new "schools" of history would make history a mere tool of contemporary polemics, and so destroy the reason for exploring our past. They would make men of all other ages into the slaves of our conceit—to be used only for our purposes. We must make our history more total by incorporating the past that people lived but that historians have not talked much about. In the United States this means an effort to make more of the history of immigrants, of the history of technology, of the history of everyday life, of business and advertising and housing and eating and drinking and clothing. Democratizing our history does not mean perverting it to the current needs of demagogic or "revolutionary" politics. It does mean enlarging its once-pedantic scope to include the whole spectrum of the ways of life of men and women.

When we allow ourselves to be imprisoned in the present, to be obsessed by the "relevant," we show too little respect for ourselves and our possibilities. We assume that we can properly judge our capacities by the peculiar tests of our own day. But we must look into the whole Historical Catalogue of man's possibilities. To be really persuaded that things can be otherwise, we must see how and when and why they have actually been otherwise.

To revive our sense of history is surely no panacea for current ills. But it surely is a palliative. It may help us discover what is now curable, may help us define the timetable of the possible, and so help us become something that we are not. If history cannot give us panaceas, it is the best possible cure of the yen for panaceas. And the only proven antidote for utopianism.

"The voice of the intellect," observed Sigmund Freud (who did not underestimate the role of the irrational) in 1928, "is a soft one, but it does not rest until it has gained a hearing. Ultimately, after endlessly repeated rebuffs, it succeeds. This is one of the few points in which one may be optimistic about the future of mankind." Beneath the strident voice of the present we must try to hear the insistent whisper of reason. It does not sound "with it." It speaks only to the attentive listener. It speaks a language always unfamiliar and often archaic. It speaks the language of all past times and places, which is the language of history.

III

**Staughton Lynd,
"Again—Don't Tread on Me"**

It is misleading to speak of the condition of the "American spirit" or of "psychic recession" in America as a nation. There are and always have been different, conflicting groups in American society which experienced life quite differently at the same point in time. The spiritual crisis of the American Indian or of the Afro-American throughout the past 350 years is something deeper and more grave than anything undergone by white Americans. Historians know relatively little even about what life felt like for the working-class white: for seamen and tenant farmers at the time of the American Revolution, for the immigrant Irish laborers on whose bodies (Thoreau said) were laid the tracks of American railroads, for the Eastern European steelworkers who worked twelve hours a day and 24 hours every other Sunday in Pittsburgh and Gary. Generalizations about national character and national spirit are usually extrapolations from documentary evidence produced by the affluent articulate, and should be suspect for this reason.

There *is* a crisis in American society, however. It is fundamentally economic, not spiritual, but it expresses itself secondarily in the realm of psyche and spirit. And no doubt certain generalizations—"alienation," for instance—do produce an incomplete description of the quite different spiritual crises experienced by different classes, races, and age groups. My friend David Harris, a draft resister, writes from a Federal penitentiary:

> It seems one of the characteristics of the insanity consuming America is that no experience is actively shared. The operational identities, the fantasies, the frustrations and all the hurts are collected in individual sockets that eventually deny any other reality and demand, in sheer desperation, to be recognized.

Doubtless George Wallace and Eldridge Cleaver could each find a part of himself in those words. But the description is too general to get at the reality of either man, or of the parts of American society they personify.

So it is superficial and falsely ponderous to speak of a crisis in the American spirit. Equally spurious is the tendency to select a single aspect of the present crisis and mechanically compare it to some counterpart phenomenon in the past. Of course it is true that the nation was at least as deeply divided in the years before the Civil War as it is today, and that after the Civil War there was an era of assassinations and industrial conflict resembling the period of racial conflict since World War II, and that young people were disillusioned and rebellious in other times, too. Comparisons of this kind nurture the implicit thesis that since there have been crises before, the good old American ship of state will also weather the storms of the present. There are some people who would be ritually repeating this adage as the waters closed over their heads.

To be helpful, analysis must avoid murky psychological generalizations and must deal with the specific character of the present crisis as a whole.

The place to begin, in my opinion, is the failure of the New Deal to overcome the Depression of the 1930s. Richard Hofstadter emphasized this 25 years ago in his "The American Political Tradition." It has recently been stressed again by Howard Zinn and Barton Bernstein. Zinn writes:

> When the reform energies of the New Deal began to wane around 1939 . . . the nation was back to its normal state: a permanent army of unemployed; twenty or thirty million poverty-ridden people effectively blocked from public view by a huge, prosperous, and fervently consuming middle class; a tremendously efficient yet wasteful productive apparatus that was efficient because it could produce limitless supplies of what it decided to produce, and wasteful because what it decided to produce was not based on what was most needed by society but on what was most profitable to business.

Bernstein concurs. The number of unemployed in 1939 was still about half the number out of work in 1933. And: "The liberal reforms of the New Deal did not transform the American system; they conserved and protected American corporate capitalism. . . . There was no significant redistribution of power in American society."

The New Deal did not overcome unemployment but World War II did. What Roosevelt had failed to accomplish in his capacity as Dr. New Deal he achieved in his role as Dr. Win The War. And the important thing is this, that ever since then American prosperity has depended on massive public defense spending in a "permanent war economy." Walter Oakes coined the phrase in an article written for Politics magazine in 1944. Said Oakes: "The fact is that the capitalist system cannot stand the strain of another siege of unemployment comparable to 1930–1940. . . . The traditional methods . . . will not be followed." Oakes was brilliantly right. Business opinion overcame its antipathy to public works so long as the produce was military, because only in this way could a recurrence of the Depression be forestalled.

I believe this to be the key fact from which the current crisis is derived. Also important is the increase in overseas private investment, now roughly ten times greater than at the end of World War II. This fact underlies American foreign policy since the 1940s just as huge government spending on "defense" is the basis of domestic policy. But the relative importance of the two economic facts, public defense spending and private investment overseas, is clear. Overseas economic expansion has helped the American economy but defense spending—the welfare program of the rich—has become essential to it.

At least as important as the export of capital and goods to other countries is the effort to make the domestic market bigger through advertising. Perhaps it could be said of nineteenth-century capitalism that it made approximately what people needed (although it did not distribute its product to those who needed it most). The situation now is that human needs are manufactured by advertising and then products of dubious social utility made "in response to demand." Thus car fins, changing women's fashions, and what young people denounce as the "plasticity" of American life. Thus also the role of TV and other instrumentalities of mass culture. People who talk about "America's spiritual crisis" see TV as a symbol. They show how violence is packaged and sold on the screen so that it is experienced as intensely immediate but also distant and artificial at the same time, with the result that a generation is readied to kill without feeling, and to have Vietnam brought into its living room without crying out in horror and stopping the war. What is not enough emphasized is that TV as a cultural phenomenon is the result of TV as an advertising medium. Mass culture is only the filler between commercials.

The overseas imperialism of Coca-Cola and napalm is accompanied by a "domestic imperialism" which tries to make people buy things which they don't really need. Yet neither of these sales programs solves the problem. The productive capacity of the American economy dwarfs the ability of people either abroad or at home to absorb its products at a profit. The fundamental way in which the United States has tried to deal with its ability to produce is by war, or more precisely, by a condition of permanent war-readiness which year by year increases the probability that wars will occur.

Because our economy is dedicated to the production of plasticity and lethal junk, young men and women grow up in America not believing that adult society has useful work it needs them to get done. Paul Goodman describes in "Growing Up Absurd" how in modern America there is no initiation to adulthood, how adolescence ceases to be an apprenticeship to becoming a full citizen, because there are so few grown-up jobs now which a person can respect himself for doing.

The root of delinquency and rebelliousness in all their forms is unemployment but this unemployment is more than an absence of a pay check, it is also the absence of useful work. Most Americans are out of work even when they are making a good living. They put money on the table but use only a fraction of their human capacity in getting it. Work for most Americans may no longer be dirty, but it is still boring, humiliating, and unworthy of what man might be. The young are right to rebel against an adulthood which insults them.

Education tires to shape the young for this unmanly and inhuman adult work-life, and so itself becomes a target. The rapid expansion of higher education since the end of World War II came about because of technological change in industry. Automatized and computerized industry requires more and more young men and women who have white-collar skills but behave with the docility expected of blue-collar workers. The thrust of the multiversity in which so many of our 7 million college students are trained is toward skilled obedience. The student, like the worker he is intended to become, uses his mind as well as his hands, but not creatively, not at his own initiative, still within limits set by orders coming down from above. That is what modern capitalist industry is like and so that is what modern higher education is like, too. And the students tell those who give them orders to practice being foremen on

Demonstrations have become a familiar part of American life, involving those of all ages and backgrounds. Here young and old, black and white, march in a peace demonstration in New York City.

someone else. In their own words, they refuse to be bent, folded, spindled, and mutilated.

Those who tell us that the crisis of America is a crisis of authority are, in a sense somewhat different than they imagine, absolutely right. In choosing to forestall depression by war spending, the United States has made the larger choice to respond to change with violence. Rather than moving with life, like a gardener or a teacher, our society rigidly confronts life like a policeman. Repression and authoritarianism are on the rise in America because at its highest levels the society insists that things stay the way they have been, remain in a form familiar and amenable to control: this society believes it is better (for other people) to be dead than different. And so in every institution, at every age, in every meeting of those with more power and those with less, there is indeed a crisis of law and order. The people who talk most about it are those who have the power, hence the law and order, and feel no need for change. They—and I am talking not of George Wallace but of the Ivy League graduates in Wall Street and government—are apparently prepared to destroy the world rather than let it become something which they don't run.

What they fear, when all is said and done, is socialism: management of the economy not by corporation executives selected by other corporation executives but democratically, by the people. The danger as perceived from Harvard Square, the Yale Green, and their various extensions is that incompetent common people in Mozambique or Muncie might take the rhetoric of the Declaration of Independence seriously and try to run the economy themselves. To prevent this, an outcome which they perceive not as the end to their accustomed power and profits but as the end to freedom, God, country, and motherhood, the decent young scions of the governing class are prepared to use any means. Marx was more right than he could have imagined when he said that the choice was between socialism and barbarism.

This choice is likely to present itself as a struggle for democracy. Cold-war ideology has led us to suppose that the choice for socialism means dictatorship, while capitalism, whatever its other handicaps, is free. Of course it is perfectly true that socialism can mean dictatorship. But the historically emergent problem which I see dominating the next generation in this country, say from 1970 to the year 2000, is the struggle to preserve and extend American democracy against repression from the right (both the genteel right of the Northeast and the rougher Southwestern variety with which the former will reluctantly ally). If America can stay democratic I believe it will become socialist. In the struggle to keep it democratic, a coalition may be formed which will have the power to make it socialist. Huey Long once said that if Fascism came to the United States it would call itself democratic. If socialism is to come, it will have to be democratic; and if democracy is to be preserved and extended, Americans will have to open their minds in a new way to what democracy would mean if applied to the economy.

Earlier, I criticized the practice of drawing comparisons between single aspects of the present and the past. Let me in closing refer to the one total moment of the American past which I think has some essential resemblance to our present situation.

A consequence of the permanent war economy has been the concentration of decisions over life and death in the hands of one man, the President, and the growing sense on the part of the American people (left and right) that government in Washington is almost a foreign power, an invader rather than a protector. We have rightly come to feel, not that we run the government, but that it runs us and we protect ourselves as best we can. The labels are different, but in effect we begin to perceive our government as a constitutional monarchy, and a capricious one at that.

Accordingly, the American Revolution which the nation will shortly commemorate jumps back into focus. The process of that revolution was of ever-escalating resistance to arbitrary power, which the people did not control, but could only petition and say No to. So today, having petitioned all too often, we are learning the salutary habit of saying No. Confronted by the authority of the Selective Service System (in a permanent war economy induction is the initiation to adulthood), of armed policemen like those who shot down unarmed "rioters" in the Boston Massacre, of a dozen contemporary variants of the customs officer without a search warrant, the contemptuous governor, and the king who would not hear, an increasing number of the American people are taking the best page from their history and responding: Don't tread on me.

IV

Arthur M. Schlesinger, Jr., "The Velocity of History"

America is unquestionably experiencing an extreme crisis of confidence. And this crisis is unquestionably not illusory, even if it coexists with affluence, social gains and scientific miracles. It is a crisis with many sources; but none is more important, I think, than the incessant and irreversible increase in the rate of social change.

Henry Adams was the first American historian to note the transcendent significance of the ever accelerating velocity of history. "The world did not [just] double or treble its movement between 1800 and 1900," he wrote in 1909, "but, measured by any standard known to science—by horsepower, calories, volts, mass in any shape—the tension and vibration and so-called progression of society were fully a thousand times greater in 1900 than in 1800." Hurried on by the cumulative momentum of science and technology, the tension and vibration of society in 1970 are incalculably greater than they were when Adams wrote. Nor, pending some radical change in human values or capabilities, can we expect the rate of change to slow down at all in the foreseeable future.

This increase in the velocity of history dominates all aspects of contemporary life. First of all, it is responsible for the unprecedented instability of the world in which we live. Science and technology make, dissolve, rebuild and enlarge our environment every week; and the world alters more in a decade than it used to alter in centuries. This has meant the disappearance of familiar landmarks and guideposts that stabilized life for earlier generations. It has meant that children, knowing how different their own lives will be, can no longer look to parents as models and authorities. Change is always scary; uncharted, uncontrolled change can be deeply demoralizing. It is no wonder that we moderns feel forever disoriented and off balance; unsure of our ideas and institutions; unsure of our relations to others, to society and to history; unsure of our own purpose and identity.

The onward roar of science and technology has other consequences. A second springs from the paradox that the very machinery civilization has evolved to create abundance for the mass also creates anxiety for the individual. The high-technology society is above all the society of the great organization. In advanced nations, the great organizations—of government, of industry, of education, of research, of communications, of transport, of labor, of marketing—become the units of social energy. These great organizations, as Professor Galbraith points out, generate a life, world and truth of their own; in all areas, the sovereignty of the consumer begins to yield to the sovereignty of the producer; and, in the shadow of these towering structures, the contemporary individual feels puny and helpless. Indeed, no social emotion is more widespread today than the conviction of personal powerlessness, the sense of being beset, beleaguered and persecuted. It extends not only to Black Panthers and members of the Students for a Democratic Society but also to businessmen, publishers, generals and (as we have recently come to observe) Vice Presidents.

A third consequence springs from the technological process itself. For the inner logic of science and technology is rushing us on from the mechanical into the electronic age—into the fantastic new epoch of electronic informational systems and electronic mechanisms of control, the age foreshadowed by television and the computer. One need not be a devout McLuhanite to recognize the force of Marshall McLuhan's argument that history is profoundly affected by changes in the means of communication. There can be little doubt that the electronic age will have penetrating effects not just on the structure and processes of society but on the very reflexes of individual perception. Already television, by its collectiveness and simultaneity, has fostered an intense desire for political self-expression and visibility, as it has spread the habit of instant reaction and stimulated the hope of instant results.

The accelerating velocity of history has, of course, a multitude of other effects. Improved methods of medical care and nutrition have produced the population crisis; and the growth and redistribution of population have produced the urban crisis. The feverish increase in the gross national product first consumes precious natural resources and then discharges filth and poison into water and air; hence the ecological crisis. Nor can one omit the extraordinary moral revolution which makes our contemporary society reject as intolerable conditions of poverty, discrimination and oppression that mankind had endured for centuries.

All these factors, as they have risen in intensity and desperation, are placing increasing strain on inherited ideas, institutions and values. The old ways by which we reared, educated, employed and governed our people seem to make less and less sense. Half a century ago Henry Adams wrote, "Every historian—sometimes unconsciously but always inevitably—must have put to himself the question: How long . . . could an outworn social system last?" This is a question which historians—and citizens—must consider very intently today.

If this analysis is correct, then the crisis we face is a good deal deeper than simply the anguish over the ghastly folly of Vietnam. For that matter, it is a good deal deeper than is imagined by those who trace all iniquities to the existence of private profit and corporate capitalism. For the acceleration of social change creates its problems without regard to systems of ownership or ideology. The great organization, for example, dominates Communist as much as it does democratic states. Indeed, more so; for the more centralized the ownership and the more absolutist the ideology, the greater the tyranny of organization. The individual stands his better chance in societies where power is reasonably distributed and diversified and where ideas are in free and open competition.

If the crisis seems today more acute in the United States than anywhere else, it is not because of the character of our economic system; it is because the revolutions wrought by science and technology have gone farther here than anywhere else. As the nation at the extreme frontier of technological development, America has been the first to experience the unremitting shock and disruptive intensity of accelerated change. The crises we are living through are the crises of modernity. Every nation, as it begins to reach a comparable state of technical development, will have to undergo comparable crises.

Is the contemporary crisis more profound than other crises in our history? This seems to me an unanswerable question, because a crisis surmounted always seems less terrible than a crisis in being. One cannot say that we are in more danger today than during the Civil War, for example, or during the Great Depression, or during the second world war. One can only say that we met the earlier challenges—and have not yet met this one. And one can add that in earlier crises in our history the quality of our national leadership seemed much more adequate to the magnitude of the challenge.

What Lincoln brought to the Civil War, what Franklin Roosevelt brought to the Great Depression and the second world war, were, above all, an intense imaginative understanding of the nature of the crisis, perceived in the full sweep of history, with a bold instinct for innovation and a determination to mobilize and apply social intelligence and a compassionate sense of human tragedy. It was this embracing vision that gave particular policies their meaning and strength and inspired the American people ro rise to their obligations and opportunities. Today, alas, our national leadership hardly seems aware of the fact we are in a crisis; in fact, it hardly appears to know what is going on in America and the world. It is feeble and frightened, intellectually mediocre, devoid of elevation and understanding, fearful of experiment, without a sense of the past or a sense of the future. This is one reason why our crisis of confidence is so acute. It is as if James Buchanan were fighting the Civil War or Herbert Hoover the Great Depression.

The basic task is to control and humanize the forces of change in order to prevent them from tearing our society apart. Our nation is in a state of incipient fragmentation; and the urgent need (along with ending the war) is a national reconstruction that will bring the estranged and excluded groups into full membership in our national community. This means social justice as well as racial justice; it means a far broader measure of participation in our great organizations and institutions; it means the determination to enable all Americans to achieve a sense of function, purpose and potency in our national life. And it means leadership in every area which greatly and generously conceives its responsibility and its hope.

I do not accept the thesis of the inexorable decline of America. No one can doubt that our nation is in trouble. But the present turmoil may be less the proof of decay than the price of progress. The cutting edge of science and technology has sliced through ancient verities and accustomed institutions; it has raised up new questions, new elites, new insistences, new confrontations. As the process has gathered momentum, the immediate result has been—was almost bound to be—social and moral confusion, frustration, fear, violence. Yet the turmoil, the confusion, even the violence may well be the birth pangs of a new epoch in the history of man. If we can develop the intelligence, the will and the leadership to absorb, digest and control the consequences of accelerated technological change, we can avoid the fate of internal demoralization and disintegration—and perhaps offer an example that will help other nations soon to struggle with similar problems and will, in time, restore American influence in the world.

But, as Herbert Croly wrote 60 years ago, we can no longer conceive the promise of American life "as a consummation which will take care of itself . . . as destined to automatic fulfillment." We face a daunting task—still not a bad one for all that. Emerson said,

> if there is any period one would desire to be born in—is it not the era of revolution when the old and the new stand side by side and admit of being compared; when all the energies of man are searched by fear and hope; when the historic glories of the old can be compensated by the rich possibilities of the new era? This time like all times is a very good one if one but knows what to do with it.

Acknowledgments

xvi, George Eastman House; p. 5, Minnesota Historical Society; p. 20-21, State Historical Society of Wisconsin; p. 24, Carnegie Library, Pittsburgh; p. 34, Carnegie Library, Pittsburgh; p. 39, New York Public Library; p. 51, George Eastman House; p. 52, left, Culver; p. 52, right, Library of Congress; p. 53, George Eastman House; p. 54, Carnegie Library, Pittsburgh; p. 55, Carnegie Library, Pittsburgh; p. 56, top, Carnegie Library, Pittsburgh; p. 56, bottom, Carnegie Library, Pittsburgh; p. 57, left, top & bottom, George Eastman House; p. 57, right, Carnegie Library, Pittsburgh; p. 58, Carnegie Library, Pittsburgh; p. 60, Library of Congress; p. 62, George Eastman House; p. 64, New York Public Library; p. 68-69, Carnegie Library, Pittsburgh; p. 75, George Eastman House; p. 78, Library of Congress; p. 80, Museum of the City of New York; p. 84, George Eastman House; p. 87, George Eastman House; p. 94, New York Public Library; p. 95, Chicago Historical Society; p. 105, Museum of the City of New York; p. 110, Granger; p. 113, Smithsonian Institution; p. 116, Nebraska State Historical Society; p. 120, New York Historical Society; p. 125, Santa Fe Railway; p. 126, New York Public Library, Rare Book Room; p. 127, Nebraska Historical Society; p. 128, top, Oklahoma State Historical Society; p. 128, bottom, Library of Congress; p. 129, top, Minnesota Historical Society; p. 129, bottom, Denver Public Library; p. 130, top, Nebraska State Historical Society; p. 130, bottom, Nebraska State Historical Society; p. 131, top, Minnesota Historical Society; p. 131, bottom, Northern Pacific Railway Company; p. 132, State Historical Society of Wisconsin; p. 135, State Historical Society of Wisconsin; p. 139, Culver; p. 145, Library of Congress; p. 150, George Eastman House; p. 157, Granger; p. 160, Library of Congress; p. 168, Franklin D. Roosevelt Library; p. 173, Brown Brothers; p. 176, Library of Congress; p. 179, Brown Brothers; p. 183, Library of Congress; p. 190, Granger; p. 193, Library of Congress; p. 197, Library of Congress; p. 200, Granger; p. 203, Library of Congress; p. 204, United Press International; p. 205, National Archives; p. 214-215, Chicago Historical Society; p. 218, United Press International; p. 223, Museum of Modern Art Film Stills Archive/RKO; p. 224, Museum of Modern Art Film Stills Archive/Wark Producing Company; p. 225, Museum of Modern Art Film Stills Archive/Metro Goldwyn Mayer; p. 226, left, Museum of Modern Art Film Stills Archive/Paramount; p. 226, right, Museum of Modern Art Film Stills Archive/Metro Goldwyn Mayer; p. 227, left, Museum of Modern Art Film Stills Archive/Twentieth Century Fox; p. 227, right, Museum of Modern Art Film Stills Archive/United Artists; p. 228, Museum of Modern Art Film Stills Archive/Paramount; p. 229, Museum of Modern Art Film Stills Archive; p. 229, bottom, Museum of Modern Art Film Stills Archive/Twentieth Century Fox; p. 230, top, Museum of Modern Art Film Stills Archive/United Artists; p. 230, bottom, Museum of Modern Art Film Stills Archive; p. 232, Library of Congress; p. 237, Chicago Historical Society; p. 240, United Press International; p. 243, Library of Congress; p. 245, Franklin D. Roosevelt Library; p. 254, Granger; p. 257, Library of Congress; p. 261, Franklin D. Roosevelt Library & *New York Times*; p. 265, National Archives; p. 268, Franklin D. Roosevelt Library; p. 271, Granger; p. 278, Library of Congress; p. 280, New York Public Library; p. 283, Granger; p. 288, Library of Congress; p. 292, Granger; p. 293, New York Public Library; p. 295, New York Public Library; p. 301, New York Public Library; p. 302, Granger; p. 305, Library of Congress; p. 311, National Archives; p. 312, Granger; p. 320, Imperial War Museum, London; p. 324, Granger; p. 327, Granger; p. 334, West Point Museum Collection; p. 336, National Archives; p. 337, National Archives; p. 341, Granger; p. 345, National Archives; p. 347, Granger; p. 351, Imperial War Museum, London; p. 355, Brown Brothers; p. 358, Franklin D. Roosevelt Library; p. 362, Museum of Modern Art; p. 369, United Press International; p. 374, United Press International; p. 380, Library of Congress; p. 384, United States Army Photograph; p. 388, United States Air Force; p. 391, National Archives; p. 393, Brown Brothers; p. 395, top, CARE Photo; p. 395, bottom, Official United States Air Force Photo; p. 401, Joint Task Force One; p. 407, United States Army Photograph; p. 411, Illingworth in the *London Daily Mail*; p. 415, *Verdens Gang* (Oslo); p. 418, New York Public Library; p. 421, United Press International; p. 427, United Press International; p. 429, Acme Photo; p. 432, United Press International; p. 436, Agency for International Development; p. 439, Rebman Photo Service, 1525 Superior Ave., Cleveland, Ohio; p. 441, Herblock, *Washington Post*; p. 447, Illingworth, copyright by *Punch*; p. 454, United Press International; p. 463, Herblock, *Washington Post*; p. 471, Wide World Photos; p. 475, United Press International; p. 491, United States Army Photograph; p. 492, Wide World Photos; p. 504, David Cupp; p. 512, Black Star, Flip Schulke; p. 518, United Press International; p. 526, Museum of Modern Art Film Stills Archive; p. 527, Museum of Modern Art Film Stills Archive; p. 534, Yale University, James Weldon Johnson Collection; p. 539, Library of Congress; p. 540, Black Star, Declan Haun; p. 541, top, United Press International; p. 541, bottom, United Press International; p. 542, left, United Press International; p. 542, right, United Press International; p. 543, top, United Press International; p. 543, bottom, United Press International; p. 544, Black Star, George Ballis; p. 544, bottom, United Press International; p. 545, left, Black Star, Matt Heron; p. 545, right, Black Star, East Street Gallery; p. 546, left, United Press International; p. 546, right, PIX, Jefferey Blankfort; p. 547, Black Star, Claus C. Meyer; p. 554, United Press International; p. 557, Black Star, Flip Schulke; p. 567, Black Star, John Launois; p. 570, Black Star, David Prince; p. 571, Black Star, Bill Reed; p. 574, Black Star, Charles Moore; p. 577, United Press International; p. 580, United Press International; p. 583, Black Star, Leo Choplin; p. 593, NBC News; p. 595, Peace Corps; p. 598, Neal Slavin; p. 603, Black Star, Ivan Masser; p. 608, Maury Englander; p. 612, Fred McDarrah; p. 616, Black Star, John Collier; p. 619, Black Star, Alan Copeland; p. 627, David Cupp; p. 633, Black Star, Vernon Merritt; p. 636, Derrick Te Paske

Index

Primary source material is indicated by italics in the index.

Acheson, Dean (1893-1971), *418-419,* 420, 425, 452, 453
Adair v. *United States* (1908), 63
Adamic, Louis (1898-1952), *81-85*
Adamson Act (1916), 154
Adler, Alfred, 200n
advertising, 180-181, 182-184
Agrarian Revolt, 108-124
Agricultural Adjustment Act (1933), 253, 533
Agricultural Revolution, 109
agriculture, 109-124,, 174, 253; and immigrants, 79-81
air power, and morality, 394-395
Alaska, 292
Aliquippa, 272-276
Alliance for Progress (1961), 480
Amalgamated Association of Iron and Steel Workers of America, 65-70
Amendments to Constitution: Fourteenth, 537; Eighteenth, 189; Nineteenth, 199; Twenty-first, 190
America First Committee (1940), 357
American character, 16-23, 85-86, 98-99, 497-498, 513, 621-637
American Communist Party 609
American Federation of Labor, 61, 63, 65, 96, 187, 217, 271, 272, 533, 535
American Labor Union (1898), 61
American Party (1886), 95
anarchists, 59
Anschluss (1938), 351-352
anti-Catholicism, 96, 192-194
Anti-Poverty Act (1964), 594
anti-Semitism, 97, 192-194
Arbenz-Guzman, Jacobo, 442-444, 445
Armour, Philip Danforth (1832-1901), 11

arms race, 290, 409, 441-442, 438, 447
Army-McCarthy hearings (1954), 455
arsenal of democracy, 354-357, 390
Arthur, Chester A. (1830-1886), 196
Associated Brotherhood of Iron and Steel Heaters, Rollers, and Roughers (1872), 65
Association for the Study of Negro Life and History, 206-207
Atlantic Charter (1941), 392-393
atomic weapons, 387, 390, 394-405
Attlee, Clement, 392
automobile, 4-5, 175-179

Baghdad Pact (1955), 440
balance of power, 318
"balancing nationalities," 96
Ballinger, Richard A. (1858-1922), 147
banking, 158, 252
Banking Act (1935), 264
Batista, Fulgencio, 469
Bay of Pigs invasion (1961), 470, 612
Bellamy, Edward (1850-1898), *27-30*
Benson, Elizabeth, *199-201*
Berger, Victor Louis (1860-1929), 61
Berlin Crisis (1948-1949), 408; (1958 and 1961), 442
Bismarck, Otto von, 267, 318
Black Manifesto (1969), 584-585
Black Muslims, 565-566
blacks, 202-221, 532; activism, 556-564; mobility, 588-590; nationalism, 587; power, 574; purpose, 573-590; separatism, 573-574. See also civil rights, Negroes, race, racism.
Bland-Allison Act (1878), 112
bloody shirt, 136
Blount, James H., 297
Bloshevik Revolution (1917), 334
Bonus Expeditionary Force (1932), 236
boondoggling, 253
Boorstin, Daniel *629-631*
Borah, William E. (1865-1940), 338
Bourne, Randolph (1886-1918), *104-107*
Boxer Rebellion (1900), 306
Bozell, L. Brent, *457-459*
Brandeis, Louis D. (1856-1941), 64
British Guiana, 302

Brotherhood of Sleeping Car Porters, 533
Brown v. *Board of Education* (1954), 535, 536-538, 556
Bryan-Chamorro Treaty (1916), 303
Bryan, William Jennings (1860-1925), 110, 113-114, 188, 325
Buchanan v. *Warley* (1917), 216n
Buckley, William F., *457-459*
Bullitt, William C. (1891-1967), *409-411*
business, 156-159, 164-167, 526-529, 529-531; and the Depression, 277; and government, 174; regulation of, 152-167. See also concentration, industry, railroads
busing, 581-584
Byrnes, James F., 397, 402, 403

capital, 31-32, 59-76, 108
capitalism, 628
captain of industry, 11
Carey Act (1894), 138
Caribbean, and American policy, 302-305
Carmichael, Stokeley, 570
Carnegie, Andrew (1835-1919), 1, 11, 33, 34, *34-37,* 38, 40, 43, 44, 46, 47, 48-50, 66-67
Carter, Robert *538-540*
Casablanca Conference (1943), 392
Castro, Cipriano, 304
Castro, Fidel, 469-471, 476
Chamberlain, Neville, 352
Chamberlain, William Henry, 373, 379
Chambers, Whittaker, 452
change, 1-2, 77-81, 122, 133, 140-142, 169-170, 175-178, 187-201, 276-279, 453, 513, 518-519, 574-575, 577-578, 614, 635, 637; in black and white relations, 202-221; economic, 3-14; social, 98, 148-149; political, 248; technological, 3-14
Chiang Kai-shek (1887-), 378, 392, 416, 421-422, 425, 426, 461
Chicago, and blacks, 212-216
Chicago World's Fair (1893), 4, 96
Chile, 298, 309
China, 306, 368, 377-379, 381-383,

411, 416-417, 420-424; and Cuba, 471; and foreign policy, 461-462; and the Korean War, 430-434; and Russia, 440
Chinese Communist Revolution (1949), 420-421
Chinese Exclusion Act (1892), 97
Chinese immigration, 93
Chou En-lai, (1898-), 430-431
Christianity, and imperialism, 290-292
Churchill, Winston (1874-1965), 378, 392, 397, 399
cities, 189-192; and blacks, 202, 203, 573; escape from, 184-186; growth of, 175; politics, 140-142; riots, 577-581
civil rights, 519, 532-590
Civil Rights Act (1960), 558
Civil Rights Act (1964), 559, 560, 594
Civil Service, 133, 134
Civilian Conservation Corps (1933), 252, 533
class, 94-95; and prohibition, 191; and racism, 213; and violence, 206
Clayton Anti-trust Act (1914), 154, 166
Clayton-Bulwer Treaty (1850), 303
Clemenceau, Georges, 286, 335
Cleveland, Grover (1837-1908), 96, 112-113, 138, 234, 297, 298-299
co-existence, 440, 451, 475
Cold War, The, 396-399, 402, 406-419, 450-451, 469-470; and Korea, 423; and McCarthyism, 452
Colombia, 303, 307, 308
Colored Alliance (c.1891), 109
Colton, David, 11-12.
Cominform (1947), 407
Commager, Henry Steele, *408-409*
commerce, and imperialism, 296, 300, 306, 309; and World War I, 323
Committee on a Sane Nuclear Policy (1957), 463
communications, 180-181
Communism, 406, 410-411; and American radicalism, 609-610; and race, 206
Communist Manifesto (1848), 406
Communist Party, in America, 187

641

community, 77-92, 625-637; and poverty, 591-607; and race, 532-590; and youth, 608-624
competition, 10, 12-14, 155; and imperialism, 293-294; 296-297, 306; industrial, 40-44, 46-50; and values, 15; and World War I, 318
concentration, business, 12, 41-44, 154-155, 156-159, 171, 174; and the Depression, 232-233; in Japan, 368, 422; and reform, 133
conformity, and McCarthyism, 457-459
Congress of Industrial Organizations (1938), 271, 533, 535
Congress on Racial Equality (1942), 562n, 575, 585
conservation, 138, 139, 146-148
consumer economy, 181-184
Containment, 414-417, 438
Coolidge, J. Calvin (1872-1933), 172-173, 350
Co-Prosperity Sphere, 379-381
"*cordon sanitaire,*" 406
corruption, 109, 133, 140, 172, 516; and China, 422
Coughlin, Father Charles, 264, 266
Crimean War, 281
Cuba, 303, 304, 469-479
Cuban Insurrection (1868-1878), 302
Cuban missile crisis, 471-479, 612
Cuban Revolution (1895-1898), 302-303; (1969), 469-470, 611
Cumming v. *County Board of Education* (1901), 537
Czechoslovakia, 352, 407

Danbury Hatters Case (1902), 63
Darrow, Clarence (1857-1938), 188
Darwin, Charles (1809-1882), 15, 188
Daugherty, Harry M., 172
Daughters of the American Revolution (1890), 289
Davies, John Patton, 459-462
D-Day (1944), 390
Debs, Eugene V. (1855-1926), 61
DeGaulle, Charles (1890-1971), 478
DeLeon, Daniel (1852-1914), 61
democracy, 634; and Latin America, 480-481; and the saloon, 191

Democratic Party, 171, 248, 279, 516; and the Populist Revolt, 112-114
Denby, Edward (1870-1929), 172
Dennis v. *United States* (1951), 453
depression, agricultural, 109; of 1873, 234; of 1893, 112, 113, 136; of 1920, 174-175; of 1929, 169-170, 222-247, 349
Dewey, George (1837-1917), 305-306
Dewey, Thomas E. (1902-1971), 515-517
"Dishonest Graft," 140
Dixiecrats (1948), 517, 535
Doheny, Edwards L. (1858-1835), 172
Dollar Diplomacy, 304-305, 469
Dominican Republic, 304, 480
domino theory, 437, 482-483
Donnelly, Ignatius (1831-1901), 112, *115-119*
Du Bois, W. E. B. (1869-1963), 202, 203, 216
Dulles, John Foster (1888-1959), 434, 435, 438, 439, 440, 442, 443, 459, 460, 461, 462
Dumbarton Oaks Conference (1944), 393
Duryea, Charles E. (1862-1938), 4

Economic Opportunity Act (1964), 602-604
economics, 3-14, 108, 109, 112, 139, 154, 184, 520-523; agrarian, 110, 111; and the Cold War, 407, 408, 470; and the Depression, 248-251; and politics, 154-156; post-War, 515-520; and warfare, 371
education, and blacks, 204-205, 217; and the Cold War, 441; and patriotism, 286-287; and racism, 323, 535-557
Eisenhower Doctrine (1956), 440, 448-450
Eisenhower, Dwight D. (1890-1969), 390, 398, 408, 434, 435, 436, 438-446, *446-448, 448-450,* 452, 454, 455, 462, 470, 515, 517-520, 551-553, 606
Elections: of 1892, 112; of 1896, 110, 113-114, 119, 136; of 1900, 136, 137; of 1912, 154; of 1920, 350; of 1924, 173, 350; of 1928, 173, 194-196, 350;

of 1932, 190, 243, 252; of 1936, 252, 264; of 1940, 252; of 1944, 252, 515; of 1948, 517; of 1952, 434, 517; of 1956, 519; of 1960, 593; of 1964, 594-595
Ellis, Havelock, 200n
Elkins Act (1903), 137-138
embargo, on Cuba, 470
Emergency Relief and Construction Act (1932), 237
Emerson, Ralph Waldo (1803-1882), 15
Engels, Friedrich, 59
England, 302; and foreign policy, 281; and the Panama Canal, 303
entrepreneurs, 10-12, 37
Epstein, Abraham *269-271*
escalation, 489
European Recovery Program (1948), 407

Fair Deal, 516
Fall, Albert B. (1861-1944), 172
family, 88; and the Depression, 241-242
Fante, John, *89-92*
farmers, 109-114; *See also* agriculture
Fascism, 350-351
Faubus, Orval E., 551-553
Federal Emergency Relief Administration (1933-1935), 253, 532-533
federal income tax (1913), 112
Federal Reserve System (1913), 154, 253
Federal Trade Commission (1914), 154, 166-167
Federal Writers Project (1935), 533
finance, and World War I, 324-325
Fisk, James (1834-1872), 11
Forbes, Charles R., 172
Ford, Henry (1863-1947), 4, 97, 178-179
Fordney-McCumber Tariff (1922), 350
foreign policy, 408-409, 412-419, 497-511
Foreman, Clark, 532
Forman, James, 584-585
Fourteen Points (1918), 335
Franco-Prussian War (1870-1871), 281
Frankfurter, Felix (1882-1965), 452

Free Speech Movement (1964), 613-615
French Revolution (1789), 286
Freud, Sigmund, 200n
Frick, Henry Clay (1849-1919), 11, 66, 67-69, 156
Fuchs, Klaus, 452
Fulbright, J. William, 455, 476, 486-487, *497-499*
Fundamentalism, 188, 201

Garfield, James A. (1831-1881), 133-134
Garvey, Marcus (1887-1940), 206, 217-219
Geneva Conference (1954), 482
Genovese, Eugene, *626-628*
Gentlemen's Agreement (1907), 97, 306
George, Lloyd, 335
Gerard, James (1867-1951), *325-326*
Germany, division of, 392
ghetto, 83, 86-89, 212-216. *See also* riots
G.I. Bill of Rights (1944), 516
Ginsberg, Allen, *612-613*
Gladstone, William E., 40
gold, 111
Goldwater, Barry, 595
Gompers, Samuel (1850-1924), 63
Gong Lum v. *Rice,* 537
Good Neighbor Policy, 469-480
Gould, Jay (1836-1892), 11
government, 137, 151, 256-257, 272-279, 307, 310; and the Depression, 234-240; and the economy, 172-175, 250-251; local, 140-142
Grange, the (1867), 109
Granger Movement, 109, 110
Grant, Madison, 97n
Grant, Percy S., (1860-1927), *100-103*
Grant, Ulysses S. (1822-1885), 234
greenbacks, 111
Grünwald, Henry, *621-624*
Grew, Joseph C. (1880-1965), *368-371, 371-372,* 373, *375-377,* 402, 403
Gross National Product, 7-9
Gulf of Tonkin, 483, 484-485, 486-487, 488-489
Great Leap Forward, the, 440

Greece, 407
Guatemala (1954), 442-445

Haiti, 217, 305
Hall, Prescott F. (1868-1921), *98-100*
Hampton Institute, 16-19
Hanna, Mark (1837-1904), 113, 137
Harding, Warren G. (1865-1923), 172, 336
Harriman, Edward H. (1848-1909), 11, 137, 158
Harrington, Michael, *596-598, 604-607*
Harrison, Benjamin (1833-1901), 296
Hawaii, and imperialism, 292-299
Hawaiian Revolution (1893), 292-293, 295
Hawthorne, Julian (1846-1934), *71-72*
Hay-Bunau-Varilla Treaty (1903), 303
Hay-Herran Treaty (1903), 303, 310-311
Hay, John (1838-1905), 303, 306, 307
Hay-Pauncefote Treaty (1901), 303
Hayes, Rutherford B. (1822-1893), 138
Haymarket Affair (1886), 95
Hearst, William Randolph (1863-1951), 302
Hepburn Act (1906), 138
Hill, James J. (1836-1916), 13, 137, 158
Hillquit, Morris (1869-1933), 61
Hiss, Alger (1914-   ), 452
Hitler, Adolph (1889-1945), 169, 350-351, 406
Ho Chi Minh, 482
holding company, 14
Holmes, Oliver Wendell (1841-1935), 149, *151*
Homestead Strike (1892), 64-76
Honduras, 443
honest graft, 140
Hoover, Herbert (1874-1964), 172, 173-174, 194, 195, 217, *234-236*, 243-245, *257-259*
Hoovervilles, 234
Hopkins, Harry L. (1890-1946), 252-253
horizontal integration, 33
House, Col. Edward (1858-1938), 324
housing, and racism, 212-213
Housing Acts (1949 and 1968), 607

Howe, Frederic C. (1864-1940), 19, *19-23*
Hughes, Langston (1902-1966), *220-221*
Hull, Cordell (1871-1955), 375-379, 381
Hume, David, 289
Humphrey, Hubert, 535, 595
Hungary, 439-440, 446
Huntington, Collis P. (1821-1900), 11
Hyde Park Improvement Protective Club (1908), 213

Ickes, Harold L. (1874-1952), 252, 532
identity, 89-92, 621-624; black, 217-221, 575-577
ideology, 412-413; and Cold War, 406
Immigration Restriction League, 98
immigrants, 59, 77-92, 187, 191, 194, 204, 350; fear of, 192; and labor, 23-26; reaction to, 93-107
imperialism, 97, 137, 281, 300-316, 317, 366, 407, 499-501
Indo-China, 379-383, 387, 425, 429, 434-437; *See also* Viet Nam
Industrial Workers of the World (Wobblies) (1905), 61
Industrial Revolution, 1, 3-4
industrialization, as a cause of World War I, 318
industry, 154-155, 178-179; automobile, 4-5; and blacks, 211; and immigrants, 78-79, 81; steel, 33-50
integration, 573-574, 585-587
internal combustion engine, 4-5
Interstate Commerce Act (1887), 111, 137-138, 152
Interstate Commerce Commission, 138, 153
inventions, 4, 182. *See also* technology
Irish, in urban politics, 96; and treaty of Versailles, 339-340
Iron and Steel Roll Hands of the United States (1873), 65
isolation, 297-298, 300-301, 349, 350. *See also* neutrality
Italians in America, 89-92
Italy, 351; invasion of, 389

Japan, 306, 313-316, 396-405; in Manchuria, 350; and U.S. relations, 366-383
Jazz Age, 188-189, 199-201
Jefferson, Thomas (1743-1826), 15
Jews, 86-89
Jim Crow, 207. *See also* civil rights, segregation
John XXIII, Pope (1881-1963), 472
Johnson, Hugh S., 260
Johnson, James Weldon (1871-1938), 216
Johnson, Lyndon Baines (1908-   ), 435-436, 472, 480, 483, 484, *484*, 499, 594-595, 602
Johnson-Reed Act (1924), 98
Jones-Laughlin Steel Corporation, 272-276
Jones, E. K., 533
Jung, Carl, 200n

Katsura, Count Taro, 313-314
Kearney, Dennis, 95
Keating-Owen Act (1916), 154
Kellogg-Briand Pact (1928), 350
Kellogg, Frank B. (1856-1937), 350
Kennan, George F., *412-414*
Kennedy, John Fitzgerald (1917-1963), 462, 470-472, 473-475, 479, 480, 499, 593-594, 611
Keynes, John Maynard (1883-1946), 250
Krushchev, Nikita (1894-1971), 438-440, 441, 471-472
Kim Il-sung, 423
King, Martin Luther, Jr. (1929-1968), 556, 559, 562, 575
Knights of Labor (1869), 60, 66, 96
Knox, Philander C. (1853-1921), 305, 316
Konoye, Prince Fumimaro, 375-377, 379
Korea, 313-314, 422-423
Korean War (1950-1953), 420, 422-434
Kristol, Irving, *502-506*
Ku Klux Klan (1915), 97, 192-194, 206, 587
Kuomintang, 421

labor, 23-26, 59-76, 138, 149-151, 175, 187-188, 516-517; and agrarian revolt, 112, 113; and blacks, 211-212, 217; and immigrants, 77-78, 96; and the right to organize, 254. *See also* unions
land reform and Communism, 422
Landon, Alfred, 264
Lansing, Robert (1864-1928), 324, *326-328*
Latin America, 281-282, 480-481; and seizure of Panama, 308, 310
Lattimore, Owen, 378-458
League of Nations (1920-1946), 282, 333, 335, 336, 338, 339-346, 350, 368
Lebanon, 440, 448
Lend-Lease Act (1941), 350
Lewis, John L., 271
Liberal Republican Party (1872), 133
Liliuokalani, Queen (1838-1917), 292-293, 294, 298-299
Lindbergh, Charles A. (1902-   ), 196-198, *357-360*
Lippman, Walter, *414-417, 506-511*
Little Rock Crisis (1957), 551-553
Lochner v. *New York* (1905), 149, 151
Lodge, Henry Cabot (1850-1924), 96, 338, *341-343*
Long, Heuy P. (1893-1935), 260-263, 264, 266
lynching, 205-206, 216, 217
Lynd, Staughton, *631-634*

MacArthur, Gen. Douglas (1880-1964), 240n, 389, 422, 424, 425, 426, 428-429, 431, 434
McCarren Act (1951), 453, 458
McCarthy, Joseph (1908-1957), 452, 453, 454, 455, *455-457*, 457, 458, 459, 460, 461, 462
McCarthyism, 452-468, 499
McCormick, Cyrus H. (1809-1884), 11
McKinley, William (1843-1901), 113-114, 302, 306
McLaurin v. *Oklahoma State Regents*, 537
McNamara, Robert, *484-485*, 486, 488-489
McNary-Haugenism, 174
machine politics, 140-142

Mahan, Alfred T. (1840-1914), 290, 300-301
Malcolm X (1925-1965), 565-568
Manchuria, 368
Mao Tse-tung (1893-   ), 422
market system, 12-13
Maroquin, José Manuel, 310-312
Marshall, George C. (1880-1959), 398, 403, 407, 416-417, 422
Marshall Plan (1947), 397, 417
Marshall, Thurgood, 538-540
Marx, Karl (1818-1883), 59
Marxism, 187, 412-413
Masaryk, Thomas 352
mass production, 9-10
Maximum Employment Act (1946), 515, 516
Maximum Freight Rate Case (1896), 153
Meat Inspection Act (1906), 138
mechanization, impact on agriculture, 109, 114-115
Medicare (1964), 594
Mellon, Andrew (1855-1937), 235, 277
Melting Pot, the, 100-103; failure of, 104-107
Mexico, 309, 328, 445
Missle East, 440, 446-450
migration, black, 211-212, 534
minimum wage, 253
mining, 108
Mississippi Summer Project (1964), 569-572
Missouri ex rel. Gaines v. *Canada*, 537
Mitchell, John (1870-1919), 138
Molly Maguire Riots, 95
money, and the agrarian movement, 111-113
monopoly, 11
Monroe Doctrine, 281, 300, 408
Montgomery bus boycott (1955-1956), 556
Moody, Anne, 560-562
morality, international, 409
Morgan, House of, 137, 325
Morgan, J. P. (1837-1913), 11, 156, 157, 158
Morse, Wayne, 485-487, 489
Moskovitz, Henry, 203
muckrakers, 156

Mugwumps, 133
Muhammad, Elijah, 565
Munich, (1938), 352
Mussolini, Benito, 351, 352
Myrdal, Gunnar, 533

Nation, Carrie (1846-1911), 199n
National Association for the Advancement of Colored People, 202, 203, 206, 216-217, 533, 535, 551, 562, 575
National Commission of Urban Problems (1969), 606
National Industrial Recovery Act (1933), 253-254, 271
National Labor Relations Act (1935), 264, 272, 273, 275
National Labor Union (1866), 60
National Liberation Front, 482
National Recovery Administration (1933), 533
national security, 289-290
National Security Council (1947), 437
National Urban League, 203, 533-534, 575
National Youth Administration, 264, 533
nationalism, 93-98, 104-107, 286-297, 318, 339-340; black, 206, 217-219; and Viet Nam, 482
nationalist societies, 287-288
Native-American party (1850s), 93
nativism, 93-98, 453
natural law, and economics, 15
Negro Renaissance, 206
Negro Revolt, the, 556
Negroes, 175, 192. *See also* blacks, civil rights, race, racism
neutrality, 282, 317, 319-321, 322-325, 325-330, 349, 352-360, 387 *See also* isolation
New Deal, 169, 248-263, 264-279, 632; and civil rights, 532-533
new immigrants, 77
New Left, the, 610-611
Newlands Act (1902), 138
newspapers, and the Cuban revolution, 302; and Hawaiian annexation, 293-297; and World War I, 318
Niagara Movement, 202-203
Nicaragua, 305, 443

Nine-Power Treaty (1922), 350
Nixon, Richard Milhous (1913-   ), 437, 452, 462, 476-477, 519, 593, 606, 625
non-violent resistance, 556
Norris, Frank (1870-1902), 114-115
Norris, George W. (1861-1944), 255
North Atlantic Treaty Organization (1949), 408, 418-419
Northern Securities Case (1904), 137
Northwest Alliance, the, 109
Nuclear Test Ban Treaty (1963), 442, 472

obsolescence, 181-182
Octopus, The, 11
Office of Economic Opportunity, 594
Office of Education, 533
"Ohio Gang, the", 172
"old immigrants," defined, 77
"Open Door" (1899), 306
Oppenheimer, J. Robert, 399, 403, 454
Order of the United American Mechanics, and nativism, 96
Organization of American States (1948), 443, 444
organized crime, 189
oriental exclusion, 97, 98; and Hawaii, 296-297
overseas expansion, 281, 284-299
Ovington, Mary White, 203

Page, Walter Hines (1855-1918), 324, 325, 328
Palestine, 410
Palmer, A. Mitchell (1872-1936), 187
Panama, 307-313
Panama Canal, 300, 303, 307-313
Panamanian Revolution (1903), 303
Panic of 1893, 112; of 1907, 97
Panikkar, K. M., 430-431
Pankhurst, Emmeline, 199n
Paris Exposition (1867 and 1900), 4
Paris Peace Conference (1898), 303
Parks, Rosa, 566
patriotism, 286-287
Pauling, Linus, 463
Peace Corps, 594
Pendleton Act (1883), 133

Perkins, Frances (1882-1965), *255-257*
Peron, Juan, 445
Pershing, John J. (1860-1948), 333, 334
philanthropy, 34
Philippines, 303, 306, 313
Pickens, William, *217-219*
Pinchot, Gifford (1865-1946), 138, *146-148*
Pinkerton, Robert A., 69
Platt Amendment (1901), 303
Platt, Thomas C. (1833-1910), 137
Plessy v. *Ferguson* (1896), 536, 537, 538
Plunkitt, George Washington (1842-1924), 140
pogroms, 86, 89
Poland, 352, 397, 439
polarization, 581
political parties, 112-114, 122-123, 519
politics, 2, 165-166, 194-196, 517, 524, 531; agrarian, 109-114; and the atomic bomb, 399; and civil rights, 535; conservative, 595; and the Depression, 243-245; and economics, 154-156; local, 140-142; and racism, 216, 217; and the Treaty of Versailles, 335; and youth, 608-624
pooling, 40-41
Populist Movement, 97, 112-114, 124
Populist (People's) Party (1892), 110, 112; platform 115-119
Potsdam Conference (1945), 392, 397
poverty, 591-608
Powderly, Terence V. (1849-1924), 72-74
President's Civil Rights Committee (1947), 535
progressive leadership, 136-137
progressive morality, 142-146
Progressive (Bull Moose) Party (1912), 154
Progressive Party (1948), 517
progressivism, 110, 112, 171, 133, 167, 243; and World War I, 323
Prohibition, 189-192
prosperity, in the 1950s, 521-523
prostitution, 191
protectorates, 303-305

public opinion, and the coming of World War II, 362-365, 372-373
Public Utility Holding Company Act (1935), 264
Public Works Administration (1933), 252
Pulitzer, Joseph (1847-1911), 302
Pullman, George M. (1831-1897), 36, 49
Pure Food and Drug Act (1906), 138

quarantine, as foreign policy, 443

racism, 19, 97-98, 207-208, 211-212, 212-216, 290-292, 306, 513, 534-535, 548-551. *See also:* riots
radio, 180-181
railroads, 113, 114-115, 158; and agriculture, 109; and monopoly, 11; regulation, 110-111, 137-138; strikes (1877), 95
Randolph, A. Philip (1899-   ), 206 533
Rauschenbusch, Walter (1861-1918), *148-149*
Recession; of 1914, 324; of 1937, 264; of 1957, 520; of 1970, 625
Reconstruction, 108
Reconstruction Finance Corporation (1932), 516
Red scare, of the 1920s, 187; of the 1950s, 452
Red Summer (1919), 206
reform, 133-151, 164-167; and American foreign policy, 444-445; financial (1933), 253
regionalism, 108, 122-123, 124
relief, 236-240, 252-253
Relief Act (1935), 264
religion, and reform, 148-149; revivalism, 22
reparations, 335-336, 350
Republican Party, 171, 172. *See also* politics, conservative
Resettlement Administration, 264
Reuther, Walter (1909-1970), 535
revolution, and foreign policy, 442; and the immigrant threat, 95; Latin America, 444-445; and the new politics, 615-618; social, 438

Rhee, Syngman, 423
riots, labor, 23, 26; race, 202-203, 205-206, 214-216, 534, 576-581
robber baron, 11-12
Robinson, Jackie, 535
Rockefeller, John D. (1839-1937), 1, 11, 156, 157, 158
Roosevelt Corollary (1904), 304
Roosevelt, Franklin D. (1882-1945), 169, 190, 243-245, *245-247*, 251-257, 264, 266-267, *267*, *352-354*, *354-357*, *360-361*, 375, 378, 392, 397, 469, 515, 532, 534-535
Roosevelt, Theodore (1858-1919), 97, *103-104*, 136, 137, 153, 154, 156, *159-162*, 195-196, 234, 290, 303, 304, 305, 306, 307, *310-313*, 313-314, *314-315*, *321-322*, 323
Rosenberg, Ethel and Julius, 452
Ross, Edward A., *144-146*
Rudd, Mark, *615-618*
Russia, and the Chinese Communist Revolution, 422. *See also* U.S.S.R.
Russian Revolution (1917), 187
Russo-Japanese War (1904-1905), 306, 366-367
Rustin, Bayard, *585-587*

Sacco, Nicolo (1891-1927), 187
Samoan protectorate (1878), 292
Sanger, Margaret, 200n
Savio, Mario, *613-615*
Schlesinger, Arthur M., Jr. *634-637*
Schurz, Carl (1829-1906), *297-298*
Schwab, Charles (1862-1939), 40, 46-48, *154-156*, 156
Scopes, John T., 188
Scopes Trial (1926), 188
Securities Act (1933), 253
segregation, 207, 217; and labor, 272. *See also* Jim Crow
Selassie, Haile, 351
Selective Service Act (1940), 350
Seligman, F. R. A., 203
"separate but equal," 536
Sherman Anti-Trust Act (1890), 64, 134, 137, 152, 153
Sherman Silver Purchase Act (1890), 112, 112n
silver, 111-112

Sinclair, Harry F. (1876-1956), 172
Sinclair, Upton, 138
Sipuel v. *Oklahoma*, 537
sit-in movement, 558, 560-562
Smith Act (1940), 457
Smith, Alfred E. (1873-1944), 190, 194, 195-196
Smith, Jesse, 172
Smoot-Hawley Tariff (1930), 350
Smyth Report (1945), 399-400
Social Darwinism, 290-292
Social Democratic Party of America (1897), 61
social gospel, 148
social security, 266-271, 519
Social Security Act (1935), 264
socialism, 187; and the depression, 248; fear of, 23; and labor, 60-63, 187
Socialist Labor Party, 61
Socialist Party, 61
Socialist Party of America (1900), 61
Soule, George, *248-250*
Southern Alliance, 109
Southern Christian Leadership Conference (1957), 575
Southern Manifesto, 556
Spain, 302-303, 317
Spanish-American War (1898), 302-303, and Hawaii, 299
Spanish Civil War (1936), 351
Spooner Act (1902), 303
Spreckles, Claus, 294, 295, 297
Sputnik (1957), 441
Stalin, Josef (1879-1953), 392, 397, 404
Standard Oil Company (1870), 12, 13, 14, 137
standardization 178-179
status revolution, 96
steel, 33, 38-40
Steel Workers Organizing Committee, 272-275
Stevens, John L., 293, 294-295, 297, 299
Stevenson, Adlai E. (1900-1965), 434, 452, 485, 517-518, 519, 611
Stilwell, Joseph W. (1883-1946), 459
Stimson, Henry L. (1867-1950), 350, 378, 396-399, 402, 403, 404, 405
Stock Market Crash (1929), 222, 234

Stone, William (1848-1918), *328-330*
Strong, Josiah (1847-1916), *290-292*
Students for a Democratic Society, 612, 615
Student Nonviolent Coordinating Committee, 558, 575, 584, 612
submarine warfare, 326-328
subtreasury plan, 112
suburbanization, 177-178
Suez Crisis (1956), 440, 446-448
summit meetings: 1955, 438-439; 1960, 442
Sumner, William Graham (1840-1910), *31-32*
Supreme Court, 149-151, 152-153, 166, 264-265, 278; and integration, 535-548
Suslov, Mikhail, 446
Sweatt v. *Painter*, 537
Swift, Gustavus F. (1839-1903), 11
symbolism, 196-198, 287

Taft-Hartley Act (1947), 516-517
Taft, Robert A. (1889-1955), 516, 517, 605
Taft, William Howard (1857-1930), 96, 146-147, 153-154, 305, 315
Tammany Hall, 134, 140
tariff, 154; and labor, 73; and reform, 113; Underwood, 154; of 1890, 124; of 1892, 124; Smoot-Hawley, 350
Teapot Dome (1927), 172
technology, 171, 182; and change, 35; and the Depression, 233, 234; impact of, 3-14, 175, 175-178, 180-181, 188, 366, 614; and poverty, 597; and unionization, 65; and values, 238; and warfare, 326
Tehran Conference (1943), 392
Teller, Edward, 403
temperance, 133
Tennessee Valley Authority (1933), 255, 533
Third Plenary Council (1884), and anti-Catholicism, 96
Thurmond, J. Strom, 517
Tillman, Benjamin (1847-1918), 216n
Timko, Joseph, 272
Tonkin Gulf Resolution (1964), 488
total war, 394-396

645

Townsend, Dr. Francis (1867-1960), 264, 266
Trade Expansion Act (1962), 594
Treaty of Versailles (1919), 282, 335-339, 350
Tri-Partite Declaration (1950), 448
Tripartite Pact (1940), 354, 379
Truman Doctrine (1947), 397, 407, 410, 416
Truman, Harry S. (1884-   ), 392, 396-399, 420, *424-426*, 428-429, *431-434*, 453, 513, 515-517, 535
trusts, 13, 41-44. See also concentration
Tweed, William M. "Boss" (1823-1878), 134
Twentieth Soviet Party Conference (1956), 439, 610
Twenty-One Demands, 367

Union Party (c.1936), 264
U.S.S.R., 406-419; and Cuba, 471-479; and revolution, 446; and the Suez Crisis, 440
unions, 23, 59, 60-64, 138, 153, 175, 187, 264, 271-275, 524-526; and blacks, 533; and immigration, 96; and racism, 217. See also labor
United Auto Workers, 535

United Mine Workers, 63
United Nations (1945), 393, 409, 410, 416-417, 443, 444, 447-448, 449, 472, 485; and the Korean War, 424
United Nations Relief and Rehabilitation Administration (1943), 393
United Sons of Vulcan, 65
United States Steel Corporation (1901), 12, 33, 41-44, 152, 153, 154, 156, 177, 273, 594
United States v. E. C. Knight Co. (1895), 153
universal military conscription, 318
Universal Negro Improvement Association (1914), 206
University of California at Berkeley, 613-615
ubanization, 1-2, 3, 6; conflict of, 188

values, American, 188-189, 194-196, 196-198, 199-201, 394-396, 409, 457-459, 498
Van Buren, Martin (1782-1862), 234
Vanderbilt, W. K. (1821-1885), 158
Vanzetti, Bartolomeo (1888-1927), 187
Vardaman, James K., 216n
Venezuelan Crisis (1895), 302; (1902), 304

vertical integration, 33
Viet Nam, 482-496, 625, 626-627, 629; and youth, 596. See also Indo-China
violence, 615-621
Volsted Act (1919), 189
Voting Rights Act (1965), 560

Wabash Case (1886), 111
Wagner Act (1935), 264
Waite, Henry, *141-142*
Wallace, Henry (1888-1965), 515, 517
Walling, William English, 203
war debts, 349, 350
Warren, Earl (1891-   ), *536-538*
Warsaw Pact (1954), 408
Washington, Booker T. (1856-1915), 16, *16-19*, 202
Weathermen, 615-618
Weaver, Robert C., 532
Weimar Republic, 335
Welsh, in America, 85-86
Western Federation of Miners, 61
white backlash, 581-584
White House Conference (1908), 138
White, Walter (1893-1955), 216, 532
White, William Allen (1868-1944), 119-122
Wilhelm II (1888-1918), 318, 323, 335

Wilkins, Roy, 533, 534
Williams, Robert F., *562-564*
Wilson, Woodrow (1856-1924), 96, 97, 136, 154, *162-164*, 282, 305, *319-321*, 322, 323-324, 325, *330-332*, 333, 334, 335, 336, *343-346*, 346-348
Wolfe, Robert, *499-501*
women's rights, 133, 143-146, 199-200
Woodson, Dr. Carter G., 206
Works Progress Administration (1935), 533, 562
World War I (1914-1918), 171, 187, 282, 312-335, 394; and blacks, 205, 211; and immigration restriction, 97; impact of, 149-150; and reform, 154
World War II (1939-1945), 170, 222, 369-383, 387-391; and morality, 394
Wright, Richard (1909-1963), *207-211*

Yalta Conference (1945), 392, 397
yellow dog contracts, 63
yellow press, 302
Young, Whitney M., 575
youth, 513, 596; and the new politics, 608-624

Zimmermann telegram, 328